1996 Medical and Health Annual

Encyclopædia Britannica, Inc.
Chicago • Auckland • London • Madrid • Manila • Paris • Rome • Seoul • Sydney • Tokyo • Toronto

1996 Medical and Health Annual

Library of Congress Catalog Card Number: 77-649875
International Standard Book Number: 0-85229-615-0 International Standard Serial Number: 0363-0366

A Few Words from the Editor...

Encyclopædia Britannica is pleased to publish the 1996 *Medical and Health Annual*—for old and new readers alike. Past readers will notice that the book has had a "face-lift"; it also has some new items in its "wardrobe."

The entire volume boasts a bold new design. Also brand-new—and visually exciting—is our "World Health Data" section, compiled by Encyclopædia Britannica's statistics-gathering experts.

The opening "Feature" article is one that we feel fortunate to include. On a blizzardy day in January 1994, the *Annual*'s editors braved the elements to see a special exhibit: artwork by children who were living near the Chernobyl nuclear power plant on April 26, 1986—the day the station's fourth reactor exploded. That exhibit was still vivid in our minds months later when we began planning this book. We learned that the works by the young artists had *not* been shown elsewhere. Thanks to the generosity of their collector, 14 paintings by Chernobyl's children are reproduced on pages 6–17. Our picture essay is followed by David Marples' assessment of the medical consequences of the nuclear disaster on its 10th anniversary.

A trio of articles we hope readers will find "fun" as well as "food for thought" includes "Hold the Mayo!," "Pass the Pâté," and "An American (Chef) in Paris." In the latter, Los Angeles restaurateur Michael Roberts takes the reader shopping in Paris' colorful street markets, visits colossal one-stop *hypermarchés,* and samples the fare (and ambience) in some Parisian eating establishments. Because we know the subjects of diet and nutrition are of ongoing interest to readers, we include other food-related reports—among them, articles that filter out the facts about coffee, rank vegetables nutritionally, explain why infants thrive on breast milk, consider a newly defined eating disorder, and speculate on the future of food irradiation.

In the 4th century AD, Saint Augustine proclaimed: "The greatest evil is physical pain." Exactly halfway through the Decade of the Brain, the *Annual* examines the large body of knowledge that neuroscientists have acquired about this *persisting* evil. Sidebars focus on the diagnosis and treatment of pain in children and effective new treatment for migraine headaches, while a companion article looks at the role of the most important *bedside* pain managers—nurses.

A four-part progress report on breast cancer begins on page 202; an equally enlightening report focuses on the leading cancer of men, prostate cancer (page 360).

Many articles offer personal insights from leading health professionals. Neurologist-writer Richard Restak explores the remarkable bond between blind people and their canine companions. He visits the Seeing Eye, Inc., where he takes a hair-raising blindfolded stroll with a guide-dog-in-training. Pediatrician Abraham Bergman considers the changes—some miraculous, some ominous—in the field of caring for children that have occurred during his 40-plus years in the profession. Compelling photographs illustrate his reflections; these include two quite unforgettable shots of medical students from the 1950s by the late Alfred Eisenstaedt.

Perhaps the toughest part of putting together an annual of medicine and health is to be current. In a field that changes daily, it would be impossible to be entirely up to date. (But we try!) The 1996 *Annual* offers more than 40 "NewsCaps" of late-breaking medical news.

The *Annual is* prepared in the manner of *Britannica* itself. Its contributors are internationally recognized experts, the articles carry their authority, and the volume is edited to be comprehensible to the layperson. Whenever possible, we avoid hard-to-swallow medicalese, but we also assist readers by including a "Glossary." Our aim is to publish a book that provides sound and practical information for health-conscious consumers; we hope we have succeeded.

—Ellen Bernstein

CONTENTS

FEATURES

WORLD OF MEDICINE

192

319

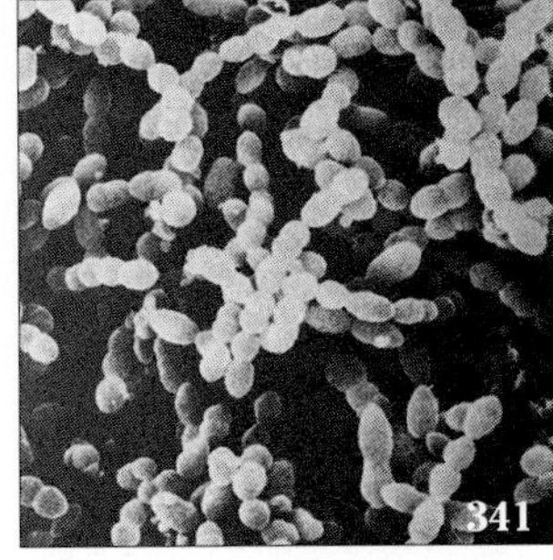
341

371

Children of Chernobyl: Their Pictures Tell the Story

On April 26, 1986, a chain reaction set off a catastrophic explosion at the Chernobyl nuclear power station north of Kiev, Ukraine (then part of the U.S.S.R.). The surrounding area, including a neighboring region in the now-independent republic of Belarus, was contaminated by radioactivity. Even today, visitors to the region are astonished by the devastation of the countryside and the abject state of those who still live there. Some fears of radiation-related diseases have been borne out, especially among children.

One Westerner who has witnessed the aftermath of Chernobyl is Christian K. Narkiewicz-Laine, founder and director of the Chicago Athenaeum, a museum of architecture and design. The descendant of a prominent Belarusian family, Narkiewicz-Laine visited the land of his forefathers in 1993. He was moved by the people's courage.

When he was shown the artwork of young Chernobyl survivors, he was struck by its level of sophistication. The pictures on these pages, never before reproduced, represent just a few of the 100 drawings that Narkiewicz-Laine selected for an exhibit at the Chicago Athenaeum in December 1993. He is now working to place these drawings in other exhibit spaces around the U.S.—as a reminder to an often forgetful world of the plight of the children of Chernobyl.

Most but not all of the artists' names and ages are known; many have since died from the effects of radiation.

—*Medical and Health Annual* editors

(Above) "Mommy, I Want Home," Sergey Kozlov, age 13; (opposite page) "Atom," Julia Berlinova, age 14.

Photographs, courtesy of The Chicago Athenaeum: Museum of Architecture and Design; photography by Jim Iska

ATOM

(Above) "Wind of Chernobyl," unidentified artist; (opposite page, bottom) "My Toys," Anna Skozetskaya, age 9

(Opposite page)
"Abandoned," Tanya Konovalova, age 10; (above) "Our Future," Sergey Krutko, age 12

"Dead Garden," Natasha Yerofevya

"We Are Still Living in the Affected Zone," Elena Antonyuk, age 14

"The Flowers of Chernobyl," Masha Samagulova, age 12

"Washing the World," Igor Blozkov, age 12.

"In the Chernobyl Forest," Larisa Maskalyova, age 13

"The Chernobyl Nuclear Power Station," Sergey Krutko, age 12

"Chernobyl Stairs," Yura Fedorin, age 11; (overleaf) "A Handful of Soil in Memory of My Native House," P. Vinga

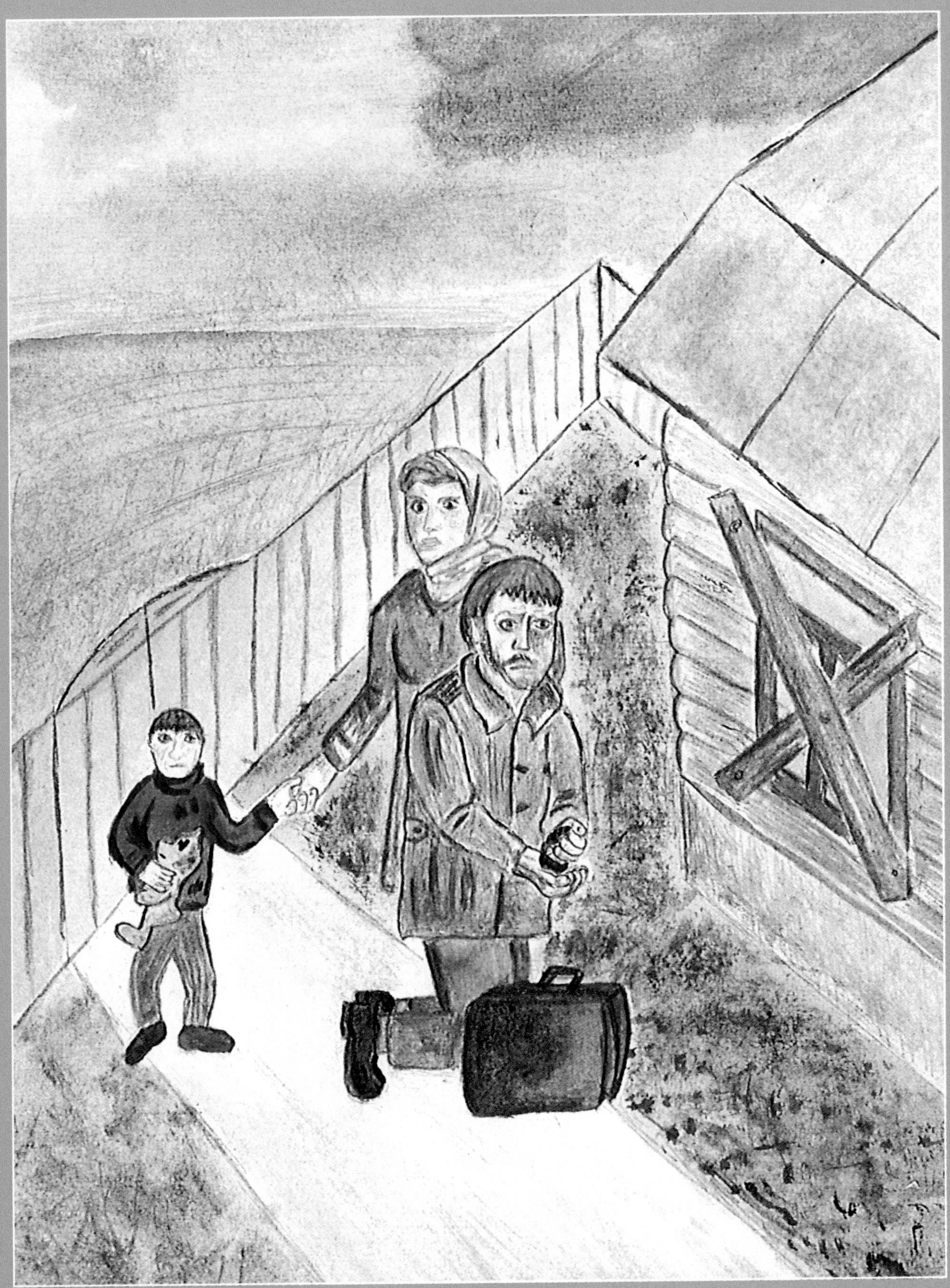

Chernobyl: Ten Years After the Catastrophe

by David R. Marples, Ph.D.

Abandoned schoolroom, Belarus, 1990

April 1996 will mark the 10th anniversary of the accident at the Chernobyl nuclear power station in the former Ukrainian Soviet Socialist Republic. Since that time, the Soviet Union has disintegrated and has been replaced by independent republics. Three of these—Russia, Ukraine, and Belarus—were significantly affected by the radioactive contamination of Chernobyl. The responsibility for the aftermath of this major industrial disaster has devolved from the Soviet government to the governments of these new republics. The Chernobyl power station itself is today under the control of the Ukrainian au-

David R. Marples, Ph.D., *is Professor of Russian History, University of Alberta, Edmonton.*

Vladimir Sichov—Sipa

Victoria Ivleva—Magnum

thorities rather than those in Moscow, as was the case in 1986–91. What has been discovered about the accident itself in the 10 years that have elapsed since the catastrophe? What has been its impact on the lives and health of the millions of people who were affected?

Even a decade after the incident, the impact of Chernobyl remains a subject of debate among scholars, scientists, and administrators. There is no consensus, for example, between the committees appointed in Ukraine and Belarus to deal with the aftermath of the accident and the Vienna-based International Atomic Energy Agency (IAEA). The latter sponsored its own investigation into the health of the affected population. Its report, *The International Chernobyl Project (ICP),* published in 1991, concluded that among those studied, no health problems could be traced specifically to the accident at Chernobyl. Local authorities, however, have tended to attribute an overall increase in disease rates in their populations directly to the accident. The truth undoubtedly lies somewhere in between.

Disputes as to the origins of certain illnesses (including cancers) that have increased notably since 1986 are complicated by the lack of an adequate disease-surveillance system in the Soviet republics before the Chernobyl incident. One Belarusian specialist observed that prior to the accident the discipline of epidemiology simply did not exist in his country; a surveillance system had to be developed from scratch. Problems of inadequate or absent records were compounded by official secrecy and the classification by the Soviet Ministry of Health of all health information relating to Chernobyl. The official figure for deaths resulting from the disaster—31 (of which 28 were due to radiation sickness)—has been steadfastly maintained since the summer of 1986 despite numerous other documented deaths. On the other hand, grassroots anger at the obvious inaccuracy of the official figures has led to inflated casualty totals from a variety of nongovernmental sources, such as the Chernobyl Union, the labor union that represents the Ukrainian workers who were responsible for cleaning up the accident site.

A twisted pine tree—its growth deformed by radiation exposure—stands outside the ruins of the fourth reactor.

A disaster waiting to happen

According to data in the possession of the KGB of the U.S.S.R., design deviations and violations of construction and assembly technology are occurring at various places in the construction of the second generating unit of the Chernobyl AES [Atomic Energy Station], and these could lead to mishaps and accidents.

The structural pillars of the generator room were erected with a deviation of up to 100 mm from the reference axes, and horizontal connections between the pillars are absent in places.

Wall panels have been installed with a deviation of up to 150 mm from the axes. The placement of roof plates does not conform to the designer's specifications. Crane tracks and stopways have vertical drops of up to 100 mm and in places a slope of up to 8°.

—1979 report by the KGB to the Central Committee of the Communist Party of the Soviet Union

The site of the ill-fated power plant was the town of Chernobyl, located some 104 kilometers (65 miles) north of Kiev (population 2.5 million), the capital of Ukraine. First settled in the 12th century, Chernobyl was home to about 10,000 people in 1986. The nuclear power plant, located 16 kilometers (10 miles) northwest of the town, was part of an ambitious nuclear energy program begun by the U.S.S.R. in the 1970s. The program centered on what is known as a graphite-moderated nuclear reactor. In this type of reactor (usually referred to by its Russian acronym, RBMK), the fuel rods and channels for coolant are housed in stacks of graphite blocks. The power station at Chernobyl had four such reactors at the time of the accident. (Similar power plants were located at Sosnovy Bor [near the city of St. Petersburg] and Kursk in Russia and Ignalina in Lithuania. This type of Soviet-made reactor was never exported from the U.S.S.R.)

After the Chernobyl disaster, scientists at the Kurchatov Institute of Atomic Energy in Moscow revealed that the RBMK reactor design had, at minimum, 32 basic flaws. Most seriously, they found that the reactor becomes unstable if operated at low power. Also, in contrast to the other Soviet reactor type, the water-cooled VVER reactor, the RBMK lacked a containment dome over the reactor core. Nevertheless, Soviet authorities noted with pride the RBMK's safety record.

The details of the accident itself are fairly well-known. In the early hours of April 26, 1986, an experiment was conducted on the fourth reactor. Its purpose was to ascertain whether, in the event of a reactor shutdown, turbines that were still spinning would produce sufficient energy to run the plant's safety equipment until emergency power became operational. In order to prevent an automatic shutdown, the plant operators purposely disconnected seven safety devices. Then, owing to a worker's error, the plant suffered a sharp loss of power. Operators responded by increasing the power, causing an energy surge that blew the roof off the reactor. It was estimated at the time that 3.5% of the reactor core was released through the open roof. More recent figures, such as those of Alexander Sich, a nuclear engineer at the Massachusetts Institute of Technology, put the percentage considerably higher, perhaps between 6% and 10%.

A fireman who suffered extensive radiation burns while extinguishing the blaze at Chernobyl receives treatment at Moscow Hospital No. 6.

Some 450 different types of radionuclides (radioactive atoms) and a total of 50 million curies of radioactive material—equivalent in force to 90 atomic bombs of the type dropped on Hiroshima, Japan—entered the atmosphere. The explosion of the reactor core propelled chunks of radioactive graphite into the machine room and other areas of the plant. The immediate danger was that posed by a graphite fire that burned for four hours and threatened to spread to the third reactor.

The response: too little too late

As [the firemen] struggled to breathe in the soot and smoke, their boots stuck in the melted bitumen on the roof. . . . Burning chunks of graphite and astronomically high radiation spewed from the reactor. A man had to leave after working for 90 seconds, because in that time he received a lifetime's permissible dose of radioactivity.

—eyewitness account from *Beyond Chernobyl: Women Respond* (1993)

At the time of the accident, neither the plant director nor the chief engineer was on hand. Both had

Novosti/Sovfoto

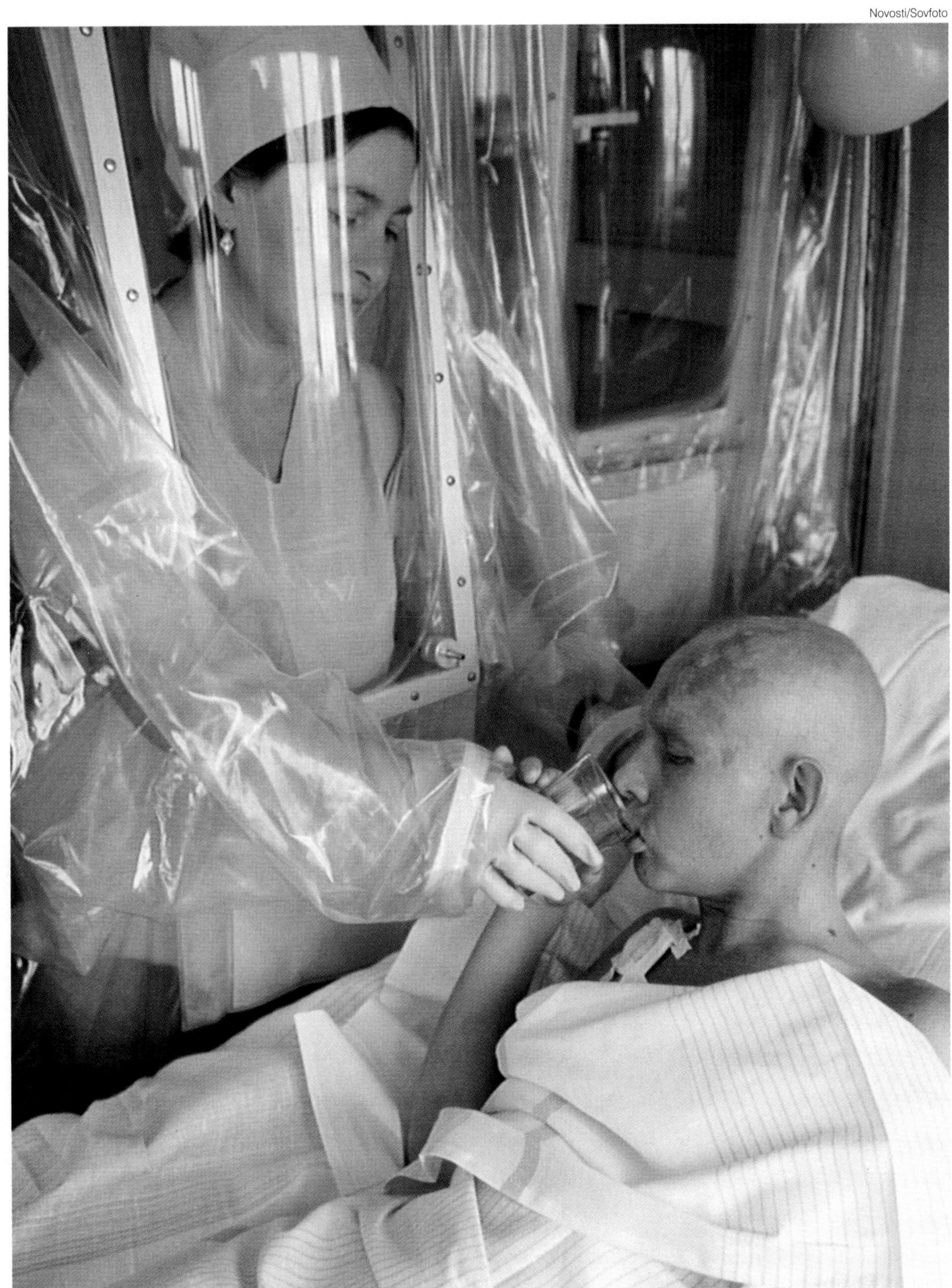

to be wakened; once at the plant, neither realized that the reactor core had exploded. A fire-fighting unit from the city of Pripyat, 3.2 kilometers (2 miles) north of the power station, faced the fire alone until the arrival of crews from Kiev and other parts of Kiev province. Both firemen and first aid workers suffered heavy casualties, and radiation levels were too high to be measured by the few Geiger counters available. Indeed, the firemen lacked even protective clothing. The most severely ill were flown to Moscow Hospital No. 6, the only institution in the Soviet Union equipped to deal with cases of radiation sickness. Despite the mayhem at the power station, life in Pripyat (population 45,000), a city built specifically for workers at the nuclear plant and their families, continued as normal on the next day, a Saturday. Not until 2 PM on April 27—some 37 hours after the accident—was an evacuation ordered. Buses were sent from Kiev to transport the residents of Pripyat, who were ordered to pack enough for a three-day absence.

By May 2 the authorities in Moscow had assumed control. Two Politburo officials, Nikolay Ryzhkov and Yegor Ligachev, were dispatched by General Secretary Mikhail Gorbachev to investigate the situation. They immediately broadened the zone of evacuation to a 30-kilometer (18.6-mile) radius around the destroyed reactor. The evacuation area thus extended north into Belarus (then the Byelorussian S.S.R.). Responsibility for sealing the exposed reactor and decontaminating the area around the plant was delegated to a government commission, led by the deputy chairman of the U.S.S.R. Council of Ministers, Boris Shcherbina. A major advisory role was played by scientists under the leadership of the vice president of the Academy of Sciences of the U.S.S.R., Yevgeny Velikhov.

Helicopters flew over the damaged reactor and dropped sand, lead pellets, and boron into the core to prevent the emission of radioactive materials. Such missions were highly dangerous—most of the helicopter pilots have since died—and wildly inaccurate, as many missed their targets altogether. Nonetheless, by May 10, just over two weeks after the accident, radioactive releases from the plant had ended. By December a concrete shell, known as the sarcophagus, had been built over the destroyed reactor. The sarcophagus was a makeshift affair. Cracks soon began to appear in it, and the Ukrainian government estimated in 1990 that it would last only another 15 years at the most.

Several other events of 1986 merit brief note. According to official Soviet figures, a total of 135,000 people had to be evacuated. They were relocated to nearby regions, to the city of Kiev, and to other, more distant areas in need of labor. Initially, some people were moved to the west, the same direction in which the radiation cloud traveled; they had to be "evacuated" a second time. The resettlement process was a lengthy one.

The authorities quickly began to publicize optimistic accounts about the cleanup effort, proclaiming that the disaster had been "contained." Even non-Soviet scientists maintained that the contaminated lands might eventually be brought back under cultivation. In August 1986 the Soviet authorities, led by Valery Legasov of the Kurchatov Institute, delivered a report on the causes of the accident to the IAEA, placing almost exclusive blame on human error. The report was misleading; within a year it was known that the accident was principally a result of the flawed reactor design. Incredibly, by November 1986 the first two reactors at Chernobyl had been restarted, and the plant continued to provide power for about 7% of Ukraine's 52 million people.

Radioactive fallout: invisible enemy

We eat everything that the earth nurtures, even though it has been contaminated by radiation. I have four children and they are all sick.

Igor Kostin—Imago/Sygma

Commission after commission visits here, but it is no use. . . . We are hostages. We have no opportunity to leave and yet it is impossible to live here.

—letter in the Kiev newspaper *Radyans'ka Ukraina,* June 22, 1989

The major health threat from the accident at Chernobyl was that posed by the fallout of radionuclides. The predominant component of the fallout was iodine-131, which was disseminated over the northern parts of Ukraine and the southern regions of Belarus. Iodine-131 has a relatively short half-life (the time required for half of the atoms of a radioactive substance to disintegrate)—only about eight days—but exposure to this element in the first weeks after the accident was widespread.

This exposure was particularly dangerous because the affected regions (known locally as the Polissya—in Russian, Polesye—area) have a naturally low level of iodine in the soil. People who live in the region, therefore, do not get sufficient iodine from the food supply and, as a result, radioactive iodine from the environment would readily accumulate in their thyroid glands. (This metabolism-regulating gland

An amusement park in the now-deserted city of Pripyat was being readied for May Day celebrations when the order to evacuate was issued on April 27, 1986.

Victoria Ivleva—Magnum

Workers wearing protective gear monitor radiation levels inside the building that houses the destroyed reactor.

has an affinity for iodine, which it requires in order to function properly.)

In some neighboring countries, such as Poland, once the news of the accident became known, potassium iodide tablets were distributed among the population. The purpose was to saturate the thyroid gland with an innocuous form of iodine and thus prevent the uptake of radioactive forms. In most parts of the Soviet Union, however, such precautions either were not taken or were adopted only belatedly. (There were a few exceptions in which local nurses handed out such tablets without official authority.) The area of iodine-131 fallout included most of Belarus and the northern oblasts of Ukraine. Another short-term radionuclide prevalent in the atmosphere after the explosion was cesium-134 (with a half-life of 2.06 years).

A more long-lasting threat was posed by strontium-90, cesium-137, and plutonium-239, which have half-lives of 29.12, 30, and 24,390 years, respectively. These radionuclides pose a danger because they enter the soil and pass into the food chain. The area affected by these elements initially was thought to be limited to the zone of evacuation. In fact, for three years after the accident, the belief prevailed in the Soviet Union that the 30-kilometer circle around Chernobyl—demarcated by an ominous barbed wire barricade—marked the outer limits of radioactive fallout. During this time unrestricted fishing was allowed in the Kiev Reservoir, which is linked by river systems to the Chernobyl plant, and berries and mushrooms from the forests of the Gomel region continued to be collected and eaten. Agricultural production continued as normal outside the 30-kilometer zone.

In the spring of 1989, however, the official secrecy was partially lifted, and *Pravda* and other newspapers published maps of the areas of radiation fallout, showing, much to the alarm of the populations involved, that these regions were considerably broader than initially thought. The new maps increased the size of the population affected by Chernobyl to 3.5 million people. In the Ukrainian S.S.R. the contaminated zone was expanded to include large parts of Zhytomyr and Chernihiv oblasts, including the town of Slavutych, which had been built to accommodate refugees from Pripyat.

Photographs, Frederique Hibon—Sygma

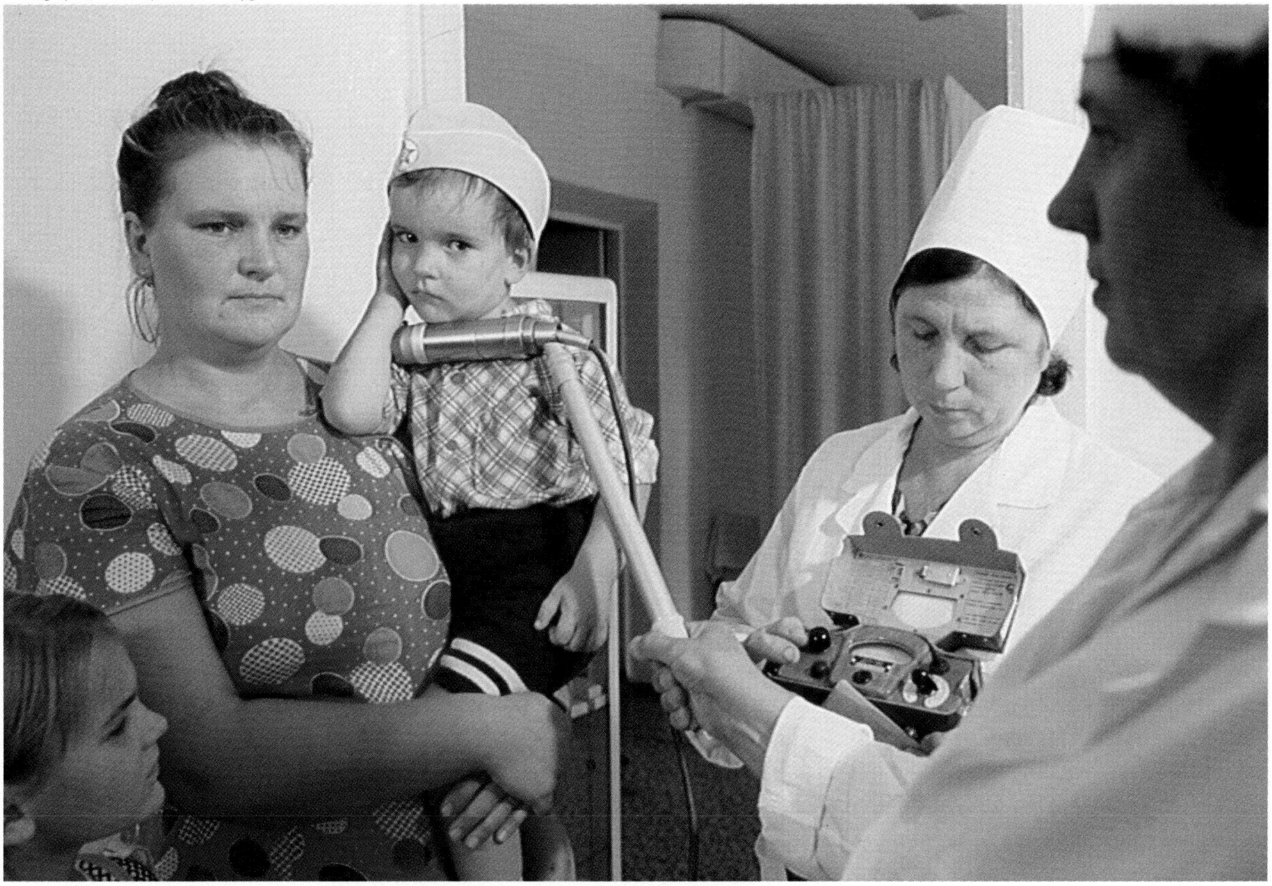

(Above) Measuring radiation exposure at a Kiev clinic a few months after the accident. (Right) Evacuees from Chernobyl in a hastily built new village.

Fishing was finally prohibited in the Kiev reservoir. In the southern half of Belarus, Gomel, Mogilev, and the eastern part of Brest oblast were included in the expanded fallout zone, in addition to a small region in the west of Minsk oblast. In Russia, Bryansk oblast was most heavily contaminated, and parts of Leningrad (St. Petersburg), Tambov, Smolensk, and the Mordovian Autonomous Republic (Mordvinia) were also included. By spring 1989, the

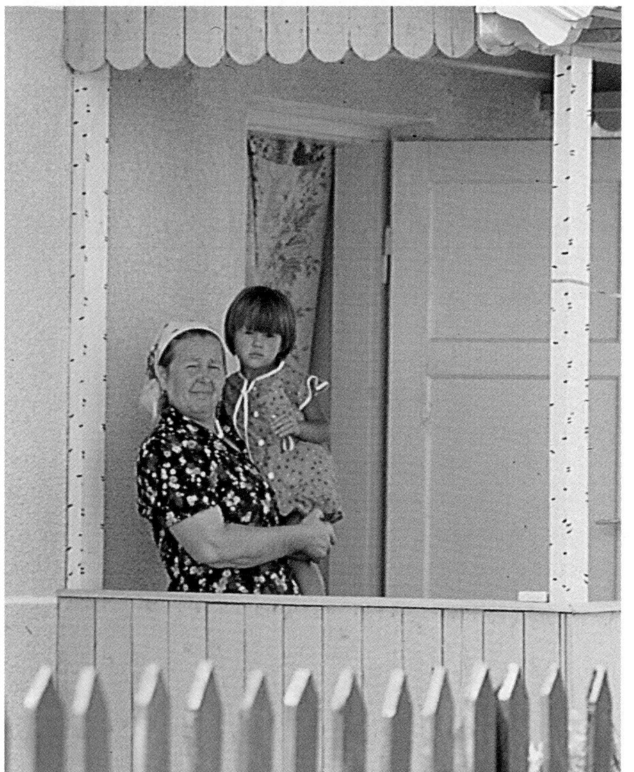

true magnitude of the disaster was becoming evident.

The Soviet Ministry of Health based its toleration levels for radiation exposure on those of the International Commission on Radiological Protection, measured in units called rems. The natural background radiation—that from the Sun and other unavoidable sources—in the former Soviet Union would have exposed the population to approximately 80 millirems (*i.e.,* 0.08 rem) per year. The average exposure of individuals ranged from 120 to 300 millirems a year. The maximum permissible dose of radiation prior to Chernobyl had been established as 500 millirems per year

(0.5 rem). Initially, therefore, taking into account international advice, the Soviet Ministry of Health set a limit of 35 rems of exposure per person over a natural lifetime of 70 years, or 0.5 rem per year, which conformed to international safety standards.

In Ukraine the environmental group Green World protested the use of the official toleration level for assessing the impact of the Chernobyl events, charging that it failed to take into account the very high immediate exposure from the accident. By 1990, when the republics had established their own committees for dealing with the effects of Chernobyl, the limit had been reduced from 35 rems to 7 rems over a natural life span, or 0.1 rem per year. The lower rate had the effect of increasing the size of the population eligible for evacuation.

In Ukraine and Belarus five "zones of concern" were designated, based on the levels of contamination of the soil and graded according to the danger to the population. Since the main aftereffects of the disaster would henceforth derive from the soil and the food chain rather than the air, scientists devised toleration levels for the public based on the amount of radioactive cesium, strontium, and plutonium that would enter the human body through food products and water. The five zones were as follows: (1) the "zone of alienation," the territory evacuated initially and a slightly broader area around it; (2) the "zone of primary evacuation," or the region that was evacuated during the period 1987–89; (3) the "zone of subsequent evacuation," the area evacuated after 1989; (4) the "zone with the right to evacuation," an area in which the population had the right to be resettled if it proved impossible to obtain sufficient supplies of uncontaminated food and water; and (5) the "zone of periodic radiation control," in which people were being closely monitored for adverse health effects.

In reality, measurement of radionuclide levels—and therefore the delineation of zones—was hampered by the limited number of Geiger counters available. Also, radiation levels could vary considerably, even from one side of a street to the other. Further, radiation hot spots (including high concentrations of plutonium) were dispersed by wind, fires, and public transport and sometimes could be found hundreds of kilometers from their source. Nonetheless, the authorities appeared to be correct in holding that the main danger was in the soil rather than in the air.

Within the territories of what is now the Commonwealth of Independent

A barbed wire fence and warning signs mark the perimeter of the zone of most intense radioactive contamination.

Conti/S. Bukowski—Sipa

States (*i.e.,* the former U.S.S.R., excluding Georgia and the Baltic republics), almost 2.5 million hectares (6.2 million acres) of land have been found to have dangerously high cesium levels (over five curies) in the soil. Of this total area, 1,350,000 hectares (3.3 million acres) are located in Belarus, 377,500 (933,000) in Ukraine, and 725,000 (1.8 million) in Russia. Belarus thus received more than

(Right and below) Uprooted residents bid good-bye to their homes in the "zone of subsequent evacuation." Four years after the accident, authorities were still identifying areas too contaminated to be inhabited.

(Top) Wojtek Laski—Sipa; (bottom) P. Le Segretain—Sygma

50% of the high-level fallout and must be considered the area of prime concern in terms of health effects. About 19% of its territory, with a population of about 2.1 million, has been affected by levels of more than one curie. Eight oblasts in Ukraine (about 10% of the republic's total territory), with a total population of 1,480,000, have been affected. Because of the size of the Russian Republic, the percentage of contaminated land is much lower (less than 0.1%), and the number of people affected, 297,400, is comparatively small. Contamination in the Bryansk region of western Russia is significant, however, and has only recently begun to receive attention. The Bryansk region also experienced significant strontium contamination of the soil; the health effect of the radiation was exacerbated by the local population's total ignorance of the extent of the irradiation in the period 1986–89.

Fate of the "liquidators"

The persons who suffered the greatest radiation exposure were the liquidators—those involved in the decontamination process. Their exact number is unknown, but it has been estimated that the entire cleanup campaign involved some 600,000 people. For the first month after the accident, their number included several hundred volunteers from as far away as the Baltic republics and even Sakhalin Island. The majority of volunteers returned home once their period of service had been completed, so it has proved impossible to develop a comprehensive register of potential medical victims. By late May 1986 the cleanup campaign was largely in the hands of military reservists, whose terms of duty often extended beyond the assigned 30 days. Though their official radiation limit was set at an emergency level of 75 rems, this level was frequently exceeded. Often the Geiger counters being used to measure exposure would record only up to 25 rems. Work on the reactor roof, in particular, involved extreme exposure to radioactive elements.

Several uncorroborated reports have noted high death rates among the liquidators. The Chernobyl Union estimates that between 8,000 and 10,000 died between 1986 and 1995, a number that has been supported by the Chernobyl committee established by the Ukrainian parliament. A figure of 5,000 deaths was cited by the former Green World chairman and Ukrainian minister of the environment, Yury Shcherbak (now Ukraine's ambassador

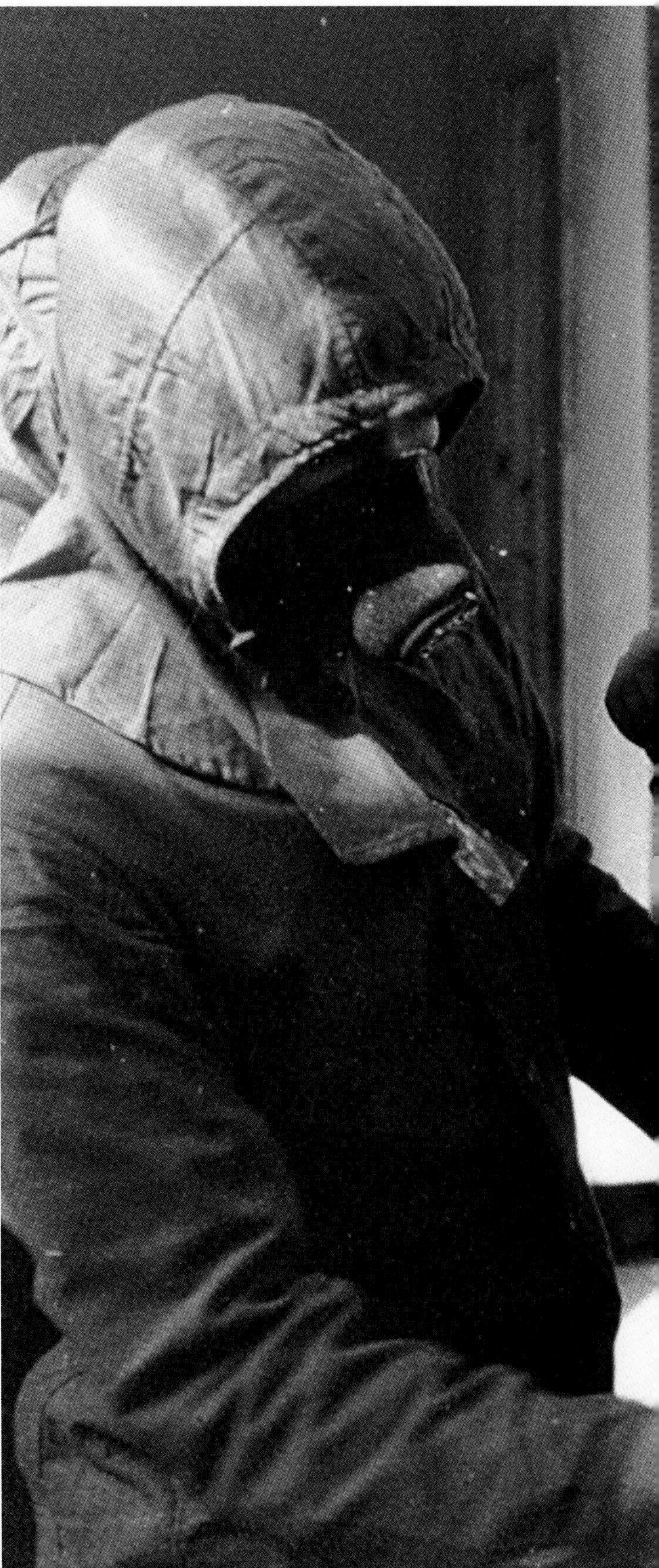

Cleanup workers prepare to ascend to the reactor roof, where the levels of radioactive elements were highest. Many thousands of these "liquidators" died as a result of such exposures.

Igor Kostin—Imago/Sygma

Robert Wallis—Saba

to the United States), and some Chernobyl officials. The highest number was that reported in the newspaper *Sovetskaya Belorussiya,* 93,000. Independent confirmation of any of these figures is lacking, however. Certainly cleanup workers were exposed to dangerous levels of radiation. In 1994 a report from Belarus asserted that 30% of those examined by means of full body scans had received a dose of 50–100 millisieverts (1 millisievert = 5–10 rems), 47% had received 100–250 millisieverts, and 7.3%, 250–500 millisieverts.

About 6% of the liquidators—approximately 38,000 individuals—are in poor health, suffering from a variety of illnesses. These include, in particular, chronic skin diseases, respiratory disorders, digestive ailments (the rate of digestive problems among the liquidators is 10–12 times higher than the average for the rest of the population), and a high incidence of heart attacks, a condition not usually associated with exposure to high levels of radiation. In addition, these workers have reported a significant number of symptoms that might be considered psychological, or psychosomatic, in origin: nervousness, insomnia, extreme irritability, and loss of libido, among others. At least one source has claimed that of those liquidators who had died since the Chernobyl disaster, one in six had committed suicide.

Leukemia: fears and reality

At the time of the Chernobyl accident, it was speculated that the first major discernible health consequence would be an increase in the incidence of leukemias. Such a development had been seen after the dropping of atomic bombs on Hiroshima and Nagasaki in 1945; an apparent rise in leukemia rates had been detected in the exposed populations as early as 18 months later, and a clearly increased rate was evident after three to four years. Despite this prognostication, 10 years after Chernobyl the increase in leukemia has been relatively small and remains within the "normal" range for the population of Europe generally. Nonetheless, a slight increase has been detected, particularly among the over-60 age group in northern Ukraine.

The most severely affected area, the Gomel region in Belarus, has had the highest number of leukemia cases. However, the correlation between exposure to high radiation levels and the development of leukemia is, at best, uncertain. Moreover, the peak postaccident year for new leukemia cases in Gomel was 1987—a time when it was probably too early for the effects of radiation exposure to be fully apparent. After Gomel the greatest number of cases in Belarus were to be found in the city of Minsk, which, although not in the fallout zone, became home to some 25,000 Chernobyl evacuees. The concentration of cases in Minsk, a city with high levels of industrial pollution, has led the chief hematologist of the republic to speculate that environmental pollution may be more to blame than radiation exposure for the local increase in leukemia. Finally, it should be noted that the current relatively high rates of leukemia in the Chernobyl-affected zones, which rank in the 75th percentile of the European average, are still lower than those of the 1970s. For example, the rate of childhood leukemia in Minsk was 48 cases per one million children in 1986–91, compared with 72.5 per million in 1979.

Pollution spews from factory smokestacks in Ukraine. Health authorities in the newly independent republics blame the depredation of the environment in the Soviet period for many of today's health problems. One expert speculated that Minsk's increased rate of childhood leukemia may be more a result of industrial pollution than one of radiation exposure.

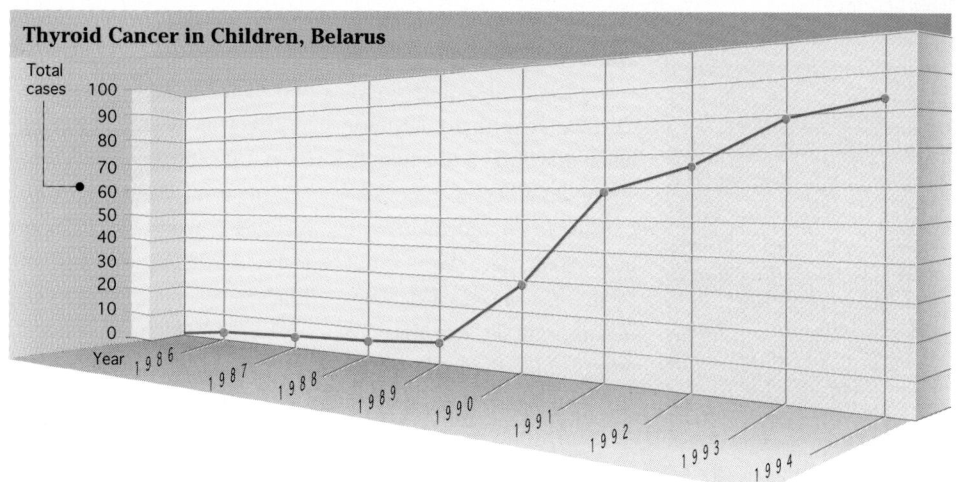

Unpredicted rates of childhood thyroid cancer

Unfortunately, our worst fears have become a reality. We know of course that the thyroid gland was affected through internal and external irradiation, and this has accelerated the rate of thyroid cancer. This increase appeared much earlier than anyone could have expected.
—Yevgeny Konoplya, director of the Institute of Radiobiology, Belarusian Academy of Sciences

The most disturbing result of Chernobyl to date has been the increased incidence of cancer of the thyroid gland among children in the exposed areas. An outbreak on the scale that has occurred was largely unanticipated and may have been worsened by the deficiency of natural iodine in the soil. Initially, the Center for Radiation Medicine in Kiev, under the jurisdiction of the Academy of Medical Sciences of the U.S.S.R., predicted that some 300 additional cases of thyroid cancer would occur in Ukraine over a 35-year period, or an increase of 1.4% over the expected level. However, the first significant increase in cases had already been noted by 1990 (though it evidently escaped the attention of the *ICP* scientists). The outbreak of thyroid cancer has been confined mainly to Belarus and, to a lesser extent, Ukraine. In Russia only seven such cases had been reported among children by early 1995.

Five years after the catastrophe, schoolchildren in Narodichi, Ukraine, were still wearing radiation-detection devices.

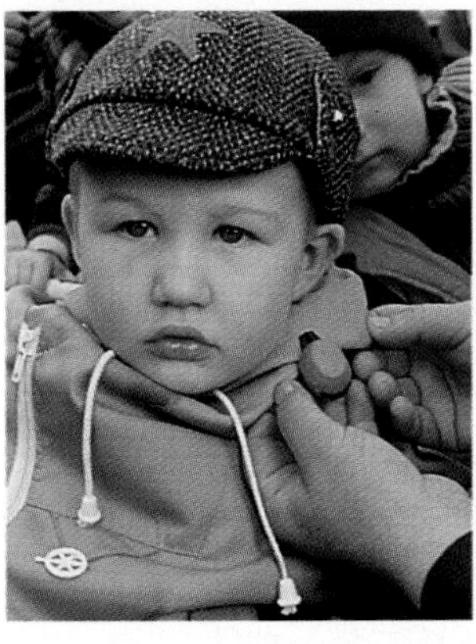

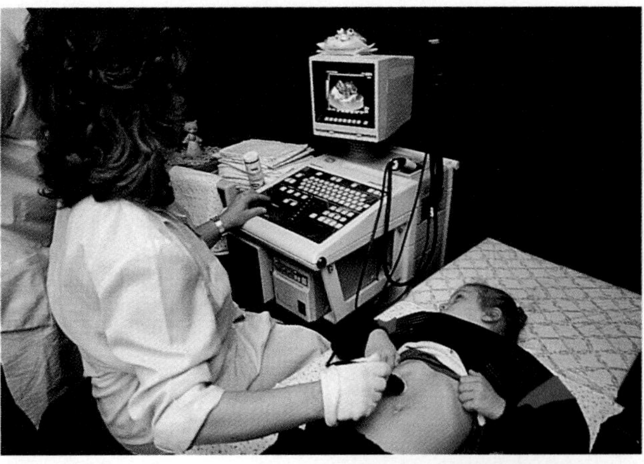

Although authorities disagree on the extent to which radiation exposure can be blamed, none dispute that there has been a significant increase in illnesses of all kinds in Ukraine and Belarus in the years since Chernobyl.

(Below left) Wojtek Laski—Sipa; (left) Gueorgui Pinkhassov—Magnum; (below right) Michael J. O'Brien—Panos

Thyroid cancer in children was a relatively rare disease in the U.S.S.R. in the 1970s and 1980s. In Belarus, E.P. Demidchik, the chief specialist at the thyroid tumor clinic in Minsk, first began to study the illness in 1966. According to Demidchik, in the late 1960s there were about 40 thyroid cancer cases diagnosed annually among both adults and children in the Belorussian S.S.R. Subsequently, an increase was seen, amounting to about one case per 100,000 inhabitants per year. Among children, however, the numbers were infinitesimal; only a total of about seven cases were detected between 1966 and 1986. After the accident, however, the numbers began to rise precipitously (*see* Graph, page 33). By the end of 1994, 333 youngsters in Belarus were suffering from this illness. The number of adult cases had also increased, from 148 cases in 1985 to 512 by the end of 1993.

Over 179 of the childhood thyroid cancer cases in Belarus, or more than 50%, were detected in the most seriously contaminated area, the Gomel region, while 76 (22.8%) were reported in Brest oblast, which also received heavy fallout. By comparison, in Vitebsk oblast, which lies north of the region of radioactive iodine fallout, only seven cases of thyroid cancer in children have been reported to date. Increased rates of other thyroid diseases have also been confined largely to the regions that received the most fallout. Thus, of the 207 cases of thyroid adenoma (a benign tumor) in Belarusian children at the end of 1994, 57 were in Gomel oblast and 40 in Brest (46.8% of the total); of 197 cases of goiter (enlargement of the thyroid gland), 82 occurred in Gomel and 32 in Brest (57.9%); and of 70 cases of thyroiditis (inflammation of the gland), the figures were 20 and 11, respectively (44.3%).

There appears to be a clear correlation between substantially increased rates of thyroid disorders and the fallout of radioactive iodine. Some notable discrepancies exist, however. A few outbreaks of thyroid cancer have occurred in areas that were not thought to have been exposed to high levels of irradiation—the Svetlogorsk region in southeastern Belarus, for example. Higher figures than reported might also have been expected in Mogilev oblast, a significant area of fallout. A U.S. radiation expert, John Jagger, has suggested that if the projected rate of increase in thyroid cancer among children was accurate, then of the 527 cases in Belarus and Ukraine in early 1995, perhaps 150 were the result of radiation fallout. Such a figure can be considered the minimum estimate; it does not explain why the number of cases has continued to rise.

What is known about the 333 young thyroid cancer patients in Belarus? First, all were born prior to the Chernobyl accident or were at the fetal stage in April 1986. Hence, the youngest of the children are now approaching the age of 10. They suffer from a highly aggressive form of cancer that can metastasize, or spread, rapidly. Indeed, these patients must be operated on shortly after diagnosis. Repeat surgery is necessary in about 40% of cases. Generally, the younger the patient, the better the chances for a complete recovery. Demidchik has noted that in the past the 10-year survival rate was 100% for patients in the 15–34 age group. Among the present victims, only one has died, a girl whose death was attributed to complications from lung metastases.

The appropriate course of treatment for thyroid cancer is a matter of debate. In contrast to Western practice, physicians in Belarus excise only the affected part of the thyroid, not the entire gland. Owing in part to the necessity of lifetime monitoring of those affected, the vast majority of these operations (unlike procedures for some other Chernobyl-related diseases) have been carried out locally rather than abroad. If the number of cases continues to rise, however, the disease may ultimately become too great a burden to be borne by the precarious health care systems of the newly independent states. In both Belarus and Ukraine, there is a notable shortage of many drugs; Moscow-supplied vaccines for newborns are often substandard; "donations" from abroad account for most of the advanced equipment in children's hospitals; and, according to a Canadian pediatrician who visited clinics and hospitals in Minsk in December 1993, medical equipment was outmoded—it was similar to that in Western hospitals of the 1930s and 1940s. A study conducted by the Institute of Radiation Medicine in Belarus showed that health problems, especially among

(Below) These two young Chernobyl victims were among many who were sent to Havana for medical treatment. (Right) A doctor at the Pediatric Center near Minsk studies photos of children born with congenital defects. All are now dead.

(Left) P. Robert—Sygma; (right) Wojtek Laski—Sipa

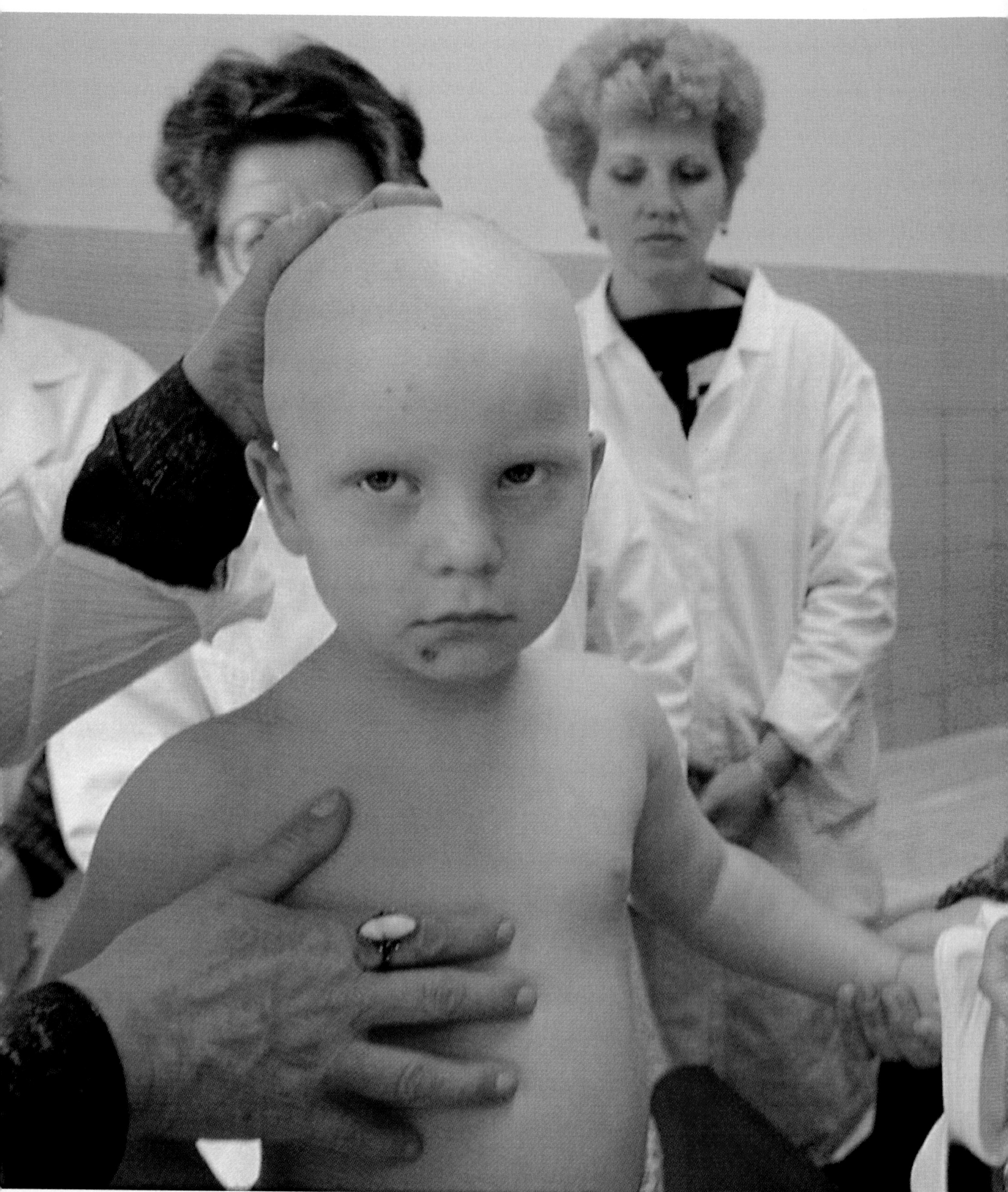

Gerd Ludwig—Visum

Doctors in Kiev are baffled by a young boy's hair loss. Outbreaks of mysterious health problems are a source of constant anxiety for those living in the shadow of Chernobyl.

children, were considerably worse in areas with heavy industrial pollution, such as the industrial Zavadsky district in Minsk. The recent increases in thyroid cancer must therefore be considered within the context of a general health crisis in which environmental hazards, outdated medical facilities and equipment, and a struggling economy all play a part.

"Radiophobia" and stress

Today more than 12,000 "Chernobylites" live in Minsk. The majority got on the list for urgent removal from the contaminated areas: the sick, the disabled, families with young children, the old and the lonely—those for whom the "radioactive AIDS" is especially dangerous. . . . However, having removed people from small villages to the capital city, our authorities consider the matter closed. They have left the Chernobyl resettlers alone with their problems, cares and troubles. These weakened people have not gained health by moving . . . they understand the old truth: the drowned have been put in the care of the drowning, especially in our new "market" era.

—article in the Ukrainian newspaper *Dobryy vechar*, Sept. 20, 1993

There is no question that both Ukraine and Belarus have experienced a significant and marked rise in illness in the decade since the Chernobyl disaster. Not only have these republics seen major outbreaks of "obsolete" infectious diseases—particularly diphtheria, cholera, and tuberculosis—but the incidence of juvenile diabetes mellitus has risen notably, and the disorder has begun to affect children at an increasingly younger age. While there is no discernible connection between childhood diabetes and exposure to radiation, doctors at the Minsk Children's Hospital No. 3, which this author visited in 1993, were convinced that the nuclear accident was responsible for the increases in this condition. Similar conclusions have been drawn about the increase in anemia, digestive and respiratory diseases, and, most of all, the disorder known in the affected areas as "Chernobyl AIDS"—lowered resistance to infection due to radiation exposure.

Some experts have dismissed the claims that radiation exposure is responsible for these ailments, labeling them as "radiophobia" (exaggerated fears of radiation). Certainly the incident provoked many fears. Yet it would be misleading to attribute increased incidence of illness solely to radiophobia. For one thing, detection of disease has improved. In the Gomel region, for example, it was noted recently that there are a sufficient number of doctors for the first time in the history of that province. In Belarus as a whole, some 2,200 new doctors are completing medical training annually. As a result of international humanitarian aid, many persons living in rural settlements have received adequate medical attention, often for the first time in their lives. Another factor affecting health is that fear of radiation, combined with awareness of the presence of radiation in the soil, has led to widespread malnutrition, some of it self-imposed. Moreover, the stress caused by evacuation—or, conversely, the anxiety of living in a radiation-affected zone—is likely to influence people's resistance to illness.

Robert Gale, a U.S. physician who performed bone marrow transplants on the earliest Chernobyl victims, noted in 1991 that every hospital bed in Kiev was occupied, although it was not clear whether all of those hospitalized were suffering from the consequences, direct or indirect, of Chernobyl. In a survey conducted in Gomel, 52% said they

Control-room personnel oversee the operation of reactor No. 3. Although declared unsafe in 1994, the Chernobyl nuclear plant continues to provide power for several million Ukrainians.

believed they were suffering from psychological tension or stress. Many attributed this stress to the unreliability of official information and their lack of faith in scientific analyses released to date. Some residents of Belarus have confided to this author their fear that as a result of Chernobyl, the health of future generations is in jeopardy and the nation itself may be doomed to extinction. Such pessimistic prognostications undoubtedly affect both mental and physical well-being.

Continuing crisis

As the 10th anniversary of Chernobyl approaches, a clear picture of the health impact of the disaster is emerging. In the areas that received the heaviest fallout, the failure of a predicted "epidemic" of leukemia to materialize has been offset by an alarming increase in thyroid cancer. Many other diseases have also increased, and thousands of those injured or made ill during the cleanup process still require medical attention.

The individual republics are economically ill-equipped to deal with a tragedy of this magnitude. Until recently, the financial burden of Chernobyl—especially the costs of evacuation, compensation payments for abandoned homes and land, and construction of new housing for evacuees—consumed 22% of the Belarusian budget and 13% of that of Ukraine. In 1994–95 both republics were facing financial and economic crises and had become dependent on international aid to deal with Chernobyl-engendered problems. Ukraine could afford neither to rebury the exposed reactor nor to shut down the Chernobyl nuclear power station, which, albeit belatedly, was declared unsafe after a 1994 IAEA inspection. Faced with a continuing energy crisis, the government of Ukraine currently hopes that the Chernobyl plant can continue to operate until the year 2000 and that a new nuclear power station will be constructed in the vicinity.

Chernobyl's impact on the well-being of the affected population of Belarus, Ukraine, and Russia must be put into perspective. The health effects of the disaster are only one aspect of a general crisis situation. Factors responsible for this crisis include the poor state of health care generally; lack of state investment in the health system dating back to the Soviet period; environmental degradation resulting from industrial expansion in the Soviet period and, es-

Gerd Ludwig—Visum

Gueorgui Pinkhassov—Magnum

pecially in the major cities, from pollution-emitting public transport; and official secrecy following the accident, which led to people's consuming contaminated food and liquid. The situation is exacerbated by the poor diet and unhealthy lifestyle of Eastern Europeans generally. (In Russia the life expectancy for males dropped from 64.9 years in 1987 to 59 in 1992, undoubtedly in part as a result of heavy smoking and alcohol consumption. By comparison, life-expectancy figures from France and Germany were 72.9 and 72.2, respectively.)

Above all, Chernobyl has affected the health of children, whose rapidly growing bodies are particularly susceptible to the effects of radiation. In Belarus in 1993 some 38 humanitarian organizations were in operation and were especially committed to serving young victims' needs. Birthrates in Ukraine and Belarus fell dramatically after 1986, and in 1992 the number of congenital abnormalities among newborns was 2.5 times higher than in 1986. In the contaminated zone of Belarus, medical authorities noted, also in 1992, that 40% of schoolchildren who were examined had diseases of the heart and blood vessels. Clearly, while both the health authorities and the general public may exaggerate the aftereffects of Chernobyl, the concern about the health of future generations is a legitimate one.

Hold the Mayo! American Attitudes About Food

by Judith Ashley, Ph.D., R.D.

Illustration by Cathy Hull

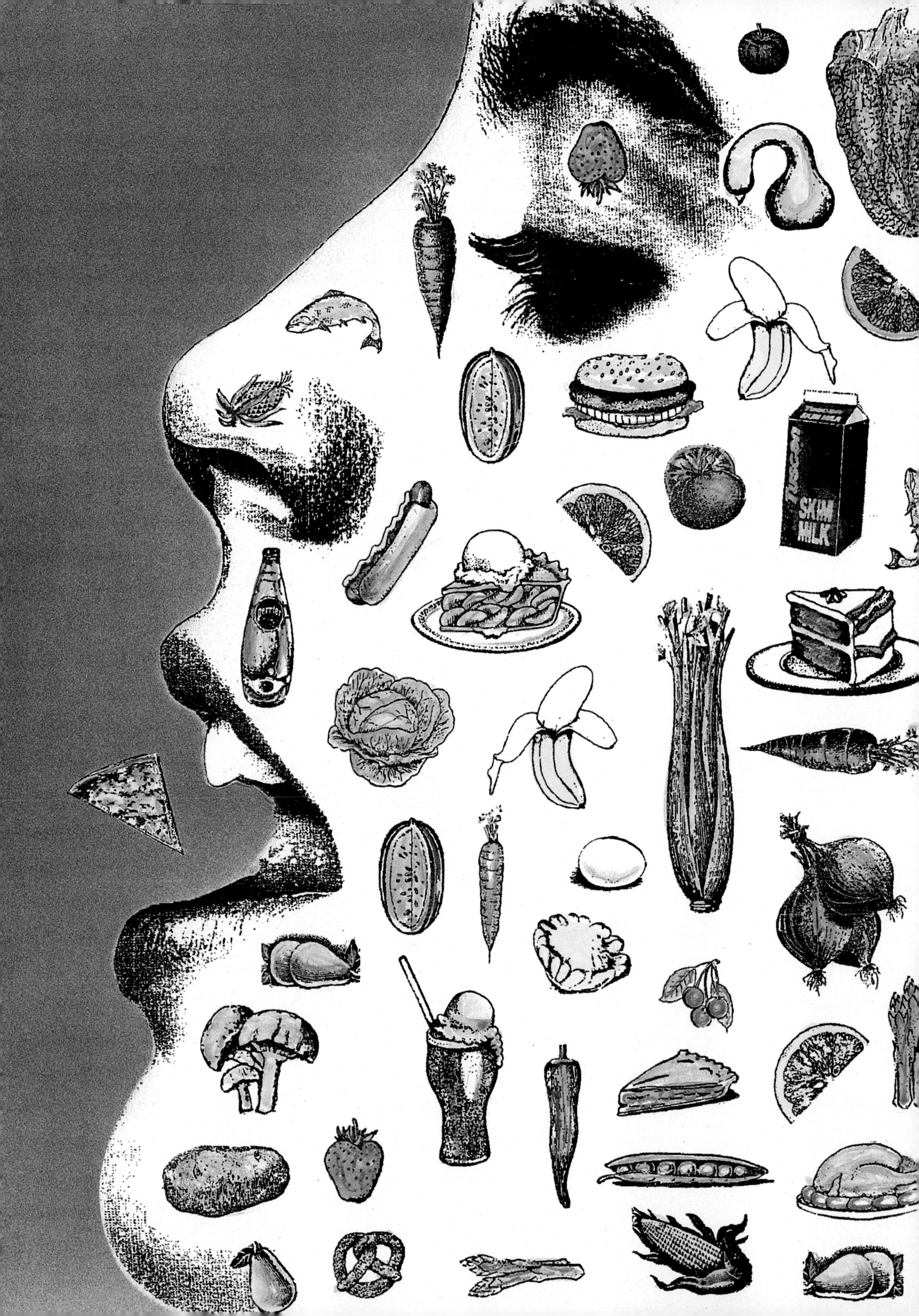
SKIM
MILK

Rickets and pellagra—vitamin-deficiency diseases that once were widespread—are virtually unknown in the U.S. today. Instead, in the 1990s the most prevalent nutrition-related health problems are conditions associated with overconsumption of nutrients. The U.S. has among the world's highest rates of atherosclerotic heart disease, as well as high rates of those cancers (*e.g.,* breast, prostate, colorectal) thought to be linked to a high-fat, low-fiber diet. Moreover, increasing numbers of Americans are developing lifestyle-related forms of diabetes, osteoporosis, and gastrointestinal disorders.

Judith Ashley, Ph.D., R.D., *is Assistant Professor, Division of Clinical Nutrition, University of California at Los Angeles School of Medicine.*

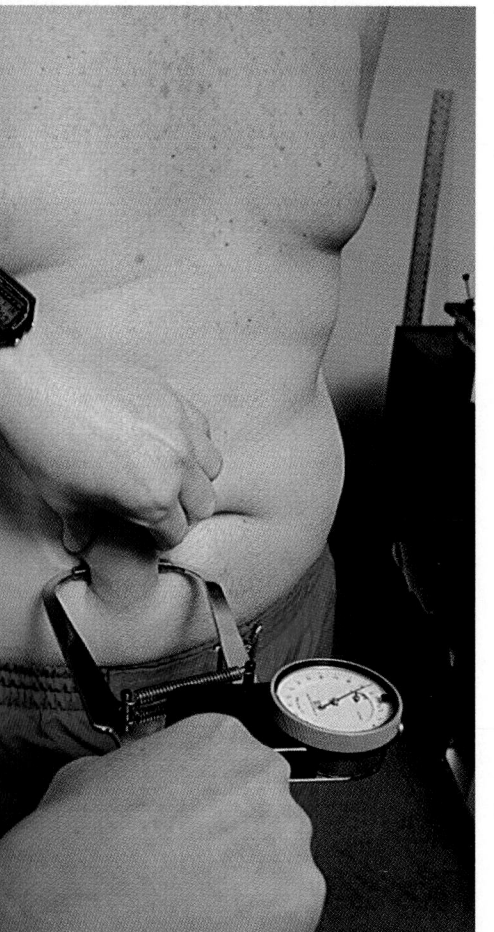

More than 30% of U.S. adults are obese—*i.e.,* 20% or more above desirable body weight. The health consequences and costs of that overindulgence are enormous.

Frank Siteman—Stock, Boston

Obesity—a predisposing factor in diabetes, high blood pressure, and many other ailments—is rampant. A recent survey by the National Center for Health Statistics (NCHS) showed that by the early 1990s one-third of U.S. adults were overweight, compared with only one-fourth a few decades earlier; the prevalence of obesity had increased 8%. A 1995 report by the Institute of Medicine concluded that more than $70 billion in U.S. health care costs was related to the population's overindulgence.

Long-term patterns in disease prevalence have complex origins, based in social and economic as well as behavioral changes. Like most developed countries, the U.S. has in the past century undergone a transformation from a sparsely populated, primarily agricultural country to an industrialized nation in which a majority of the people live in urban areas. The nature of work has changed; many Americans today are employed in professions that did not even exist at the turn of the century. Sedentary jobs and widespread ownership of cars and laborsaving appliances make for a population that engages in little regular physical activity. But of the many factors that can affect an individual's health status or risk of disease—so-called risk factors—perhaps none has changed so much as what Americans eat. The ways food is produced, purchased, stored, prepared, and consumed in the U.S. have been revolutionized in a matter of decades.

Land of too much

In the earlier part of the 20th century, Americans bought most of their food from small neighborhood grocery stores. Grocers obtained their goods directly from local growers and producers; food was sold in bulk, without brand names. By the 1950s, however, with the burgeoning of food technology and the increasing speed and sophistication of transportation, U.S. consumers had a diverse array of foods available to them. Through advertising, the food industry influenced both the marketing and the perception of food. For example, factory-produced foods were promoted—and rapidly accepted—as being more "wholesome" and "pure" than those from the bins of the corner grocery. By the 1960s food purveyors were offering not just prepackaged processed foods but so-called convenience foods designed to appeal to the needs of a fast-paced society. An entire day's menu could be built around frozen foods alone. It was not long before canned, packaged, and frozen items vastly outnumbered the fresh foods offered

Charles Osgood—Chicago Tribune

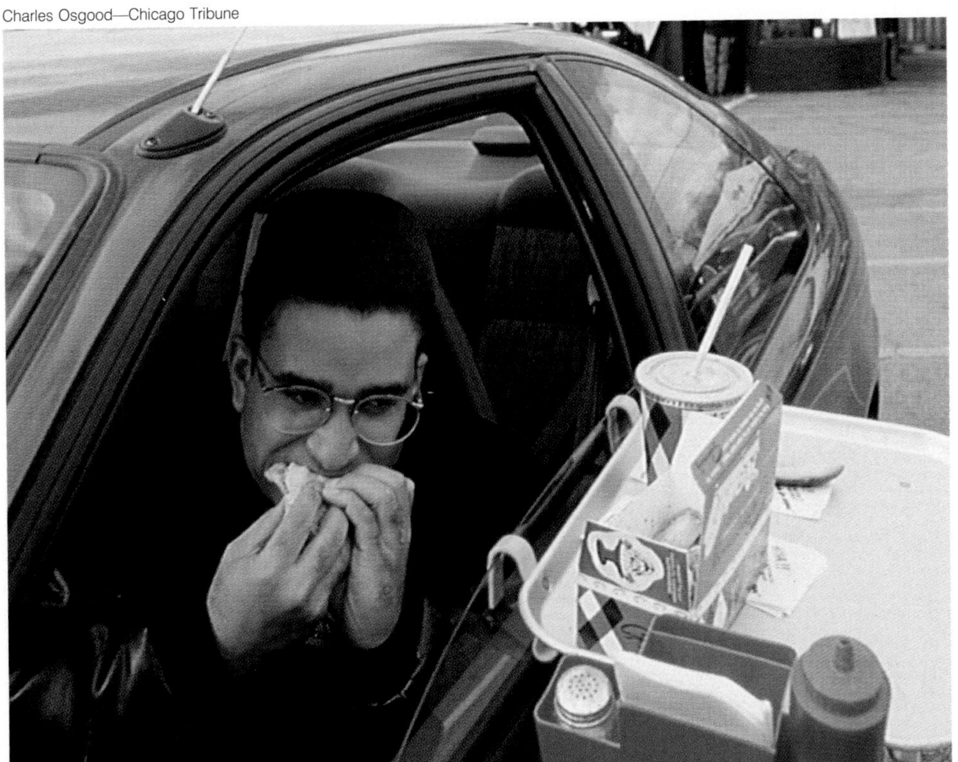

So-called fast foods represent about 35% of U.S. food sales. The easy availability of such high-fat, high-calorie fare has played an integral part in the "fattening" of America.

for sale in most stores. Then fast food arrived, growing from a mere 5% of food sales in the 1950s to some 35% in the '90s.

Availability, abundance, and variety have played a major part in fashioning American tastes and eating habits. In many ways today's overindulgence and overnutrition may be seen as natural consequences of life in the "land of plenty." Eating too much, once an occasional event, has become a national pastime.

Also a regular feature of life for many Americans is the weight-loss diet. According to some studies, half of the population is on a diet at any given time, and more than $30 billion a year is spent on weight-loss programs and products. Overeating, however, is only one manifestation of the preoccupation with food. Others, equally dangerous to health, are the eating disorders, including anorexia, bulimia, and binge eating. Anorexia nervosa, which affects primarily teenage and young adult women, doubled in incidence in the 1980s. Clearly, food and eating have become the focus of a conflict the health implications of which extend far beyond the bounds of physical well-being.

"Eat this . . . don't eat that"

In the 19th century, Americans learned of the health-promoting properties of food from "health food" enthusiasts such as Sylvester Graham (inventor of the graham cracker) and John Harvey Kellogg, a physician and vegetarian who promoted cold cereal as a "healthy" replacement for meat at breakfast. (His brother, W.K. Kellogg, established the cereal business.) Although ready-to-eat cereals have retained their popularity to the present day, interest in the relationship between diet and health waxed and waned as food fads passed in and out of vogue. Then, about 25–30 years ago, the first epidemiological investigations specifically linked heart disease to eating habits; the public's attention has been riveted on diet ever since.

As the epidemiological evidence accumulated, confirming an association between what people eat and the diseases they fall prey to, the federal government and health and nutrition professionals began to advise the public about diet. No fewer than 15 major sets of "dietary recommendations" have been issued in the past two decades—from the Senate Select Committee's *Dietary Goals for the United States* (1977) to *The Surgeon General's Report on Nutrition and Health* (1988) to the Food Guide Pyramid released in 1992 by the U.S. Department of Agriculture (USDA). Common themes run through virtually all of these guidelines: (1) eat less fat, saturated fat, and cholesterol; (2) reduce the intake of salt and sugar; and (3) increase the consumption of complex carbohydrates (fruits, vegetables, and whole grains).

Have nearly 20 years' worth of diet exhortations had any effect on what Americans eat? Overall the data show that people have made *some* dietary changes based on the experts' recommendations. At the same time, those data reflect both positive and negative trends in national eating patterns. The existence of contradictory trends indicates that Americans are either confused about the dietary advice they have been receiving or ambivalent about following it. Currently, public health authorities are concerned about some very re-

The Granger Collection, New York

Chef BOY-AR-DEE
SPAGHETTI DINNER
Sauce with Mushrooms
MEATLESS
Chef BOY-AR-DEE
SPAGHETTI SAUCE WITH MUSHROOMS
BOY-AR-DEE Grated Cheese
Chef BOY-AR-DEE SPAGHETTI
SPECIALLY MADE FROM CHOICE
When your family clamors for something different...
Delicious Mealtime Magic! Only 12 short minutes is all it takes to put this wonderful Italian-style spaghetti dinner on your table. A real taste treat to brighten up your family's meals! Everything you want in one Chef package! The finest, quick-cooking spaghetti . . . ready to heat, tomato-rich sauce with tender mushroom pieces . . . and lots of tangy, grated cheese. A dream of a meal for 3—at only about 14¢ a serving.
Quick tempting...tasty
CHEF BOY-AR-DEE
SPAGHETTI DINNER
with Mushroom Sauce or Meat Sauce
It's the specially blended sauce that makes Chef Spaghetti Dinners—and all the many other Chef products—so extra-specially good.
Try Chef Boy-Ar-Dee Ravioli, Spaghetti and Meat Balls, Sauce with Meat, Sauce with Mushrooms, Sauce with Meat Balls, Spanish Sauce, and Meat Balls with Gravy. So why not make one night a week "Chef Night"? You'll save time, save money, serve wonderful meals!

Foods that could go from package to table in a matter of minutes found a ready market in the fast-paced U.S. society of the 1950s.

cent evidence of "nutritional backsliding" on the part of the American public.

What we know versus what we do

Periodic surveys by various government and food-industry groups monitor the dietary patterns and nutritional status of the U.S. population. For the most part, these studies show that Americans have been taking the recommendations of the nutrition authorities to heart. For example, the third and most recent National Health and Nutrition Examination Study, or NHANES III (1988–91), conducted by the NCHS, showed that in the previous two decades total fat intake had been reduced from about 40% to 34% (a positive indication, even though it failed to meet the level of 30% or less called for in national recommendations). Carbohydrate intake had risen to 48% for males and 50% for females, but dietary fiber intake—at 12 grams per day for females and 17 for males—was well below the National Cancer Institute's recommended level of 20–30 grams.

The USDA's Continuing Survey of Food Intakes by Individuals (CSFII) found similar trends. Compared with data from 1977–78, the most recent CSFII (1989–91) showed that Americans were eating more grains, had replaced whole milk with low-fat and skim, and were eating less meat. However, consumption of fruits and vegetables—major sources of complex carbohydrates and fiber—had changed little.

"Trends 94," a survey by the Food Marketing Institute, a trade organization that represents the food industry, revealed that more than 60% of U.S. consumers acknowledged that their diets could be "somewhat" or "a lot" healthier and that they were "very concerned" about the nutritional content of their food. Ninety-four percent said that they had made some changes in

their eating habits; a third of this group reported having cut down on consumption of fats and oils. A smaller percentage said they were eating more fish, more fiber, and less salt.

A disparity between what Americans know about healthy eating and what they actually eat was evident in the findings of the Diet and Health Knowledge Survey that accompanied the CSFII. For example, 7 of 10 respondents who were the primary meal preparers in their households were aware of health problems related to consumption of fat, but only one-fourth of them limited their own or their families' fat intake to the recommended 30% or less of total calories. When asked to compare the levels of fat, saturated fat, and cholesterol in their own diets with healthful levels, both men and women overestimated the amount of cholesterol they consumed but underestimated their intake of fat and saturated fat.

Another recent survey, conducted by the International Food Information Council (IFIC) in conjunction with the American Dietetic Association (ADA), confirmed that most Americans have the basic knowledge needed to make healthy choices. When questioned about foods they were eliminating from their diets because of health concerns, a majority cited fat (74%), saturated fat (68%), cholesterol (67%), and fried foods (64%). Their answers also identified some major misconceptions. One in three respondents said he or she believed that high-fat foods cannot be part of a healthy diet, even if balanced with low-fat choices. Whereas the experts recommend that the diet as a whole provide no more than 30% of calories from fat, 65% of respondents thought that every food in a "healthy diet" must derive less than 30% of calories from fat.

Is overnutrition a natural consequence of life in the "land of plenty"?

(Top) © Don Smetzer—Tony Stone Images; (right) Cary Wolinsky—Stock, Boston

The joint IFIC/ADA study reaffirmed that Americans eat primarily for pleasure—more than 90% reported that they find eating enjoyable—but for many that pleasure was diminished by health concerns (about fat, cholesterol, and weight gain) or feelings of guilt. Nearly half of those questioned said they believe that the foods they like are not good for them; 36% admitted feeling guilty about eating favorite foods.

© Naoki Okamoto—Black Star

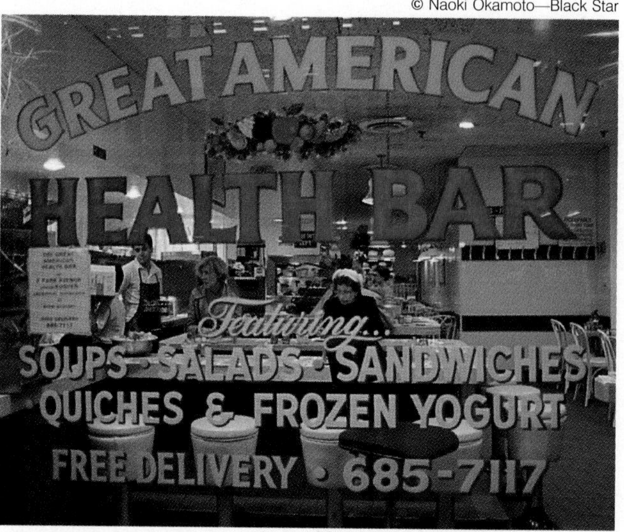

Although American consumers apparently know how to make healthy choices, they often have difficulty putting that knowledge into practice. When dining out, especially, many eschew eating "sensibly."

The urge to splurge

While the data from the late 1980s and early '90s indicate that most Americans understand the need for dietary changes—and are willing to make such changes—more recent statistics indicate a widening gap between what consumers know and what they actually do. For example, according to USDA figures, the consumption of beef was at its highest level in five years in 1994; Americans ate about 28.6 kilograms (63 pounds) of beef per person (compared with only 6.8 kilograms [15 pounds] of "heart healthy" fish and shellfish). The Institute of Shortening and Edible Oils reported that in 1994 per capita consumption of butter, lard, margarine, and oils also rose slightly over that of previous years. Some authorities interpret these data as a sign that Americans are tired of deprivation and have abandoned the goal of dietary modification. But if this is true, what explains the record sales in 1994 of reduced-fat cookies and crackers? Perhaps the purchase of such products is simply an exercise in self-delusion, or it may represent a concession, albeit a reluctance, to prudence.

Ambivalence and conflicting desires are apparent when Americans dine out. In a telephone survey published in *Restaurants and Institutions* in June 1994, consumers were asked what healthful foods they thought restaurants should offer. Almost 48% wanted more salads, vegetables, seafood, poultry, and vegetarian items; 25% requested items with reduced fat, cholesterol, sodium, and calories; and about 13% said chefs should adapt more healthful food-preparation methods such as baking, broiling, and steaming. Only 8%, however, expressed satisfaction with the healthy choices being offered, and many said that when eating out they want to splurge.

Cheeseburger on a whole-wheat bun

What kind of picture emerges from all these data? Can any conclusions about Americans' attitudes toward food be drawn from the mass of surveys and statistics? Behavioral scientists and nutrition professionals have offered several explanations for the apparent contradictions in attitudes and behavior. Some contend that Americans today, having already denied themselves much in the name of health, are simply tired of trying to be "good." A comparison of the 1988 and 1993 Annual Lifestyle surveys conducted by the market research firm Yankelovich Partners revealed that the percentage of Americans not concerned with maintaining their weight had increased (from 49% to 52%) and the number who described themselves as strongly committed to fitness had dropped (42% versus 30%). Mihaly Csikszentmihalyi, professor of psychology at the University of Chicago and an authority on human motivation, sees this apparent backlash against health-promoting behaviors as a growing realization on the part of Americans that too many restrictions can make life intolerable. To people faced with increasing social, economic, and personal pressures, he observes, matters such as diet can come to seem trivial.

Barbara Posner, director for research at Boston University and a leading investigator in the ongoing Framingham Study (a long-term investigation of lifestyle and disease in several generations of residents of Framingham, Massachusetts), has a different view of Americans' mixed success in improving their diets. She speculates that while the public may find simple dietary changes easy to make, more complex modifications are difficult for the majority to implement. Posner also thinks that the enormous array of food choices available to U.S. consumers makes it harder for them to achieve a healthy balance.

Eileen Kennedy, a nutrition policy coordinator for

© Annie Griffiths Belt—Aurora

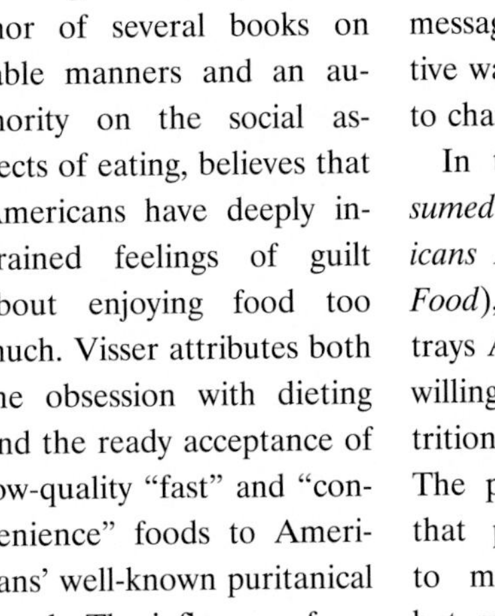

The pleasurable aspects of eating endure, although for many Americans food is also a source of guilt. In a recent survey half of the respondents acknowledged that the foods they like are not healthful ones.

the USDA, believes that nutrition professionals have failed to deliver a clear message about fat, calories, and weight control. Thus, many individuals who have cut the amount of fat in their diets mistakenly assume that they can eat all they want of reduced-fat and fat-free foods—without gaining weight. Kennedy and others in the field point to the fact that many Americans have no idea what constitutes a normal portion. Food labels typically underestimate usual portion sizes: is "a serving" of pasta 57 grams (2 ounces), as the label indicates, 113 grams (4 ounces, the amount specified in most cookbooks), or 227 grams (8 ounces, an average restaurant portion)?

Margaret Visser, the author of several books on table manners and an authority on the social aspects of eating, believes that Americans have deeply ingrained feelings of guilt about enjoying food too much. Visser attributes both the obsession with dieting and the ready acceptance of low-quality "fast" and "convenience" foods to Americans' well-known puritanical streak. The influence of puritanism is often invoked as a reason why U.S. attitudes toward alcohol swing periodically from self-indulgence to self-denial; perhaps a similar principle influences food choices.

Physician C. Wayne Callaway maintains that most health professionals, in emphasizing balanced diets and weight control, neglect the pleasurable aspects of food. In the process of promoting healthful habits, they convey negative messages about food. Many public health authorities agree that negative messages are not an effective way to persuade people to change their habits.

In the 1994 book *Consumed* (subtitled *Why Americans Love, Hate, and Fear Food*), Michelle Stacey portrays Americans as only too willing to embrace every nutrition fad that comes along. The problem, then, is not that people are reluctant to make dietary changes but rather that they do so too readily and on the basis of meager factual evidence. Stacey suggests as an alternative "enlightened hedonism," an approach to nutrition that would strike a balance between information and pleasure.

Physician, biochemist, and humanist scholar Leon Kass, author of *The Hungry Soul* (1994), argues that middle-class Americans have become alienated from the cultural and spiritual meanings of food. He sees the recent rise in incidence of eating disorders as a reflection of this alienation.

Ultimately, whether one believes that Americans are exasperated, confused, alienated, unable to resist temptation, or simply deluded about how much they really eat, the one inescapable conclusion about their attitudes and behaviors toward food is that there is an enormous gap between knowledge and practice. Is this, perhaps, the "American paradox"?

An American paradox: eating fat-free foods but getting fatter all the time.

(Top and left) © Jacques M. Chenet—Gamma Liaison

Pass the Pâté: Examining the French Diet

by Cathy J. Saloff-Coste, M.S., R.D.

"The Square in Front of Les Halles" by Victor Gabriel Gilbert (1847–1933), Musée des Beaux-Arts, Le Havre; Bridgeman Art Library, London. Copyright reserved

The French have a long and cherished relationship with food and gastronomy. Their cuisine has evolved over the centuries and undergone many changes, yet to this day it remains grounded in agricultural, rural traditions.

Historically, there are three major types of French cuisine. The "classic cuisine," or *grande cuisine,* of French restaurants includes world-renowned dishes—such as veal Orloff and eggs *à la reine*—based on standard recipes and served in a ritualized style. "Cuisine bourgeoise" relies on simpler dishes and is based on recipes passed from one generation to the next. Typical examples are pot-au-feu (a long-simmered stew of beef, bones, and vegetables), *blanquette de veau* (veal in a white wine sauce), *gigot rôti* (roast leg of lamb), coq au vin (chicken braised in wine), and *rôti de porc* (roast pork). Finally, "regional cuisine" consists of specialty dishes from different parts of France that are derived *du terroir,* or from the soil. Examples include cassoulet (a stew of legumes, sausages, and vegetables) from Toulouse and Castelnaudary in the southwest, the fish stew called bouillabaisse from Marseille, *choucroute* (sausage and sauerkraut) from Alsace in the northeast, and from Provence *soupe au pistou* (a soup of white beans, pasta, and vegetables to which pesto is added). An enormous variety of wines, cheeses, sausages, and even candy and pastries from particular regions are also well-known and appreciated.

In addition to these three distinct types of cuisine, there is also a basic, traditional French style of cooking and eating. It is organized around three

Cathy J. Saloff-Coste, M.S., R.D., *is a Nutrition Consultant in Toulouse, France.*

Magis—La Photothèque Culinaire

(Below and opposite page) Magis—La Photothèque Culinaire

(Right) The stew called cassoulet is a regional dish from southwestern France. (Far right) Hearty pot-au-feu is representative of the "cuisine bourgeoise." (Opposite page) A salmon soufflé in the tradition of the *grande cuisine* contains liberal amounts of butter, eggs, and cream. These three traditional cuisines continue to be enjoyed by the French today.

structured meals per day with a *goûter,* or afternoon snack, for children. Breakfast typically consists of bread or rolls with butter and jam and coffee with milk. Lunch is a complete meal, perhaps soup with bread and potatoes. Dinner, which is for most urban dwellers the main repast of the day, includes an appetizer, a main course of meat and vegetable, cheese, fruit or dessert, and coffee. And, of course, no dinner would be complete without bread and wine. The preparation time of meals in the traditional style is generally long; as much as two and a half hours a day might be devoted to cooking.

French cuisine: a brief history

During the medieval period and the Renaissance, the wealthy classes dined lavishly, feasting on beef, mutton, and wild game and consuming liberal quantities of wine. At the same time, Christian values influenced eating patterns. The calendar included more than 150 fast days a year, and devout Christians strove to avoid the sin of gluttony, using food merely to maintain good health or to treat illness. Spices such as ginger, cinnamon, cloves, and pepper were used regularly, as much to disguise the flavor of the food (which was often spoiled) as to complement it. In the 15th and 16th centuries, sugar and butter became more prominent in French cooking.

The 16th century marked the emergence of cooking as a culinary art in France. Indigenous condiments such as herbs, garlic, and mushrooms replaced the pungent spices favored in earlier times. Kings and the very wealthy employed their own chefs. The French nobility and aristocracy took cuisine seriously; the ability to serve well-prepared meals in a convivial atmosphere was a matter of pride. An anecdote from the second half of the century demonstrates this well. François Vatel, a chef and maître d'hôtel to the nobility, committed suicide following the humiliation of having run out of food at a party for 3,000 in honor of Louis XIV.

A series of cookbooks, beginning with the master chef La Varenne's *Le Cuisinier françois* (1652), made the case for a simpler style of cooking than had become the norm in France. This movement culminated in the "modern cuisine" of Vincent La Chapelle, author of the multivolume *Le Cuisinier moderne* (1735). The goal was to retain the culinary variety of the preceding century but to create less extravagant and pretentious dishes. La Chapelle's ideas were criticized but remained influential until the early 1800s, when Marie-Antoine (Antonin) Carême introduced a more grandiose cuisine, featuring *grandes sauces* such as béchamel

Photos, E.T. Archive

Marie-Antoine (Antonin) Carême has been called "architect of the French cuisine." (Inset) Two ornate Carême constructions from *The Art of French Cooking* (1847).

and Mornay, dishes prepared au gratin (covered with bread crumbs or cheese and browned), and flaming desserts. The proliferation of restaurants starting in the 19th century increased the demand for meals based on a fixed menu and featuring dishes that could be rapidly prepared. The culinary creations of Georges-Auguste Escoffier, premier chef of the 1920s and '30s, fulfilled these requirements.

It was not until the second half of the 20th century that the next major trend in French cooking, the so-called nouvelle cuisine, emerged. In many ways this culinary style, with its emphasis on clarity of taste and lack of artifice, resembles the "modern" cuisine of the 18th century. According to one version of the story, while dining out in the early 1970s, Henri Gault and Christian Millau, two renowned French food critics, requested a very light meal; the chef Paul Bocuse produced a green bean salad that the diners pronounced exceptional in its simplicity. With this dish a new culinary style was born. In addition to its hallmark simplicity, the major principles of nouvelle cuisine are the use of ingredients at their "peak of freshness" and the avoidance of overcooking and heavy sauces that would mask natural flavors.

City life and working wives

Beginning around 1950, profound social changes prompted a dramatic alteration in eating habits

Hulton Deutsch

Georges-Auguste Escoffier (far right in the photograph) inspects a dessert prepared under his direction by the chefs of the ship *Berengaria*. Escoffier's innovations in food preparation and service revolutionized restaurant dining.

The renowned chef Paul Bocuse is a leading practitioner of nouvelle cuisine. One of the dishes prepared in his restaurant just north of Lyon is a fillet of red mullet served in beurre blanc (butter sauce flavored with lemon juice) with finely diced tomato and zucchini and accompanied by wild mushrooms.

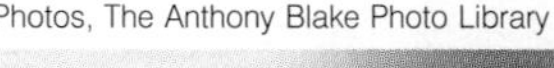
Photos, The Anthony Blake Photo Library

© Erica Lansner

Social changes in France in recent decades have increased the number of meals eaten away from home, which, in turn, has had a major impact on dietary patterns.

in France. In his book *L'Homnivore* (1990; rev. ed., 1993)—the title is a play on the word *omnivore; homme* is French for "man"—the French sociologist Claude Fischler, director of research at the National Center for Scientific Research, Paris, cites several societal developments that affected eating patterns. Chief among them was the increasing industrialization of France, which caused many people to migrate from the country to urban settings. The working class diminished as the numbers of managerial and professional jobs grew. People began buying televisions, cars, and household appliances, which led, respectively, to new ways of deciding what foods to buy, purchasing those foods, and preparing them. In the meantime, with the decline in jobs involving physical labor, physical activity decreased, and energy needs fell from more than 3,000 calories per day to 2,200 for men and from an estimated 2,400 to 1,800 for women. Further, in recent decades women have become a major element in the workforce, and as a result, they have less time for cooking than they once did. Today the average amount of time spent preparing meals is less than 40 minutes per day.

Several other factors have contributed to the altered French eating patterns. First, people eat out more often; in 1991 three meals per person per week (representing 20% of the food budget) were eaten away from home, compared with two in 1969. These meals are eaten not only in restaurants but also in fast-food establishments, as well as in school and company cafeterias.

Second, the emergence of the *hypermarchés* and *supermarchés* has revolutionized the way people shop. These extremely large grocery stores carry virtually all foods—the former have nonfood items as well—and are especially common in the suburban areas. In 1991 the average individual spent more than 62% of his or her food budget in these stores, compared with 21% in 1971. The convenience offered by "one-stop" shopping, along with the plethora of foods available at any season, has seduced the French consumer. Many people, especially Parisians, continue to buy such products as fresh fruits and vegetables and fish at small specialty shops, but other merchants have suffered greatly as a result of the shift to the supermarket. In particular, the *épicerie,* or traditional grocer's store, and the *crémerie,* or dairy shop, have lost half of their sales to the big supermarkets. The *boulangerie* (bread bakery), *pâtisserie* (pastry store), *boucherie* (butcher shop), and charcuterie (specialty store for sausages and cured meats) are surviving, however. Moreover, 35% of French households have vegetable gardens; foods raised or grown at home represent more than 5% of the average budget. Agricultural tradition remains deeply rooted.

The U.S. presence in the French food industry since 1950, and especially in the past 20 years, has raised considerable concern in culinary circles. It has been suggested by some gastronomists that French cuisine is threatened by Americanization. Certainly, classic U.S. exports have taken hold in France, from Coca-Cola to bubble gum to fast-food chains like McDonald's and Burger King. One can now find Kellogg's corn flakes,

(Left) The convenience offered by *supermarchés* and *hypermarchés* has transformed the way many French consumers shop—and eat. Are these huge, one-stop stores presenting a threat to the very existence of the small specialty food purveyors, such as the *boucherie,* or butcher shop (opposite page)?

(Left) © Paul Cherfils—Tony Stone Images; (opposite page) © Marc Garanger

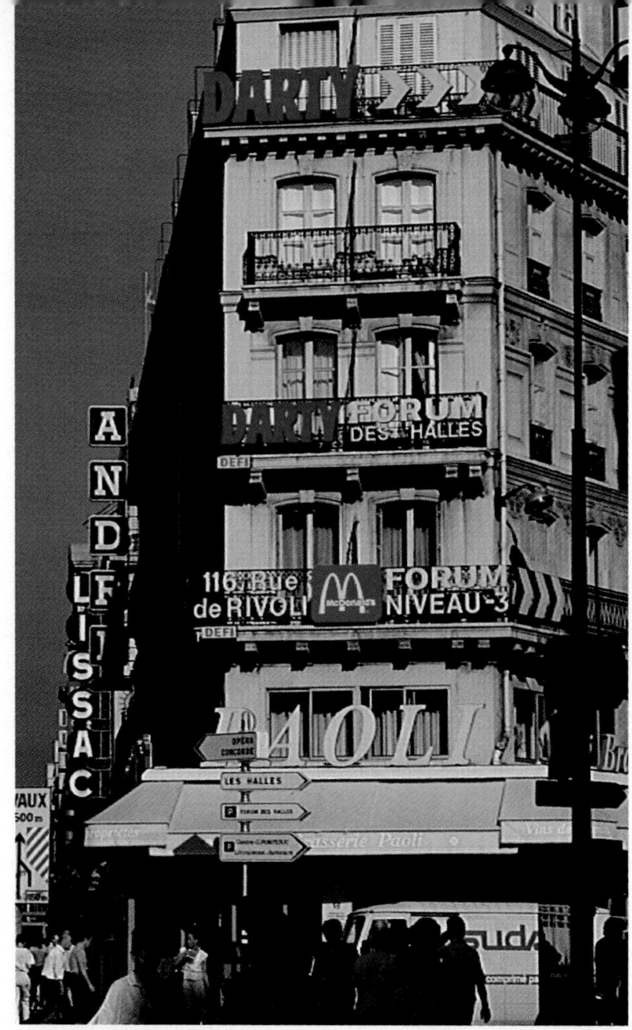

(Right and opposite page, bottom) The Americanization of the food supply is seen in French culinary circles as an ominous development.

Mars candy bars, and, more recently, Häagen-Dazs ice cream (which, contrary to popular notion, originated in the Bronx, New York, not in Scandinavia). Overall, however, the evolution of French eating patterns can be attributed more to social change and modernization in general than to Americanization.

Eating patterns: what the data show

What are the French people eating today? The National Institute of Statistics and Economic Studies in Paris has completed a series of detailed studies on food-consumption patterns in France every one to two years from 1965 to 1991 and thus has acquired a body of data reflecting a 25-year period. (It can be assumed that the patterns observed in 1991 have continued to prevail.)

In 1991 the French spent F 12,668 (F 5.27 = $1) per person on food, including food consumed at home and in restaurants. This number represents around 20% of household budgets, compared with 30% in 1969. Total consumption during this period varied, however, paralleling changes in economic conditions. For example, a decrease in food purchases occurred between 1989 and 1991.

The proportion of expenditures for each food group has varied little since 1965. There have been small increases in cereal products and fruits and vegetables. Meat, fish, poultry, and eggs have remained stable and represent about 38% of the food budget. Dairy products, cereal products, and beverages have each accounted for 11–12%. The only category that has declined is fats and oils, from 7% of the budget in 1965 to less than 3% in 1991.

Still, a great many changes in eating patterns have occurred. Most notable perhaps is the increase in the use of convenience foods. The purchase of frozen prepared dishes multiplied by a factor of six between 1979 and 1991; consumption of frozen vegetables doubled. Consumption of fresh milk decreased from 85.6 liters (22.6 gallons) per person to 66.2 liters (17.5 gallons), but at the same time, cheese intake increased from 10.4 to 15.9 kilograms (23 to 35 pounds), and yogurt intake rose from 73.3 servings per person (a serving being 125 grams) to 156. The intake of mineral water and other nonalcoholic beverages nearly doubled. And

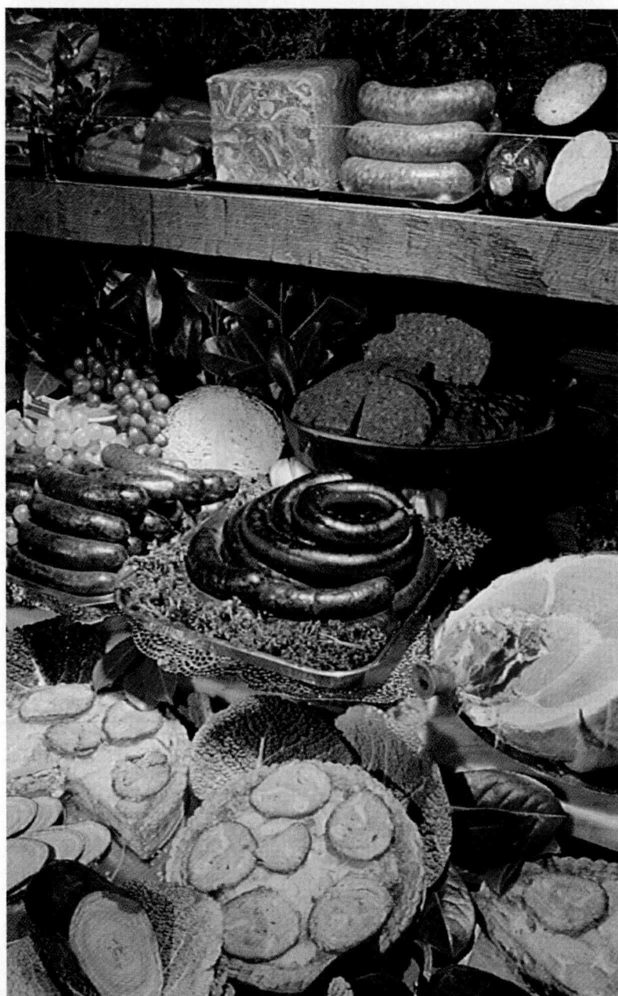

(Top) Michel Garnier—Gamma Liaison; (bottom) © Francis Jalain—Explorer

while consumption of ordinary table wine decreased by 80% over the period 1979–91, from 83.6 to 15.5 liters (22.1 to 4.1 gallons), that of more costly "vintage" wines increased by 30% (from 7 to 10.2 liters [1.85 to 2.7 gallons]). Other smaller increases were evident over the 25 years in fruit, fish, pork, poultry, and charcuterie. These items correspond to the demands of consumers for "good" foods, on the one hand, and foods that can be quickly and easily prepared, on the other. Meanwhile, the consumption of both bread and potatoes declined precipitously.

(Top and bottom) © Marc Garanger; (center) © Owen Franken—Stock, Boston

(Left, top and bottom, and opposite page, bottom) Perhaps more exacting than their U.S. counterparts, many French shoppers remain devoted to specialty purveyors for high-quality fresh foods such as fancy pastries, crusty baguettes, and charcuterie (sausages and other delicatessen products).

Different groups, different menus

In addition to individual differences in eating habits and disparities between socioeconomic classes, there are also differences between

© Stuart Cohen—Comstock

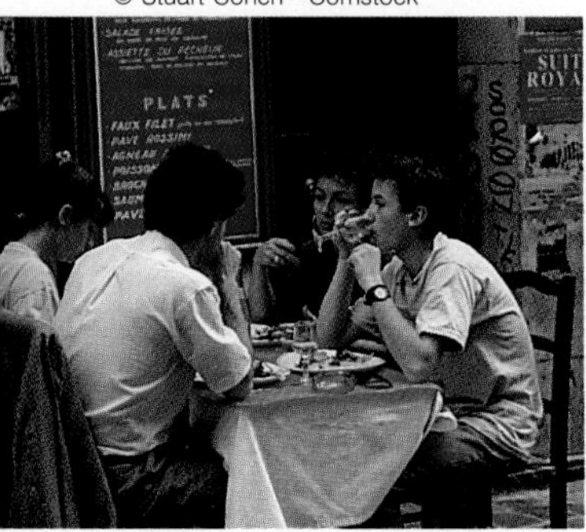

A Parisian family lunches at a neighborhood café.

people who eat a traditional-style diet and those who follow a contemporary one. At one end of the spectrum are farm families and other rural dwellers, who follow quite traditional patterns. Up to 35% of food eaten in rural households is homegrown. Generally, this population eats basic foods, such as bread and potatoes, drinks table wine, and uses fewer packaged and commercially prepared products than do other groups. Meal preparation is usually the woman's task and requires ample time and care.

At the other end are white-collar, bourgeois urban and suburban families (*cadres supérieurs*), who buy a larger proportion of the more costly food items and "upscale" (*haut de gamme*) prepared products and eat less bread, pasta, and potatoes. Time devoted to food preparation among this group is short and frequently involves the use of food processors and other "high-tech" kitchen aids. Weekend social activities often include gastronomic events.

Two other groups have their own characteristic patterns of eating: urbanites and the elderly. Young urban singles and couples generally spend little time shopping for and preparing meals and rely heavily on prepared dishes, fast food, and restaurants for their nourishment. The elderly, a category that represents about 12% of the population, either follow traditional patterns of food preparation or, especially when living alone in isolated conditions, eat basic fresh foods simply prepared. Many seniors follow diets dictated by particular medical conditions, such as diabetes and hypertension (high blood pressure). The number of people over 65 will double by the year 2040, and it is anticipated that the

© Jeff Selmer—Sygma

(Above) Though more accustomed to a traditional diet, older people are increasingly turning to modern convenience foods. (Below) In a village in southern France, a mother and daughter prepare the family's midday repast.

© Marc Garanger

preferences of this group will shift toward convenience foods that can be quickly heated in a microwave oven.

The French paradox

It is now common knowledge that France, in spite of its high fat intake, has a significantly lower rate of coronary heart disease (CHD) than all other developed countries except Japan. Fat accounts for 36–42% of total calories. Moreover, the ratio of polyunsaturated fat (which is considered "heart healthy") to saturated fat is low—44% lower than U.S. recommendations. Other countries with similar fat-intake profiles have up to four times the rate of CHD. How can this "French paradox" be explained?

Several hypotheses have been offered. The interplay of various dietary factors is complex, however, and no single dietary practice may be said to account for the low rate of heart disease in France. One factor that is often cited is the French intake of alcohol—in particular, regular consumption of red wine. Red wine (and, to a lesser extent, white) contains antioxidant compounds believed to protect against the buildup of fatty substances in the arteries. Alcohol per se has also been shown to inhibit the formation of blood clots, which play a major part in heart attacks. Authorities still do not agree whether it is red wine in particular or alcohol in general that offers protection against CHD.

Peter Turnley—Black Star

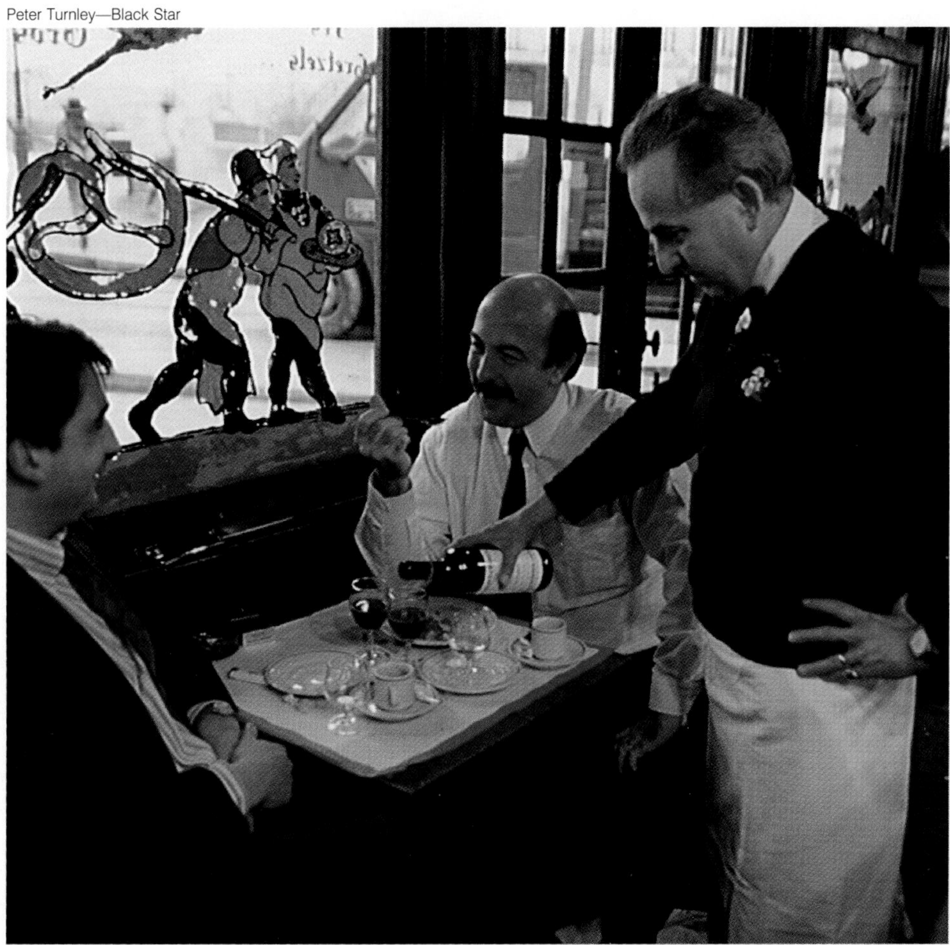

Some scientists credit the comparatively low rate of heart disease in France to wine drinking—particularly red wine—with meals, but most nutrition authorities doubt that the explanation of the "French paradox" is so simple.

The French habit of eating an abundance of vegetables and fruits—rich sources of antioxidants—may be another protective factor. Lower intake of red meat than in the U.S., reliance on vegetable oils rather than animal fats, and a high intake of cheese have also been cited to account for the low French rate of CHD. (According to one highly speculative theory, the high calcium content of cheese prevents absorption of fats and therefore minimizes the accumulation of fatty deposits in blood vessels.)

Some theorists credit the French practice of eating structured meals at fixed times. Others point to the fact that many French people still eat their major meal at midday and therefore do not consume the majority of their calories at night, when they are inactive, as most Americans do. Still other nutrition authorities note that French meals feature a greater variety of foods and smaller portions than their American counterparts.

Regional differences in food intake may shed some light on the paradox. For example, the southwestern part of the country—in particular, Toulouse—has the lowest rate of CHD. Some nutrition experts believe that goose and duck liver and their oils, prominent in the cuisine of the southwest, may explain some of the region's advantage. These foods are thought to have high proportions of the "good," or cardioprotective, fats.

Scientists continue to study the relative contributions of alcohol, diet, and lifestyle factors to the French paradox. In the meantime, French health au-

© Erica Lansner

Berries artistically displayed at a Parisian street market. Epidemiological studies around the world show that diets like that eaten in France, containing abundant amounts of fruits and vegetables, are associated with low rates of coronary heart disease.

thorities are advising people to maintain a "traditional" eating pattern.

Having their cake

How do the attitudes of the French people toward food differ from those of the U.S. public? The view of the French about "light" (*i.e.,* reduced-fat or reduced-calorie) foods is perhaps indicative of their general outlook. Whereas Americans have embraced these products with enthusiasm, and the usage of the word *light* is specifically regulated under the recently enacted U.S. labeling laws, in France *produits allégés* ("light" products), such as low-fat yogurt, cheeses, butter, and margarine, have not found the same acceptance. While the data show that these foods maintain some share of the French market, their sales seem to be decreasing. A 1992 study by the Research Center for the Study and Observation of the Conditions of Life (better known by its acronym, Crédoc) found that most people do not believe the purported health benefits of such products are significant and find them to be less tasty than the regular (higher-fat) versions.

Are the French unconcerned, then, about gaining a few extra kilograms? The prevalence of obesity in France is lower than in the U.S.—perhaps one-fourth of French adults are obese (*i.e.,* 20% or more above the desirable body weight), compared with about one-third of Americans—but the unscientific observer would not know this from looking at the myriad ads for weight-loss aids on French television. Weight loss, in fact, is a huge industry in France, and diet gurus have their devoted followers just as they do in the U.S. Moreover, as eating habits and activity patterns have changed, the prevalence of obesity has increased, especially among children. Other eating disorders may be increasing in frequency as well. A recent epidemiological study by scientists at the National Institute of Health and Medical Research in Paris found that 2% of females between the ages of 12 and 19 are at risk for bulimia—a figure only slightly lower than estimates of bulimia incidence in the United States.

Gustatory pleasures: alive and well

Will the traditional French dietary patterns—and the apparent health benefits associated with them—disappear in years to come? Will fresh vegetables from the greengrocer, warm baguettes from the corner *boulangerie,* and the meticulously ripened, creamy Camemberts and Bries purchased at the *fromagerie* simply become mere bits of nostalgia? Will the French forget their agricultural roots and their unique culinary heritage and blend into a "homogenized" Europe? French history suggests not.

Traditional values are still strong within the fabric of the French character. For instance, in a recent survey conducted by Crédoc, people were asked what it means to "eat well." Their answer: the nutritional, dietetic aspect of food is important—that is, eating healthy, balanced, and varied meals—but the gustatory and social pleasures of food are equally important.

(Top) © José Azel—Aurora; (bottom left) © Joe Viesti—Viesti Associates, Inc.; (bottom right) The Anthony Blake Photo Library

(Top) Bread is baked the old-fashioned way at the Poilâne bakery in Paris. (Above left) The gustatory and social pleasures are integral to the French concept of "eating well." A Parisian family sits down to a relaxed meal at home. (Above right) An array of cheeses at a Parisian *fromagerie* delights the eyes and palates of customers.

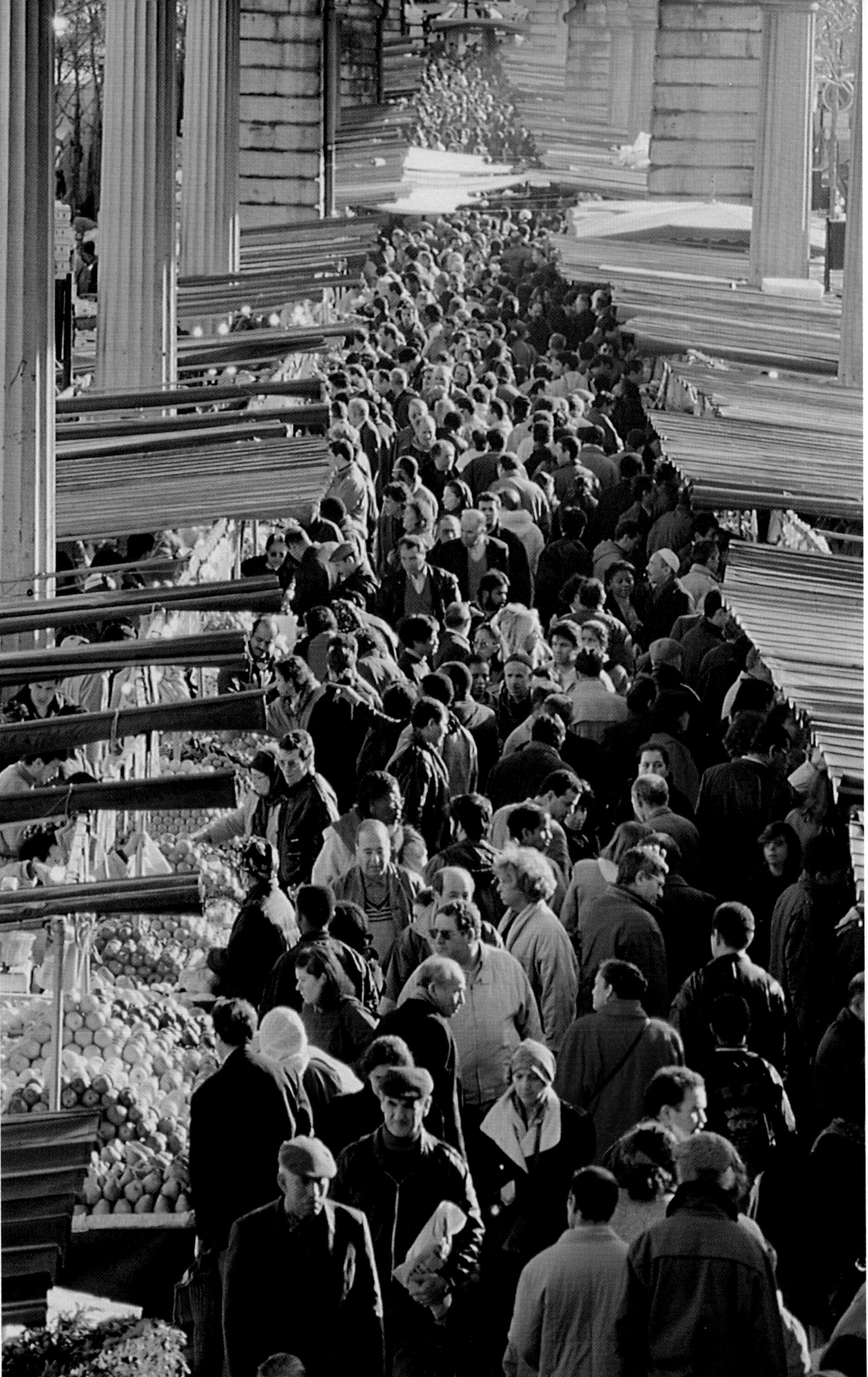

An American (Chef) in Paris

by Michael S. Roberts

Parisians readily, if ingenuously, confess that they really do not know how to cook, except for simple things—and *that,* of course, is not "cooking." "Ah, Monsieur," said one woman I spoke with while shopping for food during a recent visit to Paris. "I have no recipes."

"But," I replied, "look at all the food in this market. Certainly it is not here simply to make the neighborhood more picturesque. And, Madame, I see that your basket is full of vegetables. You obviously are not going to take them home and throw them in the trash can. Please, tell me, what do you do with these things?"

"Mind you," she said, "I'm not a cook, but here's what I do. . . ." Four ingredients and five steps later, I had what most Americans would call a recipe.

"Ah, but this is not a recipe?" I ventured, after listening to another shopper's scrumptious-sounding description of how she was going to prepare the sole she had just bought. "Mais, non, Monsieur," she insisted. "Chefs have recipes. This is just how I prepare it."

* * *

For centuries Paris has attracted immigrants from the provinces and abroad who brought with them different customs and ideas. They also brought with them vestiges of their previous lives in the form of the foods prepared in their native towns and villages. These dishes, cooked today by people who may be second-, third-, or even fourth-generation Parisians, connect the fast-paced urban present to a pastoral, agricultural past.

The routine of shopping, cooking, and dining follows a strict order in Paris and, for that matter, in the rest of France. Most people eat three meals a day at relatively fixed times, even on weekends. One Saturday while browsing at a large home furnishings store south of Paris, I noticed that around 1 o'clock the store emptied of shoppers. Everyone had gone to lunch.

(Below) Pierre-Gilles Vidoli; (opposite page) © Jean-Pierre Casaubon—Tony Stone Images

The author, Californian Michael S. Roberts, appears very much the native Parisian as he roams one of the city's roving neighborhood markets. (Opposite page) Shoppers throng the narrow aisles of the Marché de Barbès.

Although Parisians no longer devote hours to preparing the main meal of the day, they still place a high value on meals eaten at home in the company of family and friends. A leisurely dinner can be a cherished "retreat" from the hassles of daily life in a bustling city. Cooking, therefore, is perceived as a productive use of time, an activity that enhances the day.

An American observer cannot help but notice that people are rarely seen eating "on the run" in the streets of Paris, although they can be seen dining or sipping coffee and aperitifs in the many outdoor cafés. There are no vendors selling hot dogs from carts. Even the supermarkets stock little in the way of snack foods.

Depending on work schedules and family size, food shopping is done either early in the morning, during the lunch break, or on the way home from work. Roving markets—colorful street affairs that set up twice a week in many neighborhoods—are open from early morning until 1 in the afternoon. They reopen at 4 PM and remain open until 7. The same schedule is followed in the *rues commerçantes,* or neighborhood shopping streets, as well as in the large covered markets that house many inde-

***Michael S. Roberts** is Co-owner and Executive Chef, Twin Palms Restaurant, Pasadena, California. He is the author of* Secret Ingredients *(1988),* Make-Ahead Gourmet *(1990), and* What's for Dinner? *(1993) and is preparing a volume on Parisian home cooking.*

pendent vendors. Practically everything is closed Sunday afternoon and all day Monday.

This traditional schedule left a gap that has been readily filled by supermarkets and small neighborhood general stores, which remain open when everything else is closed. Today increasing numbers of Parisians can be seen shopping at all hours of the day, and even the traditional mealtimes are not as rigidly observed as they were formerly.

Suzanne Fournier—Rapho

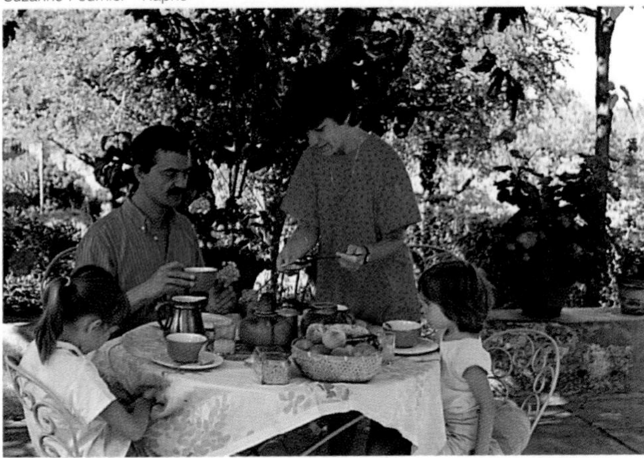

(Above) Unlike many Americans in the 1990s, the French still tend to eat three meals a day at relatively fixed times. Also unlike many Americans, they continue to uphold the tradition of the shared family meal. (Below) The sidewalk café is another Parisian institution. These establishments are crowded day and night with patrons enjoying a leisurely aperitif or cup of coffee. American visitors to the city are struck by the fact that Parisians rarely eat "on the run."

Visiting the supermarket

Parisian supermarkets are small by American standards. Cart size is modest too, which leads one to assume that Parisians do not do a whole week's shopping at once. After all, what does one do with a week's worth of food if one's refrigerator is only about half the size of the average appliance in a U.S. household? And even if Parisians had the storage space, how would they carry

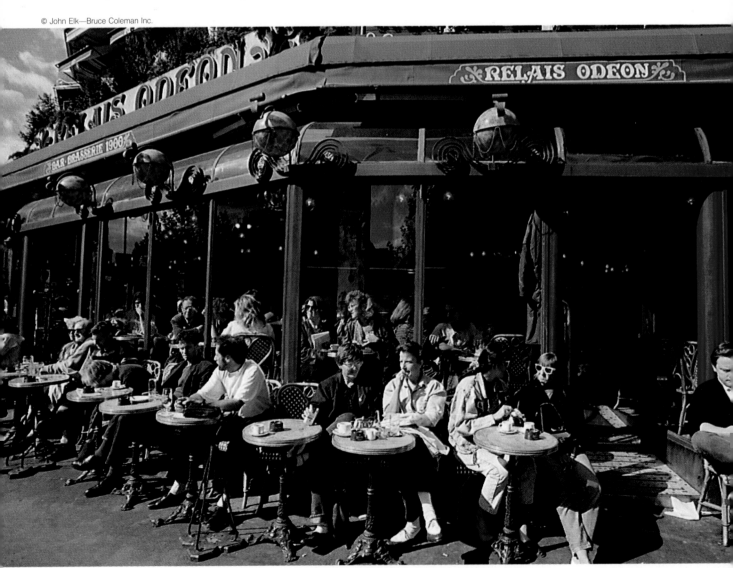

© John Elk—Bruce Coleman Inc.

home several days' worth of food?

The great innovation of the French supermarkets when they first started appearing in the 1960s was the diversity of their offerings. No longer did one have to go to several shops along the *rue commerçante* to buy the various items on one's shopping list. This in itself was a leap in convenience. And it was very popular too, at least with the younger generation of shoppers. I used to frequent the supermarket on the rue de Buci in the fashionable St.-Germain-des-Prés district. At the end of the workday, it was, and still is, always full of young, mostly single people. Most shoppers buy just enough to overload a *ficelle,* or string bag or sack, and then stop to relax with friends in a nearby café before returning home to cook dinner.

Suburban venture

Over the past several years giant supermarkets, called *hypermarchés,* have sprung up on the outer periphery of the city, mostly in the new neighborhoods. These are areas where large apartment buildings with their own parking garages are often part of a shopping complex. Rallye, on the boulevard Périphérique near the Porte d'Orléans, is such a place. People travel to the *hypermarché* by car, shop American-style, and cart home a carful of groceries and other household goods. The shoppers themselves seem quite intent about getting what they need and getting out of the store. Here shopping seems to be a chore rather than the pleasurable activity that it can be when one is selecting foods from the small, colorful city markets.

One feature of these stores that immediately impresses the U.S. visitor is the vast shelf space given over to condiments, including the usual preserves, vinegars, and mustards but also an extensive selection of olives, anchovies, capers, and even six or so different kinds of salt—sea salts, gray, white, or ground with algae; rock salt; flavored salts; and *sel de fin* or *de table* ("table salt"). The French love salt!

On the whole, suburban supermarkets and *hypermarchés* have poorer-quality meats, fish, poultry, and produce than the specialty shops. But what they lack in quality, they make up for in variety. Everything the French like to eat is available, including such items as kidneys, tongue, calf's brains, sweetbreads, and headcheese (a delicacy made from the head, feet, and other parts of the pig).

The cheese selection at the average supermarket is disappointing—mostly commercially produced Camembert and Brie—which leads one to believe that the French, who cherish cheese, still shop for it at specialty markets or the cheese shops (*fromageries*). Bread, too, is more likely to be purchased fresh daily at the corner *boulangerie,* the bakery that specializes in bread.

Despite the general mediocrity of their wares, supermarkets remain quite popular among young singles and married couples with young children. My observation, though, is that in their mature years French shoppers return to the specialty shops and outdoor markets. My French friends, who did little or no cooking while in their 20s, are now "established" with families and have become more traditional in their middle age—more like their parents in their shopping and eating habits.

A morning on the *rue commerçante*

The *rue commerçante* on the avenue Simon Bolivar in the 19th arrondissement is typical of the neighborhood shopping street. It boasts two produce stands, three butchers, two poultry shops, two fishmongers, three pastry shops, two *boulangeries,* a couple of convenience stores, some wine shops, and a general grocery store, or *épicerie.* As if this were not sufficient, at the end of the street is the Marché Sécrétan, a covered market dating from 1868, which shelters an additional two dozen or so food purveyors, including two kosher butchers and a Moroccan specialty shop. Neighbors gossip and exchange news while shopping for the day's meals—the atmosphere being akin to that of a local fair.

The *marchand des quatre-saisons,* or greengrocer, hawks tomatoes from Sicily and Anjou pears from Morocco. He is full of admonitions and advice—for example, he tells one customer simply to shell but not peel the tender young fava beans. On this balmy spring day his offerings include new (*i.e.,* freshly harvested) garlic, wild asparagus shoots, green beans, yellow wax beans, cauliflower, broccoli, cabbages, onions, zucchini, eggplant, peppers, celeriac, turnips, several varieties of potatoes, fresh herbs, and fruits too numerous to list. And the next day, he tells me excitedly, he expects a shipment of cèpes—the king of mushrooms—just in time for the weekend. On weekends, he informs me, people spend more time cooking, "*comme les amoureux*" ("like lovers").

The butcher sells all cuts of beef, lamb, veal, and pork. A reputable butcher buys whole pigs, lambs, and goats and whole or half carcasses of steers and calves. Thus, when entering the butcher shop, one does not see many ready-to-eat portions of minute steak, filet mignon, or beef for stew but the whole section of the carcass from which these cuts come. One asks the butcher for some beef stew meat, and he pulls out a 3.2-kilogram (7-pound) shank of beef. "How much would you like? How large would you like me to cut the chunks?" he asks. (And each customer is usually quite precise in his or her instructions.)

Next door, the *triperie* sells specialty meats. Prominently displayed are some eviscerated sheep's heads and *rognons blancs* ("calf's testicles"), which prompts me to inquire: "Do many people eat these items? How does one prepare them?"

"Well, they're a bit special," the vendor allows. The sheep's heads contain the tongues and brains. He advises splitting the head in half and roasting it in the oven. As for the *rognons blancs:* "You cook them in Normandy butter with lots of garlic and shallots," he instructs.

Parisians buy more liver than any other organ meat. I asked the merchant if his customers were concerned about eating liver from animals that had been fed growth hormones. "Ah, non. Not with French meat. It's not a problem," he answered.

"But don't the French worry about fat and cholesterol?" I persisted. I sensed that he was growing impatient with me. His theory, he explained, is that those who deny themselves for the sake of their health make a mistake. "You have to make your digestive organs work," he expounded. "The less they are made to work, the less they are capable of working. Okay, you have high cholesterol. So you have to cut back on fat. But you must continue to eat at least some fat so that your liver will continue to eliminate fat from the system."

On to the cheese vendor. Here, in addition to no fewer than two to three dozen different kinds of *fromages,* one also finds milk (cow's, goat's, and sheep's), yogurt, and several different kinds of butter. (Paris is among the highest butter-consuming regions of France.) I asked the proprietor if people were eating less cheese than in past years. "Oui et non," the cheese seller replied. "For a while people were concerned about fat and cholesterol. They tried low-fat cheese. They bought more factory-produced cheese. Now my clients have gone back to quality. They'd rather eat a little bit of something marvelous than a big slab of something mediocre. I buy farm-produced cheeses almost exclusively now."

Rewards of the roving market

The greatest delights of food shopping in Paris are to be found in the roving neighborhood markets. It is here that the farm-to-consumer chain is most direct and that one finds the best prices on most items, especially

Shopping for food in Paris can be a pleasure or a chore, depending on whether one chooses the bland anonymity of the *hypermarché* (top), the colorful precincts and personalized service of a covered market (above), or an open-air stall on the *rue commerçante* (below).

Photos, R.É.A./Saba; (top) © Sittler; (center and bottom) © Marta Nascimento

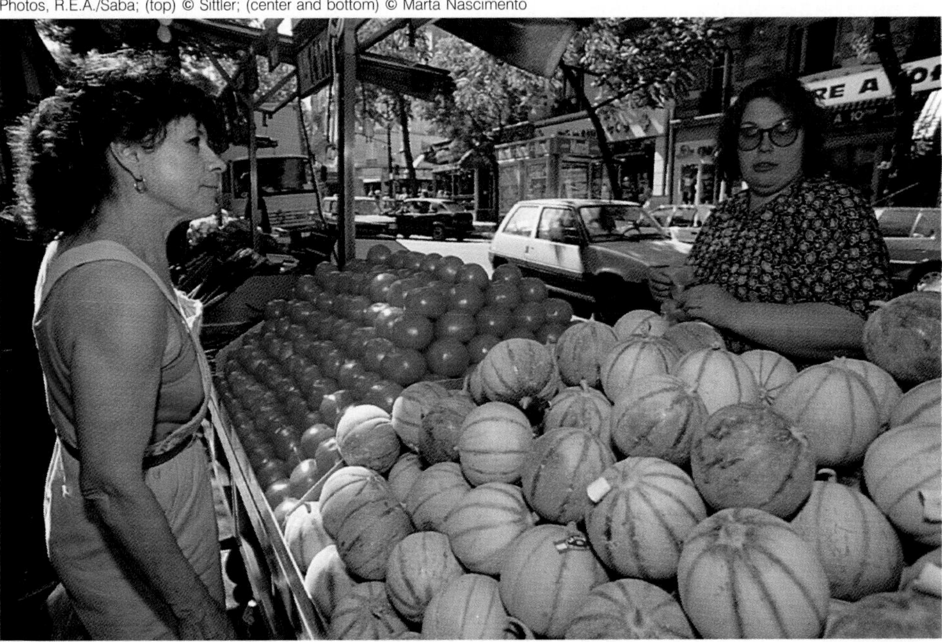

meat, poultry, fish, dairy products, spices, and vegetables. Because the vendors have a personal relationship with the growers and producers they buy from, the consumer feels an inherent trust in the freshness and quality of the food. On the day I am shopping, most of the shoppers are middleaged and older housewives. As 1 o'clock approaches, though, there is usually an influx of younger working people getting in some quick shopping on their lunch break. Despite the convenience offered by the supermarkets, many young people—especially those who were brought up in more traditional households—prefer to shop in open-air markets. As the French anthropologist Christina Nordin has observed, the intensely personal character of these outdoor, roving markets is the antithesis of the "placelessness" that characterizes the suburban malls and *hypermarchés.*

In addition to having the freshest produce, the roving markets are also the chief source of foods produced by individual artisans. In the avenue de Saxe, an upscale neighborhood not far from the Eiffel Tower, I chatted with a *charcutière,* a vendor who specializes in *demi-sel,* or brined pork products, including pig snouts, ears, and tails, as well as hams and spareribs. She admitted

A fruit-and-vegetable vendor sets up her stall in the Marché Sécrétan, a covered market in the 19th arrondissement that dates from the 1860s.

(Above) Butter, a staple of the Parisian diet. (Right) Rotisserie shop, Marché Sécrétan.

that the number of cottage producers has shrunk drastically in the past 10 years but, she told me, "More and more, people are coming back. They're willing to pay a little more for something of quality. Our products may not be as picture perfect as the industrial ones, but they are certainly tastier. My pigs, for example, are certainly among the fattest—they have to be. Fat gives the meat flavor. People who want to eat lean pork are silly. They are prisoners of their diet regimens."

Dining out

At lunchtime (from about 1 to 3) nearly all Parisian restaurants, from the most elegant four-star establishments to the neighborhood bistros and brasseries, are packed. Nowadays it is less common than in the past for people to live and work in the same neighborhood. Thus, few are able to return

(Left) © Richard Phelps Frieman—Rapho; (right) © Marta Nascimento—R.É.A./Saba

ôtisserie

home for lunch. And with more and more two-income households, there is no one to stay home and prepare a midday meal.

As a professional chef and Los Angeles restaurateur, I was curious on my recent visit to see how much "American health consciousness" had penetrated Parisian restaurant cuisine. I saw little indication that nutritional concerns are influencing the way French chefs prepare food. The traditional cream sauces remain. Chicken dishes, one of the staples of "heart-healthy" menus in the U.S., are poorly represented on menus of better restaurants. Rather, one finds duck à l'orange, *riz de veau* (sweetbreads), *foie de veau* (calf's liver), and *foie gras* (fattened goose or duck liver). There are relatively few vegetable offerings, but this is probably because people prepare a lot of vegetables at home. Portions are smaller than in U.S. eateries, but there is more variety in the meal. Among the more prominent chefs, there is an increase in Italian- and other Mediterranean-inspired cooking and therefore a prevalence of dishes that use olive oil and are tomato-based. But this trend seems to be driven more by fashion than by concerns about heart disease.

The pleasure principle

What concerns the French most today is not that eating may make them fat or lead to chronic disease. Rather, they fear the assault on the traditional routine of shared meals and the depersonalization of the modes of food production. They have a deep distrust of modern food technology, the so-called advances designed to ensure safety, purity, and uniformity. To the French consumer, a worm in an apple is not a defect but rather an indication that the fruit has not been sprayed with a chemical. If the tomatoes in the market are nearly overripe, so much the better. They are perfect for eating immediately.

When one buys poultry at the roving market, it is not hermetically sealed in plastic. The consumer chooses a chicken (there may be as many as six breeds for sale), and the vendor singes the bird's skin, then empties the cavity of gizzard, liver, heart, and kidneys. All of this is reassuring to French consumers, giving them a sense of confidence in the chain of production that begins at a farm in the provinces and ends on their kitchen tables; what they put in their mouths represents the integrity of hard-working humans along the way. The French shopper is more suspicious of the oven-ready chicken purchased at the supermarket than the farm-fresh chicken from the open market—even though the latter may have hung outdoors, unwrapped, where flies may have landed on it or a passerby may even have sneezed on it.

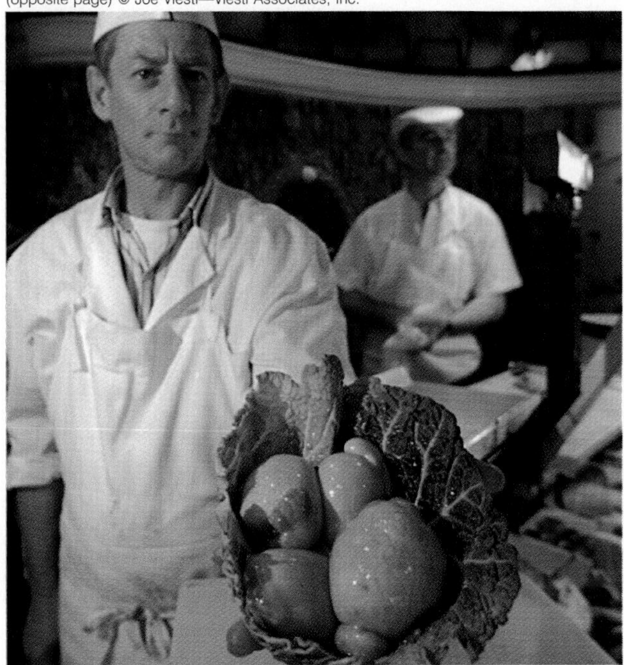

Parisians do not hesitate to buy specialty meats that many Americans would shun. Nor do they insist that their poultry be swathed in plastic (opposite page). Confidence in the food producers means more to them than the government's guarantees of purity or a health expert's stamp of approval.

Unlike Americans, the French do not imbue the food they eat with a health imperative. The average French man or woman will never be persuaded to give up espresso because scientists pronounce caffeine addictive or because a government report says that in large quantities coffee may cause bladder cancer in rats. Nor are they likely to pass up the morning croissant with butter because they fear for their arteries. There is a pleasure principle at work; the French attitude toward food, if I were to attempt to sum it up, is that all foods are created equal and all should be eaten and enjoyed (in moderation).

* * *

The French give meaning and significance to food far beyond its value for sustaining life. Alain Paton of the Centre Ferrandi, the government cooking school, holding forth on the Parisian affinity for fresh fish, told me: "Parisians are mad for fish simply because it's so perishable. Better to dine on fish while it's fresh, for life is fleeting. You could be crushed under the wheels of a speeding Métro train, or hit by a taxi, or assassinated in the street."

He threw up his arms and shrugged. "Ah, oui, Monsieur, life in Paris can be like that. Voilà. C'est tout."

POULE DINDE FINE À RÔTIR
POULET BLANC À RÔTIR CLASSE A
POULET BLANC À RÔTIR CLASSE A
CANETON EXTRA
1 KG 12F00
39 90

Unlocking Pain's Secrets

by Allan I. Basbaum, Ph.D.

COZZOLINO

The greatest evil is physical pain.

—Saint Augustine

There is chronic undermanagement of pain, from cancer to arthritis to sickle-cell anemia or migraine or anything you can think of.

—Jon Levine,
rheumatologist,
University of California
at San Francisco

Illustration by Paul Cozzolino

Why is pain so undertreated? The worst reason is that some caregivers assume that "the pain can't be as bad as the patient claims." This misconception results from the fact that pain cannot be seen. Pain is whatever the patient reports; there are no instruments that objectively measure it.

Pain is a complicated perception influenced by sensory input, mood, experience, the immediate environment, the attitude of the patient's family, and even cultural heritage. Just as a painting may be beautiful to one person and ugly to another, so the magnitude and quality of pain differ considerably in patients who have comparable injuries or illness or are subjected to similarly unpleasant stimuli.

Another reason for undertreatment of pain is the fear that addiction to potent painkilling drugs—in particular, opiates (substances derived from opium)—will occur. There is, however, almost no evidence that addiction occurs in pain sufferers when morphine—considered the safest and most effective opiate—is used. The patient may become tolerant (a higher dose is needed for relief) but does not develop a psychological craving for the drug.

There are also many different types of pain. The deep, achy pain of tissue injury, called nociceptive pain (from the Latin *nocere,* "to harm"), is very different from the burning, shooting neuropathic pain that can result from injury to the nervous system. Medications that work for nociceptive pain, such as morphine, are often ineffective for neuropathic pain. There is now evidence that the central nervous system (CNS) of the patient undergoes physical changes when injury and pain are *not* treated. These changes contribute to the quality of the pain, its persistence, and its responsiveness to analgesics (pain-relieving drugs). Physicians are only beginning to appreciate the fact that aggressive treatment of pain can prevent these CNS changes. In just the past half decade, neuroscientists have acquired vast amounts of new information about the basic biology of pain—much of it relevant to the assessment and effective management of pain in suffering patients.

Allan I. Basbaum, Ph.D., is Professor of Anatomy and Physiology and Vice Chairman, Department of Anatomy, W.M. Keck Foundation Center for Integrative Neuroscience, University of California at San Francisco.

Illustrations (Figures 1–8) by Harwin Studios.

The perception of pain is influenced by complex neural-circuit interactions in the brain and spinal cord.

Bob Daemmrich—Stock, Boston

The "pain" message

It would be a great thing to understand Pain in all its meanings.

—Peter Mere Latham, 19th-century English physician

A basic understanding of the CNS and peripheral nervous system (PNS) pathways is useful for appreciating the many recent breakthroughs (Fig. 1). In all sensory systems, information is transmitted by nerves of the PNS

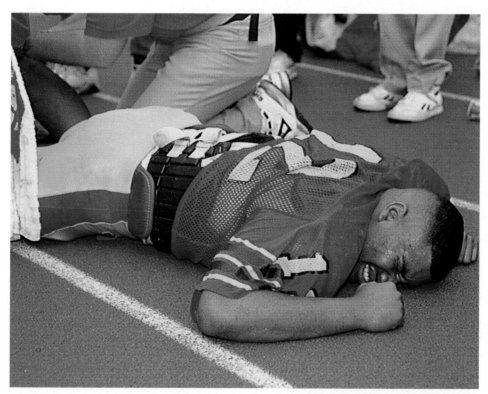

to the CNS. The PNS includes all of the nerve fibers of the body that are located outside of the spinal cord and brain. The latter two structures constitute the major components of the CNS.

Sensory information conveying the state of the body ("somatosensory" information) is transmitted by three types of nerve fibers, known as primary afferent, or first-order, fibers (Fig. 2). The largest of these, with a diameter of 5 to 12 micrometers (one micrometer equals one-millionth of a meter), are the A-beta fibers, which conduct nerve impulses to the spinal cord at high velocity (up to 60 meters per second). A-beta fibers respond to nonnoxious (nonpainful) stimuli (for example, light touch or the movement of a joint). A-delta fibers are smaller (1–5 micrometers) and thus conduct impulses more slowly (5–25 meters per second). The third type, called C fibers, are of very small diameter (one micrometer) and conduct impulses at a rate of about one meter per second.

A-delta and C nerve fibers are predominantly nociceptors; *i.e.,* they respond to noxious thermal, chemical, or mechanical stimulation. A-delta fibers mediate the first, or fast, sharp pain, such as the pain that is felt upon stubbing a toe; C fibers mediate the second, or slow, pain that follows seconds later and lasts longer—pain that is diffuse, throbbing, or possibly burning.

Both A-delta and C primary afferent nerve fibers enter and travel up the spinal cord and terminate in the area of the brain known as the gray matter; there they make connections, called synapses, with second-order nerve fibers, or neurons. The primary afferent fibers release chemical neurotransmitters at the synapse; these neurotransmitters act upon specialized receptors on the postsynaptic neurons (nerve cells that convey a wave of excitation away from a synapse). The neurotransmitters are synthesized in the cell bodies of the primary afferents located in the dorsal root ganglion outside the spinal cord. Signals from the second-order neurons are transmitted to "higher" centers in the brain stem and thalamus and from there to the cerebral cortex, the brain's outer layer (Fig. 3). How and where in the cortex the nociceptive message evokes the sensation and perception of pain is not yet entirely clear. However, there are now beginning to be some substantial clues.

There is physiological specificity in the response properties of the peripheral nerve fibers—the small-diameter C fibers having the highest mechanical and thermal threshold. That is, they respond to stimuli that often produce pain. They are activated by inflammatory mediators that are released during injury and in inflammatory disease such as rheumatoid arthritis. It

Figure 1

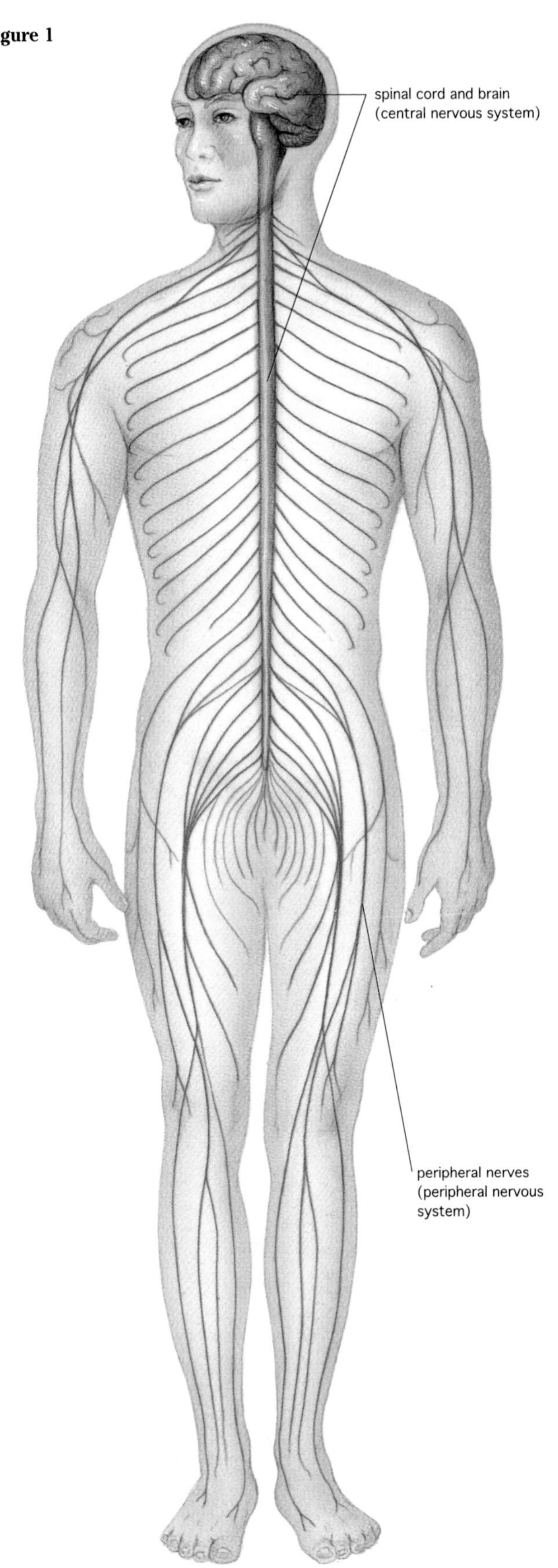

Figure 2

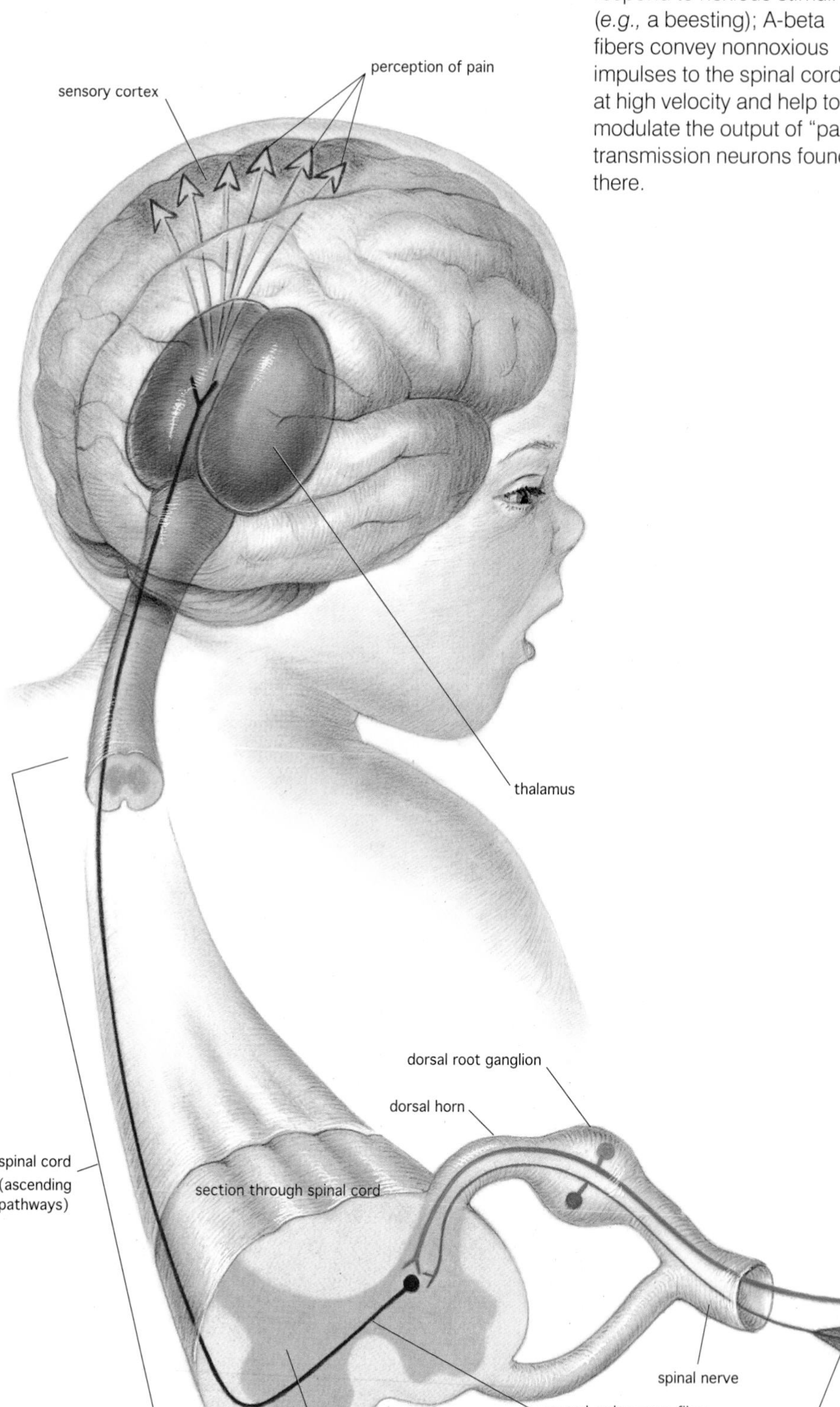

A-delta and C primary afferent nerve fibers respond to noxious stimuli (*e.g.,* a beesting); A-beta fibers convey nonnoxious impulses to the spinal cord at high velocity and help to modulate the output of "pain" transmission neurons found there.

would be inappropriate to call the C fibers "pain fibers" because that assumes that every time the C fibers are activated, pain will be perceived. Nor are there "pain pathways" along which "pain messages" predictably travel. Rather, because of complex neural-circuit interactions in the spinal cord and the brain, the perception of pain can be either blocked or enhanced. Thus, neither the magnitude nor the quality of pain is predictable from the magnitude of injury or from the amount of activity in the C fibers.

Pictures of pain

The fact that pain cannot be seen is, of course, what makes it so difficult to measure objectively. Recently, however, neuroscientists have used the imaging techniques of positron emission tomography (PET) scanning and magnetic resonance imaging (MRI) to detect regions of the cerebral cortex that are active during experimentally induced pain conditions. PET scanning detects the small increases in cerebral blood flow that are associated with increased activity of neurons; MRI provides the resolution necessary to identify the locus of the neuronal activity.

In PET scanning the subject is injected with a short-acting radioisotope of oxygen incorporated into a water solution, which can be tracked in the brain. The images produced provide a measure of blood flow. In MRI the subject is placed in a large, hollow, cylindrical magnet. The powerful magnetic field causes the body's protons (hydrogen nuclei) to align themselves in a single direction. When exposed to short bursts of radio waves, the protons are knocked out of alignment but milliseconds later realign themselves, emitting radio signals that are processed by a computer to produce a three-dimensional image.

Researchers Jeanne Talbot, M. Catherine Bushnell, Gary Duncan, and colleagues at the University of Montreal and the McConnell Brain Imaging Center of the Montreal Neurological Institute used these techniques to produce pictures of brain activity in awake, healthy human volunteers who were subjected to painful heat stimulation (*see* page 95). The eight subjects all had a noxious 48°–49° C (118°–120° F) heat pulse (described as "painful but tolerable") applied to their right forearms for five seconds. They also had nonpainful warm pulses of 41°–42° C (106°–108° F) applied. PET scans revealed that the noxious stimulation evoked increased activity of two major regions of the brain, the somatosensory cortex and the cingulate gyrus (Fig. 3).

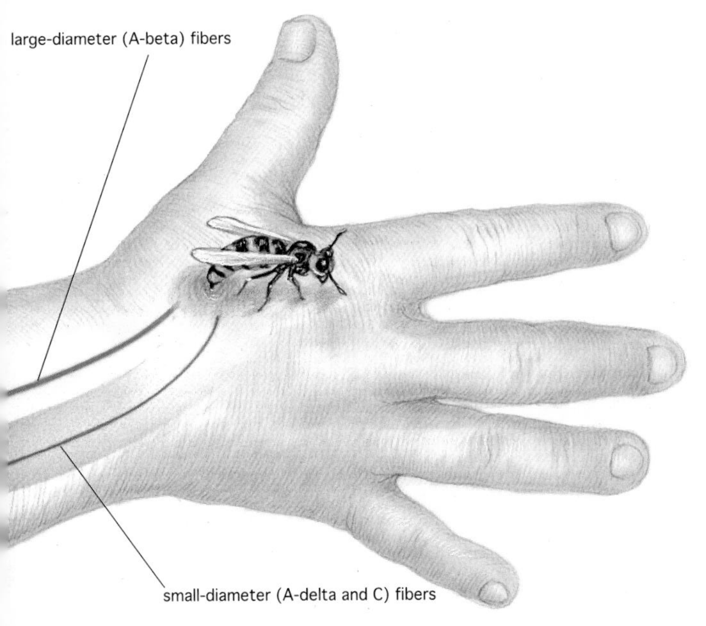

The somatosensory cortex is a brain region located near the midpoint containing nerve cells that respond to bodily sensations, including thermal stimuli. The activation of this area was not surprising. The activity in the cingulate gyrus, however, was unexpected. This forebrain area is generally associated with the regulation of emotions and would be expected to be involved in the affective (emotional) response to pain. The Montreal researchers had measured their subjects' anxiety by monitoring blood pressure during the heat-pulse delivery. Anxiety level did not change, which suggests that the cingulate gyrus activation was not "simply the result of emotional arousal." Rather, it represents a specific pain response in this part of the brain.

Monitoring pain

The problems associated with the assessment of pain in humans also exist in the laboratory. In order for the neural circuits that underlie the pain experience to be understood, effective ways to monitor their neuronal activity are needed. Scientists can monitor the behavior of animals but can only make conjectures about the actual experience of pain. The majority of animal investigations have used electrophysiological approaches to study the process of nociception, focusing on properties of single neurons. These studies have demonstrated that neurons in several regions of the spinal cord and brain stem respond to noxious stimulation. On the other hand, since these studies are performed in animals that have been anesthetized, they cannot reveal the precise relationship between the firing of a given neuron and the pain behavior that it evokes.

An exciting alternative method for monitoring and studying pain has recently been found. It is based on the fact that specific neuronal genes are induced, or "turned on," when neurons are active. In particular, the neuronal gene known as the c-*fos* proto-oncogene has proved useful for studying pain. (A proto-oncogene is a gene that has the potential to become an oncogene; an oncogene is a gene that can cause a normal cell to become cancerous.) The c-*fos* proto-oncogene codes for a protein that regulates the expression of other genes. Although increased c-*fos* expression has been implicated in the growth and differentiation of developing neurons, its function in neurons after development is not known. By monitoring gene expression with antibodies directed against the gene's protein product, however, scientists are able to identify literally thousands of neurons that are active in response to different stimuli. Most important, they can use special staining techniques to make the activity visible, which enables them to correlate the

Figure 3

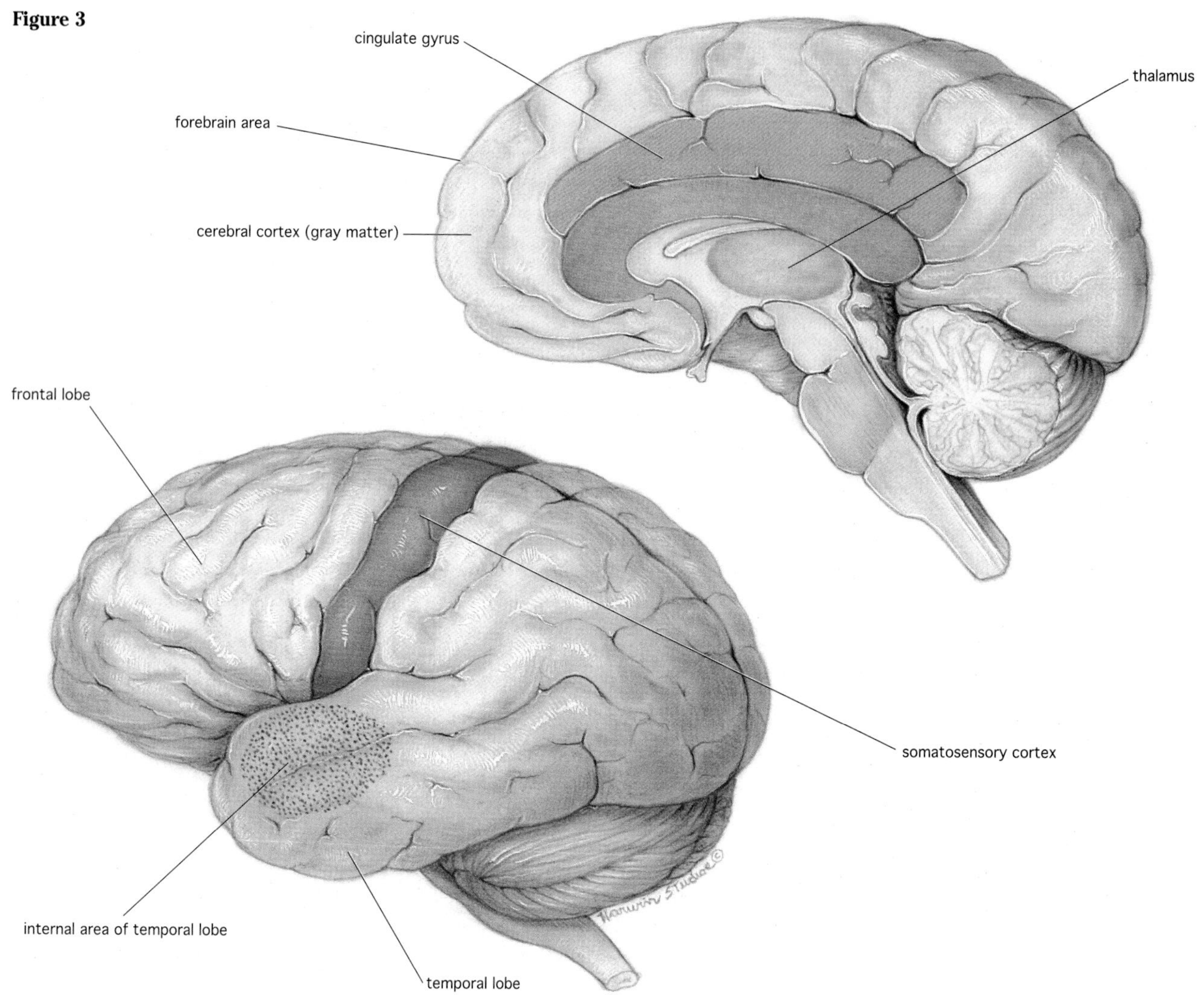

patterns of specific gene activity—in this case, the c-*fos* gene—with the CNS behavior that occurs in response to a given stimulus.

This approach has revealed that different types of noxious stimuli (*e.g.,* thermal, mechanical, and chemical) evoke activity in overlapping but not identical groups of spinal-cord neurons. It also has been used to study the effects of analgesic drugs. For example, morphine significantly reduces the expression of the gene in the spinal cord. Scientists are using this approach to understand how different populations of pain-responsive neurons are influenced by different classes of drugs—drugs that may be suitable for treating pain.

Memories in the spinal cord

C-*fos* is but one of many genes that are induced by noxious stimulation. When injury and pain persist, there are also dramatic increases in expression of genes that are involved in the synthesis and regulation of neurotransmitters. For example, there is a significant increase in the expression of the gene that codes for the precursor of substance P, a C-fiber neurotransmitter. This enhanced expression presumably contributes to enhanced transmission of the pain message to the spinal cord. In other cases peptides that are not normally expressed in C fibers appear with injury. In the dorsal horn of the spinal cord, there is a significant increase in the expression of genes that encode certain hormonelike substances, called endorphins, that are involved in endogenous (internal) pain-control circuits. Thus, it appears that pronociceptive and antinociceptive circuits are simultaneously increased in the presence of persistent injury and inflammation.

The fact that genes are "turned on" in response to painful stimulation emphasizes the complexity of the pain-transmission pathway (Fig. 4). The pathway could be likened to a voice-

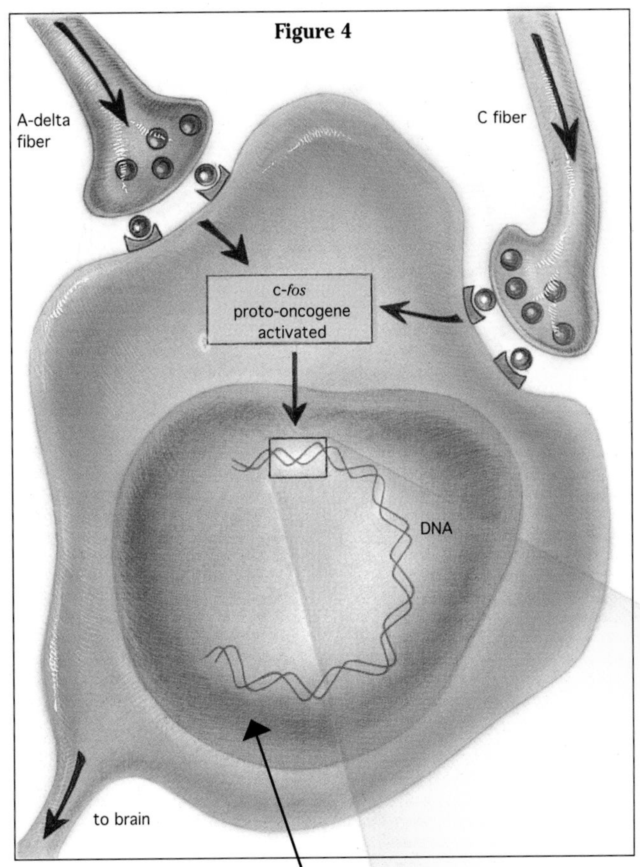

mail system. When a pain message enters the CNS, it can be stored for long periods of time. The molecular changes that occur establish a memory trace of the injury. The memory of the injury can influence the subsequent transmission of information along the pathway. How this memory trace is established and what its functional consequences are gradually are being revealed.

When C fibers are activated during injury, they release the substance glutamate from their synaptic terminals in the dorsal horn. Glutamate is the major excitatory neurotransmitter in the CNS; it induces activity in postsynaptic neurons. The triggering of a postsynaptic response by glutamate, however, is not as simple as, say, turning on an electric light. By acting at different receptors (proteins in the nerve cell membrane that mediate the effect of neurotransmitters), glutamate can evoke either short-term changes in neurons (lasting milliseconds) or long-term changes (lasting hours or days).

Among the most interesting receptors through which glutamate acts is

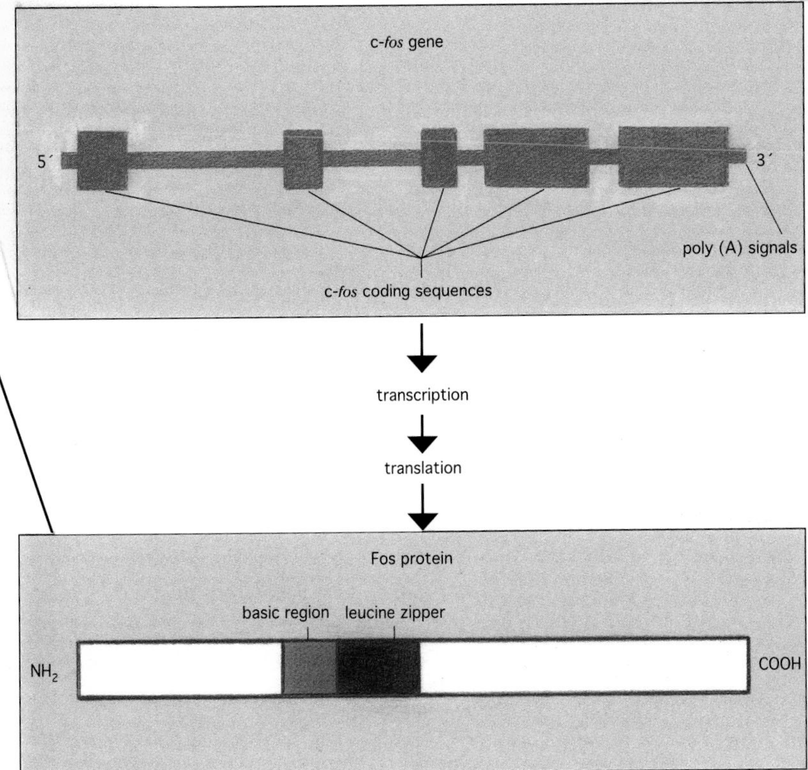

Injury produces long-term changes in the molecular machinery of spinal cord neurons. (Top left) Noxious stimulation "turns on" specific genes, including the c-*fos* proto-oncogene. C-*fos* produces messenger RNA (middle box) that leads to the synthesis of the Fos protein, which regulates other DNA molecules and establishes a "memory trace" (lower box) that can be activated by future noxious stimuli.

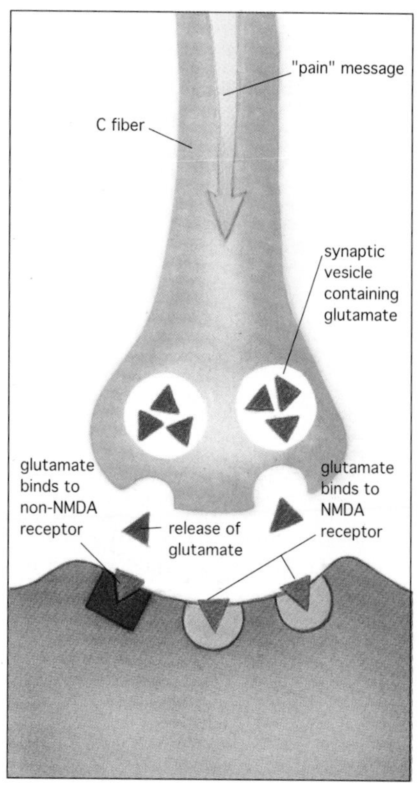

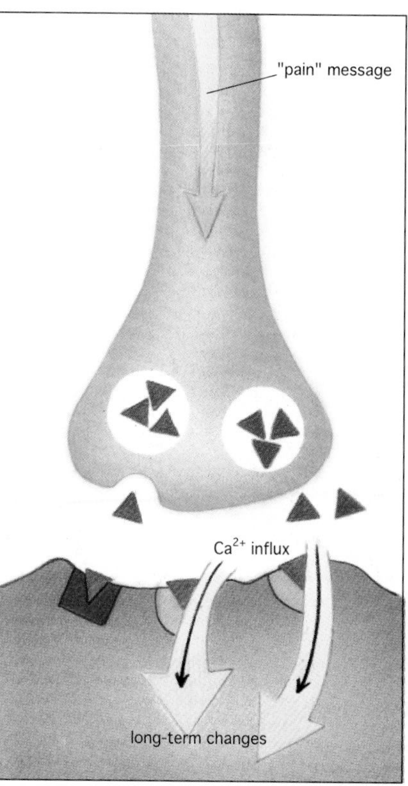

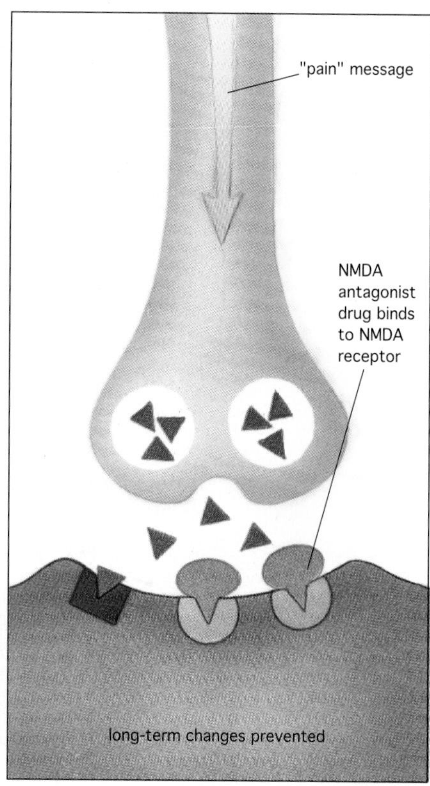

glutamate ▲ $-H_3N^+-C(COO^-)H-CH_2-CH_2-COO^-$

Figure 5

the *N*-methyl-D-aspartate (NMDA) receptor (Fig. 5). (NMDA is a synthetic analogue of glutamate that is used in experimental analysis of glutamate's actions.) In the absence of stimulation, the NMDA receptor is blocked. A severe injury, however, unblocks it.

Once unblocked, the NMDA receptor can be acted upon by glutamate. The long-term consequence of this action at the NMDA receptor is a strengthening of the connection between the C fiber and the dorsal-horn neuron. When this occurs, nonnoxious stimuli produce pain, noxious stimuli produce excessive pain, and spontaneous pain (pain in the absence of stimuli) can also occur. This heightened sensitivity to pain is referred to as central sensitization, or secondary hyperalgesia, to distinguish it from primary hyperalgesia, the acute sensitivity to pain that results from peripheral-tissue injury (for example, sunburned skin).

In the case of primary hyperalgesia, the injury evokes the release of chemicals (prostaglandins) in the skin and joints, which lower the firing threshold of the C fibers. Primary hyperalgesia can be treated with analgesics—including aspirin and related nonsteroidal anti-inflammatory drugs (NSAIDs)—that inhibit the enzyme that regulates prostaglandin synthesis. By contrast, treating secondary hyperalgesia is not so straightforward. To be effective, agents must prevent a memory trace of the injury from being established. The drugs that can do this best are so-called NMDA antagonists.

Anticipating pain: preemptive analgesia

The inadequacy of postoperative pain relief is shameful.
—A.M.S. Black, consultant anesthetist, Bristol (England) Royal Infirmary

To date, NMDA antagonists have been used only to treat or prevent secondary hyperalgesia in animals; widely applicable, clinically useful, and safe NMDA antagonists are still under development. How, then, can the recently acquired understanding of the mechanisms of central

Glutamate, a major excitatory neurotransmitter of A-delta and C fibers, is stored in vesicles in the nerve terminals and can be released by noxious stimulation. Although glutamate binds to two different receptors on the dendrites of dorsal horn neurons—the *N*-methyl-D-aspartate (NMDA) receptor and the non-NMDA receptor—only the latter is functional in the resting state. Binding of glutamate to the non-NMDA receptor depolarizes the postsynaptic neuron and thereby transmits an acute "pain" message to the dorsal horn neuron (and from there to higher centers). At the same time, the depolarization unblocks the NMDA receptor, which leads to an influx of calcium ions (Ca^{2+}) into the dorsal horn neuron. These ions trigger a host of second messengers, which, in turn, contribute to the long-term changes that characterize the NMDA-mediated memory of noxious stimulation. While NDMA antagonists do not block the acute "pain" messages, they can prevent these long-term changes from developing. (Right) The administration of anesthetic directly to spinal-cord nerves at the time of surgery significantly reduces the experience of postoperative pain.

Barry Slaven—Medical Images, Inc.

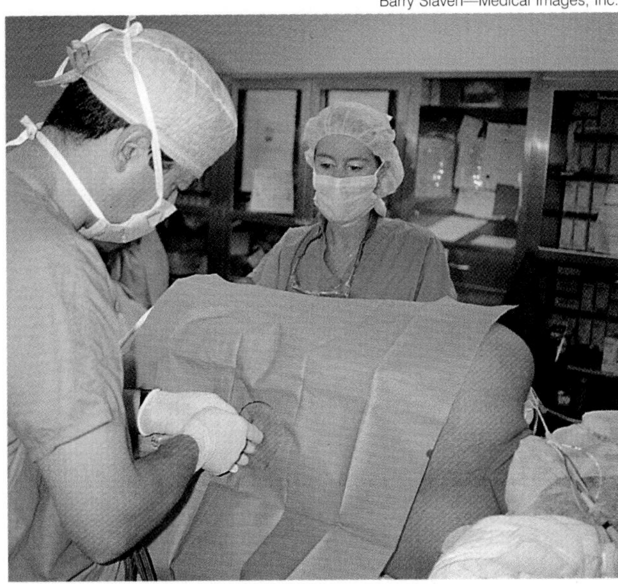

sensitization be used to treat human pain?

Consider, for example, the patient who is having surgery on a leg. When the operation is performed under general anesthesia, the brain is rendered unresponsive (in other words, the patient is unconscious); there is no pain during the procedure, and the patient will have no conscious memory of the operation. On the other hand, general anesthesia cannot prevent the spinal cord from "experiencing" the tissue injury or the consequent activation of peripheral nerves. By coadministering local anesthetics to the spinal cord or to the nerves of the limb undergoing operation, however, the anesthesiologist can ensure that the NMDA receptor is not acted upon by glutamate released from the massively activated C fibers. This prevents the establishment of long-term changes in the spinal cord. Clinical studies have, in fact, demonstrated that the magnitude of postoperative pain can be significantly reduced by so-called preemptive analgesia; that is, by anticipation—and prevention—of the barrage of pain signals to the spinal-cord neurons. In the future the development of selective, clinically applicable NMDA antagonists should permit the direct interruption of the mechanism through which the memory trace of the injury is generated in the spinal cord.

The potential of preemptive analgesia has been most dramatically demonstrated in patients undergoing surgical amputation of a limb. Blocking the spinal cord (administering anesthetic directly to spinal-cord nerves) before and during amputation makes it possible to prevent the development of phantom-limb pain. Every patient who undergoes limb amputation has a "phantom" perception of the part of the body that was removed. In other words, sensory awareness of the body part remains intact. In some cases the patient can voluntarily "move" the phantom limb. Usually the phantom disappears over time, but in about 10% to 20% of cases the phantom limb persists, and the patient experiences a severe burning or razor-sharp pain in the absent limb.

More "pain" transmitters

In addition to glutamate, many neuropeptide transmitters are synthesized by C-fiber bodies. These include substance P, an 11-amino-acid peptide, which was originally isolated in the 1930s in a powder form from horse intestine. (The *P* is for *powder,* not *pain.*) There is considerable evidence that substance P, which acts through a class of receptors called neurokinin receptors, contributes significantly to the transmission of the "pain" message. Substance P not only is synthesized by many C fibers but is also transported to the central terminals in the spinal cord, where it is stored and can be released when stimuli are activated as a result of injury. Studies in rats have shown that with prolonged noxious stimulation substance P can be recovered in the animals' spinal cords and cerebrospinal fluid.

Substance P has also been detected in patients who suffer from chronic pain. Electrophysiological studies have shown that direct injection of substance P into the spinal cord specifically excites neurons that respond to noxious stimulation. Injection of substance P into the cerebrospinal fluid of rats evokes behaviors that also suggest it is a "pain neurotransmitter." For all of these reasons, the recent discovery of highly potent

(continued on page 86)

Migraine: Relief at Last

by Allan I. Basbaum, Ph.D.

Statistics vary, but anywhere from 10% to one-quarter of the population suffers from migraine, periodic and debilitating headaches that are characteristically on one side of the head. The head pain is often accompanied by some form of gastrointestinal upset such as nausea or vomiting. In some cases an attack can last as long as three days. In "classical" migraine the headache is preceded by an aura, which may take the form of visual disturbances (blurring of objects, flashing of lights, partial blindness) or somatosensory disturbances, (tingling in the limbs, numbness), or it may be manifested by loss of speech (transient aphasia). Auras are not reported in "common" migraine.

Long thought to be of psychological origin, migraine is now recognized as a complex neurochemical disorder. Until recently it was accepted that migraine resulted from an initial constriction of the cerebral blood vessels (responsible for the aura), followed by dilatation of those vessels, which generated the head pain.

Years ago it had been suggested that the neurotransmitter serotonin (5-HT) was somehow involved in the pathophysiology of migraine. On the basis of the fact that the serotonin antagonist methysergide can be helpful in migraine, it was assumed that serotonin itself must evoke the vascular changes. Molecular biology studies, however, have identified almost 20 subtypes of serotonin receptors. It turns out that methysergide, although an antagonist at some 5-HT receptors, is an agonist (initiator of neuronal activity) at others. In fact, new drugs that selectively target the specific receptor subtype 5-HT_{1d} have proved to be remarkably effective in aborting migraine headache. Sumatriptan (Imitrex), the first of a family of highly selective agonists of 5-HT receptors, became available in the U.S. in a self-injectable form in 1993. (A 100-milligram oral form of the drug has been in use in Europe for several years and is expected to be approved soon by the Food and Drug Administration.) Most migraine sufferers obtain relief with sumatriptan within about 10 minutes.

Though sumatriptan is highly effective, its precise mechanism of action remains poorly understood. One theory argues that because the 5-HT_{1d} receptor is present on a subset of cerebral vessels, the drug blocks migraine by selectively constricting these vessels. Another theory suggests that the vascular changes are not the culprit. Neurologist Michael Moskowitz at Massachusetts General Hospital in Boston has proposed that migraine is initiated by a massive depolarization, or excitation, of neurons (known as "spreading depression") in subregions of the cortex; the particular region affected determines the qualities of the aura. The wave of depolarization in turn stimulates the peripheral terminals of C fibers that innervate blood vessels on the surface of the brain, which results in the vascular component of the headache and the pain.

In experimental studies in rats, Moskowitz and colleagues artificially produced spreading depression and found an increase of activity in C fibers, which could be blocked with sumatriptan.

C fibers also express the 5-HT_{1d} receptor on their peripheral terminals. The blockade of vasodilation by sumatriptan is presumed to result from inhibition of neurogenic inflammation, a process through which inflammatory changes are produced by peripheral release of substance P and other chemicals from C fibers. Because the new substance-P antagonists are extremely effective at blocking such neurogenic inflammation, it is likely that these drugs, too, will soon be tested in migraine patients.

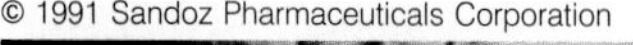

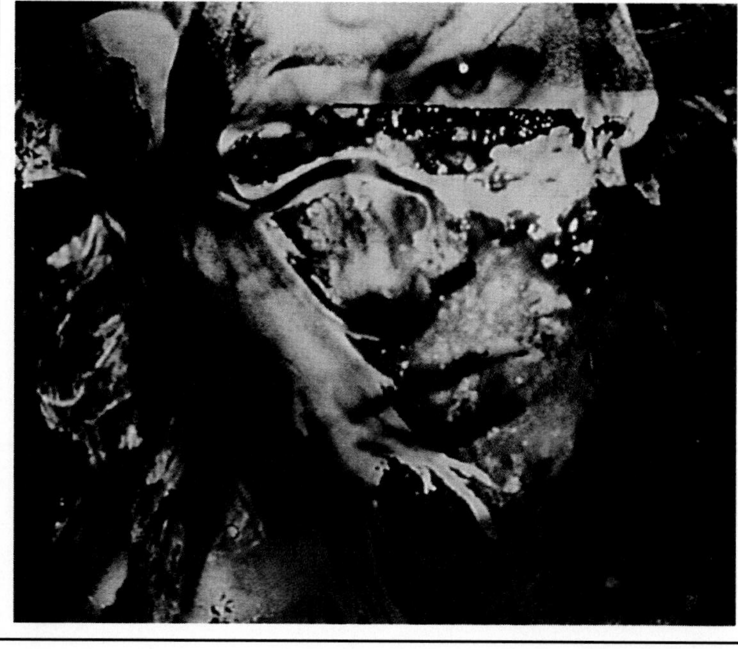

Their pain illustrated: (left) "Underworld" by Carrie Notari and (opposite page) "Gripping Headache" by Raymond Dorow.

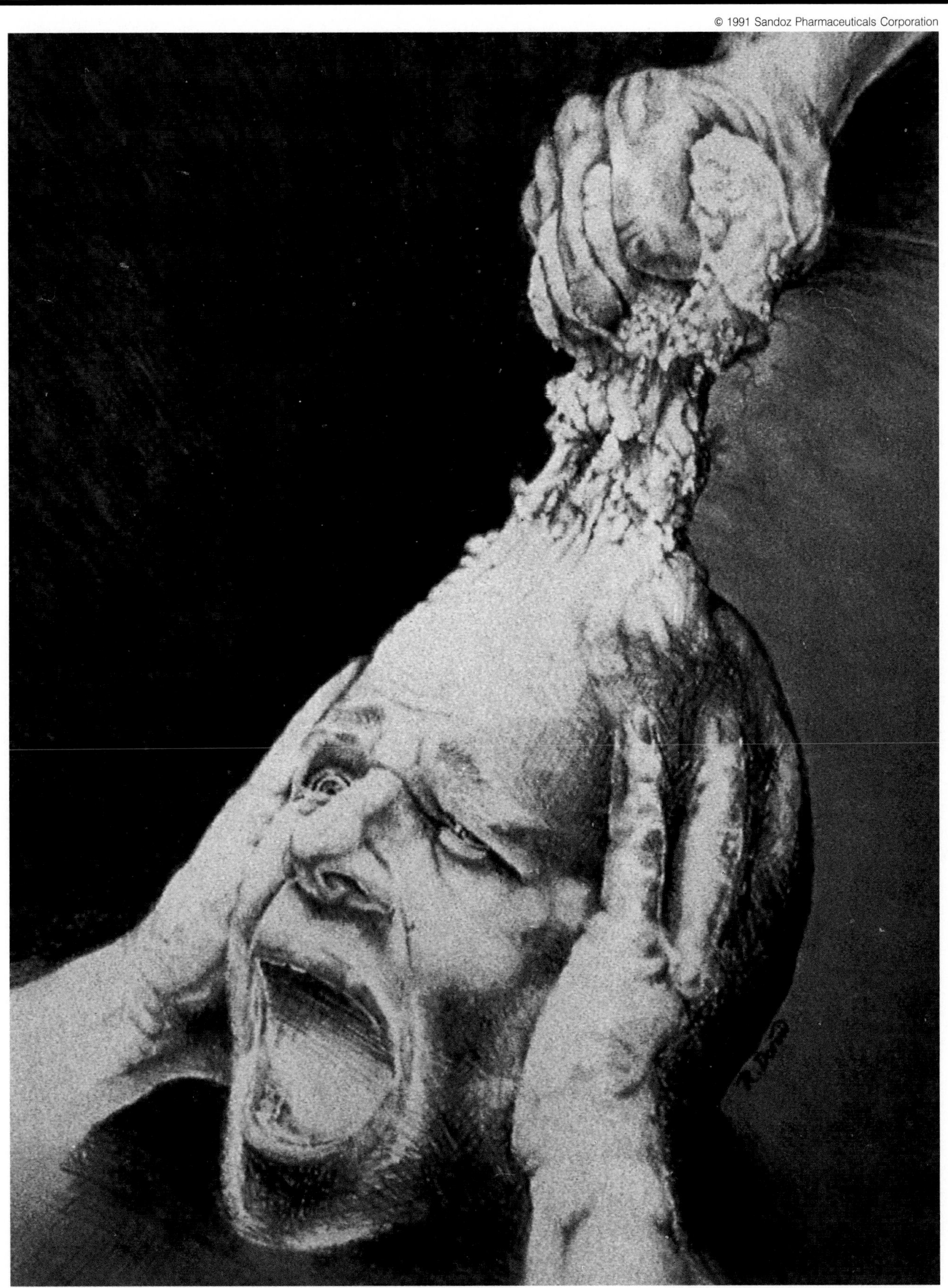

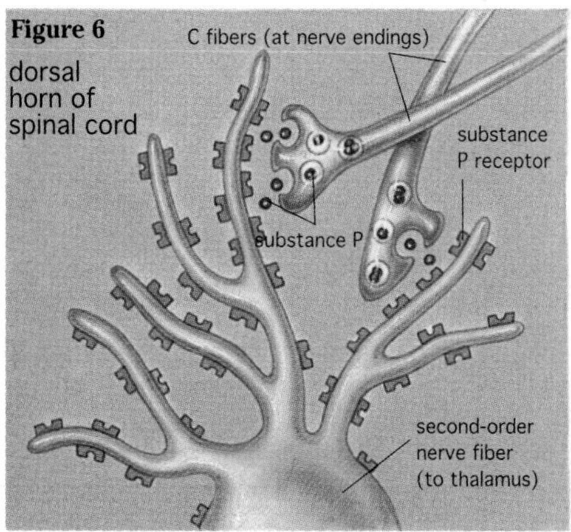

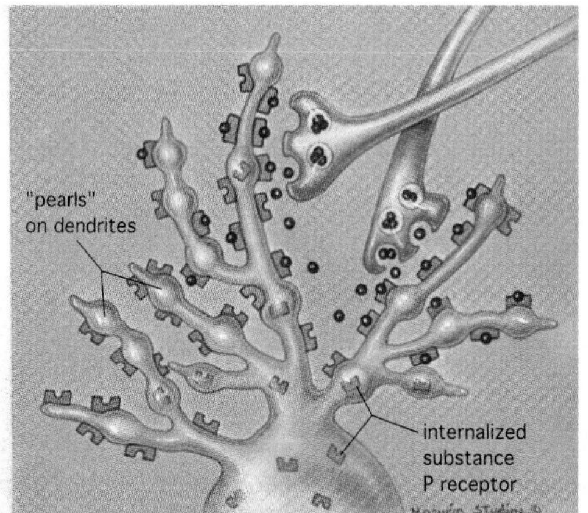

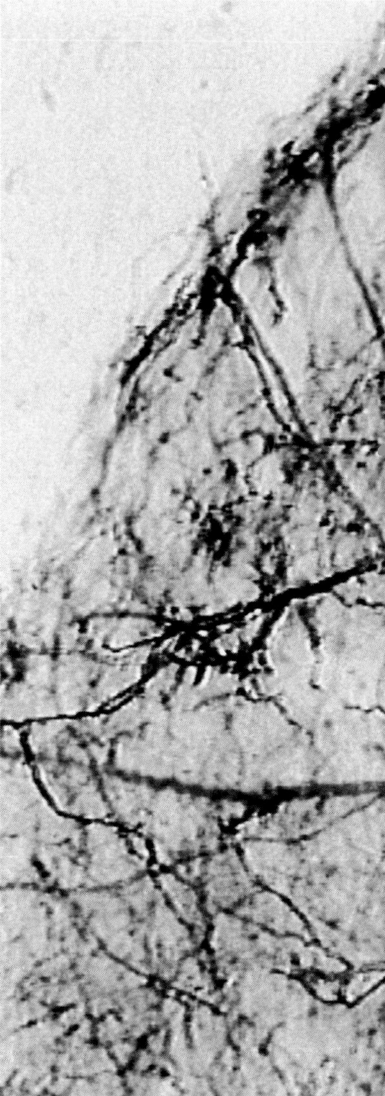

The binding of substance P to its receptors not only depolarizes the neuron but also transforms the shape of the dendrites. When the neuron is in the resting state (above left), the dendrites are smooth; after stimulation they develop numerous bulges (above right), resembling pearls on a string. These "pearls" are often filled with substance-P receptors that have been absorbed from the neuron membrane. A photomicrograph of rat spinal cord tissue (right) shows neurons whose entire surface is covered with substance-P receptors.

(continued from page 83)

and selective nonpeptide substance-P antagonists that readily cross the blood-brain barrier is extremely exciting. Several such antagonists are presently being tested in clinical trials for a variety of pain conditions.

Substance P and glutamate are not redundant neurotransmitters. Rather, substance P enhances the effects of glutamate. Furthermore, unlike glutamate, whose action is terminated by rapid reuptake into the terminals from which it is released, substance P, once released from C-fiber synapses, can diffuse long distances in spinal-cord tissue, facilitating many neurons. Substance P's action can be terminated only by enzymatic degradation, not by reuptake. Another difference is that the glutamate receptor is found close to its site of release, but the substance-P receptor is distributed over the entire surface of target neurons in the dorsal horn. As injury persists, more and more substance P is released; consequently, the number of neurons in which long-term changes may be induced is significantly increased, and the pain message is conveyed well beyond the territory of the C-fiber terminals. Thus, some pains are difficult to localize, and clearly localized injuries may result in achy sensation over a large region of the body.

Recent studies by this author and coinvestigators at the W.M. Keck Foundation Center for Integrative Neurosciences at the University of California at San Francisco have provided direct evidence that substance P generates profound long-term changes, including clear structural changes in neurons. Neurons typically have very smooth processes (projections) called dendrites. When neurons are exposed to substance P (either after direct injection into the fluid surrounding the spinal cord or secondary to release from C fibers), the structure (morphology) of the dendrites alters in such a way that they resemble a pearl necklace. The "pearls" correspond to swellings along the dendrite; these swellings contain concentrations of the substance-P receptor taken into the neuron from the surface membrane (Fig. 6). These are reversible changes, occurring under conditions of short-term stimulation. Future studies will determine whether these morphological changes persist when an injury is prolonged. An important possibility is that the structural changes in the dendrites strengthen the connection between glutamate- and substance-P-containing C fibers and dorsal horn pain-transmission neurons—and thus to the development of central sensitization.

Other neurotransmitters are involved in relaying pain messages. This suggests that multiple therapeutic targets are possible. NMDA, substance P, and other antagonists may all be useful in the treatment of pain.

Photomicrograph, Allan I. Basbaum, Ph.D., University of California at San Francisco

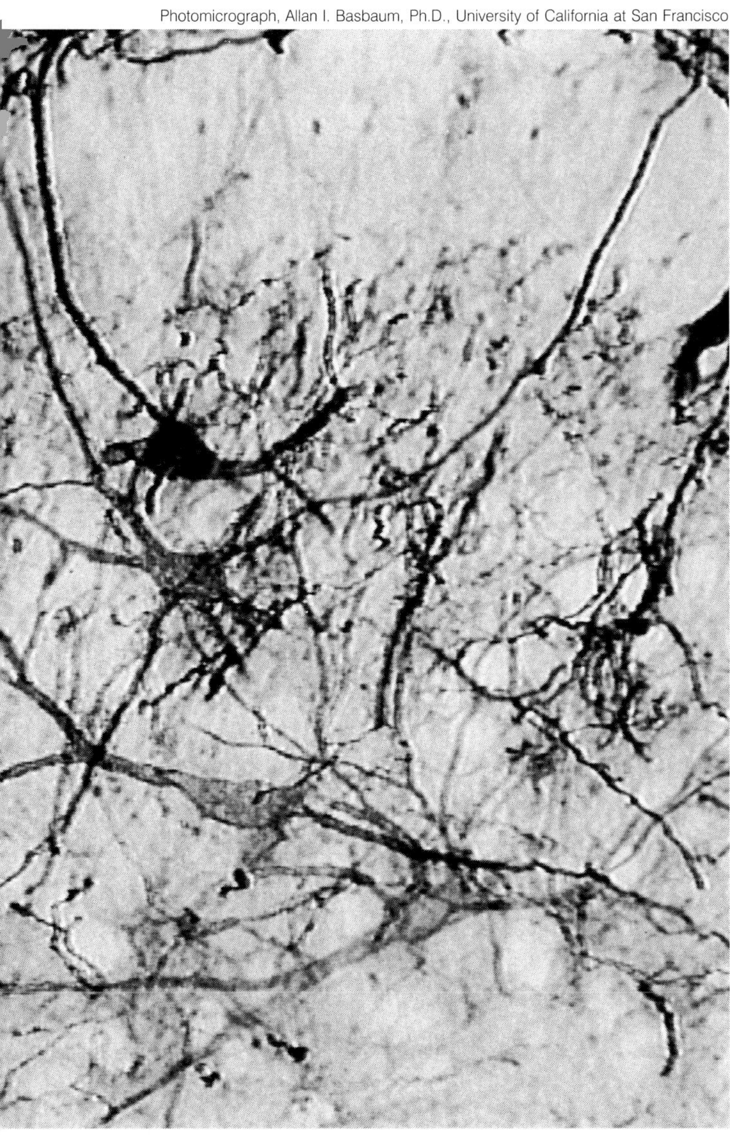

Old drugs, new appreciation

As noted above, aspirin and related drugs work by blocking the enzyme that regulates the synthesis of prostaglandins. The enzyme in question is cyclooxygenase. Until recently it was assumed that the analgesic action of NSAIDs was exclusively due to the blockade of peripheral cyclooxygenase, which prevents synthesis of the prostaglandins that lower the threshold of C fibers. Recent evidence, however, suggests that NSAIDs may also block pain via an action in the CNS.

Researchers Tony Yaksh and Annika Malmberg at the University of California at San Diego demonstrated that injection of NSAIDs into the cerebrospinal fluid produces an analgesic effect at doses that would not be effective in peripheral tissue. One potential explanation for this is that noxious stimulation evokes the synthesis of prostaglandins in nonneuronal cells in the spinal cord. The prostaglandins, in turn, act on the central terminal of the primary afferent C fiber, which results in enhanced release of glutamate, substance P, and other neurotransmitters from the C fiber. Such a process exacerbates the "pain" message that is transmitted to the neurons in the dorsal horn. The pain-relieving properties of aspirin, ibuprofen, and other anti-inflammatory medications may thus result from both PNS and CNS action.

"Unsympathetic" nervous system?

It has been known for many years that the sympathetic nervous system—namely, that component of the nervous system that normally regulates visceral organs (*e.g.,* heart, lungs, blood vessels, kidneys)—is a major player in neuropathic pain syndromes that result from nerve injury. Among the most striking examples of a syndrome in which there is a sympathetic nervous system component is the condition known as reflex sympathetic dystrophy (RSD). The pain of RSD, which can follow even mild trauma to a limb, has a terrible burning quality that is easily exacerbated by normal movement of a limb or even by very light touch. Such pain is accompanied by physical changes in the injured limb, such as cold, clammy skin or overgrown nails. The latter changes result from hyperactivity of the sympathetic nervous system and excessive release of its major neurotransmitter, norepinephrine. Often the disease is treated with sympathectomy—surgical removal of the sympathetic nerves within the affected limb. It can also be treated with drugs that block norepinephrine receptors. One way of delivering such medications is via a skin patch that slowly releases phentolamine, which blocks the norepinephrine receptors themselves, or clonidine, which blocks the release of norepinephrine from sympathetic nerves.

Animal models have provided important insights into the underlying cause of RSD (and other types of "sympathetically maintained" pain). Under normal conditions norepinephrine does not evoke activity in C fibers. However, when C fibers are injured, they become unusually sensitive to the release of norepinephrine from sympathetic nerves. This sensitivity arises in part from the induction of genes that code for the norepinephrine receptors. There is also evidence that sprouting (new growth) of sympathetic nerve terminals occurs around the cell bodies of neurons in the dorsal root ganglion, which almost certainly results in molecular changes in these cells—changes that contribute to the persistence and quality of the pain.

Figure 7

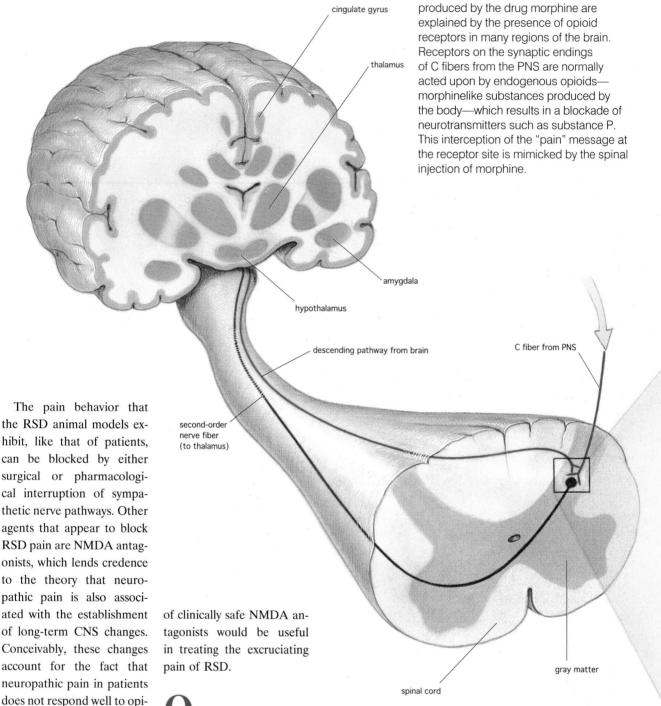

Both analgesia and the side effects produced by the drug morphine are explained by the presence of opioid receptors in many regions of the brain. Receptors on the synaptic endings of C fibers from the PNS are normally acted upon by endogenous opioids—morphinelike substances produced by the body—which results in a blockade of neurotransmitters such as substance P. This interception of the "pain" message at the receptor site is mimicked by the spinal injection of morphine.

The pain behavior that the RSD animal models exhibit, like that of patients, can be blocked by either surgical or pharmacological interruption of sympathetic nerve pathways. Other agents that appear to block RSD pain are NMDA antagonists, which lends credence to the theory that neuropathic pain is also associated with the establishment of long-term CNS changes. Conceivably, these changes account for the fact that neuropathic pain in patients does not respond well to opiates. It appears likely that the circuitry through which opiates exert their effects is disrupted during the reorganization that occurs after sympathetic nerve injury. This new understanding suggests that the development of clinically safe NMDA antagonists would be useful in treating the excruciating pain of RSD.

Opiate analgesia: powerful pain relief

Morphine is an extract of the dried milky exudate of the unripe seed capsule of the opium poppy (*Papaver somniferum*). It was first isolated by the German chemist

F.W.A. Sertürner in 1806. Owing to its power to reduce the level of physical distress, morphine is among the most important compounds useful in the treatment of cancer pain and in cases where other analgesics have failed. In the 19th century morphine was widely used to treat everything from menstrual cramps to epilepsy and was even referred to by the turn-of-the-century physician Sir William Osler as "God's own medicine" and by early 20th-century American hematologist Francis W. Peabody as "the gift of God." It also has a calming effect that protects the system against exhaustion in the case of traumatic shock, internal hemorrhage, congestive heart failure, or other debilitating conditions. Morphine can be injected to ensure rapid action but is also effective when taken orally.

Multiple mechanisms. Morphine inhibits the firing of neurons in the spinal cord that receive C-fiber input (Fig. 7). This occurs in two ways. First, morphine binds to opioid receptors in the brain, which activates powerful descending inhibitory control systems that shut off the transmission of "pain" messages at the level of the spinal cord. Second, morphine blocks pain transmission by binding to opioid receptors that are located on the central-spinal-cord terminals of C fibers, thereby inhibiting the release of glutamate, substance P, and other neurotransmitters. Direct injection of morphine into the spinal cord is, in fact, a common approach to the treatment of postoperative pain and, increasingly, cancer pain.

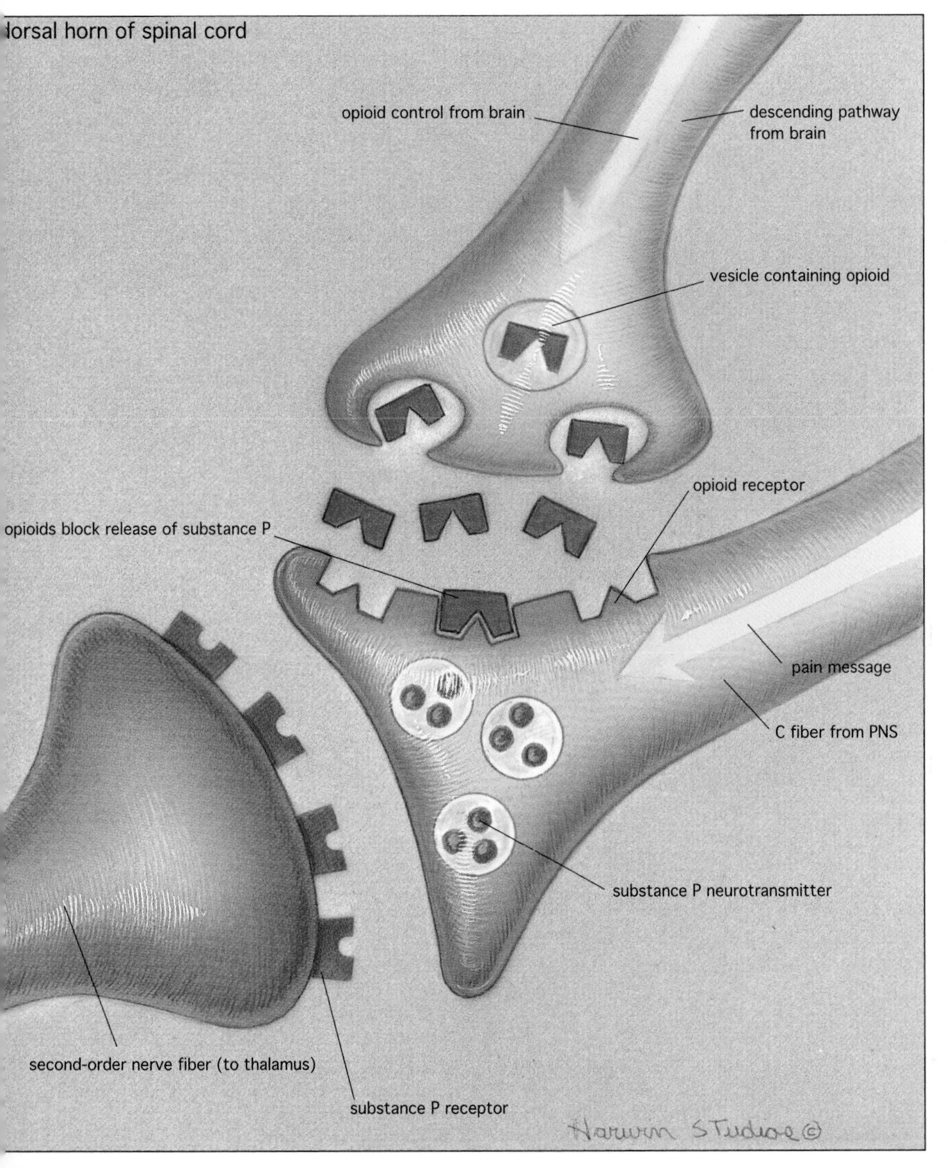

Recent investigations have shown that morphine also blocks pain outside the CNS. The morphine targets the opioid receptor that is synthesized by C fibers and transported to peripheral terminals in skin, joints, and muscle. Animal studies first established that injection of very low doses of morphine into the knee joint can block pain associated with inflammation. The same dose of morphine given intravenously is without effect, which indicates that a CNS target is not involved. Anesthesiologist Christoph Stein at Johns Hopkins University, Baltimore, Maryland, subsequently reported that a single local injection of morphine directly into the knee joints of patients who had undergone arthroscopic surgery resulted in prolonged freedom from postoperative pain. A great advantage of this route of injection is that those adverse effects of morphine that occur with direct administration into the bloodstream—*e.g.,* respiratory depression, constipation, and tolerance—can be avoided.

Morphine is an external (exogenous) substance that is introduced into the body. Naturally occurring opioids within the body also act on opioid receptors. Stein demonstrated that many cells of the immune system synthesize the endogenous opioid peptide endorphin—which suggests that under conditions of inflammation, circulating immune system cells find their way to the injury site, where they release morphinelike endorphins that act on the primary afferent opioid receptor and thus block pain transmission.

It is of interest in this regard that the medulla, or interior part, of the adrenal gland, which is activated in stress situations, synthesizes huge quantities of endorphins; conceivably, the opioid receptors on the primary afferent C fibers are a target of circulating endorphins that are released under stress. It is likely that this system comes into play in situations in which injury does not produce pain. It was once presumed that a psychological blockade of pain enables the soldier who is severely injured during combat to keep fighting through the "heat of battle" or the football player who is injured on the field to perceive no pain until the game is over.

Such natural pain relief is not 100% effective; injury that results in inflammation almost always produces some pain. In fact, if pain were to be completely blocked, one would not be aware of the injury. The acute pain experienced upon injury provides an important warning—to get away from the noxious stimulus. The pain that requires treatment is the pain that persists.

Insights from molecular biology. Although morphine is still the treatment of choice for severe pain, there unquestionably are problems associated with its use, including undesirable side effects. The side effects occur because opioid receptors are located not only in pain-related areas of the brain and spinal cord but in tissues that control respiration, in the gut, and in parts of the limbic system of the brain that influence emotions and presumably induce the "high" produced by opiate analogues such as heroin.

There are three major classes of opioid receptors—*mu, delta,* and *kappa*. Pharmacological studies have shown that the *mu* receptor is the most important for pain relief; unfortunately, most opiate analgesics, including morphine, do not selectively target the *mu* receptor.

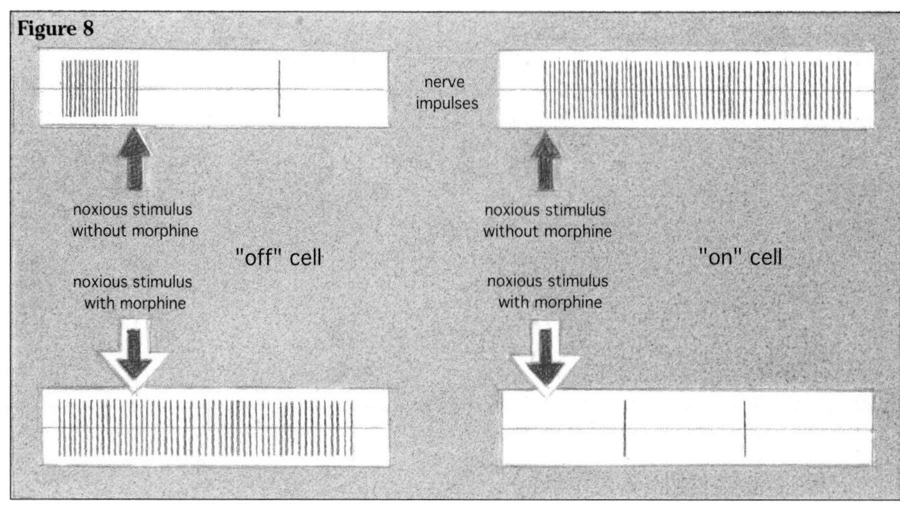

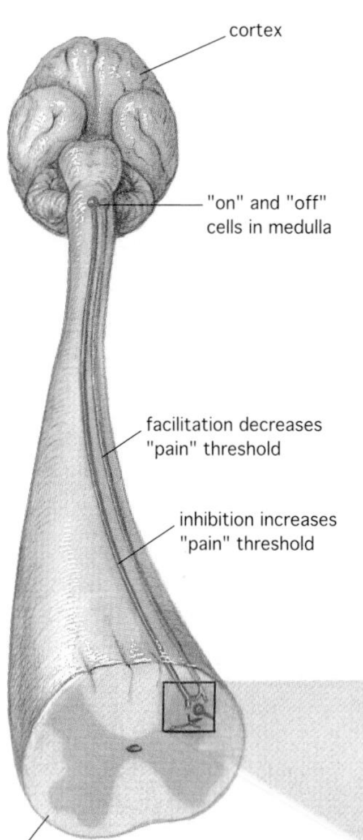

"Off" cells, which inhibit the firing of dorsal horn neurons, are normally active but are turned off when a noxious stimulus is present. "On" cells, which facilitate dorsal horn neuron function, are not normally active but fire continuously in response to a noxious stimulus. In the presence of morphine, the usual reaction of both "off" and "on" cells to noxious stimuli is blocked, which thus interferes simultaneously with two different modes of pain transmission.

In 1993, however, there was a major breakthrough in opioid research; the genes that code for the three classes of receptors were cloned (*i.e.,* genetically "copied" in the laboratory). With the genetic sequences of the receptors revealed, their individual properties now can be studied. Using genetic engineering techniques, researchers will be able to alter specific amino acids in the receptors so that the precise mechanism of opioid binding can be determined. This information then will enable pharmacologists to develop highly selective and potent molecules that target only one of the three opioid receptors. It may also be possible to develop antagonist drugs that selectively block some of the unwanted side effects of currently available opiate drugs.

Morphine tolerance: a new perspective. What about the problem of tolerance—the most frequently cited reason offered by physicians for *not* giving morphine to patients in pain? Traditional views of the means by which the nervous system becomes tolerant to morphine cannot be reconciled with the observation that a withdrawal syndrome (sweating, aches, nausea) is precipitated when the pure opioid antagonist naloxone is injected into a morphine-tolerant animal (or patient). This syndrome can even be observed at the level of single neurons, which increase their firing when naloxone is present. Since naloxone is able to displace morphine only from the opioid receptor site, when it is injected into controls (animals that have not received morphine), it exerts absolutely no effect. If morphine was *not* working, naloxone would not produce a reaction in the morphine-tolerant animal. The conclusion this leads to is that the condition of tolerance is not one in which morphine is not working but rather one in which morphine continues to function, but its effect is counterbalanced by a compensatory response that develops in the CNS.

Blocking of the compensatory response should prevent tolerance. Keith Trujillo and Huda Akil at the University of Michigan have shown that the development of tolerance in rats can be prevented with antagonists of the NMDA receptor. The naloxone-precipitated withdrawal syndrome is also prevented. Because the NMDA receptor mediates long-term changes in CNS neurons and the consequent enhanced pain associated with secondary hyperalgesia, it is possible that the compensatory response that occurs with continuous narcotic administration has features in common with the memory trace that is established in the spinal cord when a severe PNS injury is experienced. Therefore, it could be that pain is "processed" differently under conditions of opioid tolerance.

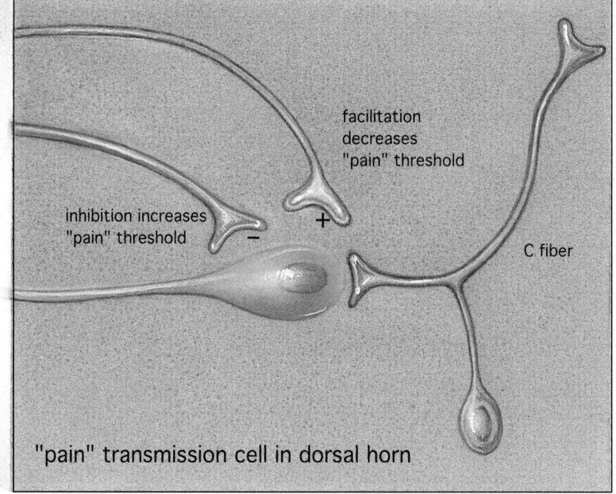

This author and colleagues Dawn Detweiler and Dana Rohde recently tested that possibility by using the c-*fos* technique referred to above. As was noted previously, injection of morphine reduces the number of spinal-cord neurons that express the c-*fos* gene in response to noxious stimulation. This technique demonstrated, surprisingly, that in morphine-tolerant rats there was a significant increase in the numbers of neurons in the spinal cord that express the c-*fos* gene, which resulted in enhanced activity of spinal-cord neurons in response to morphine. These findings suggest that with continuous use of morphine, a latent sensitization of spinal-cord neurons develops; this is manifested when the experimental rats are challenged by injury-provoking stimuli. In a similar way, there is a latent sensitization that is established by noxious stimulation, and pain is subsequently generated by stimuli that normally are not noxious.

More ways to make pain worse—and better

For every question we answer, we raise a whole set of new questions for which there are as yet no answers.

—James Campbell, neurosurgeon, Johns Hopkins University School of Medicine

Endorphin-mediated pain-control systems can be activated in a variety of ways: by morphine injection, by electrical brain stimulation, and even by psychological factors. Recent studies led by Howard Fields at the University of California at San Francisco indicated that there are also pain-facilitatory systems. Electrophysiological recordings from neurons in the brain stems of rats revealed two types of neurons: "off" and "on" cells (Fig. 8). The firing of the "off" cell was abruptly terminated by a noxious stimulus, which suggests that the "off" cells normally suppress pain responsiveness. "On" cells, on the other hand, increased their firing under pain conditions. When the firing of the "on" cells increased, the delay in response to a noxious stimulus by "off" cells decreased, which suggests that the "on" cell facilitates the transmis-

(continued on page 94)

Big Pain in Small Persons

by Allan I. Basbaum, Ph.D.

> *Large-scale studies of the prevalence and severity of children's pain really ache to be done.*
>
> —Charles Cleeland, neurologist, University of Wisconsin School of Medicine

Simon Fraser—Royal Victoria Infirmary/Science Source/Photo Researchers

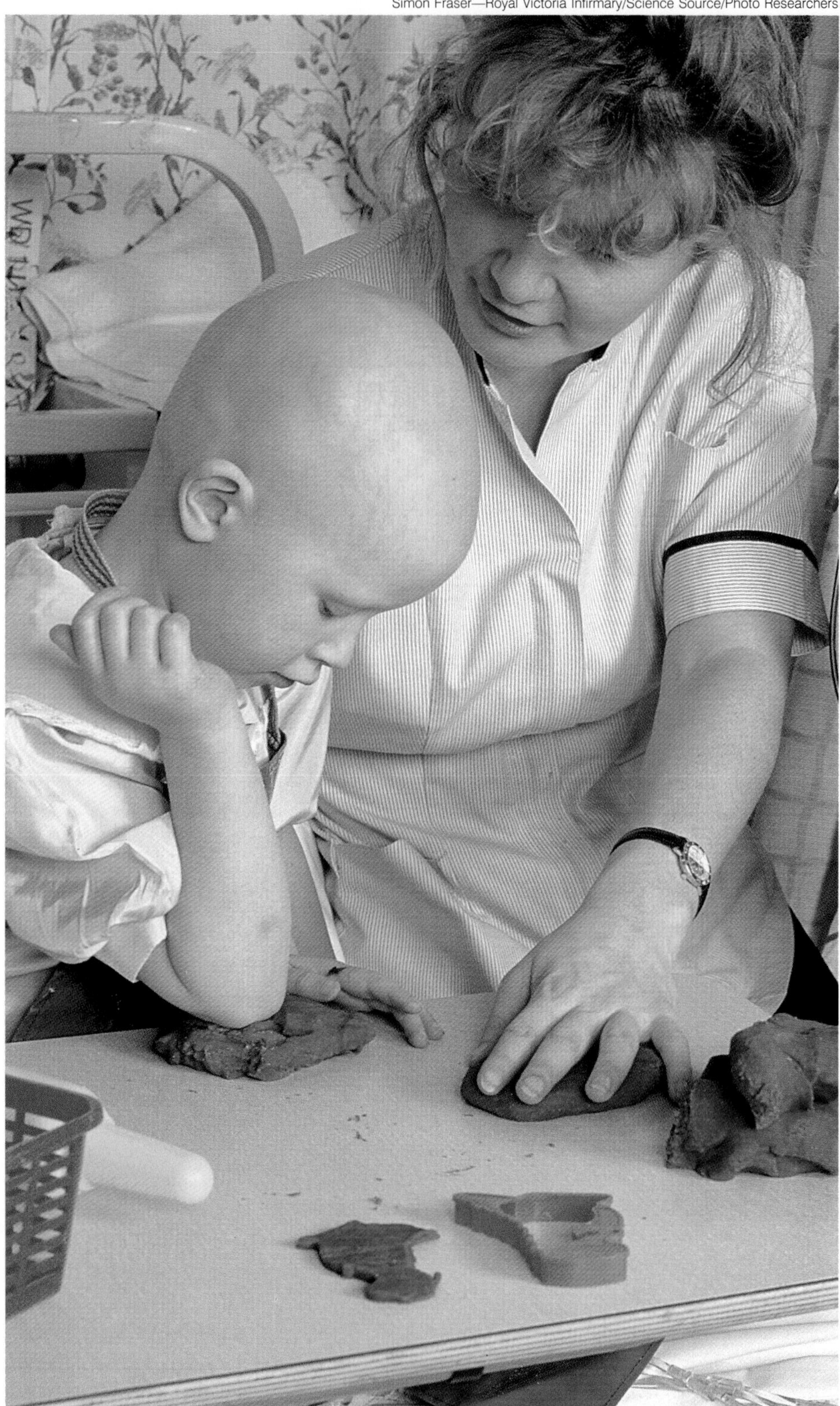

Young cancer patients experience pain caused by their illness as well as by its treatments; (above) a pediatric nurse helps distract a British child hospitalized for treatment of a rare type of bone cancer. Children often can convey the level of their pain to caregivers by selecting an appropriate face on the "Oucher" scale (opposite page).

Though measuring and assessing pain in adults is by no means an exact science, a far greater problem—and an enormous challenge to parents, pediatricians, and nurses—is the evaluation of pain in infants and children. For one thing, children may not communicate their feelings clearly (at least from an adult's perspective); further, their experience is limited. Thus, both the context and the meaning of pain may be very different to a child than they are to an adult.

Specialized tests have been developed that address this problem. Among these are various pictorial assessment methods. One is sometimes called the "Oucher" scale; designed for pediatric patients between the ages of 3 and 12, the scale consists of five simple drawings—faces with expressions ranging from happy to miserable. The child is asked to pick the one that most closely reflects what he or she feels. Children also convey their pain very lucidly in their own drawings; red seems to be the color that they most

Scale to assess pain in children developed by Ada Rogers, R.N., and Raymond W. Houde, M.D., Memorial Sloan-Kettering Cancer Center, New York City

commonly use to characterize pain. In another test, children are asked to pick up poker chips according to the intensity of their pain; the more chips they pick up, the more it hurts.

These tests are not without problems, however. Children may not understand what is asked of them, or their response may be influenced by fears or expectations. For example, if a hospitalized child thinks that admitting to pain will entail further unpleasant procedures (such as the use of needles), he or she may underrate the pain. When cognitive measures of pain are not possible (such as in preverbal children), physiological or behavioral measures are used. Measures of heart rate, blood pressure, and hormone levels in the blood may be helpful in assessing acute pain but are not very reliable in the evaluation of persistent pain. Although heart rate and blood pressure accelerate, and certain hormones (*e.g.,* adrenaline) are released upon painful stimulation, they may stabilize rapidly, an indication of the autonomic nervous system's ability to adapt to injury.

Observing the facial expressions of preverbal children when they are crying may provide some clues about the overall degree of a child's distress. However, such expressions probably do not communicate discrete feelings; a wailing, grimacing infant, for example, may be hungry or afraid rather than in pain. A more reliable means of assessing pain in infants is to study the sounds of their crying. Sophisticated sound-spectroscopy recordings enable the clinician to measure and analyze the pitch, level, and duration of individual crying sounds. Intense pain evokes extremely high-pitched, high-frequency cries and may even be a sign of underlying damage to the youngster's developing nervous system.

The difficulties of evaluating pain in children and newborns have almost certainly contributed to the long-standing assumption that babies do not experience pain at all, a belief that resulted in the performance of many surgical procedures on infants without anesthesia or analgesia. A vast amount of research in the last 10 years, however, has unequivocally established that children and neonates do experience pain. Not only do their nervous systems have the capacity to transmit nociceptive messages, but their behavior indicates that they experience noxious stimuli as "pain." Fortunately, all of this evidence has influenced surgery on children; no longer are anesthetics and analgesics withheld.

Although considerable progress is being made in understanding acute pain in children such as that associated with surgery or injury, much less is known about the child's experience of chronic, or persistent, pain and pain that is associated with illness or disease. In children with cancer the focus of treatment is usually on acute pain, probably because it is the most easily measured. Thus, the task of alleviating pain tends to be directed more toward pain that is associated with treatments and tests (bone marrow aspiration, lumbar puncture [spinal tap], and repeated blood drawing) than toward the more enduring pain produced by the cancer itself.

There is little doubt, however, that children with cancer experience pain. In spite of this, opiates are frequently avoided owing to the fear of the child's becoming addicted or receiving an overdose. While the former tends to be overemphasized, the latter can indeed be a problem. Children's bodies differ in important ways from those of adults. Their livers and kidneys function differently in relation to their size, and they metabolize drugs very differently from adults. Because most drugs are not tested in children, appropriate dosages are often unknown.

Child psychologist Leora Kuttner, who practices in Vancouver, British Columbia, has found that "mind-over-matter" approaches can be quite effective in reducing children's pain. She has demonstrated that certain methods of distraction are remarkably effective; these include blowing bubbles, taking imaginary "trips" to idyllic places, practicing Lamaze-like breathing techniques, and even undergoing hypnosis. The success of these approaches underscores the fact that pain is a complex perception that is not equivalent to the physical stimulus that produces it.

The historical undertreatment of children's pain reflects not only its complexities but the myths that have been generated about it. Better methods of both evaluating and treating chronic pain are clearly needed.

(continued from page 91)
sion of pain messages. Subsequent studies showed that manipulations to block pain (*e.g.*, administration of morphine) increased the firing of "off" cells and decreased the firing of "on" cells.

These results indicate that there are both excitatory and inhibitory mechanisms that regulate transmission of the pain message. Conceivably, such a facilitatory system evolved as a protective response—enabling an organism to react rapidly and appropriately to threatening stimuli. The presence of parallel systems that inhibit pain and facilitate pain suggests that there are previously unappreciated ways that pain is made worse; in addition, there appear to be previously unappreciated ways to eliminate or diminish it. Thus, one might treat pain not only by increasing the activity of the endogenous inhibitory system (as occurs with morphine) but also by decreasing activity of the facilitatory system. If the neurotransmitter mechanisms that underlie the two systems indeed are different, new pharmacological approaches could prove highly effective.

Overcoming "opiophobia"

Unrelieved pain is a common daily reality for many patients with cancer. This is all the more tragic because we have the necessary knowledge, if applied appropriately, to relieve even severe pain in most cancer patients.

—Richard Payne, coauthor, *Management of Cancer Pain: Clinical Practice Guideline,* 1994

It has been estimated that about 85 million persons in the United States will eventually have cancer; this year alone some 1.2 million new cases of cancer will be diagnosed. Many of these patients will have severe pain. In fact, pain is one of cancer's most common symptoms; at least two-thirds of cancer patients have pain severe enough to require treatment at some point during the course of their disease.

Among patients with advanced cancer, many will require prolonged use of morphine or a similar narcotic for treatment of their pain. It is generally less well appreciated, however, that many patients with localized and often curable cancers also experience significant pain. Furthermore, when pain is not controlled, patients may be unable to comply with treatment. Pain weakens the patient's ability to fight cancer in several important ways: by limiting physical activity, decreasing appetite, reducing sleep, and increasing fear and depression. In the future, novel means of eliminating pain will likely be developed; until then, however, it is essential to make the best use of remedies that are available.

In most cases an opium-derived analgesic is likely to be part of the treatment regimen. Morphine is the strong opiate of choice, with a well-established record of effectiveness; moreover, the dose can be tailored to the individual patient.

A growing trend is to treat pain with narcotic medication in a nonhospital setting. This not only dramatically reduces cost but significantly improves the patient's quality of life. Rather than relying on repeated injections, patient-controlled analgesia (PCA) is a self-administered alternative that permits the patient to press a button that releases medication directly into the bloodstream, only as needed. This approach is an important addition to the pain-control arsenal because pain intensity does not rise and fall according to a predictable schedule. In fact, it has been found that although patients generally get full relief this way, their total medication usage is less than if they receive injections on a set schedule in the hospital. The fact that PCA puts patients in control of their own pain has important psychological ramifications as well, and it may even influence the outcome of treatment.

There are also continuous-infusion methods that provide sustained pain relief. A reservoir of medication that is implanted under the skin is one delivery method. Another uses an ambulatory continuous-infusion pump attached to a needle in the patient's arm. Transdermal administration is still another means of providing continuous relief from pain. The morphine-like drug fentanyl, for example, readily crosses cell membranes and thus can be administered by skin patch. Prior to the development of the patch, fentanyl was used only in hospitals and was given by injection.

Despite these effective pain-control methods, most cancer patients are not being adequately treated for their pain. In a recent survey of 1,200 physicians in the United States who treat

Cancer Pain

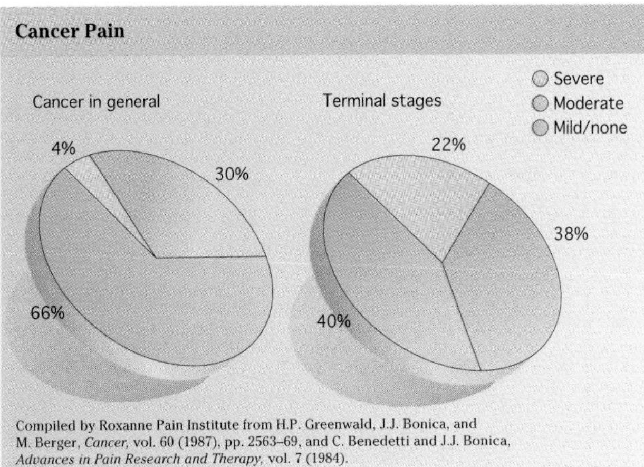

Compiled by Roxanne Pain Institute from H.P. Greenwald, J.J. Bonica, and M. Berger, *Cancer,* vol. 60 (1987), pp. 2563–69, and C. Benedetti and J.J. Bonica, *Advances in Pain Research and Therapy,* vol. 7 (1984).

Three-dimensional surface rendering by D. Gellad; photograph, courtesy of Gary H. Duncan and M.C. Bushnell, Université de Montréal and Montreal Neurological Institute

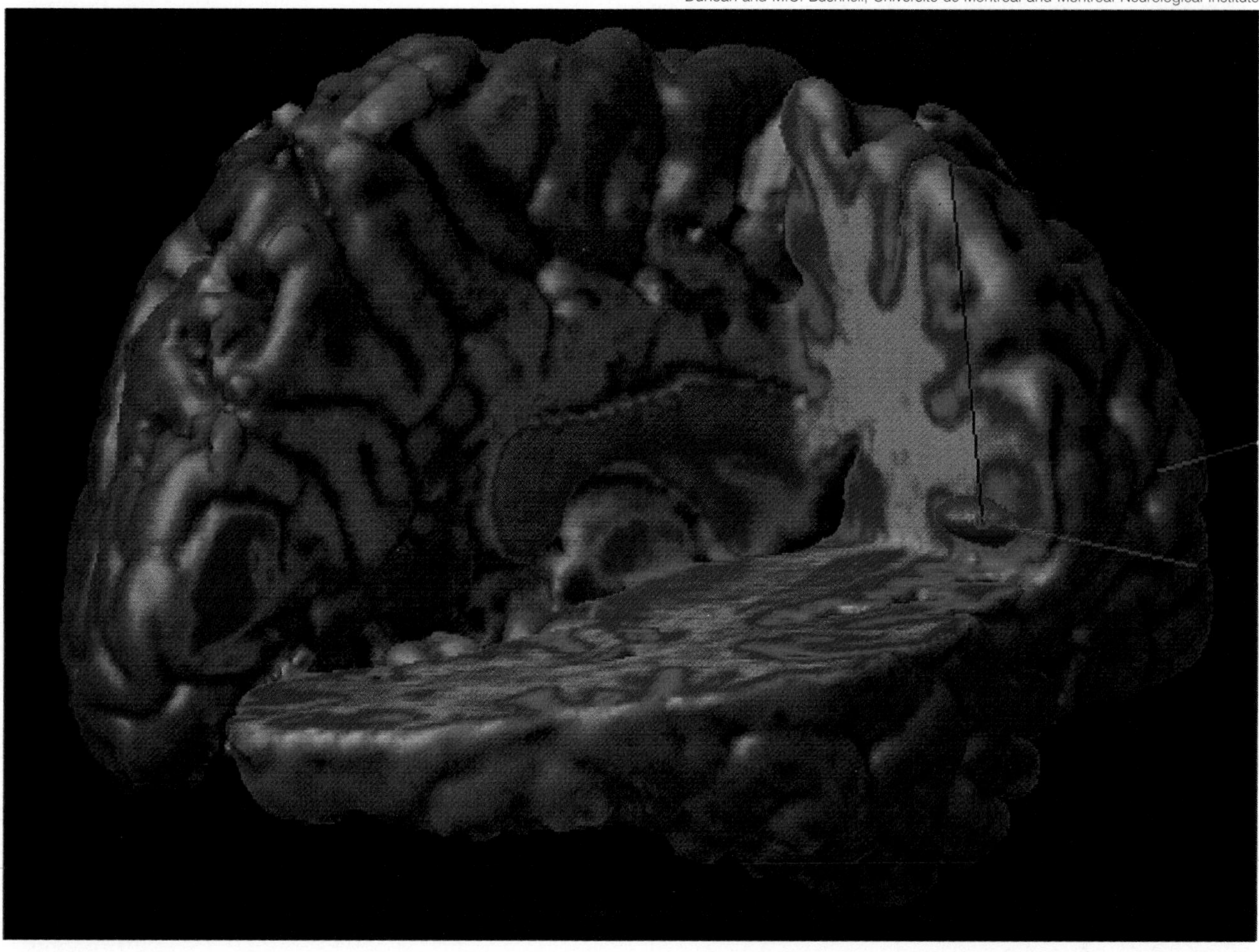

cancer, 85% of the doctors said that their patients were undermedicated for pain. Only 27% reported having had adequate pain-management training as residents, and only 11% learned about managing pain in medical school. In March 1994 the Agency for Health Care Policy and Research, a branch of the Public Health Service of the U.S. Department of Health and Human Services, issued new guidelines for physicians who treat cancer patients; these specify that early and aggressive treatment of cancer-related pain is appropriate and that opiates should not be withheld because of unrealistic fears of addiction.

No magic bullets yet

Seven or eight years ago, I could count the number of physicians with an interest in pain management on the fingers of one or two hands. Now patients who used to have to travel hundreds or thousands of miles to get relief from serious pain can find it close to home.

—Gary Feldstein, anesthesiologist, St. Luke's-Roosevelt Hospital Center, New York City

The last half decade has seen remarkable progress in the understanding of the basic mechanisms through which pain is produced. Studies carried out in both animals and humans have contributed to this rapid advance. So has recent research in molecular biology. The evidence that the nervous system of the patient in pain—whether that of a child or an adult—is *different* from the nervous system of the patient without pain has motivated caregivers to treat persistent pain much more aggressively.

Recently acquired understanding of different types of pain—including some quite surprising findings—has led to the identification of new ways of "turning pain off." Several promising new drugs are being tested in clinical trials. There is good reason to be optimistic that the next few years will bring increased relief to the millions of sufferers whose pain is *not* adequately controlled.

Pain's secrets are rapidly being disclosed. In just the past few years, vast strides have been made in the understanding of the brain's complex mechanisms. Neuroscientists can now even "take pictures" of pain.

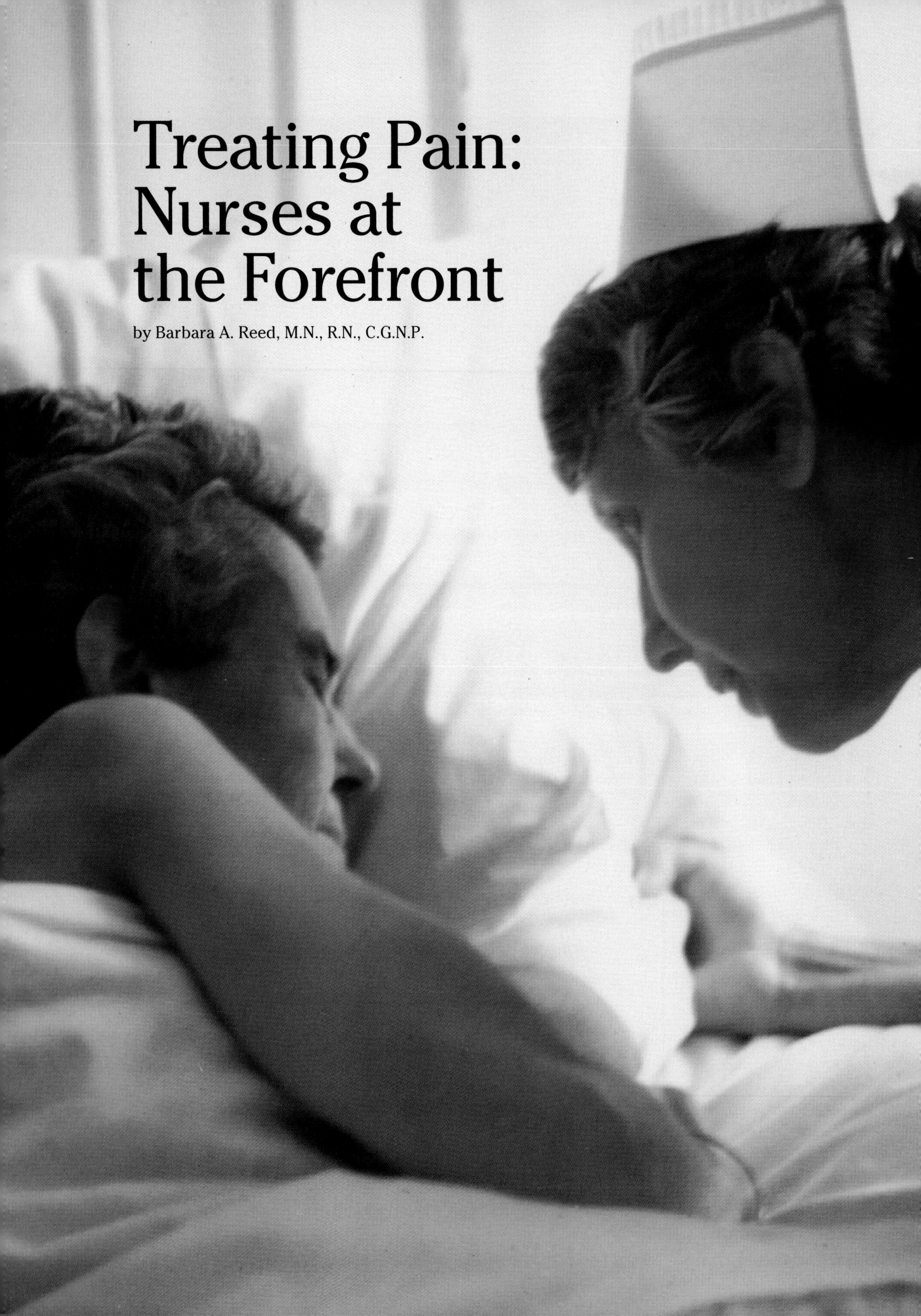

Treating Pain: Nurses at the Forefront

by Barbara A. Reed, M.N., R.N., C.G.N.P.

Pain is whatever the experiencing person says it is, existing whenever he or she says it does.

—Margo McCaffery, 1968

The acceptance of this definition of pain revolutionized nursing practice. Before that, nurses had been taught—and many sincerely believed—that they were the experts on whether a patient was really in pain. Most clinicians in the field of pain management now agree that the patient's self-report of pain is the single most reliable measure on which to base both medical and nursing pain care.

The oldest art

Nursing, which has been called the oldest of the arts and the youngest of the professions, has a long history of primary involvement with pain. While researchers and

Barbara A. Reed, M.N., R.N., C.G.N.P., *is Clinical Nurse Specialist, Pain Management, Emory University Hospital, Atlanta, Georgia, and Cofounder, American Society of Pain Management Nurses.*

Plate no. 328 from *Work of Mercy* by Grace Goldin, published 1994 AMS/Boston Mills Press, Toronto, Ontario

The Granger Collection, New York

Tending those in pain: Hôtel-Dieu, Paris (*c.* 1500).

physicians have been searching for the answers to what causes pain and how it can best be alleviated, nurses have been at the patients' side helping them cope with their pain—but most of all comforting them in their suffering.

Some of the earliest references to nurses treating pain were in Egyptian papyri that described women who dressed wounds and applied the treatments prescribed by male physicians. A crucial interrelationship between the medical practitioner and the nursing practitioner was probably established around that time.

One of the earliest nursing roles was that of the midwife, who helped women through the ordeal of childbirth. The need for that role was clearly established in the Old Testament when Adam and Eve were banished from the Garden of Eden and God said to Eve, "I will greatly multiply your pain in childbearing; in pain you shall bring forth children" (Genesis 3:16).

St. Elizabeth of Hungary (1207–31), a patron saint of nursing, is considered the forerunner of modern public health nurses. Elizabeth devoted her life to nursing those in pain. She distributed alms to the poor, fed the hungry, tended the sores of lepers, and comforted women during childbirth.

Getting organized

In the sense that Hippocrates (*c.* 460–*c.* 377 BC) was the father of medicine, Florence Nightingale (1820–1910) was the mother of modern nursing. For many, Nightingale represents the epitome of the nurse. The gulf between physicians and nurses may never have been greater than during the Crimean War (1854–56), when Nightingale took charge of nursing sick and wounded soldiers on the battlefields and in the military hospitals at Scutari, Turkey, despite the fact that military physicians tried—for all they were worth—to keep her out. But she persisted and somehow coped with overcrowded hospital wards, lack of sanitation, and shortages of even basic medical necessities.

Among Nightingale's numerous achievements was the founding of the Nightingale School for Nurses at St. Thomas's Hospital, London, in 1860. This school became a model for other nursing schools around the world, and it helped to raise the status of the nurse from that of a doctor's handmaiden to that of a member of a respectable profession.

The Granger Collection, New York

Mother of modern nursing on the battlefield, Crimea (1854).

From 1900 to 1910 almost 700 new nursing schools were established in the United States. Unpaid student nurses were used to staff hospitals while they were also in school. Such exploitation became an important issue at about the same time women were beginning to struggle in a broader way for emancipation and equality. Many nurses were among the suffragettes, outspoken advocates of women's rights. Activism on behalf of patients was a natural outgrowth of the suffrage movement, and patients' rights remain a high priority of nurses today. On March 31, 1995, nurses from across the United States marched on Washington, D.C., to bring attention to recent cuts in hospital nursing staffs and the inevitable impact that those cuts would have on patient care.

Among the biggest problems facing nursing at the turn of the century was a lack of professional standards. A few foresighted nursing leaders realized that an organization could accomplish things that an individual could not. They began to get organized. Societies with the aim of improving the education and status of nurses then developed. The largest nursing group is the American Nurses Association (ANA), the professional organization for registered nurses in the U.S., formed in 1896. The International Council of Nurses was established in 1899.

As increasing numbers of nurses joined the workforce in a variety of specialties, it became obvious that no single nursing association could speak or act for nurses as a whole. Medical care became more specialized following World War II, new nursing roles evolved, and nurses sought higher education. Although the first graduate program for nurses began in 1899, the first doctoral program did not open to them until 1920. By 1965 "nurse practitioners" had evolved. Then in 1980 the ANA formally recognized nurses with advanced degrees as "specialists" who have "become expert in a defined area of knowledge and practice in a selected clinical area of nursing."

Although specialization led to the development of new and revised curricula to enable nurses to acquire the knowledge, skills, and responsibilities consistent with their new roles, this, unfortunately, was not the case in the area of pain management. In 1960 when graduate nursing student Margo McCaffery at Vanderbilt University, Nashville, Tennessee, proposed writing her thesis on pain management, she was told to choose another topic because too little was known about pain. Fortunately, like Nightingale, she persisted, and it was her definition of pain (cited at the outset of this report) that is now internationally accepted by clinicians and by nurses.

Pain takes precedence

During the late 1960s and early 1970s, the relief of pain was not a high priority among those professionals working most closely with the patient. It seemed that if the doctor ordered medication, the nurse gave it, and the patient did *not* report relief, then there was something wrong with the *patient*. Thankfully, that is beginning to change.

During that era nurses were instrumental in the inception and growth of two types of patient care directly concerned with pain relief. One of these was childbirth education. Nurses spearheaded a movement to prepare pregnant women for labor and delivery. One of the most important topics covered in childbirth education classes was the control of pain. Such prepara-

Nurses at Bellevue Hospital, New York City, join medical students and surgeon in bedside consultation. In 1873 Bellevue was the first U.S. institution to establish a nurses' training program based on Florence Nightingale's revolutionary methods.

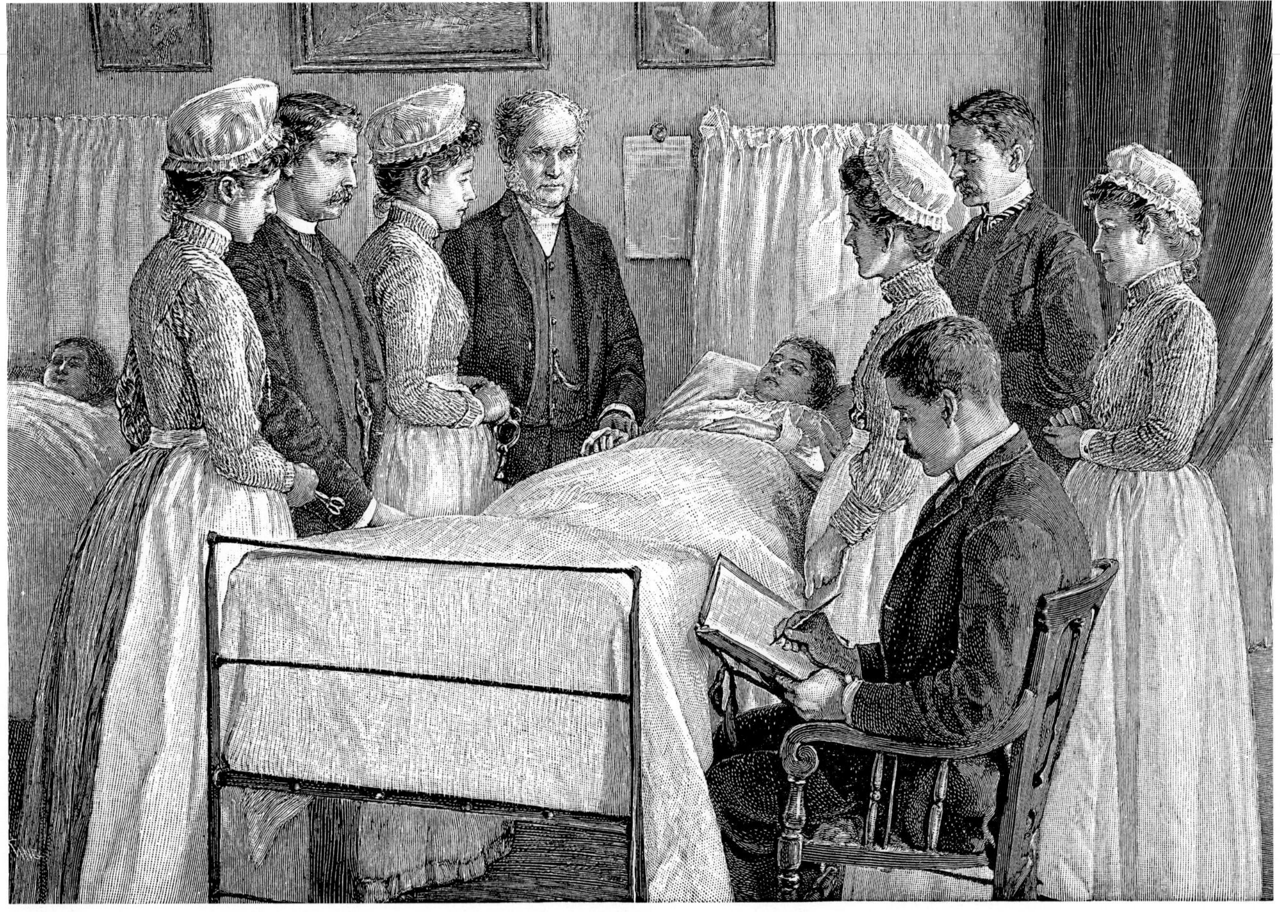

Stock Montage, Inc.

tion is now widely accepted, and classes are still primarily taught by nurses.

The second type of patient care was hospice care. Pain control is the first item on the agenda of hospices. The term *hospice* dates back to medieval times, when it described a place of shelter for sick or weary travelers on long journeys. The first "hospice" in the U.S. was started in 1899 by a small group of women in New York who began caring for destitute women with advanced cancer. It is only since 1967, however, when physician Cicely Saunders established St. Christopher's Hospice in London, that hospice programs have become an alternative kind of care for the terminally ill cancer patient. The hospice concept centers on humane and compassionate care that enables dying patients to spend the end of their lives alert, comfortable, and pain-free in a homelike setting.

In the 1970s hospice programs started becoming available across the U.S. to patients with terminal illness. Most are staffed and run by skilled nurses who have the know-how to manage even the most complex and severe pain. In many cases these nurses have more knowledge about the appropriate use of potent opiate analgesics than the physicians who traditionally write the prescriptions. Consequently, 40 U.S. states have revised their Nurse Practice Acts to give prescriptive authority to nurses who are closely involved with patients in pain.

In 1960 there were only a few clinics in the U.S. that specialized in treating chronic nonmalignant pain, and nurses then primarily assisted the physician. In 1972, however, Renee Steele Rosomoff, a registered nurse, became the first nurse to establish and direct a specialized center for pain treatment within a hospital. That center, the University of Miami (Florida) Comprehensive Pain and Rehabilitation Center, is now internationally recognized.

In 1973 the late anesthesiologist John Bonica, at the University of Washington School of Medicine, considered "the father of pain management," organized the first international symposium on pain. He also helped create the International Association for the Study of Pain in 1974. Gradually, "pain services" began to appear in general hospitals. These were staffed by teams (usually led by anesthesiologists) whose primary role was the management of acute and postoperative pain. It became evident very quickly that nurses should be an integral part of these services. Although the physician was generally the leader of the team, nurses were the ones who were with patients around the clock; they were the professionals most con-

On March 31, 1995, nurses make sure their concerns about patients are heard in Washington, D.C.

Bill Burke—Impact Visuals

sistently available to assess and treat patients' pain over a period of hours and days. They were also consistently available to provide support for and answer questions of patients' families.

Taking the lead

Although nurses were beginning to be leaders in pain management in a few hospitals, a survey of accredited baccalaureate nursing programs conducted in 1990 still found that while 81% included some formal class instruction on pain, 48% of these programs offered only four hours or less on the subject. Eighty-two percent of the schools had no pain expert on their faculty. Furthermore, the content of standard textbooks used in most nursing schools even today is largely inadequate, inaccurate, and confusing in the area of pain management. A study done in 1992 found that only 1.6% of the pages in major nursing texts were concerned with pain.

Since there was little or no formal educational preparation in pain management for nurses, they necessarily gained much of their knowledge and expertise on the job. While they were taking charge of pain on the ward, they were also scrambling to keep themselves abreast of the many stunning advances and technologies that were exploding around them. Nurses nationwide began to make contact with each other and "com-

(Top) The Granger Collection, New York; (center) Joseph Nettis—Stock, Boston; (bottom) Alain Goldeville—Rapho/Black Star

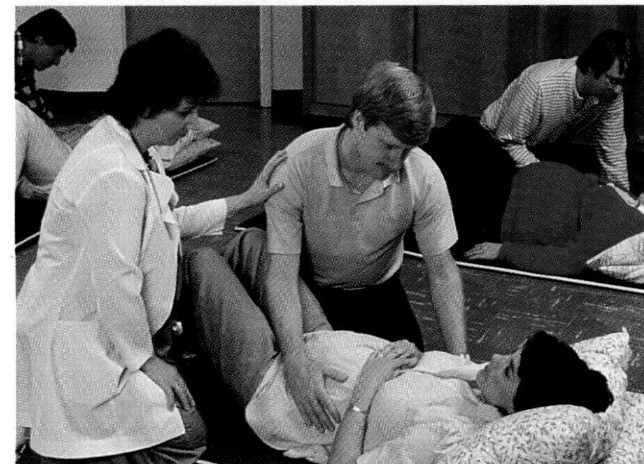

(Top) At the hour of birth the midwife is there, Baghdad (1237). (Left) Coached by a contemporary nurse-midwife, couples learn pain-reducing breathing techniques in preparation for natural childbirth. (Below) A pain-management nurse injects analgesic medication into the epidural space of the back, ensuring her patient's relief from pain without side effects.

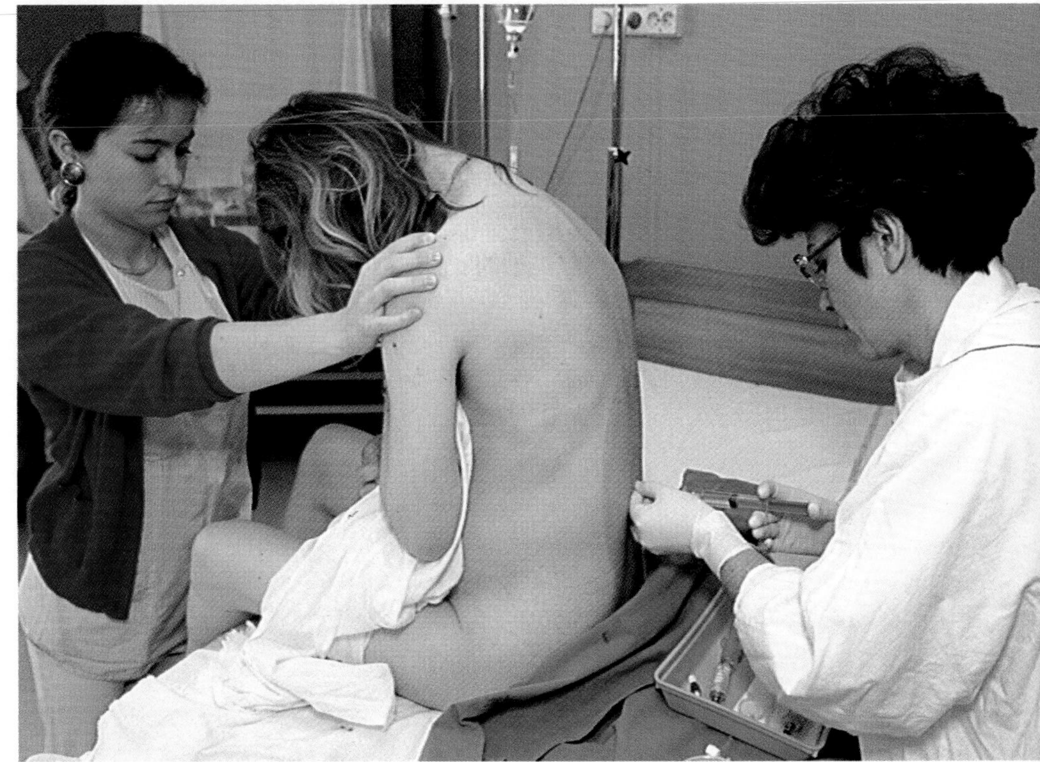

Dan McCoy—Rainbow

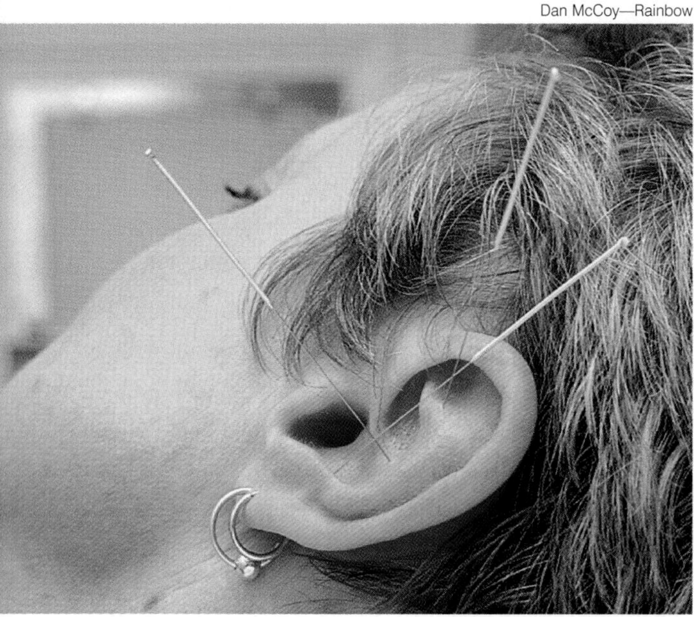

Carefully positioned acupuncture needles can eliminate pain. Many nurses today are skilled in the application of alternative treatment methods.

pare notes" on pain-control policies, procedures, and instruction. It soon became obvious that a formal network was needed to facilitate such communication.

In March 1990 seven nurses from six states met in Atlanta, Georgia, to discuss the feasibility of establishing a national organization of registered nurses who specialized in caring for patients in pain. In two days they managed to lay the foundation for the organization that became the American Society of Pain Management Nurses (ASPMN). ASPMN's membership has grown substantially; the society has over 1,200 members, including nurses from the United States, Canada, England, Australia, New Zealand, and Switzerland.

The role of nurses in the treatment of pain undoubtedly will expand as the 21st century approaches. In many hospitals, however, nurses already are the recognized experts in several areas of pain management. These include:

- patient-controlled analgesia, or PCA, which allows patients to self-administer medication directly into the bloodstream
- epidural analgesia, affording "site-specific" pain relief with the fewest possible side effects (achieved by the infusion of a minimal amount of a drug into the epidural space, outside and adjacent to the spinal canal)
- infants' and children's pain, especially in devising innovative methods to assess pain in youngsters and developing and using analgesic creams that prevent pain associated with needle sticks

While wondrous treatments cure patients, nurses will always comfort and, above all, *care* for them.

- nondrug implantable devices that offer new ways to block pain signals in patients who have chronic pain
- cancer pain, especially the organization of volunteers who actively advocate the aggressive control of pain in oncology patients
- alternative pain-control methods such as biofeedback, hypnosis, meditation, "guided imagery," and acupuncture
- pain in patients with AIDS
- episodes of severe pain ("crises") in patients with sickle-cell disease
- pain in the elderly, especially joint and muscle pain that interferes with the geriatric patient's quality of life

As new and improved technologies and methods for eliminating pain are developed, nurses will be able to do even more to reduce patients' suffering. But they will also remain a constant source of support and education for patients. Just as physicians will continue to work toward curing patients, nurses will continue to *care* for them; it is only through the promotion and practice of both care and cure that patients will be assured of the best that medicine has to offer. They expect no more. They deserve no less.

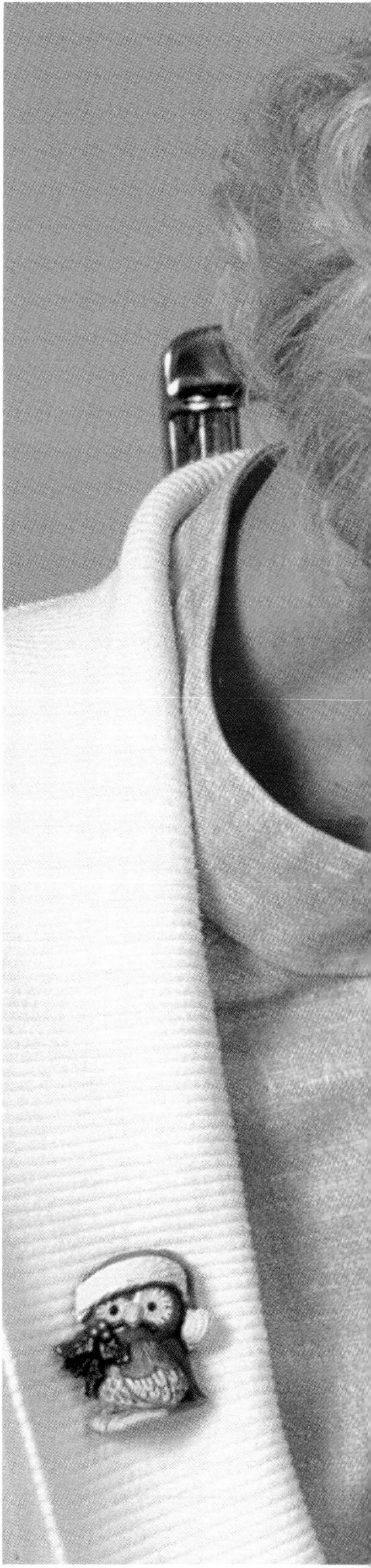

SIU Biomedical Communications/Photo Researchers

Lights, Camera, Suction! Medicine on TV

by Joseph Turow, Ph.D.

(Below, clockwise from top left) Steven Kiley (James Brolin) in "Marcus Welby, M.D."; Mary Lamont (Laraine Day), a nurse in the motion picture *Dr. Kildare's Strange Case* (1940); psychiatrist McKinley Thompson (Paul Richards) in "Breaking Point"; Ben Casey (Vince Edwards) in the series of the same name. (Opposite page) Contemplating their patient's prognosis are (left) James Kildare (Richard Chamberlain) and Leonard Gillespie (Raymond Massey).

(Top left and opposite page) Personality Photos, Inc.; (top right) Everett Collection; (bottom, left and right) Globe Photos

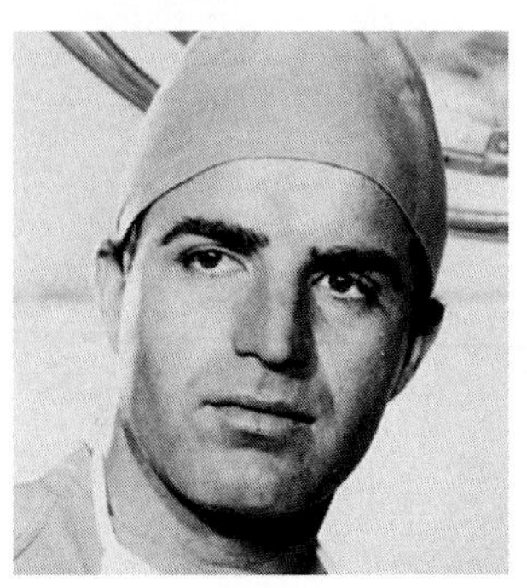

The 1994–95 United States television season introduced two prime-time series about doctors: "ER," set in the emergency room of an inner-city Chicago hospital, and "Chicago Hope," about an urban medical center known for its high-tech medicine and surgery. Not since "St. Elsewhere" aired in prime time during the 1980s had medical fiction so captured the imagination of the television audience. "ER," on NBC, rose quickly to the top of the ratings and remained among the most popular shows. Internet bulletin boards enthused about its plots and cast. George Clooney, starring as a pediatric resident in the drama, became a particular favorite. "The smoothest operator in the ER burns up the tube—and viewers catch the fever," gushed *TV Guide.*

***Joseph Turow, Ph.D.**, is Professor of Communication, Annenberg School for Communication of the University of Pennsylvania, and author of* Playing Doctor: Television, Storytelling, and Medical Power.

"Chicago Hope," on CBS, did not fare as well in the ratings. Nevertheless, it was mentioned with "ER" in the comparisons of real-life and TV doctors that filled newspapers and magazines at the beginning of the season. A number of commentators pointed out that the programs were introduced during a difficult period in U.S. health care. The Clinton health plan—the American Health Security Act—had just gone down in defeat; physicians, health policy analysts, and the public were concerned and confused about what was to come. In March 1994, 82% of those questioned in a *New York Times* poll felt that every American should receive health insurance coverage, yet such coverage appeared remote. Observers suggested that people's interest in "doctor shows" was evidence that Americans were preoccupied with medical issues more than they had been in years past. Few

critics of the health care system addressed the question: What were these doctor shows telling Americans about their health care system? And should people believe what the shows were saying?

(Below) A scene from *Dr. Kildare's Strange Case* (1940), starring Lew Ayres as Kildare and Laraine Day as Nurse Lamont.

A simple answer is that the view of American health care presented in doctor shows is often at odds with the situation acknowledged by policy analysts in the 1990s. "ER" and "Chicago Hope" inherited a tradition from early television dramas of this genre. Since the debut of "City Hospital" on CBS in the 1950s, U.S. television has seen more than 60 series and scores of prime-time movies about physicians. A sketch of the history of doctor shows will highlight why, despite any changes in these shows over the years, television's picture of health care is drastically different from the one that today's policy makers, both public and private, present.

The formative years

Programs about doctors did not just pop up out of nowhere. TV producers and writers borrowed from a formula for the medical drama that had been evolving since the 1930s. The formula reached its pretelevision pinnacle in the "Doctor Kildare" motion pictures, which portrayed the life of a young hospital intern, played by Lew Ayres, and in the "Doctor Christian" radio series about a kindly family physician, played by Jean Hersholt. Both treated the physician with utmost respect. The "Kildare" films, in particular, portrayed medical doctors as elite members of society, with great authority over their patients. Hospitals were citadels of healing where the medical elect carried out their professional duties. Physicians were masters of the hospital; nurses and other staff acted at their command.

It was against this backdrop that television entered the arena of medical storytelling. "City Hospital," in 1952, was the very first medical series on TV, but the first to receive substantial public attention was "Medic," which aired for two years beginning in 1954. The show's creator, James Moser, was a successful writer on the hit "Dragnet" radio series whose real-life friend was a medical resident at Los

Everett Collection

Angeles County Hospital. Moser reasoned that just as "Dragnet" fascinated its audience with realistic police procedure, a television drama with realistic medical plots could also succeed. Moser decided to focus his half-hour series on dramatic interventions involving lifesaving medical technology. The program followed Dr. Konrad Styner's attempts to combat the physical ailments of his patients. To achieve realism—and for budgetary reasons—Moser filmed his episodes in actual hospitals in the Los Angeles area.

The ratings of "Medic" were acceptable but not terrific. Nevertheless, Moser's experience with the show left him believing that medicine as a subject had the potential to fuel a major television hit. Trying consciously to meld the melodrama of "Doctor Kildare" movies with the technical realism of "Medic," he came up with the idea for "Ben Casey," an hour-long drama that centered on a young neurosurgeon. Around the same time, Norman Felton, head of TV production at MGM, decided to revive the "Kildare" name in a television series. Both shows debuted in the autumn of 1961, a season that also saw the debut of "The Dick Van Dyke Show," "Hazel," and "The Defenders." The "medicos" (as the Hollywood weekly *Variety* called the doctor shows) quickly climbed to the top of the ranks. So great was their popularity that the shows spawned "Casey" and "Kildare" toys, records, and fan clubs. Several other series tried to copy them in the early 1960s, with varying success. By the time they left prime time in 1966, "Dr. Kildare" and "Ben Casey" had made such an impression on producers and network executives that they defined the setting, characters, and plots of subsequent doctor shows for years to come.

Archive Photos

Richard Boone as surgeon Konrad Styner scrubs for a segment on "Medic," one of TV's first medical shows. Boone was the host of the series and starred in several episodes.

The Kildare-Casey formula

The setting was the hospital, which was portrayed as the sparkling center of medical professionalism. The stock characters tended to be a young male physician, his mentor (also a male), his patients, and assorted other doctors, nurses, and orderlies. The viewer learned little about the medical staff's personal lives, which took a backseat to their professional responsibilities. The central plot of each episode focused on one patient's problem, typically a combination of physical complaints and emotional or social difficulties. The physical problems were almost always acute rather than chronic, which allowed the plot to climax predictably in a dramatic incident (usually an operation) that cured the patient or (occasionally) led to tragic death.

By highlighting the personal problems of the patients, the producers were able to use the series as a dramatic forum in which to present timely "issues." For example, Ben Casey took care of a girl who, it turned out, had been beaten by her father—an opportunity to explore the societal problem of child abuse. Similarly, Dr. Kildare treated a dying middle-aged man who had a retarded brother who was dependent on him. The exploration of social issues gave both series validity that went beyond medical issues.

The doctors in "Kildare" and "Casey" were mostly specialists, which ensured that they were given the greatest respect. They were highly solicitous of their patients, often leaving the hospital to track down relatives and others whose presence was necessary for a patient's recovery. In addition, on these shows the physicians, not administrators, dictated hospital policy; no one worried about the cost of care. In fact, these shows presented American health care as high-tech, hospital-based, specialized medicine that appeared to be in boundless supply. In the early 1960s this view that medicine was an unlimited resource was accepted by medical associations and governmental agencies.

Encouraging the programs along these lines was the American Medical Association (AMA). The shows' producers and network executives were anxious not to antagonize the medical establishment and wanted the favorable publicity that might come with the establishment's stamp of approval. So, in return for showing their organization's seal at the end of each program, AMA representatives were given the opportunity to read every "Kildare" and "Casey" script and make certain changes—in the name of accuracy. To the AMA, however, accuracy also concerned the doctor's image. During the height of its power in the 1960s, the AMA Advisory Committee for Television and Motion Pictures tried to make sure that, with few exceptions, the physicians in these programs came off as intelligent, upright, all-caring experts.

The producers and writers of TV's doctor shows actually had motives very similar to those of the committee. On the whole, the medical establishment agreed with TV's general "picture" of contemporary health care. Medical consultants' disagreements with the TV executives tended to revolve around questions of image. The AMA was committed to extirpating even the slightest examples of haughtiness, ineptitude, or rudeness from television doctors, even physicians who were "guest stars." Often the producers and the advisory committee had to reach compromises about showing physicians in situations where they were especially angry or amorous. On the other hand, the AMA advisers were quite insistent that the cars physicians drove not be too expensive or luxurious, the way they treated patients be "proper" (which disallowed a male physician from sitting on the edge of a female patient's bed), and the mistakes doctors made be few and far between. Owing to this stringent scrutiny of scripts, TV doctors had a virtually flawless image.

(Top) Everett Collection; (bottom) Globe Photos

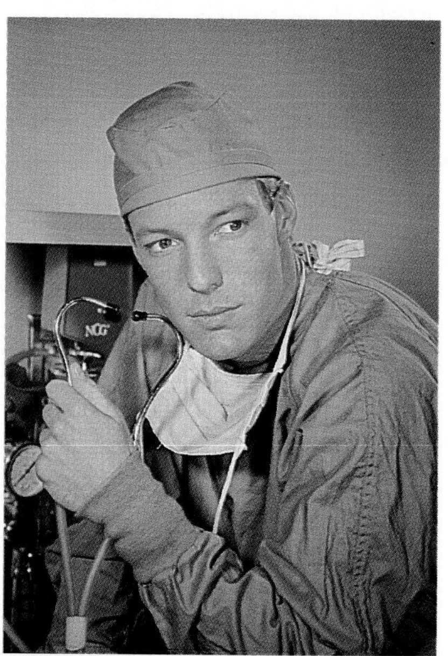

(Right) On the air from 1961 to 1966, Richard Chamberlain as James Kildare was a hero with intellect and heart. The "formula" pioneered by "Dr. Kildare" still has an impact on the doctor shows of today. (Below) Spanning the same years, "Ben Casey" also had a profound influence on what became a lasting formula for the genre. Here Vince Edwards gives guest star Sammy Davis, Jr., the news about what ails him.

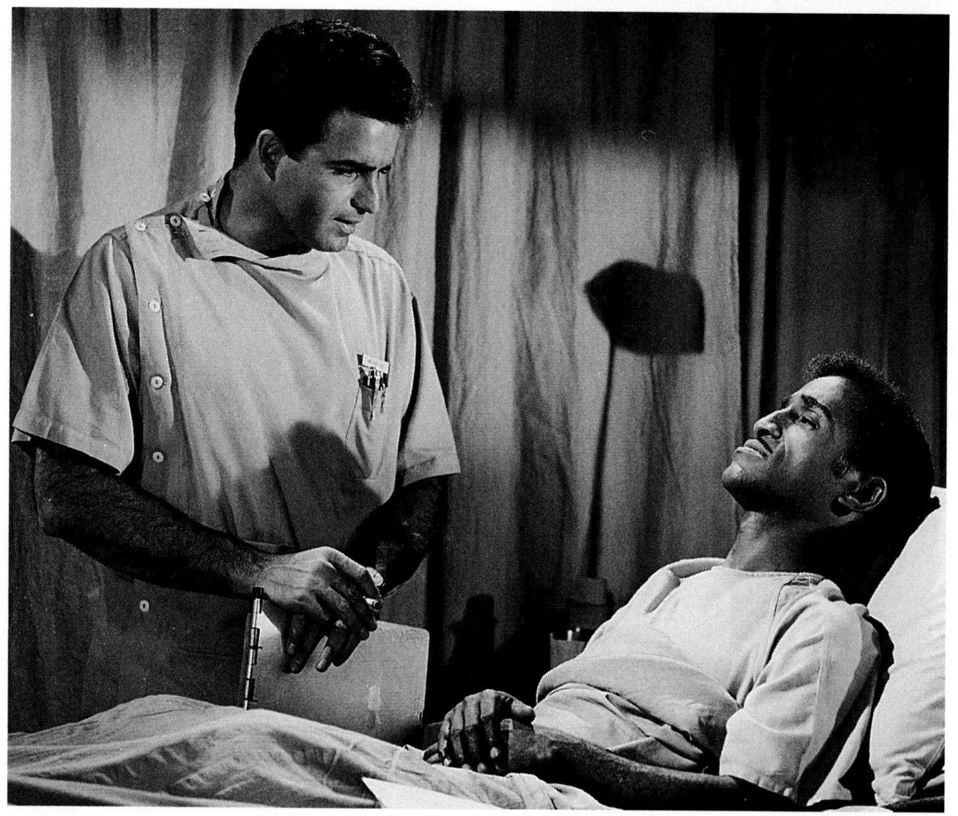

The Kildare-Casey legacy

Strict guidelines such as those set by the AMA were followed by all the doctor shows of the 1960s. In fact, most of the prime-time doctor programs that followed "Dr. Kildare" and "Ben Casey" borrowed the same ideas about setting, character, and plot that had been at the previous shows' cores. A few shows, however, during the 1960s—"The Nurses," "The Eleventh Hour," and "Breaking Point"—built medical dramas around nurses and psychologists as well as physicians. Doctors organizations became angry that these programs were giving nurses and other health professionals the same status as M.D.'s. These controversies, along with bad ratings, reinforced network programmers' belief that to be successful, medical shows would have to focus almost exclusively on physicians in hospital settings.

The trick for a show's creators was to find a variation on the tried-and-true formula—one that distinguished the new show from its predecessors, ideally by being more compelling. Two of the most popular doctor shows of the 1970s were "Marcus Welby, M.D." and "Medical Center." These and the programs that followed them in the late '70s sought to appear urgently "relevant" (a buzzword of the 1970s TV industry) without being truly controversial. "The New Doctors," "Code R," and "Emergency!" were among the shows that attempted to focus on state-of-the-art medical technology—the newest exploratory techniques, cutting-edge emergency medical procedures, experimental surgeries, and helicopter transports of deathly ill patients. A few programs introduced women and African-Americans as medical professionals. "Quincy" portrayed a swinging police pathologist who was not only a master of forensic medicine but a natural at crime detection.

Still another way that producers tried to gain audiences was by confronting hot-button issues, such as abortion, homosexuality, drug addiction, venereal disease, and rape. During the 1960s ABC, CBS, and NBC executives would never have allowed such issues on TV. Now, in the heat of ratings competition and with their social antennae attuned to the changing mores, they did. Arguments between producers and network censors shifted from deciding whether a topic was acceptable to making sure that a script's approach to a "relevant" but potentially volatile topic would not offend the viewing audience.

Diverging from policy and patients

While doctor shows were changing to accommodate the needs of ratings-conscious executives, medical policy was evolving in a way that diverged strongly from the formula that shows continued to employ. By the mid-1970s many health care experts had begun to worry that the cost of medical care was rising out of proportion to inflation. Private firms became concerned that the cost of insuring their employees was forcing up the

(Below) Marcus Welby, M.D. (Robert Young), southern California's most hospitable physician, makes his rounds on the series that ran from 1969 to 1976.

Movie Still Archives

price of their goods, which would make them less competitive with products manufactured outside the U.S.

During the late '70s and throughout the '80s, as the cost of medical care continued to rise, it became clear to policy makers and bureaucrats that U.S. society could no longer consider medicine an unlimited resource available to all those who needed it in the amount that they desired or required. "Managing" medical care became a major focus of government and private-sector economists as health maintenance organizations (HMOs) and other managed-care facilities began to spring up. The cost of high-tech care was questioned, as was the overabundance of physician specialists. At the same time, economists and ethicists became concerned about the problems that such a rethinking of health care might cause. Should only certain hospitals be allowed to buy certain kinds of expensive equipment? Should specialization be discouraged in favor of an increase in the number of primary care physicians? Would managed care inevitably mean rationing? If so, on what basis might care be rationed—age? socioeconomic status? race? Who should make rationing decisions—legislators? insurance executives? physicians? some combination of these? What might the implications be for medicine and society when physicians no longer saw themselves in full control of medical care?

Television's doctor shows, however, steered clear of probing these contentious issues. They continued to portray their high-tech, hospital-focused medical worlds as if the problems of scarcity and out-of-control costs did not exist. The formula of the 1960s changed, but in a very different direction from the one policy makers were taking. Health care experts were preoccupied with the cost of patient care and ways that the hospital and physicians might keep costs low. Television doctor shows, by contrast, were continuing to de-emphasize or ignore the rising cost of care and began to move away from a focus on the patient and his or her needs.

Among the most highly lauded programs in American television history, "M*A*S*H" was also one of the first shows to depart from the patient-focused format. Based on a book that had been made into a movie, the TV series highlighted the lives of physicians in a mobile army surgical hospital (MASH) unit during the Korean War. While the Korean War had taken place 20 years before "M*A*S*H" aired, the show's producers and writers assumed that viewers saw the program as a reflection of the national angst about the Vietnam War, which was raging at the time the series debuted. Vietnam, they felt, was still too close to the collective national consciousness and therefore was too painful or too controversial to be dealt with directly. The "M*A*S*H" creators believed that Korea made a good surrogate.

In a MASH unit physicians and nurses were continuously on call to patch up soldiers wounded in combat. The series frequently focused on the strangely comic responses of the MASH physicians to the continual onslaught of desperately injured or dying patients. At the core of the show was the realization that the only way for medical personnel to keep their sanity amid the chaos of war was to view their situation as hopeless and crazy and act accordingly. The program alternated between high humor and dark pathos. A number of "M*A*S*H" episodes—for example, one in which a reporter interviews the physicians about their experiences and another in which Lieut. Col. Henry Blake is killed in a helicopter crash—became television classics.

When considered outside its combat-based locale, "M*A*S*H" had subversive implications for the doctor-show formula. In previous programs the physicians had been authority figures dedicated to treating patients. When physicians had personal problems, these problems were, for the most part, irrelevant to their ability to take charge of a sick or injured person's care. In "M*A*S*H," however, the steady stream of patients was the source of continual personal problems for the physicians. The rigors of the field hospital not only brought the doctors worry and lack of sleep but placed them in constant personal danger. Moreover, unlike previous doctor shows, which explored patients' personal lives along with their physical infirmities, "M*A*S*H" viewers rarely got to know the patients. Most patients either died or were sent home or back into combat, so the army hospital was in a constant state of flux. The patients and their care under duress simply served as vehicles through which the physicians' personalities could emerge.

During the late 1970s this perspective began to filter into other doctor series. Initially, producers tried to bring the "M*A*S*H" attitude into new half-hour situation comedies, such as "House Calls," "A.E.S. Hudson Street," "AfterMASH," and "E/R." It was "St. Elsewhere," launched in 1982, that showed that a "M*A*S*H"-like perspective could be applied with success to an hour-long urban dramatic medical series. The setting was a teaching hospital in a run-down urban area. But the "St. Elsewhere" writers did not use the poverty of the location and the inadequate technology to explore the crisis of care in the inner city or to highlight its effect on the patients. Indeed, the patients and the decrepit hospital served primarily as a backdrop for the personal disturbances frazzling the workaday lives of "St. Elsewhere" physicians. Television's traditional heroic doctor–helpless patient relationship was pushed to the side in favor of an examination of the personal problems and relationships of the medical professionals themselves.

This major shift in the formula was encouraged by network executives. They saw "St. Elsewhere" as reaching prosperous baby boomers who enjoyed watching people with similar problems to their own. The deteriorating hospital with out-of-date equipment did not become a mainstay in the doctor-show formula, however. In shows created in the late 1980s—"Kay O'Brien" and "Heartbeat" are examples—the physician's domain was modern and efficient. An exception was "Northern Exposure," set in a remote Alaskan town. In making the central character a doctor, its producers (who also had created "St. Elsewhere") seemed to have been searching for a role that would realistically thrust an outsider (a New York Jew) into the center of a rural, communal life that was foreign to him. From the standpoint of portraying medical care, though, the result was no different from other shows of the 1980s. "Northern Exposure," in putting its focus on strong characterization, naturally emphasized the physician's personal (and sometimes physical) problems rather than those of the patients or the medical system.

Acting out health care in 1995

To a large extent this latter approach persists in "ER" and "Chicago Hope." While health care reformers agonized over the political, economic, and ethical aspects of medicine, the television dramas did not. How, then, did these two shows act out the state of health care in the U.S. of 1995? Note how news reports reflect three propositions (of this author). Then look at the extent to which the two series reflect them.

(Below) Crisis management on "The Nurses," one of the few hour-long dramas in the 1960s to focus on other key members of the medical team.

Everett Collection

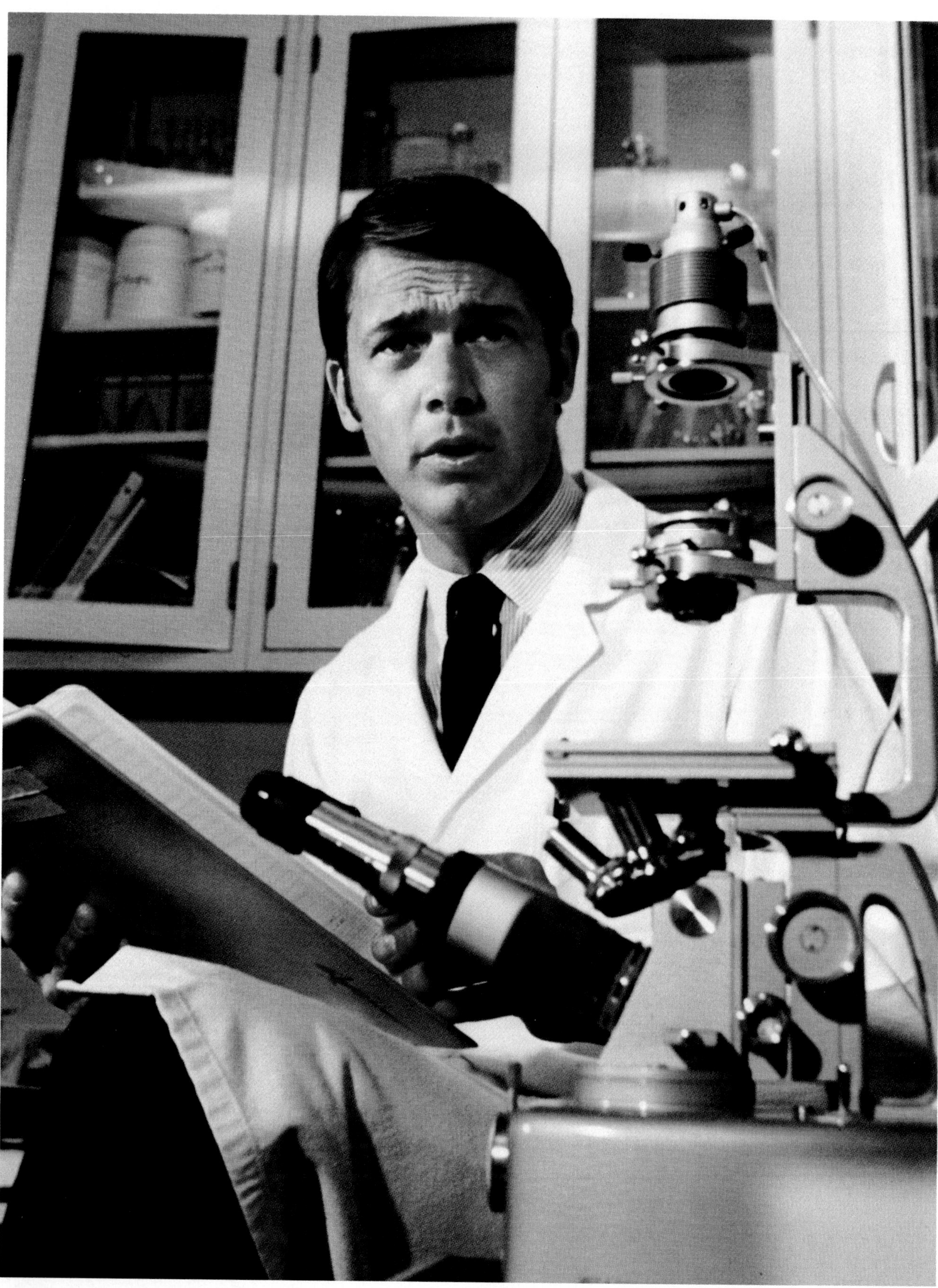

(Opposite) Chad Everett played Joe Gannon, a skilled young surgeon, on "Medical Center."

Personality Photos, Inc.

> *The hospital's 90 skilled nursing beds have been close to 100 percent full and are slated to increase as more [$1,000-a-day] acute-care beds are closed... [leaving] the uninsured even worse off unless the government acts to protect them.*
>
> —*New York Times*, Jan. 29, 1995

Proposition 1: *Many major U.S. hospitals are struggling to take care of large numbers of uninsured individuals who are flooding emergency rooms and filling expensive beds.* What struggles? Both of these TV hospitals look and sound upbeat. Floors shine, equipment is terrific, morale is high. The ER is a busy, even frenetic, place, but the program does not reflect reformers' claims that in some real-life hospital emergency departments, waits for care are interminable, infectious diseases rampant, and demands on staff overwhelming.

"ER" never shows crowds at the admissions desk of an emergency room waiting while their insurance forms are processed. It never shows ER personnel seeking confirmation from an HMO that the person's care will be paid for. One way or another, the patients of "ER" are admitted and receive help.

As for "Chicago Hope," one gets the sense that this is an urban medical center where other specialists who have run out of options send their patients. "Chicago Hope" uses the issue of money to heighten drama fairly frequently, but money is always available, regardless of the procedure's cost or the patient's situation. In one episode the hospital's budget director and some of the board of directors prattled on about the high costs of certain nonreimbursable surgical procedures that a surgeon wanted to perform. In the end, though, the medical director overruled them, angrily declaring that he would recoup the million-dollar cost from the research grants of some of the prestigious physicians in his charge. At "Chicago Hope" it seems that there is always some pot of gold at the end of a patient's rainbow, even when the plot twists in quite unrealistic and unfeasible ways.

> *All the studies show that the uninsured get less care and end up sicker than people with insurance. Insurance per se makes a huge difference.*
>
> —Drew E. Altman, president of the Henry J. Kaiser Family Foundation, *New York Times*, July 11, 1994

Proposition 2: *Uninsured Americans suffer owing to lack of care.* Rarely, if ever, on these shows. Nobody asks anybody for an insurance card, and health professionals who do not treat all people equally have to face negative consequences.

In "Chicago Hope," for example, a resident was reprimanded severely by a surgeon for hesitating to treat a bleeding prostitute who admitted to having HIV. Not only did the resident apologize, but the surgeon carried out a hugely expensive experimental bone marrow transplant in an attempt to improve her condition. At the end of the episode, she lay on a gurney next to a middle-aged African-American man who also had undergone a hugely expensive experimental operation (transplantation of an ape's heart for his own defective one until a human donor could be found).

The implication—that there is equal-opportunity caregiving here—reinforces the traditional formula's theme of medicine as an unlimited resource. In the real world, though, experimental surgical procedures, which most health insurance policies will not support, are usually available only to those who can af-

NBC/Globe Photos

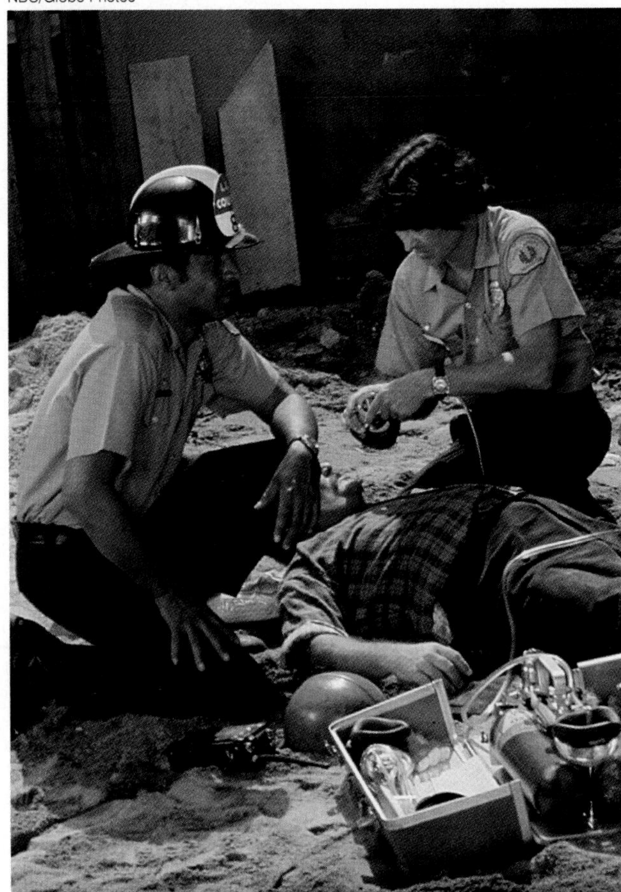

State-of-the-art technology was the forte of the show "Emergency!" Here paramedic John Gage (Randolph Mantooth, kneeling right) comes to the rescue; the series aired from 1972 to 1977.

(Clockwise from top left) Los Angeles medical examiner Quincy (Jack Klugman) scrutinizes a crime scene; despite being the only doctor in Cicely, Alaska—the setting for TV's "Northern Exposure"—Joel Fleischman (Rob Morrow) seems to have plenty of time for reading; Capt. Benjamin Franklin ("Hawkeye") Pierce (Alan Alda) and Maj. Margaret ("Hot Lips") Houlihan (Loretta Swit) suit up for combat medicine on "M*A*S*H."

(Top left and bottom right) Everett Collection; (bottom left) Personality Photos, Inc.

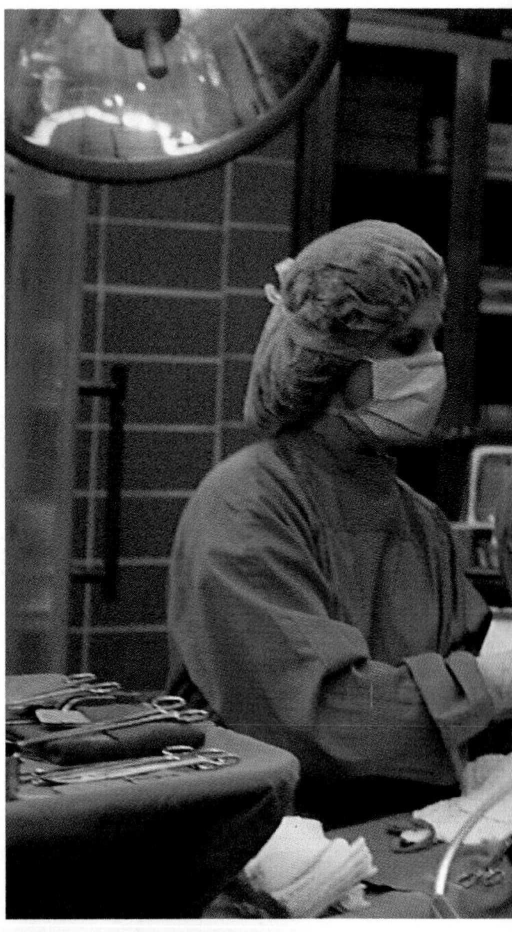

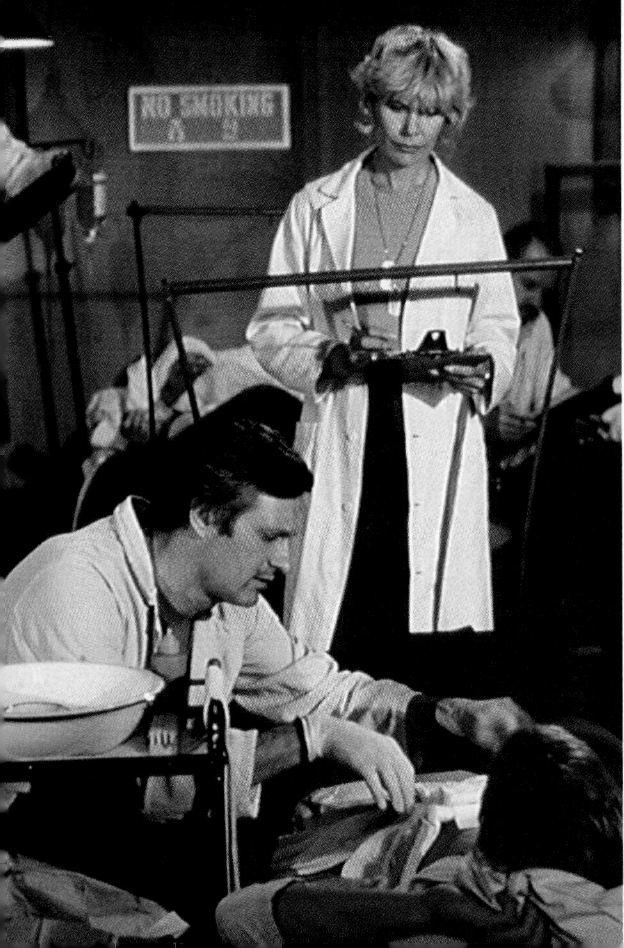

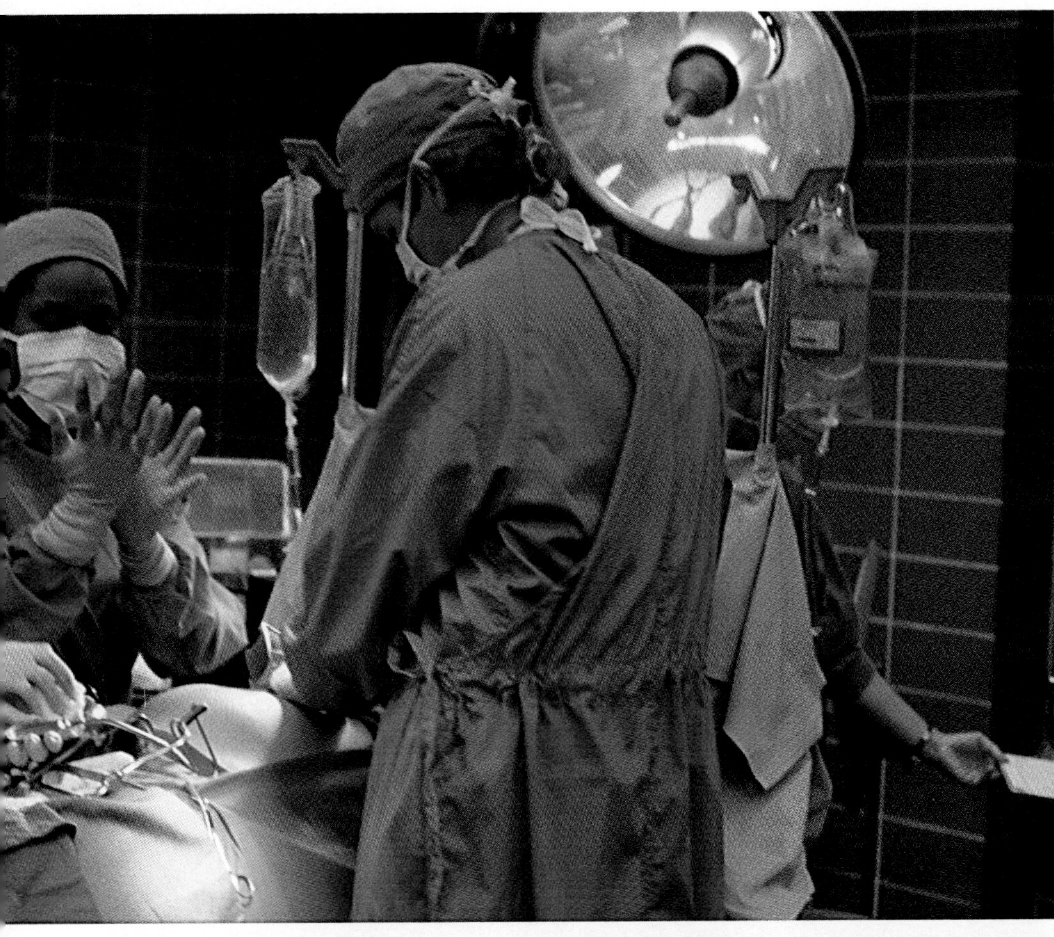

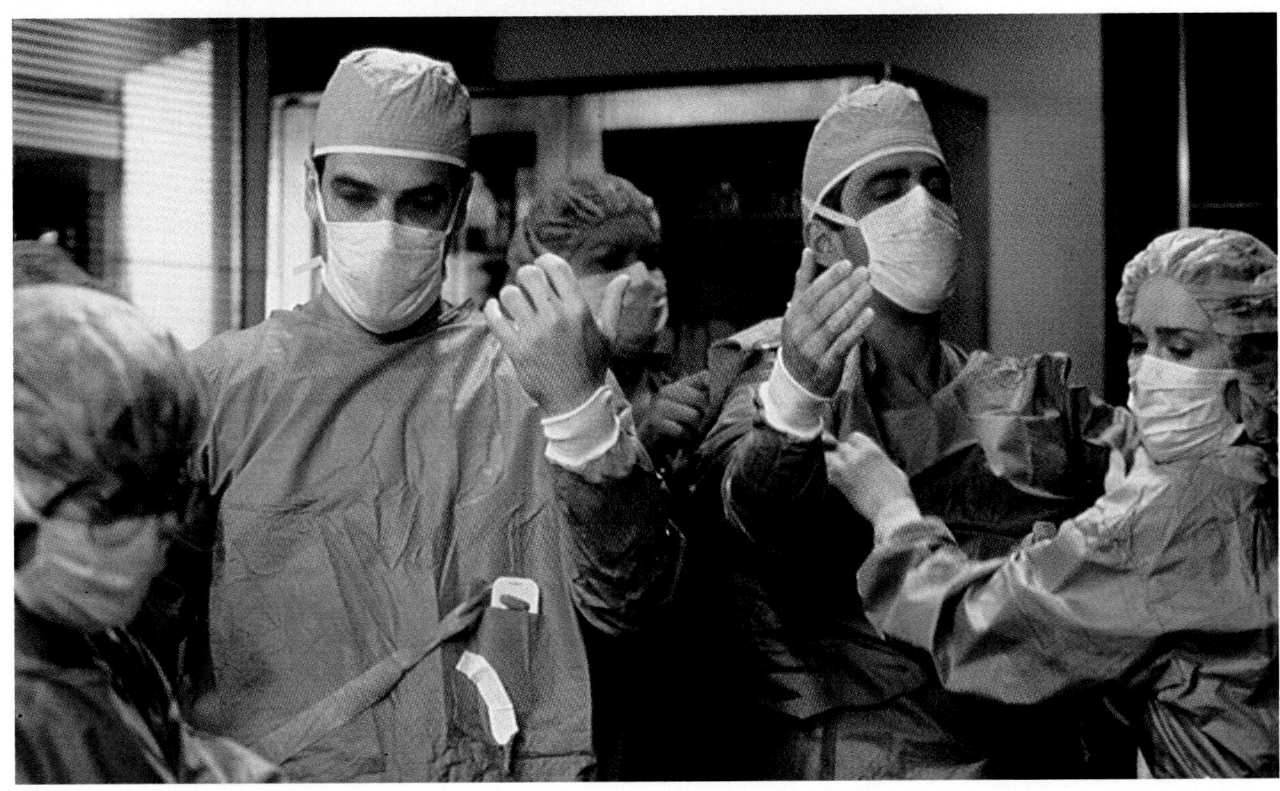

(Left) A surgery scene from the popular drama "St. Elsewhere," where curative medicine often took a back seat to character-driven, physician-focused plotlines. (Below) A sterile situation from the new drama "Chicago Hope," starring Mandy Patinkin (left) as Jeffrey Geiger and Adam Arkin (right) as Aaron Shutt.

(Top) NBC/Globe Photos; (bottom) CBS/Everett Collection

ford the exorbitant cost. Physicians also make choices about whom to treat—criteria include patients' general physical health, tendency toward alcoholism or drug addiction, and age. By not emphasizing this aspect of medical decision making or the insurance company's denial of coverage, "Chicago Hope" is turning away from some of the most difficult and controversial realities of cutting-edge medicine.

Membership in health maintenance organizations has exploded in the last 10 years, to 45 million in 1993 from 12.5 million in 1983.
—*New York Times*, Feb. 15, 1994

Proposition 3: *To get the most out of scarce medical resources, high-tech medicine must be de-emphasized in favor of primary care.* Here, of course, is where the debate about health care policy gets dramatic. Is it good that government and corporate policy makers want teaching programs to turn out fewer specialists and more family practitioners, general internists, and general pediatricians? Should the public at large be comfortable that companies are channeling their employees into HMOs, where primary physicians are coordinators of care and gatekeepers to specialists?

"ER" and "Chicago Hope" very seldom join the raging debate. For these shows, high-tech hospital-based medicine is not just the best medicine; it is the only medicine worth dramatizing. In their worlds primary care doctors simply do not exist, and HMOs hardly rear their heads. What counts on "ER" are multiple crises that shift back and forth with pulsating, MTV-like tension at the edge of chaos, where life hangs in the balance and *cost* is a dirty word. In "Chicago Hope" what counts is the pristine operating room, where state-of-the-art doctors use state-of-the-art machinery to advance science. When an HMO did try to dictate care to a "Chicago Hope" surgeon, its representatives were coldly put in their place. This runs counter to the real trend in U.S. health care of moving away from smaller ERs and large research hospitals toward hospital conglomerates and HMOs. Modifications in the delivery of health care have steadily increased in the '90s as everyone has felt the heat of the health care crisis.

NBC/Globe Photos; photo, Chris Haston

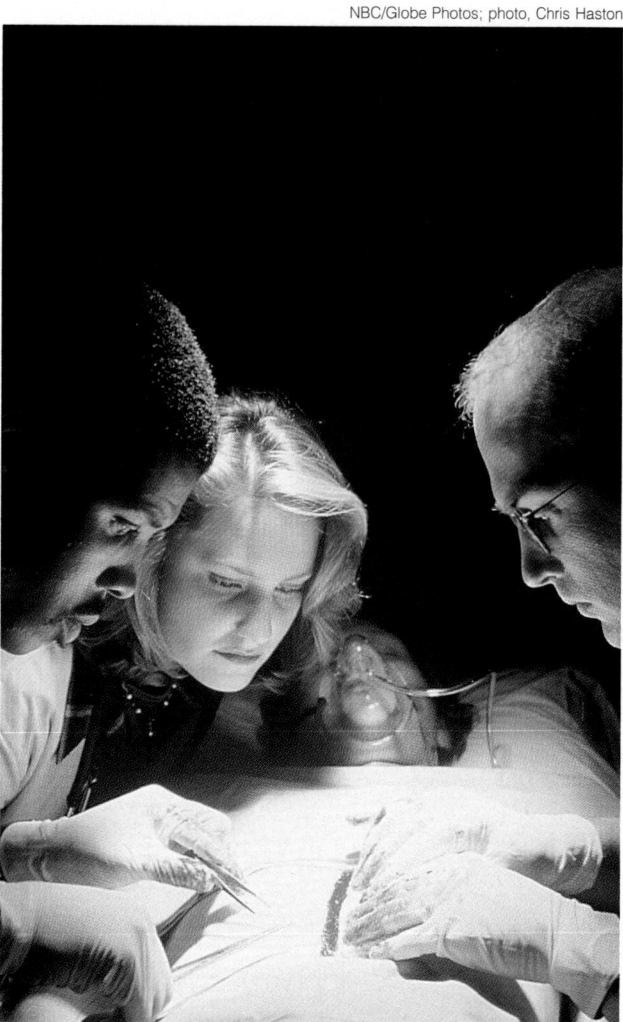

(Above) With the surgical precision typical of "ER," Peter Benton (Eriq LaSalle), Susan Lewis (Sherry Stringfield), and Marc Greene (Anthony Edwards) suture a stressful situation.

Yet the emergency room setting of "ER" was a shrewder choice for a contemporary medical drama than the gleaming surgical center of "Chicago Hope." While the latter concerns itself with life, death, and health care, its plots make the process appear almost leisurely compared with the frantic activity of an emergency room. On "Chicago Hope" the physicians often seem more interested in their self-aggrandizement than in their patients. Toward the end of the 1994–95 season, in fact, some "Chicago Hope" episodes appeared almost surrealistic in their treatments of petty rivalries and affairs among the staff. The principals became increasingly difficult to like—or believe.

Emergency rooms, on the other hand, are at their core the place where medical care often must be given first and questions asked later. The more mundane aspects of ER work (such as insurance forms and long lines) are de-emphasized in favor of that basic fact. The essential high-pressure realism of "ER" is part of its success. Viewers can find heroes in physicians acting correctly under great stress. Economic issues are put on hold when a patient is wheeled in spurting blood from a gunshot wound. The hectic pace of the show seems legitimate. The patient's story and the larger societal questions take a backseat to the superlative actions of the doctors, whose sole focus is to provide immediate, responsible care.

It is difficult to know whether story lines that emphasize medical heroics to the exclusion of the politics of medicine reflect a principled stand on the health care debate by the programs' creators and producers. It is more likely that these story lines flow out of the long history of doctor show plots from "Ben Casey" to "The Bold Ones," from "Emergency!" to "M*A*S*H" to "St. Elsewhere." In other words, today's shows lack a strong precedent for tackling difficult health care issues.

Nevertheless, in the context of the present health care debate, there are at least a couple of ways to weigh the TV drama's picture of medicine against the realities people have to deal with in their everyday lives.

One approach, the more pessimistic, is that by failing to encourage viewers to consider the ethical and legal issues of the changing medical world, television doctor shows are keeping many key issues behind closed doors, where lobbyists, legislators, and special interest groups can deal with them unencumbered by public scrutiny. Another, more optimistic perspective is that by showing how medicine *should* be practiced, rather than how it necessarily is, television is holding the medical community up to high standards that the public will come to expect, even under conditions of scarcity.

As the Hospital Turns

Daytime TV shows also provide big doses of medicine. Virtually all of the hit soap operas currently on the air have story lines set in hospitals and doctors as principal characters. Here are some of the dramatic medical moments from the 10 "soaps" airing in the summer of 1995.

All My Children

Sped to the hospital after falling from scaffolding, Erica is in such terrible pain that she persuades her doctor, Anton, to give her more medicine.

Another World

Justine gives Spencer something for his headache. Later, when Spencer has collapsed, Christophe suspects that Justine has drugged him. Christophe is afraid that Justine might also harm Rachel; he phones her psychiatrist, who quickly sends medication.

As the World Turns

Tony appears to have committed suicide, and pills are found at his bedside. Barbara falls in the middle of a restaurant and must be rushed to the emergency room.

The Bold and the Beautiful

Everyone is ecstatic to hear that Ridge's eye surgery was a success. His eyesight has been fully restored.

Days of Our Lives

During Austin and Carrie's engagement party, Marlena, who has been possessed by the devil, sends in a swarm of bees. Shawn Douglas, who is allergic to bees, is stung and makes a trip to the emergency room.

General Hospital

In a fit of rage, Joe aims a gun at Sonny. His dad, Mike, throws himself in the line of fire, taking the bullet intended for his son. He then is rushed to the hospital for surgery.

Guiding Light

Eve discovers that her rare blood disease (which will eventually be diagnosed as leukemia) is worsening. Fearing that her prescription medication is not working, she turns to a home remedy.

Loving

After much deliberation, Deborah decides to sue Alden Enterprises for discriminating against female heart attack victims, since the company's research on heart disease focuses only on men and thereby ignores thousands of women who suffer from the disease.

One Life to Live

While stranded at the Mountain Sunset Lodge in a rainstorm, Luna gives birth to boy-girl twins with Max's assistance. Luckily, both mother and children are healthy and happy.

The Young & the Restless

Paul, recovering from a freak hit-and-run accident, begins to wonder if the attack was intended for Chris instead.

Dana Belcher

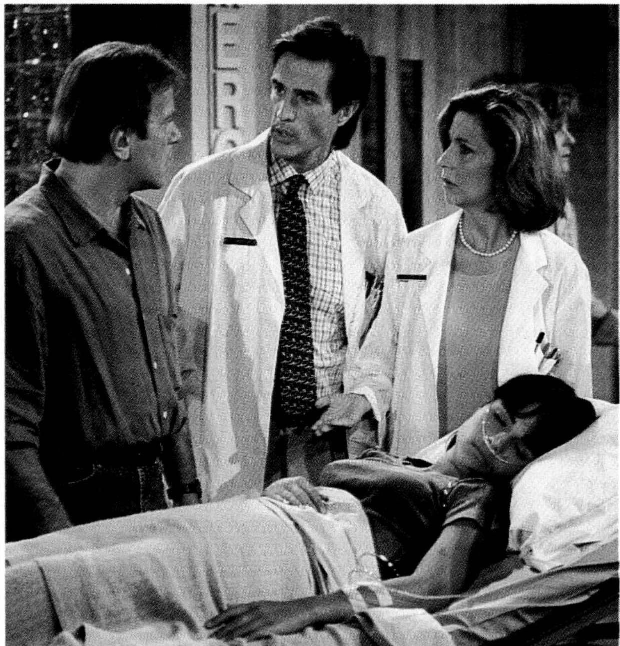

"As the World Turns": Nikki (Jordana Brewster) is hospitalized after a car crash. Bedside are her father, Hal (Benjamin Hendrickson, left); Larry (Ed Fry); and Susan (Marie Masters).

Culture, Class, and Health

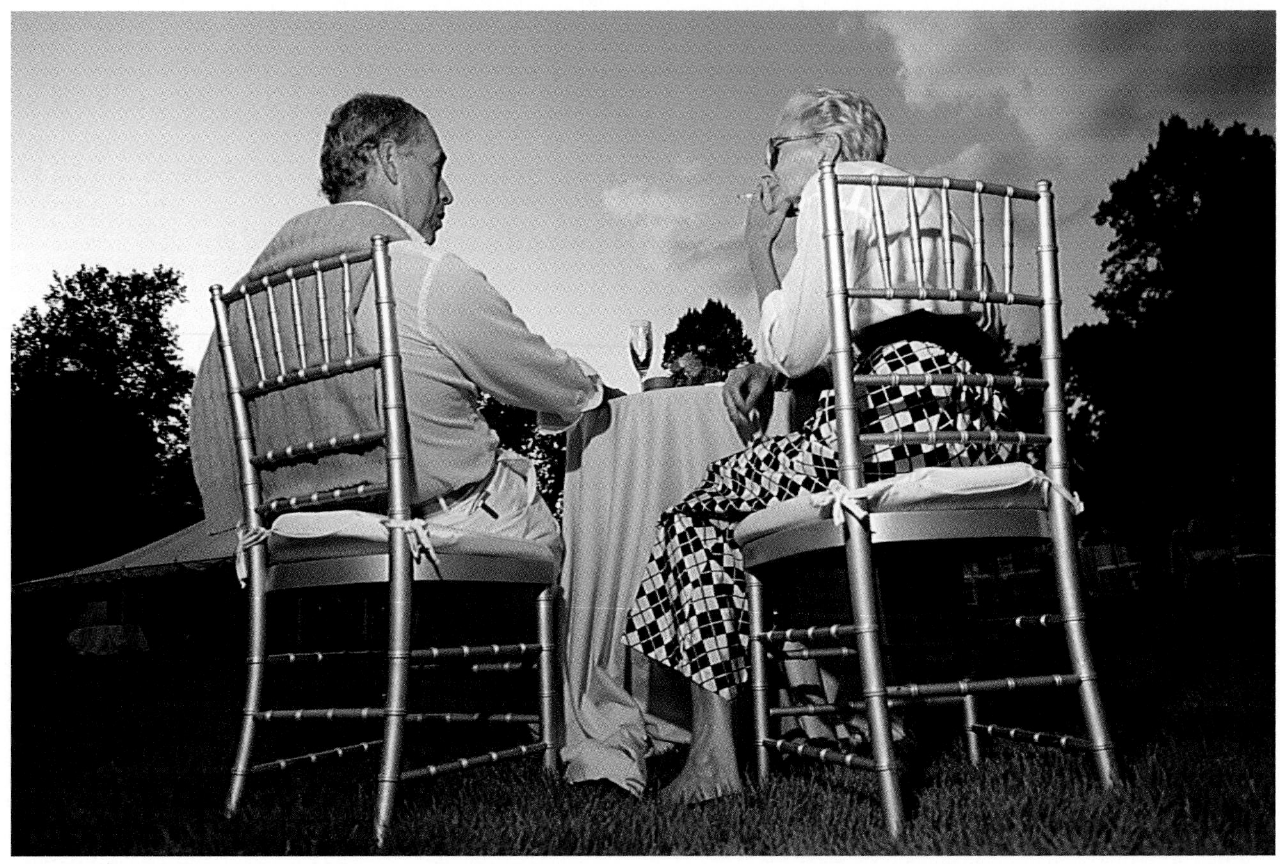

Mark Peterson—Saba

In his preface to *The Doctor's Dilemma,* George Bernard Shaw put forward his formula for achieving a long life: "Take the utmost care to get born well and well brought up." The playwright had a point. While it is impossible for anyone to exert an influence over the circumstances of his or her birth, evidence has long been accumulating that there are substantial differences in the health and longevity of rich and poor people. In study after study it has been shown that those at the bottom of the social scale have much poorer health than those at the top. Even in the wealthiest industrialized countries, a child born to a lawyer can expect to live 7 to 10 years longer on average than the child of a manual laborer. Exceptions are rare.

***Bryan Christie** is Health Correspondent for* The Scotsman, *Edinburgh, and Correspondent for the* British Medical Journal.

It is not a new revelation that wealth and health—more often than not—go hand in hand.

Long life for the wealthy

Health inequalities have been studied closely only in recent times, but they are far from being a new phenomenon. Indeed, they are deep-rooted and abiding. Research conducted in the late 1970s looked at the records of certain Florentine

by Bryan Christie

Andrew Lichtenstein—JB Pictures

Healthwise, smokers at the lower end of the social scale are likely to pay a very high price for their tobacco habit.

families from the 15th century and compared dowry investments for the daughters. Women from the wealthiest families—those with the largest dowries—lived the longest. Similar conclusions have been drawn from studies of Victorian graveyards in Scotland. Researchers measured the height of obelisks in cemeteries in Glasgow and checked that against the age at death of the people buried there. The tallest and most elaborate monuments, commemorating the wealthiest people, belonged to the longest-lived.

Although life expectancy in the developed world has risen steadily throughout the 20th century, the social class differences in health have not disappeared. In many countries they are worsening. A recent editorial in *The New England Journal of Medicine* noted that the latest available figures from the U.S. National Center for Health Statistics had shown that in spite of an overall decline in death rates in the United States between 1960 and 1986, the gap between poor and less educated people and those who are wealthier and more educated had grown steadily wider. In 1986 Americans with a yearly income of less than $9,000 had a death rate three to seven times higher than those earning more than $25,000. Those who had not graduated from high school had a death rate two to three times higher than those who graduated from college. Such disparities have not disappeared in the 1990s.

Disease for the disadvantaged

Disadvantage is associated not only with earlier death but with a higher incidence of disease throughout life. Studies in Finland have shown that chronic illness affects 18% of middle-aged men in the highest income groups; among those with the lowest incomes, the chronic-illness rate is 42%. In Australia the poorest third of men were found to have rates of serious illness 65% higher than those of the wealthiest third. The Mental Health Foundation in Britain recently found that people living in socially deprived areas were three times more likely to suffer from mental disorders and be admitted to psychiatric hospitals than were people from more affluent communities. It has also been shown that people from lower socioeconomic groups survive for a shorter period with serious conditions such as cancer, even when they receive the same level of treatment as their advantaged counterparts.

Hierarchies of health

Health inequalities affect more than just the extremes of society. They occur throughout the social scale; at any point at which differences are examined, those earning more money will, on average, enjoy better health and better prospects. Compelling evidence of a gradient in health from the bottom to the top of the social scale has come from the Whitehall study, an ongoing investigation of 17,500 British civil servants. It found that the higher the grade of employment, the better the health of that group of individuals. Michael Marmot, director of the Centre of Health and Society at University College, London, who led the study, said at a European Commission-sponsored conference, "Action on Social Inequalities and Health," in May 1994: "Men and women in the second highest grouping of employment grades are not poor, yet they have worse health than those in the highest grades. There is a social gradient—each grade having worse health than the one above it in the hierarchy. Poverty affects the minority at the bottom. The lesson from these data is that health inequalities run right across the whole of society."

The Granger Collection, New York

Slum housing in London, as seen by rail, 1872.

Sickness and Status in Civil Servants

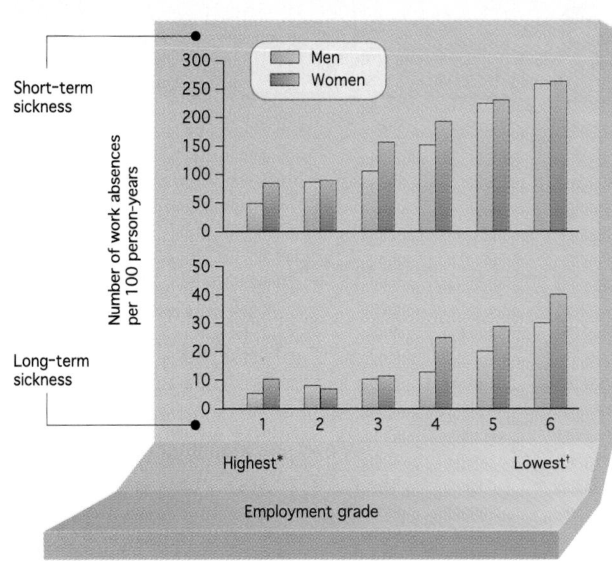

*Grade 1 = highest executive officers.
†Grade 6 = clerical and office support staff.
Adapted from M.G. Marmot *et al.*, "Explaining Socioeconomic Differences in Sickness Absence: The Whitehall II Study," *British Medical Journal*, vol. 306, no. 6874 (Feb. 6, 1993), pp. 361–366.

Hiroshi Nakajima, director general of the World Health Organization (WHO), expressed alarm in early 1995 that those disparities were widening worldwide. Later that year, in its first World Health Report, *Bridging the Gaps,* WHO identified poverty as "the world's most ruthless killer and the greatest cause of suffering on earth. . . . Poverty wields its destructive influence at every stage of human life from the moment of conception to the grave." Much of the illness suffered by the world's population is preventable and tied to ever-widening gaps in health, education, and access to care, the health report shows. In its foreword, Nakajima wrote of "stark and often shocking inequities in health and in access to even basic health care."

Conditions of extreme poverty in the less developed world mean that children are dying because of the lack of simple medicines. In industrialized countries the problems are not so basic, but they are no less worrisome. WHO's regional European office has declared that reducing inequalities is at the top of its priority list of 38 targets for improving the health of Europeans by the year 2000. The aim is to reduce the differences in health status between countries in Europe—and between groups of people within those countries—by 25%. One of the leading researchers in the field, Richard Wilkinson of the Trafford Centre for Medical Research at the University of Sussex, Brighton, England, puts it succinctly: "In Britain, as in many other countries, the scale of the excess mortality associated with lower social status dwarfs almost every other health problem." One study, conducted in the north of England, found that death rates for people under the age of 65 are four times higher in the poorest residential areas than they are in the most affluent neighborhoods. A child of an unskilled manual laborer is twice as likely as one from a professional background to die before the age of 15; researchers suggest that there would be 42,000 fewer deaths a year in Britain if manual workers enjoyed the same health as the nonmanual workers. As Wilkinson commented in an editorial in the *British Medical Journal* (April 30, 1994), "If risks as great as these resulted from exposure to toxic materials then offices would be closed down and populations evacuated from contaminated areas."

Peter Turnley—Black Star

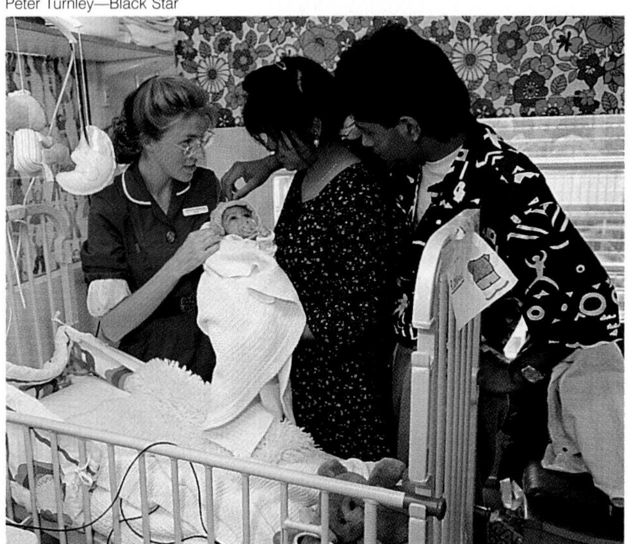

Will this baby, born in the U.K., live a long and healthy life?

Life and Death Around the World: A Matter of Income *

Income range (in U.S. $)	Life expectancy (in years)	Infant mortality (per 1,000 live births)
15,000 and above	70-79	5-26
10,000-14,999	72-78	7-22
5,000-9,999	63-77	9-68
1,000-4,999	51-76	10-93
500-999	45-72	24-133
100-499	43-71	27-158

*Some less developed low-income countries have achieved life expectancies and infant mortality rates comparable to those in developed market-economy countries.
Source: World Health Organization, *The World Health Report 1995*.

Explaining disparities

Why should poorer people have poorer health? One suggestion is that social position, at least in part, is determined by the health of the individuals involved. People in poor health have limited employment opportunities and drift downward on the social scale. In the same manner, the fittest move upward. A number of studies have examined this concept, and while they suggest that health "selection" does occur, it has only a minor effect.

Another possible explanation concerns the access people have to health services. The rich, not surprisingly, have greater access. Yet poorer people make less use of preventive services even, it appears, when these services are provided at no cost to themselves. Steven Katz and Timothy Hofer of the University of Michigan carried out a study in which usage rates for breast and cervical screening among women in Ontario and women in the United States were compared. The researchers expected to find more Canadian than U.S. women from lower socioeconomic groups using these services because in Canada they are provided to everyone at virtually no cost. By contrast, women in the U.S. need adequate health insurance to benefit, and about 40% of the population is either uninsured or underinsured. To the investigators' surprise, however, very little difference was found between the two countries. "These results suggest that even universal coverage and the elimination of insurance-related barriers is not

Born in a poor country without sophisticated medical services, this Guatemalan child (left foreground and below) spent her first 12 years suffering from a congenital heart defect. Her prospects brightened when a team of pediatric cardiologists from New York City performed lifesaving open-heart operations on dozens of ailing Guatemalan youngsters.

Photographs, Eugene Richards—Magnum

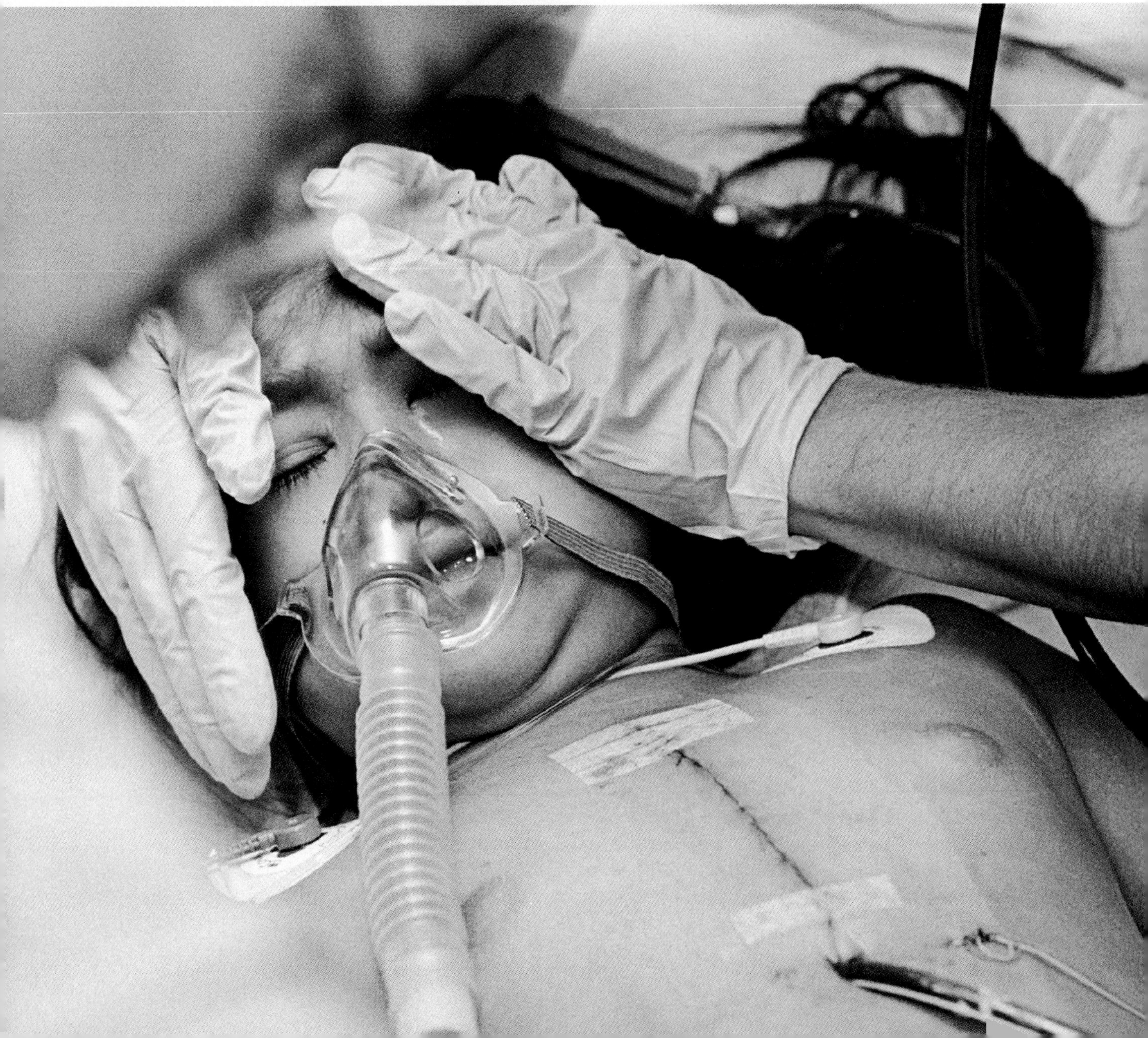

sufficient to overcome the large disparities in screening demonstrated in both countries," Katz and Hofer concluded.

A study of schoolchildren living in an impoverished inner-city neighborhood in Chicago found that those students did not receive adequate dental care even when it was offered at no cost. Susan Diamond, who did the study, wrote in the *Chicago Dental Society Review* (December 1994): "Only the occurrence of pain alerts many students' parents to bring them to the dentist. Dental care appears to be a low priority. . . . Many students do not own toothbrushes, and others must share them with family members."

There is ample other evidence that the provision of health services plays only a small part in influencing the health status of individuals. The pioneers of the British National Health Service (NHS) believed that the universal provision of free health care for all at the time of need would lead to rapid improvements in the health of the population and a consequent reduction in demand on the service. Unfortunately, over the past four and a half decades, they have been proved wrong. The demands today are greater than ever before, and the social-class differences are as apparent as they were in 1948—the year the NHS began. People from higher-income groups repeatedly have been shown to benefit most from health services; they know how to use them better, and studies have established that some doctors are more responsive to patients from the same social class as themselves.

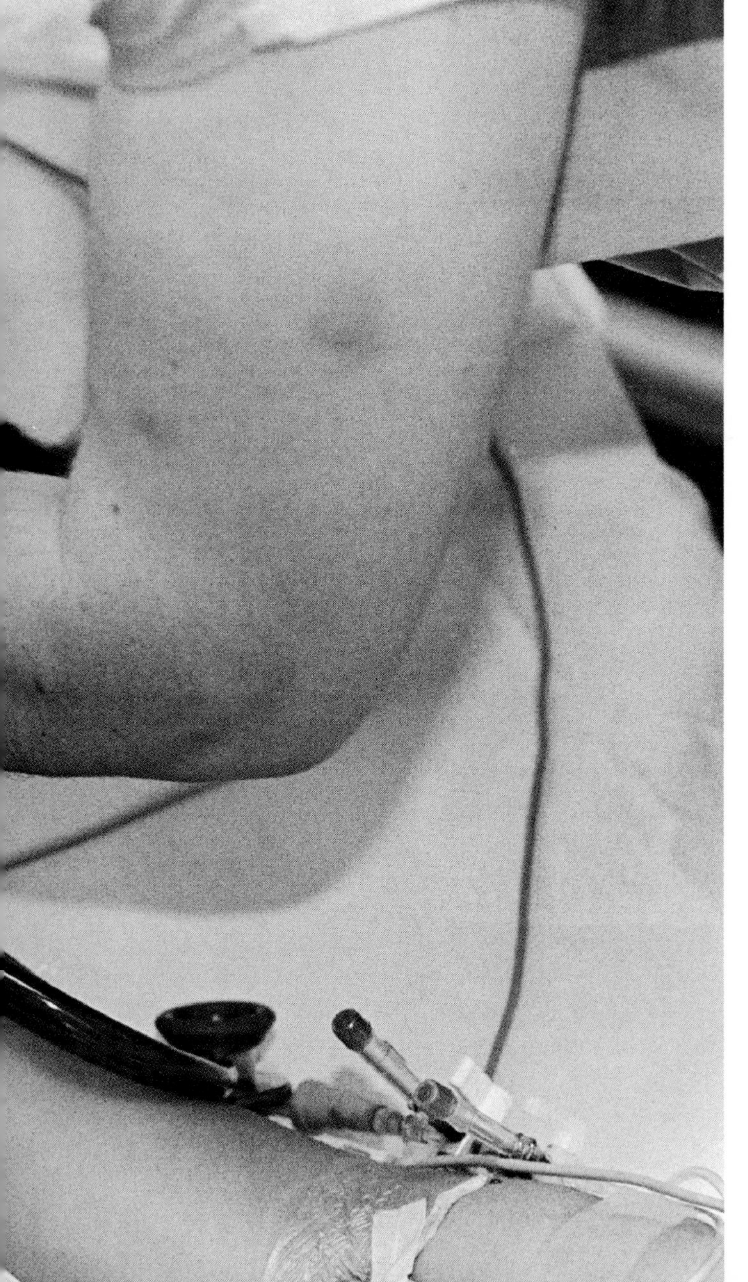

The two explanations for health inequalities that have attracted the most attention have to do with personal behavior and material circumstances. First, there are substantial differences in the lifestyles adopted by lower and higher socioeconomic groups. Poorer people generally lead unhealthier lives. Their diet is poorer, their smoking rates are higher, and alcohol and drug addiction are more common among poorer people. It is accepted that these habits will all have an adverse effect on health, but social-class gradients are even evident for the same self-damaging behaviors. For example, smokers at the bottom of the socioeconomic scale have been found to pay the highest toll for their habit. When lung function is compared among smokers from all social groups, those whose material circumstances are lowest fare worse than those with the best circumstances.

Although personal lifestyle plays a part in disparities, it does not offer a complete answer. A study in Alameda county, California, compared the overall health of well-to-do people and poor people. Although the researchers took the health-damaging behavior of all the subjects into account, they still found that those in the poorest groups had 1.5 times the risk of dying prematurely that those in the richest group had. These findings led the investigators to conclude that the general living conditions and the environment poor people live in are more important than the habits in which they indulge.

People in lower socioeconomic groups are also more likely to live and work in hazardous physical environments. Their homes may be of poor quality, located in built-up, overcrowded areas, where levels of air pollution are high. In one of New York City's poorest sections, Harlem, in March 1995 an apartment building with 70 units collapsed, killing three residents. Tenants who survived claimed that there were leaking pipes, a major crack in an outside wall, a flooded basement, sloping floors, and other structural and upkeep problems that

(Top left) Van Cappellen—REA/Saba; (bottom left) Dan Habib—Impact Visuals; (right) Alon Reininger—Contact Press Images

Children's health depends on many factors, including their parents' economic circumstances, the food they have to eat, and the environment in which they grow up. (Opposite page) A manual laborer in a plastics factory is at greater risk than his boss of becoming ill or injured on the job.

had been ignored by inspectors and owners.

Increasing evidence shows that poor housing conditions can adversely affect health. A study of public-housing projects in London, Edinburgh, and Glasgow found that rates of illness were substantially higher among children living in damp houses. Dampness, the researchers concluded, was an important public health issue that deserved greater attention. Residents of Glasgow set up a "dampness task force" to investigate the problem. They found that about 250,000 people living in 84,000 homes in that city alone lived in damp housing without central heat. The task force estimated that 10 million people throughout the U.K. shared their plight.

Again, dangerous and damp housing is likely to be part of the explanation but not the whole story. In the previously mentioned study of British civil servants, all of the subjects worked in "clean," white-collar jobs, and none could be described as "poor." Still, the investigators found clear differences in sickness and premature-death rates among ranks of employees; office-support

Health Services : Greater Access, Greater Use?

Insurance status	Ontario (percentage)	U.S. (percentage)
None	—	13.1
Medicaid	—	6.8
Private	—	61.1
Medicare	—	19.0
Universal coverage	100	—
Women having Pap test* (age group)	**Ontario (percentage)**	**U.S. (percentage)**
18-29	74.9	82.6
30-39	82.8	81.1
40-49	75.2	73.9
50-59	65.0	67.2
60-69	53.9	58.6
≥70	38.6	47.9
Overall	74.0	76.4

* Within the past two years.

Adapted from Steven J. Katz and Timothy P. Hofer, "Socioeconomic Disparities in Preventive Care...," *JAMA*, vol. 272, no. 7 (Aug. 17, 1994), pp. 530–534. Copyright 1994, American Medical Association.

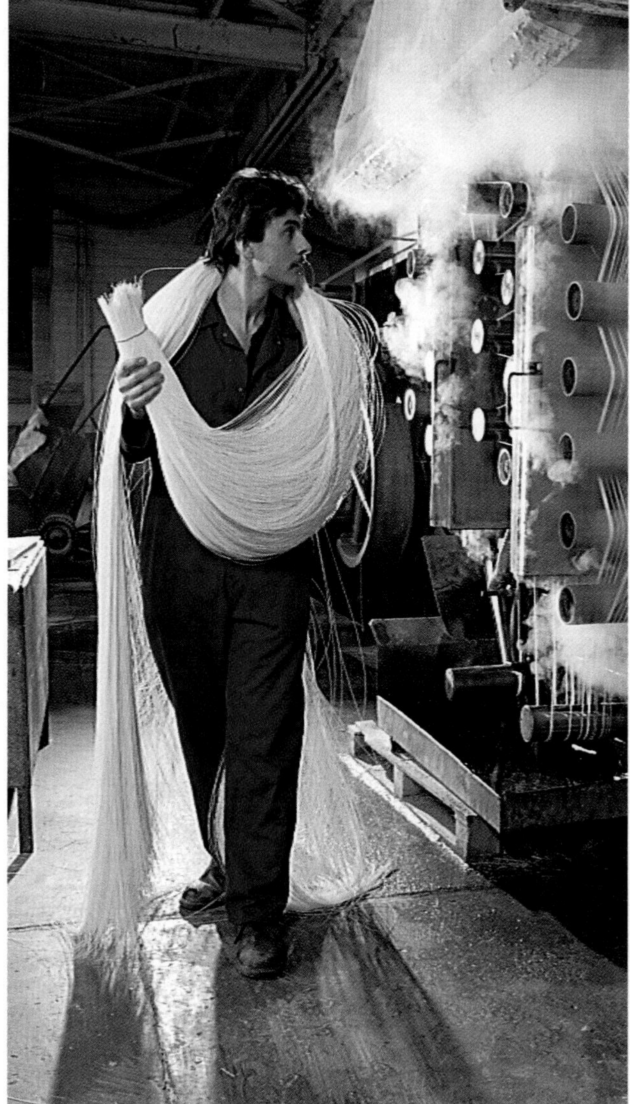

Penny Tweedie—Panos Pictures

staff and messengers, for example, had much higher rates of morbidity (sickness) and mortality (death) than senior administrators.

Personal behavior is often dictated by material circumstances. A low-income mother who wants to buy fruit to improve the diet of her children may find that the only local shop she has access to does not stock it or charges a price she cannot afford. Julian Le Grand of the London School of Economics, speaking at the European Commission-sponsored conference on inequalities, said that any attempt to distinguish between the behavioral and materialist explanations is misguided. "In practice, people's behavior is greatly influenced both by the material constraints they face on their activities, including income and prices, and by their tastes and preferences. Individuals brought up in poor households whose parents found it cheaper to buy white bread rather than brown or to smoke a packet of cigarettes rather than take a walk in the country are likely to develop tastes that accord with their situation."

Programmed for health?

Another theory that has emerged in recent years suggests health inequalities are rooted in the biological makeup of the people affected rather than in the practices—healthy or unhealthy—that they adopt. Studies have borne this out. Graham Watt, professor of general practice medicine at the University of Glasgow, notes that his city has the highest rate of lung cancer in the developed world: "Glasgow produces more lung cancer per pack of cigarettes smoked than any other city. It is not the level of smoking. There is something about the people who smoke which gives this high incidence."

What could that something be? David Barker of the British Medical Research Council's environmental epidemiology unit at the University of Southampton, England, has found that developments early in life—even before birth—can have an impact on disease later in life. Barker has been tracking a group of people born in England in the early part of the 20th century for whom precise records were kept of birth weight and subsequent health and development. The research has shown a clear association between low-birth-weight babies and disease and premature-death rates in adulthood. Barker's hypothesis is that lung function, glucose tolerance, blood pressure, and cholesterol metabolism are all influenced by the manner in which the fetus and young infant develop. People may be "programmed" from their earliest days to face a premature death. As Watt has said, "If you get a bad start in life, it may be that you just don't recover."

Differences in health status are also apparent between ethnic groups. Mortality rates of African-Americans are higher at every level of income compared with those of nonblacks in the U.S. In a report in *The Lancet* (Aug. 13, 1994), hypertension expert Norman M. Kaplan at the University of Texas Southwestern Medical Center at Dallas said that a third of the excess mortality can be explained by lower socioeconomic status and another third by higher rates of hypertension among blacks, with the remainder remaining unexplained. It has been suggested that biological differences, including increased sodium sensitivity, may explain why hypertension is more common among black people. They also suffer greater cardiovascular and renal damage at any level of blood pressure than white Americans, and they do not respond to certain antihypertensive drugs in the same way as whites. U.S. researchers are currently seeking the genes that may predispose African-Americans to diseases such as hypertension, diabetes, and kidney failure. In 1994 they set up the Genomic Research in African American Pedigrees project to make cell lines from large, multigenerational black families available for study.

Research is also revealing that the conditions of adult life can have profound effects on health. Studies in both Sweden and the U.S. have shown that people who are under pressure at work but feel they have little control over what they do have higher rates of coronary heart disease. The Whitehall study has found that civil servants with stressful jobs but little power are the most likely to have low levels of "good" cholesterol—high-density lipoprotein—in their blood; they also have high rates of non-insulin-dependent (adult) diabetes. Living or working in a stressful or poor social environment is thought to produce adverse changes in the en-

Children's health and well-being may be "programmed" from their very earliest days. (Opposite page) Weighing just 1,200 grams (2.6 pounds), a three-week-old infant in Germany requires around-the-clock care in a neonatal intensive care unit just to survive.

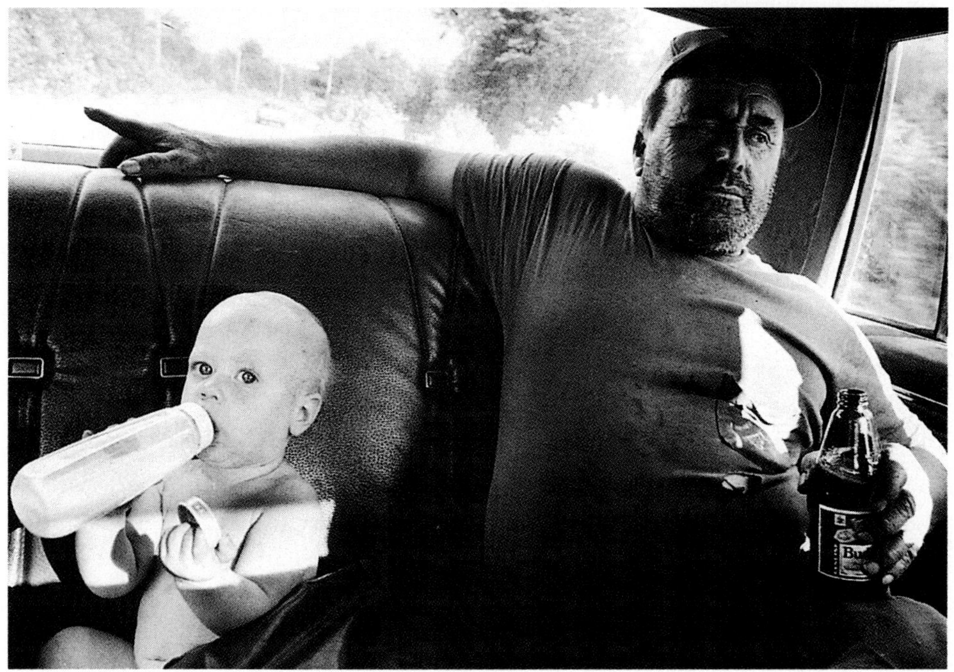

(Opposite page) Ronald Fromann—Laif/Saba; (top) Elizabeth Rappaport—JB Pictures; (bottom) Steven Rubin—JB Pictures docrine and immune systems that increase susceptibility to the development of infectious and chronic disease.

Quite clearly, health inequalities are not caused by a single factor but result from the interplay of genetic inheritance, personal behavior, environmental conditions, and psychosocial influences. In a recent report published in the *European Journal of Public Health,* three British researchers—George Davey Smith, David Blane, and Mel Bartley—explained how those factors can come together in a "cluster of disadvantage":

> *A woman in a low-income household is more likely to be poorly nourished during pregnancy and to produce a low birthweight or premature baby. A child growing up in a low income household is more likely to be disadvantaged in terms of diet, crowding, safe areas in which to play and opportunities for educational achievement. An adolescent from a low-income household is more likely to leave education at the minimum school-leaving age before entering a low paid, insecure and hazardous occupation, with no occupational pension. An adult working in this sector of the labour market is more likely to experience periods of unemployment, to raise a family in financially difficult circumstances and to retire early because their prematurely expended health can no longer cope with the physical demands of their work. A retired person who does not have an occupational pension is more likely to experience financial deprivation in the years leading up to their death.*

Melissa Ciano

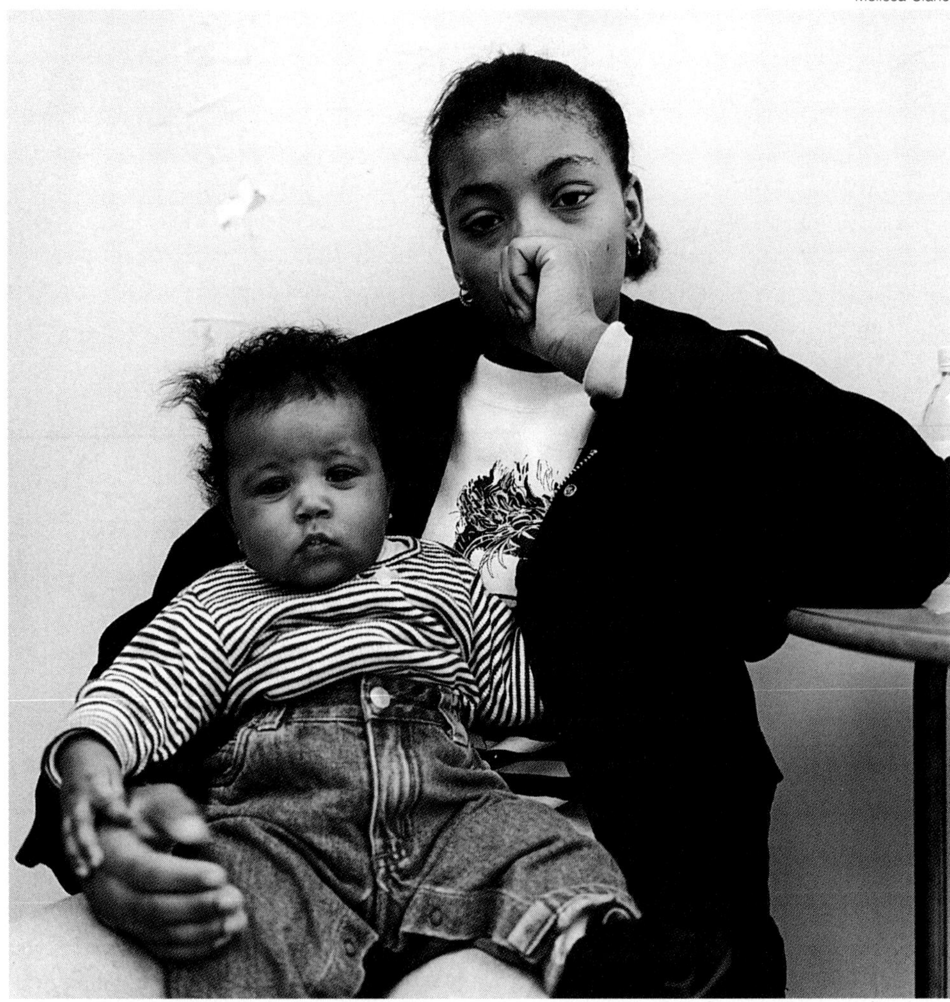

Closing the gap

The problem of health inequalities has been tackled very differently around the world. In Britain, where much of the early research into disparities took place, the government for many years refused to recognize that health inequalities deserved attention. A report produced in 1980 by a working party chaired by Sir Douglas Black, a former chief scientist at the Department of Health and president of the Royal College of Physicians of London, detailed the extent of the problem but was virtually ignored by government administrators. A follow-up report, "The Health Divide," in 1988 received an equally dismissive official reception. Only in 1994 did this position change, with the government's acceptance that health inequalities existed and merited examination. It then set up an interdepartmental working party to examine the factors involved and consider what effective action might be taken.

While the British argued, the Dutch acted. In the mid-1980s the government of The Netherlands accepted WHO's targets for reducing differences, and the issue of equity in health was placed firmly on the political agenda. Governmental agencies established a national research program on inequalities in 1989, and since that time various policy initiatives have addressed the problem. Coordinated pro-

(Top) Melissa Ciano; (bottom) Stephen Shames—Matrix

Their own youth cut short by childbearing, teenagers from an urban ghetto in New York City (opposite page and above) have little chance of escaping their own disadvantaged backgrounds. (Right) An elderly woman, living alone and without social supports, is not likely to enjoy a long and rewarding old age.

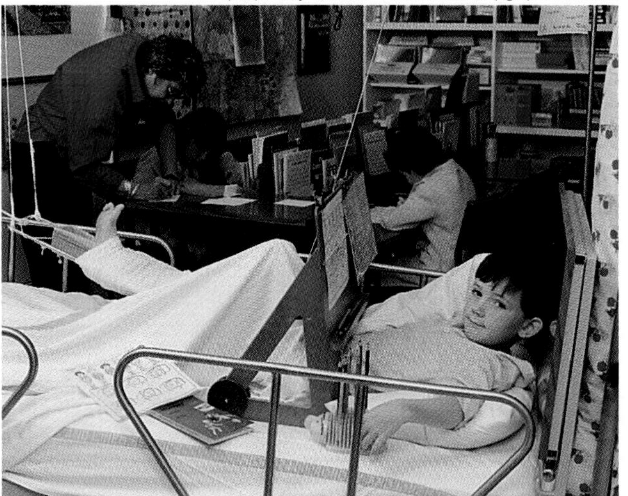

(Left) Penny Tweedie—Panos Pictures; (right) Photo Index

Australia is now working hard to redress the social disparities that have existed for so long between Aborigines and their more privileged Caucasian counterparts.

grams have been developed to improve living conditions in impoverished areas. Many towns are experimenting with urban renewal, major health-education campaigns have been launched, and attention is being directed toward improving job prospects and reducing the threat of violence in high-crime areas.

A report entitled *National Health Strategy: Enough to Make You Sick—How Income and Environment Affect Health,* detailing the scale of health inequalities in Australia, was issued, and without much foot-dragging, programs addressing those inequalities were set up and endorsed at the highest political level. In particular, the government made preventive health strategies a top priority. The disadvantaged status of the Aborigines is recognized as the number one public health problem in the country. The Aboriginal people constitute the poorest segment of the population, have the least access to health care services, and suffer from the highest incidence of chronic and acute diseases. Infant mortality among Aboriginal children is 3–5 times greater than among non-Aboriginal children, and adult Aborigines in their 30s have premature-death rates 10–11 times higher than those of their non-Aboriginal counterparts. The government established the National Aboriginal Health Strategy and has allocated substantial funds toward improving the social and economic conditions of the country's poorest and most disadvantaged people. It is widely acknowledged, however, that there is a long way to go.

Most attempts to tackle health inequalities are still in their infancy. Some of the most progressive policies are being pursued in Nordic countries. In Finland, for instance, programs have been established to improve environmental conditions in the workplace and residential areas, and information is being directed at individuals through health education. In Sweden all national public agencies are required to set specific goals to reduce inequalities and to analyze the impact of policies on health. Norway was the first nation in the world to adopt a national food policy with the aim of making reasonably priced nutritious food available to everyone. Although evaluations have shown that progress toward that goal has been mixed, the policy itself has won international acclaim.

Canada has also recognized the importance of tackling inequalities. In Ontario the Council on Health Strategy published a report saying, "In the past, the approach to health has been to protect people from hazards—usually infectious disease organisms—in the environment. We now realize that for people to be healthy, they must live in a healthy environment." Five specific goals for creating "healthy environments" have been established.

Rapid strides in health and wealth

Japan has demonstrated in the last 50 years that health inequalities are not an inevitable consequence of economic growth. The Japanese now have the highest life expectancy in the developed world, and substantial improvements in health status affect all socioeconomic groups (without the kind of steep gradients that exist in many other countries). The country has seen both its health and its wealth improve and has made a substantial investment in sustaining the quality of social environments. Evidence from other countries in Asia that have gone through rapid economic growth in the last few decades also suggests that income equity and investments in "human capital"—*i.e.,* in the health and well-being of the entire population—are equally important in creating and sustaining health equity.

The relative rather than the absolute level of income appears to be the most influential factor. Sweden, for instance, has a lower per capita income than does the U.S., but it distributes that income more evenly across its population through the taxation system. Perhaps as a consequence, the Swedish population enjoys a higher life expectancy than does the population as a whole in the United States.

"A society that handicaps large segments of its population during periods of major technological change may be handicapping its future economic growth," conclude John Frank and Fraser Mustard of the Canadian Institute for Advanced Research, writing in the fall 1994 issue of *Daedalus,* the journal of the American Academy of Arts and Sciences. It is not the level of wealth that a country has that improves the health of the population but its commitment to allocating resources to key programs that affect key sectors. The provision of good education and proper nutrition for all women and children is a prime example.

Rations for all

Health inequalities pose a direct challenge to the traditional system of health care in which large sums of money are invested in biomedical research to improve treatments directed at individuals. Accumulating evidence makes it clear that greater gains are achieved by investigating the social circumstances that lie *behind* ill health and then *addressing* the problems that are identified. As Ken Judge, director of the King's Fund Institute, a London-based health policy research center, commented in the leading editorial in the Dec. 3, 1994, issue of the *British Medical Journal:*

> *Most of the available resources go into the invention of new technologies even though their aggregate contribution to the population's health is modest. Relatively little effort goes into assessing the effectiveness of the existing health care system, and almost nothing is invested in looking at the nonmedical influences on health. What's urgently needed is a more systematic programme of research to improve our understanding of the socio-environmental determinants of health and of how to design public policies that will prevent or ameliorate poor health. . . . A sustained effort should be made to persuade not only politicians and patients but also those who earn their living in the health care industry that it makes economic and social sense to limit spending on health care to free resources for other policies that promote health.*

In the earlier part of this century, Britain proved that such policies have appreciable value. During World Wars I and II, civilian life expectancy in England and Wales increased two to three times faster than at any other times in the 20th century—the increase being most marked among the poorest sectors of society. Although policies were not designed to promote health (and few at the time would have thought they would have that effect), the gains that were seen have been put down to the fact that there were full employment and substantial redistribution of income *populationwide.* While rationing meant that people were eating a bland diet, healthful, nutritious food was available to all for the first time.

The world's future depends on the health of its youngest generation.

Ralf-Finn Hestoft—Saba

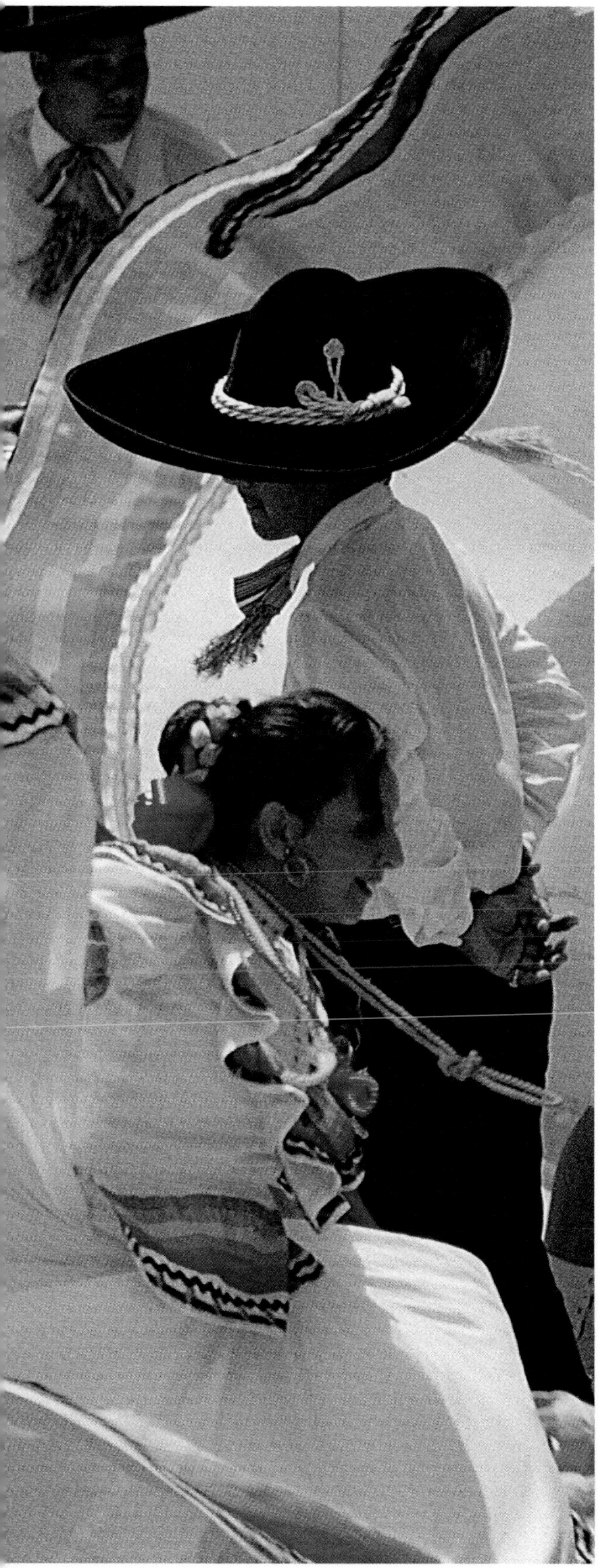

Spotlight: Latino Health

by Carlos W. Molina, Ed.D., and Marilyn Aguirre-Molina, Ed.D.

The term Latino, *as used in this article, has the same meaning as the official U.S. census designation* Hispanic, *encompassing all those in the U.S. whose ancestry can be traced to Spain, Mexico, Puerto Rico, Cuba, the Dominican Republic, or any of the Spanish-speaking Latin-American countries. The authors prefer the word* Latino *to* Hispanic *because it acknowledges the influence of both the Indian and African cultures of Latin America. Moreover, the terms* Hispanic, Spanish-surnamed, *and* Spanish-speaking *can be misleading, as they would seem to include many who are not of Latin-American heritage (such as Filipinos, who are not Latinos but Asians) and would exclude many others who are of Latin-American heritage or descent—for example, those whose surnames have been changed through marriage.*

* * *

Festival, San Antonio, Texas

Bob Daemmrich—The Image Works

Latinos are the fastest-growing ethnic/racial group in the United States today. In 1994 the Bureau of the Census estimated their number at 26 million (approximately 10% of the U.S. population)—representing a more than 50% increase over the total reported in the 1980 census. Moreover, the actual number of Latinos is probably several million higher; the uncounted include those overlooked in the census and those who are undocumented immigrants. Approximately 64% of the Latinos counted in the 1990 census were born in the U.S.

Unity in diversity

Although Latinos living in the U.S. have come from

Carlos W. Molina, Ed.D., *is Associate Professor of Health Education, York College of the City University of New York, Jamaica, New York.* ***Marilyn Aguirre-Molina, Ed.D.,*** *is Senior Program Officer, Robert Wood Johnson Foundation, Princeton, New Jersey. They are coeditors of* Latino Health in the U.S.: A Growing Challenge *(1994).*

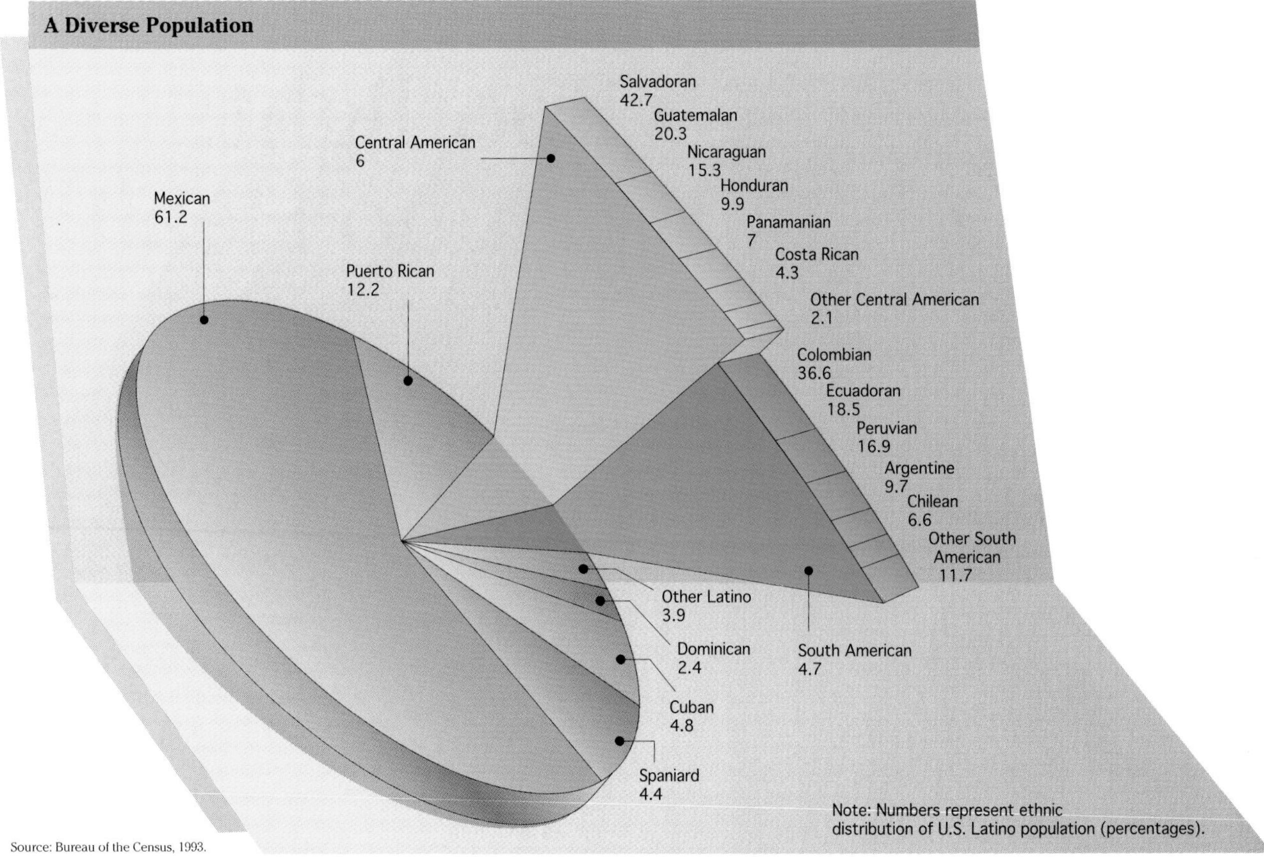

Source: Bureau of the Census, 1993.

many different countries, from varied social classes, with sundry expectations, and during different periods in history, they share numerous common experiences and conditions. For example, in addition to being a rapidly growing population, Latinos are also a young population. The median age of U.S. Latinos is only 26.2 years, compared with 33.7 years for whites. There is considerable variation between the Latino subgroups, however, ranging from a median age of 24.3 years among those of Mexican heritage to 39.3 among Cubans.

The national vital statistics show that Latino women have the highest birthrates of all U.S. women, although, again, notable variations exist between the subgroups. In general, however, Latinos have larger families than whites.

According to 1993 figures, more than twice as many Latinos as whites live in poverty—12.2% for whites, compared with 30.6% for Latinos (and 33.1% for African-Americans). The disparities were even greater for the percentages of children living in poverty—17.8% for whites, compared with 40.9% for Latinos (and 46.1% for African-Americans).

Latinos living in the United States are primarily concentrated in the central cities of the largest metropolitan areas. About 92% of U.S. Latinos live in urban areas (compared with 73% of non-Latinos), and two-thirds of the Latino population live in just 16 metropolitan areas. The largest U.S. Mexican community is in Los Angeles and the next largest in Chicago; the biggest Puerto Rican population lives in New York City, the second biggest in Chicago; the major Cuban community is in Miami, Florida, followed by that in New York City.

As a young, fast-growing, largely poor, and predominantly urban population, Latinos have distinctive health needs and concerns. Their unique demographic characteristics, along with the many sociocultural barriers that inhibit their access to the formal health care system, have far-reaching implications for public health in the U.S.

La familia

Latino families tend to be extended rather than nuclear and traditional in terms of age and sex roles, parenting practices, and respect for authority. In addition to parents and siblings, the traditional Latino family may include aunts, uncles, cousins, close family friends who are often referred to as honorary uncles or aunts, and *padrinos* ("godparents"). Family members have a strong sense of mutual obligation and are expected to provide reliable and dependable social support, even in old age. When economic, health, or other problems threaten the children in one nuclear family, someone in the extended Latino family will care for them and, if necessary, rear them to adulthood. These children are lovingly referred to as *hijos de crianza* ("raised sons and daughters").

Latinos generally depend more on the family than on health professionals for health services and advice and for emotional support in times of illness. Responsibility for the healing process is placed on the entire family. Latinos often consult other family members and close family friends on matters of health, illness, and treatment and will ask family members to accompany them to medical appointments. Not all Latinos hold the same attitudes toward health or engage in the same health practices, of course. Beliefs and behaviors prevalent among some subgroups may be more or less dominant among others. Even among members of the same subgroup, the strength of traditional health beliefs varies with the individual's level of acculturation and educational attainment.

The strong social support provided by the cohesive Latino family is a factor that promotes and maintains health. Moreover, the family's beliefs about disease, ideas on how to cope in times of illness, and collective knowledge about various treatments—its "family health culture"—shape the individual's opinions about health and disease and choice of treatment.

***Personalismo* in health care**

The values that guide Latino culture influence the nature of interactions in the health care setting. Latino social interactions are guided by the value of *personalismo*—the trust and rapport that is established with others by developing warm, friendly, and personal relationships. Latinos favor and respond better to a congenial, respectful, personal manner than to a formal, businesslike one. In health care they expect the doctor, nurse, or therapist to take a personal interest in their problems and to be warm, sympathetic, and reassuring. When health providers meet these expectations, family mem-

Erica Lanser—Black Star

The Latino population in the U.S. is predominantly young and urban, as well as relatively poor. The youthful family above lives in the Williamsburg neighborhood in Brooklyn, New York.

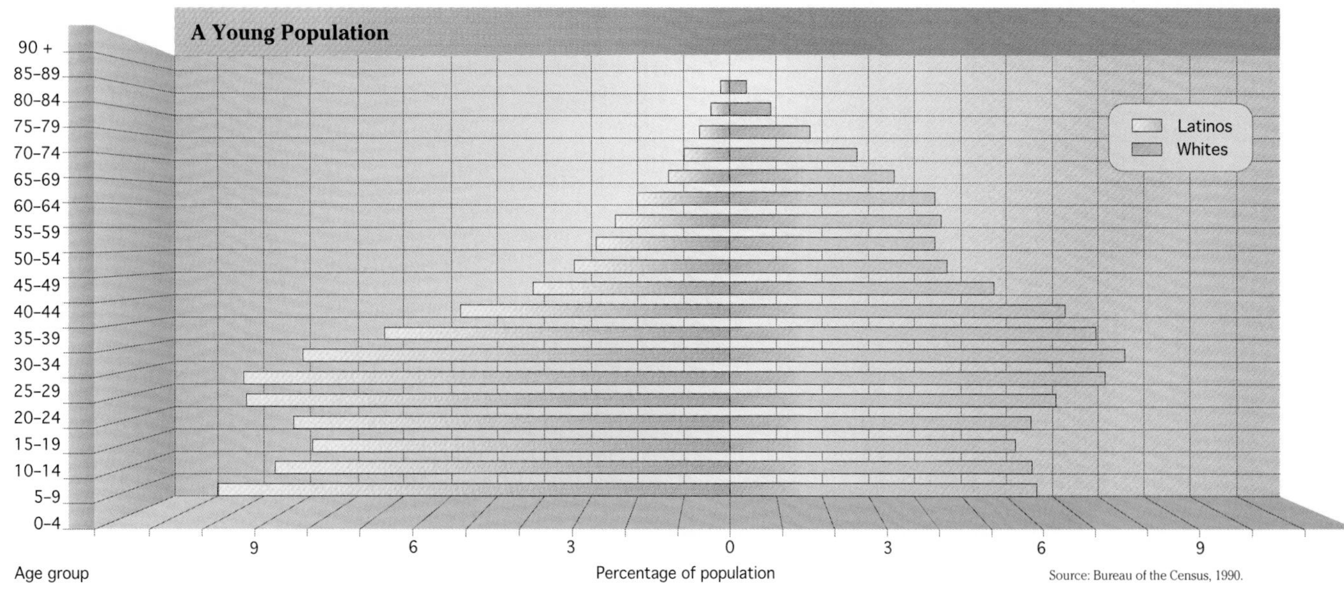

Asnin—Saba

Latino families tend not only to be large but also to have strong bonds of affection and mutual obligation. Family cohesiveness undoubtedly has a positive impact on health.

bers are likely to respond in kind, sometimes greeting them with hugs or bringing home-cooked foods as tokens of appreciation.

Respeto and *dignidad* are other important values in the Latino culture. While people everywhere enjoy and expect respect from others, the language and symbols of respect vary from one cultural group to another. For example, white or African-American patients might appreciate a doctor who dresses casually to appear more human and accessible, whereas to a Latino patient such informality might be seen as a signal that the health care professional cannot be taken seriously and may not be respectful of his or her patients. Such behavior may connote *una falta de respeto* ("a lack of respect").

The preeminence of the family in Latino culture and the traditional view of sex roles need to be taken into consideration by anyone who treats Latino patients. The health care provider who seeks to gain the confidence of the patient should make a point of soliciting opinions from other family members, especially the "man of the house."

Health status of Latinos today

- Of all persons in the U.S. who report that they have a regular source of health care, Latinos are least likely to have a private physician and are more likely than both whites and African-Americans to go to public health facilities or clinics, hospital outpatient clinics, or hospital emergency rooms.
- Nationwide, nearly 33% of Latinos did not have health insurance in 1993, compared with approximately 13% of whites and 20% of African-Americans. Moreover, the average annual growth in the uninsured population (from 1977 to 1992) was higher among Latinos—9.7%—than

The teenage friends below, of Honduran, Dominican, and Cuban heritage, epitomize the ethnic diversity of U.S. Latinos. Despite their varied backgrounds, Latinos share a common culture.

Tony Aruza—The Image Works

among African-Americans (2.8%) or whites (1.9%)

- In 1992 only about 64% of Latino mothers began their prenatal care in the first three months of pregnancy—considerably lower than the rate for white mothers (81%) but essentially the same as that for African-Americans (63.9%). Some 10% of all Latino mothers had only late prenatal care or none at all, compared with about 4% of whites and 9.9% of African-Americans.
- The risk for tuberculosis (TB) in the Latino population was five times that in the white population in 1993; Latinos accounted for 19% of TB cases reported in the U.S.
- A review of AIDS cases reported to the U.S. Centers for Disease Control and Prevention in 1994 revealed that the rate of AIDS among Latinos was three times that among whites.

The Latino population is so diverse that any statements about Latino health as a whole are necessarily generalizations (*see* Table, page 139, for a comparison of causes of death among the different subgroups). The predominant public health problems of Latinos concern maternal and child health, lifestyle-related disorders such as diabetes and cirrhosis of the liver, and occupational illness and injury.

Bob Daemmrich—The Image Works

A family in Texas shares a Thanksgiving meal. While ethnic origins and acculturation levels vary, all groups living in the U.S. are influenced by the customs of their adopted country.

Chronic diseases such as coronary heart disease and cancer cause proportionately fewer deaths among Latinos than among whites, in part because the Latino population is young, and these and other chronic diseases are conditions that are associated with aging. Other as-yet-undetermined protective factors—genetics, lifestyle, cultural factors such as the strong family—probably play a role in the comparatively lower Latino death rate from heart disease and cancer, although there has been little scientific study of how these factors protect against chronic disease or enhance survival in this particular population. Moreover, public health authorities predict that over the next 20 years the impact of these chronic diseases on the Latino population will intensify as greater numbers of Latinos enter the older age groups. The following is a brief profile of the health status of the Latino population.

Cardiovascular disease. Overall, Latinos of the three major subgroups in the U.S. (Mexicans, Puerto Ricans, and Cubans) have lower death rates from heart disease and stroke than either whites or African-Americans. Public health authorities consider this comparatively lower mortality rate an epidemiological paradox. The Latino population as a whole ranks high in several well-established risk factors for cardiovascular disease—low levels of high-density lipoprotein, or HDL (the "good" cholesterol, believed to have a cardioprotective effect), elevated triglyceride levels, a marked prevalence of diabetes, and disadvantaged socioeconomic status. On the other hand, compared with the rest of the U.S. population, fewer Latinos are heavy smokers, and high blood pressure is less prevalent among Latinos. The reasons for the lower Latino rate of cardiovascular disease remain to be fully elucidated.

Diabetes. Latinos living in the U.S. have a higher-than-normal prevalence of diabetes. The rate among Mexicans is two to three times that among whites. This disease is the third leading cause of death among Latino women and the fifth leading cause of death among Latino men (it ranks seventh among non-Hispanic men and women).

Two factors that undoubtedly play a part in the high Latino rate of diabetes are obesity and family history of the disease, both of which are well recognized as strong risk factors for diabetes. Like heart disease, however, diabetes is an extremely complex condition, and the reasons for its unusual prevalence in the Latino population are probably equally complex.

Alcohol-related problems. Although drinking patterns and rates of alcohol-related disease and death vary considerably between the different Latino subgroups, death rates from cirrhosis of the liver are greater among Latinos as a group than among the general U.S. population. Alcohol also plays a significant part in violence and homicides; the latter are the 5th leading cause of death among Mexicans and Puerto Ricans and the 6th among Cubans but rank 15th among whites.

Occupational health. The available evidence suggests that Latino workers are disproportionately exposed to hazardous substances and conditions on the job and have a higher incidence of occupational illness and injury than other workers in the general population. The hazardous industries and occupations that employ many Latino workers include construction, meat packing and processing, apparel manufacturing, agriculture, health care, and those that involve

Stephen Fiorella—Gamma Liaison

(Above) A worker from a Philadelphia maternity clinic's outreach program schedules a prenatal care appointment for a pregnant woman out shopping. (Below) A toddler gets a checkup at an East Los Angeles clinic.

exposure to airborne dusts and toxic chemicals such as vinyl chloride, benzene, and formaldehyde.

Undocumented status, in particular, is a risk for occupational exposure; undocumented workers are not in a position to complain or to report unsafe conditions to the authorities. Poverty and unemployment also play a part in influencing Latinos to take jobs despite substandard, or even dangerous, working conditions. Inability to speak English is also a factor in employment in hazardous work—English literacy may be required for the office, managerial, and supervisory positions in manufacturing but not for the production jobs that involve persistent exposure to toxic substances.

Infant mortality. The infant mortality rate for Latinos, 8.5 deaths per 1,000 live births, is slightly higher than that for whites, 6.8 (1992 figures). The relationship between low socioeconomic status and high rate of infant mortality that is well established for the white population has not been found among Latinos overall. The infant death rate among Latinos is low even when socioeconomic status is low and does not decrease when socioeconomic status rises. This finding lends credence to the theory that among Latinos cultural factors mitigate the effects of urban poverty on pregnancy.

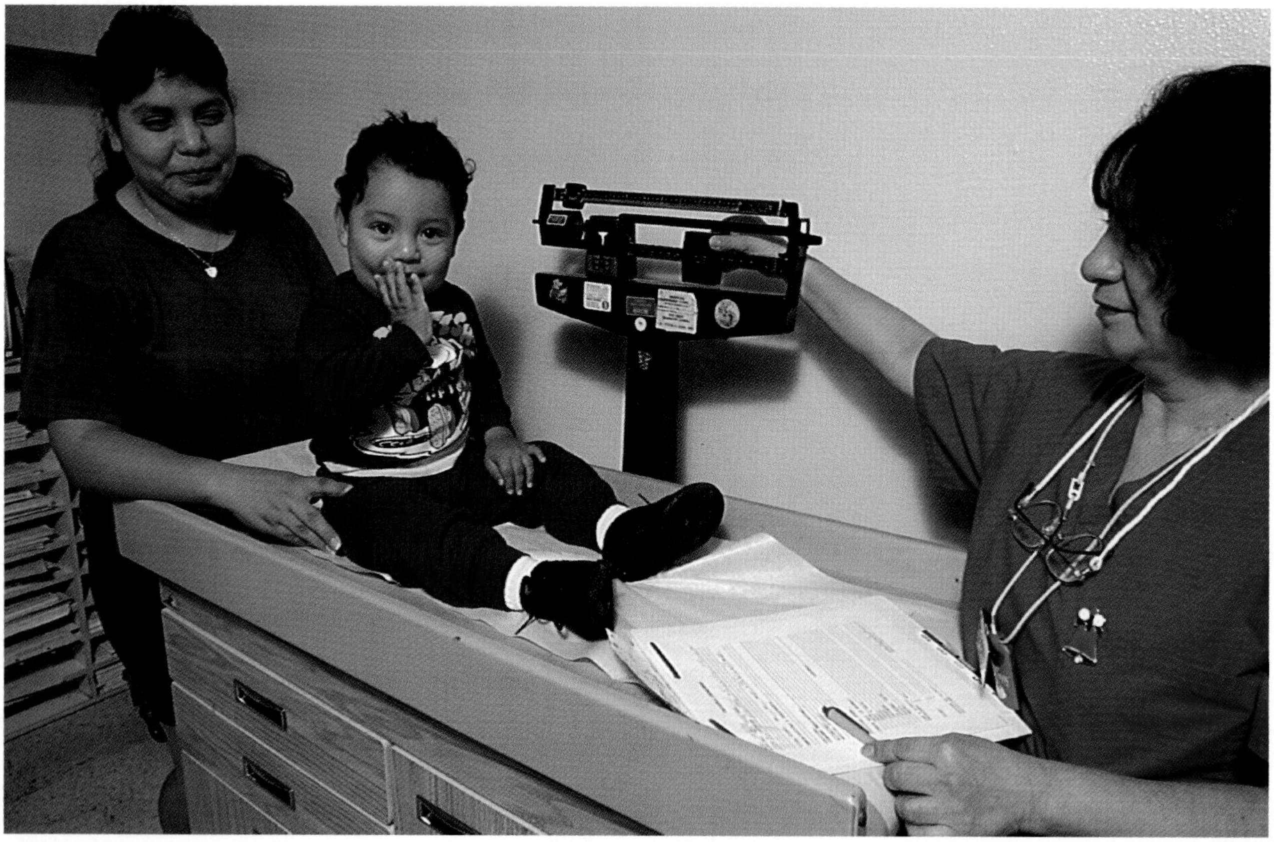

Alon Reininger—Contact

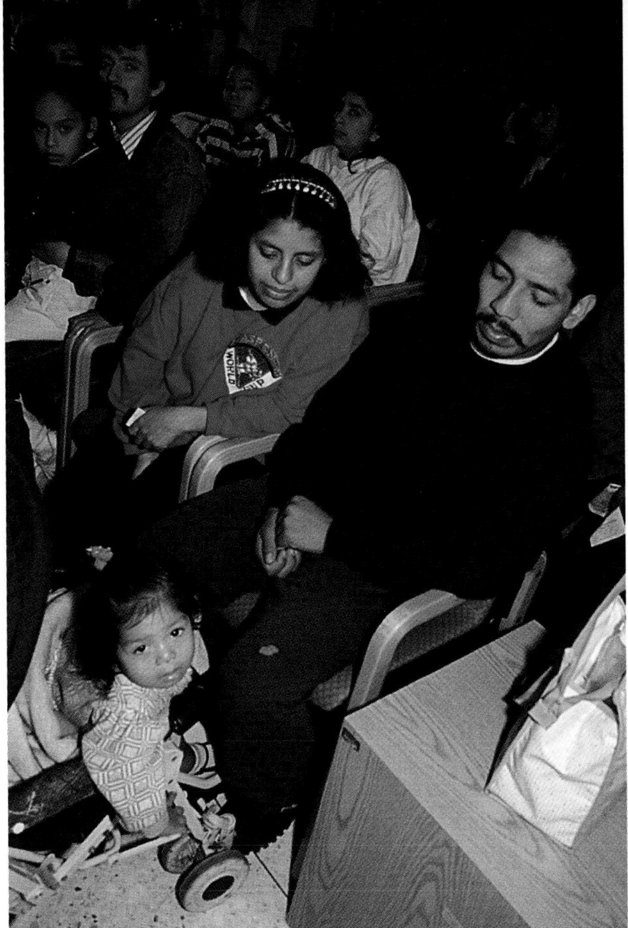

Lester Sloan—Gamma Liaison

Of all those in the U.S. who have a regular source of health care, Latinos are the least likely to have a private physician.

Immunizations. Latino children tend to live in inner-city areas, where only about 50–60% of two-year-olds have the required immunizations—far below the national objective of 90%. In recent years a few notable outbreaks of measles have occurred in the inner-city neighborhoods of major U.S. metropolitan areas. Public health authorities examined one such epidemic in Chicago and found that more than 25% of students in schools with predominantly Latino enrollment did not receive the measles vaccine until they started school, compared with 7% of children in schools with predominantly white enrollment. (The current U.S. schedule of immunization calls for the measles vaccine to be administered at 12 to 15 months of age.)

Not surprisingly, epidemiological studies in specific urban Latino communities have shown that the rate of immunization is highest for those children who have a regular source of health care or are covered by health insurance. Compounding the problem of low immunization rates in these communities is the regular arrival of immigrants from countries where the vaccination requirements are different from those in the U.S. These individuals are a continuing source of exposure to vaccine-preventable diseases.

What Kills Whom: U.S. Latino and White Populations Compared

	Mexican		Puerto Rican		Cuban		Central and South American		Other Latino		White	
Cause of death	Percentage	Rank	Percentage	Rank	Percentage	Rank	Percentage	Rank	Percentage	Rank	Percentage	Rank
Diseases of the heart	24.1	1	24.0	1	33.6	1	19.4	1	25.9	1	35.5	1
Cancers	16.9	2	14.4	2	23.0	2	19.1	2	17.9	2	23.6	2
Unintentional injuries	11.6	3	5.2	4	3.8	5	11.1	3	8.3	3	4.0	5
Cerebrovascular disease	5.4	4	3.8	6	5.2	3	4.7	7	4.8	4	6.9	3
Homicide and related violence	4.5	5	4.5	5	2.1	9	10.8	4	3.6	6	—	—
Diabetes mellitus	3.8	6	2.6	9	2.8	6	—	—	2.9	9	2.0	7
Chronic liver disease and cirrhosis	3.3	7	3.2	8	1.9	10	2.5	8	2.9	9	1.1	9
Pneumonia and influenza	3.1	8	3.3	7	2.8	6	2.1	10	3.1	7	3.7	6
Conditions affecting fetus and newborn	3.0	9	—	—	—	—	2.4	9	3.0	8	—	—
Suicide	2.0	10	—	—	—	—	6.5	5	—	—	1.5	8
AIDS/HIV	—	—	11.3	3	3.9	4	5.7	6	4.3	5	—	—
Chronic obstructive pulmonary disease	—	—	2.6	9	2.8	6	—	—	—	—	4.3	4
Atherosclerosis	—	—	—	—	—	—	—	—	—	—	1.0	10

Source: *Latino Health in the US: A Growing Challenge*, Carlos W. Molina and Marilyn Aguirre-Molina, editors, © 1994 American Public Health Association; statistics from National Center for Health Statistics, May 1992.

Bob Daemmrich—The Image Works

A mural in the Mirasol housing project in San Antonio, Texas, educates the residents about AIDS risks. The incidence of the disease is three times higher among Latinos than whites.

Barriers to care

Socioeconomic circumstances are perhaps the major determinant of how people respond to health concerns. Among poor populations survival—food, shelter, employment—takes precedence over health needs. Accordingly, economic reality has much to do with whether a Latino turns to home remedies or the formal health care system. For many Latinos, lack of health insurance is a major barrier to obtaining care.

Cultural and linguistic factors also play a part in deterring Latinos from using the formal health care system. For example, in a survey designed to determine the primary reasons why Mexicans in the U.S. have difficulty obtaining health care, the first 6 of 13 obstacles cited by the respondents had to do with economics (*e.g.,* high cost of service, loss of pay from work) and convenience (long waits for appointments, lack of transportation). The remainder, however, were cultural and linguistic: lack of knowledge about where to seek care; lack of confidence in the staff; no Spanish-speaking staff; disrespectful staff members; no Latino staff members.

The inability to speak English is a significant barrier to the use of health services by Latinos, just as English proficiency is a major predictor of the use of services. Equally important deterrents exist in the social and racial discrimination and cultural insensitivity that pervade the medical care system. Providers who are predominantly white and middle class tend to have little familiarity with diverse cultural groups within American society. In one study, for example, researchers at the University of Illinois at Chicago sent a questionnaire to 1,000 directors of hospitals and clinics in urban Latino neighborhoods. More than half of the health care providers who responded reported a lack of knowledge about Latino health status and the heterogeneity of the Latino population. In addition, 50% of the respondents said they felt that Latinos should learn English instead of expecting bilingual services to be provided. In another study researchers in California found that obstetricians at two major teaching hospitals on the West Coast held stereotypical views of particular ethnic/racial groups, especially those that are on the lower end of the socioeconomic scale; pregnant Latino women, for instance, were perceived as being noisy, passive, and uninformed.

Future needs

The process of treating disease and promoting health is an interactive one. It involves a relationship between patients and health care providers. Whenever the cultural backgrounds of these parties are widely divergent, the effectiveness of the interaction may be hindered. For this reason, any measures that would enhance the relationship between Latino patients and their health care providers—for example, greater numbers of bilingual staff and interpreters or increased sensitivity to cultural differences on the part of providers—would be a step forward for Latino health.

Because Latinos in the U.S. are predominantly young and have large families, they stand to benefit from public health policies that improve their access to primary care and maternal and child health services. And since they are both a young and a largely poor population, they would benefit from better schools, increased opportunities for young adults entering the workforce, and improved family housing—all of which have a direct impact on health and well-being.

(Opposite, top and bottom) Graduation, East Harlem, New York City, and shopping, Los Angeles. From coast to coast, nothing matters more than the health and well-being of *all* of America's children.

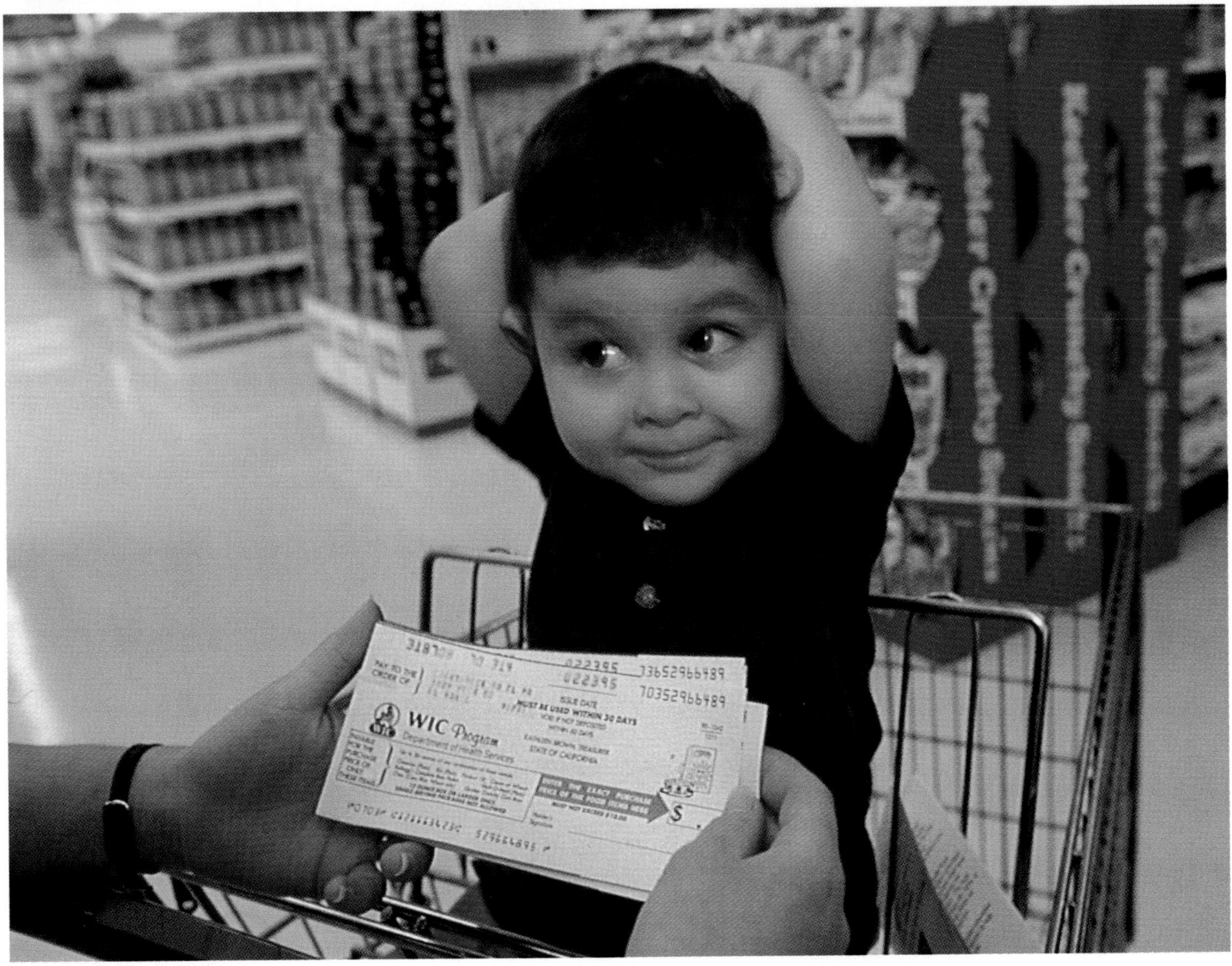

(Top) Joe Rodriguez—Black Star;
(bottom) Steve Lehman—Saba

Mental Health: Cultural Contexts

by Allen Frances, M.D., and Stacey Donovan

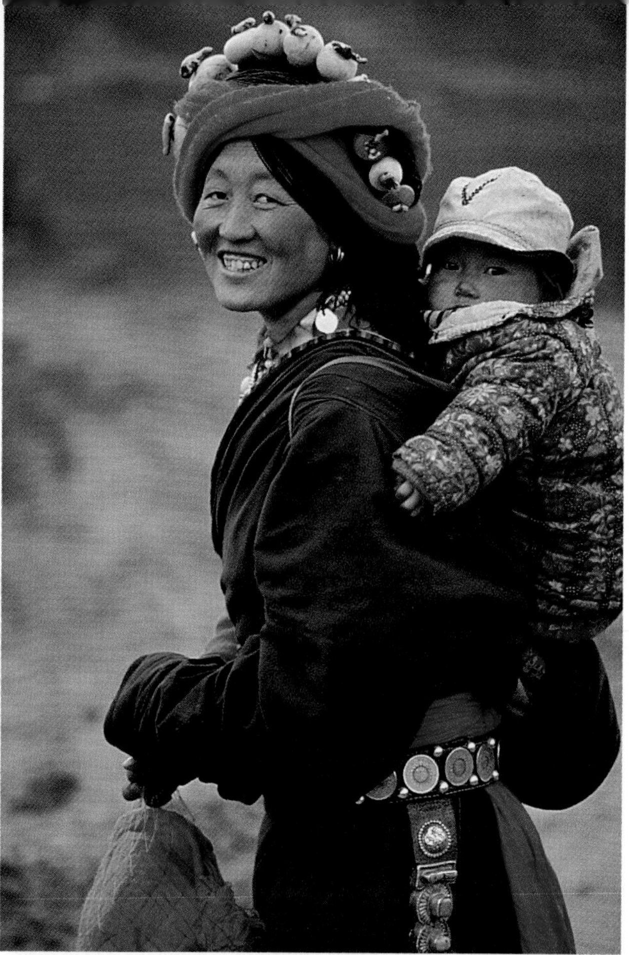

Human beings are clearly much more alike than they are different. Regardless of what part of the world they come from or what their early developmental and cultural experiences have been, all people probably share a basic vulnerability to the same variety of mental illnesses. Despite this similarity among people, cultural factors provide an important framework for understanding mental disorders and may determine which symptoms are most prominent. It follows that there can be significant cross-cultural confusion when it comes to interpreting those symptoms.

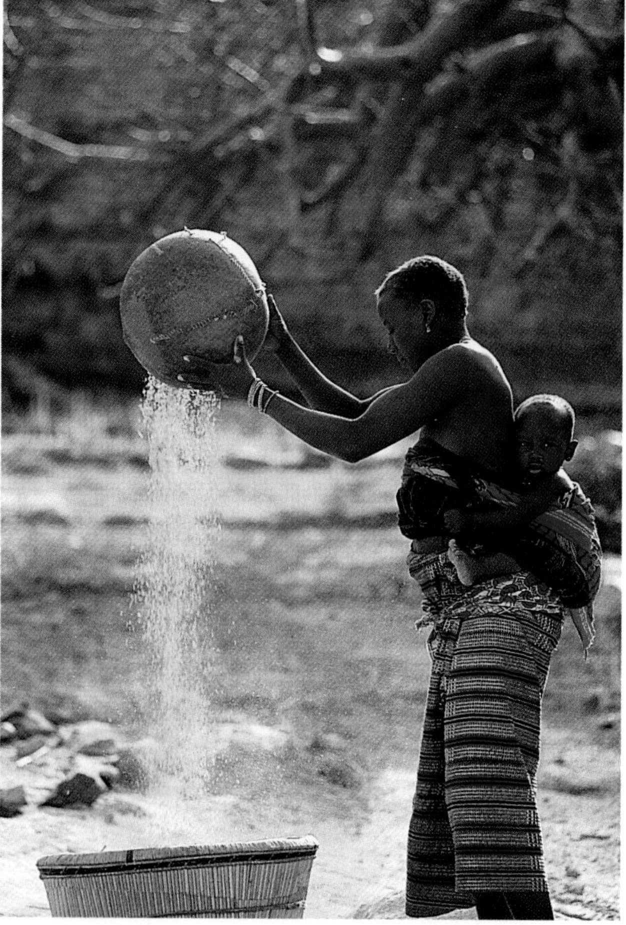

Allen Frances, M.D., *is Professor and Chairman, Department of Psychiatry and Behavioral Sciences, Duke University Medical Center, Durham, North Carolina, and Chairperson, Task Force on the* Diagnostic and Statistical Manual of Mental Disorders, fourth edition.
Stacey Donovan *is Research Assistant, Department of Psychiatry and Behavioral Sciences, Duke University Medical Center.*

More alike than different: women around the world carrying their infants. Babies on their mothers' backs in Tibet and Mali (opposite page, top and bottom); and (clockwise from below) in The Gambia; Northwest Territories, Canada (Inuit mother and child); Bolivia; and the U.S.

(Opposite page) Photographs, (top) Cary Wolinsky—Stock, Boston, (bottom) Nik Wheeler. (This page) Photographs, (below, top right, and center right) Wolfgang Kaehler, (bottom right) Robert Winslow—Viesti Associates

The problems inherent in cross-cultural diagnosis prove especially formidable when one considers that almost every society holds numerous culturally sanctioned beliefs that could undoubtedly be considered delusional or in some way psychopathological if they occurred in an individual in another culture. Certainly there are religious influences on behavior that could be misconstrued by a culturally uninformed outsider. Experiences such as hearing or seeing a deceased relative during bereavement; practices such as voodoo, speaking in tongues, and shamanism; and beliefs in life beyond death, the evil eye, and magical forces might all be misdiagnosed as indications of a psychotic disorder.

Depression and schizophrenia

People's cultural backgrounds affect the way symptoms are experienced and communicated. Societal responses to particular symptoms are also influenced by local culture. In some societies depression may be experienced primarily in somatic (physical) terms; in others depression primarily affects mood. Complaints of "nerves" and headaches are common expressions of a depressed state in Latino and Mediterranean cultures. Weakness, fatigue, and "imbalance" are more commonly seen in Chinese and other Asian cultures. In Middle Eastern cultures one who is depressed is said to have a problem of the "heart"; "heartbroken" is the term for depressive illness among Hopi Indians. Background may also affect how one views another's symptoms; irritability, for example, may provoke greater concern than sadness or withdrawal among family and friends in some cultures than it would in others.

Cultural differences are noted in the presentation, course, and outcome of schizophrenia. For example, catatonic behavior, characterized by psychomotor abnormalities (*e.g.,* stupor, rigidity, purposeless agitation, extreme negativism, refusal to speak), is relatively uncommon among individuals with schizophrenia in the United States but is seen frequently in non-Western countries. Individuals with schizophrenia in less developed nations tend to have a more acute course of illness but a better outcome than individuals in industrialized nations.

Cognitive and perceptual distortions (hallmark manifestations of schizophrenia) are largely influenced by culture; consideration of cultural context is therefore crucial in the assessment of symptoms. In some cultures visual or auditory hallucinations (among the most prominent symptoms of schizophrenia) may be a normal part of a religious experience. The assessment of disorganized speech can

Stock Montage, Inc.

be difficult owing to linguistic variations across cultures. Cultural differences in styles of emotional expression and the use of eye contact and body language may further complicate the diagnosis of this major mental disorder.

Problems with labels

Cultural values make the determination of which behaviors are labeled psychopathological even more nebulous. In some societies there is an emphasis on passivity, politeness, and deferential treatment of others, but in others these types of behavior can be misinterpreted as "dependent personality disorder." Similarly, wide variations in concepts of self, styles of communication, and coping mechanisms make it difficult to apply criteria for "personality disorder" across societies.

Some cultural or ethnic groups restrict the participation of women in public life, but those women should not be diagnosed as having agoraphobia, a mental disorder characterized by anxiety about leaving home and being in public places.

Anorexia nervosa, an eating disorder characterized by extreme weight loss, appears to be far more prevalent in industrialized

A Haitian woman is gently restrained during a voodoo ritual; those unfamiliar with other cultures' religious practices could misjudge worshipers' behavior.

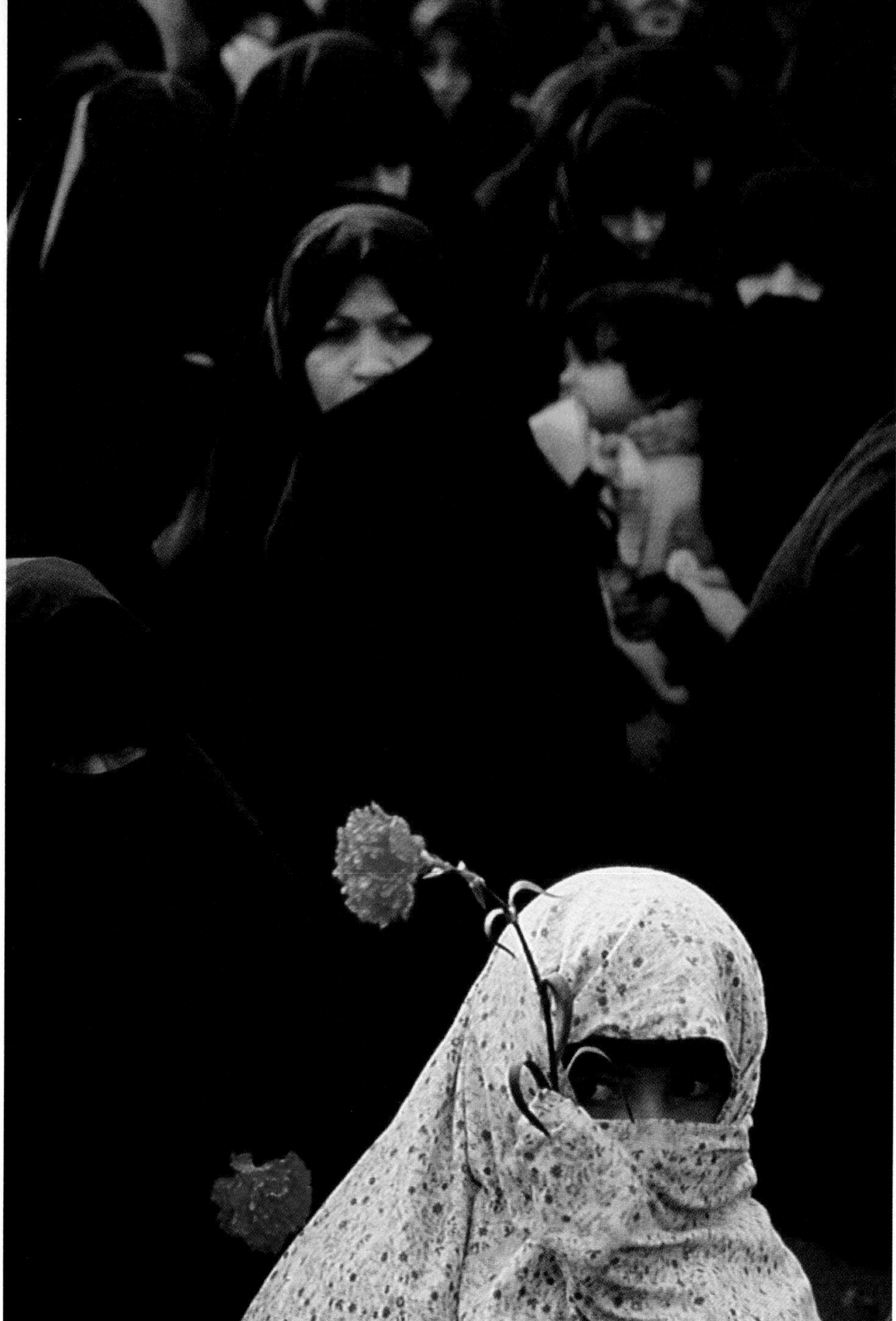

Alain Keler—Sygma

Muslim women in Iran (above), whose participation in public life is restricted, wear veils and traditional dress. Some cultures have sharply defined customs and conventions to which members of society must strictly adhere.

societies, where being considered attractive is linked to being thin, especially among females. Immigrants who move from countries in which the disorder is rare to those in which it is prevalent may develop anorexia nervosa in the process of assimilating "thin-body ideals. In the U.S. there are major differences between white women and African-American women in perception of the body. A recent study sponsored by the National Institute of Child Health and Human Development found that 90% of white junior-high and high-school girls were dissatisfied with their weight, and a large proportion were obsessed with dieting. Among their African-American counterparts, 64% thought it was better to be overweight than underweight, while 70% were perfectly satisfied with their body size.

Cultural considerations come of age

Marked differences characterize the quantity, frequency, and patterning of alcohol consumption in the countries of the world. In most Asian cultures, the overall prevalence of Alcohol-Related Disorders may be relatively low, and the male-to-female ratio high. These findings appear to relate to the absence, in perhaps 50% of Japanese, Chinese, and Korean individuals, of the form of aldehyde dehydrogenase that eliminates low levels of the first breakdown product of alcohol, acetaldehyde. When such individuals consume alcohol, they experience a flushed face and palpitations and are less likely to consume large amounts. In the United States, whites and African-Americans have nearly identical rates of Alcohol Abuse and Dependence. Latino males have somewhat higher rates, although prevalence is lower among Latino females than among females from other ethnic groups. Low educational level, unemployment, and lower socioeconomic status are associated with Alcohol-Related Disorders, although it is often difficult to separate cause from effect.

—*Diagnostic and Statistical Manual of Mental Disorders*, fourth edition (1994)

Diagnostic assessment can be especially challenging when a clinician from one ethnic or cultural background uses the American Psychiatric Association's *Diagnostic and Statistical Manual of Mental Disorders* (*DSM*) to evaluate an individual from another cultural group. The *DSM* provides the standard nomenclature for psychiatric disorders and is used in the U.S. and many other parts of the world. Owing to the wide international acceptance of this nomenclature, special efforts were made to incorporate an awareness of ethnic and cultural differences in the newly revised, fourth, edition of the manual, *DSM-IV*, published in 1994.

In an effort to steer clinicians clear of the pitfalls that may be encountered in cross-cultural diagnosis, *DSM-IV*'s editors incorporated several new features specifically intended to elucidate cultural considerations. For instance, the manual points out in the section on "Disorders Usually First Diagnosed in Infancy, Childhood, or Adolescence" that "immigrant children who are unfamiliar with or uncomfortable in the official language of their new host country may refuse to speak to strangers in their new environment. This behavior should not be diagnosed as Selective Mutism." Throughout the nearly 900-page volume, there are discussions of culture-specific aspects of most mental disorders. The text describes the ways in which varied cultural backgrounds affect the form of symptoms, and it suggests preferred idioms for describing distress.

Another type of information aimed at enhancing the cross-cultural applicability of *DSM-IV* is an "Outline for Cultural Formulation" that was expressly designed to assist clinicians in evaluating the impact of patients' cultural backgrounds on their present symptoms. The cultural identity of the individual, cultural explanations for specific symptoms, and cultural elements of the relationship between the individual and the clinician, for example, can all have an effect and therefore should be considered.

The volume also refers to specific "culture-bound syndromes" that have been noted in just one or in a number of the world's societies. Some of these locality-specific patterns of aberrant behavior are used as examples throughout the manual, while a list comprising 25 syndromes can be found in a glossary at the end of *DSM-IV*.

From *amok* to *zar*: a world of syndromes

The term *culture-bound syndrome* is defined by *DSM-IV* as recurrent, patterned, and troubling sets of experiences and observations that are generally limited to specific societies or cultural areas. Many of these patterns are indigenously considered to be "illnesses," or at least afflictions, and most have local names. There is seldom a one-to-one equivalence of any culture-bound syndrome with a standard *DSM* diagnostic category.

A condition known as *amok* in Malaysia is a "dissociative episode"—a disruption in the usually integrated functioning of consciousness, memory, identity, or perception of the environment—that is often characterized by a period of brooding followed by an outburst of violent, aggressive, or homicidal behavior directed at people and objects. The episode tends to be precipitated by a perceived slight or insult and seems to be prevalent only among males. A similar behavioral pattern has been seen in Laos, the Philippines, and Polynesia (referred to as *cafard* or *cathard*); in New Guinea and Puerto Rico (*mal de pelea*); and among the Navajo (*iich' aa*).

Another example of a culture-bound syndrome is *ataque de nervios,* an idiom of distress that has been principally reported among Latinos from the Caribbean but is also recognized among many Latin-American and Latin Mediterranean groups. Such "attacks" are characterized by uncontrollable shouting, crying bouts, trembling, and verbal or physical aggression. A common feature of an *ataque de nervios* is a sense of being out of control, usually following a precipitating stressful event.

Dhat is a folk diagnostic term used in India to refer to severe anxiety and hypochondria that are associated with the discharge of semen, whitish discoloration of the urine, or general feelings of weakness and exhaustion. Similar syndromes occur in Sri Lanka and China.

Ghost sickness, a preoccupation with death and the deceased, has frequently been observed among members of many American Indian tribes. The various symptoms that may be attributed to this malady include bad dreams, weakness, hallucinations, loss of consciousness, confusion, feelings of futility, and a sense of suffocation.

Pibloktoq, observed in Arctic and sub-Arctic Eskimo communities, is an abrupt dissociative episode accompanied by extreme excitement of up to 30 minutes' duration and frequently followed by convulsive seizures and coma lasting up to 12 hours. The individual may be withdrawn or mildly irritable for a period of hours or days before the attack and will typically report amnesia for (*i.e.,* no memory of) the attack. During the episode the individual may tear off his or her clothing, break furniture, shout obscenities, eat feces, flee from protective shelter, or perform other irrational acts.

Shen-k'uei and *shenkui* describe a syndrome seen in Taiwan and China, respectively. *DSM-IV* notes that somatic complaints include dizziness, backache, fatigability, general weakness, insomnia, frequent dreams, and sexual dysfunction that "are attributed to excessive semen loss" and represent a potentially life-threatening "loss of one's vital essence."

Susto is a folk illness describing "fright" or "soul loss" most often seen among some Latinos in the United States and among people in Mexico, Central America, and South America. The disorder can also be called *espanto, pasmo, tripa ida, perdida del alma,* or *chibih. DSM-IV* specifies that *susto*'s "typical symptoms include appetite disturbances, inadequate or excessive sleep, troubled sleep or dreams, feeling of sadness, lack of motivation to do anything, and feelings of low self-worth or dirtiness. Somatic symptoms accompanying *susto* include muscle aches and pains, headache, stomachache, and diarrhea." Treatment for *susto* involves "ritual healings . . . calling the soul back to the body and cleansing the person to restore bodily and spiritual balances."

Zar is a culture-bound syndrome experienced primarily in Ethiopia, Somalia, Egypt, The Sudan, Iran, and some other African and Middle Eastern societies, in which persons are said to be "possessed by a spirit." Such individuals may shout, laugh, bang their heads against a wall, sing, weep, show apathy, or refuse to eat, but these behaviors are "not considered pathological" locally.

R. Ian Lloyd—Westlight

Culture in perspective

It is important neither to ignore the role culture plays in psychiatric diagnosis nor to overemphasize it. A proper balance takes into account the fact that culture influences how people behave both when they are well and when they are ill. On the other hand, most psychiatric disorders seem to be an element of the human condition that transcends the particularities of specific cultures. It is hoped that the new features of the *DSM-IV* will increase sensitivity to variations in how mental disorders may be expressed in different cultures and will reduce the possible effect of unintended bias stemming from the clinician's own cultural background.

Within a culture various ethnic groups may have quite different beliefs and perceptions. African-American teenagers tend to feel much better about their own appearance and body size than their white peers; those feelings may profoundly affect the behaviors and self-concepts of individuals within those groups.

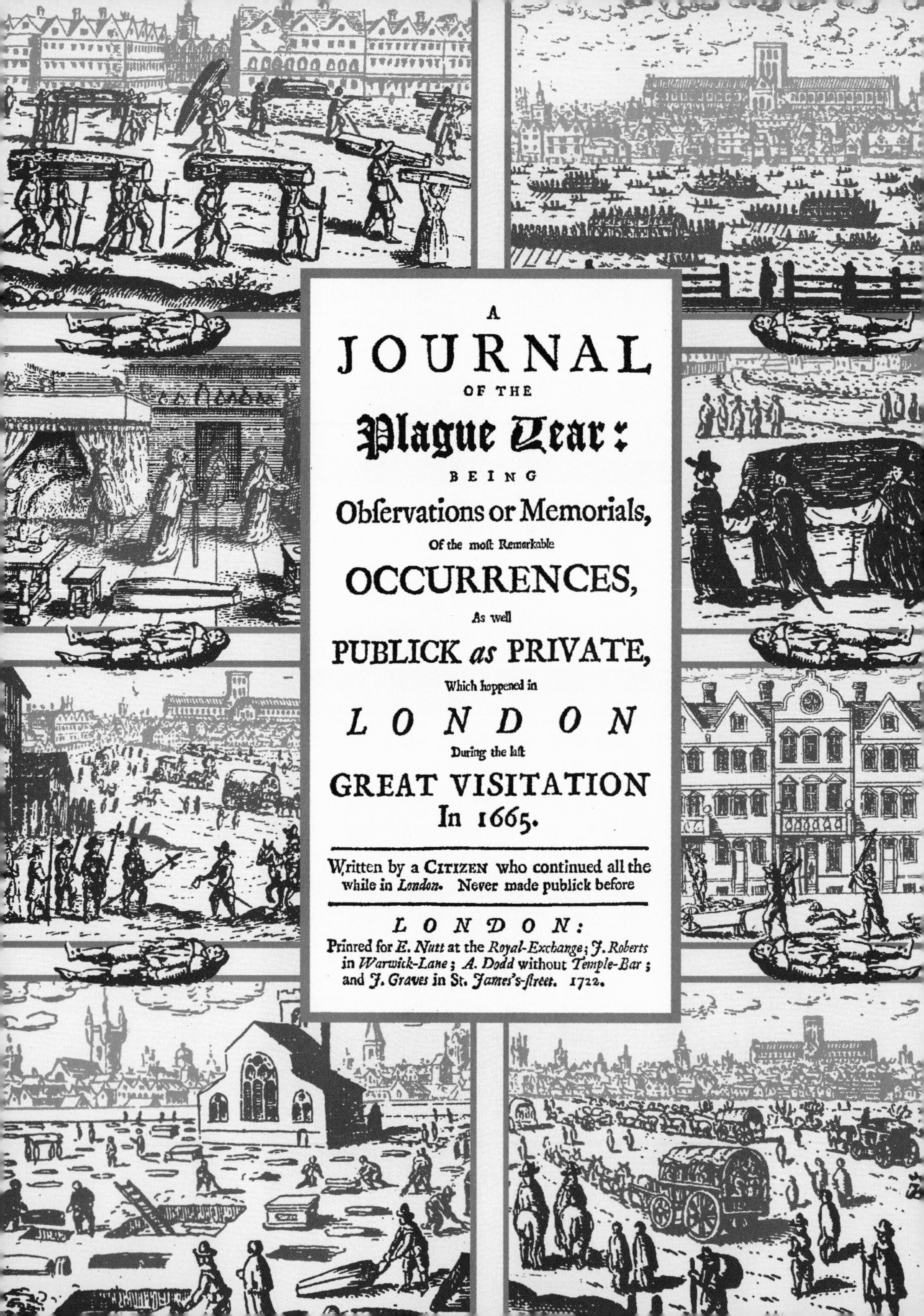

A

JOURNAL

OF THE

Plague Year:

BEING

Obſervations or Memorials,

Of the moſt Remarkable

OCCURRENCES,

As well

PUBLICK *as* PRIVATE,

Which happened in

LONDON

During the laſt

GREAT VISITATION

In 1665.

Written by a CITIZEN who continued all the while in *London*. Never made publick before

---

LONDON:

Prinred for *E. Nutt* at the *Royal-Exchange*; *J. Roberts* in *Warwick-Lane*; *A. Dodd* without *Temple-Bar*; and *J. Graves* in St. *James's-ſtreet*. 1722.

Sir Walter Scott observed that even if Daniel Defoe had not been the author of *Robinson Crusoe,* he still would have deserved immortality for the genius displayed in *A Journal of the Plague Year,* published in 1722. Author of some 500 books and pamphlets, Defoe not only was the most prolific writer of his time but was considered by many scholars to be the first true novelist. Though the author was only five years old at the onset of the Great Plague of London in 1664, Defoe's narrative, constructed from numerous sources, very accurately recounts the last and worst of London's epidemics. Beginning in the city's suburbs, the plague took its toll, killing more than 75,000 in a population estimated at 460,000. The plague was often referred to by the author as "distemper" (an illness that destroys physical, mental, or spiritual functions), as its origins, causes, and cures were widely misunderstood in Defoe's time. Even today when it strikes, the plague presents a unique and formidable adversary, as it did in India in September 1994.

(Opposite page) Facsimile of title page from the first edition; vignettes from a print in the Mansell Collection

London in tears

The face of London was now indeed strangely altered . . . sorrow and sadness sat upon every face; and though some parts were not yet overwhelmed, yet all looked deeply concerned; and, as we saw it apparently coming on, so every one looked on himself and his family as in the utmost danger. Were it possible to represent those times exactly to those that did not see them, and give the reader due ideas of the horror that everywhere presented itself, it must make just impressions upon their minds and fill them with surprise. London might well be said to be all in tears . . . nobody put on black or made a formal dress of mourning . . . but the voice of mourners was truly heard in the streets. The shrieks of women and children at the windows and doors of their houses, where their dearest relations were perhaps dying, or just dead, were so frequent to be heard as we passed the streets, that it was enough to pierce the stoutest heart in the world to hear them. Tears and lamentations were seen almost in every house, especially in the first part of the visitation; for towards the latter end men's hearts were hardened, and death was so always before their eyes, that they did not so much concern themselves for the loss of their friends, expecting that themselves should be summoned the next hour. . . .

The apprehensions of the people were likewise strangely increased by the error of the times; in which, I think, the people, from what principle I cannot imagine, were more addicted to prophecies and astrological conjurations, dreams, and old wives' tales than ever they were before or since. . . .

Possessed

The imagination of the people was really turned wayward and possessed. And no wonder, if they who were poring continually at the clouds saw shapes and figures . . . which had nothing in them but air and vapour. Here they told us they saw a flaming sword held in a hand coming out of a cloud, with a point hanging directly over the city; there they saw hearses and coffins in the air . . . and there again, heaps of dead bodies lying unburied, and the like, just as the imagination of the poor terrified people furnished them with matter to work upon.

So hypochondriac fancies represent
Ships, armies, battles in the firmament;
Till steady eyes the exhalations solve,
And all to its first matter, cloud, resolve.

I could fill this account with the strange relations such people gave every day of what they had seen; and every one was so positive of their having seen what they pretended to see, that there was no contradicting them without breach of friendship, or being accounted rude and unmannerly on the one hand, and profane and impenetrable on the other. . . .

There are two churchyards to Bishopsgate church or parish; one we go over to pass from the place called Petty France into Bishopsgate Street, coming out just by the church door; the other is on the side of the narrow passage where the almshouses are on the left; and a dwarf-wall with a palisado on it on the right hand, and the city wall on the other side more to the right.

In this narrow passage stands a man looking through between the palisadoes into the burying-place, and as many people as the narrowness of the passage would admit to stop, without hindering the passage of others, and he was talking mighty eagerly to them, and pointing now to one place, then to another, and affirming that he saw a ghost walking upon such a gravestone there. . . .

This ghost, as the poor man affirmed, made signs to the houses, and to the ground, and to the people, plainly intimating, or else they so understanding it, that abundance of the people should come to be buried in that churchyard, as indeed happened; but that he saw such aspects I must acknowledge I never believed, nor could I see anything of it myself, though I looked most earnestly to see it, if possible.

Illustration by George Cruikshank; photograph, Ann Ronan Picture Library/Image Select

"'I am a waterman . . . and what I get I lay down upon that stone' says he, showing me a broad stone . . . 'and then' says he, 'I halloo, and call to [my family] till I make them hear; and they come and fetch it.' "

These things serve to show how far the people were really overcome with delusions; and as they had a notion of the approach of a visitation, all their predictions ran upon a most dreadful plague, which should lay the whole city, and even the kingdom, waste, and should destroy almost all the nation, both man and beast. . . .

One mischief always introduces another. These terrors and apprehensions of the people led them into a thousand weak, foolish, and wicked things, which they wanted not a sort of people really wicked to encourage them to: and this was running about to fortune-tellers, cunning-men, and astrologers to know their fortune, or, as it is vulgarly expressed, to have their fortunes told them, their nativities calculated, and the like; and this folly presently made the town swarm with a wicked generation of pretenders to magic, to the black art, as they called it, and I know not what; nay, to a thousand worse dealings with the devil than they were really guilty of. And this trade grew so open and so generally practised that it became common to have signs and inscriptions set up at doors: 'Here lives a fortune-teller', 'Here lives an astrologer', 'Here you may have your nativity calculated', and the like. . . .

People might be heard, even into the streets as we passed along, calling upon God for mercy through Jesus Christ, and saying, 'I have been a thief', 'I have been an adulterer', 'I have been a murderer', and the like, and none durst stop to make the least inquiry into such things or to administer comfort to the poor creatures. . . . Some of the ministers did visit the sick at first and for a little while, but it was not to be done. It would have been present death to have gone into some houses. The very buriers of the dead, who were the hardenedest creatures in town, were sometimes beaten back and so terrified that they durst not go into houses where the whole families were swept away together, and where the circumstances were more particularly horrible, as some were; but this was, indeed, at the first heat of the distemper. . . .

Cruel confinement

The locking up the doors of people's houses, and setting a watchman there night and day to prevent their stirring out or any coming to them, when perhaps the sound people in the family might have escaped if they

Illustration by George Cruikshank; photograph, Ann Ronan Picture Library/Image Select

"The cart had in it sixteen or seventeen bodies; some were wrapt up in linen sheets, some in rags, some little other than naked, or so loosely wrapped that what covering they had fell from them."

had been removed from the sick, looked very hard and cruel; and many people perished in these miserable confinements. . . .

Those that did thus break out spread the infection farther by their wandering about with the distemper upon them, in their desperate circumstances, than they would otherwise have done; for whoever considers all the particulars in such cases must acknowledge, and we cannot doubt but the severity of those confinements made many people desperate, and made them run out of their houses at all hazards, and with the plague visibly upon them, not knowing either whither to go or what to do, or, indeed, what they did; and many that did so were driven to dreadful exigencies and extremities, and perished in the streets or fields for mere want, or dropped down by the raging violence of the fever upon them. Others wandered into the country, and went forward any way, as their desperation guided them, not knowing whither they went or would go: till, faint and tired, and not getting any relief, the houses and villages on the road refusing to admit them to lodge whether infected or no, they have perished by the roadside or gotten into barns and died there, none daring to come to them or relieve them, though perhaps not infected, for nobody would believe them. . . .

And I know it so well, and in so many several cases, that I could give several relations of good, pious, and religious people who, when they have had the distemper, have been so far from being forward to infect others that they have forbid their own family to come near them, in hopes of their being preserved, and have even died without seeing their nearest relations lest they should be instrumental to give them the distemper, and infect or endanger them. If, then, there were cases wherein the infected people were careless of the injury they did to others, this was certainly one of them, if not the chief, namely, when people who had the distemper had broken out from houses which were so shut up, and having been driven to extremities for provision or for entertainment, had endeavoured to conceal their condition, and have been thereby instrumental involuntarily to infect others who have been ignorant and unwary.

This is one of the reasons why I believed then, and do believe still, that the shutting up houses thus by force, and restraining, or rather imprisoning, people in their own houses, as I said above, was of little or no service in the whole. Nay, I am of opinion it was rather hurtful, having forced those desperate people to wander abroad with the plague upon them, who would otherwise have died quietly in their beds. . . .

Flee if you can

It was thought that there were not less than 10,000 houses forsaken of the inhabitants in the city and suburbs. . . . This was besides the numbers of lodgers, and of particular persons who were fled out of other families . . . it was computed that about 200,000 people were fled and gone. . . . It was a rule with those who had thus two houses in their keeping or care, that if anybody was taken sick in a family, before the master of the family let the examiners or any other officer know of it, he immediately would send all the rest of his family, whether children or servants, as it fell out to be, to such other house which he had so in charge, and then giving notice of the sick person to the examiner, have a nurse or nurses appointed, and have another person to be shut up in the house with them (which many for money would do), so to take charge of the house in case the person should die. . . .

However, the poor people could not lay up provisions, and there was a necessity that they must go to market to buy, and others to send servants or their children; and as this was a necessity which renewed itself daily, it brought abundance of unsound people to the markets, and a great many that went thither sound brought death home with them.

It is true people used all possible precaution. When any one bought a joint of meat in the market they would not take it off the butcher's hand, but took it off the hooks themselves. On the other hand, the butcher would not touch the money, but have it put into a pot full of vinegar, which he kept for that purpose. The buyer carried always small money to make up any odd sum, that they might take no change. They carried bottles of scents . . . and all the means that could be used were used; but then the poor could not do even these things, and they went at all hazards. . . .

Suckling death

One of the most deplorable cases in all the present calamity was that of women with child, who, when they came to the hour of their sorrows, and their pains come upon them, could neither have help of one kind or another; neither midwife or neighbouring women to come near them. Most of the midwives were dead, especially of such as served the poor; and many, if not all the midwives of note, were fled into the country; so that it was next to impossible for a poor woman that could not pay an immoderate price to get any midwife to come to her—and if they did, those they could get were generally unskilful and ignorant creatures; and the consequence of this was that a most unusual and incredible number of women were reduced to the utmost distress. Some were delivered and spoiled by the rashness and ignorance of those who pretended to lay them. Children without number were, I might say, murdered by the same but a more justifiable ignorance: pretending they would save the mother, whatever became of the child; and many times both mother and child were lost in the same manner; and especially where the mother had the distemper, there nobody would come near them and both sometimes perished. Sometimes the mother has died of the plague, and the infant, it may be, half born, or born but not parted from the mother. Some died in the very pains of their travail, and not delivered at all; and so many were the cases of this kind that it is hard to judge of them. . . .

I could tell here dismal stories of living infants being found sucking the breasts of their mothers, or nurses, after they have been dead of the plague. Of a mother in the parish where I lived, who, having a child that was not well, sent for an apothecary to view the child; and when he came, as the relation goes, was giving the child suck at her breast, and to all appearance was herself very well; but when the apothecary came close to her he saw the tokens upon that breast with which she was suckling the child. He was surprised enough, to be sure, but, not willing to fright the poor woman too much, he desired she would give the child into his hand; so he takes the child, and going to a cradle in the room, lays it in, and opening its cloths, found the tokens upon the child too, and both died before he could get home to send a preventive medicine to the father of the child. . . . Whether the child infected the nurse-mother or the mother the child was not certain, but the last most likely. Likewise of a child brought home to the parents from a nurse that had died of the plague, yet the tender mother would not refuse to take in her child, and laid it in her bosom, by which she was infected; and died with the child in her arms dead also. . . .

Consumed by calamity

An order was published by the Lord Mayor, and by the magistrates, according to the advice of the physicians, that all the dogs and cats should be immediately killed, and an officer was appointed for the execution.

It is incredible, if their account is to be depended upon, what a prodigious number of those creatures were destroyed. I think they talked of forty thousand dogs, and five times as many cats; few houses being without a cat, some having several, sometimes five or six in a house. All possible endeavours were used also to destroy the mice and rats, especially the latter, by laying ratsbane and other poisons for them, and a prodigious multitude of them were also destroyed. . . .

After the funerals became so many that people could not toll the bell, mourn or weep . . . as they did before; no, nor so much as make coffins for those that died; so after a while the fury of the infection appeared to be so increased that, in short, they shut up no houses at all. It seemed enough that all the remedies of that kind had been used till they were found fruitless, and that the plague spread itself with an irresistible fury; so that as the fire the succeeding year spread itself, and burned with such violence that the citizens, in despair, gave over their endeavours to extinguish it, so in the plague it came at last to such violence that the people sat still looking at one another, and seemed quite abandoned to despair; whole streets seemed to be desolated, and not to be shut up only, but to be emptied of their inhabitants; doors were left open, win-

(Opposite) "I heard of one infected creature, who running out of his bed in his shirt in the anguish and agony of his swellings . . . ran downstairs and into the street."

Illustration by George Cruikshank; photograph, Ann Ronan Picture Library/Image Select

Ann Ronan Picture Library/Image Select

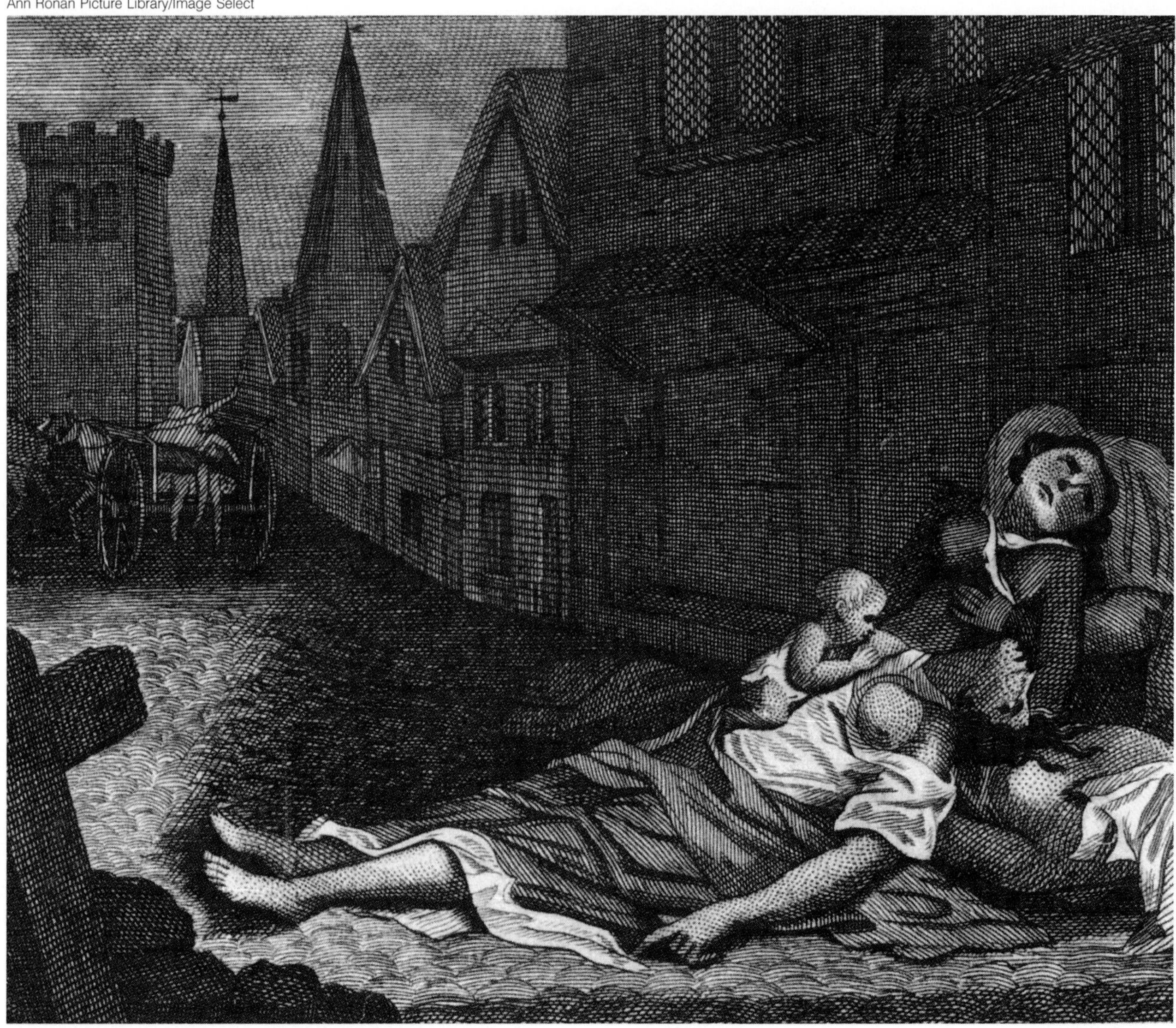

"I could tell here dismal stories of living infants being found sucking the breasts of their mothers, or nurses, after they have been dead of the plague."

dows stood shattering with the wind in empty houses for want of people to shut them. In a word, people began to give up themselves to their fears and to think that all regulations and methods were in vain, and that there was nothing to be hoped for but an universal desolation. . . . It was indeed one admirable piece of conduct in the said magistrates that the streets were kept constantly clear and free from all manner of frightful objects, dead bodies, or any such things as were indecent or unpleasant—unless where anybody fell down suddenly or died in the streets, as I have said above; and these were generally covered with some cloth or blanket, or removed into the next churchyard till night. All the needful works that carried terror with them, that were both dismal and dangerous, were done in the night; if any diseased bodies were removed, or dead bodies buried, or infected clothes burnt, it was done in the night; and all the bodies which were thrown into the great pits in the several churchyards or burying-grounds, as has been observed, were so removed in the night, and everything was covered and closed before day. So that in the daytime there was not the least signal of the calamity to be seen or heard of, except what was to be observed from the emptiness of the streets, and sometimes from the passionate outcries and lamentations of the people, out at their windows, and from the numbers of houses and shops shut up. . . .

I knew a man who conversed freely in London all the season of the plague in 1665, and kept about him an antidote or cordial on purpose to take when he thought himself in any danger, and he had such a rule to know or have warning of the danger by as indeed I never met with before or since. How far it may be depended on I know not. He had a wound in his leg, and whenever he came among any people that were not sound, and the infection began to affect him, he said he could know it by that signal, viz., that his wound in his leg would smart, and look pale and white; so as soon as ever he felt it smart it was time for him to withdraw, or to take care of himself, taking his drink, which he always carried about him for that purpose. Now it seems he found his wound would smart many times when he was in company with such who thought themselves to be sound, and who appeared so to one another; but he would presently rise up and say publicly, 'Friends, there is somebody in the room that has the plague', and so would immediately break up the company. This was indeed a faithful monitor to all people that the plague is not to be avoided by those that converse promiscuously in a town infected, and people have it when they know it not, and that they likewise give it to others when they know not that they have it themselves; and in this case shutting up the well or removing the sick will not do it, unless they can go back and shut up all those that the sick had conversed with, even before they knew themselves to be sick, and none knows how far to carry that back, or where to stop; for none knows when or where or how they may have received the infection. . . .

Rumours

You may be sure, also, that the report of these things lost nothing in the carriage. The plague was itself very terrible, and the distress of the people very great, as you may observe of what I have said. But the rumour was infinitely greater, and it must not be wondered that our

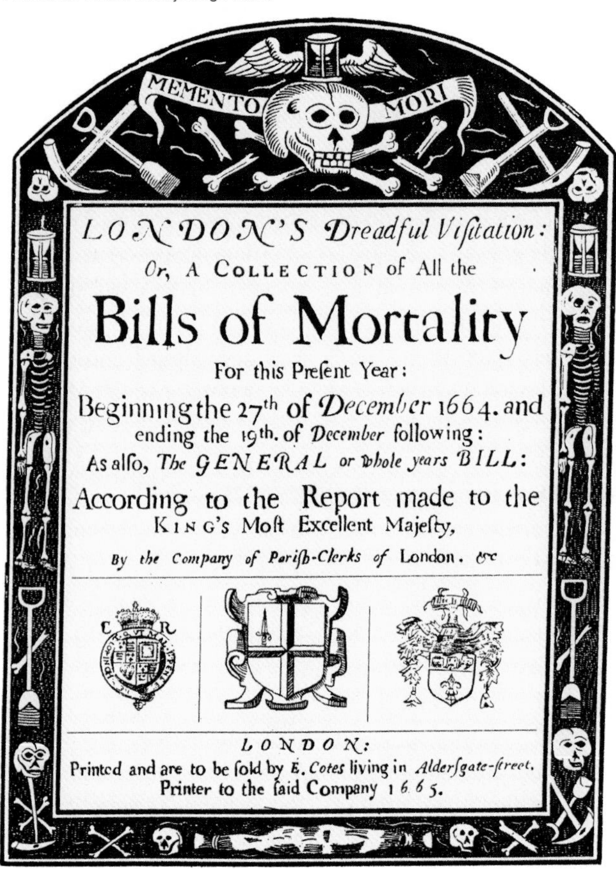

LONDON'S Dreadful Viſitation:
Or, A COLLECTION of All the
Bills of Mortality
For this Preſent Year:
Beginning the 27th of December 1664. and ending the 19th. of December following:
As alſo, The GENERAL or whole years BILL:
According to the Report made to the KING's Moſt Excellent Majeſty,
By the Company of Pariſh-Clerks of London. &c

LONDON:
Printed and are to be ſold by E. Cotes living in Alderſgate-ſtreet, Printer to the ſaid Company 1665.

"And thus great numbers went out of the world who were never known, or any account of them taken, as well within the bills of mortality as without."

friends abroad . . . said that in London there died twenty thousand in a week; that the dead bodies lay unburied by heaps; that the living were not sufficient to bury the dead or the sound to look after the sick; that all the kingdom was infected likewise, so that it was an universal malady such as was never heard of in those parts of the world; and they could hardly believe us when we gave them an account how things really were, and how there was not above one-tenth part of the people dead; that there was 500,000 left that lived all the time in the town; that now the people began to walk the streets again, and those who were fled to return, there was no miss of the usual throng of people in the streets, except as every family might miss their relations and neighbours, and the like. . . .

Not in the streets only, but in private houses and families, great quantities of coals were then burnt, even all the summer long and when the weather was hottest, which was done by the advice of the physicians. Some indeed opposed it, and insisted that to keep the houses and rooms hot was a means to propagate the distemper, which was a fermentation and heat already in the blood; that it was known to spread and increase in hot weather and abate in cold; and therefore they alleged that all contagious distempers are the worse for heat, because the contagion was nourished and gained strength in hot weather, and was, as it were, propagated in heat.

Others said they granted that heat in the climate might propagate infection—as sultry, hot weather fills the air with vermin and nourishes innumerable numbers and kinds of venomous creatures which breed in our food, in the plants, and even in our bodies, by the very stench of which infection may be propagated; also that heat in the air, or heat of weather, as we ordinarily call it, makes bodies relax and faint, exhausts the spirits, opens the pores, and makes us more apt to receive infection, or any evil influence, be it from noxious pestilential vapours or any other thing in the air; but that the heat of fire, and especially of coal fires kept in our houses, or near us, had a quite different operation; the heat being not of the same kind, but quick and fierce, tending not to nourish but to consume and dissipate all those noxious fumes which the other kind of heat rather exhaled and stagnated than separated and burnt up. Besides, it was alleged that the sulphurous and nitrous particles that are often found to be in the coal, with that bituminous substance which burns, are all assisting to clear and purge the air, and render it wholesome and safe to breathe in after the noxious particles, as above, are dispersed and burnt up.

The latter opinion prevailed at that time, and, as I must confess, I think with good reason; and the experience of the citizens confirmed it, many houses which had constant fires kept in the rooms having never been infected at all; and I must join my experience to it, for I found the keeping good fires kept our rooms sweet and wholesome, and I do verily believe made our whole family so, more than would otherwise have been. . . .

All in the air

The mercy of God was greater to the rest than we had reason to expect; for the malignity (as I have said) of the distemper was spent, the contagion was exhausted, and also the winter weather came on apace, and the air was clear and cold, with sharp frosts; and this increasing still, most of those that had fallen sick recovered, and the health of the city began to return. There were indeed some returns of the distemper even in the month of December, and the bills increased near a hundred; but it went off again, and so in a short while things began to return to their own channel. . . .

The people of London thought themselves so plague-free now that they were past all admonitions; they seemed to depend upon it that the air was restored, and that the air was like a man that had had the smallpox, not capable of being infected again. This revived that notion that the infection was all in the air, that there was no such thing as contagion from the sick people to the sound; and so strongly did this whimsy prevail among people that they ran all together promiscuously, sick and well. Not the Mahometans, who, prepossessed with the principle of predestination, value nothing of contagion, let it be in what it will, could be more obstinate than the people of London; they that were perfectly sound, and came out of the wholesome air, as we call it, into the city, made nothing of going into the same houses and chambers, nay, even into the same beds, with those that had the distemper upon them, and were not recovered.

Some, indeed, paid for their audacious boldness with the price of their lives; an infinite number fell sick, and the physicians had more work than ever, only with this difference, that more of their patients recovered; that is to say, they generally recovered, but certainly there were more people infected and fell sick now, when there did not die above a thousand or twelve hundred in a week, than there was when there died five or six thousand a week, so entirely negligent were the people at that time in the great and dangerous case of health and infection, and so ill were they able to take or accept of the advice of those who cautioned them for their good. . . .

A plague is a formidable enemy, and is armed with terrors that every man is not sufficiently fortified to resist or prepared to stand the shock against. It is very certain that a great many of the clergy who were in circumstances to do it withdrew and fled for the safety of their lives; but 'tis true also that a great many of them stayed, and many of them fell in the calamity and in the discharge of their duty. . . .

God be praised

Nothing but the immediate finger of God, nothing but omnipotent power, could have done it. The contagion despised all medicine; death raged in every corner; and had it gone on as it did then, a few weeks more would have cleared the town of all, and everything that had a soul. Men everywhere began to despair . . . people were made desperate through the anguish of their souls, and the terrors of death sat in the very faces and countenances of the people.

In that very moment when we might very well say, 'Vain was the help of man', — I say, in that very moment it pleased God, with a most agreeable surprise, to cause the fury of it to abate, even of itself; and the malignity declining, as I have said . . . fewer died, and the very first weeks' bill decreased 1843; a vast number indeed!

The Granger Collection, New York

The Diſeaſes and Caſualties this Week.

Abortive	4	Impoſthume	8
Aged	45	Infants	22
Bleeding	1	Kingſevil	4
Broken legge	1	Lethargy	1
Broke her ſcull by a fall in the ſtreet at St. Mary VVoolchurch	1	Livergrown	1
Childbed	28	Meagrome	1
Chriſomes	9	Palſie	1
Conſumption	126	Plague	4237
Convulſion	89	Purples	2
Cough	1	Quinſie	5
Droptie	53	Rickets	23
Feaver	348	Riſing of the Lights	18
Flox and Small-pox	11	Rupture	1
Flux	1	Scurvy	3
Frighted	2	Shingles	1
Gowt	1	Spotted Feaver	166
Grief	3	Stilborn	4
Griping in the Guts	79	Stone	2
Head-mould-ſhot	1	Stopping of the ſtomach	17
Jaundies	7	Strangury	3
		Suddenly	2
		Surfeit	74
		Teeth	111
		Thruſh	6
		Tiſſick	9
		Ulcer	1
		Vomiting	10
		Winde	4
		Wormes	20

Chriſtned { Males — 90, Females — 81, In all — 171 } Buried { Males — 2777, Females — 2791, In all — 5568 } Plague — 4237

Increaſed in the Burials this Week — 249

Pariſhes clear of the Plague — 27 Pariſhes Infected — 103

The Aſſize of Bread ſet forth by Order of the Lord Maior and Court of Aldermen,
A penny Wheaten Loaf to contain Nine Ounces and a half, and three half-penny White Loaves the like weight.

"It was observed with great uneasiness by the people that the weekly bills . . . increased very much during these weeks."

It is impossible to express the change that appeared in the very countenances of the people that Thursday morning when the weekly bill came out. It might have been perceived in their countenances that a secret surprise and smile of joy sat on everybody's face. They shook one another by the hands in the streets, who would hardly go on the same side of the way with one another before. Where the streets were not too broad they would open their windows and call from one house to another, and ask how they did, and if they had heard the good news that the plague was abated. Some would return, when they said good news, and ask, 'What good news?' and when they answered that the plague was abated and the bills decreased almost two thousand, they would cry out, 'God be praised!' and would weep aloud for joy, telling them they had heard nothing of it; and such was the joy of the people that it was, as it were, life to them from the grave. I could almost set down as many extravagant things done in the excess of their joy as of their grief; but that would be to lessen the value of it.

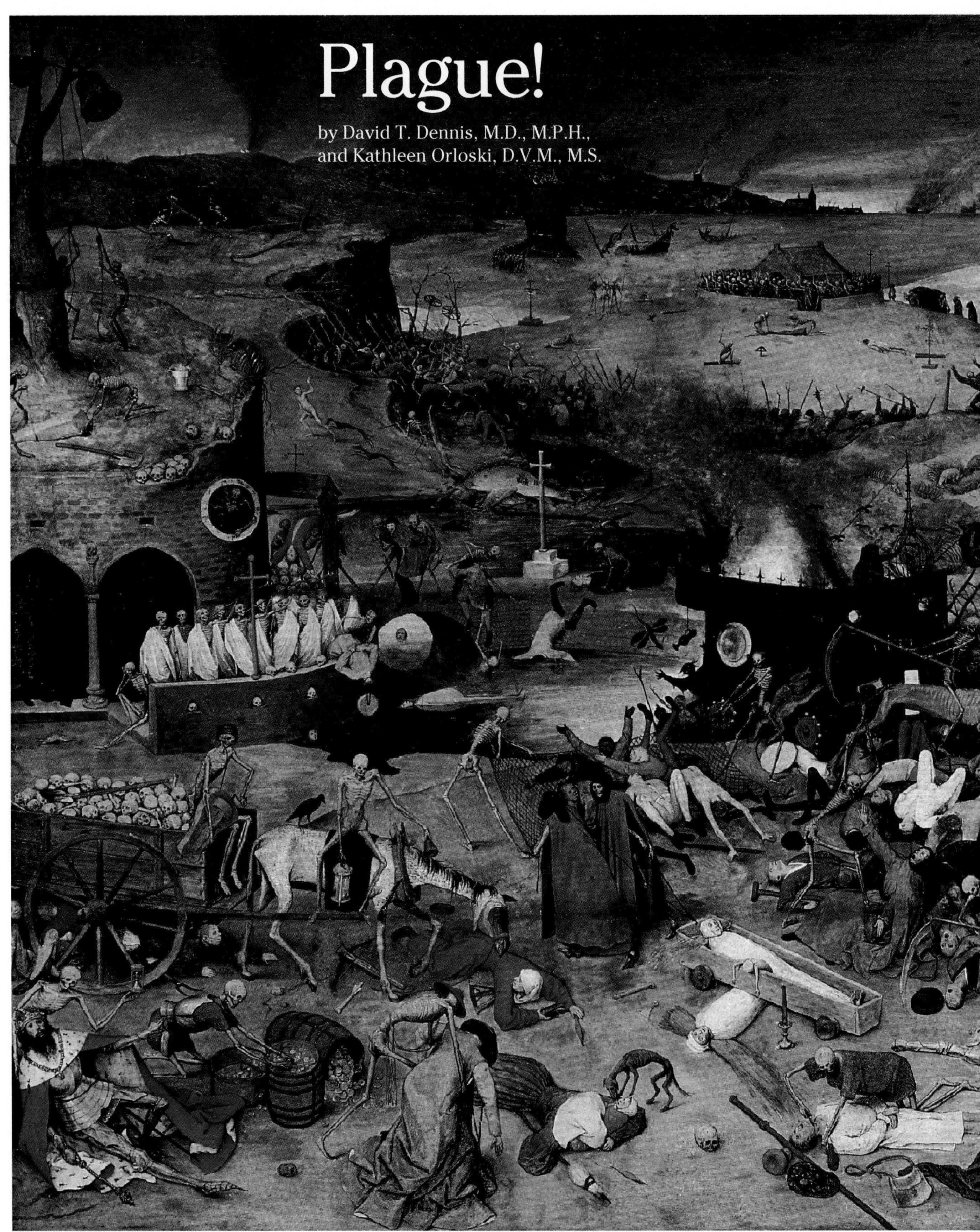

Plague!

by David T. Dennis, M.D., M.P.H.,
and Kathleen Orloski, D.V.M., M.S.

Plague ravages Europe in Pieter Bruegel the Elder's "Triumph of Death."

Prado, Madrid; photograph, E.T. Archive

On Sept. 19, 1994, an unexpected fax from India slid into the receiving tray at the federal Centers for Disease Control and Prevention (CDC) laboratory in Fort Collins, Colorado. The fax came from the Southeast Asian Regional Office (SEARO) of the World Health Organization (WHO), in New Delhi. It was asking for highly specialized reagents to be used in diagnostic tests for plague.

Requests for assistance in making the laboratory diagnosis of exotic diseases at distant sites around the globe are not unusual at the Fort Collins laboratory. The lab serves as headquarters for CDC scientists responsible for preventing and controlling certain vectorborne infectious diseases—in particular, those transmitted by the bites of insects, such as fleas and mosquitoes, and other arthropods, such as ticks and lice. The CDC collaborates in this effort with WHO. Throughout 1994, as in other years, requests

David T. Dennis, M.D., M.P.H., *is Chief, Bacterial Zoonoses Branch, National Center for Infectious Diseases, Division of Vector-Borne Infectious Diseases, Centers for Disease Control and Prevention (CDC), Fort Collins, Colorado.*
Kathleen Orloski, D.V.M., M.S., *is Epidemic Intelligence Service Officer, at the CDC, Fort Collins.*

for plague diagnostic materials were processed at the CDC lab. These came from countries in South America, Africa, and Asia. What was unusual about the request from New Delhi was that plague had not been reported anywhere in India since 1966 and was no longer considered a public health threat there.

More disturbing than the initial request was one that came two days later, accompanied by press clippings describing an outbreak of suspected bubonic plague in the district of Beed, situated in rural Maharashtra state, about 300 kilometers (185 miles) east of Bombay. Almost simultaneously, the CDC received telephone calls, E-mail messages, and other communications alerting it to the possibility that a second, much more ominous outbreak of pneumonic (respiratory) plague was occurring in Surat, a large coastal city about 200 kilometers (125 miles) north of Bombay.

Hastily arranged conference calls between Fort Collins scientists, officials at WHO headquarters in Geneva, and SEARO personnel in India confirmed that two simultaneous outbreaks of suspected plague were being reported by the Indian government. The CDC promptly sent plague-detection tests. Within days, it also dispatched a team of medical scientists with expertise in plague so they could provide on-site assistance to WHO and the Indian government. By that time plague was being reported in the capital, New Delhi, where schools and theaters were closed and the government was broadcasting messages warning people to avoid public places, such as bus terminals, that normally were crowded.

Dread disease

Plague is among the most acute fulminant (*i.e.,* sudden and severe) infectious diseases known; its cause is the rod-shaped bacterium *Yersinia pestis.* It is widely feared because without prompt antibiotic treatment, the fatality rate even for the milder bubonic form can approach 60%, while the pneumonic form with-

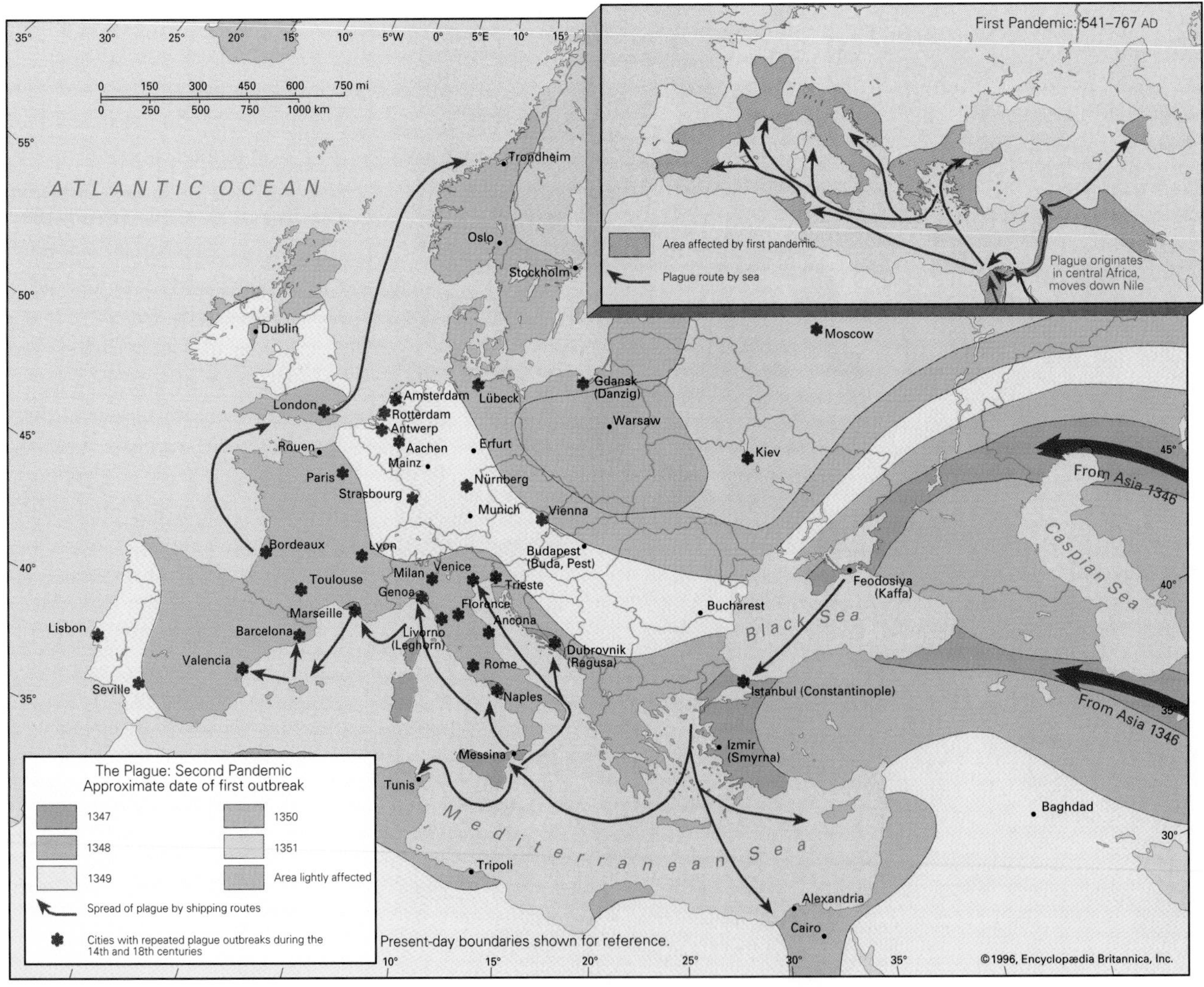

out treatment is almost universally fatal. Historically, plague has distinguished itself as a scourge that sweeps across countries and continents and even traverses oceans, decimating whole populations in its wake.

The earliest reliable accounts of plague are from AD 542, the start of the first recorded world pandemic (the so-called Justinian pandemic). The disease entered Byzantium (Constantinople), probably from infected rats aboard grain ships. At its peak the epidemic killed 10,000 people per day in Byzantium alone. The ill were "covered with black pustules or carbuncles, the symptoms of immediate death."

Over the next 50 years, the disease spread via the Mediterranean Sea to Europe, including Italy and France. Some 40 million people died. Then plague disappeared. For the next six centuries, the world was free of the dread disease.

Pestilence in the Old Testament (1 Samuel)—divine punishment of the Philistines.

Prolonged pandemic

A second pandemic began in the early 1300s, when plague spread out of central Asia, probably moving by caravans and then by ship. By 1346 there were reports of devastating plague outbreaks in China and India. In October 1347 the disease entered the port city of Messina, Sicily. Within five years it had spread from Sicily to most of Europe, including France, Spain, Germany, England, Denmark, Sweden, and Norway.

In June 1348 plague reached Paris and London and came to be known as the Black Death. It is estimated that 25 million people died in Europe alone between 1347 and 1352.

The second pandemic ravaged the continent and the British Isles in successive waves until the late 1700s. It is said to have killed a quarter of the population of Europe during that time. Not surprisingly, the impact on society and the economy of such a prolonged pandemic was enormous.

(continued on page 171)

"The Plague at Ashdod" by Nicolas Poussin, 1630, Louvre, Paris; photograph, Giraudon/Bridgeman Art Library

Photographs, The Granger Collection, New York

(Opposite, top) Coffin making and burial of plague victims at Tournai, Belgium, 14th century. (Opposite, bottom) Jews, blamed for the Black Death, are burned alive, *c.* 1493. (Right) St. Roch of Montpellier, France, points to the bubo (lymphatic swelling) on his groin. Afflicted by the bubonic plague on a pilgrimage to Rome in the early 14th century, the "patron saint of plague" recovered and lived another five years. When he died, he left the farewell message, "All those who are stricken . . . and who pray for aid through the merits and intercession of St. Roch, the servant of God, shall be healed."

"St. Roch" by Carlo Crivelli, Gallerie Dell'Accademia, Venice; photograph, Cameraphoto-Arte, Venice/Art Resource

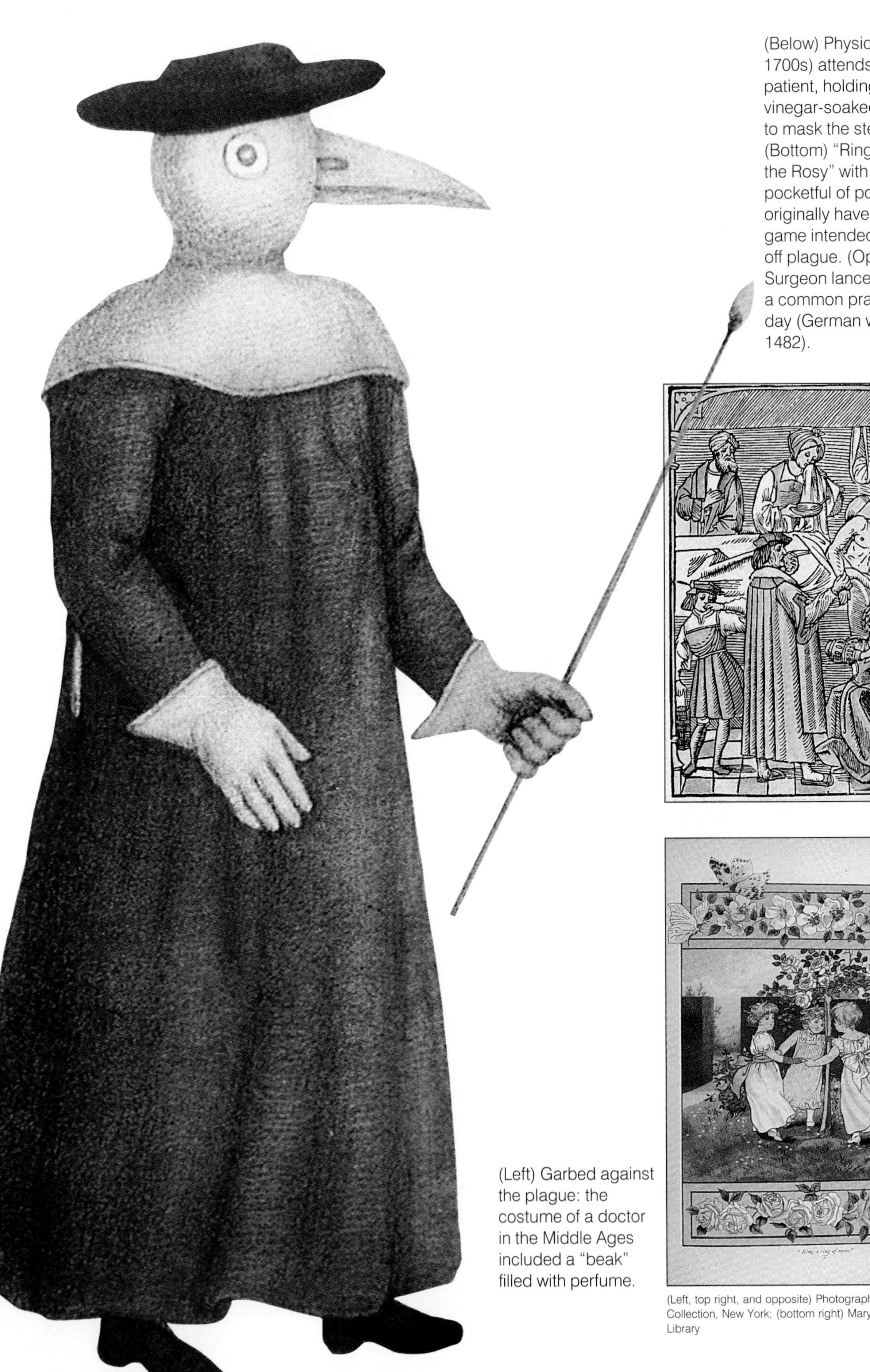

(Below) Physician (*c.* 1700s) attends plague patient, holding a vinegar-soaked sponge to mask the stench. (Bottom) "Ring Around the Rosy" with "a pocketful of posies" may originally have been a game intended to ward off plague. (Opposite) Surgeon lances a bubo, a common practice of the day (German woodcut, 1482).

(Left) Garbed against the plague: the costume of a doctor in the Middle Ages included a "beak" filled with perfume.

(Left, top right, and opposite) Photographs, The Granger Collection, New York; (bottom right) Mary Evans Picture Library

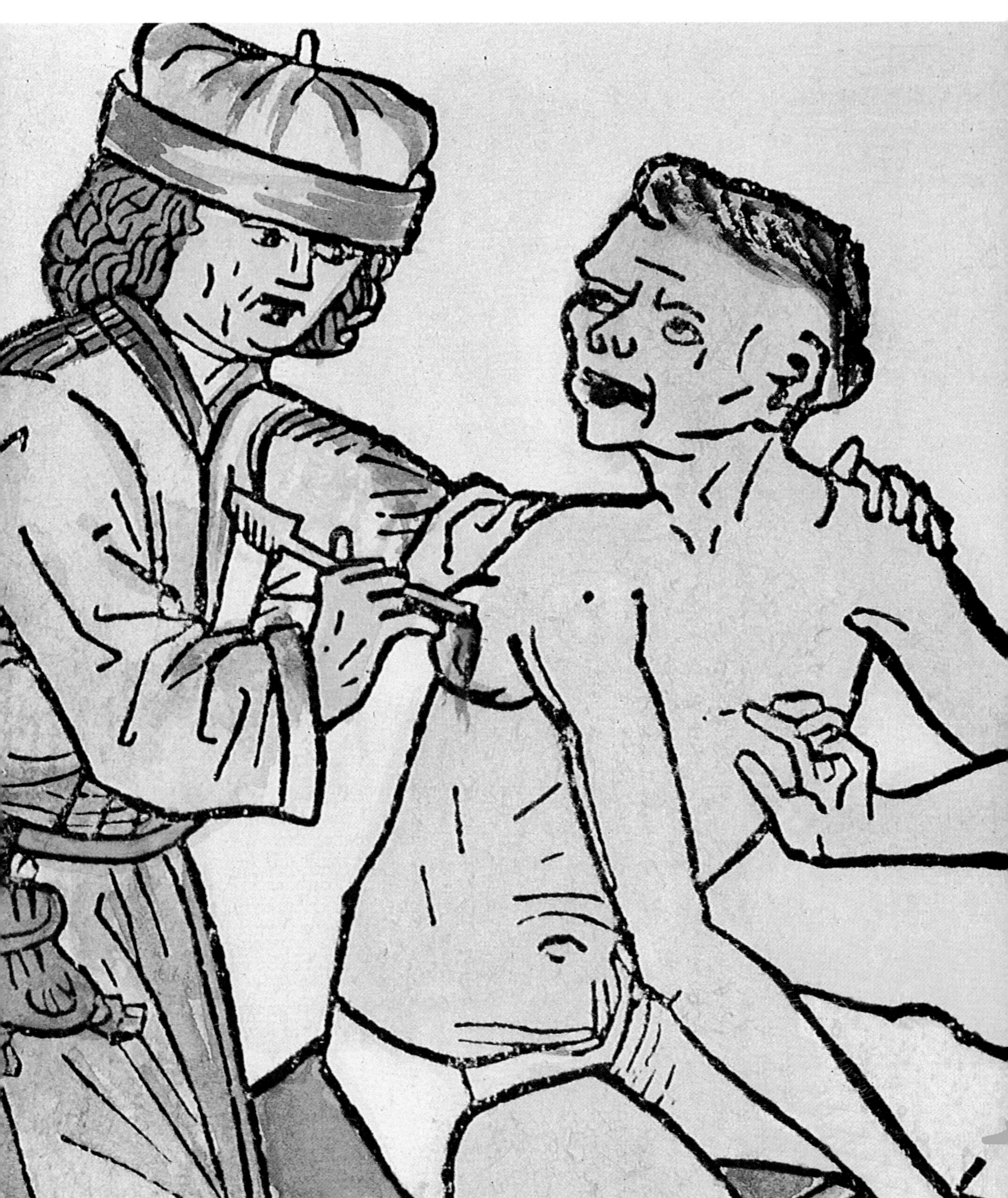

Culver Pictures

The Granger Collection, New York

(Opposite) The bishop of Marseilles amid the plague stricken, 1720. (Above) City dwellers flee London to escape plague, *c.* 1630. (Right) To quell the terror of his soldiers, Napoleon dares to touch the plague afflicted at Jaffa, 1799.

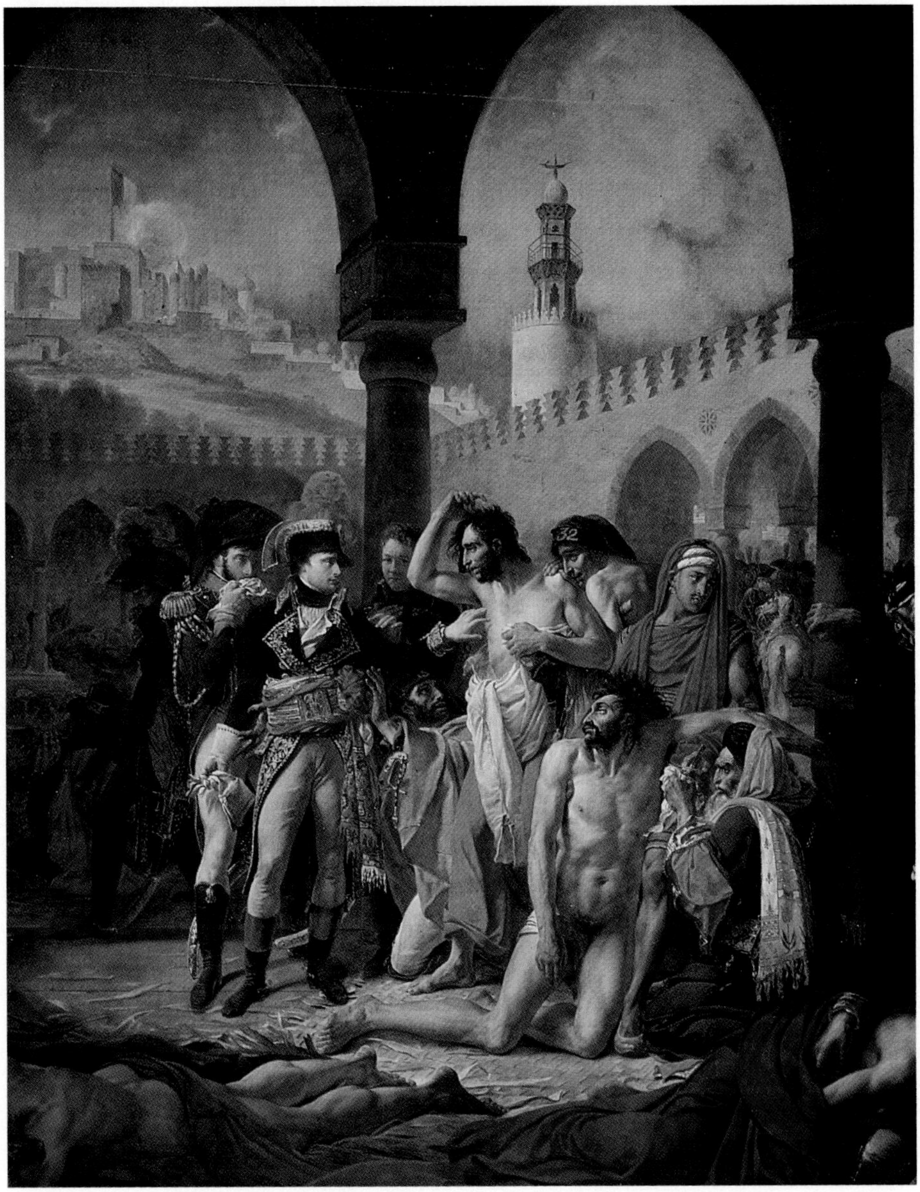

"Bonaparte Visiting the Pest Ridden of Jaffa" by Antoine-Jean Gros, 1804, Louvre, Paris; photograph, SuperStock

"The Plague" by Arnold Böcklin, 1898, Oeffenliche Kunstsammlung Basel, Kunstmuseum; photograph, Martin Bühler

(continued from page 163)

Glimpses of understanding

By the late 1800s a third plague pandemic was under way. Emerging once again in central Asia (1855), it was subsequently carried on rat-infested ships to major port cities; none of the world's major inhabited land masses was spared.

When plague reached Hong Kong in 1894, quickly killing 10,000 people, a young Swiss disciple of Louis Pasteur was sent to investigate. Alexandre Yersin erected a makeshift laboratory on the grounds of a small general hospital, where he began examining tissue specimens from plague patients. Under the lens of his microscope, he identified the causative bacterium, named *Yersinia pestis* in his honor.

The next breakthrough came in 1898, when a French scientist, Paul-Louis Simond, was sent to investigate an overwhelming epidemic of bubonic plague in Bombay. Working out of a tent, Simond dissected rats and found the plague bacillus in their tissues; he also made the critical observation that fleas transmitted the disease among rats and probably from rats to people.

There was still no effective treatment for plague, however, and by 1908 it was estimated that more than six million deaths had occurred as the third pandemic swept the world.

The third pandemic was particularly devastating in India. Between 1898 and 1928 it moved through the entire subcontinent, leaving an estimated 12 million people dead, mostly from the bubonic form of the disease but occasionally from brief bursts of the pneumonic form. Hardest hit of all was the city of Bombay. Plague entered the port of Bombay in 1896 and quickly became established in the large rat population there.

India suffered from recurring, if diminished, epidemics of plague until the disease dissipated in the early 1950s, the last confirmed human case occurring in 1966 in Karnataka state in southern India. In retrospect, scientists now believe there may have been more recent clusters of cases, unconfirmed by laboratory tests, among some remote rural communities and that plague activity continued undetected among wild rats.

Plague today

Since the late 1960s the majority of cases of plague in humans have been reported from limited areas of four continents: Africa, Asia, and North and South America. There has been no plague in Western Europe or in Australia since the early part of the century.

Because of its potential for rapid introduction and spread around the world, plague is designated (along

(Opposite) Plague riding through medieval city, painting by Arnold Böcklin.

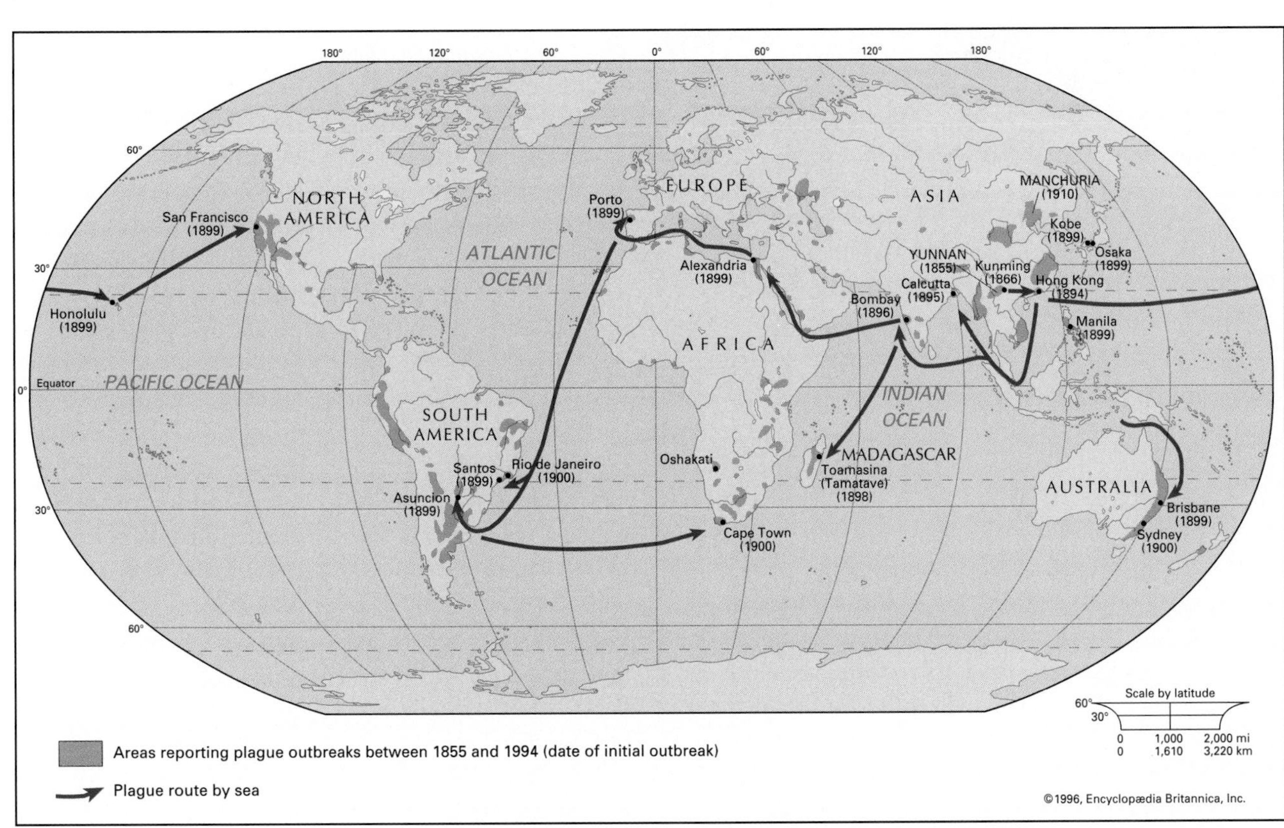

with cholera and yellow fever) as one of the three remaining "class 1" internationally quarantinable diseases (smallpox was removed from this designation after being eradicated in the 1970s). During the second pandemic, people who were suspected of being infected were isolated until it had been established that they were not bearers of the disease. The practice was first applied in Venice in the 14th century; when ships arrived, they were kept at port for a specified period—usually 40 days. *Quarantine* is derived from the Italian word *quarantina* (a 40-day period).

From 1969 through 1993, 36,643 cases of plague were reported to WHO. That number is undoubtedly an underestimate, since in many countries case detection and reporting are inadequate. In 1993 (the most recent year for which complete data are available) 10 countries reported 2,065 cases of plague, 191 of which were fatal: Zaire (636 cases, 89 deaths), Peru (611 cases, 31 deaths), Vietnam (370 cases, 20 deaths), Uganda (167 cases, 18 deaths), Madagascar (147 cases, 23 deaths), Myanmar (Burma; 87 cases, 0 deaths), Mongolia (21 cases, 7 deaths), China (13 cases, 1 death), the United States (10 cases, 1 death), and Kazakhstan (3 cases, 1 death).

The Burns Archive

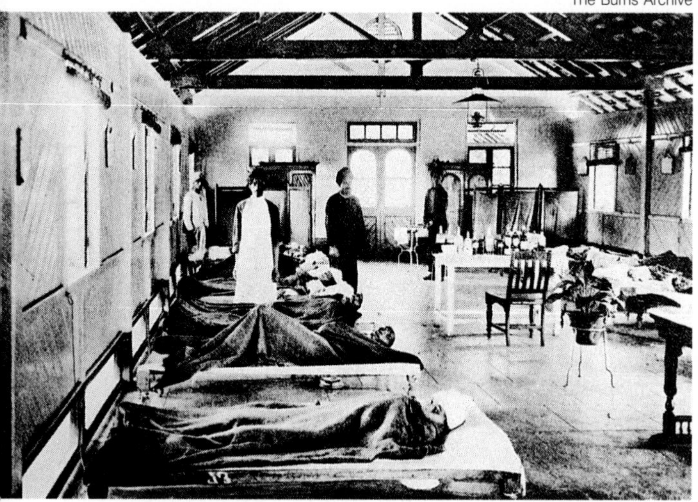

Plague patients, Bombay. The third pandemic ravaged the Indian subcontinent.

Rodents, fleas, and people

Rodents and their fleas are the usual hosts of the plague bacillus, *Y. pestis.* The fleas responsible for transmitting the disease among rodents can also transmit the disease to other animals and to humans. Worldwide up to 200 species of rodents and 100 species of fleas have been found to be natural hosts. For reasons that are not understood, plague frequently undergoes quiescent periods in nature, where it is maintained in relatively disease-resistant wild rodent populations at low levels—a situation that results in only sporadic human exposure and disease. Owing to complex, poorly understood combinations of circumstances—which include certain environmental conditions, relative availability of food, and other unpredictable factors—however, the disease periodically spreads among wild rodents, sometimes resulting in catastrophic outbreaks of disease (called "epizootics"). If a wild-rodent epizootic occurs near an area of human habitation, there is a risk of spillover of plague into rats that live in close association with humans, including the common house (or roof) rat (*Rattus rattus*), the sewer rat (*R. norvegicus*), and in Asia the large bandicoot rat (*Bandicota bengalensis*). Once this has happened, humans themselves are at high risk of becoming infected.

There are three principal ways in which people contract plague: (1) bites by fleas from plague-infected rats; (2) direct contact with infected animals, such as rats, squirrels, prairie dogs, rabbits, and cats; and (3) intimate contact with pneumonic plague patients. Animals susceptible to plague infection experience high mortality; fleas then leave these dead animals in search of fresh blood meals.

Typically, epidemics of human plague are preceded by large die-offs of rat populations. These sudden, sharp declines in populations of domestic rats are commonly called "rat falls" because dead and dying rodents fall suddenly to the ground—often from rafters and other elevated rat runways in houses, warehouses, granaries, etc.

Once a flea ingests the plague bacillus in the blood of an infected rat or other animal, the bacillus multiplies in the flea's digestive tract—sometimes blocking the passage of food, causing starvation, and stimulating a ravenous appetite. Finding a new host, the flea bites its victim and proceeds to feed vigorously. At the same time, the flea regurgitates infected material, which deposits plague bacilli into the wound and thus "inoculates" the new host.

In addition to the direct inoculation of infectious material into cuts and other breaks in the skin when people handle infected animals, plague can be spread through the air. This form of transmission occurs by inhalation of infected respiratory droplets expelled when patients with pneumonic plague cough or sneeze. Because the bacillus is spread by means of droplets that do not become truly aerosolized, only persons in very close contact with the sick person (usually within 1.8 meters [6 feet]) are at risk of acquiring pneumonic plague. Typically, victims are household members and caregivers.

Signs and symptoms

More than 90% of plague cases in the world are of the bubonic form. The manifestations include fever, prostration, and the characteristic formation of a bubo (an infected, swollen, and very painful lymph gland) near the site of the flea bite, most often in the groin, armpit, or neck. These symptoms begin within seven days after exposure. Sometimes the patient experiences nausea, vomiting, abdominal pain, and diarrhea. If the disease is not treated within one to two days, the infection rapidly spreads and invades the bloodstream, producing a severe illness called septicemic plague, which is often accompanied by shock, bleeding, and blockage of small blood vessels of the extremities (leading to poor circulation and sometimes gangrene in the fingers and toes).

Septicemic plague may lead to a secondary infection of the lungs, called secondary pneumonic plague. At this stage the plague

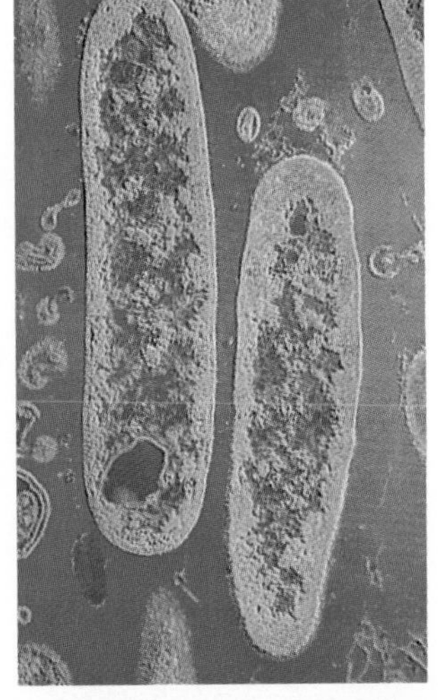

(Far left) *Rattus rattus* in grain store; (left) *Yersinia pestis,* the bacterium that causes bubonic plague and is carried by fleas; (below) a rat flea clings to its host's fur.

(Top left) Andrew J. Purcell—Bruce Coleman Limited; (top right) CNRI/Science Source/Photo Researchers; (bottom) Tony Brain—Science Source/Photo Researchers

bacillus can be transmitted to other persons. Persons infected by droplet inhalation will develop primary pneumonic plague, which has a shorter incubation period than bubonic plague, usually from one to three days. Symptoms include fever, cough, bloody sputum, shortness of breath, and terminal respiratory failure. Without prompt treatment (within 24–48 hours after the onset of symptoms) pneumonic plague is rapidly fatal in most cases.

Treatment

Once diagnosed, plague must be treated immediately with the proper antibiotics. Beginning in the early 20th century, crude vaccines and methods to control rats and their fleas were used to protect exposed populations; however, it was not until the 1940s and the discovery of sulfonamide antibiotics that an effective treatment for plague became available. A short time later, in 1947, the newly discovered antibiotic streptomycin brought about dramatic cures for all forms of plague; even now, streptomycin remains the antibiotic of choice. Other drugs that cure plague and are used today include tetracycline, chloramphenicol, and gentamicin. Fortunately, with plague there has been no clinical documentation of antibiotic resistance (as there has been with many other infections, such as tuberculosis). Most plague patients respond well if treatment is not delayed.

Vaccines against plague are available but are recommended only for very limited use, such as in laboratory personnel working with the plague bacillus and in persons whose occupations or fields of study bring them into close contact with potentially infected animals and their fleas—for example zoologists doing fieldwork in epizootic areas. Short courses of prophylactic antibiotics are recommended for persons thought to be at risk for infection through exposure to respiratory secretions of plague patients or through direct contact with the tissues of infected animals or their fleas. Infrequently, antibiotic prophylaxis may be recommended for persons living in or traveling through an area where there is a known outbreak of human plague.

Swapan Parekh—Black Star

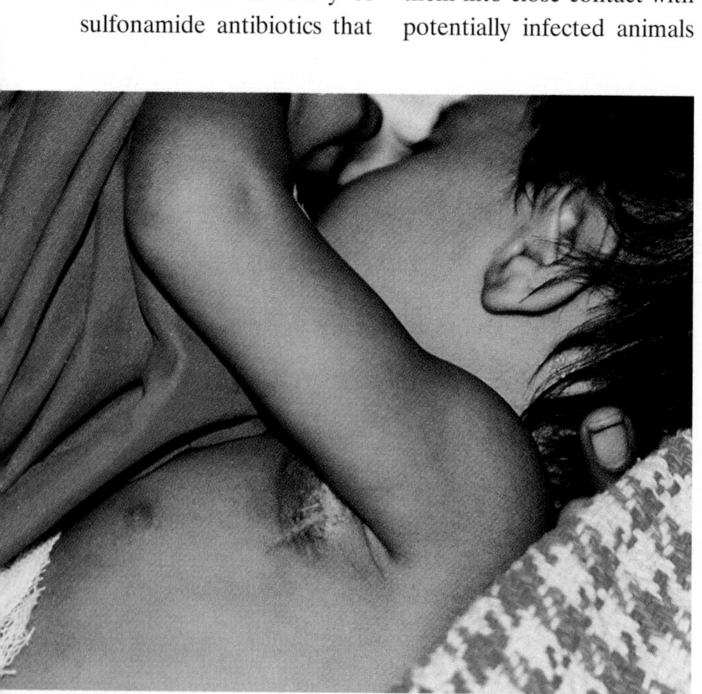

World Health Organization

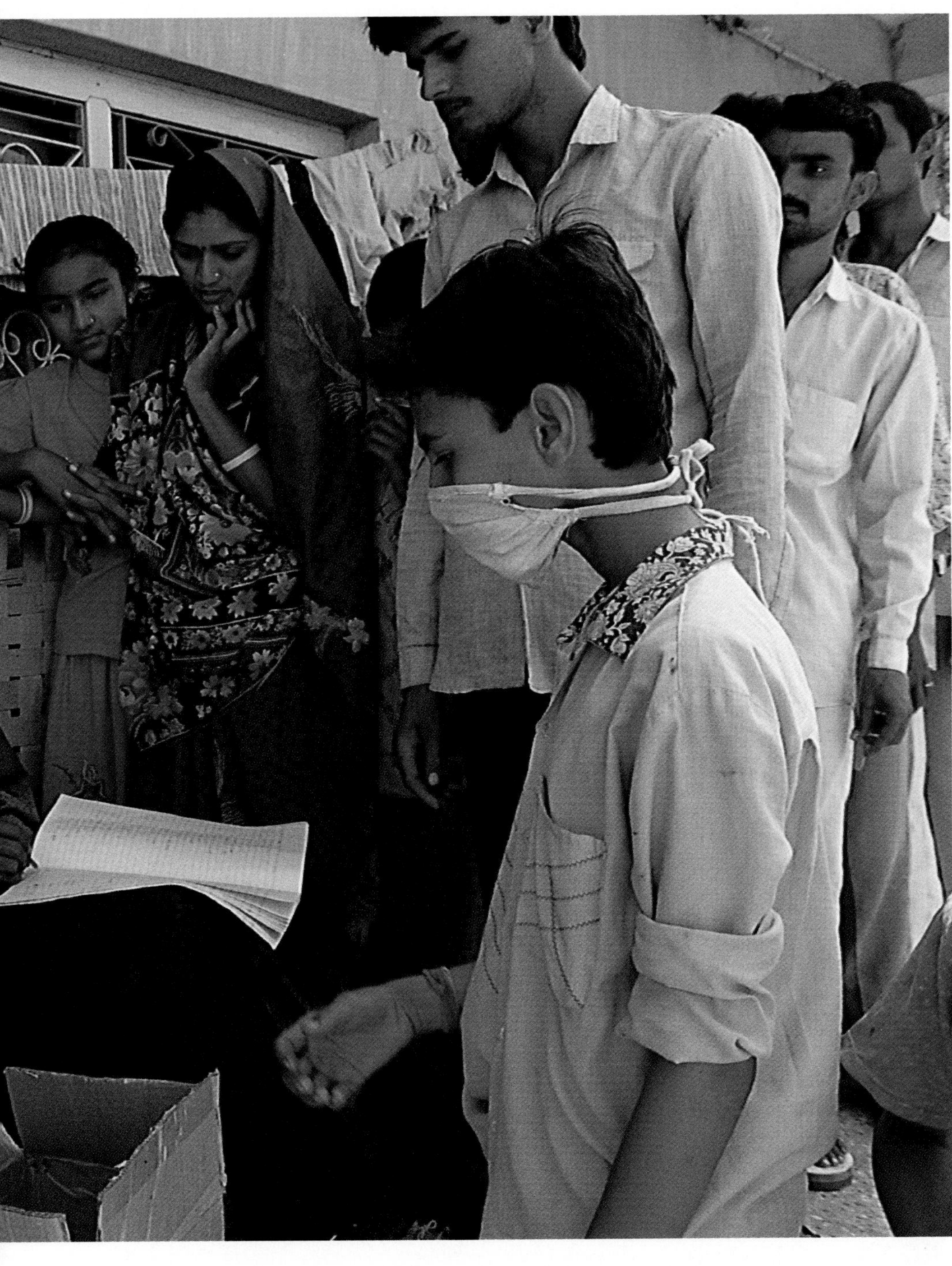

(Opposite page, bottom) Indian child with an underarm bubo.
(Left) All suspected plague patients in Surat receive tetracycline.

Reducing the risk

Global plague eradication is not considered possible, but surveillance for rodent outbreaks and human plague *is.* Timely preventive measures greatly reduce the risk. Those living in plague-endemic areas can protect themselves by avoiding known plague "hot spots"; removing rodent harborage and food sources, especially in urban residential areas; and using insect repellents on themselves and on pets.

Today when plague is newly discovered in an area or makes its reappearance in one where it has been absent for a long time, it is reported to WHO without delay. Local and regional public health officials monitor wild rodent populations for evidence of epizootics, alerting the local medical community when there is the potential for human cases and advising persons living near or visiting epizootic areas of potential risks and of the need to take necessary personal precautions. Prompt reporting of all human cases is required.

India: 1994

The first known plague patient ("index case") in India in 1994 was Abhimanyu, an 18-year-old male farmer living in Mamla, a small rural village with 400 or so inhabitants in the southeastern Beed district, about 250 kilometers (150 miles) east of Bombay. In late August Abhimanyu developed a pain in his right groin, mild weakness, and fever. His illness progressed over the next day or so to a high fever, sweats, chills, and a tender swelling at the site of the pain in his groin. The swelling grew to the size of "a small lemon," his other symptoms worsened, and soon he was too weak to tend his crops. Accompanied by friends with a similar but milder illness, he went to the nearest clinic (about eight kilometers [five miles] away), where each was given tetracycline. Over the next days and weeks, they recovered.

The Bettmann Archive

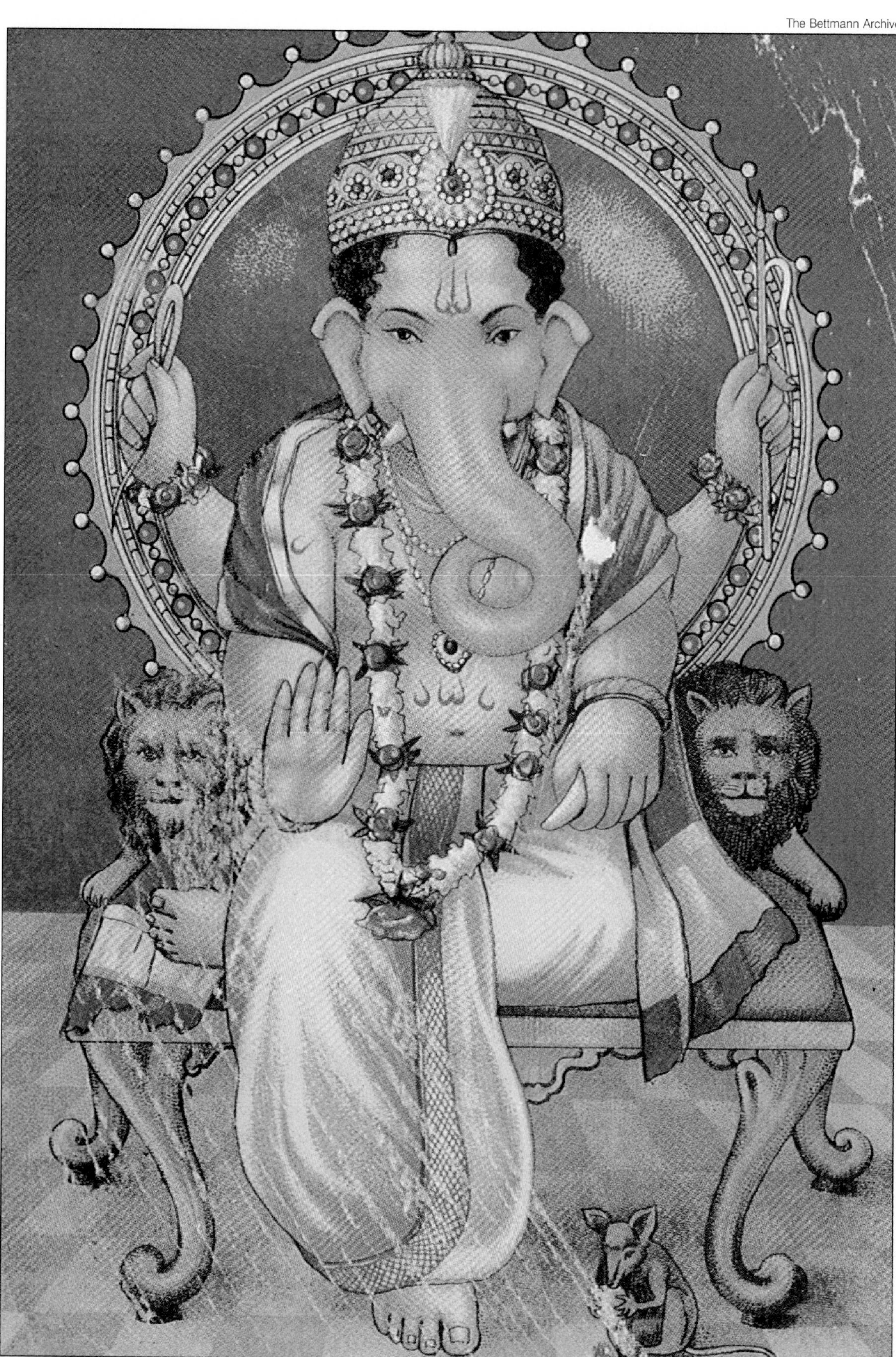

Health workers at the local clinic remembered that Abhimanyu's village had recently reported a flea nuisance. A health team was sent to Mamla to investigate and search for additional people with fever and swollen glands. The medical team identified 33 persons with some recent history of fever and swollen and tender lymph nodes. However, none of these persons was as ill as would be expected from typical bubonic plague. Blood samples were taken, all patients were promptly treated with antibiotics, and the village was dusted with insecticides.

The local health authorities treated persons in Mamla and surrounding villages who had fever and swollen glands as if they might have mild plague but did not officially report the disease as plague until word came back from the Indian National Institute of Communicable Diseases in New Delhi that some of the blood specimens had tested positive for antibodies to the plague bacillus. That report, relayed to the state medical authorities, set off a large-scale systematic search for new cases throughout Beed district. All cases and their family members and neigh-

Marc Deville—Gamma Liaison

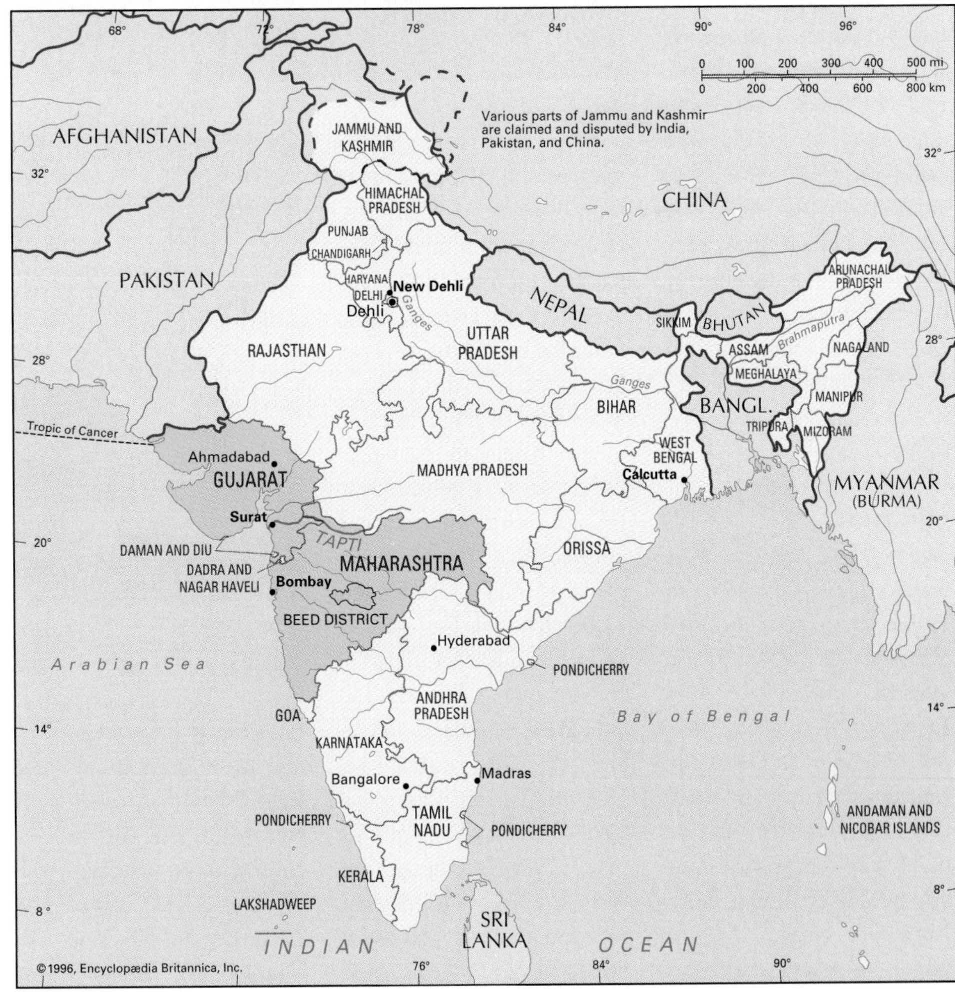

(Opposite) The Hindu god Ganesha is celebrated with particular enthusiasm in Maharashtra; (top right) Ganesha icon stands amid toppled homes after 1993 earthquake.

Village of Mamla: a home with rat holes (left); a bountiful harvest (below) serves as a rich source of rat food; rodents proliferate (below right), spreading plague. (Opposite page) A child with suspected bubonic plague recovers from a fever and swollen lymph glands.

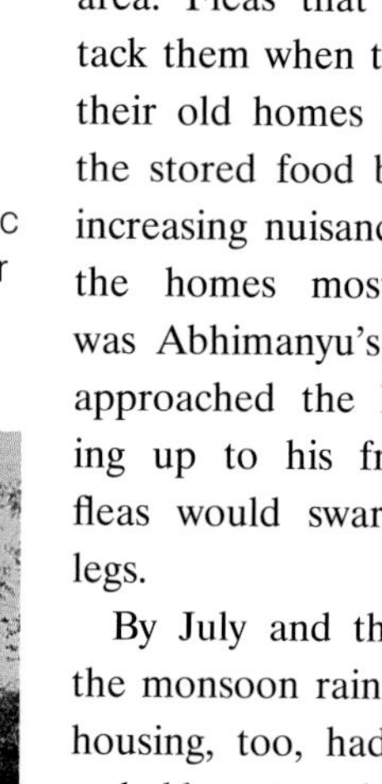

bors were promptly treated with tetracycline. By mid-September, newspapers in Maharashtra and surrounding states were reporting the occurrence of limited outbreaks of suspected bubonic plague in rural villages.

Although in retrospect the situation was alarming, there was almost no panic by the public—because the disease being treated as plague was mild, and there were apparently no associated deaths. This differed greatly from outbreaks in 1948–49, when villagers in the same area, fearing sudden and terrible illness and death from bubonic plague, fled from their homes into the surrounding fields.

Stage set for an outbreak

The story of plague in Beed district actually began a year earlier, in September 1993. Earthquakes had destroyed villages and killed more than 10,000 persons in a neighboring district. At that time and for several weeks thereafter, the inhabitants of Mamla felt mild tremors and heard "groaning" noises from the earth. Walls of homes in Mamla had been constructed in the traditional manner of stacking stones on top of one another and covering them with mud. Thick sod roofs topped the homes. In 1993 the residents rightly feared the collapse of their homes should the tremors increase in strength. Mindful of the tragedy in the neighboring district when similar stone-walled homes had crushed their sleeping occupants, Mamla village leaders requested that the government provide materials for constructing temporary, less dangerous housing. Poles and tin for roofing began arriving in December 1993; construction of the new housing continued until June 1994, by which time the whole village had abandoned its old homes.

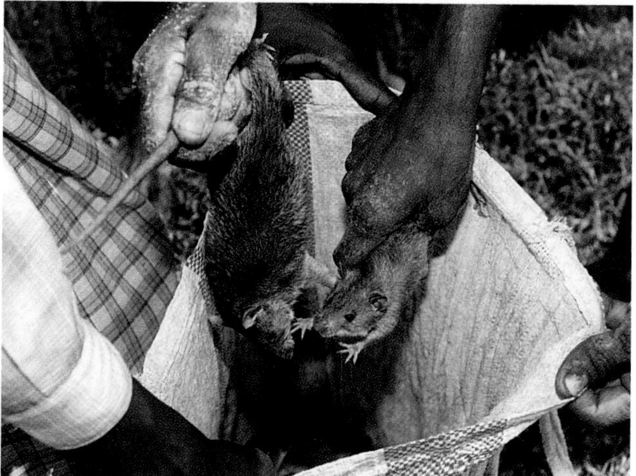

During the construction process, the villagers stored their newly harvested grains and groundnuts (peanuts) in their old homes, which soon became overrun with rats, including large bandicoot rats (*B. bengalensis*), which normally live in the fields. By March 1994 villagers had begun to notice occasional dead rats in the evacuated area. Fleas that would attack them when they visited their old homes to recover the stored food became an increasing nuisance. One of the homes most affected was Abhimanyu's; when he approached the lane leading up to his front door, fleas would swarm on his legs.

By July and the start of the monsoon rains, the new housing, too, had been invaded by rats and their fleas, and an occasional rat would be seen running in circles or staggering before dying. Several rats died in this manner in Abhimanyu's new home.

After the first cases of human plague were discovered in Mamla and neighboring villages, a general survey in September and early October throughout Beed district turned up hundreds of other cases of mild illness with low-grade fever accompanied by some swelling and mild tenderness of lymph nodes. The story was the same throughout the district; the problem of increasing numbers of rats in the fields had been building for two years. This led to the destruction of crops; in villages rats fed on stored grain. When flea nuisances and rat deaths were identified, whole village populations were treated and villages dusted with insecticides. Although WHO testing found the fleas to be resistant to most insecticides, at least one available formulation, benzene hexachloride, *was* effective in reducing flea numbers. Only then were efforts made in selected villages to control rats by poisoning. (There is always the risk in killing rats during plague outbreaks that fleas will abandon rat corpses in search of human blood to consume.)

Surat: very different circumstances

A much more terrifying set of events was unfolding in Surat, situated on the banks of the Tapti River, in Gujarat state, about 20 kilometers (12 miles) inland from the coast of the Arabian Sea. This city of more than two million persons is well known throughout India as a center of the country's diamond-cutting industry and the base of many textile factories. The city had grown at a rapid, uncontrolled rate without regulation of housing, sewers, garbage disposal, and piped water. The busy city had large pockets of slums and filth but was attractive to rural villagers seeking jobs and the chance for upward mobility. Because cases of plague had not been identified in Surat for 60 or more years, no one was monitoring the city's enormous rat population.

The greatest immediate concern to the residents and the government authorities of Surat in mid-September 1994 was the cleanup from severe flooding of large areas of the city earlier in the month. The monsoon season had dumped more than 200 centimeters (80 inches) of rain on Surat, which necessitated the opening of floodgates. Whole slum areas had been inundated by muddy water 2.5 to 3 meters (8 to 10 feet) deep, and damage to housing and shops had been severe. The receding waters left raw sewage and drowned animals as flotsam in its wake. Surat had already been experiencing high numbers of cases of typhoid fever, malaria, dysentery, and dengue fever (an acute viral illness sometimes called "breakbone fever," causing severe headache, joint pain, and rash). Indeed, the flooding promised to make the health situation even worse.

One of the hardest-hit slums was the Ved Road area, where 30,000 of the city's poorest residents lived. There had been a recent

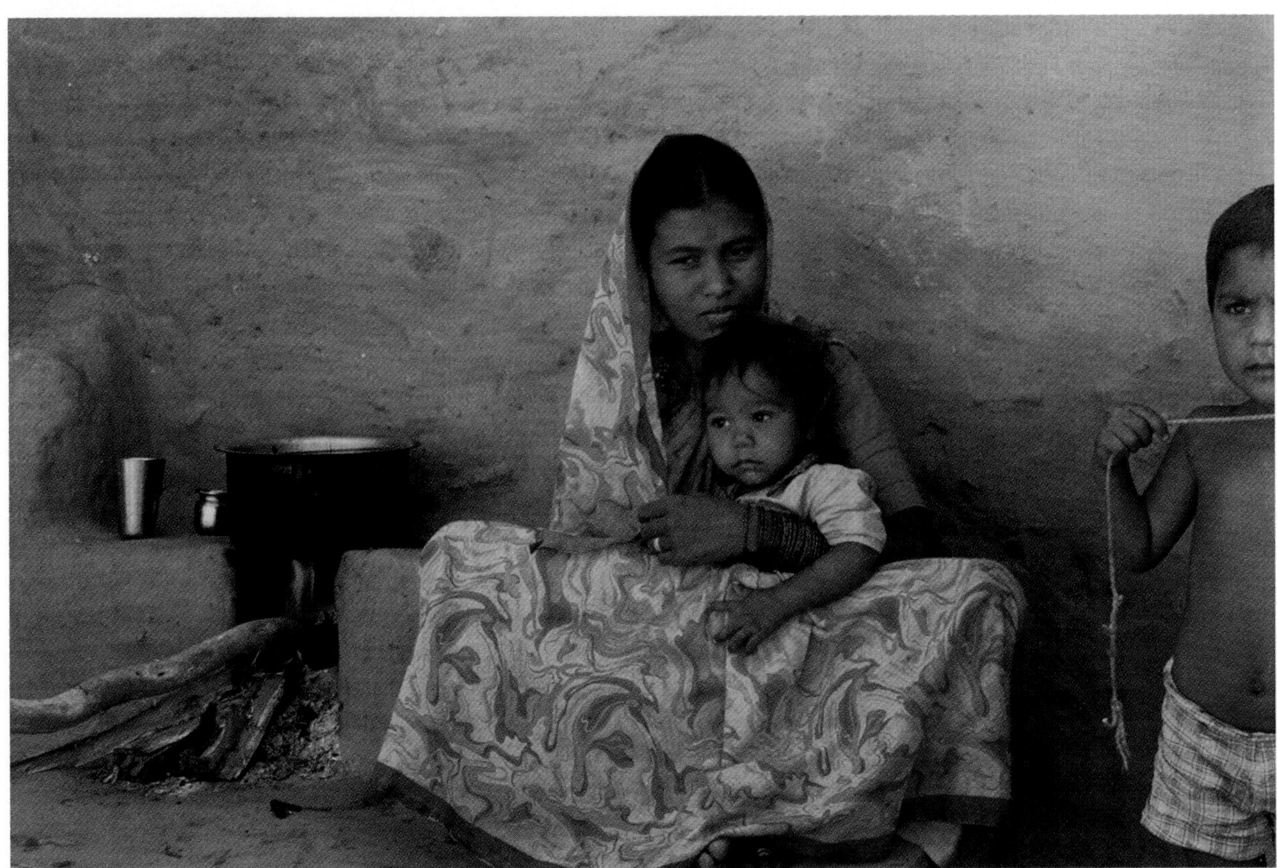

(Above, opposite page, top and center) David T. Dennis, M.D., Centers for Disease Control and Prevention, Fort Collins, Colorado; (opposite page, bottom) Latha Ananpharaman—Gamma Liaison

Garbage on the streets of Surat. The city's slums are a breeding ground for organisms that cause disease. (Opposite) Surat Civil Hospital is filled with acutely ill plague patients and their frightened relatives.

influx of young men from rural farming areas of Maharashtra to help prepare for one of the most important Hindu holidays of the year, the festival celebrating the birth of the beloved elephant-headed god, Ganesha. Traditionally, large effigies of Ganesha were built in poor areas of the city, taken in festive processions to the edge of the Tapti River, and immersed. The processions were made up mostly of young men. That year the celebration was held on September 18, only days after the floodwaters had receded.

The joy of the festival was soon superseded by events in the city's hospital. On September 20 doctors admitted seven patients suffering from pneumonia to the Surat Civil Hospital emergency room; by 3 AM the next day, despite treatment with penicillin antibiotics, two patients had died, and the rest were desperately ill. New patients with similar symptoms arrived in the emergency room. Almost all were young men from slum areas, especially the Ved Road slum. One was a farmer from Beed district with bilateral pneumonia (infection in both lungs), cough, and bloody sputum. By the afternoon of September 21, 13 patients had been admitted with severe pneumonia, and 7 patients had died. Examination of the sputum of some of these patients revealed rod-shaped bacilli with a "safety pin" appearance (characteristic of the plague bacillus but also typical of other, more common bacilli).

Government authorities were notified by the hospital that Surat could be facing an outbreak of pneumonic plague. One of the first notified was J.C. Gandhi, chief epidemiologist of Gujurat state. Receiving the information on the evening of September 21, Gandhi rushed from the state capital, Ghandinagar, to Surat for a late-night meeting with the city's physicians, administrators, and politicians. Calls to physicians at other hospitals in Surat revealed that, beginning on September 19, they too had been caring for cases of severe pneumonia that had an unexpectedly high fatality rate.

The decision had to be made: Was the outbreak to be managed as plague or not? At that point the diagnosis by isolation of *Y. pestis* had not been confirmed. A false alarm of plague would create panic and risk a crisis of confidence. On the other hand, to wait for laboratory confirmation from New Delhi (which could take a week or more) would probably cost lives. Once the machinery of control and prevention had been set into motion, the government's suspicion of an outbreak of plague would be obvious.

Given the presumptive evidence, Gandhi, not a man of indecision, declared that the disease was to be treated as plague until proved otherwise. All suspected plague patients would be admitted to the one government hospital, and a uniform treatment, tetracycline and streptomycin, would be instituted. The public would be alerted and told to report to health authorities immediately if they had an illness with fever and respiratory signs. Contacts of cases would be identified and treated with prophylactic antibiotics immediately. Prophylactic antibiotics would be dispensed to all susceptible people, and affected areas would be blanketed with insecticide. At the same time, epidemiological and microbiological surveillance would be carried out by a team of scientists.

Public health at its best and worst

What followed over the next two weeks was some of the best—and less than best—in public health. All the actions that Gandhi called for were executed with extraordinary rapidity and thoroughness (India's ability to respond expeditiously to crises is widely acknowledged). On the other hand, large segments of the population of Surat, remembering epidemics of plague in the preantibiotic era, panicked. Tens, perhaps hundreds, of thousands fled in fear for their lives. This raised the specter of spread of the disease to other areas, even to large cities such as Bombay and Calcutta. Efforts to halt the exodus were only partially successful. The public was suspicious, hostile, and doubtful of the ability of the authorities to control the spread of the disease.

Fear was also aroused because the "case definition"—the criteria for considering a patient to be plague-infected—was intentionally a loose one, so as to be inclusive rather than exclusive and so that as few cases as possible would go untreated. Hospitals were soon crowded with patients who had fevers and respiratory symptoms and were cough-

(Opposite page) Leonard Freed—Magnum;
(top) Baldev—Sygma; (bottom) Swapan Parekh—Black Star

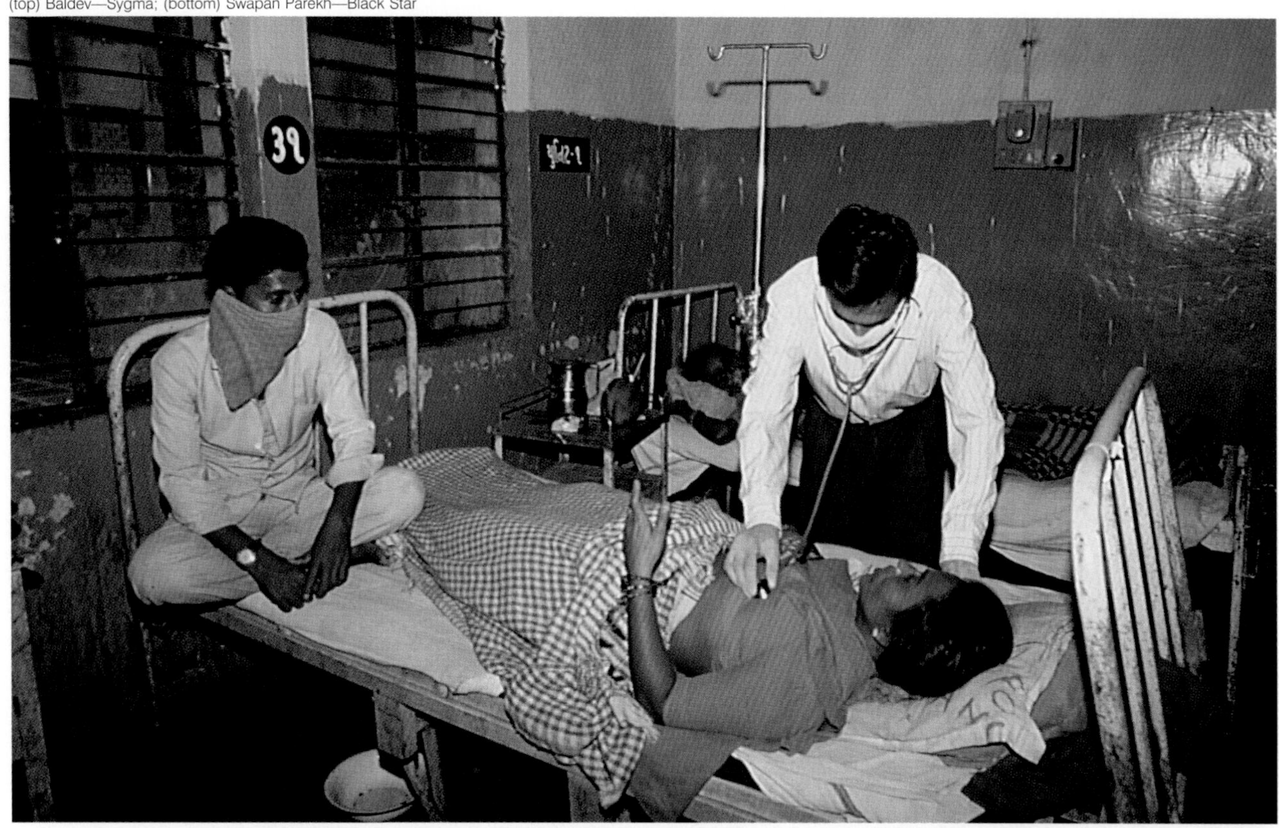

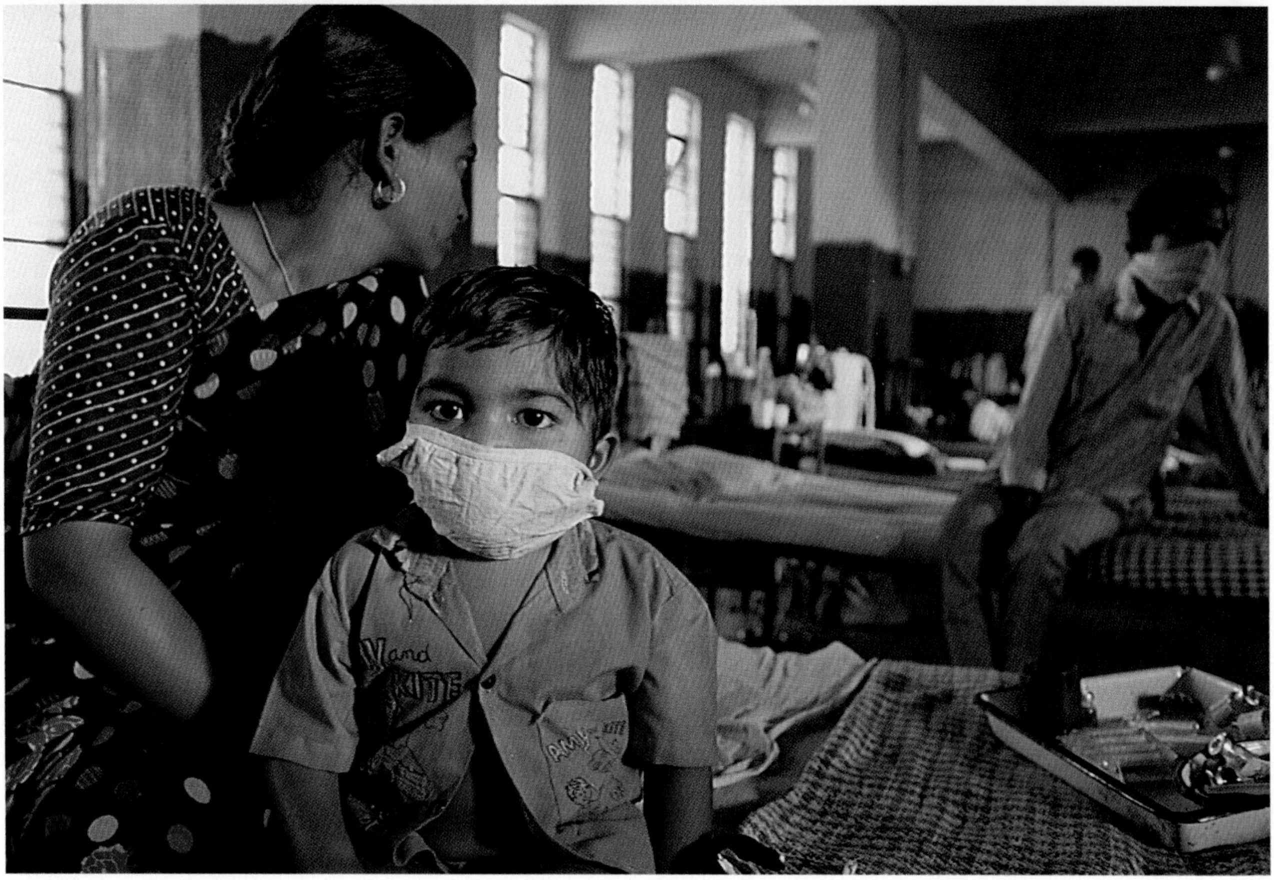

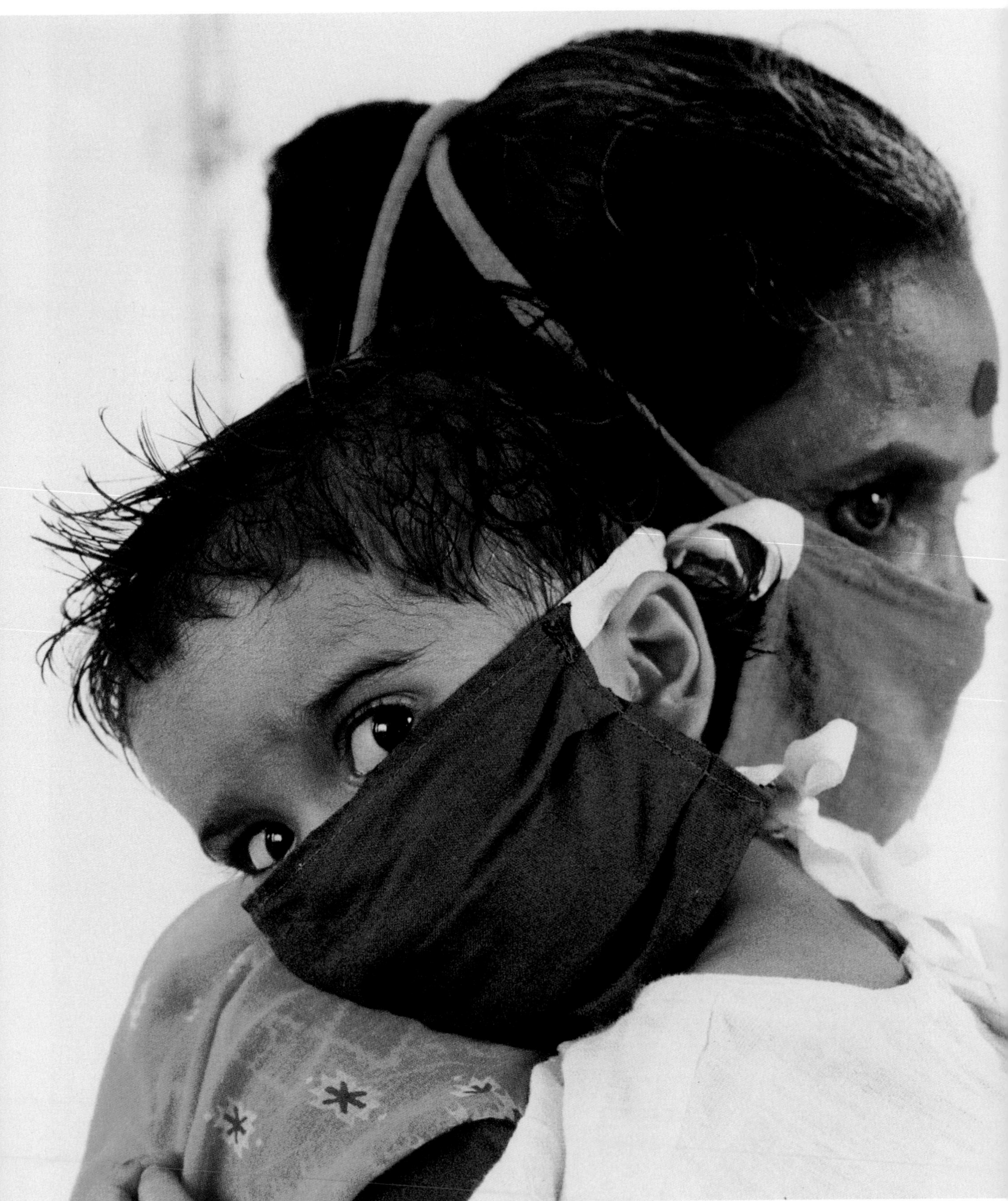

(Opposite page) Jay Ullal—Stern/Black Star; (below) Sankalan—Asiaweek

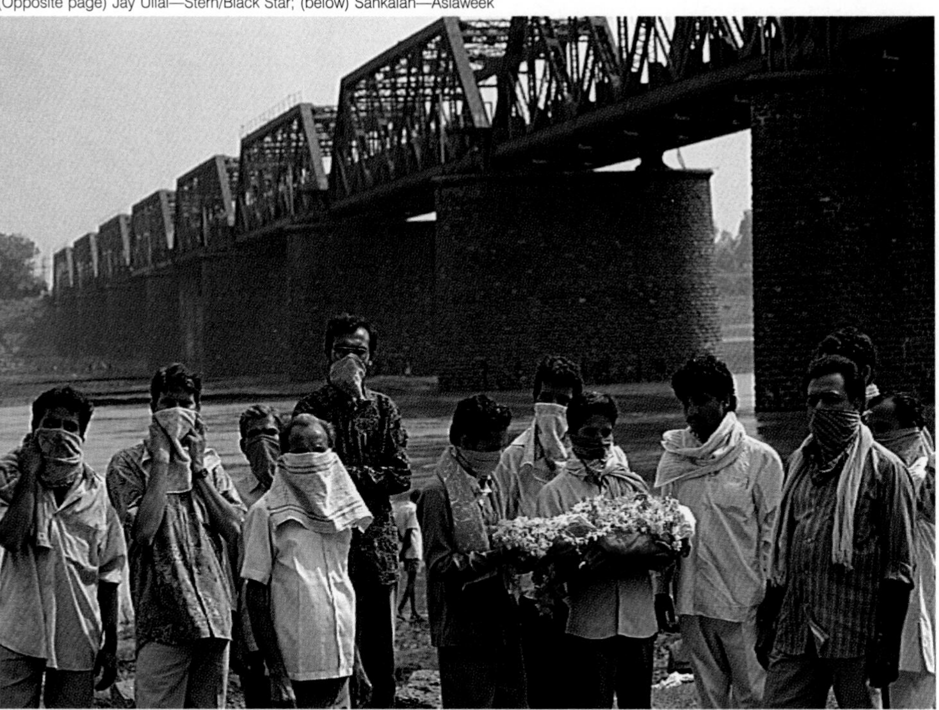

ing up blood. Many did not have plague but were suffering from other conditions such as malaria, typhoid fever, and tuberculosis.

Swift spread

Within the first weeks of plague's appearance, suspected cases were starting to be identified in a number of major cities throughout India and in rural areas surrounding the original focus. By the end of the second week, a total of 5,150 cases of suspected pneumonic or bubonic plague and 53 related deaths had been reported to WHO from eight states in India.

(Opposite) A mother and child at the hospital in Surat. (Above) Residents of the city mourn a young victim of the deadly pneumonic plague.

Countries around the world responded with efforts to prevent importation of the disease through travel or freight. The United States, Canada, and Great Britain continued normal travel and trade, relying on advisories and heightened surveillance of all travelers arriving from India. At all major seaports in India, outgoing vessels were inspected for rodents and insects, and before leaving the country, all ships were required to have a certificate showing they were free of rats. On the other hand, some governments discontinued all travel to and from India, stopped trade, and withdrew their embassy personnel. From the end of September well into October, the press throughout the world highlighted the extraordinary international public health emergency occasioned by a disease thought to have been relegated to history.

On October 7 Hiroshi Nakajima, director general of WHO, announced the formation of an independent international team of eight scientists to investigate the plague situation in India. It was quickly established by the team that plague had probably not spread beyond its original foci in rural Maharashtra and the city of Surat. Only a single case of bubonic plague was confirmed among suspected plague patients hospitalized in New Delhi; this was a young man who had traveled from Beed district to the capital during the incubation period of his disease.

After the third week of the outbreak, no new cases were confirmed in Surat. Studies conducted at the Civil Gen-

Photographs, Swapan Parekh—Black Star

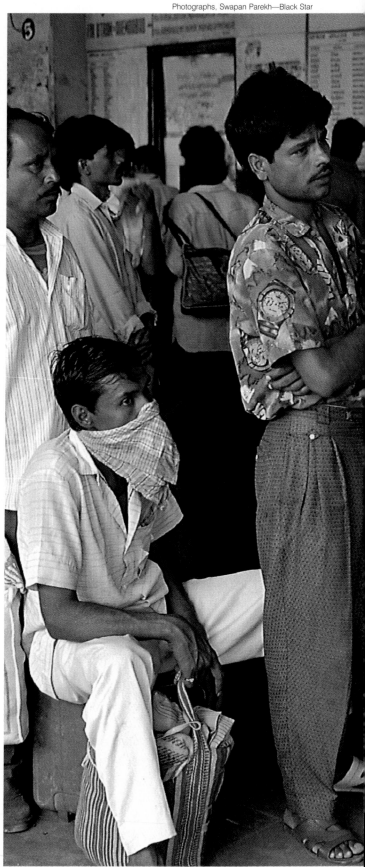

eral Hospital and the Surat Medical College ascertained that a cluster of a hundred or more cases admitted to hospitals during the first few days were likely to be pneumonic. Autopsy tissues from some of the fatal cases demonstrated typical features of acute plague, including enlargement of and bleeding into the spleen and liver and bleeding into the lungs. Although the air sacs of patients' lungs were filled with fluid and red blood cells, they contained very few inflammatory cells of the type usually seen with the more common bacterial pneumonias. Epidemiologists tracked these cases back to their homes in the slums and interviewed survivors or family members. Evidence supported earlier observations that the illness had affected mostly slum-dwelling young men. Some lived in the same immediate neighborhood in the

(Right) Gripped by their fear of the most ominous form of plague, many Surat inhabitants flee by rail. (Above) Scene at the city hospital.

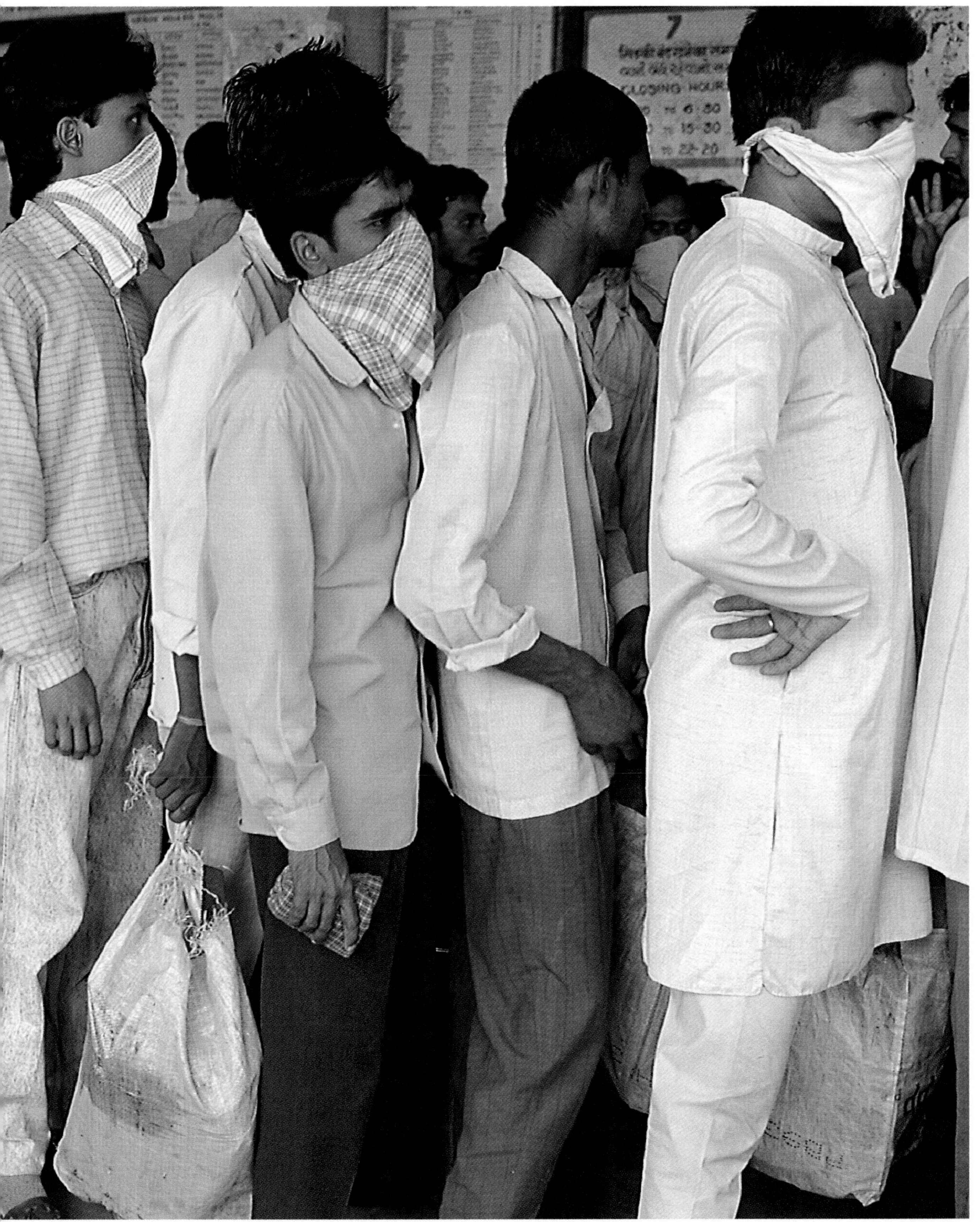

AMBULANCE

(Below) AP/Wide World; (right) Dayanita Singh—JB Pictures

Ved Road slum area but only rarely within the same household. Although most residents had participated in the Hindu festival, so had most of their healthy neighbors. Four of 27 cases and one healthy control were found to have antibodies against the plague bacillus. Antibodies were also found in 2 of 10 neighborhood dogs tested. (Dogs may become infected with the plague bacillus by eating infected rodents or being bitten by their fleas; they develop antibodies but usually do not sicken or die. Dogs, therefore, serve as excellent sentinels of plague.)

There are continuing mysteries surrounding the Surat outbreak. How, for example, did pneumonic plague arise in the first place? Pneumonic plague outbreaks that have been studied in the 20th century can almost always be traced back to an individual with bubonic plague whose illness has progressed to the pneumonic form of the disease. That person can readily spread the infection to close contacts by coughing or sneezing.

The incubation and infectivity periods for pneumonic plague are short, and the disease is severe and easily recognized. Such outbreaks are thus recognized for what they are and brought to a halt quickly by isolating sick individuals and treating all cases and their contacts with appropriate antibiotics.

In Surat epidemiologists were unable to find any convincing evidence of underlying bubonic plague in the city. It seemed likely, therefore, that someone went to Surat incubating plague acquired elsewhere, such as Maharashtra, developed the secondary pneumonic form of the disease, and spread it to unsuspecting contacts in the city. A similar scenario had been documented in Tanzania in 1991. Such an explanation made sense to epidemiologists, who generally try to link two rare events that occur simultaneously rather than assuming that the two situations arose independently.

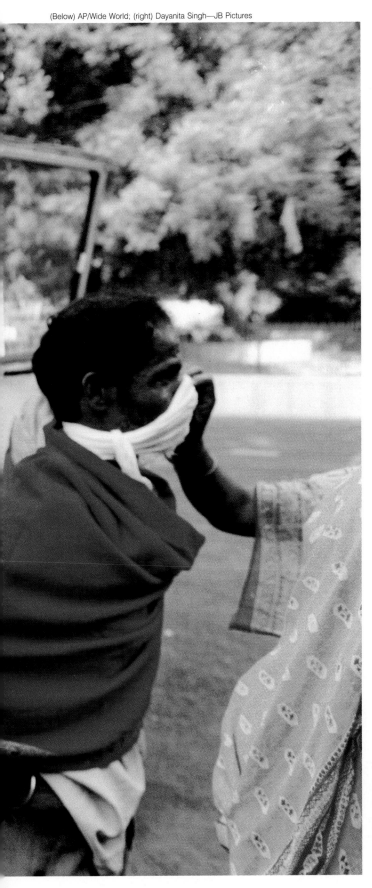

Panic spreads to India's capital, New Delhi; although many were hospitalized, only one case of bubonic plague was confirmed.

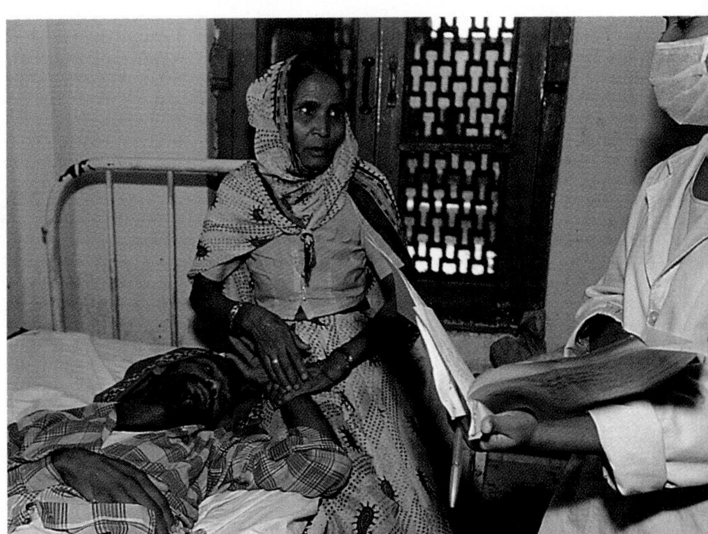

Lingering uncertainties

While the epidemiologists on the international team were attempting to reconstruct events in Surat, a CDC entomologist with expertise in disease ecology was doing a quick reconnaissance of the situation in Mamla, with the assistance of colleagues from the Ministry of Health. Interviews of persons living in Mamla and surrounding villages were conducted. Blood specimens were taken from recovered suspected plague patients and healthy controls. Dogs in plague-affected and unaffected villages were also tested. Rats were collected and their fleas harvested.

Specimens collected in the field were taken to laboratories in New Delhi, where they were examined by the microbiologists. Blood taken from some suspected plague cases and some dogs from affected villages tested positive for antibodies to the plague bacillus, while blood from people who had not been ill and from both people and dogs from unaffected villages tested negative. Some of the antibody levels were very high, which indicated recent infection. The plague bacillus itself was not found in rats or their fleas, however.

The inability of scientists to confirm plague at the time of the outbreaks and some of the unusual features of the outbreaks themselves led to serious doubts in the minds of some medical practitioners, scientists, and the press that the disease reported as plague was really that. Other potential diagnoses were considered, including hantavirus and melioidosis, a severe bacterial infection with clinical features similar to those of plague. The controversy raged for weeks in the Indian press, while scientists around the world disputed the matter in medical journals. The WHO investigative team concluded that limited outbreaks of both types of plague had occurred. The team recommended continuing field and laboratory investigations that would elucidate the genetic characteristics of the causative agent and determine whether natural cycles of plague might pose an ongoing risk of infection among persons living in Maharashtra and Surat.

The final chapter on plague in India in 1994 is still being written, and for epidemiologists, at least, it makes fascinating reading. Cultures of sputum from suspected pneumonic plague patients and autopsy tissues from some fatal cases were obtained from the Surat Medical College at the time of the investigations in October. Through weeks of painstaking laboratory work, pure isolates of *Y. pestis* from three patients were confirmed by scientists from the CDC and two other independent investigating groups. These were found to be typical plague organisms but with distinct "genetic fingerprints" that could serve as useful epidemiological markers. The remarkable bioengineering method known as the polymerase chain reaction (PCR) was used to amplify many thousands of times a tiny fragment from chromosomal DNA from the plague bacillus extracted from the autopsy tissues. This confirmed the presence of *Y. pestis* in tissue from each of the five fatal cases examined. This was the first time PCR had been used to confirm the presence of plague infection.

Follow-up investigations by CDC and Indian scientists in Maharashtra in March 1995 provided some intriguing leads to unanswered questions. Epidemiological and ecological studies identified continuing widespread conditions of large numbers of rodents and fleas that were ideal for the spread of diseases such as plague and typhus in villages in Beed district. In addition, the trapping of rodents and the mapping of the distribution of their hosts led

The Indian gerbil, *Tatera indica* (below), a known plague carrier. (Opposite) One day's rodent collection, Bombay.

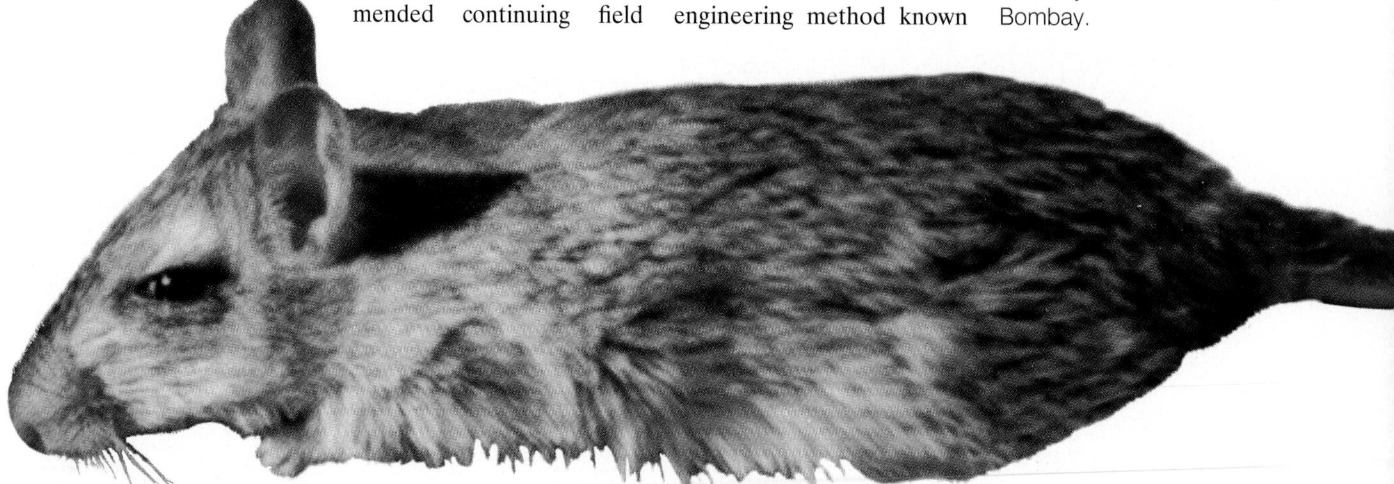

David T. Dennis, M.D., Centers for Disease Control and Prevention, Fort Collins, Colorado

AP/Wide World

Scott Camazine—Science Source/Photo Researchers

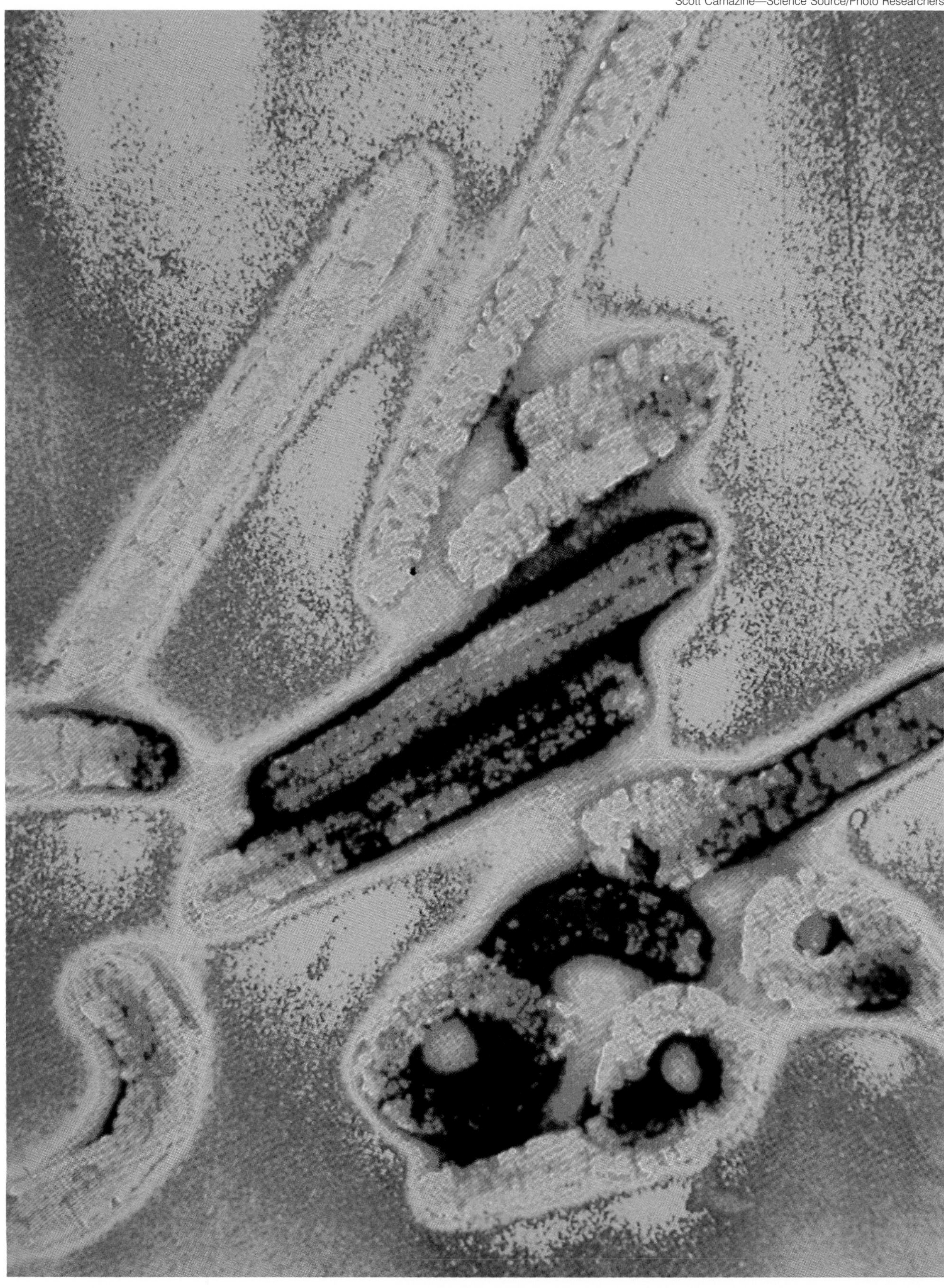

to the discovery of flea-infested Indian gerbils, *Tatera indica,* within Mamla village itself. Decades earlier this gerbil had been identified as the probable silent source of plague in India, but it had not previously been discovered within village confines in situations of close contact with rodent species such as bandicoots and the roof rat. The flea species infesting the gerbils was *Xenopsylla cheopis,* the classic plague vector. This finding may be the missing link between plague that has persisted silently for decades in wild rodents in south-central India and plague in village rats that resulted in human illness. Continued scientific investigation in the coming months and years should clarify these and the many other intriguing features of the Indian plague outbreaks of 1994.

(Opposite and below) In the spring and summer of 1995, the rare Ebola virus killed several hundred in Zaire. Like the plague in India, the situation alarmed the world about the possibility of future deadly disease outbreaks.

Global omen?

The reported outbreaks of plague in India created a perceived international health crisis that cost India an estimated $2 billion in lost tourist and trade revenues and caused an enormous disruption of normal international and national activities. The political costs were also high, and the opposition Indian press took full advantage of the situation to discredit the government and its attempts to explain and control the outbreaks. To the world community, plague in India was a dramatic reminder of the threat that emerging and reemerging diseases can pose anytime anywhere on the globe—in this age of massive intercontinental travel and commerce. Spurred on by Indian plague, hantavirus, Ebola hemorrhagic fever, and other recent outbreaks, health agencies involved in responding to these crises, such as WHO and the CDC, have made preparedness planning for new and emerging diseases a top priority for international action.

AP/Wide World

Saying Farewell to a Friend

by George H. Pollock, M.D., Ph.D.

December 1994

Dear Friends,

. . . Having survived fires, mud slides, and an earthquake, we have finally met our match. It seems that time pardons no one, not even cocky Californians. In this case, time is measured in dog years and our beloved Martha has recently served the last of these on this earth. At the age of 13½ human years, Martha had a rapid functional decline, was diagnosed with end-stage renal failure, and passed all within a 10 day period in early December. Such is the injustice of species-specific life span. Since Martha was the perfect dog, both of us are devastated. We can't believe how still a dogless house can be. It's simply going to take some time and a great deal of Kleenex to work through this. I know that many of you cannot envision us without her; neither can we. Those of you with dogs, please give them an extra hug tonight for Martha and cherish every day with them. . . .

Gail and Dave

[Annual Christmas letter]

People cherish their pets. It is neither abnormal nor surprising that they are deeply affected by an animal companion's death. Traditionally, mourning and bereavement are associated with the death of a significant other *person*—especially a close family figure (a mother, father, spouse, child, or sibling). These reactions, however, can extend to other losses—for example, of one's country, a body part, a home, a job, or a treasured object. A former patient of this author was enormously grieved when a tree that he had planted in his yard and nurtured over many years was struck by lightning and destroyed. Young children frequently mourn the loss or destruction of a special blanket or teddy bear that has functioned as a close companion. So, too, can the loss or death of an animal companion be a cause for profound grief and mourning.

Pets on a pedestal

Today more households have pets than have children. According to recent statistics, there are about 229 million pets (cats, dogs, birds,

George H. Pollock, M.D., Ph.D., *is the Ruth and Evelyn Dunbar Distinguished Professor of Psychiatry and Behavioral Sciences, Emeritus, Northwestern University Medical School, Lecturer in Psychiatry, Rush Medical College, and Psychiatrist and Psychoanalyst in part-time practice in Chicago. He is also Clinical Professor of Psychoanalysis, the Medical College of Wisconsin, Milwaukee, and the author, coauthor, and editor of many books, articles, and monographs in his field.*

June Evelyn Atwood—
Contact Press Images

WICK
KB/MDK
GARIBALDI
AMONGST
BOOTS AND
Merry Christmas

fish, horses, and small mammals) living in United States households alone, and pets are just as popular—or more so—in many other countries.

Pet-human attachments date back to prehistoric times, when animals served the purpose of protecting cave dwellers and alerting them to dangers. In ancient Egypt religion was based on the worship of animals, especially cats and dogs, and sacred dogs and cats were mummified when they died. Special dog cemeteries have been uncovered from ancient China; Pekingese dogs were entombed with their royal masters. Pets have been the subjects of great artistic works. The "Aesop" fables and many other classics of literature center around animals. European painters often included pets as central figures in family portraits. In more contemporary times, most U.S. presidents have had celebrated "first pets" living with them in the White House (*see* Table, page 196).

The importance of pets in people's lives should not be underestimated. The meaning and function of pets vary; some see pets as family members comparable to children, parents, siblings, or spouses; others see them as companions, confidants, and loyal and constant friends; still others rely on them as personal bodyguards. Pets provide constancy and stability, especially during times of stress and transition. In many instances the relationship with a beloved pet is the most important tie an individual has. This may be especially true for the elderly, disabled, widowed, divorced, childless, or single persons living alone. For an only child a pet may serve as a surrogate sibling.

Research has shown that pets can contribute to the health of their owners. They can help lower the blood pressure of hypertensive patients and aid in the treatment of the chronically ill or those who have physical disabilities.

Victoria and Albert Museum/E.T. Archive

Intimate pet-human attachments have been the subject of artistic works for centuries. The Flemish illustration above dates to about 1450.

Death of a "significant other"

A new interest for this author was sparked when I was asked to appear as a professional consultant on a television documentary. The topic of the program was "pet bereavement." During the course of my long career as a psychiatrist, I had done extensive research and writing on death and bereavement. Although I had not investigated the subject of *pet* bereavement per se, I agreed to participate. First, I decided to look into the subject further.

I began my research by looking for pertinent literature. I soon discovered, however, that very little was available. While volumes have been written about human death and the reactions to it, almost no clinical material existed on mourning after a pet's death. There were a few published studies, but these were hard to obtain. I was surprised that so little professional attention had been paid to the subject of pet bereavement—particularly because so many people go through it.

Owing to the lack of available literature, I recalled the contact I had had with patients, friends, and family members who had endured the death of a pet. I also consulted colleagues, who shared their own professional experiences with me. I was especially interested in cases in which pet bereavement occurred in the course of therapy for more serious psychiatric conditions.

Coming to terms with the pain

I had Freddie, my pet schnauzer, for 15 years. He became ill, and the vet said his kidneys were badly damaged. Despite various treatments, Freddie and I knew he was going to die. I remember the last time I saw him at the animal hospital. I looked into his eyes, and he looked into mine—we both knew it was the end. Freddie was put to sleep. I knew this was the best way, but nonetheless, I cried and cried for a long time afterward. I did not get another dog—none could ever replace him. I will always love Freddie—and I still think of him virtually every day.

The importance of pets in the lives of people—young and old—should not be underestimated.

So related Freddie's bereaved owner, a middle-aged man, a number of months after his schnauzer's death. Though he had accepted the death, he was still deeply saddened (and in mourning). Mourning is a normal process following a major change, loss, or disappointment; when the result is death, the act of mourning is known as "bereavement." Typically, there are accompanying feelings of pain, grief, sorrow, remorse, and even anger. Under normal circumstances these feelings evolve into memories and fond recol-

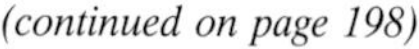

(continued on page 198)

(Top left and center right) Norvia Behling; (top right) Joel Dexter—Unicorn Stock Photos; (bottom left) Tommy Thompson—Black Star; (bottom right) Jane Burton—Bruce Coleman Limited

Presidential Pets

ALLIGATOR
John Quincy Adams
ANTELOPE
Calvin Coolidge
BADGER
Theodore Roosevelt
BEAR
Thomas Jefferson
Theodore Roosevelt
Calvin Coolidge
BIRD
Canary
Rutherford B. Hayes
Grover Cleveland
Calvin Coolidge
John F. Kennedy
Chicken
Theodore Roosevelt
Woodrow Wilson
Eagle
James Buchanan
Gamecock
Andrew Jackson
Ulysses S. Grant
Goose
Calvin Coolidge
Mockingbird
Thomas Jefferson
Rutherford B. Hayes
Grover Cleveland
Calvin Coolidge
Mynah bird
Calvin Coolidge
Owl
Theodore Roosevelt
Parakeet
John F. Kennedy
Parrot
George Washington
James Madison
Andrew Jackson
Ulysses S. Grant
William McKinley
Theodore Roosevelt
Calvin Coolidge
Partridge
Thomas Jefferson
Peacock
Thomas Jefferson
Pheasant
Thomas Jefferson
Pigeon
Rutherford B. Hayes
Thrush
Calvin Coolidge
Turkey
Abraham Lincoln
Warren G. Harding
Unknown species
Benjamin Harrison
Woodrow Wilson
BOBCAT
Calvin Coolidge
CAT
Angora
William McKinley
Siamese
Rutherford B. Hayes
Gerald Ford
Jimmy Carter
Unknown species
Theodore Roosevelt
Woodrow Wilson
Calvin Coolidge
Harry Truman
John F. Kennedy
Bill Clinton
COW
William Henry Harrison
Andrew Johnson
William Howard Taft
Calvin Coolidge
DEER
Thomas Jefferson
John F. Kennedy
Gerald Ford
DOG
Airedale
Warren G. Harding
Beagle
Lyndon B. Johnson
Bird dog
Calvin Coolidge
Bulldog
Calvin Coolidge
Bull terrier
Theodore Roosevelt
Chesapeake Bay retriever
Theodore Roosevelt
Chow chow
Calvin Coolidge
Cocker spaniel
Harry Truman
Richard Nixon
Collie
Calvin Coolidge
Lyndon B. Johnson
Elkhound
Herbert Hoover
English mastiff
Rutherford B. Hayes
Eskimo
Herbert Hoover
Fox terrier
Herbert Hoover
French hound
George Washington

Photographs, Stock Montage, Inc.

(Left) Pres. Theodore Roosevelt's second son, Kermit, with his dog Jack, and (above) his fourth son, Archibald Bulloch ("Archie"), on his pony, Algonquin—both photographed in 1902, their dad's second year in office.

Brown Brothers

President and Mrs. Calvin Coolidge with just two of the dozens of animal companions that shared their White House residency (1923–29). Some of their more exotic pets were boarded at the zoo.

German shepherd
John F. Kennedy
Golden retriever
Gerald Ford
Greyhound
Rutherford B. Hayes
Irish setter
Harry Truman
Richard Nixon
Irish water spaniel
John F. Kennedy
Irish wolfhound
Herbert Hoover
John F. Kennedy
Italian wolfhound
John Tyler
King Charles spaniel
Ronald Reagan
Newfoundland
James Buchanan
Ulysses S. Grant
Pekingese
Theodore Roosevelt
Police dog
Herbert Hoover
Poodle
Grover Cleveland
Richard Nixon
Scotch collie
Herbert Hoover
Scottie
Franklin D. Roosevelt
Setter
Herbert Hoover
Sheepdog
James Monroe
Calvin Coolidge
Ronald Reagan
Spaniel
James Monroe
Terrier
Theodore Roosevelt
Calvin Coolidge
Welsh terrier
John F. Kennedy
Weimaraner
Dwight D. Eisenhower
Yorkshire terrier
Richard Nixon
Unknown species
George Washington
James Garfield
Benjamin Harrison
Theodore Roosevelt
Franklin D. Roosevelt
Lyndon B. Johnson
Jimmy Carter
George Bush
DONKEY
Calvin Coolidge
ELEPHANT
James Buchanan
FISH
James Garfield
Richard Nixon
GOAT
Abraham Lincoln
Rutherford B. Hayes
Benjamin Harrison
Harry Truman
GUINEA PIG
Theodore Roosevelt
John F. Kennedy
HAMSTER
John F. Kennedy
HIPPO
Calvin Coolidge
HORSE
George Washington
John Adams
Andrew Jackson
John Tyler
James Polk
Zachary Taylor
Ulysses S. Grant
Benjamin Harrison
Franklin D. Roosevelt
John F. Kennedy
Ronald Reagan
HYENA
Theodore Roosevelt
JACKASS
George Washington
LAMB
John F. Kennedy
LION
Calvin Coolidge
LIZARD
Theodore Roosevelt
MOUSE
Andrew Johnson
MULE
George Washington
Franklin D. Roosevelt
OPPOSUM
Benjamin Harrison
Herbert Hoover
PIG
Abraham Lincoln
Theodore Roosevelt
Dwight D. Eisenhower
PONY
Abraham Lincoln
Ulysses S. Grant
Theodore Roosevelt
John F. Kennedy
RABBIT
Abraham Lincoln
Theodore Roosevelt
John F. Kennedy
Jimmy Carter
RACCOON
Calvin Coolidge
RAT
Piebald
Theodore Roosevelt
Kangaroo
Theodore Roosevelt
SHEEP
James Madison
Woodrow Wilson
SILKWORM
John Quincy Adams
SNAKE
Theodore Roosevelt
SQUIRREL
Theodore Roosevelt
Dwight D. Eisenhower
TIGER
Martin Van Buren
WALLABY
Calvin Coolidge

From *Presidential Pets* by Niall Kelly © 1992 Abbeville Press, New York City

FLUFFY
MY BABY
1975——1983

BUTTONS
MY DEAREST LITTLE POODLE
SO SUPER-TRUE-AND SWEET
YOU ARE ONLY REALLY SLEEPING
TIL IN HEAVEN WE MEET
BELOVED BY OWNER
ROSEMARY GRIFFIN
1960 1974

Commemorating a cherished pet in some formal way can help the bereaved human companion come to terms with the overwhelming sense of loss.

(Left) Jane Evelyn Atwood—Contact Press Images; (top right and bottom right) Paul A. Hein—Unicorn Stock Photos

(continued from page 195)
lections, facilitated by the mourning process. Mourning enables the individual to "work through" the loss in a systematic manner. In other words, it is an adaptive, coping mechanism that ultimately is self-liberating.

Losses may be permanent or transitory and are different from each other depending upon who or what is lost, when the loss occurs, and whether it is sudden and unexpected or anticipated and prolonged. The significance of the deceased in a person's life is one of the determinants of the severity, duration, and subsequent course of the bereavement process. Reactions are also dependent upon the age and maturity of the mourner and his or her experience with previous losses and deaths.

When the mourning-bereavement process occurs, it may have various physical, psychological, emotional, social, and religious manifestations. In instances where the owner or family elected to "put the pet away," there may be reactions of guilt and shame. If the bereaved witnessed an accident or some other tragedy that caused the pet's death, he or she may feel responsible. When a pet has disappeared or died for unknown reasons, a person's fantasies about what may have happened can be very troubling. Was the animal stolen? Was it hit by a car? Did someone leave the door open and let the pet out? Such questions and fantasies may reinforce guilt, anxiety, and shame, or they may arouse feelings of anger, victimization, and revenge.

The mourning-bereavement process has several phases. There may first be an awareness of circumstances that will result in death (*e.g.,* realizing that a pet's illness is terminal; seeing a fast-approaching train just as a cat jumps onto the tracks). Next comes the recognition of the reality of the loss and of death's finality. Often, shock or denial will follow. Grief may be manifest in any number of ways, including crying; depression; anxiety; sleep, appetite, or bowel disturbances; emotional and social withdrawal; or a strong need to talk about the pet to other people who are empathic. When reactions are severe or persistent, it may be helpful to consult a grief counselor or join a pet-bereavement group. Finally, the bereaved may wish to commemorate the death in some formal way—making burial arrangements (*e.g.,* in the family yard or a pet cemetery), displaying photographs of the deceased pet, or memorializing the beloved animal with poems, songs, or favorite stories about its escapades.

The decision about whether to replace the deceased pet with another varies from individual to individual. Thus, a bereaved owner, unlike Freddie's owner, may wish to get another dog of the same breed, same color, and same temperament right away. Others look not for a "replacement" but for a "successor" that may be quite unlike the lost or dead pet.

When an animal that serves as a hearing ear or guide dog dies or is lost, the deaf or blind person loses not only a meaningful companion but also a vital function and perhaps the ability to get along in life. These are often cases where replacement of the animal is a necessity rather than a matter of choice.

In some instances so-called anniversary reactions—"reexperiencing" the loss and going through "mini-mourning"—occur at specific times that are meaningful to the owner. Recognizing them as such helps

Pet cemeteries in California (top left) and Maryland (left); (above) grave site unknown.

(Top left) Mike Yamashita—West Light; (left) Mark C. Burnett—Stock, Boston; (above) James Schnepf—Gamma Liaison

the individual get through these times of turmoil.

Some years ago this author was consulted by a man whose parents were both deaf. The patient had no such impairments. When asked how he communicated with his mother, particularly as an infant and a young child, he said he had had a hearing ear dog. In further explanation, he spoke of this canine caretaker as if it had been a nanny. When he was in bed at night and needed something, for example, his "doggie" would get up and go to his mother and gently nudge her. If this did not arouse her, the dog would pull on the blanket or tug at her nightgown. The awakened mother would then go to her child.

Obviously, the dog had played a vital role in this patient's upbringing. When the dog became terminally ill years later, the man was extremely bereaved. In fact, it was on the occasion of a profound anniversary reaction to the dog's death that the patient initially sought psychiatric counsel.

Vets and pets

Pet bereavement does not often result in serious psychiatric problems, and rarely is it a cause for seeking professional help. The professional who plays the most important role is usually the veterinarian. The vet may have to break the news that an ill or injured pet has died, and he or she may be present when the owner is most aggrieved. Thus, the veterinarian more than any other professional is the "pet bereavement specialist." In fact, veterinarians directly experience the death of their animal patients about five times more often than physicians experience the death of their human patients.

In the introduction to *Pet Loss and Human Bereavement* (1984), one of the few available sources on the subject, William J. Kay, a veterinarian and one of the volume's editors, emphasized the key role of the vet in both recognizing and dealing with "the profound distress experienced by pet owners faced with the death of a pet."

Although studies on pet bereavement are lacking, much literature exists on the attachment theory and principle as they relate to human relationships. When separation occurs or attachments are broken, distress is experienced, and later mourning-bereavement occurs. Veterinarians are increasingly involved in helping owners understand the nature of human-pet attachments and why grief is profound when those relationships are disrupted. Continued contact with the veterinarian may be helpful to the bereaved individual.

And animals mourn animals

Mourning occurs not only in humans for animals but also in animals for animals. In the book *The Human Nature of Birds* (1993), author Theodore Xenophon Barber cites the example of a female mandarin duck that "displayed the strongest marks of despair" when her mate was taken away. The duck's bereavement was exhibited in her behavior, which included "retiring into a corner

Frank Siteman—Stock, Boston

Animal companions enrich the lives of residents of nursing homes (left and below).

and altogether neglecting food and drink, as well as the care of her person." Later, the drake was returned to the aviary, and "the most extravagant demonstrations of joy were displayed by the fond couple."

Veterinarian Kay points out that grief related to pet death involves not only the owners and family members who lived with and cared for the pet but also other surviving pets in the household. This is well illustrated in the case of Chema.

Chema was a Burmese cat given to a young bride by her husband. The cat was in the family for 11 years, through several moves and the birth of three children. As the children came into the family, they too became closely attached to Chema. Several times Chema had litters. All but one of her kittens were given to family friends that could give them a good home. The kitten that remained was named Eleanor. Chema and Eleanor were rarely apart. Then one day Eleanor disappeared. The family wondered if she had been "catnapped" or had run away. Chema brooded for days, searching all over the house, crying out, sleeping poorly, and eating little. Chema clearly was in mourning. Several days after Eleanor's disappearance, Chema was found strangled on a clothesline in the basement. The mother cat apparently had jumped, got caught in the rope, and thereby "hanged herself." Was this suicidal behavior? Probably not, but Chema's reaction to the loss of Eleanor was indicative of the impact that the loss of one family pet can have on another.

Pets grieve for presidents and other people

It is evident, too, that animals are deeply affected by the death of humans. The case of Hachi is one example. In 1923 a professor at the University of Tokyo acquired a puppy named Hachi. The pet soon formed the habit of going to the railroad station with his master each morning and waiting there until he returned from the university on the evening train. When the professor died in 1925, his family moved to another part of Tokyo, taking Hachi with them. Hachi, however, returned to the railroad station each day to wait for the master who would never return. Hachi made his daily trip to the station for 10 years—until *he* died. Hachi was so well known at the Tokyo railway station that a statue was erected in his honor with the inscription "The Faithful Dog, Hachi." And in 1953 Japan issued a commemorative stamp for Hachi.

In the book *Presidential Pets* (1992), author Niall Kelly, a pet fancier who was born and raised on a farm, recalls the close attachment between U.S. Pres. Franklin Delano Roosevelt and his Scottie, Fala.

When Roosevelt died in Georgia a few months after his fourth inauguration, Fala seems to have sensed it back at the White House. On the day of the death, the dog had been dozing in a corner of the room when suddenly he hopped up, ran to the door, and bashed his head against the screen. The screen broke and Fala, crawling through, ran snapping and barking onto a hill where he reportedly sat for hours all alone.

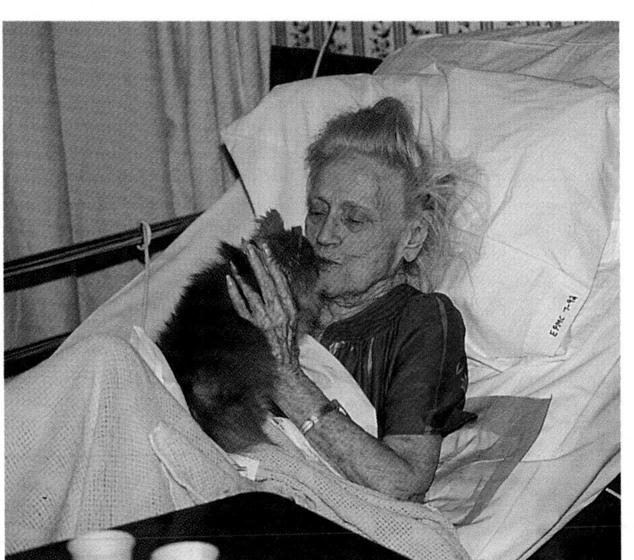

Kent and Donna Dannen

(Above) "First pet" Fala—the devoted Scottie of U.S. Pres. Franklin Delano Roosevelt—attends his master's funeral in Hyde Park, New York, in 1945. (Right) Laddie Boy, faithful Airedale companion to 29th U.S. Pres. Warren G. Harding (1921–23), not only cheered the beleaguered chief executive but charmed the American public.

Photos, Brown Brothers

Ceremony and ritual

Memorializing a deceased pet is one way to cope with the feelings of bereavement. Kelly writes about the ceremonial tribute that Lyndon Baines Johnson paid to his beloved Little Beagle Johnson. When the dog died, before his human companion became president, Johnson had him cremated. At first, he kept Little Beagle's ashes in an urn on top of the refrigerator. Eventually, however, Johnson gave in to his cook's objections and sent the ashes to his Texas ranch, where they were properly buried.

Monuments and statues, such as the one in Tokyo for Hachi, are another way to memorialize a pet. After U.S. Pres. Warren G. Harding's death in 1923, the Newsboys' Association collected pennies from paper carriers across the U.S. to celebrate Laddie Boy, Harding's cherished Airedale. Every newsboy in the country was asked to donate one penny to the fund. "After Laddie nobly endured fifteen sittings," Kelly relates, "19,134 donated pennies were melted down and molded into a statue by a sculptor named Bashka Paeff. Unfortunately, before the statue could be presented to Mrs. Harding, the former first lady died, so it went instead to the Smithsonian, where it still stands."

The writer Cleveland Amory wrote three books about his pet cat Polar Bear. All were best-sellers. In the final volume, *The Best Cat Ever* (1993), Amory says that when he first learned his feline companion was seriously ill, it felt "like being stabbed." In the end, he buried Polar Bear on a ranch in Texas beneath a headstone inscribed with these words:

> *Beneath This Stone*
> *Lie the Mortal Remains of*
> *The Cat Who Came for Christmas*
> *Beloved Polar Bear*
> *1977–1992*
> *'Til We Meet Again*

Ultimately, Amory believed that "the best place to bury your animal is your heart."

Progress Report: Breast Cancer's Genetic Origins

by Edward P. Cohen, M.D.

Hundreds of thousands of women throughout the world will develop breast cancer this year. Although age-adjusted incidence and mortality rates vary from country to country—the British Isles having among the world's highest rates and Japan and Mexico among the lowest—breast cancer is not only a common disease but a leading killer of women. In the United States alone, approximately 182,000 new breast cancer cases are detected each year, and 46,000 women die annually from the disease. This means that one in nine American women will be affected at some point in her life. Until 1989 the number of deaths from breast cancer had remained essentially unchanged for nearly 40 years. Then, in only three years, the overall breast cancer death rate for women in the U.S. dropped nearly 5% (*see* "Optimism on the Breast Cancer Front," page 218). During the same period, however, breast cancer deaths among African-American women increased nearly 3%.

***Edward P. Cohen, M.D.**, is Professor, Department of Microbiology and Immunology, College of Medicine, University of Illinois at Chicago.*

Fortunately, in the past several years, great leaps have been made in the understanding of breast cancer and its causes. Research teams led by Steven Narod of McGill University, Montreal, Barbara Weber and Francis Collins at the University of Michigan, Ellen Solomon at the Imperial Cancer Research Fund, London, and Mary-Claire King at the University of California at Berkeley have discovered many of breast cancer's closely guarded secrets. They and others played vital parts in discovering breast can-

(Opposite) "Beauty out of Damage" (1993), self-portrait by Matuschka, a photographer, writer, activist, and recipient of many prestigious photographic and humanitarian honors, including the World Press Photo's Gold Award, the Rachel Carson Award, and the Gilda Radner Award.

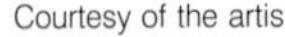
Courtesy of the artist

Breast Cancer Deaths

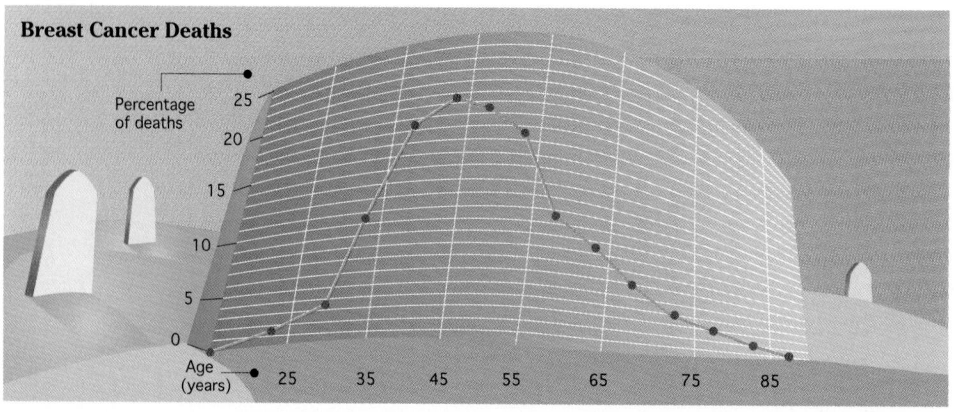

Around the World: Breast Cancer Deaths in Women

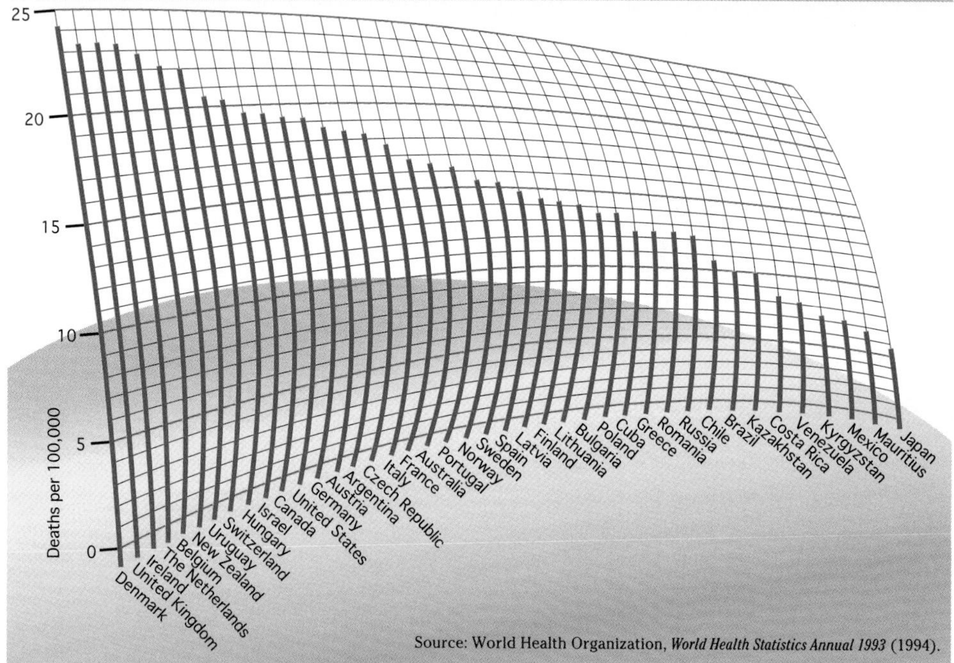

Cancer of the breast is the most common form of cancer in women worldwide and the single most common cause of death in women aged 40–50.

cer's genetic basis. Comparisons of the chromosomes of breast cancer cells with the chromosomes of normal cells led to the finding that a portion of one chromosome—chromosome 17—was missing or altered in the cancer cells in a large proportion of cases. Then, in September 1994, Mark Skolnick and his colleagues at the University of Utah Medical Center identified the precise gene that was often altered. The defective gene was dubbed *BRCA1.*

The isolation and characterization of the "breast cancer gene" will lead to more precise means of preventing the disease, the identification of healthy women who are at greater-than-average risk of developing the disease at some future time, and more effective therapies. The new findings also raise difficult ethical questions regarding the determination and notification of individuals who are at risk. These issues will have to be taken carefully into account by physicians and others involved in the care of cancer patients and by women themselves and members of their families.

What causes cancer?

For generations, little was known about the cause of cancer, although many environmental and dietary factors were known to be associated with the development of malignant dis-

Courtesy of the artist

"The Illusion Was to Think She Had Any Control over Her Life," oil pastel on paper with painted frame (1992) by Hollis Sigler, from her *Breast Cancer Journal: Walking with the Ghosts of My Grandmothers.*

ease. Women who begin menstruating at an earlier-than-average age and enter menopause later than most, for example, have a higher-than-average risk of developing breast cancer. Patients with colon cancer often are people who exercise infrequently and eat a diet rich in animal fats and deficient in fiber. It has been well known for the past 30 or more years that cigarette smoking is associated with lung cancer. Smoking has also been related to the development of bladder and other cancers. Chewing tobacco leads to cancer of the mouth, and excessive exposure to sunlight's harmful rays results in skin cancer in many individuals. These are only some of the external and hormonal influences that are common in cancer patients. Exactly how these factors influence the development of cancer—just

"Grief Masks I–IV," stained porcelain (1989) by Paulette Carr, conveys the impact that having cancer had on the artist. "When the nightmare confronts you, you want to scream, but can't," says Carr.

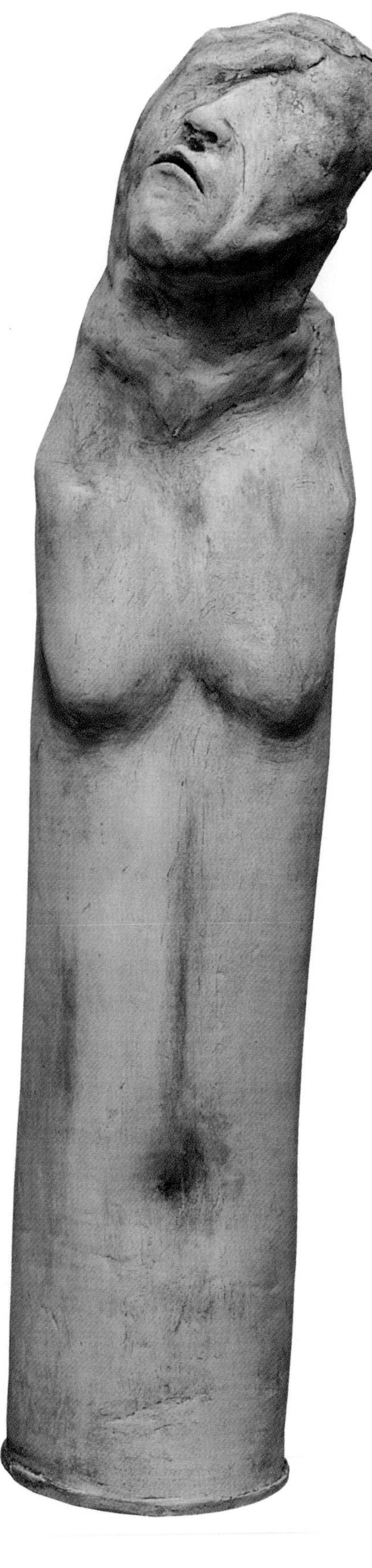

Courtesy of the "Healing Legacies" arts registry, Breast Cancer Action Group, Burlington, Vermont what changes occur within the body and cause cells to transform from normal to malignant—was unknown until relatively recently.

Now medical scientists have determined that cancer results from damage to certain genes, precise segments of DNA within an individual cell of the body. It is this genetic damage that causes a normal cell to become malignant. The genes in question are responsible for controlling mitosis—*i.e.,* cell division, or new-cell formation. Without such controls the cell divides continually and is no longer responsive to the usual body influences that limit the extent of cell proliferation. A malignant tumor, an accumulation of cancer cells, results when these critical genes are damaged.

Cells normally divide during natural growth, in response to injury, and to maintain the body's health. The growth process depends on the formation of new cells to replace older ones that are no longer functional. The average life span of a red blood cell, for example, is 120 days; the old ones are then replaced by young ones, and the proliferation of immature red blood cells is required for generation of the new ones. The repair of a wound requires cell proliferation as well. The number of white cells in the blood is also carefully controlled. It increases in response to an infection.

Photographs, David Spector, M.D.—Peter Arnold, Inc.

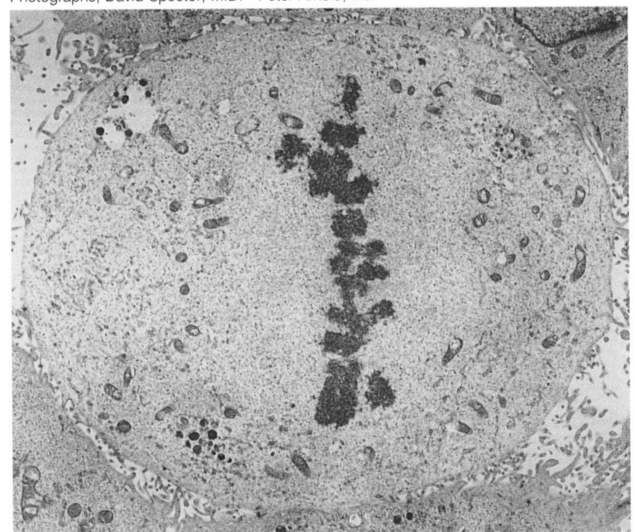

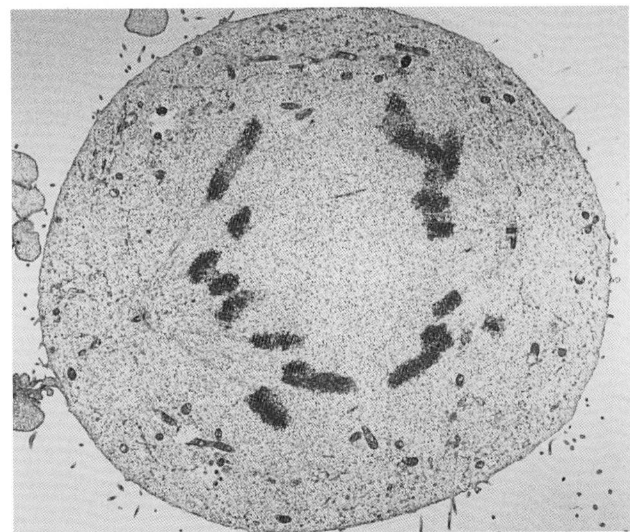

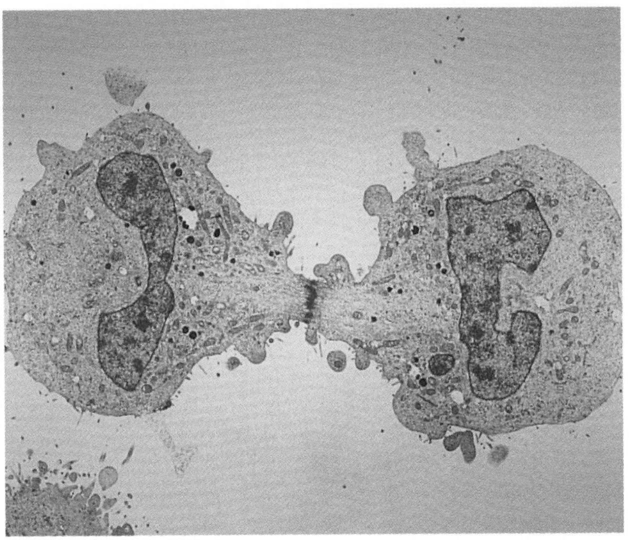

A cell undergoes mitosis in three phases. Cell division nears completion as new nuclei form in the two daughter cells (bottom).

Cells divide when they receive special external signals from other cells. The "proliferation signal" comes from naturally occurring chemical substances in the body that interact with specific receptors on the surfaces of the cells. The stimulus for cell division is transmitted from outside the cell through the cell's cytoplasm to its nucleus, where genes that regulate proliferation are found. A complex set of signals inside the cell results in the activation of genes that are responsible for regulating mitosis, and cell division continues until the stimulus subsides. Thus, when sufficient growth has occurred, a wound has been repaired, or an infection has cleared, the specialized cells cease dividing and return to their prior resting state.

These complex controls that maintain the health of the body do so in a carefully orchestrated manner. If the genes that are responsible for the control of cell division are damaged—that is, if they undergo mutation—or if the genes are broken and rearranged abnormally with other genes in the cell, the usual signals will not be received properly. Rather than ceasing when the need for cell division is no longer present and the cell-proliferation signals normally disappear, mitosis will continue.

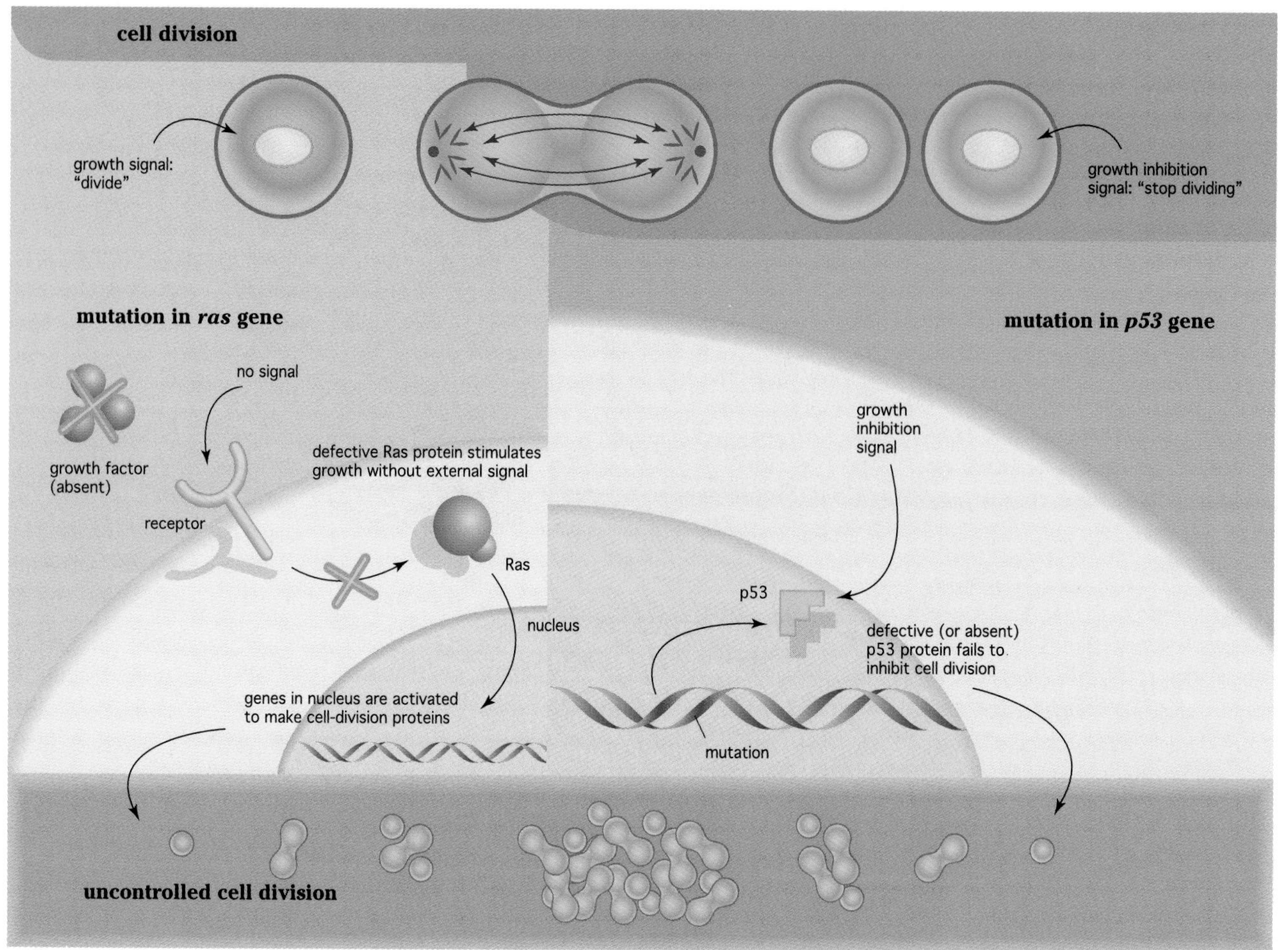

Breast cancer develops when genes responsible for the control of the division of cells in the breast are damaged, or mutate. Other malignancies form when genes in the cells of other body tissues are damaged. Leukemia, for example, results when there is an abnormal, sustained proliferation of white blood cells. Colon cancer follows the mutation of so-called growth-regulating genes in the cells of the large intestine. A tumor, or neoplasm ("new growth"), then develops.

Two main classes of genes control mitosis. The first, known as tumor-suppressor genes, control the extent of cell proliferation. The second, growth-stimulating genes, or proto-oncogenes, initiate cell division. Both work in concert to initiate and control the extent of cell growth. Genes in either class can be damaged. A damaged proto-oncogene is known as an oncogene, a gene that causes cancer.

Once cell transformation has taken place, further genetic changes (mutations in various other genes of the malignant cells) enable cancer cells from the primary neoplasm (the site of the original proliferation of abnormal cells) to

(Above left) When a mutation occurs in the *ras* proto-oncogene, its protein product, Ras, can issue signals for cell proliferation even in the absence of stimulation by external growth factors; the result is uncontrolled cell division. (Above right) The *p53* gene is a tumor-suppressor gene that is defective or missing in many inherited cancers. A damaged or absent p53 protein cannot carry out its normal function of inhibiting cell growth in response to the appropriate signal; again, the result is uncontrolled cell division.

invade surrounding tissues, migrate into blood and lymphatic vessels, and spread, or metastasize, to various other, often distant, organs of the body.

Often when primary tumors are treated with chemotherapeutic drugs, many cancer cells are killed. Some genes in cancer cells, however, confer resistance to chemotherapeutic drugs. These cells escape destruction and continue dividing. Other genes enable cells from one organ to grow in a specific "foreign" site. Malignant breast cancer cells, for example, may spread to the bones or the liver. Ma-

NCI/CNRI—Phototake

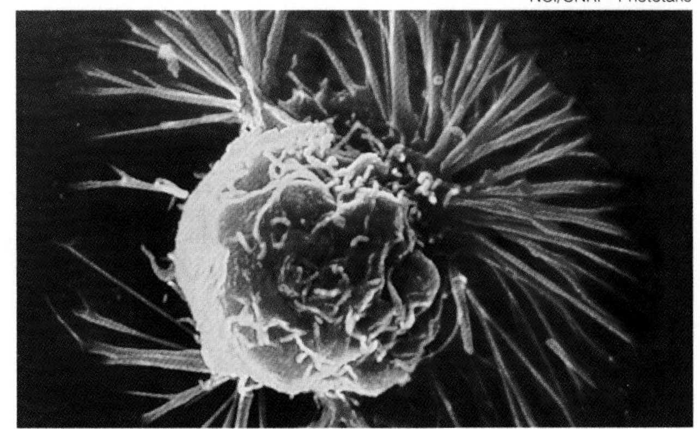

lignant skin cancer cells may migrate to the brain, where they form a metastatic tumor. The spread of the malignant cells throughout the body often results in death of the cancer patient.

Fortunately, cancer does not develop each time damage to a gene controlling cell division takes place. Random mistakes in DNA replication occur from time to time not only in genes controlling cell proliferation but in a variety of genes responsible for other properties of the cell as well.

Because genetic damage is common, cells have a mechanism for "correcting" the mistakes. Special replication-error-repair (RER) enzymes "read" the DNA, detect the damaged portions, excise them, and then repair the deleted portions of the genes. Ultraviolet (UV) rays from sunlight, for example, damage the DNA of skin cells. RER enzymes in skin cells detect the DNA damage, and the altered portions of the gene are then enzymatically excised and the missing portions replaced. With the error thus repaired, the cell functions normally.

Some individuals inherit defective RER enzymes, and those people have an unusually high incidence of skin cancer (because some damage to DNA from daily exposure to UV rays is common). In people with such defective RER enzymes, skin cancer may form even in childhood. In other instances damage to RER enzymes occurs by chance. Notably, defective RER enzymes have been found in cancer of the colon. When RER enzymes are defective, whether owing to inheritance or to chance,

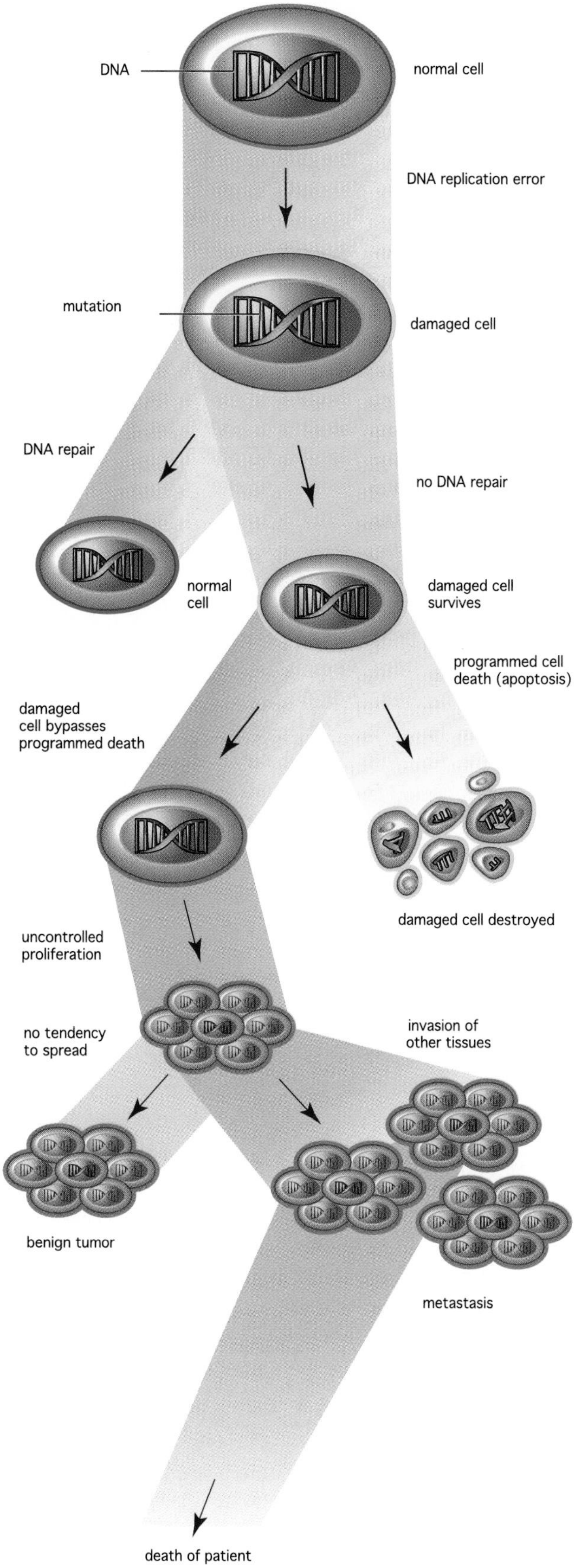

(Right) Occasionally during mitosis a mutation—an error in DNA replication—occurs. Usually the damage is repaired or the cell dies (through the process known as programmed cell death, or apoptosis). When neither happens, the cell can accumulate more mutations, eventually forming a malignant tumor. (Above) A color-enhanced photomicrograph captures a breast cancer cell as it begins to metastasize.

DNA
normal cell
DNA replication error
mutation
damaged cell
DNA repair
no DNA repair
normal cell
damaged cell survives
programmed cell death (apoptosis)
damaged cell bypasses programmed death
damaged cell destroyed
uncontrolled proliferation
no tendency to spread
invasion of other tissues
benign tumor
metastasis
death of patient

Gopal Murti—Science Source/Photo Researchers

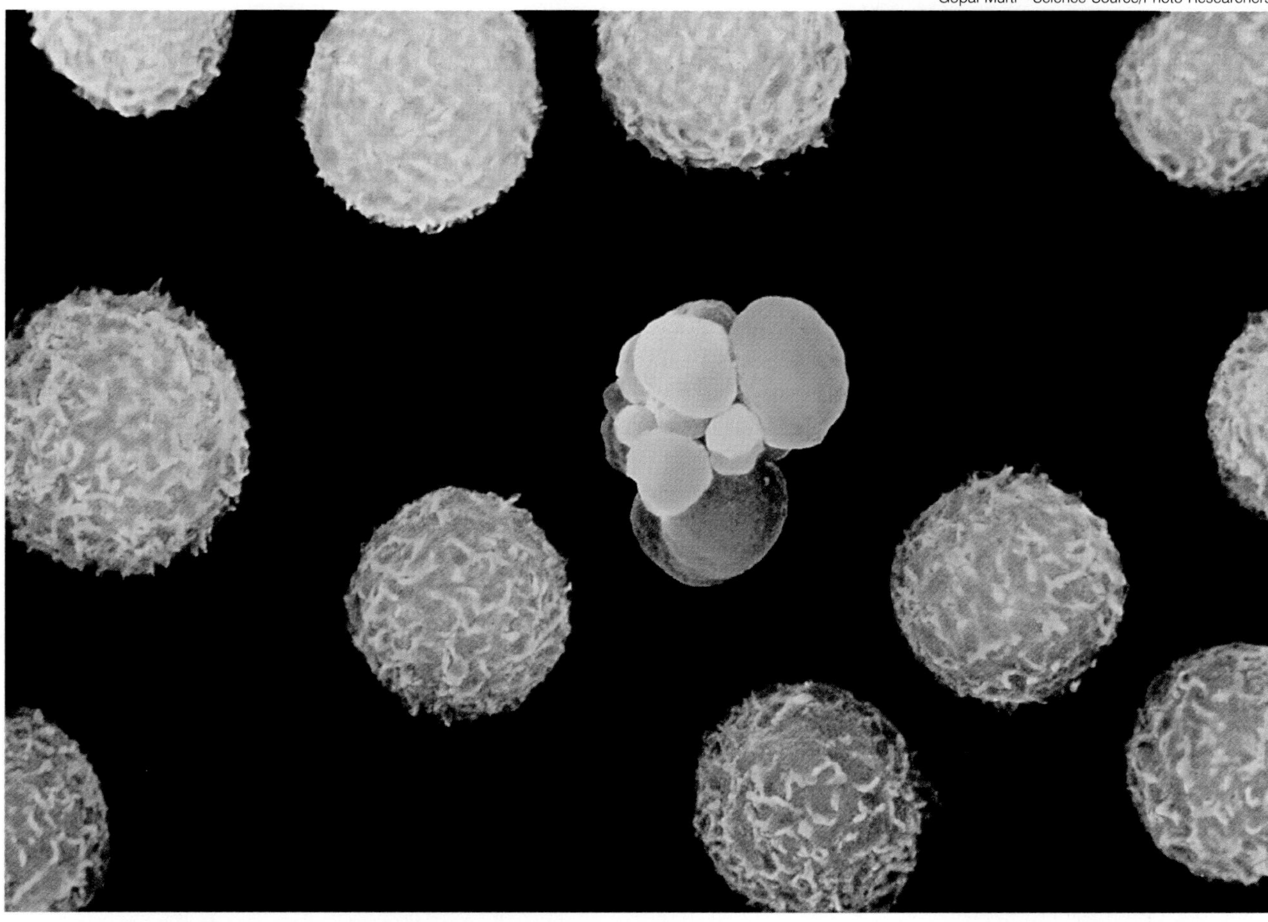

A damaged cell, surrounded by healthy ones, undergoes cell suicide (apoptosis); scavenging white blood cells eventually will absorb the debris from the destroyed cell.

random genetic errors, including errors in growth-regulating genes, cannot be repaired.

If damage to the DNA is so severe that the altered genes cannot be repaired, the cell may "commit suicide." It will die through a process known as programmed cell death, or apoptosis. At the same time, other mechanisms to prevent further damage to DNA are also activated. In the case of damage to the skin from UV rays, melanin (dark pigment) forms so as to protect further genes in skin cells from sun damage. The end result is maintenance of healthy cells and preservation of the integrity of the cells' DNA.

Mistakes in DNA replication and other forms of genetic damage occur most often when cells divide. Each time mitosis occurs, the cell's DNA is replicated and a faithful copy of the gene is passed on to each daughter cell. On rare occasions, in about one in one million cell divisions, an error in DNA replication takes place and a gene is damaged. In most instances the damaged gene is repaired or the cell dies. On one hand, then, since there are so many genes—thousands are required for maintenance of the cell—the chance is slight that a growth-regulatory gene in an individual cell will be damaged and not be repaired; the damage in that case will be of no consequence to the body. This process takes place continually. On the other hand, because the body contains so many cells (in the range of 10^{14}) and because millions of cell divisions occur daily in various organs and tissues, over time a critical growth-regulatory gene in an individual cell may be damaged. For example, excessive cell proliferation resulting from years of exposure to sunlight or the smoking of thousands of cigarettes increases the likelihood that cancer will develop. Likewise, prolonged hormonal stimulation, as occurs with early menarche (menstrual onset) and late menopause, is associated with excessive proliferation of cells in the breast and a higher-than-average risk of breast cancer.

Insights into the cancer process

In 1970 Robert DeMars, at the University of Wisconsin,

Photograph, Colin Hamilton

Works by contemporary artists (left to right) Ann Ferrer, Hannah Wilke, and Nancy Fried, shown in the exhibit "Diagnosis: Breast Cancer," curated by Mary Ann Wadden.

hypothesized that damage to two growth-regulatory genes within an individual cell was required for the normal cell to be transformed to a cancerous one. (All mammalian cells contain two, usually identical, copies of each gene. The identical copies that are present at the same relative position on chromosomes are known as alleles.) According to DeMars, damage in the same cell to both allelic copies of genes controlling cell proliferation is required for transformation.

Support for DeMars' "two-hit" hypothesis followed when Alfred G. Knudson, Jr., of the Institute for Cancer Research, Philadelphia, described families in which the incidence of retinoblastoma, a rare childhood malignancy of the retina, was unusually high. The retina is the pigmented tissue in the back of the eye that receives light. The fact that the disease was common in certain families, affecting both eyes in some individuals, suggested that it was inherited—that families with a high incidence of retinoblastoma had inherited a gene that caused the disease. Using a mathematical formula relating the frequency and incidence of the disease in the affected families, Knudson postulated that originally one of a pair of genes in the retina was inherited (*i.e.,* passed on) in a defective form from either the mother or the father. (At conception one set of chromosomes carried by a sperm joins a second set of chromosomes present in the egg. The 23 chromosomes from each parent—22 autosomes plus one sex chromosome—are duplicated as the cell divides. The fertilized egg and each cell of the body, therefore, contain copies of both sets of chromosomes.) In the case of retinoblastoma, damage to the remaining, normal gene within an individual cell in the retina occurred randomly during growth—usually during the first six years of a child's life. The cell is then converted from normal to malignant, and retinoblastoma results.

Most tumors form in individuals who are not members of families with an inherited predisposition to developing cancer. Common cancers such as cancer of the breast, lung, and colon are most often caused by damage to both alleles within the same cell. The damage occurs by chance.

Though a rare childhood tumor of the eye may seem quite a different thing from a common disease that strikes one in nine women, these findings were indeed significant; they provided greater insight into cancer's cause. For the first time, medical scientists had proof that cancer is a genetic disease—*i.e.,* it occurs at the level of a single cell of the body. The role of environmental and hormonal influences could then be unraveled.

Further support for the notion that genes normally responsible for the control of cell proliferation are defective in cancer cells came from studies of "cancer-prone" families. Frederick Li and Joseph Fraumeni, Jr., of the National Cancer Institute described a group of families in which the incidence of several kinds of cancer was unusually high—severalfold higher than might be expected among individuals in the general population. These included cancers of the breast and brain, soft-tissue sarcoma, osteosarcoma (bone cancer), leukemia (cancer of the blood-forming organs), and adrenocortical carcinoma (cancer of the adrenal glands). The fact that cancer occurred so frequently within members of the same family suggested that some of the family members had inherited the tendency to develop malignant disease, just as people inherit a predisposition for eye color. Since the malignancies first appeared when members of the cancer-prone families were adults (most were over 30 years of age), it was likely that only one of several genes required for transforming the cell from normal to malignant had been inherited in a defective form. Further damage to other growth-regulating genes would be necessary to cause cancer, the additional genetic damage occurring randomly as cell proliferation took place.

The defective growth-regulating gene that was inherited in the so-called Li-Fraumeni families has now been identified and its precise chromosomal location shown. The gene is known as *p53,* and it has been mapped precisely to 17p. The designation p53 simply means that the product of the gene is a protein of average size with a molecular weight of 53,000; 17p designates the number and short arm of the chromosome. (In humans the chromosomes from each parent are numbered arbitrarily from 1 to 22, in addition to the two sex chromosomes, X and Y.)

In Li-Fraumeni families one of the two alleles for p53 was found to be missing or defective at the time of conception. Members of the families developed cancer at a higher-than-average

"The Road Back (Self-Portrait I)," photograph (1991) by Susan B. Markisz, from a series done shortly after the artist had a modified radical mastectomy.

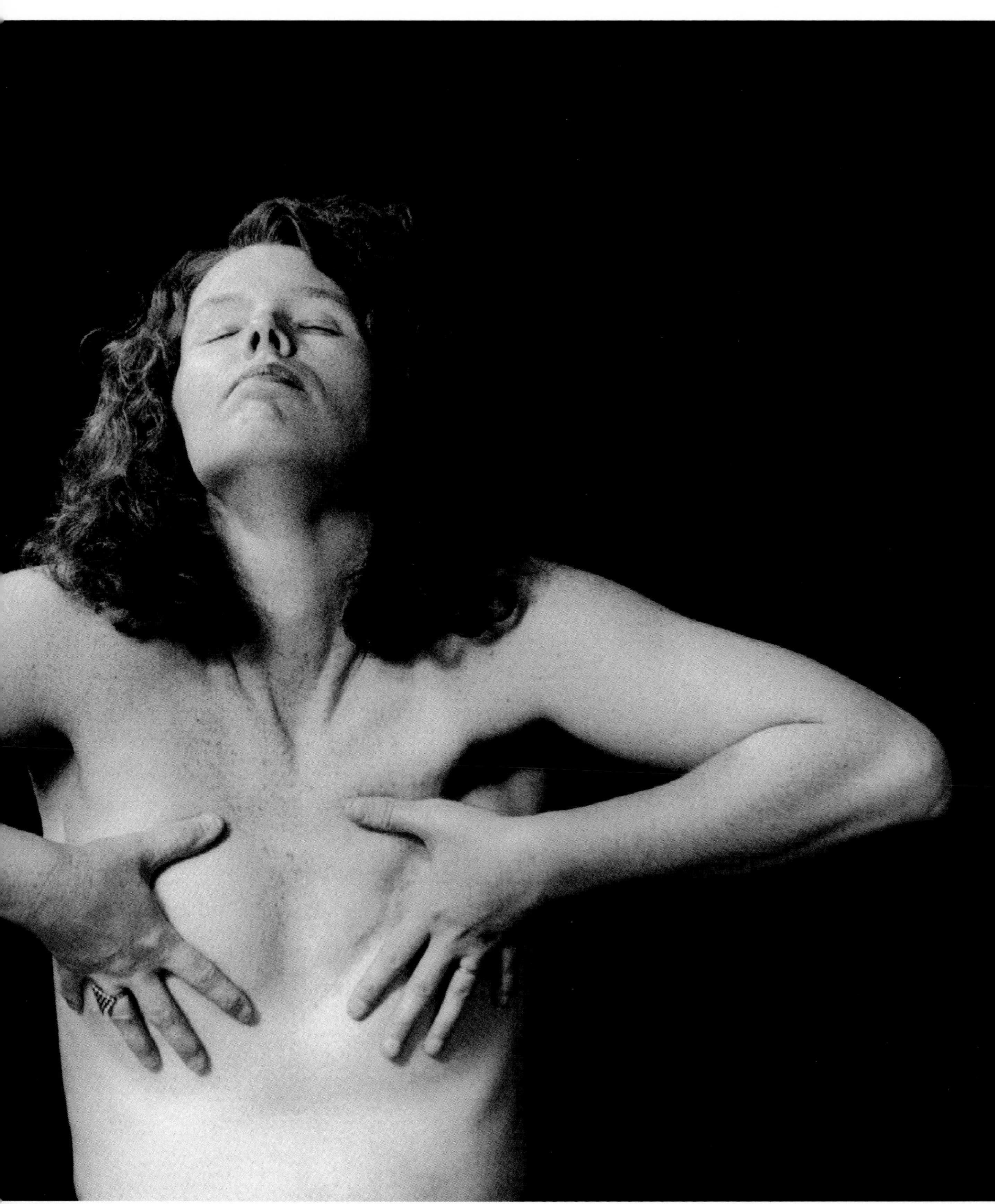

Courtesy of the "Healing Legacies" arts registry, Breast Cancer Action Group, Burlington, Vermont

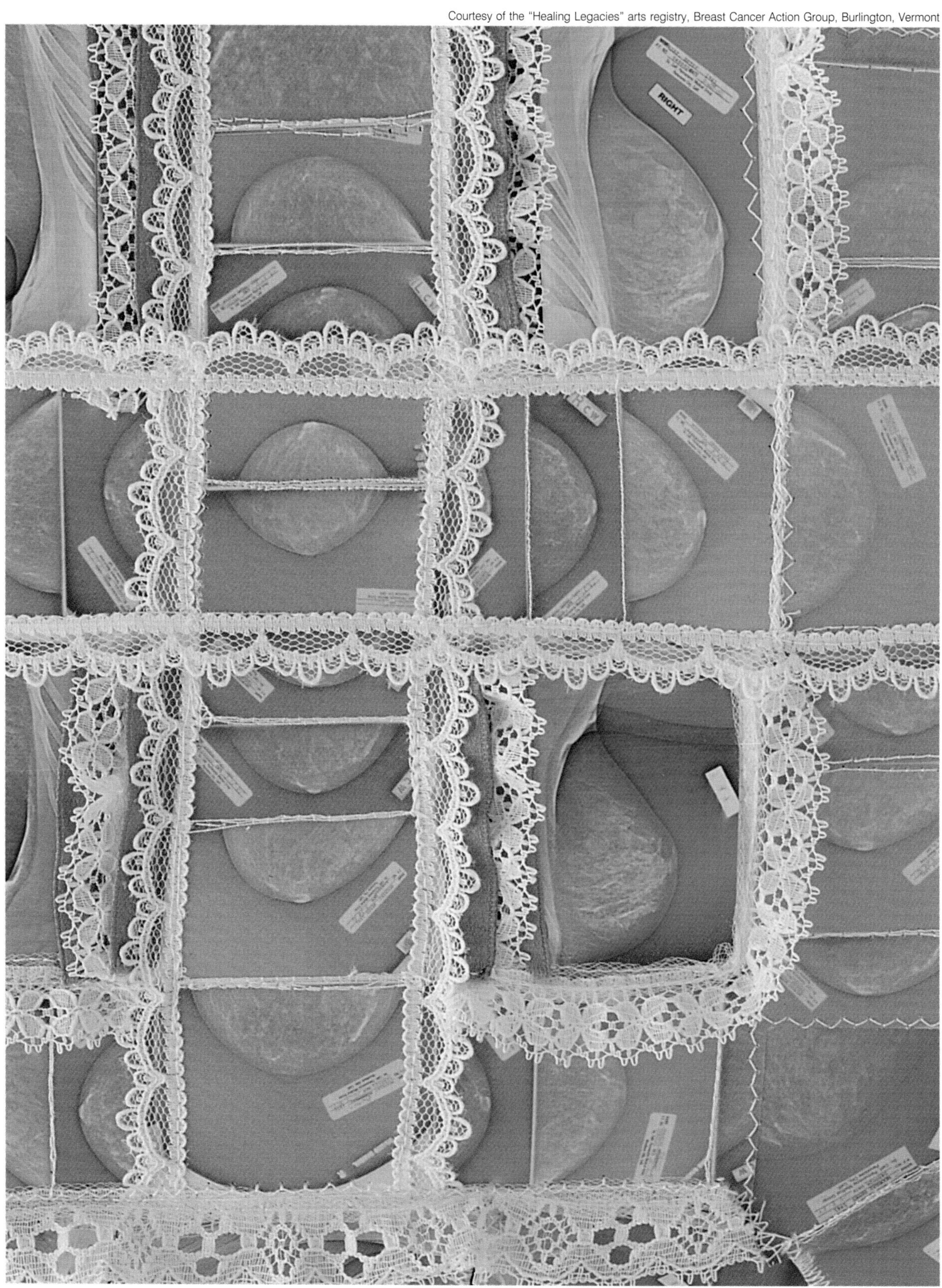

rate because the likelihood was great that damage to the remaining, normal copy of the gene for p53 in an individual cell would occur. The earlier-than-average age for tumor development in members of Li-Fraumeni families reflects the shorter period of time it takes to sustain damage to one, rather than two similarly situated, or homologous, alleles in the same cell.

The genes for p53 are altered in only about one-half of cancer patients in Li-Fraumeni families. Since the gene for p53 is normal in the tumor cells of many patients, it is likely that *p53* is only one of a number of as-yet-unidentified tumor-suppressor genes responsible for certain inherited forms of cancer.

Further clues

Bert Vogelstein and his colleagues at Johns Hopkins University School of Medicine, Baltimore, Maryland, determined that the process of cell transformation requires the alteration of multiple genes within the same cell. Vogelstein and his team compared specified genes in colon cancer cells with the analogous genes in premalignant and in normal, nonmalignant cells from the colon. Colon cancer often develops from smaller, premalignant growths in the colon known as adenomas. (Because such growths are a common finding, periodic examination of the colon to detect these generally small, nonmalignant tumors is recommended for people over age 50.) The adenomas often form a stalklike mass of cells, a polyp. The proliferation of cells forming the adenoma is partially uncontrolled, but the cells do not invade surrounding tissues. Their removal at the premalignant stage is important because cells in the adenomas frequently become malignant, and the malignant cells then metastasize.

Vogelstein found that damage to genes on chromosomes 5, 17, and 18 was present in the malignant cells, that a lesser number of genes were damaged in adenoma cells, and that the genes were undamaged in normal cells. Greater numbers of genes were damaged as the adenoma cells advanced closer to malignancy.

One gene that was altered in about 47% of cases of colorectal cancer cells is known as *ras*. *Ras* is a cancer-promoting proto-oncogene that stimulates cell proliferation. Since the gene was not damaged in all cases, other growth-promoting and growth-suppressing genes must also be involved. Clearly, development of a fully malignant tumor requires damage to multiple genes.

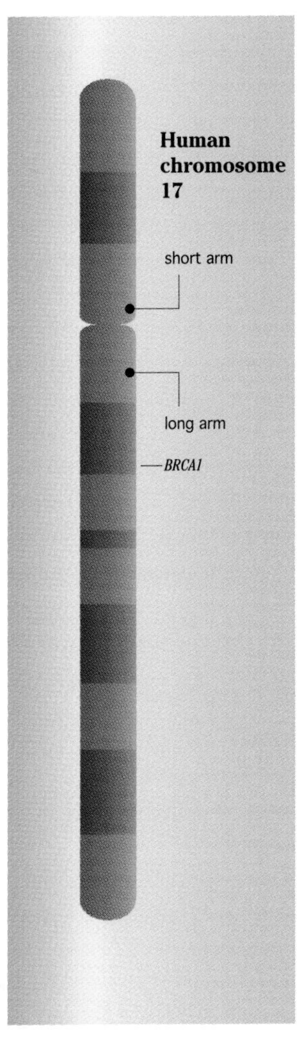

(Right) Identifying and sequencing the *BRCA1* gene on chromosome 17 was a major research breakthrough. (Below) A "breast cancer-prone family." Most inherited breast cancers strike women in susceptible families before menopause.

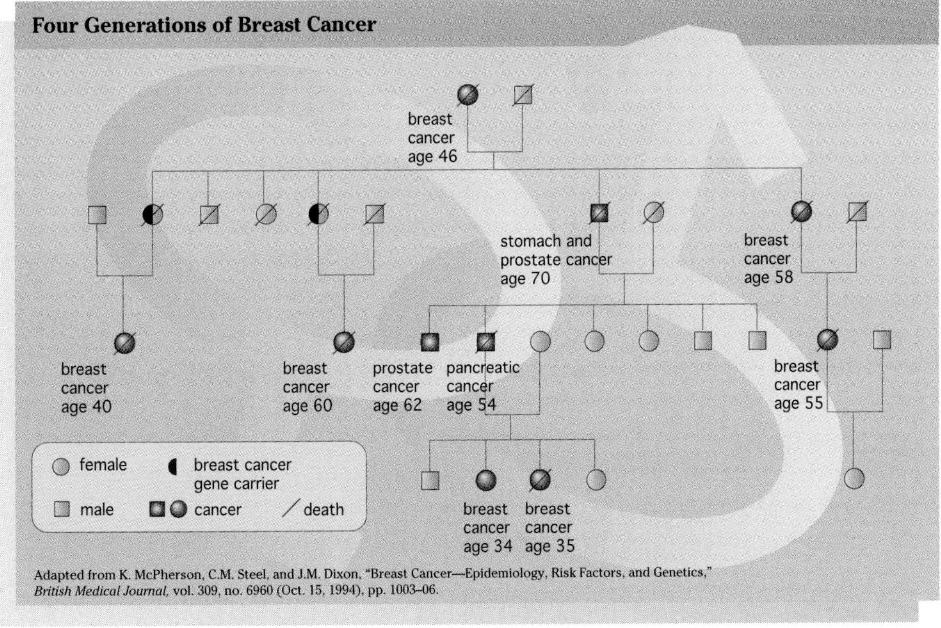

Adapted from K. McPherson, C.M. Steel, and J.M. Dixon, "Breast Cancer—Epidemiology, Risk Factors, and Genetics," *British Medical Journal*, vol. 309, no. 6960 (Oct. 15, 1994), pp. 1003–06.

(Opposite page) "Mammogram Mandala Pillow" (1994) by Betsy Carol Stock Noorzay, lace-enhanced photographs of the artist's mammogram films.

Thus, cancer is a complex, many-stepped process, resulting from an accumulation of genetic changes within an individual cell, some of which may be inherited in a defective form. The transformed cell must bypass programmed death, grow without the stimulus provided by growth factors, ignore signals that limit the extent of cell proliferation, stimulate the formation of new blood vessels to nourish the tumor mass, migrate through surrounding tissues, and finally colonize other organs at distant sites in the body.

Detection of a breast cancer gene

In an era in which the importance of a scientific advance often appears to be measured by the amount of media coverage it generates, the level of reporting of the recent identification of BRCA1, *a susceptibility gene for breast cancer on chromosome 17 and the first such gene to be isolated, suggests that this discovery is the most exciting breakthrough in modern times.*

—Barbara L. Weber, *The New England Journal of Medicine,* Dec. 1, 1994

Breast cancer is unusually common in members of certain families, which suggests that the tendency to develop the disease is inherited. Daughters of women who developed breast cancer before the age of 45 and who also have a sister with the disease have a 14-fold greater likelihood of developing breast cancer than women without such affected relatives. In the Nurses' Health Study, Graham Colditz, Walter Willett, and their colleagues at Harvard Medical School and Harvard School of Public Health associated the ages and family histories of almost 118,000 women with the risk of developing breast cancer. They found that about 6% of women with breast cancer had close family members who also had the disease. Not all women in the "breast cancer families" were affected, however. Some remained cancer-free throughout their lives, dying from other causes.

The realization that there were breast cancer families led to a search for a breast-cancer-susceptibility gene. It was likely that such a gene was inherited in a defective form. The search was carried out by medical scientists who employed molecular "probes" that bind precisely to certain segments of DNA on different chromosomes. By comparing the binding of the probes to chromosomes in both unaffected families and breast cancer families, investigators discovered that a region on the long arm of chromosome 17 was absent in a large proportion of both nonmalignant and malignant cells in women from the breast cancer families. (The gene for p53 on the short arm of the same chromosome was not involved.) Since deletion of a segment of a chromosome involves the loss of thousands of genes, the finding indicated only the general region of the chromosome in which the breast cancer gene resides. Nevertheless, this was a key first step toward the identification and cloning (*i.e.,* laboratory replication) of the breast cancer gene.

The identification of the precise breast cancer gene required the isolation and cloning of a vast number of genes contained in the general chromosomal region. Each gene had to be identified and its nucleotide sequence (the precise order of its chemical subunits) determined. The sequence was then compared with the homologous gene—the gene having the same relative chromosomal position—in members of affected as well as unaffected families (males as well as females). The pres-

(Continued on page 218)

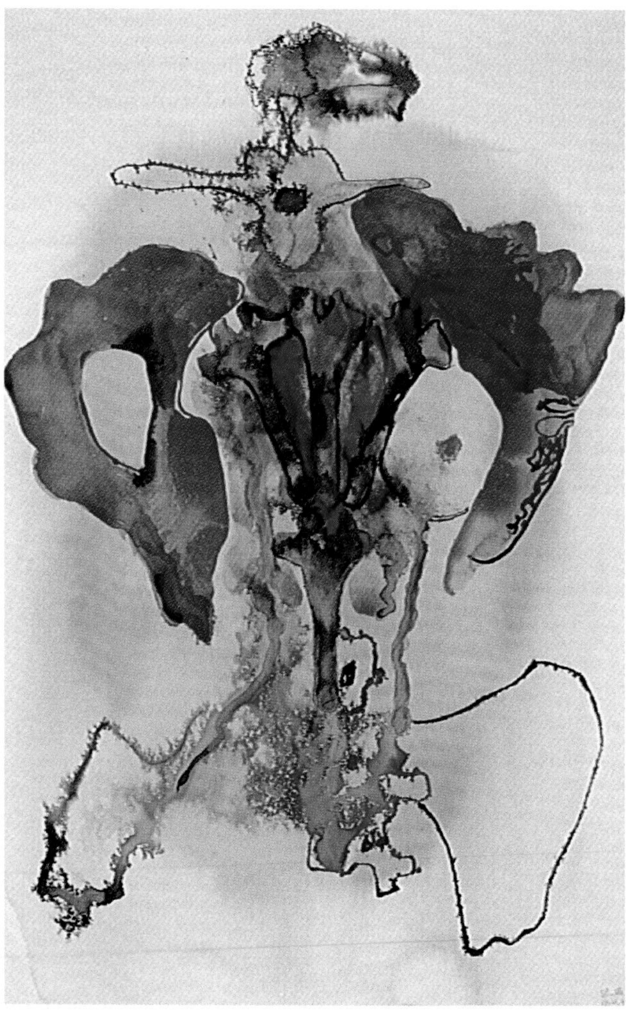

"Self-Portrait," bodyscape in watercolor, ink, and acrylic on paper (1993) by Susan Shatter.

Courtesy of the artist

Making the Most of Mammography

Because early detection of breast cancer can save lives, it is important that mammography facilities offer women high-quality mammograms. To help ensure that women get the best care, the Agency for Health Care Policy and Research (AHCPR), a branch of the United States Public Health Service, in cooperation with the Food and Drug Administration (FDA), recently issued guidelines on "Quality Determinants of Mammography," based on the recommendations of a panel of experts. The following summary of the recommendations was adapted from the 12-page AHCPR booklet Things to Know About Quality Mammograms, *Publication Number 95-0634, October 1994.*

—*Medical and Health Annual* editors

Facts about mammograms

- A mammogram is a safe, low-dose X-ray picture of the breast.
- A *screening mammogram* is a quick, easy way to detect breast cancer early, when treatment is more effective and survival is high. Usually two X-ray pictures are taken of each breast. A physician trained to read X-ray pictures—a radiologist—examines them later.
- A *diagnostic mammogram* may be done if there is a problem getting a good picture (for instance, in women with breast implants). Diagnostic mammography takes somewhat longer than screening mammography because more X-ray pictures are usually taken. A radiologist may then check the X-ray pictures while you wait.

When to call the doctor

You should call your doctor if you notice:

- a lump or thickening of the breast
- a discharge from the nipple that stains your bra or bedclothes
- dimpling of the skin of the breast

The above changes may be normal, but you should always have them checked as soon as possible.

Choosing a mammography facility

- A new law called the Mammography Quality Standards Act (MQSA) requires all U.S. X-ray facilities that do mammograms, except those that are part of the Veterans Health Administration, to be certified by the FDA. The act took effect Oct. 1, 1994.
- To find a certified mammography facility, ask your doctor, call the National Cancer Institute's Cancer Information Service toll free at 1-800-4-CANCER, or write to the FDA, MQSA Consumer Inquiries, 1350 Piccard, (HFZ-240), Rockville MD 20850.

Scheduling your mammogram

- Make your appointment for a time of month when your breasts will be least tender.
- Be prepared to answer questions the mammography facility may ask over the phone, such as whether you are pregnant, the date and place of your last mammogram, and so forth.
- Make sure you get *your own* questions answered at the same time.

Going prepared

- Wear a two-piece outfit.
- Don't use deodorant, talcum powder, or lotion under your arms or near the breasts that day (these products can show up on the X-ray).
- Bring a list of the places and dates of previous mammograms, biopsies, or other breast treatments.
- Try to relax. Studies show that most women do not find a mammogram painful.

Following up

- Always find out the results of your mammogram.
- Do not assume that your mammogram is normal just because you have not received the results.

If a mammogram uncovers a problem or a need for something to be checked further, take the following steps.

- Make sure you understand what is in question and exactly what you need to do next.
- Follow your doctor's recommendations for follow-up and schedule diagnostic mammography, if needed, as soon as possible.

Taking charge

- Ask your doctor to check your breasts as a part of any regular physical examination.
- Check your breasts yourself carefully and thoroughly each month.
- If you have a breast lump or notice a change at any time, even if your last mammogram was normal, see a doctor as soon as possible.
- Schedule any subsequent screening mammograms at the intervals recommended by your doctor; don't delay calling.

To get more information

- For general information on breast cancer and mammography, contact:
American Cancer Society
1-800-227-2345
- To obtain a copy of the booklet *Things to Know About Quality Mammograms* (English- and Spanish-language versions available), call or write:
Agency for Health Care Policy and Research
Publications Clearinghouse
PO Box 8547
Silver Spring MD 20907
1-800-358-9295

Erica Berger—Newsday

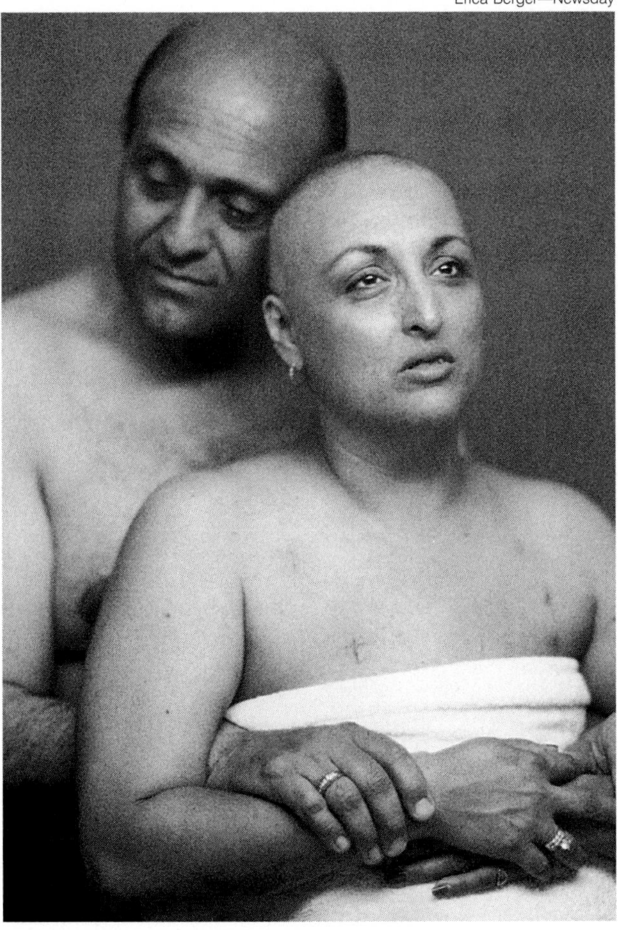

"Fran and Jerry Lenzo" (left) and "Fran in Radiation" (opposite page), photographs (1994) by Erica Berger for a *Newsday* series of profiles on women with breast cancer.

(Continued from page 216)

ence of a damaged gene only in members of the affected families would indicate that the gene was at least partly responsible for the development of breast cancer.

It was Skolnick and his coinvestigators at the University of Utah who found that a *BRCA1* gene was damaged or absent in three female members of a breast cancer family. In two healthy women in the same family, the gene was normal. The gene Skolnick identified was found to be a protein of 1,863 amino acids distributed over a large region of chromosome 17q. The mutated gene was expressed in cells in not only the breast but the ovary, thymus gland, and testes of family members.

About 0.5% of women have inherited a mutation of *BRCA1* and have an 85% lifetime risk of developing breast cancer. About half of these women—an extraordinarily high number—will develop the disease before they reach the age of 50. *BRCA1* is implicated in the development of ovarian cancer—another commonly fatal, malignant disease—as well. About 30% of women with a defect in the gene will develop ovarian cancer at an earlier-than-average age.

Breast cancer is extraordinarily rare in men because of a lack of hormonal stim-

(Continued on page 220)

Optimism on the Breast Cancer Front

For the first time in four decades, American women can celebrate winning a battle in the war against breast cancer.

The good news is that the death rate from breast cancer is finally dropping. A report from the National Cancer Institute shows that overall death rates declined nearly 5% from 1989 to 1992. And for those women between the ages of 30 and 39 who developed breast cancer, death rates fell even more—18% since 1987. Now we must build on this progress.

There are multiple reasons for our success. Advances in treatment such as chemotherapy and hormonal therapy after breast cancer surgery may be responsible. Adjuvant chemotherapy—which attacks minuscule deposits of cancer—is widely available but is not used enough, especially for women without health insurance. In addition, increased public awareness about self-examination and mammography screening, coupled with changes in diet and exercise, may have improved survival rates.

These gains did not happen by accident. During the 1980s women called for society to open its eyes and recognize the pain and misery inflicted by this disease. Women demanded more research, more national public education campaigns, and a comprehensive federal effort to find answers about the causes of the disease and to discover new treatment and prevention strategies.

In the last year, there have been major breakthroughs, including the discovery of the *BRCA1* gene, which will help us understand hereditary risks and possibly more.

We found that mammography screening rates were far too low. We added funds for education and outreach efforts. Screenings, however,

Erica Berger—Newsday

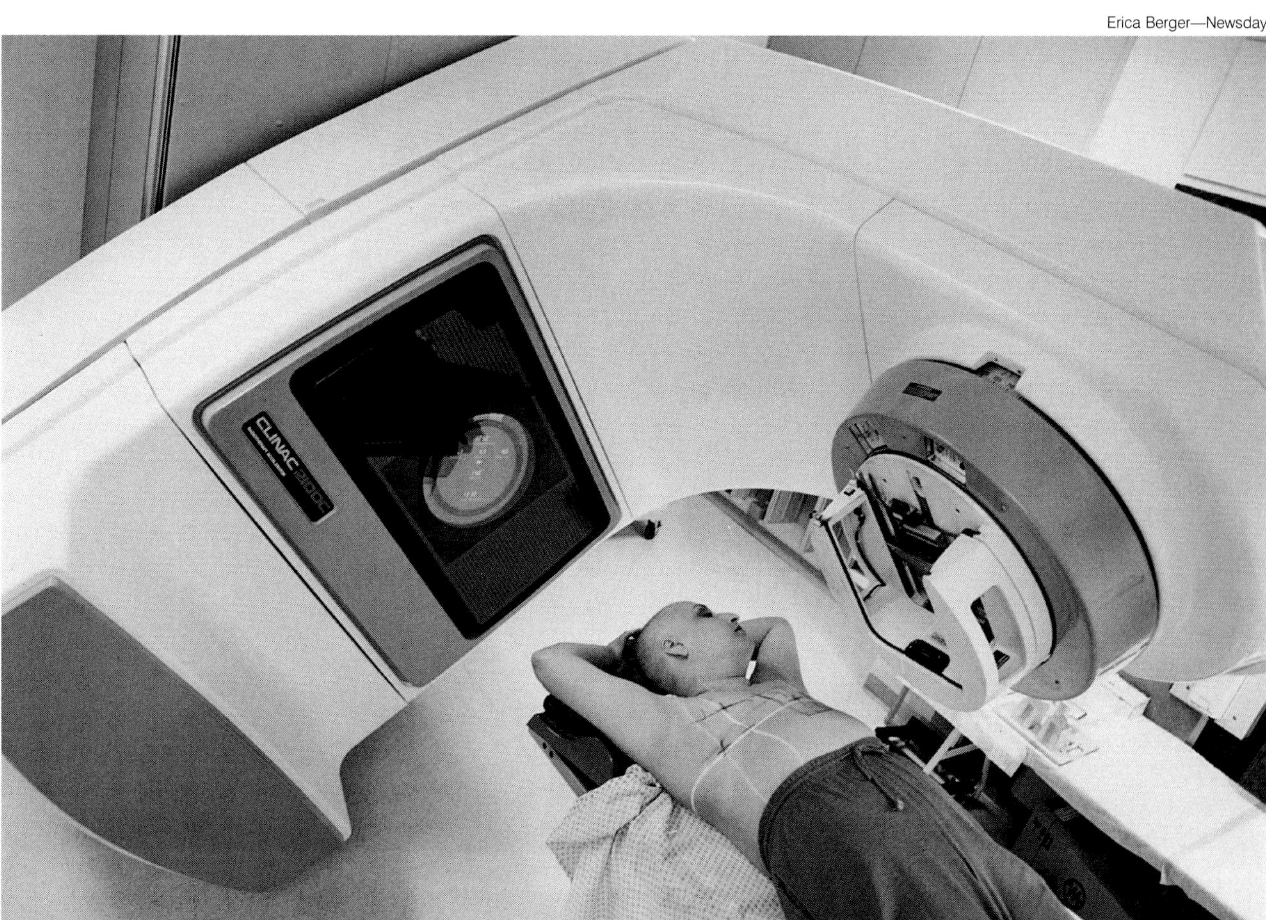

remain too low among the very women most likely to benefit; only 50% of older women in the U.S. have had a mammogram in the past year. To turn that around, we are launching a national initiative to increase older women's use of the lifesaving mammography benefit provided by Medicare.

We also found that women were receiving unreliable mammograms and were not getting appropriate exams, and we stepped in. The 10,000 mammography facilities around the country must now be certified by the Food and Drug Administration. But we did not stop there. We also developed guidelines for the prompt notification of mammography results, so women get notice within 10 days.

In addition, we saw the need for greater partnership in research in both the public and private spheres. Imaging technology that first made it possible to spot missiles from thousands of miles above the Earth is now being adapted to detect tiny tumors in the breast.

And finally, we convened government policy makers, consumer advocates, and scientists to craft a National Action Plan on Breast Cancer. Implemented by the Public Health Service's Office on Women's Health, this landmark plan has laid out the first nationwide strategy to explore and expand research into the causes of breast cancer. It has sought to involve more women, especially minority women, in clinical research trials, and among other projects it is developing a tissue and data resource bank to increase scientific knowledge.

Yet even as we celebrate our successes, there is much more to do. While it is true that the overall death rate for breast cancer declined, breast cancer death rates among African-American women increased 2.6%. This disparity must end.

About 46,000 American women will die from breast cancer in 1995. That may include someone you know. There may be something you can do to help.

In the months ahead, as we continue to debate the role of the federal government, we are certain to find even greater strength and success in situations where we lock arms in partnership. By working together, we can realize safer, healthier futures for all Americans.

—Donna E. Shalala,
U.S. Secretary of Health
and Human Services

Photograph, Dean E. Johnson

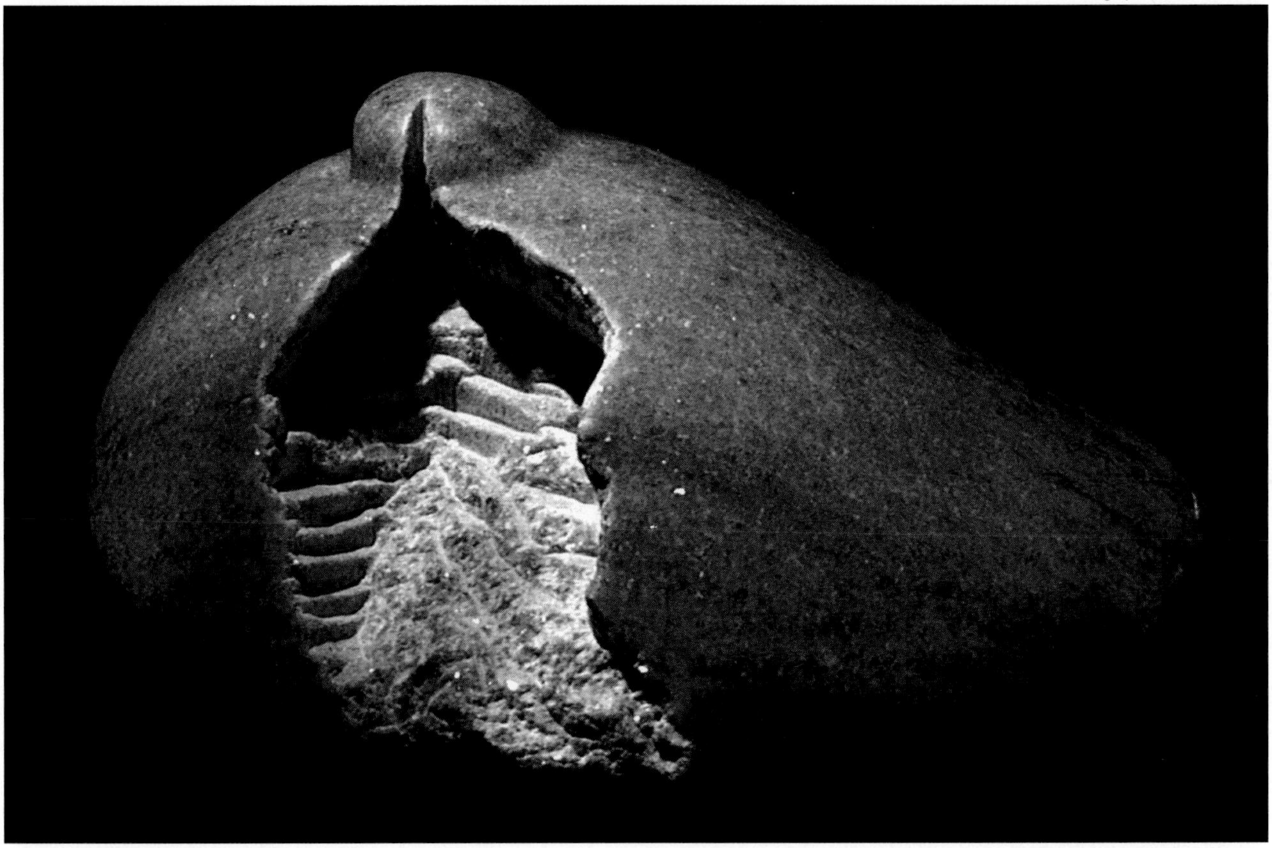

"Abandoned Quarry" (1994), carved from Brazilian green marble by Susan Falkman, from the solo sculpture show "Body Memories," a traveling exhibition dedicated to the artist's close friend Jean Scott, whose breast cancer was diagnosed in 1993.

(Continued from page 218)
ulation and proliferation of cells in the breast.

Mutation or deletion of the *BRCA1* gene has not been found in women who have the most common, noninherited (*i.e.,* sporadic) forms of breast or ovarian cancer, so it is not responsible for the most common forms of these two cancers of women. Other, as-yet-unidentified growth-regulating genes therefore must also be involved. Moreover, as not all cases of breast cancer in breast cancer families are accompanied by a mutation of *BRCA1* (as noted above, the gene is damaged in about one-half of the cases), a second breast cancer gene must be present in these individuals, and there may be others as well.

In 1994 a second susceptibility gene was mapped to chromosome 13 by Michael Stratton and Doug Easton and colleagues at the Institute of Cancer Research, Sutton, England, and David Goldgar and colleagues at the University of Utah. The precise chromosomal position of the gene, however, has yet to be specified. Known as *BRCA2,* the gene is defective in about 70% of breast cancer cases in which *BRCA1* is not involved. *BRCA2* has also been associated with a slightly, but significantly, increased risk of breast cancer in men. Mutations of *BRCA2* are not found in patients with ovarian cancer. Just how the *BRCA1* and *BRCA2* genes are able to control the proliferation of cells in the breast is still unclear but under active investigation.

A susceptibility test: the next step?

> *The goal is to help the next generation of women not have to face death from breast cancer.*
>
> —Mary-Claire King, Ph.D., Sarah Rowell, M.P.H., and Susan M. Love, M.D., *Journal of the American Medical Association,* April 21, 1993

The identification of breast-cancer-susceptibility genes makes possible a test to detect individuals who are at risk of developing breast cancer—to "screen" for a predisposition to the disease. Such a screen could identify now-healthy individuals who, owing to their inheritance, are at high risk of developing the disease at some future time. Women in breast cancer families could also learn if they were *not* at greater-than-average risk.

Such a test could be readily performed; scientists

now have the tools and the skills. DNA would be extracted from white blood cells of presently healthy women. The sample would be analyzed for a mutation of *BRCA1* and *BRCA2*.

The development of a genetic screen to predict which women will develop breast cancer at some future time would be of immense value. Women who knew that they were likely to develop the disease could have frequent mammograms and periodic examinations to detect tumor development at the earliest possible time. Removal of malignant lesions before metastasis has occurred can cure the disease. The early removal of a cancer of the breast, however, does not mean that another tumor will not occur; tumors might still appear in the remaining breast tissue.

In some circumstances women who are members of breast cancer families and are found to be at high risk might choose to undergo removal of both breasts in early adulthood. In instances in which *BRCA1* was found to be damaged, they might wish to have both ovaries removed as well. These are obviously very radical steps that involve difficult choices. Removal of breasts and/or ovaries would not be considered in women without mutations of *BRCA1* or *BRCA2*.

The proponents of a breast cancer test point out that the decision to have prophylactic ovary and breast removal could be made by a susceptible woman after she has had children and her family is under way. Still, the psychological harm that might occur in women who learn that they are at risk could be severe. They would live with the knowledge that they are likely to develop the disease and that their daughters might also; the choice would be having disfiguring surgery to prevent cancer versus taking the chance of developing a possibly fatal disease in the near or distant future. Women who learned they were not likely to develop cancer might suffer guilt and have great anxiety about affected sisters.

For certain serious inherited diseases, such predictive tests are already available. Huntington's disease is an example. In some instances healthy members of a family in which a disease is commonly present have chosen not to have a predictive test performed; they prefer not to know. Unlike breast cancer, however, in the case of Huntington's disease, nothing can be done to prevent the disease if a mutation in the critical gene is found to be present.

In addition to psychological considerations, predictive tests for breast cancer susceptibility present certain technical problems because the gene is relatively large and the site of mutation varies. Numerous tests would have to be performed in each woman in order to be certain that a mutation did not exist and she was not at risk. The possibility of "false negatives" is an important concern; women at risk might be told—wrongly—that no excessive danger was present. Furthermore, such a test would not be able to predict breast cancer in the vast majority of women—those who do not have a familial predisposition.

Much has yet to be learned about breast cancer and its development and prevention. Nonetheless, because so many women in the world are affected, the importance of these new discoveries cannot be overemphasized.

Howard Sochurek—Medical Images, Inc.

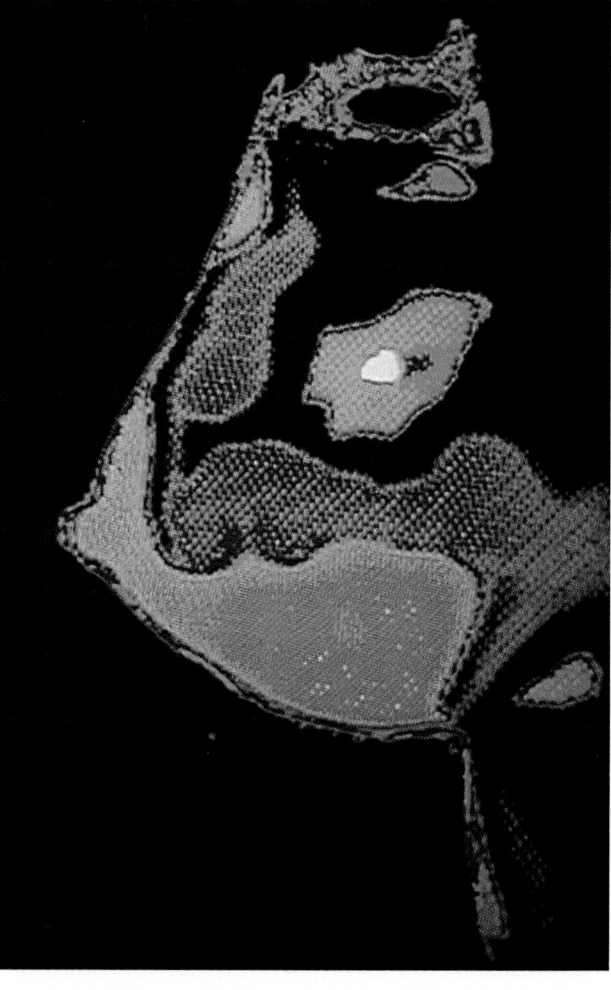

High-quality mammograms can save lives. (Above) A color-enhanced X-ray shows an early tumor (white spot in center of breast).

Coping with Breast Cancer: A Message for Men

When Jim Feldman, a Chicago-area businessman, learned that his wife, Susan, had been diagnosed with breast cancer, he wanted to do all he could for her. But he, too, needed help coping. When he looked for support, he found that "nothing was available for the man." All of the literature he could find "was geared to the medical or psychological problems of the woman." Feldman established a fund at the Y-ME National Breast Cancer Organization to remedy that situation. The 16-page booklet When the Woman You Love Has Breast Cancer *(1994)—Feldman's "living memorial" to Susan, who died in 1989—was the result of their joint efforts. The following text is adapted from that publication with the kind permission of Y-ME. Unlike other resources, it addresses the emotional struggles of* men *and the important ways that they can help their partners through the crisis of breast cancer.*

—Medical and Health Annual editors

An important role

If your wife or partner has been diagnosed with breast cancer, it is important that you become an integral part of her healing. Of course, your partner must make the final decisions regarding her treatment with her doctor. It is important, however, that you listen to her feelings and fears, learn about treatment options, and become involved in her care.

You may feel a lot of conflicting emotions right now. The traditional male role—solving problems and acting knowledgeable, protective, and in charge—may be causing you turmoil. You may even be experiencing guilt over worrying about your own emotional pain. These feelings are normal as you and your partner try to come to terms with the diagnosis of breast cancer.

Initial doctor's visit/diagnosis

When first confronted with a breast cancer diagnosis, your wife or partner may experience fear, denial, frustration, isolation, confusion, guilt, anxiety, and a sense of betrayal. Many women understandably change their everyday priorities, putting themselves first. This new attitude may be confusing or disturbing to you. She may distance herself from you, physically and emotionally, to protect you from potential loss. Her feelings of helplessness, hopelessness, or despair may be compounded by her need to change from being the family caretaker to becoming the one who needs care. She may be afraid of becoming a burden on you, your children, other family, and even her health care team. She will also fear changes in appearance and sexuality. Some suggestions: cry together, encourage her.

You may also be feeling fear, anger, denial, and a sense of betrayal. You may

Illustrations by Jody Hewgill

"Husbands or partners of women with breast cancer often do not know others in the same situation because it is not something that is discussed. Men are supposed to be strong. We have often been brought up to believe that we are capable of handling setbacks, that 'real men don't cry.'"

feel that you have to adopt the stereotypical role of the man who is "strong." And as a man, you may not be oriented toward expressing or even acknowledging your deepest feelings. Critical issues for you are likely to be anxiety over the future and the possible loss of your wife or partner. Such thoughts may trigger fears regarding your own mortality. Many men feel guilty over this, so it is important to recognize that your fears and feelings of guilt are normal and common.

It is also normal for you to worry. Studies conducted with husbands of breast cancer patients found that the husbands went through a variety of emotional and psychosomatic problems—including eating and sleeping disorders. They also had a significant amount of anxiety before and after their partner's surgery.

You may feel overwhelmed—that the news has come so quickly that you have had no time to prepare. You may be in great pain and not want your loved ones to see you this way; you may even want to seek counseling without your wife. Support groups for men, though still relatively rare, are available.

You may also have needs that are quite strong at this point—for information as well as for choice and control. State openly what you need, and give yourself permission to experience these feelings fully.

Sometimes keeping a journal may help to give you a sense of control. This may be especially useful during treatment and subsequent doctor's visits. It can be helpful to record every doctor's visit—to write down the date and time, anything that needs to be checked or followed up on later, and every procedure suggested or performed. Write down what you are *feeling* as well. At this point you may also want to tape-record consultations, request photographs of women after surgery, request printed information regarding treatment options, and carefully prepare your own questions. During treatment you can be supportive in a number of important roles: coordinator of social support, monitor of normal functioning, patient advocate, and even physician's assistant.

Whenever one partner gets sick, a couple's usual patterns of give and take and dependence and independence are altered. Serious illness can bring a couple closer together. However, like any crisis, it can also disclose shortcomings in your relationship.

Once your partner has been diagnosed with cancer, your relationship very likely will change. With open, trusting communication, that change can be positive. Tell your wife or partner what you are feeling. Establish clear and open communication; avoid mind reading and do not make assumptions.

"I don't care how well you're put together, you never imagine the best; you always imagine the worst. So you're immediately devastated. You feel hopeless; you don't even have time to think reasonably."

Talk in specifics, and attempt to feel comfortable with a free exchange of ideas. Express your feelings and "own" them; that is, use "I" messages. When your partner tells you something, listen without becoming defensive. Make sure you understand her message. Give feedback so that she knows how you feel about what was said—express your viewpoint during the conversation, not several days later.

Communication can also be physical—as simple as holding hands. Comforting your partner in this manner may make you feel better.

Build on the strong, positive areas of your relationship to help feel closer and enjoy each other. Strive for cooperation coupled with independence, and place a high value on flexibility:

- demonstrate mutual love, respect, and understanding
- maintain independent identities, and accept each other as separate individuals
- give each other privacy
- trust each other
- make a commitment to tough it out together

Direct, open communication should also be extended to the family so that you and your wife have as large a support system as possible. Family and friends cannot offer help if they do not know you are in a crisis. If children are not told, they will sense that something is wrong, and confusion will be added to their concern.

Cancer is not contagious, and sexual activity will not make cancer worse. You cannot "catch" it by kissing, hugging, or having intercourse; a cancer cell from one person's body cannot take root in another's.

Treatment options

You and your partner may feel pressured to decide on a course of treatment in a brief period of time. This can make you feel powerless and confused. Give your wife the opportunity to communicate her feelings and fears. Become involved with her doctors and nurses. Take an interest in her treatments as well. Such support can help her better tolerate the necessary treatments.

Become informed; read and talk with your partner and her doctors about all possible therapies. Sometimes you and your partner will interpret what you read or hear differently. This very difference can become the basis of intelligent decision making. By becoming informed, you and your loved one can make important decisions together with confidence. Information is available from libraries, doctors' offices, the National Cancer Institute's Cancer Information Service, and the Y-ME National Breast Cancer Organization (*see* below).

After surgery

After surgery—whether radical or partial mastectomy or lumpectomy—your partner may have feelings of embarrassment or low self-esteem, as well as physical discomfort. Though she needs emotional support at this point, she may find it tiring to deal with too many well-meaning friends. She may have to conserve her energy and screen out those individuals whose interaction is not helpful. You may have to mediate between your partner and her friends and relatives; when she is tired, explain to others that she appreciates their concern but is not up to seeing them that day.

"Ask every question that crosses your mind. Do not be intimidated by a doctor. If you don't understand the answer, ask your question again. Tell the doctor, 'I don't understand what you're saying' or 'Can you explain that to me again?' Every time any doctor says, 'We're going to do such-and-such,' you need to ask the question 'Why?'"

Try to be at the hospital as much as possible. Be optimistic, but do not promise miracles. Reinforce genuine hopes and promise her what you can guarantee; for example, let her know that you will not abandon her. Acknowledge her anger, confusion, and frustration. And because a positive attitude may actually aid her fight against cancer, help her keep an optimistic frame of mind.

Many men have trouble acting as a support system for their partner while coping with their own emotions. While you need to be strong for her, you may be feeling guilty, lonely, or abandoned. You may be afraid of what would happen if you were to become ill now, since everyone depends on you.

You may have feelings of fear and even repulsion—these are natural. Generally, however, it is not your partner's superficial change

"By going through these monumental concerns one after the other–discussing my wife's breast cancer with Y-ME and with doctors–I put the whole thing in a better perspective. I realized that it's something you can handle–it isn't beyond you; it isn't bigger than you."

in appearance that affects you so strongly but rather its psychological significance to you. The fear of losing your wife or partner may cause you to withdraw affection and sexual intimacy as part of a larger, more harmful process of withdrawal. In other words, if you cannot look at her scar, you may be expressing deeper feelings—perhaps anger over suddenly being responsible for the children or fear at being reminded of your own vulnerability.

Many men also feel a real sense of loss. It is unrealistic to expect a man to have no reaction whatsoever when his lover loses part or all of her breast. For these reasons, you may have to make as many adjustments as she does.

Couples should go through the entire process—diagnosis, treatment, and recovery—as partners. Communication is important; silence on either of your parts may be misinterpreted as a lack of interest.

During recovery, men may feel cut off from the information flow, and this may leave them isolated and angry. Just as you helped your partner gather information before treatment, however, you can continue to take a proactive role during treatment, especially with physicians. This can be very valuable, as your partner may forget to bring up an important point. For example, one man whose wife has kidney disease questioned the doctor about the use of chemotherapy drugs, which are metabolized through the kidneys. The husband arranged for her oncologist and kidney specialist to talk to one another, and a modified chemotherapy program was used.

Communication and information are also very important for sexual health after cancer treatment. When you know what to expect, it is easier to have a meaningful discussion about potential challenges to this aspect of your relationship.

Perhaps nothing can prepare your partner (and you) for the shock of what her chest may look like. Acknowledging that the loss of a breast is very sad for both of you begins the grieving and promotes the healing process.

Looking at the scar together will help you both adjust to the physical changes. The sooner a couple can look at the scar—preferably before leaving the hospital—the sooner they can deal with the fact that the breast is gone (or, in the case of a lumpectomy, that a scar is present). Remember that most scars are at first red and raw, but with time they fade and are much less frightening.

Sexual issues can arise after surgery because the loss of a breast can damage a woman's sense of attractiveness and self-esteem. She may be embarrassed in certain sexual positions, such as the woman on top, since the scar is more noticeable in that position. Or she may have pain or stiffness in her arms and shoulders, especially after axillary dissection (surgery involving her armpit area). You may want to avoid positions that put weight on her shoulders or arm. It can be helpful to support these areas with pillows during intercourse.

Sexual activity is usually safe during and after cancer treatment. Check with your doctor if you have questions.

Coming home after surgery, your wife may suddenly feel lonely or disoriented because her extensive medical and psychological support team at the hospital is not immediately available. Discuss these concerns with her. Help her develop new sources of support among family and friends. Many women find it helpful to develop a buddy system with another breast cancer survivor at this time.

She may be emotionally distant; her body mobilizes all of its resources to combat infections and restore strength, and her mind focuses on how bad she feels and what she must do to get better. These things can change the way she feels about her body, herself, or her sexual activity.

New priorities

You may feel overwhelmed by the changes in your partner and in your own household responsibilities. You cannot do everything; do

what you can. Help your wife with household chores, but encourage her to do what she can because a regular schedule can be very therapeutic.

It is very important to let your partner know that you accept her because of who she is. Be understanding. Love her. Reassure her. Be kind and sympathetic. Help change dressings and give back rubs. And encourage her to begin or maintain an exercise routine. Regular exercise is very helpful both physically and emotionally.

Contrary to myth, few marriages in which the wife had breast cancer end in divorce, and most of these divorces are due to preexisting problems. Typically, relationships that were strong before the diagnosis of breast cancer remain strong after surgery and treatment.

Nonetheless, you should expect a shift in her priorities and a change in your roles. Very likely, nothing will be as it was. You may find yourself less attracted to your wife yet still so in love that it hurts. Perhaps you will find yourself treating her too delicately. In some cases the adjustments you have to make—both sexual and in daily life—may disturb or annoy you.

Be ready to make changes. Examine what is important. Relax housekeeping standards, prepare simpler meals, and have children take on additional chores. Other family members can also help. Sort out necessary tasks from those that can go undone.

Be honest with your wife. Tell her that while she may have changed physically, your love for her is unchanged. Share how you would feel if you lost her.

Communication should also extend to sexual intimacy. Both of you should talk about your sexual feelings and desires. Your wife may feel that her sexuality has been diminished, and she may think that you feel that way too. She may have trouble communicating her fears, and if you wait for signals from her to talk about it, no one will take that first, necessary step. Communication can overcome feelings of isolation and rejection.

Reestablishing a sexual relationship is essential to your relationship and to your wife's healing process. Remember that what is normal for you and your wife is whatever gives you pleasure together. One-fourth to one-third of couples have sexual difficulties following surgery, so reestablishing a sexual relationship may take time.

After your partner has come home from the hospital, increase nonsexual intimacy. Physical contact in general—a hug, a touch, hand-holding, kisses on the lips—can take place for its own sake, not as a prelude to sex.

A woman's sexual feelings may be changed by her perception of her altered body image as well as by overt depression or even unconscious mood changes. Women say that their most pressing need at this time is to be held, but they are concerned that their husband will be offended if this is not an invitation to lovemaking.

Typically, a man will be relieved to discover that his partner is not rejecting him. And he is often pleased that he can offer something of value to his wife—by showing affection, he can make her feel more secure, loved, and protected. When you spend intimate time together, try to put day-to-day problems on hold.

You may have a fear of hurting your wife during lovemaking. In that case, you should talk with her about sexual positions that are more comfortable for her.

"Every time she looks in the mirror, goes into the bath, holds her children, is in bed with her husband, cancer faces her. The woman sees the reaction in the faces of her family members. Nothing but love and understanding can help."

Further treatments

Chemotherapy is given in cycles; a regimen is repeated every few weeks. Each chemotherapy agent has its own side effects, most of which are temporary—lasting hours to days. Some women will have none, others many. This does not reflect the severity of the disease, only the individual's tolerance to these drugs.

There are medications that can relieve some of these side effects, but some doctors do not routinely prescribe them. If your partner's side effects seem particularly severe, ask the doctor whether intervention is available to relieve the symptoms.

Many women feel fatigued. Encourage your wife to be active, to see friends, to work if possible, but allow her extra time to rest. Let her know you understand how she feels by volunteering to do tasks she normally does without making her feel guilty. Nausea can make her even less active. Medications can help. A change in diet often helps.

"I think that, on the whole, men do the right thing. There are stories of men who have walked out, but I would like to think that's rare. I think basically that if a man loves the woman, he knows what he's going to do."

Not all chemotherapy causes hair loss, and some women experience only partial baldness. Ask the doctor what can be expected on her particular drug regimen. Hair loss, when it occurs, is devastating to most women. With breast cancer, personal body image concerns are already present—but baldness lets the world know. Remind your partner that her hair will grow back, that she is beautiful to you, and that she is still very much loved. Go with her to shop for wigs.

Subtle side effects can occur with chemotherapy: dry skin, cracked nails, and mouth sores. All are temporary, but these small inconveniences can become a major irritant. Remind her that hair loss and other chemotherapy side effects are generally temporary. If she develops menopausal symptoms, loss of menses, hot flashes, or vaginal dryness, she may be dealing with one more issue—she may feel a loss of "femininity." Hot flashes come unexpectedly and can disturb sleep and normal activities.

A cancer patient can reduce the nausea from chemotherapy by learning relaxation skills. By making sure that when she comes home from treatment she is not overwhelmed by food smells, you can help reduce nausea brought on by chemotherapy. You might also want to have herbal teas, crackers, and other bland things to eat available.

For the woman undergoing it, radiation therapy can be fatiguing—it is given every day for five to seven weeks after lumpectomy. Every treatment is a reminder to the woman of her diagnosis and her mortality, which makes this a stressful time.

Often, because the immediate side effects are milder, radiation therapy is easier than chemotherapy. Most women have a skin reaction, which is something like a bad burn that constantly aches. The breast can swell and may hurt and feel heavy. Sexual breast play can be very uncomfortable at this time.

Radiation therapy or surgery can also cause lymphedema, swelling around the breast, or under and down the arm, caused by a buildup of lymphatic fluid. It may occur suddenly after radiation, or it may be brought on by physical exertion following treatment.

For some women, especially those with severe cases, lymphedema can be devastating; their arms may not fit

"During my wife's illness we became closer mentally and less close physically. She was embarrassed. She did not want to be touched in a sexual way. We held each other, we talked, we watched TV, listened to music . . . as close friends."

"Support, participation, and discussion are needed during these times. Women have told me that they could face the hair loss, the skin changes, and all the other side effects if they just knew that their loved ones would stand by them."

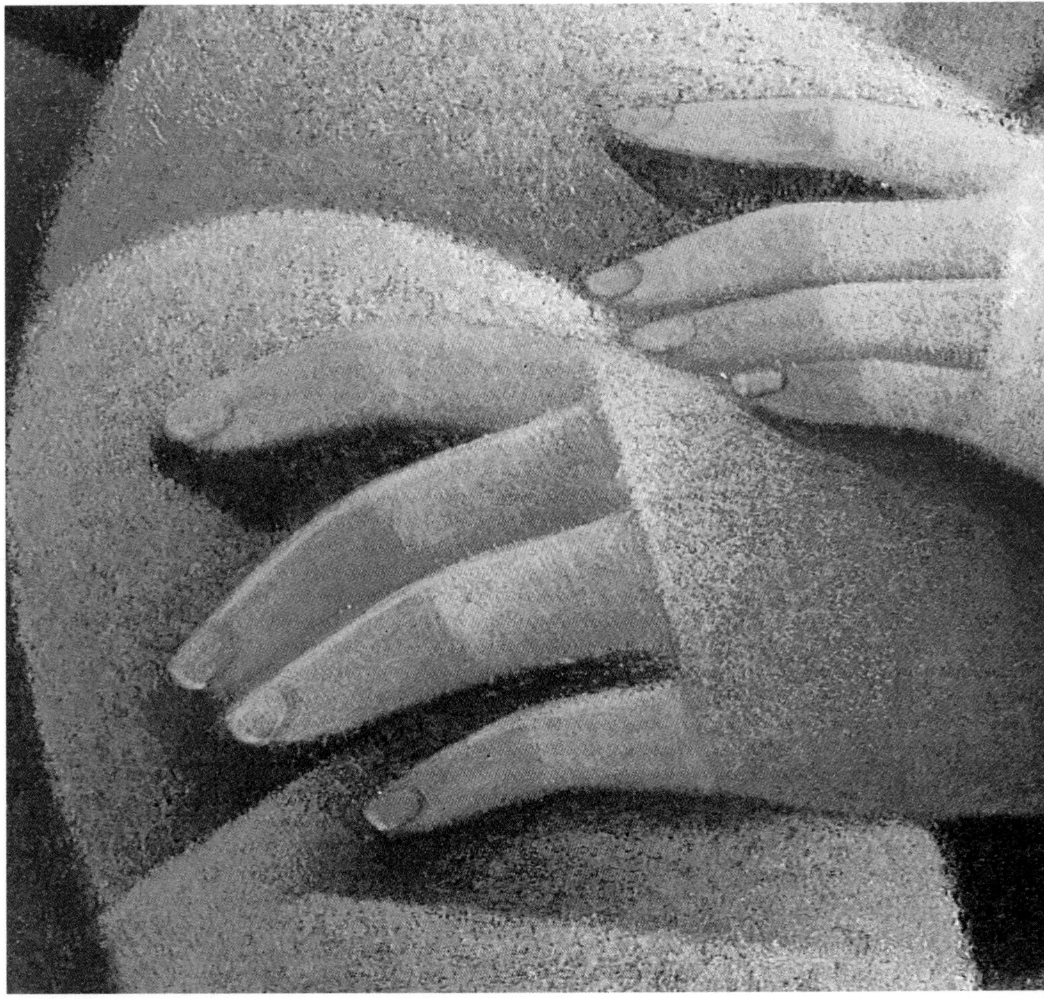

into their clothes, and they may have to wear a special elastic sleeve. To keep swelling to a minimum, encourage your wife to perform appropriate exercises and to avoid heavy lifting and working long hours near a hot oven. Severe lymphedema should be discussed with the doctor because there are certain procedures that can help relieve symptoms.

You may be feeling frustrated and helpless, especially because follow-up therapy can go on for months. Support your wife by accompanying her to her chemotherapy or radiation therapy appointments. Help pick out some interesting hats. If she comes home with a novel scarf or turban, compliment her on it. Dare her to be different!

Chemotherapy may leave your lover tired, nauseated, anxious, or depressed for periods of time. Radiation therapy can cause irritation or swelling in a woman's breast or arm. As a result, she may not be interested in intercourse. During this time you can be physically intimate in other ways—through kissing, stroking, cuddling, hugging, massaging, or exchanging loving words.

Chemotherapy can also bring about changes that directly affect your partner's interest in sex. It can directly or indirectly induce the development of menopause, even if she is quite young. Many of the physical changes she experiences can be addressed directly. For example, vaginal dryness can be reduced with a vaginal lubricating jelly (purchased over the counter). A gynecologist may recommend other products to help. Remember that sexual activity does not expose you to the effects of chemotherapy or radiation.

Fears about the future

After treatment your loved one will always wonder whether the cancer is going to come back. (You may remain just as worried.) She may interpret every little ache and pain as new cancer.

Such fears can linger indefinitely and intensify. Your wife may also show a dependence on doctors and experience "anniversary" symptoms around the date of the original diagnosis. You should understand which symptoms are significant and make sure she checks them with her doctor.

Even in the most loving relationship, a woman may reach out to other women with breast cancer through a hot line or support group so that she can share common concerns. Do not think that she is moving away from you. There are times when

a woman needs reassurance and solace from someone to whom she can reveal her innermost thoughts. This is healthy. When talking with other survivors, she will not need to be overly concerned with their feelings, whereas she may be so with yours.

After your partner has completed her chemotherapy or radiation treatments, sexual desire can bounce back for both of you. So add romance to your life: have special dinners together, leave each other notes, send cards, or give gifts.

If she has had breast reconstruction, she may enjoy sex more because of the boost that her "new" body gives to her feelings of attractiveness and self-esteem. Reconstruction, however, will probably not completely restore the pleasure she used to feel from having her breast caressed.

It is important to realize that while great strides are being made in plastic surgery, a reconstructed breast is not identical to the breast that has been lost. A reconstructed breast may be harder, parts of it may be numb, and the shape may be different. Massaging, squeezing, or caressing a reconstructed breast will not cause any harm, but there is generally a lack of sensation in the area, so the breast may no longer be a great source of sexual stimulation. Most women are pleased with the reconstructed breast, however, especially when they are realistic about the surgical outcome.

Enriched by the experience

Many who not only have survived breast cancer but have turned it into a positive, even enriching, experience have done so because they had an ally in their partner. In fact, most couples are drawn closer together by the experience. If you and your loved one make a commitment to go through diagnosis, treatment, and recovery as partners, her recovery may occur more quickly.

* * *

Y-ME National Breast Cancer Organization acknowledges all who helped bring When the Woman You Love Has Breast Cancer *to fruition: Jim Feldman and the Susan Feldman Memorial Fund, for providing the necessary impetus and funding; Bill Bloch, Ray DeLuca, Jim Feldman, Marvin Goldberg, Jimmy Gole, and Kenneth Suhanek for their frank and open discussions of living with a partner who has breast cancer; Debra Pawlik for conducting interviews and for her careful editing; the medical advisers who reviewed the text for accuracy; Thomas Croak and Michael Scott for their long hours spent in organizing a large mass of information and interviews and finally putting together a coherent, educational text; and, finally, the creative communications group Marcus, Inc., for the writing, layout, and design of the published booklet.*

RESOURCES:

- Y-ME National Breast Cancer Organization
  212 W Van Buren
  Chicago IL 60607
  1-800-221-2141
  (weekdays, 9 to 5)
- Cancer Information Service of the National Cancer Institute
  1-800-4-CANCER
  (1-800-422-6237)
- National Alliance of Breast Cancer Organizations (NABCO)
  9 E 37th Ave 10th floor
  New York NY 10016

"The Pediatrician's Office" by Stevan Dohanos, 1955; collection, Lucille and Walter Rubin, © The Curtis Publishing Company

Reflections on Four Decades in Pediatrics

by Abraham B. Bergman, M.D.

Recently I examined a three-year-old girl whose parents were concerned about her increasing paleness and tendency to bruise easily. They had also noticed that she had swollen lymph glands. A blood test confirmed a diagnosis of acute lymphocytic leukemia. As I joined the oncologist to discuss our findings with the parents, I reflected on what they might have been told in 1954, the year I entered medical school. The words were chilling: "Leukemia is a treatable but not curable disease." Anticancer drugs newly available at that time might have allowed a child to live for 12 months at most. Today I am able to assure these stricken parents that the cure rate for this type of leukemia is 85%.

The change in outlook for childhood leukemia is only one of scores of miracles I have been privileged to witness during my 40-plus years in pediatrics. During this astonishing period, more changes have occurred in medicine than took place in the previous four centuries. Dreaded diseases such as rheumatic fever, poliomyelitis, and epiglottitis (a bacterial infection that can result in suffocation) have virtually disappeared. Others such as leukemia and bacterial pneumonia can be controlled and cured. All but the most complex heart defects can be surgically repaired, even in infancy. Some entities that were often overlooked or misdiagnosed—*e.g.,* sudden infant death syndrome (SIDS), child abuse—have become well recognized, and considerable attention is given to them by pediatricians. At the same time, however, new scourges such as HIV have emerged. Disintegration of the family, widespread substance abuse, and societal violence now pose greater threats to the health of children than germs do.

A look back

I started medical school at Western Reserve University School of Medicine (now called Case Western Reserve) in Cleveland, Ohio, in 1954. Upon graduation I continued my training in pediatrics at Boston Children's Hospital (1958–60) and St. Mary's Hospital in London (1961–62) and then served as a pediatric fellow at the State University of New York Health Science Center at Syracuse (1962–64).

In 1964 I returned to my hometown of Seattle to work at Children's Hospital and teach at the University of Washington School of Medicine. I moved across town in 1982 to another university hospital, Harborview. I have spent my entire career teaching general pediatrics to medical students and residents and caring for the children of mostly low-income and minority families. The following are reflections on some of the stunning changes I have witnessed over that more than 40-year period.

1954–64

Prior to World War II, drugs that were effective and safe were few and far between. In the absence of reliable treatments, conscientious physicians spent much of their time attempting to make accurate diagnoses and helping families cope with the effects of childhood illnesses. The situation changed radically in the 1950s with the appearance of a succession of "wonder drugs"—antibiotics, corticosteroids, and anticonvulsants—that finally provided physicians with powerful tools for the treatment of such disorders as meningitis, kidney disease, and epilepsy.

Traditions die hard. Up until the early 1960s, most children's hospitals had very restrictive visiting policies, allowing parents to see their children only a few hours once a week. The rationale was that visitors brought in harmful germs and also that the children became "too upset" when their parents left. Then medical scientists discovered that the most dan-

Abraham B. Bergman, M.D., is Chief of Pediatrics, Harborview Medical Center, and Professor of Pediatrics, University of Washington School of Medicine, Seattle.

gerous germs were those that lived in hospitals. Moreover, doctors came to recognize that separation from parents could have devastating effects on sick children, sometimes even resulting in an almost catatonic state termed hospitalism. These realizations eventually led to a liberalization of visiting practices. When my colleague Thomas Oliver, director of neonatology at the University of Washington, not only allowed but encouraged parents to reach into incubators to touch and feed their premature infants, he was regarded as a revolutionary.

The absence of effective treatments in the preantibiotic era led to the pervasive practice of prescribing bed rest for practically anything. An image that remains vivid in my mind is of wards at Rainbow Convalescent Hospital in Cleveland full of children confined to their beds for one to two years. These were youngsters recovering from poliomyelitis, rheumatic fever, rheumatoid arthritis, and Legg-Calvé-Perthes disease, a common disorder producing temporary degeneration of the hip joint. Within a short time, however, the medical profession came to learn that bed rest was not only unnecessary for those youngsters but harmful.

Operating-room schedules in the 1950s and '60s were booked with orthopedic procedures to "correct" flatfeet and turned-in and turned-out legs, conditions that are now known to be perfectly normal. There were always babies in the hospital with severe eczema (skin inflammation) until the practice of feeding eggs as an infant's first solid food was stopped.

Saving lives. My first year of residency was the most thrilling of my career. Though we complained mightily—as residents always have and always will—we saw ourselves as soldiers fighting in "war zone." All residents at Boston Children's Hospital were on duty every other night; our work shifts could be as much as 36 hours long. Ours was also the last hospital in the coun-

(Below and opposite)
Photographs, Alfred Eisenstaedt, *Life* Magazine © Time Warner Inc.

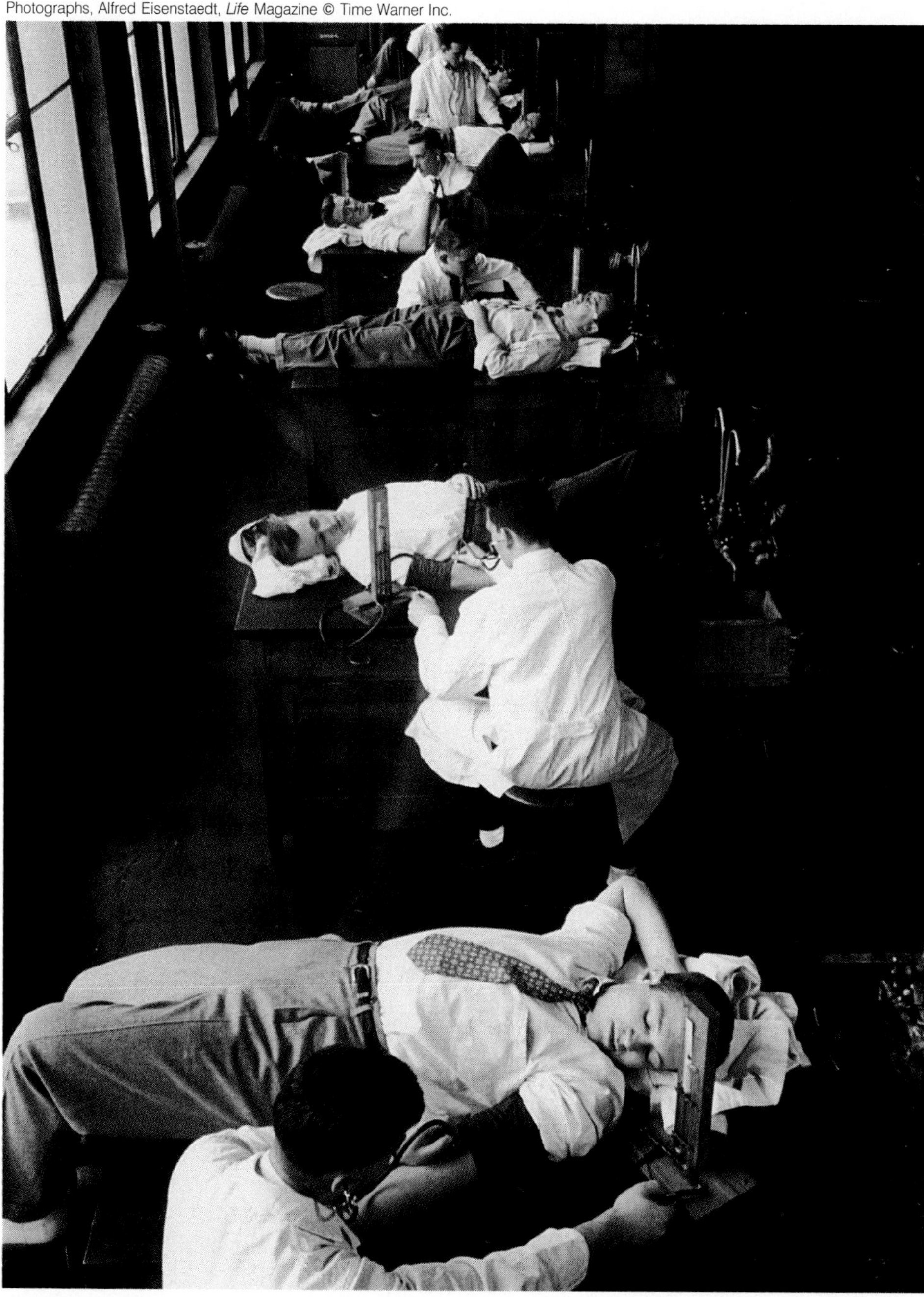

By the 1950s U.S. medical education had already acquired its reputation as a test of will, intellect, and physical endurance. (Above) Medical students of the period practice the art of physical examination by using their fellow pupils as patients. (Opposite page) Meals, like sleep, take second place to studies.

Ross Madden—Black Star

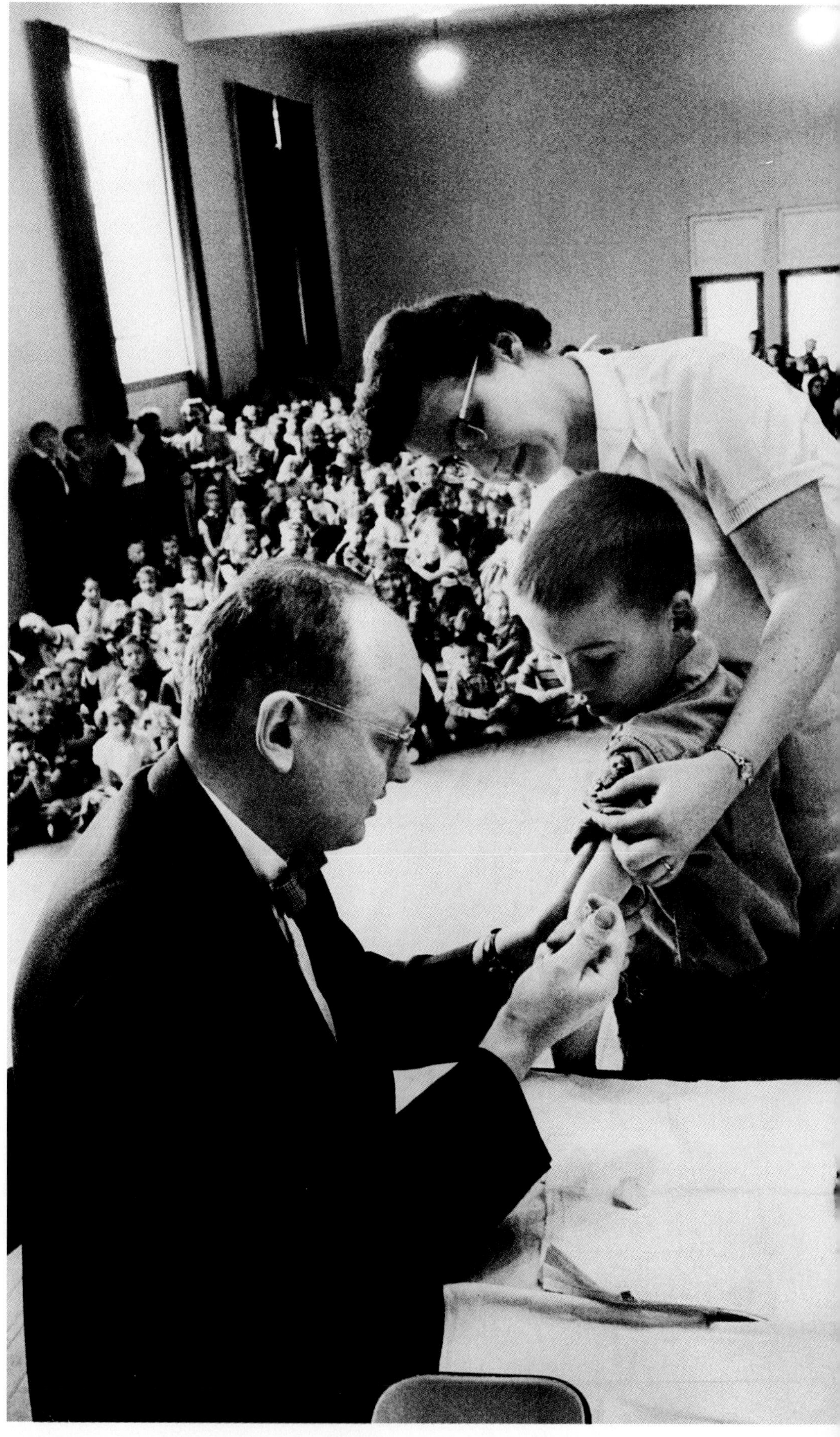

A youngster is vaccinated against polio as part of a mass inoculation of schoolchildren in the late 1950s. The Salk vaccine was released for general use in 1955; by 1960 more than 450 million doses had been given, and paralytic poliomyelitis had virtually disappeared from the U.S.

try where interns received no pay. We were, however, provided with free sleeping rooms, uniforms, and meals in the hospital cafeteria.

Although the work was physically hard, it was relatively uncomplicated. Most of the children who were hospitalized in those days had acute illnesses for which treatments were available. Infants who were dehydrated from diarrhea and vomiting were revived with intravenous fluids. Those with Rh-hemolytic anemia (a potentially fatal condition resulting from incompatibility of the maternal and fetal blood types) were treated with exchange blood transfusions. Babies with meningitis were given intravenous antibiotics. It was immensely satisfying to carry out all the diagnostic and therapeutic procedures for a patient with the knowledge that one was, quite literally, saving lives. I feel a particular pride in having cared for victims of acute rheumatic fever and poliomyelitis—experiences that younger physicians can only read about. I can still hear the hissing noise made by the huge negative-pressure ventilators (iron lungs) used in the last major polio epidemic in 1959.

Another memory I retain from that time is of a conference where X-rays were shown of an infant with a mysterious condition involving multiple bone fractures—some recent, others of earlier origin. The prevailing opinion among the learned professors was that the child had a metabolic defect that was causing weakness of the bones. Only the radiologist dissented; he believed the fractures were caused by trauma. It would be another 10 years before "battered baby" syndrome was recognized as a medical entity.

1964–74

Poliomyelitis disappeared by 1960, thanks to the vaccines first of Jonas Salk and then of Albert Sabin. Rheumatic fever also practically disappeared. The most notable feature of this decade, however, was the remarkable growth of pediatric subspecialties, especially neonatology, cardiology, and hematology.

In the '60s a much more aggressive approach was developed toward treatment of the various afflictions that affect preterm infants. Prior to that time preemies were placed in incubators to maintain their body temperature and given oxygen to assist their breathing. The brakes were put on oxygen therapy, however, when it was discovered that high levels of oxygen were associated with retrolental fibroplasia (later renamed retinopathy of prematurity), a condition that produces blindness. The death in 1963 of the prematurely born son of President and Mrs. John F. Kennedy helped focus attention on hyaline membrane disease (now called respiratory distress syndrome), the condition of preterm infants born with undeveloped lungs. General pediatricians no longer handle the care of small preemies and sick newborns; rather, subspecialists whose domain is the neonatal intensive care unit now attend these cases.

March of Dimes Birth Defects Foundation

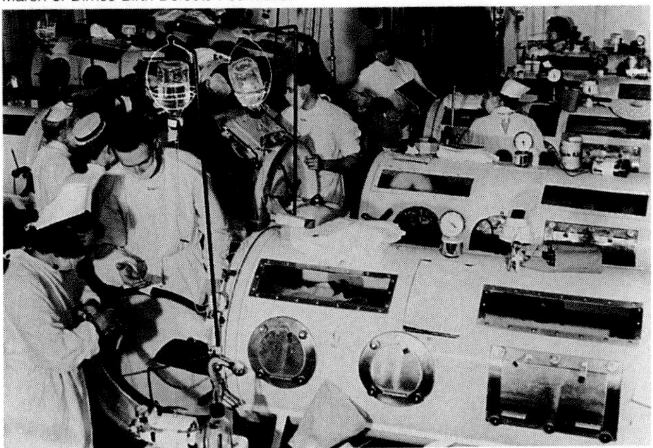

The hissing noise of the iron lung, a device that enabled paralyzed polio victims to breathe, was an all-too-common sound for physicians in 1950s hospital wards.

From gloom to elation. When I went to work at Children's Hospital in Seattle in 1964, congenital heart disease was the greatest single cause of death among infants and children. Open-heart surgery supported by the heart-lung machine, which temporarily takes over breathing and heart function, was just coming into its own. Which children to recommend for major heart repairs had always been a dilemma. Those with the most complicated heart defects were also the smallest and sickest and thus at greatest risk of dying during the procedure. Without the surgery, however, their deaths were inevitable. It was technically impossible to operate on children who weighed less than 9 kilograms (20 pounds), which put a lot of children, especially those with cyanotic heart disease (so-called blue babies), into the "hopeless" category. I recall the gloom pervading our hospital when 10 successive open-heart operations ended in failure and then the elation as more and more children began to survive. Today such surgery is undertaken on the smallest of infants, even those with very complex heart defects. Most survive.

Though I have always been a pediatric generalist, I did practice the "subspecialty" that might best be termed political medicine—the effort to improve public health by means of the political process. In the 1960s I hated to look into my patients' mouths; most of them had severely decayed teeth, and dental care was unavailable for poor families. My biggest political victory came in 1968 when I helped organize a successful campaign to fluoridate Seattle's water. Within 8–10 years rampant dental caries in children became rare.

In those days the children's hospital was still the gathering place for the community's pediatricians, and they exercised considerable influence over its operation. The quality of medical practice was monitored only in informal ways. I recall when the questionable practices of a certain local physician were raised at a meeting of the hospital's medical executive committee. The chief of staff, Vernon Spickard—a distinguished, soft-spoken, white-haired figure—terminated the heated discussion by saying, "Perhaps I will give Dr. ———— a call." The questionable practices ceased. Spickard ruled by moral suasion; no pediatrician would think of ignoring his "suggestions."

Teamwork. As medical and surgical treatments for acute illnesses continued to improve, the care of children with chronic disabling con-

Matt Herron—Take Stock

In addition to giving preschoolers from poor families an academic advantage, Project Head Start—one of many ambitious social programs of the 1960s—also sought to provide for their nutritional needs. The societal achievements of the decade were especially heartening to pediatricians and others committed to the cause of child public health.

ditions required more attention. This resulted in a relative diminution of the role of physicians and a substantial increase in the role of other professionals. For example, because of their problems with mobility, children with cerebral palsy had traditionally been cared for by orthopedic surgeons; orthopedists provided braces for affected limbs and performed operations to relieve muscle contractures. But many of these children also had difficulties with nutrition, speech, and education, as well as the ordinary problems of growing up. The solution that emerged was a multidisciplinary clinic where orthopedists, pediatricians, neurologists, and specialists in rehabilitation medicine were joined by physical and occupational therapists, psychologists, social workers, and educational counselors, all of them functioning as a team. Similar multidisciplinary teams were created to care for children with cleft lip and palate and meningomyelocele (a spinal-cord defect).

The civil rights spirit of the '60s was contagious. The parents of retarded and handicapped children and the professionals who treated them banded together to campaign for passage of the Education for All Handicapped Children Act of 1975. This monumental achievement ensured that the public education system would provide services to all children, no matter what their intellectual or physical limitations. Thanks in part to the influence of the Kennedy family, mental retardation centers became established in most communities.

"Can-do" spirit. Pres. Lyndon B. Johnson's now largely derided "War on Poverty" was a boon to those of us involved in caring for poor children. Medicaid, by releasing them from the gloomy corridors of public clinics, enabled the poor to be treated in better-staffed and better-equipped facilities. Funds became available

Rick Friedman—Black Star

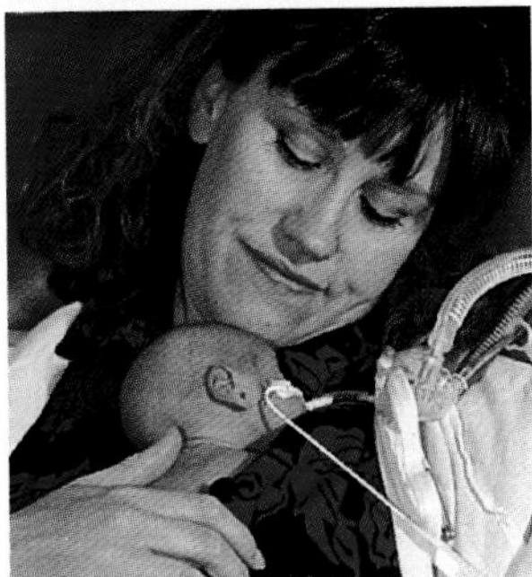

With advances in the care of premature infants in the 1960s, the prospects for survival of these babies vastly improved.

to address the broad health problems of communities—decayed housing, infrequent trash collection, absence of playgrounds, and, especially, inadequate, poorly functioning schools—all of which have as much effect on the health of children as the ministrations of physicians, or perhaps more. During the Johnson years laypeople from the community, trained as health aides, helped to reduce childhood illness and death in urban ghettos as well as in isolated rural areas such as American Indian reservations. The Special Supplemental Food Program for Women, Infants, and Children, which provides nourishment for pregnant women, nursing mothers, and children under five, sharply reduced the prevalence of iron-deficiency anemia in the United States.

What sticks in my mind most about this era is the "can-do" attitude—a general societal willingness to tackle the problems of the less fortunate, especially children. This spirit dissipated when funds for the "War on Poverty" were sapped by the war in Vietnam.

Much of my time in the 1970s was spent in a national campaign to gain recognition for SIDS, the unexplained death of apparently healthy babies in the first year of life.

Alexander Tsiaras—Science Source/Photo Researchers

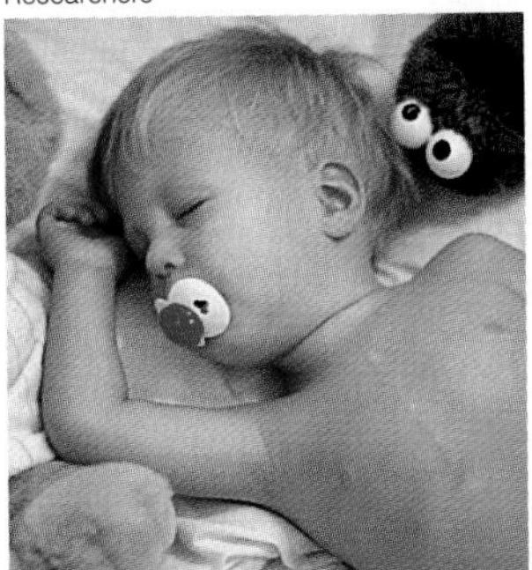

Thanks to developments starting in the 1970s, heart surgery can now be performed successfully on even the smallest, sickest infants.

Even though "crib death," as it was formerly called, claimed about 8,000 lives a year in the U.S., it was not discussed in medical schools or mentioned in pediatric textbooks. Nor was any research being conducted to find the cause or to devise a means of prevention. Because of the unexpected nature of such deaths and because of ignorance on the part of both health professionals and the public, parents felt themselves to be responsible. I joined a small group of bereaved parents in an organization called the National SIDS Foundation. Its purpose was to lobby for research funds, to educate health professionals and the public, and to provide emotional support to families. While the cause of SIDS is still unknown, and no means of prevention is at hand, the existence of the entity is recognized, a modest research effort is under way, and, most important, parents are no longer made to feel responsible.

1974–84

My most profound recollections of the period from the mid-1970s to the mid-'80s are of the enormous advances in technology, the changes in the patient population of children's hospitals, and the altered patterns of pediatric practice. Nowhere have the benefits of technology been more apparent than in the field of diagnostic imaging. Traditional radiographs—X-rays—were fine for detecting lesions of the bones or lungs but had limited value in identifying abnormalities of the brain, heart, abdomen, and blood vessels. Attempts to diagnose tumors, heart defects, malformed blood vessels, or bleeding in the brain involved complicated and painful procedures, and even then the results were often inconclusive. When I first

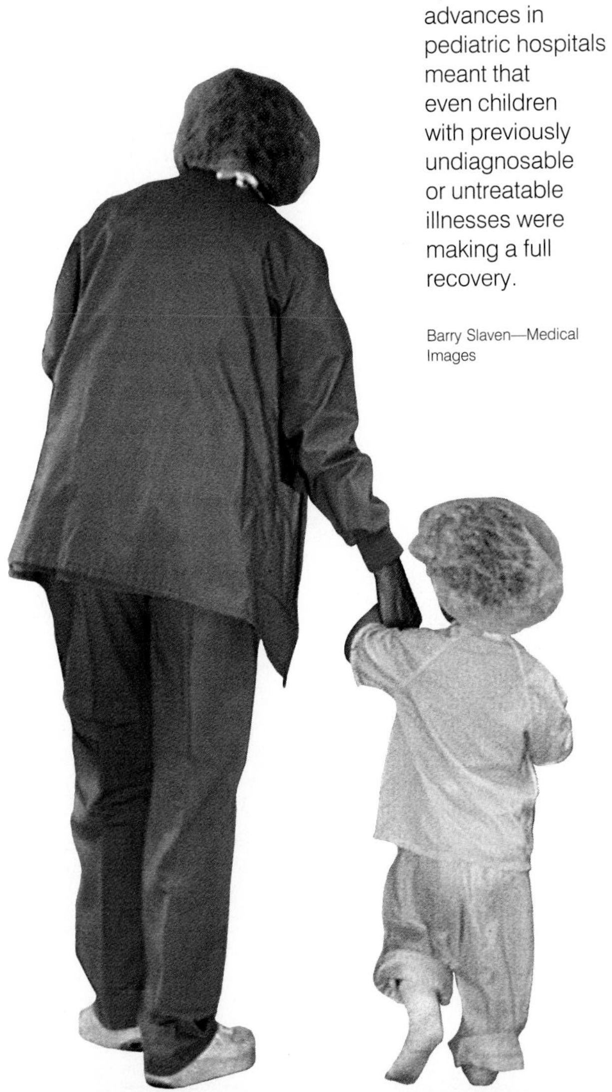

By the 1970s, advances in pediatric hospitals meant that even children with previously undiagnosable or untreatable illnesses were making a full recovery.

Barry Slaven—Medical Images

saw a computed tomography (CT) scan, it was as if I had been bestowed with mystic powers. CT and the other innovations that are now in common usage—ultrasound, echocardiography, and magnetic resonance imaging—provide a degree of diagnostic precision that was not dreamed to be possible when I started in medicine.

Technology also had mixed blessings. Improved methods of life support altered the demographics of children's hospitals. Innumerable infants and children were saved who in previous decades would have died. This development, in turn, gave rise to difficult ethical dilemmas such as the propriety of temporarily maintaining heart and lung functions in a child with a hopeless condition. For example, victims of drowning who are pulseless and without respiration when rescued invariably die or suffer devastating brain damage regardless of the emergency care they receive. I always wonder how much of a resuscitative effort should be made when such a child arrives in the emergency room. I do not, however, act on my doubts. If a heartbeat can be restored, the youngster is connected to a respirator and sent to the intensive care unit. Another difficult decision facing virtually every pediatrician is whether to employ mechanical ventilation in children with progressively deteriorating lung function, such as occurs in

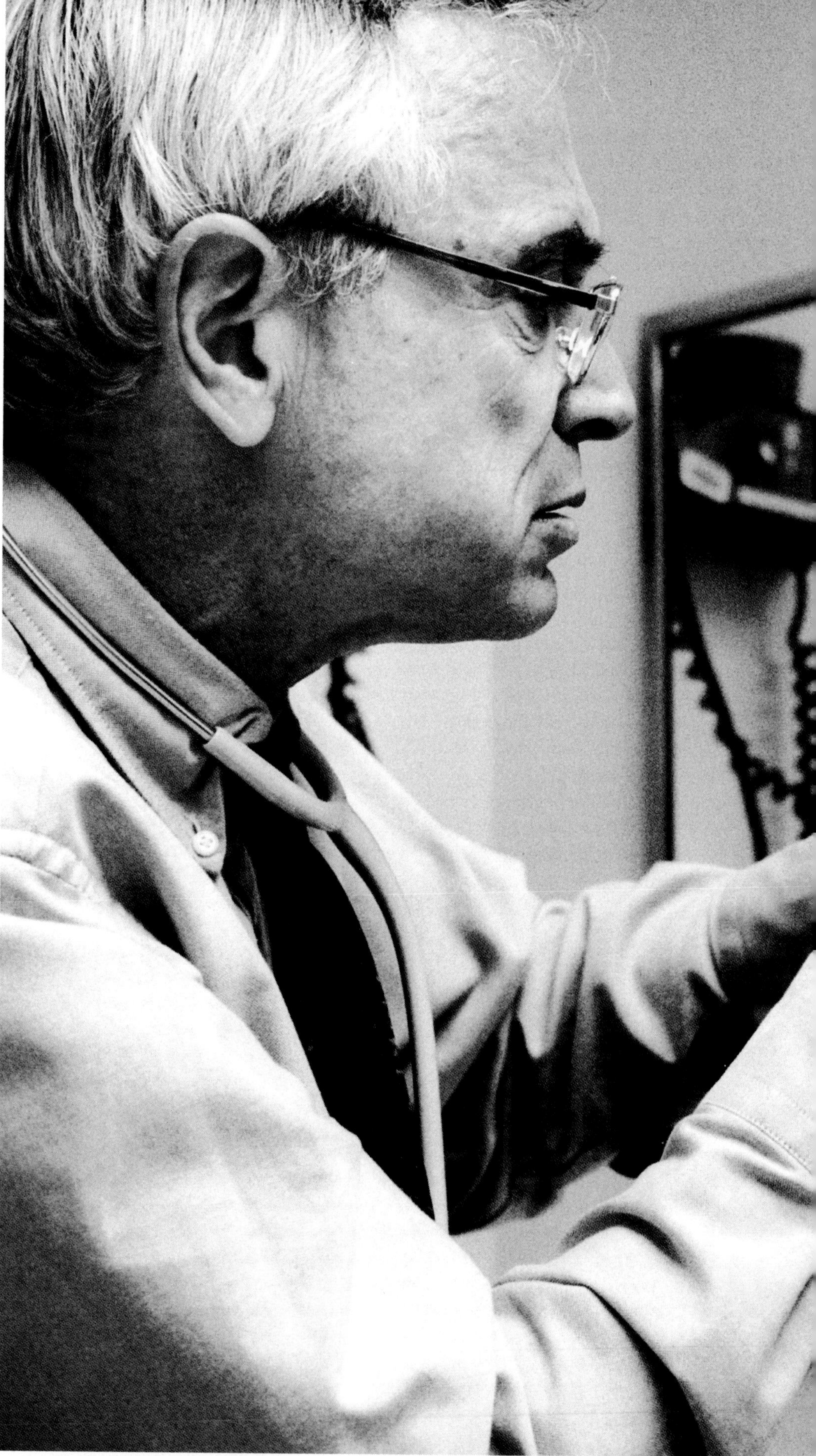

(Above and opposite) Photographs, Dan Lamont—Matrix

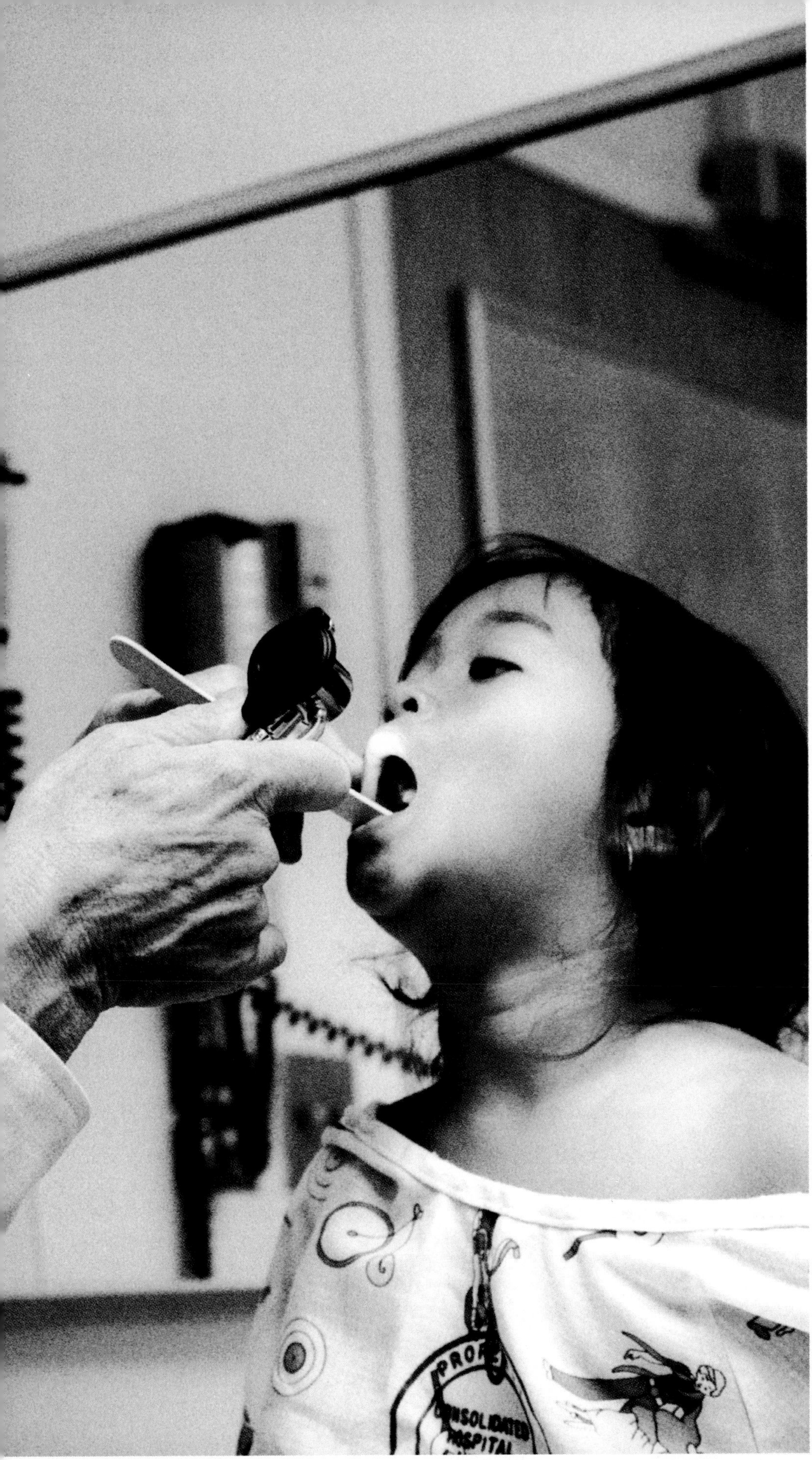

cystic fibrosis and muscular dystrophy.

A new category of patients requiring long-term intensive care began to consume a high proportion of the physical and mental energy of the hospital staff, to say nothing of financial resources. Many of these children, "graduates" of the neonatal intensive care unit, had severely damaged lungs and required mechanical ventilation indefinitely.

Children having children, a drug "culture," and other ominous trends. In the 1960s an average pediatrician might have three, four, or more patients in the hospital at any one time; in the '80s the number dropped to one or two a month. Pediatricians were increasingly taken up with social and behavioral ills, especially as they began to care for more teenagers. Single-parent families were no longer unusual. Sexual abuse, learning problems, eating disorders, substance

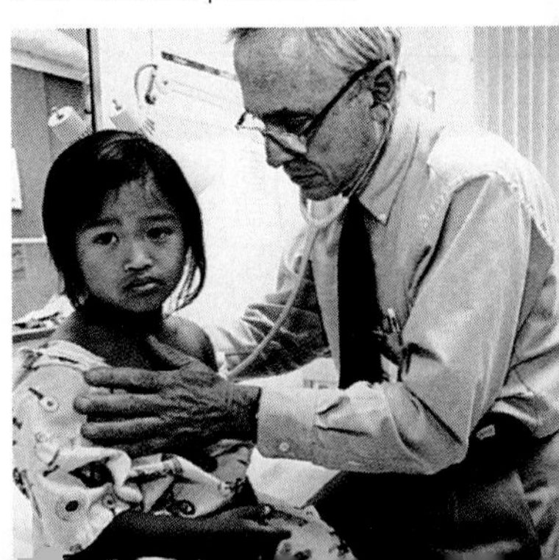

Abraham Bergman examines a Cambodian child at the drop-in clinic of Harborview Medical Center in Seattle, Washington. Her family are recent immigrants who speak no English. Nowadays Bergman spends nearly as much time dealing with patients' social needs as with their medical problems.

Bergman checks a 14-week-old infant who has been crying and fussing incessantly. After examining the infant, he will face the task of reassuring the mother, herself only a teenager, who is anxious about coping with a colicky baby.

abuse, and teenage pregnancy became as regular in pediatric practice as viral infections and booster shots.

In the U.S. the fee-for-service system of medicine worked against conscientious pediatricians. Handling behavioral and social problems was a time-consuming business, but that is not what we were getting paid to do. Though the work in earlier years was more physically demanding, coping with these "modern" conditions—on which the traditional tools of medicine have much less impact—has made the job of the pediatrician more difficult and, perhaps, less rewarding.

1984–94

While marvelous innovations in imaging allowed doctors to see in great detail what the insides of the body looked like, it was not until the mid-1980s that knowledge gained in molecular biology laboratories began to reach into the clinical arena, providing detailed information on how the body functions. To me, "medical genetics" had always meant calculating the odds of heritable disorders by compiling vast family trees. Now, through the use of the tools of molecular biology, it is possible to detect abnormalities of DNA and thus to directly determine whether a healthy individual has a particular genetic mutation. It is possible to detect unaffected "carriers" of cystic fibrosis, sickle-cell anemia, Duchenne muscular dystrophy, Huntington's disease, retinoblastoma (a malignant eye tumor), and a host of metabolic disorders.

"Bottom-line" medicine. Recombinant DNA technology has produced biological products to treat growth failure, the anemia of prematurity, and many other illnesses. The biotechnology boom has its drawbacks, however. The financial incentive for companies to produce "breakthrough" products is enormous, which means that drugs are developed and tested with sales potential rather than human benefits in mind. For example, no new drug to treat children's cancer has been developed in 20 years because the sales potential of such an agent is minimal. Yet expensive, heavily promoted new antibiotics to treat minor illnesses such as middle ear infection and sore throat hit the market at a dizzying pace. I continue to treat the latter ailments with amoxicillin, a cheap and effective antibiotic that has been in use for 25 years.

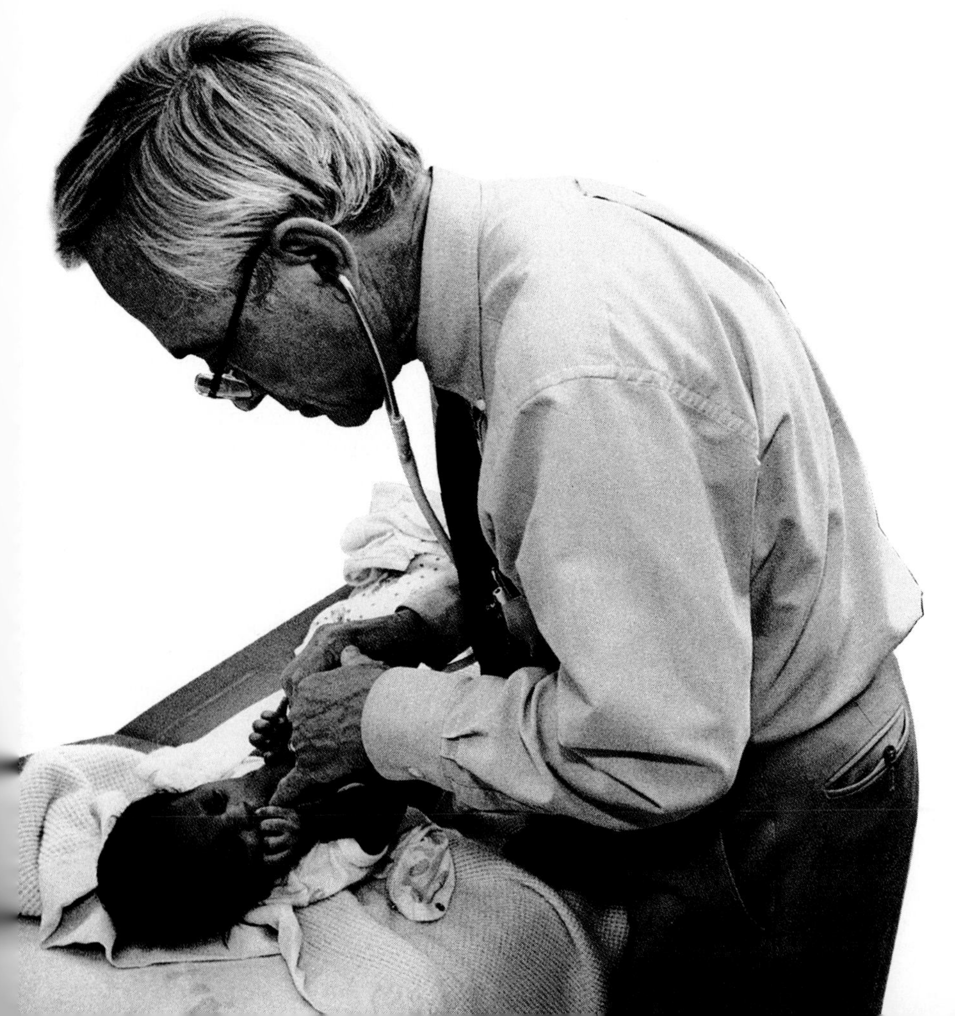

The "bottom line" mentality has profoundly affected medical practice. In many

(Opposite and top) Photographs, Dan Lamont—Matrix; (bottom) Jerry Berndt—Stock Boston

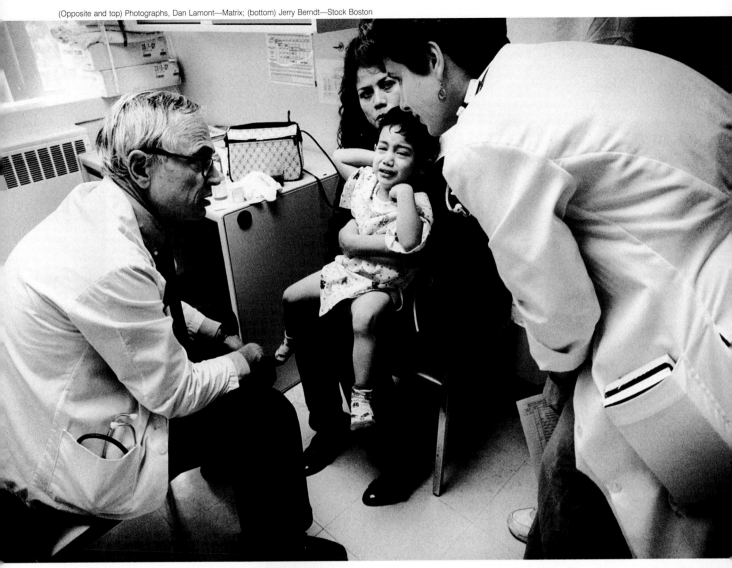

(Above) Bergman provides guidance for Jill Sells, a pediatric resident at Harborview. His role as an adviser and mentor to young physicians is one of the most rewarding aspects of his career in medicine. (Right) In the 1990s the reality of teen pregnancy is a routine part of the pediatrician's practice.

circles "health care reform" is nothing but a euphemism for "cost cutting." Undoubtedly improvements can be made in our health care system, and unnecessary costs need to be trimmed, but when insurance companies and government functionaries control the provision of medical care, the interests of children and their families are rarely at the fore.

Pediatricians are now required to discharge the newborn infant of a 15-year-old mother within 24 hours after delivery, with no opportunity to watch for complications or assess the success of maternal-infant bonding. When I supervise a ward at the children's hospital, I must answer five or six phone calls a day from "utilization-review specialists" of insurance companies asking me to justify keeping a particular child in the hospital or having that child undergo a particular treatment.

The injury "epidemic." Working at a major trauma center brings me into contact with the injuries, both intentional and unintentional, that are virtually epidemic in our "overdeveloped" society. While I can come to terms with serious natural illnesses over which humans have no control, I find it hard to accept death as the outcome for a three-year-old who exercises his natural curiosity and wanders into the street. Likewise, I am unnerved by seeing a four-year-old who has been permanently paralyzed because the seat belt of the car she was riding in was designed for adults. I am horrified by the increasing number of preteens who have access to loaded guns at home and are brought into the emergency room after having been "accidentally" shot in the head while "playing."

1994–2004

Despite the enormous changes in medical practice—many of them clearly not for the better—would I like to see one of my five children become a pediatrician? Decidedly yes! His or her experiences would be different from mine but no less rewarding.

The opportunity I have had to interact with (and perhaps have some influence on) several hundred young pediatric residents who have gone on to establish their own careers has given me great optimism. It hardly seems possible, but each successive class of residents seems more talented and more idealistic than the one before. It is these outstanding young physicians who give me confidence that the health needs of future generations of children will be well served.

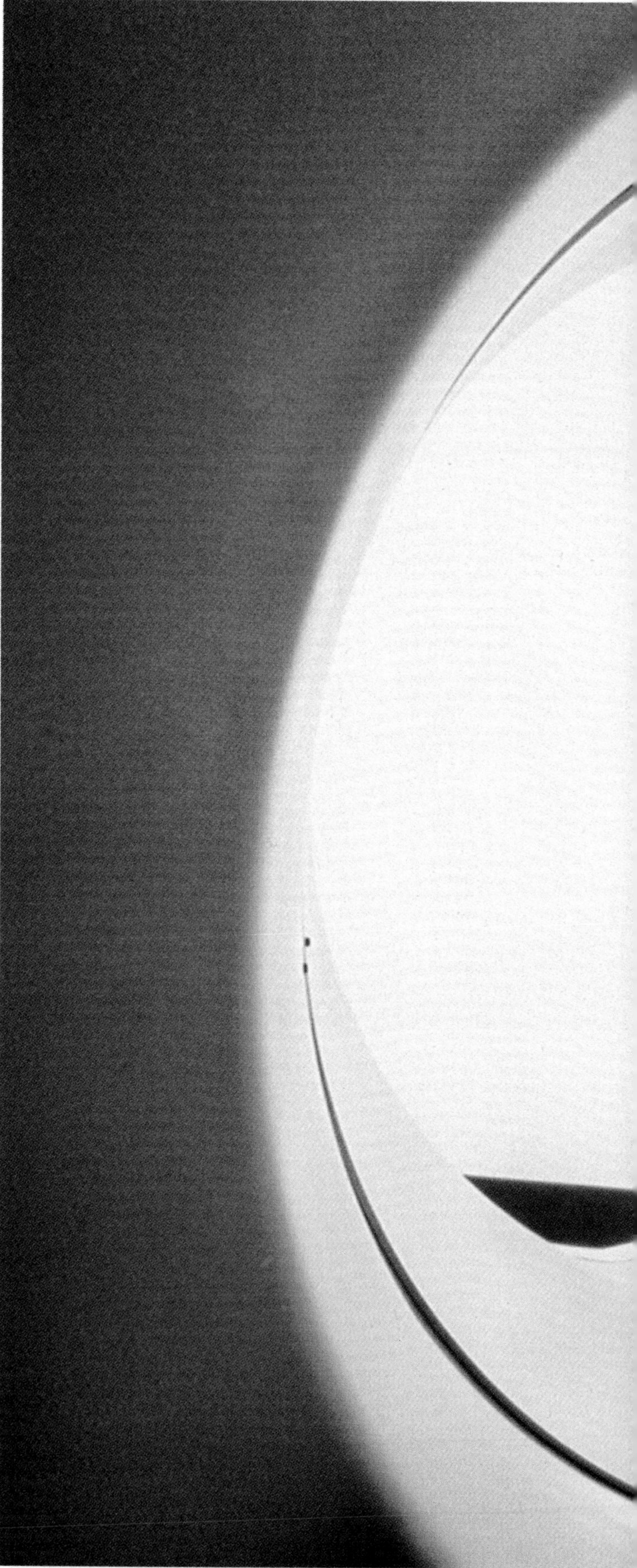

Innovations like computed tomography scanning are taken for granted by those entering medicine today. Practitioners of Bergman's generation fully appreciate the wonders of such technologies and the enabling powers they grant to the physician.

Alexander Tsiaras—Science Source/Photo Researchers

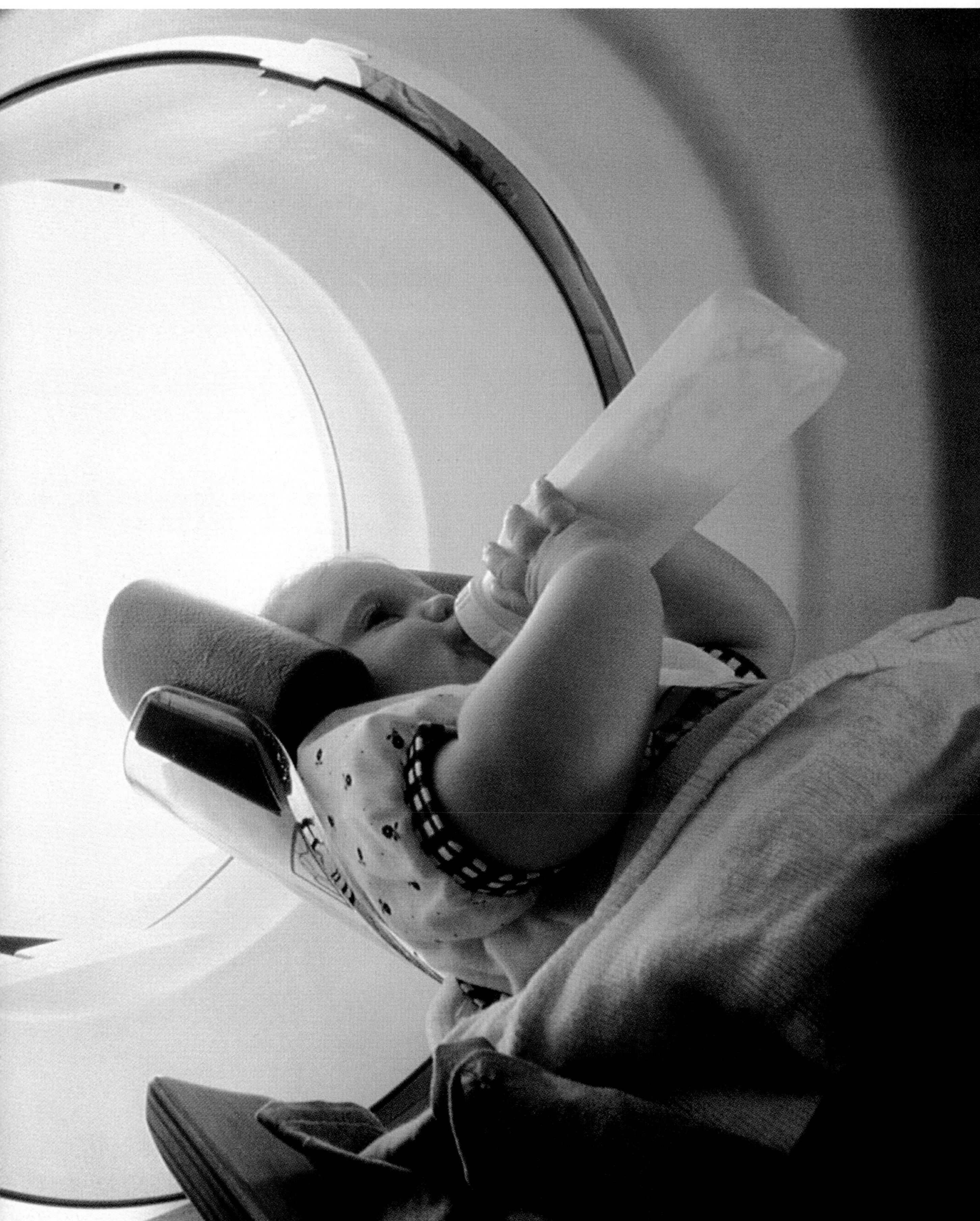

World Health Data

The information presented here reflects the most recent published statistical figures that were available to the editors of *Medical and Health Annual* in 1995. Sources include principal intergovernmental organizations—*e.g.,* the World Health Organization (Geneva), the United Nations (New York City), and their regional offices and affiliated organizations; national statistical offices worldwide; principal U.S. authorities—the National Center for Health Statistics, the Centers for Disease Control and Prevention; and on-line resources of the Internet.

Most of the figures provided are "best estimates" and may conceal the considerable range of variation—geographic, economic, or demographic—within any single national value. Because the scope and priorities of national data-collection systems differ greatly, coverage of some subjects may be incomplete.

Certain terms used in this section have specific meaning in a public health context:

incidence New cases of a disease or condition diagnosed during a specified period of time; may be reported as the "total number of cases," or as a "rate per [1,000, 10,000, or 100,000]," when referred to a specified population.

prevalence Total cases, including new and all existing cases; may be reported as a total or as a rate.

eradication Complete destruction of a disease organism in human populations and potential animal vectors (though the organism may be preserved for research purposes—*e.g.,* the smallpox virus).

elimination Reduction of new cases of a disease to the lowest practicable level by suppression of human transmission or control of animal vectors.

The application of other terms may differ in their national contexts–availability of "health services within one hour's travel" means availability of *appropriate* services (different for the U.S. and, say, India) in one hour's travel (travel services differing as much as health services). Some common alternative names for the same condition are shown parenthetically—*e.g.,* Machupo (Bolivian hemorrhagic fever).

Symbols and abbreviations:

...	not available	AIDS	acquired immune deficiency syndrome
<,>	less than/greater than	DALY	disability-adjusted life year
≤	equal to or less than	FAO	Food and Agriculture Organization
≥	equal to or greater than	HIV	human immunodeficiency virus
		WHO	World Health Organization

Health Indicators

Region/bloc	Life expectancy		Other			
	Male (years)	Female (years)	Persons per doctor	Infant mortality per 1,000 births	Pop. having safe water (%)	Food (% FAO recommended minimum), 1988–90
WORLD	64.1	68.2	730	64.3	77	114
AFRICA	53.9	57.1	4,180	94.8	50	100
Central Africa	51.0	54.4	12,870	100.1	42	91
East Africa	49.1	52.2	13,070	107.5	40	85
North Africa	62.1	65.7	1,900	69.0	74	122
Southern Africa	61.4	67.3	1,430	50.9	56	124
West Africa	51.8	54.6	6,830	100.8	46	95
AMERICAS	68.2	74.3	560	38.1	86	123
Anglo-America[1]	72.5	79.2	400	8.2	100	136
Canada	74.0	80.6	460	6.8	100	122
United States	72.3	79.0	390	8.3	100	138
Latin America	65.6	71.4	760	48.6	78	114
Caribbean	65.5	69.9	520	52.4	77	114
Central America	64.1	69.1	1,490	47.9	66	103
Mexico	66.5	73.1	890	41.0	76	131
South America	65.5	71.2	730	51.1	79	110
Andean Group	66.2	71.7	900	44.5	75	98
Brazil	63.5	69.1	850	60.0	87	114
Other South America	71.5	77.7	360	34.0	62	126
ASIA	64.2	67.0	1,000	64.7	75	109
Eastern Asia	69.3	73.0	640	24.3	76	114
China	68.6	71.8	650	26.0	72	112
Japan	76.1	82.1	580	4.5	97	125
South Korea	69.0	76.0	900	15.0	97	120
Other Eastern Asia	70.2	75.7	520	18.2	99	121
South Asia	59.6	60.3	2,410	93.8	80	99
India	60.4	61.2	2,190	88.0	85	101
Pakistan	59.3	60.7	2,240	104.7	56	99
Other South Asia	55.3	55.2	5,890	109.6	71	89
Southeast Asia	60.6	64.7	2,650	66.3	55	112
ASEAN[2]	61.4	65.4	2,490	67.6	65	114
Non-ASEAN	58.5	63.0	3,210	63.2	28	106
Southwest Asia	64.8	69.3	600	49.9	86	126
Central Asia	64.6	72.0	280	36.2	100	132
Gulf Cooperation Council	69.4	72.8	560	23.1	95	123
Iran	64.4	66.2	2,000	62.1	89	125
Other Southwest Asia	64.0	69.1	720	53.8	78	124
EUROPE	68.7	77.1	290	11.6	98	134
Eastern Europe	63.3	74.1	270	16.8	97	132
Russia	59.0	73.2	230	18.1	100	132
Other Eastern Europe	66.5	74.8	320	15.9	95	132
Western Europe	73.4	79.8	310	6.8	100	135
EFTA[3]	73.6	80.2	340	6.3	99	122
European Union (EU)	73.3	79.8	300	6.9	100	136
France	72.9	81.1	370	6.4	100	143
Germany	73.2	79.6	310	6.1	100	132
Italy	73.6	80.2	190	7.4	100	139
Spain	74.6	80.5	260	7.4	100	141
United Kingdom	73.2	78.6	450	6.6	100	130
Other EU	73.0	79.1	340	8.1	98	136
Other Western Europe	73.2	78.6	520	7.9	100	131
OCEANIA	70.7	76.0	520	21.7	88	123
Australia	75.0	80.9	440	6.1	99	124
Pacific Ocean Islands	63.4	67.3	780	36.5	67	122

[1] Anglo-America includes Canada, the United States, Greenland, Bermuda, and St. Pierre and Miquelon.
[2] Association of Southeast Asian Nations; excludes Vietnam.
[3] European Free Trade Association.

Emerging Infectious Diseases

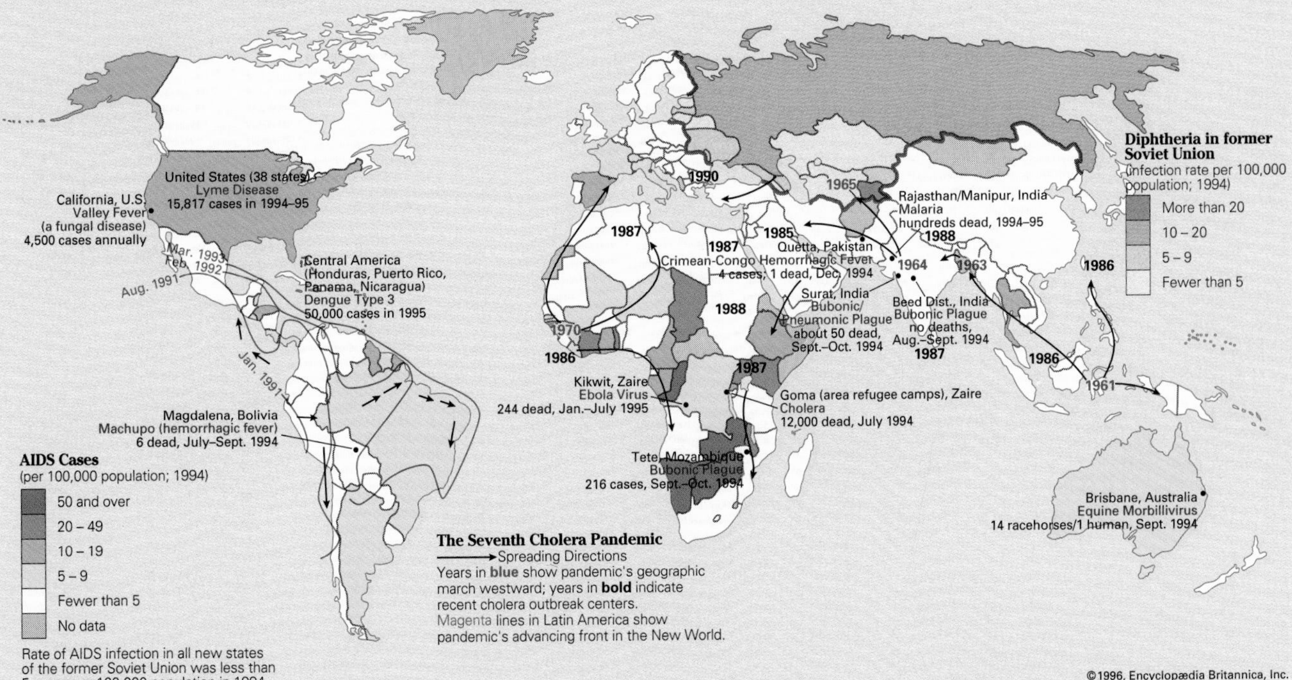

Progress Toward the World Health Organization's Health for All by the Year 2000 Targets (189 WHO Member States)

Health indicator	1980	1990	2000[1]	Target
HEALTH STATUS				
Life expectancy at birth (in years)				
• Global figure	61	64	67	
• Number of countries reporting a figure of 60 years or over	86	103	111	In all countries life expectancy at birth will be 60 years or over
Infant mortality (per 1,000 live births)				
• Global figure	82	65	54	
• Number of countries reporting a figure of 50 per 1,000 live births or under	70	83	99	In all countries infant mortality will be 50 per 1,000 live births or under
Mortality under 5 years (per 1,000 live births)	117	92	74	
DISEASE STATUS				
Poliomyelitis incidence	630,000	116,000	0	Eradication of poliomyelitis
Dracunculiasis prevalence (adults)	12,000,000	3,000,000	0	Eradication of dracunculiasis
Leprosy prevalence	10,500,000	5,500,000	300,000	Elimination of leprosy
Neonatal tetanus incidence	1,000,000	500,000	negligible	Elimination of neonatal tetanus
Hepatitis B carriers among children	...	350,000,000	400,000,000	Control of hepatitis B
Tuberculosis deaths	2,900,000	2,900,000	3,500,000	Control of tuberculosis
Malaria deaths	1,450,000	2,250,000	1,950,000	Control of malaria
HEALTH CARE COVERAGE (%)				
DPT (third dose)	8	83	98.5	
Poliovirus vaccine (third dose)	8	85	99	
Safe water	52	75	86	Primary health care available to whole population
Sanitation	24	71	92	
Delivery of babies by trained personnel	...	55	60	
HEALTH RESOURCES[2]				
Percentage of GNP expended on health	3.2	3.0		
Per capita health expenditure (in U.S. $)	111	135		

[1] Projections for 2000 based on actual figures for 1992.
[2] Central government expenditure only.
DPT=diphtheria/pertussis/tetanus vaccine; GNP=gross national product.

Source: WHO, *The World Health Report 1995.*

Maternal Health (Selected Countries)						Infant/Child Health (Selected Countries)					
	Percentage of deliveries				Deaths per 100,000 live births	Deaths per 1,000 live births		Percentage of children immunized (age 12 months and under)			
	Prenatal care	Attended by trained personnel	Tetanus toxoid vaccine (pregnant women, 2 or more doses)	Babies of low birth weight (less than 2,500 grams[1])	Maternal mortality	Infant mortality rate (deaths in first 12 months)	Child mortality rate (deaths in first 5 years)	Bacillus Calmette-Guerin (TB) vaccine	Diphtheria/ pertussis/ tetanus vaccine (3rd dose)	Oral polio vaccine (3rd dose)	Measles vaccine
AFRICA											
Egypt	40–59	35	78	10	100–249	55	55	95	89	89	89
Ethiopia	40–59	10	13	16	≥500	...	208	46	28	28	22
Nigeria	60–79	37	33	16	250–499	95	191	40	29	29	34
South Africa	≥90	90	26	12	25–99	52	70	66	79	79	85
Zaire	...	...	29	15	≥500	93	188	65	32	31	31
NORTH AMERICA											
Canada	≥90	100	...	6	<25	7	8	...	85	85	85
Mexico	60–79	69	42	12	25–99	35	33	95	91	92	91
United States	≥90	99	...	7	<25	8	10	...	83	72	83
SOUTH AMERICA											
Argentina	40–59	92	...	8	25–99	29	24	96	79	80	95
Brazil	60–79	73	62	11	100–249	56	65	90	69	92	78
Colombia	60–79	71	14	10	25–99	37	20	94	83	85	94
Peru	60–79	60	21	11	100–249	76	65	87	84	86	75
Venezuela	60–79	97	...	9	25–99	33	24	82	69	75	63
ASIA											
Bangladesh	<40	7	73	50	≥500	107	127	95	74	92	71
China	80–89	95	2	9	100–249	27	43	93	95	95	94
India	40–59	32	78	33	250–499	86	124	92	90	90	85
Indonesia	60–79	40	67	14	250–499	65	111	94	89	95	93
Iran	40–59	70	82	9	100–249	42	58	100	99	99	96
Japan	≥90	100	...	6	<25	5	6	93	87	94	69
Korea, South	80–89	89	...	9	25–99	21	9	72	74	74	93
Pakistan	<40	35	46	25	250–499	98	137	87	74	74	71
Philippines	60–79	55	70	15	100–249	39	60	90	88	89	88
Saudi Arabia	80–89	90	62	7	25–99	31	40	94	94	94	92
Thailand	60–79	66	75	13	100–249	27	33	96	88	88	78
Turkey	40–59	76	20	8	25–99	57	87	59	65	65	62
Vietnam	≥90	90	71	17	100–249	38	49	94	91	91	93
EUROPE											
France	≥90	...	...	5	<25	7	9	78	89	92	76
Germany	≥90	100	...	6	<25	7	8	...	75	90	70
Italy	≥90	100	...	5	<25	8	10	...	95	98	50
Poland	≥90	...	...	8	<25	15	16	95	95	95	95
Romania	≥90	...	...	7	25–99	23	28	93	91	91	99
Russia	...	...	...	...	25–99	...	32	87	65	82	88
Spain	≥90	...	...	4	<25	7	9	...	87	88	90
Sweden	≥90	100	...	5	<25	6	7	...	89	95	83
Ukraine	...	...	...	...	...	...	25	89	90	91	94
United Kingdom	≥90	100	...	7	<25	8	9	...	91	93	92
OCEANIA											
Australia	≥90	99	...	6	<25	8	9	...	95	72	86
New Zealand	≥90	100	...	6	<25	9	10	20	81	68	82

≥ equal to or greater than; < less than

[1] Approximately 5½ pounds.

Source: WHO, *The World Health Report 1995.*

Lifestyle-Related Mortality per 100,000 Population (Selected Countries)

	Cirrhosis of the liver	Diabetes mellitus	Suicide	Motor vehicle accident	Homicide
AFRICA					
Egypt	8.1	9.0	0.1	6.6	0.5
Ethiopia	...	...	...	2.3	6.7[1]
Nigeria	...	...	...	8.3	2.4[1]
South Africa	...	...	...	35.3	...
Zaire	...	...	...	11.7[2]	...
NORTH AMERICA					
Canada	8.2	15.7	13.2	12.7	2.3
Mexico	21.6	31.4	2.4	16.4	17.5
United States	10.4	19.7	12.4	18.4	9.9
SOUTH AMERICA					
Argentina	9.6	17.3	6.7	9.1	5.0
Brazil	11.7	18.0	4.6	29.6	29.6
Colombia	4.1	11.3	3.5	17.4	74.4
Peru	10.4	6.6	1.0	7.9	5.2
Venezuela	8.0	15.3	4.8	20.7	12.1
ASIA					
Bangladesh	...	...	...	...	2.2[1]
China[3]	10.4	8.1	8.6	8.5	2.4
India[4]	3.4	2.6	7.7	.12.3	3.0
Indonesia	...	...	...	6.0	0.8[1]
Iran	...	...	...	6.4	...
Japan	13.8	8.0	16.9	11.8	0.6
Korea, South	30.4	13.8	8.9	38.9	1.4
ASIA (cont'd)					
Pakistan	...	...	...	4.8	5.3[1]
Philippines	...	...	...	0.7	36.9[1]
Saudi Arabia	...	...	...	22.0	0.7[1]
Thailand	...	6.2	12.4	14.4	9.3
Turkey[5]	4.9	8.5	0.7[1]	10.1	3.2[1]
Vietnam	...	...	...	...	...
EUROPE					
France	17.0	11.1	20.2	16.5	1.1
Germany	24.5	24.5	17.5	13.6	1.2
Italy	26.8	33.6	7.6	15.8	2.6
Poland	11.2	15.8	14.9	19.2	2.9
Romania	39.2	10.1	11.6	15.0	4.9
Russia	13.6	7.1	26.7	26.1	15.4
Spain	5.3	23.1	7.5	20.5	1.0
Sweden	3.7	17.9	15.6	7.9	1.3
Ukraine	16.9	15.3	56.6	63.2	7.4
United Kingdom	6.2	14.8	8.0	14.5	0.9
OCEANIA					
Australia	5.9	20.2	12.0	10.8	1.6
New Zealand	3.4	11.9	14.0	19.4	2.0

[1] Crime-based statistics; may include attempted homicide.
[2] Kinshasa only.
[3] Selected rural areas.
[4] Rural sample survey.
[5] Province and district capitals only.

Source: WHO, *World Health Statistics Annual* (1994); national statistical offices.

Total HIV Infections, Late 1970s/Early 1980s Through Mid-1995
(Estimated Distribution for Adult Cases by WHO Region)

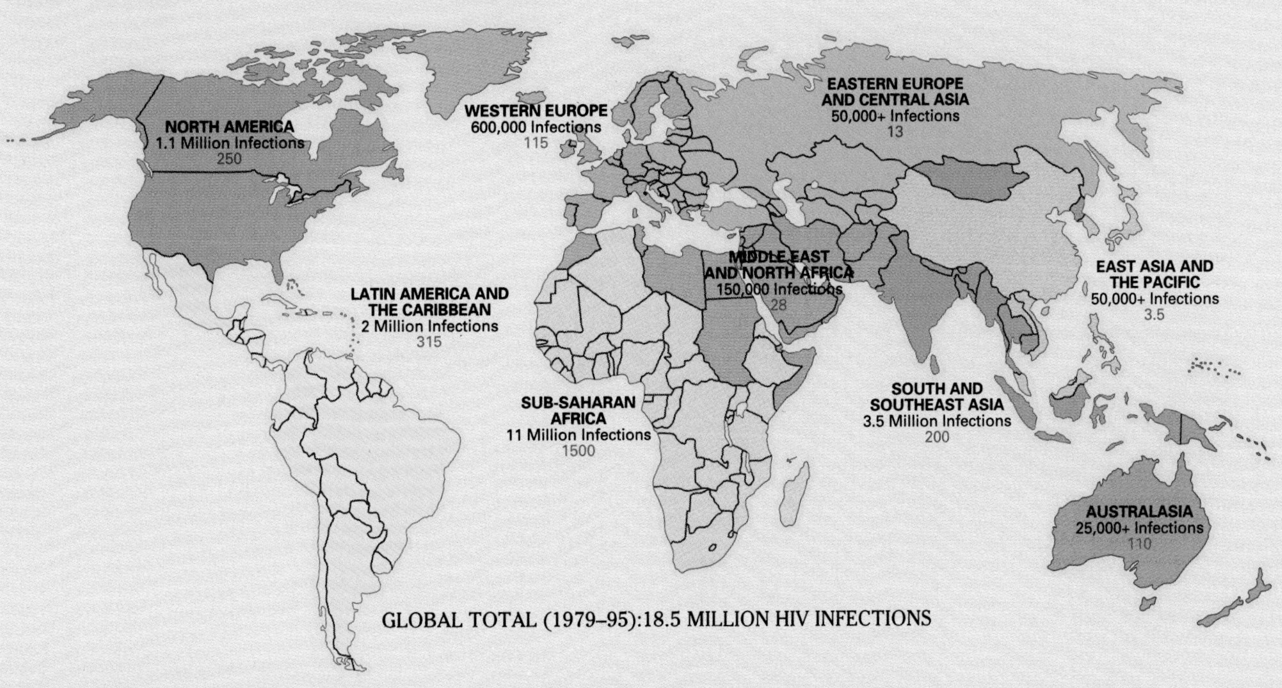

Values shown in red represent the approximate number of HIV-infected adults per 100,000 population as of mid-1995.

Global Health Situation: Mortality and Morbidity, Selected Causes, 1993 Estimates[1]

Diseases/conditions	Deaths (in 000s)	Incidence (cases per 100,000)
Infectious and parasitic diseases (selected)	**16,445**	
Acute lower respiratory infections under age 5	4,110	2,483[2]
Diarrhea under age 5, including dysentery	3,010[3]	18,210[2]
Tuberculosis	2,709	83
Malaria	2,000	...
Measles	1,160	452
Hepatitis B	933	22
AIDS	700	6.2
Whooping cough	360	431
Bacterial meningitis	210	...
Schistosomiasis	200	...
Leishmaniasis	197	72
Congenital syphilis	190	...
Tetanus	149	3.0
Hookworm diseases (ancylostomiasis and necatoriasis)	90	...
Amebiasis *(Entamoeba histolytica)*	70	...
Ascariasis (roundworm)	60	...
African trypanosomiasis (sleeping sickness)	55	0.6
American trypanosomiasis (Chagas disease)	45	4.0
Onchocerciasis (river blindness)	35	...
Meningitis (meningococcal)	35	...
Rabies	35	...
Yellow fever	30	2.0
Dengue/dengue hemorrhagic fever	23	5.6
Japanese encephalitis	11	0.4
Foodborne trematodes	10	...
Cholera (officially reported figures only)	6.8	3.8
Poliomyelitis	5.5[4]	1.1
Diphtheria	3.9	0.8
Leprosy	2.4	6.0
Plague	0.5	0.05
Giardiasis	...	5.0
Trichomoniasis	...	940[5]
Chlamydial infections (sexually transmitted)	...	970[5]
Genital warts	...	320
Gonococcal infections	...	780[5]
Genital herpes	...	210
Other syphilitic infections	...	190[5]
Chancroid *(Haemophilus ducreyi)*	...	90[5]
Endemic treponematoses	...	2.0
Dracunculiasis (guinea worm disease)	...	20
Perinatal and neonatal causes (selected)	**3,180**	
Birth asphyxia	840	...
Congenital anomalies	660[6]	36
Neonatal tetanus	560	6.7
Birth trauma	420	...
Prematurity	410	...
Neonatal sepsis and meningitis	290	...
Maternal causes (selected)	**508**	
Hemorrhage	126	143
Indirect causes	101	135
Sepsis	75	120
Abortion	67	199
Hypertensive disorders during pregnancy	62	71
Other direct obstetric causes	39	36
Obstructed labor	38	73

Diseases/conditions	Deaths (in 000s)	Incidence (cases per 100,000)
Diseases of the circulatory system (total)	**9,676**	
Ischemic heart disease	4,283	...
Cerebrovascular disease	3,854	...
Other heart diseases[7]	1,133	...
Rheumatic fever and rheumatic heart disease	406	...
Chronic lower respiratory diseases (selected)	**2,888**	
Chronic obstructive pulmonary disease	2,888	...
Malignant neoplasms/cancer (total)	**6,013**	**90**
Cancer of trachea, bronchus, and lung	1,035	...
Stomach cancer	734	...
Cancer of colon and rectum	468	...
Cancer of lip, oral cavity, and pharynx	458	...
Liver cancer	367	...
Breast cancer	358	...
Esophageal cancer	328	...
Cervical cancer	235	...
Lymphoma	221	...
Cancer of pancreas	214	...
Leukemia	207	...
Cancer of prostate	182	...
Cancer of bladder	135	...
Ovarian cancer	123	...
Cancer of uterus	64	...
Skin cancer	37	...
Other cancers	853	...
Intentional and unintentional injuries (total)	**3,996**	
Falls, fires, drowning, etc.	1,810	...
Motor- and other road-vehicle accidents	885	99
Suicide	779	...
Homicide and violence	303	86
Occupational injuries due to accidents	220	1,200
Occupational diseases	...	690
Other (selected)	**170**	
Diabetes mellitus	170	...
Hemophilia	...	0.2
Hemoglobinopathies	...	3.0
Unknown	**8,124**	
Disability (selected)		
Trachoma-related blindness	...	205
Glaucoma-related blindness	...	33
Cataract-related blindness	...	109
Alcohol and substance abuse (selected)		
Alcohol dependence syndrome	...	115
Substance abuse (drug dependence syndrome)	...	94
All causes (total)	**51,000**	

[1] Estimates for some diseases may contain cases that are also included elsewhere; for example, estimates for acute lower respiratory infections and diarrhea under age 5 include those associated with measles, pertussis, malaria, and HIV.
[2] Incidence figures refer to episodes.
[3] Deaths from dysentery are estimated at 450,000.
[4] Estimate based on case-fatality rate for paralytic cases only.
[5] Based on maximum estimates.
[6] Includes 440,000 deaths among children under age 5.
[7] Includes heart failure, nonrheumatic endocarditis, diseases of pulmonary circulation, cardiac dysrhythmias, and other ill-defined conditions.
[8] Global data not available or not applicable.

Source: WHO, *The World Health Report 1995.*

Physicians by Specialty:[1] United States,[2] 1993

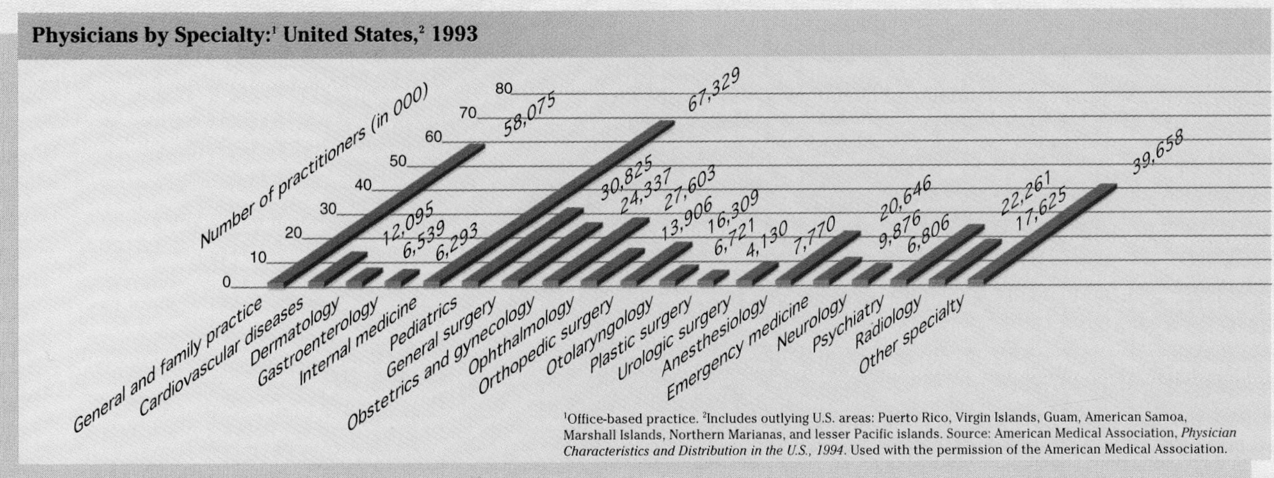

[1]Office-based practice. [2]Includes outlying U.S. areas: Puerto Rico, Virgin Islands, Guam, American Samoa, Marshall Islands, Northern Marianas, and lesser Pacific islands. Source: American Medical Association, *Physician Characteristics and Distribution in the U.S., 1994*. Used with the permission of the American Medical Association.

Human Resources for Health Care, Most Recent Data (Selected Countries)

	Persons per doctor	Persons per dentist	Persons per nurse	Persons per pharmacist	Persons per midwife
AFRICA					
Egypt	1,698	9,253	1,242	5,595	...
Ethiopia	30,195	...	12,815	123,080	...
Nigeria	4,692	77,432	1,306	15,839	1,608
South Africa	1,264	9,698	250	4,179	...
Zaire	15,584	913,073	1,356	634,508	...
Zimbabwe	7,371	74,275	1,591	28,040	3,670
NORTH AMERICA					
Canada	464	1,923	107	1,271	...
Mexico	924	18,425	599	...	...
United States	295	1,427	138	1,290	85,136
SOUTH AMERICA					
Argentina	328	1,505	1,734	44,493	...
Brazil	848	1,464	...	3,376	...
Colombia	1,078	2,263	695	...	...
Peru	952	4,000	1,316	3,703	6,249
Venezuela	590	2,392	36	3,385	...
ASIA					
Bangladesh	5,264	211,386	11,451	...	14,334
China	648	...	1,120	2,819	19,491
India	2,170	78,226	2,535	...	4,401
Indonesia	6,861	45,025	1,804	96,816	...
Iran	2,000	11,942	1,443	...	...
Japan	583	1,668	171	820	5,388
ASIA (cont'd)					
Korea, South	1,007	4,457	482	1,155	5,609
Pakistan	2,072	56,639	4,704	34,221	7,302
Philippines	849	43,377	4,714	95,905	5,674
Saudi Arabia	523	8,258	338	8,970	...
Thailand	4,372	23,348	719	12,975	5,313
Turkey	1,108	5,336	1,249	3,552	1,844
Vietnam	2,843	...	1,149	5,161	4,569
EUROPE					
Bulgaria	298	1,478	163	3,563	1,226
France	374	1,496	185	1,120	5,248
Germany	313	1,430	114	1,902	...
Italy	193	5,264	334	1,055	...
Poland	459	2,315	189	2,354	1,627
Romania	531	3,547	...	3,600	...
Russia	226	...	88	...	...
Spain	257	3,460	241	1,034	6,227
Sweden	394	1,769	105	1,600	...
Ukraine	227	...	84	...	...
United Kingdom	667	3,228	308	3,207	...
OCEANIA					
Australia	438	2,539	88	1,506	...
New Zealand	323	1,875	80	1,005	...

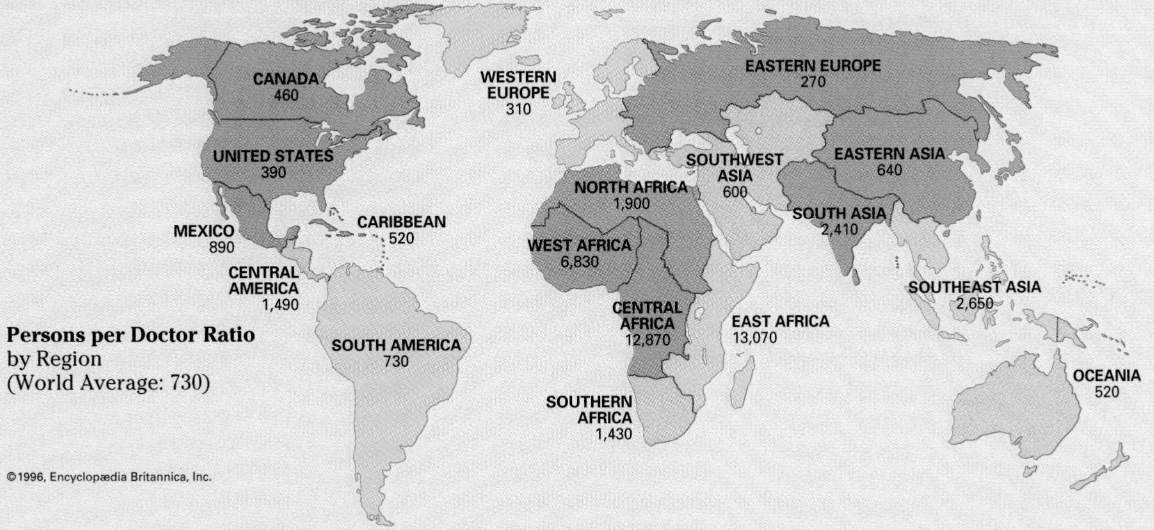

Persons per Doctor Ratio
by Region
(World Average: 730)

Hospitals, Most Recent Data (Selected Countries)

	Hospitals (number)	Hospital beds per 10,000 population	Admissions per 10,000 population	Bed-occupancy rate (%)	Average length of stay (days)
AFRICA					
Egypt	1,521	20	...	...	...
Ethiopia	86	3	...	...	...
Nigeria	11,588	12	...	...	...
South Africa	737	43	1,597	71.7	8
Zaire	942	21	1,249	64.1	7
NORTH AMERICA					
Canada	1,079	70	1,677	75.7	13
Mexico	772	8	403	64.7	5
United States	6,639	46	1,220[1]	65.6[1]	7[1]
SOUTH AMERICA					
Argentina	3,189	48	...	...	...
Brazil	35,701	37	1,277	...	...
Colombia	947	14	614	57.2	6
Peru	427	17	416	88.2	14
Venezuela	610	26	1,587	80.7	7
ASIA					
Bangladesh	890	3	853	...	...
China	63,101	26	460	80.9	16
India	25,452	9	...	...	...
Indonesia	985	6	...	...	...
Iran	581	15	...	...	...
Japan	10,066	136	643	83.3	56
Korea, South	924	23	519[2]	80.6[2]	13[2]
ASIA (cont'd)					
Pakistan	10,905	6	...	...	...
Philippines	1,695	13	...	...	...
Saudi Arabia	229	21	749	...	...
Thailand	1,064	17	...	...	...
Turkey	857	22	568	44.1	9
Vietnam	10,768	25	1,587	80.7	7
EUROPE					
France	3,819	122	2,318	83.0	16
Germany	2,411	83	1,823	83.8	15
Italy	1,886	68	1,491	70.0	12
Poland	775	66	1,288	72.5	14
Romania	...	95	...	...	...
Russia	12,700	135	...	...	...
Spain	830	43	946	76.9	12
Sweden	...	56	1,998	77.1	8
Ukraine	3,900	135	...	...	...
United Kingdom	2,423	64	1,220	65.6	7
OCEANIA					
Australia	1,071	50	...	...	...
New Zealand	337	77	1,293[3]	80.3[3]	8[3]

[1] 5,292 community hospitals only.
[2] General and specialized hospitals only.
[3] Government hospitals only; excludes psychiatric hospitals.

Source: national statistical offices.

Health Expenditures by Origin (Selected Countries), 1990

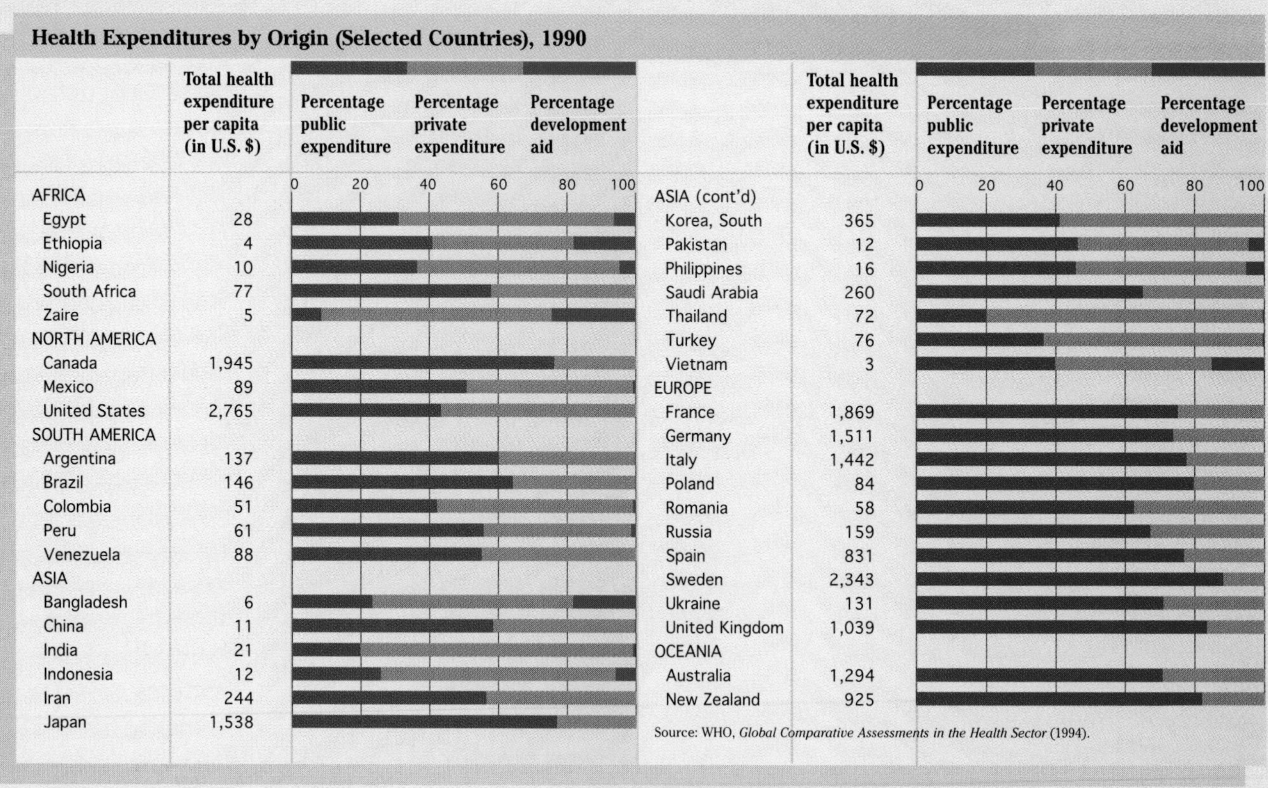

	Total health expenditure per capita (in U.S. $)
AFRICA	
Egypt	28
Ethiopia	4
Nigeria	10
South Africa	77
Zaire	5
NORTH AMERICA	
Canada	1,945
Mexico	89
United States	2,765
SOUTH AMERICA	
Argentina	137
Brazil	146
Colombia	51
Peru	61
Venezuela	88
ASIA	
Bangladesh	6
China	11
India	21
Indonesia	12
Iran	244
Japan	1,538
ASIA (cont'd)	
Korea, South	365
Pakistan	12
Philippines	16
Saudi Arabia	260
Thailand	72
Turkey	76
Vietnam	3
EUROPE	
France	1,869
Germany	1,511
Italy	1,442
Poland	84
Romania	58
Russia	159
Spain	831
Sweden	2,343
Ukraine	131
United Kingdom	1,039
OCEANIA	
Australia	1,294
New Zealand	925

Source: WHO, *Global Comparative Assessments in the Health Sector* (1994).

Per Capita Health Expenditures, Selected Countries, in U.S. Dollars, 1960–92

1960 1965 1970 1975 1980 1985 1990 1992

$3,000 2,750 2,500 2,250 2,000 1,750 1,500 1,250 1,000 750 500 250 0

United States $3,086
Switzerland 2,068
Canada 1,949
Germany 1,775
France 1,745
Sweden 1,317*
Austria 1,576*
Luxembourg 1,550
Iceland 1,456*
Italy 1,497*
Belgium 1,485*
Norway 1,468*
Australia 1,451
The Netherlands 1,449
Finland 1,363*
Japan 1,376*
Denmark 1,163
United Kingdom 1,151
New Zealand 1,079
Ireland 879*
Spain 895*
Portugal 585
Greece 452
Turkey 156

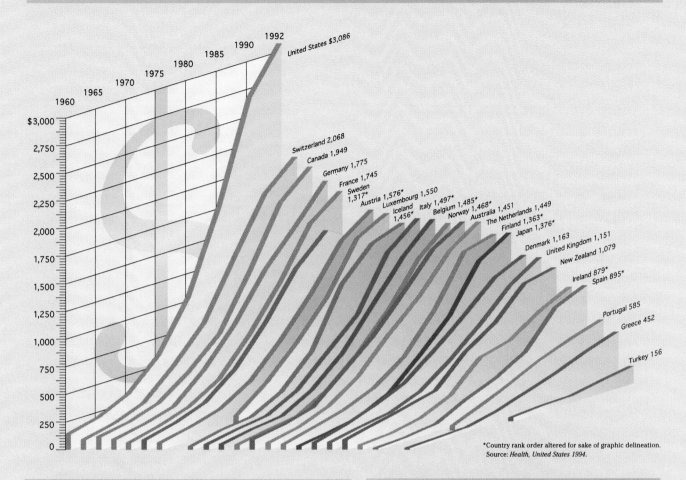

*Country rank order altered for sake of graphic delineation.
Source: *Health, United States 1994.*

World Distribution of DALYs[1] Lost to Disability, 1990

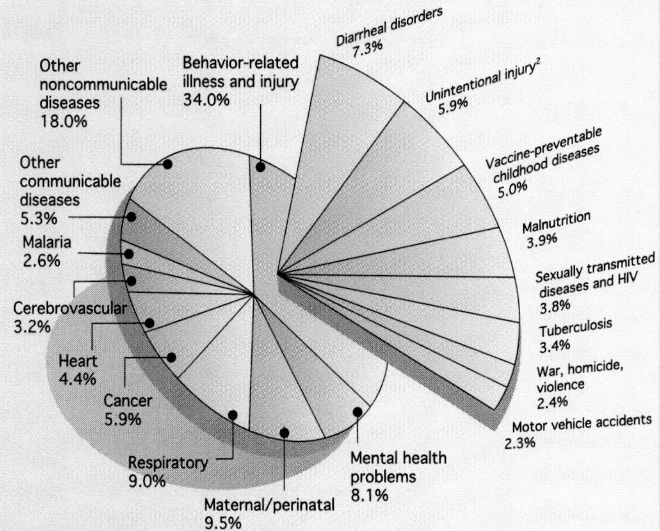

[1] Based on the concept of the Disability-Adjusted Life Year (DALY), a combined measure of years of life lost through premature death and years of healthy life lost through disability.
[2] Excluding motor vehicle accidents.
Source: World Bank, *World Development Report* (1993), as adapted by R. Desjarlais *et al.*, *World Mental Health* (1995).

United States, National Health Expenditures by Kind, 1993

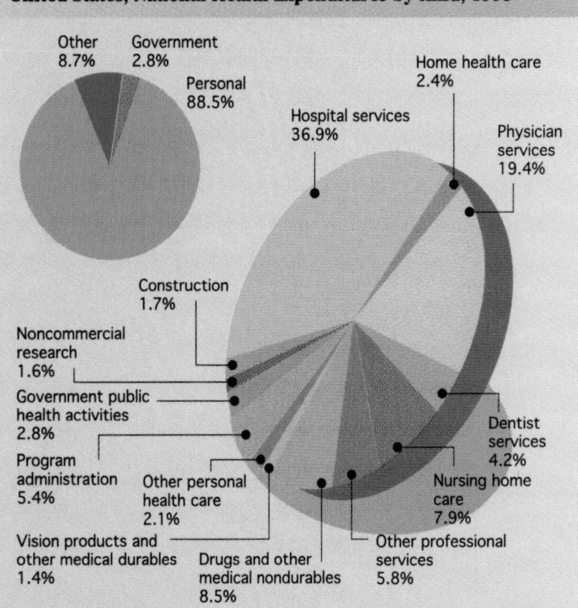

Sources: Office of National Health Statistics; Office of the Actuary, *National Health Expenditures* (1993); Health Care Financing Administration, *Health Care Financing Review*, vol. 16, no. 1, HCFA Pub. no. 03361 (1994).

Household and Community Health Indicators (Selected Countries)

	% persons in communities having:			% households having:	
	Health services (one hour's travel)	Safe water	Sanitary waste disposal	Inside toilet/ water closet	Refrigerator
AFRICA					
Egypt	99	88	51	...	...
Ethiopia	46	28	16	55.2	...
Nigeria	72	50	15	7.0	...
South Africa	...	...	...	...	...
Zaire	40	33	25	...	...
NORTH AMERICA					
Canada	100	100	...	99.4	99.6
Mexico	90	77	55	45.0	...
United States	100	100	...	98.9	99.8
SOUTH AMERICA					
Argentina	...	64	89	95.1	...
Brazil	...	86	78	...	71.1
Colombia	100	93	63	77.9	...
Peru	95	56	59	78.0	70.3[1]
Venezuela	...	90	94	84.4	74.2
ASIA					
Bangladesh	60	78	32	2.6	...
China	90	83	97	25.2	3.1/56.7[2]
India	100	74	15	20.0	...
Indonesia	80	51	44	26.6	...
Iran	87	61	51	43.6	...
Japan	100	...	...	65.8	98.9
Korea, South	100	92	100	51.3	93.1
Pakistan	90	56	24	25.1	...

	% persons in communities having:			% households having:	
	Health services (one hour's travel)	Safe water	Sanitary waste disposal	Inside toilet/ water closet	Refrigerator
ASIA (cont'd)					
Philippines	75	82	69	35.0	...
Saudi Arabia	98	93	82	...	...
Thailand	70	76	74	40.9	25.7
Turkey	100	92	...	70.6	83.1
Vietnam	90	27	18	...	...
EUROPE					
France	...	100	100	93.5	97.9
Germany	...	...	...	98.3	76.6
Italy	100	100	100	94.0	91.0
Poland•	100	100	100	68.9	97.7[3]
Romania	100	100	100	...	...
Russia[4]	100	100	100	...	95.0
Spain	95	100	100	97.1	...
Sweden	100	100	100	98.0	...
Ukraine	100	100[5]	100	...	...
United Kingdom	100	99	100	99.8	99.0
OCEANIA					
Australia	100	...	...	92.2	99.6
New Zealand	100	97	100[5]	97.1	76.5[6]

[1] Metropolitan Lima.
[2] Rural households/urban households.
[3] Households of employed persons.
[4] Data refer to former U.S.S.R.
[5] Urban households.
[6] Combined refrigerator-freezers only.

Sources: UNDP, *Human Development Report* (1994); WHO, *Progress Towards Health For All* (1994); national statistical offices.

Environmental Pollution

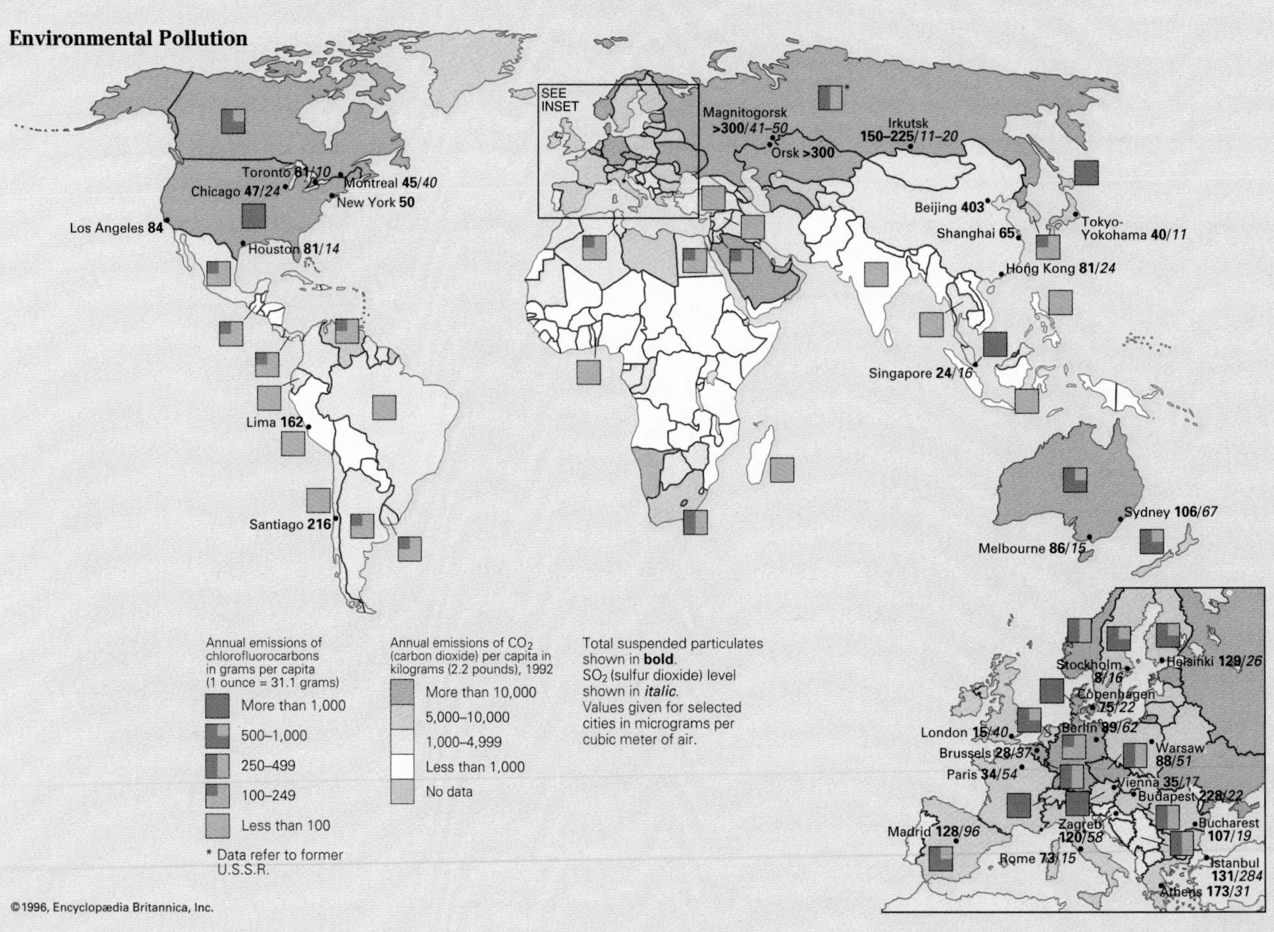

Deaths due to Injury, United States, 1992

Selected causes by type of accident or manner of injury	
TOTAL DEATHS DUE TO INJURIES	145,655
UNINTENTIONAL INJURIES/ACCIDENTS	86,777
Transport accidents	40,982
Railway	642
Highway	40,982
Water	837
Air and space	1,094
Poisoning and medical misadventure	7,082
Drugs (licit and illicit), medications, and biologics	5,951
Gases and vapors	633
Complications of medical and surgical care	2,669
Falls	12,646
Fire	3,958
Lightning	53
Other accidents	16,455
Drowning	3,524
Inhalation and ingestion of food or other object	3,128
Firearm	1,409
Handgun	233
Other firearm	1,176
Explosive material	189
Hot substance or object, corrosive material, and steam	131
Electric current	525
Adverse effects of drugs in therapeutic use	156
SUICIDE	30,484
HOMICIDE	25,488
Assault by firearm	17,488
Assault by cutting and piercing instrument	3,528

Source: National Center for Health Statistics.

Occupational Injury and Illness Rates per 10,000 Workers,[1] Selected Industries, United States, 1992

Industry	Annual average employment (in 000s)	Injuries	Occupational illnesses							
			Total	Skin diseases	Dust diseases of the lungs	Respiratory conditions related to toxic agents	Poisoning	Disorders due to physical agents	Disorders associated with repeated trauma	Other
PRIVATE INDUSTRY	90,459.6	830	59.8	8.2	0.3	3.1	0.9	2.9	36.8	7.5
Agriculture, forestry, and fishing	1,224.3	1,100	61.7	26.7	0.2	3.8	1.4	3.9	14.8	10.9
Mining	631.0	700	29.2	3.8	9.0	1.3	0.7	1.3	10.6	2.4
Construction	4,471.0	1,290	26.4	6.0	0.3	2.4	1.2	2.9	5.5	8.0
General building contractors	1,063.8	1,200	21.5	4.2	...	3.0	2.0	2.4	4.0	5.5
Special trade contractors	2,696.0	1,350	27.8	5.4	0.3	2.1	0.9	2.8	6.7	9.6
Manufacturing	18,040.0	1,080	165.0	17.6	0.6	5.6	2.0	6.3	124.1	8.8
Durable goods	10,237.0	1,170	169.7	18.1	0.5	6.5	2.7	8.1	124.4	9.5
Fabricated metal products	1,322.3	1,540	142.4	18.3	0.3	5.1	1.7	16.2	92.4	8.5
Industrial machinery and equipment	1,922.4	1,010	96.4	18.7	0.4	3.2	1.3	2.9	63.2	6.8
Electronic and other electric equipment	1,525.7	680	159.2	13.8	0.3	6.5	2.1	2.5	125.0	9.0
Transportation equipment	1,822.2	1,480	388.1	34.7	0.9	15.2	6.9	19.2	295.7	15.7
Nondurable goods	7,804.0	970	158.7	16.9	0.6	4.5	1.0	3.9	123.8	8.0
Food and kindred products	1,654.8	1,540	344.1	33.8	0.8	6.1	1.3	9.9	281.8	10.5
Apparel and other textile products	1,005.0	750	197.6	18.4	...	...	...	2.0	164.5	7.9
Printing and publishing	1,503.8	670	65.6	4.4	...	1.4	0.3	1.0	51.6	7.0
Chemicals and allied products	1,082.7	530	73.7	16.6	0.9	5.7	1.8	2.4	39.4	6.8
Transportation and public utilities	5,709.0	880	31.0	5.5	...	2.1	0.8	1.6	16.2	4.6
Trucking and warehousing	1,605.9	1,320	16.3	1.6	...	1.2	0.4	0.9	8.5	3.5
Communications	1,267.5	300	35.0	4.9	...	1.4	...	0.8	25.3	2.4
Wholesale and retail trade	25,391.0	820	21.9	2.8	0.1	1.6	0.5	...	10.1	4.8
Wholesale trade	6,045.0	730	23.6	2.5	...	2.9	0.4	1.2	11.2	5.5
Wholesale trade—durable goods	3,469.0	660	17.2	2.4	...	1.5	...	...	7.4	4.3
Wholesale trade—nondurable goods	2,576.0	830	32.5	2.5	...	4.7	...	1.0	16.4	7.2
Retail trade	19,346.0	850	21.2	2.9	0.1	1.2	...	...	9.6	4.5
General merchandise stores	2,422.2	1,020	23.6	2.3	0.1	1.5	...	0.4	12.8	3.9
Food stores	3,179.5	1,160	33.7	...	0.3	1.2	...	...	25.9	...
Automotive dealers and service stations	1,973.9	780	17.0	6.1	0.1	1.5	...	...	2.3	5.6
Apparel and accessory stores	1,131.0	420	9.9	0.4	...	...	...	...	7.4	...
Eating and drinking places	6,601.7	890	...	3.8	...	1.6	...	...	2.7	5.6
Finance, insurance, and real estate	6,571.0	270	27.1	1.8	...	1.4	0.2	1.3	19.2	3.2
Depository institutions (banks)	2,103.3	200	11.0	...	...	...	0.1	...	6.4	2.5
Real estate	1,282.0	650	26.1	7.2	...	4.8	...	3.9	4.8	4.9
Services	28,422.3	680	32.0	7.7	0.2	3.1	0.6	1.7	7.9	10.7
Hotels and other lodging places	1,572.0	1,090	27.8	9.9	0.5	2.9	...	1.4	6.2	6.6
Personal services	1,111.4	480	23.5	7.8	0.1	...	...	...	8.8	5.6
Business services	5,312.6	520	20.3	3.7	...	1.5	...	...	8.0	5.9
Amusement and recreation services	1,169.4	980	33.3	12.5	1.1	1.5	...	...	7.7	...
Health services	8,523.3	970	52.2	14.4	...	4.3	...	2.4	9.6	20.2
Educational services	1,699.5	540	16.1	2.7	0.2	2.8	0.4	...	4.3	2.7
Social services	1,958.0	780	25.0	6.4	...	2.8	...	2.6	2.0	10.3
Engineering and management services	2,469.4	220	24.5	3.2	...	...	...	0.5	8.2	7.0

[1] Incidence of nonfatal events or conditions, for full-time workers.

Source: U.S. Department of Labor, *Occupational Injuries and Illnesses: Counts, Rates, and Characteristics, 1992* (1995).

Disease Eradication: The Global Effort

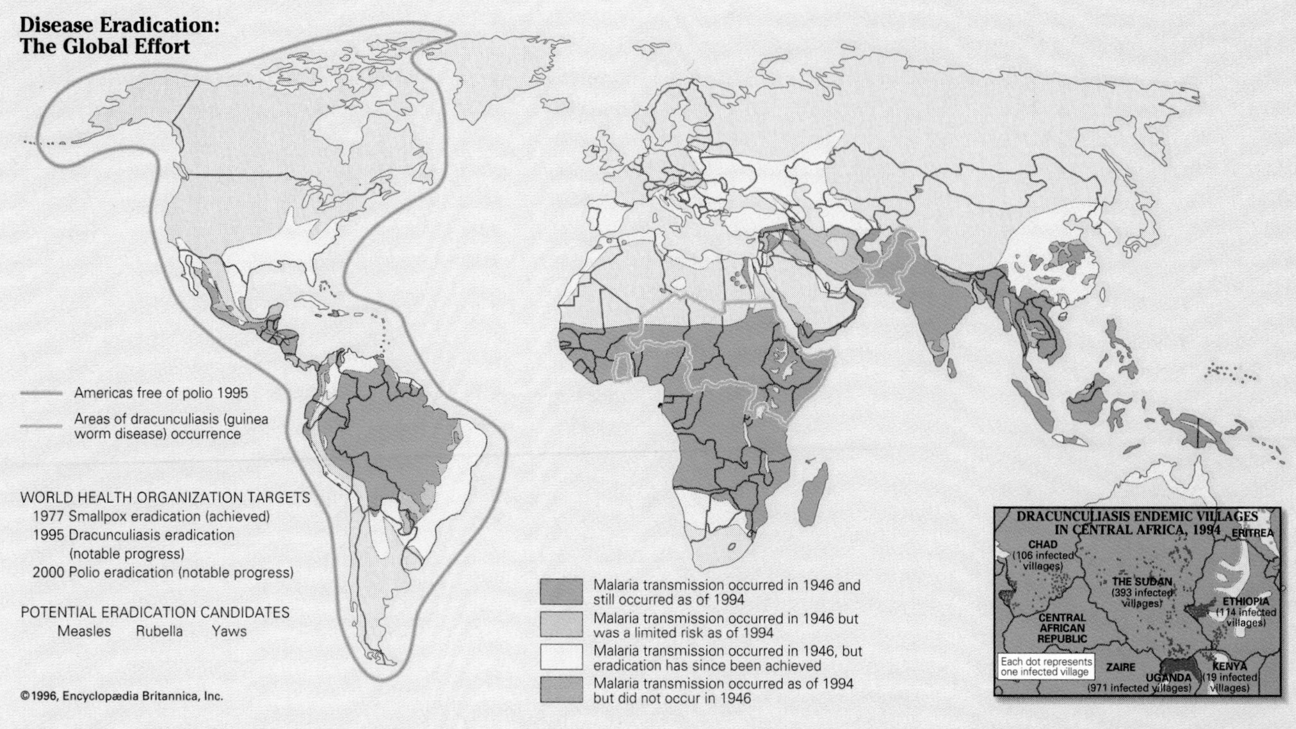

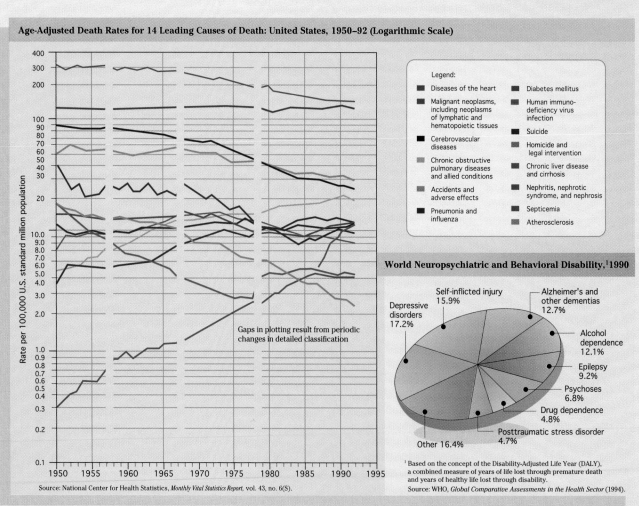

Age-Adjusted Death Rates for 14 Leading Causes of Death: United States, 1950–92 (Logarithmic Scale)

Rate per 100,000 U.S. standard million population

400, 300, 200, 100, 90, 80, 70, 60, 50, 40, 30, 20, 10.0, 9.0, 8.0, 7.0, 6.0, 5.0, 4.0, 3.0, 2.0, 1.0, 0.9, 0.8, 0.7, 0.6, 0.5, 0.4, 0.3, 0.2, 0.1

1950 1955 1960 1965 1970 1975 1980 1985 1990 1995

Gaps in plotting result from periodic changes in detailed classification

Legend:
- Diseases of the heart
- Malignant neoplasms, including neoplasms of lymphatic and hematopoietic tissues
- Cerebrovascular diseases
- Chronic obstructive pulmonary diseases and allied conditions
- Accidents and adverse effects
- Pneumonia and influenza
- Diabetes mellitus
- Human immunodeficiency virus infection
- Suicide
- Homicide and legal intervention
- Chronic liver disease and cirrhosis
- Nephritis, nephrotic syndrome, and nephrosis
- Septicemia
- Atherosclerosis

Source: National Center for Health Statistics, *Monthly Vital Statistics Report,* vol. 43, no. 6(S).

World Neuropsychiatric and Behavioral Disability,[1] 1990

- Depressive disorders 17.2%
- Self-inflicted injury 15.9%
- Alzheimer's and other dementias 12.7%
- Alcohol dependence 12.1%
- Epilepsy 9.2%
- Psychoses 6.8%
- Drug dependence 4.8%
- Posttraumatic stress disorder 4.7%
- Other 16.4%

[1] Based on the concept of the Disability-Adjusted Life Year (DALY), a combined measure of years of life lost through premature death and years of healthy life lost through disability.

Source: WHO, *Global Comparative Assessments in the Health Sector* (1994).

Recent Developments from the World of Medicine

The Changing World of Medicine and Health

A basic challenge facing all countries is to create systems that improve the health of their people. In most Western industrialized nations, this means creating public and private policies and institutions that finance and deliver "medical care." But "health" depends on many factors beyond medical ones. Social, economic, psychological, environmental, and biological phenomena all contribute to the status of the public's health. This is not a new realization. In the late 19th century, the public health movement in Great Britain emphasized the importance of clean air, sanitation, and nutrition as key factors not only in reducing the spread of communicable diseases such as cholera, tuberculosis, and smallpox but in improving general health and increasing longevity.

Throughout the last century and well into this one, many less developed countries were struggling just to provide their populations with a basic public health infrastructure. Many still are. Even in many developed nations, the challenge is reemerging. A combination of poverty, global immigration, limited access to basic public health measures such as immunization, and even societal complacency are creating an alarming increase in diseases thought to have been long overcome. The AIDS epidemic is a striking example of a global problem—one that is drawing attention to the inadequacy of the public health infrastructures in both developed and less developed nations.

As science clarifies human understanding of the complex relationship between health and environment, the notion of health care will inevitably be enlarged. Interventions that derive from the broader definition of health care (such as investments in prenatal care, infant nutrition, and injury prevention) can go a long way toward improving the population's general health. *Lack* of attention to the broader definition could be catastrophic.

Yet to most citizens of the developed world, health care still means medical care. Rightly or wrongly, a good medical delivery system is perceived as the minimum requirement for any country that wants to improve the health of its people. A fully developed medical system requires adequate financing and delivery of physician, hospital, and diagnostic services; pharmaceutical interventions; and long-term care. Worldwide, as the baby boom generation ages, with its sheer force of numbers, higher education levels, and larger incomes, the financing and delivery of health care will change—dramatically.

Basic trade-offs

In order to provide high-quality health care services to all its citizens, a country's health care system must consider a series of trade-offs. The basic issues that all health care systems must juggle are: cost (how much is paid and by whom), access (who gets what range of services under what circumstances), and quality (the caliber and outcomes of health care services provided). In the United States there is a fourth dimension—security of benefits. Depending on their social, economic, and employment status, Americans can lose and gain health care benefits several times in the course of their lives.

Cost. Most developed nations spend between 7% and 10% of their gross domestic product (GDP) on health care. Most health care systems in Europe, Canada, Australia, and New Zealand have managed to contain costs as a share of GDP for 5-to-10-year periods. They do so by managing costs from the top down through aggressive budget mechanisms. The United States, on the other hand, has continually expanded its share of the economy devoted to health care over the last 70 years. At least in part, this is because the U.S. is unique among developed nations in attempting to contain costs through market mechanisms. Despite having the highest and fastest-rising costs in the world, the U.S. maintains a strong ideological commitment to so-called user fees. These cost-control mechanisms include co-payments, deductibles, coinsurance, and patient out-of-pocket expenses. Consequently, the country has the highest proportion of costs borne directly by the consumer.

Quality. The quality of medical care is often thought to be a function of the caliber of inputs: training level of physicians and other professionals, technological sophistication, government investment in health, and the availability of highly specialized care. Increasingly, however, evidence shows that the returns gained from ever-increasing resources are often nonexistent or so negligible that they do not warrant further investment. In the U.S. the RAND Corporation has found that anywhere from a third to a half of medical procedures performed are unnecessary. Medical care is thus being called to task. What has it done with all the money? Where is the improved health status as indicated by such factors as longevity, mobility, quality of life, and so forth?

Access. Virtually all developed countries (the countries that make up the Organisation for Economic Co-operation and Development) have achieved universal coverage for health care for all their residents, with the notable exceptions of the U.S. and South Africa. In the former more than 40 million people are uninsured at any time, and as many as 60 million people are uninsured at some point in any two-year period. Inadequate access to health care is particularly acute in the case of children. At any given time more than 10 million American children lack even basic care.

Security of benefits. While the elderly in the U.S. enjoy guaranteed coverage through Medicare and certain groups with low incomes have access to health care through Medicaid, most Americans receive health insurance through an employer. Consequently, the uninsured population is a highly volatile one; as people change jobs or move in and out of employment, they go on and off insurance.

Global diversity

Different mechanisms exist for managing cost, quality, access, and security. Four basic models prevail:

- *Socialized medicine.* In this system the state owns or has virtual monopsony control (as the only payer) of all the factors of production in health care. The British National Health Service and the Danish and Swedish systems are the prime examples of socialized medicine. In the United Kingdom private insurance does exist, and approximately 10% of citizens avail themselves of this option, but the private-sector delivery mechanism is much smaller than the public one. Even the most complex medical cases are cared for in publicly financed facilities. Cost containment in socialized medicine is achieved by direct budget control.

- *Socialized insurance.* In this system the state acts as a monopoly insurer on behalf of all its citizens. The Canadian system is the prime example. Having economies of scale in administration and huge monopolistic power, a single payer purchases health services from independent providers. This concentration of purchasing power is the key to cost control.
- *Mandatory insurance.* In this system all citizens are covered by a variety of state-sponsored health insurance, independent employer or union-sponsored plans (often called sickness funds), and private health insurance. The systems of France, Germany, the Benelux countries (Belgium, The Netherlands, and Luxembourg), and Japan operate this way. Cost control is achieved by careful coordination of purchasing power among these different groups.
- *Voluntary insurance.* In the U.S. and South Africa, access to health insurance is not government-mandated. While the U.S. government sponsors insurance coverage for the elderly and the poor, the vast majority of citizens receive health insurance as a benefit of employment or by directly purchasing it themselves. There is, however, no requirement that either occurs, and many employed people pay on a fee-for-service basis. Because there is no single mechanism for control, the U.S. system has not been able to contain its costs. The hope is that competition between providers and the growth of managed care will help contain costs. The idea behind managed care is to change the incentives for delivery of health care services and to systematically oversee, evaluate, and micromanage medical care. Managed care has not done this so far; until it does, there is little hope of containing costs in the U.S.

Health care systems around the world have very different cultural roots and thus show a substantial variation in details of financing and the nature of services provided. In Britain and Germany, for example, there are sharp divisions (*i.e.,* very little overlap) between those doctors who work in hospitals and those who have community practices. In Canada there is no such discontinuity of care. Germans believe in treating low blood pressure, while the rest of the world is obsessed with high blood pressure and its treatment. The French are Europe's most avid consumers of pharmaceuticals, and French doctors prescribe more drugs aimed at treating "liver ailments" than does any other nation.

Global convergence

Despite cultural differences, health care systems are beginning to converge. The socialized medicine, socialized insurance, and mandatory insurance systems are all importing some tenets of managed care and competition. Generally, they are doing so not as a mechanism to contain costs but as a means to encourage improvements in quality and in customer service and responsiveness. Similarly, despite social democratic objections to charging citizens directly for health care, many

Dutch parents get a first glimpse of their newborn, delivered by cesarean section. All citizens of The Netherlands enjoy medical coverage through the country's mandatory insurance scheme, to which state, employer/union, and private sources contribute.

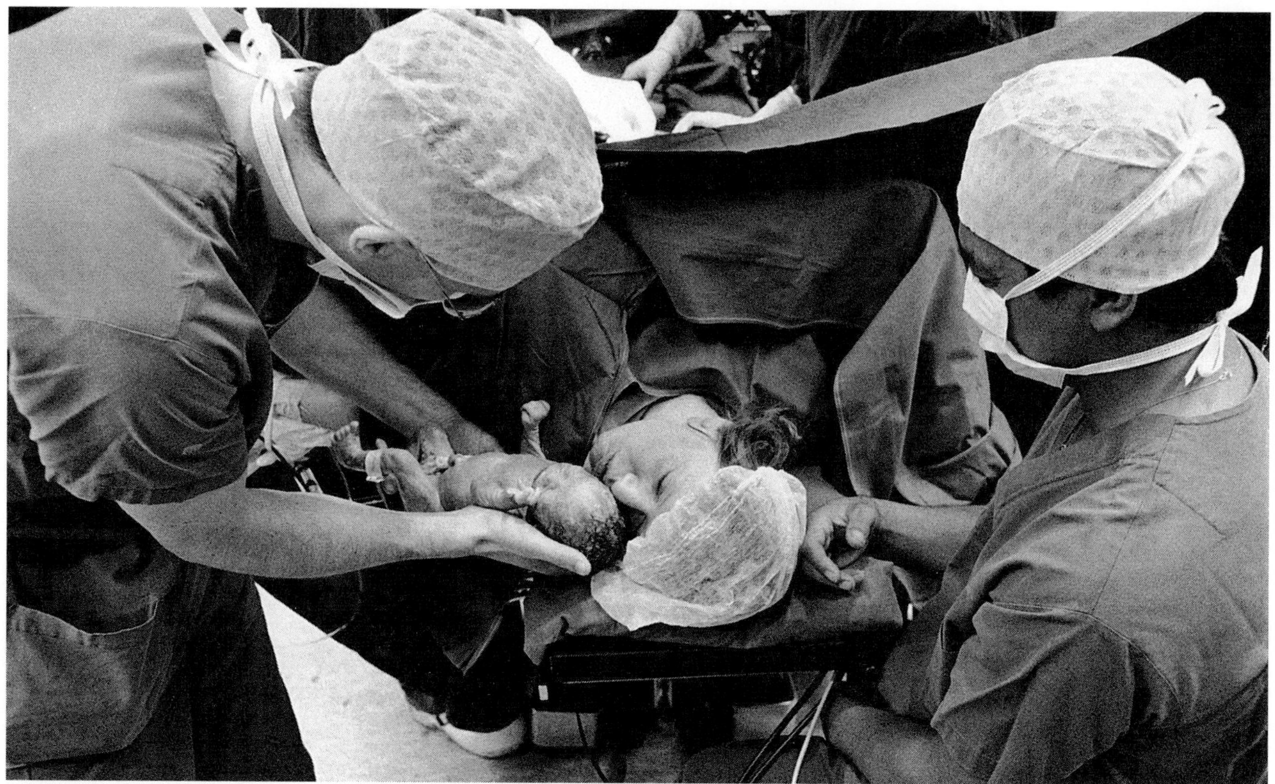

Rob Huibers—Panos Pictures

European systems are now looking to user fees, private insurance, and supplemental insurance to raise additional funds.

The United States, too, is showing signs of convergence. Had it been passed, the Clinton administration's health plan would have brought the U.S. system much closer to the German or Japanese systems. While large-scale reform on the federal level is clearly dead for the immediate future, some form of meaningful health care reform undoubtedly will be enacted in the next 15 years. Otherwise, the enormous growth of the population over age 65, which will begin to occur in 2010, will tax the system beyond its limits. Until then, however, it is not inconceivable that the U.S. will bury its head in the sand and ignore the plight of the uninsured and underinsured, which would mean that early in the next century, more than 50 million Americans would be without health insurance or access to good medical care.

"I have no objection to alternative medicine so long as traditional medical fees are scrupulously maintained."

"Big, ugly buyers"

The payers in the world's health systems—government, private payers, and individual patients—are merging their forces for a much more practical reason: to contain costs and increase value from their investments. Whether they are health care coalitions or large employers in the United States or regional health authorities in Great Britain, power is shifting to the purchasers. These powerful purchasers could be dubbed the "big, ugly buyers."

Funding private-sector style. Large American employers funded the health care cost excesses of the 1980s. When profits were high, there seemed little reason to get tough. With the 1990 recession, fierce global competition, and a wave of reengineering, American employers woke up to the need to contain health care costs. As a result, they are beginning to join forces to create more effective business coalitions. These coalitions have negotiated tougher contracts and raised employees' contributions. In response, health plans are consolidating to increase their own purchasing power with their contracting providers.

These purchasing coalitions recognize that it is in their collective interest to get *total* health costs under control. So far no one has found a good answer. It is clear that by pressuring plans and providers to keep costs down, big purchasers will

NEWS*CAP*

Americans: Feeling Pretty Healthy

A recent national survey found that nearly 87% of Americans over the age of 18 rate their health as good, very good, or excellent. The telephone survey, conducted by the Centers for Disease Control and Prevention (CDC), questioned over 100,000 Americans. Four questions were asked:

- Is your health generally excellent, very good, good, fair, or poor?
- How many days during the previous 30 days was your physical health not good because of injury or illness?
- How many days during the previous 30 was your mental health not good because of stress, depression, or problems with emotions?
- How many days during the previous 30 did your physical or mental health prevent performance of your usual duties?

Among the intriguing, but unexplained, findings were differences in the responses by state: Alaskans felt best, with 91.6% saying their health was good to excellent; residents of New Hampshire (90.8%), New Jersey (90.8%), Iowa (90.7%), Washington (90.5%), and Connecticut (90%) followed. At the bottom of the list were five adjacent south-central states: Tennessee (81.5%), Arkansas (80.3%), Kentucky (79.9%), Mississippi (78.4%), and West Virginia (76.6%). Also curious was the fact that the residents of Washington, D.C., a highly urban area where one might expect the population to suffer from higher-than-average environmental pollution, crime and accident rates, stress, and other problems of modern living, topped the list for the number of days on which residents considered themselves in good physical or mental health (28.4), compared with West Virginia's low of 24 good-health days.

The four questions have been added to the CDC's Behavioral Risk Factor Surveillance System, an ongoing annual survey in which state and federal health officials gather pertinent data on factors that could influence public health among Americans.

be able to contain their own costs. It is a fallacy, however, to presume they will be successful in containing wider system costs at the same time. In the absence of a total budget limit, as in Canada or Europe, the buyers in the U.S. may serve only to amplify the cost-shifting cascade.

Public-sector funding. Increasingly in the U.S. but certainly in the U.K. and Canada, "big, ugly buyers" reign supreme in the public sector. In the U.S., Medicare—perceived by many as the biggest and ugliest buyer of all—can cut what it pays its providers in order to get more services for less. The Medicaid program cannot cut prices any more than it already has without severely affecting access to care for the low-income citizens it serves. Instead, it resorts to capitation (whereby providers are paid a fixed monthly fee for all the care they provide or for a defined set of services per capita per month)—an obvious incentive to minimize the clinical services for the patient and a way for managed care to keep its costs down.

Over the last five years, a new class of big, ugly buyer has emerged in the U.S. public sector—the public employee group purchaser. The California Public Employees' Retirement System (CalPERS), which covers over one million employees and dependents, is perhaps the best example of a public-sector entity concentrating its purchasing power through a relatively limited number of managed-care plans. While short-term cost containment has been achieved by these purchasers, it is not known what their wider effects will be.

Big, ugly buyers, by concentrating their purchasing power, are forcing health plans to lower rates and consolidate horizontally. In fear of becoming lackeys to intermediaries, providers are beginning to integrate. In the U.S., hospitals, health plans, and physicians are reorganizing themselves in a myriad of contractual, organizational, and economic relationships that attempt to align incentives of each of the parties to contain costs and improve quality. Similar shifts are occurring in Sweden and Great Britain.

One unifying theme in the reintegration of health care is an attempt to shift the basic incentives of medical care from fee-for-service (whereby medical care providers get paid each time they perform a clinical service, an obvious incentive to do more) to capitation.

As a consequence, more actual patient care is being put in the hands of primary care physicians, who act as "gatekeepers" to the specialized services provided by hospitals and medical specialists. In effect, these primary care doctors become general contractors on behalf of their patients.

The creation of fund holders in the U.K. (groups of physicians who receive capitated contracts) or capitated medical groups in the U.S. is an attempt to give providers significant financial incentives to lower the costs of treating entire populations rather than maximizing the services they provide. Because the stock of U.S. physicians is dominated by specialists, however, it is questionable that this model can provide the majority of health care services. In Great Britain almost 50% of doctors are in general or family practice. By contrast, fewer than 20% of doctors in the U.S. are engaged in these disciplines. Moreover, because of the long lead time required for training physicians, it will be virtually impossible to change this mix in a substantial way anytime soon.

Threats to academic medicine

Traditionally, university-affiliated medical centers have been the crowning glory of health care systems, providing the highest form of medical care. In the U.S. and most of Europe, academic medicine has enjoyed massive cross-subsidy from faculty practitioners (whose services are billed out at much higher rates than their individual remuneration) and from the provision of esoteric, complex, and expensive clinical services such as organ transplantation and open-heart surgery. In the U.S. the 1980s were the golden years of academic medicine. But the world of the big, ugly buyer is shortsighted, and few employer coalitions, health plans, or fund holders today are likely to underwrite the excessive cost of medical education. Many academic medical centers could be in real jeopardy.

Academic medicine is starting to respond. Many of the prestigious New York City academic medical centers, for example, are on a buying spree—in hopes of building a "feeder network" of community-based institutions that can, in turn, support the high-technology medical palaces of Manhattan. But such strategic moves ignore the key questions of who is going to pay for research, teaching, and service innovation.

Ultimately, academic medicine will have to transform itself. It will have to produce fewer specialists and more generalists; focus on the creation of cost-reducing, not cost-increasing, technologies; and be more responsive to community needs in the provision of clinical services. Worldwide, it remains to be seen whether academic medicine will be able to meet these enormous challenges.

Health care's future face

For the developed nations, designing health care financing and delivery mechanisms that maximize access and quality

The new government of South Africa, elected in April 1994, will establish a national health service that is intended to redress the sharp disparities that existed for decades under apartheid rule.

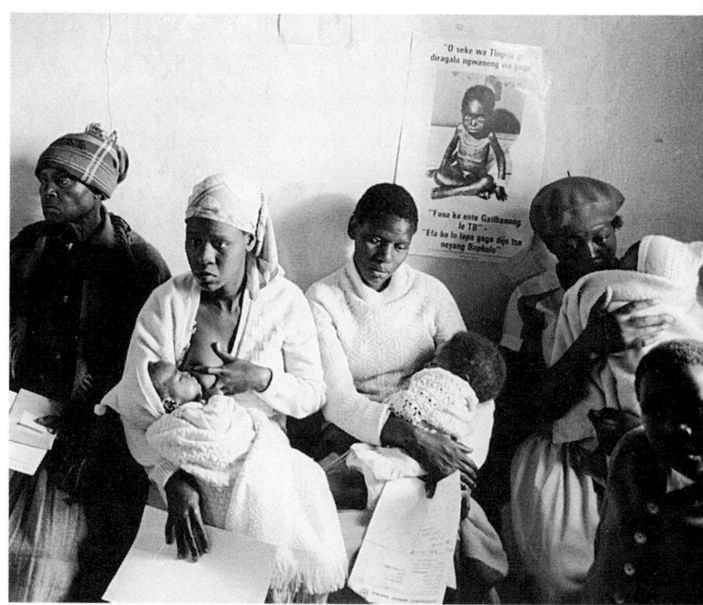

Gisèle Wulfsohn—Panos Pictures

while minimizing cost remains the key challenge. That task will become increasingly difficult because of the potent forces that are driving change. These include:

- *Sophisticated consumers.* Today's knowledgeable consumers are challenging the unique authority of physicians and insisting on a greater role in clinical decision making. Patients are neither passive nor docile. Increasingly, they are as educated as their doctors.
- *Shift to corporatism.* Medicine has historically been dominated by the self-regulated professional. Doctors take the Hippocratic oath to do no harm and serve the patient. Across the globe, medicine is being transformed from a professional to a corporate activity. Whether they are the American for-profit health plans and hospital chains or British fund holders, health trusts, and regional health authorities, the principal institutions of the future will be run more like corporations than professional practices.
- *Measurement and accountability.* As the shift from professional to corporate practice occurs and medicine confronts the demands of sophisticated consumers and corporate buyers, there will be an increasing need for better information on value in medical care. This requires systematic methods of collecting, reporting, and analyzing scientifically sound data on the costs, processes, and outcomes of care. This field of outcomes-oriented research is still in its infancy and, thus, no single tried-and-true means of evaluating the cost-effectiveness of health service has been developed.
- *Technology explosion.* Molecular biology and information technology, singly and in combination, will transform medicine in the next century. Mapping of the entire human genome will provide new insights into disease and possibly reveal long-hidden secrets that will lead to new, better, and more effective therapies for a host of diseases. But perhaps more powerful will be the application of computers and communications to the practice of medicine and the coordination of care. Medical practice is an information-based activity, yet it has lagged far behind other industries for decades (some say for centuries) in the appropriate use of information technology. The most significant transformations will come from a combination of large patient databases, "intelligent" knowledge-based systems to aid diagnosis, and satellite communications in remote areas, as well as various types of wireless communications and telemedicine.
- *Ethical questions.* New technologies, cost pressures, and sophisticated consumers are a powerful and potentially toxic combination. Death and dying issues, including euthanasia and medical futility, will become a major focus of societal debate in the next century as the baby boom generation confronts its mortality. The legitimacy of rationing care will come under enormous scrutiny. Because debates about the ethics of rationing will not be solved easily by technical analyses, the battles will often be political and confounded by issues such as race and poverty. Knotty questions will be asked about the rights of human beings to control and shape their own biology and that of the unborn. Indeed, deep-seated beliefs about life, disease, personality, and death will be challenged by the new biology.

Globally, health care systems will be challenged by all of these forces. Although convergence will increase, the health care systems of the near and distant future are likely to remain diverse, reflecting as they do the variations in the cultures in which they originated.

—J. Ian Morrison, Ph.D.

NEWS*CAP*

America's Deadliest Epidemic

A series of reports published in the *Journal of the American Medical Association* (June 14, 1995) offered ample evidence of violence as a public health emergency in the U.S. Guns remained central to the problem.

- A team of California researchers projected the cost of medical care for firearm-related injuries in 1995 at $4 billion.
- A study by the Centers for Disease Control and Prevention revealed that for every person killed by firearms in the U.S., nearly three persons were wounded. Information obtained from emergency rooms in 91 large and small hospitals nationwide showed that persons aged 15 to 24 years and African-Americans were four times as likely to be wounded by guns as to be killed.
- A study of homicides in New Orleans, La., indicated that the mortality rate for blacks was six times that for whites; this disparity, however, "generally disappeared" when socioeconomic status was taken into account. These findings contradicted assumptions that the psychological effects of racism are responsible for a presumed "predilection" for violence in black culture.
- A study conducted in Atlanta, Ga., appeared to counter one of the principal arguments for gun ownership—namely, that guns play an important role in preventing home-invasion crimes. Fewer than 2% of individuals who resisted home invasion used guns to do so.
- Another component of the nationwide epidemic of violence—domestic violence—was the focus of a study of women who received care in emergency departments of three hospitals and two walk-in clinics in Denver, Colo. While only 11.7% of the women surveyed had sought treatment as the result of domestic violence, more than 54% had been "assaulted, threatened, or made to feel afraid by partners at some time in their lives."

Rejuvenation Through Exercise

If I had known I was going to live this long, I'd have taken better care of myself.
—Eubie (James Hubert) Blake, pianist and ragtime composer, Feb. 7, 1883–Feb. 12, 1983

Many people fear old age. They worry about being sick or in pain. They worry about becoming debilitated. They worry about their ability to pay their medical bills. They dread the day when they might be helpless or dependent.

"See, the problem with doing things to prolong your life is that all the extra years come at the end, when you're old."

Growing old and feeling it

On the one hand, people work hard to prepare for those contingencies. They contribute to pension plans, pay off mortgages, buy supplemental medical insurance, and, if they live in the United States, sign up for Medicare and join the American Association of Retired Persons. Yet those same people often ignore a way of preparing for old age that would help ensure that their "golden years" are rewarding—exercise!

Not only are sports and exercise fun, but they offer a way to stave off many of the effects that are commonly assumed to be "inevitable" with aging. As they age, people discover that it is harder to do the activities they took for granted when they were younger. So they cut back even more; they accept rides instead of walking a short distance, and they often give up walking for pleasure. This, unfortunately, starts a vicious circle of disuse that makes them even weaker.

Too many people accept the stereotype of the hunched-over old woman who wears sweaters in the summer and can no longer open a jar of pickles or the man whose walk has turned into a shuffle and who is so stiff he can barely bend over to tie his shoelaces. These and other activities of daily living—such as people's ability to walk across a room, do simple grooming chores, feed themselves, get to the washroom, and transfer themselves from a bed to a chair—are the types of activities that gerontologists typically inquire about when assessing the functional capacities of the elderly.

But are these declines in functioning inevitable? What really happens to the body as a person ages? In the book *Biomarkers: The 10 Keys to Prolonging Vitality* (1991), physiologist William J. Evans and physician Irwin H. Rosenberg of the Human Nutrition Research Center on Aging (HNRCA) at Tufts University, Boston, identified 10 determinants of aging:

- lean body (muscle) mass
- strength
- resting metabolism
- body fatness
- aerobic capacity
- insulin sensitivity
- blood fats (cholesterol)
- blood pressure
- bone density
- body temperature

While some decline in physiological functions may be inevitable, all of the factors, or "biomarkers," cited by Evans and Rosenberg can be favorably affected by exercise. Exercise, of course, is not the whole answer to staving off declines. Nutrition is another important factor, and some conditions such as high blood pressure and high blood cholesterol may require drug therapy. Nonetheless, regular exercise is an important component in the prevention of conditions usually associated with old age, and therefore each of the biomarkers merits attention.

Another approach to aging

The Framingham Heart Study, which has discovered many things about the links between lifestyle and health, found that about half of women over age 65 cannot lift 10 pounds.

Muscle mass and strength. Between ages 20 and 70, people lose about 30% of their lean body tissue (muscle mass). After age 30, people lose both muscle cells and the nerve cells that tell muscles to contract. Even though people lose muscle mass as they age, they can increase the strength of the remaining muscle cells. Researchers have shown that people who do some form of progressive resistance exercise, or weight training, can improve their strength at any age. Possibly the most striking example was a study done by Maria A. Fiatarone and colleagues from the HNRCA. The researchers studied a group of 10 frail, elderly men and women who ranged in age from 87 to 96 at the Hebrew Rehabilitation Center for the Aged, a chronic-care nursing facility near Boston. The subjects participated in an eight-week program of high-intensity strength training of the lower body. All but one subject completed the program; the nine remaining participants made the following improvements:

- increased muscle strength by an average of 174%
- increased walking speed by an average of 48%
- increased size of mid-thigh muscles by an average of 9%

The researchers concluded that exercise enables dramatic strength gains even in very old and frail people.

In a subsequent study, Fiatarone and her associates studied 100 elderly residents of the same institution. The subjects, whose average age was 87 years, were assigned to four study groups for a 10-week period. A first group did lower-body resistance exercise; a second took a multivitamin nutritional supplement; a third group exercised and took a supplement; while a fourth group did not engage in resistance training and took a placebo instead of a supplement. The subjects who exercised, compared with those who did not exercise, again showed dramatic improvement:

Kevin Horan

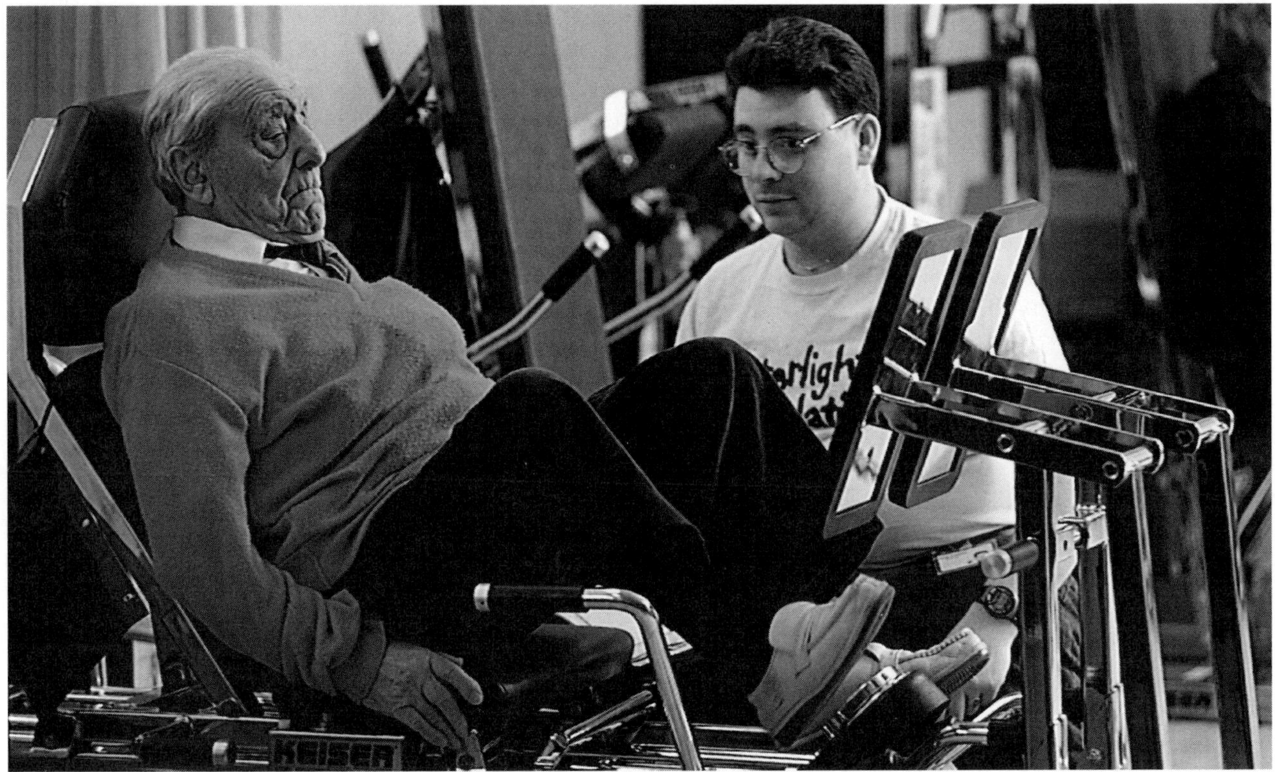

A nonagenarian works out on weight-training equipment at a Boston rehabilitation center for the aged. Even frail, very elderly nursing home residents can vastly increase their strength and enhance their daily functioning with progressive resistance exercise.

- increased muscle strength by 113%
- walked almost 12% faster after the study
- improved stair-climbing ability by 28%
- increased thigh muscle size by an average of 2.7%

The multivitamin supplementation apparently had no effect on the outcome of the study, so the researchers concluded that exercise, not nutrition, counteracts muscle weakness in older people. Furthermore, the improvements in walking and stair climbing and the enhanced strength in the exercisers translated to an increased ability to perform activities of daily living. The researchers also reported that four of the subjects who had used a walker before the study were able to walk comfortably with a cane after the study. On the other hand, one of the nonexercisers who had used a cane before the study required a walker *after* the study.

Resting metabolism. The rate at which the body burns calories just to maintain vital functions (such as breathing) is called resting metabolism, or basal metabolic rate. As people age, their caloric need decreases because less oxygen is required for fueling the decreased muscle mass. On average, people need about 100 fewer daily calories with each passing decade after about age 20. Resistance exercise, however, counteracts some of the muscle loss and thus the tendency to require fewer calories. The explanation for this is that muscle, as opposed to fat, is active tissue, and it therefore requires more calories to maintain itself.

Body fatness. The body of the average 25-year-old woman is 25% fat. That of the average 65-year-old sedentary woman is 43% fat. In 1985 a panel of experts convened by the National Institutes of Health issued a consensus statement on the health implications of obesity. That document defined obesity as 20% above ideal body weight and concluded that being obese is a major health hazard.

Such excess fat is a risk factor for heart disease and stroke. The Harvard Alumni Health Study followed more than 10,000 men, aged 45 to 84, for eight years and showed that the more overweight men were, the higher their risk of death from "all causes" and from coronary heart disease in particular. In 1995 Harvard researchers conducting the Nurses' Health Study, an ongoing investigation of diet, lifestyle, and health of more than 115,000 female registered nurses, reported that higher levels of body weight within the "normal" range, as well as modest gains in weight during adult life, increased the risk of fatal and nonfatal heart disease in women. The weight that the women had attained at midlife (ages 30–55) and the degree of excess body fat appeared to be factors that had the most to do with whether they developed coronary disease.

It is well established that regular physical activity can decrease body weight and fat stores, whereas calorie restriction alone leads to the loss of muscle mass. Thus, the most effective way to reduce total body fat is to combine regular exercise with a low-calorie diet; the best way to cut caloric intake is to limit the percentage of daily calories from fat.

Aerobic capacity. Maximal oxygen consumption, also called aerobic capacity, describes the body's ability to take in and use oxygen. It is a key indicator of an individual's heart-lung function and capacity to produce energy. Physiologists measure such physical capacity in workload units known as metabolic equivalents, or METs. (One MET equals the amount of oxygen required for sitting at rest.) Average men and women have an 8- to 12-MET capacity. This means that at a maximal level of exercise, they consume 8 to 12 times the amount of oxygen that they take in at rest. Older or unfit persons and heart patients generally average 5 to 8 METs. In contrast, highly trained endurance athletes have been measured at 15 to 20 METs or more.

When aerobic capacity improves, the following physiological changes generally occur:

- The amount of air the lungs can take in increases owing to increases in the rate and depth of breathing.
- The amount of oxygen that moves from the lungs to the blood increases.
- The heart pumps more oxygen-rich blood to the muscles with each beat.
- Oxygenated blood reaches the muscles faster.
- The muscles are able to extract more oxygen from the bloodstream.

High aerobic capacity is obviously important to a young athlete who wants to compete in a marathon, but how does increased maximal oxygen consumption help the elderly woman who wants to tend her garden? A given task (like gardening) requires a relatively constant supply of oxygen. In gardening, a woman who is not aerobically fit may use her entire aerobic capacity; the aerobically fit woman may use the same number of METs for gardening, but since she has a higher capacity, she will have greater "energy reserve." This means that she can accomplish other strenuous tasks of daily living with less fatigue.

Another example of how increased aerobic capacity increases performance level is the cardiac patient who has an extremely low aerobic capacity of 4 METs. After just three months in a supervised walking program, he increases his maximal oxygen consumption to 6 METs. As a result, the relative oxygen cost of a 4.8-km (3-mi)-per-hour walk (3 METs) decreases from 75% of that man's capacity to 50%. He, like the gardener, is able to manage the tasks of daily living with less fatigue.

At one time the standard means of recovery after a heart attack was bed rest. A classic study in the late 1960s, however, showed that the effect of prolonged bed rest on aerobic fitness is the opposite of that of exercise. After three weeks of bed rest, active and inactive (but presumably healthy) subjects had a 27% lower maximal oxygen consumption. That amount approximates the decrease in fitness that normally occurs from age 30 to 60. In other words, three weeks of bed rest resulted in the same decrease in heart-lung fitness as aging 30 years! Fortunately, the fitness of those subjects returned within weeks of resuming physical activity.

After the age of 20, maximal oxygen consumption typically declines by about 1% per year. An aerobic exercise program can lead to a 20% increase in heart-lung fitness, which translates to a 20-year functional rejuvenation. In other words, a physically trained 60-year-old can achieve the same fitness level as an inactive 40-year-old.

Insulin sensitivity/glucose tolerance. The ability of the body to regulate the level of sugar in the blood is called blood sugar tolerance, or glucose tolerance. When blood sugar tolerance declines, the concentration of sugar in the blood increases. By age 70 about one in four adults is at risk of developing adult-onset, non-insulin-dependent diabetes. These people are said to be "insulin resistant." That is, a larger-than-normal amount of insulin is required for lowering blood sugar. Physiologist Arthur Leon, at the University of Minnesota Medical School, speculates that the decline in blood sugar tolerance with aging is probably related to weight gain and physical inactivity. As muscle mass decreases and body fat increases with age, the tissues need more insulin to do the same amount of work. Studies show that regular exercise increases insulin sensitivity or enhances the ability of the body to use the insulin it produces, and thereby normal blood sugar levels are maintained.

To improve blood sugar tolerance, a regular exercise program should be combined with a diet that is low in fat and high in fiber. Preventing diabetes is an important goal in itself, but diabetes also affects the vascular system and contributes to high levels of blood cholesterol, which is a major risk factor for heart disease.

Blood fats. The relationship between high blood cholesterol and high rates of heart disease has been substantiated in numerous scientific investigations, including the Framingham Heart Study, which began in the late 1940s and has continued to track lifestyles and disease development in nearly 5,000 residents of Framingham, Mass. Heart disease is virtually nonexistent in men with total cholesterol values below 150 mg/dL (milligrams per deciliter). Assessment of coronary risk, however, must also consider total cholesterol, which includes both low-density lipoprotein (LDL) cholesterol (the "bad" cholesterol that clogs blood vessels) and high-density lipoprotein (HDL) subfractions. HDL, the "good" form of cholesterol, helps to clear blood vessels.

Blood cholesterol values tend to increase with age. According to the American Heart Association (AHA), approximately one-third of Americans aged 20 to 34 have a serum cholesterol level of 200 mg/dL or more. About 64% of people over age 75 have this level of serum cholesterol. While LDL levels generally increase with aging, HDL values generally decrease or remain unchanged. The severity of atherosclerosis and the risk of coronary heart disease increase with levels of total cholesterol above 200 mg/dL, LDL values above 130 mg/dL, and HDL levels below 40 mg/dL. On the other hand, HDL values above 60 mg/dL are now considered a "negative risk factor"—one that protects against heart disease.

The combined results of 95 research studies that evaluated subjects who gained, maintained, or lost body weight showed that regular exercise produced modest changes in total and LDL cholesterol. When body weight decreased or remained unchanged, total cholesterol and LDL cholesterol levels decreased significantly. Conversely, when body weight increased, cholesterol and LDL cholesterol levels increased. These findings suggest that exercise-mediated reductions in total cholesterol and LDL cholesterol are greatest when concomitant body weight losses occur.

While numerous studies have shown that vigorous physical activity is associated with increased HDL cholesterol, more recent studies indicate that regular low-intensity, long-duration physical activity such as walking several kilometers most days also increases HDL levels. An additional energy expenditure of approximately 1,000 calories per week, equivalent to walking or jogging 13–16 km (8–10 mi) per week, appears to be the minimum level needed for raising the HDL level.

Maximum functional benefit can be achieved when exercise, dietary modification, and weight loss are combined. The best way to reduce body weight and fat stores is through sensible caloric restriction (especially of dietary fats) and regular endurance exercise that uses large muscle groups in a repetitive manner—walking, jogging, swimming, bicycling, rowing, cross-country skiing, etc.

Blood pressure. A person has hypertension when he or she has a resting systolic blood pressure (during the heart's contraction) of 140 mm Hg (millimeters of mercury) or higher and a diastolic pressure (during the heart's relaxation) of 90 mm Hg.

The incidence of high blood pressure increases with age. The AHA reports that in the United States about 9% of men and 3% of women aged 20 to 34 have hypertension; after age 75 about 64% of men and 75% of women are affected.

High blood pressure kills nearly 40,000 Americans annually, and it contributes to the death of many more who have fatal strokes, heart attacks, or heart failure. The risk of developing high blood pressure is related to physical activity and fitness levels. Persons who are less active have a 30% to 50% higher risk of high blood pressure.

Scientists at the Cooper Institute for Aerobics Research in Dallas, Texas, report that their clients who maintain fitness as they age have a 34% lower risk of developing high blood pressure. Regular aerobic exercise also lowers blood pressure in persons who already have high blood pressure, especially when there is concomitant weight loss.

A recent meta-analysis of 25 relevant studies conducted over the last 20 years strengthens the case for exercise training in the treatment of mild hypertension. The studies generally involved men between 15 and 70 years of age, and training programs varied from one to 12 months in length. About two-thirds of the subjects in the exercising groups had statistically significant decreases in blood pressure, averaging about 10 mm Hg for both systolic and diastolic blood pressure. Moreover, low-intensity training such as walking seemed to be just as effective as high-intensity training such as running—and possibly more so.

Although these results are encouraging and suggest that greater numbers of sedentary people might now be motivated to exercise, it should be emphasized that the antihypertensive effects of exercise, like pharmacological therapy for high blood pressure, depend on continuation of the treatment. In other words, hypertension returns soon after the cessation of a regular exercise program.

Bone density. A decrease in bone mineral density, or bone loss, is inevitable as people age. Until about age 20, bone growth outpaces bone breakdown (resorption). But as people age, this process reverses, which causes bone loss. Osteoporosis means "porous bone." It is defined by the National Osteoporosis Foundation as "a disease characterized by low bone mass and structural deterioration of bone tissue, leading to bone fragility and an increased susceptibility to fractures of the hip, spine, and wrist." Type I osteoporosis is the accelerated loss of bone density that occurs when women reach menopause. Type II osteoporosis occurs in both men and women after about age 70. One-third to one-half of all postmenopausal women and nearly half of all persons over age 75 will be affected by one of these types of bone loss. Not surprisingly, women are affected at a much higher rate than men; 80% of persons with osteoporosis are women. Osteoporosis is responsible for about 1.5 million bone fractures in the U.S. annually. Fractures of the hip and wrist are the most common; fractures of the hip, however, are the most devastating. Persons who have hip fractures have a 5% to 20% greater risk of dying within a year than do others their age, and 15% to 25% or more of those who have lived independently before a hip fracture need long-term care after the fracture.

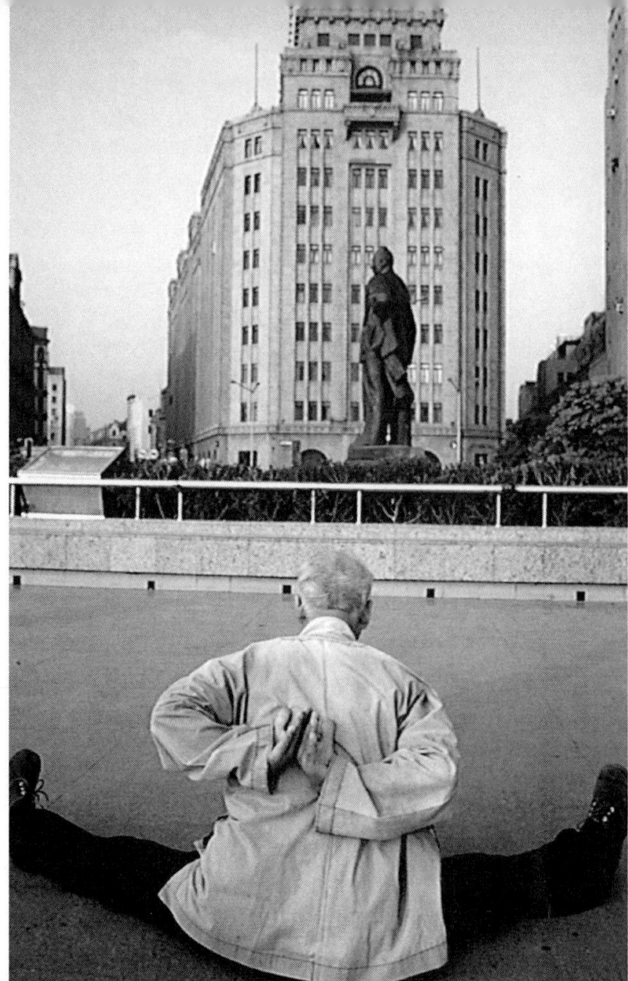

A T'ai Chi ch'uan practitioner in Shanghai begins each day with an early-morning routine of meditative exercise. At the age of 84 he has lost neither his vitality nor his flexibility.

Fritz Hoffmann—JB Pictures

It is well documented that weight-bearing exercise such as walking, jogging, or aerobic dance helps maintain bone density. Although bone density improvement generally is small, it appears that exercise also helps prevent further bone loss in women who are already affected. Even small improvements may help prevent bone fractures.

Calcium intake is also important in the prevention of osteoporosis but is not enough. In a recent study of 55- to 70-year-old women, in which all participants took a 1,500-mg calcium supplement per day, half of the subjects participated in an exercise program of walking, jogging, and stair climbing.

The women who exercised had a 5.2% increase in bone mass in the lumbar vertebrae (lower spine). Those who took the calcium but did not exercise had no change in bone mass.

In recent years investigators have studied the effect of resistance training on bone density. A study of postmenopausal women who participated in a weight-training program showed they had an average 1.6% increase in bone mineral density in the spine. During the same time period, those who did not exercise lost an average of 3.6% of bone density.

Experts who have studied the effects of exercise on bone mineral content caution women not to assume that exercise and increased calcium intake alone will prevent bone loss. Bone loss in postmenopausal women is related to the decrease in estrogen levels, and for some women hormone replacement therapy is recommended. Women should discuss these interventions with their doctors.

Body temperature. Healthy persons have a core body temperature close to 37° C (98.6° F); this is maintained because the body has an internal "thermostat." Sweating in response to heat and shivering in response to cold are the mechanisms that regulate this internal body temperature.

Older people are more susceptible to problems with temperature regulation because as they age, they lose some of their ability to sweat and shiver. The heart pumps less blood to the skin; thus, less internal heat is lost in the form of sweat. Shivering is the rapid contraction of muscles to produce body heat, but because older persons have less muscle mass, they do not shiver effectively. Aerobic exercise improves the ability to sweat, and resistance exercise increases muscle mass, which thereby enables normal shivering.

Joints, muscles, and the passing of the years

Evan W. Kligman, at the Arizona Center on Aging, University of Arizona College of Medicine, and exercise physiologist Eric Pepin describe two hallmark conditions that are usually associated with aging: lack of flexibility and osteoarthritis (degeneration of bone and cartilage). Flexibility is defined as the range of motion around a joint. Kligman and Pepin suggest that decades of inactivity cause an astonishing loss of flexibility and consequent motor limitation; this is especially true among men.

Although flexibility has not been studied as extensively as other components of fitness, such as strength, it is known that persons who are not flexible are at risk for posture and low-back problems. Older people who are not flexible have a hard time with many daily activities such as bending over to tie their shoes. Daily stretching exercises, however, will help counteract the loss in flexibility that comes with age.

Osteoarthritis is a "wear-and-tear" disease of the weight-bearing joints—especially the hips, knees, and lower spine. The cartilage, which cushions the end of the bone, becomes rough and wears away. When this happens, the person experiences pain, swelling of the affected joint, and stiffness.

Osteoarthritis can occur at any age but is typically a disorder of the elderly. According to one estimate, as many as 85% of 70- to 79-year-olds have osteoarthritis. Exercise helps the joints move more easily. It also decreases pain and stiffness and makes it easier to perform daily living tasks. Persons with osteoarthritis benefit from two types of therapeutic exercise. Range-of-motion exercise (*e.g.,* shoulder shrugs) decrease stiffness and prevent loss of motion. Resistance exercise increases the strength of muscles around joints. Moreover, contrary to previous thinking, weight-bearing exercise seldom causes further harm to joints and generally improves their functional capacity. Patients with osteoarthritis are now urged to exercise; most will benefit from a program of walking, calisthenics, jogging, or other weight-bearing aerobic activity.

Courtesy of Cooper Aerobics Center

Vigorous walkers lower their blood pressure and maintain an enviably high level of fitness at the renowned Cooper Aerobics Center and Institute for Aerobics Research in Dallas, Texas.

Aging: not to be taken sitting down

Several years ago a study by Steven N. Blair and colleagues at the Cooper Institute found that a low level of aerobic fitness is an important risk factor for death from all causes. The researchers studied over 10,000 men and 3,000 women who were given a preventive medical examination and a maximal treadmill exercise stress test to assess their aerobic capacity. Over an average follow-up period of slightly more than eight years, 240 men and 43 women died. The study revealed the following:

- Higher initial levels of aerobic fitness, expressed as METs, translated to lower death rates from cancer and heart disease (the relationship plateauing at a fitness level of 9 to 10 METs).
- No additional benefit (that is, further reduction in death rate) was associated with higher levels of fitness (highly trained distance runners were at no lower risk of death than were individuals with average to slightly above-average fitness).
- The greatest reduction in risk for both men and women occurred as they progressed from the lowest level of fitness (≤ 6 METs) to the next level (7 METs), which suggests that even a slight improvement in aerobic fitness among the most unfit confers a substantial health benefit.

Blair's research emphasized that the fitness level associated with the lowest mortality could be easily achieved by most men and women by simply walking briskly for 30 minutes or more every day. This recommendation was recently echoed in a position statement issued jointly by the Centers for Disease Control and Prevention and the American College of Sports Medicine: "Every American adult should accumulate 30 minutes or more of the moderate-intensity physical activity on most, preferably all, days of the week."

In 1995 Blair and co-workers reported on the relationship between changes in aerobic fitness and the risk of death in men. Participants included nearly 10,000 men, ranging in age between 20 and 82, who were given two preventive medical examinations, which included assessment of physical fitness by maximal exercise testing, about five years apart. Approximately five years after the second examination, deaths from all causes and from cardiovascular disease were determined. The highest death rate occurred in men who were unfit at both examinations; the lowest death rate was in men who were physically fit at both examinations. Men who improved from the unfit to the fit category between the first and second examinations had an intermediate death rate, even after adjustments were made for age, health status, and other risk factors. These important new findings on the relationship between changes in fitness and risk of death support the hypothesis that regular physical activity improves health and delays death.

Investigators have carefully documented the physiological changes that come with age. Less studied but perhaps as important are issues of self-image and well-being. Many older people find that their opportunities to socialize are limited. Numerous studies have shown that social isolation is associated with a poor general health prognosis. Engaging in group activities such as dancing, bowling, and synchronized swimming not only brings older people together but makes life more interesting and fun. And those are just a few of the activities that have no age limits!

A recent study by the National Institute on Aging's Gerontology Research Center in Baltimore, Md., concluded:

> *Aging is a highly unique, individualized process. There is no such thing as a typical elderly person. People age at markedly different rates. Some individuals even show improvements over time for certain physiological functions. Declines in older men and women occur most frequently during incidents or periods of stress.*

—Barry A. Franklin, Ph.D., and Frances Munnings

AIDS Update

The year 1995 was a watershed for AIDS/HIV research. The development of a highly sensitive method for measuring the amount of virus in the blood provided the basis for experiments that led to key advances in the understanding of how HIV causes disease. At the same time, efforts to design better agents for inhibiting viral replication began to bear fruit. Significant advances were also made in the prevention and treatment of major complications of HIV infection. Although the numbers of HIV-infected individuals worldwide continued to mount, the pessimism that had prevailed for the past several years among AIDS researchers, clinicians, and persons infected with HIV was giving way to cautious optimism.

The U.S. epidemic

Nearly a half million cases of AIDS had been reported in the United States by the start of 1995. Approximately 80,000 cases were reported during 1994, compared with about 100,000 in 1993. The larger number of cases in 1993 reflected the impact of the change that year in the official case definition for AIDS (the criteria for determining who has the disease). The revised case definition included, in addition to HIV-infected persons with certain specific "AIDS defining" diseases, asymptomatic individuals with severe depletion of the immune system cells called T-helper lymphocytes, also known as T-helper cells or CD4+ cells. (Healthy people have from 800 to 1,200 T-helper cells per cubic millimeter of blood. Under the expanded case definition, those with 200 or fewer cells per cubic millimeter can be classified as having AIDS.) The Centers for Disease Control and Prevention (CDC) projected in 1994 that the rate of new U.S. AIDS cases had reached a plateau and would remain roughly constant for the next several years.

In 1994 AIDS became the leading cause of death for U.S. men and women aged 25–44 years. Slightly more than half of all cases reported in the U.S. since the beginning of the epidemic had occurred in homosexual men. Of the new cases reported in 1994, however, only 43% occurred among homosexual men; the majority of new AIDS cases occurred among intravenous drug users and their female sexual partners. Women represented nearly 20% of new cases. While the rate of homosexually transmitted AIDS cases declined among white men in the major urban centers of New York, Los Angeles, and San Francisco, it rose among urban black and Hispanic men and among all men in suburban and rural areas. Heterosexual transmission accounted for nearly 10% of new cases in 1994.

Worldwide: 10,000 new infections daily

Although the incidence of AIDS was apparently stabilizing in the U.S., the virus continued to spread inexorably on a global scale. According to the 1994 estimate of the World Health Organization (WHO), 18 million people worldwide were infected with HIV. Four million people became infected that year alone—a rate of 10,000 new infections per day. The disease had taken the greatest toll in sub-Saharan Africa, where its impact has been particularly devastating among the young. In Uganda 80% of deaths among young adults and people in early middle age are attributed to AIDS. WHO estimates that nearly 10 million African children eventually will be orphaned because of AIDS.

The burgeoning of the HIV epidemic in Asia also continued unabated. According to WHO, three million Asians were infected with HIV at the end of 1994—with nearly two-thirds of the cases in India, 27% in Thailand, 5% in Myanmar (Burma), and 8% elsewhere in Southeast Asia. The commercial sex industry has been a major factor in the spread of the virus in Asia.

Pathogenesis: a clear picture emerges

Recent advances in molecular biology have led to the development of new techniques for measuring the amount of HIV in an infected individual's blood. The new assays detect viral genetic material (RNA); they are far more sensitive and precise than previous methods, which relied on the ability to culture (grow) HIV from blood samples.

Virus versus immune system. Large numbers of HIV particles are found in the blood during initial, or primary, HIV infection (*i.e.,* shortly after a person becomes infected). HIV levels then decline as the body mounts an effective immune response to the virus. In studies published in January 1995, investigators at the Aaron Diamond AIDS Research Center in New York City and the University of Alabama at Birmingham demonstrated that the amount of virus in the blood at any given time is a result of a dynamic equilibrium that is established between production of HIV in the lymphoid tissues (lymph nodes and vessels) and continuous clearance of the virus by the immune system. Moreover, the number of new virus particles being produced is roughly equal to the number of T-helper cells being replaced.

Both teams of investigators gave patients potent experimental anti-HIV drugs of the class known as protease inhibitors (*see* below). The result was near-total inhibition of HIV replication. This was reflected in a dramatic decline in HIV levels over several days after drug therapy was initiated. By monitoring the rate of disappearance of HIV from the blood, the researchers were able to estimate that the half-life of circulating HIV is approximately two days—in other words, the HIV content of the blood is constantly turning over, with approximately half of the virus particles being replaced every two days. About two billion virus particles are produced and cleared each day; several trillion are produced in an infected individual over the usual 10-year course of the disease.

The researchers also observed that profound reductions in circulating HIV were associated with equally dramatic increases in the number of T-helper lymphocytes, in some cases to near normal levels. Further analysis of these data suggested that the massive production of HIV in an HIV-infected individual is tightly coupled with the destruction and replacement of nearly two billion T-helper lymphocytes each day. This new information provided strong evidence in support of the hypothesis that the loss of T-helper cells in HIV infection is a direct consequence of viral replication rather than a result of indirect immune mechanisms.

Indian women who have tested positive for HIV wait to be seen by doctors at an AIDS clinic. Some public health authorities predict that within the next five years Asia—and in particular, India—will replace Africa as the epicenter of AIDS.

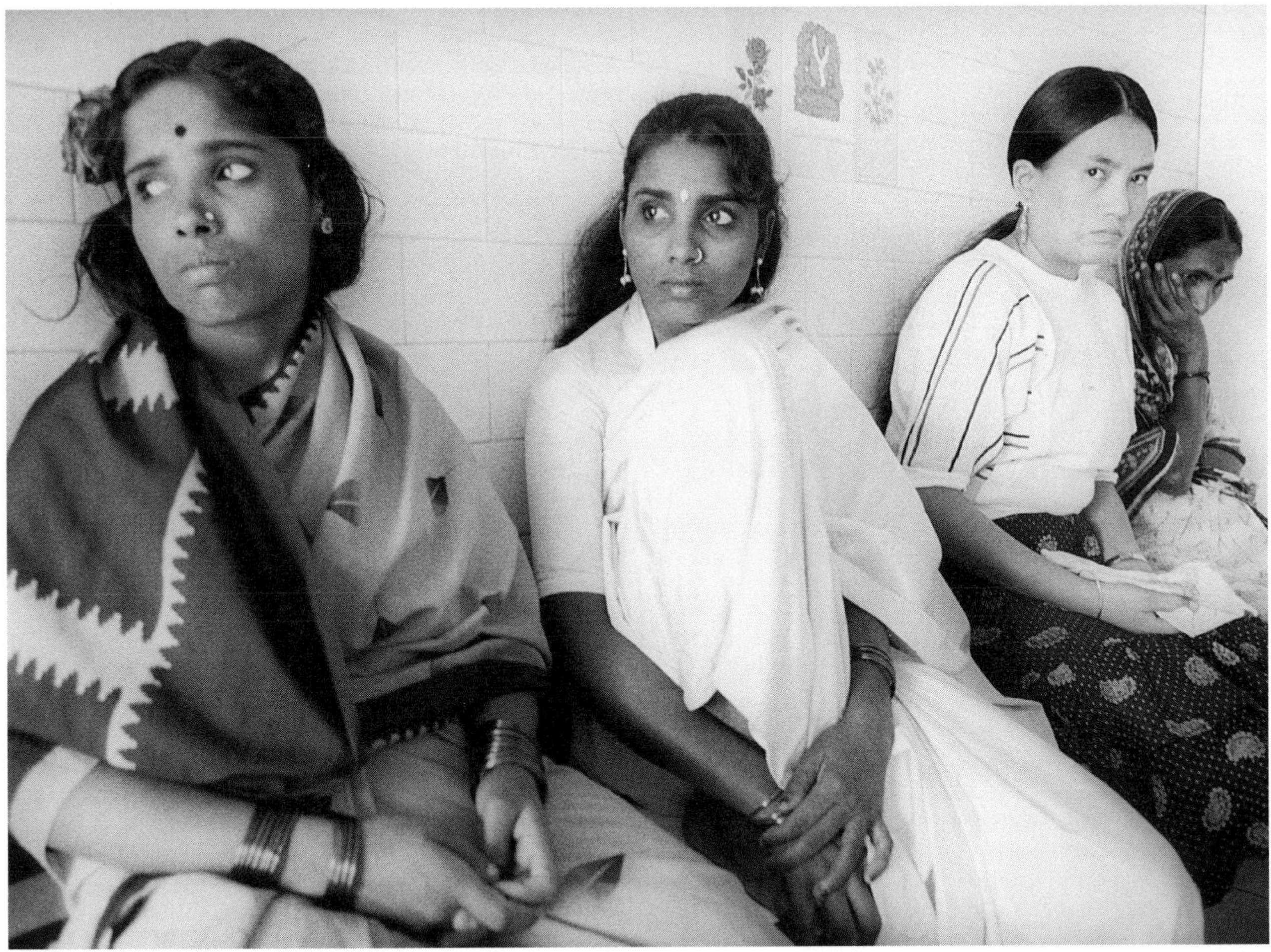

Dayanita Singh—JB Pictures

The Immune System Overwhelmed

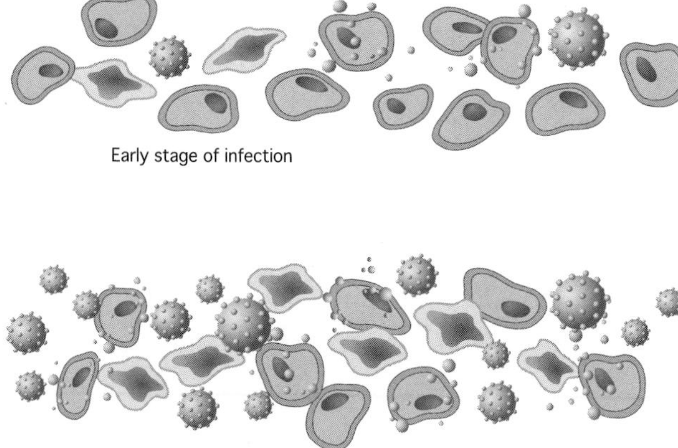

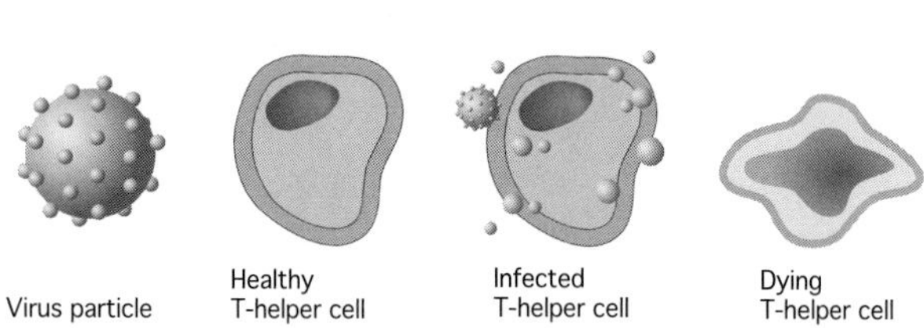

According to recent understanding of the progression of HIV infection, T-helper cells infected by the virus churn out huge numbers of new virus particles daily. Although the infected cells eventually die, the body replaces them with new ones, which, in turn, become infected by new virus particles. Eventually, the immune system's capacity to generate new T-helper cells is overwhelmed by the production of new virus particles.

An important implication of these findings is that even late in the course of disease, T-helper cells can be replenished if HIV replication can be halted. The goal of AIDS clinical trials, therefore, should be to identify therapies that will suppress HIV replication effectively and lastingly.

Secrets of long-term survival. Some AIDS researchers are focusing their efforts on individuals who have remained healthy for many years after initial HIV infection. Whereas the median time from initial infection to the development of AIDS is about 10 years, approximately 8% of those who are infected progress to AIDS within two years. A small proportion of infected persons, however—fewer than 5%—show no signs of disease progression even 15 years later. This category of "long-term nonprogressors" includes individuals who have no HIV-related symptoms at least 10 years after infection, have T-helper cell counts in the normal range, and have very low levels of viral RNA in their blood.

Some long-term nonprogressors harbor variants of HIV that are genetically defective, which possibly accounts for the low levels of virus found in this group. Whether such defective strains of HIV are truly avirulent (incapable of causing disease) or simply cause disease more slowly than other viruses remains to be proved. Other long-term nonprogressors carry strains of HIV that are indistinguishable from strains isolated from individuals who have progressed to AIDS. These nonprogressors appear to have unusually vigorous immune responses to HIV. Better understanding of the biological mechanisms that induce and sustain this robust immunity may lead to more effective strategies for vaccines against HIV and for immune-based therapies for HIV infection.

Anti-HIV drugs

Several significant advances in anti-HIV therapy were announced during the past year, and promising new agents were being readied for clinical trials. The recent findings about the pathogenesis of AIDS gave added impetus to the effort to develop drugs capable of interfering with HIV replication.

Lamivudine. In clinical trials the experimental drug lamivudine (trade name 3TC) has been well tolerated by patients and has not caused the side effects associated with other currently available agents of the same class, such as zidovudine (AZT), didanosine (ddI), zalcitabine (ddC), and stavudine (d4T). Although lamivudine is a more potent inhibitor of HIV than AZT, early studies suggested that the rapid development of resistance might limit the drug's effectiveness.

More recent data, however, indicate that despite the development of lamivudine resistance, patients who received the combination of lamivudine plus AZT had significant reductions in virus levels, persisting for up to 52 weeks, as well as long-lasting increases in T-helper cell counts. The changes in response to combination therapy were significantly greater than those observed in patients treated with lamivudine or AZT alone. Analysis of HIV from patients treated with the lamivudine-AZT combination suggested that treatment with lamivudine prevented the development of AZT resistance, which thereby prolonged the effects of AZT. If lamivudine is licensed by the U.S. Food and Drug Administration, the lamivudine-AZT combination could become the first combination regimen approved for use in HIV-infected individuals who have no symptoms but have T-helper cell counts below 500 per cubic millimeter.

The promise of protease inhibitors. Protease inhibitors fileetimes called proteinase inhibitors) belong to a class of drugs that inhibit HIV by acting at a different stage in the virus's life cycle from the other available anti-HIV agents—the latter all being reverse transcriptase inhibitors. Reverse transcriptase is an enzyme required for the synthesis of DNA from viral RNA, a crucial early step in the infection process. The newly formed DNA is then integrated into the DNA of the host cell and uses the cell to make new virus particles. The HIV protease is an enzyme required at a later stage for the maturation of new virus particles. When HIV protease is blocked, the newly created particles are incapable of causing infection. Although protease inhibitors are very effective in the laboratory, their complex chemistry and poor solubility have slowed their development for clinical purposes.

Recently, clinical trials with three protease inhibitors have sparked hopes that this class of drugs may represent a significant advance in the treatment of HIV infection. In a study conducted by the AIDS Clinical Trials Group (ACTG) of the U.S. National Institutes of Health (NIH), patients who received the protease inhibitor saquinavir in combination with AZT plus ddC had greater reductions in HIV levels compared with patients who received AZT plus ddC or saquinavir alone. A separate study at Stanford University demonstrated that the activity of saquinavir could be improved by giving substantially higher doses than were used in the ACTG trial.

The results of preliminary trials with two experimental protease inhibitors, indinavir (formerly called MK-639) and ritonavir (formerly called ABT 538), suggested that these drugs are far more active than saquinavir. As described above, the administration of these drugs resulted in profound reductions in blood levels of HIV and similarly dramatic increases in T-helper cell counts. The extent of virus suppression reported for these new products was far greater than that observed with currently available drugs such as AZT. Resistance to the protease inhibitors develops over four to six months, however, eventually limiting their effectiveness. Current research is investigating combinations of protease inhibitors plus reverse transcriptase inhibitors, as well as combinations of different protease inhibitors, in hopes of achieving greater inhibition of HIV replication and delaying the emergence of drug-resistant variants. Several other protease inhibitors were expected to enter into clinical trials by the end of 1995.

Combination therapy: two drugs better than one? The clinical trials conducted to date have consistently shown that antiretroviral agents produce greater immunologic and virological improvement (*i.e.,* increased levels of T-helper cells and decreased levels of circulating virus particles) when used in combination than when taken singly. So far, however, these studies have not proved that combination therapy delays disease progression more effectively than monotherapy. The results of three large clinical trials designed to resolve this issue were expected by the end of 1995. Two of these involved adults and the third, children. One arm of the latter study was halted ahead of schedule in February 1995 when researchers found that AZT alone was less effective in children than regimens involving ddI alone and ddI plus AZT.

Immune-based therapies

Whereas agents such as AZT and the protease inhibitors directly target the virus, immune-based therapies attempt to boost immune function in infected individuals. Immune-based therapies may be HIV-specific or general. The former seek to enhance the capacity of the immune system to contain HIV infection, whereas the latter seek to stimulate the immune system more broadly so as to prevent the opportunistic diseases that characterize advanced HIV infection and AIDS.

The therapeutic vaccine approach. One example of HIV-specific immune-based therapy is therapeutic vaccination—*i.e.,* vaccination of those already infected for treatment purposes (as opposed to preventive immunization of uninfected persons). This approach was pioneered by the late Jonas Salk, developer of the first polio vaccine, who proposed that HIV-specific immune responses could be stimulated in infected individuals by administering components of the virus or whole, inactivated virus in the form of a vaccine. Researchers have demonstrated that such vaccines can indeed boost immunity against HIV, but whether therapeutic vaccination slows disease progression remains doubtful. The biotechnology firm Genentech abandoned efforts to develop a therapeutic vaccine based on the HIV envelope protein (gp120) after a large controlled clinical trial failed to show any benefit in patients in the early stages of HIV infection. Undeterred, Salk's colleagues at Immune Response Corp., Carlsbad, Calif., were forging ahead with a controlled trial of their own inactivated HIV vaccine in patients with moderately advanced infection.

Photograph by Carolyn Jones from her book, *Living Proof: Courage in the Face of AIDS*

Researchers hope that the study of long-term survivors like Zoe Lorenz (right), who remains well 12 years after becoming infected with HIV, will yield new therapies for AIDS or even a vaccine against the virus.

Interleukin-2 therapy. Interleukin-2 (IL-2) is one of several cytokines produced by the immune system cells called T lymphocytes. (Cytokines are proteins that regulate immune responses.) Individual cytokines have the capacity to stimulate or inhibit the proliferation of immune system cells and therefore may have positive or negative effects on immune function. In a study published in March 1995, investigators from the NIH demonstrated that intermittent infusion of high doses of IL-2 resulted in sustained increases in T-helper cell counts in HIV-infected persons. This effect was observed only in patients who had T-helper cell counts greater than 200 per cubic millimeter to start with. Treatment with IL-2 was poorly tolerated in patients with more advanced disease and did not lead to improvement in T-helper cell counts.

A number of important questions must be answered before IL-2 can be recommended for routine clinical use. For example, it is unclear whether treatment with IL-2 leads to increased production of T-helper cells or simply causes cells in the lymph nodes to migrate into the blood and thereby produce an increased T-helper cell count. Moreover, it is unknown whether the T-helper cells stimulated artificially by IL-2 can function normally to generate an immune response. In addition, IL-2 administration is associated with transient increases in the level of HIV in the blood, perhaps as a result of direct stimulation of virus production by IL-2. Clinical trials to address these questions are currently under way.

Progress against complications of HIV

Great strides have been made in the prevention and treatment of many of the diseases that typically develop in those infected with HIV. For example, *Pneumocystis carinii* pneumonia, which used to occur in nearly 80% of patients with advanced HIV infection, is now readily prevented by prophylactic drug treatment. During the past year important advances were made in the management of cytomegalovirus (CMV) infections, disseminated infection due to *Mycobacterium avium* complex (MAC), and AIDS-related wasting syndrome.

CMV infection. Approximately 25% of patients with AIDS develop complications due to CMV infection. The most frequent clinical manifestations are retinitis (inflammation of the retina of the eye), which can lead to blindness, and colitis (inflammation of the colon), which is commonly associated with bloody diarrhea. After initial treatment of CMV infection in persons with AIDS, lifelong maintenance therapy is usually necessary to prevent a relapse. Until recently this treatment required surgical placement of a permanent intravenous catheter (a tiny plastic tube connecting a portal on the skin surface directly to a vein) since the drugs used to treat CMV infection—ganciclovir and foscarnet—are ineffective when given orally. In 1994 a clinical trial of a new oral formulation of ganciclovir demonstrated that this agent is effective in preventing episodes of retinitis and can be used in place of intravenous maintenance therapy, which frees patients from the inconvenience and potential complications (such as infections) of intravenous therapy. Another study showed that a ganciclovir-releasing membrane implanted directly into the eye was effective in preventing relapses of CMV retinitis and had fewer systemic side effects than intravenous ganciclovir.

MAC infection. *M. avium* and related mycobacteria—collectively called *M. avium* complex, or MAC—are organisms commonly found in water and soil. They generally cause disease only in immunocompromised persons. The infection may be limited to the lungs, or it may be disseminated throughout the body. Disseminated disease due to MAC occurs in up to 50% of patients in the later stages of AIDS. Treatment is complicated by resistance of these organisms to most standard antibiotics.

In the past two years, clinical trials have demonstrated that prophylactic treatment with either rifabutin or clarithromycin is effective in reducing the incidence of MAC infection among patients with advanced HIV infection. As a result of these findings, many experts now think that the use of either rifabutin or clarithromycin should be standard in the care of HIV-infected individuals with T-helper cell counts below 100.

AIDS-related wasting syndrome. Infection with HIV is often associated with unintended weight loss. Unlike starvation, in which protein stores and lean muscle mass are conserved while fat deposits are broken down for energy, wasting entails loss of lean body tissue. Wasting syndrome is the major manifestation of AIDS in many HIV-infected individuals. As with the wasting that occurs in some cancer patients, the wasting syndrome in AIDS is due to basic changes in metabolism and cannot be reversed by increased food intake. In October 1994 researchers at the University of California at San Francisco reported the results of preliminary trials of a genetically engineered human growth hormone. The study showed that the treatment can reverse the effects of AIDS-related wasting syndrome, and thus lead to an increase in lean body mass. The preliminary trials did not address the question of whether such treatment improves survival.

NEWS*CAP*

MTV Makes Health Hip

Music Television (MTV), the network that has been taking the youth culture's electronic pulse since the early 1980s, surprised many in 1995 by offering several innovative programs that explored health issues, sandwiched between music videos and its standard 20-somethingish fare. Most notably, "Out of Order: Rock the Vote Targets Health Care" comprised six half-hour installments that dramatized issues such as drug and alcohol abuse, hospitalization crises, child abuse, eating disorders, and sexually transmitted disease. Among other things, the network championed safe sex with a "no glove, no love" admonishment. Even MTV's interview/home-shopping program, "The Goods" (normally a clearinghouse for Rolling Stones tour jackets and the like), presented a program—called "Think Positive"—that marketed a package of popular consumer items, with profits going to the AIDS cause.

In a more dramatic and personal way, MTV viewers were confronted with the harsh realities of AIDS during the 1994–95 airing of the series "The Real World." This popular, if somewhat contrived, documentary focused on seven young people brought together under one San Francisco roof and the unrelenting scrutiny of MTV's cameras. One member of the group, Pedro Zamora, was charming, gay, and HIV-positive. He was also a nationally known activist who, after learning at age 17 that he was HIV-positive, carried his plea for AIDS awareness to young people across the U.S. and to Congress.

As viewers witnessed Zamora's interactions with his roommates, his marriage, and his AIDS activism, they came to care about a young man whose life would be claimed by his disease in November 1994. Indeed, "The Real World" was never more illuminating than in the programs in which Zamora was most prominent.

New direction for AIDS research?

Throughout the past year a recurring theme in the debate over priorities for AIDS research has been the suggestion that funds be shifted from clinical research to basic research. Those in favor of such a shift hold that significant progress in the treatment and prevention of AIDS will come only through basic laboratory research that provides a better understanding of human immunity and the pathogenesis of HIV infection. William Paul, director of the NIH Office of AIDS Research, has stated his intention to move funds from large-scale clinical research programs to smaller, investigator-initiated basic research grants. One result of this new policy is a projected decrease in the ACTG budget from $68 million in 1995 to $60 million in 1996, with a consequent reduction in the number of adult AIDS clinical trial units around the U.S. (About 35 such units were in operation in 1995.) Despite this trend, the fact remains that there is no animal model for AIDS. Therefore, clinical research on infected individuals is likely to continue to be the major source of insights into the pathogenesis of AIDS.

—Daniel R. Kuritzkes, M.D.

Report from France

France has more reported cases of AIDS than any other country in Europe and the largest number of HIV-positive individuals on the continent. Since a national surveillance system was established in 1982, more than 35,000 cases of AIDS had been reported by midyear 1995; about 60% of the patients had died. Currently, it is estimated that there are 110,000 French HIV-infected individuals. About 80,000 of them benefit from medical follow-up, while an estimated 30,000 do not know they are seropositive. In Paris, AIDS is now the leading cause of death of young men aged 20 to 34 years. Many factors are believed to have contributed to this unhappy record.

HIV discovery

The AIDS epidemic as it exists in France today is a paradox that may never be fully elucidated. It is a paradox because from the start, French science has been at the forefront of AIDS research.

In January 1983 Luc Montagnier, head of viral oncology at the Pasteur Institute in Paris, received a small piece of a lymph node from a patient diagnosed as having an immune deficiency disorder. With co-workers Françoise Barré-Sinoussi and Jean-Claude Chermann, Montagnier produced a laboratory culture in which he identified a type of virus known as a retrovirus, or RNA tumor virus, that he and his codiscoverers first called lymphadenopathy-associated virus (LAV).

A test developed a few weeks later showed the same type of virus to be present in other patients with similar immune

Luc Montagnier, who headed the scientific team that in 1983 first isolated the AIDS virus, remains at the forefront of international AIDS/HIV research. In 1995 Montagnier called for France to step up the fight against the epidemic that affects an estimated 110,000 French people.

Florence Durand—Sipa

(Left) Stevens/Chesnot—Sipa; (right) Nahassia—Sipa

(Above) In 1992 Michel Garretta, the former director of France's National Blood Transfusion Center, was convicted of having knowingly allowed the distribution of contaminated blood and was sentenced to four years in prison. (Right) Angry citizens demonstrate outside the courthouse where Garretta and three other former health officials are on trial and charge the French government with complicity at the highest level in the "tainted blood affair."

deficiency symptoms, and by June 1983 laboratory research at the Pasteur Institute had showed that the virus selectively attacks a special population of lymphocytes (white blood cells) called T4 cells, which, in Montagnier's words, are the "headquarters cells" for the immune system.

About a year later Robert C. Gallo, director of the National Cancer Institute's Laboratory of Tumor Cell Biology in the U.S., reported identifying another AIDS virus, which later turned out to be essentially the same as the one that had been identified in France. Since then, these viruses have been renamed human immunodeficiency viruses (HIV). A dispute over whether Montagnier or Gallo was the actual discoverer of HIV dragged on for 10 years. In July 1994 the U.S. Department of Health and Human Services recognized that Gallo had used a virus sent to his lab from Montagnier's lab to develop an important blood test. (The widely used test uses pieces of the virus to detect HIV antiviral antibodies in infected persons.) At stake in the Gallo-Montagnier dispute were lucrative patent rights to the test. The U.S. agreed to give France a substantially larger share of the test royalties than it had previously received.

Tainted blood affair

As early as Aug. 29, 1983, Montagnier wrote to Philippe Lazar, director of the French Institute of Health and Medical Research (INSERM), warning of the existence of a potentially dangerous new virus. At the same time, he appealed for funds for the development of diagnostic techniques. Montagnier's recommendations were largely ignored at the time. Such authorities as veteran hematologist Jean Bernard, at the Saint Louis Hospital in Paris, considered that AIDS represented less of a risk than hepatitis and stated that the principle of gratuity (*i.e.,* blood donations were voluntary) protected the blood supply of the Centre National de Transfusion Sanguine, or CNTS (the National Blood Transfusion Center), from contamination. (The supply was not protected. The volunteer donors included drug addicts and prison inmates, who had not been tested for HIV or hepatitis viruses.)

The CNTS was created as a nonprofit public trust underwritten by the state but independent in its operation. Michel Garretta, deputy director in charge of commercial activities of the CNTS, became the center's director in 1984. Garretta wanted to turn it into a profit-making industry and had a blood-processing factory built in Les Ulis, 24 km (15 mi) west of Paris. Early in 1985, when it became known that the process of heating blood samples neutralized HIV, the CNTS still had stocks of unheated blood and blood extracts, which it continued to distribute until late in the year. Moreover, the CNTS continued its practice of collecting blood in state prisons, sometimes offering inmates certificates of good behavior if they donated blood. This was done in spite of warnings that inmates were at high risk of infectious diseases and should not be included among blood donors. By October 1985 only one of nine penitentiary administrations had banned such donations; it was estimated that blood from untested prisoners accounted for a quarter of HIV-contaminated blood collected in France.

The so-called *affaire du sang contaminé* ("tainted blood affair") finally brought four former blood officials to trial for "deception over the quality of a product," a charge usually associated with breaches in commercial law. A "correctional tribunal" sentenced Garretta to four years in prison in 1992; he was released in April 1995. Jean-Pierre Allain, Garretta's former assistant, also received a four-year sentence, but two of those years were suspended, and he was released in August 1994. A third official received a suspended sentence, and a fourth was acquitted.

The scandal, however, was not over. Garretta and several people who were government officials in 1985 (including Laurent Fabius, then prime minister, and François Gros, former Pasteur Institute director and permanent secretary of the French Academy of Sciences) were recently charged with "poisoning." In May 1995 Louis Schweitzer, chief executive officer of the Renault automobile manufacturing company, was also placed under examination. As director of Fabius's Cabinet in May 1985, Schweitzer had asked that the acceptance of a test developed by Abbott Laboratories in the U.S. be "held up" at the National Laboratory of Health, apparently to give priority to a French test prepared by Diagnostics Pasteur, the commercial subsidiary of the Pasteur Institute.

In April 1995 a confidential report by the French High Committee on Public Health aroused new controversy. The report, leaked to the press, underlined collective rather than individual responsibility, stating that "unlike their foreign colleagues French transfusion doctors generally did not take advantage of epidemiological knowledge that had been solidly acquired by 1983." French hematologists failed to do systematic clinical screening that would have allowed them to track donors who were more likely than others to be infected and whose blood would not have been used. In addition to HIV, blood transfusions transmitted the hepatitis C virus, and according to another report, up to two million French people may be infected with that virus owing to tainted blood.

In June 1995 Jean-Baptiste Brunet, an internationally respected AIDS expert who since 1987 had directed the European Center for the Epidemiological Monitoring of AIDS, near Paris, was also charged with "complicity in poisoning." Detailed accusations against him were not revealed, but they arose from complaints filed by patients who had received contaminated blood. The charges against Brunet drew protests from leading AIDS researchers, including Montagnier, who said he planned to bring together parties involved in the scandal to reach some kind of settlement that would put an end to prosecutions. By July, 15 people had been charged with poisoning or being accessories to it.

Widespread drug abuse

In the late 1980s and early 1990s, the epidemiological situation did not improve. Drug addiction was widespread, a situation that favored the spread of HIV through shared needles. It took time for health authorities to react by making clean syringes and needles available to addicts. It is currently estimated that there are as many as 300,000 injecting drug users in France, and a quarter to a third of them may be HIV-positive.

A 1970 law had criminalized even occasional uses of narcotic substances, establishing jail terms and fines for such offenses. In a report to the prime minister in 1994, Montagnier contended that "criminalizing the user drives him underground, which makes it harder to identify him or to provide him with access to health care services." In September 1994 Philippe Douste-Blazy, who served as deputy minister of health from 1993 to May 1995, came out in favor of decriminalization, and the Gaullist leader and mayor of Paris, Jacques Chirac, supported a more humane approach toward intravenous drug users. As the French capital is a hub of drug trafficking and addiction, Chirac was quite familiar with the problem. His election to the French presidency in May may help establish drug addiction and AIDS as national priorities.

Machine-dispensed kits—containing sterile syringes, a condom, and an HIV-prevention message—are part of an effort to curtail the spread of AIDS among the large drug-injecting population in France.

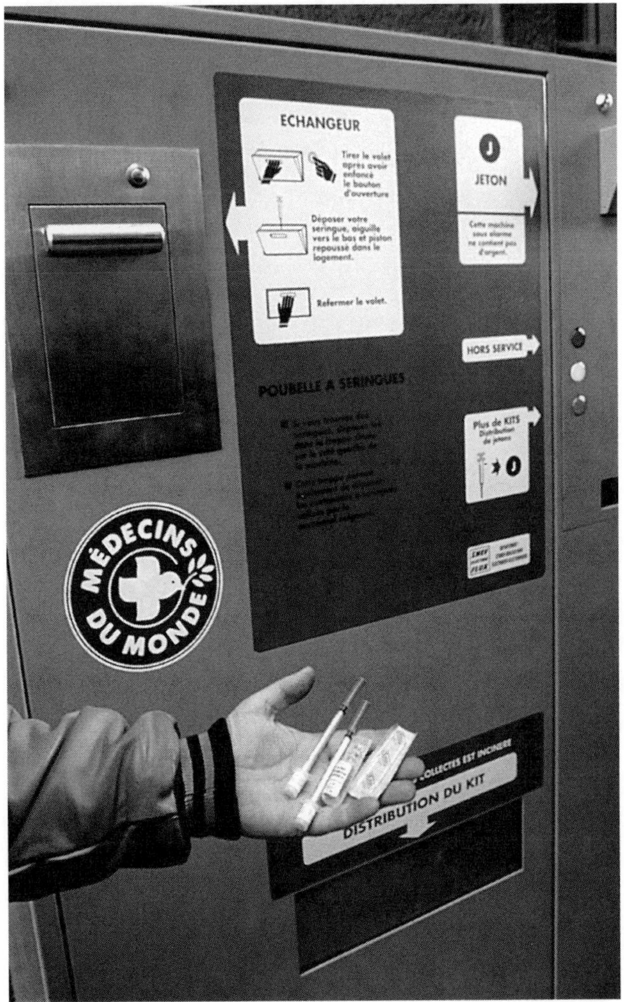

Nicolas Le Corre—Gamma Liaison

Condom rejection and uninformed physicians

Other, historical factors probably contributed to the French AIDS epidemic. France lags behind most other countries in the European Union in the use of condoms. Pro-life legislation adopted at the beginning of the century made it illegal to advertise contraceptives; this legislation was repealed only in 1987. The use of oral contraceptives, favored by many young people, further limited the use of condoms. Moreover, public prejudice often associated condom use with prostitution and illicit sex.

A vigorous campaign in recent years has started to reverse this trend. Douste-Blazy launched a campaign called *opération préservatifs jeune* ("condoms for the young") and made the device, also known as *la capote anglaise* ("the English coat"), available in pharmacies for the price of F 1 (about 20 cents). Condoms are also issued in prison pharmacies and wards, and in 1994 their delivery to inmates who asked for them became mandatory (even though sexual relations in jail are forbidden). According to a study completed in 1995, the use of condoms by teenagers during their first sexual experience increased from about 57% of couples in 1989 to about 85% in 1993. Condom use, however, is less frequent among older people.

Another survey, ordered in 1995 by Director General for Health Jean-François Girard, showed that French doctors know little more about the AIDS epidemic than the general public and probably less than the average 15- to 18-year-old. Thirteen percent of French general practitioners believed that HIV could be transmitted by saliva, 7.2% that it could be transmitted during a stay in the same ward as an infected patient, 6.1% by donating blood, and 2% by mosquito bites. Doctors who are over 45 years old and who have no seropositive patients are particularly likely to underestimate the risk of infection and order fewer tests than younger doctors who are better informed.

Infected children

It is estimated that 2,000 French children are HIV-positive, and over 500 are suffering from AIDS. About one-fifth (largely children treated for hemophilia) were infected by transfusion of contaminated blood extracts; four-fifths were infected by the so-called vertical route (from mother to infant, either in the fetal stage, at the time of birth, or through breast milk).

The Ministry of Health suggests that French doctors recommend to all pregnant women that they take an HIV test, but many doctors do not. However, when such testing is proposed by a physician, it is hardly ever refused. Most women who learn they are infected choose to have a legal abortion rather than take the 20% to 30% risk of giving birth to a seropositive child. (This approximate risk varies somewhat among countries.) It has also been shown that the risk of vertical transmission increases with the progression of maternal infection, doubles if the mother breast-feeds, and is associated with the mother's age (risk is 16% for mothers under 25 but increases to 30% for those over 30). A further problem is that many seropositive mothers do not benefit from France's well-organized maternal and child health care system; about 45% of seropositive mothers are Africans, many of them without residency permits or a permanent home and many of whom receive no medical care.

In 1994 another study, cosponsored by the U.S. National Institutes of Health and the French Agence Nationale de Recherches sur le SIDA (National Agency of AIDS Research), showed that the HIV-transmission rate to children dropped from 20% to about 8% when both the mothers and their babies received the antiviral drug zidovudine (AZT). Other studies have confirmed that finding, and AZT administration is now recommended for all seropositive pregnant women who do not select abortion. There continue to be concerns, however, about possible, though as yet undetermined, long-term effects of AZT therapy. In April 1995 one of the last official decisions made by the outgoing minister of social affairs and health, Simone Veil, was to issue a directive that children born to seropositive women and treated with AZT be monitored medically "for life."

Home delivery of condoms is part of a campaign aimed at encouraging the practice of safer sex. France has the highest incidence of HIV and among the lowest rates of condom use in Europe.

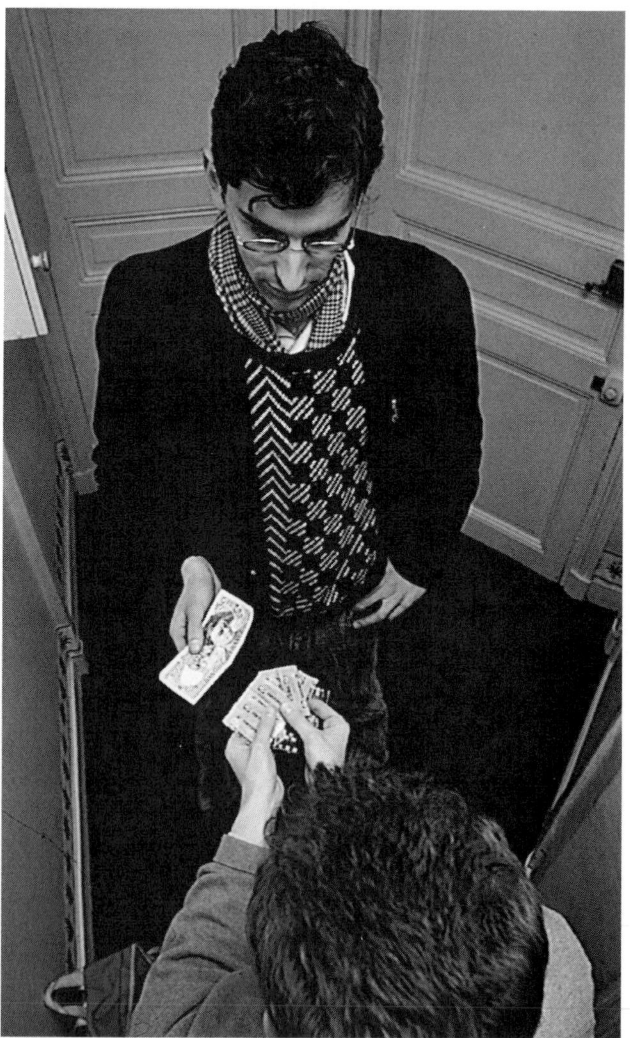

Dupuis/Sebelliard—Gamma Liaison

Inadequate testing

Another hitch in the AIDS-prevention campaign has come from the use of unreliable antibody tests to diagnose HIV seropositivity. The Société Nationale de Transfusion Sanguine, which replaced the ill-fated CNTS, showed that 9 of the 30 antibody tests used in France had only moderate sensitivity; in July 1993 Douste-Blazy announced that the potentially inaccurate tests would be withdrawn from the market. One of them was a test called Génie HIV-1-HIV-2, developed by Diagnostics Pasteur and promoted as a diagnostic method that used elaborate technology to provide quick results (within nine minutes). The withdrawal of Génie HIV-1-HIV-2 came as a surprise. SIDA Info Service, a nationwide telephone service providing information on AIDS, learned of the measure from a television news broadcast and was swamped with more than 500 telephone calls an hour from health professionals who had not been informed of the measure and from people concerned that they may have been given false-negative results. Others called to ask whether their seropositive diagnosis could be wrong. (All of the latter were disappointed, because seropositivity is always verified by several tests.)

Now, about eight million individuals annually (about one-seventh of France's population) are screened for HIV. Once testing of blood donors was instituted, the number of seropositive donations fell sharply (from 6.4 per 10,000 in 1985 to 0.47 per 10,000 in 1994). In some cases, particularly before surgery, screening is done without patients' knowledge, an ethical violation of an individual's rights.

Outlook improving

The epidemiological pattern of HIV infection in France has definitely taken a turn for the better. The number of cases of declared AIDS had increased by 79% from 1986 to 1987 but rose only by 7.8% from 1993 to 1994. The peak of the epidemic appears to be over. Prevention campaigns, sometimes criticized as insufficient, have been broadened, and health authorities are aware that the effort should not be relaxed. After the presidential election in May 1995, there was hope that an interministerial committee to step up the fight against AIDS (a plan proposed by Montagnier) would be established. Such a committee would bring together clinicians, scientists, and policy makers, perhaps doing away with the current French anti-AIDS agency, l'Agence Française de Lutte contre le SIDA, which has been widely criticized for its lack of effectiveness.

Meantime, researchers in France, and elsewhere, are disappointed with the lack of new tools to fight the disease, as well as the declining hope for a vaccine in the near future. In 1993 Pasteur Institute biologist Ara Hovanessian believed he was close to a breakthrough when he identified a molecule that appeared to promote the entry of HIV into the cell it infects. HIV attacks a cell by latching on to a protein receptor, named CD4, on the cell's surface. Normally the CD4 molecule mobilizes the immune system's defenses, but the virus somehow fools the receptor. Hovanessian reported that another receptor, called CD26, helps the virus infect the cell after it has latched on to CD4, and he hoped to devise a drug treatment that would block access to the CD26 receptor. His report, highly touted in the French press, was viewed with skepticism by the international scientific community. Thus far, additional research has not resolved the legitimacy of the theory, but the hope of treatment via CD26, even in France, has waned.

Earlier, another researcher at the Pasteur Institute, Mirko Beljanski, had developed a novel antiviral drug known as PB-100. The formulation was based on extracts from the Brazilian tree *Pao pereira* that presumably inhibited the activity of reverse transcriptase, an enzyme that catalyzes retroviruses (as do AZT and other drugs used to treat AIDS). After a conflict with officials at the Pasteur Institute, Beljanski left to set up his own laboratory. He did not apply for authorization to market PB-100, arguing that patients under threat of death should not be kept waiting by the normal protocol—involving laboratory tests, animal experiments, toxicological evaluation, and clinical trials.

Hundreds of patients with AIDS and cancer were treated with PB-100, reportedly including former president François Mitterrand, who suffers from cancer of the prostate. In 1994 Girard ordered a series of tests to verify the alleged activity of the product; those studies, carried out by several laboratories, showed no specific activity against HIV—except when PB-100 concentrations were so high they triggered massive cellular toxicity. Beljanski's PB-100 was later submitted for testing to Douglas L. Mayers, a scientist at the Walter Reed Army Institute of Research in Rockville, Md. His report has since been submitted to French health authorities, but as of July 1995 those results had not been disclosed.

Cracking down on quackery

A 1995 government report commissioned by Douste-Blazy estimated that thousands of French AIDS sufferers are treated by unauthorized and probably worthless drugs promoted by self-styled researchers and therapists. Some of the promoters act through bona fide associations; others claim to be medical pioneers who have been persecuted by the official scientific establishment. Some alleged therapeutic practices are carried out solely for commercial reasons and were described in the report as "pure charlatanism."

Twenty-five specific cases were cited, some of which are being prosecuted under charges of illegal practice of medicine or pharmacy or deceitful advertising. The report also details, without giving names of individuals or companies involved, numerous dubious practices that are believed to be spurred by the medical community's sense of powerlessness against the disease and its lack of effective therapies or vaccines.

Perhaps the most striking aspect of the report is that for the first time it revealed the scope of unauthorized treatments. One pharmacy had filled over 15,000 prescriptions written by about 500 doctors for 8,000 patients. Another, selling pills for the "treatment of immunity," listed 250 prescribing doctors and 4,000 patients. Until now the government has been very hesitant about tackling such cases. The judicial apparatus to handle them is complex, and in the past the fines that were meted out were too small to be dissuasive.

—*Alexander Dorozynski*

Cardiovascular Health Update

Disease of the heart and blood vessels continues to be an important scientific focus because of its widespread occurrence and severe consequences. This update considers selected issues in the prevention and treatment of coronary heart disease (CHD), recent findings about the prevention of stroke, the progress in understanding and treating hypertrophic cardiomyopathy (a heart-muscle disorder), and the impact of a nation's health care system on the waiting times for cardiovascular procedures.

Cholesterol and coronary heart disease

Evidence supporting the importance of cholesterol reduction in the prevention of CHD continues to accumulate. Lowering of serum cholesterol prevents nonfatal heart attacks as well as deaths from CHD. Much of the research in this area has focused on primary prevention.

Primary-prevention research. "Primary prevention" refers to the forestalling of a heart attack or cardiac death in individuals who have not yet experienced any overt symptoms or signs of CHD. For research purposes it is difficult to carry out a study that treats a group of CHD-prone people with a cholesterol-lowering diet and shows a reduction in coronary events. In such a study there would need to be a control group with similar predisposition to CHD that would be on a moderate- to high-fat diet, which could prove dangerous to the control group's health. A meaningful comparison would not be possible without phenomenal compliance by study participants, many thousands of enrollees, and several years of observation. But, over a number of years, how could investigators be sure that study participants had adhered strictly to a specified low-fat, low-cholesterol diet? What if the control subjects, of their own volition, adopted a lipid-lowering diet and thus skewed the results?

The ideal approach to preventing atherosclerosis—the buildup of fatty deposits in arteries—on a populationwide basis would be the promotion of a diet low in saturated fat, total fat, and cholesterol. In research trials, however, it has been more possible to demonstrate the preventive role of cholesterol-lowering drugs.

The Lipid Research Clinics Coronary Primary Prevention Trial enrolled 3,806 middle-aged men at high risk for coronary disease but without symptoms. A combination of a change in diet and the cholesterol-lowering agent cholestyramine was shown to lower cholesterol levels by 11.8% and low-density lipoprotein (LDL; the artery-clogging cholesterol) levels by 18.9%. Controls, following the same diet but taking a placebo, showed reductions of only 5% in total cholesterol and 8.6% in LDL cholesterol.

Over a follow-up period of about seven years, those treated with cholestyramine had a 19% reduction in nonfatal myocardial infarctions (heart attacks) and a 24% reduction in deaths from cardiovascular disease, which demonstrated only a modest benefit for cholestyramine. Though moderately helpful, cholestyramine is dispensed as a powder that must be mixed with a liquid and consumed two or three times daily with meals. It is mildly distasteful, has a gritty texture that some patients liken to sand, and can cause abdominal bloating and constipation. Patient compliance is therefore a significant problem with this cholesterol-lowering preparation.

The Helsinki Heart Study, the results of which were released in 1988, set out to validate the effectiveness of the drug gemfibrozil, a tasteless tablet taken twice daily that has fewer side effects than cholestyramine. The study randomly assigned 4,081 middle-aged men to take either gemfibrozil or a placebo. In comparison with the placebo group, treated subjects had a 10% reduction in total cholesterol and an 11% reduction in LDL cholesterol. Moreover, gemfibrozil raised the high-density lipoprotein (HDL) cholesterol by 11%. HDL is the "good" cholesterol, which protects against coronary disease. The clinical result of treatment with gemfibrozil turned out to be more statistically significant than that of the cholestyramine trial, with a 34% drop in cardiac events.

Secondary-prevention research. Patients with angina pectoris (transient chest pains caused by coronary disease) or who have had a previous myocardial infarction have an accentuated risk of suffering a subsequent heart attack or cardiac death. Such high-risk patients are especially useful for studying the clinical effect of cholesterol-lowering medications.

A drug first marketed in 1991, simvastatin, inhibits the activity of an enzyme (HMG-CoA reductase) that regulates the body's ability to produce cholesterol. Drugs acting in this way appear to promote the greatest reductions in serum cholesterol. The Scandinavian Simvastatin Survival Study, which focused on this newer medication, is the most encouraging secondary-prevention trial to date. In this study 4,444 men and women aged 35 to 70 who either had chest pain or had previously had a heart attack were given either simvastatin or a placebo. When compared with a placebo, simvastatin reduced total cholesterol by 25% and LDL cholesterol by 35%. The HDL cholesterol was raised by 8%. Patients treated with simvastatin showed a 37% decrease in nonfatal heart attacks and a 30% decrease in deaths over an average follow-up period of about five years.

Angiographic studies. The effects of cholesterol reduction can also be studied by means of coronary angiograms (X-ray motion pictures) of treated patients. Several studies employing various methods of vigorous cholesterol reduction have recently been completed. They demonstrate a very effective slowing in progression of buildup in the coronary arteries. In addition, there is a slight reversal in the severity of some

Clear Benefits of a Cholesterol-Lowering Drug

	Simvastatin (2,221 patients)		Placebo (2,223 patients)	
DEATHS	Number of patients	Percentage	Number of patients	Percentage
Women	27	6.6	25	6.0
Men	155	8.5	231	12.8
Under age 60	55	5.2	89	8.1
Aged 60 and older	127	11.0	167	14.8
MAJOR CORONARY EVENT				
Women	59	14.5	91	21.7
Men	372	20.5	531	29.4
Under age 60	188	17.6	303	27.6
Aged 60 and older	243	21.0	319	28.3

Adapted from Scandinavian Simvastatin Survival Study Group, "Randomised Trial of Cholesterol Lowering...," *The Lancet*, vol. 344, no. 8934 (Nov. 19, 1994), pp. 1383–89.

coronary artery narrowings; the average observed reduction in the degree of narrowing, however, is only 1% to 2%.

The effects of high cholesterol. Although cholesterol reduction yields only very minor physical change in the arterial areas that have been damaged by atherosclerosis—such coronary lesions are known as plaques—it is associated with a major reduction in adverse cardiac events, including heart attack. This clinical benefit may result because the reduction of cholesterol can stabilize a patient's clogged vessels, rendering them less "overloaded" with lipids and making them less metabolically active and less likely to rupture. In the worst cases, spontaneous rupture of a plaque at the artery wall exposes the lipid-laden surface of the wall to the bloodstream and can lead to the formation of a blood clot. Indeed, most patients who have a fatal heart attack show postmortem evidence of plaque rupture.

Even without plaque rupture, high cholesterol levels can upset the function of the endothelium, the cellular lining of the artery. Elevated serum cholesterol increases the oxidative stress (a form of chemical injury to cells produced by oxidized LDL cholesterol) on the vessel wall and may thereby disturb the cell lining. Endothelium-derived relaxing factor (EDRF) is a chemical product of endothelial cells that aids in the regulation of cell activity. EDRF controls normal endothelial cell function, including opening the artery and preventing the clot-producing blood cells (platelets) from adhering to artery walls. Endothelial cells that are not functioning properly do not produce normal amounts of EDRF; as a result, the diseased artery begins to close and platelets can clot, which can lead to an occlusive thrombus (a blood clot that obstructs the artery) and myocardial infarction.

The "quick fix." The dietary intake of cholesterol and saturated fat in the United States and many other Western industrialized countries has been, and remains, high. Most cardiovascular experts consider this lipid profile of the population *too* high.

Most dietary habits (including the adoption of a high-fat diet) are established in childhood, but concerns about serum cholesterol levels generally do not develop until people approach middle age and become increasingly fearful of heart problems. By middle age, however, coronary artery disease is already well advanced in the typical individual. Current therapeutic efforts tend to focus on those individuals with high cholesterol levels, even though medical science has not established a threshold cholesterol level at which cholesterol buildup is most likely to lead to a coronary event.

Accordingly, diet and drug therapy for possible elevated cholesterol levels associated with heart problems is often initiated after age 50, when adults typically begin to see a physician on a more regular basis and have blood tests more frequently. Treatment to lower serum cholesterol levels of people in their sixth decade of life, however, is only partially effective. While cholesterol-lowering drugs help, they provide only a partial solution, or a quick fix.

In the United States the four drugs that inhibit the body's ability to manufacture cholesterol—lovastatin (Mevacor), simvastatin (Zocor), pravastatin (Pravachol), and fluvastatin (Lescol)—have been aggressively marketed by pharmaceutical manufacturers. They are expensive medications—a starting dose costs about $2 per day. It is important for consumers to recognize the therapeutic advances made possible by the drugs that inhibit cholesterol production, but those advances need to be put in perspective. Dietary and lifestyle modifications starting at an early age are even more important to the overall cardiac health of the general population.

"*I* never *think about cholesterol when I'm on vacation.*"

Cholesterol and the elderly. Special attention has recently been given to the significance of elevated cholesterol levels in the elderly. It stands to reason that if elevated cholesterol is associated with the risk of heart problems in young adults and middle-agers, then the same should hold true for those over age 70. Yet reports in 1993 from the ongoing Framingham (Mass.) Heart Study and from the Epidemiologic Study of the Elderly (EPESE) in 1994 suggest otherwise. In the former study, elevated serum cholesterol did not appear to increase the risk of death from heart disease in older individuals. The recent EPESE study evaluated elderly patients to ascertain their total serum cholesterol levels and HDL-cholesterol levels. Low HDL levels were not found to be associated with a higher CHD mortality rate or with more frequent hospitalizations for heart attack or angina among individuals over 70 years of age. A larger and more recent study, however, did show a correlation of low HDL-cholesterol levels with accentuated coronary risk in elderly persons.

The results of these studies of heart disease have led some investigators to make preliminary recommendations discouraging routine screening and treatment of higher serum cholesterol in the elderly population. There is some concern that cholesterol-lowering therapy may do more harm than good in older people. For example, lower blood cholesterol has been associated with an increased risk of cancer.

The question of whether the lowering of cholesterol produces an overall benefit or harm may be better answered by a study that is currently under way, the Antihypertensive, Lipid-Lowering to Prevent Heart Attack Trial. In this trial, involving 20,000 elderly men and women, death due to myocardial infarction and other manifestations of coronary disease in two populations is being compared: one treated with the cholesterol inhibitor pravastatin and the other given only dietary-restructuring advice.

The promise of coronary stenting

Balloon angioplasty of the coronary arteries, in which a balloon compresses plaque against the artery wall and opens a channel through a diseased arterial segment, is a widely performed cardiovascular procedure. There is, however, one persistent drawback; restenosis (renarrowing of the artery) occurs in 30% to 40% of treated patients, usually within six months of the initial angioplasty treatment. The medical profession has anxiously awaited the results of several research trials involving so-called coronary stents, hoping that implantation of these small metallic supports at the site in the artery where the obstruction has been reduced can decrease the occurrence of restenosis.

The results of two large trials of coronary stents published in August 1994 suggest a significant reduction in the rate of restenosis among patients receiving the recently introduced PALMAZ-SCHATZ stent. When stents are implanted in the artery wall, restenosis is one-fourth to one-third less frequent. A larger initial vessel diameter is achieved with stenting, which has the potential to decrease abrupt closures and myocardial infarctions. Stents can also repair the torn vessel walls that often complicate otherwise successful angioplasty procedures. The restenosis problem, however, is not fully solved. The benefits of coronary stenting are often achieved at the cost of more difficult procedures and longer hospital stays. Nonetheless, stenting is still perceived by the majority of cardiologists today as the most promising treatment currently available.

Prevention of strokes

Ischemic stroke is a major cause of prolonged disability or death in the elderly. It occurs when one of the arteries supplying the brain closes, cutting off its flow of oxygenated blood. The affected region of brain tissue is permanently damaged. Among the possible consequences of stroke are paralysis or numbness on one side of the body, loss of coordination, and impaired speech.

Some risk factors for ischemic stroke are similar to those that are recognized for coronary heart disease. Hypertension, cigarette use, elevated cholesterol levels, diabetes, and advanced age all contribute to the risk. Controlling the alterable risk factors can decrease the incidence of stroke. Following are some of the newest and most innovative methods of stroke prevention.

Atrial fibrillation. An abnormal heart rhythm, known as atrial fibrillation, is characterized by a lack of organized contractions of the atrial chambers of the heart. Slowing of blood flow along the motionless walls of the left atrium can lead to the buildup of a thrombus (blood clot). If a fragment of thrombus detaches and travels in the bloodstream, eventually blocking an artery in the brain, a sudden stroke results. An

The recently approved PALMAZ-SCHATZ expandable stent is a metal support used in conjunction with angioplasty to open and hold open a section of coronary artery. This particularly promising new device is shown below in its four basic positions (from top to bottom): undeployed; with angioplasty balloon inserted; with angioplasty balloon expanded; and deployed.

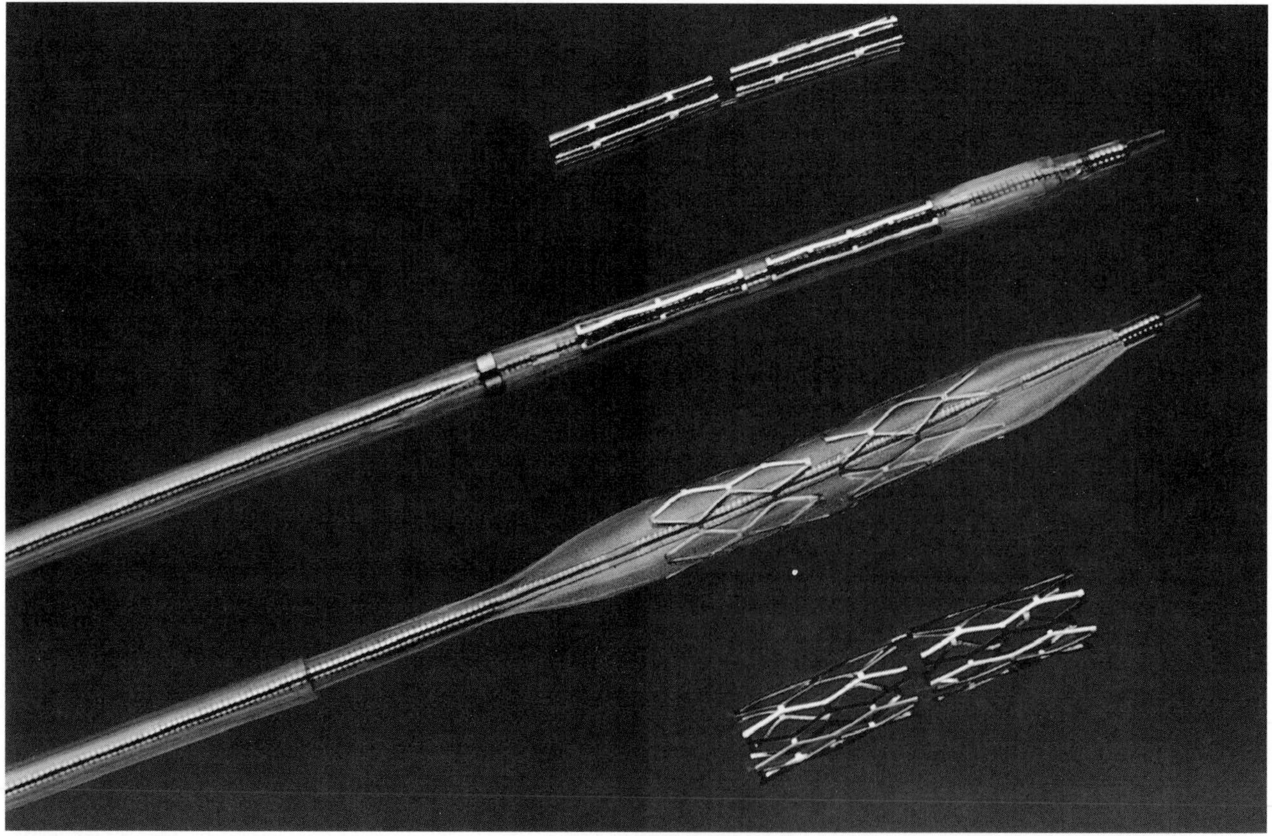

Johnson & Johnson Interventional Systems Co.

Computer-generated images, Cleveland Clinic Foundation

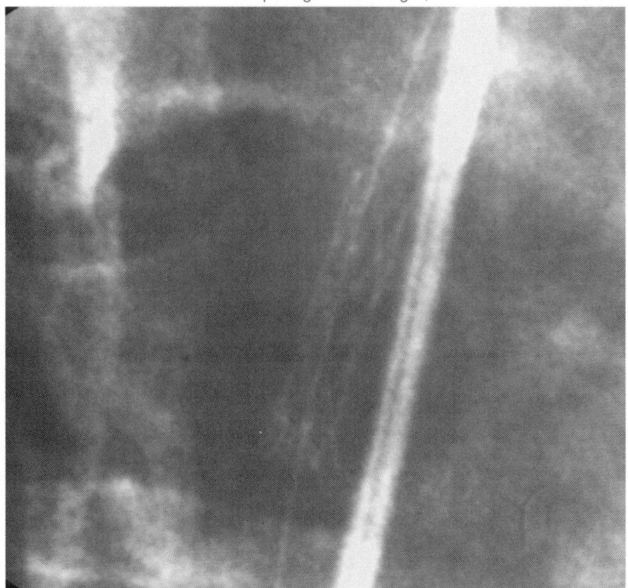

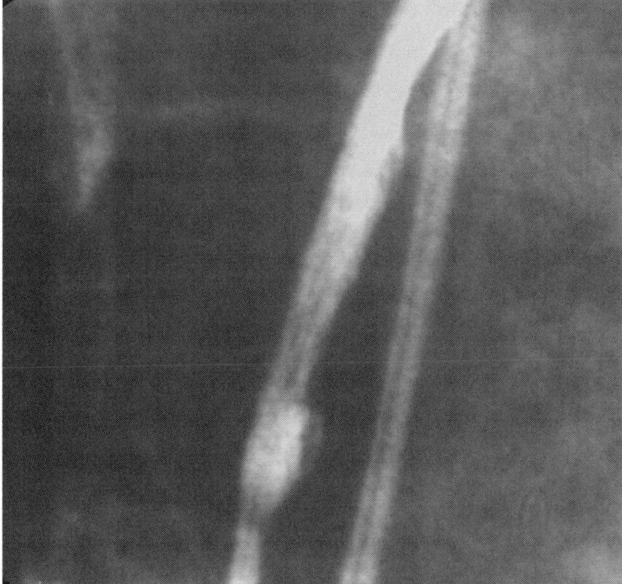

(Top) Coronary angiography (an X-ray motion picture) reveals a PALMAZ-SCHATZ expandable stent deployed in a saphenous vein graft to the right coronary artery. In the angiogram (above), the stent and lesion (narrowing) in the artery in the same patient are illuminated.

ischemic stroke caused by such a fragment is known as an embolic stroke. The risk of embolic stroke for patients with atrial fibrillation is greatest in people over the age of 60, as well as for patients with a history of congestive heart failure.

Several research trials have demonstrated the effectiveness of the drug warfarin, which keeps the blood from clotting and prevents embolic stroke in high-risk patients. Warfarin interferes with the action of vitamin K in the liver cells; vitamin K produces certain proteins that promote clotting. In most cases the benefits of preventing clotting outweigh the risk of serious bleeding sometimes associated with warfarin. Careful monitoring of the degree of anticoagulation is essential for assurance that the therapy is safe. Patients with atrial fibrillation who have strong medical reasons to avoid the use of warfarin, such as gastrointestinal bleeding or frequent bleeding injuries, can alternatively be treated with aspirin, a less-effective but reasonable substitute. Aspirin also may be the treatment of choice for younger patients without congestive heart failure.

Antiplatelet drugs. Most ischemic strokes are caused by clots that are formed from blood platelets and fibrin (an insoluble protein) and originate in the arteries supplying the brain. A platelet-fibrin clot can block an artery at the site of its formation or can detach and move downstream farther into the brain. A logical therapeutic step for preventing this type of ischemic stroke is to administer drugs that inhibit platelet activity.

The effectiveness of aspirin as a platelet inhibitor has been well demonstrated in patients with brief symptoms that warn of an impending stroke and in patients who have already experienced a small stroke. Although low-dose aspirin (150 mg) seems to be effective in preventing heart attacks, the prevention of stroke may require a higher dose of up to 650 mg (two standard tablets) daily.

In two large research trials, ticlodipine, a new platelet inhibitor, has also been shown to prevent stroke in patients with warning symptoms or minor strokes. Ticlodipine causes more side effects than aspirin, however, including diarrhea, nausea, rash, and a suppression of the white blood cell count. A patient's white cell count must be monitored every two weeks for the first three months of therapy. These drawbacks become minor, however, when compared with potential benefits. Data collected in research trials suggest that ticlodipine may be more effective than aspirin in women, in patients who have already had a stroke despite the use of aspirin, and in those with symptoms originating in the back of the brain (*i.e.,* in the posterior circulation).

Carotid endarterectomy. The right and left carotid arteries, which run along each side of the neck, provide the major blood supply to the brain. Distribution of carotid blood flow into the cerebral tissue is known as the anterior (front of the brain) circulation. Many of the most devastating strokes are associated with stenosis of a carotid artery. Surgical reopening of a carotid stenosis is thus expected to reduce the likelihood of a stroke, yet use of this surgical procedure, known as carotid endarterectomy, has been tempered by an unacceptably high rate of complications. Ironically, the most common major complication of the surgery is a stroke, either during or soon after the operation and at rates as high as 10% in some studies. Two large research studies, however, one in North America and one in Europe, have recently demonstrated a lower occurrence of stroke after carotid endarterectomy when compared with medical treatment (aspirin). These studies also concluded that symptomatic patients benefit from endarterectomy most when their carotid stenosis is severe (70% to 99%). It has been widely recognized that carotid endarterectomy will be an acceptable treatment *only* when complication rates are low and the operative stroke risk is significantly reduced.

The potential benefits of this surgery in patients with asymptomatic carotid stenosis have been more difficult to establish. Three research trials, the results of which were

Carotid Endarterectomy for Stroke Prevention

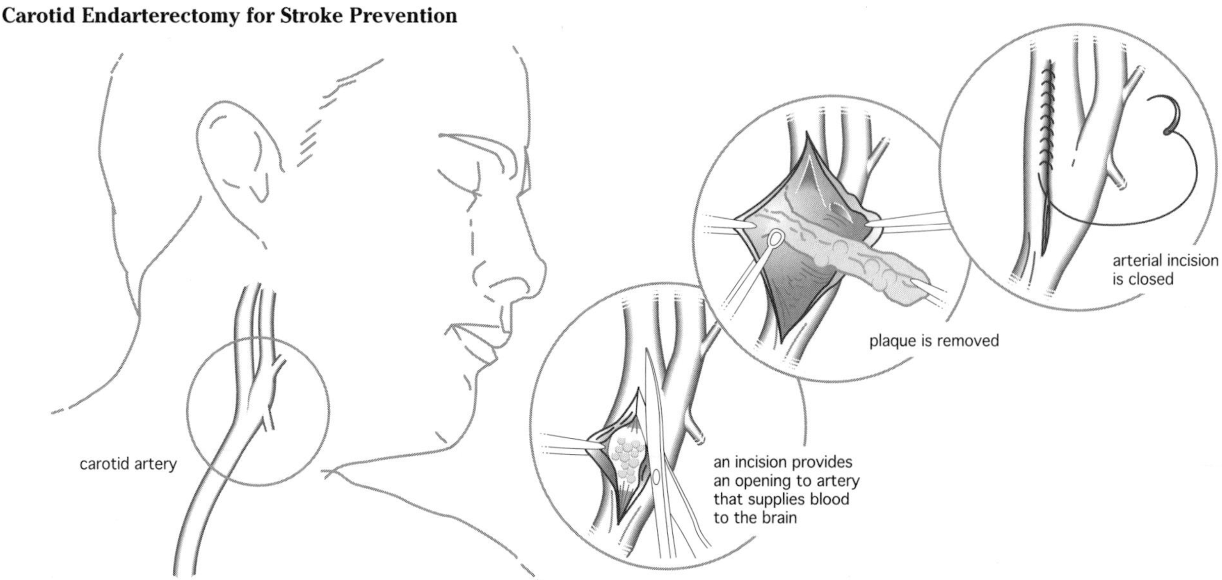

Adapted from June 1995 *Mayo Clinic Health Letter* with permission of the Mayo Foundation for Medical Education and Research, Rochester, Minn.

published as recently as 1993, failed to show the advantages of surgical treatment when patients had no symptoms. International attention was again focused on this procedure in late 1994, when results of the Asymptomatic Carotid Atherosclerosis Study showed surgical treatment to be advantageous when the carotid artery had narrowed by at least 60%. In the end, however, the benefit of carotid endarterectomy in such patients was quite small, with a reduction in the risk of stroke of about 1% per year.

Insight into a deadly heart-muscle disorder

Familial hypertrophic cardiomyopathy is an inherited disorder of heart-muscle structure and function. Although rare, this condition has long fascinated cardiologists, who believe that an understanding of the disease might yield knowledge about the normal functions of the heart. In addition to recent clarifications of the genetic and biochemical basis of hypertrophic cardiomyopathy, there have also been advances in treatment.

An abnormal gene from just one parent is enough to cause the disease; 50% of offspring of an affected parent will inherit the gene, although not all develop symptoms. Early detection can prevent the deaths of young adults, particularly athletes, who can thereafter avoid placing undue stress on their hearts. There is often exaggerated thickening of the interventricular septum (the segment of muscle separating the two ventricles), which obstructs the outflow of blood from the left ventricle. The thickening may also extend to the remainder of the left ventricular wall and cause patients to experience chest pains, fainting spells, and shortness of breath from congestive heart failure. The risk of sudden death from ventricular arrhythmia (particularly, an abnormally rapid but regular rhythm) greatly increases in these patients.

Traditional treatments. Over the past few decades, both medical and surgical treatments for hypertrophic cardiomyopathy have been offered. Drug therapy often reduces the vigor of cardiac contraction, minimizes obstruction of the blood flow out of the left ventricle, and facilitates relaxation and filling of this heart chamber. Surgically restructuring a portion of the interventricular septum, a procedure known as septal myomyectomy, relieves the ventricular obstruction and has the potential to restore normal blood flow and reduce symptoms of congestive heart failure. These traditional approaches have limitations, however. Medication may yield an inadequate response. Some patients require additional medication to control arrhythmia, and most are advised to avoid exertion, which can worsen symptoms, precipitate fainting spells, and lead to sudden death.

Pacemaker therapy. A recently identified simpler approach to relieving hypertrophic cardiomyopathy that is both safe and reliable is the implantation of a pacemaker. Pacemaker systems combine a power source that contains a battery and circuiting with a coated wire (lead) that conducts the electrical stimulus from the battery to the cardiac muscle. These leads are implanted through the subclavian vein to the right heart chambers. The pacemaker is programmed to pace the atria and the ventricles in close succession. The pacemaker also initiates the contraction of the right ventricle slightly earlier than that of the left. These alternations in the activation of cardiac muscle favorably change the motion of the septum, which permits unobstructed outflow of blood. Symptoms are then reduced.

In a recent study of 84 patients, pacemaker therapy eliminated such symptoms as breathlessness caused by exertion in a third of patients and reduced symptoms in 56% overall. Forty percent of patients experienced fainting spells before the insertion of a pacemaker, and only 6% fainted during the two- to three-year follow-up period. Pacemaker therapy is now highly favored for hypertrophic cardiomyopathy, especially because these encouraging results were achieved with a simple, low-risk procedure.

(continued on page 284)

NEWS*CAPS*

Fishy Findings

There is probably nothing unhealthful about eating fish, but a diet rich in fish does not prevent the development of coronary heart disease, as many health authorities had hypothesized.

In a large-scale epidemiological study, researchers monitored 44,895 men—all health professionals aged 40–75 and all initially free of cardiovascular disease—for six years to find out whether those who ate the most fish had the lowest incidence of heart disease. The results, reported in *The New England Journal of Medicine* (April 13, 1995), showed that whether the men ate fish once a month or six times a week, their rate of heart disease was not affected. Nonetheless, people who eat a lot of fish may have better *overall* dietary and lifestyle habits that may reduce their disease risk.

New Culprit in Cardiovascular Disease

Both women and men consume inadequate amounts of the important B vitamin folate, and this nutritional deficiency may increase their risk for cardiovascular disease. It has been known for some time that women of reproductive age need folate (also called folic acid or folacin) to prevent certain birth defects. Folate's basic role is to assist the body in the manufacture of DNA, the genetic material of human cells. If pregnant women do not get enough of the vitamin, especially during the first 28 days after conception—when fetal cells divide rapidly to form the neural structures that become the baby's spinal cord and brain—spina bifida and related birth defects may result.

Now it appears that a lack of the vitamin also contributes to the development of coronary artery disease in adults of both sexes. Folate reduces levels of the amino acid homocysteine in the blood. High homocysteine levels are associated with atherosclerosis (accumulation of fatty deposits in the arteries), which can lead to heart attack and stroke.

Four reports presented at the annual meeting of the American College of Cardiology in March 1995 and a study published in *The New England Journal of Medicine* (Feb. 2, 1995) focused on homocysteine's role in heart disease. These recent findings indicated that men with damage to their coronary arteries also had high blood levels of homocysteine; moreover, the higher the level of homocysteine, the more arterial lesions (fatty deposits) present. While previously a link had been suspected between elevated levels of homocysteine and the early development of coronary disease in men, one of the recent studies found that high homocysteine levels triple the risk for atherosclerosis among female and older patients. Assessing the recent research, Meier Stampfer, professor of epidemiology and nutrition at Harvard Medical School, said that homocysteine ranks "in the same league as cholesterol" as a risk factor for heart disease and stroke.

A new way to lower heart disease risk may be to increase folate intake. The U.S. Public Health Service recommends that adults, especially women of reproductive age, consume about 400 mcg (micrograms) of folate a day, but a 1994 government survey found that the average daily consumption of folate is only 236 mcg. Foods rich in folate include green leafy vegetables (*e.g.,* spinach and turnip greens), fortified instant oatmeal, orange juice, certain organ meats, and legumes (*e.g.,* chickpeas and great northern beans).

To Your Health?

Moderate drinking may reduce death rates in some women, according to a 1995 study—the first to find that alcohol consumption may hold benefits for women.

Over a 12-year period, researchers studied the drinking habits and death rates of more than 85,000 women aged 34–59. Their findings, published in *The New England Journal of Medicine* (May 11, 1995), indicated that:

- Death rates among women who consumed one to three alcoholic beverages per week (1.5–4.9 grams of alcohol per day) were 17% lower than among women who consumed no alcohol or drank more than 5 grams per day. The survival benefit was seen only in women at greatest risk of coronary heart disease—*i.e.,* those over age 50 and those with at least one major risk factor for heart disease.
- Younger women without risk factors derived no benefits.
- Having two or more drinks per day was associated with *higher* mortality.

The researchers cautioned that apparent benefits must be balanced against obvious risks of excessive consumption, which include increased risk of breast and other cancers, cirrhosis of the liver, and intentional and unintentional injuries.

(continued from page 282)

Waiting times for cardiovascular procedures

Prior to the ebbing of the U.S. health care reform debate (in September 1994), considerable attention was focused on the nationalized health care systems in other countries and their comparatively long waiting times for cardiovascular procedures. A recent survey of physicians in four industrialized countries looked at this issue. Hospitals in the United States (excluding Veterans Affairs hospitals) reported no waiting times over three months for elective coronary arteriography (a procedure in which a catheter is inserted into the coronary arteries to assess blockage in the artery), while 16% of patients in Canada, 15% in Sweden, and 23% in the United Kingdom waited over three months for the same procedure. Waiting times for coronary artery bypass surgery were similarly prolonged. U.S. patients who elect to have coronary bypass usually are operated on within six weeks of their decision. The majority of Canadian patients wait six weeks to six months for their bypasses; Swedish patients wait six weeks to three months; and patients in the U.K. wait three to nine months.

Although what constitutes an acceptable waiting time for cardiac procedures is frequently debated, increased illness and death rates from prolonged waiting periods are to be expected. Since limited disease is routinely treated medically or by angioplasty (or another direct intervention) of the coronary arteries, patients referred for surgical treatment usually have extensive coronary disease, and surgery is often recommended in hopes of gaining a survival advantage.

These differences in waiting times for cardiovascular procedures may be due to differences in how funds are appropriated rather than to the type of health care system per se. Canada, Sweden, and the U.K. all spend comparatively smaller percentages of their gross national products on health care than does the U.S.

—Marc K. Effron, M.D.

Medical Informatics

A 13-year-old boy is taken to the emergency room (ER) by the county emergency medical service (EMS) after the motorist who hit him calls 911 on his cellular phone. The EMS finds the boy at the side of the road unconscious. His lips are swollen, and he has several large erythematous (red and inflamed) areas, suggestive of hives. His breathing is labored and irregular. He was wearing a bicycle helmet, but it is shattered.

On the way to the ER, the paramedics swipe the magnetically coded medical ID card they find in the boy's wallet through a transmitter linked to a national medical registry. Meanwhile, an abstract of the boy's medical history, obtained from his hometown more than 1,200 km (750 mi) away, is downloaded from a computer terminal at the hospital.

Ten minutes later in the ER, the boy is found to be responsive only to painful stimuli, but his pupils are equal and reactive to light. He has an abnormally shaped head that has some boggy (spongy) areas. A bone protrudes from the front of his right thigh, and he has multiple diffusely distributed abrasions but no other evidence of trauma. Laboratory tests show a moderately elevated serum glucose (blood sugar) level and an abnormally low hematocrit (ratio of red blood cells to whole blood).

His past medical history provides several pieces of lifesaving information: (1) a severe allergy to beestings; (2) panhypopituitarism (a nonfunctioning pituitary gland), for which he requires regular hormone replacement therapy; and (3) congenital skull anomalies, for which he had several corrective surgeries as a small child. Closer physical examination reveals a possible sting site on his left cheek. He is treated for anaphylactic shock and given appropriate pituitary hormone replacements.

X-rays reveal a right femur fracture. A computed tomography (CT) scan of his head is ordered. To determine whether there is internal bleeding, suggested by the low hematocrit and multiple abrasions on his torso, a CT scan of his abdomen is ordered. A computer alarm goes off, indicating an allergy to iodine; a non-iodine-containing contrast material is used instead for the scan, which thus avoids a potentially lethal allergic reaction.

A CT scan taken after his last surgery (at age two) was part of his medical file. That scan is "aged" on a computer, which enables the current doctors to estimate what his skull should look like today. The complexity of this extrapolation and comparison requires consultation with specialists at a regional radiology laboratory. Images are transmitted and viewed in real time by the consultant radiologists as well as by radiologists and neurosurgeons at the current hospital. This allows the neurosurgeons to plan a skull operation with great precision. The surgery, decompression and reconstruction of the skull, is completed successfully, and the patient does well.

The current hospitalization is indexed in the national medical registry, and a discharge summary is E-mailed to the regional health information network (RHIN) in the patient's hometown, which E-mails copies to his parents' managed-care plan and the boy's pediatrician. His parents and pediatrician then receive detailed instructions on his follow-up care.

The make and model of the bicycle helmet are E-mailed to the national office of the Consumer Product Safety Commission. That particular model shows up as one that has failed several times; two days later the manufacturer issues a recall of all the helmets of that model sold over the past three years. A copy of the trauma report is automatically transmitted to the local highway safety department; a month later improved paths for bicyclists are installed near the accident site.

Technology's wonders

Science fiction? Not at all. In fact, all of the technology needed to realize the above scenario is available today. While the foregoing hypothetical situation occurred within a 1,200-km area, it could have happened on a global scale, using technologies that link distant countries.

Wonders of the kind described above are the domain of a field called "medical informatics." The term came into use in the 1970s as a variety of technologies were developing and health professionals were beginning to apply them. Those in the burgeoning field searched for a term that conveyed its breadth and depth; "medical computing" seemed much too narrow.

In an article in the *Journal of the American Medical Association* in 1990, Robert A. Greenes and Edward Shortliffe defined medical informatics as "the field that concerns itself with the cognitive, information processing, and communication tasks of medical practice, education, and research, including the information science and the technology to support these tasks. An intrinsically interdisciplinary field, medical informatics . . . addresses a number of fundamental research problems as well as planning and policy issues."

John Shaw Billings, the first director of the National Library of Medicine (NLM) in Bethesda, Md., might be called the father of medical informatics. In 1879 Billings established a monthly listing of references to the biomedical literature called the *Index Medicus*. In 1964 the *Index Medicus* was computerized and the Medical Literature Analysis and Retrieval System (MEDLARS) established. MEDLINE, which made MEDLARS available on-line, followed in 1971. MEDLINE is a resource that helps today's health professionals navigate through mountains of published literature.

In 1978 the International Medical Informatics Association (IMIA) was established. Originally a special-interest group within the International Federation for Information Processing, IMIA is now a separate nongovernmental organization devoted to: "the promotion of informatics in medicine, health care, and biomedical research; the advancement of international cooperation; the stimulation of research, development, and routine applications; the dissemination and exchange of information; and the representation of the health and medical informatics field in the World Health Organization and any other relevant professional or governmental organization." The American Medical Informatics Association, established in 1988, is a member of IMIA. In 1990 the University of Maryland created a database on medical informatics training programs worldwide. By early 1993 there were close to 100 educational programs identified.

The electronic medical record

A central component of any health information network is the electronic medical record (EMR), sometimes known as computerized medical record or computerized patient record. EMRs eventually will replace paper records. A report by the Institute of Medicine (IOM) in 1991 identified "improved patient records" and "information management of health care data" as "essential elements of the infrastructure of the nation's health care system." The IOM report noted that the technology to develop a robust EMR was already available in the early 1990s but that relatively few health care facilities had yet computerized their records or even developed the means to exchange information electronically. If fact, in an era when most fast-food franchises computerize every aspect of every client transaction, it is estimated that only 5–10% of U.S. health care records are maintained electronically.

The EMR is more than a static picture of a patient's medical history. It depends on an "intelligent" system that closely monitors patient care. For example, when a pharmaceutical order is placed, the system must analyze the patient's history of allergies and possible contraindications and potential interactions with other drugs.

The Joint Commission on Accreditation of Healthcare Organizations (JCAHO) has recently established requirements and guidelines for the management of computerized health data, and all institutions accredited by JCAHO will be required to meet its specifications by 1996. Moreover, expenditures for health care information systems are expected to increase from $7.5 billion in 1993 to $11 billion in 1996.

Telemedicine

Telemedicine is one of the most exciting areas under development. The term refers to a system that allows a physician located at one site to participate in the care of a patient at another. This consultation usually involves the transmission of images, which may range from full-body videos to internal radiographic or ultrasonographic images. In some instances telemedicine systems allow real-time interactive applications.

Above all, telemedicine can improve access to health care in remote and underserved locations. Telemedicine decreases the professional isolation of rural physicians, facilitates continuing medical education, and provides a mechanism for coordination and continuity of care. Telemedicine thus far has been used for health services delivery in isolated sites such as rural settings, on military bases, in referral hospitals in less developed countries, and on maritime vessels. Because telemedicine facilitates correct diagnosis through consultation with experts, transport of sick or injured patients to distant medical centers may not be necessary, and scarce resources are thus conserved.

There remain many challenges to the large-scale implementation of telemedicine. These include: (1) establishing its cost-effectiveness, (2) licensing the practice of telemedicine across state lines, (3) credentialing of physicians to practice telemedicine and act as consultants nationally and internationally, and (4) resolving a number of medical liability issues. A big concern involves diagnostic imaging. Telemedicine is too new to have established clear standards on the quality of teletransmitted images. A misdiagnosis *could* occur owing to poor-quality image resolution. Currently, though, having a physician at the other end of a camera is probably better than

A patient in rural Georgia consults an orthopedist in Augusta about a problem in her right hand. Telemedicine allows him to diagnose and treat her; in future videoconferences he can evaluate her progress.

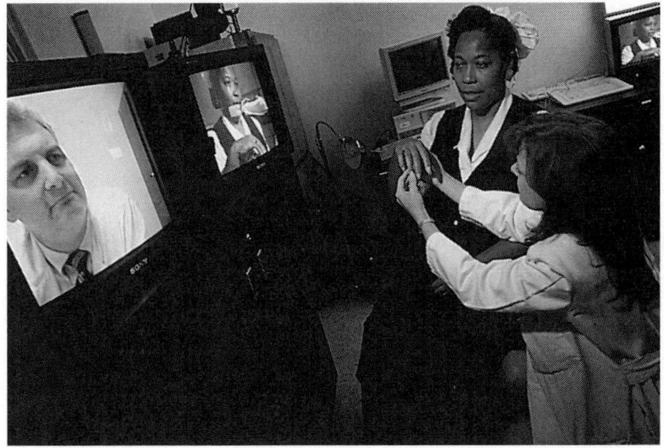

Ann States—Saba

having no physician at all—the alternative for many rural communities.

The Egleston Children's System of Healthcare at Emory University, in conjunction with the Children's Heart Center, both in Atlanta, Ga., is establishing one of the first systems capable of transmitting real-time echocardiographic images of newborns and pediatric patients. This system will allow pediatric cardiology subspecialists hundreds or thousands of kilometers away to guide and interpret critical diagnostic examinations for babies with heart defects, regardless of the time of day or night. Because time is critical, appropriate therapy based on this examination can be lifesaving.

NEWS*CAPS*

Cyberspace Addicts

With the proliferation of on-line communications has come a new kind of addiction—a habit labeled by one expert as "computerism." Increasing numbers of reports are appearing about individuals—in most instances men—who have become compulsive users of on-line services and who display behaviors that are clearly similar to those of people "hooked" on addictive substances.

Addiction results from indulgence in a substance or an activity that alters one's mental state and sense of reality. Howard Shaffer, a psychiatrist and addiction disorder specialist at Harvard Medical School, contends that an on-line service, while "not as reliable as cocaine or alcohol," nonetheless fulfills the same consciousness-shifting function. He has observed that, like those addicted to drugs, some on-line users begin to display tolerance and thus must increase their "dose"—*i.e.,* computer time. Eventually they can become isolated and ignore other aspects of life, also typical of other addicts.

The number of on-line users more than doubled between 1992 and 1994. CompuServe reported that its membership grew from 1.1 million to 2.7 million during that time. As such services continue to grow, so does the number of people who cannot resist spending hour after hour on-line despite negative physical and emotional consequences. Paul Gillin, editor of *Computerworld,* a weekly trade magazine, notes that it is people with addictive, obsessive tendencies who gravitate toward computers in the first place.

Whether a true addiction or not, excessive indulgence in on-line activities has negative consequences for many. Not only do they become isolated from friends and family, but the habit sometimes results in neglect of work, which may have economic repercussions. It can also cause orthopedic problems such as carpal tunnel syndrome.

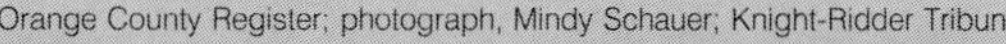

Orange County Register; photograph, Mindy Schauer; Knight-Ridder Tribune

Predicting Sneezes

Although it may not bring much actual relief to allergy sufferers, a new pollen-reporting system developed by the American Academy of Allergy, Asthma, and Immunology in Milwaukee, Wis., will at least help these patients and their doctors pinpoint the cause of their allergy symptoms. Because pollen counts have always been issued the day after they were taken, allergists have been able to tell sufferers only what caused *yesterday's* problem. Furthermore, published and broadcast pollen counts have never been collected and analyzed in a systematic way.

To remedy these shortcomings, the academy has established a nationwide network of scientifically trained and certified pollen counters. They issue reports weekly to headquarters in Milwaukee, where trends are analyzed and correlated with national weather patterns, climatic shifts, and changes in land use. By mid-1995, 100 certified pollen-counting stations were in operation nationwide, all using standardized methods for collecting, analyzing, and reporting on pollen.

Harriet Burge, an aerobiologist at the Harvard School of Public Health and manager of the network, said that with the new system, pollen counts will have practical application. Allergists will be able to use the data to manage their patients' treatment and monitor the effectiveness of desensitization therapy.

RHINs and CHINs

In today's competitive and complex health care marketplace, it is essential to avoid fragmentation of clinical, financial, and administrative data. Several factors are driving the integration of data: (1) the decentralization of care and utilization of outpatient services (*e.g.,* those provided by outpatient surgical facilities, rehabilitation centers, home health care companies—currently the fastest-growing segment of the health care marketplace); (2) the emergence of managed-care organizations and capitated reimbursement (uniform payments scales); and (3) the increased emphasis on cost containment.

There are many models and names for systems that enable health data sharing among providers, employers, financial institutions, government agencies, and ancillary service providers such as pharmacies and medical supply retailers. Perhaps most central to what transpired in the hypothetical case presented above is the existence of a RHIN. The RHIN is a computer network connecting insurers, purchasers of health care, providers of health care, pharmacies, financial institutions, and patients to enable the sharing of vital health care data. The RHIN incorporates digitized imaging, telemedicine, the EMRs' medical information storage capacity, access to the Internet, and data-transmission protocols that enable data sharing across disparate computer systems. The 13-year-old's bike crash also demonstrated how government agencies can be integrated with the private sector. While lifesaving tertiary care services were provided—neurosurgery, for example—preventive care and public health actions were also initiated (recall of helmets and installation of bicycle paths). In addition to RHINs, there are community health information networks (CHINs) and community health management information systems (CHMIS). Community or regional networks may be publicly sponsored, provider-owned, or vendor-owned.

Notable progress in the development of such networks is being made in several U.S. cities. In New Orleans, for example, the medical schools of Louisiana State University and Tulane University, the Department of Public Health, and several city outpatient clinics and private providers are working to establish the New Orleans Health Information Network. A major goal of the network will be to carry out outcomes research (the determination of which treatments work best in practice). This ability to document cost-effective and good health outcomes has become critical in the current era of managed care.

An important unresolved issue for the evolving health care networks is: Who owns the data? The clinic that collected it? The current repository? The referring physician? It is a settled matter of law that patients own and can control the release of personal data, but it is not yet clear who owns aggregate data. The participants in the New Orleans network are planning to form their own jointly held corporation to "own" the data; others will be charged for access.

The information age

"Health care reform" in the U.S. has turned out to mean the very rapid development of new types of organizations for health care delivery. Diverse organizations today are often bound together more by their information systems than by anything else. Controlling these valuable data therefore is a key corporate strategy.

The notion that one doctor can have one's entire medical history in a single manila folder is fallacious—people just move around too much. Because so many people receive medical care at a multiplicity of sites today, and because health care information is needed and collected in all of those sites, linkages between them are essential. This is especially true in the case of the medically indigent. Often they are bounced around from one facility to the next—public clinic to municipal hospital to some other treatment facility. Unfortunately, this is often the very population that is at highest risk for diseases such as tuberculosis, AIDS, and other infectious diseases that need vigilant follow-up care. When there is no continuity of care, patients are at high risk for severe long-term complications from chronic conditions such as diabetes, sickle-cell disease, and hypertension. RHINs and CHINs are just beginning to provide a paradigm to support the delivery of health services to all people.

Disaster response

Because CHINs and RHINs have such large databases, they will allow public health and environmental protection agencies to plan health-related outreach and prevention programs, such as childhood vaccination campaigns and drunk-driving prevention. The systems will also enable quick responses to disasters.

Evidence that CHINs can be valuable in managing disasters was demonstrated by the use of the information system CDC WONDER when floods ravaged Iowa in 1993. The Federal Emergency Management Agency funded the Iowa Department of Public Health to buy microcomputers and modems for each of its 99 county health departments. In about three weeks, teams from the department and the Centers for Disease Control and Prevention (CDC) in Atlanta were able to set up the equipment and train public health personnel statewide to use it. These largely novice computer users immediately began communicating valuable information about potential outbreaks of disease, contaminated wells, and locales where supplies were most urgently needed.

In essence, a "virtual" CHIN was set up statewide. Disaster-management and county health officials found that it greatly contributed to the most efficient use of resources. It also had the effect of jump starting Iowa's investment in a robust statewide computer network to provide ongoing monitoring of the health of all Iowans.

Grand challenges

Standardization in medical informatics is critical to its success. An editorial—"Grand Challenges in Medical Informatics?"—in the September–October 1994 issue of the *Journal of American Medical Informatics Association* outlined fundamental scientific or technological problems whose solutions require significant increases in current levels of scientific knowledge and/or technical capabilities. Among the goals were: a unified, controlled medical vocabulary; complete computer-based patient records; automatic coding of patient data—medical histories, hospital discharge abstracts, etc.; automated analysis of medical records, yielding the expected (most common) clinical course and outcome for patients with a given diagnosis; and global access to a complete three-dimensional digital representation of the human body. Such a model made its debut in November 1994 at the annual meeting of the Radiological Society of North America in Chicago (*see* below).

Other grand challenges might include: (1) a set of methods to evaluate the costs and benefits of developing and installing medical informatics systems; (2) techniques to help unify/integrate the full range of medical practice settings—from public health prevention programs to the outpatient clinic to the referral center—in a way that ensures maximum collaboration and efficiency among program managers, providers, and patients; and (3) the development of low-cost, portable techniques and technologies that are appropriate for traditionally underserved populations—in the U.S. and abroad.

"Visible man"

Joseph Jernigan, a 39-year-old Texas murderer who was put to death by lethal injection in 1993, willed his body to science. Scientists examined some 2,000 bodies before selecting Jernigan's as the anatomically representative male that would provide the most detailed "atlas" of the human body ever created.

The $1.4 million project, sponsored by the NLM, is called "Visible Man." This remarkable resource is now accessible to researchers and medical schools worldwide via the Internet. The virtual cadaver is composed of about 15 gigabytes of data, about 50 times as much as the entire *Encyclopædia Britannica.*

Pictures of Jernigan's body were taken from head to toe by X-ray, CT scan, and magnetic resonance imaging by a team at the University of Colorado School of Health Sciences Center in Denver. The body was then frozen and sliced with a laser-guided instrument into 1,870 wafer-thin segments. Each exposed layer was photographed and scanned into a computer, and the images were reduced to digital data.

The various "maps" of anatomic parts of the body can be rotated, viewed in any plane, dissected, and reassembled. The Visible Man is expected to be especially useful in training medical students in surgery in the same way that flight simulators are used to train pilots. It also can be used as a "crash dummy" in automobile safety tests and for designing artificial organs and joints. This technological wonder will be joined by a "Visible Woman" in late 1995.

—Dale Nordenberg, M.D., and Andrew Friede, M.D., M.P.H.

After being X-rayed, scanned, divided, and sliced into wafer-thin segments, the body of executed murderer Joseph Jernigan is immortalized as the "Visible Man," an "atlas" of the human male. Detailed cross-sections from this remarkable anatomic resource are shown below.

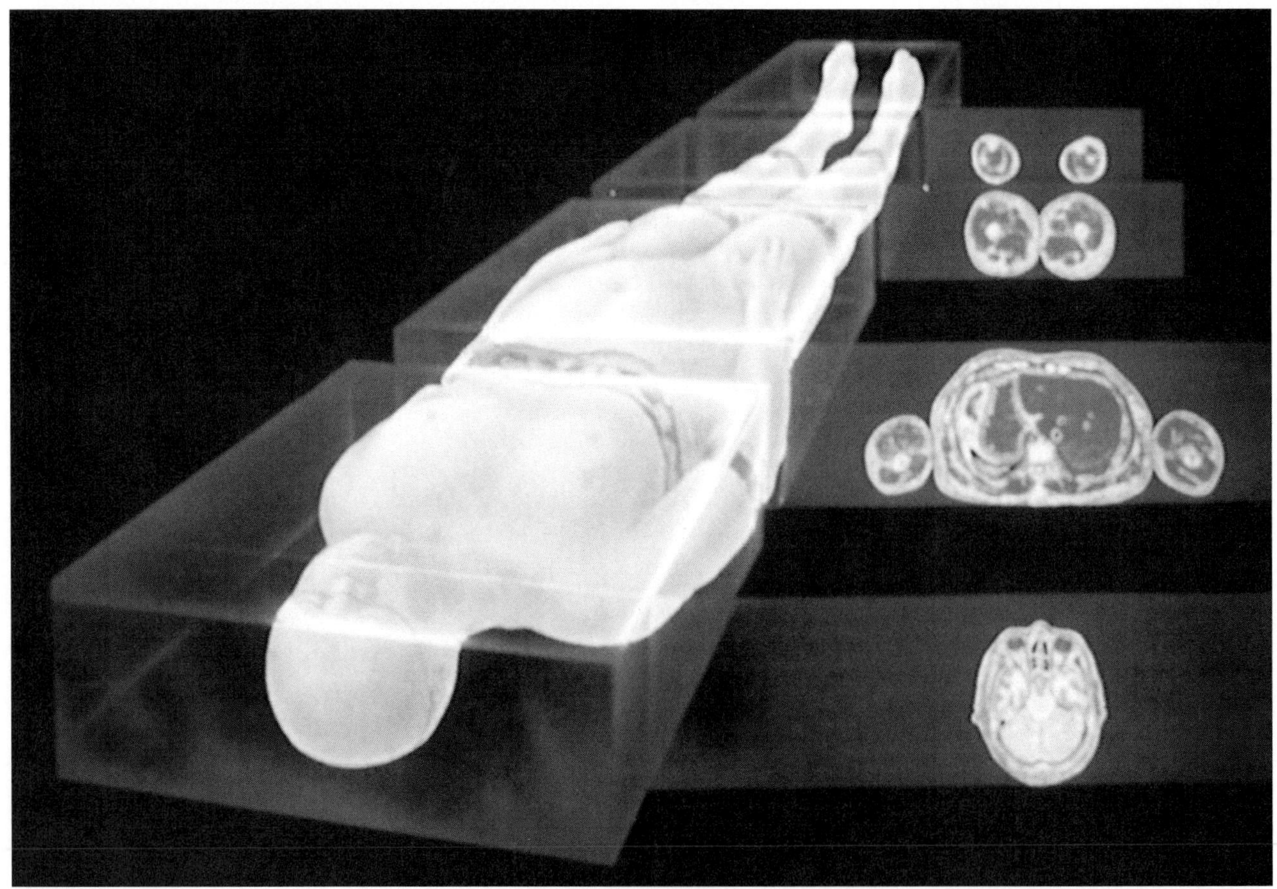

Ron Laytner

Vegetables: Rating the Healthiest

One of the most important steps toward reducing the risk of chronic disease and improving overall diet is to eat more vegetables. Eating five servings a day of fruits and vegetables should be a minimum goal. Currently, most Americans eat about half this amount. Many health experts suggest that seven or eight daily servings are an even better target.

While all vegetables are "healthy," a few stand out for their exceptional nutritional value, their disease-fighting properties, or both. Some are common if not universally beloved; this group includes spinach, carrots, and former president George Bush's nemesis, broccoli. Others, such as bok choy and the sea vegetable nori, are less familiar to many Americans. Before examining the benefits of several of these nutritional "stars," it is important to understand the many healthful substances they contain.

Nutrients and nonnutrients: both needed

Vegetables have long been appreciated for their superior nutrient content. They tend to be high in vitamin C, beta-carotene, vitamin E, folic acid, iron, calcium, and potassium. Vegetables are also an important source of fiber. What many people do not know is that vegetables are also rich in substances known as *phytochemicals* (from the Greek *phyto,* "plant"). Unlike vitamins and minerals, phytochemicals are not nutrients. That is, they are not required for growth and maintenance of body tissues and are not essential for life in the way that vitamins and minerals are. Nonetheless, they may be extremely important for optimal health.

In the past several years, scientists have come to realize that all plant foods are abundant in these potentially beneficial substances (which are found only in plants). The presence of phytochemicals probably helps to explain why people who eat more vegetables and fruits have lower rates of cardiovascular disease, cancer, and other illnesses. When analyzing the compounds that give vegetables their health-promoting properties, it is therefore important to consider both nutrients and nonnutrients.

Why fiber?

Nutrition authorities agree that Western diets are much too low in fiber, a type of indigestible carbohydrate that is found only in plants. The average intake of fiber in the United States, for example, is around 12 g per day, whereas the National Cancer Institute recommends that people consume between 20 and 30 g per day. Vegetarians and others who eat predominantly plant-based diets typically consume 25–50 g of fiber per day.

There are two types of fiber in foods, soluble and insoluble. Although most fiber-rich foods contain a mixture of both, individual foods tend to be higher in one or the other. Whole grains, for example, contain mostly insoluble fiber, while some fruits and vegetables contain relatively more soluble then insoluble fiber.

Insoluble fiber promotes bowel regularity and is thought to protect against colon cancer. The theory is that by promoting frequent elimination, fiber reduces the duration of contact between the lining of the colon and potential carcinogens present in the feces. It has been estimated that colon cancer in the U.S. could be reduced by as much as one-third if people increased their fiber intake by 13 g per day, the amount in three to four servings of fiber-rich vegetables.

Soluble fiber has been shown to reduce blood cholesterol levels. The exact mechanism for this effect is not known for certain, but scientists believe that soluble fiber binds to substances called bile acids in the intestines. Bile acids, which are composed of cholesterol, are needed for nutrient absorption in the digestive tract. When fiber binds to bile acids, the acids are excreted; consequently, cholesterol in the body is used to make new bile acids. The net effect is to lower the level of cholesterol circulating in the blood. Soluble fiber also plays a part in regulating blood glucose levels and is important for people with diabetes.

The antioxidant advantage

Many vegetables are high in vitamins C and E and the provitamin beta-carotene. (Beta-carotene is not a vitamin in the strictest sense, but the body converts it into vitamin A.) These three nutrients have received considerable attention in recent years because of their role as antioxidants. Antioxidants are substances that protect the body against damage by free radicals—unstable molecules (especially oxygen molecules) that form as a result of both normal metabolic processes and exposure to substances such as ionizing radiation. Free radicals seek to achieve stability by giving up electrons. This process causes cellular damage that can increase the risk of heart disease, cancer, cataracts, and other conditions. The same kind of damage is also involved in the aging process.

Protection against heart disease. In two studies involving thousands of subjects, those individuals who supplemented their diets with vitamin E were one-third less likely than the others to experience a heart attack. The likely explanation for this protective effect of vitamin E has to do with its antioxidant properties.

The risk of heart disease is elevated in people who have atherosclerosis, a condition in which fatty, cholesterol-laden plaques form in the arteries. A major factor in the development of atherosclerosis is high blood cholesterol. In order for cholesterol in the bloodstream to form into plaques, however, it must first be oxidized. Recent evidence shows that preventing the oxidation of blood cholesterol (*i.e.,* the formation of free-oxygen radicals) is just as important as lowering cholesterol levels in reducing the risk of heart disease. Not all antioxidants are beneficial in reducing heart disease risk, however. Both vitamin E and vitamin C seem to be effective in this regard, but beta-carotene, although a powerful antioxidant, has not been shown to prevent the oxidation of cholesterol.

Combating the common cold. Vitamin C has long been advocated as a means of preventing the common cold, although its use for this purpose remains controversial. While it has not been shown to actually prevent colds, in large doses vitamin C can reduce cold symptoms by approximately 25%. Again, antioxidant properties may hold the key. In response to infection by a cold virus, blood cells called neutrophils release oxidizing compounds that are toxic to other cells and are thought to be responsible for at least some of the symptoms of the common cold. Vitamin C may interfere with this process. Scientists have also found that the white blood cells known as leukocytes, which are associated with the immune system, have lower-than-usual concentrations of vitamin C during a cold.

Cancer fighters. Epidemiological studies consistently show that people who have high dietary intakes of vitamin C are less likely than others to develop cancer. Vitamin C consumption in these studies is determined by dietary assessment—that is, by measuring food intake. Therefore, what these investigations really show is that people who eat foods rich in vitamin C have some measure of protection against cancer. These same foods contain other substances that may be protective as well. For this reason, consuming foods rich in vitamin C is a much better approach to cancer prevention than taking vitamin C supplements.

Beta-carotene is another potent antioxidant that may reduce cancer risk, particularly cancer of the lungs or esophagus. As noted above, in the body beta-carotene is converted into vitamin A.

Both vitamins E and C can inhibit the formation of compounds containing nitrosamine, carcinogens produced by the nitrites found in some preserved meats, such as bacon. In addition, the various antioxidants can work together to reduce cancer risk. In animal studies a mixture of vitamins C and E, beta-carotene, and glutathione (another antioxidant) more effectively inhibited oral cancer than the same substances administered individually.

Counting calcium

To most Americans, who are accustomed to equating calcium with dairy products, the high calcium content of many vegetables comes as a surprise. In fact, anthropologists theorize that prehistoric humans, who did not eat dairy products, had more calcium in their diets than people do today. The prehistoric diet included an abundance of wild greens, an excellent source of calcium. Vegetables in the contemporary Western diet that are especially calcium-rich include the dark-green leafy ones (such as kale, collards, and turnip greens), broccoli, and bok choy. Many other calcium-rich green vegetables are not common in the diets of industrialized, Westernized countries but are popular in other parts of the world. Examples include komatsu (mustard greens) and kelp, eaten in Asian countries.

In some vegetables the presence of oxalates (compounds containing oxalic acid) can make calcium unavailable for absorption by the body. This is true of spinach, beet greens, and Swiss chard. The calcium in most other vegetables, however, appears to be very well absorbed.

Adequate lifelong calcium consumption is associated with strong bones and a reduced risk of osteoporosis. In Western populations, where the incidence of hypertension (high blood pressure) and colon cancer is high, a diet rich in calcium may also lower the risk for these disorders. Calcium consumption is less important in populations whose risk for these diseases is generally low. For example, many groups that eat no dairy products and have comparatively low calcium intakes also have comparatively low rates of hypertension and colon cancer.

Iron and other nutrients

Vegetables are an important source of iron, which is necessary for the synthesis of hemoglobin, the constituent of red blood cells that carries oxygen to body tissues. Although iron is an essential nutrient, excessive levels in the body are toxic; the body has no mechanism for excreting iron. Body levels of iron are regulated strictly by absorption. The type of iron found in vegetables and other plant foods is called *nonheme* iron; it is much more sensitive than *heme* iron (found in meat) to the factors that regulate iron absorption. Moreover, iron acts as a catalyst in the oxidation process and thus may increase the risk of certain chronic diseases. Recent evidence suggests that nonheme iron is less likely than heme iron to be involved in free-radical formation.

Vegetables are rich in many other important nutrients that have a wide range of functions in the body. These include potassium, the B-vitamin folic acid, magnesium, and copper.

A close look at phytochemicals

All plants contain phytochemicals, substances that have the potential to protect against diseases such as cancer and heart disease. One important group of phytochemicals is the carotenoids. As many as 600 different carotenoids exist in nature. Carotenoids actually encompass both phytochemicals (nonnutrients) and nutrients, since beta-carotene is a carotenoid.

Carotenoids are the pigments that give plants a yellow or orange color, although in some cases the presence of chlorophyll overshadows the carotenoids, which results in a green-colored plant. Many carotenoids are potent antioxidants. Lycopene, the main carotenoid in tomatoes, is just as effective an antioxidant as beta-carotene and may protect against both colon and bladder cancer. Alpha-carotene, found in carrots, and lutein, found in broccoli, greens, and spinach, may reduce the risk of lung cancer.

Some of the healthful properties attributed to beta-carotene probably are actually due to the presence of other carotenoids. In fact, some scientists have come to view beta-carotene as an "indicator nutrient"—one present in foods that are rich in a variety of carotenoids. It may be the presence of a group of carotenoids rather than of beta-carotene alone that reduces disease risk. It is also possible that carotenoids are more powerful in combination with one another and with other plant chemicals than when consumed in isolation. As is the case with vitamin C, taking supplements of beta-carotene is probably much less beneficial than eating beta-carotene-rich vegetables and fruits.

The cruciferous vegetables (broccoli, cabbage, kale, and related vegetables) have been in the forefront of discussions about phytochemicals because they contain the compounds called glucosinolates, isothiocyanates, and indoles, all of which have been studied for their anticancer effects. Much of the research related to these compounds has focused on colon cancer. Animal experiments show that these substances inhibit the development of colon tumors, and some studies in humans have found that people who eat more cruciferous vegetables are at a reduced risk for colon cancer. The possible anticancer effects of cruciferous vegetables are not limited to colon cancer. For example, sulfurophane, another compound isolated from broccoli, has been shown to reduce breast tumors in experimental animals.

Both phenolic acids and flavonoids are plentiful in vegetables. These phytochemicals have been the focus of research, in part, because of their antioxidant effects. Recently, a 16-country survey found that flavonoid intake partially explained the differences in the death rates from coronary heart disease between the countries. The flavonoids in red wine may account for the relatively low rate of heart disease in France despite a relatively high intake of saturated fat—the so-called French paradox. The flavonoids, in addition to functioning as antioxidants, also inhibit the activity of enzymes thought to be involved in converting normal cells into cancer cells.

Isoflavones, also called isoflavonoids, are another group of phytochemicals with a wide range of protective effects. Soybeans are among the only commonly consumed foods that are rich in this group of compounds. Isoflavones have a weak estrogenic effect, which may help to explain why decreased blood cholesterol levels, improved bone density, and relief from menopausal symptoms (hot flashes, night sweats) are associated with the consumption of soy-based foods.

Of all of their putative beneficial health effects, the potential anticancer effects of isoflavones have attracted the most interest. Isoflavones are thought to reduce risk of breast cancer by replacing estrogen on certain cell receptors and thereby blocking its activity. One isoflavone found in soybeans, genistein, has been shown to inhibit the growth of cancer cells in laboratory cultures. It appears to act against a number of different cancers, including colon and lung cancer, and may also play a role in cancer treatment. Although still speculative, evidence suggests that as little as one serving of soybeans or soy-based food (tofu, tempeh, miso) per day lowers risk for a wide range of cancers.

Soybeans also contain certain protease inhibitors (substances that block the activity of the enzyme protease) that have demonstrated anticancer properties and are now being tested in human subjects for their ability to prevent oral cancer. Saponins, another group of phytochemicals found in soybeans and other legumes, are being studied for their ability to prevent colon cancer and to lower cholesterol.

NEWS*CAP*

No Percentage in 30%?

According to an eminent British investigator—and some leading nutrition experts in the United States—diets that limit fat to no more than 30% of calories may not be as widely beneficial as the *Dietary Guidelines for Americans* suggest. Cardiologist Michael F. Oliver, emeritus professor at the National Heart and Lung Institute, London, presented his findings in April 1995 at the first International Conference on Fats and Oils and Human Disease, held at Rockefeller University, New York City.

Oliver's analysis of the medical literature revealed that limiting fat to 30% of calories was not effective in lowering blood cholesterol levels and that 30% fat consumption did not reduce heart disease rates. Diets that were *lower* in fat *were* effective, Oliver found, but because such diets tend to be so restrictive, they are of limited practicality.

Neil J. Stone, chairman of the American Heart Association's nutrition committee, said that many U.S. experts share the concern that the so-called population diet (*i.e.,* the one recommended to reduce the risk of heart disease and other chronic disease in a majority of the population) "may not be strict enough to make a difference for high risk people or it may be too strict for healthy people." Jules Hirsch, physician in chief at Rockefeller University, concurred, citing studies carried out at his institution that found that when dietary fat content drops below 20%, the body starts making fat out of carbohydrates. Moreover, the fat produced by the body is saturated fat—the kind that is the most unhealthy for the heart and blood vessels. He speculated that people may reach a point of diminishing returns in their efforts to reduce fat intake.

Another American at the conference, Walter Willet, professor of epidemiology and nutrition at Harvard School of Public Health, pointed out that the effects of dietary fat reduction depend upon *which* fats are reduced. If people preferentially reduce the saturated fat in their diets, the consequence is a reduction in the proportion of high-density lipoprotein (HDL), the blood lipid believed to exert a protective effect against heart disease. Substituting carbohydrates for fats also reduces HDL and at the same time increases triglyceride levels—the consequence of which is an increased risk of heart disease. Willet concluded that some of the dietary changes being recommended could actually be deleterious for some people.

All of the experts assembled for the conference agreed upon two points, however—that the current understanding of dietary factors in heart disease is imperfect and that it is far from complete. Thus, more research is needed.

The Healthiest Vegetables: A Nutrition Scorecard*

	USRDA†	Bok choy	Broccoli	Carrots	Kale	Nori	Green soybeans	Spinach	Sweet potatoes
Calories	—	20	43	108	41	35	254	41	344
Protein (g)	63	2.6	4.6	2.6	2.4	5.8	22.2	5.3	5.4
Fat (g)	—	0.2	0.5	0.4	0.5	0	11.5	0.4	0.9
Fiber (g)	—	na	4	6.4	4.3	na	na	3.9	9.8
Vitamin A (RE)‡	1,000	436	215	5,887	962	520	28.8	1,474	5,594
Vitamin C (mg)	60	44	116	5.5	53	39	30	17.7	56
Calcium (mg)	800	160	71	74	93	70	261	245	70
Iron (mg)	15	1.7	1.3	1.5	1.2	1.8	4.5	6.4	1.8
Beta-carotene (RE)‡	—	na	239	5,857	956	na	173	1,210	5,559
Phytochemicals	—	glucosinolates, isothiocyanates, indoles	glucosinolates, isothiocyanates, indoles, sulfurophane, carotenoids	carotenoids	glucosinolates, isothiocyanates, indoles, sulfurophane, carotenoids	unknown	isoflavones, protease inhibitors, saponins	carotenoids	carotenoids

* Serving size= $\frac{1}{2}$ cup, cooked.
† U.S. Recommended Daily Allowance.
‡ Retinol equivalents.
na = not available.

Illustration by Jody Williams

Vegetable scorecard

There is really no such thing as an unhealthy vegetable. Challenged to produce a list of those that provide good sources of multiple nutrients and phytochemicals, these authors came up with the following.

Bok choy. A popular vegetable in Asian cuisine and a member of the Chinese cabbage family, bok choy, also spelled pak choi, is rich in calcium, vitamin C, and iron. As a cruciferous vegetable, it is also a good source of glucosinolates, isothiocyanates, and indoles.

Identifying this vegetable can be problematic since a wide variety of related vegetables are often referred to as "Chinese cabbage." Bok choy actually is easier to recognize by appearance than by name: it has long, fat white stalks, topped by very dark-green leaves similar to those of Swiss chard.

When buying bok choy, one should choose narrow stalks for stir-fried dishes; larger, fatter, stalks are preferred for soups. The stalks should be crisp, not limp. Bok choy keeps well for only two or three days and should be stored unwashed, in a perforated plastic bag, in the refrigerator. Typically, the whole vegetable—stalk and leaves—is used in Asian cuisine. It can be stir-fried, steamed, simmered, or added to soup. Because bok choy cooks very quickly, it is usually the last ingredient added to a dish. Regardless of cooking method, bok choy will become mushy if cooked more than three or four minutes. The leaves should be just wilted, and the stalks should be crisp.

A delicious, simple dish can be made by stir-frying bok choy in a small amount of peanut oil with freshly shredded ginger, minced garlic, and a dash of soy sauce. For an authentic Chinese soup, bok choy can be added along with chunks of tofu to a miso (soybean paste) broth flavored with ginger. Or it can be simmered in a beef stock to which some shredded meat is added.

Broccoli. Well-known to U.S. cooks, broccoli also has a long history in other parts of the world. The Greeks and Romans were cultivating it over 2,000 years ago. It is also a member of the cruciferous vegetable family and is abundant in the phytochemicals that may reduce risk for colon and breast cancer. Broccoli is rich in carotenoids, including beta-carotene, and is an excellent source of calcium, iron, and other nutrients.

When purchasing broccoli, one should select bunches that are heavy and brightly green or that have the purplish tinge that is typical of some varieties. The buds, or florets, should be compact. Broccoli that is limp, is yellowing, or has tough, woody stems should be avoided. Fresh broccoli should also have a mild odor since the smell becomes stronger with cooking. It should be stored unwashed, wrapped in plastic, in the refrigerator. It will keep up to a week if the bunch is broken apart and the stems placed, with florets upright, in a pitcher of water; the florets should be covered with a plastic bag.

Stems are more tender if they are peeled before cooking. Broccoli can be simmered for about five minutes or steamed for about 10 minutes. It is also a good addition to stir-fried dishes. The flavor of broccoli is complemented by a number of different seasonings, including flavored vinegars; fresh herbs such as basil, thyme, or oregano; freshly squeezed lemon juice; freshly grated ginger; or a dressing of olive oil, lemon juice, and Dijon mustard.

Many people enjoy broccoli uncooked, and it is widely believed that the raw vegetable provides greater nutritional benefits. While there may be more vitamin C in raw broccoli, beta-carotene is probably better absorbed from broccoli that has been cooked.

Carrots. Carrots were first cultivated in Afghanistan, where ancient cults that worshiped the Sun believed that eating orange and golden foods brought about righteousness. Not all carrots are yellow, however. Dutch farmers once grew purple carrots, and small crops of these vegetables are still produced in The Netherlands. Carrots are among the richest sources of beta-carotene. They are also abundant in other carotenoids and provide fiber and calcium.

Carrots should have smooth skins and should be free of tiny white roots—a sign of age. If the green, leafy tops are still attached, they should be removed before storing the carrots to maintain freshness. Carrots should be stored in a plastic bag in the refrigerator. Miniature, pale-colored carrots are much lower in beta-carotene than full-size carrots.

Most people prefer to peel carrots before cooking. They can then be sliced, julienned, or cooked whole. They can be steamed or simmered until just tender-crisp or until they are completely tender, depending on the diner's preference. When stir-fried, carrots are usually cooked just to the crisp stage. Carrots are delicious eaten raw as a snack or in salads, but the beta-carotene is better absorbed from cooked carrots than from uncooked ones. Carrots can be seasoned with nutmeg, fresh dill, thyme, or basil or glazed with a small amount of margarine and brown sugar.

Kale. Yet another member of the cruciferous vegetable family, kale is rich in phytochemicals like glucosinolates, isothiocyanates, and indoles. It is also abundant in beta-carotene, is a very rich source of well-absorbed calcium, and provides substantial amounts of iron and vitamin C.

Kale grows as a loose head of curly dark-green leaves. Some types of kale have a bluish tint. Although it is available all year long, kale is at its best in the winter since its flavor is improved by exposure to frost. The leaves should be small and dark in color and not dry, brown, or yellowed. The head should be compact, the stem slender. Although kale can keep an appearance of freshness for a week or so, it actually can be stored successfully for only a few days. After that, even though the leaves may still look fresh, the taste becomes bitter. Kale should be stored unwashed, wrapped in plastic, in the coldest part of the refrigerator.

Baby kale leaves can be used raw in salads mixed with other greens. Larger leaves, which are generally too strong-tasting and chewy to be eaten raw, can be steamed, stir-fried, or braised in stock. Traditionally, kale is cooked for 15 to 20 minutes until it is very soft and tender. It cooks down significantly, so a cooked portion will be considerably smaller than the same amount raw. Tender, young leaves can be cooked more quickly and eaten while still crunchy.

Stir-fried kale can be flavored with fresh ginger and garlic. Steamed kale can be seasoned with caraway or fennel seeds or hot peppers or sprinkled with Parmesan cheese or lemon juice.

Nori. Also called laver, nori is one of a number of sea vegetables that are commonly consumed in many parts of the world. Sea vegetables (sometimes called seaweeds) are among the most nutritious foods available. In Asian countries they are standard fare. In Japan nori is widely used as a wrapping for sushi rolls. Nori is very high in protein, B vitamins, calcium, and iron. The phytochemical content of sea vegetables is not known.

Nori is generally preroasted and sold in very thin, flat sheets that are dark greenish-brown in color. It can be crumbled and sprinkled into soups, grain dishes, and salads or over popcorn to give these foods a pleasant, briny taste.

Green soybeans. Often called by their Japanese name, *edamame,* green soybeans are a nutritious vegetable that is extremely popular in Asian countries, particularly Japan. These are fresh soybeans that are harvested at the immature stage, before they turn brown and begin to dry. They are a rich source of very high-quality protein and also provide calcium, iron, and B vitamins. Soybeans are most notable, however, as an outstanding source of a wide variety of phytochemicals. In particular, soybeans are the only commonly consumed food that contains genistein.

Fresh green soybeans are generally available only in markets that serve large Asian populations and then only in season. However, frozen green soybeans contain all the nutritional benefits of the fresh product. The flavor is also well preserved in the frozen beans. Green soybeans must be cooked before serving. One common technique is to simmer them in salted water for 10 to 15 minutes. They should be tender but have a slight crunch. They can be served warm, lightly salted, or chilled and added to salads.

Spinach. Spinach was first cultivated in Persia after it was found growing wild in desert regions. The Chinese used it in soups and called it "Persian herbs." Later it was adopted into Indian cuisine and called "China flower." Spinach is rich in beta-carotene and other carotenoids, vitamin C, and iron.

It is usually sold either as loose leaves tied together in a bunch or packaged in cellophane. The bunched spinach tends to be quite sandy and requires thorough washing, while the packaged spinach, which has already been cleaned, contains more stems (which are less desirable than the leaves) and more bruised leaves.

Before storing spinach, one should carefully pick through it and remove any bruised or rotten leaves. It can be kept in the refrigerator unwashed, wrapped in plastic. Even packaged spinach, which is usually labeled "prewashed," should be washed before cooking. Bunched spinach needs to be untied, rinsed, and then left to soak in a basin of cool water. The water should be changed several times to make sure all of the sand and gritty dirt are rinsed away.

Spinach can be served raw in salads or can be steamed or simmered. It requires just a few minutes of cooking—not more than five. Spinach cooks down considerably, so two to three pounds of fresh spinach will yield just two cups cooked.

The time-honored way to season spinach is with a dusting of ground nutmeg. It can also be served with herbs such as marjoram or sprinkled with red wine vinegar or freshly squeezed lemon juice.

Sweet potatoes. The sweet potato—which is not actually a true potato—is native to Central America and grows best in hot tropical climates. Although sweet potatoes rarely appear on European menus, they are very popular throughout Asia and the Americas. They are extremely rich in beta-carotene and other carotenoids and are a good source of the soluble fiber that helps to reduce blood cholesterol levels and normalize blood glucose. Sweet potatoes also contain calcium and minerals. Small to medium-sized sweet potatoes have the best flavor and texture. They should be free of cuts, scars, mold, and wet spots. They will keep for up to two weeks when stored in a cool, dry area (*not* in the refrigerator).

The most common way to prepare sweet potatoes is to bake or boil them, but they can also be diced and eaten raw in salads. In a very hot oven (about 205° C [400° F]), sweet potatoes should bake for about 45 minutes. Because they can leave a sticky residue on the bottom of the oven, it is best to bake them on a cookie sheet. Sweet potatoes can be served with a sprinkling of freshly grated ginger or with freshly squeezed lime juice. They are also delicious added to spicy stews or curried dishes.

Runners-up

All vegetables are rich in nutrients and a variety of phytochemicals. Other excellent choices include the following (listed alphabetically rather than according to nutritional merit):

- **asparagus** (rich in vitamin C, folic acid, potassium)
- **Brussels sprouts** (vitamin C, potassium, indoles)
- **cabbage** (vitamin C, indoles)
- **cauliflower** (vitamin C, potassium, indoles)
- **greens such as collards, turnip greens, and mustard greens** (beta-carotene and other carotenoids, vitamin C, calcium, iron)
- **potatoes** (vitamin C, iron)
- **pumpkin** (beta-carotene and other carotenoids, iron)
- **red bell peppers** (beta-carotene and other carotenoids, vitamin C)
- **sea vegetables, including kelp, Irish moss, and wakame** (iron, calcium, zinc)
- **tomatoes** (beta-carotene and other carotenoids, vitamin C)

—Mark Messina, Ph.D., and
Virginia Kisch Messina, M.P.H., R.D.

Coffee: Filtering Out the Facts

Strolling down Broadway on the Upper West Side of Manhattan, Filmore Street in San Francisco, or just about anywhere in Seattle, Wash., one cannot help but be struck by the enormous number of coffeehouses. Virtually every major city in the United States has areas crowded with such establishments. Coffee is served in every restaurant, diner, and fast-food outlet in the country, in most gas stations, and even in many bookstores. At movie theaters cappuccino is becoming as common as Coke. Every supermarket, corner grocery, and bodega sells coffee—regular coffee, instant coffee, decaffeinated coffee, and decaffeinated instant coffee. This beverage is the national drink of adult Americans and, indeed, of adults in nearly every country in the Western world.

(Top) © 1995 Nina Barnett; (bottom) Maurizio Cargnelli, Trieste, Italy

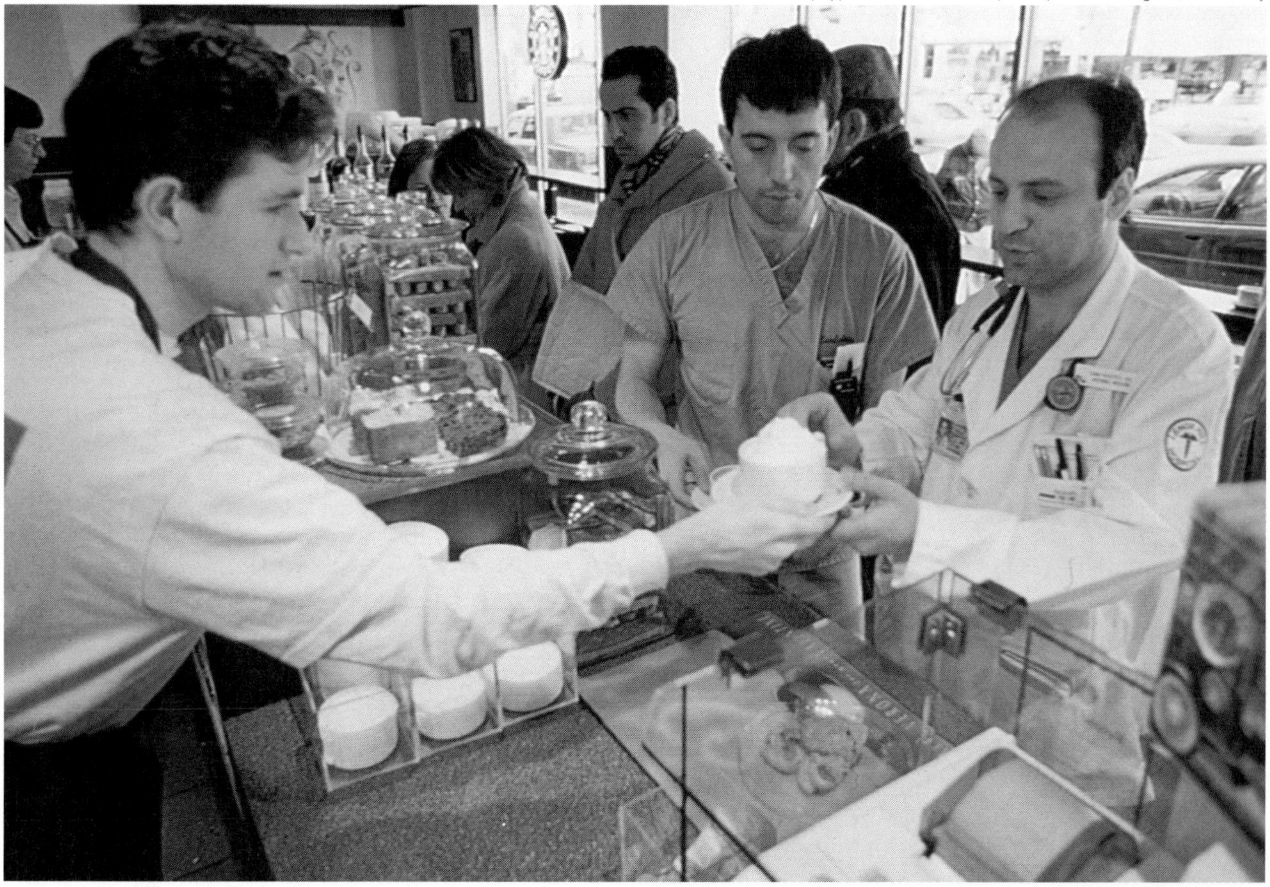

Exactly what is this drink that is consumed in such great quantities, and why do most Americans, Latin Americans, Europeans, and Middle Easterners like it so much? Coffee is a water extract of the coffee bean. Although this definition sounds very simple, it is not. There are many varieties of coffee grown in different countries throughout the world and many ways to prepare the coffee extract. The kind of bean and the type of extraction determine what substances are actually present in a given cup of coffee. Each roasted coffee bean contains more than 700 chemical components, some of which differ considerably from one variety of coffee to another. Extracting the coffee by filtration, as is most common in the United States, or by boiling, as is done in many European countries, will yield chemically different products.

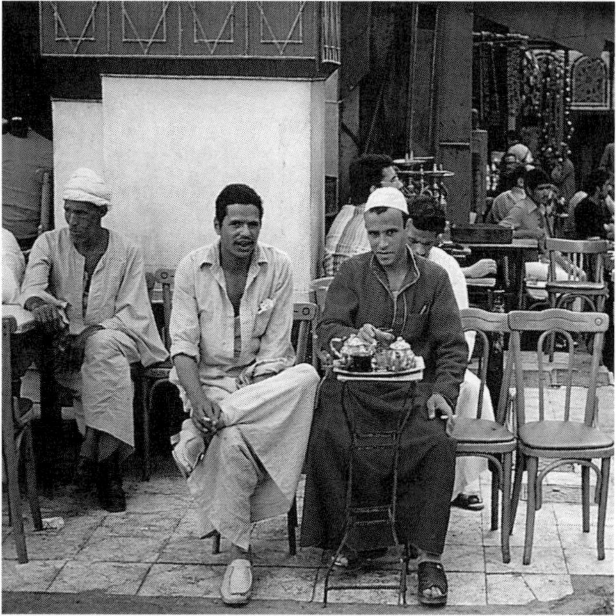

Java aficionados enjoy a satisfying cup: from a trendy Manhattan Starbucks to a timeless open-air café in Cairo. Coffee is the favorite beverage of adults in countries around the world, consumed with food as well as in between meals. Some coffee drinkers are attracted by the wonderful aroma and unique flavor; others are primarily interested in the stimulant effects of the caffeine.

Caffeine: where the "kick" comes from

People enjoy coffee because of its aroma and taste. But perhaps more important, they drink coffee because of its "kick." Coffee increases their alertness and their ability to perform mental and physical tasks. It also reduces the amount of sleep they need, or so they think. Caffeine, the odorless, bitter-tasting compound that is alleged to produce these effects, is found in all coffee beans and, unless it has been intentionally removed, in every cup of coffee.

Caffeine is metabolized by the body into more than 25 compounds, which have a variety of actions. Its pharmaco-

logical effects have been widely studied. Probably the most important, particularly to coffee drinkers, is central nervous system stimulation. This effect accounts for the "lift" that many people get from coffee and also for the difficulty some people have in falling asleep if they drink it in the evening. Pills designed to ward off drowsiness, such as NoDoz, are mostly caffeine in relatively high doses. (One NoDoz tablet contains 100 mg of caffeine, or nearly as much as a five-ounce cup of coffee.) Caffeine has many other effects, however, including an increase in the strength of contraction of the heart, dilation of the bronchi in the lungs, relief of pain—particularly headache—when used in conjunction with other painkillers, and diuresis (an increased excretion of water by the kidneys). Because of these pharmacological properties, caffeine is used as an ingredient in many medications. Many of the pharmacological effects of caffeine last only a few days, as people tend to develop a tolerance to repeated exposure. However, the central nervous system effects may persist.

Because of the body's ability to develop a tolerance to many of the effects of caffeine, habitual coffee drinkers experience withdrawal symptoms when coffee intake is discontinued. The daily dose at which withdrawal occurs is approximately 250 mg of caffeine, roughly the amount contained in 2–2½ cups of drip-brewed coffee. Withdrawal symptoms may include headache, drowsiness, fatigue, decreased mental performance, decreased physical endurance, mood changes, muscle pain and stiffness, nausea and vomiting, anxiety, and caffeine craving. At worst, these symptoms last only a few days. Thus, consumption of caffeine or coffee for a long period of time, like the use of tobacco or alcohol, is addictive. Compared with these other habits, however, the caffeine habit is much easier to break because the symptoms of withdrawal are much milder and last for a shorter time. Moreover, the symptoms of caffeine withdrawal may be avoided by gradual reduction in caffeine intake.

Caffeine: Grounds for Concern?

Beverage	Serving size (oz)	Caffeine (mg)
Coffee, drip	5	110-150
Coffee, percolated	5	60-125
Coffee, decaffeinated	5	2-5
Coffee, instant	5	40-100
Espresso	0.7	74
Cappuccino	8	74
Tea, brewed	5	20-110
Tea, instant	5	25-50
Cocoa	5	2-20
Soft drink	12	36-45
Food		
Milk chocolate	1	1-15
Baker's chocolate	1	26
Dark chocolate, semisweet	1	5-35
Over-the-counter drug	**Dose**	
Anacin	1 tablet	32
Excedrin	1 tablet	65
NoDoz	1 tablet	100

Health consequences: extensive studies

Because caffeine has strong pharmacological effects and because a very large segment of the population consumes it on a regular basis—not only in coffee but in tea (about 40% of the caffeine content of coffee per cup) and certain soft drinks (cola drinks, for example, contain about one-third the caffeine of a cup of coffee), concern has been mounting for years about the long-term health consequences of coffee in general and caffeine in particular. Heavy caffeine users are almost always heavy coffee drinkers, so it can be very difficult to separate the effects of coffee from those of caffeine. Over the years, however, scientists have been able to draw certain conclusions about the relationship between coffee, caffeine, and various medical conditions.

Cardiovascular disorders. Heart disease, particularly coronary artery disease (CAD), is the leading cause of death in the Western world. As noted above, caffeine is known to affect the heart directly by increasing the force of contractions. It also affects the heart indirectly by increasing blood pressure, at least transiently, and high blood pressure is known to increase the risk for CAD. Thus, there is theoretical reason to be concerned that high caffeine consumption may lead to heart disease. The evidence, however, is contradictory. Some studies show an increased risk of CAD in people who drink four or more cups of coffee per day; others do not. A detailed examination of these studies reveals that those demonstrating an increased risk were done in Scandinavia, whereas those demonstrating no increased risk were carried out in the United States. Scandinavians make coffee by boiling the ground coffee beans in water. Americans generally pour the water over the coffee grounds and let the resulting brew drip through a filter. It turns out that the method of preparation is crucial. It is not the caffeine that is the culprit in CAD—American coffee may actually contain slightly more caffeine than European coffee—but a fatty acid that is removed by filtration. Like any food or beverage derived from plants, coffee contains no cholesterol. However, it does contain a number of fatty acids, some of which can increase the coffee drinker's cholesterol level. Some, if not all, of these fatty acids are removed by filtration. Hence American coffee drinkers do not have an increase in serum cholesterol levels as a result of their habit, but apparently many European coffee drinkers do. (The French method of adding water to ground coffee and applying pressure to separate the grounds from the liquid does not remove the fatty acids from the beverage either.) Caffeine, even at the level of 300 to 400 mg per day, does not seem to increase the risk for CAD. There is some evidence that heavy coffee consumption (more than five cups a day) may increase the risk for heart attack, although it is not clear how much behaviors such as smoking and inactivity, often associated with coffee drinking, contribute to the increased risk.

Although, as noted above, caffeine can temporarily increase blood pressure, drinking caffeinated coffee is not a cause of persistent high blood pressure. Neither coffee nor caffeine has been shown to cause arrhythmias (abnormal heart rhythms);

nonetheless, some doctors recommend that people diagnosed with these conditions avoid caffeinated coffee.

Cancer. Periodically, reports have appeared purporting to link consumption of coffee or caffeine with certain cancers, including cancer of the pancreas, bladder, prostate, and breast. Each of these reports has raised alarm among medical professionals and spread anxiety among the general public. Because the findings have been so worrisome, the studies have been repeated to see if the results could be confirmed. The subsequent investigations, which employed more refined methods than the originals, have demonstrated that neither coffee nor caffeine increases the risk of any type of cancer. What, then, accounts for the perceived association of coffee and various cancers? A population that consumes large quantities of coffee may also be one that tends to smoke and drink alcohol and eat a less nutritious diet than non-coffee drinkers, and these differences may increase cancer risk. If there is any increased risk of cancer among coffee drinkers, it is probably due not to coffee or caffeine but to other factors that the early studies failed to take into account.

Fibrocystic breast disease. Fibrocystic breast disease is a benign condition in which multiple fibrous cysts form in the breasts. The cause is not known. A few studies in the past have associated fibrocystic breast disease with excessive coffee intake. More recent research, again more carefully designed than the earlier investigations, has failed to confirm such an association. The preponderance of evidence suggests that neither coffee nor caffeine consumption increases a woman's risk for fibrocystic breast disease.

Female reproductive health. A number of reports have suggested that caffeine may have adverse effects on various aspects of female reproduction. Some have not been substantiated upon further scrutiny; others seem to be valid.

There is no good evidence that consumption of either coffee or caffeine is associated with any types of malformations of the human fetus. The original research suggesting that caffeine might increase the risk for congenital malformations was done in rats; subsequent human studies have failed to substantiate the finding. Other experiments in rats have suggested transient behavioral abnormalities in the offspring of mothers fed coffee in relatively large amounts during pregnancy. Again, these results have not been duplicated in numerous human studies. Mild caffeine-withdrawal symptoms have been reported in human infants born to mothers who consume large amounts of coffee, but these symptoms disappear shortly after birth with no treatment.

While miscarriages (spontaneous abortions) have not been shown to be associated with heavy consumption of coffee or high intakes of caffeine, recent studies suggest a link between high coffee or caffeine intake and retarded fetal growth. Women who consume four or more cups of coffee per day throughout pregnancy give birth to smaller babies than women who drink less coffee or none. The effect of coffee drinking on birth weight is slight but significant; it is not nearly as pronounced as the effect of smoking on birth weight. However, if a woman consumes more than four cups of coffee a day *and* smokes during pregnancy, the effects of the two habits are synergistic, and birth weight can be reduced significantly.

Tony Duffy—Allsport

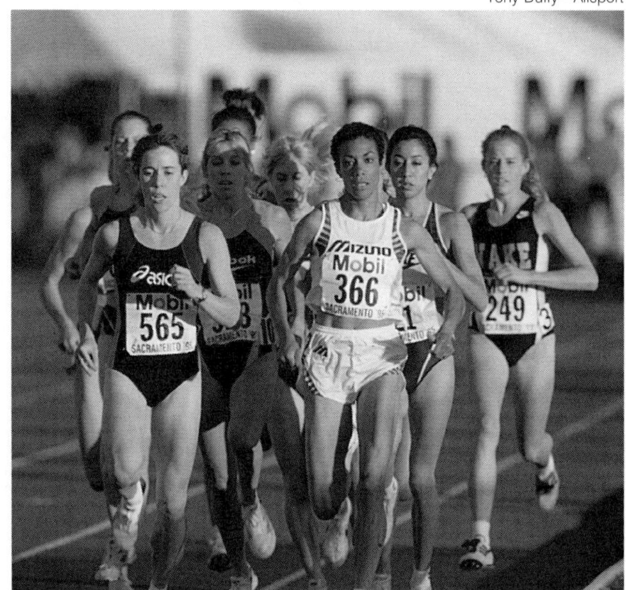

Although scientists do not agree about caffeine's potential to enhance athletic performance, some amateur sports organizations limit or even ban caffeine use prior to competition.

Coffee may have detrimental effects on fertility. Women who drink more than three to four cups of coffee per day take longer to conceive than women who do not drink coffee. The exact cause of this delayed conception—and whether coffee consumption is an important factor—is not known. Nonetheless, prudence would dictate that such women reduce their coffee consumption or even eliminate coffee altogether. Recent data also suggest that caffeine in relatively high amounts may affect male fertility by reducing sperm motility. While the research has not yet proved that wives of men who consume large quantities of coffee or caffeine actually have more difficulty conceiving, the data on reduced sperm motility are impressive. Therefore, if a couple is having trouble conceiving, it would probably be advisable for both members to cut back on or eliminate coffee consumption.

Osteoporosis. Loss of bone density after menopause is a problem facing every woman as she gets older. Caffeine accelerates excretion of calcium in the urine slightly and thereby increases the rate of bone loss. Therefore, a high intake of caffeine is a risk factor for osteoporosis. Just how important a risk factor is not known, but it appears that other factors—stature (small frame or above-average height), heredity, smoking, calcium intake, and exercise level—are more influential than caffeine intake. For this reason, it does not seem appropriate to recommend that all women reduce their caffeine or coffee consumption to reduce their risk of osteoporosis. By contrast, curtailing coffee and caffeine intake may have a small but important positive effect in women who are at high risk for osteoporosis or already suffer from the disease. Such women probably should consume less than 400 mg of caffeine per day from all sources.

Other health effects. Authorities do not agree about the purported ability of moderate amounts of caffeine to enhance athletic performance, especially in endurance events. Initially

Drawing by Mort Gerberg; © 1993 The New Yorker Magazine, Inc.

"Nowadays, Hal is ninety-nine per cent caffeine-free."

the evidence suggested that consuming several cups of coffee before an event was beneficial. More recent data suggest little if any effect. Nonetheless, many athletes are convinced of positive effects, and some sports organizations, such as the National Collegiate Athletic Association, ban the use of caffeine prior to competition.

Some people suffer from heartburn after they drink coffee. Caffeine probably is not the culprit, as symptoms often persist even when decaffeinated coffee is substituted. Coffee itself stimulates the release of stomach acid and may also relax the muscles of the digestive tract, actions that could account for the stomach discomfort people typically attribute to caffeine. Coffee consumption has been reported to alleviate asthma, and caffeine itself has been used to treat the disorder, although better asthma drugs exist. Caffeine is often used in conjunction with more potent drugs in the management of migraine headaches and is an ingredient in many over-the-counter pain remedies.

Decaf: drink all you want?

Some people find that the problems they experience in connection with coffee disappear if they drink decaffeinated coffee. Switching to decaf is certainly the answer for those who are kept awake by regular coffee. Decaffeinated coffee does not have the stimulant effect of regular coffee. Decaf also lacks the calcium-depleting effect of regular coffee, so it is a better choice for women who are at high risk for osteoporosis.

As noted above, decaffeinated coffee can be a stomach irritant; therefore, making the switch to decaf may not help those who develop heartburn after drinking coffee. Still, if they are reluctant to give up coffee altogether, they may want to try a decaffeinated brew to see if they get any relief. While studies have evaluated the effects of caffeinated coffee on female fertility and fetal growth, no such research has examined decaffeinated coffee, so it would be premature to recommend decaf as an alternative for women with fertility problems or those who are at risk of delivering low-birth-weight infants. On the other hand, since the research on reduced sperm motility has definitely implicated caffeine, decaffeinated coffee is an appropriate choice for men who have concerns about fertility.

Does decaffeinated coffee pose health risks in and of itself? Most of the processes used to extract the caffeine from coffee beans are not suspected of having any effects on health. The sole exception is the process that uses methylene chloride, a substance that is known to be a carcinogen. However, the amount of methylene chloride actually found in coffee decaffeinated by this process is minuscule. Consumers may find that the method of decaffeination affects the taste of the resulting brew, but they need not worry that decaffeination has harmful effects.

Summing up

For most people, consuming up to around four cups of filtered coffee (400 mg of caffeine) a day poses no increased risk for any major diseases. In pregnant women, however, this otherwise harmless level of coffee consumption can cause slight fetal growth retardation. Others who should moderate or even eliminate their coffee and caffeine intake include women at risk for osteoporosis and both male and female partners in a couple having difficulty conceiving. As for the millions of Americans frequenting the ever-increasing number of coffeehouses, most of them can be reassured that when consumed in moderation this drink, which has been enjoyed for thousands of years, will have no detrimental effects on their health or well-being.

—Myron Winick, M.D.

A Future for Irradiated Food?

In 1994, I enjoyed my first irradiated turkey sandwich. It was delicious!... Each modern food-processing advance—pasteurization, canning, freezing—produced criticism. Food irradiation is no different.... The technology of food irradiation has languished too long.

—Philip R. Lee, assistant secretary for health, U.S. Public Health Service

The subject of food irradiation has been hotly debated for many years. On the one hand, its potential to reduce foodborne illness, prolong shelf life, and thus increase the food supply worldwide while reducing the use of agricultural chemicals has promise. The concerns, however, are several. One is that irradiation, like all forms of processing—even cooking—lowers the amounts of some nutrients such as vitamins in food, but this effect is minimal at lowest doses. Also, some chemical changes in food occur with irradiation. So-called radiolytic products form when foods are exposed to a radiation source; examples are glucose, formic acid, and carbon dioxide—none of which has been shown to be unsafe. Not all radiolytic products are known, but numerous tests and studies have not demonstrated any negative impact from irradiation.

The long-term impact of chemical changes induced by irradiation processing has not been fully elucidated. Although there has been no clear evidence of genetic damage to humans, scientists in India in the 1970s reported an increase in the development of abnormal chromosomes (a condition known as "polyploidy") in laboratory animals and some malnourished children after consumption of irradiated wheat-based products. However, a number of national scientific committees and independent researchers from several countries have evaluated the alleged incidence of polyploidy. These reviewers failed to replicate the results and concluded that the Indian study's results were not reliable. Finally, food irradiation adds some cost to products, although it also has the potential to lower costs. For example, it has been estimated that the current cost of disinfestation of fruit in the United States is 10–20% more costly than irradiation would be.

Irradiation's potential benefits are not presently being fully utilized owing to ongoing concerns about the safety of the process. What has been clearly established is that irradiation has the potential to minimize foodborne illness worldwide. Because it extends product shelf life, it would make more good food available for feeding undernourished populations. Thus far, few food manufacturers or retailers have been willing to sell irradiated food, largely because of their impression that the majority of the public distrusts anything even remotely related to "nuclear energy" and thus will never buy or accept irradiated food.

To the extent that this perception has been challenged, it does not appear to be accurate. It is not supported by market research or consumer-attitude surveys. When consumers are presented with attractive, high-quality products, and when they are given reliable, scientific information about the food-irradiation process, they are quite likely to buy and trust such foods.

A carefully controlled process

Food irradiation is a food-preservation process capable of destroying microorganisms that cause food spoilage and foodborne illness. Irradiation utilizes ionizing energy; the food is exposed to radiation that frees electrons from atoms or molecules and creates ions (electrically charged particles). It is these ions that cause the chemical changes in the structure of microbial pests that render them inactive, making the product safer.

Irradiation of consumer products is not new. It is widely used to sterilize medical, surgical, and dental supplies and consumer products such as tampons and plastic bandages. It is used to destroy bacteria in cosmetics, coat nonstick cookware, purify wool, and inspect luggage at airports.

Nor is food irradiation a new concept. On the basis of many studies and safety tests over the past 40 years, the U.S. Food and Drug Administration (FDA) approved several uses for irradiation beginning in the early 1960s. (The FDA defines the application of ionizing radiation to food as an "additive.") Since 1972, when American astronauts sampled irradiated ham on their Apollo 17 space mission, irradiated food has been a staple of spaceflight diets.

Irradiation does not make food radioactive. In the United States the process has undergone considerable review for safety and efficacy, and tests have been done to assess the nutritional impact and potential toxicity of irradiation. Carefully defined process controls ensure that the proper dose is absorbed. "Absorbed dose" is the amount of energy imparted by ionizing radiation to a quantity of a product. It is measured in kiloGrays (kGy). Delivered as gamma rays, X-rays, or electrons, ionizing energy can be carefully controlled to deliver a precise range of absorbed dose to a product. The absorbed dose alters the chemical makeup of microbial pests, parasites, or ripening factors that may be present in the food. The genetic material of the living tissue is partially or totally inactivated, or the chemical bonds associated with the ripening factors are partially or totally broken. Toxicological testing has demonstrated that these changes are typical of what occurs with other processing methods, such as heating.

The energy source (usually cobalt-60 but in some cases cesium-137) is stored inside an irradiation chamber under a shield of deionized water when not in use. The walls of the irradiation chamber are composed of thick concrete that prevents gamma rays from escaping into the surrounding work environment. When ready for use, the energy source is hoisted up through the water into a stationary position above the water, and the food product is transported past the source. Generally, the product is rotated in the chamber so that both sides are directly exposed. Because the source strength is known and the distance from the source is constant, a precise range of absorbed dose is delivered to the food in question over a calculated period of time. The efficient penetration capacity of gamma rays allows many thousands of kilograms of a product to be irradiated at one time. (X-rays and electron beams have lower penetration capacities.)

Most countries that allow food irradiation have established minimum and/or maximum absorbed doses for each food commodity. Generally, low-dose irradiation is used to inhibit sprouting in potatoes and onions, inactivate insects in cereals and parasites (such as *Trichinella spiralis*) in pork, and delay physiological processes such as ripening of fresh fruits. Medium-dose irradiation is used to extend shelf life by reducing levels of pathogenic and spoilage microorganisms such as *Salmonella* in poultry, eggs, and meat. High-dose irradiation is used to sterilize hospital diets, spaceflight diets, and pet foods for research.

In 1981 a joint committee of experts from the Food and Agriculture Organization of the UN, the World Health Organization (WHO), and the International Atomic Energy Agency concluded that the irradiation of any food at an average absorbed dose of up to 10 kGy is toxicologically safe.

Irradiation of meat and poultry. Raw meat and poultry are perishable products that provide a nutrient-rich environment for growth of pathogenic and spoilage organisms. Slaughter and processing systems are not capable of excluding these organisms, but measures can be taken (*e.g.,* proper sanitation and refrigeration) to significantly reduce the numbers of microorganisms. Irradiation is a technology that is applied to a product after it has been processed in a sanitary manner. It cannot make spoiled food edible, nor can it be used to "clean up" improperly processed products.

Because raw poultry is a highly perishable commodity, the United States Department of Agriculture (USDA) requires that it be maintained in refrigerated storage before and after the irradiation process. Although the irradiation process causes only an insignificant rise in internal product temperature (usually less than 1.1° C [2° F]), the processing facility must take steps to ensure that the poultry is not temperature-abused. In addition, poultry must be packaged in materials approved for direct food contact and for irradiation, such as polyethylene film overwrap. Packaging the product prior to irradiation provides added assurance that the poultry will not become recontaminated by pathogenic microorganisms after the irradiation process.

Labeling. Unlike most food additives, irradiation currently cannot be detected in a product. Consequently, mandatory labeling of irradiated products informs consumers that food has been "treated with radiation" or "treated by irradiation." In addition, the product carries the international green and white "radura" symbol—green leaves (representing food) and a solid circle (the energy source) inside a broken circle (the rays from the energy source). Meanwhile, researchers are making significant strides in identifying markers that may someday be used to determine whether food has been irradiated and, if so, at what absorbed dosage level.

Nonirradiated strawberries and mushrooms (far left) are compared with irradiated samples of the same; the higher the absorbed dose (measured in kiloGrays [kGy]), the fresher the product. Irradiation of any food at an average absorbed dose of up to 10 kGy is considered safe.

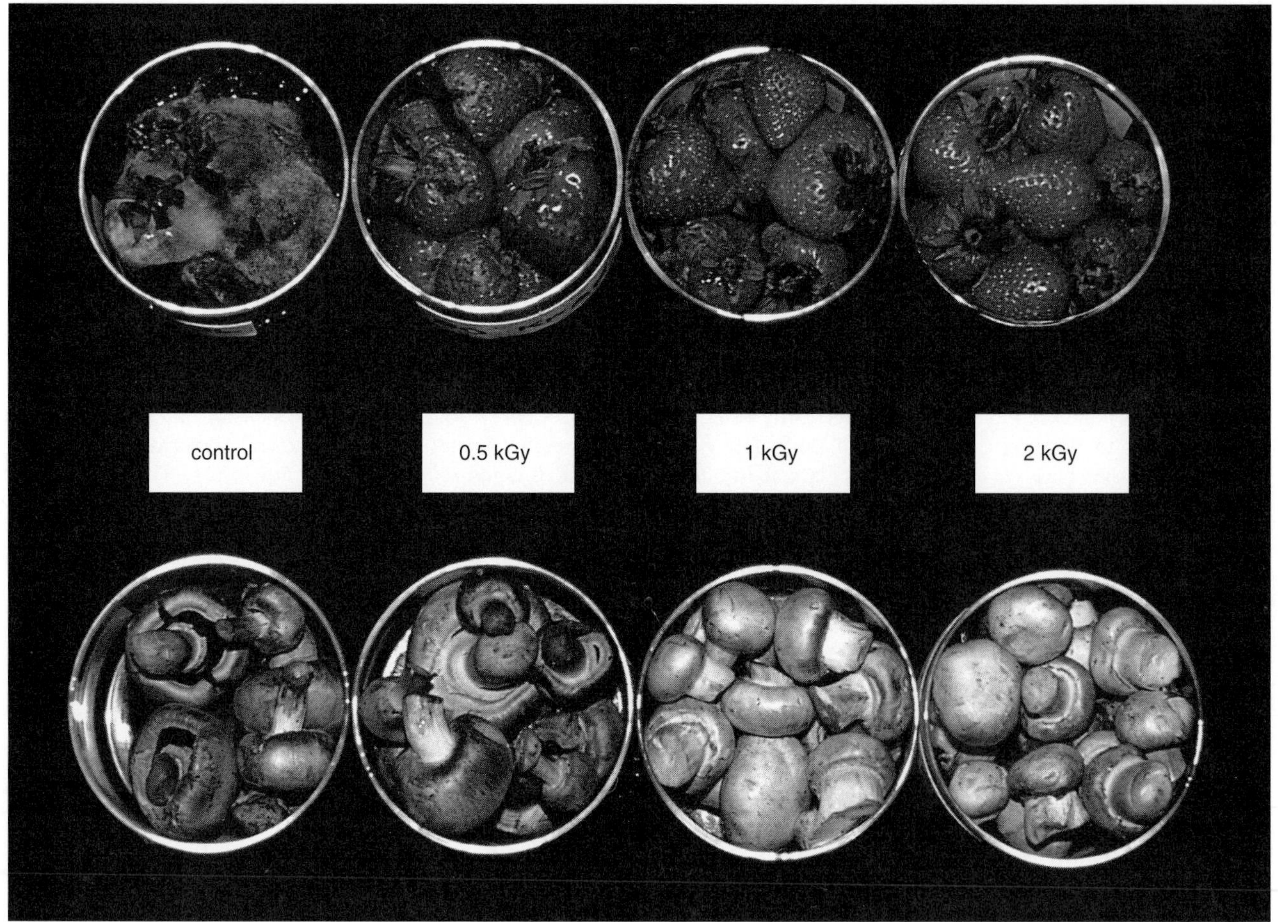

Nordion International, Inc.

Cathy Melloan

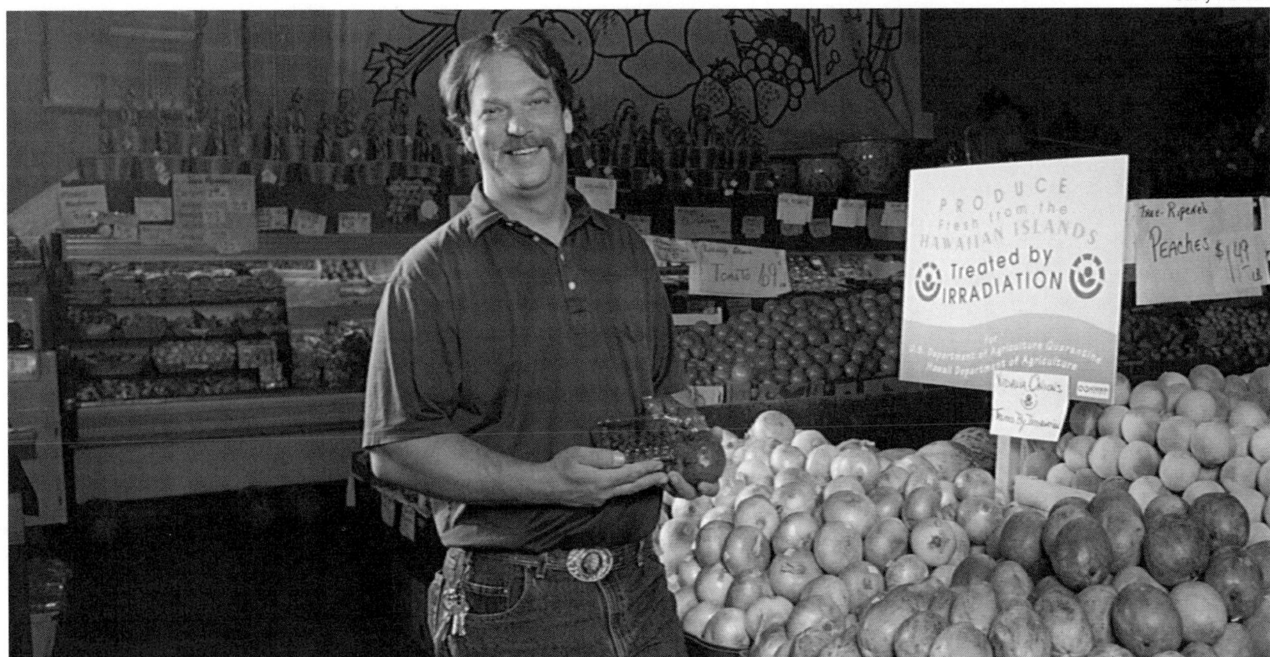

Grocery store proprietor James Corrigan is a firm believer in irradiated foods. Carrot Top, Inc., his market in Glenview, Ill., introduced irradiated fruit in 1992. Corrigan now carries a wide assortment of irradiated fruits, vegetables, and poultry; all sell well to his regular, appreciative customers.

The experience of Carrot Top, Inc.

Carrot Top, Inc., is a grocery and produce market in Glenview, Ill., one of Chicago's northern suburbs. Its owner is James Corrigan. As a produce marketer, Corrigan became interested in irradiation's potential about six years ago; the limited information he had about the process suggested that the technology had promise, but he was also aware that media coverage and consumer reactions had been fairly negative.

In February 1990 Corrigan conducted a survey of his customers through a company newsletter. Almost 75% of the respondents reported that they had seen or read something about irradiation, but over 90% felt they had not received enough information to develop an opinion. About 50% said they would be willing to try irradiated products.

Over time Corrigan learned all he could about food irradiation and provided information to his customers. In March 1992 Carrot Top began to sell irradiated fruits; irradiated vegetables followed. All irradiated produce continues to be popular among his customers.

Corrigan became such a believer in the potential of food irradiation to reduce the likelihood of foodborne illness that he decided that his grocery had to be the first in the United States to offer irradiated poultry. When irradiation was approved for poultry in 1992, Carrot Top sold it. Prior to that time, Carrot Top was basically a produce market and had never sold meat or poultry; it still does not sell nonirradiated poultry, but irradiated chicken is a proven winner. Corrigan has become an irradiation spokesperson, traveling nationally and internationally to speak about his own marketing experiences and his commitment to irradiation's potential to reduce what he calls "the triple threat"—foodborne illness, the use of pesticides on food, and world hunger.

Consumers: curious but uninformed

Many consumer-attitude surveys have tallied consumer acceptance of irradiated foods. Studies conducted in the 1980s showed that the public had little awareness of or knowledge about the process and that people needed more information to make decisions. In one study only 30% had heard of the technology. It became clear that education could increase the potential for acceptance.

The first significant study was done in 1984 by the U.S. Department of Energy in conjunction with the National Pork Producers Council. This study collected information from consumers to be used in the planning and development of educational materials. In a 1986 market test, a Miami, Fla., grocer sold Puerto Rican mangoes labeled "irradiated." Nonirradiated mangoes were also available. Sales of the irradiated mangoes totaled two tons in one month, outselling the nonirradiated fruit.

Other early market tests included the sale of irradiated papayas and apples. Consumer surveys were conducted during these tests, and information about irradiation was provided. Participants in these studies were, on the whole, curious to try the fruit; a majority preferred the irradiated fruit and judged it to be of better quality in terms of freshness and appearance than nonirradiated fruit, and up to 80% of those who had purchased the foods said they would buy irradiated produce again.

In January 1992 a Florida food-irradiation plant began treating strawberries. Antiradiation groups threatened massive demonstrations and predicted consumer boycotts, but the irradiated berries were reported to have sold briskly their first day on the market—five pints for every three of nonirradiated strawberries.

A look at a large body of early consumer-attitude research indicates that consumers, while very unfamiliar with food irradiation, are quite likely to view it positively when provided with information about its benefits. At the same time, 5% to 10% appear to be "rejecters" who, for a variety of reasons, seem unwilling to change their minds. This group tends to worry about environmental hazards in general.

Apprehensions: to be expected

Early researchers stressed that it was unrealistic to expect no concern. Studies also showed that many consumers had major reservations about freeze-dried foods, canned foods, frozen foods, and microwaved foods when they were first introduced. Irradiation was simply another new technology.

Researchers at the University of Georgia conducted a large survey in which consumers expressed greater concerns about issues such as pesticides, antibiotic residues, bacteria, and additives in the food supply than they did about food irradiation. When asked if they would buy properly labeled food treated with approved doses of radiation, 45% said "yes," 17% said "no," and 38% were "undecided."

A study conducted by researchers at Purdue University, West Lafayette, Ind., in 1992–93 consisted of 178 people in two focus groups. The purpose was to determine their acceptance levels and to see how having both information about and experience with irradiated products influenced them. First, both groups were questioned about their attitudes toward knowledge of food irradiation. At that time 54% indicated they were ready to buy irradiated food. Then one focus group was shown a videotape about the process. The other group was shown the tape and sampled irradiated strawberries. After viewing the video, 90% of the first group said they were ready to buy irradiated food. Of the group that saw the video and actually ate the strawberries, 99% reported that they were ready to buy.

If studies and market tests show that consumers will buy and accept irradiated foods, why is there a general perception of nonacceptance? To a large extent, opponents of food irradiation are quite vocal about it, while other consumers who may not be opposed are not demanding irradiated food (even though they might accept it—if they knew more and if it was readily available). Also, it appears that many industries, citing consumer concerns as a reason, have taken a "wait-and-see" position, while a few more-daring companies test-market irradiated products.

Hamburger alarm

There are indications, however, that this hesitancy on the part of food processors is diminishing. In 1992–93 a virulent form of the bacterium *Escherichia coli* (*E. coli 0157:H7*) in

NEWS*CAP*

Informed Cookie Consumers

Does knowledge about nutrition alter people's eating habits? Not much, apparently. In May 1995, one year after new food-labeling requirements went into effect in the U.S., a national survey found that Americans had not significantly changed their food choices on the basis of the new label information. In fact, consumption of some not-so-healthy foods—such as chocolate chip cookies and ground beef—actually increased.

The 15-month survey was conducted by the NPD Group, a market research company based in Park Ridge, Ill., which looked into the dietary habits of a national sample of 2,500 households. The families were first questioned three months before the new labeling went into effect.

The Food and Drug Administration (FDA) spent 10 years developing the new labeling regulations at a cost to food manufacturers of about $2 billion. In addition the federal government spent about $1.5 million on advertising in a three-year public service campaign. The Nutrition Labeling and Education Act imposes strict standards for the amount and kind of information to be provided by food manufacturers and processors. It also requires that the listed amounts of a product's nutrients, sodium, and fiber be presented as a percentage of a "Daily Value" based on a 2,000-calorie diet. A primary objective of the revised labels is to make people aware of the amount of fat in their diets.

Survey participants were asked to keep a two-week record of what they ate, to rate more than 300 foods on a "goodness" (*i.e.,* healthfulness) scale, and to take a short nutritional quiz. Even though the participants became more knowledgeable about the nutritional content of their diets as the new labels started appearing, they continued to eat high-calorie and high-fat foods.

Critics of the NPD survey contend that it is too early to fully realize the impact of the new labels on Americans' buying and eating habits. Moreover, they argue that as a result of the new regulations, today's children will grow up knowing more about what they eat and will adjust their eating habits accordingly. FDA Commissioner David Kessler noted that the law had at least succeeded in its goal of providing thorough information on which to base food choices. Whether knowledge, in the long run, will affect behavior remains to be seen.

undercooked hamburgers served in fast-food restaurants in four West Coast states led to the deaths of 4 people, hospitalized close to 200, and caused severe illness in another 700. Subsequent to that outbreak, a federally appointed panel of 15 independent experts was convened to study the problem and consider options for making the food supply safer. The panel concluded that *E. coli 0157:H7* posed a serious threat to the public health, with children being at greatest risk, and voiced support for radiation processing for at least some of the ground beef sold in the U.S.

After the West Coast outbreak, the American Meat Institute (AMI) began seriously considering food irradiation as one way to reduce the threat of foodborne bacteria in meat. The institute undertook a three-part investigation. In the first part a Gallup Poll of 1,000 consumers showed that 73% of respondents had heard of irradiation, but most had little knowledge about the process and its potential benefits. After being given information about food irradiation, 7 of 10 people saw irradiation as necessary for meat products. About half said they would buy specific irradiated foods; 52% would buy irradiated poultry, 50% irradiated beef, and 48% irradiated pork. Over 60% said that they would pay a 5% premium for irradiated hamburger. This survey also found that the endorsement of the American Medical Association (AMA) was an important factor in their acceptance of the technology. In 1993 the AMA's Council on Scientific Affairs found food irradiation "a safe and effective process that increases the safety of food when applied according to governing regulations."

In the second part of the AMI's study, interviews of participants in three consumer focus groups indicated that they had little understanding of the irradiation process. Interviews further revealed that information provided must be simple and readily comprehensible to be influential. The most successful information linked irradiation with a familiar and proven-safe process, such as the pasteurization of milk.

Part three of the AMI's research was a grocery-store intervention study. Selected shoppers were given money to purchase ground beef. Ground beef labeled "irradiated" was offered for sale along with nonirradiated ground beef. Before receiving information about food irradiation, 52% of the shoppers selected irradiated ground beef. After the shoppers were given information, 71% selected it. The AMI concluded that U.S. consumers are ready to accept food irradiation if properly informed about it.

The next hurdle

What will it take for irradiation to become accepted? More than anything else, it will take public education about this unfamiliar technology. The general public typically lacks knowledge of science and therefore mistrusts it. A recent study by the National Institutes of Health found that only 20% of Americans have enough knowledge of basic science to understand research findings and make informed choices.

Before the products become widely available, it is possible that they will be introduced through selected populations. Those at risk for foodborne illness, such as immunocompromised patients, would benefit most. Hospitals and nursing homes are looking into serving irradiated foods to

Who Irradiates What

● Unconditional
▲ Conditional

	Argentina	Bangladesh	Belgium	Brazil	Bulgaria	Canada	Chile	China	Denmark	France	Hungary	Israel	Japan	Netherlands, The	Norway	South Africa	Thailand	United States
Spices	●	●	▲	●		●	●		●	●	●	●		●	●	▲	●	●
Dried Indian jujubes	●				▲			●		●		●		●		●	●	●
Dates	●				▲		●	●		●		●		●		●	●	●
Dried fruits	▲				▲			●		●		●		●		▲		●
Onions	●	●	▲	●	▲	●	●	●		●	●					▲	●	●
Potatoes	●	●	▲	●	▲	●	●	●		▲	▲		●			▲	●	●
Garlic	●		▲		▲			●		●							●	●
Strawberries	●		▲	●			●			●	▲	●					●	●
Mushrooms	●							●			▲	●						●
Fish		●		●			●									▲	●	
Condiments		●					●											
Wheat		●		●		●	●	●				●					●	●
Papayas		●		●			●					●					●	●
Pulses		●					●					●		●				●
Shrimps		▲	▲							●				●			●	
Poultry				●						●		●		●		▲		●
Legumes		●					●					●		●				●
Frog legs		●								●				●				
Rice		●		●	▲		●	●				●				●	●	●
Mangoes		●					●					●				●	●	●
Shallots			▲							●								●
Herbs			▲			●			●	●				●	●	●		●
Arabic gum			▲							●				●				
Dried vegetables			▲							●		●		●		▲		●
Maize (corn)				●	▲			●		●								●
Cereal grains					▲			●		●		●						●
Nuts												●				▲		●
Peaches					▲							●						●
Cherries					▲						▲	●						●
Tomatoes					▲			●				●						●
Grapes					▲						▲	●						●
Apricots					▲			●				●						●
Raisins					▲					●		●		●		●		●
Raspberries					▲							●						●
Cocoa beans							●					●					●	●
Apples								●				●						●
Pork								●										●
Litchis								●				●						●
Pears											▲	●						●
Dried vegetable seasonings						●				●		●		▲	●	●		●
Sterile meals														●		▲		
Egg whites										●								
Camembert cheeses										●								
Coffee beans												●						●
Fish products		●		●			●										●	
Wheat products		●		●		●	●					●					●	●
Beans, dry		●		●													●	●
Dried fish		●		●			●										●	
Herbal teas																●		
Potato chips, raw and cooked																▲		
Corn flour																▲		
Bacon																▲		
Cold meats																▲		
Rolled oats																▲		

Source: Based on information from the joint Food and Agriculture Organization/International Atomic Energy Agency/World Health Organization International Consultative Group on Food Irradiation, August 1994.

some patients requiring a sterile diet. Studies conducted with cancer patients showed that they could safely consume "fresh" irradiated meat even when their diets were restricted to canned, sterile foods. It will also take retailers like Corrigan who are innovative, who inform their clientele about issues, and who are willing to take the risk of possible short-term public resistance and skepticism.

The future?

At the end of 1994, WHO issued a 161-page report, *Safety and Nutritional Adequacy of Irradiated Food,* which concluded that irradiated foods are safe. About 30 countries worldwide are now using the technique on a limited commercial scale for more than 40 products, including spices, grains, potatoes, onions, garlic, poultry, pork, beef, frozen seafood, fruits, and vegetables. The U.S., Denmark, Sweden, the United Kingdom, and Canada are among the countries that have endorsed or approved irradiation. The countries that have employed the technology have found it to decrease spoilage and waste and to reduce health care costs associated with foodborne illness.

WHO statistics indicate that up to 70% of diarrheal illness, which causes 25% of deaths in less developed countries, is the result of foodborne illness. In the U.S. there are 6 million–33 million cases annually and about 10,000 deaths caused by pathogenic bacteria such as *Salmonella, Campylobacter, Shigella, E. coli,* and *Vibrio* and by *Trichinella,* tapeworms, and other parasites. The USDA estimates that in the U.S. alone foodborne illness costs some $5 billion to $6 billion in annual medical and lost-productivity costs. The Centers for Disease Control and Prevention recently estimated that 20,000 people in the U.S. are affected by *E. coli 0157:H7* each year.

In the wake of the hamburger scare on the West Coast, the red-meat industry began actively pursuing irradiation to reduce pathogens in beef. The U.S. seafood industry recognizes that irradiation could boost seafood sales; in particular, sales of raw seafood (clams, oysters, sushi) have suffered in light of reports of food poisoning. Research is currently being conducted by the Southeastern Poultry and Egg Association on irradiation to reduce the threat of *Salmonella enteritidis* in eggs. Not only does the process have the potential to reduce illness caused by this increasingly prevalent form of the bacteria, but a side benefit of the research appears to be lighter, fluffier angel food cakes!

Some government agencies, such as the Cooperative Extension Service of the USDA, are already providing basic information to the public. The Food Safety and Inspection Service, the agency within the USDA that inspects meat and poultry in processing plants, also provides information through its toll-free Meat and Poultry Hotline (1-800-535-4555). The FDA has a 24-hour seafood help line (1-800-332-4010). The American Seafood Institute, a trade association, also has a help line (1-800-EAT-FISH/1-800-328-3474; 9 AM–5 PM Eastern Standard Time).

What is the future for food irradiation? Ultimately, consumers will have the final vote on the matter with their food dollars.

—Susan D. Conley
and Daniel L. Engeljohn

It's a Dog's Job

On an unseasonably warm and misty afternoon in early December, I am walking, blindfolded and at a rapid pace, along a narrow path just outside Morristown, N.J. Alongside me, to the left, is Topher, a black Labrador retriever. Following us is Doug Roberts, director of Programs of the Seeing Eye, Inc., the oldest facility in the U.S. for the training of guide dogs for the blind.

Topher is exerting a powerful pull on the harness, propelling both of us along at what seems to me an alarming pace. "Trust Topher," Doug repeats from behind on several occasions. Despite his reassurance, I find it hard to control my growing sense of panic and heed his advice to resist pulling back on the harness. ("Shoulders back and with the stride of a soldier" is how one instructor described the correct gait and manner of a blind person when walking with a dog.) Rather than a soldier, however, I feel like one who is either recoiling from a tangle of rattlesnakes or recklessly charging forward only to trip and almost fall, were it not for Doug gently touching my arm and thereby communicating the message, "Stop!"

* * *

My walk in the dark

I traveled to the Seeing Eye in December 1994 for the express purpose of learning about the very special relationship between blind people and their dogs. My interest in this subject was sparked some 40 years ago, when at age 12 I took magic lessons from a blind magician in my home town of Hanover, Pa. Even more interesting to me than the tricks I learned (now long forgotten) was the intimate psychological bond I observed between this middle-aged man (who had lost his sight a decade earlier in an industrial accident) and the German shepherd that led him along the sidewalks of our small community.

Gradually during my walk with Topher, I learned to respond to the right and left turns and subtler changes in direction communicated to me by his pulls on the harness. Once, though, when he halted suddenly at a curb, I lost my balance and would have fallen had it not been for Doug's steadying hand on my arm.

As Doug later tactfully explained, the fault was all mine; Topher had given me ample warning of his intention to stop, but I was not paying sufficient attention to his "message," transmitted to me through the harness. At the time, as if in response to some unconscious realization of my lack of expertise, I felt a vague fright. Part of me wanted to yank off the blindfold, while another part remained fascinated and wanted to continue on the walk. As Doug explained, there was nothing unusual about my reaction. "You experienced firsthand what goes into the formation of the basic trust every blind person must develop for his or her guide dog."

Negotiating a world of obstacles

The use of dogs to guide blind people can be traced back at least two thousand years. A blind Germanic king is said to have used a guide dog in 100 BC. A wall painting at Pompeii shows a dog leading a blind man through the marketplace.

In later centuries the painters Tintoretto, Rembrandt, and Thomas Gainsborough depicted blind men with dogs. The animals used in those days were small and had no special training. Apparently they were not always effectual—in one painting a guide dog is shown leading its master into a ditch, while in another the dog calmly watches its charge fall from a bridge. The image, as Edward Allen, an early director of the Perkins School for the Blind in Watertown, Mass., once described it, was that of "a dirty little cur dragging a blind man along at the end of a string, the very index of incompetence and beggary."

In 1819 Father Johann Klein, a Viennese priest, suggested that guide dogs be trained by sighted instructors. Nearly a century passed, however, before Klein's idea was put into practice. In 1916 a school was opened in Oldenburg, Germany, for the training of guide dogs for blind people, human guides being in short supply (owing to the numbers of able-bodied persons who were involved in fighting World War I, as well as the increasing numbers of those blinded as a result of the war).

Around the same time, Dorothy Harrison Eustis, a wealthy socialite from Philadelphia then living in Switzerland, started breeding German shepherds for desirable character traits such as alertness, responsibility, and stamina. Soon many of her canine "graduates" were providing valuable services to the Swiss army and to police units in several European cities. Eustis herself realized the dogs' full potential, however, only after visiting a school in Potsdam, Germany, that trained dogs as guides for blind people. She wrote of this experience in *The Saturday Evening Post* (Nov. 5, 1927):

> *Because of their extraordinary intelligence and fidelity, Germany has chosen her own breed of shepherd dog to help her in the rehabilitation of her war blind, and in the lovely city of Potsdam she has established a very simple and business-like school for training her dogs as blind leaders. . . . The school consists of dormitories for the blind, kennels for the dogs, and quarters for the teachers, the different buildings framing a large park laid out in sidewalks and roads with curbs, steps, bridges, and obstacles of all kinds, such as scaffoldings, barriers, telephone poles, and ditches, everything, in fact, that a blind man has to cope with in everyday life.*

Buddies to the blind

Eustis' article elicited this response from Morris Frank, a blind 20-year-old living in Nashville, Tenn.: "Thousands of blind like me abhor being dependent on others. Help me and I will help them. Train me and I will bring back my dog and show people here how a blind man can be absolutely on his own."

Frank got his wish—in the form of an invitation to Switzerland, where a dog (Buddy) was selected and trained for him. (Over his lifetime he owned five more dogs, all German shepherds and all named Buddy.) True to his word, he returned to the United States and devoted the rest of his life to demonstrating in towns and cities across the country that guide dogs could enable blind people to have freedom and independence.

The Seeing Eye

The training of guide dogs in the United States was pioneered by Morris Frank, a blind youth from Tennessee, and philanthropist Dorothy Harrison Eustis, who was an established dog breeder in Europe.

In 1929 Frank, together with Eustis and Jack Humphrey, an expert on the genetics and training of German shepherds, established the Seeing Eye at Nashville. Two years later the school moved to the Morristown area. In the 66 years since its founding, the organization has placed more than 11,000 dogs.

Breeding the best

In addition to German shepherds two other breeds, Labrador retrievers and golden retrievers, are chosen for this most responsible and demanding job. Since 1941 the Seeing Eye has bred its own dogs, as do a majority of the other nine approved guide dog training schools in the U.S. And thanks to the establishment in 1976 of a scientific breeding station at the Seeing Eye, complete records detailing the physical characteristics and temperament traits of several generations of dogs are available. When a litter is born, information about each puppy is entered into a computer. This can be compared

Leader Dogs for the Blind, Rochester, Mich.

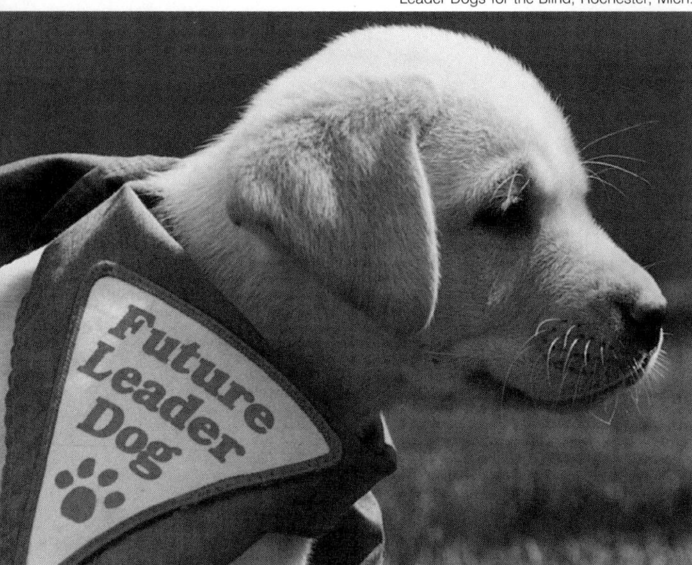

This Labrador retriever puppy is about to join the foster family that has volunteered to raise him. In just over a year he will return to Leader Dogs for the Blind in Rochester, Mich., to begin formal training.

with data about the pup's dam and sire and their previous litters. Such information can be used later by the staff at the breeding station to select the best mate for each dog. Among the current genetic research projects under way at the Seeing Eye is the effort to mate shepherds and retrievers in the hope of obtaining the best traits of each breed.

Much more than just a good breeding program is needed to produce the "ideal" guide dog, however. First, a dog must be socialized and grow accustomed to living with people; thus, at six to eight weeks of age, puppies to be trained at the Seeing Eye are placed in foster homes, where they remain for a year. Many of the puppy raisers are teenagers and 4-H Club members. Living in a family atmosphere, the pups learn to socialize and bond with humans and to conform to simple obedience training. The adoptive families are encouraged to expose their charges to many of the situations they will later encounter; the animals are taken on trains and planes and walked on crowded, noisy streets and into shops, supermarkets, and other public places.

At about 16 months of age, the dogs are returned to the school, where their formal training begins. (The other U.S. guide dog schools follow a similar regimen.) During the first 16 weeks, the dogs are worked, fed, and exercised by a single instructor, who works with up to 10 dogs at a time. The program begins at the Seeing Eye campus with basic obedience training and learning to wear the harness. Next, the training shifts to a residential route through Morristown, where the dogs learn to lead in the harness and stop at curbs along heavily trafficked streets. Weather does not alter the training schedule. On the misty December day that I visited the Seeing Eye, I observed several blind students, dressed in yellow rain slickers, walking along with their trainers and dogs.

After four months of rigorous training, each dog is given a "final exam" consisting of leading a blindfolded instructor through the streets of Morristown while a supervisor evaluates its performance. If the dog passes the exam, it is matched with one of the 250 or more blind applicants who go to the Seeing Eye each year for a 20–27-day training program.

The ideal guide dog, as defined by Humphrey, the original trainer at the Seeing Eye, must possess good health and stamina, be big enough to exert a strong pull on the harness but not so big that it cannot fit under a table or chair, exhibit willingness and intelligence, and remain absolutely "gun-sure" (*i.e.,* it must not be startled by loud noises or sudden changes in the environment). Guide dog users, too, must have specific traits. They must be healthy, mobile, and agile enough to require no more than a light touch while walking with a human guide. They must be prepared for the mental and physical strain that accompanies the transition from the use of a cane or dependence on others. They must be capable of understanding, assimilating, and remembering the instructor's advice. Finally—and this is perhaps the most important quality—they must be genuinely fond of dogs and unafraid of them. Not every blind person fits this description—one of the reasons why fewer than 3% of them use a guide dog.

Learning and *un*learning

Although guide dogs are bred for temperament and intelligence, their willingness to please is a prime asset. " 'My goal in life is to be your best friend and dedicate myself to your well-being' is the attitude we strive to achieve in a guide dog," says Pete Jackson, one of the trainers at the Seeing Eye. "But like people, few dogs are perfect, and we often have to settle for a dog whose attitude could be summed up: 'I like working for you, and I'm going to do an honest job, but you can't expect me to give up staring at the occasional pigeon or sniffing at a fire hydrant.' Working as a guide dog is a very unnatural state for a dog," says Jackson. "Natural tendencies like the instinct to chase other animals must be kept continuously suppressed."

Probably the most difficult thing for guide dogs to *un*learn is the instinct to sniff at scent trails left by other dogs. In contrast to humans, dogs possess highly evolved olfactory systems, and urine "markers" are a form of universal canine communication. Anyone who has ever walked a dog can attest to the natural attraction of these scent markers. A guide dog must learn to ignore these and other distractions, including, of course, all other animals. In a photograph familiar in guide dog training circles, Fred Maynard of Guide Dogs for the Blind in San Rafael, Calif., is shown gently restraining (by word and reassuring pats on the back) a German shepherd that is watching a cat slink along directly in front of them. The dog appears curious and hypervigilant, yet from the look on its face and Maynard's, one senses that this is probably the last time that dog will ever really look at a cat.

The blind people who go to the Seeing Eye have equally rigorous training. They attend classes in canine psychology and behavior. They also learn to remain alert to the dog's natural tendency to become distracted and to recapture the animal's attention verbally or with a timely but gentle jerk on the leash. In fact, the blind person must work continuously to keep the dog motivated and its attention focused on the master's needs and commands.

(Left) Guide Dogs for the Blind, Inc.; photograph, Thom Ainsworth; (right) The Seeing Eye

(*Above left*) *A San Francisco neighborhood, with its intriguing sights, sounds, and smells, is a training ground for a dog learning the importance of ignoring distractions while working.* (*Above*) *The active blind person needs an equally energetic canine companion. With help from an instructor at the Seeing Eye, a blind commuter and her dog learn to meet the challenges of using public transportation.*

For the dogs this part of the training involves nothing less than a restructuring of their senses, replacing smell with vision as the dominant sensory source of information. As Jackson explains it, "The dog must learn to relinquish the preeminence of smell, take in more of the world visually, and interpret what is seen."

Cues that communicate

Contrary to the popular notion, a blind person does not order the dog to take him or her to a specific location. While the guide dog can lead its master almost anywhere he or she wants to go, the dog, except along familiar, frequently traveled routes, is not aware of the intended destination. In order for the team to successfully reach the destination, the blind person must know exactly how many blocks to go and which way to turn. Thus, every blind person who wishes to remain mobile must develop a finely honed directional sense. The dog merely obeys a series of commands such as "forward," "right," and "left." The dog is trained to stop at *all* curbs and wait for the command to go forward.

At the Seeing Eye blind people learn to construct mental maps of their surroundings. By running their fingers over a scale model of the facility's main building, they familiarize themselves with their immediate environment. Later they will memorize by touch a relief map of the streets of Morristown. Like anyone relying on a map, however, they sometimes take a wrong turn. When blind people lose their way, they resort to the same time-honored method used by the sighted: asking directions from others.

Although the dog responds to the directional commands and the encouragement of the phrase "good boy" (or "good girl") when things are going well—or the disapproving term "phooey" when a mistake is made—much of the communication between master and dog is nonverbal. The harness is the primary conduit of this communication. Indeed, the harness is the key to understanding what guide dogs are all about. A guide dog outside of harness is like any other dog. When in harness, however, the dog must concentrate on its "work" and be sheltered from unnecessary or avoidable distractions. The dog is trained to take orders exclusively from its master, and anything that interferes with this single-minded focus detracts from the bond between the two. This is one reason guide dogs should never be petted or otherwise fussed over by strangers unless permission has first been obtained from the owner.

Intelligent disobedience

Also contrary to popular belief, guide dogs cannot distinguish between red and green traffic signals (dogs are essentially color-blind). Instead, given the command to go forward at a particular crossing, the dog will assess the situation and will *disobey* the command to cross if—and only if—the dog determines that it would be unsafe to proceed. This capacity for "intelligent disobedience" is perhaps the most important quality of a guide dog. If an obstacle suddenly looms up after the command "forward" has been given, the dog must stop and refuse further commands to proceed. Failure of this test could cost the lives of both dog and owner. At Guide Dogs for the Blind, the dogs are put to a particularly challenging test of this ability. On a route the dog and instructor have walked many times before, a car driven by a staff member turns at an intersection directly in front of the dog. The dog is expected to stop and step backward. If the dog merely stops but does not retreat, the test is repeated later, but this time the dog is gently bumped by the car. After the dog has learned the correct "stop-and-back-up" response, the test will be repeated with different cars and drivers so that the dog does not associate the situation with a particular vehicle or individual.

Intelligent disobedience comes hard for many dogs because of their innate desire to please. Here a delicate balance must be struck; if the dog is not highly motivated to please its owner, it would not be selected as a guide dog. Yet if that desire to please is not tempered by a capacity for judgment, the end result can be disastrous. Frank recounted one such near calamity that occurred while he was visiting Dayton, Ohio, in the 1930s:

> *I was scheduled to address a large convention that evening; the train had arrived late, and I was pressed for time. With Buddy . . . I rushed up to my room on the 14th floor. . . . I had only 15 minutes to get to the convention hall. I had to hurry downstairs and find a cab.*
>
> *I hustled along the corridor to the elevator foyer. There Buddy stopped stock-still. She, who always walked up to an elevator and pointed with her nose to the call button for my convenience, would not approach this one. She ignored completely my "Forward" command. Then, in my great haste, I did what no Seeing Eye owner should ever do—I dropped the harness and started forward alone.*
>
> *Buddy immediately threw herself across my legs, pushing so hard against me that I could not move. At that moment a maid coming out of one of the rooms let out a terrified shriek.*
>
> *"Don't move!" she shouted. "The elevator door's open, but the elevator's not there. There's only a hole!"*
>
> *My knees all but buckled. Had Buddy let me take two or more steps I would have disappeared down the empty shaft!*

Canine judgment

In humans the frontal lobes of the brain, which make up 40% of the volume of the cerebral hemispheres, play the predominant role in judgment. Damage to these areas disrupts the ability to appraise a situation correctly and respond appropriately. In dogs, however, the frontal lobes are small—constituting only 10% of the brain's volume—and are not at all as dominant as they are in humans. How then does the dog learn to exercise judgment?

In essence, the process involves the transfer to the dog of a limited amount of human judgment. Thus, the dog will learn to appraise whether an overhanging branch is so low that it could strike the head or face of its human companion. On other occasions the dog will be called upon to decide from a block away how best to negotiate various obstructions in its path. The animal must at all times be prepared to respond to sudden changes in the environment and alter its course accordingly. Frank described an occasion when Buddy's acute observational abilities and quick reaction saved the day:

> *As we walked down the narrow sidewalk the feel of the harness told me Buddy . . . had deftly swung out to the left, then back in line again. I felt no presence of person or building nearby. I put my hand up and at about eye level hit an iron pipe, the framework support of an awning. . . . It would have struck me right in the face but for Buddy. This seemed to me the most amazing guiding she had done. Traveling alone she would hardly have noticed that heavy structure, so far above her. But with me in tow her eyes had measured it against my six feet. She had received no command; she acted entirely on her own. When she did that, she was thinking!*

Such feats of observation and reasoning cannot be accomplished by every dog, which is one of the reasons that only 50% of dogs successfully complete the training and qualify as guide dogs.

Lessons from a Labrador

Part of my exploration of the relationship between guide dogs and their owners involved interviews with blind people. Typical of the comments I heard were those of public relations specialist Susan Morgan about her Labrador retriever, Louise. "It's difficult some days to figure out where I end and she begins. Louise has assimilated some of my attributes, and she's so inspiring I'm happy to take on some of her qualities." Morgan, who lost her sight gradually to retinitis pigmentosa (a hereditary degenerative disease of the eye), particularly appreciates Louise's ability to respond when Morgan feels unhappy by putting her head on Morgan's knee and reassuring her.

As Charles Kaman, director of the Council of U.S. Guide Dog Schools in Bloomfield, Conn., has observed, the bond between blind people and their dogs sometimes even transcends that between husband and wife. It is not surprising, then, that minor jealousies and conflicts may arise. "My fiancé knows my dog [is] more to me than just a pet," one blind woman told me. "Sometimes I think he even feels a little jealous about the very special relationship I have with my dog. I suspect that's because he recognizes that neither he nor *any* other person could duplicate that bond. My dog and I spend literally every waking hour together—and do so without getting too much on each other's nerves."

As the communication between dog and owner evolves, a single word or phrase may be sufficient to direct the dog to a familiar site. As noted above, this is not how dogs are trained or how their owners are taught to use them, but with long experience many dogs learn to go with a minimum of direction to certain often-visited locations. One blind woman told me of her dog's enthusiasm for a certain restaurant where quite a fuss is made over him. Whenever the pair approach the restaurant, the dog indicates by a slight pull on the harness that he would like to go inside. She laughs and tells him, "Not today. Maybe tomorrow."

Such closeness is the consequence of the careful compatibility matching that is done at the training schools. At Guide Dogs for the Blind, the instructors who train the dogs also select dogs for the individual students and teach the students how to use them. The size of the person and the dog, the blind person's home environment and job, and his or her activity level are all taken into consideration.

"Louise loves the excitement of accompanying me to speaking engagements," says Morgan, who travels extensively to educate business and community leaders about hiring qualified job applicants who are blind. "In fact, during those periods when I travel less she pouts a little because she clearly misses the excitement." For a less active person, a more placid dog probably would be a better match.

The enduring bond of affection and trust between guide dog and master is like no other relationship. As one blind woman put it, "People may let you down, but your dog doesn't."

Guide Dogs for the Blind, Inc.

Faithful to the end

Since the guide dog is the key to the blind person's independence, parting with a dog that has become too ill or aged to work is an extremely painful process. At the same time, however, plans must be made for the dog's successor. "Even during the period of mourning you have to think ahead to the new dog and the opportunity it will provide for your continued independence," observed Michele Drolet, a blind woman who won a medal in cross-country skiing at the last International Games for the Disabled (Paralympics).

At the Seeing Eye, Drolet counsels blind people who have lost their dogs to illness or old age. When I spoke with her, she was undergoing a difficult transition herself. Her nine-year-old dog Tessa had just been diagnosed with hip dysplasia, a crippling degenerative bone disease. Drolet believes the relationship of dog to master or mistress is closer than any other. "Your dog follows you through every phase of your life, thick or thin, for better or worse. And they don't let you down; people may let you down, but your dog doesn't. And if that sounds exaggerated, think of it this way," she added with a smile; "no husband is going to lie under a rack of clothes while I try on one dress after another."

After only a few moments spent with them, it was obvious to me that Drolet and Tessa were united by a remarkable bond. The dog frequently turned and looked toward her, as if seeking some kind of reassurance. And although I do not consider myself an expert in interpreting the expression and moods of animals, Tessa seemed sad to me. "She is depressed because she knows that I am not using her as much as I did," Drolet said. "As the dysplasia has advanced, she moves much slower and stumbles a lot, and I can't totally depend on her. . . . As a result, I am now much less physically active that I was only a few months ago."

Drolet is waiting for a new dog that is scheduled to finish training in two months. In the meantime, she describes her feelings as "ambivalent"; she is looking forward to greater independence but is apprehensive about the prospect of accustoming herself to her new dog's personality. And, of course, she must deal with the sorrow of the gradual separation from Tessa.

* * *

My blindfolded walk completed, I am only too aware that my experience of temporary, voluntary deprivation of sight cannot begin to compare to the experience of a blind person or provide more than just a hint of the difference that a guide dog makes in his or her life. Although I now know more than I did before about the intimate bond between them, I remain separated from the experience by the miracle of sight.

—Richard M. Restak, M.D.

Injury-Prevention Messages: View from the Other Side

Among the steps that a society takes to protect its citizens from injury are the setting of highway speed limits, the enforcement of blood alcohol limits for driving, and the requirements that motorcyclists wear helmets and gun owners register firearms. Such legislation is consistent with an approach to health that identifies problems within the environment rather than within the individual. This "public health" perspective contends that the risk of becoming disabled through injury is unacceptable—and that disability is preventable. Yet, even as the purpose of public health is to protect people from harm, could it be that such efforts inadvertently do harm by stigmatizing people who already possess the attributes targeted for prevention? As a case study, this report considers the extent to which health education approaches to preventing injury—with their implicit message, "Don't let this happen to you!"—may portray people with disabilities in a stigmatizing way.

Too many injuries

In the United States more than 140,000 people die from injuries every year. Among people aged 1–44, injury not only is the number one cause of death but exceeds all major categories of disease as a cause of premature loss of years of life. According to the National Safety Council, in 1994 fatal and nonfatal unintentional injuries cost Americans an estimated $410.6 billion. That amount included wage and productivity losses, medical expenses, administrative costs, employer expenses, and costs associated with motor vehicle and property damage.

To a large extent, public health measures are taken in response to the high number of injuries and the travails of survivors of disabling injuries. But while rightly contending that becoming disabled is an unacceptable risk, the public health ethic may convey a message that *being* disabled is an unacceptable status. (*Disability* is defined as a motor or cognitive deficit that in some way impairs or incapacitates the individual. In the United States alone there are an estimated 43 million individuals who fit that description.)

Another voice, another message

Health educators and policy makers seek to prevent affliction; others—disability rights advocates—have a different goal. They champion laws and programs that support personal autonomy. They view such physical limitations as the inability to walk, hear, learn, or lift as but single characteristics among the many that give an individual his or her personal identity.

The author showed both posters below to two groups to see what impact their injury-prevention messages had. The reactions of able-bodied college students differed strikingly from those of people who had disabilities and needed to use wheelchairs.

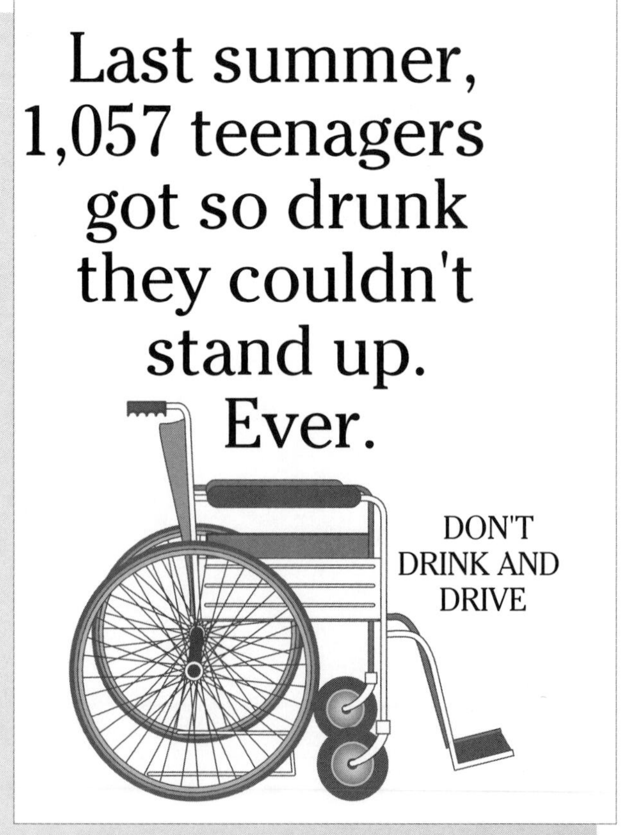

In 1979 the American Psychiatric Association rejected the use of stigmatizing labels in its official nomenclature, the *Diagnostic and Statistical Manual of Mental Disorders* (*DSM*). Expressions such as *schizophrenic* and *alcoholic* were avoided; instead, *DSM* uses the descriptors "person with schizophrenia" and "person with alcohol dependence." It does so in order to define and classify the *condition*—and not the person. For over a decade, AIDS activists have recognized the significance of dehumanizing labels; thus, persons who have the disease reject sensational expressions such as "AIDS victim" and "AIDS patient" and consider themselves "persons living with AIDS." A disability rights activist, addressing the same issue, put it simply: "I'm a person with a disability. But I'm a *person* first."

It is not surprising that many people with disabilities resent the mythology of helplessness that they must contend with on a daily basis—programs of health and social agencies that pathologize individuals as helpless, defective, and incapable of meeting their own needs. They must continually struggle against discrimination in the public arena. This includes their efforts to use public transportation, obtain adequate insurance and fair housing, pursue an education, and get jobs in occupations they are well qualified for. When the stigma of disability influences public policy, it can have profound consequences on all aspects of their lives.

"Don't let this happen to you!"

Eliciting fear represents one classic approach to prevention. A poster aimed at teenage drivers serves as an example. The universally recognized symbol for wheelchair access marks a parking spot. The poster's headline reads: "Drink and drive and you could have the choicest parking spot at school." It continues at the bottom of the poster: "But who cares? You'll lose your spot on the football team. The marching band. The prom dance floor. You'll sure be giving up a lot just because you didn't give up your keys." Another anti-drinking-and-driving poster shows a young person in a wheelchair with his back to the camera. "Become a big wheel around school," it says.

Those posters were produced by the advocacy group Mothers Against Drunk Driving (MADD). MADD's goal is to reduce the exceptionally high incidence of fatal automobile crashes that involve alcohol. The organization contends that drunk driving is not "an accident" but a crime—in fact, the most frequently committed violent crime in the U.S. Through its influential health education campaigns, MADD fights to prevent drunk and drugged driving. Few would argue with the fact that the organization has been very effective in spreading its message, in working for the passage of stringent legislation, and in providing assistance for the injured through its

Members of a group home in Queens, New York City, have not been warmly welcomed to their middle-class residential neighborhood. Like many with physical or mental impairments, they are stigmatized at almost every turn and must struggle for acceptance daily.

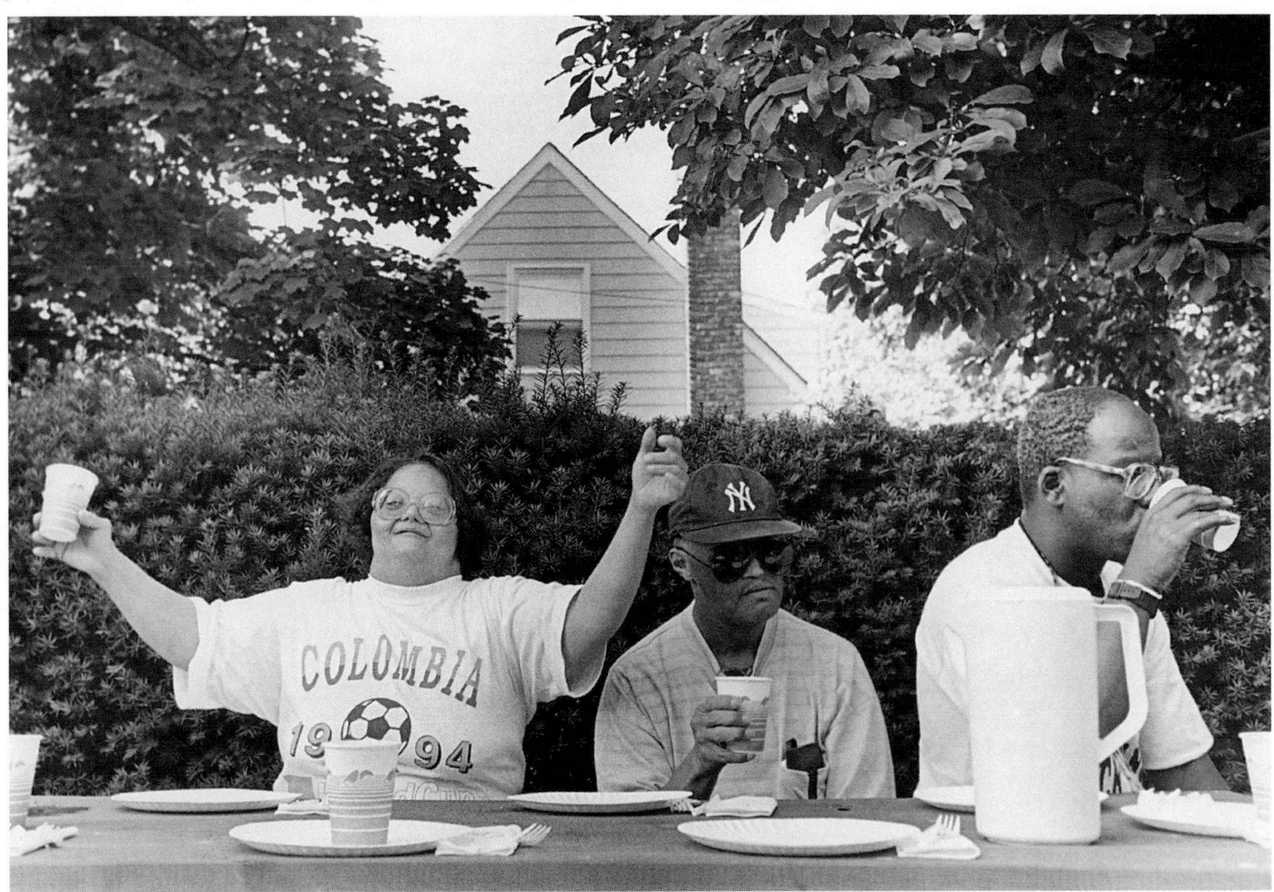

Edward Keating—The New York Times

National Victim Services Office. Nor would many criticize the group's noble intention: to prevent injury. But could posters that scare promote stigma as well as health?

To determine how different audiences might view injury-prevention ads that carry the implicit message "Don't let this happen to you!" this investigator showed two posters to two groups—college students enrolled in a health education course and people who had mobility impairments and used wheelchairs. One poster had no frightening image—just a buckled seat belt and the advice to "Buckle up." But it also carried the statement "If you think seat belts are confining, think about a wheelchair." One in the first group remarked:

> *To me it still sends shivers up my spine, like, "God, if I was in a wheelchair."*

Her comment conveys the fear evoked by words alone. Reacting to the same public service ad, a 27-year-old woman with a disability said:

> *You know, frankly, I'll look at an ad like this and say, "What's so bad about using a wheelchair? Here we go again getting the message that we're not "okay" as wheelchair users or people who are blind or deaf or people who use crutches or whatever. It might be effective for people who buy into the whole idea that disability is negative and significantly diminishes one's quality of life. It's devaluing to the rest of us, who know better.*

The second poster paired a picture of an empty wheelchair with the words "Last year, 1,057 teenagers got so drunk they couldn't stand up. Ever." One man with an acquired disability reacted, "It's holding us up as someone to avoid." Another said, "I feel it's an attack on my self-esteem and dignity."

A high-school health education program attempted to give able-bodied students a sense of what it is like to live with disability. The students were strapped into the type of surgical collar worn by some quadriplegics. One's reaction was:

> *I would rather die than have to live that way.*

The paradox of prevention

A biomedical approach to health seeks to localize and then treat disease (or disability) within the individual. By contrast, public health is committed to the active promotion of health in general population groups. The approach of proponents of public health implicitly supports the minimization of disability through prevention. Although biomedical and public health professionals are often at odds with each other over their respective approaches and use of resources, both subscribe to the common view of disability as a deficit and an often-preventable tragedy.

The meaning of "disability," however, is shifting—partly through sweeping civil rights legislation, such as the Americans with Disabilities Act (ADA) of 1990, and partly through the use of new language and labels. Disability rights activists in-

NEWS*CAP*

Miss America

Heather Whitestone of Birmingham, Ala., was not only a talented, bright, poised, and pretty contestant in the 1994 Miss America pageant but the first winner with a major disability. Deaf since the age of 18 months, Whitestone has triumphed over her limitation. Although she knows American Sign Language well, she is an adept lip-reader who prefers speaking. As Miss America 1995 she often addressed both hearing-impaired and non-hearing-impaired audiences across the country.

Whitestone's deafness was the result of nerve damage, a complication of *Haemophilus influenzae,* formerly the most common cause of pediatric meningitis and permanent neurological damage in tens of thousands of U.S. children. A heartening example of a vaccine's potential to eliminate illness is the dramatic reduction that has occurred in pediatric meningitis since an *H. influenzae* vaccine was introduced in 1989. Had the vaccine been available when Whitestone was a child, many in her generation would not be deaf today.

AP/Wide World

sist that the biological condition of disability be distinguished conceptually from "handicap," a social limitation imposed by societal barriers or personal outlook. People with disabilities have long had to deal with such labels as "deviant," "defective," "crippled," "invalid," and "handicapped." The drafters of the ADA even rejected "disabled" in favor of "person with a disability." A man who has a mobility impairment and uses a wheelchair told this author that like most people in his position, he reacts against all such labels, which make him feel "frustrated and angry" every time he hears them. Another man who is paralyzed below the neck, uses an iron lung, and requires attendant care around the clock, said:

> *Some of us have a lot of trouble, but you can look out on any street and you can say, "That person's more disabled than I am." There's lots of ways to be screwed up.*

Only recently have research efforts been directed toward studying not just the effectiveness but the consequences of health promotion campaigns, including consequences that may be unintended. This approach examines health education strategies from different perspectives, including those of people with impairments. Such research suggests the extent to which society is capable of truly accepting people with disabilities. In addition, studying the effects of various health education approaches aimed at preventing injuries provides a framework for examining other conditions that are typically viewed as ones worth avoiding—AIDS, homelessness, and even growing old, for example.

As participants in the struggle to reduce injuries, trauma survivors can be powerful spokespersons for prevention. James Brady, the press secretary who was shot in an assassination attempt on former U.S. president Ronald Reagan, has used the authenticity of his experience in a wheelchair to rivet the nation's attention on the need for handgun control.

In recognizing the stigmatizing effects of certain prevention methods, trauma survivors, along with the medical professionals who treat them, can play a role in designing prevention campaigns that do not alienate those with disabilities. By contrast, comedian-actor Jerry Lewis' muscular dystrophy telethons are sometimes criticized for portraying people with disabilities as helpless and dependent. Even as telethons raise research money for cures, they compound the struggle of people with disabilities for acceptance. Historian Paul Longmore of San Francisco State University notes that telethons serve as national rituals to define who is normal, complete, and authentic—and who is not.

To what extent do public health professionals paradoxically enforce the notion of people with disabilities as "others"—people one should not become? How do those with disabilities experience the popular culture's interpretation of their conditions? In an era in which health education is sought as a remedy for an unprecedented array of health issues, public health workers ought to understand fully the consequences of prevention strategies. In so doing, they may continue to discourage preventable injuries without stigmatizing people with disabilities.

—Caroline Wang, Dr.P.H.

Eating Disorders Update

Human beings have an inherent desire to feel good about themselves and to take charge of their lives. Sometimes people judge themselves—or feel judged by others—on the merit of attributes beyond their control. Most world cultures have prevailing standards of beauty and can be aggressively intolerant of people who do not meet the prototype. Consequently, many individuals feel an overwhelming sense of anxiety because of biological features they cannot alter. Few experiences are more demoralizing.

If advertising and the popular media are any reflection, a body type that is highly revered by many today is an extremely lean one. For the majority, however, that ideal is neither reasonable nor genetically possible. When ideals of thinness become confused with judgments about personal accomplishment, people turn against themselves in frustration. Feeling compelled to conform at all costs, they make relentless attempts to lose weight; in the process some deprive their bodies of sound nutrition. Others simply overeat, insulating themselves with fat and abandoning all pretense of conformity. In the United States the current standard of leanness is so oppressive and unrealistic that an estimated 13 million Americans "feel fat." Many go on unsensible diets or even abuse food to life-threatening extremes; an estimated eight million have eating disorders.

A gender gap

Although men and women both feel society's pressures to conform, the development of disordered eating patterns is a predominantly female phenomenon. That is not to say that men are immune to eating disorders; generally, however, unless a man is genetically predisposed to obesity or has a weight-focused vocation (*e.g.,* a jockey or a wrestler), the societal pressure on him to be slender is not as harsh.

The drive for women to do something abnormal to their bodies to make themselves more appealing is neither new nor unusual. At various periods throughout history, starting in the 2nd millennium BC, women have used corsets, girdles, and brassieres to bind their torsos and cinch their waistlines. Often without regard to their own well-being, they have raised, flattened, and surgically altered or accentuated various body parts according to vogue.

Regardless of the ordeals through which women may put themselves, as the biological childbearers of the species, they are predisposed to carrying an extra supply of fat in the hips and thighs. Starting at puberty, and especially during pregnancy, women tend to accumulate fat in the lower part of the torso.

Although men traditionally have participated in physical activity to prove their strength and to validate their masculinity, women often attempt to solve their social and interpersonal problems by manipulating their looks. Often, to cope with stress, they eat. When challenged with the current ideal of thinness, they can feel a terrorizing disharmony in relation to food and body weight. For any woman whose dietary and lifestyle patterns revolve primarily around the desire to be slim, the results may be disastrous.

Anorexia nervosa: dying to be thin

Ninety percent of those who suffer from anorexia nervosa (literally "nervous loss of appetite") are female. In Japan, Europe, Canada, and the U.S., approximately 1% of the young adult female population is affected. The majority range in age from 12 or 13 to 35, but increasingly 8- to 11-year-olds are exhibiting symptoms. To some extent, anorexia has been brought to public attention because celebrities (like singer Karen Carpenter and gymnast Christy Henrich) died from the disorder. Though most women with anorexia are not famous, they are obedient and perfectionistic and have difficulties adapting to adulthood.

Abnormally preoccupied with a fear of gaining weight, anorexics starve their bodies and may refuse to eat anything except minute quantities of a few "allowable" foods. They often engage in excessive exercise. As a result of feeling controlled by their environment and unable to be their own person, they turn to their bodies to experience a sense of control they feel they have lost or never had. They think they are fat—and even see themselves in mirrors as fat—when, in fact, they are extremely thin.

(Top) The Granger Collection, New York; (bottom) Ogust—The Image Works

The desire of women to be attractive is not a new one, nor is the drive to do unnatural things to their bodies in order to attain an idealized look. The waist-cinching corset at right was advertised in English newspapers in the late 1800s. (Below) If ads and fashion designs are a fair reflection of what a society considers "attractive," then it is not surprising that many women find current standards oppressive. Those who feel compelled to conform to today's concept of beauty may end up compromising both their health and their well-being.

Kansas City Star

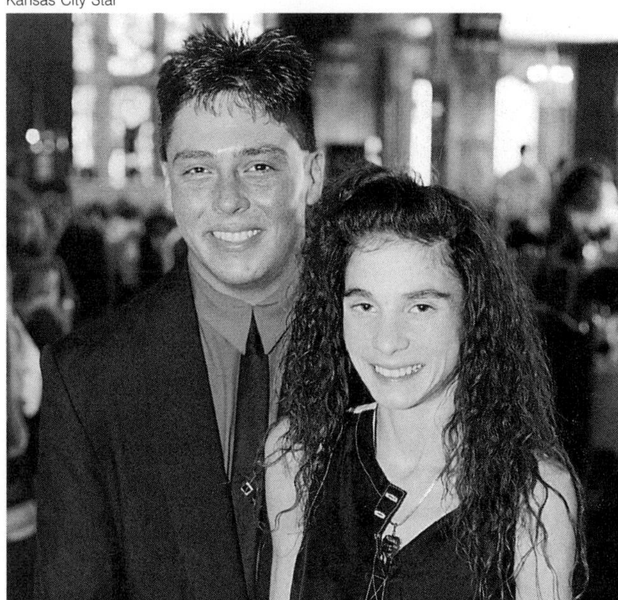

Champion U.S. gymnast Christy Henrich poses with her fiancé, Bo Moreno, 11 months before her untimely death from multiple organ system failure. An anorexia nervosa and bulimia sufferer, Henrich died on July 26, 1994, at age 22, weighing under 27 kg (60 lb). In 1988, when she narrowly missed qualifying for the Olympics, she had weighed a relatively healthy 43 kg (95 lb). The gymnast's mother attributed "99% of what happened" to Christy to her sport, where "all the focus is on the body."

Typically, an active, seemingly well-adjusted adolescent girl who does well in school and is considerate of others will start dieting, perhaps to attain "just the right look" or because someone has made a comment about her "figure" or her friends are doing it. Almost always, she has been influenced by images in the popular media. Because she is successful at shedding a few pounds or kilograms, she attempts to reinforce self-esteem by losing more weight and gets "hooked" on the "high" of dieting. For some young women, the first diet can be as influential—and detrimental—as an alcoholic's first drink.

Obsessive dieting can push body weight to levels that are neither healthy nor attractive. (The condition anorexia nervosa is defined as weight under 75–85% of the healthful standard for age and height.) Chronic starvation can lead to malnutrition, which causes both physical and mental changes. Those changes affect drive and motivation and are likely to bring on still further dieting and often a refusal to admit to needing help. The young woman with anorexia rarely chooses to go for evaluation or treatment without the intervention of parents, spouse, or friends.

Some signs of anorexia nervosa are obvious, such as food refusal, marked weight loss, and social withdrawal. Lack of adequate nourishment can cause dehydration and constipation; irregular or slowed heartbeat and thyroid function; lowered body temperature and blood pressure; slowed reflexes; dry, brittle, thinning hair; and low blood sugar and sodium and potassium levels, any of which can be life-threatening. Anorexics may grow a coating of downy fuzz (called lanugo) on the face, limbs, and body. Mood changes are common. Insufficient nourishment impairs brain function and clarity of thought and contributes to a misperception of the environment.

Because a certain amount of body fat is necessary for menstruation, anorexics also experience hormonal deficiencies and the absence or interruption of periods (secondary amenorrhea). This may lead to osteoporosis and increased risk of fractures and, in severe, long-term cases, to atrophy (arrested development and function) of the reproductive organs. Few anorexics have suicidal intentions from the start, but between 5% and 20% eventually die as a result of vital organ failure. Because genetics, culture, nutrition, education, brain chemistry, and even childhood experiences contribute to the pattern, approaches to therapy must be dynamic (*see* below).

Bulimia: hungry as an ox

Bulimia (also known as bulimia nervosa, binge-purge syndrome, or "ox hunger") affects 3% to 5% of women living in the United States between the onset of puberty and age 30. In addition, as many as one-third of all anorexics eventually develop bulimia; thus, the two illnesses often coexist or succeed one another. Rarely, however, do bulimics develop anorexia nervosa.

About 85% of all diagnosed bulimics are female. According to the *Campus Health Guide,* published by the College Entrance Examination Board, 20% of all U.S. college women develop symptoms of bulimia nervosa. They generally are within 5 to 7 kg (11 to 15 lb) of normal weight. To counteract weight gain they fast, induce vomiting, exercise excessively, and abuse laxatives, diuretics, and diet pills. In contrast to individuals with anorexia nervosa, people with bulimia fully recognize their abnormal behavior. They are usually quite secretive and ritualistic about these behaviors and feel depressed and shameful after each episode. Because of the secretive and remorseful nature of the disorder, symptoms can exist for a long time—even years—before anyone but the bulimic knows. Bulimics become locked into a cycle of overeating, guilt, self-deprecating thoughts, and depression—a pattern from which they appear powerless to escape.

If not treated, bulimia can be physically and emotionally catastrophic. Being unable to stop eating voluntarily often leads to fear and frustration and thence to self-loathing and intense social alienation. Repeated self-induced vomiting can have severe physical consequences; these include internal bleeding, erosion of dental enamel, chronic throat irritation, and swollen glands under the jaw. Often bulimics develop heartburn, abdominal pain, and a variety of irritable bowel complaints, which accompany regular self-purging. Though weight is not abnormally low, cessation or irregularities of menstruation may develop as well.

The long-term effects of bulimia can be as devastating as those of anorexia. Dehydration leads to an irregular heartbeat; and fatigue, dizziness, muscle spasms, and poor concentration signal electrolyte imbalance (particularly, low sodium and potassium levels), which heightens the risk of liver and kidney damage and may lead to severe cardiac problems and even death.

(Right and opposite page) Photographs, Brian Plonka—Impact Visuals

Neither anorexia nor bulimia

Although reckless dietary habits are increasingly common, not everyone develops eating behaviors that are diagnosable as life-threatening disorders. The largest and least-researched category of self-destructive food problems has only recently been recognized. In the recently revised (fourth) edition of the American Psychiatric Association's *Diagnostic and Statistical Manual of Mental Disorders* (*DSM-IV*), compulsive overeating (called "binge eating disorder") is defined as a psychological syndrome that encompasses people who have clinically severe food problems but who do not meet the diagnostic criteria for anorexia or bulimia.

Binge eating, as defined in *DSM-IV,* is associated with some combination of the following:

- eating very rapidly
- eating until uncomfortably full
- eating large amounts when not hungry
- eating alone owing to shame or embarrassment
- feeling disgusted, depressed, or guilty after overeating

Like anorexics and bulimics, people who suffer from binge eating disorder are not happy with their bodies. They typically eat in secret, feel ashamed of their eating habits, and feel inadequate in view of society's emphasis on slimness. Often they lose and gain weight repeatedly. They restrict and avoid food and thus make themselves so hungry that they overeat compulsively. With the experience of being out of control around food, they fall into a repetitive cycle. Although people with binge eating disorder may or may not overeat at mealtimes, they turn to food not to satisfy physical hunger but to relieve stress and numb painful feelings. They tend to prefer high-sugar, high-fat "comfort foods" and may nibble and snack for hours at a time.

Binge eaters often demonstrate all the symptoms of bulimia nervosa except for the frequency or duration of binges and the use of compensatory behaviors such as purging to offset weight gain. *Overview of Eating Disorders,* published by the National Eating Disorders Organization, cites studies that estimate up to 7% of the general population and 10% of the student population fall within the definition of binge eating disorder. Persons of average weight as well as approximately 25% to 50% of all obese individuals eat in ways that meet these diagnostic criteria.

Like other eating disorders, binge eating disorder is more prevalent in women than in men (by about 1.5 times), and generally the problem develops in late adolescence or early adulthood. It is not uncommon for people with binge eating disorder to suffer from other psychiatric conditions, such as depression, alcohol- or drug-abuse disorders, or personality disorders.

Vicious circles

Eating disorders almost always have their roots in dieting. An estimated 40% of all U.S. women are on some kind of weight-loss program at any given time. The Centers for Disease Control and Prevention (CDC) recently reported that one in six children between the ages of 13 and 15 has tried diet pills at least once.

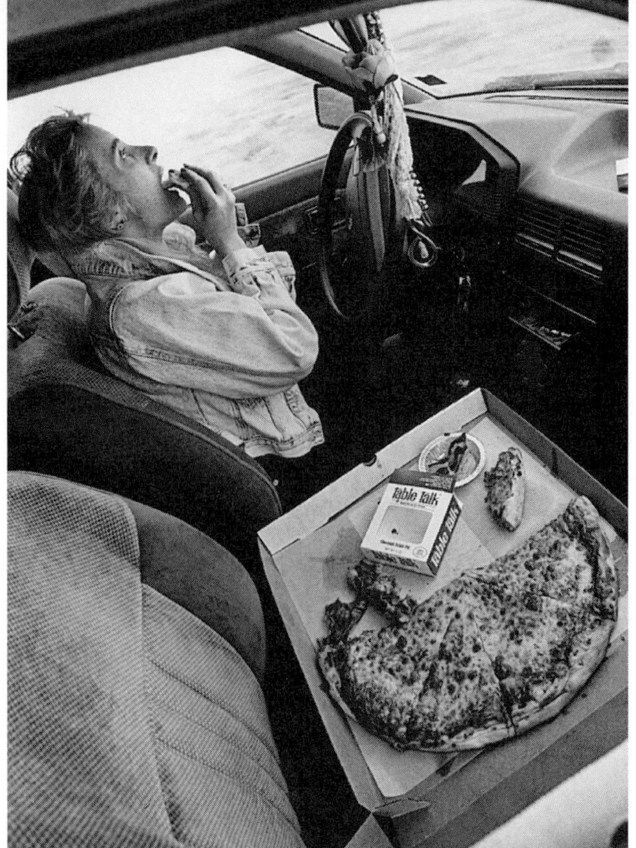

Binge eating followed by vomiting is an activity that bulimics usually hide from others. Susan Sanborn (above) suffers from both anorexia nervosa and bulimia. She agreed to be photographed for a newspaper feature story.

Since body weight increases in proportion to the number of excess calories consumed, it seems reasonable to attempt weight control by limiting caloric intake. Research indicates, however, that the human body perceives a reduction of 500 or more calories a day (enough to trigger a weight loss of about one-half kilogram [one pound] a week) as deprivation. The body lowers its metabolic rate in response, to conserve fuel and allow survival, a reaction that makes dieting increasingly futile. This physical response, in combination with a depletion of essential nutrients, affects the balance of chemicals in the brain and interferes with the ability to think clearly.

Because caloric intake and body-fat ratios regulate the rate at which the body burns calories, low-calorie dieting also contributes to a progressive cycle of weight gain. When a person stops dieting and returns to former eating habits, a sluggish metabolism may temporarily or permanently fail to resume burning calories as efficiently as it once did. In addition, muscle tissue, though difficult to acquire, is lost to excessive dieting. To adjust to these changes, the metabolism regulates itself to a slower-than-prediet rate.

Cutting calories is a key trigger of eating disorders in certain individuals, but not everyone who diets gets caught up in the vicious circle of eating disorders. People who suffer from clinically severe eating disorders often come from families in which addiction and depressive disorders are prevalent. Familial patterns of perfectionism and obsessional characteristics, with adherence to rigid standards in place of conflict resolution, predispose some individuals to the disorder. Experts suggest that these people may suffer from inherited neurochemical imbalances.

There is also a psychological/emotional "vicious circle" in eating disorders. Body size and physical hunger generally have little to do with food abuse. Rather, it is the accompanying feelings of guilt, shame, confusion, and worthlessness that trigger the urge to eat even more.

Only in the past decade has research begun to study and interrelate the underlying biochemical factors and predisposing social and behavioral events that precipitate patterns of disordered eating. It is now appreciated that many who receive treatment for eating disorders suffer from anxiety and depression of clinical significance. And several recent studies have found that people with eating disorders survived abusive, traumatic, or stressful childhoods.

One increasingly accepted theory is that because overeating elevates blood sugar levels, it stimulates hormones that generate feelings of calm; thus, bulimics may eat large quantities of food in an attempt to induce calm or maintain emotional equilibrium. Studies carried out by investigators at the Massachusetts Institute of Technology suggest that bulimics may even crave carbohydrates as a means of self-regulating abnormally low levels of serotonin, a vital mood- and appetite-balancing chemical in the brain. (The neurotransmitter serotonin, as well as norepinephrine, has also been associated with anorexia.) Whether due to genetics or to dietary deprivation, abnormally low levels of this "natural antidepressant" cause the brain to become lethargic and the individual to become anxious and depressed. All of these factors make it difficult for those who suffer from eating disorders to overcome their irregular eating patterns.

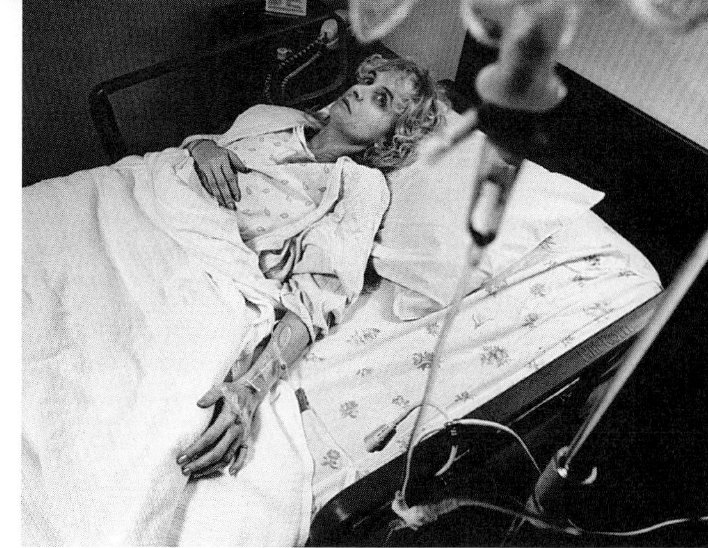

Eating disorders can take a very grave physical toll. When Susan Sanborn's body became so deprived of vital nutrients that her very life was at risk, she was hospitalized and fed intravenously.

Evidence also suggests that irregular levels of the hormones cortisol and vasopressin may put certain individuals at risk for destructive eating patterns. These brain chemicals also have a role in clinical depression and obsessive-compulsive disorder.

Advances in treatment

Recovering from an eating disorder, whether anorexia nervosa, bulimia nervosa, or binge eating, requires more than just giving up inappropriate behavior around food. To eliminate starving, vomiting, or compulsive eating patterns permanently, a person must substitute more effective ways of coping with underlying needs that food alone cannot satisfy. This demands the development of self-confidence.

Effective treatment usually involves a blend of professional services that provide physical, mental, emotional, and spiritual care to the patient and often to the patient's family. Response to treatment varies. Chances of recovery improve greatly with prompt treatment and thorough evaluation, but anorexics rarely seek intervention on their own, and bulimics, though they recognize that they have a problem, may wait years before finding help.

For people with eating disorders, group and individual psychotherapies are the most frequently used forms of treatment. Unless a person is in acute medical danger, the emphasis is not on weight control and modification of eating habits but on learning that body weight and shape and other aspects of appearance are not indicators of personal worth or determinants of personality.

Behavior modification therapy directs the patient to learn alternative ways to cope with circumstances around food, eating, and body weight. Cognitive behavioral therapy (focusing on replacing maladaptive thought patterns) works to resolve conflicts, build self-esteem, and improve body attitude.

A recently developed cognitive approach is called "narrative therapy" and is based on the premise that people interpret rather than directly perceive their environments. In other words, they provide a narrative structure, or stories, to give their world order. If the dominant stories in a person's life focus on problems, those problems become emotional prisons, reflected in maladaptive behaviors. Therapy centers on finding new narratives and "rewriting" stories.

Other measures and types of care have proved successful in the treatment of eating disorders, often in combination with group or individual psychotherapy. Among these are:

- **medical care:** to deal with physical problems such as bloating, low weight, and abnormal menstrual periods
- **hospitalization:** to provide a safe environment for patients in medical danger or at risk of suicide or to help patients stabilize eating patterns and bodily functions when outpatient efforts have failed
- **dental work:** to repair or minimize the damage to teeth and gums and oral health in general that is caused by starvation and vomiting
- **nutritional counseling:** to correct food myths, to educate about nutrition and the medical consequences of disordered eating, and to construct a nutritionally sound eating program
- **family therapy:** to help family members understand eating disorders and to change destructive patterns of family interaction that contribute to the disorder
- **support groups:** to benefit from sharing experiences, coping methods, setbacks, etc., with other patients and families that have similar problems

The majority of people who address their emotional and physical problems and get treatment for an eating disorder before it develops into a severe or irreversible illness usually recover in less than a year. By contrast, the success rate for the treatment of obesity is only in the vicinity of about 5%. Many patients with eating disorders, however, fail to stay in treatment long enough to achieve lasting results.

About one-third of those with anorexia nervosa recover completely, a third demonstrate significant improvement, but a third remain chronically ill. In more than 30 studies of approximately 500 bulimic patients treated with some form of psychotherapy, 35% to 50% of patients were free of bingeing and vomiting at the end of treatment; approximately one-half experienced a 50% to 75% reduction in bingeing and vomiting. Similar results were seen in bulimics who took antidepressant medication. Long-term treatment outcomes for binge eating disorder are not yet known.

Recovery from eating disorders generally extends beyond issues of food and body weight. Improved attitudes toward sex, money, career, and other abused substances usually accompany the overcoming of food and body weight difficulties.

—Zae Zatoon, Ph.D.

NEWS*CAP*

Metabolism: Myths Debunked

Obesity is not caused by "slow" metabolism, investigators at Rockefeller University, New York City, have shown. Their research, reported in *The New England Journal of Medicine* (March 9, 1995), indicated that the body has a natural weight toward which it gravitates, and the metabolism adjusts to maintain that weight.

Using male and female volunteers ranging in age from their 20s to their 40s, the researchers established that the body burns calories more slowly than normal after weight loss and faster than normal following weight gain; therefore, it is harder either to lose or to gain weight than to maintain the same level of weight.

The metabolism of those who gained weight during the study accelerated by 10–15%, while the metabolic rate of those who shed excess body fat was 10–15% slower than normal. The body adjusts its metabolism by making muscles more or less efficient in burning calories. Understanding this process could be the key to successful weight-loss programs.

Another myth debunked by the study was that excessive dieting deranges the metabolism. Equally disturbed metabolic function was found in subjects who gained and those who lost weight, regardless of whether they had ever dieted or whether they were fat or thin.

SOURCES OF INFORMATION

Anyone who wants to learn more about eating disorders and their treatment may contact the following:

American Anorexia/Bulimia Association (AABA)
293 Central Park West, Suite 1R
New York NY 10024
(212) 501-8351

Anorexia Nervosa and Related Eating Disorders (ANRED)
PO Box 5102
Eugene OR 97405
(541) 344-1144

Center for the Study of Anorexia and Bulimia
One W 91st St
New York NY 10024
(212) 595-3449 or (212) 595-3444

Anorexia Nervosa and Associated Disorders (ANAD)
PO Box 7
Highland Park IL 60035
(708) 831-3438

Overeaters Anonymous World Service Office (OA)
PO Box 44020
Rio Rancho NM 87174-4020
(consult phone book for local chapter)

Bulimia, Anorexia, and Binge Eating Services (BABES)
PO Box 3012
Kailua-Kona HI 96745
(808) 325-0222

National Eating Disorders Association (NEDO)
PO Box 470207
Tulsa OK 74147-2027
(918) 491-8100

Hormones, Hormones Everywhere

When the U.S. Environmental Protection Agency (EPA) set out to review the health effects of dioxin in 1991, it was hoping to resolve a straightforward question: Does this chemical compound, a pollutant found in trace quantities in meats and dairy products, increase the human risk of cancer? Indeed, EPA scientists found evidence suggesting that this ubiquitous compound—actually, a group of chemical by-products of waste incineration and paper manufacturing—probably acts as a weak carcinogen (cancer-causing substance). As the researchers sifted through a mass of dioxin studies from the late 1980s and early '90s, however, they discerned another health risk, one that was quite surprising. In a draft report released in September 1994, the EPA proposed that dioxin may have subtle effects on the human reproductive system, triggering problems such as endometriosis (abnormal growth of the tissue that lines the womb) in women and decreased sperm count in men. In essence, dioxin often appears to act much like the estrogens, the major female sex hormones, stimulating or muting various bodily processes.

A debate begins

Dioxin is not the only chemical with hormonal actions. Over the past few years, environmental scientists have implicated several prominent pollutants as potential disrupters of the endocrine system. This system is the source of hormones, substances that regulate vital bodily functions such as growth, digestion, and reproduction. In January 1994 scientists from around the world convened in Washington, D.C., to review research on the health effects of chemicals that have estrogen-like actions. The consensus among the scientists was that certain synthetic chemicals, including some that are commonly released into the environment as pollutants, may be affecting human hormonal equilibrium, perhaps leading to health problems ranging from infertility to breast and testicular cancers. The conference and the EPA's subsequent dioxin report ignited a firestorm of public concern, which prompted U.S. officials to begin to reassess federal regulations governing these environmental chemicals. At the same time, many scientists remain unconvinced that these substances present any health hazard. The following looks at some of the evidence on both sides of this debate.

Unexpected exposures

One of the first indications that synthetic chemicals may act like hormones appeared in the early 1970s, when researchers found that diethylstilbestrol (DES)—a synthetic estrogen given to millions of pregnant women between the 1940s and the '60s to prevent miscarriage—was linked to a rare form of vaginal cancer in the daughters of women who took it. Later it was also discovered that the sons of women who took DES had unusually high rates of genitourinary abnormalities. In recent years scientists have been accumulating evidence against dozens of hormonelike chemicals, including polychlorinated biphenyls (PCBs), industrial compounds often used as coolants (now being phased out of use in the United States); bisphenyl A, a chemical formed during the degradation of many kinds of plastics, including those used in baby bottles; and DDE, a breakdown product of the once widely used pesticide DDT.

Howard K. Suzuki—Aquatic Life Sculptures

Wildlife such as this Florida alligator has provided some clues to the possible effects of common environmental pollutants on human hormonal equilibrium.

Not all human exposure to extrinsic estrogens (*i.e.,* those originating outside the body) comes from synthetic compounds. Several estrogen-like substances, including the phytochemicals (from the Greek *phyto,* "plant") known as indoles and flavanones, occur naturally in certain edible plants. Phytochemicals that have estrogenic properties are referred to as phytoestrogens.

A lesson from alligators

The most compelling evidence of the health effects of environmental hormones comes from wildlife studies. In one celebrated example, shortly after a DDT spill at Florida's Lake Apopka in 1980, the birthrate of alligators in the lake plummeted to about 10% of the previous year's rate. A research team led by Louis Guillette, Jr., a reproductive physiologist at the University of Florida, found that alligator eggs from Lake Apopka hatched at only about one-third the rate of eggs from nearby lakes. Moreover, young male alligators in Lake Apopka appeared to have smaller penes than alligators of similar age in other lakes. To test their theory that exposure to DDE (produced by degradation of the spilled DDT) might have wreaked havoc on the animals' reproductive systems, Guillette's team treated alligator eggs from a lake near Apopka with DDE and found that these eggs hatched about as infrequently as Lake Apopka eggs. In October 1993, testifying at a congressional hearing on estrogen-mimicking pesticides, Guillette warned that his studies had only begun to address what he and his colleagues believed to be a serious, widespread threat to wildlife populations.

Led by toxicologist L. Earl Gray, EPA scientists began studying DDE after learning about the investigations in Florida. The alligator studies reminded them of their own earlier work with a pesticide called vinclozolin, which binds to cellular receptors for androgens (a group of male hormones that includes testosterone). Gray's team found an eerie parallel between vinclozolin's actions and DDE's. Male rat fetuses exposed to vinclozolin developed reproductive abnormalities such as delayed puberty and small penes, which were strikingly similar to the abnormalities seen in the alligators. The EPA researchers have suggested that DDE may exert its feminizing effects by blocking the masculinizing actions of androgens.

Marine mammals also may be vulnerable to the harmful effects of environmental hormones. At the previously mentioned international conference on the health implications of estrogens in the environment, Canadian researchers presented data showing that two-thirds of the beluga whales autopsied after becoming stranded in the St. Lawrence estuary had adrenal gland lesions. This gland produces a variety of hormones, including both androgens and estrogens. The scientists also found that the whales' fat tissue contained high concentrations of PCBs, DDT, and heavy metals such as mercury and lead. They concluded that the adrenal lesions probably arose from exposure to environmental hormones.

In addition, the whales suffered from a high rate of opportunistic infections. These are infections that occur only in organisms whose immune function is impaired; their presence, therefore, is a sign of compromised immunity. Further evidence of the potential of PCBs and other environmental hormones to damage the immune systems of marine mammals came from a Dutch study published in 1994. This study suggested that a distemper virus that killed thousands of seals in the North and the Baltic seas in 1988 was abetted by the presence of PCBs and dioxin in the waters. The pollutants and the virus appeared to work together to impair the animals' immune systems.

Are humans next?

The above findings support evidence of disturbing trends in wildlife health that were reported in 1991 at a gathering of experts from a range of disciplines, from anthropology to wildlife management. Meeting in Racine, Wis., these scientists heard anecdotes about wildlife populations suffering from a variety of health problems, including defects in many species of birds, fish, and turtles; feminization in male birds and fish; and impaired immune function in birds. Many of the accounts came from researchers working in the Great Lakes, in which tons of PCBs, DDT, and dioxin have accumulated since World War II.

The problems afflicting many of the region's birds and aquatic life fit a pattern of illness the researchers dubbed "Great Lakes embryo mortality, edema, and deformities syndrome," or GLEMEDS. Its manifestations include eggshell breakage in double-breasted cormorants, embryo death in herring gulls, and birth defects in a range of fauna, including Caspian terns and black-crowned night herons.

In a consensus report, the conferees in Racine agreed that the problems in wildlife foreshadowed potential dangers to human life, noting that in the U.S. population the concentrations of a number of environmental hormones are already well within the range that produces noticeable effects in wildlife. The potential hazard of these known "endocrine disrupters" to both animals and humans is, therefore, great.

Corroborating these observations are laboratory studies of rodents exposed to a range of doses of environmental hormones. Perhaps the most scrutinized such compound is dioxin. Compared with offspring of nonexposed female rats, the male offspring of females exposed to dioxin during pregnancy take longer to become sexually mature, have smaller genitals, produce fewer sperm, and are less inclined to mate. One of the more disturbing aspects of these findings is that these reproductive problems can result from exposure to only tiny doses of dioxin—doses comparable to the levels of dioxin and similar chemicals that have been found in human body fat. The EPA, taking these findings seriously, is considering ordering industries to reduce their dioxin emissions.

Equivocal evidence

Despite the provocative evidence that environmental hormones trigger reproductive problems in animals, the threat to human health is unproven—that is, no study has yet provided a conclusive link between exposure to environmental hormones and the subsequent development of severe human health problems. Nonetheless, several findings suggest that more attention should be paid to a possible association between environmental exposures and conditions such as breast and testicular cancers, decreased sperm counts, and learning deficits in children.

The DDT-breast cancer link. In 1993 a study by researchers at the Mount Sinai School of Medicine of the City University of New York suggested that women exposed to DDT may have a higher risk of breast cancer than women not exposed to the pesticide. The investigators measured DDE levels in blood samples from 58 women diagnosed with breast cancer and compared them with DDE levels in a control group. The cancer patients had significantly higher DDE levels. Like other organochlorine chemicals, ingested DDE is stored in breast tissue and other fatty tissues. According to one theory, by blocking the actions of androgens, DDE may remove one restraint on the actions of estrogens. One of these actions is to stimulate cell proliferation in the breast, which could precede the development of a tumor. It has also been posited that DDE may bind to cellular estrogen receptors, which are unable to distinguish it from natural estrogen. DDE exposure would thus have the effect of increasing a woman's lifetime exposure to estrogen. Women with greater lifetime estrogen exposure are believed to be at greater risk than others of developing breast cancer. Indeed, some studies have found a link between high doses of estrogen (in the form of birth control pills and postmenopausal estrogen replacement therapy) and an elevated risk of breast cancer. It would follow then that exposure to high levels of DDE also could increase breast cancer risk.

Confirmation of this suspicion has proved elusive, however. A study published in the *Journal of the National Cancer Institute* in 1994 analyzed 150 breast cancer cases—nearly three times as many as the earlier study—and found no correlation between DDE levels and breast cancer. In an accompanying editorial Brian MacMahon, professor emeritus of epidemiology at the Harvard School of Public Health, urged researchers to interpret the data cautiously. He noted that early studies showing an association between an exposure and a disease often are not confirmed by subsequent research.

Environmental factors in testicular cancer. To many scientists, a link between environmental hormones and testicular cancer is more credible than the association with breast cancer, even though there are as yet few data to support such a connection. In the past half century, the incidence of testicular cancer has at least doubled in industrialized countries. Whereas the increased rates of many cancers can be attributed to the aging of the population, the same cannot be said of testicular cancer, which typically strikes men between the ages of 20 and 40. Therefore, an environmental exposure would seem to be a likely suspect. Studies in laboratory animals have fueled this speculation. In several experiments in mice, for instance, the male offspring of animals exposed to high doses of estradiol (the predominant natural estrogen) during pregnancy had a high rate of testicular cancer. Several pesticides and other industrial chemicals mimic the actions of estradiol. Long-term studies of human males who were exposed prenatally to estrogenic substances are currently under way at the National Cancer Institute and elsewhere; the men will be followed medically to determine it they have a higher-than-expected rate of testicular cancer.

NEWS*CAP*

Chicago Heat

More than 550 persons died when a record-setting mid-July heat wave engulfed the Chicago area—better known for its subzero temperatures. (By contrast, only about 250 people died in the Great Chicago Fire of 1871.) Temperatures soared to 41° C (106° F) on July 13, and in the days that followed, the Cook county morgue filled so rapidly with corpses that nine massive refrigerated trucks had to be used for the overflow. The unbearable temperatures took the greatest toll on the elderly and those who were already in poor health.

Not only had heat victims lacked air conditioners, but many had kept windows closed, fearing break-ins. Concerns about crime may also have kept others from venturing outdoors when the apparent temperature, or heat index (a measure combining the effects of temperature and humidity on the body), climbed to 48.3° C (119° F).

The tragedy in the Windy City quickly escalated into a political storm, with Mayor Richard M. Daley charging that the medical examiner's office had overstated the role of the heat in the rash of deaths. But when officials from the Centers for Disease Control and Prevention, Atlanta, Ga., investigated, they concluded that the coroner's count of heat-related fatalities was reliable.

Criticized for not responding adequately to the crisis, the city government established a new heat-emergency plan that included setting up air-conditioned "cooling centers," a special system for checking on elderly residents, delivery of ice to shut-ins, and provision of electric fans for residents with no other cooling source. In the wake of the July heat, the city instituted a three-level (watch/warning/emergency) heat-advisory system, but on the hot July and August days that followed, some critics of the system felt that *too many* alerts were being issued and that the public might begin ignoring them.

AP/Wide World

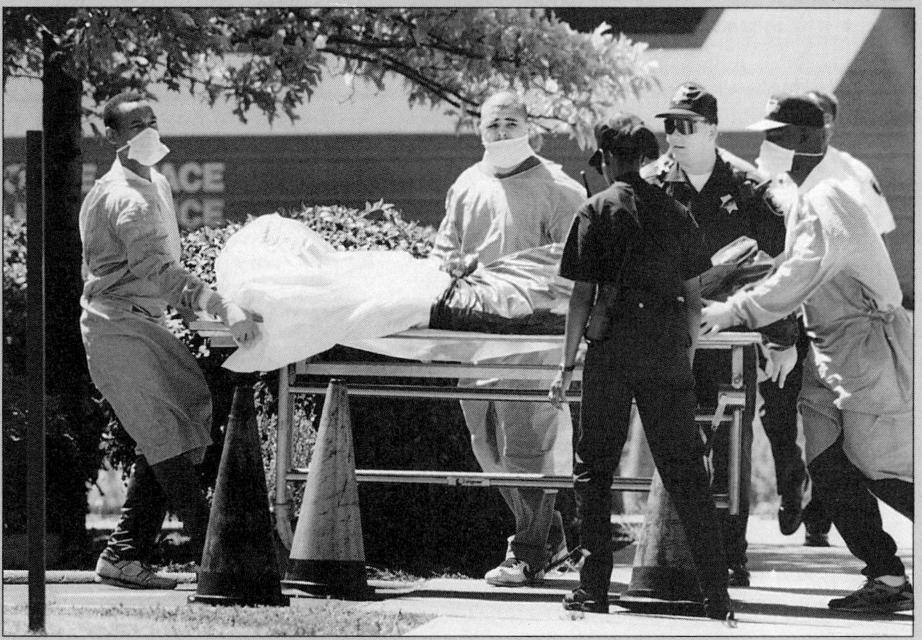

Fewer sperm?

Perhaps the most contentious of the links between environmental hormones and human health problems is the claim of a global decline over the past half century in the number of sperm produced by healthy men. In the May 1993 issue of the British journal *The Lancet,* reproductive biologists Niels E. Skakkebaek of National University Hospital in Copenhagen and Richard M. Sharpe of the British Medical Research Council Reproductive Biology Unit in Edinburgh published a meta-analysis of 61 studies of sperm counts conducted over a 50-year period. (Meta-analysis is a statistical technique used to draw conclusions from multiple studies addressing similar questions.) The data showed that the mean concentration of sperm in healthy adult men had decreased from 113 million per milliliter of semen in 1938 to 66 million per milliliter in 1990. The authors speculated that environmental estrogens, which have been shown to suppress sperm production in laboratory mice, may have played a role in the decline of human sperm counts.

Some scientists point out that the drop in sperm counts over the past 50 years does not appear to have been continuous. Several analyses published since 1993 suggest that for the past 25 years—when most of the data on sperm count were collected—human sperm production has remained relatively stable. Other scientists speculate that a factor other than environmental change, already in operation before 1970, caused a sharp decline in sperm counts and that these lowered counts persist today, but the situation has not worsened. Some even suggest that the mystery influence is the change in men's underwear fashions from boxer shorts to the more tight-fitting briefs. (Briefs may keep the testicles warmer than boxers. The extra warmth could suppress sperm production, which depends on the testicles' being a few degrees cooler than the average body temperature.)

Possible effects on cognitive development. If it is difficult to prove an association between a specific disorder and an environmental factor, it is even more problematic to evaluate claims that some pollutants may cause gradual, progressive deterioration in normal functioning. For example, there is some evidence that PCBs in the environment may cause subtle abnormalities in children. In a study published in 1990 in *The Journal of Pediatrics,* researchers from Wayne State University, Detroit, Mich., and the Michigan Department of Public Health tested the cognitive development of babies born to women who ate fish from Lake Michigan two or three times a month. Fish from the Great Lakes often are contaminated with trace amounts of PCBs and other pollutants; the theory was that PCBs would accumulate in the breast milk of the women who ate fish, and the chemical would be passed on to their children through breast-feeding. Indeed, the breast-fed infants had elevated concentrations of PCBs in their blood, and this slight exposure appeared to have had an effect on their cognitive development. Compared with infants with no evidence of PCB exposure, they scored lower on tests of psychomotor function and visual recognition; even at age four, the pollutant-exposed children had impaired verbal and memory abilities. A study of North Carolina children with only trace amounts of PCBs in their blood noted similar deficiencies, although by age three these children had normal test results.

Express News Papers/Archive Photos

"I've warned your dad about the female hormones in the water supply—but he won't listen."

Alcohol, phytoestrogens, and feminization. As noted above, synthetic chemicals are not the only source of environmental hormones. Scientists have identified dozens of phytoestrogens, and some of these substances have also been shown to affect human health. At the Oklahoma Medical Research Foundation, Oklahoma City, researchers sought to discover why severely alcoholic men with cirrhosis of the liver also suffered from feminization, marked by loss of facial hair, accumulation of fatty deposits in the chest, atrophy of the testes, and, in severe cases, impotence. The scientists isolated two phytoestrogens from bourbon whiskey that appear to have been responsible for the feminization.

A critical look at the data

Recent headlines proclaiming the possible dangers of environmental hormones have elicited a skeptical response from scientists who challenge the relevancy of animal data to humans. One of their strongest arguments is that most known environmental estrogens are very weak. The ability of these compounds to exert their estrogenic effects inside cells—by binding to a molecular receptor for estrogen—is hundreds to thousands of times weaker than that of the body's own estradiol. This fact alone casts doubt on the ability of environmental hormones to cause harm to women—or, for that matter, to most men, whose bodies convert testosterone and other androgens to estradiol. Because the blood levels of hormone-mimicking pollutants are overwhelmed by those of the body's own estradiol, some scientists argue, the pollutants have little chance of exerting an effect. An exception might occur when people or wildlife are suddenly exposed to massive doses of environmental hormones, as in the case of the Lake Apopka alligators. Even smaller amounts could be damaging if exposure occurred during fetal development and childhood, when timing of exposure may be just as critical as dosage.

This argument, however, fails to address the demonstrated effects of low doses of environmental hormones in laboratory animals. This discrepancy may be explained by biochemical differences between humans (and their primate relatives) and other mammals. In the human body a chemical modifier—

a sulfate group composed of sulfur and oxygen—attaches to estrogens as they circulate in the blood. This change in chemical structure deactivates the estrogens. Rats and mice, on the other hand, use a protein to deactivate estradiol.

Still another argument, advanced primarily by toxicologist Stephen H. Safe of Texas A&M University, is that the environment is a virtual sea of hormonelike chemicals—estrogens and antiestrogens, androgens and antiandrogens—that may mitigate or cancel out each other's actions. For instance, antiestrogens such as indole-3-carbinol, found in broccoli, cauliflower, and related vegetables, inhibit the formation of breast tumors in lab animals. These compounds appear to work by binding to a cellular receptor that triggers the release of chemicals that, in turn, block the ability of estrogens to bind to their receptor.

Resolving the questions

Before scientists can determine the magnitude of the threat posed by hormonelike pollutants, they must first refine their understanding of how these substances affect human health. Dioxin is a case in point. This widely studied chemical inhibits breast tumors in rats and mice, but it increases the incidence of liver tumors in these animals. The fact that dioxin causes a range of health problems in fish, birds, and mammals suggests that it could do the same in humans. At the same time, the data on dioxin's effects in humans are equivocal. Several research programs are attempting to clarify these issues.

The questions about dioxin underscore the biggest challenge facing researchers: how to determine the relevancy to human health of the harmful effects documented in animals. Scientists on both sides of the debate agree that much research remains to be done to persuasively confirm—or disprove—the theory that environmental hormones pose a risk to human health.

—Richard Stone

Service and Sickness: Persian Gulf Puzzle

In the late summer and fall of 1990, a massive military deployment was carried out to counter the August 2 invasion of Kuwait by Iraqi forces. Nearly 700,000 U.S. troops were sent to the Persian Gulf region, along with forces from various other nations under the authorization of the United Nations.

The first troops to arrive were housed in camps in the desert. In these field camps, military personnel lived in tents. Electricity was provided on-site by diesel engines; water and food were shipped in. Human and material wastes were burned in open pits. Dust and sand, a particular problem in the desert environment, were suppressed on occasion by aviation fuel spread on the campgrounds. In February 1991 the Iraqi military, as they withdrew from Kuwait, detonated explosives in the oil fields, touching off massive smoky oil-well fires that burned for months, darkening the skies over the desert even at midday.

Because of the very real risk that the Iraqis would make use of biological and chemical weapons, troops departing for the Persian Gulf theater were immunized against the most common and expected biological warfare pathogens; many were also provided with a drug to be taken as a prophylaxis in the event of a nerve-gas attack. These medical preparations and the enemy propaganda that the ground war would be the "mother of all battles" may have created a "psychological environment" of terror for the U.S. and allied troops. In short, the unfamiliar desert terrain, the surreal smoke-darkened skies, the fear of weapons of mass destruction, and the social isolation caused by the segregation of military from native civilian personnel combined to make the Persian Gulf War experience unique in the annals of U.S. warfare.

A mystery illness?

During the months of deployment in the Persian Gulf, and for months and even years after discharge from the armed services, veterans of this experience began to report vaguely defined but, in some cases, severely debilitating illness. About 43,000—or some 6%—of the Gulf War veterans have reported ailments. Many attribute their symptoms to their service in the Gulf region and, particularly, to specific agents such as chemical warfare agents, radiation from spent (*i.e.,* depleted) uranium used in armor-piercing shells, pollutants from the oil-field fires, pesticides, or the vaccines and chemopreventives against biological and chemical weapons.

The primary symptoms of this so-called Gulf War syndrome are: generalized fatigue; headaches; irritability; difficulties with sleep, memory, concentration, and cognitive function; joint pain and muscle aches; skin rashes and hair loss; gastrointestinal symptoms (nausea, diarrhea, abdominal pain); and shortness of breath, cough, and other respiratory symptoms. Although a few instances of miscarriages, birth defects, and illness in family members have been attributed to veterans' experience in the Persian Gulf area, studies of these populations have not demonstrated a higher-than-expected incidence of reproductive abnormalities.

Most of the symptoms cited above are characteristic of a number of common ailments. Nonetheless, many veterans are convinced that their health problems are a direct result of their Persian Gulf service, and others who currently are well fear that they may become ill in the future. The apparent similarity between the Gulf veterans' complaints and the health effects attributed to exposure to Agent Orange during the Vietnam War has given rise to the concept that a single, specific "mystery illness" may be associated with service in the Persian Gulf.

To date, no such illness has been identified. Still, health problems and related disability persist among Gulf War veterans. This situation has prompted extensive efforts to pinpoint a cause (or causes) and to develop suitable remedies.

Exploring possible causes

The wide range of possible causes of this unexplained illness can be understood only in the complex context of the physical, chemical, biological, and psychological environment of the Persian Gulf War. The decision to send U.S. forces to the Gulf was sudden and the deployment of troops rapid. Several hundred thousand of the troops were reservists who were abruptly removed from their jobs, families, and communities. As noted above, on arrival many were housed in rudimentary camps with few amenities. Later the camps were made more comfortable, and some troops were billeted in buildings with air-conditioning and modern sanitary facilities; conditions in the field remained primitive, however. The following is an enumeration of the many exposures that have been cited as possible causes of illness in returnees from the Gulf War.

Infectious agents. A major source of anxiety to troops in the Gulf was the possibility of exposure to the biological warfare agents known to be in the Iraqi arsenal. These included botulin (the deadly toxin produced by the bacterium *Clostridium botulinum,* which causes botulism) and spores of the anthrax bacillus, highly infectious to humans. According to the Department of Defense (DOD), there is no evidence of troops' exposure to such agents. Nevertheless, the administration of vaccines against botulin and anthrax lent reality to the threat. Gulf-bound personnel were also given other routine immunizations, including vaccines against hepatitis and tetanus.

An additional concern for the troops was the possibility of exposure to indigenous infectious agents such as *Leishmania tropica* (a parasite transmitted by the bite of the sand fly). Ordinarily, infection with *L. tropica* is manifested as a skin disease called cutaneous leishmaniasis. Another species of the parasite causes what is known as visceral leishmaniasis, which is sometimes characterized by fatigue, abdominal pain, cough, and other complaints like those reported by the veterans. Several dozen cases of *L. tropica* infection have been diagnosed in Gulf War returnees by means of special investigative techniques, and it is possible that less-sensitive tests may have missed other cases. However, if *L. tropica* is responsible for the veterans' symptoms, these cases represent an unusual manifestation of leishmaniasis. (In India, where outbreaks of visceral leishmaniasis occur periodically, researchers recently found a few patients who had evidence of *L. tropica* infection. Thus, it is possible that a new form of the disease is emerging.)

Nonetheless, it is unlikely that *L. tropica* is the cause of the unexplained illness in all or even most of the veterans. The army set up sophisticated laboratory stations in the field to monitor the biological environment and to respond to infectious disease outbreaks. As it turned out, the majority of such illnesses resulted from a combination of poor sanitation in the field, crowding of personnel (which facilitates the rapid spread of food- and airborne disease), and ordinary interpersonal contact.

Physical agents. Extremes of temperature, low humidity, wind, and sandstorms caused physical discomfort among the

Conditions in the field in Saudi Arabia—including sandstorms, extremes of temperature, primitive sanitation, and social isolation—challenged the morale of the troops in the Persian Gulf. They also presented a possible health hazard.

Kenneth Jarecke—Contact Press Images

Chris Stewart—Black Star

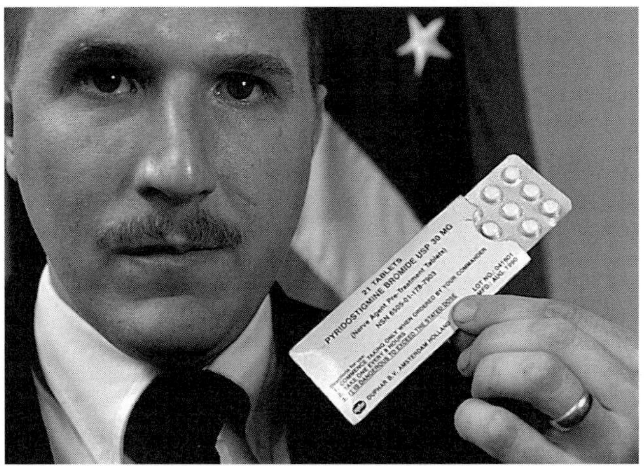

Kent Sayles, a Persian Gulf War veteran, testifies before Congress in 1994 about the use of the anti-nerve-gas agent pyridostigmine, which some vets claim may have caused their symptoms.

troops and put them at risk of dehydration and respiratory tract ailments from inhaled particles. What is less certain is the nature and degree of possible exposure to mineral and organic material in the thousand-year-old surface crust of the desert, which was pulverized into particulate matter by trucks and tanks and liberated into the atmosphere by periodic sandstorms.

Ionizing radiation from the spent uranium used in armor-piercing shells was also considered—and ruled out—as a health concern. Repeated assessments by radiation experts have concluded that the level of exposure of military personnel from such warheads was below accepted levels set for occupational radiation exposure.

Chemical warfare agents. The principal concern of the U.S. military regarding potential chemical exposure of the troops was the Iraqi military's large stocks of chemical warfare agents, primarily mustard gas and the nerve gas sarin. Along with demonstrating a willingness to use such weapons, the Iraqis also had a fairly effective delivery vehicle in the form of the Scud missile. Therefore, the U.S. troops were equipped with protective garments, which they donned when warned of impending Scud attacks. As another protective measure, they intermittently took pyridostigmine, a drug that can mitigate the effects of nerve gas but also has adverse effects, including nausea, diarrhea, and respiratory problems. The prescribed dose was 30 mg every eight hours, a minuscule amount in comparison with the dosage prescribed for medical treatment of the degenerative neuromuscular disorder myasthenia gravis. Because much larger amounts of pyridostigmine cause no symptoms in patients taking the drug therapeutically, most medical authorities discount this agent as a cause of the illness reported in returnees from the Gulf.

Veterans have told of repeated chemical alerts, during which they were instructed to don protective gear and take the preventive agent. On occasion the alert would be followed by an actual missile attack. Some have testified that they smelled a distinctive "bitter almond" odor after the attack. (Sarin is odorless.) The DOD, however, has repeatedly insisted that chemical-detection equipment, which was widely deployed, indicated no significant exposure to chemical warfare agents in any U.S. troops.

Petroleum products. The use of petroleum products in many forms offered opportunities for widespread exposure of military personnel to vapors, fumes, aerosols, and products of combustion. Crude-oil products released in the oil-field fires were the most notorious potential source of exposure and the one most often identified by the veterans. When the retreating Iraqi troops blew up wellheads and set fire to the effusion of oil and gas, this material was released under great pressure as gas, vapor, and liquid aerosols (*i.e.,* tiny airborne drops of petroleum), mostly in unburned form. This mixture, when ignited, produced dense black clouds of partially combusted hydrocarbons, various gases (NO_2, SO_2, H_2S, CO, CO_2), metals, and a variety of other compounds contained in fossil fuels.

While these fiery black infernos were awesome in appearance, their contribution to the exposure of ground troops to particulate and gaseous materials appears to have been small. Air-sampling measurements indicated that the larger droplets settled out quickly and the respirable particles were carried aloft by the intense heat of the fires. Postmortem studies on 85 battlefield casualties showed no evidence of the metals vanadium and nickel, which are found in crude-oil

NEWS*CAP*

Dirty Air

The risk of death is 15% higher in those U.S. cities with the dirtiest air. This was the conclusion of one of the largest studies of air quality ever conducted in the country. The work was carried out jointly by investigators from the Harvard School of Public Health and Brigham Young University, Provo, Utah, who monitored the health records of more than 550,000 people in 151 cities over a seven-year period.

The researchers attributed the higher death rates in the dirty-air cities to fine-particle pollution. Microscopic particles—smaller than 2.5 microns in diameter—emitted from automobiles, power plants, and other sources in the form of dust, soot, smoke, or tiny droplets of acid cause damage to the lungs when inhaled. People suffering from respiratory diseases such as asthma and bronchitis are the most susceptible to the effects of fine-particle pollution. The results, published in the *American Journal of Respiratory and Critical Care Medicine* (March 1995), confirmed numerous previous investigations that had shown this form of pollution to be a significant health hazard. Not all of the cities included in the study were named in the report, but the authors cited Steubenville, Ohio, as one with the dirtiest air and Topeka, Kan., as one with the cleanest.

smoke; therefore, it is unlikely that these troops had significant exposure to smoke from the oil fires. Seven individuals had elevated blood lead levels, but since lead is not typically released when crude oil burns, this finding suggests some environmental exposure other than the oil-well fires, possibly even predating military service. Ingestion of or skin contact with the oil could have led to absorption of potentially toxic hydrocarbons. Overall, the authorities believe that the oil fires were not responsible for exposures extensive enough to explain the apparently widespread distribution of the unexplained illnesses.

Troops involved in fueling, maintaining, and repairing aircraft, tanks, and other mobile vehicles also were exposed to petroleum products. Because heavy vehicle use is a major component of modern mechanized warfare, such exposure may have been significant. The practice of using fuels as dust and sand suppressants in the camps made for yet another source of exposure to petroleum liquids and vapors. Absorption of such liquids via the skin or inhalation of the fumes could have led to significant exposures to benzene, toluene, xylene, and ethylbenzene. These substances, in turn, may produce such symptoms as irritation of mucous membranes, light-headedness, fatigue, and mental (cognitive) dysfunction. (Some of these compounds also are known carcinogens.)

A plume of dense black smoke rises from a burning Kuwaiti oil well. Some who served in the Persian Gulf attribute their health problems to exposure to the sooty fumes emanating from such fires.

Peter Turnley—Black Star

Combustion products. Fuel combustion must be considered as a possible source of significant pollutant exposure of military personnel. Such pollutants would have included: carbon particles; carbon monoxide, carbon dioxide, sulfur dioxide, and nitrogen oxide gases; and aldehydes, aromatic organic compounds, and a variety of other volatile hydrocarbons. Gasoline and diesel engines were widely used in the Persian Gulf in military armored and transport vehicles and electricity generators. In addition, liquid-fueled heaters were used in the tents, which may have been poorly ventilated. Fuel was also used daily to incinerate solid waste at campsites. Exposures from all of these sources could well have exceeded civilian standards. These combustion products principally affect the respiratory tract, but they also may produce some central nervous system symptoms.

Pesticides, insecticides, and rodenticides. Extensive use of agents such as DEET, resmethrin, chlorpyrifos, *d*-phenothrin, Malathion, methomyl, lindane, pyrethroids, and others might have given rise to symptoms of neurotoxicity (such as memory loss, mood changes, and impaired performance) and irritability in troops who were exposed. These agents were widely used on skin and clothing, in tents and around camps, and in broader applications to control disease-carrying insects, rodents, and other pests and to establish reasonably hygienic conditions. Levels of exposure were not measured, and some probably were excessive. Delayed and long-term effects like those reported by some of the veterans would not ordinarily be expected, however.

Troops serving in the Persian Gulf operation are likely to have experienced multiple chemical exposures at levels higher than are usual in civilian life. Some of these exposures could have acted in combination with others to produce health effects not found with single-agent or lower-level exposures.

Psychological stressors. The nonspecific, multisystemic symptoms reported by many Persian Gulf veterans are compatible with the psychosomatic manifestations of psychological stress. Several psychological factors may have caused—or at least contributed to—the illnesses reported in this group.

The first of these is the suddenness of the changes that occurred in the lives of many of the military personnel, particularly the large number of reservists and National Guard troops who were called up on short notice. Second is the harsh physical environment and living conditions of the desert. Third is the social isolation, not only separation from family and community but also alienation from Kuwaiti society. Troops were not allowed to interact with local residents because of the Kuwaiti concern that Western customs would be an undesirable cultural influence. Fourth is the ever-present terror of biological and chemical weapons. Fifth is the enhanced credence lent to that threat by actions such as distribution of protective gear and anti-nerve-gas pills. Sixth is the Iraqi resolve to employ overwhelming destruction, exemplified by the oil-field fires. Finally, the visibility of the Scud missiles (which were the expected delivery system for chemical weapons), the finding of dead animals, the smelling of unusual odors, and similar ominous events are likely to have added to the fears of the troops.

The known and the unknown

Despite government inquiries (discussed below), no firm conclusions have been drawn about either the nature or the causes of the unexplained illnesses reported by veterans of the Persian Gulf conflict. Are their complaints legitimate? Many who have cared for ailing veterans believe that the illnesses are genuine but have been inadequately evaluated and are poorly understood. Some diagnostic and treatment centers have performed detailed workups of veterans referred for evaluation. These centers report that approximately 85% of the illnesses can be accounted for by known factors but that 15% remain unexplained.

It is becoming increasingly apparent that in most instances these illnesses were not triggered by exposure to a single, known substance. In some cases there is no evidence of any such exposure, while in others the reported symptoms do not fit the diagnostic criteria for a disease that occurs as a result of the exposure in question. In still other cases the distribution of the reported ailments does not match the distribution of the alleged causative agents. An important exception may be the discovery of an unusual form of leishmaniasis. However, this condition has been diagnosed in only about 30 individuals and, as noted above, is not likely to be responsible for most of the unexplained illnesses.

A variety of occupational and environmental exposures could have produced symptoms of acute illness and could have lingering effects on health. Some of the illnesses are well recognized—for example, skin rashes due to contact with irritating chemicals—but the absent or limited data on exposure make such causal relationships difficult to prove.

It is well recognized that symptoms connected with vivid experiences, especially those that occur under psychologically stressful conditions, tend to be attributed to those experiences even when the symptoms do not appear until later. This phenomenon is exemplified in posttraumatic stress disorder (PTSD), a psychological condition seen in troops who have witnessed horrifying scenes in battle and in civilians who have survived similarly vivid and disturbing events. Most mental health professionals acknowledge that PTSD is a real phenomenon, although its manifestations are highly variable, and much remains to be learned about it.

The 82nd Aerial Brigade for Chemical Decontamination holds a chemical-warfare-response drill. The potential use of chemical weapons in the Persian Gulf War was clearly a major source of psychological stress for U.S. military personnel.

Jacques Langevin—Sygma

Despite the many unanswered questions, a number of initiatives have been launched to deal with the health problems reported by the Persian Gulf veterans. In 1994 Congress passed legislation providing a three-year period of special medical benefits to veterans of the Persian Gulf operations. These benefits will allow those afflicted to receive diagnostic evaluation and treatment pending a more complete understanding of the illnesses. Ailing veterans may be evaluated by their own private physicians or by their local Department of Veterans Affairs (VA) hospital. In addition, the VA has established three regional centers in Washington, D.C., New Orleans, La., and Los Angeles for the further evaluation of these patients by a detailed, standardized protocol.

NEWS*CAP*

Not a Drop to Drink

More than 53 million Americans drink tap water that fails to meet the safety and health standards established under the Safe Drinking Water Act, according to reports released in June 1995 by two environmental watchdog groups, the Environmental Working Group (EWG) and the Natural Resources Defense Council. On the basis of data compiled by the Environmental Protection Agency and local water utilities in 1993–94, the reports cautioned that further deterioration of the water supply could result if Republican proposals to weaken the Safe Drinking Water Act are passed. According to the EWG report, fecal coliform bacteria, organisms normally found in human waste material and capable of causing severe gastrointestinal illness, were present in 1,172 U.S. water systems. Cryptosporidium, a microbial contaminant found in the water systems serving 45 million Americans, had been responsible for illness in some 400,000 in Milwaukee, Wis., in 1993 and had possibly contributed to more than 100 deaths.

Topping the list of the 20 U.S. cities with the most suspect tap water was New York City. Other locales with "drinking water to watch" were:

- Tucson, Ariz.
- Greenville, S.C.
- Utica, N.Y.
- Elizabeth, N.J.
- New Port Richey, Fla.
- Decatur, Ill.
- Lansdale, Pa.
- Joliet, Ill.
- Springbrook township, Pa.
- Ft. Bragg, N.C.
- Altoona, Pa.
- Rock Hill, S.C.
- Oak View, Calif.
- Bloomington, Ill.
- Shamokin, Pa.
- Camden, N.J.
- Davis, Calif.
- Danbury, Conn.
- Merchantville-Pennsauken, N.J.

Toll-free telephone numbers have been established for Gulf War veterans and eligible family members who wish to register for medical examination and treatment. The VA number is 1-800-749-9387; the DOD number is 1-800-796-9699. (The DOD has also set up a separate number for veterans to report details of incidents they believe may be associated with health problems experienced since their return from the Persian Gulf region.)

Ongoing search for answers

The DOD, VA, National Institutes of Health (NIH), and Institute of Medicine (IOM) have all set up blue-ribbon panels to evaluate exposures, illness, medical care, and research related to the health effects of service in the Persian Gulf. In April 1994 the NIH Office of Medical Applications of Research held a two-day workshop entitled "The Persian Gulf Experience and Health." Workshop participants recommended further epidemiological studies of the military personnel who served in the Persian Gulf area. They also suggested the development of a standardized protocol for medical evaluation of veterans seeking treatment for ailments possibly attributable to military service.

An IOM committee that was established to review the health consequences of service in the Gulf published its preliminary findings and recommendations in early 1995. It proposed, among other measures, that epidemiological studies be undertaken to compare the frequency of unexplained illness in Persian Gulf personnel with that in the civilian population.

Both of these expert panels concluded that the major barrier to explaining the illnesses reported by Gulf War vets is a lack of adequate data. They also cited the failure of the agencies involved to coordinate data collection. In response, Congress has authorized $10 million to be spent on research. The DOD has established a comprehensive registry of all veterans of the Persian Gulf operation, their times of service, and locations of assignment. The VA has established a registry of all Gulf War service personnel who have complaints of illness. Data on specific environmental and occupational exposures are still needed, however, and comprehensive medical data on those reporting symptoms are being gathered according to a standardized protocol. It will also be necessary to develop a better understanding of the psychological stresses of modern warfare and their impact on subsequent illness.

Epidemiologists know that disease typically occurs in populations at regular and fairly predictable rates. When the reported rate of illness clearly exceeds the predicted rate, public health authorities declare an epidemic. To declare an "epidemic" of illness in Gulf War veterans, these authorities must first develop a precise definition of the illness. Then they must determine whether it is occurring at a greater-than-expected rate and decide whether the illness can be attributed to agents or conditions to which the victims have been exposed.

Studies are now under way to answer each of these basic questions. The answers are important not only for the well-being and peace of mind of veterans of the Persian Gulf War but also for the conduct of future military interventions.

—Gareth M. Green, M.D.

Medical Sleuths in Kathmandu

"I'm seeing a particle in the stool exams that I can't identify." With that announcement Ramachandran Rajah, a lab technician at the Canadian International Water and Energy Consultants (CIWEC) Clinic in Kathmandu, Nepal, set in motion what was to be a several-year-long investigation that would culminate in the discovery of a new cause of diarrheal disease in travelers throughout the world.

The CIWEC Clinic is a unique Western-operated medical facility that serves the expatriate and tourist populations in Nepal. Nepal's Himalayan setting makes it a favorite destination for tens of thousands of travelers from developed countries annually, and the Kathmandu clinic is arguably the busiest travel clinic of its kind in the less developed world. The three American physicians who serve it see over 5,000 patients per year, of whom 1,200 are evaluated for a gastrointestinal illness.

Disease of travelers

Fear of diarrhea leads the list of reasons why residents of developed countries do not wish to travel to less developed ones. If this fear could be eliminated, millions of dollars in tourist revenues could be generated, which would help further the development of many fascinating places in the world.

From 1987 to 1988 the clinic had collaborated with the Armed Forces Research Institute of Medical Science (AFRIMS), Bangkok, Thailand, in a yearlong study of traveler's diarrhea. Stool samples from diarrhea patients in Nepal were processed and shipped on ice to the AFRIMS laboratory, where they were analyzed for all known causes of traveler's diarrhea. The yield of pathogens (disease-causing organisms) was higher than in any similar previous study. However, a specific cause of diarrhea was found in only 80% of the samples. That finding raised a question: Were there other, as-yet-undiscovered pathogens lurking in the samples?

In earlier times traveler's diarrhea was not distinguished from other forms of diarrhea. The organisms that caused it could be found all over the world, wherever fecal material could find its way into food and water. The problem was essentially solved in developed countries by creating sewerage systems that kept fecal waste far from the food chain. The disease is now associated mainly with travel to destinations where these hygiene problems have not yet been solved.

Half a century ago a specific cause of diarrhea could be found in only about 20% of cases. Over time new organisms were discovered, and the role of already-known organisms was more clearly defined. This led to today's situation, in which a precise pathogen can be found in at least half the cases.

Traveler's diarrhea is not an innocuous problem limited to vacationing tourists. The military has long been concerned with the condition because it is often the main reason that troops are unable to fight and carry out their missions after arriving at their destination. It was the single most widespread illness among Western troops stationed in Saudi Arabia during the Persian Gulf War in 1991.

The organisms that cause diarrhea in visitors to less developed areas are also a major affliction of local children; these children are often undernourished and at high risk of dying from diarrhea. In countries where mortality rates range from 20% to 50% of all children under five years of age, diarrhea is the leading cause of death.

Early clues

The curious particle that baffled Rajah in Kathmandu that summer day—June 26, 1989—resembled another organism that was known to cause diarrhea: cryptosporidium. This organism was first identified over 15 years ago but did not attain prominence until 1993, when it was discovered in the water supply of Milwaukee, Wis. There it caused as many as 400,000 cases of diarrhea and may have contributed to 40–100 deaths. In laboratory studies the new organism absorbed stain the same way that cryptosporidium did, but it was larger and had more elaborate internal structures. On the day the new particle was first noticed, the staff of the CIWEC Clinic started recording the presence of the organism whenever it appeared in stool samples. Their hope was that the mystery organism could be associated with particular symptoms.

Earlier that spring (1989) the doctors at the clinic had started to see people who were suffering from a prolonged

In Kathmandu, Nepal, Ramachandran Rajah sits at the microscope through which he first spotted a "mysterious particle" in a stool sample—one that proved to be a new cause of traveler's diarrhea.

David R. Shlim, M.D., CIWEC Clinic, Kathmandu

diarrheal illness but did not respond to the usual antibiotic medications. Patients reported profound fatigue, loss of appetite, and weight loss of as much as 7–9 kg (15–20 lb). Yet the stool exams of these patients were always negative for known pathogens. Suddenly, however, the doctors noticed that this strange particle was present in virtually every patient who came in with this severe unexplained illness.

The clinic's doctors decided to send some of the stool samples in question to Beth Ungar, a well-known cryptosporidium expert at the Uniformed Services University of the Health Sciences, Bethesda, Md. Ungar agreed that this was not a known organism but suspected that it fell into the broad category of protozoans known as coccidia (which includes cryptosporidium). Willadene Zierdt, parasitologist at the adjacent National Institutes of Health, concurred. Because coccidia often cause illness in farm animals, a specimen was sent to a veterinarian as well. He was certain that it was *not* a coccidium.

The puzzle appeared to be solved when Ungar obtained a copy of a manuscript being prepared for publication by microbiologist Earl G. Long at the Centers for Disease Control (now the Centers for Disease Control and Prevention; CDC), Atlanta, Ga. Long, who had previously received eight specimens from around the U.S. that were identical in appearance to the organism that came from Nepal, argued that the organism was actually a cyanobacterium, or blue-green alga. Although no cyanobacterium had been known to invade the human intestine, it was known that a form of blue-green algae could produce a toxin that could cause intestinal illness in people and cattle when they drank from algae-filled ponds.

By November 1989, 55 patients with the unknown organism had been seen at the CIWEC facility. The organism then was not seen again until the following summer. The physicians reported on these 55 cases in an article that was published in the *American Journal of Tropical Medicine and Hygiene* (September 1991). They had found that people were ill when the organism was present in stool and recovered only when it was not present. None of the broad-spectrum antibiotics they tried (norfloxacin, metronidazole, tinidazole, quinacrine) shortened the illness. In both treated and untreated patients, the illness lasted from one to 12 weeks—the average duration being 6 weeks. Symptoms would then clear spontaneously, and complete recovery was usual. There were a few people, however, who continued to have symptoms although the organism was gone. These patients eventually responded to treatment for the condition known as tropical sprue.

Significantly, the organism was never found in anyone who did not have the typical symptoms of profound fatigue, loss of appetite, and diarrhea. Unlike other diarrhea-producing organisms, which may be present in the human intestine without producing symptoms, there appeared to be no asymptomatic carriers of this infection.

The following summer, in July 1990, an outbreak of the illness was reported in Chicago among house staff at Cook County Hospital. All those affected had attended a party in an office building associated with the hospital. Ten cases were identified; the symptoms and clinical course were similar to the illness reported in Kathmandu. Drinking water in the building was eventually implicated as the source of infection, and corrective measures were taken.

In all cases, although the organism could be seen in stool samples under a microscope, it defied efforts to be grown in a test tube. Experts around the world continued to debate whether it was a coccidium or an alga. The CDC's suggestion to refer to the unspecified organism as a "Cyanobacteria-like body," or CLB, was adopted. Meanwhile, it was learned that an identical-looking organism had been described by medical researchers in Papua New Guinea as far back as 1979. Because no one else had subsequently seen the organism, that report had been forgotten.

Getting closer

In 1991 the authors of this report were both attending an international conference on travel medicine in Atlanta. At the conference one of them, David Shlim, director of the CIWEC Clinic, delivered a paper on CLB. The other, Bradley Connor, a New York gastroenterologist, thought the symptoms that were described sounded like those of an upper intestine (small bowel) infection. If that were so, endoscopic examination, which would visualize the interior of the small bowel, might elucidate the type of organism. It was agreed that Connor would transport his endoscopy equipment, which was not available at the CIWEC Clinic, to Kathmandu.

In June 1991 Connor was able to examine 16 patients in one week, 9 of whom had the CLB in their stool. Those nine patients all had moderate to severe inflammation of the upper intestine (duodenum), and the normally absorptive surface of the organ appeared to be flattened. This explained the lack of appetite and weight loss. The organism was seen in intestinal fluid in two of the nine patients, but there was no evidence of it in any of the intestinal biopsy sections that were later analyzed by electron microscope. Although it was clear that the organism caused marked changes in the upper intestine, no one knew how it caused those changes. Was it through the production of a toxin that could damage the lining of the intestines? Or did the organisms invade directly, inducing an inflammatory response?

British researchers shed some light on the matter in March 1993 in an article published in *The Lancet*. R.P. Bendall and colleagues did biopsies of the jejunum, the intestinal segment just beyond the duodenum. Samples from two patients showed what appeared to be minute bodies known as sporozoites, which occur as a result of repeated divisions of a coccidian protozoan. (The life cycle of a coccidian protozoan involves the process of dividing into new bodies, called sporulation. Algae, on the other hand, do not exhibit this behavior.) It remained unclear, however, why sporozoites had not been present in the CIWEC patients.

Compelling evidence

Was the organism a coccidium after all? The previous autumn, Charles Sterling and colleagues had presented some new information on CLB at the annual meeting of the American Society of Tropical Medicine and Hygiene. This information was based on their studies of infected children in Peru. Unlike previous researchers, they had succeeded in getting the organism to divide (sporulate) while incubating in

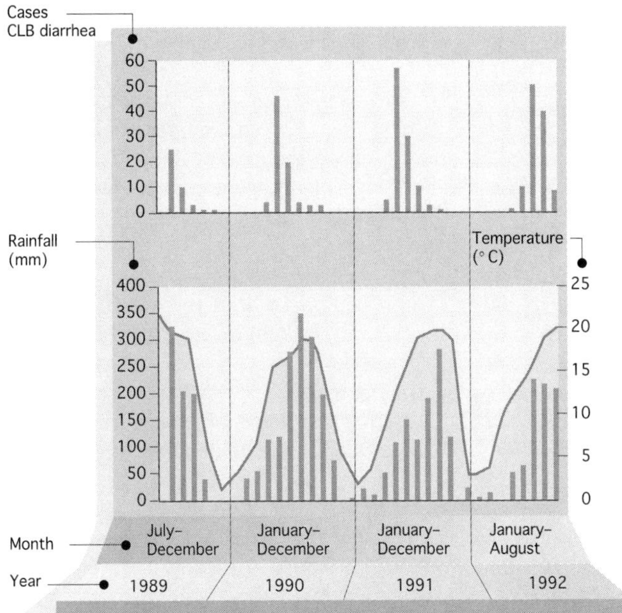

Adapted from Charles W. Hoge *et al.*, "Epidemiology of Diarrhoeal Illness...," *The Lancet*, vol. 341, no. 8854 (May 8, 1993), pp. 1175–79.

(Above) Average minimum temperatures (line) and total rainfall (bar) recorded in Kathmandu monthly from July 1989 through August 1992; (top) number of cases in which cyanobacteria-like bodies were diagnosed at Kathmandu clinics during the same period.

a laboratory solution of potassium dichromate. When Sterling and his colleagues left the organism in potassium dichromate for an extended period of time—from 5 to 13 days—they were rewarded with unequivocal evidence of sporulation. This confirmed that the organism was indeed a coccidium. In appearance the organisms seemed most closely related to a genus called *Cyclospora,* which was first described in 1870 but occurred mainly in rodents, reptiles, and insects.

While the researchers in Peru were making headway, investigations at the CIWEC Clinic continued. Each year the *Cyclospora* outbreaks were intensely seasonal, occurring only from April to November, with most of the cases occurring in a four-week period from mid-June to mid-July. Nepal has monsoon rains each year, starting in mid-June and lasting until mid-October. The diarrheal illness would appear before the start of the monsoons and start to subside as the rains reached their full intensity in July, but a few cases occurred as late as November, after the monsoons had ended.

The CIWEC physicians had already observed that the incidence of diarrhea among expatriates and tourists in Nepal increased dramatically in the spring, beginning in March and peaking in June each year. This increase in traveler's diarrhea in the spring coincided with Nepal's fly season, which extends from March to June. The arrival of the heavy rains in June then dispatches most of the flies, which leads to a decrease in diarrhea among foreigners. The organisms that cause traveler's diarrhea in Nepal—such as *Escherichia coli, Shigella, Campylobacter, Salmonella, Giardia lamblia, Entamoeba histolytica,* and cryptosporidium—are present throughout the year. *Cyclospora* was unique in disappearing completely between epidemics, which suggested that there was some particular source of the infection that appeared every year.

In 1992 Shlim consulted Charles Hoge, an infectious disease specialist who had worked as an epidemiologist for the CDC before joining the staff at AFRIMS. They designed a yearlong epidemiological study of diarrhea among foreigners in Nepal. Patients who went to the CIWEC Clinic with diarrhea were randomly recruited into the study, as were all clinic patients who had *Cyclospora* in their stools. In addition, the investigators recruited an equal number of controls—people who did not have diarrhea but from whom stool samples were collected. All participants in the study filled out a 10-page questionnaire on their eating habits in the week before they became sick or the week before they gave a stool sample.

Cyclospora accounted for over 10% of the diarrhea patients seen at the CIWEC Clinic in the 1992 season. Ninety-three of them completed the questionnaire, as did 96 controls. *Cyclospora* was detected in the stool samples of only one of the asymptomatic controls, but that person became ill three days later with typical *Cyclospora*-related illness.

From the questionnaire it was determined that drinking untreated water or unpasteurized milk was associated with acquiring *Cyclospora* infection. Further evidence of waterborne transmission was found when one sample of unprocessed tap water from the home of a *Cyclospora* patient proved to have *Cyclospora* organisms in it. But only 28% of the *Cyclospora* patients reported drinking untreated water or unpasteurized milk, so it appeared that there had to be other ways of acquiring the infection.

The cure

Despite this apparent progress, however, there was still no information on whether the infections could be shortened by treatment. In July 1993 Sterling's group reported that five of their *Cyclospora*-infected patients had been treated and were cured by the antibiotic trimethoprim-sulfamethoxazole (TMP-SMX), which is commonly known by the trade names Bactrim and Septra. Initially a lab technician who worked with Sterling had developed diarrhea and had treated himself with TMP-SMX before obtaining the results of a stool examination. The stool sample confirmed that he had a *Cyclospora* infection. With the medication, however, his symptoms improved rapidly. A subsequent stool examination was negative. Four Peruvian children were then treated, with a similar result.

After learning of this, the CIWEC physicians began treating *Cyclospora* patients with TMP-SMX; in all cases symptoms resolved, and the organism disappeared from stool in the ensuing week. It was not known, however, whether some or all of the patients would have gotten better on their own over the same period. Hoge and Shlim then spent the winter designing a treatment study that would take place the following *Cyclospora* season (1994).

A total of 40 patients with *Cyclospora* were enrolled; 21 were given TMP-SMX, and 19 received a placebo (inert pill). All subjects took one pill twice a day for a week and had their symptoms and stools monitored closely. Because the trial was double-blind, neither the patients, physicians, nor lab technician knew which patients were taking the antibiotic and which were taking the placebo.

Of the TMP-SMX-treated patients, 94% had a negative stool exam for *Cyclospora* after seven days, compared with only 12% of the placebo patients. Patients who still had *Cyclospora* in their stools after a week were then knowingly treated with TMP-SMX, and all were cured. Subsequently, researchers in Haiti reported that double the usual dose of the antibiotic was an effective cure for *Cyclospora* infections in HIV-positive patients, in whom the illness tended to be chronic and unremitting.

TMP-SMX, a sulfa drug, had been the main antibiotic used to treat other forms of traveler's diarrhea through the mid-1980s. Gradually, however, many diarrhea-causing bacteria had become resistant to it. The CIWEC Clinic, along with most other travel medicine clinics around the world, then began to use quinolone antibiotics such as norfloxacin and ciprofloxacin to treat most suspected bacterial-caused traveler's diarrhea. The emergence of *Cyclospora* as a cause of diarrhea coincided with the decreasing use of TMP-SMX. It now would appear that *Cyclospora* infections were present but were probably being accidentally cured by the wide use of TMP-SMX for diarrhea. Only when TMP-SMX was abandoned did *Cyclospora* become more prevalent. No one thought to try TMP-SMX again until its accidental rediscovery.

NEWS*CAP*

A Deadly Relative of Measles Down Under

A new virus capable of causing a fatal respiratory disease was discovered in Brisbane, Australia, in September 1994. The outbreak killed 14 racehorses and their trainer. A stablehand who also was infected contracted an influenza-like illness but survived.

The newly identified organism is a morbillivirus, a group that includes the measles virus and others that affect only animals.

The Australian scientists who tracked the outbreak reported their findings in *Science* (April 7, 1995). They speculated that the virus had existed for some time in an as-yet-unidentified native Australian animal without causing disease. Why it suddenly became transmissible to horses—and then to humans—is a mystery. The researchers tested 1,600 horses and 90 humans in the vicinity of the outbreak for antibodies to the virus and found no further infections. Within a month after the disease was identified, new cases had ceased to appear.

Meanwhile, veterinarians in Brisbane were trying to identify the natural animal reservoir of the virus and cataloging and testing all other animal species living near the site of the first equine infections.

A sprue connection?

Until 1994, diagnosing *Cyclospora* in patients in Nepal had been like passing a sentence on them. They were destined to be quite ill over the next two to six weeks. Now, thanks to a serendipitous series of events, *Cyclospora* is simply another diagnosable and treatable diarrheal illness. The exception is that no effective alternative treatment has yet been found for people who are allergic to sulfa drugs and who cannot take TMP-SMX.

Among physicians, however, one more mystery surrounded *Cyclospora:* its possible connection with the condition known as tropical sprue. The first summer that the CIWEC Clinic began to see what came to be called *Cyclospora,* all but three patients recovered when the organism vanished from the stool exams. Those three patients, however, continued to feel tired, lose weight, and have intermittent diarrhea even when *Cyclospora* was no longer detectable. Their illness now closely resembled tropical sprue. Moreover, like the intestines of sprue patients, theirs showed poor absorption of d-xylose, a sugar that is used to evaluate the nutrient-absorbing capacity of the gut.

Tropical sprue is a poorly understood condition associated with diarrhea, weight loss, fatigue, and malabsorption of food by the upper intestine. The infection occurs in some countries but not in others. It occasionally occurs in epidemics among local inhabitants, but both natives and foreign visitors are susceptible. No specific organism that is consistently associated with the infection has been isolated. Was *Cyclospora* the real cause of tropical sprue?

Probably not. Unlike the *Cyclospora* patients, tropical sprue patients do not tend to get well without specific treatment. Moreover, the CIWEC Clinic continued to see people with tropical sprue who did not have *Cyclospora,* and their infections could be diagnosed at any time of year, not just during the *Cyclospora* season. The three patients who had spruelike illness following their *Cyclospora* infection responded rapidly when they were given the antibiotic tetracycline and the vitamin folic acid—the standard treatment for suspected tropical sprue. The CIWEC physicians had tried that combination in people who had *Cyclospora* present in their stool but found it had no benefit.

It now appears that *Cyclospora* may trigger certain changes in the intestine or that some other unknown pathogen may be involved, setting the stage for tropical sprue in some individuals. A few CIWEC patients recovered completely from *Cyclospora* infections only to come down with tropical sprue in the following year. Researchers in the U.K. had noted a similar phenomenon.

Although *Cyclospora* has been added to the host of pathogens that cause woe in travelers, a lot of details remain to be filled in. Whether future investigations of *Cyclospora* will eventually help explain the remaining mysteries of tropical sprue is unclear. It is worth noting, however, that a great deal is not known about most diarrhea-causing organisms, even the most common ones such as cryptosporidium and *G. lamblia.*

—David R. Shlim, M.D., and Bradley A. Connor, M.D.

NEWS*CAPS*

Of (Fat) Mice and Men

The discovery within the past year of a gene for obesity has already begun to offer at least the promise of a treatment for this frustrating and seemingly intransigent problem. Scientists immediately hailed the accomplishments as "fabulous."

First, in a report in *Nature* (Dec. 1, 1994), researchers at Rockefeller University, New York City, announced that they had discovered and replicated a gene that contributes to obesity in mice. The gene, dubbed *ob,* was detected in a strain of specially bred mice that reach three to five times their normal body weight. The gene functions by directing fat cells to secrete a protein that alerts the brain to suppress appetite when fat stores in the body are sufficient. When both copies of the *ob* gene (*i.e.,* one inherited from each parent) are either missing or defective, no protein is produced, no satiety message reaches the brain, and appetite goes unchecked. A search of the entire human genome revealed a gene that was 84% identical to the one found in mice; the researchers, therefore, presumed it had the same function.

Seven months later, in a report in *Science* (July 28, 1995), three research teams, including the gene discovery scientists at Rockefeller, published studies of the *ob* gene's protein product, a hormone they named leptin (after the Greek word for "thin"). When the genetically obese mice were injected with leptin, they lost 30% of their body weight in two weeks. Not only did the animals eat less, but their metabolism also increased. Lean mice that had been fed a high-fat diet also lost weight when given leptin.

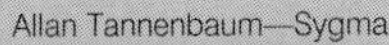
Allan Tannenbaum—Sygma

The investigators noted that while their discovery offers encouragement for those struggling to lose weight, it is far from having a direct application. Years of testing would be required for determining if leptin treatment is safe in humans. And since the lost weight is regained when leptin treatment is discontinued, obese individuals would have to take leptin indefinitely.

It is important to note that mutations in the *ob* gene, which are rare in mice and so far unknown in humans, are *not* believed to be the fundamental cause of most human obesity. Nonetheless, the identification of the gene made possible the isolation of leptin, and the study of leptin, in turn, is expected to yield clues to the origin and treatment of obesity.

Still More Alzheimer's Genes

In the summer of 1995, two groups of scientists announced that they had found genetic mutations associated with early-onset Alzheimer's disease (AD), bringing to three the number of different genes that may be responsible for forms of the progressive dementia that develop before age 65. First, an international research team reported in *Nature* (June 29, 1995) that they had isolated a gene that causes a rare but very aggressive form of AD that affects some victims as early as in their 30s. The investigators, from institutions in Canada, France, Britain, Italy, and the U.S., studied 21 families with a history of AD's developing at an early age. A mutated gene called *S182* located on chromosome 14 accounted for more than 70% of AD cases in six of the families. Moreover, inheriting the mutation virtually guaranteed than an individual would be affected. Because 15 families in the study did not show mutations in *S182,* the researchers theorized that in some cases other genes must be involved in the early development of AD.

A gene on chromosome 1 was implicated in another study (reported in *Science,* Aug. 19, 1995). Conducted by scientists at the Massachusetts General Hospital, Boston, and the Veterans Affairs Medical Center in Seattle, Wash., this study also focused on families with a high incidence of early-onset AD. The gene on chromosome 1 codes for a protein that is very similar to the one encoded by the gene on chromosome 14, but the function of the proteins had not yet been determined.

NEWS*CAPS*

The very first mutation associated with early-onset AD, identified in 1987, involved the gene for amyloid precursor protein (APP), located on chromosome 21. APP contributes to the formation of amyloid, a substance that accumulates in characteristic lesions found in the brains of Alzheimer's sufferers.

AD affects about four million people in the U.S. and is the fourth leading cause of death. Only about 10% of cases develop in individuals younger than 65, but scientists expect that insights into the early-onset forms of the disorder will shed light on the disease process in general.

Giant Steps: Genetics and Dwarfism

A series of recent studies have pinpointed the genetic mutations underlying some types of dwarfism. Early in 1994 scientists determined that the gene responsible for achondroplasia, the most prevalent genetic form of dwarfism in most parts of the world, is located on the short arm of human chromosome 4. Building on that work, researchers at the University of California at Irvine identified the specific gene involved, the so-called fibroblast growth factor receptor 3 (*FGFR3*) gene, and described how it became mutated (*Cell,* July 29, 1994). Subsequently, a team in Paris reported that a single amino acid change in the protein product of the *FGFR3* gene was all that was necessary to cause the characteristic deformities of achondroplasia (*Nature,* Sept. 15, 1994). Finally, researchers at the National Center for Human Genome Research reported that another, less severe form of dwarfism, called hypochondroplasia, also stems from a mutation of the *FGFR3* gene but involves a different subunit of the gene (*Nature Genetics,* July 1995).

While achondroplasia occurs in between one in 15,000 and one in 40,000 live births worldwide, another skeletal disorder, diastrophic dysplasia (DTD), is the most frequent genetic cause of dwarfism in Finland and the third most prevalent cause in the U.S. After studying the DNA of 18 Finnish families with at least one affected member, researchers at the Whitehead Institute for Biomedical Research, Cambridge, Mass., and the University of Helsinki were able to narrow the search for the gene to a region of chromosome 5. They then determined the precise location of the gene, which encodes a protein that transports sulfate in and out of cells (*Cell,* Sept. 23, 1994). Certain sulfate compounds are necessary for the creation of tough, resilient bones. Individuals who inherit defective DTD genes from both parents develop twisted bones and arthritis.

A Gene Linked to Bed-Wetting

Since the mid-1980s some scientists have believed that genetics, not psychological factors, is primarily responsible for persistent bed-wetting (*i.e.,* into adolescence). Now, however, in a report in *Nature Genetics* (July 1995), researchers at the University of Copenhagen have announced the discovery of the general location of a gene—on the long arm of chromosome 13—that may confirm the theory. Of 400 families included in the Danish study, 11 were found to have at least one child and one parent who had a history of primary nocturnal enuresis—persistent bed-wetting three or more times a week beyond the age of seven years. This finding suggested a pattern of genetic transmission in which the gene responsible for the trait is dominant (*i.e.,* only one parent has to pass it on for a child to be affected).

Although the Danish scientists were unable to specify the exact site of the gene or to explain how it brought about bed-wetting, they believed the discovery would make it easier for those affected and their families to accept the condition. While noting that a genetic connection may be helpful in treating some children, some child development experts view genetics as but one factor among several (including slow development of motor control and the presence of allergies) that contribute to the involuntary passage of urine while sleeping.

Bed-wetting, which for unexplained reasons is more common in boys than girls, is considered normal for two- and three-year-olds. By age 4, however, 60% of children have stopped; by age 6, 90% have stopped; and by age 18, the problem persists only among 1%.

One-quarter of those who experience nocturnal bed-wetting have secondary enuresis (infrequent instances of bed-wetting after at least a six-month problem-free period). The Danish researchers found no evidence that the secondary form of enuresis is inherited; rather, they attributed it to "anything from epilepsy to psychologic tension in the family."

U.S. Health Reform: Dead but Not Buried

A little more than a year ago, expectations were high in the United States for the passage of legislation that would result in comprehensive health care coverage for all citizens. Not only did that not occur, but after two years of headlines, page-one stories, and voluminous coverage on television and radio, no consensus was reached in regard to the content of that legislation.

The decade of the 1990s in the United States could well become known as the "Decade of Reform." Indeed, virtually every aspect of society was, is, or will be in some way "reformed." In 1995 Congress was in the process of "reforming" not only the criminal justice system, the welfare system, and the legal and internal revenue systems but also government itself, including the Congress. While 1993–94 was the year of health care reform, 1994–95 seemed to be the year of reform for everything *but* health care. How is it possible that an issue could drop from number one on the policy hit parade to barely being on the charts?

In the coming years, volumes will be written analyzing the many wrong turns taken on the "Road to Health Care Reform." As one Washington pundit put it, had the saga been filmed, it would have seemed more like a Bob Hope–Bing Crosby "road" picture than a serious attempt to address a major societal problem.

But is health care reform really as dead as members of Congress and the media declared in September 1994? Or should it be regarded as only a case of "reformus interruptus"?

Confusion over definitions

Part of the answer to the above question depends on what is meant by "health care reform" and whether *reform* is the appropriate word to have been applied to health care in the first place. *Reform* means "the amendment or altering for the better of some faulty state of things; the improvement in form, structure, and quality and the removal of defects and errors"—the emphasis being on beneficial change.

When considering the Democratic and Republican health care reform proposals of 1993–94, it would be hard to say that any of them was designed to truly amend or alter "for the better" the overall health care system. Such an effort would have entailed some improvement in the actual delivery of that care to people. While the president's and several other proposals did focus on increasing access to care and controlling costs, there was little focus on the care itself. Other proposals not only ignored the issue of the provision of care but would have done little to improve access significantly; they were primarily proposals to change the mechanism for financing health care.

Perhaps a more suitable term for the proposals around which the 1993–94 health care debates revolved would have been health care *restructuring.* Whether a particular "restructuring" proposal would truly lead to "reform" would then become a matter for debate.

Reforming the "care" in health care

The need to reform the manner in which health care is actually provided to the U.S. population was recently spelled

Senior citizens lobby for a single-payer system of health care. When then presidential hopeful Bill Clinton was in search of a health plan, he considered a single-payer approach but knew it would have little chance of acceptance in the United States.

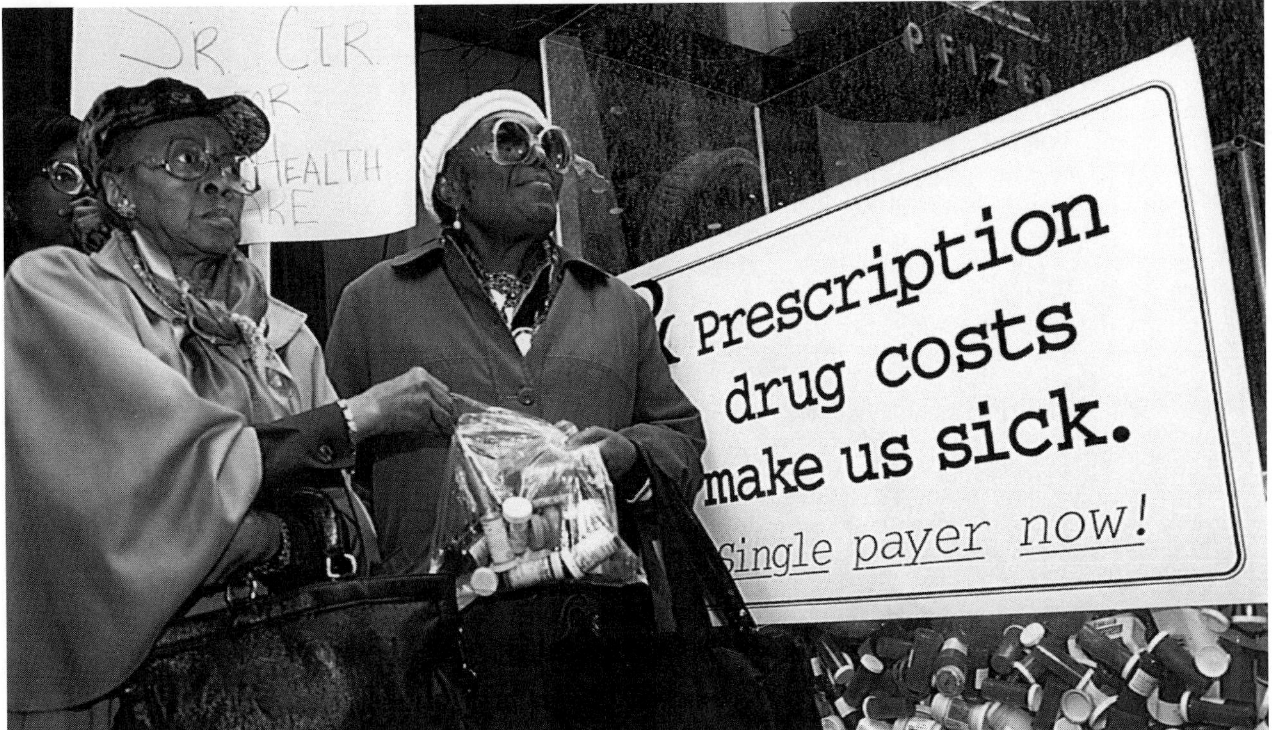

Steven Rubin—JB Pictures

out by Jody Heymann, a Boston-based physician and public policy analyst. In 1994 Heymann attended a Harvard Medical School Alumni meeting at which a speaker had said, "Sooner or later, every single one of you will become a patient. I dare say, you will not particularly like being on the other side of the fence." Shortly thereafter, Heymann became a hospital patient—an experience she recounted in the book *Equal Partners* (1995). Among the kinds of medical practices that she discovered to be in need of reform were:

- routine actions that regularly cause patients to suffer
- ignoring of patients' descriptions of experiences that are related to their conditions
- increasing control of medical practice by insurers, which results in less and less time for physicians and patients to talk with each other
- physicians' daily denials that patients are equals
- physicians' discouraging patients from making decisions about their own care
- hospitals' ignoring patients' needs in everything from making patient-discharge arrangements to scheduling the institution's spring-cleaning activities
- hospital staff members' treating patients' families as invisible

Heymann concluded that "many of the insults are small—doctors not giving local anesthesia for temporarily painful procedures or nurses not calling a doctor when a hospitalized patient grows sicker and asks to be seen—but taken together, these regular wrongs are a stronger indictment of our current system than the less frequent acts of malpractice or rare acts of malevolence."

Though the public's concern about the reforming of care itself was seldom reflected in the many polls on health reform conducted during 1993 and 1994, a small, informal survey of about a hundred Minnesota residents was conducted by this author in the summer of 1993. The purpose was to determine whether the "person in the street" with health insurance saw health care reform in the same light as Pres. Bill Clinton did—that is, reducing national health care costs and achieving universal coverage. Only about 5% of the surveyed population mentioned either universal coverage or cost containment. The problems that the respondents cited most often were:

- having to wait a long time to get an appointment to see a doctor
- having to wait an hour to see a doctor for a five-minute visit
- having to leave a doctor's office without clearly understanding what the diagnosis is or how the medical problem should be treated
- doctors' explaining things in terms the patient does not understand
- having to change physicians because one's chosen doctor is not a participating provider in a particular managed-care plan
- not being able to see a specialist when needed
- being discharged from the hospital before being well enough to function
- having to pay increasingly larger out-of-pocket costs for care
- hospitals' and insurance companies' placing financial imperatives above patients' health needs

Andrew Lichtenstein—JB Pictures

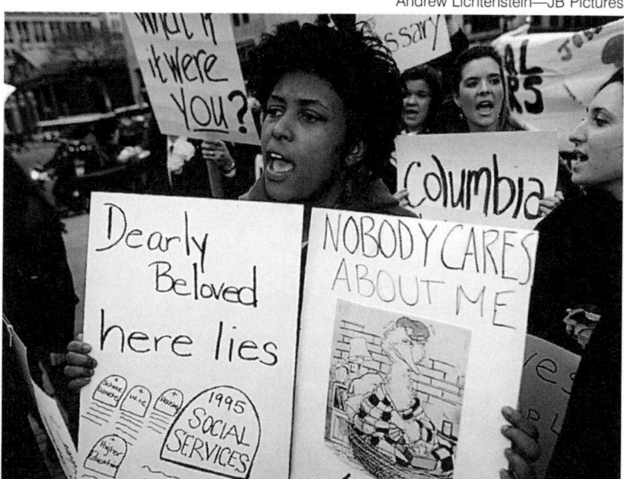

In May 1995 protesters in Washington, D.C., denounce Republican-proposed budget cuts in social programs—cuts the Democrats viewed as "mean-spirited."

If the results were indicative of how the majority of the public viewed health care reform, the conclusion of this pollster was that passage of a meaningful health care reform bill—that is, meaningful to the public—was most unlikely. Moreover, once the public discovered that the health care reform proposals, including that of the president, did not address *its* concerns, it would turn against the administration, as would members of Congress when it came to actually passing any legislation.

A doomed plan

The debate on health care reform in the United States has been going on without resolution since 1910, when a compulsory system of health insurance was first called for. After the failure of health care reform in September 1994, an interesting bit of recent history came to light. In 1991 presidential hopeful Clinton was in search of a health care policy. He invited two health policy analysts to meet with him and a group of his advisers. The policy experts were Theodore Marmor, professor of public policy and politics at Yale School of Management, and Ronald F. Pollack, the head of Families U.S.A. Foundation, a Washington, D.C.-based advocacy organization. Marmor was an advocate of a Canadian-style single-payer plan, while Pollack supported a "play-or-pay" system built on the existing health care system but requiring employers to either provide health insurance for their employees (play) or contribute to a pool that would provide it (pay). Each expert argued in favor of his preferred plan. At the end of the discussion, Clinton turned to Marmor and said, "Ted, you win the argument." Then, pointing to Pollack, he said, "but we're going to do what he says." Everyone in the room agreed that even considering a single-payer system would prompt immediate Republican cries of "socialized medicine," which the press then would faithfully report, spelling doom for any such proposal.

On Sept. 26, 1994, Senate Majority Leader George J. Mitchell officially declared the president's health care reform bill (the American Health Security Act) and health care reform itself "dead" for the year. But from September 1992, when President Clinton addressed Congress outlining his plan, to January 1993, when he appointed Hillary Rodham Clinton to head the President's Task Force on National Health Care Reform, to the day in September 1994 when the plan took its last breath, health care reform was the most prominent public policy issue in the country. No single factor was responsible for the downfall. As Robin Toner suggested in "Autopsy on Health Care" in the *New York Times,* the demise of health care reform could be compared to the death in *Murder on the Orient Express,* where most of the suspects had their hands on the knife at one time or another.

After the 1992 presidential election, there was political and public like-mindedness in regard to health care reform; almost no group, whether special-interest or political, wanted to be cast as an opponent, and most members in both houses of Congress initially were convinced that a health reform bill would come out of the 103rd Congress. That support, however, was not for all aspects of the president's plan. For example, even though the American Medical Association (AMA) leadership joined Hillary Clinton in a September 1993 White House Rose Garden ceremony, toasting the plan and expressing support of universal coverage, employer mandates, and reform of the insurance industry, the organization was opposed to "premium caps" and other cost-control measures. By the end of 1993, when the promise of an overhauling of the country's health care system had been turned into a 1,342-page act, virtually no group was a firm supporter of the plan, and by D-Day (Death Day) a year later, it was difficult to find anyone who had anything good to say about the plan.

Assessing the failure

The factors that contributed to the demise of health care reform could be categorized as follows:

The Clinton plan itself. It might have been a predictor of things to come that in the president's September 1993 speech to Congress, in which he outlined his six reform principles—"security, simplicity, savings, choice, quality, and responsibility"—it took him longest to explain simplicity. With health care reform the president attempted to do something grand to redeem his campaign promise of a government devoted to the "forgotten middle class." His plan, however, was a compromise between the conventionally liberal and conservative approaches to addressing the problems of the health care system. This resulted in his displeasing both the liberal single-payer advocates and the conservative free-market advocates. He also appeared to be defending just the kind of big bureaucratic program he ran against as a "new Democrat" at a time when the public was developing a distrust of government and an antipathy toward government bureaucracy.

Whether the plan the president proposed was in reality any more complex than the existing system is debatable, but it is clear from polls that the public thought it was. A hallmark of the plan was the establishment of a new administrative body known as the regional health alliance. Among other things, these alliances would have eliminated insurers' opportunities to select the families and individuals they preferred to enroll. In February 1994 only 25% of Americans surveyed claimed to know what a "health alliance" was. To this day the contents of the president's plan remain a mystery to the public at large.

The news media and public opinion. It is generally agreed that the media failed to clarify the issues and adequately educate the public so it could understand the arguments made by both supporters and opposers. Nor did the media do enough to evaluate the arguments made in regard to the plan's reliability and validity. Public confusion and cynicism prevailed.

While the early poll results indicated that half the public wanted a radical change in the health care system, it has been suggested by policy analysts that those results were taken too literally by the Clinton administration. The public was primarily concerned with "radical" improvement of the system that delivered its own care, while to those in the capital, radical meant something far different. For example, Bill McInturff, a Republican pollster, reported that when people were asked exactly what they meant by radical change, they said, "If I lose my job, I don't want to lose my coverage, and I don't want it to cost so much." McInturff added, "What they were really talking about was portability. So what in Washington was considered incremental change was to people out in the country radical."

By 1994 the improved U.S. economy meant that Americans were less fearful of losing their jobs and health insurance than they had been when the president was elected. This took much of the urgency out of the debate; crime and urban problems then took the limelight.

NEWS*CAP*

Doctors in the House—and Senate

When the 104th U.S. Congress opened in January 1995, five physicians took their places, the most in the nation's history. Bill Frist, a thoracic surgeon and a Tennessee Republican, became the first doctor in 20 years to sit in the Senate. Three physicians were elected to the House on the Republican ticket: Dave Weldon, a Florida internist; Greg Ganske, an Iowa reconstructive surgeon; and Tom Coburn, an Oklahoma family practitioner. One Democratic representative, Jim McDermott, a psychiatrist from the state of Washington, was reelected to his fourth term.

Two other physicians, Jerry Labriola, a pediatrician from Connecticut, and Ben Clayburgh, an orthopedic surgeon from North Dakota, were defeated for Senate seats, while three physician-aspirants to the House lost their bids: Eugene Fontenot, a surgeon and hospital administrator from Texas; A. John Elliot, an orthopedic surgeon from Rhode Island; and Kevin Vigilante, an internist, also from Rhode Island. Earlier, 12 physicians had been defeated in primaries.

Steve Greenberg; reprinted courtesy of the Seattle Post-Intelligencer

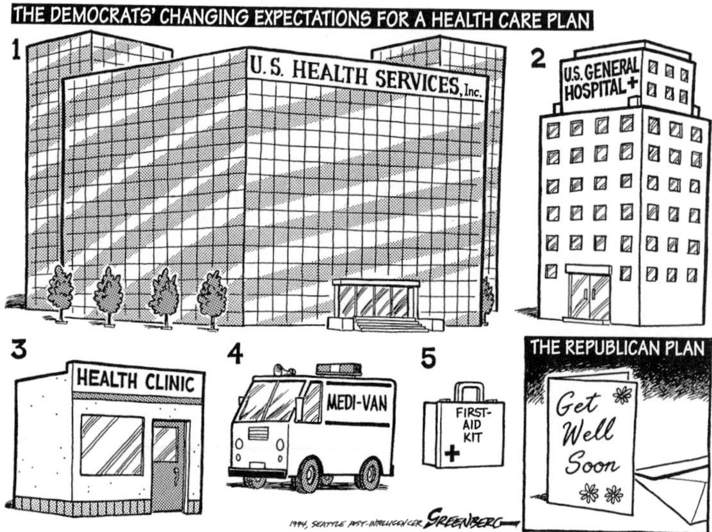

In a large poll conducted in September 1993, 75% of respondents said they favored a guarantee of universal coverage. Eventually, however, individuals with coverage came to believe that universal coverage would mean higher costs, rationing of care, and lack of personal choice about care, and their enthusiasm waned. As Drew Altman, president of the Henry J. Kaiser Family Foundation, said in August 1994 about a fundamental underlying dynamic that guides the public's support of social programs, "The American people want change as long as it doesn't cost them too much or affect them too much personally."

Special-interest groups. When the public was polled as to *why* health care reform failed, it said that special-interest groups and lobbyists were primarily to blame. The Center for Public Integrity reported in the spring 1995 issue of the journal *Health Affairs,* a volume devoted entirely to health reform, that health care reform was the most heavily lobbied initiative in recent U.S. history. In fact, it has been estimated that special-interest groups spent an estimated $120 million to $300 million to defeat the plan, while only $12 million to $15 million was spent in support of it. The National Federation of Independent Business (NFIB), representing 600,000 small businesses, was reported to have spent $40 million alone fighting the plan.

Big business. Big business's response to health care reform was initially positive because it thought the president's plan would help control its own rising health care costs. By May 1993, when it appeared that not only would it be quite a while before businesses might see such a reduction but that their own increasingly successful efforts to keep costs down were being jeopardized, opposition began to surface. Employers' skepticism centered on fears that they would end up subsidizing the cost of reform. In February 1994 the Business Roundtable, representing 200 of the nation's largest corporations, threw its support behind a more modest rival plan, that of Rep. Jim Cooper, which was dubbed "Clinton lite." At the same time, both the National Association of Manufacturers and the U.S. Chamber of Commerce came out against the Clinton plan.

Small business. While small business, arguably, became the most potent special-interest group opposing the Clinton plan, it is not true, as was often reported, that its opposition was monolithic. Most of the small business community's opposition to the plan stemmed from its distrust of the president's claims that there would be sufficient subsidies for small businesses to pay for their employees' health coverage and that workers would not have to be laid off because of the cost of the employer mandates.

The NFIB was able to mobilize the majority of its members against the plan. Among other things, the lobby put pressure on the U.S. Chamber of Commerce to reverse its original position in support of employer mandates, a critical element of the plan.

The insurance industry. Given that the Clinton plan included mandatory purchasing alliances, which would have provided individuals and businesses with a menu of insurance choices, many independent insurance agents would have been edged out of selling health insurance. Thousands of agents then informed their clients that the Clinton administration wanted to replace the personalized services with a giant, impersonalized bureaucracy, which thus added many of those clients to the chorus of complainers about the plan. It was also expected that if the Clinton plan were to pass, most of the nation's 500 or so health insurers would be driven out of the business, with the major beneficiaries being the five monoliths of the industry—Prudential, Cigna, Aetna, Travelers, and Metropolitan Life—as well as the more than 70 Blue Cross and Blue Shield plans.

Thus, it was the smaller insurance companies, represented by the Health Insurance Agency of America (HIAA), that felt they had the most to lose. Soon after the president's September 1993 address to Congress, the HIAA began its notorious "Harry and Louise" television commercial campaign, which featured a typical middle-class working couple fretting, among other things, about the likelihood that they might have to switch doctors under the president's plan. That campaign cost $17 million and generated 250,000 calls and letters to Congress. Some policy analysts believe that next to small business, Harry and Louise had more impact on the failure of health care reform than any other force.

Politics. At a White House meeting in February 1994 attended by Democratic leaders of both houses of Congress, House members, flush with optimism, reassured the president that they could get the bill through their chamber that year but cautioned him not to expect any Republican support. Sen. Daniel Patrick Moynihan, however, pointed out that for any health care bill to pass in the Senate, there would need to be a 60-vote filibuster-proof majority and that without Republican support a bill would not get through. This suggested that President Clinton should seek a compromise with the Republicans rather than exclude them. Apparently, however, that advice was lost on the president and his congressional allies. The decision to forgo a bipartisan, less-confrontational approach set the scene for a series of political fiascoes that contributed not only to the demise of health care reform but to the Republicans' gaining control of both houses of Congress in the 1994 midterm elections.

The initial response of the Republican leadership to the Clinton plan was to leave open the possibility that it would be willing to negotiate with the president on the crafting of a bill that could receive bipartisan support. The main exception was 1996 presidential candidate Sen. Phil Gramm, who had taken an implacable position against the plan. Gramm claimed that "if people understood that this bill took away something more important than their money, their job, their health care, if they understood it took away their freedom, that [would be] the little stone with which we could slay Goliath." As conservative criticism mounted, other Republicans rushed to take Gramm's position, and public support for the president and his plan began to erode.

An additional problem was that Democrats, upon whom the president had set his hopes for victory, could not agree among themselves on the content of a health care reform bill, and many started jumping off the health care reform train, which thus destroyed any pretext of a unified democratic caucus. The desertion by members of his own party made Clinton look weak, and the weaker he seemed, the more they deserted him.

Perhaps the most ironic aspect of the demise of the president's proposal was that the public joined with Republicans in believing that health care choices would be reduced for the average American. Now, however, with an ever-increasing number of employed people covered by limited- or no-choice managed-care programs, it appears that the public might well have had more choice under the Clinton plan than it has without it.

Is health reform really dead?

It is understandable that there has been a reluctance on the part of many in the 104th Congress to reopen the health care debate. Moreover, it is unlikely that the two major factors responsible for the nation's health care "crisis"—a lack of access to comprehensive health care and the escalating cost of care—will be seriously addressed within the next five years.

In the Republicans' Contract with America, the words *health* or *health care reform* were not even mentioned. Moreover, balancing the budget by the year 2002, a cornerstone of the contract, would require a reduction in the growth of or a cut in the $176 billion Medicare program and the $90 billion Medicaid program—both politically risky steps.

It had become clear even prior to the demise of health care reform that trends in the health care marketplace were such that the health care system of the future would be in striking contrast to the system most Americans had envisioned or even the one they once had.

After the federal government pulled back from health care reform, the business community stepped up its reform efforts. Those activities were largely responsible for:

- a slowing of the rise in premium costs and a lowering of employer health care costs
- an increase in the number of employees enrolled in managed-care plans from 29% in 1988 to 51% in 1993
- a decrease in the proportion of employees with conventional insurance plans (non-managed-care plans) from 73% in 1988 to 33% in 1993
- an increase in the share of health care costs paid by employees

State action

With the lack of attention to health care reform at the federal level, action has recently moved to the states. While some states are directing their efforts toward increasing access to care, only a few will enact comprehensive reforms that approach universal coverage. Instead, most states will focus on incremental legislation and build on the momentum of market-based reforms that are already under way. In 1994, 47 states were experimenting with some type of cost-containment measure to curb Medicaid outlays. In May 1995 Delaware, Massachusetts, and Minnesota were added to the nine states that already have Medicaid waivers allowing them to shift Medicaid beneficiaries into managed-care plans and use projected savings to expand coverage. Massachusetts will expand coverage to 400,000 uninsured persons. Minnesota will extend Medicaid eligibility to children up to age 19 who live in families with incomes below 275% of the poverty level, and Delaware will expand Medicaid to an additional 8,000 low-income adults and children.

To date, the only state that can be said to have implemented both Medicaid and statewide reform through a mandated insurance program is Hawaii. Since 1974 Hawaii has required all businesses to provide a basic benefits package with employees required to chip in a maximum of 1.5% of wages for premiums. Medicaid covers the poorest Hawaiians, and a separate state program covers part-time workers, low-wage earners, and others who are not covered by Medicaid or employer plans. Approximately 95% of Hawaiians enjoy health coverage.

In 1993 a Washington state health reform plan was approved by the legislature. It was patterned after President Clinton's managed-competition model. The plan required all employers to offer health insurance, required every insurer to offer minimum state-defined policies, and placed limits on increases in medical premiums. After the Republican landslide in 1994, the new legislature rescinded these requirements.

Before the governor signed the replacement legislation, he was assured that it would preserve the insurance portability and preexisting-condition regulations of the 1993 act.

Under a law that took effect in New Hampshire in 1995, insurers cannot deny coverage for preexisting conditions, and rates must be based on the expected utilization of health services by subscribers as a whole, not on an individual's health status, sex, age, or profession. Previously when insurers have used such factors in determining premiums, the high cost has often put coverage out of reach of smaller companies.

In spite of the limited emphasis on health care, approximately 15 health-care-related bills were introduced quietly in the early part of first term of the 104th Congress. None would have ensured universal coverage, controlled overall health care costs, or imposed employer mandates. Rather the reform issues the Republicans addressed were those that appeared to be of concern to most of the voters. They included restricting "cherry picking" (the denial of coverage to people with preexisting health conditions), "portability" (the worker's ability to retain health care coverage when switching jobs), and the political hot potato of cost reductions to specifically targeted programs such as Medicare and Medicaid.

Formerly it was the conservative Republicans who had either extolled the virtues of the status quo or denied there was a health care crisis. Now that the Republicans were in power, however, they were trying to persuade the public that there *was* a crisis and that the status quo was too expensive to sustain.

In fact, there were more uninsured Americans in 1995 (41 million) than the 37 million there had been when the president called for universal coverage. As for the cost of care, the 1995 national health expenditures were for the first time projected to surpass a trillion dollars, accounting for over 14% of the country's gross domestic product.

Summing up

In the health care debates of 1993–94, instead of a reasoned discussion in which accurate, truthful, and reliable data were presented, what occurred was a confusing, biased, and misleading discussion of an unwieldy and complex issue that was not amenable to a debate of sound bites. Evidence was offered for just about any claim or charge that was made, and the opportunity was provided for both sides to stir up fears and resentments in an attempt to make people feel threatened or cheated.

It would have been much healthier if there could have been an honest, open, and informed debate on one of the most important public policy issues ever to face the country. Arguably the only truly successful health care program in the U.S. in 1994 was NBC's top-rated "ER."

—*Lester E. Block, D.D.S., M.P.H.*

Pres. Bill Clinton and Hillary Rodham Clinton attempt to sell their health care plan to the American public on June 30, 1994. On Sept. 26, 1994, the American Health Security Act was officially proclaimed "dead."

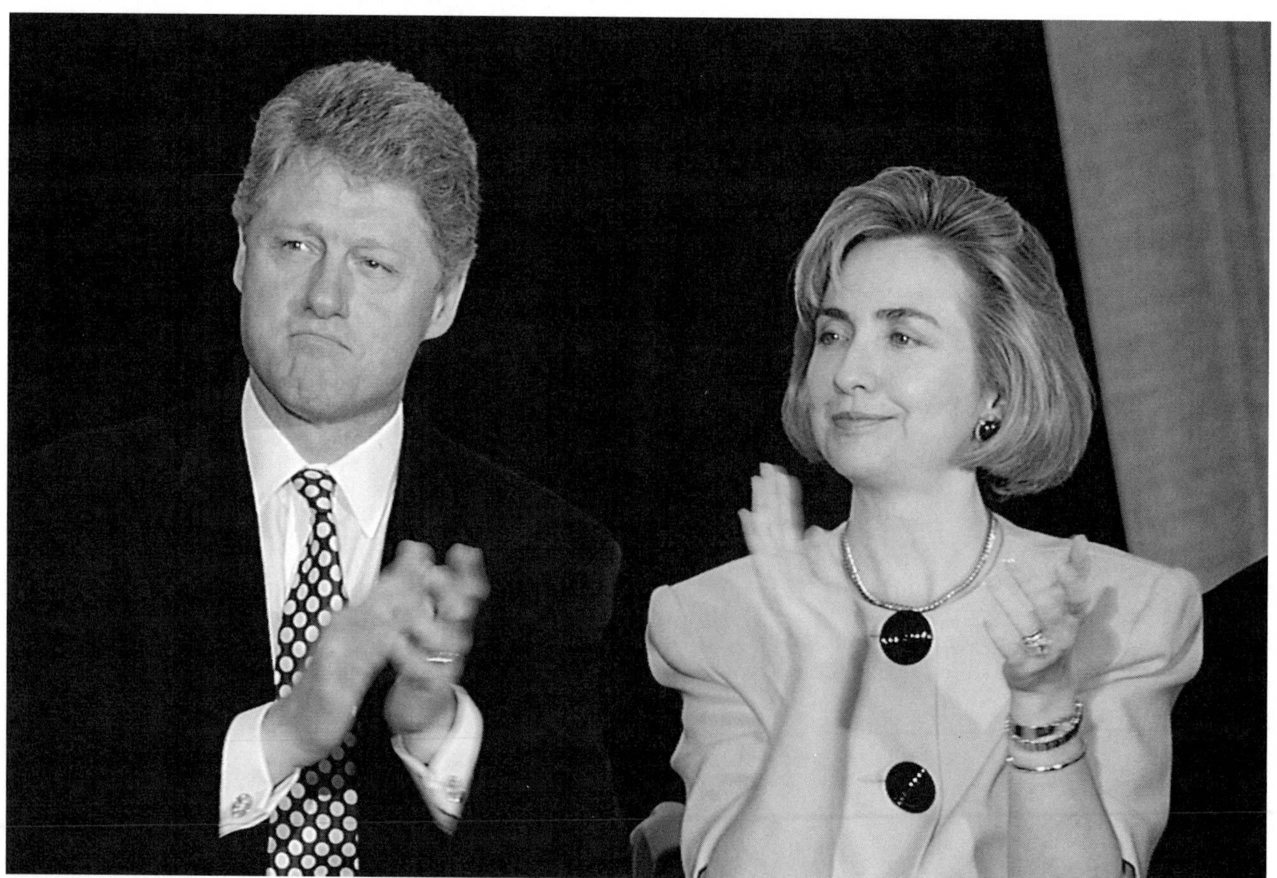

Larry Downing—Sygma

Strep: Growing Deadlier?

"Killer bug ate my face," proclaimed the headline in one British tabloid. "Dither—and you die," cautioned another. In May 1994 reports from England of a cluster of cases of a "flesh-eating" disease—a group A streptococcal infection capable of destroying body tissues in a matter of hours—raised an alarm around the world. Physicians and health departments across the U.S. received calls from anxious individuals inquiring whether they or their children were at risk. Some even expressed concern that travel to England might be unsafe. In response to sensationalistic news coverage, the World Health Organization, the U.S. Centers for Disease Control and Prevention, and other disease-surveillance agencies attempted to reassure a fearful public that invasive strep infections had not increased in prevalence in recent years, despite their increasing preeminence in the news. Some authorities in the field disagreed with this assessment.

Whether severe, life-threatening group A strep infections are on the rise or not, there is no doubt that cases have been reported recently from around the world. These dramatic infections—collectively called streptococcal toxic shock syndrome (strep TSS)—attack people of all ages, affect many organs of the body, and lead to shock and death in as many as 70% of patients. Beyond these facts, many questions remain. Has strep TSS always existed, or is it a relatively "new" disease? Is it more common today than in the past? Is it growing more lethal?

George Phillips—Sipa

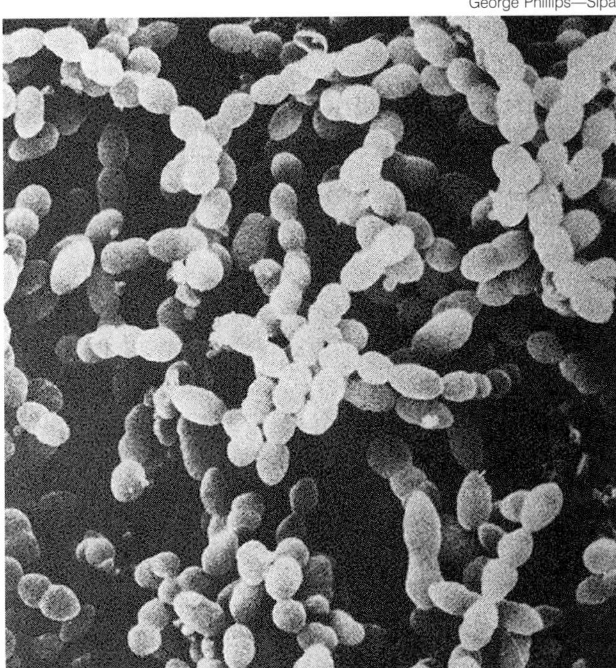

The group A streptococcus, viewed through a scanning electron microscope, reveals its characteristic string, or chain, of round, berrylike structures.

The many faces of Group A strep infection

The group A streptococcus (scientific name, *Streptococcus pyogenes*) is one member of a large family of bacteria, the streptococci. This single bacterium is capable of causing many different diseases. The name streptococcus is derived from two Greek words, *streptos* ("twisted") and *kokkos* ("berry"), and alludes to the organism's appearance under the microscope. Currently, more than 80 different subtypes of group A streptococcus, or GAS, are recognized. They are distinguished by minor structural differences in a protein, called M protein, on the surface of the bacterial cell.

GAS is a uniquely human pathogen. Only rarely is it found in other animals, and even when present, it does not cause disease. It lives on the skin and mucous membranes and has a variety of special qualities that enable it to interact in highly specific ways with various components of the human immune system.

As mentioned above, group A streptococcus causes a remarkable variety of diseases. The most important are:

Strep throat. Streptococcal pharyngitis, or strep throat, is the most common type of group A streptococcal infection. The symptoms include chills, fever, and an extremely painful sore throat, particularly when the person swallows. When examining a patient with suspected strep throat, doctors look for evidence of swelling of the tonsils (tonsillitis), redness of the mucous membranes lining the throat, whitish-yellow accumulations of pus on the back of the throat, and swelling of the lymph nodes beneath the skin of the neck and under the chin. With appropriate antibiotic treatment, strep throat usually clears up in four to five days. Untreated, however, this condition may lead to the development of rheumatic fever (*see* below).

Because there are many other causes of sore throat—including the common cold, influenza, and infectious mononucleosis—it is necessary to test for the presence of GAS in order to determine the course of treatment. First, a cotton swab is gently rubbed on the back of the throat. Next, this swab is used to inoculate a culture medium in a laboratory dish. Organisms removed from the throat can thus be grown in the laboratory, a process that takes about 24 hours. Alternatively, the material collected from the throat can be mixed with antibodies against group A streptococcus and a result obtained within a few minutes. Since the rapid test is sometimes inaccurate, it is usually used in conjunction with the slower but more reliable laboratory culture. If group A strep is confirmed, the physician will prescribe an antibiotic, usually penicillin.

Scarlet fever. Scarlet fever, also called scarlatina, most commonly occurs in association with strep throat but can also result from infection of surgical wounds by *S. pyogenes.* The infection is characterized by a widespread, bright red skin rash accompanied by high fever. Temperatures of 39.4°–40° C (103°–104° F) are typical and, prior to the availability of antibiotics and antifever (antipyretic) medications (*e.g.,* aspirin, acetaminophen, and the nonsteroidal anti-inflammatory agents), children often died of severe complications of high fever, such as dehydration and seizures.

Epidemics of scarlet fever killed thousands of people in Europe in the 15th and 16th centuries. Over the past century, however, scarlet fever has declined in incidence, and today, when it does occur, it is a very mild disease.

Rheumatic fever. Following a streptococcal infection of the throat, some patients develop muscle aches, pain and swelling of the joints, and, less commonly, a red skin rash and pea-sized nodules beneath the skin. St. Vitus' dance, also known as Sydenham's chorea, characterized by involuntary movements of the face and extremities, may also develop. These signs and symptoms are transient and are not immediately life-threatening. The major serious complication of rheumatic fever is heart disease or, more specifically, damage to the heart valves. Though some patients die during the acute stages of rheumatic fever, most live relatively normal, symptom-free lives for several decades but then develop heart failure.

In the past 30 years, replacement of diseased human heart valves with mechanical or porcine valves (*i.e.,* from pig hearts) has allowed those with rheumatic heart disease to live normal lives. The incidence of rheumatic fever has declined dramatically in the past 50 years in the United States and Western Europe. In certain parts of the world, however, such as India, rheumatic fever continues to be prevalent and is a leading cause of death in adults under age 40.

Impetigo and poststreptococcal glomerulonephritis. Impetigo, a superficial infection of the skin, may be caused by GAS or the unrelated organism *Staphylococcus aureus.* It occurs most commonly in children living in tropical environments. Poor hygiene may be a predisposing factor, which accounts for the appearance of impetigo among homeless adults.

NEWS*CAP*

TB Aloft

The first cases of infectious tuberculosis (TB) transmitted aboard a commercial airliner were reported in 1995 by the Centers for Disease Control and Prevention (CDC). Four persons were infected while sitting near an individual with active TB during a flight from Chicago to Honolulu. In another case a flight attendant transmitted TB to fellow crew members and four passengers who had been on several of the attendant's flights.

While the risk for TB transmission on aircraft is no greater than in other confined spaces, the CDC nonetheless issued a recommendation that persons known to have infectious TB not travel on commercial planes or other forms of commercial transport. The agency also said that airlines should notify all potentially exposed passengers when it is discovered that an individual with TB was infectious at the time of the flight and exposure was prolonged and occurred on a flight lasting longer than eight hours. Priority should be given to notifying passengers and flight crew who—on the basis of their proximity to the infected traveler—were at the greatest risk for exposure.

Group A Strep Infections: Patterns over Time

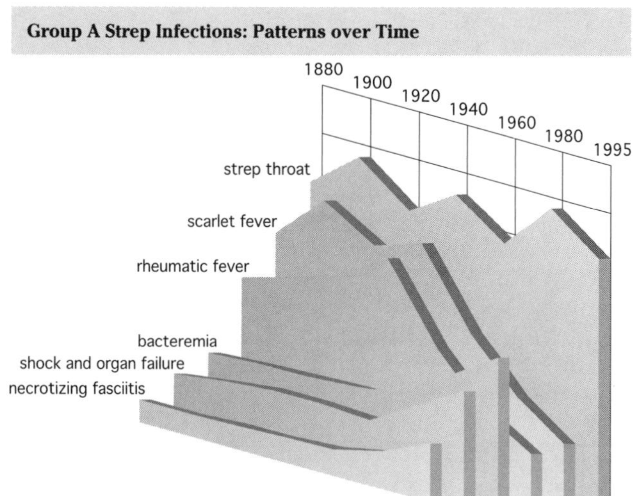

A small number of patients with impetigo due to GAS may develop a severe kidney disease, called poststreptococcal glomerulonephritis, two to three weeks after the onset of the skin infection. Epidemics of this form of nephritis have occurred in the U.S. and elsewhere, but today it is a very rare complication of GAS infection.

Erysipelas and cellulitis. Superficial infections of the skin resulting in a brilliant red or salmon-colored raised rash (erysipelas) or a smooth area of pinkish-colored skin (cellulitis) may be due to GAS. When red streaks extending up an extremity are associated with either of these streptococcal skin infections, the condition of lymphangitis (inflammation of the lymph channels) is present; a more common name is blood poisoning. True blood poisoning—infection of the bloodstream—will occur if lymphangitis is allowed to progress, since the lymph channels ultimately empty into the bloodstream at a point near the heart.

Necrotizing fasciitis. Necrotizing fasciitis is a deep-seated infection of the tissue beneath the skin that results in rapid destruction of the fascia, the connective tissue covering the muscle, or, in some cases, the muscle itself (a condition called myonecrosis or necrotizing myositis). The latter is the disease that caused Canadian political leader Lucien Bouchard to lose his left leg in December 1994.

Necrotizing fasciitis was first described in the medical literature in 1924 by F.L. Meleney, a U.S. physician working in China. It was termed streptococcal gangrene and was probably similar to some of the cases of so-called hospital gangrene reported by military surgeons during the French revolutionary and Napoleonic wars (1792–1815) and the American Civil War (1861–65). From 1924 until the mid-1980s, necrotizing fasciitis caused by group A streptococcus was relatively rare. In the past 10 years, however, many reports have documented an increase in the frequency and severity of this condition. Not all tissue-destroying infections are caused by group A streptococcus. Therefore, it is extremely important that a specific diagnosis be established as soon as possible so that if GAS is indeed present, an appropriate antibiotic (penicillin, clindamycin, or both) can be prescribed and dead (necrotic) tissue removed.

Streptococcal toxic shock syndrome (strep TSS). Strep TSS is a severe, life-threatening infection first described in the 1980s. It is characterized by the rapid onset of shock and multiple organ failure. Many patients develop bacteremia (*i.e.,* bacterial infection of the bloodstream) and suffer severe pain at sites where bacteria have become established in the deep tissues. The fatality rate is high, ranging from 30% in the U.S. to as high as 70% in other parts of the world. Many victims are previously healthy individuals in the prime of life.

Disease patterns: highly variable

The primary reservoir of the group A streptococcus in nature is the human throat—roughly 5% of adults and 15–20% of children may harbor GAS in their throats at a given time. During the winter months in temperate climates, this figure may be as high as 70% in schoolchildren. Not all of these children will have sore throats—they are simply carriers of the bacterium.

Several different strains of GAS are often present in a given community at a given time. When a new strain enters a community, a small but predictable epidemic of strep throat generally occurs. In fact, in the Northern Hemisphere the number of cases of strep throat remains quite constant from year to year. Despite this consistency, the incidence of complications of GAS—rheumatic fever, scarlet fever, severe tonsillitis—has decreased markedly over the past 50 years. This reduction can be attributed at least in part to the availability of penicillin.

Even before the discovery of penicillin, however, significant variations occurred in the incidence and severity of a variety of GAS infections. For example, 4,000 deaths were associated with a major outbreak of scarlet fever in Boston in 1735–36. This epidemic spread westward and gradually dissipated over the ensuing five or six years. In the 1870s the fatality rate from scarlet fever in New York City was 35%, yet by 1900 it had dropped to only 1–2%. Although the number of cases of scarlet fever continues to wax and wane, the seriousness of the disease has remained constant for the past several decades; it rarely, if ever, causes death today. Some authorities speculate that major changes in the virulence of the group A streptococcus occur in a regular cycle every 100–150 years. Within that time span other cycles may occur, affecting the incidence but not the severity of infection. For example, the German microbiologist Werner Kohler has demonstrated that from the 1950s to the present, a specific strain of GAS associated with scarlet fever has appeared and disappeared regularly every four to seven years.

At any rate, from about 1875 to 1985 there was a gradual decrease in both the frequency and the seriousness of severe streptococcal infections, including scarlet fever and rheumatic fever. In the mid- to late 1980s, however, severe life-threatening GAS infections began to reemerge. Most authorities believe that the incidence of these severe infections has remained constant in the past few years, although no definitive epidemiological studies have been performed. (Most Western countries do not keep official statistics on group A strep infections, largely because of the absence of severe cases in recent history.) Nonetheless, the cases reported in the past decade appear to be much more severe than those described initially—the fatality rate in the 1924 Chinese outbreak was 20%, compared with today's 30–70% range—despite antibiotic therapy and major advances in critical care.

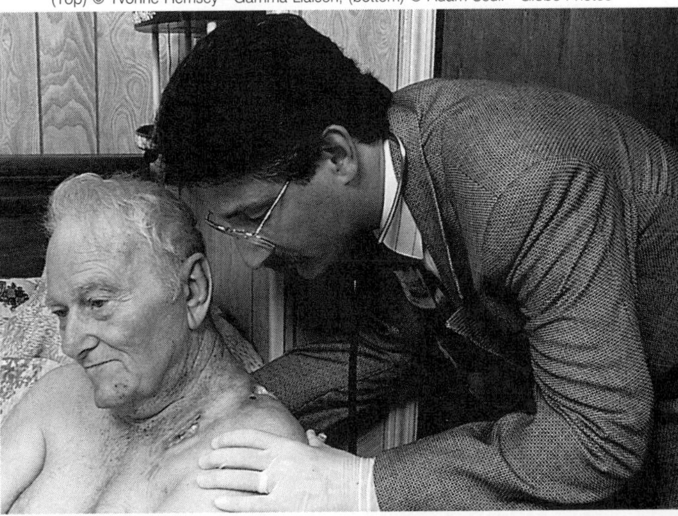

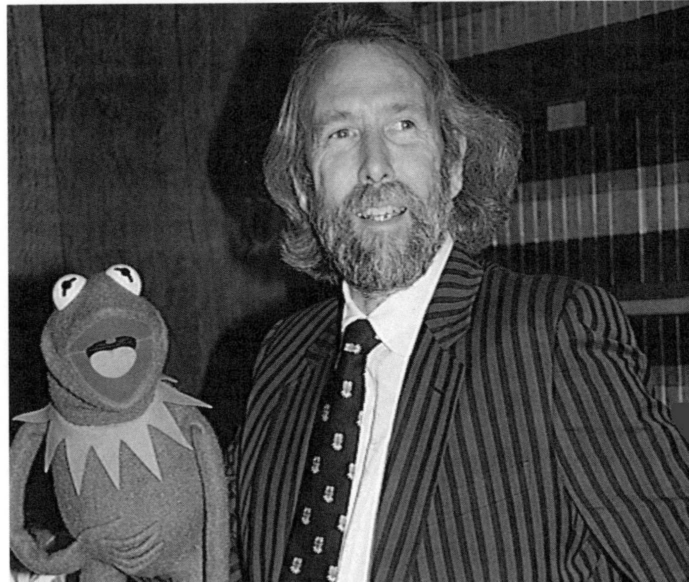

(Top) A doctor examines the lesions of necrotizing fasciitis, a form of group A streptococcus (GAS) infection that rapidly destroys tissue and may be fatal. This patient was saved by prompt treatment. Streptococcal toxic shock syndrome, a severe, invasive GAS infection, took the life of Muppet creator Jim Henson (above) in 1990.

Recognizing life-threatening infections

Any group A strep infection associated with the rapid onset of shock and organ failure can be considered strep TSS—a potentially fatal disease. Approximately 50% of cases of strep TSS are associated with necrotizing fasciitis. In the remaining cases, strep TSS is present along with pneumonia, sore throat, peritonitis (inflammation of the abdominal lining), septic arthritis (joint infections), or eye infection.

Pain is the most common initial symptom of strep TSS. It is abrupt in onset, is severe, and usually precedes the development of tenderness. The pain most commonly affects an extremity, but it may resemble the abdominal pain of peritonitis or pelvic inflammatory disease or the chest pain of acute heart attack. Before the onset of pain, 20% of patients have had an influenza-like illness characterized by fever, chills, body aches, and diarrhea. Recently, this author has also seen individuals with nausea, vomiting, and diarrhea associated with fever who subsequently developed strep TSS.

Fever is the most common physical sign (*i.e.,* objective finding, as distinct from a symptom, such as pain, which is subjective), although 10% of patients with strep TSS have profound hypothermia (subnormal body temperature) and are in shock at the time of admission to the hospital. Confusion is present in 55% of patients; others may be combative or comatose.

Eighty percent of patients who have strep TSS develop evidence of soft-tissue infection, such as localized swelling and redness of the skin. An ominous sign is the progression from swelling to the formation of vesicles (blisters) and then bullae (larger blisters), the latter appearing blue or violet in color. About 70% of patients with soft-tissue infection may develop necrotizing fasciitis or myositis. The tissue destruction may proceed extremely rapidly—in a matter of hours. Surgical removal of the affected tissue is frequently required. In some cases amputation of an affected limb is necessary.

Group A streptococci most commonly enter the body via cuts, abrasions, burns, slivers, insect bites, chicken pox lesions, or surgical incisions. In about half of patients who develop necrotizing fasciitis, however, the bacterium's portal of entry into the body cannot be identified. In analyzing many of these cases, this author and his colleagues have found that most of the patients had sustained a bruise to the muscle (without breaking the skin) and that the infection developed at the precise location of the prior injury. They hypothesize that the bacteria travel to the injury site via the bloodstream; the source of the bacteria, they believe, is an inapparent strep throat. These cases are particularly hard to diagnose because both patient and physician attribute the pain and swelling to the injury itself rather than to a coexisting infection elsewhere in the body.

Whether or not a break in the skin is evident, the combination of severe pain and swelling or pain plus fever and chills should be sufficient to cause one to suspect a diagnosis of necrotizing fasciitis. Another clue in youngsters with chicken pox is the persistence of fever for more than four days. A child with chicken pox who still has a fever on day six of the illness should be taken to the doctor. If this child also has increasing pain in an extremity or increasing redness around a pox lesion, he or she may have a serious group A strep infection of the skin or necrotizing fasciitis.

Approximately 20% of those diagnosed with strep TSS have no soft-tissue infection. A variety of other types of infections may be present in these patients, including infection of the eye (endophthalmitis), liver (perihepatitis), abdominal cavity (peritonitis), or heart muscle (myocarditis). A small percentage of strep TSS patients have overwhelming infection of the bloodstream.

Wreaking havoc on the body

Group A streptococci adhere to the mucous membranes of the throat by means of components on the surface of the organism's cell wall. M protein is one such component. If an individual has antibodies against M protein, he or she is able to ward off infection. In the absence of such antibodies, a localized infection such as a sore throat may develop. Such infections are usually of a mild nature. In a small percentage of people who lack antibodies, a more serious, invasive infection may develop.

M protein molecules vary in structure and, as noted above, these variations allow group A streptococci to be divided into over 80 different M protein types. A person may have immunity against several types and still be susceptible to others. Therefore, an individual can develop strep throat many different times. Immunity is acquired over time through infection by different strains of the bacterium. Consequently, strep throat is most common in childhood and is quite rare in individuals over age 35.

Strains of group A streptococci associated with strep TSS and necrotizing fasciitis produce toxins, harmful proteins that can affect the function of the immune system. Normally when immune system cells such as macrophages and lymphocytes respond to infection, they produce minute quantities of cytokines, proteins that enhance the function of other immune system components and thereby improve the body's defense against infection. Some streptococcal toxins interact with macrophages and lymphocytes to cause massive production of cytokines. In large quantities these otherwise beneficial substances have the ability to cause shock and organ failure. In essence, then, the streptococcal toxins cause the body to self-destruct. Scientists are convinced that these toxins play an important role in the disease process in strep TSS. It is not yet clear whether the present-day outbreaks of infection are due to new, more virulent toxins or increased production of previously existing toxins.

Combating strep: weapons of the future

Many strategies are being studied for combating severe group A streptococcal infections. One possibility is the development of antibiotics capable of preventing the synthesis of toxins. Penicillin, currently the drug of choice for these infections, acts by disrupting the formation of new bacterial cells, but it does not prevent existing cells from producing toxins. Clindamycin, on the other hand, has been found to stop bacterial toxin production in the laboratory and is effective against severe GAS infections in animals. It has not been thoroughly studied in these severe infections in humans, however. Clearly, there is room for new antibiotics against the group A streptococcus.

Other strategies include neutralizing the toxins circulating in the blood or decreasing the production of cytokines. Still another involves the use of monoclonal antibodies (synthetic antibodies that can target specific proteins) directed at cytokines that have formed in the tissue or blood. In addition to drug therapy, patients will continue to require oxygen, massive amounts of intravenous fluids, dialysis for kidney failure, and aggressive surgical treatment to remove nonviable tissue.

In the meantime, scientists are continuing to explore the interactions between the human immune system and the streptococcal surface components and toxins in hopes of discovering how one bacterium can cause such an array of diseases. The challenge for the future will be to devise ways to alter the body's response to the organism and to develop vaccines capable of preventing infection.

—*Dennis L. Stevens, Ph.D., M.D.*

Aid-in-Dying: Society's Dilemma

Should physicians help their patients die? Several harrowing cases have recently raised that question in the United States and elsewhere. There have also been muddled efforts in the U.S. to develop public policies addressing the question, as well as two failed state ballot initiatives—in Washington and California—to legalize "aid-in-dying," as physician-assisted suicide is called by its proponents. A third initiative, in Oregon, won the support of voters but was halted by a court injunction and was subsequently declared unconstitutional.

Meanwhile, U.S. health care providers and medical ethicists have followed with interest events in The Netherlands, the only country with a quasi-legal program of physician-performed euthanasia. (Euthanasia is the practice of killing or permitting the death of the hopelessly ill in a painless manner. It may be voluntary or involuntary.) For the members of a bioethics commission in New York state, The Netherlands' experience only confirmed their suspicions about the perils of legalizing physician assistance in suicide. Together these developments suggest that the struggle over public policy on euthanasia will continue to be intense. At the same time, they illustrate the complex relationship between moral judgments and public policies.

"Sanctity of life"

Sue Rodriguez, a 43-year-old British Columbian woman, suffered from amyotrophic lateral sclerosis (ALS), a progressive degenerative disease that renders the muscles useless but leaves the mind intact. Rodriguez wanted to end her life and requested a physician's help. Her case was notable for two reasons: it was taken up by the Canadian Supreme Court, and it became widely publicized as a result of Rodriguez' appearance on television. Despite a five-to-four ruling against her request, Rodriguez committed suicide in February 1994 with the aid of a physician and with a member of Canada's Parliament, Svend Robinson, in attendance. Robinson said that she died "with incredible courage and dignity."

Expressing the majority opinion, Supreme Court Justice John Sopinka argued that granting Rodriguez' request would compromise Canadians' "fundamental conception of the sanctity of life." The denial of the request reflected "the state's interest in protecting the vulnerable." In one of the dis-

Despite a ruling against her by Canada's Supreme Court, Sue Rodriguez, a 43-year-old amyotrophic lateral sclerosis patient, committed suicide in 1994 with a physician's help. She is pictured below with Svend Robinson, a member of Parliament who supported her decision to end her life.

Canapress; photograph, Chuck Stoody

senting opinions, Justices Claire L'Hereux-Dube and Beverly McLachlin wrote that making a distinction between suicide (which is not against Canadian law) and assisting in suicide denies "some people the choice of ending their lives solely because they are physically unable to do so, preventing them from exercising the autonomy over their bodies available to other people." Justice Peter Cory, another dissenter, wrote that "the right to die with dignity should be as well protected as is any other aspect of the right to life. State prohibitions that would force a dreadful, painful death on a rational but incapacitated terminally ill patient are an affront to human dignity."

Rodriguez was exactly the kind of person for whom the case in favor of physician-assisted suicide is most convincing. She was articulate, determined, and courageous; her mind remained sharp even as her body deteriorated and her suffering increased. Nonetheless, a majority of Canada's Supreme Court justices remained unconvinced.

Controversy in Michigan

The activities of one person—pathologist Jack Kevorkian—have made Michigan a principal focus of the U.S. debate over physician-assisted suicide. Kevorkian, who prefers the term *medicide,* had admitted to involvement in the deaths of 25 persons between June 1990 and August 1995. In 1992 the Michigan legislature passed a law that declared assisting in suicide illegal. The law was only temporary, however; it was set to expire in November 1994, at which time the state's Commission on Death and Dying, which the legislature had also created, was to make its recommendation on Michigan law regarding suicide.

The commission had a brief but contentious existence. The legislature determined its membership; the views of the members ranged from those of the right-to-life movement to those of the Hemlock Society, the group led by Derek Humphry that had lobbied for aid-in-dying laws in Washington, California, and Oregon. Advocates for persons with disabilities disrupted a March 1994 hearing, denouncing assisted suicide as "extermination without representation." Kevorkian himself dismissed the commission as "corrupt." Ultimately, on the question of whether physician assistance in suicide should be legal under certain conditions, the commission was split, with nine in favor, six opposed, and seven abstaining.

On Nov. 26, 1994, within hours after the expiration of the temporary law, Kevorkian assisted in the suicide of 72-year-old Margaret Garrish. In a televised broadcast eight months before her death, Garrish complained of severe pain—she had lost both legs and suffered from rheumatoid arthritis, advanced osteoporosis, and other disorders—and said she wished to end her life. In response to the broadcast, two physicians contacted Kevorkian and his attorney, seeking to dissuade him from helping her commit suicide and recommending more effective treatment for her pain.

According to Kevorkian, Garrish's family had asked him to wait until the law expired. He, however, did not feel constrained by the temporary statute, which he claimed was unconstitutional. "If these immoral idiots want to try and jail me, that's fine," he said. "I'm ready to make fools out of them again." Kevorkian had been both tried and imprisoned previously for his medicide practices. In December 1994 the Michigan Supreme Court upheld the statute that makes assisting in a suicide a criminal offense. Kevorkian petitioned the U.S. Supreme Court to reverse this decision, but on April 24, 1995, the high court refused to hear the case.

Changing the law: three states' attempts

In 1991 voters in the state of Washington defeated a referendum known as Initiative 119, which had been drafted by the Washington state chapter of the Hemlock Society. The official question on the ballot was: "Shall adult patients who are in a medically terminal condition be permitted to request and receive from a physician aid-in-dying?" Aid-in-dying was defined as "a medical service, provided in person by a physician, that will end the life of a conscious and mentally competent qualified patient in a dignified, painless, and humane manner, when requested voluntarily by the patient through a written directive." The initiative was vague enough to encompass active euthanasia by physicians. Active euthanasia occurs when an individual, in this case a physician, causes death—for example, by administering a lethal dose of drugs. In assisted suicide, by contrast, the physician supplies the means of death—in Kevorkian's recent cases, a canister of carbon monoxide—but the patient sets into motion the chain of events that results in his or her own death (*e.g.,* turning on poisonous gas or taking lethal drugs). Fifty-four percent of the voters opposed the initiative.

The following year California voted on a ballot initiative modeled on a Hemlock Society proposal. Like Washington's failed initiative, California's Proposition 161 would have legalized both physician-assisted suicide and active euthanasia, but it would have limited its application to people with six months or less to live. California's attempt was rejected by the same margin—54% to 46%—despite having more safeguards than were specified in the Washington initiative.

Only in Oregon, where active euthanasia was excluded and stringent conditions imposed, was a ballot initiative to legalize physician-assisted suicide successful. Known officially as Oregon Ballot Measure 16, the Death with Dignity Act was approved on Nov. 8, 1994, by a margin of 53% to 47%. The act stated:

> *An adult who is capable, is a resident of Oregon, and has been determined by the attending physician and consulting physician to be suffering from a terminal disease, and who has voluntarily expressed his or her wish to die, may make a written request for medication for the purpose of ending his or her life in a humane and dignified manner in accordance with this act.*

The measure was scheduled to become law on Dec. 8, 1994.

One provision specified that two doctors had to agree that the patient had six months or less to live. Patients had to make at least three separate requests for assistance in suicide, the last one in writing. Mandated waiting periods were also required; the second oral request had to be at least 15 days after the first one, and at least 48 hours had to elapse between the written request and the prescribing of the drugs that would be the means of committing suicide. Other protections were built in as well. The patient could rescind his or her request at any time. If either physician believed that a psychiatric disorder was present, the patient had to be referred for counseling. Residents of long-term-care facilities had to have a witness to their request who met the qualifications specified by the Oregon Department of Human Resources. Complete records of all assisted suicides were to be kept, and a sample of them were to be reviewed annually. And physicians were required to ask patients to notify their next of kin, although patients could choose to decline that request. If physicians demonstrated "good faith compliance" with these requirements, they would be exempt from civil or criminal liability. That is, they could neither be sued nor be charged with a crime.

Reactions to the Oregon measure were strong and varied. The American Medical Association declared that "physician-assisted suicide, even under the limited scope of the Oregon measure, is unethical and goes against the unalterable role of physicians as healers." Oregon's own medical association, on the other hand, was unable to achieve a consensus either to support or to oppose the measure and opted instead to appoint a task force to consider issues for dying patients. The Hemlock Society described the measure's passage as "a ground breaking victory for the people of Oregon," while an attorney for Kevorkian declared, "It's just the first domino to fall." The Vatican characterized it as "a day of mourning for all humanity." By Dec. 27, 1994, opponents of the new law were able to get a preliminary injunction against it, and six months later a federal judge declared the law unconstitutional, saying it violated the 14th Amendment's guarantee of equal protection.

The Dutch break new ground

Physicians have performed active euthanasia openly in The Netherlands since 1973, although the practice received increasing legal scrutiny in the 1980s. At that time Dutch courts articulated guidelines that, if followed by physicians, would exempt them from punishment for an act still considered a crime under Dutch law. In 1993 the Dutch parliament stopped short of legalizing active euthanasia, but it did codify the earlier guidelines into four "carefulness requirements": (1) the patient must be the source of the request, which must be completely voluntary; (2) the request must be consistent and repeated; (3) the patient must be told of alternatives; and (4) the suffering must be "perpetual, unbearable and hopeless." Physicians who complied with these conditions would be given immunity from prosecution.

In October 1994 a Dutch religious television network aired *Death on Request,* a documentary film that recorded the act of euthanasia. The patient, Cees van Wendel de Joode, was a 62-year-old man with ALS who died by lethal injection. The film caused a sensation in Europe. The filmmakers said they wanted to show the impact of such decisions on all the parties involved. They denied requests to allow the death scene to be broadcast in isolation from the rest of the film. The documentary was shown in its entirety in England in March 1995.

Dutch public opinion has increasingly accepted voluntary active euthanasia. Nearly half of those polled in 1966 said that physicians should not give lethal injections to patients who requested them. By 1991 only 9% in a similar poll were against euthanasia. A survey of more than 400 Dutch physicians in 1990–91 found that 49% had practiced active euthanasia, 22% in the previous two years; 38% said they had never done so but could imagine a situation in which they would. Only 13% said that they could not imagine circumstances under which they might practice active euthanasia. A majority—61%—reported that their views of active euthanasia had not changed during the course of their professional careers. Those who had changed their opinions were likely to have become less, rather than more, restrictive.

Critics of euthanasia are quick to cite the "slippery slope" argument—that is, once society sanctions the killing of certain patients, the circumstances under which such action is approved will gradually and inevitably broaden. Those critics can point with satisfaction to the case of Boudewijn Chabot, a Dutch psychiatrist who assisted in the suicide of a 50-year-old woman described as healthy and competent but despondent over the deaths of her two sons. Chabot claimed that the woman's suffering was genuine and deep, though not the product of any psychiatric disorder. She refused treatment with antidepressant drugs. Before acting, Chabot had discussed the case with four psychiatrists, a psychologist, and a general practitioner, all of whom agreed with his diagnosis, although none of them actually saw the patient. Chabot was acquitted by two lower courts, but the prosecution appealed the decisions. The case was finally heard by the Dutch Supreme Court in June 1994. This court found Chabot guilty of assisting in suicide but declined to punish him. The court did not take exception to the fact that Chabot had acted to relieve psychological rather than physical pain, nor did it object because the patient was not terminally ill. Rather, the court's objection was that no other physician had personally examined the woman. If one had, Chabot presumably would have been found innocent.

Compassion tempered by caution

The latter Dutch experience proved influential in New York. In May 1994 the New York State Task Force on Life and the Law unanimously recommended against proposals that would legalize assisted suicide and euthanasia, arguing that "the dangers of such a dramatic change in public policy would far outweigh any possible benefits." The report continued, "In light of the pervasive failure of our health care system to treat pain and diagnose and treat depression, legalizing assisted suicide would be profoundly dangerous for many individuals who are ill and vulnerable. The risks would be most severe for those who are elderly, poor, socially disadvantaged, or without access to good medical care."

The task force noted that adequate treatment for depression or pain frequently obviates the desire for suicide. On the other hand, if the prohibition against assisting in suicide or performing active euthanasia were abolished, the impetus for providing more effective pain relief and better diagnosis of depression would be diminished. A number of people might choose to die who would not have chosen to do so if they had been properly diagnosed and treated.

Further, the task force predicted that euthanasia of those incapable of consent would be a "likely, if not inevitable, extension of any policy permitting the practice for those who can consent." In support of this conclusion, the report cited a Dutch study showing that although an explicit request for euthanasia is supposedly required in The Netherlands, in nearly one-third of cases of death by active euthanasia, no such explicit request had been made. Another study estimated that 1.8% of all deaths in The Netherlands were from voluntary euthanasia, while 0.8% were from involuntary euthanasia—that is, killing "without a contemporaneous request from the patient." Still another study asked Dutch doctors whether the patients on whom they performed involuntary euthanasia were competent; 56% of patients were described as incompetent, 8% as possibly competent, and 36% as competent.

The New York task force expressed "deep compassion" for the suffering of terminally ill people, but it concluded that there are "better ways to give people greater control and relief from suffering than by legalizing assisted suicide and euthanasia." There is no contradiction in this combination of compassion for patients with determination not to legalize physician aid-in-dying; rather, the judgment sought to balance a variety of moral considerations in order to create a reasonable public policy.

Legitimate fears

The intellectual and political struggle over the control of death seems likely to persist. Much of the opposition to physician aid-in-dying has come from people who acknowledge that in certain cases physicians who assist in suicide or perform active euthanasia probably do nothing morally wrong. Their concern is that legalizing physician aid-in-dying will make matters worse rather than better. Given that public policies virtually always fall short of perfection in their implementation, a policy sanctioning physician aid-in-dying inevitably would have its share of errors. Undiagnosed cases of depression and abuses such as active euthanasia of incompetent persons are among them. Moreover, such a policy could divert attention from the search for more skillful and compassionate means to care for dying persons.

The fear of a slow, painful, and degraded death, coupled with powerful convictions about individual self-determination, will continue to activate supporters of physician-assisted suicide and active euthanasia. Likewise, fears about the consequences of a public policy sanctioning these acts will continue to energize the opposition.

—Thomas H. Murray, Ph.D.

Managed Care: Raising New Issues

How best to allocate limited medical resources is a dilemma as old as medical ethics itself. Today, however, the focus of questions about rationing has shifted from whether treatment is medically futile for the patient to whether it is financially futile for the payer. What kind of treatment patients are entitled to, how much they should be told, and what kind of care hospitals owe the dying are related ethical issues of current concern. All have in common the need for individual and personal resolution at the patient's bedside, rather than in a boardroom, committee room, or courtroom.

The case of "Baby K"

Babies who are born dying are among the most poignant cases any physician encounters. Perhaps because they represent new life, because they cannot speak for themselves, or because their parents are often terrified, these babies—for whom there is no hope of survival—usually receive intensive and very costly care. Yet if society cannot agree to limit sophisticated, expensive treatment for babies who cannot benefit from it, there seems little possibility of containing costs rationally. The recent case of the infant girl known to the courts and the media as "Baby K" exemplifies this dilemma.

Baby K was born on Oct. 13, 1992, with anencephaly—congenital absence of the brain cortex, which enables higher functions such as thought. The brain stem, the part of the brain that controls involuntary functions such as heartbeat and respiration, remained intact. Baby K was thus born in a "persistent vegetative state," or coma. Anencephalic babies cannot see or hear and are essentially unconscious. Without mechanical life support, very few live longer than a week. Many survive only a few hours.

Baby K's mother requested that everything possible be done to keep the infant alive, in keeping with the mother's strong Christian belief that all life should be protected. Fairfax Hospital, in Falls Church, Va., and its physicians could see no point in subjecting the permanently unconscious baby to continued mechanical ventilation. The hospital asked the federal district court in Richmond for permission to discontinue treatment. The judge denied permission, and so did a federal appeals court, the latter citing a constitutional amendment and three federal laws that would be violated if treatment were withdrawn. The infant's father wanted to discontinue intensive treatment, but his relationship with the mother had ended even before the birth, and the courts found his opinion to be "unpersuasive." In June 1994 the case was appealed to the U.S. Supreme Court, which declined to hear it.

In the meantime, the infant was transferred to a nursing home, although she required periodic readmission to the hospital for treatment of infections. She survived until April 1995. The costs of hospitalization were fully covered by Kaiser-Permanente, the mother's health maintenance organization (HMO). Some of the nursing home care was paid for by Medicaid.

From a medical ethics perspective, the case of Baby K represents a long series of missed opportunities. First, because an ultrasound scan had revealed the fetus's condition during the second trimester of pregnancy, many questions about her future could have been decided well before the birth. Such questions could have been resolved by the clinicians and the parents as medical and ethical concerns instead of by courts and judges as legal issues. Even after birth, the mediation process could have focused on whether treatment would improve the baby's quality of life or the function of her organs rather than concentrating solely on the psychological and emotional benefits to the mother. The issue of treatment choice could have been resolved by following accepted standards for medical care of the terminally ill, already practiced in hospices worldwide. A decision to provide compassionate care for the dying infant would have prevented the parents' disagreement and the standoff between the mother, on one hand, and the doctors, the hospital, and the baby's court-appointed guardian, on the other.

The case also raises the question of whether medical care is different from other consumer goods and services. In restaurants or hotels, for example, anything a consumer wants and can pay for, he or she gets. George J. Annas, a lawyer and medical ethicist at Boston University Schools of Medicine and Public Health, has written about Baby K:

> *It is impossible for physicians to argue credibly that treating patients in persistent vegetative states is contrary to standards of medical practice, because most physicians actually provide continuing treatment if the family insists. Treating medical care as a consumer good is a central reason why medical costs are out of control and why a national health plan that gives physicians financial incentives not to treat seems attractive to many policy makers.*

In the U.S., unlike France, Spain, and several other European countries, anencephalic infants are not considered "brain dead." Potential donor organs may not be removed until the infant's heart or brain function has ceased, by which time the organs are likely to have deteriorated. Some authorities would like to change the U.S. law to allow donor organs to be removed from these infants while they are still alive, as was recommended by the Ethical and Judicial Council of the American Medical Association (AMA) in 1995. Others, including many AMA members, strongly oppose such a step.

Futility: a matter of definition

In February 1995 Gregory Messenger, a Michigan dermatologist, was acquitted of manslaughter charges for turning off the respirator supporting the life of his 82-minute-old premature son. Michael Ryan Messenger, born 15 weeks premature on Feb. 8, 1994, weighed only 0.77 kg (1 lb 11 oz). Messenger and his wife had been told that the chances were less than fifty-fifty that the baby would live and that if he did survive, he might have severe disabilities. The Messengers had requested (prior to delivery) that the baby not be placed on life support.

Both of the cases discussed above show the legal authority that parents have over decisions regarding the care of their infants. Yet few physicians, attorneys, or medical ethicists believe that Messenger acted ethically; likewise, few authorities supported Baby K's mother in her insistence on life-sustaining treatment. Without clearly delineated standards of medical care for the terminally ill, and with cost containment growing in importance, it seems likely that regulators and third-party payers—not parents or doctors—will be making crucial medical decisions for the Baby K's and Michael Ryan Messengers of the future.

Both of these cases also highlight the continuing ethical debate about "futile" treatment. Different people define futility differently, depending on their own goals and values. If the goals of treatment (*e.g.,* cure, prevention, education, rehabilitation, or palliation) are unclear or disputed, however, then futility is in the eye of the beholder. Only if the goals of treatment are clear and agreed upon at the outset will those involved be able to agree whether a given treatment is indeed futile.

To cover or not to cover?

Managed care—a system of medical treatment in which the financing and delivery of care are integrated—is growing in popularity in the U.S. because it appears to be a way to control expenditures. At the top of the list of ethical issues in managed care are the type and extent of coverage to be provided. Which services are basic? How much coverage should employers offer their employees? Should managed-care plans or physicians inform patients about the limitations in coverage? Because financial incentives exist for physicians to "undertreat" patients, "Caveat emptor" is an increasingly necessary warning for patients and families.

Whether such plans should cover the costs of experimental treatment is another hotly debated issue. For one thing, the authorities may disagree as to whether a particular therapy or procedure is innovative or standard. For another, experimental treatments may be very expensive and risky and may increase the expectations and frustrations of the patient, the physician, and the health plan manager. Organ-transplant cases clearly illustrate these dilemmas.

In one such case, *Ralph Barnett* v. *Kaiser,* a 50-year-old Californian with a highly infectious form of hepatitis needed a liver transplant to survive. The transplant advisory board of the Kaiser Foundation Health Plan, Barnett's HMO, denied his application, saying that the transplant would fail. He paid for the procedure privately and then sued the health plan to recover the costs. The U.S. Court of Appeals for the 9th Circuit ruled against Barnett. The court found that Kaiser had exercised appropriate medical judgment; moreover, it held

The husband and daughters of a breast cancer victim sued her managed care plan for refusing to cover the costs of a treatment the plan deemed "experimental." A California jury ruled in favor of the family.

that the medical group should be allowed to make decisions about transplantation candidates.

In another case a California jury ordered the HMO Healthnet to pay more than $89.3 million to the estate of a woman who had died of metastatic breast cancer after being denied a bone marrow transplant. The woman had been diagnosed in the summer of 1991; by fall her disease had spread, and she was treated with surgery and chemotherapy. A few months later her oncologist suggested that a transplant might improve her chances of survival. Healthnet refused to pay for the procedure, calling it "experimental." The patient's family raised the money, and she had the transplant but subsequently died. The case was eventually settled for much less than the initial award, but the ruling stands.

In July 1994 an Idaho jury awarded more than $26 million, including $25 million in punitive damages, to a woman whose husband was refused coverage for transplant surgery. His HMO, Lincoln National, had advertised organ-transplant coverage in its marketing brochure but did not include the procedure in its contract with patients. This family, too, raised the money privately, and this patient also died.

In all three of the above cases, the transplant surgery could have been considered "innovative"—the term used to describe a treatment or procedure approved for one purpose but prescribed for another. The transplants also could have been considered "marginal"—*i.e.,* having only a slight chance of benefit or effectiveness. Labeling a treatment "innovative" or "marginal" may dampen the enthusiasm of health plan managers, but it usually does not discourage the terminally ill, who see such treatment as their last chance.

In the name of research

Many people would assume that another incident like the Tuskegee (Ala.) Syphilis Study—the infamous "experiment" in which several hundred black men with syphilis were followed medically for 40 years but given no treatment for their disease—could not happen in the 1990s. In 1994, however, another study was revealed in which patients were unknowingly used for information-gathering purposes. For five years, beginning in 1989, the hospital of the Medical University of South Carolina tested pregnant women for drug use without their consent, collected confidential information from them, and then turned it over to the police. Those who tested positive for illicit drugs were jailed if they did not agree to complete the hospital's prenatal care and drug-treatment programs. As in the Tuskegee study, race allegedly played a part; black women apparently were routinely imprisoned, while white women were referred to rehabilitation programs.

The Office of Civil Rights of the Department of Health and Human Services (HHS) ruled in 1994 that the women's civil rights had been violated. After the hospital agreed to stop the testing and referral practices, HHS placed the university on probation for violating ethical standards in medical research. (The hospital had consistently denied that the program was "research.") The university could, as a consequence, lose $32 million in federal research grants and $302 million annually in other federal funds.

In August 1994 a Minnesota physician, the drug manufacturer Genentech, and the drug distributor Caremark, Inc., were indicted in a case involving the unwitting participation of research subjects. The doctor, David R. Brown, allegedly accepted $1.1 million in kickbacks for prescribing Protropin, a genetically engineered growth hormone that has been approved exclusively for treatment of children with growth failure due to inadequate levels of growth hormone. Protropin must be taken regularly and can cost patients as much as $40,000 annually. Brown reportedly received 5% of Caremark's revenues for each prescription he wrote for Protropin during 1986 and '87. Most of these prescriptions allegedly were for children who were small for their age but had no hormone deficiency. Brown also received more than half a million dollars for participating in postmarketing research (*see* below). In the meantime, Genentech voluntarily discontinued its sponsorship of school-based height-screening programs, which identified youngsters of short stature and referred them to physicians as possible candidates for growth hormone treatment.

© Andy Levin—Science Source/Photo Researchers

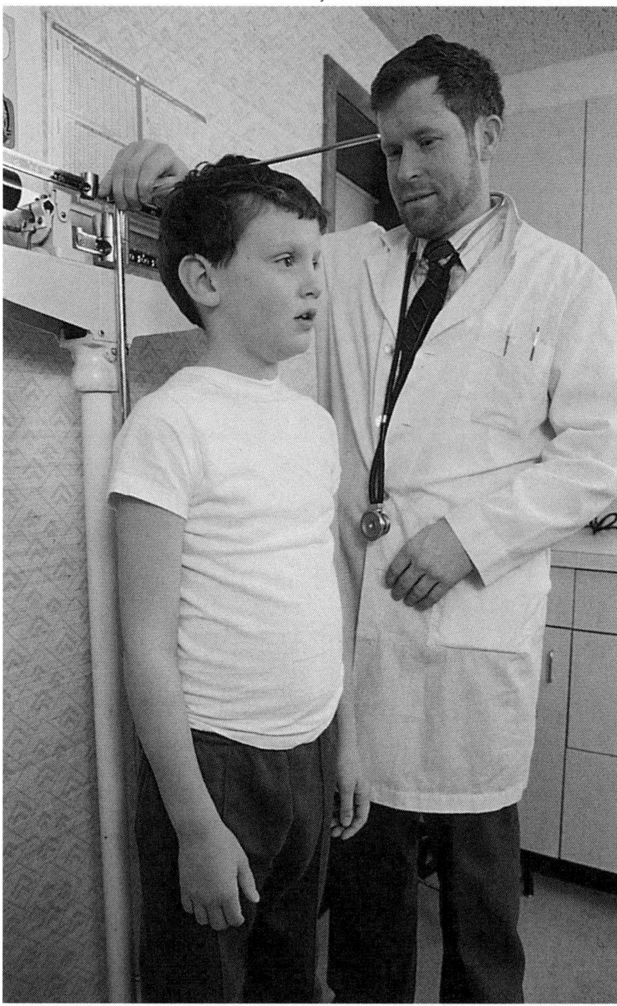

A boy's height is measured during a routine physical. Recently, unethical practices were uncovered in a program to identify youngsters as potential candidates for recombinant human growth hormone therapy.

Postmarketing research—the continued gathering of data on a drug after it has been approved for marketing—poses difficult ethical dilemmas for physicians. Most such studies are not "research" but rather attempts to familiarize doctors with products that are, for the most part, duplicates of medications already on the market (known in the trade as "me-too" drugs). The "data-gathering" process is usually sponsored by a drug company. Doctors are paid to enroll patients in a "study" of a given drug, perform basic laboratory tests assessing the drug's actions and efficacy, and report these "research data" to the drug company. The company pays the costs of the patient's lab tests, medication, and, sometimes, office visits. The doctors involved may have a financial interest in the drug company, act as salaried consultants, or simply receive a fee for each patient enrolled.

Unlike the controlled clinical trials in which drugs are tested prior to marketing, postmarketing research typically does not involve a research protocol. Often there is no genuine scientific hypothesis to be tested, nor are there any control groups. The patient may or may not be asked to give informed consent to research. In fact, the patient may not even know he or she is in a study. Certainly, the patient is unaware that the doctor is getting paid for enrolling study participants.

Even more worrisome, the doctor-researcher is sometimes paid twice for the same visit—once by the patient's insurer and once by the drug company. This system of compensation raises the specter of conflict of interest. It is not clear if the doctor is working for the best interests of the patient, the drug company, or him- or herself.

Postmarketing research could be conducted differently—and ethically. Large safety trials could be designed to catch a rare adverse drug effect, which is one legitimate purpose of postmarketing studies. Trials could include control groups. They could be retrospective rather than prospective—*i.e.,* they could recruit subjects from among many patients who have already taken the new drug and thereby remove the financial incentive for doctors to prescribe the medication. Informed consent from patients could be a standard part of the postmarketing research process and could include disclosure of the physician's financial ties to the pharmaceutical industry. Reforms advocated in the *British Medical Journal* in the summer of 1995 focused on physician disclosure and patients' right to know.

Ethics standards: fostering better communication

In difficult cases the hospital's clinical ethics consultant may be as important a member of the treatment team as the primary care physician. Standing up for a family's beliefs, interpreting a living will, and ensuring adequate attention to pain and discomfort are part of the ethics consultant's charge. Under the 1995 accreditation standards of the Joint Commission on Accreditation of Healthcare Organizations (JCAHO), all managed-care organizations, hospitals, and long-term-care facilities must, to be accredited, have an established process for addressing certain clinical ethical issues. Accreditation is crucial to many of these institutions because without it, they would not be eligible to receive reimbursement for treating Medicare and Medicaid patients. Thus, health care organizations have a compelling reason to comply with JCAHO requirements.

The following specific situations are those in which such organizations are required to employ or provide the services of a clinical ethics consultant if needed by the patient, family, or provider:

- a patient requests that life-sustaining treatment (*e.g.,* dialysis, blood transfusion) not be instituted
- a disagreement arises—either between patient and family or between patient and provider—about the care to be provided
- a patient decides to forgo emergency resuscitation
- a patient requests (or requires) the appointment of a surrogate decision maker
- a patient must decide whether to participate as a subject in research
- a provider wishes to share confidential information about a patient with another institution or individual
- a patient requests (or requires) information, advice, or a referral for the preparation of an advance directive
- a decision must be made about organ donation

Why is a relationship emerging between accreditation and ethics? The answer is that everyone in the health care system—health plan managers, health care providers, patients, families—wants better communication. One study of malpractice cases showed that patients cite issues of communication in more than 70% of their depositions. A recent *Consumer Reports* survey of 70,000 people revealed that 29% said their physicians had not talked with them about potentially beneficial lifestyle changes, and 26% were dissatisfied with the explanation of the possible side effects of medication or did not receive any such explanation.

Ethics services appear to improve communication and enhance medical decision making. Institutional ethics committees, headed by clinical ethics consultants, are instrumental in the process. In the U.S. such committees function chiefly to educate hospital staff, to propose policies and guidelines, and often to provide the clinical assistance patients need. (Hospital ethics committees are also gaining favor in Germany and the U.K., although clinician-consultants in ethics are still rare.)

The role of the ethics consultant is likely to grow in importance as medical decision making becomes increasingly influenced by pressures to contain costs and as patients discover the limits of their coverage under managed-care plans and appeal constraints on care. At the same time, cost containment will certainly restrict the amount of money available for ethics services. Patients who need help may not find a medical ethicist on their HMO's panel.

What, then, is the future of medical ethics in the era of managed care? The answer lies with patients, physicians, and health plan managers and their collective motivation to ensure that scarce resources are allocated fairly. With consumers demanding a greater say about how plans operate, and with accrediting bodies looking more closely at the plans' practices and policies, managed-care plans may ultimately seek the counsel of medical ethics. Paradoxically, the plans themselves may eventually pay for ethics services that help to resolve disputes about treatment—if only to avoid the more costly alternative of litigation.

—*John La Puma, M.D.*

Commemorating the Country Doctor

The illustrious Valentine Mott (1785–1865) of New York, pioneer in vascular surgery and a bold operator on the bones and joints, frequently remarked to his colleagues and students that he feared meeting a country physician in consultation. Not only did he find them "well-posted and abreast of the times," but they were able to give *him* valuable suggestions. To the dismay of his colleagues, he proclaimed that the average city physician was not nearly the equal of the country doctor in either knowledge or skill. The city practitioner, said Mott, was accustomed to relying on the experience and expertise of other members of his profession—especially in difficult cases. Not so the country practitioner.

Fully cognizant of their state's rich medical history—and of the slow-but-sure demise of the type of "country doctor" that Mott held in high regard—a group of eight enterprising women from North Carolina (three physicians among them) dreamed of establishing a museum in honor of their medical forefathers. Fund-raising began in 1967—not without raised eyebrows and setbacks—as the determined women begged, borrowed, and cajoled. But the response was overwhelming.

Within months a museum site in the town of Bailey (population 996), 51.5 km (32 mi) east of Raleigh, had been chosen, and two still-standing but dilapidated buildings that formerly served as physicians' offices for country doctors Howard Franklin Freeman (1849–1915) and Cornelius Henry Brantley (1860–1942), both from nearby towns, had been donated. These were duly hauled (by truck) to Bailey, and soon restoration of a composite "country doctor's office" was begun.

The Country Doctor Museum Foundation was chartered in 1967, and the museum opened in December 1968. In 1994 the museum attracted more than 5,000 visitors, from across the United States and other countries as well. With each passing year, the relics in the museum's unique collection become true treasures of a bygone era.

Medicine in a new nation

Physicians played a significant part in the shaping of colonial America. Because America was a new land, a raw wilderness far away from the European continent, the practice of medicine—of necessity—evolved in its own special way. Colonial medical practitioners might have had as little background as merchants who sold herbs or as much education and training as the finest European universities and medical apprenticeships could offer. By 1775 there were about 3,500 Americans who practiced some sort of medicine for a living—about one "doctor" for every 600 colonists.

One of the first American colonies, North Carolina encompassed a large territory (including what became South Carolina). It remained largely rural and sparsely populated until about 1880; its physicians therefore were true "country doctors."

During the American Revolution, North Carolina's doctors were surgeons at the battle sites, officers on the line, and statesmen in legislatures and congresses. One luminary among them was Hugh Williamson, a framer and signer of the Constitution, who was frequently referred to as the "Ben Franklin of North Carolina." Like most of his contemporaries, Williamson first adhered to the "doctrine of miasmas," the belief that "bad air" (swamp air, night air, sickroom air, and air from excrement) caused and spread disease. Later, however, he became convinced that attention to diet, dress, lodging, and drainage was important to good health. He was able to test that belief during the Revolution, when he served as surgeon general of the North Carolina troops. Following his rigorous instructions, 1,200 well-provisioned soldiers camped in the "bad air" of Dismal Swamp for six months; only two soldiers died, and no others were ill enough to warrant medical furloughs. Williamson could then claim:

> *When men shall have the prudence to keep themselves dry and clean, and shall be provided in all their excursions, during the winter, with clothing fitted to cold weather, and when they shall exchange the use of grog and ardent spirits for beer well seasoned with hops, or water that is less dangerous than either, we may be assured that many useful lives will be saved.*

Distinction for North Carolina

On Dec. 23, 1799, the North Carolina legislature chartered the state's Medical Society, the first in the Union to establish official panels charged with regulating and licensing physicians. According to medical historian J. Wesley Long, members of the 19th-century North Carolina Medical Society

> *stood for all that was good but set their faces like a stone wall against all that was evil; against quacks and empiricism; against secret remedies and the giving of certificates for them; against patentees; against advertising and against the contract practice. To say of these pioneers that many of their theories and practices have proven to be erroneous, is only to anticipate what posterity shall say of us. They lived up to the best lights, the most advanced science of their day.*

North Carolina's country doctors were, perhaps more than anything else, great improvisers. With enviable skill, little equipment, enormous courage, and unequaled determination, they had a "mission" to combat ignorance, disease, and death. As Thomas C. Parramore, professor of history at Meredith College, Raleigh, has said:

> *The rural medical practitioner was a jack-of-all-medical trades. He delivered babies, treated illnesses and injuries, pulled teeth, set bones, compounded remedies, nursed those who responded and comforted those who did not. Often as not he was the man appointed to serve as the local justice of the peace, sheriff, militia surgeon, vestryman, postmaster, or state legislator. . . . [He was] a venerated figure among his rural neighbors . . . whose art and whose dedication helped America to fulfill its promise as a haven for the oppressed and a refuge to the afflicted.*

Stepping into the past

Entering the Country Doctor Museum, one first crosses the threshold of the authentically furnished (*c.* 1860) "Apothecary Shop." Its handcrafted wild cherry and glass shelves house a complete collection of apothecary jars and stock-medicine bottles, dating from 1750 to 1900. There are pharmacy scales (*c.* 1800–85). Numerous "show globes" are displayed. These hand-blown glass apothecary bottles of varying sizes, shapes, and designs were filled with colored liquids and illuminated by an oil lamp or candle. In the era before gas and electric lights, the seller of medicines depended on these beacons to mark his shop at night.

One corner of the apothecary is occupied by the drug counter, where medicines were compounded. The compounding process involved mixing proper ingredients and bringing them to a doughy consistency with a mortar and pestle, then rolling and cutting the dough into strips on the "pill machine," a grooved wooden device invented in the 18th century to replace pill rolling by hand. Individual pills were cut and measured for proper dosage on the "pill tile." Finally, pills were polished in a small lignum vitae bowl ("pill polisher").

Proceeding into the "Doctor's Office," one finds the Matthew Moore Butler and Thomas H. Avera collections, both of Civil War vintage. Avera had served as a Confederate army surgeon, and Butler was a surgeon from Tennessee. The Butler collection includes many surgical instruments, including those that were used to amputate the left arm of Gen. Thomas J. ("Stonewall") Jackson on May 2, 1863. During the Battle of Chancellorsville (Va.), the general was wounded by fire from his own Confederate troops. Butler and Hunter McGuire of Richmond, Va., performed the necessary amputation. (Though Jackson survived the drastic operation and his army won the battle, the patient's overstrained immune system did not protect him from catching pneumonia. A week later he succumbed to overwhelming infection.)

In the main room of the museum are a multitude of medical artifacts used by Southern country doctors. These include microscopes and stethoscopes. One of the stethoscopes belonged to Joseph Hollingsworth, who was the personal

*The country doctor (*c. *1870) was a venerated figure who traveled long distances in any weather to treat the ill, bring babies into the world, perform surgery on the spot, pull aching teeth, set broken bones, or simply comfort his patients.*

Culver Pictures

Courtesy of the Country Doctor Museum; photograph, Anthony of Wilson

A composite of two authentic 19th-century doctors' offices housing a unique collection of medical memorabilia, this quaint museum in the town of Bailey, N.C., commemorates a vanished era of American medicine.

physician of the celebrated Siamese twins Chang and Eng. Born in Siam and congenitally joined at the chest, Chang and Eng immigrated to the United States, and for many years they traveled and performed with the P.T. Barnum circus. Never having been separated, the twins both married, and each had a large family. The families settled in North Carolina, making their home in Surry county, where Hollingsworth served as the entire family's doctor.

The humoral doctrine of disease, espoused for many centuries by Hippocrates and his followers, was still a prevailing theory in the early 19th century. Accordingly, most Southern country doctors believed disease was the consequence of a "morbid state of the humors" (blood, bile, etc.), and phlebotomy, or bloodletting, was among the most widely utilized therapies. The release of "bad humors" through bleeding was presumed to be curative.

For centuries leeches offered the most convenient method of "bleeding" a patient. Leeches placed on the skin release the potent anticlotting chemical hirudin as they suck the blood. The leech's bite is made painless by the release of another chemical that acts as a local anesthetic. Only recently have medical scientists again turned to the leech for its therapeutic potential; leeches are being used to treat cardiovascular disease, inhibit cancers, and prevent complications in plastic surgery.

"Cupping" and "lancing" were other phlebotomy methods; the former relied on a cup or bowl to draw small amounts of blood to the body's surface. Physician H.B. Shields (1853–1938) of Carthage, N.C., described the latter:

> *The operation was a simple one, and the information that a patient must be bled did not indicate any unusual fear or disturbance. Every doctor of the old school carried in his pocket instrument case a lancet, two kinds of which were in use. One was the thumb lancet: a single, sharp double edged thin blade that tapered to fine point. The other was a spring lancet set to spring a concealed knife so quickly into the flesh of a patient that he had no time to meditate on the coming pain. The quantity of blood drawn depended upon the effect it had on lowering the pressure of the pulse.*

Not surprisingly, the museum has a large collection of phlebotomy implements—including scarifactors (spring lancets), pocket lancets, brass bleeding bowls, and leech jars—some of which contain live leeches.

Every 19th-century country doctor had a portable medicine chest that he carried with him wherever he went. These had special compartments for stock medicines and surgical instruments; separate drawers for bandages, dressings, medicine labels, and disinfecting agents; and a "secret" sliding panel that concealed the doctor's precious supply of narcotics and alcohol. Several beautiful examples of these meticulously designed cases are on display in the Country Doctor Museum.

Scientific tomes to advice on "bedside manner"

Having access to medical texts and other resources has always been essential to any practicing physician; it is fitting, therefore, that a library is an integral part of the Country Doctor Museum. Until the 19th century the textbooks in general use in U.S. medical schools were the works of European physicians and surgeons of earlier centuries. As a rule, the medical student relied on the copious notes he took in lectures; these notebooks, or journals, later served as valuable practice guides. In addition to an extensive collection of 18th-, 19th-, and early 20th-century books on medicine and pharmacy, the museum boasts 12 lengthy journals kept by Southern country doctors.

The library also has manuals on doctors' decorum—among them, D.W. Cathell's *The Physician Himself and Things That Concern His Reputation and Success* (1897). Cathell preached that "every physician's dress, manner and bearing should agree with his noble and dignified calling." He admonished all physicians to "keep up your medical studies, or the knowledge which you have already acquired will soon become misty and ere long slip from your memory." Cathell further instructed country doctors not to "borrow books, instruments, umbrellas, [or] money, especially if you keep them beyond the proper time, or return them in bad condition"—a habit that he assured them would "deprecate you more than you would suppose."

House calls

> *Doctors traveled on horseback to see their patients. Folks rarely went to the doctor's office. . . . Bills were not sent, and fees were from fifty cents to a dollar. Many paid their bills with a cabbage head or a pound of butter.*

He used a surrey, with a boy in front, so that he could read along the road. Many hours a day did he spend thus, acquiring information which he was ready at a moment's notice to put to use. In a flap on the dashboard he kept a bag in which were stored a medical library and a miniature instrument shop.

As these descriptions suggest, the Southern country doctor of the 19th century made house calls. In fact, he often traveled quite long distances to see his patients. It is fitting, therefore, that adjacent to the museum is a "Carriage House."

Well-worn leather saddlebags filled with medicines and other tools of the doctor's trade are displayed. So, too, are blankets that kept the country doctors warm on chilly winter days in open buggies. The assiduous curators of the museum were even lucky enough to obtain a doctor's buggy, a surrey, and a 1912 Model T Ford Motor Run-About, all used by country physicians in their medical practices.

Nor has the museum forgotten the heroic horses that transported the dedicated doctors to their ailing patients. A scale-model horse and buggy, complete with leather bridle, reins, and whip (*c.* 1852), bears the inscription: "They also serve who only stand and wait."

Plants, potions, and pills

On Aug. 29, 1971, the museum's "Medicinal Herb Garden" was officially opened. Nineteenth-century country practitioners relied frequently on herbals, manuals describing age-old medicinal remedies. Most doctors compounded their own drugs. Some grew plants themselves, but most depended on collectors. History records large botanical supply houses in the mountains of North Carolina. Indeed, the state had such a bounty of medicinal plants that it became necessary to impose legal restrictions on random collecting.

It is documented in the early 19th-century records of the North Carolina Medical Society that prizes were awarded for the cultivation of certain nonnative plants as crude-drug sources. These included foxglove (*Digitalis purpurea* and *D. lantana*), rhubarb, opium poppy, and castor bean.

Pines are among the most important trees both economically and medically in the southern United States. Although all pines produce sap when tapped, those yielding the finest tar, pitch, and turpentine are long-leaf pines; both *Pinus palustris,* a coastal tree, and *P. strobus,* the eastern white pine, grow prolifically in the South. The pine was the source of many Southern folk remedies, and all parts of the trees were used: twigs, tops, inner bark, buds, cones, and needles.

Turpentine, an antiseptic, diuretic, and antirheumatic, was a valuable drug in veterinary and human medicine. It was used in inhalants for bronchitis, as a plaster for burns and stings, and as an "antihelminthic" to expel parasitic worms from the body. Tar, distilled from the pine's roots, was effective in a compound for psoriasis (especially that occurring in the scalp area), as well as for burns, itch, and cough. Pitch was used to treat kidney and bladder complaints.

By the latter part of the 19th century, most drugs were manufactured from synthetic chemicals rather than being derived from plant extracts. Lack of demand caused a general decline in herb cultivation; only recently has there been a resurgence of interest in the potential of plants as sources for new drugs.

Courtesy of the Country Doctor Museum; photograph, Anthony of Wilson

The museum's drug counter displays two "show globes"—beacons that marked the "Apothecary Shop" at night—and all the implements the pharmacist needed to compound drugs and grind, mix, roll, cut, measure, weigh, and polish pills.

May the spirit live on

The Country Doctor Museum not only commemorates those fine physicians of yesteryear but is also intended as an inspiration for young physicians to take up the mantle to become true family physicians. In no other way can the dire prediction of the oft-quoted sobriquet "the vanishing breed" be dispelled. This sentiment was eloquently expressed by Edgar T. Beddingfield, Jr., president of the North Carolina Medical Society, at the museum's dedication ceremony.

While no physician today could practice with the equipment and methods illustrated by the fine collection of memorabilia in this museum, we do have another heritage handed down to us from our courageous forebears, and this heritage is just as useful, and just as essential in the care of sick people today as it was a century ago. . . . I refer to the spirit of the country doctor, *his feeling of concern for the patients and their families in sickness and health, his industry, ingenuity, and resourcefulness, his availability, his sense of empathy with the patient and the community, his dignity, his calm and reassuring influence as he entered the sickroom, his appreciation of the* art *as well as the* science *of medicine.* This is the country doctor.

—Josephine E. Newell, M.D.

NEWS*CAP*

A Tribute to the Father of Vaccines

The year 1996 marks the momentous 200th anniversary of the first modern vaccine, developed and championed by the English country physician Edward Jenner. As a youth Jenner had a great love of nature; as a young man he was an eager learner and experimenter. He was considered by his surgical colleagues to be capable, skillful, and astute.

Early in his career Jenner began to notice that people who suffered an attack of cowpox—a relatively harmless disease contracted from cattle—did not become infected by the deadly smallpox virus. In May 1796 Jenner extracted live cultures from a cowpox lesion on the hand of Sarah Nelmes, a local dairymaid. He then inoculated eight-year-old James Phipps, who promptly developed a mild case of cowpox. On July 1 of that year, Jenner inoculated the boy again, this time with smallpox matter. Young Phipps was fully protected against smallpox.

Jenner's finding, privately published in 1798 in a small volume entitled *An Inquiry into the Causes and Effects of the Variolae Vaccinae, a Disease Discovered in Some of the Western Counties of England, Particularly Gloucestershire, and Known by the Name of the Cow Pox,* did not gain much attention at the time. Yet Jenner prophetically predicted that "the annihilation of the Smallpox, the most dreadful scourge of the human species, must be the result of this practice." He waged a tireless crusade to protect the public through vaccination, and by the time of his death, he not only had been recognized by England's Parliament for his accomplishment but also had spurred a hot debate in the medical community about the use of vaccines.

In Jenner's day smallpox was a devastating pestilential disease worldwide. Today it does not exist. Truly, the global eradication of smallpox—achieved by the World Health Organization in 1977—is one of the greatest achievements the world has known.

Jenner has not been forgotten. He is acknowledged worldwide as the father of immunology and virology. Visitors to Gloucestershire can tour the Jenner Museum in his hometown of Berkeley and see the "temple of vaccinia"—a thatched-roof hut where Jenner gave free vaccines to the poor. More significant, thanks to the recent establishment of the £10 million Edward Jenner Institute for Vaccine Research at Compton, Berkshire, England, the work that Jenner began well over 200 years ago will continue, and many new and better immunizations to benefit humanity will be the result.

(Top) Centers for Disease Control and Prevention, Atlanta; (bottom) Culver Pictures

(Above) Edward Jenner gives one of the first smallpox vaccinations in 1796; (Top right) Ali Maow Maalin, the world's last known smallpox victim, in Merka, Somalia, in October 1977.

Bedside Reading: An Opus from Oxford

Crammed full of fascinating titbits of information on a hugely broad range of topics while containing trustworthy and comprehensive reviews, the book displays medicine as a broad house in which each can surely find his or her niche from the molecular to the historical, sociological, and global scale. I challenge you to squeeze it into your Christmas stocking.

—Jocelyn Brookes, *The Lancet*, Dec. 24–31, 1994

Just in time for Christmas in the United Kingdom, and in plenty of time for Valentine's Day (1995) in the United States, an exciting new book was published. On the face of it, there was nothing unusual about that, yet there was. Oxford University Press, publisher of the venerable Oxford Companion series, had chosen to undertake what amounted to a drastic revamp of an earlier companion (so major that a new title was called for). The new *Oxford Medical Companion* (title changed from the *Oxford Companion to Medicine*) is much more than a heavily revised "new edition." Not only is its scope now fully international, its contents bang up-to-date, and its size (and price) half that of the original, but its target audience has shifted from that of mainly health professionals to general readers, making it now truly akin to the other *Oxford Companion*s.

All indications were that the first, two-volume medical opus, published in 1986, was a success; it was widely welcomed by medical professionals, received overwhelmingly complimentary reviews, and sold out on a print run that many publishers would envy. In the preface to the original volumes, the editors had clearly stated their objectives: "We hope first to make the volume meaningful to students and practitioners of medicine whatever their specialty, so that, for instance, a plastic surgeon wishing to learn more about the role and responsibilities of a psychiatrist might turn with profit to the article on psychiatry to seek the information he [sic] required." At the same time, they "also hoped that the essays would be written in language sufficiently clear and simple to make them meaningful to the intelligent layman."

A revered predecessor (with some problems)

Despite those aims, several commentators wondered whether the original text had actually been pitched too high. To be sure, the needs of the target readership—doctors, nurses, and other health professionals—had been met. Those readers would have had little difficulty understanding the concepts and technical terms that were used in articles characterized by depth and rigor and written by experts. But was the original treatment really comprehensible to the layperson?

Though sales were robust and there was no question that both the content and the quality of the writing were high, nonprofessionals did not flock to buy it in the same way that they had virtually every other *Oxford Companion.* The series, which began in the 1930s, now totals 32 (five in paperback), with several other paperbound versions in the works. Most of the early *Companion*s have been revised at various intervals, usually sufficiently intensively to be considered new editions. The *Oxford Companion to English Literature* and the *Oxford Companion to American Literature,* for instance, are both currently in their fifth editions. The *Oxford Companion to Music,* which was first published in 1938, is now in its 10th edition. (That volume, which this author bought in 1947 and devoured cover to cover, inspired a lifelong passion for music.)

Probably any blurring of the focus in the original medical *Companion* can be explained by a single tragic event—the death of the original editor and conceiver of the project, Sir Ronald Bodley Scott, in a car accident in Italy in 1984. A physician to the queen of England, Sir Ronald first discussed the idea of an *Oxford Companion* devoted to medicine in the late 1970s with Paul Beeson, an American physician who had left his senior appointment at the University of Washington School of Medicine to take up the Nuffield professorship of medicine at the University of Oxford.

The project was soon under way. By the time a replacement editor had been appointed, many of the articles had already been commissioned, and it was too late to make major changes to the volume's format. The new editor was Sir John Walton (later Lord Walton of Detchant), a distinguished neurologist and public figure.

Bodley Scott and Beeson began their undertaking by constructing an initial list of "head words" (key terms of subjects in alphabetical order), graded into five categories (A through E), according to importance and length. That rank-

Now Oxford University Press offers just about everything most people would want to know about medicine—from "Abbott, Maude Elizabeth Seymour," to "Zygote"—in one "friendly" 1,038-page volume.

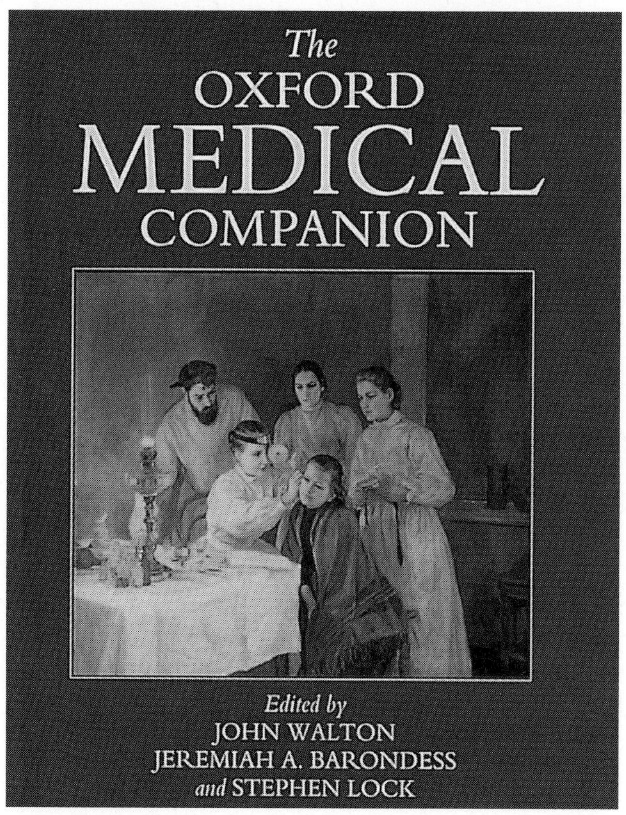

The Oxford Medical Companion, edited by John Walton, Jeremiah A. Barondess, and Stephen Lock, 1994; by permission of Oxford University Press ing system specified A entries of up to 10,000 words and E entries of no more than 100. In addition, a list of notable names in medicine and medical science was drawn up for inclusion, with the proviso that no living person would be given a biography. The latter policy is one that applies to most Oxford University Press reference books. One can argue—and rival publishers, such as the Cambridge University Press, do—that merely being alive should not prevent important contemporaries from being included. The Oxford view, however, certainly makes life a lot easier for editors (who otherwise might be prone to invidious judgments).

The original medical *Companion* took only four years from the time of Walton's appointment to publication and contained 150 main entries, as well as over 1,000 biographies of physicians—mainly those who had made important contributions to medicine (from cardiologist Maude Abbott to anatomist Emil Zuckerkandl) but also some doctors who had achieved notoriety in other ways, such as Hawley Harvey Crippen (1862–1910):

> *Crippen is notorious as the doctor who murdered his wife and dismembered her, burying the remains in the basement of his house in London. He fled by ship with his mistress, Ethel Le Neve. He was apprehended because the vessel on which he chose to travel was equipped with the new wireless telegraphy, and the police were able to radio the master and the police in the USA, so that they arrested him as he landed. Two facts make him interesting: he was the first person to be caught by radio; and he belongs to the comparatively rare group of doctors who are known to have committed murder.*

A "reader-friendly" reference

Plans for the new *Oxford Medical Companion* started in 1991. Fortunately, continuity was ensured when Walton agreed to continue as editor. Walton then recruited as coeditors Jeremiah A. Barondess, an American internist and president of the New York Academy of Medicine, and this author, the recently retired editor of the *British Medical Journal.*

The guidelines that Sir John had agreed upon with the publisher were clear-cut. The length was to be more than halved, which enabled the contents to be contained in a single volume and the price cut from £55 to £40 in the U.K. and from $120 to $49.95 in the U.S. Paradoxically, however, the

NEWS*CAP*

Contemplating AIDS

Two physicians, one involved in the care of AIDS patients and one in HIV prevention, won critical praise for their 1994 books.

Author of *My Own Country: A Doctor's Story of a Town and Its People in the Age of AIDS,* Abraham Verghese hardly fits the stereotype of the country doctor in the rural American South. Born to an expatriate Indian family in Ethiopia and educated in India, he did postgraduate training in medicine in the U.S. Ultimately, he set up practice in Johnson City, Tenn., far from the urban centers where AIDS was taking its relentless toll. As young gay men who had fled the Bible Belt for big cities began returning home with HIV-related illnesses, Verghese found himself almost alone in caring for them. AIDS awareness was slow to arrive in the heartland: "I saw AIDS *everywhere* in the fabric of the town; I wanted to pick up a megaphone as I stood in a checkout line and say, 'ATTENTION K-MART SHOPPERS: JOHNSON CITY IS A PART OF AMERICA AND, YES, WE DO HAVE AIDS HERE.' " Verghese speculates in his book on how his outsider status contributed to his effectiveness in treating those regarded as aliens in their own hometown. Despite his single-minded devotion to his patients, Verghese saw them die, one after another. The experience took its toll—on both his family and his career. He moved to Iowa to attend a writing workshop, then returned to medical practice in Texas.

Although equally personal in its perspective on AIDS, Ronald O. Valdiserri's *Gardening in Clay: Reflections on AIDS* is a very different kind of book, a loosely organized collection of essays about subjects as seemingly disparate as sex education and science fiction. The unifying element is the author's unfailing optimism in the face of adversity and loss, including the 1992 death of his twin brother, Edwin, from AIDS.

Like Verghese, Valdiserri found his life utterly changed by the AIDS epidemic. He abandoned the practice of pathology to study public health: "I had been content to study disease from a distance, behind a microscope. . . . But after the epidemic took hold, my interest in abnormal physiology waned. . . . No longer satisfied with identifying disease, I wanted to learn how to prevent it from occurring." He went on to become deputy director of the division of HIV/AIDS prevention at the Centers for Disease Control and Prevention in Atlanta, Ga.

Throughout the book, gardening—a passion the author shared with his brother—provides a metaphor for the human condition. "Gardens do not grow without weeds, and life does not unfold without misfortune," Valdiserri writes.

editors reached a consensus that more rather than fewer main entries were needed; hence, the length of even major articles had to be slashed to no more than 3,000 words. The original authors were instructed to update but also to cut their original contributions by at least a third. This particular editorial travail has been aptly dubbed "filleting" by *The Lancet;* although most authors find such self-censorship painful, they generally come to agree that the result is worthwhile.

Despite the formidable task they took on, the editors' and publisher's aims were achieved; the number of words now totals 500,000, compared with 1,250,000 previously. The new volume retained all of the 150 main entries of the first edition, though all were shortened and updated. No fewer than 150 of the shorter D and E entries were cut out as individual entries (mostly biographies but also certain institutions and drugs); at least a third of those, however, resurfaced within one of the 25 newly commissioned main entries.

Among the new main entries is one entitled "Fraud and Misconduct in Medical Research." Though not unheard of in the 1980s, fraud and misconduct in medicine had become issues of growing ethical and public concern (including congressional concern in the U.S.). Other new main entries are "AIDS and HIV" and "Genetic Engineering."

The 1986 *Companion* included a main entry on "Fringe Medicine, Cults, and Quackery," which read: "Of the unorthodox systems of medicine, those with some pretence of a rational basis have been called fringe, alternative medicine, or complementary." The text goes on to describe the dubious methods of "unqualified practitioners" and "quacks," who "act solely from commercial motives."

The editors of the 1994 *Companion* commissioned a new article of comparable length, entitled "Complementary (Alternative) Medicine," written by Sir Douglas Black (emeritus professor of medicine at the University of Manchester and former president of the Royal College of Physicians of London). Sir Douglas writes:

> *"Complementary medicine" is a term of comparatively recent origin and of growing currency, which is used to denote a number of systems of medicine which were previously described as "alternative medicine," or even as "fringe medicine." This change in nomenclature is not trivial, for it expresses a welcome recognition that in matters as complex as the pursuit of health or the treatment of disease there is room for diverse approaches, which may complement one another, depending on the nature of the problem and on the physical and psychological "make-up" of the actual or potential patient.*

He then goes on to describe selected complementary treatments "that enjoy wide currency; are legally permitted in a number of countries or states; and have recognized training programmes, codes of practice, and registers of qualified practitioners."

Some important deficiencies in the first version had been pointed out by reviewers at the time—for instance, the omission of the role of self-experimentation in medical discovery. Others became obvious to the second edition's editors upon scrutiny of the list of head words. Skimped in the 1986 edition, for example, was *osteoporosis,* which is currently the principal cause of hospitalization for women over age 65 in the U.K., while in the U.S. osteoporosis-associated hip fractures consume an estimated $6 billion in primary medical care costs annually. Yet other subjects clearly were in need of much fuller treatment—for example, the continuing health havoc in the world wreaked by cigarette smoking.

Some reviewers had previously detected an Anglo-American bias, and others noted a tendency for Anglo ascendancy over the American. The latter was not intended, though, admittedly, a few of Bodley Scott's short, tongue-in-cheek biographies might have given that impression. Thus, sacrificed in the new edition were such engagingly dotty accounts as that of Adolphe Abrahams (1883–1967), English gastroenterologist and brother of the Olympic athlete Harold Abrahams. Adolphe "regularly ran round Regent's Park many years before such activities became commonplace," wrote Sir Ronald. The biography further revealed that Abrahams was a great "upholder of traditional medical dress and manners."

One answer to the charge of British imperialism was to recruit several more American authors for some of the principal articles. Another was the decision to use American as well as British spellings of all medical terms (*edema* as well as *oedema,* for instance). Of course, there was more to achieving internationalism than settling Anglo-American differences, real or perceived. Thus, the editors recruited distinguished authors from many countries, and the new *Companion* includes individual entries on medicine in Africa; Australia; France; Germany, Austria, and Switzerland; Greece; Italy; Japan; New Zealand; the Arab world; the European Community; the former Soviet Union; and the Indian subcontinent.

Encyclopedic, but not an encyclopedia

None of the *Oxford Companions* has ever been intended to rival an encyclopedia or specialized dictionary. And neither edition of the medical *Companion* was meant to compete with any of the host of excellent medical and family health encyclopedias published in the past few years by such institutions as the American Medical Association, the British Medical Association, the Mayo Clinic, and Columbia University College of Physicians and Surgeons. To be sure, there is a growing demand for such sound, up-to-date, "reader-friendly" information for consumers, but a "companion" seeks to do more. Facts are complemented by history, background, and, as Brookes said in her *Lancet* review, "fascinating titbits." The editors hope that they have achieved what Sir David Weatherall, Regius professor of Medicine at the University of Oxford, so generously said of the 1994 publication: "Like all good *Companions* it offers both hours of pleasurable browsing and a valuable work of reference."

It is fully anticipated that future editions will evolve as organically as those of the other *Oxford Companions* have. Indeed, if the editors accomplished what the *Companion to Music* achieved in both breadth of learning and simplicity, this editor of the new *Oxford Medical Companion,* for one, would regard the effort that went into it as one of the most personally rewarding ventures of a lifetime.

—Stephen Lock, M.D.

Focus on Prostate Cancer

Carcinoma of the prostate is a growing health problem throughout the Western world. It is now the most common cancer—and the second most common cause of cancer-related death—in American men. The prostate is a walnut-shaped gland located just below the bladder and in front of the rectum. The urethra (urinary channel) passes from the bladder through the prostate and then continues through the penis. The main function of the prostate is to provide a fluid that supports sperm and contributes to fertility. Attached to the prostate are the seminal vesicles, which also provide fluid that contributes to male fertility. (*See* diagram, page 362.) Men can live normally without the prostate or seminal vesicles, although they lose their reproductive ability.

For a number of reasons, a great deal of attention is currently focused on prostate cancer. One is that well-known personalities, such as U.S. Gen. Norman Schwarzkopf, former French president François Mitterrand, and U.S. presidential hopeful Sen. Robert Dole, have been diagnosed with it, while others, such as musician Frank Zappa and actor Bill Bixby, have died from it. Furthermore, over the past five years in the U.S. alone, the number of diagnosed cases of prostate cancer has more than doubled, from slightly over 100,000 in 1990 to an expected 250,000 in 1995. And finally, new methods of diagnosis and treatment have been developed, and these have received considerable coverage in the press.

Unfortunately, many unresolved issues complicate the management of this particular type of cancer. The decision about treatment, for example, is a difficult one because the disease usually occurs in older men who will die of other causes, the rate of disease progression in individuals is quite variable, and the complications of treatment can have a devastating effect on a man's quality of life.

Current understanding of tumor biology

A striking feature of prostate cancer is its high prevalence compared with its relatively low mortality. Approximately 18% of men aged 30–40 have microscopic evidence of prostate cancer; the proportion increases to over 50% for 80-year-olds. Nevertheless, current estimates are that perhaps one of every 9 men will be diagnosed with this disease during his lifetime, while only one in 30 will die from it. There are wide statistical variations between groups of men, however. Japanese men living in Japan have only one-tenth the risk of dying from prostate cancer that American men and Japanese men living in the United States have. African-American men have the highest mortality from the disease in the world, whereas prostate cancer is very uncommon among Africans in African countries.

What accounts for these wide differences? A number of explanations have been offered:

- Diets high in animal fat and red meat or low in fresh fruits and vegetables have been associated with an increased risk of prostate cancer. The possibility that the disease can be prevented, or its progress slowed, through diet modification is one that warrants intensive investigation.
- It was recently discovered that glutathione S-transferase (GSTP1), an enzyme that helps detoxify carcinogens, is missing or dysfunctional in cancerous prostate cells. At some time in the future, it may be possible to correct this genetic abnormality with chemicals that augment GSTP1's activity.
- A gene that blocks the spread of prostate cancer—known as *KA11* on chromosome 11—has been identified, and efforts are now under way to develop a clinically useful test that would predict the course of the disease.
- Most important, an increased risk has been associated with a family history of prostate cancer; men with one affected first-degree relative have a higher risk by a factor of two, while men with two affected first-degree relatives have an eightfold-higher risk than men without a family history of the disease.
- Vasectomy does *not* appear to increase a man's risk of developing prostate cancer.

Early detection

A general principle of cancer management is that early detection offers the best chance for cure. Screening, which means testing for a disease in people without any symptoms of that disease, potentially offers the best chance to find a cancer before it becomes advanced. Since most cancers, including prostate, lack effective therapy for advanced disease, screening would appear to be ideal. The use of mammography for early detection of breast cancer in women between the ages of 50 and 69 is a good example; in those women screening results in a 30% reduction in breast cancer deaths.

The value of screening for prostate cancer, by contrast, is highly controversial. The most commonly performed test to detect prostate cancer is the digital rectal examination (DRE), which a physician performs by placing a gloved index finger into the patient's rectum (with the patient either bending over a table or positioning himself on both hands and knees on the examining table). Because of the prostate's location adjacent to the rectum, the physician is able to feel the back of the gland. During the exam the physician searches for irregularities in the prostate's size and shape. Simply having an abnormality, such as an enlarged prostate, is not an indication of cancer. Actually, only one in four men with an abnormal result from a DRE will be diagnosed with the disease.

One of the most important recent advances in diagnosis is the development of a test for prostate specific antigen (PSA). PSA is a protein that is produced only by cells located in the prostate gland. Although both benign and malignant cells produce this protein, generally the larger the prostate, the higher the level of PSA, even in the absence of cancer. Noncancerous conditions that can cause an abnormally high PSA level include benign prostatic enlargement, infection or inflammation in the prostate, and trauma. Even bicycle riding has been associated with high PSA levels. Consequently, while normal levels have been defined, certain adjustments must be made to account for a patient's age and prostate size.

Currently, the approved use for the PSA test is in monitoring patients already diagnosed with prostate cancer; a rising PSA usually means that the cancer is progressing. Interest in the test for screening purposes arose because the PSA in men

(Top left) UPI/Bettmann; (bottom left) Robert Trippett—Sipa; (top right and bottom right) Reuters/Bettmann

with prostate cancer may be abnormal even when a DRE is normal. In fact, the majority of cancers diagnosed today are in men with a normal DRE and an abnormal PSA. Most of the time, however, an abnormal test is due not to cancer but to a benign enlargement. Cancer is present in only about 30% of patients with an abnormal PSA. When the DRE and PSA both are abnormal, however, the probability of having cancer increases to 65%.

Another recent development is the ability to measure two different forms of PSA—one that circulates freely in the bloodstream and one that is bound to another protein called alpha chymotrypsin. Patients with cancer have a low ratio of free PSA to total PSA, whereas men with a benign condition have a higher ratio. In the future this test may be used to decide which patients with an abnormal total PSA level can avoid a biopsy—the only definitive way to diagnose prostate cancer.

Over the past several years, transrectal ultrasonography (TRUS) has played an important role in improving early diagnosis of prostate cancer. The test involves placing a probe about the thickness of the thumb into the rectum. Sound waves pass from the probe into the prostate, then bounce back to the probe and are recorded on a machine. Because

Carcinoma of the prostate is the leading cancer among U.S. men. (Above left) Persian Gulf War hero Gen. Norman Schwarzkopf (top) and Senate Majority Leader Robert Dole (bottom) have been diagnosed with it; rock star Frank Zappa (top right) and actor Telly Savalas (above) both were its victims.

cancer cells often differ from noncancer cells in the way they absorb sound waves, distinct patterns frequently are seen when cancer is present. Unfortunately, many false positives (*i.e.,* suggestions of cancer when there is none) are seen with TRUS, which makes it a poor screening tool. Its major value is in directing a biopsy needle into specific areas of the prostate. Generally, if either the PSA or DRE is abnormal, then an ultrasound-guided biopsy is performed. In some cases physicians direct the biopsy needle into abnormal areas seen on the TRUS in addition to performing a number of random biopsies to sample the entire gland. A negative biopsy, however, does not mean that cancer is absent, and approximately 10% of the time when the biopsy is repeated, cancer may be found.

Asymptomatic men: to screen or not to screen?

Most doctors usually perform a DRE as part of a normal male checkup even though there is no evidence that routine DRE will save lives. The question that has raised the most controversy is whether to perform the PSA in a man who has no signs or symptoms of abnormality. Organizations that support PSA screening include the American Cancer Society, the American Urological Association, and the American Radiological Society. In contrast, the National Cancer Institute and the U.S. Public Health Task Force do not endorse routine PSA screening.

The argument against screening is that there is no statistical evidence that it saves lives. The fact that more early-stage cancers are detected with the PSA does not guarantee that

Prostate Location

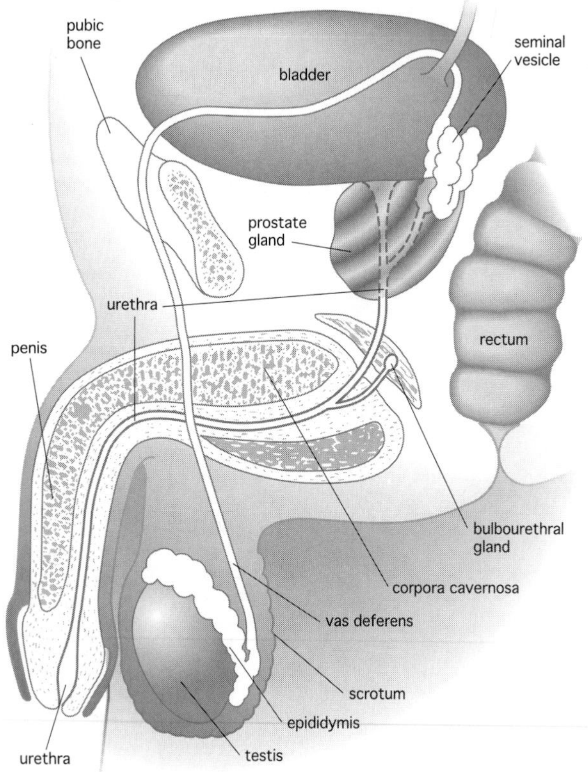

Prostate Specific Antigen: Normal Levels

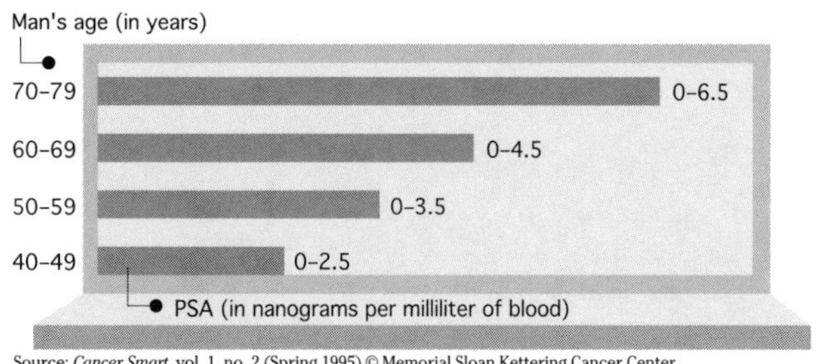

Source: *Cancer Smart,* vol. 1, no. 2 (Spring 1995) © Memorial Sloan Kettering Cancer Center.

fewer men will die of the disease. Similar questions often are raised about routine screening for lung cancer and screening for breast cancer in women aged 40–49. The chance of dying from cancer is identical in people screened and those not screened for those cancers.

This apparent paradox is best shown with a case history: A man first develops prostate cancer at age 60. It is not diagnosed at the time because there are no symptoms. As the years pass, the cancer grows and eventually is diagnosed when the patient, at age 68, experiences difficulty with urination and consults his family doctor. He then has cancer treatment. Seven years later, at age 75, he dies. How long did he survive after diagnosis? Seven years (from age 68 until 75). How long did he live after the cancer developed? Fifteen years (from age 60 to 75).

Now suppose that this same individual was tested with the PSA at age 65. Although the man's DRE was normal, his PSA was abnormal and cancer was detected. He then undergoes treatment but still dies at 75. How long did he live after the diagnosis? Ten years, or three years longer than if the screening test had not been performed. Nonetheless, the length of time from the beginning of his cancer until his death (15 years) was unchanged. Screening, therefore, had no impact on the final outcome. In addition, since prostate cancer is present in many men who will not die of their disease, screening could result in detecting and treating some men unnecessarily. Clearly, on the basis of data that are presently available, the value of general screening for prostate cancer remains unsubstantiated.

Is screening then a waste of time and money? Not necessarily. First, the mortality rate of prostate cancer has not declined in the past 30 years. Second, only early-stage cancers can be cured, and conventional methods infrequently detect early stages of the disease. Third, although no study has proved unequivocally that screening will reduce the death rate, postponing diagnostic studies could result in many potentially avoidable deaths. Just as breast cancer screening appears to be successful for women over 50, screening in the case of prostate cancer could have distinct merits.

For now, the best approach is for patients to participate in the decision. They should know the potential benefits and risks of screening and of the various treatments. Men should be aware that screening offers the best chance to avoid developing advanced prostate cancer and dying from the disease, while not screening is the best way to maximize individual quality of life and avoid unnecessary treatment and complications. The older the patient, the smaller the potential benefit from screening. With this information, each man can make his own choice. The next decision he must make is about treatment.

Grading tumors

The conventional treatment options for localized (early-stage) prostate cancer include watchful waiting, radical prostatectomy, radiation therapy, and hormone therapy. The choice of treatment is determined largely on the basis of the appearance of the cancer cells under the microscope, which is known as the tumor grade.

One of the most commonly used methods of categorizing prostate tumors is the Gleason scoring system, which assigns a number (from 1 to 5) to the tumor according to the degree of differentiation between cancer cells and normal prostate cells. The cells of a Gleason grade 1 tumor are well-differentiated—small, basically uniform in shape, and tightly packed. Gleason grade 5 tumors are highly irregular in size, shape, and arrangement and have little resemblance to normal prostate cells. A Gleason score is assigned to each patient by combining the tumor grades of the two most common types of cells on the biopsy. If all the cells appear similar, then the Gleason grade is doubled. Thus, patients may have a tumor with a Gleason score from 2 to 10. The results of treatment are also frequently assessed by Gleason scoring. Recent studies show that patients with a tumor containing any Gleason grade 4 or 5 highly undifferentiated cells have a worse prognosis than patients with moderately or well-differentiated cells.

Watchful waiting

Watchful waiting is often the treatment of choice for older patients with localized, low-grade prostate cancer. This means that no immediate treatment for the prostate gland is initiated after the diagnosis is made. Instead, patients are monitored with regular exams (usually twice a year) and blood tests until symptoms develop, which indicates the cancer has progressed. At that time treatment to reduce symptoms is begun.

Considerable controversy surrounds this treatment option, especially in the United States. Not providing immediate treatment goes against the grain of standard American medical practice. Prostate cancer, however, is different from other cancers in that it is often slow-growing, and men with localized prostate cancer may die of some other cause before the cancer causes any problems. Depending on a man's health, life expectancy, and personal goals, watchful waiting may be a reasonable option. The benefits of watchful waiting are that a patient can maintain and prolong his quality of life (because the cancer is usually asymptomatic) and that the potential complications of surgery, radiation, or pharmaceutical therapy are avoided. The primary disadvantage of watchful waiting is that a patient may miss an opportunity to be cured of a disease that could shorten his life and cause much suffering when it spreads to other parts of the body.

NEWS*CAP*

Their Bodies, Their Ignorance

Judging by a survey conducted for *Reader's Digest* by Market and Opinion Research International Ltd. (MORI), London, the average British man is more likely to know the location of, say, Wembley Stadium than he is to know precisely where his own prostate is found. That survey—conducted among nearly 2,000 Britons aged 15 and over and reported in the magazine's April 1995 issue (British edition)—investigated men's (and women's) attitudes about health. The study revealed a "lamentable" knowledge by men of illnesses that affect their gender in particular.

Among the more disturbing findings was the revelation that only 11% of men were able to locate the prostate on a diagram of the male body (women fared slightly better—16%). Other health-related ignorance revealed:

- Nearly half of men (47%) were unaware that prostate cancer affects only men.
- When presented with a series of true-false statements, only 44% of men recognized that pain or a burning sensation while urinating can be a symptom of prostate cancer.
- Almost half of men (47%) admitted to knowing nothing about prostate cancer.
- Forty-four percent of men knew nothing about testicular cancer.
- Nearly one in four men (23%) had not seen a doctor in the previous year, compared with only 15% of women.
- Twenty-two percent of men said they delayed visiting a doctor because they were afraid of wasting the doctor's time; almost 18% said they were too busy to see a doctor.
- Only around half (53%) of the men had had their blood pressure taken the previous year (compared with 68% of women)—despite the fact that two of Britain's most common illnesses, stroke and cardiovascular disease, are caused by hypertension.
- Twenty-seven percent of men had not had their blood pressure taken in the previous two years.
- Nearly one-fifth of men (19%) believed they drank too much alcohol, more than double the percentage of women reporting drinking too much (8%).

The higher the Gleason score, the greater the risk that the cancer will spread and shorten a man's life if managed by watchful waiting. Two large studies of watchful waiting found that 10 years after diagnosis 18% of patients with a Gleason score of 2–4 developed metastases to other parts of the body (while 82% did not); 9–13% died of prostate cancer, but 87–91% did not. Among patients with a Gleason 5–7 score, 42% developed metastases (56% did not) and 13–25% died of prostate cancer (75–87% did not). On the other hand, among patients with a Gleason 8–10 score, 75% developed metastases and 52–66% died from prostate cancer.

Although the best candidates for watchful waiting are men who are likely to live only another 10 to 15 years, men with a longer life expectancy may choose watchful waiting because the gain in survival from surgery or radiation may not be worth the risk of complications.

If cancer spreads, most patients either have no symptoms initially or may have symptoms that can be relieved by hormone therapy (described below). Once the cancer has spread to other parts of the body, approximately 50% will live at least an additional three years after hormone therapy is initiated, while half will die from the disease within three years. The risk of eventually developing pain and discomfort with cancer once it has spread, however, is quite high, and most patients with metastatic disease ultimately die of their disease.

Radical prostatectomy

If cancer is localized—*i.e.,* no cancer cells are present outside the prostate—then surgery will cure the disease. Unfortunately, because some cancer cells may have spread beyond the prostate but are not yet detectable by any tests, not every patient is cured by surgery. A new test under investigation is called reverse transcriptase polymerase chain reaction (RT-PCR). This test can detect even a single cancer cell circulating in the bloodstream. Investigators hope that this test can identify patients who would be unlikely to be cured by aggressive treatment. A potential problem of such a test is that the presence of prostate cancer cells in the bloodstream does not necessarily mean that the patient is incurable; thus, basing therapy on the results of RT-PCR could result in an incorrect treatment decision.

Studies indicate that the results of radical prostatectomy after 10 years are as follows: 4–12% of patients with a Gleason 2–4 score will develop metastases, and 5–10% will die of prostate cancer. Sixteen percent to 25% of patients with a Gleason 5–7 score will develop metastases, and 10–15% will die; and 35–50% of men with a Gleason 8–10 score will develop metastases, and 18–30% will die from their prostate cancer. Thus, the higher the Gleason score, the greater the potential gain from surgery. Estimating the potential benefit of radical surgery among men who are likely to live for longer than 10–15 years, however, is not presently possible.

Studies are under way to determine the appropriate approach for patients undergoing surgery who have tumor cells outside the prostate. One such approach is to interfere with the normal growth of prostate cells by reducing or blocking testosterone, the male sex hormone. Since lowering the testosterone level will kill some cancer cells, some patients are receiving this treatment for a few months prior to undergoing surgery. Hormone therapy alone, however, does not cure prostate cancer. Preliminary results show that patients who have hormone treatment have fewer cancer cells near the outer edge of tumors that are removed during surgery, which suggests a potential benefit, although some researchers believe that the cells are merely harder to identify and that eventually the outcome will be the same. Furthermore, since some cancer cells are resistant to hormone therapy, those cells would have additional time to spread before surgery is performed; thus, the patient might be at a disadvantage.

Martin Simon—Saba

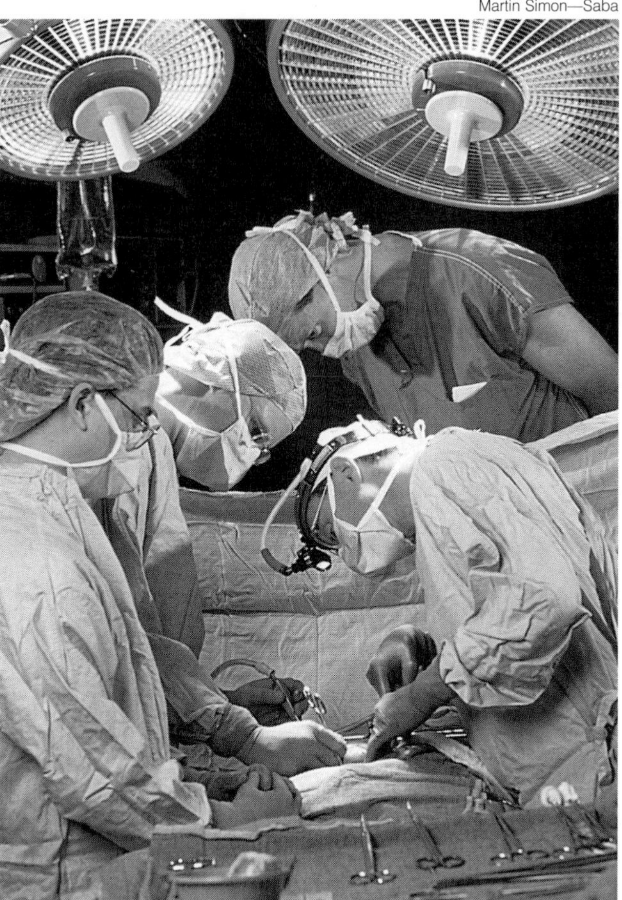

Radical prostatectomy cures cancer if no cancer cells remain outside the prostate gland. Patients who undergo this aggressive form of treatment, however, tend to report high complication rates.

Potential complications of surgery include impotence, urinary incontinence, scarring of the urethral channel, blood clots in the leg, bowel injury, and death. The likelihood of these events depends on many factors, including the age and health of the patient at the time of surgery and the skill of the surgeon. Although reports by surgeons indicate low complication rates, recent surveys of patients suggest much higher rates.

Radiation therapy

An alternative treatment to radical prostatectomy for patients who have localized prostate cancer is external beam radiation therapy. Studies indicate that 10 years after treatment, the percentage of men alive after radiation is similar to the percentage alive after radical prostatectomy. The advantage of radiation is that it may prevent further growth of the cancer while permitting a patient to avoid some of the complications of radical prostatectomy. Some cancers, however, that might have been cured by surgery will not be cured by radiation; moreover, if the patient is not cured by radiation, additional treatments, such as surgery, have a much higher complication rate and are less likely to be successful when the cancer is more advanced.

In general, the best candidates for radiation are men (usually those aged 68 or older) with life expectancies that are limited to 10 or 15 years. Other patients who may benefit from radiation treatment are those men who, for one reason or another, are not good candidates for surgery.

Outcomes according to Gleason score are as follows: the chance of dying from prostate cancer within 10 years after radiation therapy is approximately 10% for patients with Gleason 2–4 tumors, approximately 24–32% for those with Gleason 5–7 tumors, and 50% for those with Gleason 8–10 tumors.

Recent studies have found that if the initial PSA is fairly high—above 15 or 20 ng/ml (nanograms per milliliter of blood)—then within two years of completing radiation therapy, more than 80% of the patients have a rising PSA (which indicates that the radiation probably was not successful). As a result, many doctors now believe that radiation is not a good choice when the PSA is above these levels, particularly for younger men (under 65). In an effort to improve the results, studies giving hormone therapy before and during radiation are under way. Preliminary results of this combined treatment approach are promising, but the impact on survival will not be known for many years.

In addition to certain of the same complications associated with surgery, radiation may also result in chronic diarrhea or blood in the stool. Again, patients tend to report higher complication rates following radiation than physicians' reports would suggest.

A new method for administering radiation is called conformal therapy. This process limits the damage to tissues surrounding the prostate and may allow higher radiation doses to be administered and thus cause more cancer cells to be killed. Many years will be needed for the overall effect and survival rate of the treatment to become known.

An alternative to external radiation therapy is the use of radioactive seed implants. With this treatment tiny radioactive seeds, or pellets, are placed through the skin into the prostate. They stay in place forever, but the radioactivity decays, or declines, over time. The radioactivity affects only the tissues very close to each seed, which prevents injury to organs outside the prostate and thereby reduces potential side effects. Until recently, the seeds were implanted during an operation. Now, however, they can be put in place through the skin, using an ultrasound probe in the rectum. The treatment is both safe and easy to deliver. The total procedure takes only a few hours, and the patient can usually go home the same day. Unfortunately, the seeds have a tendency to move out of position, which leaves portions of the prostate untreated. It is too soon to know what the overall effectiveness of the new technique will be; at present, patients with the least life-threatening tumors are generally selected.

Hormonal therapy

The goal of hormonal therapy is to lower testosterone levels. Testosterone is produced in the testicles and the adrenal gland. In one approach the female hormone estrogen is given, either orally or by monthly injection. Estrogen treatment lowers the amount of testosterone produced by the testicles. Another approach is surgical removal of the testicles (castration). The treatments appear equally effective, although estrogens produce slightly more side effects—the most common being hot flashes, a diminished sex drive, and sometimes breast enlargement.

Another medication, flutamide, works by blocking the action of testosterone. Its most common side effects are mild diarrhea in 10% of patients and breast tenderness in 50%. Some patients can also have potentially more serious liver changes. Flutamide used alone is generally not as effective and therefore is frequently used in combination with hormonal or surgical castration. Studies have shown that in men whose tumors have metastasized, there is a small increase in survival when both flutamide and castration are used compared with castration alone.

Usually, hormone therapy is given when the cancer has progressed. Its value in men with localized prostate cancer remains unclear. Older men may do well with hormone therapy as a primary treatment because the growth of their cancer is slowed and they die of some other cause before developing problems from prostate cancer. The potential disadvantage of hormone therapy is that resistant cells may grow more rapidly, which thus reduces a patient's survival time.

Cryosurgery

Another treatment that is not new but recently has been improved and reintroduced for prostate cancer is cryosurgery, which involves freezing the prostate. The treatment is performed by passing small needles, called cryoprobes, through the skin near the rectum. The patient is given a general or spinal anesthetic. The probes are guided into the prostate by means of an ultrasound device. Usually five probes are placed to enable the entire prostate to be treated. Liquid nitrogen that has been chilled to −190° C (−310° F) or a gas is circulated through the probes. The procedure takes under three hours. After the treatment a small tube, or catheter, is left in the bladder, passing through the abdomen to facilitate urination. After one to two weeks, when the patient can urinate normally, the catheter is removed. The advantage of the operation is that it is easily performed. The major complications are impotence, which occurs in over 75% of the patients, and incontinence. Three months after cryosurgery, over 85% of patients have a negative prostate biopsy, although the PSA level rises in nearly 50% of patients after 12 months, which suggests the cancer may be regrowing. Although a patient treated by cryosurgery can be retreated with the same procedure, long-term survival rates are currently

(Top) Dan Lamont—Matrix; (bottom) Hank Morgan—Rainbow

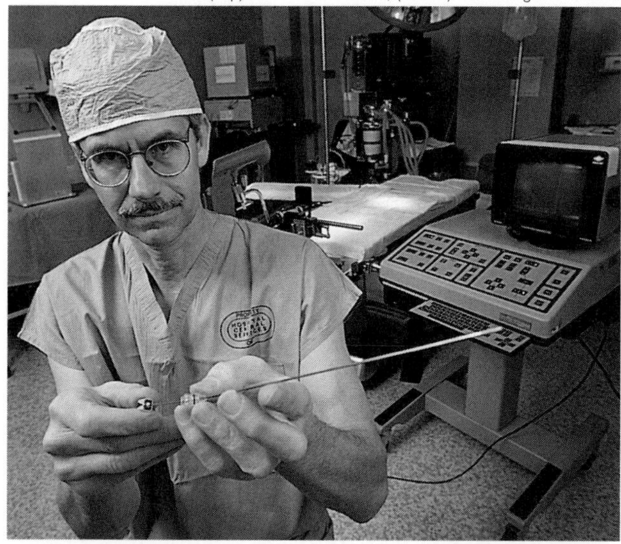

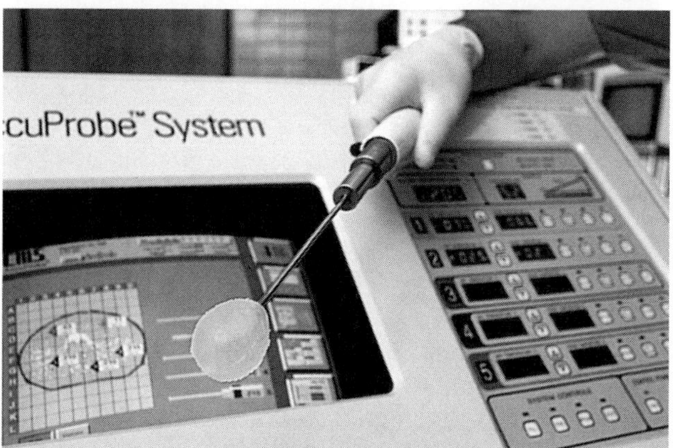

Radioactive seed implants (top) offer an alternative to the more traditional external-beam radiation therapy. Though the seed method is cheaper and less invasive and has fewer complications, it is too soon to know what its long-term effectiveness will be. The cryoprobe (above) freezes the prostate, which potentially arrests the cancer.

unknown. Consequently, it will be a number of years before cryosurgery as a primary treatment can be reliably compared with either radical prostatectomy or radiation therapy. For now, cryosurgery is probably not the treatment of choice for men under age 65 unless they are part of an experimental protocol.

Ongoing search for solutions

Currently in progress are studies that are addressing the many unresolved issues about and shortcomings in the diagnosis and management of prostate cancer. One such study is PIVOT, or the Prostate Intervention Versus Observation Trial, in which patients are randomly assigned to have either radical prostatectomy or watchful waiting. For now, patient education is critical to making informed choices. The trade-offs between benefit and risk can be assessed only for and by each individual patient.

—Gerald W. Chodak, M.D.

Hypnosis: Treatment in a Trance

Does the word *hypnosis* conjure up images of a magician-like figure dangling a gold watch in the face of a stuporous subject while giving the command to "sleep deeply"? Though hypnosis has been used as a form of cheap entertainment and is often linked with the practice of the occult, it is far more than that. Hypnosis today is a valuable therapeutic tool used by health care professionals to treat a wide variety of serious medical and psychological problems.

Establishing efficacy

Although hypnosis has been the object of interest for centuries, only in recent years has there been serious research on the phenomenon. Hypnosis is not easy to define, nor has the hypnotic state been definitively measured or identified, either biochemically or neurologically. Because conducting research on such a subjective modality is difficult, most of the knowledge thus far acquired about hypnosis comes from case studies, clinical anecdotes, and systematic observations of hypnotic phenomena.

The emphasis in the entire field of medicine today is on "outcome studies"—controlled investigations designed to isolate and demonstrate the effectiveness of one particular intervention or treatment versus another. Though not yet abundant, such outcome studies provide objective support for the application of hypnosis in such diverse areas as pain control, the amelioration of bad habits, and the enhancement of cognitive-behavioral therapies for depression and anxiety. Meanwhile, active research is being conducted on the potential of hypnosis in the treatment of a wide range of additional mental and physical problems.

Suggestibility and influence

Formal hypnosis takes place when a clinician helps focus a client's attention on some suggested thought, feeling, or sensation. Anything absorbing can serve as an "induction," including the proverbial dangling-watch, "you're getting sleepy" routine.

"Suggestibility" is an openness to accepting new ideas or information. It is not the same as "gullibility." Everybody is to some degree open to suggestion. The suggestibility of each individual makes change possible and allows growth to take place. It is through experience that people discover that their information is wrong or incomplete. Such discovery enables them to accept the ideas or viewpoints (suggestions) of others—especially those they consider experts.

It is the task of the clinician to establish rapport with the client in order to influence him or her in some beneficial way. Without that rapport, hypnosis is unlikely to be effective.

Psychopathologies (emotional disorders) arise because people think arbitrary and hurtful things (whether about themselves, others, or some aspect of their lives). They also come to believe those things. Therapists typically hear only about the hurtful things people tell themselves, such as, "I'll never be able to do this." People can come to believe helpful things they tell themselves as well ("I can do this, even though I'm a little intimidated by it"). Ernest Hilgard, a distinguished hypnosis researcher, has described hypnosis as "believed-in imagination."

Consider the individual who has a phobia about speaking in public. People who are fearful of public speaking typically create vivid mental pictures of themselves standing before a roomful of people (or even just a few others)—an audience that seems bored, irritated, or otherwise antagonistic. They visualize themselves, in great detail, "messing up" their presentation and looking foolish in the eyes of everyone present. Such images summon up all the anxious and terrified feelings of a real experience.

The direction in which people focus their attention determines how they respond to life experiences and, ultimately, how they feel about themselves. Hypnosis involves shifting focal points. Hypnosis helps people build the frame of mind to do whatever it is they are trying to do; it connects them with the necessary resources to accomplish their goals.

Building frames of mind

Essentially, hypnosis can be used as a tool in the treatment of any human condition in which a person's attitude is a factor. Clinical interventions employing hypnosis will almost always involve some or all of the following classical hypnotic ("trance") phenomena. These represent the basic ways that the mind can be focused for therapeutic benefit.

- *Age regression.* Age-regression techniques are based on an intense absorption in memory. The therapist guides the client back in time to some experience. The client either remembers the experience as intensely as possible (called "hypermnesia") or relives it as if it were happening in the here and now ("revivification"). Age-regression strategies can be employed in at least two distinct ways. The first involves "going back" in time to redefine negative or traumatic experiences. The second involves rediscovering and making use of a client's hidden abilities that have been demonstrated in past situations but are not currently being used—unfortunately, to his or her own detriment.
- *Age progression.* One can think of the phenomenon known as age progression as gaining hindsight while it is still foresight. This happens through intense absorption in expectations about the future. A therapist guides the client into the future. The client imagines the consequences of current changes or choices. This makes it possible to obtain an "overview" of his or her life situation.
- *Amnesia.* Amnesia means "loss of memory." One can consciously forget something but still be influenced by it. Its use in hypnosis can be most simply described as "deliberate forgetting"; thus, one can consciously forget receiving a suggestion that can still have a beneficial impact on one's life.
- *Hypnotically induced analgesia and anesthesia*. These two trance phenomena are on a continuum of diminishing bodily sensation. *Analgesia* refers to a reduction in the sensation of pain that nonetheless allows associated sensations that orient the client to his or her body to remain. *Anesthesia* refers to a complete or near-complete elimination of sensation in all or part of the body.
- *Catalepsy*. The cataleptic state inhibits voluntary movement while the individual intensely focuses on some thought or feeling (*i.e.,* one becomes "frozen with fascination").
- *Dissociation*. The ability to break an experience into its component parts is known as dissociation. It involves amplifying one's awareness of one part while diminishing awareness of the others. Through dissociation, people can detach themselves from their immediate environment; they can "go through the motions" but not really "be there." The conscious mind can be one place, preoccupied with whatever has its attention, leaving the unconscious free to respond in whatever way it chooses. Dissociation allows for spontaneous responses. Forgotten experiences can be remembered. The hand can lift involuntarily. The body can "forget" to notice pain.
- *Hallucinations*. A hallucination is, by definition, a sensory experience that does not arise from external stimulation. Hypnotically created hallucinations can be characterized as being either positive or negative. A positive hallucination is evident when one has the experience (visual, auditory, kinesthetic, olfactory, gustatory) of something that is not objectively present—for example, hearing someone call one's name when one is alone. A negative hallucination is the failure to experience something sensorially that is objectively present—for example, not hearing the phone ring.
- *Time distortion*. The phenomenon of time distortion involves the alteration of one's perception of time. The passing of time can seem much longer or much shorter than is objectively true, depending on one's focus of attention. Common therapeutic uses of distortion include decreasing one's sense of time in order to endure a painful, long, or otherwise difficult medical procedure or increasing one's sense of time so as to enjoy restful imagery and thereby reduce tension.

Medical hypnosis

Hypnosis can be a useful adjunct to traditional medical treatments for several reasons. One is that it takes advantage of the so-called mind-body relationship. Attitudes and emotions have a powerful influence on bodily (somatic) conditions. In the medical literature there are many descriptions of patients who get the "upper hand" over their disease and of "miracle cures" that defy medical explanation. Patients who have an intense will to live and refuse to give up are more likely to survive than those who think of themselves as doomed.

A second reason for using hypnosis is that it places an emphasis on the responsibility of each person for his or her own health and well-being. Because hypnosis allows people to attain a significant degree of control over seemingly uncontrollable physical processes, it can be used very effectively to reduce or eliminate pain, both chronic and acute.

The potential to reduce pain constitutes one of the most meaningful applications of therapeutic hypnosis. Even pain emanating from clearly organic causes has psychological components—particularly the way in which the individual experiences it (its relative intensity, its capacity to debilitate, etc.). Many hold the misconception that if one can reduce or eliminate pain with hypnosis, then the pain is not "real." On the

Philippe Plailly—Science Source/Photo Researchers

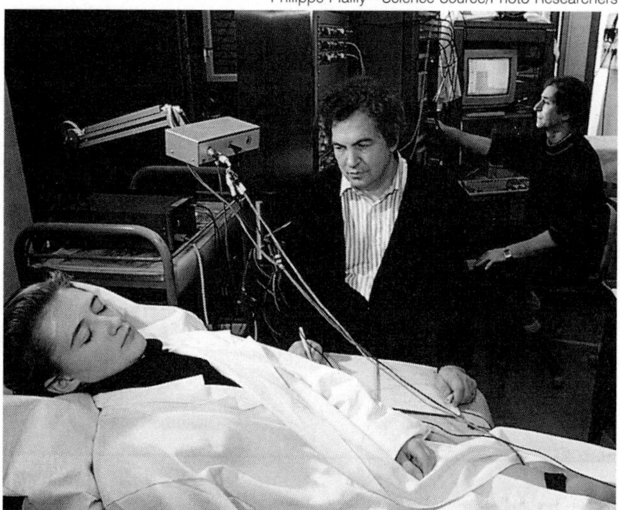

A hypnotized subject participates in pain research. Like most other treatments today, hypnosis is the focus of carefully designed research studies that are evaluating its therapeutic validity.

contrary, hypnosis has even been used as the principal anesthetic in major surgical procedures, where the pain is very real but is hypnotically "filtered out" of awareness.

Hypnotic pain reduction can curtail patients' overreliance on medications. Such pain-management techniques can be used before, during, and after surgery; to facilitate childbirth; and to help manage physical trauma. Hypnosis can be valuable in the management of very serious diseases such as cancer and AIDS. By its very nature, hypnosis is "holistic"; hypnotism recognizes the importance of the whole person by addressing patients' emotional needs as a part of treatment.

The exact mechanism whereby a doctor can offer hypnotic suggestions and effect changes in the patient is unknown, but the answer is thought to reside in the branch of medicine known as psychoneuroimmunology. Current research in this area suggests that people are more likely to develop a serious disease during or after a highly stressful period of their lives. Stress is known to reduce the capacity of the body's natural defenses (the immune system) and thus enable malignant cells or disease-causing organisms (bacteria, viruses, fungi) to multiply in the weakened person. Hypnosis, by diminishing stress, is thought to strengthen the body's immunologic functions and thereby assist in fighting off the disease. In some studies cancer patients who participate in stress-reduction classes, for example, are more likely than controls (nonparticipants) to have remissions.

Dental applications

Many of the desired outcomes sought in medical contexts are also desirable in the dental setting. The teeth, gums, and associated structures are simply parts of the body. Attached to every mouth under treatment is a whole person, whose attitudes about the work being done, about himself or herself, and about the dentist will affect the outcome of the intervention. Hypnosis can help a patient reduce his or her anxiety about receiving dental treatment. Furthermore, one good session in the dentist's chair will serve as a blueprint for future positive dental experiences.

Many dental patients either cannot or choose not to have local chemical anesthesia (such as novocaine or nitrous oxide). Basic hypnotic techniques can reduce the degree of discomfort experienced; some patients are able to eliminate the discomfort altogether.

Hypnosis can also enhance healing after treatment. Imagining the healing process can both shorten the recovery period and make the recovery time more comfortable. For example, one imagines the gums mending after a wisdom tooth has been removed.

Advantages in psychotherapy

The main advantage of using hypnosis in psychotherapy lies in its ability to marshal the many extraordinary resources of the unconscious mind. The unconscious mind contains a lifetime of experiences and learnings. Feelings, values, memories, understanding, and beliefs are all perceptions that guide the client's current choices. Because perceptions are subjective, they can change. Hypnosis simply permits greater access to the unconscious mind's resources so that they can be used to make a desired change.

Procedures that involve simply inducing hypnosis formally and then giving suggestions directly related to a single problem ("you will stop smoking") represent the most superficial use of hypnosis. This kind of symptom-oriented hypnosis is widely employed by lay hypnotists and many lesser-trained psychotherapists. For some clients who have uncomplicated problems or single symptoms, it can be effective.

Clinical hypnosis aimed at the interruption of more pervasive patterns and problems requires a clinician with skill and training in the use of dynamic therapeutic techniques—techniques that recognize the client's multiple dimensions. For example, smokers may need to improve their relationships with their bodies so that smoking becomes inimical to their "well-being." This kind of dynamic hypnosis can help the client clarify misperceptions about early or recent experiences, learn creative and positive ways to meet special needs, or discover abilities he or she has had all along but never knew how to use.

Specialized applications

There are other uses of hypnosis—some with established efficacy, some that remain controversial. Among these are:

- *Education.* Many creative instructors at all academic levels are using hypnosis in their teaching—particularly to make the classroom conducive to learning and encourage student participation. Many students are using self-hypnosis techniques to manage anxiety, enhance concentration, become better organized, and gain confidence in competitive learning situations.
- *Business.* Effective communication can either make or break a company. Communication skills are needed in such interactions as presenting a marketing plan, handling a troublesome employee or supervisor, conducting a job interview, evaluating employee performance, establishing

work standards, and creating a pleasant and motivating work atmosphere. Because the essence of hypnosis is influencing through effective communication, hypnotically based techniques are being used—and are paying off—in many businesses and industries.

- *Sports.* Engaging in athletics requires a large measure of physical control and mental concentration. Hypnosis is a tool that can foster both. Intensive concentration and control enable athletes to push themselves to the limits of their abilities.

  In addition to building concentration and physical control, hypnosis can help athletes manage the stress inherent in competing. Formal or informal (*i.e.,* focusing methods used without the formality of an induction procedure) hypnosis can be a boon to the slumping athlete (or team). Though hypnosis does not increase talent, it can turn an individual's athletic performance around, or it can give a losing team new spirit that may enable it to gain the "winning edge."
- *Courtrooms.* The use of hypnotically obtained testimony in courts of law is highly controversial, and the laws governing its admissibility in courts vary widely from one jurisdiction to the next. Experts are at odds over such testimony because of the known potential for memories and perceptions to be contaminated or distorted through hypnosis and suggestion. A witness giving testimony under hypnosis may deliberately lie, fill in missing details with imagined details and misinformation (called confabulations), or accept misinformation that is contained in subtle questions of investigators.

Recovered memories

Probably the most highly charged and questionable use of hypnosis is in so-called recovered-memory therapy. Consider a woman who seeks psychotherapy because she is having difficulties in her interpersonal relationships, especially with men. Her psychotherapist tells her that her symptoms suggest she may have been sexually abused as a child, even though she has no memories, or even hints of memories, of any such events. Through hypnosis she "remembers" vague instances of being sexually abused by her father at a very early age. Did these episodes actually occur? Might they have been manufactured unintentionally in order to accommodate the expectations and suggestions of the psychotherapist? Is it possible to lead someone to believe he or she was sexually abused when no such abuse actually occurred?

There has been an increasing effort made through research to determine how responsive to suggestion memory might be. Numerous studies have lent support to the recognition that memory is "reconstructive," not "reproductive." Thus, the accuracy of memory can be influenced by many factors, including suggestion and misinformation.

Without objective corroborating evidence such as a photograph or videotape, how can one distinguish a real memory from a confabulation? At present, unfortunately, no objective method for doing so exists. There have been several widely publicized cases in which adults have recovered memories of childhood sexual abuse through hypnosis and then leveled

NEWS*CAP*

Mental Illness: A Global Problem

An alarming increase in mental illness in poor countries threatens the social stability of the less developed world. So concluded an international team of 88 health authorities from 30 countries in their report on global mental health. The group's findings were issued in May 1995 at United Nations headquarters in New York City. According to the leader of the international study, Arthur Kleinman, an anthropologist and psychiatrist in the department of social medicine at Harvard Medical School, the problems are broad and include "not just neuropsychiatric disorders but also behavioral problems like substance abuse and violence."

Among the specific findings were:

- The elderly, in particular, suffer from the stresses of the rapid social and economic changes occurring in many less developed countries.
- Rates of mental retardation and epilepsy are up to five times greater in poor nations than in more affluent ones. In some African and Asian countries, up to 90% of persons with epilepsy receive no treatment because medications are not available or are too expensive.
- The number of reported cases of schizophrenia in poor countries is expected to rise from 16.5 million in 1985 to 24.4 million by the year 2000. By 2025 three-fourths of dementia cases will be in less developed nations.
- In less developed countries 20% to 75% of married women are victims of domestic violence. And in many parts of the world, child prostitution and slavery are becoming "endemic," as is the abandonment of unwanted children.
- War and political upheaval are contributing to a high incidence of depression, anxiety disorders, and other forms of mental distress among the more than 40 million refugees and displaced persons in the world.

The published report, *World Mental Health: Problems and Priorities in Low-Income Countries* (Oxford University Press, 1995), called for a major initiative to improve mental health services in Africa, Asia, Latin America, and the Middle East, with particular emphasis on training more mental health workers. Follow-up studies are under way.

R. Netelev—Itar-Tass/Sovfoto

A Russian hypnotherapist has gained wide popularity for his televised group treatments of obesity. When it is used by competent professionals, hypnosis can be a very useful therapeutic tool. It can also be misused by untrained individuals.

charges against a perpetrator (usually a parent). Although a few alleged abusers have been convicted, many of these cases have been highly questionable, and many experts agree that recovered-memory therapy lacks support.

Hazards

Is hypnosis dangerous? As with any tool, hypnosis can be used well—or badly. The outcome depends on all the variables in the interaction. These include the relationship between clinician and client, the goal and expectations of each, the communication style employed, and the content of the specific suggestions. The danger that hypnosis will precipitate psychosis, neurosis, hysteria, or suicide, however, has been exaggerated.

One of the most common concerns about the use of hypnosis is the potential for "symptom substitution"—the onset of a new symptom in the place of the symptom that is the focus of the hypnotic treatment. As noted above, simple suggestions aimed at a single target symptom may be used by untrained laypersons who have no real understanding of the role of the symptom in a person's life. In such a case, symptom substitution can occur.

Another common concern about hypnosis is that suggestions made will not be removed, and the client will be left in a vulnerable state. This is unlikely. There is rarely negative carryover of the hypnotically obtained responses into the client's "waking" state. Generally, the hypnotist will carefully bring the subject out of the hypnotic state—a deliberate procedure that encourages "bringing back," into the waking state, only what is therapeutically useful. If the clinician does not remove suggestions at the end of the session, the suggestions are likely to dissipate automatically. If the exception occurs, it is possible that the client has somehow given himself or herself posthypnotic suggestions.

Probably the greatest potential hazards of hypnosis are "spontaneous regression" and "abreaction." The former describes the experience of repressed or forgotten past experiences' suddenly coming into awareness (a "flashback"). Abreaction is the expression, or unleashing, of previously pent-up emotions (rage, envy, self-blame, etc.).

Together, these two phenomena account for the often-unexpected strong emotions that make hypnosis such a powerful tool. In some cases, during something as simple as a general relaxation procedure, a client may flash upon some word or image that is associated with an emotionally charged memory. Even the most experienced clinician cannot know what "land mines" are in a client's unconscious waiting to be tripped during therapy or hypnosis. Each human being has a unique personal history. What seems like a neutral term to one person may be the trigger to some volatile issue for another. Therefore, the possibility of a practitioner's performing hypnosis without ever producing an abreaction is highly unlikely. Abreactions are dramatic events, but they can also facilitate true healing.

Caveat emptor

The hazards described above underscore the importance of selecting a competent professional. Unfortunately, a powerful tool like hypnosis can be placed in the hands of poorly trained people who are not in a position to appreciate the full implications of its use.

Fortunately, there are reliable organizations that can provide names of qualified hypnotists. A prospective client in the U.S. may contact the American Society of Clinical Hypnosis (708-297-3317) or the Society for Clinical and Experimental Hypnosis (315-652-7299) for specific referrals in his or her geographic area.

—Michael D. Yapko, Ph.D.

Contemporary Contacts

For more than 50 million persons worldwide—28 million of them in the United States—the wearing of contact lenses is a safe and acceptable alternative to eyeglasses. If they are used properly, contact lenses, which are medical devices regulated by the U.S. Food and Drug Administration (FDA), may be worn without problems. The most important factors in deciding whether contact lenses will work well for a given patient are motivation; a good fit; patient education in, and compliance with, lens care and wear routines; and meticulous follow-up.

In the U.S. some 20 million people currently wear soft lenses—up 12% from 1993—while 7 million wear rigid gas-permeable lenses. Recent trends indicate that prescriptions for disposable lenses—the latest innovation—are increasing at a fast pace. Women account for more than 75% of U.S. contact lens wearers.

Though small compared with the 100 million Americans who wear conventional eyeglasses, the growing number of contacts wearers testifies to some inherent benefits in using a lens fitted directly to the eye's surface. Contacts can eliminate problems that eyeglass wearers have, such as reflections, distortion, frame discomfort, and restricted peripheral vision. Most wearers additionally appreciate contacts for their convenience and their recreational and cosmetic advantages. Though refractive eye surgeries—reshaping of the eye's surface—are becoming a more and more common and acceptable way of correcting vision, many physicians consider contacts a safer and more conservative alternative.

For some the wearing of contact lenses is the only way to see well. Besides aiding vision, contacts may protect corneas damaged by injury or disease. Contacts may also help some patients recovering from cataract surgery. Those with severely impaired vision may use contacts in combination with low-vision aids such as telescopic lens systems and specially designed eyeglasses. Others who require unusually high-power corrections for hyperopia (farsightedness), myopia (nearsightedness), or astigmatism (distorted vision) can achieve better and more accurate vision by wearing contact lenses. Contact lenses are not for everyone, but today the scope and variety of lens options are making contacts available to more people than ever before.

Contact lens history

As early as 1508 Leonardo da Vinci sketched a lens that fitted against the cornea, providing a new refracting surface for the eye. But it was not until 1887 that a blown-glass contact lens was produced by Mueller-Friedrich Mueller of Wiesbaden, Germany, a member of a world-famous firm of makers of artificial eyes. Mueller designed a shell-shaped glass lens to protect the eye of a patient whose eyelid had been destroyed by cancer. Mueller's brother, August, later wore a similar lens as a spectator at games and was very satisfied with it. Mueller's "medical device" was also used by Adolf Fick, a German physiologist, to correct a malformation of the cornea (astigmatism). These large "scleral" glass lenses fitted over the entire eye—cornea and sclera (white portion of the eye)—

Everett Collection

Special-effects contact lenses transform actor Keye Luke into blind Master Po, martial arts whiz on the popular "Kung Fu" TV series.

but could be worn for only short periods owing to discomfort and poor optical performance.

In the 1940s Hollywood optometrist Reuben Greenspoon used glass, and later Plexiglas, contact lenses to create special eye effects and to change the color of movie actors' eyes—the most common silver-screen ocular transformations being for vampires and werewolves. Greenspoon's son, optometrist Morton Greenspoon, later prescribed contacts for performers in the television series "Kung Fu" and "The Incredible Hulk," both in the 1970s.

Lens fitting

The surface of the human eye is perpetually lubricated by fluid from the tear ducts. A contact lens fits over this tear film and provides a new refractive system to correct vision. The tear-film "sandwich" between the parallel curvatures of the lens and cornea creates a capillary attraction similar to that of two adhering plates of wet glass. The lens adheres to the eye, which allows the wearer to blink freely and to look in any direction. Each lens moves with the eye, so the wearer is always looking through the lens's optical center. The optics of correcting for nearsightedness, farsightedness, and astigmatism are essentially the same as they are for eyeglasses. That is, convex lenses (which are thicker in the center) correct for

Dan McCoy—Rainbow

A hard plastic lens adheres to the surface of the eye, allowing adequate oxygen to reach the cornea. The lens moves with the eye so that the wearer is always looking through its optical center and seeing clearly.

farsightedness and concave lenses (thinner in the center) correct for nearsightedness, while lenses for astigmatic problems correct for a misfocus in two different directions, vertically and horizontally, and thus allow light to be focused onto a single point on the retina.

Perhaps the most important physiological determinant in the successful wearing of contact lenses is the adequate exchange of oxygen from the air to the eye. The lenses must be fitted so that they cause little or no significant change in the amount of oxygen that reaches the cornea—a standard that virtually all lenses today meet. Other important lens-performance factors are adequate movement, comfortable edge design, resistance to buildup of deposits, and lens size. The health of the cornea, the adequacy of the tear film, and particular anatomic aspects of each individual eye are still further parameters to be considered.

Hard lenses

In 1947 a nontoxic plastic lens material, called PMMA, was introduced for optical use, replacing glass. Smaller corneal lenses were later improvements that increased the popularity and production of contact lenses during the 1950s and 1960s. While these hard lenses were made from material that was so durable that the lenses could last for years and were resistant to deposit buildup, they did not allow adequate oxygen to the cornea. Though occasionally still prescribed and fitted today, such hard plastic lenses have largely given way to oxygen-permeable rigid lenses.

Gas-permeable lenses

Oxygen-permeable hard contact lenses made of rigid plastic combined with other materials such as silicone were introduced in the 1980s, with dramatic results. Because they allowed high oxygen exchange, they offered improved wearability over earlier hard contact lenses. Gas-permeable lenses also provide the best vision correction of all contact lens types and correct most forms of astigmatism. Easier to handle and requiring less-frequent replacement than soft lenses, their main disadvantage is their thinness, which can cause them to warp and scratch. Most gas-permeable hard lenses are prescribed for daily wear, though some can be worn for extended and overnight wear. Like earlier hard lenses, gas-permeable lenses are quite durable and can last for several years.

Soft lenses: ever-evolving

In 1970 researchers in Czechoslovakia developed plastic contact lenses (called hydrogel lenses) that were soft and flexible enough for daily wear. With a 38% water content, these large, flexible lenses provided more initial eye comfort without the long adaptation period commonly required with hard plastic lenses. Because of their larger size, soft lenses are much less likely to pop out, or dislodge from the eye. Owing to deposit formation on the lens surface, however, soft lenses entail a more cumbersome cleaning regimen, and the lenses themselves are easily damaged. The normal life expectancy of conventional soft lenses is about one year. They are also less effective than hard or gas-permeable lenses in correcting astigmatism.

The next major development in soft lenses was an increase in water content to as much as 75%, which permitted extended wearing periods. The prospect of being able to leave the lenses in the eyes for days and forget about the daily-care routine was enormously attractive to many consumers. It was the closest thing available to permanent restoration of "normal" vision.

But such a prospect also proved too good to be true. It soon became apparent that a major disadvantage of extended-wear soft lenses was eye inflammation. The most commonly encountered problems were papillary conjunctivitis (irritated inner lids) and acute red eyes with small corneal changes. A more serious but less-frequent problem was ulcerative keratitis (ulcerated cornea); the risk of this eye infection was found to be up to 10 times greater in those who wore their lenses overnight compared with users of daily-wear lenses. The risk was nine times greater in elderly patients. Moreover, cigarette smokers showed a threefold-greater risk for ulcerative keratitis than nonsmokers, regardless of the type of soft lens worn. The wearers of daily soft lenses—and, to a lesser degree, hard-lens wearers—also experienced these problems but much less frequently and often because of misuse. In May 1990 the FDA issued guidelines that recommend that extended-wear lenses not be worn for more than seven days without removal and thorough cleaning.

Cathy Melloan

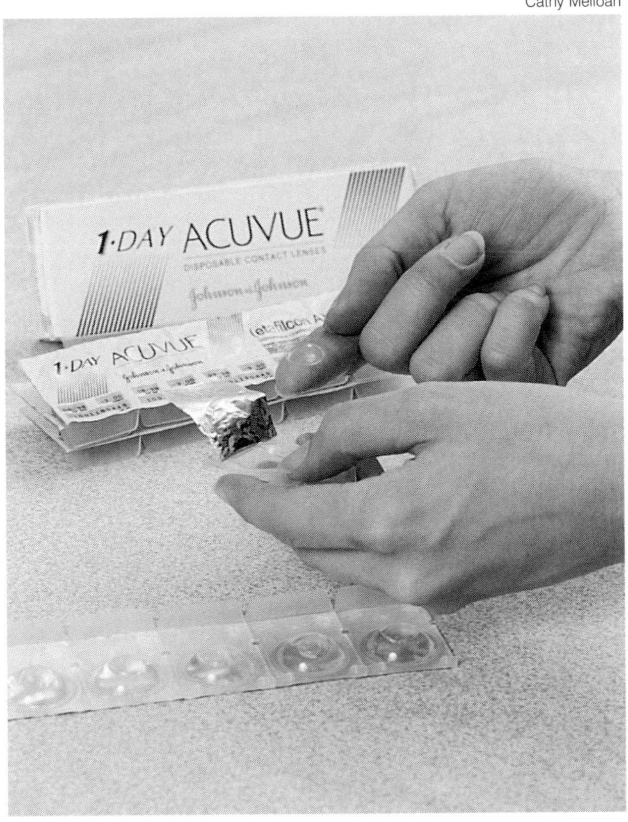

One of the latest innovations in contacts is the one-day disposable soft lens. The distinct advantage of daily disposables is that they eliminate time-consuming and, some would say, tedious, lens care.

Here today, gone tomorrow

A development of the 1990s is the disposable contact lens. Disposable soft lenses that are left in the eyes for one to two weeks and then discarded are rapidly gaining acceptance. The main advantages of this type of lens are convenience and the elimination of the time-consuming daily cleaning and insertion routines that are required for conventional soft and hard contacts. Because such lenses come in "six-packs," wearers can enjoy the security of always having a spare. Very recently one-day disposable soft contact lenses were introduced. Disposable (as well as extended-wear) lenses still do not provide any significant astigmatism correction, and whether the public will accept their higher cost is uncertain.

Special types of contacts

There are numerous specialized types of lenses available today, and the options are ever expanding.

Multifocus lenses. As the number of baby boomers over age 40 increases, more and more middle-aged people are seeking multifocal contacts for presbyopia (literally, "old-man eyes"). Presbyopia is a condition that commonly develops as people age and the lens of the eye becomes less flexible, which makes it more difficult for the muscles of the eye to accommodate for close-up vision. The fitting of hard or soft bifocal contact lenses requires the utmost skill on the part of the practitioner. Despite the growing demand, some specialists believe that high motivation and determination on the part of the individual are even more important than lens design in ultimate wearer satisfaction. Lengthy fitting sessions are needed, and the lenses take more "adjusting" time than single-correcting lenses. Consequently, many practitioners offer trial programs for presbyopic patients, allowing three to four weeks for patient and practitioner to reach a mutual decision as to whether to proceed with contacts.

Because of the fitting and adjustment difficulties associated with bi- and trifocal lenses, many presbyopic contact lens wearers opt for "reading" spectacles, worn over their regular lenses. Others prefer a special approach called "monovision." This technique requires that one eye be fitted for distance viewing while the companion eye is fitted for close-up vision. (The brain eventually adapts to the alternating focus between the two eyes.) Although monovision lens fittings have become an increasingly popular option for presbyopics, the technique often does not work well for higher-power reading corrections because it fails to provide adequate distance vision (especially in subdued lighting). Further, there may be interference with binocular vision and depth perception because of the unbalanced focusing required.

For those whose work or lifestyle demands precise binocular vision and depth perception—for example, pilots and certain kinds of technicians—bifocal contacts are probably the lens of choice over monovision. Far more costly and complicated in design than traditional contacts, hard and soft bifocals have been greatly improved in the past few years; they are easier to fit and more comfortable to wear.

Lenses for astigmatism. Recent developments have eased the fitting for those with astigmatism. Contacts that correct astigmatism, known as "toric" lenses, are available in rigid and soft materials. Soft disposable astigmatic lenses are under development and will soon be introduced to the public. Toric lenses require considerable skill in fitting as well as patience and motivation on the part of the wearer.

Ultraviolet-blocking lenses. True ultraviolet (UV) protection can be achieved only with sunglasses that fully cover the eyes. Nonetheless, UV contacts are being prescribed for some patients who have recently had cataracts removed, for those with medication-induced UV hypersensitivity, and for some albinos (individuals whose skin, hair, and eyes lack pigment).

Contacts for sports. Many athletes choose contacts because of eyeglass-related safety or breakage concerns. Other factors such as dirt, rain, snow reflections, perspiration, and lens fogging also put conventional eyeglass wearers at a disadvantage. The preferred contacts for sports are usually soft lenses that have a large surface area, which makes them unlikely to pop out during strenuous activity. They also increase peripheral vision.

Swimmers competing in the Olympic Games, as well as recreational swimmers, have worn contact lenses successfully, both with and without watertight goggles. There is a risk, however, of losing contacts in the water. Also, chlorine levels in the pool will affect the eyes with or without lenses. If lenses are worn for swimming, it is recommended that they be worn with goggles and removed after swimming to rest the eyes. Generally, the lenses that are worn most successfully for swimming, diving, and water polo are larger lenses made from soft-lens material.

Tinted contacts. Some 2.5 million persons in the U.S. wear contact lenses that enhance or change the color of their eyes. Some wear them solely for cosmetic purposes, others for cosmetic reasons and vision correction. The soft colored lenses that are available today permit the alteration of eye color from the darkest hues to stunningly light tones. Generally, today's lenses have a much more natural look than early tinted ones. Most are available in the newer soft lens or even disposable forms. Trial fittings are important to allow the consumer to "see" the color changes.

Corneal shaping. An alternative to surgery is known as "orthokeratology," a special fitting therapy using hard contact lenses to reshape the eye's surface over a period of weeks or months and thereby "naturally" reduce refractive errors. Although this technique is not new, modern lens materials have increased its popularity. The eye care specialist uses a series of specially curved lenses to alter the curvature of the eye and improve visual acuity so that eyeglasses or contacts are not needed. There have been few reports of eye complications with orthokeratology. For most patients, however, the improvement in vision is temporary and requires some continued wearing of a lens during at least part of the day and at night as a "retainer."

Anatomy of the Eye

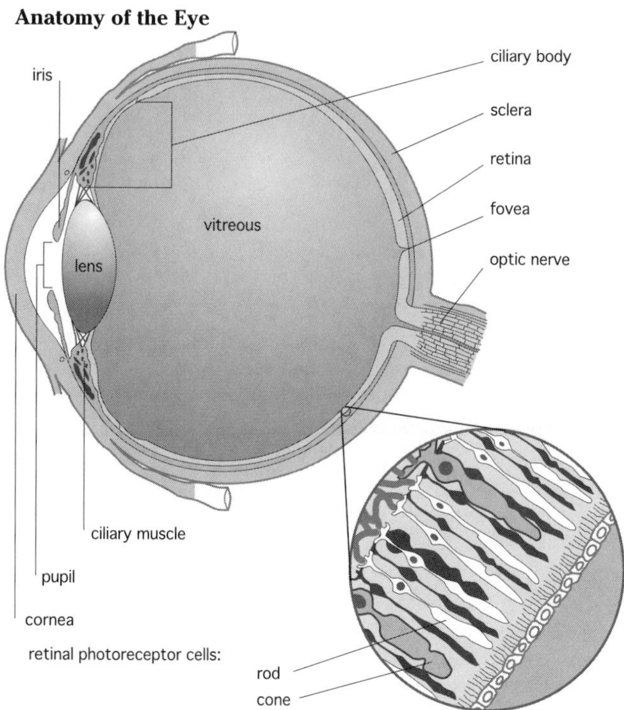

NEWS*CAP*

Shortsighted

Surgery intended to save the sight of people suffering from nonarteritic anterior ischemic optic neuropathy (NAION), a common ocular disorder among the elderly, is ineffective and may even be harmful. The surgery, called optic nerve decompression, was introduced in 1989 after researchers reported that incising the optic nerve sheath in patients with a progressive form of NAION had relieved pressure on the nerve that, in turn, was impairing vision. As no other therapy was known to be effective at that time, optic nerve decompression quickly gained acceptance.

Because the operation was done regularly but had never undergone controlled scientific study, a panel of experts was convened to assess the surgery's benefits and risks. The findings were published in the *Journal of the American Medical Association* (Feb. 22, 1995).

More than 240 patients with NAION were examined at 25 eye centers. After six months only 33% of those who had surgery to correct the disease had significantly improved vision, while 43% who had no surgery improved equally. Further, 24% of the patients who had the surgery lost a significant degree of vision within six months, compared with 12% who did not have the surgery. Patients in both groups had visual acuity of 20/64 or worse prior to the study. In light of these findings, the National Eye Institute issued a clinical alert advising all U.S. eye surgeons of the ineffectiveness and potential harm of this widely performed operation.

Lens care

Not surprisingly, there is a strong link between ocular health and the "satisfied" contact lens wearer. Although major complications are extremely rare, they occasionally do arise because of poor fit or user noncompliance—*e.g.,* failure to use proper solutions, imprudent wearing habits, and cavalier attitudes about lens care and cleaning. Instruction about proper lens care and appropriate wearing schedules should begin in the office of the eye care specialist.

Following each wearing, the lenses should be cleaned, rinsed, and disinfected. One need only visit the contact lens care section of a drugstore to see the myriad products available to the wearer. For both soft and hard lenses, there are four basic uses of solution: wetting, cleaning, soaking, and lubricating. The various cleaning and storage solutions for soft and hard lenses are not interchangeable.

Wetting solutions are formulated to make the lens amply moist, allowing an optimum flow of tears around and through the lens. Formerly, soft-lens wearers were instructed to use salt tablets dissolved in distilled water to prepare their own saline solution. Owing to the risk of acanthamoeba keratitis, a very serious and hard-to-treat infection associated with homemade saline, the FDA banned the sale of salt tablets for such solution in 1988. Today the FDA recommends that all soft-lens wearers use commercially prepared sterile saline for both wetting and soaking their lenses. Because of inherent impurities, tap water should never be used with soft lenses of any type. Hard-lens wearers must use a special and more viscous wetting solution than basic sterile saline.

Contact lenses must be cleaned and disinfected daily after removal from the eyes. Studies have shown that the mechanical rubbing motion, together with the proper cleaning agent, produces the best results. Daily cleaning solutions help mitigate the buildup of dirt on the lens. They also keep mucus and protein debris in the tears from accumulating on the lens. A separate enzyme cleaning agent that is usually used once a week is available for both soft and hard lenses to maintain an extra-clean lens.

Soaking (disinfecting) solution is necessary as a germicidal agent to reduce the likelihood of microbial contamination of the lenses during storage. The lenses must be stored at least several hours at a time, and solutions must be changed each time. Another very effective disinfecting solution for soft lenses is nonsensitizing hydrogen peroxide. Eye care specialists generally recommend hydrogen peroxide solution over heat disinfection, especially when the contacts have a very high water content or if patients are prone to excessive deposits or allergies.

Special lubricating eyedrops for contacts (also called comfort drops) act as both artificial tears and lens-rewetting agents to alleviate symptoms and irritations caused by dry-eye conditions as well as adverse environmental situations. Although many soft-lens wearers use sterile saline as drops, that practice is not recommended. Excessive use of any kind of drops can lead to other problems. Some lubricating tears or nonprescription drops contain eye-whitening chemicals to clear up mild redness, and most contain a special preservative to keep the solution sterile; some people are sensitive to these chemicals, so only a product recommended by a lens fitter or eye care practitioner should be used.

To simplify lens care and handling, some manufacturers have recently formulated "all-in-one" wetting, cleaning, and disinfecting agents. Specific cleaning products may, however, do a more thorough job than the multipurpose solutions now on the market.

Tips for wearers

Contact lens users are likely to be content if they follow these simple tips:

- Expect an adaptation period of a few days to a few weeks—which may include tearing, increased blinking, and greater sensitivity to light—especially for first-time contact lens wearers.
- Each morning take the "see well, feel well, look well" test. Cover one eye at a time. The vision in the uncovered eye should be clear, the lens should feel comfortable, and the eye should not be irritated or red.
- Before handling lenses, wash hands with a nonoily soap, and dry them with a lint-free towel.
- Whenever eyes are tired from wearing lenses for an extended period, use warm, damp compresses over eyes after removal of lenses.
- Use cold compresses over eyes after lens removal when eyes are itchy or irritated from allergies.
- Wait at least 15 minutes after waking up before putting lenses in; remove lenses at least 15 minutes prior to sleeping. This gives the eyes a chance to get more oxygen.
- Do not reuse lens solutions or share bottles with someone else.
- Refrain from wearing lenses while suffering from a bad head cold.
- Do not wear lenses during extended air travel or when weather conditions are unusually dry, dusty, or windy.
- Always build up wearing time after not wearing lenses for three or more days.

Who should not wear contacts?

The American Academy of Ophthalmology specifies certain conditions that make contacts inappropriate. Those for whom contact lenses are not a good choice include:

- people with frequent eye infections
- those with severe allergies
- those with "dry eye" (inadequate tear film)
- those whose work environment is extremely dusty or dirty
- those who are unable to handle and care for lenses properly

—Weylin G. Eng, O.D., and Robert C. Yeager, M.J.

Technology for Teeth

Dental materials and procedures continue to evolve, offering greater treatment opportunities and improved results. More durable and aesthetically acceptable materials are replacing older ones for traditional applications such as fillings and crowns, while previously irremediable problems—for example, very small or widely spaced teeth—are yielding to innovative techniques. Moreover, conditions not formerly defined as within the realm of dentistry, such as snoring, are now being controlled with oral appliances.

Amalgam fillings: lingering controversy

Amalgam, the silver-colored material that most fillings are made of, has been widely used for more than a century. It consists of a mixture of silver (about 35%) and mercury (up to 50%), along with smaller amounts of zinc, tin, or tin mixed with copper. The mercury component has long been a source of health concerns. Mercury is known to be toxic when ingested, inhaled, or absorbed via the skin. Prolonged exposures can lead to a variety of disorders, including neurological conditions and autoimmune diseases. Traditionally, mercury poisoning was an occupational disease of hatmakers, who incurred significant exposures to mercury salts used in the manufacture of felt. The personality and behavioral changes produced by chronic mercury poisoning probably inspired the expression "mad as a hatter."

Because dental mercury is bound up with silver and other metals when it is placed in a tooth, it is not readily available for reaction with body tissues. Nonetheless, periodic reports have

Photographs, George A. Freedman

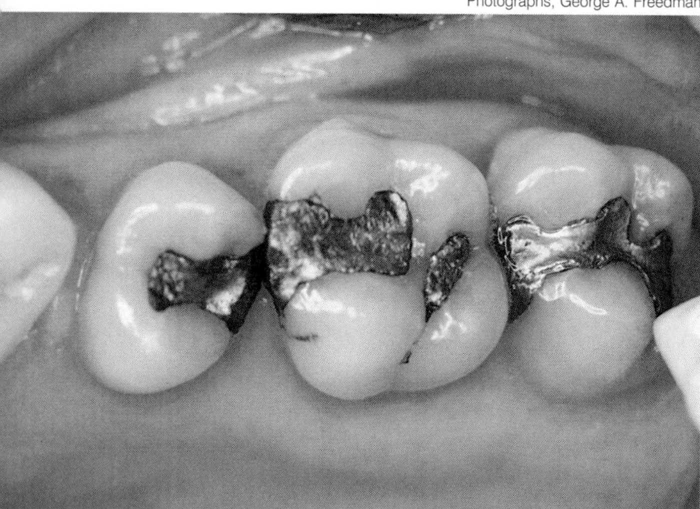

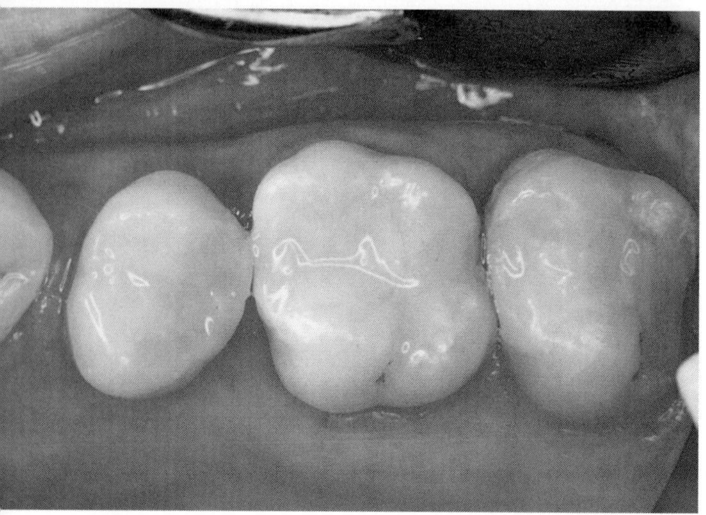

Amalgam fillings (top) can break down with wear. Ragged edges allow food and bacteria to get under the filling. Bonded composite resin fillings (above) provide attractive and extremely durable replacements; well-sealed edges form a strong barrier against further decay.

raised alarms about health risks linked to mercury amalgam fillings. Some authorities have proposed that tiny particles of amalgam can break away from fillings and enter the digestive tract, where they are attacked by acids that release elemental mercury into the body. Others have contended that mercury vapor given off by dental fillings may pose a health risk.

Solid scientific evidence of harm due to amalgam fillings has been hard to find. Researchers have demonstrated that mercury does indeed escape from fillings and that it accumulates in body tissues, but no diseases have been consistently linked to this exposure. In fact, the reports of illnesses caused by fillings are almost exclusively anecdotal. Scientific experiments that seem to implicate—or exonerate—amalgam are routinely criticized by those of the opposing view. Dentists have been hard-pressed about which side to take.

For many dental practitioners the dilemma may soon be resolved by law rather than by science. Sweden has largely banned the use of mercury amalgam, and dentists in Germany may not use amalgam fillings in children and pregnant women. Canada's Health and Welfare Department is considering limiting the number of amalgam fillings that may be placed in a patient's mouth. In the United States, bills to limit or discourage the use of amalgam have been introduced into the California and Minnesota state legislatures. Despite the dearth of scientific evidence, the movement to abandon the use of amalgam fillings clearly is gaining momentum, and a search for alternative filling materials is under way.

Tooth-colored fillings

Composite resin fillings, also known as tooth-colored fillings, have been in use for about 25 years. The material has undergone many improvements. Early composites had a tendency to shrink, leaving a gap between the tooth and the filling. The composite resins now in use, however, are quite comparable to amalgam in terms of strength and longevity and in several other respects are superior.

First, today's composites are bonded to the remaining tooth structures; because both primers and bonding agents are used, both chemical and mechanical attachments are formed between the filling material and the natural tooth. Amalgam fillings, by comparison, rely on the correspondence in shape of the filling to the cavity and the gradual corrosion of the filling to prevent gaps and further decay. Second, because composites are bonded to the tooth and can fill spaces of any shape and size, they involve far less removal of healthy tooth structures than is necessary with amalgam. Many studies also indicate that tooth-colored fillings wear down at a slower rate than amalgam fillings. In fact, composites are designed to withstand virtually the same forces and wear as natural enamel, which makes them extremely durable. Finally, tooth-colored fillings look better than amalgam; they resemble the natural tooth not only in color but in texture and reflectance.

As patients become more involved in decisions about dental treatment, they are increasingly demanding more aesthetically pleasing results, and composites provide these better results. While the jury is still out on the health risks of amalgam, a growing number of dentists are turning to composite filling materials exclusively, a trend that is likely to continue.

Light curing: distinct advantages

One feature shared by many of today's composite materials is that they are hardened, or cured, by exposure to a special form of light. The filling materials are supplied in a paste or gel form. The dentist places small dabs of several different composites on the tooth surface to evaluate their color and translucency. When a satisfactory match is found, the composite material is shaped to fill the appropriate space, and light is applied to harden the composite. Generally, the hardening process requires between 20 and 40 seconds of light curing for every 2-mm (0.08-in) layer of filling material. A small filling requires up to four 20–40-second curing sequences; a large filling may need 10 or more.

There are several advantages to using light-cured materials. Because the material does not begin to harden until the light is applied, the dentist has ample time to ensure that the color

Drawing by Leo Cullum; © 1995 The New Yorker Magazine, Inc.

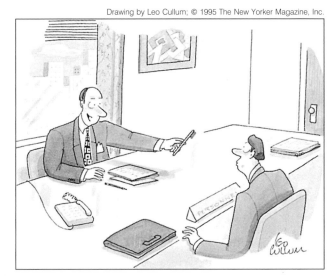

"Before I forget, Detrick, here's the dental plan."

and shape of the restoration are correct. Thus, the dentist is able to create the most artistic and aesthetically satisfying restoration.

Consistent quality is another advantage of light-cured materials. Some composite filling materials do not employ light curing. Typically, they require that two or more components be mixed together to initiate the hardening process. These ingredients can be measured only approximately at best, and minor changes in the proportions can affect the quality of the filling rather dramatically. Light-cured materials, on the other hand, require no mixing. They are expressed from a tube or a syringe in a factory-mixed, quality-controlled formula that guarantees the best possible results.

As the advantages of light-curing technology have become recognized, more and more materials and techniques that employ this process have been introduced. Moreover, in less than 15 years since its introduction, light-curing equipment has become more and more common in most dentist's offices.

A leap—with lasers

The sole drawback associated with light curing is the amount of time involved. For a larger filling, in addition to the time required for tooth preparation, the placement of the filling, and the polishing, there may be as much as seven minutes of curing time per tooth. This additional time can be exasperating for the dentist and inconvenient for the patient. It also adds to the cost of the procedure. The recently introduced argon curing laser solves this problem. The argon wavelength was selected because it is specific to those photochemical initiators used in dental composite resins. Since the laser output is very intense, the curing time is only 10–20% of that required for curing by the traditional light source. And because the argon laser beam is more concentrated than that of the regular curing light, it penetrates more deeply and completely into the filling material and produces a harder composite resin. Laser-cured composites are, in fact, 15% harder and stronger than other composites.

Regular curing lights have a tendency to heat the tooth that is being treated. While in most situations this does not present a problem, prolonged curing of a single tooth may cause postprocedure sensitivity. The majority of the heat from the regular curing light is created by the infrared and other noncuring wavelengths that are part of the spectrum. By contrast, laser light output is coherent, or limited to a very narrow range of the spectrum. Thus, the nonproductive heat-

The argon curing laser offers many advantages over conventional curing lights; it requires less time, is more comfortable for the patient, and produces better bonding and a harder, more durable composite resin.

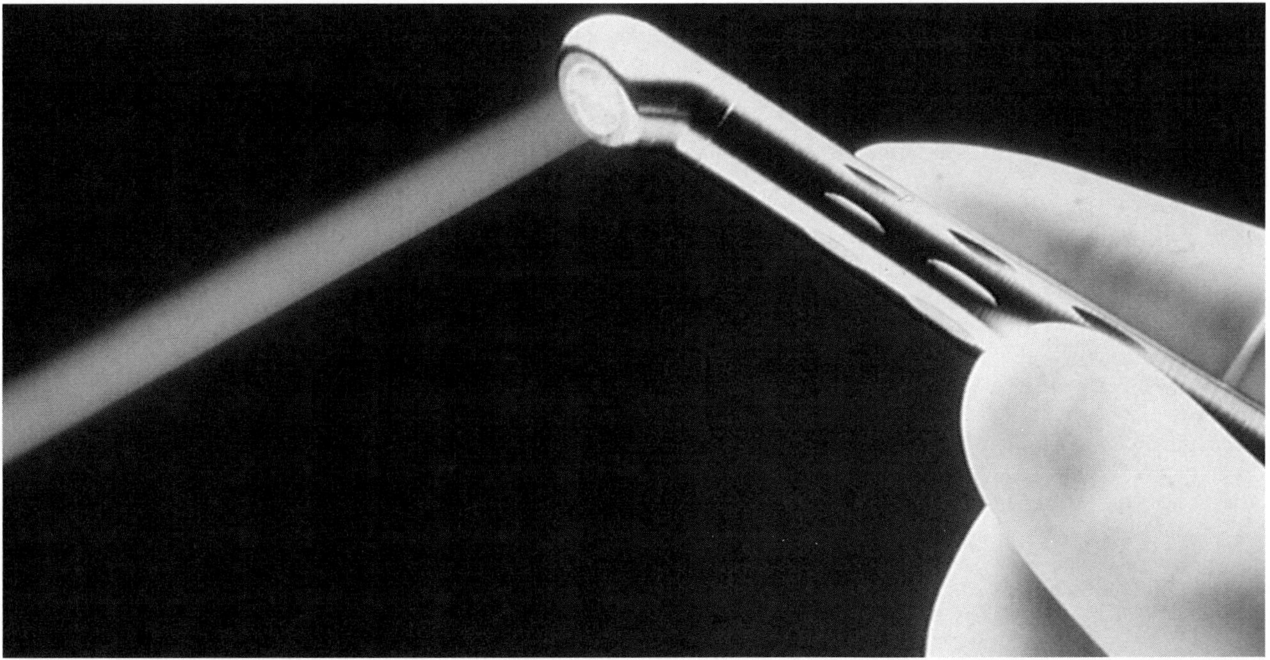

Ion Laser Technology, Salt Lake City, Utah

ing wavelengths simply are not present in argon curing lasers, and the teeth do not become warm during the procedure. As with exposure to any intense light source, it is important to protect the eyes from the light of the argon laser. Orange-tinted goggles are usually worn by both the patient and the dental staff while the laser is in operation.

The addition of lasers to the equipment of the dental office represents a tremendous leap forward in technology. In the near future, lasers may be used for many other dental purposes—to harden the natural enamel and dentin, to eliminate decay-causing bacteria inside a tooth, to remove decay without drilling, and possibly even to clean and whiten tooth surfaces.

To the snorer's rescue

While snoring and snorers are often the butt of jokes, snoring is no laughing matter. It is a common problem; more than 25% of males and 20% of females are snorers. Moreover, the prevalence of snoring increases with age—compared with those under 60, twice as many people over 60 snore.

In some people the uvula (the fleshy structure that projects into the back of the oral cavity) and the muscles of the soft palate sag as the body relaxes during sleep. These tissues then obstruct the airway, making breathing difficult and noisy and, in some cases, blocking breathing entirely. As the pressure to breathe builds, the muscles of the diaphragm work harder, eventually forcing the throat open and momentarily awakening the sleeper. Such episodes may occur hundreds of times each night, not only interfering with sleep but also causing fatigue that affects the individual's ability to function normally during the day.

This condition of frequent cessation of breathing during sleep is called obstructive sleep apnea. Each time breathing stops (episodes may last more than 10 seconds), the individual's heart must work harder to supply oxygenated blood to the tissues; the blood pressure rises, and it may remain elevated for extended periods of time. Eventually, sleep apnea can lead to attacks of arrhythmia (irregular heart rhythm), persistent high blood pressure, and permanent narrowing of the blood vessels. Not all snorers have sleep apnea, of course, but because snoring is a prelude to apnea, it should not be ignored.

Just as snoring may be damaging to the health of the snorer, it is very disruptive for those individuals who are within hearing range of the noise. Snores as loud as 90 decibels have been recorded—comparable in noise level to a motorcycle. It is common for individuals to refuse to share a bed or even a room with someone who has a serious snoring problem.

Many treatments for snoring have been tried over the years, some effective and some preposterous. Currently, medicine and dentistry are able to offer three effective options. The nasal continuous positive airway pressure (CPAP) technique involves a compressor that delivers a gentle stream of pressurized air via a mask worn over the nose. The airstream enters the sleeper's nasal passages and flows into the airway, which thus keeps the airway open and allows normal breathing and sleeping. The system is effective but cumbersome and difficult to get accustomed to.

Silent Knights Ventures Inc., Vancouver, B.C.

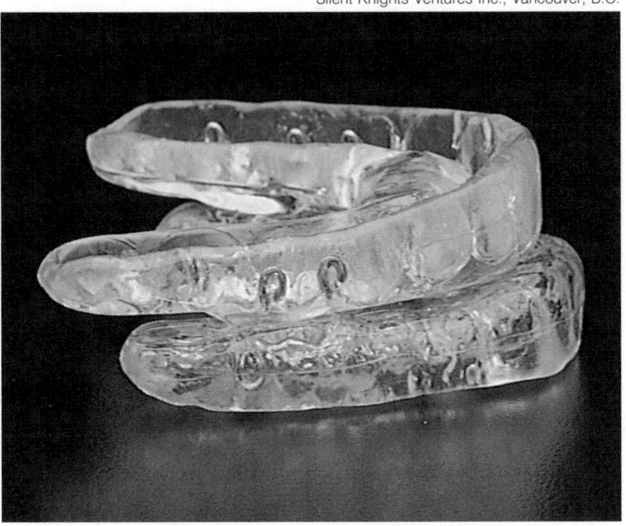

By repositioning the lower jaw and tongue, this small plastic device, worn in the mouth during sleep, can silence snoring and prevent the potentially serious breathing problems sometimes associated with it.

Alternatively, surgery can be performed on the soft palate to eliminate the fleshy tissue at the back of the mouth. Such surgery may be performed by either an oral surgeon or an otolaryngologist. The procedure, typically done with a carbon dioxide laser under local anesthetic, is invasive and requires a recovery time of two or more weeks. The success rate of this surgical procedure ranges from 50% to 70%.

The third alternative, dental appliance therapy, has the advantages of being a nonsurgical approach and being one that does not involve the support equipment or discomfort of CPAP. A small plastic device (similar to a retainer or night guard) consisting of two custom-fitted plates is made for the snorer's mouth. One plate fits snugly over the lower teeth, the other over the upper teeth. They are connected by a titanium support device mounted within a track that allows a certain amount of movement of the jaws during sleep. The device repositions the lower jaw and the tongue in a slightly more forward position than normal. Moving the tongue forward has the effect of opening up the airway and preventing the tissue collapse that causes snoring. Most patients find that a properly designed antisnoring appliance significantly reduces or completely eliminates snoring and the daytime fatigue that often accompanies it.

On the horizon

No sooner do dentists become comfortable with a new material or procedure, it seems, than even better alternatives emerge. Carbon fiber materials like those used to build the Stealth bomber are just beginning to appear in dental restorations. Video technology is enabling patients to understand their dental problems better and to become actively involved in treatment decisions. Biostimulation of the oral tissues with "cold" lasers offers the promise of improved healing after oral surgery. Surely there are undreamed-of innovations just over the horizon.

—George A. Freedman, D.D.S.

Oral Health 2000: An American Initiative

C. Everett Koop, former U.S. surgeon general, has observed that the first step most children take in learning to care for their own health is picking up a toothbrush. Indeed, dental health is a necessary part of total health, and dentistry plays an integral role in primary health care. The nationwide initiative Oral Health 2000 was launched in the early 1990s, with Koop serving as honorary chairman, to bring the public, private, and not-for-profit sectors together for the purpose of educating the public, promoting dental research, and improving the health—and lives—of Americans.

Although the U.S. remains among the world leaders in oral health care, each year approximately half of all Americans fail to visit the dentist for preventive care. Traditionally, the dental "team"—dentists, hygienists, and dental assistants—has emphasized prevention, making the retention of healthy teeth and gums a priority equal to tooth restoration. The campaign for the fluoridation of community water supplies in the 1950s and '60s—a practice that dramatically reduced the incidence of cavities—demonstrated the commitment of these professionals to prevention and provided a model for the pursuit of Oral Health 2000's goals.

Lawrence Migdale—Photo Researchers

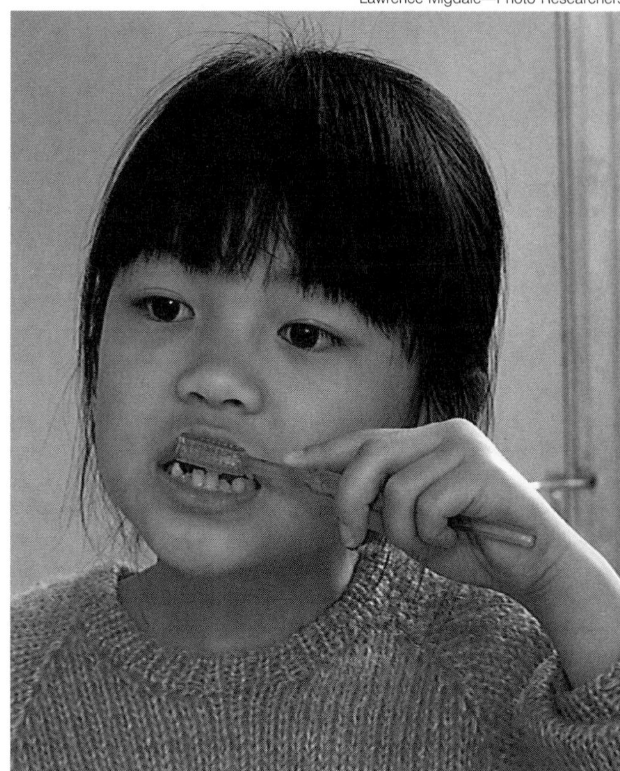

Brushing their teeth is for most children the first step in learning to care for their own health. Many of the specific objectives of Oral Health 2000 target young people.

Raising dental awareness

In 1955, responding to an anticipated shortage of dentists, individuals from the American Association of Dental Schools, the American Dental Association, and the American Dental Trade Association (representing manufacturers of dental equipment and materials) established the American Fund for Dental Education. Together, these groups worked to attract capable students into U.S. dental schools. With the threatened shortage alleviated, the organization broadened its scope in 1973, revising its name to the American Fund for Dental Health (AFDH), to reflect its broader purpose. The stated mission of the AFDH was to:

- raise public awareness of oral health as essential to overall health and a vital component of primary health care
- expand and improve access to effective oral care services
- stimulate innovative projects that improve the effectiveness of dental education
- support oral health research

Healthy People 2000: a nation's health agenda

In 1990 the Public Health Service (PHS) of the U.S. Department of Health and Human Services released its agenda for improving the health of the American public. Entitled "Healthy People 2000: National Health Promotion and Disease Prevention Objectives," the plan outlined a series of goals to be reached by the turn of the century. Among the major objectives is improved oral health. Specifically, the oral health goals are:

- reducing tooth decay so that the proportion of children with one or more cavities is no more than 35% among those 6 through 8 years of age and no more than 60% among 15-year-olds
- reducing untreated tooth decay so that the proportion of children with untreated cavities is no more than 20% among 6- through 8-year-olds and no more than 15% among 15-year-olds
- increasing to at least 45% the proportion of people aged 35 through 44 who have never lost a permanent tooth as a result of tooth decay or periodontal (gum) disease
- reducing to no more than 20% the proportion of people 65 and older who have lost all of their natural teeth
- reducing the prevalence of gingivitis (gum inflammation) among those 35 through 44 to no more than 30%
- reducing the incidence of destructive periodontal disease (progressive loss of connective tissues under the gum line, leading to receding gums and weakened tooth attachment) to no more than 15% among people 35–44
- reducing deaths due to cancer of the mouth and throat to no more than 10.5 per 100,000 among men 45 through 74 years of age and 4.1 per 100,000 among women in the same age group
- increasing to at least 50% the proportion of children who have received protective sealants on the chewing surfaces of permanent molar teeth
- increasing to at least 75% the proportion of people served by community water systems that provide optimal levels of fluoride
- increasing the use of professionally or self-administered topical or dietary fluorides to at least 85% of those people not receiving optimally fluoridated public water

Harvey Finkle—Impact Visuals

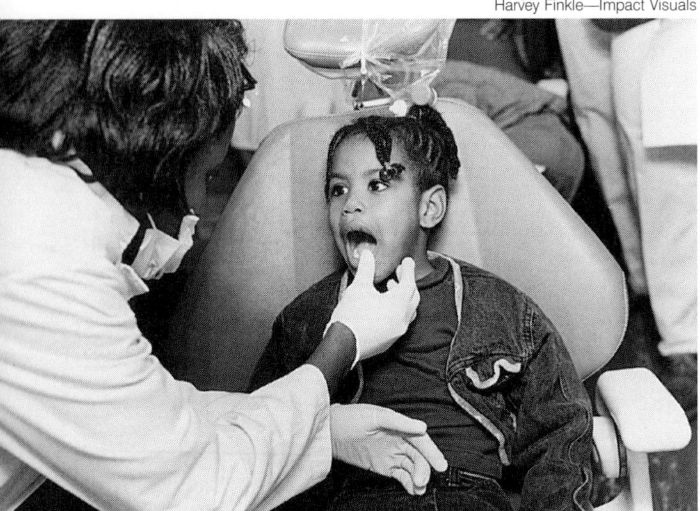

A youngster receives a dental checkup in a mobile facility that travels to low-income neighborhoods. Providing care for special populations is an important mission of Oral Health 2000.

- increasing to at least 75% the proportion of parents and caregivers who use feeding practices that prevent "baby-bottle tooth decay" (cavities that form when infants are allowed to sleep with a bottle of formula or juice propped in their mouths)
- increasing to at least 90% the proportion of all children entering school programs (including Head Start, prekindergarten, and first grade) who have received an oral health screening and follow-up for necessary diagnostic, preventive, and treatment services
- extending to all long-term institutional facilities (including nursing homes and prisons) the requirement that oral examinations and services be provided to all residents no more than 90 days after their entry into these facilities
- increasing to at least 70% the proportion of people 35 and older using the oral health care system each year
- increasing to at least 40 the number of states that have an effective system for recording and referring infants with cleft lips and/or palates to medical teams trained to correct these defects
- extending the requirement for the use of effective head, face, eye, and mouth protection to all organizations, agencies, and institutions sponsoring sporting and recreation events that pose risks of injury

The National Institutes of Health (NIH) chose the AFDH to address the oral health objectives of Healthy People 2000. The AFDH established and oversees Oral Health 2000.

The collaboration at work

The Oral Health 2000 initiative has attracted strong corporate partnerships from pharmaceutical and consumer product companies, such as SmithKline Beecham Consumer Healthcare; Procter & Gamble; Henry Schein, Inc.; Block Drug Co. Inc.; 3M Health Care; Eastman Kodak Co.; Johnson & Johnson Consumer Products; and Colgate-Palmolive Co. and Colgate Oral Pharmaceuticals. Partnerships were also forged with nonprofit entities. Oral health information aimed at older adults has been disseminated through the American Association of Retired Persons. The National Foundation of Dentistry for the Handicapped, supported each year by the AFDH, provides dental care for the homebound and other individuals with disabilities. Special Olympics International has sponsored a dental-screening program, "Special Athletes, Special Smiles," for the participants at a number of state Summer Games and has provided referral services so these individuals would have access to a dentist skilled in handling their special needs. Government agencies, including the Centers for Disease Control and Prevention (CDC), the PHS, and the NIH, have provided crucial guidance for the collaborative effort through the National Institute of Dental Research.

Through Oral Health 2000, dentists have been made increasingly aware of the role they can play in identifying abused children. Approximately two-thirds of abuse injuries occur near the face and neck, and while abusive parents may be reluctant to visit the same physician or emergency room twice, they generally take their children to the same dentist. This ongoing contact can allow dentists to develop a relationship with families and possibly recognize injury patterns.

Spreading the word

The close association between oral health and total health was emphasized by the appointment of Koop, a pediatrician rather than a dentist, as the initiative's spokesperson. Public-service announcements nationwide in print media and on television have featured him delivering the messages "You're not healthy without good oral health" and "Just filling cavities is leaving a hole in your oral health." Koop, a noted advocate of disease prevention, has praised dentistry for its active role in preventive care, suggesting that physicians could learn a lesson from the emphasis dentistry places on health maintenance.

Oral Health 2000 News, a quarterly newsletter, disseminates information on the initiative to the dental profession and to other interested individuals and organizations. Articles keep readers apprised of programs around the country that are endorsed by the initiative and encourage members of the dental profession to engage in practices that further its goals.

National consortium meetings have been held in Irvine, Calif. (1991), Washington, D.C. (1993), and Chicago (1995). From these meetings have sprung state-based consortia modeled after the national initiative, bringing together community members to address the problems prevalent in their state or locality. States from Connecticut to California have established local Oral Health 2000 consortia.

The young, the old, and the Alaskans

Some of Oral Health 2000's programs target specific groups. For example, the AFDH, working with universities, nursing organizations, and federal Women, Infants, and Children (WIC) Special Supplemental Feeding programs, has sought to instruct parents and other caregivers on appropriate oral hygiene for small children and on feeding practices that do not promote decay. It has sponsored educational programs to instruct parents about baby-bottle tooth decay and has encouraged early oral care, beginning with regular wiping of an infant's gums and newly erupted teeth with a piece of clean gauze.

Some programs have specifically addressed the needs of the older population. In concert with Harvard University, the Massachusetts Veterans Administration, and local insurance companies and nursing organizations, the AFDH funded a project to assess the oral health care status of individuals in long-term-care facilities in Massachusetts and to inform their administrators about the need for routine care. The group's findings, when presented to the state legislature, prompted changes in state policy.

Oral Health 2000 has collaborated with numerous local groups nationwide to encourage good oral hygiene practices and regular professional care. This approach was exemplified in the "Smile Alaska Style" program. In the Yukon-Kuskokwim Delta, a 207,000-sq km (80,000-sq mi) region in southwestern Alaska, dental problems are common, professional care is often distant, and health advice from nonnatives may be viewed as patronizing. In 1990 a public health clinic there received an AFDH grant to develop a culturally sensitive program emphasizing the importance of good oral health. Through a "smile" contest and dental-screening program, dental professionals identified local individuals with excellent oral hygiene and attractive smiles to serve as regional spokespersons and educators.

C. Everett Koop, honorary chairman of Oral Health 2000, and Special Olympian Jonathan Derr promote the "Special Athletes, Special Smiles" program, which targets Special Olympics Summer Games participants.

Oral Health America; photograph, Mattox Commercial Photography

In step with NSTEP

Recognizing that the link between baseball and smokeless tobacco use is as strong as the sport's link with peanuts and Cracker Jack, the AFDH has teamed up with Little League Baseball, Inc., and a group of former major league players to spread the message to young boys that the use of smokeless (chewing) tobacco, or "spit tobacco," is not a safe alternative to smoking.

On Oct. 6, 1994, baseball greats Joe Garagiola, Hank Aaron, Mickey Mantle, and Bill Tuttle, joined by National League president Len Coleman, kicked off the National Spit Tobacco Education Program (NSTEP) at a national press conference with representatives of the AFDH and then U.S. surgeon general M. Joycelyn Elders. The former players, who call themselves Joe Garagiola's AFDH No-Spit All Stars, spoke out against the use of smokeless tobacco by youngsters who wish to emulate baseball players.

An AFDH grant awarded to Little League Baseball will fund an educational video for coaches. Educational brochures will also be available both for adults, such as teachers, coaches, or parents, who have influence over potential users, and for girls, who may persuade their male friends to avoid the addictive, health-jeopardizing substance.

Eleven states have been chosen as initial targets for the program. Current plans include a media tour of the target states by former Detroit Tiger Bill Tuttle, who became a smokeless tobacco user in the 1950s and in 1993 underwent major surgery to remove a malignant growth from his mouth. As spokesman for the group, Tuttle will offer personal testimony about the horrors that can result from chewing tobacco.

Sealants: the prevention invention

Dental sealants can prevent 90% of tooth decay, but only 10% of children have these plastic coatings applied to the chewing surfaces of their molars, where decay is most likely to occur. To spread the word about sealants, the AFDH has adopted a multifaceted approach aimed at creating demand in patients and educating dentists about the advantages of the process.

Sealants cost about \$25–\$40 per tooth—less than a filling—and last about 10 years. Moreover, they maintain the healthy tooth structure, whereas fillings must be replaced occasionally over the years, with the cavity size increasing with each replacement. Eventually the tooth may have to be crowned or pulled.

In August 1994 the AFDH cosponsored a national conference on the establishment of sealant programs in public schools. Such programs have proved to be an effective means of increasing the number of children with sealants on their teeth and are especially effective in reaching lower-income children, who are less likely than their more affluent peers to visit a private practitioner. The conference set up a network of individuals to create and run school-based sealant programs nationwide.

In addition, a public relations campaign aimed at parents is intended to increase demand for sealants. With the support of Dentsply International, a leading manufacturer of dental products, the AFDH has launched a national program encouraging parents to talk to their children's dentist about sealant application. Daily newspapers, consumer magazines, school administration magazines, and public health publications will feature articles on the important role sealants play in preventing decay in children's teeth.

Eye on the new millennium

In 1995, while continuing its support for research and education, the AFDH for the first time provided funding for the direct provision of dental services. Under a new name, Oral Health America: America's Fund for Dental Health, the foundation is now working to carry into the next century its mission of better oral health for everyone.

—Ann M. Charbonneau

New Outlook on Back Pain

About 50% of people in their most productive years of life remember being limited by back symptoms for at least one day in the past 12 months. Twenty-five percent remember back symptoms lasting a month within the last year. In fact, by age 30 about one-third of all people are limited to some extent by their backs, and by age 40, 75% experience such limitation. Whereas surveys reveal that by age 50 about 80% of people remember having back symptoms, there is evidence that indicates the other 20% simply do not remember. By 50 years of age, virtually no one has a back that tolerates life as it did in early adulthood; indeed, very few 50-year-olds could lay a driveway over the weekend and then play basketball on Monday, as they once could.

How much people are bothered by or remember back symptoms may depend upon what they demand of their backs on an everyday basis. Back problems that threaten people most are those that limit work and normal, daily activities. The symptoms that may only interfere with a racquetball game or tennis match of an attorney, a telephone receptionist, or an administrator can halt the work of a hod carrier or furniture mover, thus threatening a family's financial future.

A national concern

Back problems bother people worldwide and are among the most costly of physical problems in most countries. Because so many suffer and because in the United States so many dollars are spent on "bad backs" annually—often with no effect—the Agency for Health Care Policy and Research (AHCPR), a branch of the U.S. Public Health Service, convened a panel of experts to come up with guidelines for the assessment and treatment of patients with back problems. Acute low-back problems were defined as activity limitations due to lower-back or back-related leg symptoms that last less than three months. Using the most scientific methods, the panel searched over 10,000 abstracts of published studies on low-back pain and its treatment before categorizing over 4,600 reports for careful scrutiny.

The federally appointed panel, guided by two scientific methodologists, attempted to put the data from all the scientific articles on so-called evidence tables. The panel members then reviewed these evidence tables, weighing potential benefits of widely used diagnostic and treatment methods against potential risks and costs of those procedures. The experts could then decide whether there was sufficient information available for a given method to be considered predictable.

This monumental effort was justified because back ailments are currently among the most expensive health care problems in the United States. Back problems resulting from occupational injury are the most expensive musculoskeletal problem, causing the greatest amount of disability and productive time lost among working people under 45 years of age. Moreover, there are widespread differences in the methods used to evaluate and treat back problems in different parts of the country, which suggests that many sufferers may be receiving less than adequate care.

The need for such an assessment of methods is especially important for problems that are neither emergencies nor life-threatening and where the true decision maker is the patient. Patients' understanding of what medical science supports and what it cannot yet support because of lack of evidence can greatly help them make "good" decisions.

This search for evidence was but another step to ensure that patients understand what care is predictably helpful. The training of doctors and other medical personnel in the U.S. began to change radically after Abraham Flexner issued his landmark report on American medical education in 1910. From then on, medicine was focused away from selling snake oil off the back of a wagon and toward having a sound scientific basis.

After their three-year scientific review of existing treatments, in December 1994 the 23 experts on the AHCPR panel and 7 international consultants chose to change the paradigm of care from only treating the symptoms to focusing therapy on helping the patient to either avoid debilitation (primarily from resting too much) or regain a comfortable activity level through exercise. With the new guidelines, clinicians are now armed to help back-pain sufferers be more comfortable while they resume normal activities as soon and as fully as possible. Back-pain sufferers should now get optimum care and be able to limit the amount of reconditioning they need to resume their lives comfortably and experience the fewest future interruptions. Comfortably returning to any activity, of course, depends upon how long the patient has been away from it and what he or she has been doing to stay in shape.

The expert panel emphasized the measures medical science has found predictably beneficial for the patient. However, the absence of a particular therapy from the panel's recommendations does not mean it does not work. Rather, there may have been no studies conducted on the method in question, or there was insufficient evidence to judge its potential. In some cases the present evidence may show that the potential benefit is outweighed by potential risks or costs. In such instances further research will help clarify a treatment's usefulness.

Seeking help

While a patient with a minor back problem may have the luxury to choose the latest untested or unproven fad or gimmick, he or she needs to understand what medical science finds most predictable—especially if a decision about one option or another could have an impact on a family's livelihood and future. It will be much easier for future research to establish that an inexpensive method of little risk to the patient is beneficial than it will be to prove the value of a complicated and costly procedure, or one that carries many risks and complications. In what situations should one seek professional care for back symptoms? The experts recommend that sufferers consult a clinician if:

- they cannot do their normal work
- they need to alter their daily routine for more than a few days
- they are young and find themselves limited in their activities after a fall from a height or high-impact trauma (*e.g.,* a car crash)
- they are elderly and have recently done something particularly strenuous
- chills or a fever accompanies back symptoms
- symptoms seem related to changes in other bodily functions (*e.g.,* bowel or bladder dysfunction) or to numbness
- back symptoms begin during or following intravenous (IV) treatment for another medical condition

Back's Basic Anatomy

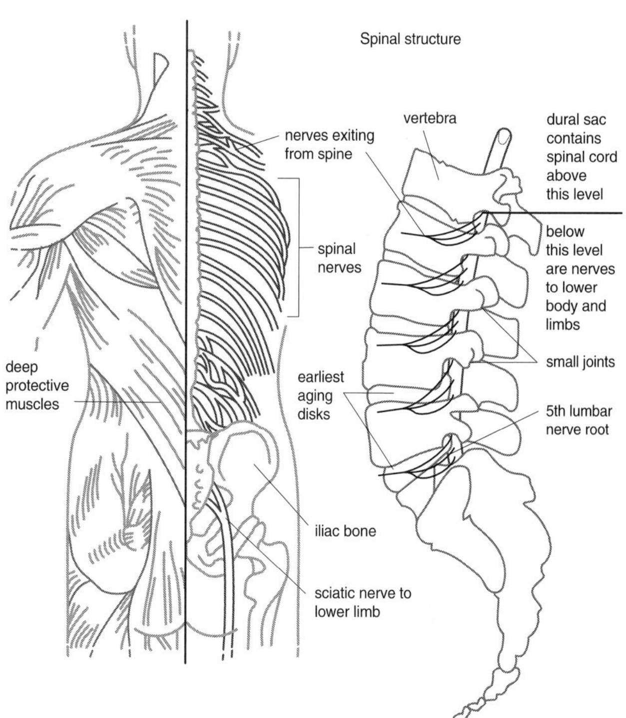

Why rest is wrong

Would a boxer who has been out of the ring for weeks or months try to box 15 rounds? Would a "couch potato" run a marathon without having trained for it? Does a coach ever rest a team for a month before the first game? When back problems are considered in this light, it makes sense that bed rest is *not* the best course for rehabilitation.

To understand why bed rest does not work, it is important to understand the back's basic anatomy. The human spine (or backbone) is made up of small bones called vertebrae, linked together by three joints. One large disk joint is in the front, and two small facet joints behind form a canal for the nerves that they protect. Nerves from the spinal cord travel down the canal before branching out and leaving the spine through the spaces between the vertebrae. The muscles are very important in supporting and protecting this column of stacked vertebrae linked together by joints.

The lower part of the back ages faster than most other parts of the body, and as people age they naturally lose muscular protection unless they exercise. By age 50 no one has a "young" back. In the absence of muscular protection, problems can arise without much of a reason and cause back pain. Less often, a problem with a disk or smaller joints can irritate or choke off nerves, causing pain that runs down the leg (sciatica).

Activity is the answer

The two most important elements that enable the back to tolerate specific activities are the individual's general stamina and the endurance capacity of specific back muscles. Why is staying active the best approach? There are several reasons. Muscles protect the bones and joints of the body. The fastest way to make a muscle too weak to do its normal protective job is to fatigue the muscle itself or its owner. If one gets generally tired or uses muscles until they fatigue, muscles cannot respond normally or quickly.

Where does general fitness level, or stamina, come in? Consider a few analogies: If one observes a professional tennis player, one notices that he or she has one larger, muscular arm and one that is less muscular. Yet once the tennis player becomes generally exhausted, neither arm works very well. Those who recall the prizefight between George Foreman and Muhammad Ali in 1974 will have no doubt who was the stronger of the two in the first round; by the eighth round, however, that stronger fighter, Foreman, was so tired that he almost collapsed in the ring. The lesson here is that general fatigue reduces the effectiveness of *all* muscles.

Once generally tired, even the most conditioned back muscles may not be able to do their normal job. This is similar to the way that the thigh muscles protect the knee. In the case of the leg, it makes no difference what the diagnosis is or if an operation is required, one who experiences knee pain will not recover until the thigh muscles have been reconditioned to the point of being able to compensate for whatever the knee has lost. This usually means conditioning the thigh muscles to a higher level than before the onset of the knee problem. If conditioned properly, some patients return to professional athletics—not because they have a normal knee but because they have conditioned the thigh muscles sufficiently to compensate for whatever knee problem remains. This is true of perhaps as many as two-thirds of National Football League players. Until the muscles have been conditioned to that point, the knee continues to be painful and cannot tolerate even normal activity; moreover, pain and even swelling can be triggered by any minor incident.

The muscles of the spine seem to carry out a similar role for the back, which is why rest does not help and can eventually make things worse. Even though a person with a "bad back" may seem to stay active, he or she is likely to avoid many routine activities, such as lifting, bending, reaching, and twisting. Such avoidance is logical because those activities can hurt, but it also substantially weakens the back muscles over time, reducing their effectiveness. With inactivity, muscles quickly become debilitated and shrivel. Only retraining of those muscles—and even conditioning of them to a higher level—provides a chance for a comfortable return to normal functioning. Staying active, despite symptoms, helps prevent the loss of muscular capacity and can reduce the need for extensive retraining or reconditioning.

Evaluating the problem

Before prescribing a treatment regimen for a true back problem, a trained clinician not only will want to hear about one's present back problems but will seek specific information to rule out rare, potentially dangerous conditions. By looking for certain "red flags," a well-trained professional can usually rule out any serious or dangerous illness without performing special tests. In fact, assuming that none of the "red flags" is evident, 9 of every 10 people will get well naturally, and X-rays and other time-consuming, costly studies can be avoided.

Among the questions the person with back symptoms may be asked are the following:

- Where are the symptoms, and how long have they been present?
- Which of your daily activities are you unable to do because of your pain?
- What do you normally do to stay in shape?
- Have you had a problem with your back in the past?
- Around the time your symptoms began, did you have a fever or symptoms of pain or burning when urinating?
- What medical illnesses have you had (for example, cancer, arthritis, or diseases of the immune system)?
- What medications do you use regularly?
- Have you ever used intravenous drugs?
- Have you recently lost weight without trying to?

Ensuring comfort

While pain can rarely be eliminated totally, there are safe methods that will take the edge off. What many people *think* are strong medications generally will not be prescribed because they do not help more than safer medications do, and their side effects may make things worse. Over-the-counter analgesics such as acetaminophen along with ibuprofen or aspirin may help assuage pain during the recovery process, but even prescription medication and manipulation will not do the whole job.

A knowledgeable clinician will prescribe safe exercises for the patient who cannot stay active. In some cases it will be necessary to find milder alternatives in order to avoid irritating activities, but it still remains important to avoid debili-

NEWS*CAP*

A Close Look at Pain in the Neck

Standard treatments for whiplash are not beneficial and may do more harm than good. The results of a two-part investigation, the most comprehensive study of whiplash ever undertaken, were published in the journal *Spine* (April 15, 1995). The study was headed by Walter O. Spitzer, chairman of epidemiology at McGill University, Montreal. In the first part of the study, 25 independent experts reviewed more than 10,000 scientific articles and concluded that whiplash remains poorly understood and ineffectively treated. The second part of the study consisted of a review of the medical records of nearly 5,000 motorists who had filed claims for compensation for whiplash injury in Quebec province in 1987.

The vast majority of the published studies lacked scientific rigor and were "flawed, uninterpretable, or inadequate," the experts found. Their report said that even the few therapies that had been scientifically evaluated, such as the use of cervical collars and the administration of muscle relaxants and other drugs, appeared to be ineffective. Unproven therapies for whiplash include rest, traction, cervical neck pillows, acupuncture, electrical stimulation, ultrasound, lasers, shortwave diathermy, heat, ice, massage, injections, and certain kinds of physiotherapy.

Whiplash injuries are often the consequence of motor vehicle crashes that cause a sudden, sharp back-and-forth whipping motion of the head and neck. About 90% of such injuries heal on their own in days or weeks, and rarely are X-rays or treatment needed. Yet many whiplash injuries come to be regarded as chronic conditions because of the wide use of ineffective therapies, the poor training of doctors, and the overstatement of the seriousness of the injury.

As a result of the new findings, a Quebec task force on the treatment of whiplash-associated disorders proposed new treatment guidelines—guidelines that emphasize "watchful waiting."

Tom Sobolik—Black Star

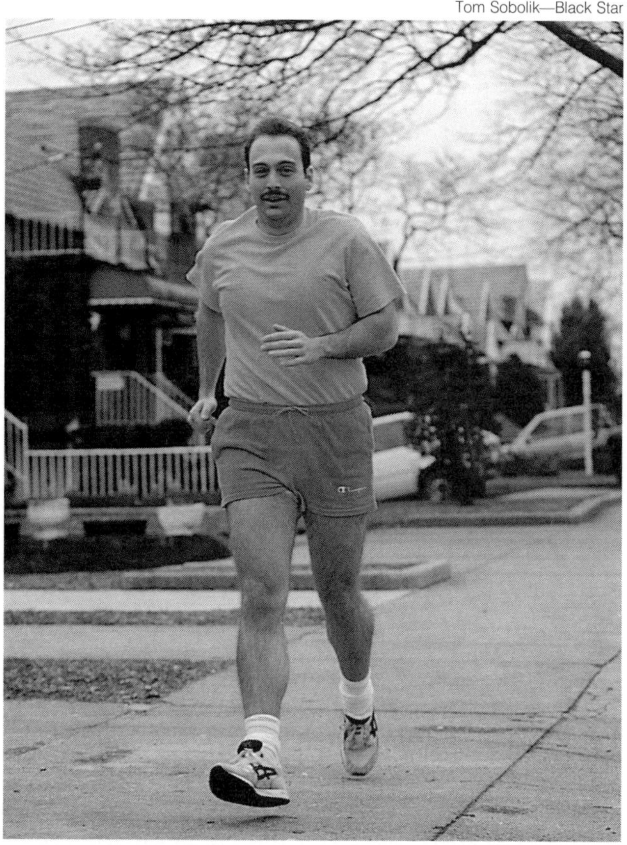

In December 1994 a panel of orthopedic experts revised the U.S. guidelines for the treatment of acute lower back problems. The new recommendations stress activity *and advise strongly* against *bed rest.*

tation. Suitable exercises include walking, cycling, swimming, and even jogging. These are all nonimpact aerobic exercises that can build stamina without stressing the back (any more than sitting on the side of the bed before getting up in the morning). Anything lifted should be kept close to the navel, and bending and twisting should be limited. Sitting may be something to avoid, especially for long periods.

A return to vigorous activities may need to be gradual. Any exercise program should be commenced slowly, then built up in both speed and duration. For example, one can work up to walking 20–30 minutes at a brisk pace over several weeks. At first, one may find that symptoms worsen with exercise. Usually this is nothing to worry about. Abrupt changes in activity can irritate the back; when people work in a garden for the first time in the spring, they suffer because they have not used certain muscles all winter, as do cyclists when they take their bikes out for the first ride of the season. Unused muscles tire easily, and then the back gets sore. The discomfort of gardening or biking, however, will go away once muscles have become used to the activity again. Likewise, one will be able to adjust to a mild exercise regimen prescribed for the back.

The older one is, the more important muscular conditioning becomes. By age 50 most people may have lost as much as half the strength in their large muscles that they had at age 20. This helps explain why a 20-year-old who is immobile for a few months will be doing pretty well after being up and around for a week, whereas a 50-year-old who is laid up in bed for a week may take a month to get going again. Obviously, younger people have much greater muscular reserve than do middle-aged and older people. As people get older, they need to exercise more to keep their muscular reserve. Even after back symptoms have been experienced, specific back-muscle conditioning may be needed to regain the muscular protection that has been lost but may be vital to a comfortable toleration of daily activities without back symptoms.

Symptoms that linger

Special studies are likely to be considered to determine why a patient does not recover within about four weeks. The ordering of tests may also depend upon the individual's general health and progress. X-rays and more sophisticated imaging studies alone are unlikely to identify the cause of a lingering problem. Physiology-based studies that may help are: a careful physical examination; laboratory (blood or urine) studies; electromyography (EMG), which measures electrical activity in affected leg muscles; and perhaps a bone scan. If a physiological change is measurable, imaging studies may help define the problem. Without a physiological hint to guide the way, however, diagnostic imaging can be confusing. In as many as 30% of those who undergo imaging after age 30, abnormalities will be reported, even without pain. In some cases anatomic changes revealed by diagnostic imaging can be confused with normal aging-associated changes. Moreover, if imaging is utilized before some guidance has been gained in the form of a specific measure of dysfunction (*e.g.*, EMG or lab tests), it can lead to surgical procedures that not only are ineffective and unnecessary but may make matters worse.

Once people experience symptoms that linger for more than a few weeks, they will probably need to face the fact that they will never have the back that they had when they were younger—one that would tolerate almost anything they asked of it. The Boston Celtics undoubtedly would have paid almost any amount of money to get one more year out of star player Larry Bird. Yet at age 34, after 13 seasons, Bird was forced by chronic back pain to face the fact that his career as one of the National Basketball Association's most valuable players was over.

If simple exercises do not enable one to perform normal activity comfortably, it may be time to question how realistic it is to expect to stay at what was once a normal level of function. In some cases, like Bird's, one may need to consider a career or occupational-task change. This is especially true if work involves heavy labor.

No Nobel Prizes

The bad news is that medical science is limited to only helping an individual with a back problem. There are no miracles. Nowhere on the horizon is it likely that any doctor or medical specialist will have the ability to make a back brand new again.

Clinicians who treat back symptoms can find the precise cause of symptoms in only 12 of every 100 patients; 88% of the people seeking treatment will never have a clear answer. While medical science is very effective in detecting many rare and serious conditions, no one has yet picked up the Nobel Prize for Medicine or Physiology for either assessing or curing back pain. Candid health care providers will admit when they "do not know." They will not blame symptoms on sprain, strain, myofasciitis, fibromyalgia, subluxation, dislocation, internal disk derangement, degenerative disk disease, or some other vague problem that truly means they "don't know." Unfortunately, those terms are used all too often by clinicians who are afraid that the back-pain sufferer might seek help elsewhere—from someone who is presumably "more knowledgeable."

The good news is that heath care providers can help reduce the frequency and intensity of back problems. Better yet, they can help keep back symptoms from interfering with daily life. The better the patient understands back treatments—what medical science finds predictable—the better decisions he or she will be able to make about back care.

What may help

Above all, the 23 experts who served on the AHCPR panel on acute low-back problems recommended knowledge and exercise.

When members of the panel looked at spinal manipulation (particularly chiropractic methods that apply the force of the hands to the back), they concluded that such therapy can help some people be more comfortable in the first month of low-back pain. Such treatment, however, should be done only by a professional with experience in manipulation. Application of cold or heat at home is unproven but safe and may provide some comfort.

A number of other "comfort" treatments are sometimes used. While these methods have their devotees—and may provide temporary relief for some people—none has been found to speed recovery or keep acute back problems from returning, and some may increase risks or be expensive:

- traction
- TENS (transcutaneous electrical nerve stimulation)
- massage
- biofeedback
- acupuncture
- injections into the back (*e.g.,* steroids, numbing agents)
- back corsets
- ultrasound
- diathermy (shortwave or microwave treatment of deep tissue)
- shoe lifts

Final caveats

Even acute back-related leg pain does not by itself indicate the need for surgery. In fact, surgery has been found to be helpful for only one in 100 people seeking help with low-back problems. If one has no symptoms other than back pain, surgery will rarely be effective and is likely to cause further problems. One should seek a knowledgeable clinician who focuses on helping people with back problems regain comfortable tolerance for activity through exercise instead of a practitioner who focuses on symptoms and emphasizes surgery, medications, or unpredictable treatments.

Finally, certain things may interfere with getting relief, such as stress (extra pressure at home or work), personal or emotional problems, depression, or drug or alcohol abuse. Patients should be aware of these factors and should tell their health care provider about them.

—Stanley J. Bigos, M.D.

John Mayer—Stock, Boston

When people work in a garden for the first time in the spring, it is normal for them to experience some strain and pain—because certain muscles have not been used all winter. The older people get, the more *they need to exercise just to maintain their muscular reserve.*

Fundamentals of Feeding Infants

The first year of life is crucial to the future health and well-being of every child. During this period it is extremely important that parents feed their children correctly. Mistakes in infant feeding are responsible for many nutrition-related childhood health problems, ranging from tooth decay to infections to iron-deficiency anemia (a potentially serious condition that can lead to impaired mental development and poor school performance later in life). Following the guidelines in this article will help a mother give her baby the best possible start toward a healthy, happy life.

Breast is still best

One of the most important decisions an expectant mother must make is whether to breast-feed her baby. This question should be answered during the pregnancy and not, as often is the case, in haste after the baby is born. Moreover, it should be answered only after the woman has learned the facts about the benefits of breast milk versus infant formula. The scientific evidence clearly establishes that breast milk is best for the baby from every possible perspective: physical, emotional, and mental. It provides newborns with all the nutrients they need for optimal health and development. For those mothers who cannot or choose not to breast-feed, an iron-fortified infant formula is a reasonable and acceptable alternative. Properly fed infants thrive on either.

In terms of nutritional value, breast milk is the "gold standard" against which infant formulas must be measured, as it is without doubt the "perfect" first food. With the sole exception of vitamin D, it has everything that a baby needs for optimal growth and development. (A vitamin D supplement is therefore routinely recommended for all breast-feeding babies.)

Immunologic benefits. Breast milk provides more than just nutrients. Numerous studies have demonstrated that breast milk contains disease-fighting antibodies that help protect a baby against a range of infections, both bacterial and viral. A 1990 study that tracked 668 Scottish-born babies from birth to two years of age found significantly less gastrointestinal illness among those who had been breast-fed than among babies who had been formula-fed. This protection against gastrointestinal infections continued well beyond the time the infants were weaned.

Another investigation, carried out collaboratively by researchers in the U.S. and Denmark, concluded that breast-fed babies had fewer episodes of otitis media (middle ear infection) during the first few years of life than formula-fed infants. Again, this protection lasted long after breast-feeding had been discontinued.

Breast-fed infants are also less likely than others to develop asthma and allergies, including hay fever and skin rashes, again because of immune-system constituents contained in the milk. This protection against allergic reactions is a great advantage, especially when there is a family history of such problems.

There is even some evidence that breast milk may provide protection against certain types of cancer. A study from the National Institute of Child Health and Human Development in Bethesda, Md., examined the incidence of childhood cancer in a group of Colorado children and found that those who had been breast-fed for at least six months were significantly less likely to develop lymphoma (cancer of the lymphoid tissues), a common cancer of young people. Other research has shown similar results. This finding does not mean, of course, that breast-fed children never get cancer later in life, but breast-feeding appears to improve the odds against contracting certain types of cancer.

How long should breast-feeding be continued in order to derive the maximum immunologic benefits? Current evidence indicates that most of the protective effects have become established after the first three months. Therefore, a minimum of three months of breast-feeding is recommended.

Neuropsychological benefits. Researchers in The Netherlands examined the neurological status of a group of children shortly after birth and again at age nine. They found that youngsters who were formula-fed as babies were twice as likely to have some neurological problems by the age of nine as those who were exclusively breast-fed for at least the first three weeks of life. The neurological problems ranged from minor abnormalities such as poor coordination to severe ones such as paralysis.

In recent years a number of separate investigations have concluded that breast-feeding enhances intellectual development. In a study of nearly 700 18-month-olds, breast-fed infants scored higher than their non-breast-fed counterparts on two different tests measuring mental development, even after the results were adjusted for factors such as birth weight and the parents' socioeconomic status. The breast-fed babies had an advantage equivalent to about 4.5 IQ points on one test and 4.3 points on the other. Similarly, a recent study in Cambridge, England, showed that compared with premature babies who were breast-fed, those who were formula-fed had significantly lower IQ scores when tested at the age of eight.

What constituent of breast milk could be responsible for these benefits? The current consensus is that one class of fatty acids, called long-chain polyunsaturated fatty acids, present in breast milk but not in infant formulas, is essential for developing nervous-system tissue. These components of breast milk may play a role in intelligence.

The emotional advantages of breast-feeding are obvious. It practically guarantees that the infant's needs for physical warmth and contact and loving attention will be met. Breast-feeding fosters an immediate, strong bond between mother and infant, and this emotional factor may be the most important benefit of all.

Despite the fact that the multiple benefits of breast-feeding are well established, a study published in February 1995 found that American physicians in three specialties—pediatrics, obstetrics-gynecology, and family practice medicine—were "ill-prepared" to counsel women about breast-feeding. The researchers, a team from the University of North Carolina, based their conclusions on a nationwide survey of U.S. doctors' training, experience, knowledge, and attitudes about breast-feeding. Women who sincerely desire to breast-feed should make this intention clear to their doctors and should be persistent in seeking the necessary information and support. (For further sources of information, *see* below.)

Peter Menzel

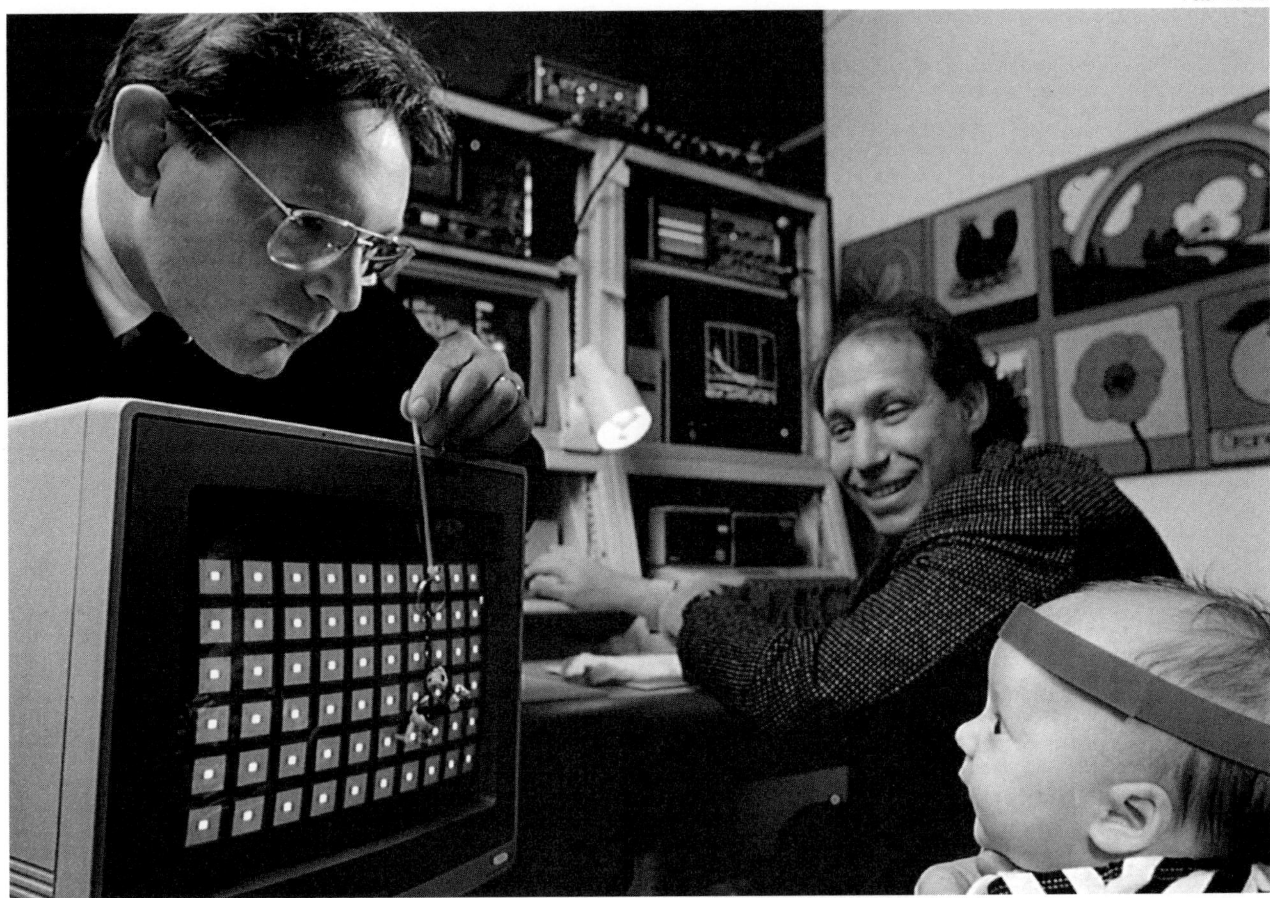

Researchers assess an infant's ability to perceive visual stimuli, one indication of neurological development. Such studies consistently indicate that breast-fed babies have an advantage over their bottle-fed peers.

Ensuring successful breast-feeding

A mother who is truly motivated to breast-feed will almost always be successful. The more often the baby is allowed to suckle, the more quickly an adequate milk supply will be established. Frequent breast-feeding during the first few days has the additional advantage of reducing the incidence of jaundice in newborns (yellowish discoloration of the skin due to an accumulation of a substance called bilirubin). Most authorities in the field, including pediatricians and lactation consultants, agree that it is best not to offer any water to a breast-feeding infant during the first few weeks of life.

The mother can feel assured that breast-feeding is going well when the baby nurses every 2 to 3 hours for at least 10 minutes, has at least three wet diapers daily during the first few days and six per day by one week, and is producing one or more yellow, loose bowel movements per day by the time he or she is one week old. Other signs of successful breast-feeding are that the mother's full breasts will feel noticeably softer after a feeding and the baby will act as if he or she is satisfied.

The following are signs of a possible problem:

- The baby is irritable and cries immediately after a feeding.
- The baby is not having one or more bowel movements per day.
- The baby has fewer than six wet diapers per day by one week of age.
- Evidence of milk production (*e.g.,* breast fullness, leaking of milk) is absent even after four to five days of trying to breast-feed.
- The nipples are very sore, cracked, or bleeding.

If any of these signs is present, it is important to contact the baby's doctor immediately.

The current U.S. trend toward earlier and earlier hospital discharges of new mothers, often before breast-feeding can properly be established, makes it imperative that feeding problems and possible failures be identified as early as possible so that the problem can be corrected or bottle-feeding substituted before the infant suffers from inadequate weight gain, dehydration, or starvation.

Weaning: when and how

Many mothers are unsure how long to continue breast-feeding. The answer is simple—for as long as she and the baby are happy with the experience. As stated above, the first three months of breast-feeding will confer most of the protective immunities. Breast-feeding beyond three months will continue to give the baby the emotional and developmental advantages previously discussed.

Weaning usually is accomplished without much difficulty when breast-feeding is allowed to run its natural course. In the end, most babies simply tire of it and begin to wean themselves, somewhere between one year and 18 months of age. There is no "best" or "right" time for weaning, and there certainly is no nutritional reason to stop breast-feeding at any particular age. Breast-feeding for the entire first year of life and beyond is ideal. Breast milk is an excellent food, even for the two-year-old who still wants it.

When initiating the weaning process before a baby is one year of age, the mother should start by substituting one bottle of iron-fortified formula for one of the regular breast-feedings each day. Some breast-fed babies take to the bottle more readily than others, and some may balk, but they all get used to drinking from a bottle sooner or later. The next step is to substitute two bottles of formula each day for two of the breast-feedings, and so on. Many babies who are nine months of age or older accept formula from a cup more readily than from a bottle.

Any abrupt change in what has been a comfortable, established pattern may be upsetting to both mother and baby. Therefore, weaning slowly over a period of weeks is the answer. A gradual transition will give the baby a chance to adjust to the change, and the mother's milk supply will diminish steadily as the demand lessens.

Myths and misconceptions

Contrary to popular belief, breast size is not a factor in the success of breast-feeding. The fatty tissue in the breasts, which is what determines their size, plays no role in milk production. Rather, milk production is based solely on supply and demand: the more often the baby suckles, the more milk is produced by the mother's body. Inverted nipples need not prevent a woman from breast-feeding. The practice of gently pulling on and lowering the nipples between thumb and fingers before feedings and the use of special nipple shields worn in the bra during pregnancy can correct the condition.

In addition to providing newborns with all the nutrients needed for optimal growth and development, breast-feeding also has emotional benefits, fostering the intimate bond between mother and child.

Monique Manceau—Photo Researchers

As for the notion that sagging breasts are an inevitable result of breast-feeding, this too is a myth. Sagging, when it does occur, is due to gravity and is caused by the weight gain and stretching of the skin that are the normal consequences of pregnancy itself. If the woman gets proper nutrition and adequate exercise after delivery, her breasts will usually return to their prepregnancy contour and appearance.

Another common misconception is that women who must return to work should not start breast-feeding or, at least, will inevitably need to discontinue it. Nothing could be farther from the truth. Mothers who must go back to work can comfortably continue to breast-feed. A simple device called a breast pump enables them to express milk at regular intervals. This milk can be safely stored in the refrigerator for up to 24 hours. The baby can be fed pumped breast milk (or infant formula) by bottle while the mother is away and breast-fed when she is at home. During the workday it may be necessary for her to express milk from the breasts if they become excessively engorged. Over time, however, milk production will decrease because of the less frequent feedings, and pumping the breasts during working hours will become less necessary.

If a mother chooses to discontinue breast-feeding before her infant has reached the age of one year, it is important that the baby be switched to an iron-fortified formula rather than to regular cow's milk. (The reasons why cow's milk is inappropriate for human infants are discussed in detail below.) After the first year, however, a baby can safely be switched to regular whole milk.

Facts about formula

For those women who cannot breast-feed or who, for whatever reason, choose not to breast-feed, there is a reasonable and appropriate alternative, namely, the commercially available iron-fortified infant formulas. These infant formulas are almost identical in their nutrient mix to breast milk. Therefore, women who cannot or choose not to breast-feed need not feel guilty. From the nutritional point of view, infants do beautifully on an iron-fortified formula. The guilt that many mothers feel about formula feeding is in large measure due to the widespread media coverage of the consequences of formula feeding in impoverished Third World countries. In these countries infants who were fed formula rather than breast milk had much higher rates of death than breast-fed infants. These reports, while true, are misleading, since they implied that formula feeding itself—rather than abject poverty and unhygienic conditions—was the major cause of the infant deaths. Many of these babies died from filevation because their parents, who could not afford to buy sufficient formula, overdiluted the product with water. Because this water was often contaminated, many infants died from various forms of dysentery. These circumstances are unlikely to apply in the United States or other industrialized countries. Since the inception of the federally funded U.S. Special Supplemental Food Program for Women, Infants, and Children (WIC), even the very poorest families are assured of an adequate supply of infant formula.

The choice of a particular formula should be discussed with the baby's doctor. Formula companies market two versions of their products: low-iron and iron-fortified. The low-iron formulas have practically no iron and do not supply nearly enough of this vital nutrient to meet an infant's daily requirements. The iron-fortified formulas, on the other hand, contain sufficient iron to prevent iron-deficiency anemia. The Committee on Nutrition of the American Academy of Pediatrics (AAP) has taken a strong stand against low-iron products, saying that it sees "no role" for these formulas in infant feedings. Nonetheless, about 20% of all bottle-fed babies in the U.S. are still fed low-iron formulas. This statistic reflects the long-standing but completely unfounded belief that the added iron in iron-fortified formulas causes gastrointestinal symptoms such as vomiting, colic, gas, constipation, and diarrhea. A number of controlled studies comparing babies fed both types of formula do not support this notion.

NEWS*CAP*

Baby Diets: The Fat Question

A Finnish study has concluded that babies under the age of two benefit from a low-fat diet. This is contrary to the prevailing opinion of most American pediatricians, who counsel parents that fat and cholesterol are necessary for normal growth and development and should not be restricted before age two. Nutritionists in Finland, however, reported in *The Lancet* (Feb. 25, 1995) that even babies 7 to 13 months old appear to benefit from a diet limited in saturated fat.

Over a six-month period, the researchers compared the diets of two groups of more than 500 babies. One group was fed a low-fat but nutritious diet (the "intervention" group); the other was allowed an unrestricted diet. The diet of the intervention group provided 30–35% of calories from fat and contained equal amounts of polyunsaturated, monounsaturated, and saturated fat. Cholesterol consumption was limited to 200 mg per day. (Adults who have high blood cholesterol levels are advised to have no more than 300 mg a day.) The parents of this group received special counseling from nutritionists. The unrestricted diet contained the same percentage of calories from fat but a larger proportion of saturated fat.

At the end of the study period, growth was the same in the two groups, but the cholesterol levels of babies on the unrestricted diet had risen. Cholesterol levels were largely unchanged in the intervention group.

The Finnish scientists contend that infants and young children who eat a fat-rich diet early in life will have difficulty accepting a lower-fat diet when they get older. Nonetheless, the majority of U.S. physicians and nutrition authorities stand by the recommendation not to limit fat in the diets of children under age two.

The following are some practical tips for proper bottle feeding:

- Make certain that the nipple hole is the correct size. When the bottle is upside down, the formula should flow out one drop at a time and not in a steady stream.
- Offer the formula at a comfortable temperature. The parent or caretaker can check the temperature before feeding by sprinkling a drop or two from the bottle onto his or her wrist.
- Do not use a microwave oven to heat the formula. There have been cases of scalding an infant's mouth as a result of microwaves penetrating and heating the liquid in the interior of the bottle while leaving the exterior feeling just comfortably warm.
- Never prop a bottle on a pillow or other object and leave the baby alone to feed him- or herself. It is very important always to hold the baby during feedings. This contact contributes to the bonding process.
- Hold the baby upright rather than supine while feeding. Babies should never feed while lying down, a practice that promotes prolonged contact between formula and the teeth, leading to tooth decay.

The current recommendation of the AAP's Committee on Nutrition is to avoid regular cow's milk entirely during the first 12 months of life. In fact, switching a baby from formula to cow's milk before 12 months is considered a prime example of faulty feeding. The three main reasons to withhold regular milk until that time are:

1. Cow's milk has practically no iron as compared with breast milk or iron-fortified formula. Inadequate intake of iron may lead to iron-deficiency anemia.

2. Regular milk causes some bleeding in the intestinal tract in babies under one year of age; this blood loss also can result in iron deficiency.

3. Regular milk contains much more salt and protein than either breast milk or formula. To eliminate excess salt and protein, the infant's body must increase the volume of water it excretes, putting an added strain on the kidneys. If the infant then develops any illness that results in the loss of large amounts of water—for example, a bout of diarrhea—he or she will be even more vulnerable to the effects of dehydration.

A small percentage of babies are allergic to a protein in cow's milk, which is the basic ingredient of standard infant formulas. Among the symptoms that may indicate a milk allergy are forceful vomiting right after feeding, chronic, often bloody diarrhea, excessive irritability, and chronic cough and wheezing. If parents suspect an allergy, they should consult the pediatrician. If the doctor determines that the symptoms are indeed due to milk allergy, the baby should be fed a non-cow's milk formula, such as a soybean or protein hydrolyzed formula. At one year of age, the formula-fed baby may be safely switched to regular whole milk. The baby's kidneys are now mature enough to handle the extra salt and protein, and gastrointestinal bleeding due to milk ingestion does not occur in one-year-olds.

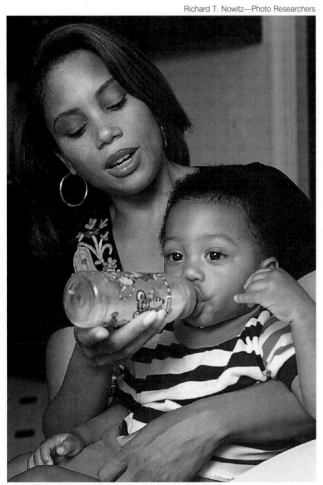

Richard T. Nowitz—Photo Researchers

Weaning can usually be accomplished without too much difficulty if breast-feeding is allowed to run its course and bottle-feeding is introduced gradually. Sooner or later, all babies get used to the bottle.

Drugs and other health concerns

Breast-feeding may not be an option for a woman who must take certain medications. These include some cancer chemotherapy drugs, radioactive compounds (especially radioactive iodine, used in thyroid disease), lithium, and some anticoagulants. Many other drugs (*e.g.,* antidepressants, anticonvulsants, some antibiotics), although not contraindicated, are not recommended for breast-feeding women. If a drug is needed for a limited period, as in the case of an antibiotic, temporary discontinuation of breast-feeding may be an option. Before taking any medication while breast-feeding, a woman should consult her physician or the pediatrician. Women who are addicted to heroin or cocaine should not breast-feed, nor should women who have certain medical conditions, including HIV/AIDS, hepatitis B, and active tuberculosis.

—*Alvin N. Eden, M.D.*

FOR FURTHER INFORMATION:

La Leche League International
1400 N Meacham Rd
PO Box 4079
Schaumburg IL 60168-4079
1-708-455-7730
1-800-LALECHE

International Lactation Consultants Association
201 Brown Ave
Evanston IL 60202
1-708-260-8874

Children's Care Comes Home

Electrocardiograms are flashed over telephone lines. Laboratory test results on blood drawn that morning are faxed to the pediatrician. Ventilator pressures are adjusted. Intravenous (IV) medication orders are rewritten.

The hospital intensive care unit? No, home care. It is now widely recognized that both high- and low-technology care can be safely and appropriately delivered in the home setting. This is true for a wide range of patients, including the very youngest and the very oldest.

In the past century, care of the pediatric patient has come full circle: from home births and house calls, quarantines, and visiting nurses to life-sustaining technology and complex treatments delivered in the hospital—and now back to the home. Today's health care professionals arrive at a child's home not only with a little black bag but with virtually all the wonders of modern medicine that just a few years ago could be found only in the pediatric intensive care unit of large urban medical centers. In 1994 the American Academy of Pediatrics (AAP), representing almost 50,000 North American pediatricians, formally acknowledged the rapid evolution of pediatric home care and set up a new section of the academy devoted exclusively to this increasingly important type of specialized care.

The purpose of home care is to promote and facilitate maximal comfort, function, and health of the patient at home. Pediatric home care involves clinical management of acute, self-limited, or chronic illness in children of all ages. The ultimate goal of home care is to provide optimal support of the child's growth and development within the home environment. Financial, medical, and psychosocial considerations are all essential components.

Home care for youngsters evolves

Presently, children represent one of the fastest-growing segments of the home-care patient population. As a consequence of recent advances in hospital-based treatments and technologies, children now survive premature delivery, low birth weight, acute medical complications, and chronic illness at increasing rates. This means a large population of children currently requires long-term care. In the United States alone, approximately 20 million children live with some type of chronic illness, and approximately 12 million children have major physical or mental disabilities; not surprisingly, these children are consuming an ever-larger share of health care resources.

Amy Kunhardt—Impact Visuals

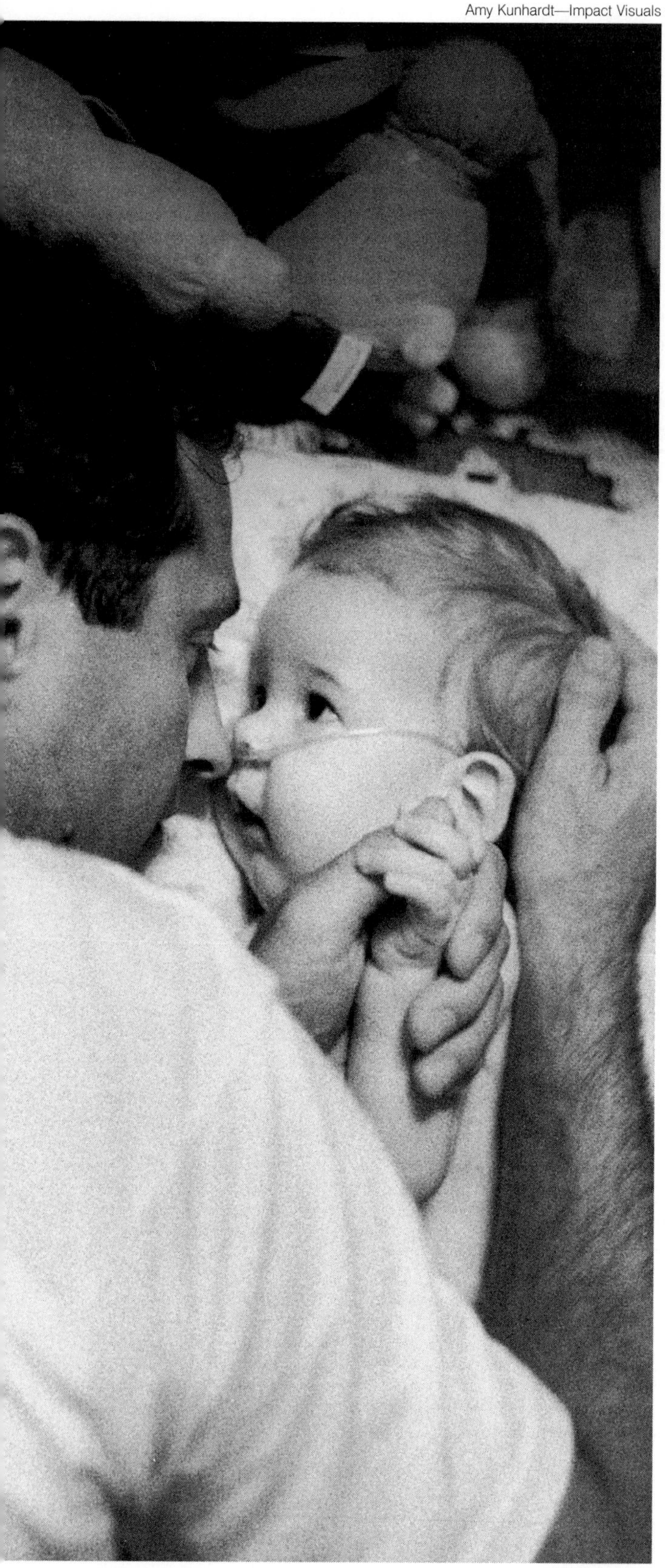

A father comforts his critically ill son, who is cared for at home. Now even the sickest youngsters can be spared the anxiety of prolonged separation from parents.

The acute-care setting is a less-than-ideal environment for children with long-term needs. It is now recognized that the goals of care are best achieved in the least-restrictive environment possible. Extended hospitalization deprives children of important family interaction and the normalizing experiences of childhood.

A changing economy is also responsible for the gradual shift from institutional to community-based and home care. The cost of health care has soared dramatically in the past several decades, with increases in hospital care rising at rates far exceeding inflation. Numerous attempts have been made at curtailing these costs. For example, in the 1980s the federal government established a system of diagnosis-related groups (DRGs), by which hospitals were reimbursed for "expected" rather than actual costs. Because costs are so high, shorter and shorter in-hospital stays are encouraged. Managed-care organizations such as health maintenance organizations (HMOs) and preferred provider organizations (PPOs) have burgeoned, also in an effort to reduce the costs of health care.

In addition to utilizing home care as an alternative to more costly hospitalization for chronically ill children, managed-care organizations are looking to home care for demonstrably cost-effective care of acute illness and even for the delivery of prevention-oriented and educational services—for example, for children with diabetes or asthma. In the 1990s hospitals and managed-care organizations are finding that home care offers a good solution to mounting costs, while families and professionals laud home care as a psychosocially sound approach.

Family centered

Successful pediatric home care always requires the intimate involvement of parents and family members in the planning of care; thus, they must be willing to provide care for the child at home and capable of doing so, whether during an acute episode of illness or in the context of a long-term, chronic disease. In a family-centered model of care, professionals view families as "partners." In this partnership family strengths and individuality, as well as different methods of coping, are recognized. At the same time, ethnic, cultural, and socioeconomic differences between families are respected, and the developmental needs of all infants, children, and adolescents in the family must be both understood and incorporated into the delivery of services. Families need to be given complete and accurate information—in terms they understand—about the care plan that has been chosen for their child.

In recognizing that the family remains stable in the child's life while the personnel who provide the care and types of treatment often change, professionals then serve the family as well as the child, ultimately assisting them toward independence.

Thanks to technology

Technological interventions that originated in hospitals have filtered down to the pediatric age group, so more technology-dependent children can be treated at home. Each breakthrough brings many new children into the potential realm of home care. Of course, these technologies need to be appropriately oriented to the home situation. Even some of the most easily accomplished hospital procedures take on new meaning when transferred to the home. "Telemedicine" and the miniaturization of infusion pumps and respiration and heart-monitoring devices have permitted some children to be fully ambulatory and even to attend school.

Pediatric situations in which home care has proved useful are too numerous to cite. In part, the services employed have derived from early concepts in adult home care, such as home meal delivery (Meals-on-Wheels) and daytime "elder care." The services have expanded to include ventilatory support and procedures such as home peritoneal dialysis that are now geared specifically to children. Children with AIDS, Lyme disease, and chronic asthma are benefiting from therapeutic and supportive home care. Neonatal jaundice, a frequent perinatal disorder, used to require extended hospital stays for phototherapy (light treatment). Such therapy has now yielded to home care, not only eliminating two to three days in the hospital but significantly enhancing crucial early maternal-infant bonding. Certain low-incidence but extremely costly long-term blood and metabolic disorders such as hemophilia and hepatic (liver) failure have been particularly difficult to treat at home, but new monitoring and infusion therapy techniques are now brightening the horizon for children with these conditions so that their lives can be maintained and enhanced outside of institutions.

Communication between the members of the multidisciplinary team managing home care is extremely important. So-called telemedicine now enables remote monitoring, transmission of sonogram and X-ray images over phone lines, the rapid dissemination of laboratory results, and doctor-to-doctor consultations across the city or even across the world. The ability to track records and information and measure outcome and quality of care has contributed greatly to the creation of an integrated delivery system.

Not all interventions are easy to evaluate. Monitoring of children at home still has a way to go. For example, apnea monitors used for children with apparent life-threatening episodes that may presage SIDS (sudden infant death syndrome) greatly reassure many parents, but such monitoring may also lead to "false alarms" and thereby provoke additional anxiety.

Hospital to home: ensuring a smooth transition

Typically, the discharge-planning process begins early in a child's hospitalization. The process is often coordinated by a "discharge planner" or social worker. Medical and nursing staff, the child's family, the home-care provider, the insurance company's case manager, and various others are also involved. A basic plan of care is established early, with necessary modifications made just prior to discharge. The type, frequency, and duration of home-care services should be agreed upon by all members of the team prior to discharge. The training of family caregivers is paramount in a planned transition from the hospital to the home setting. Thus, the family's willingness and ability to care for the child are assessed, and instruction is begun while the child is still in the hospital.

Even parents with no prior medical training often amaze the professionals with their ability to master complex procedures. Frequently, family members are trained in many procedures, including cardiopulmonary resuscitation and tracheostomy and IV catheter care. Transition from the acute-care setting can occur only after the parents and other family members have received the appropriate instruction and are capable of assuming responsibility for the child's care at home (with support and backup from the home-care provider).

When can the child go home? Several criteria determine when it is appropriate for pediatric home-care services to take over. The child cannot be discharged until medical stability has been achieved, the need for home-care services established, and a funding source identified. The home environment must be safe and have adequate electrical power, especially if certain types of equipment are required. And, of course, a telephone must be available for communication in an emergency. These details may seem trivial, but they often determine whether home care succeeds or fails.

The "right" provider

In the U.S., companies providing pediatric home care are regulated by laws, which vary from state to state. The patient's

Examples of Pediatric Situations in Which Home Care Has Proved Successful

Early discharge of newborns

Prematurity with persistent lung disease

Monitoring for sudden infant death syndrome (SIDS) and acute life-threatening episodes (ALTE) of infancy

Phototherapy for neonatal jaundice

Infusion therapy for delivery of antibiotics, other medications, blood products

- AIDS
- Lyme disease
- Osteomyelitis
- Sepsis
- Lead poisoning
- Hemophilia

Comprehensive services

- Neuromuscular disorders (e.g., cerebral palsy, muscular dystrophy, spina bifida)
- Metabolic disorders (e.g., liver and kidney-failure disorders, diabetes)

Respiratory support and management

- Short term (asthma)
- Long term (neurological disorders)

Nutritional support

- Complex trauma
- Crohn's disease
- Cystic fibrosis
- Childhood cancer
- Prematurity
- Short bowel syndrome
- Pain control
- Prevention services

Brian Smith

A young cancer patient and his mother receive instructions about treatment via a home computer. Interactive computers and other technological advances have vastly increased the feasibility of pediatric home care.

insurance company may have the option to limit the choice of companies to one with "preferred-provider" status.

In the past, nursing services were primarily provided by visiting nurse associations, and equipment and supplies had to be obtained from home medical equipment companies. Highly technical or disease-specific aspects of care sometimes were provided by companies with expertise in a limited range of specialized services, such as companies that specialize in supplying home IV therapy.

Services today are delivered by either a single large national home care company, a local independent agency, a hospital-based agency, or a network of companies. It is both desirable and cost-effective, whenever possible, to obtain all services, supplies, and equipment from a single manager capable of coordinating all aspects of care. Increasing numbers of home-care companies play this expanded role. Many large providers now even maintain their own pharmacy services.

When choosing a provider, the consumer should consider other aspects. The provider should have a mechanism in place to assess quality and should have an outcome-oriented approach to care. That is, it should offer services and methods of care that have been shown to be both safe and effective. The consumer should select a company that specifies, in writing, the parameters within which care will be delivered. All procedures should be fully defined. The chosen provider should have a philosophy of care that emphasizes integration rather than fragmentation of services.

It is extremely important that the company selected have experience in caring for children, especially if those patients are medically fragile and technology-dependent. The providers of care must understand the psychosocial issues that affect a family's ability to care for an ill child at home. Acceptance of a family-centered care approach is the cornerstone of pediatric home care; the provider, therefore, must accept a role of advocacy and collaboration.

Who's in charge?

The successful delivery of pediatric home care requires that professional roles outside the hospital hierarchy be redefined. A multidisciplinary approach, in which a variety of health care professionals collaborate with the family, has evolved. Because the home-care approach is relatively new, many professionals are not yet accustomed to the collaborative practice model. To date, roles and responsibilities remain poorly defined. Professional members of the care team often fail to recognize the important status of the child's parents, and families may thus feel that they have lost control or that they are in competition with professional caregivers.

The pediatrician's role is central to the success of pediatric home care. Ideally, the child's regular pediatrician helps establish the medical plan of care and remains responsible for home medical management. In this age of ultraspecialization, many pediatricians are narrowly focused on one particular disease or organ system, which may result in fragmentation of services. For the pediatrician to be effective, he or she must be educated in the special circumstances of home care. Some pediatricians feel that they are not properly reimbursed for the additional responsibility, paperwork, and telephone calls, not to mention home visits. Many still prefer to render care in the traditional office or hospital setting. They may be ill at ease in a supervisory role. At present, many medical liability issues in home care remain unclear. The AAP and most professionals agree, however, that once the value of pediatric home-care services is fully clear to pediatricians, most will be eager to participate.

Medical management of chronically ill children must include routine kinds of care such as immunizations, assessment of growth and development, hearing and eye tests, dental care, and assessment of potential school problems. Timely evaluation of acute or emergent medical problems depends on information supplied to the pediatrician by members of the family and other members of the care team who have regular contact with the child.

In the past, pediatric nurses in the home setting often did not have the same level of skills and expertise as their counterparts in the hospital. Many nurses considered pediatric home care a "dead end" rather than an opportunity for career growth. In fact, the pediatric home-care nurse must possess broad knowledge and be skilled in the use of state-of-the-art technology. The nursing professional must be able to function autonomously but also act as part of the multidisciplinary team. The successful pediatric home-care nurse will also serve as an advocate for the child while providing guidance and support for the family.

Currently, national certification is available in pediatric nursing as well as in home-health nursing. In addition, certification in specific interventions such as IV-catheter insertion has become standard for pediatric nurses involved in infusion therapy in the home. Skill in the use of phototherapy equipment for infants with jaundice, apnea monitors for those whose breathing needs to followed during sleep, and equipment used for nutritional support and respiratory management are essential for the pediatric home-care nurse. Fortunately, more and more pediatric nurses, including those holding master's degrees in advanced practice, are finding home care both to be rewarding and to offer opportunities for career advancement.

Ultimately, the team approach means that at various times the hospital discharge planner, the pediatrician, the parents, the home-care nurse, and the economic case manager may consider themselves "in charge." Ideally, each of the team

NEWS*CAP*

Kids' Wisdom on Diet and Exercise

A Gallup Poll released in 1995 asked 410 children between the ages of 9 and 15 about their attitudes toward food and physical activity. The survey, cosponsored by the American Dietetic Association, the International Food Information Council, and the President's Council on Physical Fitness and Sports, produced a mixed bag; some responses were encouraging, while others decidedly were not. Eighty-eight percent of the youngsters said they would change or arrange their schedules to incorporate physical exercise, but fewer than half said they eat meals with their families every day. Here are some other responses of the younger generation:

- 97% agreed that it is very important for good health to eat a balanced diet
- 33% believed it is okay to eat anything they want whenever they want (up from 18% in a similar Gallup Poll conducted in 1991)
- 52% were aware of the Food Guide Pyramid
- 95% agreed that foods like ice cream, cookies, and chips are okay to eat but not all the time
- 71% believed their favorite foods are not good for them
- 73% were tired of hearing about what foods are good and bad for them
- 98% agreed that for good health it is very important to have regular physical activity
- among those who had not played outdoors with friends in the last six months, 91% said they would do so if they had time (among those who had played outside with friends in the last six months, only 23% had done so as often as two or three times a week)
- 49% had gone swimming in the six months prior to being polled
- 75% felt they spend about the right amount of time participating in physical activity, and 93% thought they were physically fit
- 19% spent time playing computer/video games
- 28% read during their free time
- 28% watched TV during their free time
- of those who had reported no physical activity in the last seven days, 39% had "no time" or were "too busy" to exercise

members should be working within the context of achieving the best possible care for the child in a cost-effective manner. Each player needs to have independence of judgment but also the requisite skills to understand the total scope of the problem. The team that works well avoids conflicts of interest, shows flexibility, and adequately manages "in-the-trenches" problems.

Financing and public policy

Funding for pediatric home care comes from a variety of sources. The providers include traditional insurance plans, HMOs and other managed-care plans, and federal and state programs. It is important for families to understand the scope of services allowed within each plan or program—exactly what services are covered, in what amounts, and for how long. Public-sector financing is available for children whose families meet certain requirements and cannot otherwise afford medical services. More than 80,000 chronically ill children in the U.S. receive medical assistance through the federal Medicaid program. Medicaid waiver programs are now available in many states and, by eliminating certain obstacles to Medicaid eligibility or by increasing the range of services covered by Medicaid to include home care, can assist families caring for a chronically ill child at home. Such waivers are often referred to as "Katie Beckett" programs (after the widely publicized 1981 case in which the parents of a ventilator-dependent child struggled to take her home following three years of hospitalization).

Historically, third-party payers have been biased in favor of hospital reimbursement and have inadequately reimbursed those supplying home-care services. At times during the home-care industry's evolution, scandals and abuses have been reported. Legislation, regulation, and setting of guidelines for care and reimbursement, fortunately, have done much to alleviate problems that once tarnished the reputation of the industry.

Remaining wrinkles

Although increasing numbers of children successfully receive care for both acute and chronic conditions in the home setting, there remain a number of unresolved problems related to financing and availability of community resources. Even if insurance covers most costs, there are often unanticipated, or hidden, costs, such as parents' time away from the job. Furthermore, home-care provision and resources vary greatly from one geographic location to another; wide differences, for example, may be seen between inner cities and rural settings.

With the costs of hospitalization becoming prohibitive, many see some roles of the traditional hospital as becoming obsolete. Some foresee the day when hospitals will function as giant intensive care units providing only sophisticated medical and surgical procedures. Decisions regarding keeping a child at home or in an institution, however, should not be made on cost alone.

More creative ways to finance and deliver home care are certainly required. Currently a new concept known as "cluster care" is being evaluated. In this approach a team of home health aides from a single contracted agency serves many patients in a defined residential area. Thus, one care provider may have a team consisting of a nurse, doctor, physical therapist, nutrition therapist, and dentist who work solely in one large housing project. Many more new ways to include children whose families are, at present, unwilling or unable to participate in home care must still be found.

The dimensions of the task of a family caring for a chronically ill child at home are invariably underestimated. Families consistently agree that although they would not change a home-care arrangement, no amount of counseling could have prepared them for the initial overwhelming responsibility. Parents of a chronically ill child requiring home care often feel that they are in a continuous life-and-death situation in which they are responsible for the health of their own child. Families repeatedly express concern about the limited time they have to devote to their other children. They may worry that they are neglecting them or that other family responsibilities are not being met. Such worries are frequent sources of anxiety. Parents also voice feelings of isolation and may seek parent-to-parent networking opportunities. Increasingly, there are such means of support available. The Oley Foundation, founded in Albany, N.Y., in 1983, plays a major role in support of home-care nutrition. Some organizations may be disease-specific, such as those for children with cystic fibrosis, Crohn's disease, sickle-cell disease, diabetes, or cerebral palsy. Many other groups now see their role enlarging to include home care.

With more and more families caring for chronically ill children at home, there is an ever-greater need for "respite," or temporary relief, services. No matter how dedicated they are, families become tired and overwhelmed. The ability to change focus temporarily or attend to the needs of other children in the family and to neglected household matters is essential for long-term success. When these services are not available, rehospitalization of the child may then be the only available means for the family to obtain respite.

Another very important need is for the education of professionals who care for the pediatric population to be broadened. Schools of medicine and nursing are beginning to incorporate the art and science of home care into basic curricula. The AAP intends for its newly created section on home care to become a national clearinghouse for information and education of professionals.

The future of home care for children looks bright but will depend on many factors. In this era of managed care, pediatric home care must demonstrate its cost-effectiveness while still combining the best of technology and compassion. Home care represents one aspect on the continuum of good, total pediatric care—an enhancement of care—not a compromise or an alternative.

Caring for acutely or chronically ill children at home can test the mettle of any parental caregiver. Most find, however, that the rewards can be just as profound as the responsibility. Ultimately, the success of pediatric home care will depend on the unpressured willingness and ability of the family to be part of this approach.

—Arnold Schussheim, M.D., and Lynn Gardiner Seim, R.N., M.S.N.

Immunization Update

In 1991 the World Health Organization (WHO) and UNICEF announced that their goal—to immunize 80% of the world's children—had been realized. That accomplishment made it possible to aim even higher—toward universal childhood vaccination.

Early in 1995 the Advisory Committee on Immunization Practices (ACIP), under the jurisdiction of the United States Public Health Service, issued a recommended schedule for children from birth to age 16 to receive six vaccinations protecting them against nine infectious illnesses. Additionally, owing to the licensing of a long-awaited varicella virus (chicken pox) vaccine (Varivax) early in 1995, the ACIP issued a statement recommending routine chicken pox vaccination for children between 12 and 18 months of age, preferably at the same time as the first measles, mumps, rubella (MMR) vaccination. One dose of the vaccine is recommended for immunization of all children from age 19 months to 13 years who have not previously been immunized and who have yet to contract the disease. The new timetable, which includes a routine immunization visit at 11–12 years of age, will also allow for the administration of the new vaccine to any children who were not immunized at some previous time in childhood. For children over 13 years, two doses of the vaccine are recommended because the severity and complications of chicken pox increase in young adults.

In August 1995 the Centers for Disease Control and Prevention issued a statement advising Americans aged 20–37 to get a second measles vaccination. Measles protection did not take hold in 5% of vaccinated children in this age group, which puts many of them, especially college students, at risk of contracting the disease.

With these immunization-awareness measures, the United States joins many other countries in helping WHO and UNICEF achieve their new goals: to eradicate polio and eliminate neonatal tetanus globally and to reduce measles deaths by 95% by the year 2000.

F.M. Kearney—Impact Visuals

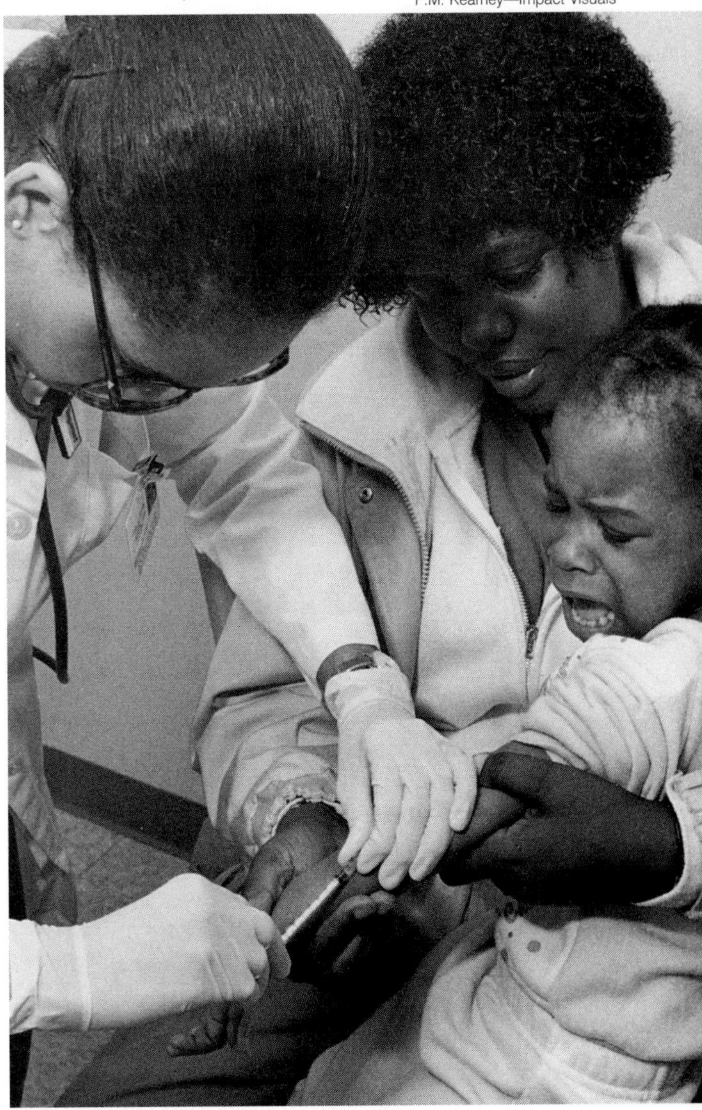

Recommended Childhood Immunizations — U.S. 1995

Vaccine	Birth	2 months	4 months	6 months	12 months*	15 months*	18 months	4-6 years	11-12 years	14-16 years
Hepatitis B (HB)†	HB								HB§	
		HB		HB						
Diphtheria, tetanus, pertussis (DTP)‡		DTP	DTP	DTP	DTP or DtaP at ≥15 months			DTP or DTaP	Tetanus-Diphtheria	
H. influenzae type B (Hib)		Hib	Hib	Hib	Hib					
Oral poliovirus (OPV)		OPV	OPV	OPV				OPV		
Measles, mumps, rubella (MMR)					MMR			MMR or	MMR	
Varicella zoster virus vaccine (VZV)					VZV				VZV §	

* Vaccinations recommended in the second year of life (*i.e.*, 12-15 months) may be given at either one or two visits.

† All pregnant women should be screened for hepatitis B surface antigens during an early prenatal visit.

‡ The fourth dose of DTP may be administered as early as 12 months of age, provided at least six months have elapsed since the third dose of DTP. Combined DTP-Hib products may be used when these two vaccines are administered simultaneously. Diphtheria and tetanus toxoids and acellular pertussis vaccine (DTaP) are licensed for use for the fourth and/or fifth dose of DTP in children aged 15 months and older and may be the preferred vaccine for these older children.

§ Those childern who lack a reliable history of hepatitis or chicken pox and have not been vaccinated previously should receive vaccinations at the routine immunization visit.

Sources: Centers for Disease Control and Prevention, Advisory Committee on Immunization Practices, American Academy of Pediatrics, and American Academy of Family Physicians.

What's in a Name?

Does an asthma medicine called Brethine work better than a chemically identical compound called Bricanyl? Does the ease with which doctors can remember and spell the name of a given drug increase the likelihood of its being prescribed? Can a consumer comparing similar cough-and-cold remedies draw any useful conclusions from the advertising claims implicit in such trade names as NyQuil, Kwelcof, and Theraflu? Just what *is* in a name?

A language of its own

The thousands of names that appear in the *United States Pharmacopeia* (*USP*), the official register of pharmaceutical products approved by the Food and Drug Administration (FDA), constitute a veritable language—one of several that every physician must master in the course of acquiring a medical degree and a license to practice. Laypeople, if they think about the origins of this language at all, are likely to labor under many misconceptions. They may believe that drug names are scientific terms, coined, like the names of bones and muscles, from Greek and Latin. They may think that drug names are similar to chemical names, determined automatically by the product's composition. Or they may assume that drug names are simply part of the mysterious jargon of the arcane art of medicine. To the uninitiated, some names seem to be pure fabrications, designed to generate a favorable impression in the hearer without actually conveying information.

While there is a grain of truth in each of these ideas, they are all largely false. The trade, or brand, name of a drug is a carefully designed creation of the manufacturer (or the manufacturer's advertising agency or public relations advisers) that becomes part of the overall identity and public image of the product. It distinctively identifies that product, and the manufacturer's exclusive right to use it is protected by law. Moreover, the brand name conveys a selected amount of information about the product, along with a positive, attractive message, much of it perhaps subliminal.

One substance, many names

Tracing the etymology (linguistic origin) of an English word generally involves going back to its roots in Anglo-Saxon, Norman French, or medieval Latin. Similarly, the analysis of drug names usually uncovers preexisting words or word elements. The quest for a drug name's origins can be both challenging and frustrating, much like deciphering a "lost language" of antiquity. And, just as in the study of a natural language, examination of the patterns of word formation and manipulation of semantic elements in the language of drug names provides insights into the psychology of those who "speak" it.

At the outset it is necessary to distinguish the three different kinds of names that drugs bear: (1) chemical names; (2) nonproprietary, or generic, names; and (3) brand names. Although every drug theoretically has one of each kind of name, for some products the three are identical.

The most basic name given to a drug is its chemical name. This is an exact description, according to internationally accepted principles, of its chemical nature and molecular structure. Because chemical names can be unwieldy—for example, (±)-2-(*p*-isobutylphenyl) propionic acid—it is often convenient to have a more concise way of referring to a drug. Moreover, assigning chemical names to some drug products simply is not feasible—some are natural substances that have not been fully analyzed, while others are complex mixtures that defy chemical description. Hence, for most drugs there is a generic name that is different from the chemical name, although it is often a simplified version of the chemical name. The generic name is the one under which all brands and forms of a drug are listed in the *USP.* It is also the name under which the drug is discussed in most of the scientific literature and in textbooks of pharmacology and medicine. In the case of the above-mentioned compound, (±)-2-(*p*-isobutylphenyl) propionic acid, the chemical name has been whittled down for convenience to ibuprofen.

Generically speaking

Ordinarily the generic name of a new drug product is proposed by its developer or manufacturer. In the U.S. generic names must be approved by the United States Adopted Names (USAN) Council, formed in 1964 under the joint auspices of the American Medical Association, the American Pharmaceutical Association, and the United States Pharmacopeial Convention, Inc. (which publishes the *USP*). The principal function of the USAN Council is to establish and enforce standards for the creation of convenient, meaningful, and distinctive names for new drug products. These standards, which are based on guidelines set by the FDA, are intended to keep generic names as simple as possible while preserving consistency in the way chemical names are abridged. They also seek to distinguish certain classes of drugs by including a common one- or two-syllable element in their names. A major concern of the council is to avoid new generic names that look or sound too much like existing names.

Some cynical observers have suggested that the manufacturer of a new drug may willingly accept an awkward or unpronounceable generic name in hopes that physicians will be more likely to prescribe the brand name of the drug than its generic equivalent. In the U.S., however, the laws of all states allow pharmacists to substitute a generic product for a prescribed brand-name drug unless the prescribing physician has specifically countermanded such substitution.

The USAN Council recommends standard patterns of simplification for turning chemical names into generics. For example, the syllable *chlor,* which indicates the presence of one or more atoms of chlorine, is regularly shortened to *clo,* and the names of certain organic molecular components such as *ethylenediaminetetraacetate* and *glucoheptonate* are abridged, respectively, to *edetate* and *gluceptate*. The council also works with other national and international agencies, particularly the World Health Organization, to promote worldwide standardization of drug names. One way of achieving this goal is to use spelling rules that accord with the practices of most of the languages that use the Roman alphabet. Another

Illustration by Rupert Howard

aspect of the effort to ensure international acceptability of generic names is the avoidance of combinations of syllables that are ludicrous or perhaps even obscene in one language or another.

Guidelines for deriving generic names from chemical names are not rigidly enforced, however, and even far-fetched derivations may gain approval. For example, the generic name of the antibiotic tetracycline alludes to the structural formula of the chemical compound: four (the Greek *tetra*) cycles, or ring-shaped configurations of atoms, in a row. The term *tetracycline* might with equal justice be applied to thousands of other compounds, from cortisone to cholesterol, that contain four cyclical components, but it happens to be the official generic name of a particular antibiotic.

Clues to origin or function

The generic names for some biological products, including plant extracts, hormones, antibiotics, and vaccines, are not based on chemical names, often because the substances in question, some of which have been used medicinally for centuries, have never been analyzed. Plant derivatives used as drugs are usually named after their sources: atropine, an antispasmodic, comes from *Atropa belladonna* (the deadly nightshade). Names of plant-derived products such as castor oil and cocoa butter, which have been in the medical vocabulary for generations, also serve as generic names.

All natural antibiotics are produced by living microorganisms, and many derive their generic names from the names of the organisms that make them: penicillin from *Penicillium notatum,* the common green mold found on bread and fruit; streptomycin from the bacterium *Streptomyces griseus.* Hormones usually bear names referring to their physiological functions, even when their chemical composition is known—hence, the name of oxytocin (from the Greek *oxytokos,* "swift birth"), the pituitary hormone that stimulates uterine contractions during labor.

A number of generic names refer to pharmacological action; examples are acyclovir, a drug active against the herpes simplex and chicken pox viruses, and filgrastim (neutro*phil*ic *gra*nulocyte colony *stim*ulating factor), used to treat a blood disorder associated with cancer chemotherapy. The list of generic names even includes some eponyms; the antifungal drug nystatin, for example, was discovered by workers at the New York State Department of Health.

Meet the *barb* and *cort* families

USAN standards include recommendations that certain families of drugs be identified by a common word element. For example, the names for all barbiturates are expected to contain the syllable *barb,* and cortisone derivatives are identified by the syllable *cort.* These family names do not necessarily indicate chemical similarities. Thus, names for beta-adrenergic blocking agents (used in the treatment of high blood pressure, coronary artery disease, glaucoma, and other conditions) end in *-olol* or *-alol* even though not all are chemically related to the patriarch of the family, propranolol.

While one reason for standardizing generic names is to ensure a stable and permanent nomenclature for drugs, generic names are not absolutely immutable. From time to time, authorities agree to make a simplified chemical name even simpler. In recent years the name of the AIDS drug azidothymidine (AZT) has been changed to zidovudine; glyceryl guaiacolate, an expectorant, has been renamed guaifenesin; and the epilepsy drug diphenylhydantoin has become phenytoin.

Brand names: strictly business

The chemical name and the generic name of a drug are spelled with a lowercase first letter; in contrast, the brand name, because it is a trademark registered with the U.S. Patent and Trademark Office, is capitalized. It is important to recognize the distinction between a patent on a drug and a registered trade name for that drug. The company that develops a new pharmaceutical product obtains a patent granting it the exclusive right to manufacture and market that product for a period of 20 years. At the same time, the manufacturer assigns a brand name to the product and, if the name receives the approval of the FDA, registers it as a trademark, which thus secures permanent rights to that name.

When the patent expires, other manufacturers are free to produce and sell the product, but they may not use the original brand name. A drug company that proposes to market another firm's product on which the patent has expired may devise and register its own brand name for the product, or it may choose to sell the product under the generic name. The holder of a patent has the right to sell the patent outright or license another firm to manufacture or sell the product. In addition, the owner of a trade name may sell its rights to the name to another firm.

Established brand names are rarely altered. When diphenylhydantoin was shortened to phenytoin, the brand name Dilantin, which was derived from the older generic name, remained unchanged. The brand name of another anticonvulsant, clonazepam, was changed from Clonopin to Klonopin, however, because the earlier name was being misread as Clonidine (a blood pressure medication) in prescriptions. Losec (an inhibitor of gastric acid secretion) was renamed Prilosec to avoid confusion with the diuretic Lasix.

A few brand names that began as trademarks have gradually evolved into generic names in fact, if not in law. While *adrenaline* (with the final *e*) is used interchangeably with *epinephrine* as a name for the hormone produced by the adrenal gland and for pharmaceutical formulations of it, the word *Adrenalin* is a registered trademark.

A marriage of science and slogan

As with any consumer product—from laundry detergent to antiperspirant—the ideal brand name for a drug is a sort of concentrated slogan, fraught with subliminal hype and free of negative connotations. Achieving this goal with a single word that is also brief, distinctive, euphonious, and memorable presents an enormous challenge to the coiner of a new brand name, particularly as the number of remaining combinations of syllables still available dwindles. The challenge is all the greater when the manufacturer seeks to include both some reference to the nature or purpose of the drug and an allusion to the name of the firm or a tie-in with the names of some of its other products.

Tracing the origins of pharmaceutical brand names is often a remarkably illuminating study, uncovering many twists and turns in the complex psychological relationship between producers and consumers. Just as the English language includes words (such as *gremlin* and *quiz*) whose origin nobody knows, there are a few drug brand names whose genesis is a mystery, even to the firms that currently own them. Determining the etymology of a drug's brand name demands a familiarity with both the pharmacology of the product and the often unruly principles of scientific terminology. Even armed with such knowledge, however, one is likely to encounter a host

NEWS*CAP*

Regulating Drugs in Europe

Europe now has its own version of the U.S. Food and Drug Administration (FDA), called the European Agency for the Evaluation of Medicinal Products. This long-awaited pharmaceutical-regulating center opened in London in 1995. The agency will centralize evaluation and registration of drugs and oversee their marketing throughout the European Union (EU).

The agency aims to ensure that uniform standards are used to evaluate the safety of new drugs throughout the 15-member union. Previously the requirements varied widely from one country to another. The agency also intends to speed up the approval of pharmaceuticals by streamlining regulatory procedures. The goal now is that the approval process take no more than 300 days, compared with the years it previously took in some countries.

One reason for establishing the new centralized facility was that many countries lacked the expertise to evaluate the safety of drugs created by biotechnology (genetically engineered, or recombinant, drugs). Approval of all new genetically engineered pharmaceutical products by the agency is now compulsory. On the other hand, the European Agency for the Evaluation of Medicinal Products does not plan to become a large bureaucracy like the FDA. Rather, it will utilize and rely on the facilities that already exist. Thus, manufacturers of nonrecombinant products can seek approval from one of the existing national regulatory agencies, and approval in one country will permit a drug to be sold throughout the EU.

of inconsistencies: spelling conventions that are deliberately exotic, a wacky sort of tongue-in-cheek grammar, and a stock of lexical elements as devious as a secret code.

Cracking the code

Many brand names are inventive abridgments of generic names. The generic name may lose its beginning (as when ceftazidime becomes Azidime), its middle (as when indomethacin is contracted to Indocin), or its end (as when ciprofloxacin is cropped to Cipro). Both beginning and end may be excised (thus, metoprolol becomes Toprol), or selected letters may be retained and the rest discarded: amoxicillin is refashioned as Amoxil and methylergonovine as Methergine.

When the generic name is a phrase, selective deletions may be combined with fusion to yield a brand name. Thus, ferrous gluconate becomes Fergon; isosorbide dinitrate, Sorbitrate. A variety of alternative methods may be used to trim a generic or chemical name. A brand of pediatric vaccine against infection with the bacterium *Haemophilus influenzae* type b, abbreviated as Hib, is marketed as ProHIBiT. Bewon is a formulation of thiamine (*i.e.,* vitamin B_1).

References to pharmacological action appear in the brand names of numerous prescription products, some of these names fabricated with the same wry humor as those of cosmetics and kitchen gadgets: Nestab and Pramilet are prenatal vitamins; GoLYTELY, a laxative designed to preserve normal electrolyte balance. The name of the pharmacological class to which a drug belongs may simply be abbreviated or altered: ANSAID, a nonsteroidal anti-inflammatory drug (NSAID); Blocadren, a beta-adrenergic blocking agent; Bronkodyl, a bronchodilator.

A brand name may indicate the condition the drug is intended to induce—for example, Akineton (the Greek word for "motionless"), a drug to control the movement disorders of parkinsonism, and Cylert, to improve alertness in attention deficit disorder. A name may also refer directly to the disease or microorganism the drug is intended to combat: Azmacort for asthma, Tinver for tinea versicolor (a fungal infection of the skin). Many drug names include word elements that consistently denote particular drug actions or medical conditions. For example, heart medicines are often identified by the syllable *card* (Greek *kardia,* "heart")—Cardene, Procardia, Tonocard—or *cor* (Latin for "heart")—Inocor, Mevacor, Vascor.

Lexical elements found in some brand names refer to mode of administration: *or*al (Dymelor, Orinase), *nas*al (Nasalide, Nasacort), or *opt*ical (Betoptic, Optipranol). The pharmacodynamics of a drug (particulars of its absorption, distribution, and excretion) may be suggested by its name in a variety of ways. For instance, names of drug products formulated to provide a long duration of action may include the syllable *dur* (Duraquin, Theo-Dur) or *span* (Aristospan, Cerespan) or may be followed by the abbreviation LA (long-acting) or SA (sustained action). When the prolongation of action is achieved by delay of the absorption of the drug, this may be indicated in the name by the syllable *slo* or *slow* (Slo-Niacin, Slow-K) or by the suffix *-SR* (sustained release). The names of drugs that are administered only twice a day may include the syllable *bid* (from *b.i.d.,* the abbreviation of the Latin phrase *bis in die,* "twice a day"): Cefobid, Lorabid.

Quirks and ambiguity

Among the discreet quirks that coiners of pharmaceutical brand names allow themselves, spelling oddities loom large. A favorite device is putting one or more capital letters into the middle of a name (BuSpar, ParaGard, RhoGAM).

Ambiguity is rampant. A quick perusal of a directory of prescription medicines reveals that the names of a dozen or so such products end in the syllable *-stat* and about the same number end in the syllable *-ase*. It might seem reasonable to conclude that each of these syllables has a specific and consistent meaning and that all of the drugs whose names have the same ending make up a sort of family whose members are similar in chemical nature or pharmaceutical action.

A comparison of members of each "family" quickly reveals that the likeness is illusory. One subset of names ending in *-stat* derives its significance from the medical jargon *stat* (from Latin *statim,* "immediately"). Its members are drugs that act rapidly, such as Ergostat (ergotamine tartrate), used to avert a migraine attack. Another group of *-stat* names refers to the control of infection by inhibition of the growth of microorganisms—that is, drugs that are bacteriostatic or fungistatic, such as Monistat, an antifungal effective against *Monilia* (an older name for the ubiquitous yeast *Candida*). In yet another class of brand names ending in *-stat,* the reference is to the hemostatic effect of the drugs (*i.e.,* their ability to stop bleeding), such as Instat, an absorbable protein material used to control bleeding in surgery.

Similarly, at least three unrelated groups of drugs end in the suffix *-ase*. They include enzyme preparations (whose names contain the suffix *-ase* in its biochemical sense of "enzyme"), oral medicines that control blood sugar in some cases of diabetes mellitus, and drugs administered by nasal inhaler.

Encountering a number of drug names incorporating the syllable *cal,* one might reasonably assume that all of these drugs contain calcium. Some, such as Calcet (calcium gluconate) and Citracal (calcium citrate), do indeed contain various salts of calcium as a dietary supplement. However, Calan is not a calcium supplement but a calcium antagonist, and Calcimar, a formulation of the hormone calcitonin, is used to treat bone disease. The name Calcimar also contains the syllable *mar,* the Spanish word for "sea," inspired by the fact that the calcitonin in Calcimar is derived from salmon. Since the same syllable appears in the name of Marezine, a drug for nausea, it might be logical to infer a connection here with the Spanish *mareo* ("seasickness"), and this would be correct. Another drug for nausea is called Marinol. It would seem a foregone conclusion that this is yet another reference to the sea, but Marinol actually has nothing to do with seasickness; rather, it is named after its source, marijuana.

OTC drugs: more hope and hype

Any systematic inquiry into pharmaceutical brand names must include a consideration of the names of over-the-counter

(continued on page 403)

Origins of Some Brand Names

Connotes strength or efficacy

DRUG	CLASS
Augmentin Fortaz	antibiotic
Maxair	bronchodilator
Maxaquin	anti-infective
Maxzide	diuretic
Primaxim Suprax Vancocin Zithromax	antibiotic

Refers to action in the body

DRUG	ACTION
Duraquin Duricef K-Dur Theo-Dur Aristospan Cerespan Meprospan Span FF	long duration
Slo-Niacin Slo-Phyllin Slow-K	prolonged absorption
Cefobid Lorabid Nolobid Pavabid	twice-a-day dosing

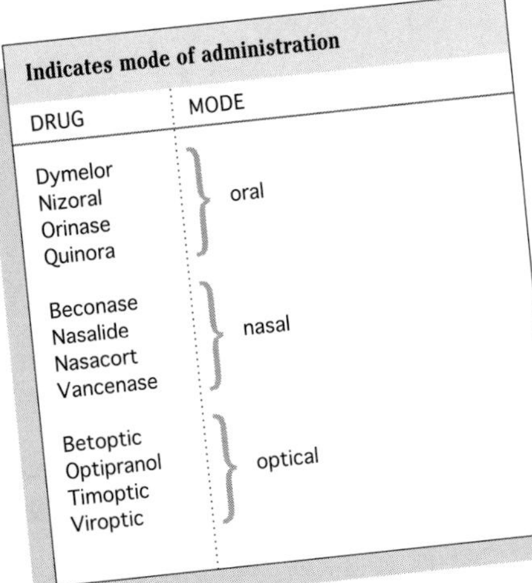

Indicates mode of administration

DRUG	MODE
Dymelor Nizoral Orinase Quinora	oral
Beconase Nasalide Nasacort Vancenase	nasal
Betoptic Optipranol Timoptic Viroptic	optical

Eponyms

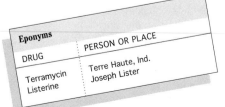

DRUG	PERSON OR PLACE
Terramycin	Terre Haute, Ind.
Listerine	Joseph Lister

Suggests condition drug is intended to induce

DRUG	CONDITION
Akineton	relief of movement disorders (parkinsonism)
Cylert	improved alertness (attention deficit disorder)
Rythmol	normal cardiac rhythm
Halcion Placidyl Restoril	sedation
Asendin Elavil Zoloft	improved mood (depressive disorders)

Specifies condition being treated

DRUG	CONDITION
Azmacort	asthma
Dymelor	diabetes
Endep	endogenous depression
Lariam	malaria
Parlodel	parkinsonism
Tinver	tinea versicolor (fungal infection of skin)
Cardene Cardura Cardizem Mevacor Procardia Tonocard Inocor Vascor	heart problems
Apresoline Capoten Catapres Combipres Loniten Minipress Tenex Tenormin	hypertension
Accutane Benzac SalAc Xerac	acne
Flexeril Norflex Paraflex Salflex	muscle spasm
Asbron Bronkephrine Bronkometer Quibron	bronchospasm
Anatuss Hycotuss Robitussin Tussionex	cough

Alludes to source of drug

DRUG	SOURCE
Lanoxin	*Digitalis lanata*
Premarin	pregnant mares' urine

Identifies target organism

DRUG	ORGANISM
Bactroban	bacteria
Elimite	mites (scabies)
Flagyl	flagellate parasites
NegGram	gram-negative bacteria
Vermox	worm infestations

Variations on generic name

DRUG	GENERIC NAME
Aftate	tolnaftate
Aldomet	methyldopa
Amoxil	amoxicillin
Azidime	ceftazidime
Azulfidine	sulfasalazine
Carafate	sucralfate
Carfusin	carbol fuchsin
Ceredase	alglucerase
Cipro	ciprofloxacin
D.H.E. 45	dihydroergotamine
E.E.S.	erythromycin ethylsuccinate
Fergon	ferrous gluconate
Haldol	haloperidol
Indocin	indomethacin
Mebaral	mephobarbital
Methergine	methylergonovine
Metopirone	metyrapone
Midamor	amiloride
Molixin	amoxicillin
Nubain	nalbuphine
PCE	particles of coated erythromycin
Pen Vee K	penicillin V potassium
Sorbitrate	isosorbide dinitrate
SSD Cream	silver sulfadiazine
Sulamyd	sulfacetamide
TACE	tri-para-anisylchloroethylene
Ticar	ticarcillin
Toprol	metoprolol

Derived from phonetic spelling of generic name

DRUG	GENERIC NAME
Bewon	thiamine (vitamin B_1)
Kay Ciel	potassium chloride (chemical formula KCl)

Based on chemical name or active ingredient(s)

DRUG	NAME OR INGREDIENT
Sudafed	pseudoephedrine
Campho-Phenique	camphor and phenol

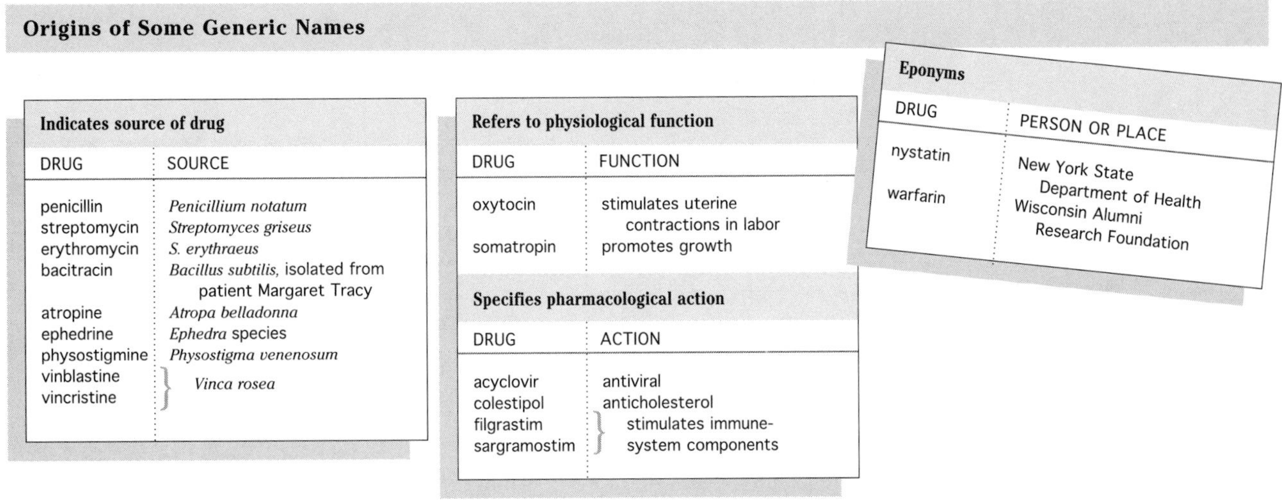

Origins of Some Generic Names

Indicates source of drug

DRUG	SOURCE
penicillin	*Penicillium notatum*
streptomycin	*Streptomyces griseus*
erythromycin	*S. erythraeus*
bacitracin	*Bacillus subtilis,* isolated from patient Margaret Tracy
atropine	*Atropa belladonna*
ephedrine	*Ephedra* species
physostigmine	*Physostigma venenosum*
vinblastine, vincristine	*Vinca rosea*

Refers to physiological function

DRUG	FUNCTION
oxytocin	stimulates uterine contractions in labor
somatropin	promotes growth

Specifies pharmacological action

DRUG	ACTION
acyclovir	antiviral
colestipol	anticholesterol
filgrastim, sargramostim	stimulates immune-system components

Eponyms

DRUG	PERSON OR PLACE
nystatin	New York State Department of Health
warfarin	Wisconsin Alumni Research Foundation

(continued from page 401)
(OTC), or nonprescription, remedies, which television commercials and other advertising have made only too familiar. Some of these refer to the product's chemical composition or echo the generic names of active ingredients—Campho-Phenique from camphor and phenol. A few are eponymous; Listerine, for example, refers to Joseph Lister, the 19th-century British surgeon who developed and promulgated antisepsis (*i.e.,* the prevention of infection by means of antiseptics). But the majority of brand names for OTC medicines refer to pharmacological action (Gas-X, Rid Lice, Sinarest).

The process of inventing names for OTC drugs includes many of the techniques that are commonly used in naming other consumer products, including cute variations in spelling (*creme, lite, nite*), pretentious terms like *formula, medication,* and *therapeutic,* and generous rations of frivolity and banality. One brand of nasal spray is called Ayr, while a long-acting nasal decongestant is called Nostrilla. Cheater's Delight is a nutritional supplement for dieters; Kick Start, a vitamin supplement laced with caffeine.

Also evident is an abundance of boosting and boasting words and phrases such as *plus, mega, fast-acting, advanced formula, high potency*—all of which (like the food producers' *grade A, fancy, select, special*) mean absolutely nothing. At least, they have no consistent reference to the quality or quantity of the active ingredients in the pharmaceutical product.

Manufacturers sometimes invent names that capitalize on the popularity of established but pharmaceutically unrelated products. The names Liquiprin (which is acetaminophen) and Nuprin (which is ibuprofen) plainly echo the name of aspirin, once the unrivaled best-seller among nonprescription pain and fever medicines. Still more often, nonprescription drug names mimic the names of prescription drugs used for the same purposes. Selsun Blue and Selsun Gold for Women, dandruff shampoos containing 1% selenium sulfide, were placed on the market after the prescription-strength (2.5%) product had achieved popularity under the name Selsun. On the other hand, Upjohn Co.'s Progaine Shampoo for Thinning Hair does not contain minoxidil, the active ingredient in Rogaine, the same manufacturer's prescription product for the treatment of baldness.

Formula for success?

The number of possible combinations of letters or sounds in a name having a manageable number of syllables is finite. How close drug manufacturers are to the limit is illustrated by the increasing number of brand names containing "rare" letters such as *q, x,* and, particularly, *z.* Whimsical spelling variations may stretch the resources of language and make brand names more distinctive or memorable, but they can also generate confusion and even error, to say nothing of being difficult to pronounce. As an example of the latter problem, a new biological product approved in 1994 was given the generic name *abciximab.*

One expedient that can enhance the availability of names for new products or new formulations is recycling existing names. As mentioned above, the patent on a drug remains in effect for only 20 years, whereas a trademark becomes the registrant's property forever. There is another and more profound difference between a patent and a trademark, one that is only dimly appreciated by most laypersons and to which some react with incredulity and even indignation. Although the registration of a trade name limits the use of that name to the registrant, it confers no obligation on the registrant to apply the name to any particular substance or material. This means that a drug company may change the formula of a product repeatedly without changing its name.

Clearly, this provision of the law serves the interests of the holder of a trade name, who is free to improve the quality of a product, avert litigation by eliminating potentially harmful ingredients, or reduce costs by substituting cheaper ingredients—all without the sacrifice of reputation and goodwill that would result if the brand name of the product had to be changed as well. Just as clearly, this practice places consumers at a certain disadvantage, particularly those who are not in the habit of comparing lists of ingredients from one purchase of a product to the next. The current formulations of Doan's Pills, Four-Way Cold Tablets, and Murine Eye Drops are as different from those of a generation ago as orange juice is from chicken soup.

In fairness to manufacturers, it must be conceded that most changes in formula are made to improve the safety or efficacy of products by introducing ingredients with more specific actions or by eliminating dubious or possibly harmful ingredients. For example, during the 1950s it became evident that the pain-and-fever medicine phenacetin, a component of several OTC remedies, posed an unacceptable risk of kidney damage for people who used it on a regular basis. Some products containing phenacetin were withdrawn from the market. In the case of Anacin, however, phenacetin was simply eliminated from the formula, leaving the aspirin and caffeine, with no change in the name of the product. Complete revamping of the formulas of prescription drugs without change of name sometimes occurs but is less common than removal or substitution of a single ingredient.

Z and *Q* words

The recycling of existing brand names is feasible only to a limited extent. A name is not likely to be reused as long as the product it represents is still serviceable and marketable. New pharmaceuticals are developed at a much faster rate than old ones are discarded. Moreover, a drug company that never released products with new names might be thought to have fallen behind the competition in research and development.

For all of these reasons, consumers can expect to see an increasing number of names beginning with *z* or ending with *q* or containing letter sequences that are uncharacteristic of English—and perhaps even unpronounceable. More and more drug names will incorporate stray letters, numerals, and symbols. Whimsy and drollery will continue to flourish. Physicians and their patients may someday have to get used to brand names of five or six syllables; they may even have to learn the Russian or Arabic alphabet. What is certain is that pharmaceutical manufacturers will continue to come up with distinctive names for new products at least as long as they keep coming up with new products needing names.

—John H. Dirckx, M.D.

Targeted Cancer Treatment

At the time that a human egg is fertilized by a sperm cell, a complex program of development is initiated. This program directs the daughter cells of the fertilized egg to take on new and distinct characteristics—characteristics that eventually give rise to the myriad of different cell types necessary to form a human being. As the cells divide and take on their new responsibilities, they communicate with each other to maintain organization of the different tissues and organs. Certain changes may take place that can cause cells to lose their ability to communicate correctly with their neighbors; they begin growing independently, forming a tumor. If the cellular alterations are severe enough, they may allow for some cells of the tumor to escape from their original tissue, flow through the blood and lymph systems, and invade other organs and tissues, which thereby impairs their function. This process is referred to as *metastasis* and distinguishes a malignant tumor from one that is benign and does not invade other tissues.

Benign tumors can often be left alone or removed by surgery, but malignant tumors are harder to treat because they can spread to many distant sites. A treatment for an already metastasized tumor must be able to distinguish cancerous from noncancerous tissue. Radiation therapy and chemotherapy evolved because tumor cells tend to be more sensitive than normal cells to their effects. The problem in treatment then becomes one of degree; a race ensues to eliminate the cancer cells without irreversibly damaging normal tissue *before* the tumor cells become altered in ways that make them insensitive, or resistant, to therapy.

An exciting recent advance in cancer treatment is the development of new drugs that are more potent against cancer cells and at the same time less toxic to normal cells. This approach, known as *targeted therapy,* makes use of toxic agents that are very precisely directed to accumulate at specific sites such as tumors. It has been understood for some time that as a normal cell undergoes the transformation toward malignancy, it changes several of its characteristics, some of which may become manifest, or expressed, at the cell's surface. Tumor cells may "express" new receptors that are not seen on their normal counterparts; in some situations they may overexpress specific receptors such as those for growth factors that are not prevalent on normal cells. Also, tumor cells can express molecules on their surface that functioned during the embryonic development of tissues but have since been "shut off."

Any of these changes in characteristics of cells could potentially be used as "targets" that would increase the specificity of a therapeutic agent. Essentially, this occurs because the agent is attached to a molecule that binds sufficiently well to the tumor cell surface. Thus, the therapeutic agent becomes preferentially retained in tumor tissue. The desired result is to maximize localization of the therapeutic agent in tumor tissue while minimizing its exposure to normal cells.

The idea of creating such a "magic bullet" is not new; the approach was first realized in the early 1900s by the German physician and scientist Paul Ehrlich. Although to date, magic bullets have shown only limited success in the treatment of humans, recent developments suggest that targeted therapies have a bright future.

Monoclonal antibodies: refining a weapon

The advent of monoclonal antibody technology has greatly facilitated the identification of markers that tend to appear more prominently on certain types of tumor cells. This technology makes use of the "humoral arm" of the immune system, which generates antibodies that recognize "foreign invaders" (tumor cells) and bind to certain of their cell-surface features. The way that this is usually accomplished in the laboratory is that an animal—most often a mouse or rat—is "immunized" with either human tumor cells or a preparation containing tumor-cell membranes. The animal's immune system is then alerted to the presence of a foreign invader and produces antibodies in response. The antibodies are directed toward a variety of structures or determinants that are different from the animal's own cell-surface molecules. The animal is then sacrificed and the spleen removed. The B cells from the spleen that produce specific antibodies are "immortalized," or "cloned" (fused to a tumor-cell line that will grow continuously in a laboratory culture).

Clones that produce an antibody that recognizes markers that are present on tumor cells but less prevalent on normal cells are rare. Once an antibody of interest has been identified, extensive studies must be performed to determine how selectively the antibody binds to tumor cells versus normal cells. In almost all cases there is some reactivity with normal cells, but this can be acceptable as long as there is preferential binding to tumor cells. Once selected, monoclonal antibodies can be linked to tumor-cell-killing agents, which thereby creates highly specific, targeted toxic agents.

Although there are several different kinds of antibody molecules, monoclonals typically are made up of four protein chains: two identical heavy chains and two identical light chains, which are held together by disulfide bonds. The pairing of each heavy and light chain forms a binding site for the specific "antigen," or substance that will stimulate an immune response. This stimulation occurs because the antigen is "recognized" by the antibody. Because the "tail" of the antibody contains a binding site for certain molecules and cells of the host defense system, early monoclonal-antibody research (in the 1970s) led to the hope that once attached to tumor cells, antibodies themselves might be able to stimulate the host defense system in such a way as to cause the cells to die. It has become clear, however, from clinical trials (*i.e.,* testing of agents in humans) that antibodies alone are not potent enough to cause regression of most tumors, even though they can be very efficient at localizing at tumor sites.

More recently, genetic engineering techniques have enabled scientists to manipulate the structure of antibody molecules to make mouse proteins more like those of humans. Proteins that are "humanlike" are tolerated for longer time periods than proteins that are foreign. Additionally, genetic engineers are able to take just the antigen binding site of a monoclonal antibody and genetically link it to other protein sequences such as toxins or other so-called effector molecules. Similar engineering may also make it possible to coat tumor cells with molecules that can stimulate a patient's own immune system to recognize tumor cells as foreign invaders and to mount a response to destroy them.

Biotechnology has provided a highly refined and potent weapon, or targeted missile, for the anticancer arsenal. Scientists are now exploiting this technology and making use of monoclonal "artillery" in a number of ways.

Targeted radioisotopes

Antibody molecules specific for tumor-related antigens have been chemically conjugated, or joined, to radioisotopes (radioactive substances) that can be used as both imaging and therapeutic agents. In diagnostic imaging, radioisotopes emit energy that enables structures inside the body to be detected; thus, a tumor can be located and visualized. Therapeutically, targeted radioisotopes can damage the genetic material of a cell, which ultimately leads to the cell's destruction. The closer in proximity an isotope is to a cell, the more pronounced its effect is. Coating a tumor cell with an antibody labeled with a radioisotope therefore takes the source of destructive power directly to the surface of tumor cells. This approach may compensate for the fact that not all tumor cells within a lesion necessarily bind to the antibody equally well; the

NEWS*CAP*

Sickle-Cell Breakthrough

The drug hydroxyurea, used for many years to treat some forms of cancer, has been found to be the first effective therapy for sickle-cell disease (also called sickle-cell anemia). In 1992 a controlled clinical trial of hydroxyurea in adults with sickle-cell disease was begun under the auspices of the National Institutes of Health. The trial was halted four months ahead of schedule, in January 1995, because the results were so compelling that investigators wanted patients in the control group as well as the treatment group to benefit from the drug.

Sickle-cell disease is an inherited blood disorder that affects an estimated 70,000 to 80,000 people in the United States, most of them African-Americans. It also occurs in people of Mediterranean, Indian, and Middle Eastern descent. Individuals with sickle-cell disease have an abnormal variety of hemoglobin, the oxygen-carrying protein in the blood. Because red blood cells containing abnormal hemoglobin molecules are sickle-shaped rather than disk-shaped, they can obstruct small blood vessels, causing pain and, ultimately, organ damage.

The study showed that while "crises" (episodes of severe pain) did not disappear entirely among those in the treatment group, they occurred less frequently, and those subjects had longer crisis-free intervals than did controls. Sickle-cell crises and hospitalizations were reduced by about 50% among patients receiving daily doses of hydroxyurea. Those taking the drug also required approximately 50% fewer blood transfusions.

Because hydroxyurea has not been tested in pediatric patients or women who might become pregnant, the researchers cautioned against its current use in these groups. As of late summer 1995, hydroxyurea had not been approved by the Food and Drug Administration as a treatment for sickle-cell disease; such approval, however, was being considered by the agency.

energy of the radioisotope that is present on a well-coated cell may also be effective at destroying a neighboring tumor cell that expresses less of the tumor antigen. While it is true that neighboring normal cells could also be affected, scientists are refining their weapons in the hope that normal cells will not be destroyed in sufficient numbers to cause harm.

B-cell lymphomas (malignant tumors of the lymphoid tissue) are good candidates for targeted radioisotope therapy because they are very responsive to conventional radiotherapy and display many relatively selective cell-surface antigens; among them are those known as *CD19, CD20,* and *CD22.* Many antibodies that strongly bind to these structures have been identified. The distribution of these molecules on normal tissue is limited to B cells, which if destroyed can usually be regenerated within one to two months. A patient with B-cell lymphoma can survive without normal B cells, albeit in an immunocompromised state (immunity is suppressed, which makes the patient more vulnerable to infections). Patients with intermediate and high-grade non-Hodgkin's lymphoma respond extremely well to standard chemotherapeutic drugs, and some patients are even cured by them. Often, however, patients with low-grade lymphoma or lymphomas that have recurred following treatment fail to respond to conventional chemotherapy. Thus, new approaches such as targeted therapy with radiolabeled antibodies are needed.

In a recent study at the University of Washington School of Medicine, oncologist Oliver Press used a specific radiolabeled antibody (an anti-CD20 antibody labeled with iodine-131) coupled with bone-marrow transplantation to treat patients whose lymphomas had recurred. The procedure involved removing and treating the patient's own marrow to remove tumor cells, administering the potent radiolabeled antibodies systemically, then reinfusing the cancer-free marrow into the patient. More than 80% of treated patients went into complete remission for an average of 11 months, and some experienced remission for over four years. The side effects observed in patients treated with radiolabeled-anti-CD20 antibody included toxicities of the cardiopulmonary and gastrointestinal systems. These and other adverse effects were seen only at the highest doses, however, and those doses were found not to be necessary for effective therapy.

While this approach appears to be highly effective for treatment of B-cell lymphoma, more commonly occurring solid tumors, such as those of the breast, colon, and lung, are not likely to be as sensitive to it. Also, the fact that the University of Washington study involved bone-marrow transplantation limits its potential. There are further drawbacks to the widespread use of radiolabeled antibodies; these include mandatory isolation of the patient, technical difficulties associated with radiolabeling and the distribution of high-level radioactivity, and the generation of substantial amounts of radioactive waste. Nonetheless, the study represents a major advance in the treatment of one form of cancer.

Antibodies linked to chemotherapeutic drugs

Antitumor antibodies have also been used to deliver such traditional chemotherapeutic drugs as doxorubicin (DOX), methotrexate, and mitomycin C to tumors. These drugs are routinely used for cancer therapy because they tend to have more selective effects on rapidly dividing tumor cells than on normal cells. Their toxicity to normal tissues, however, clearly limits their effectiveness. Selective delivery of anticancer agents at the local tumor site by chemically conjugating them to antibodies may increase the drug's therapeutic efficacy and/or decrease its normal-tissue toxicity. Such a strategy is maximally effective if the antibody-drug conjugate recognizes a cell-surface structure, binds to it, and then is taken inside the cell, or "internalized." Most therapeutic drugs must be released from the antibody in order to exert their effect, but when a cell internalizes a surface molecule, that molecule has a greater chance of ending up in a compartment that is destined for degradation. The drug can be released from the antibody and allowed to diffuse throughout the cell and reach its target. In designing effective means of linking antibodies and drugs, it is important for the "linker" to allow the drug to be held stably to the antibody while it passes through the patient's circulating blood and tissues before binding to and getting inside the tumor cell.

Recent work directed by immunologists Karl Erik and Ingegerd Hellström at Bristol-Myers Squibb Pharmaceutical Research Institute in Seattle, Wash., has demonstrated that the use of a particular internalizing antibody, BR96, to deliver the drug DOX results in the complete cure of tumors of the breast, lung, and colon in laboratory animals. This is true even when the targeted marker is present on normal tissue. The BR96 antibody was specifically generated and selected for targeted therapeutic purposes. It binds to a carbohydrate antigen that is found on the surface of a variety of cancers, including breast, colon and rectal, lung, and prostate cancers.

Example of Antibody Delivering Anticancer Drug

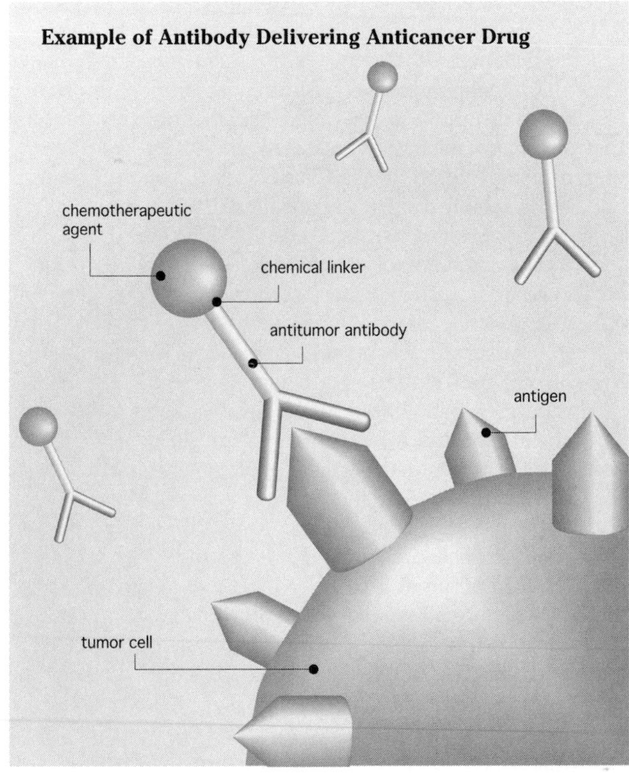

Similar to most other antitumor antibodies, BR96 is not totally tumor-specific, however, and therefore binds to some normal cells (specifically, those of the stomach, esophagus, intestine, and pancreas). To date, no antibodies have been found to bind exclusively to tumor tissue, and many bind to very vital normal cells such as stem cells, nerve cells, and cells of the heart muscle, which precludes their clinical use. BR96 represents a very desirable antibody for delivery of drugs or toxins—in particular, because of its relatively low normal-tissue cross-reactivity and its rapid internalization following binding to the cell surface. Owing to its potent antitumor activity in rodents with implanted human tumors, BR96-DOX has recently entered human trials.

Local activation of drugs at the tumor site

Another novel use of tumor-targeting antibodies is to localize an enzyme at the surface of tumor cells. After sufficient time has elapsed to allow for the antibody-enzyme to clear from the circulating blood, a chemotherapeutic drug that has been substantially inactivated (known as a *prodrug*) is administered; once it has reached the targeted enzyme, it becomes reactivated on the cancer-cell surface. Although this means of delivery is quite complicated and thus far has not been optimized, it has the potential to provide maximal amounts of a drug to a tumor while minimizing toxicity to normal tissue. The approach has been used successfully to activate various prodrugs in animals, but it is just beginning to be evaluated in humans.

Enter immunotoxins

As mentioned above, tumor cells can continue to change characteristics, and many failures of therapy are the result of cancer cells' acquisition of inherent resistance to the effects of chemotherapeutic drugs. Additionally, the ultimate effectiveness of a targeted therapy may be limited primarily by the potency of the therapeutic agent. Protein toxins are powerful toxic agents produced by a variety of living organisms and can be extremely effective tumor killers once inside a cell. To kill cancer cells, toxins first bind to specific receptors on cell surfaces. Once bound, the toxin must then gain entry into the cell and find its way to the cell's cytoplasm in order to exert its ultimate function of stopping protein synthesis, which results in cell death.

Through use of the tools of biotechnology, toxins can be designed to retain their ability to halt protein synthesis but lose their capacity to bind to cells. Because such chemically engineered agents do not bind to normal cell-surface structures, they can pass through the body without causing much harm. By attachment of a desired tumor-reactive antibody to a protein toxin devoid of its native binding ability, a potent and specific targeting agent is formed. These antibody-toxin hybrids are termed *immunotoxins*.

Protein toxins have been isolated from a variety of plants, bacteria, and fungi. The toxin ricin, isolated from the beans of the castor-oil plant, *Ricinus communis,* is an example. Ricin consists of two chains: one that carries out the catalytic activity necessary for inhibiting protein synthesis (the A chain) and a second that promotes cell binding (the B chain). When the B chain is removed, a relatively nontoxic form of ricin is left. Owing to its wide availability and its high potency once inside a cell, the ricin A chain has been useful for the construction of immunotoxin conjugates. Many chemotherapeutic agents have been produced by chemical linking of the ricin A chain to antibodies with linkers that are relatively unstable and from which the toxin can be cleaved, or detached, upon internalization, which thereby "intoxicates" target cells.

Bacterial toxins, including *Pseudomonas* exotoxin A (PE) and diphtheria toxin (DT), are similar to ricin in that they have cell-binding capability, which makes them active against most cell types. PE is produced by the bacterium *Pseudomonas aeruginosa* and has distinct structural domains that encode, or orchestrate, cell binding, translocation into the cytoplasm, and the blocking of protein synthesis. Once inside a cell, PE is cleaved in a way that allows its enzymatic portion to inhibit protein synthesis. The released domain is then transferred into the cytoplasm by a translocation process that is not fully understood. The genetic removal of the domain that controls cell binding results in a relatively nontoxic form of PE, PE40, which, when linked to tumor-reactive antibodies, forms a potent anticancer immunotoxin.

DT, produced by the bacterium *Corynebacterium diphtheriae,* also has distinct domains that can be cleaved and thus used in the construction of immunotoxins. Immunotoxins have been shown to be highly selective agents for the elimination of cancer cells and are approximately 1,000 times more potent than standard drugs but are not limited by multidrug resistance, which often follows therapy using conventional chemotherapeutic agents.

Encouraging clinical results in treating B-cell lymphoma have been obtained with the use of anti-CD22 antibody linked to the A chain of the toxin ricin. A group headed by immunologist Ellen Vitetta and biochemist Philip Thorpe of the University of Texas Southwestern Medical Center at Dallas pioneered the construction and evaluation of this immunotoxin in the treatment of humans with lymphomas that have failed to respond to conventional therapy. Administered intravenously, the immunotoxin resulted in a tumor-mass reduction of more than 50% in 38% of patients. Vitetta and colleagues have also evaluated a second immunotoxin, anti-CD19 linked to the ricin A chain, which also targets B-cell malignancies. The response rate with anti-CD19 immunotoxin was similar to that seen with the anti-CD22 immunotoxin in patients who were unresponsive to other therapies. In their next clinical trial, the investigators will combine the two immunotoxins. Their previous work with treating lymphoma in animal models showed that when both anti-CD19 and anti-CD22 immunotoxins were used together, malignancies in the animals were completely eradicated.

Ricin A-chain-based immunotoxins that target breast and colon cancer as well as malignant melanomas have been evaluated in clinical trials, although with much less success than that achieved in treating lymphoma. Hematologic malignancies (cancer of blood cells), of which lymphoma and leukemia are representative, are likely to be more responsive to targeted therapy owing to their accessibility via the bloodstream. In contrast, solid tumors such as those of the breast, colon, lung, prostate, and ovary are generally less accessible vascularly and consequently are more difficult to treat with novel (as well as conventional) chemotherapeutic drugs and/or with radiation.

Immunotoxins genetically engineered

A major advance in the immunotoxin field came in 1986 when molecular biologist John Murphy of Boston University succeeded in splicing together genes encoding α-melanocyte-stimulating hormone and a nonbinding form of DT. In doing so, Murphy engineered the first single-chain immunotoxin fusion protein. The fusion protein consisted of a binding domain able to interact with the α-melanocyte-stimulating-hormone receptor on melanoma cells and an enzymatic domain that was able to block protein synthesis on a single molecule. While this fusion protein did not prove to be clinically useful, it demonstrated that genetic engineering could be used to create immunotoxins; the advantage of genetically engineered immunotoxins is that they are single, uniform products of minimal size, which should facilitate their penetration into tumor tissue.

The antigen-binding portion of antibodies, referred to as *variable regions,* can also be cloned and genetically linked by a short, flexible linker to generate a small antigen-binding molecule. This form of genetically engineered binding site is referred to as a *single-chain antibody* (*sFv*), and when it is fused to the enzymatic domain of a toxin molecule, a single-chain immunotoxin is created. These immunotoxin fusion proteins have been shown to be highly potent and are potentially more effective than classical chemically conjugated immunotoxins that use the whole antibody linked to a toxin. Molecular biologist Ira Pastan of the National Cancer Institute, Bethesda, Md., has pioneered this research. Many sFv-immunotoxins have been tested in animal models, and recently trials with human cancer patients were begun. In rodents that had been implanted with human tumors, single-chain immunotoxins were found to be as much as 10 times more effective in causing tumors to regress than were their chemically conjugated counterparts.

Many different cancer-reactive markers have been targeted by single-chain immunotoxins. One of these is the oncogene HER2, which is prevalent on approximately 30% of breast cancers. Although HER2 is a normal molecule that is also expressed on noncancerous cells, its overexpression on tumor cells suggests that it may contribute directly to the process of some tumors' becoming malignant. Therefore, it is a promising target. Anti-HER2-sFv-toxin fusion proteins have been effective in treating human breast and gastric tumors in rodents; clinical trials are likely to begin in the near future.

These new recombinant immunotoxins offer hope not only in the treatment of cancer but in cases of graft rejection after transplantation and in the treatment of certain autoimmune diseases, such as rheumatoid arthritis. The ability of recombinant immunotoxins to cause tumor regression at lower doses than the relatively bulky immunotoxin conjugates may allow for treatment with fewer side effects. (With any targeted therapy, and especially with highly potent immunotoxins, it is essential to investigate the toxicities associated with human treatment fully in advance.) Meanwhile, oncologists eagerly await the results of clinical trials with genetically engineered single-chain immunotoxin fusion proteins.

Immunotoxins Genetically Engineered

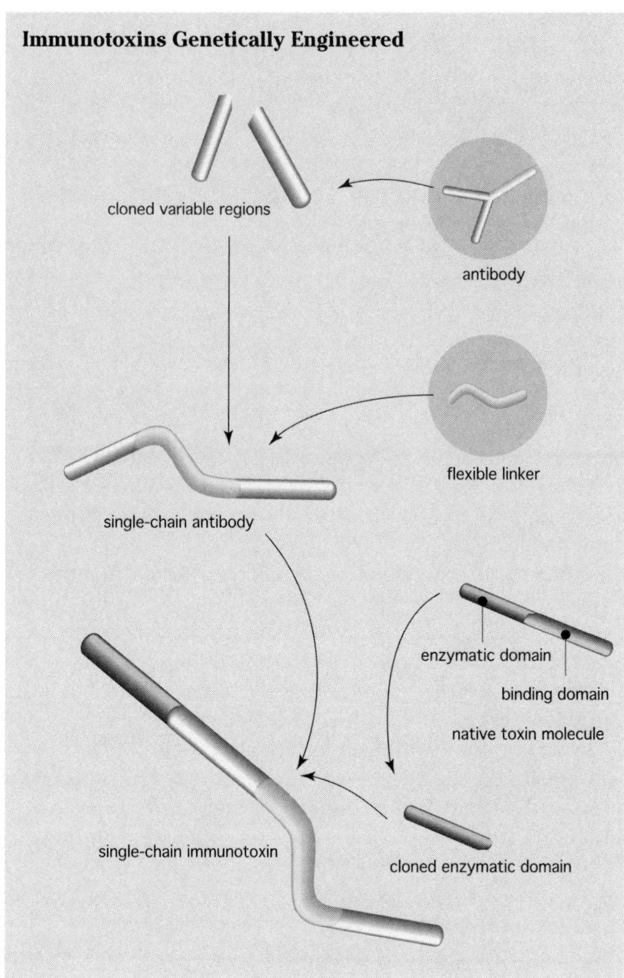

Innovations in perspective

Targeted radioisotopes, toxins, and drugs have been tested extensively in animal models. Although these studies have provided some tantalizing results, for the most part it is not likely that they will be as effective at eliminating large tumor burdens in humans. Targeted therapy in some form is likely to provide improvements in the continuing struggle to eliminate tumor cells while minimally harming the patient. In most cases, however, it will need to be coupled with surgery and forms of conventional chemotherapy in order to achieve maximum utility in the treatment of humans.

Therapy that targets cancer cells for elimination and at the same time minimizes negative effects on normal tissue is an exciting prospect. It remains to be determined whether this therapeutic approach will ultimately provide meaningful advantages over conventional treatments when it comes to conquering cancer in humans.

—*Clay B. Siegall, Ph.D., and H. Perry Fell, Ph.D.*

New Drugs Approved by the Food and Drug Administration, January 1994–July 1995			
Generic name (brand name)	**Manufacturer**	**Use**	**Selected side effects**
		PRIORITY APPROVALS*	
cysteamine (Cystagon)	Mylan	nephropathic cystinosis (a rare inherited kidney disease)	nausea; vomiting; loss of appetite; drowsiness; rash
dexrazoxane (Zinecard)	Pharmacia	cardiac toxicity associated with doxorubicin therapy in breast cancer	injection-site pain
dorzolamide (Trusopt)	Merck	glaucoma and intraocular hypertension	sulfonamide-sensitivity reactions; eyelid inflammation; ocular burning and stinging; corneal inflammation; blurred vision; light sensitivity
fludeoxyglucose F18 (no brand name)	Downstate Clinical PET Center (Peoria, Ill.)	medical imaging for diagnosis of epileptic seizures	low blood pressure; increased or decreased blood sugar
imiglucerase (Cerezyme)	Genzyme	type 1 Gaucher disease	headache; nausea; abdominal discomfort; dizziness; rash
indium-111 pentetreotide (OctreoScan)	Mallinckrodt Medical	medical imaging for diagnosis of neuroendocrine tumors	dizziness; facial redness; headache; low blood pressure; changes in liver enzymes; joint pain; nausea; sweating; weakness
iobenguane sulfate I 131 (no brand name)	CIS-US	medical imaging for diagnosis of adrenal gland tumors and nervous system sarcomas	transient high blood pressure; fever; chills; low blood pressure
metformin (Glucophage)	Bristol-Myers Squibb	non-insulin-dependent (type II) diabetes	lactic acid buildup; diarrhea; nausea; abdominal bloating; weight loss; metallic taste; decrease in blood level of vitamin B_{12} and folic acid
mycophenolate mofetil (CellCept)	Syntex/Roche	prevention of organ rejection in kidney transplantation	diarrhea; low white blood cell count; sepsis; vomiting; increased susceptibility to infection; increased risk of developing lymphoma
rimexolone (Vexol)	Alcon	inflammation following cataract surgery; anterior uveitis (inflammation of the uvea of the eye)	blurred vision; ocular discharge, discomfort, and/or itching; increased ocular pressure
salmeterol (Serevent)	Allen & Hanburys (division of Glaxo)	asthma	respiratory infection; nasal and pharyngeal inflammation; rapid heartbeat; palpitations; hives; rash; bronchospasm; headache; tremor; nervousness
stavudine (Zerit)	Bristol-Myers Squibb	HIV infection	peripheral nervous system disturbance; changes in liver enzymes; headache; nausea; diarrhea; chills and/or fever; muscle weakness; abdominal pain; malaise; upset stomach
tacrolimus (Prograf)	Fujisawa USA	prevention of organ rejection in allogeneic liver and kidney transplantation	tremor; headache; diarrhea; high blood pressure; nausea; kidney dysfunction; high potassium levels; low magnesium levels; excess uric acid; high blood sugar
vinorelbine (Navelbine)	Burroughs Wellcome	lung cancer	low white blood cell count; nausea; vomiting; hair loss
		STANDARD APPROVALS†	
acrivastine/pseudoephedrine (Semprex-D)	Burroughs Wellcome	seasonal allergic nasal inflammation	drowsiness; nervousness; inability to sleep; dry mouth
budesonide (Rhinocort)	Astra USA	seasonal and perennial allergic and nonallergic nasal inflammation	nasal irritation; sore throat; cough; nosebleed
dalteparin sodium (Fragmin)	Pharmacia	prevention of deep vein thrombosis in abdominal surgery	bleeding and swelling at injection site
famciclovir (Famvir)	SmithKline Beecham	acute herpes zoster (shingles)	headache; nausea; diarrhea

New Drugs Approved by the Food and Drug Administration, January 1994–July 1995

Generic name (brand name)	Manufacturer	Use	Selected side effects
		STANDARD APPROVALS (CONTINUED)	
fluvoxamine (Luvox)	Solvay Pharmaceuticals	obsessive-compulsive disorder	drowsiness; inability to sleep; tremor; nausea; weight loss; vomiting; abnormal ejaculation; weakness; indigestion; sweating; nervousness
iopromide (Ultravist)	Berlex	medical imaging for diagnosis of disorders of blood vessels, urinary tract, head, and neck	nausea; vomiting; decreased blood pressure; premature ventricular contractions
lamotrigine (Lamictal)	Burroughs Wellcome	epilepsy (adult)	dizziness; loss of muscular coordination; sleepiness; headache; double vision; nausea; vomiting; rash; blurred vision
lansoprazole (Prevacid)	Takeda-Abbott Pharmaceuticals	duodenal ulcer, erosive esophagitis, and persistent hypersecretion of stomach acid	diarrhea; abdominal pain; nausea; headache
losartan (Cozaar)	Merck	hypertension	dizziness; leg pain; upper respiratory infection
moexipril (Univasc)	Schwarz Pharma	hypertension	cough
nefazodone (Serzone)	Bristol-Myers Squibb	depression	nausea; dizziness; inability to sleep; muscle weakness; agitation; constipation; blurred vision; confusion; drowsiness; low blood pressure
nelmefine (Revex)	Ohmeda	opioid drug overdose	nausea; vomiting; rapid heart rate; high blood pressure; fever; dizziness
nisoldipine (Nisocor)	Miles	hypertension	swelling of extremities; headache; dizziness; palpitations; chest pain; nausea; rash; sore throat; blood vessel dilation; sinus inflammation
rocuronium (Zemuron)	Organon	relaxation of skeletal muscles during surgery	abnormal heartbeat; nausea; asthma; rash
sevoflurane (Ultane)	Abbott	general surgical anesthesia	nausea; vomiting; cough; slow heart rate; low blood pressure; rapid heartbeat; agitation; throat spasm; dizziness; sleepiness
spirapril (Renormax)	Sandoz	hypertension	cough; headache; dizziness; rash
technetium 99m bicisate (Neurolite)	DuPont Merck	medical imaging for diagnosis of stroke	headache; dizziness; seizure; anxiety; drowsiness; disruption of sense of smell; hallucinations; rash; nausea; fainting; cardiac failure; hypertension; chest pain; breathlessness
		BIOLOGICS OR VACCINES[†]	
abciximab (ReoPro)	Centocor	prevention of complications in angioplasty patients	bleeding; decreased platelet counts; hypotension; slowing of heart action; vomiting; anemia; pneumonia; pain; swelling of extremities
bubonic plague vaccine	Greer Labs	prevention of bubonic plague	malaise; headache; mild swelling of lymph glands; high fever
hepatitis A vaccine (Havrix)	SmithKline Beecham	prevention of hepatitis A	headache; fatigue; fever; malaise; nausea
pegaspargase (Oncaspar)	Rhône-Poulenc Rorer	acute lymphoblastic leukemia	allergic reactions; changes in liver enzymes; nausea; fever; malaise; increased blood sugar levels; blood clots; pancreatitis
Rho(D) immune globulin (WinRho SD)	Univax	idiopathic thrombocytopenic purpura (a hemorrhagic disease); treatment of Rh incompatibility in pregnancy	slight fever; potential for allergic reaction
typhoid vaccine (Typhim Vi)	Connaught	prevention of typhoid fever	fever; flulike symptoms; headache; tremor; abdominal pain; vomiting; diarrhea

New Drugs Approved by the Food and Drug Administration, January 1994–July 1995

Generic name (brand name)	Manufacturer	Use	Selected side effects
		BIOLOGICS OR VACCINES (CONTINUED)	
varicella-zoster virus vaccine (Varivax)	Merck	prevention of chicken pox	injection-site pain; mild chicken pox-like rash; fever; upper respiratory illness; cough; irritability; diarrhea; joint pain
		NEW INDICATIONS, FORMULATIONS, OR COMBINATIONS	
adenosine (Adenoscan)	Fujisawa USA	pharmacological substitute for exercise stress testing in diagnosis of coronary artery disease (formerly approved for restoration of normal heart rhythm in one form of arrhythmia [paroxysmal supra-ventricular tachycardia])	flushing; headache; chest discomfort; low blood pressure; changes in electrocardiogram; shortness of breath; dizziness; nausea
butorphanol tartrate (Stadol NS)	Bristol-Myers Squibb	migraine headache pain (nasal spray formulation)	drowsiness; dizziness; nausea; vomiting; nasal congestion; inability to sleep; potential for abuse
captopril (Capoten)	Bristol-Myers Squibb	kidney damage due to diabetes (formerly approved for hypertension, congestive heart failure, and left ventricular dysfunction after heart attack)	cough; rash; upset stomach
cimetidine (Tagamet HB)	SmithKline Beecham	over-the-counter heartburn treatment (formerly prescription only)	interaction with other drugs, including theophylline, warfarin, and phenytoin
conjugated estrogens/ medroxyprogesterone acetate (Prempro, Premphase)	Wyeth-Ayerst	hormone replacement therapy; treatment of osteoporosis (new combination)	breakthrough bleeding; breast tenderness; nausea; skin discoloration; weight gain or loss; changes in libido
dinoprostone (Cervidil)	Forest	promotion of cervical ripening prior to child-birth (vaginal insert formulation)	fetal heart rate abnormality; uterine contractile abnor-mality; drug interaction with oxytocin
divalproex (Depakote)	Abbott	manic depression (formerly approved for epilepsy)	vomiting; nausea; sleepiness; dizziness
doxazosin (Cardura)	Roerig (division of Pfizer)	benign prostatic hyperplasia (formerly approved for hypertension)	dizziness; weight gain; drowsiness; fatigue
enoxaparin (Lovenox)	Rhône-Poulenc Rorer	prevention of deep vein thrombosis follow-ing knee-replacement surgery (formerly approved for use following hip-replacement surgery)	low platelet count; fever; pain; bleeding; nausea; swelling of extremities; confusion
famotidine (Pepcid AC)	Merck	over-the-counter heartburn treatment (formerly prescription only)	headache; dizziness; constipation; diarrhea
fluoxetine (Prozac)	Lilly	obsessive-compulsive disorder (formerly approved for depression)	anxiety; inability to sleep; drowsiness; muscle weak-ness; tremor; sweating; weight loss; nausea; diarrhea; dizziness; rash
fluticasone (Flonase)	Allen & Hanburys (divi-sion of Glaxo)	allergy symptoms (nasal spray formulation)	nasal burning; nosebleed; headache; sore throat
ganciclovir (Cytovene)	Syntex	AIDS-related cytomegalovirus retinitis (oral formulation)	diarrhea; fever; low white blood cell count; nausea
granisetron (Kytril)	SmithKline Beecham	nausea and vomiting associated with chemotherapy (oral formulation)	headache; constipation; muscle weakness; diarrhea; abdominal pain
ibuprofen (Children's Motrin)	McNeil	over-the-counter analgesic for children six months and older (formerly prescription only)	aspirin-sensitivity reaction
leuprolide acetate (Lupron Depot)	Takeda-Abbott Pharmaceuticals	anemia caused by benign uterine tumors (formerly approved for endometriosis, advanced prostate cancer, and precocious puberty)	muscle weakness; headache; hot flashes; swelling; joint disorder; depression; vaginal inflammation

New Drugs Approved by the Food and Drug Administration, January 1994–July 1995			
Generic name (brand name)	**Manufacturer**	**Use**	**Selected side effects**
NEW INDICATIONS, FORMULATIONS, OR COMBINATIONS (CONTINUED)			
loratadine/pseudoephedrine (Claritin D)	Schering	allergy symptoms and nasal congestion (new combination)	headache; inability to sleep; dry mouth; sedation; nervousness
losartan/hydrochlorothiazide (Hyzaar)	Merck	hypertension (new combination)	swelling; palpitations; dizziness; upper respiratory infection; cough
lovastatin (Mevacor)	Merck	retardation of atherosclerosis (formerly approved for lowering cholesterol)	constipation; upset stomach; muscle pain; headache; diarrhea; rash; dizziness; abdominal pain; changes in liver and kidney enzymes
naltrexone (ReVia)	DuPont Merck	alcohol abuse (formerly approved for drug abuse)	nausea; inability to sleep; anxiety; abdominal cramps; joint and muscle pain; headache; liver damage at high doses
ondansetron (Zofran)	Cerenex (division of Glaxo)	nausea and vomiting associated with radiotherapy (formerly approved for use in chemotherapy)	headache; bronchospasm; constipation; diarrhea; severe allergic reaction; rash
paclitaxel (Taxol)	Bristol-Myers Squibb	breast cancer (formerly approved for ovarian cancer)	low white blood cell count; numbness in extremities; muscle and bone pain
ranitidine (Zantac)	Glaxo	erosive inflammation of the esophagus (formerly approved for ulcers)	headache; constipation; diarrhea; nausea; abdominal discomfort; changes in liver enzymes; rash
rifampin/isoniazid/pyrazinamide (Rifater)	Marion Merrell Dow	tuberculosis (new combination)	rash; nausea; muscle and joint pain; dizziness; changes in liver enzymes; headache; sweating; chest tightness; diarrhea
somatropin (Bio-Tropin)	Bio-Technology General	short stature caused by human growth hormone deficiency (formerly approved for treatment of short stature associated with chronic kidney failure)	headache; injection-site pain and/or bruising
somatropin (Norditropin)	Novo Nordisk	short stature caused by human growth hormone deficiency (formerly approved for treatment of short stature associated with chronic kidney failure)	nausea; headache; muscle pain and/or weakness; mild increases in blood sugar and urinary sugar
somatropin (Nutropin)	Genentech	short stature caused by human growth hormone deficiency (formerly approved for treatment of short stature associated with chronic kidney failure)	headache; nausea
sumatriptan (Imitrex)	Cerenex (division of Glaxo)	migraine headache (oral formulation)	tingling; nasal discomfort
warfarin (Coumadin)	DuPont Merck	prevention of death, recurrent heart attack, and stroke after heart attack (formerly approved for prevention and treatment of blood clots)	bleeding; skin and tissue degradation
DUPLICATE OF AVAILABLE PRODUCT			
menotropins (Humegon)	Organon	female infertility (duplicate of Pergonal)	pulmonary and vascular complications; increased incidence of multiple births; abdominal pain; nausea; rash; dizziness; rapid heartbeat

* New compounds (*i.e.,* new molecular entities) to treat serious illnesses for which no adequate alternative therapy exists.
† New compounds that provide some, little, or no therapeutic gain over products already available.
‡ Products such as serums, toxins, blood components, etc., used to prevent, treat, or cure disease.

NEWS*CAPS*

Secondhand Smoke: Impact on Infants

Infants exposed to secondhand smoke even before birth have a three-times-higher risk of dying in the first year of life than infants whose parents do not smoke. These were the findings of epidemiologists who compared factors surrounding the deaths of 200 babies who died between 1989 and 1992 of sudden infant death syndrome (SIDS) with factors in the lives of 200 healthy infants born during the same period in the same hospitals. Although the results, published in the *Journal of the American Medical Association* (March 8, 1995), did not indicate that secondhand smoke *causes* SIDS, they suggested that adult smoking is a significant risk factor for this puzzling syndrome, which annually claims the lives of 6,000 U.S. infants under age one.

SIDS victims were likely to have been exposed to tobacco smoke from a mother, father, live-in adult, day-care provider, or some combination of smoking adults. Moreover, infants who were exposed to the most smoke had the highest likelihood of dying, and the effect of secondhand smoke greatly increased when the adult smoked in the same room with the baby. The investigators also found that breast-feeding reduced the risk of SIDS in infants of nonsmokers but was not protective if the mother smoked.

Recognizing that the "emotional impact of sudden infant death is profound and devastating to the family," the researchers recommended that obstetricians, family practitioners, and pediatricians advise all prospective and new parents to abstain from smoking. They also urged that widespread public health measures be instituted to prevent environmental tobacco exposure in general.

Tobacco Industry on Trial: Who Knew What When?

In 1995 the $45 billion tobacco industry found itself facing what would probably be the largest class-action suit in history, on behalf of Americans addicted to cigarettes. (There are an estimated 40 million smokers and some 50 million ex-smokers in the U.S.) In June 1995 a New Orleans, La., federal judge allowed the "discovery process" to go forward in a suit against seven tobacco companies. That process permitted plaintiffs' lawyers to collect internal tobacco company documents. Philip Morris Companies Inc. documents, obtained by the *New York Times* in the spring of 1995, revealed that the company not only manipulated nicotine levels in its cigarettes but did so while conducting research into the "pharmacological effects" of nicotine. Company spokesmen denied that nicotine-enhanced cigarettes had ever been marketed, but the revelations appeared to support Food and Drug Administration Commissioner David A. Kessler's argument that cigarettes should be regulated as a controlled drug. It was also revealed that research had included subjects as young as 14.

More damaging evidence came to light in August. A document entered in the *Congressional Record* revealed that in 1969 Philip Morris knew that the "pharmacological effect of smoke" was so strong that the smoker's craving for cigarettes even "preempts food in times of scarcity." The same company had also studied more than 6,000 hyperactive youth whom it viewed as "prospective smokers." Meantime, an R.J. Reynolds document, obtained by the *New York Times,* referred to nicotine as a "potent drug."

Indicting documents from Brown & Williamson Tobacco Co. were sent anonymously to several news organizations and a professor at the University of California at San Francisco in May 1994. The company alleged that the documents had been stolen in 1989, but its petition to block their publication was legally denied in July 1995. Soon after, the documents were made available to the public on the Internet's World Wide Web (http://www.library.ucsf.edu/tobacco).

By permission of Mike Luckovich and Creators Sydicate

Women's Health Update

By the mid-1990s women's health issues were prominent concerns in most industrialized nations. In the United States this was evident in both medical research and public health. Not only were more research dollars being earmarked for studies of conditions that affect women exclusively, but gender differences were being taken into consideration in the evaluation of therapies for diseases common to both sexes. Both the federal government and private insurers were beginning to look more favorably upon paying for preventive services and medical treatments—from contraception and mammography to bone marrow transplantation in breast cancer—once considered nonreimbursable.

Eliminating bias in drug trials

David Kessler, U.S. Food and Drug Administration (FDA) commissioner, announced early in 1995 that the agency would henceforth require that women of childbearing age be enrolled in all trials of new drugs for AIDS and other life-threatening conditions. Kessler said the approval of new drugs would be automatically delayed if too few women were included in their evaluation and the FDA would halt trials by any drug company that did not correct female underrepresentation.

The FDA's tough new stance strengthened previous guidelines (issued in 1993) on the evaluation of gender differences in studies of new drugs. Those guidelines called for but did not require the inclusion of women in clinical trials. Starting in 1977, women of childbearing potential had been specifically excluded from the earliest trials of new drugs because manufacturers were fearful of being sued if a woman became pregnant during the study and gave birth to a child with congenital defects. Moreover, because the 1977 guidelines did not require that data on efficacy and safety be broken down by sex, researchers often did not provide gender-specific information on a new drug even when adequate numbers of women had participated in the trials.

Owing to these exclusions, there has typically been a dearth of information on the effects of drugs in women, which can be markedly different from effects in men. The 1993 guidelines, as well as the 1995 requirements for testing of AIDS drugs, were intended to ensure that trials would evaluate the different ways in which factors such as age, sex, ethnic background, individual metabolism, body-fat content and distribution, and body size affect the way a drug works in an individual.

Focus on menopause

The results of the first multicenter controlled clinical trial to test the effects of hormone replacement therapy (HRT) in postmenopausal women, reported in January 1995, confirmed that HRT appears to reduce some risk factors for heart disease. The Postmenopausal Estrogen/Progestin Interventions (PEPI) trial was conducted over three years at seven U.S. clinical centers. The participants were 875 healthy women between the ages of 45 and 64. The PEPI investigators determined that estrogen supplementation significantly raised blood levels of the so-called good cholesterol—that believed to offer protection against atherosclerosis (accumulation of fatty deposits in the arteries). Treatment with the hormone also appeared to reduce levels of the bad cholesterol and

Delegates from around the world met in Cairo in September 1994 at the third United Nations International Conference on Population and Development. Family planning—particularly the availability of contraception and abortion—was the subject of heated debate.

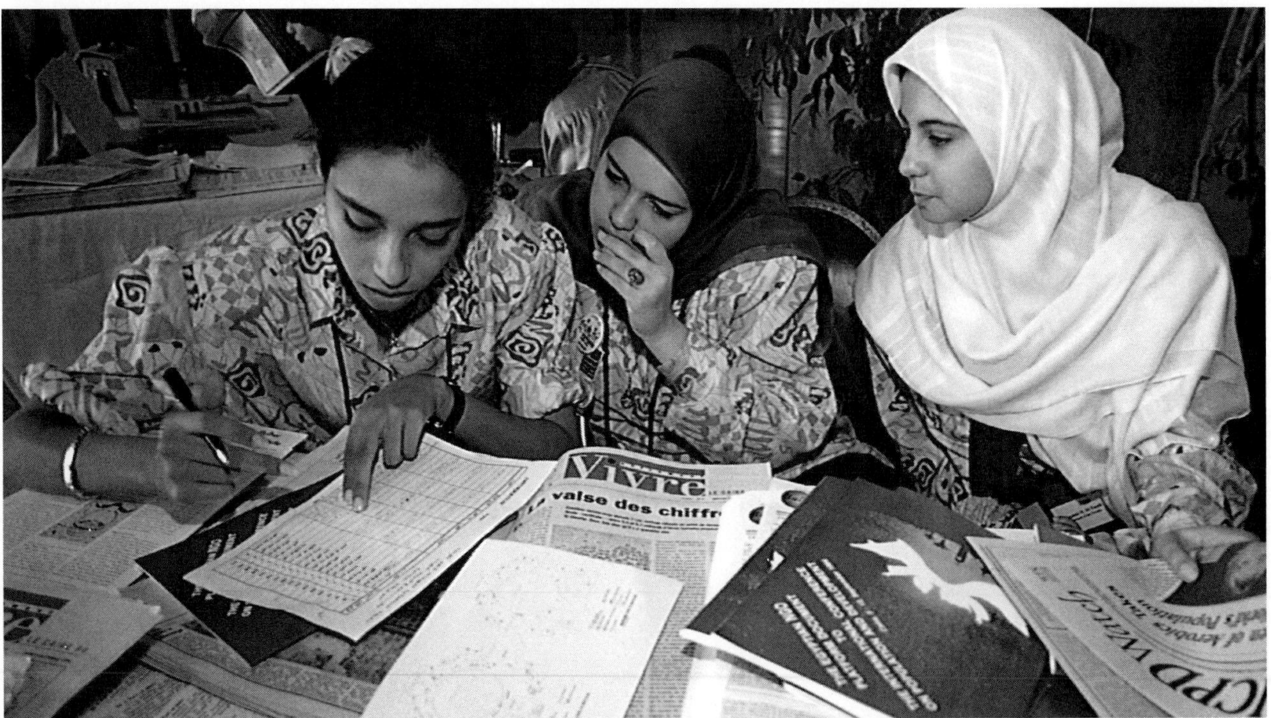

Donna DeCesare—Impact Visuals

the protein fibrinogen, which is instrumental in blood clotting and may contribute to heart attack risk. Moreover, estrogen replacement also appeared to provide these benefits without adversely affecting insulin levels or blood pressure, as some authorities had speculated it might.

Another significant finding was that the addition of progesterone, either natural or synthetic, to the regimen did not negate estrogen's impact on heart attack risk, another effect that had been suspected. Moreover, the PEPI data confirmed that the progesterone component in HRT prevents estrogen-associated overgrowth of the endometrium, or uterine lining, which can lead to endometrial cancer.

The PEPI trial was undertaken to resolve a question raised by earlier observational studies. These studies, which compared postmenopausal hormone users with women who forgo hormone therapy, found that the women on HRT were healthier. Some authorities felt that the apparent benefits of hormone use were only coincidental to better preventive health practices among HRT users—more frequent visits to the doctor, regular exercise, and so forth. Thus, the benefits of HRT might simply represent "healthy user" syndrome. The PEPI researchers eliminated this potential source of error by randomly assigning participants to receive either one of four hormone regimens or a placebo, so that those who took hormones and those who did not began on an equal basis.

Although the PEPI study provided conclusive evidence that HRT reduces risk factors for heart disease, its three-year duration was not long enough to determine whether the women who took hormones actually had fewer episodes of chest pain (angina) or fewer heart attacks or strokes than those who did not take them. The larger and longer-lasting Women's Health Initiative (WHI) should answer these questions. The WHI, which by mid-1995 was under way at 40 U.S. medical centers, was designed to monitor a total of about 160,000 postmenopausal women for nine years in three separate controlled trials and an observational study. The 25,000 women enrolled in the Hormone Replacement Therapy Study will receive either HRT or a placebo and will be followed medically to see how many in each group develop heart disease or breast cancer. On the basis of the experience of the PEPI trial, in which one-third of the women who still had a uterus and were taking estrogen alone developed overgrowth of endometrial tissue, the WHI investigators modified the hormone replacement study. Thus, only women who have had a hysterectomy receive estrogen without progesterone.

The other WHI studies will evaluate the effects of diet in preventing heart disease, cancer, and osteoporosis. Women in the Dietary Modification Study will be randomly assigned to two groups, both of which will be regularly monitored for the development of breast or colon cancer. One group will be required to limit fat intake to 20% of calories. Participants in the Calcium and Vitamin D Supplementation Study will receive both 1,000 mg of calcium and 400 IU (international units) of vitamin D or two placebos a day and will be monitored for the development of osteoporosis or colon cancer.

The observational arm of the study will entail an additional 100,000 women, who will fill out annual questionnaires on their living habits and undergo periodic physical exams. The information obtained will go into a women's health database.

Two seemingly contradictory reports published in the summer of 1995 contributed to the climate of uncertainty about the possible relationship between HRT and the risk of developing breast cancer. While most previous investigations have found comparable rates of breast cancer in hormone users and nonusers, a few have suggested that women who take hormones may be at moderately increased risk for the disease. A June 1995 report from the Nurses' Health Study found the risk among hormone users to be slightly higher than previous estimates. The following month, however, researchers at the University of Washington published results suggesting no increased risk among women on HRT.

The Nurses' Health Study, which was instituted in 1976, is an ongoing observational investigation that monitors the health status and lifestyles of more than 121,000 female nurses. The researchers are scientists at Harvard Medical School and the Harvard School of Public Health. The recent report was based on an analysis of questionnaires completed by the subjects between 1976 and 1992. The primary purpose was to determine whether use of either estrogen or progesterone alone or the two in combination affected breast cancer risk. The researchers found that the type of hormone regimen did not have a significant impact on risk, but the women's ages and the duration of hormone use did. Breast cancer risk increased 40% in women aged 50–64 and 70% in women aged 65–69 who were on HRT for more than five years. There was no increased risk in those who took hormones for five years or less, and excess risk seemed to disappear two years after HRT was discontinued.

In the University of Washington study, the investigators interviewed 537 breast cancer patients between the ages of 50 and 64, as well as 492 randomly selected women in the same age group with no history of the disease. The subjects answered questions about lifestyle, health, and HRT regimen, if any. An analysis of the data revealed no increased risk of breast cancer with either current or long-term HRT use.

Neither of these studies was a randomized, controlled trial—the kind most authorities consider the best method of evaluating medical treatments. In such studies people with similar characteristics are randomly assigned to receive either a treatment or a placebo; in other respects their care is as nearly identical as possible. By contrast, in studies like the two described above, the subjects who received the treatment in question may have had different risk factors from those who elected not to take it, or the former may have received different care from the latter. Given the limitations inherent in this methodology, the data from the Nurses' Health Study are considered to be the more important because of that investigation's longer duration and larger number of participants. The debate about the effects of HRT on breast cancer risk is far from over, however.

Alternatives to surgical abortion

The only legal methods of abortion currently available to U.S. women are invasive surgical procedures, such as vacuum aspiration or dilatation and curettage, which must be performed by a physician. Although the number of women seeking these procedures has remained relatively constant (24 abortions per 1,000 women aged 15–44) in recent years, the number of physicians providing abortions has been declining steadily for over a decade. Approximately 84% of U.S. counties now are without abortion services of any kind. This decline has stimulated interest in medical, or drug-based, methods of abortion, which, if available in the U.S., would increase access to abortion for women in rural areas, where the shortage of physician providers is most acute.

RU-486 (mifepristone), the best-known of the drugs that induce abortion, has been shown in European clinical trials to be safe and effective. But because U.S. antiabortion activists had threatened to boycott other products made by Hoechst-Celanese Corp., Summerville, N.J. (formerly Roussel-Uclaf SA), the manufacturer of RU-486, the company was unwilling to test the drug in the U.S. In May 1994, however, Hoechst-Celanese relinquished its rights to RU-486 to the Population Council, a nonprofit research organization based in New York City. Clinical trials involving 2,100 women began in October 1994 at 16 sites and were expected to be completed by July 1995. As of June 1995, however, the Population Council had been unable to find a pharmaceutical company willing to manufacture and market the drug in the U.S.

With the controversy over RU-486 capturing the spotlight, other medical means of inducing abortion have been largely ignored. Methotrexate, an anticancer drug that is also used in the treatment of rheumatoid arthritis, severe asthma, and psoriasis, has been shown in numerous studies to be a safe, effective means of treating ectopic, or extrauterine, pregnancies. Methotrexate works by destroying certain cells needed to help the developing embryo implant in the endometrium during the early weeks of pregnancy. Thus far, the use of methotrexate as an abortifacient (an agent that causes abortion) has been too limited to determine whether it is safe for widespread use.

Controversies and costs in contraception

Since June 1993 the FDA has allowed a deferment of the physical examination previously required for the prescription of oral contraceptives. Some women's health advocates want the FDA to go a step further and allow the drugs to be sold routinely without any prescription whatsoever. Those who favor over-the-counter (OTC) availability argue that today's low-dose contraceptives have been shown to be safe and effective enough for general use without a doctor's supervision. Moreover, they point to birth control pills' multiple beneficial effects: reducing the risk of endometrial and ovarian cancer, benign ovarian cysts, benign breast disease, fallopian tube infections, and ectopic pregnancy; lessening menstrual pain and bleeding; and possibly relieving premenstrual syndrome, reducing the risk of rheumatoid arthritis, and preventing bone loss. In 1990 the FDA began including a statement on oral contraceptive packages that for healthy nonsmokers over age 40, the benefits of oral contraceptives "may outweigh the possible risks."

Opponents of OTC availability of the Pill maintain that the hormones in oral contraceptives are potent drugs that should be taken only under medical surveillance. They also point out that a woman's visit to the doctor to obtain a prescription is an important opportunity to discuss benefits and risks of and alternatives to birth control pills for the individual patient and to test for sexually transmitted diseases and disseminate information about safe sex.

In 1994–95 the American Medical Women's Association (a group of women health professionals), Planned Parenthood of New York City, the American Public Health Association, and other groups mounted a campaign to educate physicians about the use of birth control pills as emergency contraceptives and petitioned the FDA to approve the drugs for that use. If the groups are successful, manufacturers of "combined" oral contraceptives (containing both estrogen and progesterone) would be obliged to inform both physicians and consumers (through labels and patient package inserts) that their products can be used for postcoital birth control. Interest in emergency contraception was not confined to the U.S. An international group of experts in women's health, meeting in Italy in April 1995, issued a consensus statement calling for greater availability of emergency services. The group's message to reluctant health care providers: "Emergency contraception is not abortion."

The costs of some of the most reliable reversible forms of contraception—*e.g.,* oral, injectable, and implanted hormonal contraceptives and intrauterine devices—are not covered by many health plans, although most pay for surgical sterilization. A report in the April 1995 issue of the *American Journal of Public Health* demonstrated that by preventing unintended pregnancies—which number about 3.5 million annually—contraception cuts health care costs. The average cost of full-term pregnancy care and delivery in the U.S. is $3,200. The new study showed that even the least effective birth control methods, if used faithfully, could yield substantial cost savings for health plans. In an editorial accompanying that report, Philip R. Lee, assistant secretary for health, U.S. Public Health Service, and Felicia H. Stewart, director of the Office of Population Affairs, called for broader insurance coverage for all forms of reversible contraception.

Breast implants: hazards prove elusive

The controversy over the health effects of silicone gel breast implants shows no sign of resolution. In April 1992, after reviewing reports of certain autoimmune diseases among women with implants, the FDA virtually removed the devices from the market, making them available only to women who were willing to enter clinical trials to determine the long-term outcomes of implantation.

Two years later, after being named in numerous individual legal suits, three principal implant manufacturers—Dow Corning Corp., Bristol-Myers, and Baxter Healthcare Corp.—entered into a class-action settlement, establishing a fund of $4,250,000,000 to compensate women with implants who develop specific, well-defined autoimmune diseases. Under the agreement the women, who forfeit the right to make additional claims against the companies, are entitled to compensation if they develop any of the following conditions within 30 years after implantation: rheumatoid arthritis, ankylosing spondylitis, polymyositis, scleroderma, systemic lupus

(continued on page 418)

NEWS*CAPS*

Experts Convene on Ovarian Cancer

Approximately 24,000 new cases of ovarian cancer were diagnosed in the U.S. in 1994, and some 13,600 women died of the disease. This grim picture prompted the National Institutes of Health (NIH) to assemble an expert panel that met in April 1994 to provide physicians with a current consensus on screening, prevention, diagnosis, and treatment. In its report the panel concluded that there is no evidence that the currently available screening methods—measurement of CA-125 (a serum tumor marker) and transvaginal ultrasonography—are effective tools for screening of apparently healthy women; such screening would not reduce ovarian cancer deaths. Moreover, the inadequacy of these methods prompted the panel to recommend against routine screening, emphasizing that it may result in needless anxiety for women, as well as unnecessary surgery.

While the survival rate of women with early-stage ovarian cancer is significantly higher than that of women with advanced disease, the vast majority of ovarian cancers are diagnosed at an advanced stage. Thus, scientists have good reason to try to develop methods of early detection. Early ovarian cancer, however, may produce no symptoms or only very mild, nonspecific ones; thus, by the time symptoms are present, the disease is usually advanced.

The cause of ovarian cancer is unknown, but several risk factors have been identified. These include advancing age; nulliparity (*i.e.,* never having borne a child); being of North American or northern European descent; having a personal history of endometrial, colon, or breast cancer; and having a family history of ovarian cancer.

Reviewing current treatment protocols, the NIH panel concluded that adjuvant chemotherapy following surgery is unnecessary for women whose ovarian cancer is detected and treated at an early stage but is recommended for those with advanced disease.

Mediterranean Diet: Four Stars?

New evidence supports the notion that a diet rich in fruits and vegetables protects against some kinds of cancer. Researchers at the Harvard School of Public Health, in collaboration with scientists in Athens, compared the diets of 820 Greek women who had breast cancer with those of 1,548 Greek women who did not have the disease. Reporting in the *Journal of the National Cancer Institute* (Jan. 18, 1995), the investigators said that women who consumed an average of five servings a day of vegetables had a 46% lower risk of breast cancer than those who ate vegetables only once or twice a day. Women who ate six servings of fruit a day had a 35% lower risk of breast cancer than their counterparts who ate fruit only once a day.

The researchers also found that women who reported consuming olive oil more than once a day had a reduced risk of breast cancer compared with women who consumed olive oil less frequently. Two earlier studies in Spain had also noted that olive oil consumption had a protective effect, although an Italian study found no such benefit. U.S. nutrition authorities were cautious in interpreting the Harvard study's findings about olive oil, pointing out that all oils are high in fat and calories and should be used only in moderation.

More than a Fashion Statement

American advertising, fashion, and retail industries have collaborated in a campaign to raise awareness of one of the country's leading killers. In October 1994, in observation of National Breast Cancer Awareness Month, the Council of Fashion Designers of America Foundation, Inc., introduced the bull's-eye T-shirt, a white T-shirt bearing a blue target and the slogan "Fashion Targets Breast Cancer." Some 2,000 department and specialty stores around the country sold the $15 limited-edition shirt; $5 from each sale went to breast cancer research. The campaign, chaired by Ralph Lauren, sold 400,000 T-shirts, raised $2 million, and is now licensed internationally.

Courtesy of the CFDA Foundation; photograph, Andrew Macpherson

(continued from page 416)
erythematosus, Sjögren's syndrome, vasculitis, or polychondritis. They will not be required to demonstrate that the disease occurred as a consequence of receiving the implants. By May 1995 more than 400,000 women had filed claims; others, who had opted out of the settlement, continued to bring individual suits against the manufacturers. Dow Corning, claiming it was overwhelmed by lawsuits, filed for bankruptcy.

Researchers, in the meantime, continued to seek scientific evidence linking breast implants to the diseases but had little success. In June 1994 investigators at the Mayo Clinic in Rochester, Minn., published the results of a study that compared about 750 implant recipients and some 1,500 controls. They did not find an elevated risk for the diseases in question among the women with implants. The following month the medical devices agency of the U.K.'s Department of Health reviewed 270 studies on implant-related autoimmune disorders published in the worldwide medical literature between 1991 and 1994. The reviewers concluded that there was no evidence of an increased risk of connective tissue disease among implant recipients, although they acknowledged that the data did not conclusively prove that implants do not cause autoimmune illnesses. A moratorium on the devices was lifted in Italy in 1994 and in France in 1995, making silicone breast implants available in all European countries.

HIV in pregnancy: to test or not?

One of the most promising recent developments in AIDS research was the 1994 finding that the drug zidovudine (AZT) dramatically reduces the risk of HIV transmission from pregnant women to their babies. In the U.S. the rate of mother-to-child transmission has been estimated at about 25%. (The rate varies from country to country.) Currently, nearly all cases of AIDS in U.S. children—or about 1,800 new cases per year—are the result of maternal transmission. Pregnant women in the U.S. are not routinely tested for HIV; thus, many may be unaware that they are infected. In February 1995, on the basis of the recent finding about zidovudine, the Public Health Service drafted guidelines suggesting that physicians offer HIV testing to all pregnant patients. Under the proposed guidelines, doctors would offer the test to women after first counseling them on the options available should the results indicate that they are infected.

While a plan to increase the availability of HIV testing for pregnant women might seem uncontentious, the proposal aroused immediate controversy. Some AIDS activists viewed the guidelines as a step toward mandatory maternal testing. They maintain that at the very least the guidelines are likely to be construed in some states as supporting proposals for mandatory maternal testing.

Opponents also fear that women demonstrated to be HIV-positive will be strongly urged to take zidovudine. There is some evidence that using zidovudine early in the course of infection can reduce the drug's effectiveness at a later, more advanced stage of the disease. Thus, women who took the drug during pregnancy might not be able to benefit from it when their illness became more severe. Finally, some opponents of the guidelines caution against putting too much confidence in the single study upon which the new guidelines were based, pointing out that there are no data on the long-term effects of zidovudine treatment on either mother or child.

Breast cancer news

In recent years breast cancer research has begun to yield insights into the development of the disease. In 1994 investigators identified mutations of at least two genes, dubbed *BRCA1* and *BRCA2,* that appear to be responsible for the disease in 5–10% of all cases (and in about 85% of all cases of inherited breast cancer). Although blood tests can identify many mutations in these genes, such testing is advised only for women with a strong family history of the disease, and then only in the setting of a research project.

Environment, diet, and breast cancer risk. While heredity is still considered to be the strongest risk factor for breast cancer, population-based research is beginning to hint at a role for environmental and lifestyle factors. In detailed epidemiological studies, the habits of women in populations with low rates of breast cancer have been compared with those of women in populations with higher rates of the disease. The findings suggest that diet is a factor in the development of the disease. Dietary fiber and soy foods, both of which may affect the levels of estrogen in breast tissue, may be protective; a high intake of saturated fat and hydrogenated polyunsaturated fatty acids—but not high-fat diets per se—may increase breast cancer risk.

There is growing concern about a potential association between breast cancer and exposure to substances in the environment that have estrogenic actions. The National Cancer Institute (NCI) has mounted five studies to evaluate exposure to estrogen-like compounds—chemicals such as polychlorinated biphenyls (PCBs)—contained in pesticides. The researchers will compare the levels of these compounds in blood and breast tissue from women who have developed breast cancer and those who are free of the disease.

Tamoxifen: role in prevention. The drug tamoxifen is an effective treatment for certain breast cancers and is also used to prevent recurrence in women who have been treated for breast cancer. Through the Breast Cancer Prevention Trial arm of the National Surgical Adjuvant Breast and Bowel Project (NSABP), tamoxifen is being used experimentally to prevent the disease in healthy women. For several years, however, some authorities have argued that the risks posed by the drug—an increased incidence of endometrial and liver cancers and a greater tendency to form blood clots—do not justify the possible benefits. Two reports published in the past two years addressed these risks. A report from Sweden indicated that breast cancer patients who took tamoxifen were only 68% as likely to be hospitalized for heart problems as their counterparts who did not take the drug. The risk continued to decline with longer duration of tamoxifen use. A subsequent report from the NSABP showed that the risk of developing endometrial cancer increased 2.3 times for breast cancer patients on tamoxifen treatment; rates of liver cancer, however, did not rise. Further, the endometrial cancers that occurred were not more aggressive than usual, as was once hypothesized. Both the Swedish and U.S. studies confirmed

Marty Heitner—Impact Visuals

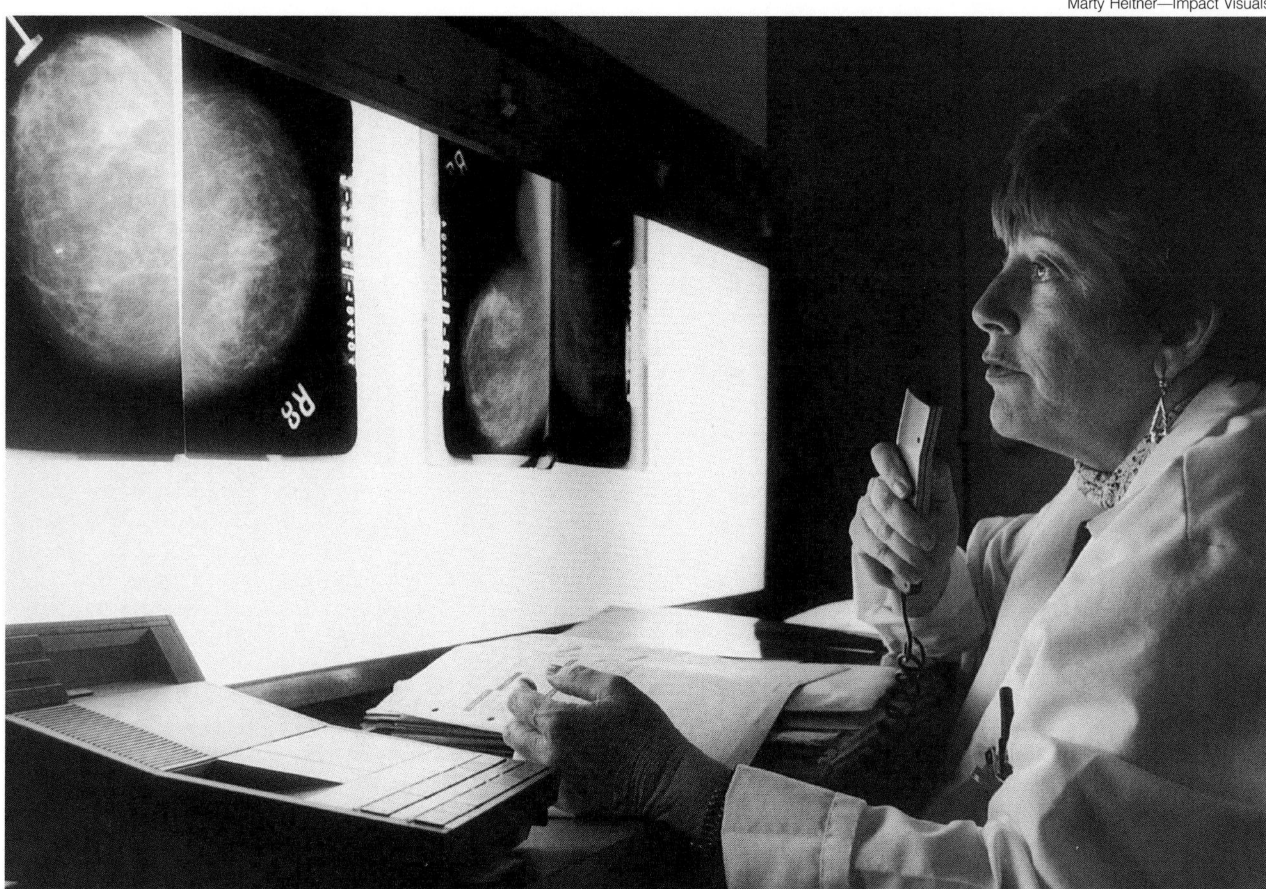

A radiologist studies a patient's mammogram films for abnormalities. While most authorities agree that mammography is an important screening tool for breast cancer, there is considerable dispute over whether such screening reduces deaths from the disease in women younger than 50.

that tamoxifen treatment significantly reduced the risk of breast cancer recurrence. Tamoxifen use by healthy women remains controversial, however.

Controversy over mammography. While mammography in conjunction with clinical breast examination is considered the best method of detecting malignant lesions in the early stages, how often mammograms need to be performed is a matter of considerable debate. Most experts agree that women aged 50 and older should have the procedure every year; however, opinion concerning women in their 40s varies. Several major studies have indicated that annual screening does not reduce breast cancer mortality among women who are younger than 50, but this finding has been disputed by some, who criticized the researchers' methodology. Nonetheless, on the strength of those studies, in December 1993 the NCI discarded recommendations that had called for all women in their 40s to have a mammogram every one or two years. Instead, the NCI advised these women to make the decision about frequency of screening on an individual basis after discussing the matter with their doctors. The American Cancer Society and the American College of Radiology continued to recommend regular mammograms for the under-50 group.

On the treatment front. In March 1994 it was disclosed that one of the investigators participating in the NSABP had submitted falsified data. Even after the suspect data were eliminated, however, the overall results of the study were still deemed valid. These results demonstrated that breast-sparing surgery, in conjunction with radiation and chemotherapy or tamoxifen when necessary, is as effective as mastectomy in extending the lives of women with cancers confined to the breast.

For women with advanced breast cancer (*i.e.,* disease that has metastasized), the prognosis was slowly improving. With conventional chemotherapy the percentage of patients who survive disease-free for five years is only 5%. The technique of very high doses of chemotherapy combined with autologous bone marrow transplantation—that is, removal and reinfusion of the patient's own bone marrow—enables 20% of those treated to live for five years disease-free. The procedure used today involves isolation and removal of stem cells (precursor cells from which all immune system constituents and blood cells develop) from the patient's bone marrow. (Earlier procedures involved transplanting the bone marrow itself.) After receiving doses of chemotherapy massive enough to destroy widespread cancer, patients are given infusions of their own stem cells, along with doses of growth factors, proteins that stimulate the stem cells to produce new populations of blood and immune system cells. The use of growth factors has expedited recovery, substantially reducing the length of the hospital stay and thus the cost of treatment. As the costs for bone marrow transplantation have come down, and refinements in the procedure have improved the outcome, insurers have become increasingly willing to cover the treatment, just as they do such other costly but widely performed procedures as hip replacement and coronary artery bypass surgery.

Heart disease: unequal treatment

The results of a survey published in October 1994 of all cardiac procedures performed in New Jersey over a two-year period showed that women who go to a hospital with heart attack symptoms are less likely than their male counterparts to undergo cardiac catheterization (a diagnostic procedure) or to have angioplasty or coronary artery bypass surgery. The women also had a higher death rate within the ensuing three-year period. Several earlier studies had also shown this apparent gender bias.

A report in April 1995 based on findings from the Coronary Artery Surgery Study (CASS)—an ongoing multicenter investigation—indicated that 15-year survival rates after bypass surgery are comparable in men and women. This was in contrast to several earlier reports suggesting that women have worse outcomes than men after such procedures. Some experts viewed the CASS data as showing that men and women receive equal treatment for cardiac disorders. On the other hand, women constituted only 16% of the CASS subjects, which may be evidence that beneficial procedures are less likely to be offered to women than to men. In both the New Jersey and the CASS studies, the women who were treated were generally older and sicker than the men.

—Beverly Merz
and Ashley Melton Stinson

Birth and the Blues

Until the 20th century, childbirth posed grave risks to a woman's physical well-being and even her life. In industrialized countries today, the chances that a woman will die in childbirth or become physically disabled are extremely small. There has been much less progress, however, in reducing the psychological risks for new mothers. For many families the joyful occasion of welcoming a new life is marred by serious emotional disturbance. One couple's experience with postpartum depression serves as an example.

Linda and Manuel were thrilled when, after an uncomplicated full-term planned pregnancy, she gave birth to their first child, Ana, a healthy girl. The couple took Ana home from the hospital the next day. Manuel took advantage of his company's one-week family leave and so was able to help with the baby, but because Linda was breast-feeding, she was the one who had to get up at night when Ana cried.

Three days after Ana was born, Manuel mildly observed that the house was a mess. Linda immediately burst into tears and began screaming that he had no right to criticize her. Perplexed by her overreaction, he explained that he had not meant it as a criticism, and he offered to clean the house. Linda calmed down and apologized. A few hours later, a love song on the radio triggered an outburst of tears from Linda. She was surprised at herself for getting emotional over such a "corny" song. She went on happily to nurse Ana while Manuel turned on the television news. Upon seeing a story about a dying child, Linda again burst into tears and screamed, "How do you expect me to nurse when I hear those stories?"

Within a week, however, Linda felt she was getting into a comfortable routine with Ana. She no longer felt prone to crying spells, irritability, or sudden changes in mood. Then, a month later, her mother fell ill, and Linda had to juggle hospital visits with caring for the baby. Manuel, now back at work, was unable to provide much relief. Linda herself was due to resume work in two weeks and was having mixed feelings about leaving Ana.

Around this time, Linda began to have trouble falling asleep and staying asleep, even when Ana was sleeping soundly. She became preoccupied with Ana's health, though the pediatrician reassured her that the baby was thriving. Linda was losing her appetite and felt that she could not keep up with Ana's nutritional demands. Exhausted and forgetful, she was unable to keep track of where she had put Ana's things. She became convinced that she simply was not up to the job of mothering. She cried every day, not sure why she was crying. Even Ana's first smiles could not elicit a smile from Linda.

One evening, when Manuel had stayed late at work and Ana was crying incessantly, the thought crossed Linda's mind that it would be a relief simply to drop the baby and let her die. Horrified, she held Ana tightly and protectively. Later, when Ana had finally fallen asleep, Linda pondered whether her husband and baby might not be better off without her.

Not a new phenomenon

Recognition of the postpartum period as a time of heightened emotional vulnerability dates at least as far back as the 4th century BC, when Hippocrates described the dramatic psychological changes he observed in some women after childbirth. Galen, a Greek physician, and Celsus, the Roman author of a treatise on medicine, also noted postpartum emotional disturbance. The first systematic study of postpartum psychiatric disorders was made in France in the early 19th century by Jean-Étienne Esquirol, one of the most influential psychiatrists of the day. Esquirol noted an increased incidence of postpartum depression with the invasion of France and the fall of Napoleon (1815) and wondered if the stress of political and social upheaval was a factor. A comprehensive early study linking childbirth to depression, titled *Traité de la folie des femmes enceintes* ("Treatise on Madness in Pregnant Women"), was published in 1858 by another French psychiatrist, Louis-Victor Marcé.

After that, however, psychiatry went through a phase of regarding postpartum disorders as no different from any other psychiatric problems. Because many such problems were known to be triggered by stress, many psychiatrists believed that having a baby was a stressful life event like any other—for example, losing a loved one or being fired from a job. This viewpoint was reflected by the fact that until 1994 the American Psychiatric Association's *Diagnostic and Statistical*

Mark Antman—The Image Works

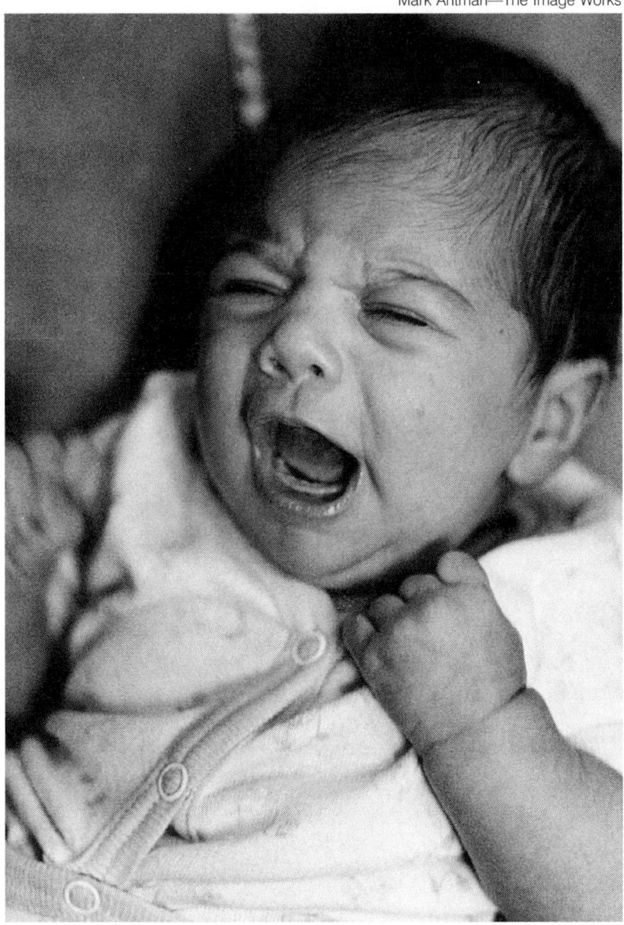

The realities of caring for a demanding newborn can be quite different from the idyllic visions of motherhood entertained by so many women when they are expecting.

Manual of Mental Disorders (*DSM*) did not include postpartum disorders as a separate category.

The fact that the diagnosis did not officially exist made the condition no less real for women who suffered from it, and their plight prompted researchers to investigate postpartum disturbances more systematically. In the 19th century most practitioners believed that emotional problems after childbirth resulted from a combination of hereditary, physical, and so-called moral (in today's parlance, stress-related) factors. Some authorities were struck by the fact that the onset of mood changes coincided with the beginning of breast milk production; this observation led to the epithet "milk fever." Current research is continuing to weigh the relative contributions of genetic vulnerability, hormonal changes, stress, and inadequate social support in the genesis of postpartum disturbance.

"Baby blues": common but confusing

The most common type of postnatal mood change is what has come to be known as the "baby blues." The initial mood changes experienced by Linda, in the case history above, are typical of this condition: tearfulness, irritability, a tendency to overreact. Linda's mood was not uniformly sad, however. She was happy and capable of enjoying the baby much of the time.

About 50% of women who give birth experience this tearful, emotionally labile (*i.e.,* changeable) state. It usually reaches a peak between the third and fifth days after birth and then gradually fades away on its own within weeks. The phenomenon of the baby blues has been observed in many diverse cultures and among all socioeconomic classes. Most studies do not find that the condition is triggered by stress or that it is more likely to occur in women who have had past episodes of depression.

No one is certain what causes the postpartum blues. Some new mothers attribute their mood changes to sleep deprivation, but while lack of sleep may intensify irritability, it does not seem to be the sole explanation for the baby blues. For one thing, women who experience sleep deprivation due to other causes do not report this unique constellation of feelings with such regularity.

Researchers have hypothesized that postpartum mood changes are a by-product of the profound hormonal changes that occur shortly after birth. Most notably, estrogen and progesterone, which are dramatically elevated throughout pregnancy, plummet to their prepregnancy levels within about three days after delivery. Typically, it is at this time that the blues reach their peak. One hypothesis is that the rate of change from prepartum to postpartum hormonal levels determines whether a woman will experience the blues. There is some experimental evidence to support this theory, but studies have produced contradictory findings.

Another hypothesis, as yet untested, hearkens back to the notion of "milk fever." While pregnancy-related hormones are dropping after birth, prolactin and oxytocin, the hormones responsible for lactation, are rising whether or not the woman breast-feeds. Studies in nonhuman mammals have demonstrated that oxytocin promotes the initiation of maternal behavior. Female rats, for example, not only nurse their newborns but also lick, carry, and build nests for them. When the oxytocin-producing cells in the rats' brains are experimentally destroyed, these maternal behaviors do not occur. On the other hand, if oxytocin is injected into the brain of a female rat that has not given birth, she will act maternally. Further, scientists have found that certain parts of the brain must be intact for maternal behavior to occur. For example, all mammals (but no other animals) have a section of the brain called the anterior cingulate gyrus. If this part of the brain is destroyed in a mother rat, she will behave normally in other respects but will not exhibit uniquely mammalian maternal behaviors such as nursing and communicating and playing with her babies.

What does this research have to do with the baby blues? No one is certain, but an intriguing possibility is that like other mammals, humans have neurobiological systems that promote responsiveness between mother and baby. New mothers may experience the activation of these systems as a heightened reactivity to all stimuli in their environments, resulting in sudden emotional changes. Regardless of cause, the blues are probably not an illness but rather a normal part of the experience of having a baby.

True postpartum depression

In about 10% of U.S. women who give birth, postpartum mood changes are more serious and prolonged than those characteristic of the baby blues. These women have what is often called clinical depression, or major depression, with postpartum onset. (The older term for this kind of depression is *melancholia,* from the Greek words for "black bile"; an excess of bile was once thought to cause depression.) Linda began to experience major depression after her mother fell ill. Women with this condition feel depressed nearly all the time. Other symptoms may include inability to experience pleasure (anhedonia), difficulty sleeping, fatigue, feelings of guilt and inadequacy, difficulty concentrating, increase or decrease in appetite, and suicidal thoughts. Although most women find their sexual drive diminished after giving birth, depressed women experience a more profound and enduring lack of interest in sex. This, combined with the depressed new mother's emotional withdrawal and irritability, can be misinterpreted by her partner as loss of interest in him, which leads to further estrangement.

What these women find most frightening, however, is the effect postpartum depression can have on their thoughts and feelings about their babies. Some clinically depressed mothers know intellectually that they love their babies, yet they have trouble feeling anything but apathy, irritation, or disgust. Others have thoughts of harming or even killing their babies. Typically, these thoughts are what psychiatrists term *ego-dystonic*—that is, they are experienced as alien, not reflecting the mother's true feelings and not at all something she wishes to enact. It is rare for a nonpsychotic acutely depressed woman to carry out these thoughts and actually harm her baby. (The sole exceptions are suicidal women who feel they must take their babies with them if they kill themselves.) In most cases the baby suffers no physical harm. If the depression goes untreated, however, it can persist for months, interfering with the mother's emotional availability to her infant. Unless other caregivers are present to provide the necessary love and attention, the child's emotional and behavioral development can suffer.

Unlike the baby blues, postpartum depression does not have a uniform time of onset. It can begin at birth or within a few weeks to months afterward. Sometimes what starts as the blues deepens into major depression. Sometimes, as in Linda's case, the blues come and go, and then a stressful life event triggers depression. Other times, women become depressed after having had no previous episodes of the blues.

Cross-cultural considerations. Because expressions of depression can vary in different cultural contexts, it is difficult to know whether postpartum depression occurs in all cultures. Anthropological studies suggest that the condition is uncommon in certain cultures and common in others. Groups vary greatly in the amount and type of rituals they observe to mark a woman's transition to motherhood. In Western cultures, pregnancy and motherhood tend to be idealized. Girls as young as two years of age begin to develop a repertoire of parenting skills and a set of attitudes toward motherhood. The experience of mothering is expected to be nothing short of blissful. Often these expectations are abruptly shattered with the birth of the child. For one thing, virtually all postpartum rituals in Western cultures center on the baby, not on the mother. While some women receive help from family members, for many others either close relatives are unavailable or their presence in the household is perceived as stressful. Therefore, the new mother may find herself isolated and alone at this critical time. To make matters worse, compared with their counterparts in traditional cultures, new mothers in Western societies have relatively little prior experience in caring for children; moreover, there tends to be less societal agreement about what constitutes good parenting than exists in traditional cultures.

Often a woman goes from being the object of special consideration and solicitousness because of her pregnant status to perceiving herself as an exhausted, overweight frump who will be criticized if she fails to meet her baby's every need perfectly. Fears about inadequacy can be intensified by the high expectations expressed by health care providers during prenatal checkups, the rapidity of hospital discharge after delivery, and the abrupt cessation of the relationship established with providers during pregnancy. (In the U.S. today most women have only one brief checkup six weeks after delivery.) There is no evidence that the incidence of depression has increased in the U.S. as hospital stays for new mothers have become shorter. Nonetheless, the longer maternity hospitalizations of previous eras (and still offered in some European countries) allowed for extended contact with nurses, which thus provided emotional support for the new mother and enabled the timely detection of postpartum depression.

In contrast to the practices in the U.S. and other Western countries, some cultures—for example, the Chinese and Nepalese—have formal rituals to acknowledge a woman's transition to motherhood. These may include seclusion; ceremonial baths, massages, and heat treatments; special foods; purification ceremonies; and exemption of the new mother from certain duties. These rituals promote individual well-being and enhance mother-infant bonding. In spiritual terms, they ensure safe passage for a major life transition. Anthropologists believe that such rituals also ward off postpartum depression, which appears to be much less common in these cultures.

Linda's experience exemplifies that of many new mothers today. She was discharged from the hospital less than 24 hours after Ana was born. Manuel's employer was relatively liberal by current U.S. standards, allowing him a week of family leave. After that, though, Linda had only very limited support. When her mother's illness added to her stress and reduced her social support system even further, it set in motion a process that led to clinical depression.

Biological factors. An unanswered question is whether biological vulnerabilities may predispose some women to becoming clinically depressed during the stressful postpartum period. Research so far supports this possibility. Some biological vulnerability is probably genetic. If a woman has had a previous clinical depression or if she has a family history of depression, her likelihood of experiencing postpartum depression increases.

As already noted, the role of hormones is unclear. Postpartum depression often begins after hormonal levels have stabilized. A number of studies have attempted to correlate postpartum hormonal changes with clinical depression, but no connection has yet been convincingly demonstrated. Nonetheless, the possibility remains that in women who are vulnerable because of heredity or unusual stress, hormonal changes after birth contribute to the likelihood of developing major depression.

One in a thousand

The most extreme postpartum reaction is psychosis, a break with reality. In these cases women experience hallucinations and develop delusions (irrational beliefs that are unresponsive to logic). Typically, these new mothers may seem reasonable and logical for a few hours or even days but then suddenly and unpredictably lose touch with reality. Their moods are quixotic, ranging from giddy elation to profound depression to both extremes simultaneously. They may become intermittently disoriented and confused.

Postpartum psychosis poses potential dangers to the woman and her baby. The mother may hear voices telling her to harm herself or the baby or both. She may begin to believe that the baby is the devil and should be destroyed. In her lucid moments she may appear so rational that others are unaware how deeply disturbed her thoughts and feelings are. For all these reasons a woman with postpartum psychosis is more likely to enact dangerous thoughts than is a woman with nonpsychotic depression.

Postpartum psychosis closely resembles the psychiatric disorder officially called bipolar mood disorder (popularly known as manic-depression). People with this disorder have episodes of clinical depression, but they also experience periods of euphoria, irritability, grandiosity, racing thoughts, rapid speech, insomnia, impaired judgment, and impulsivity. In postpartum psychosis either mania or depression can predominate, but often there is a mixture of both. Symptoms usually begin within the first three weeks after the baby's birth.

Compared with other postpartum disorders, psychosis is rare; about one in 1,000 new mothers experiences it. However, women with a personal or family history of bipolar mood disorder are far more vulnerable; about 25% of such women will have an episode postnatally. Postpartum psychosis occurs in many diverse cultures, although in some societies it is interpreted as possession by evil spirits. The disorder does not seem to be brought on by stress or lack of social support. Genetic vulnerability, perhaps triggered by hormonal changes, seems to be the most influential factor. In a few cases a specific medical cause can be found, such as a vitamin deficiency, a drug reaction, an enzyme deficiency, an infection, or inflammation of the thyroid gland.

If undetected and untreated, postpartum psychosis can lead to the tragedy of infanticide—killing of the baby. (Most

As a result of shortened maternity stays—now lasting perhaps only 24 hours after birth—new mothers may leave the hospital feeling exhausted and ill-prepared to cope with the newborn's needs.

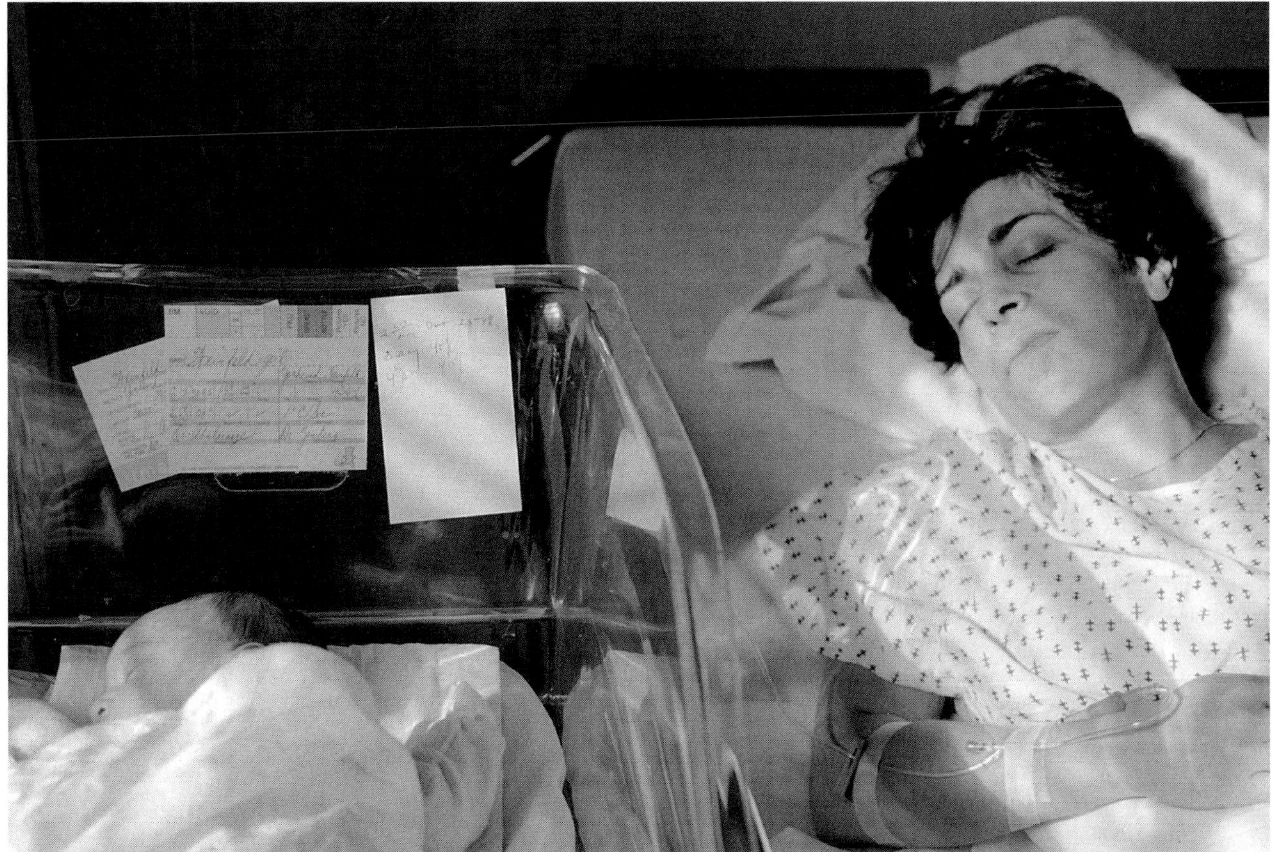

Steven Kasher—Impact Visuals

women who kill their newborns are not psychotic, however.) With effective treatment most women quickly recover from postpartum psychosis, and their children suffer no lasting harm.

Treatment

Obstetricians, midwives, and childbirth instructors are becoming increasingly aware that education about postpartum disorders is the first step in treatment and prevention. Prospective parents who know about these potential problems can recognize them more quickly than those who are uninformed and therefore are more likely to seek help when needed. The baby blues require no professional intervention but are better tolerated when the women and their families understand what is happening. Both postpartum depression and psychosis are highly responsive to treatment, and treatment for both is more effective the earlier it begins.

Treatment of postpartum depression takes into account the contributions of biological and psychosocial factors. A form of psychotherapy called interpersonal psychotherapy is effective for women whose depression is linked to difficulty with the role changes that ensue after birth. This type of therapy lasts approximately 16 weeks and is conducted by specially trained psychiatrists or psychologists. During the sessions the therapist helps the woman trace her depressive symptoms to maladaptive patterns of thoughts or behavior that are complicating the transition to motherhood or causing excessive pressures. For example, a woman who had persuaded her reluctant husband to have a third child felt driven to provide perfect care for her newborn and two older children, without making any demands on her husband. This impossible set of expectations contributed to her depression.

A logical extension of individual therapy is couples therapy, where both parents together examine how each is reacting to the new baby and how parenthood has affected their relationship. The therapy may also include exploring how the new mother can enlist further help and support, whether from members of the extended family, community resources, or agencies that send specially trained individuals into the homes of depressed new mothers to serve as caregivers. Postpartum support groups for women are available in many areas, and a few pioneering support groups for new fathers have also been established.

When postpartum mood changes are more serious than those experienced with the "baby blues," psychotherapy may help the woman understand and come to terms with her symptoms.

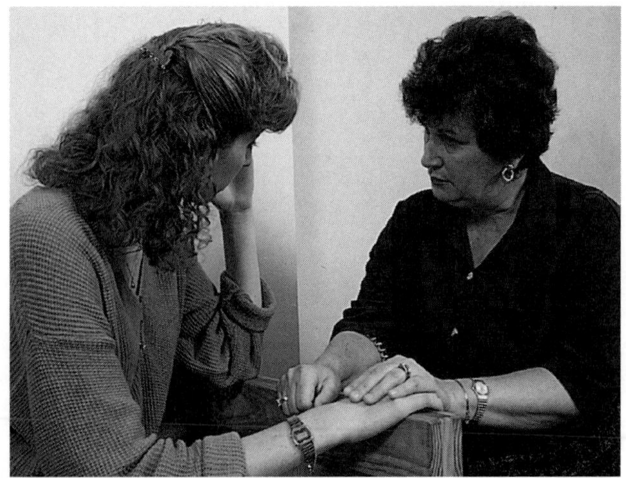

C.C. Duncan—Medical Images, Inc.

For some women the depression is so profound or its biological basis so apparent that supportive measures and psychotherapy are insufficient. In these cases a comprehensive evaluation by a psychiatrist can identify possible treatable medical conditions that may be contributing to depression. The psychiatrist also can determine whether a given individual's constellation of symptoms is likely to be alleviated by antidepressant medication and can advise the patient about the risks and benefits of breast-feeding while taking such medication. A variety of antidepressants are effective for postpartum depression; the best medication for an individual woman depends on the pattern of her symptoms, the presence of any coexisting medical conditions, and whether she is breast-feeding.

In cases of profound, suicidal depression, psychiatric hospitalization may be necessary to protect the mother and, sometimes, the baby. A few hospitals have mother-baby units where depressed mothers can keep their infants with them. In most hospitals, though, this is not possible, and active measures must be taken to maintain the mother-infant relationship. Hospital stays, which range from two to three days to two to three weeks, can be shortened by the use of intensive posthospital support, perhaps including the help of a trained caregiver. Another way to speed recovery from profound depression is through the use of electroconvulsive therapy, which, as it is now administered, is as safe and effective as antidepressant drugs but usually works faster.

The risks of postpartum psychosis are such that hospitalization, along with medication or electroconvulsive therapy, is nearly always necessary. Hospitalization can be relatively brief if a satisfactory level of posthospital support can be arranged.

Does one episode lead to another?

Women and their families who have gone through the grueling experience of a postpartum disorder are often frightened of undertaking a subsequent pregnancy. For this reason a high priority in current research is the prevention of recurrences. In the case of postpartum psychosis, preliminary results suggest that lithium, a mood-stabilizing medication, helps prevent future episodes. Intensive psychological preparation and advance planning for social support have shown promise for preventing postpartum depression. Women who have had several past episodes of depression or who seem vulnerable because of family history may require antidepressant medication. Usually, medication can begin after the baby has been born, but in some cases it is needed during all or part of the pregnancy. Since some of these drugs can be harmful to the fetus, women at risk of postpartum depression often elect to consult a psychiatrist who specializes in treating pregnancy-related mental illness.

In Linda's case it was Ana's pediatrician who suspected clinical depression and persuaded Linda to see a psychiatrist.

Suzanne Arms—The Image Works

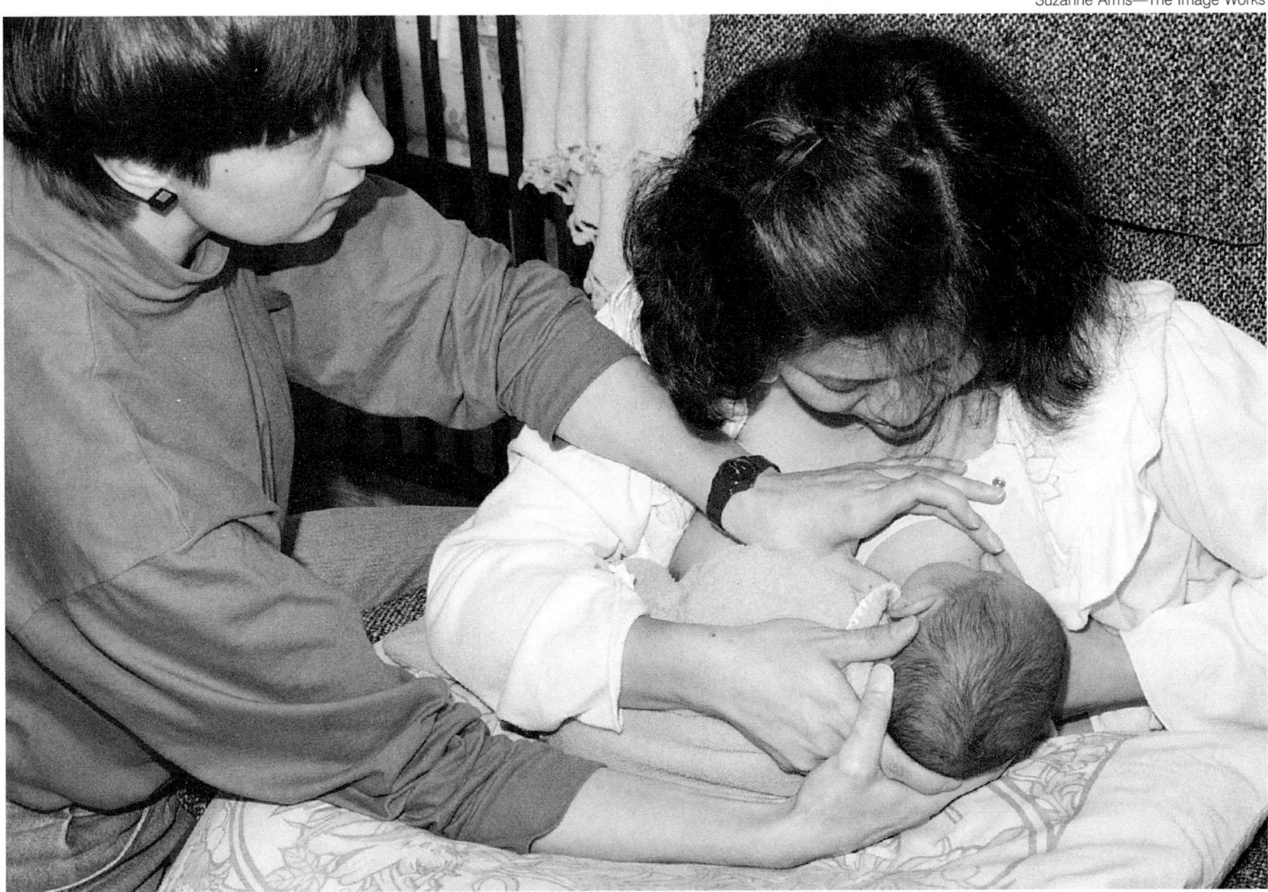

A midwife shows a new mother how to position her baby for successful breast-feeding. Many women today do not have the kind of social support that earlier generations relied upon during the postpartum period.

Psychiatric evaluation and treatment, combined with support from her extended family and a support group she found through the national organization Depression After Delivery, helped her to recover fully.

Parenthood without peril?

Because they occur at such an influential time in the life of a family, postpartum disorders warrant scientific attention and concern. The inclusion of postpartum mood disorder in the fourth and most recent edition of the official psychiatric diagnostic manual, *DSM-IV,* has spurred interest in research on these problems; it has also provided an impetus for adding postpartum disturbances to the curricula of schools that train doctors, nurses, and therapists. The Marcé Society, an international organization named after the above-mentioned 19th-century psychiatrist, promotes collaboration between researchers and clinicians in the area of postpartum mood disorders. Other organizations, such as Depression After Delivery and Postpartum Support International, disseminate information and help women find support groups and mental health professionals with experience in treating pregnancy-related problems. Midwives are at the forefront of a move to provide continuing support and education to new mothers after delivery instead of abruptly ending the relationship established during prenatal visits. A recent increase in media coverage of postpartum problems has helped some depressed women feel less shame and overcome their reticence in seeking help.

With a sustained and collaborative effort by health care providers and health educators, the psychiatric risks of giving birth may be substantially diminished, just as the physical perils have been. Being the mother of a newborn may not measure up to the idyllic expectations, but with the specter of postpartum depression removed, new families contending with sleepless nights, inconsolable crying, and other travails of parenthood at least have a fighting chance of enjoying the experience.

—Laura J. Miller, M.D.

FOR FURTHER INFORMATION:

Depression After Delivery
PO Box 1282
Morrisville PA 19067
1-800-944-4773 or 1-215-295-3994

Postpartum Support International
927 North Kellogg Ave
Santa Barbara CA 93111
1-805-967-7636

Thinking Globally

The walls between nations are now very thin curtains.
—Carol Bellamy, executive director of UNICEF

Nongovernmental organizations, or NGOs, have been active in providing humanitarian assistance around the world for nearly a century. In the past 20 years, NGOs have moved beyond providing medical relief, assisting in disasters, and distributing food toward alleviating the causes of poverty and improving the quality of life in the Third World. At the same time, many governments are ill-equipped to handle mounting health problems, and the capacity of leading multilateral international health agencies, such as the World Health Organization, to address today's international health challenges is increasingly being questioned. NGOs are thus being called upon to work with governments and multilateral organizations, and they are consistently proving their worth.

What are NGOs?

NGOs (also known as private voluntary organizations, or PVOs) often originate as the vision of a single person who, committed to a particular health problem, brings together private- and public-sector resources in order to develop sustainable capabilities. NGOs vary considerably in their goals, methods, and capabilities. What follows is an overview of the range of activities and philosophies that characterize several leading NGOs today. A brief survey of this kind can be neither representative of all such organizations in existence nor comprehensive in its coverage of the current global health problems.

Some NGOs focus on reducing human suffering from a single disease or the injury of a single organ system. Helen Keller International and Orbis International focus their services on the eye. Other NGOs provide a single type of specialty care. Interplast, for example, sends plastic surgeons to less developed countries to repair facial deformities and other anatomic defects. Yet other NGOs have targeted a specific region of the world. Africare (with branches in Burkina Faso, the Central African Republic, Malawi, Mozambique, Nigeria, and Togo) is one such entity, dedicated to improving the health and living conditions of Africans.

Some NGOs are defined by a particular type of technology. One of these is SatelLife, committed to improving health communications and information systems in less developed countries. Conceived in 1989 by U.S. and Soviet physicians, SatelLife has launched a 50-kg (110-lb) microsatellite that orbits the globe and receives up-to-date medical reports from large databases. Medical personnel in areas of the world where access is limited by poor communications, economic conditions, or disaster are able to retrieve information from ground stations that rely on inexpensive computer linkup systems. SatelLife's pilot project targeted the African nations Tanzania, Uganda, Mozambique, Zambia, Kenya, Ghana, Zaire, and Zimbabwe. These countries now have access to the latest published medical information and can link up with specialists from major medical institutions.

The world's many ills

Today's global health challenges are overwhelming; while life expectancy in most industrialized countries exceeds 70 years, people in the majority of less developed nations still have life expectancies below 50 years. In the area of maternal and child health, almost four million infants die annually within hours or days of birth. Over a half million women die each year from complications of pregnancy and childbirth, but a woman in sub-Saharan Africa is 75 times more likely to die under those circumstances than is a woman in either Western Europe or the United States.

Infectious and parasitic diseases account for almost half of all deaths in the Third World. Over one billion people are infected with roundworm, 900 million have hookworm infection, and 500 million are affected by *Trichuris,* or whipworm. The protozoan *Giardia lamblia* affects every third person in the world. This infection of the small intestine, spread by contaminated water or food or by personal contact, was once common mainly in the less developed parts of the Tropics but now is increasingly prevalent worldwide. One-third of the world's population (some 1.7 billion people) are at risk for tuberculosis. Malaria has eluded effective control measures. Moreover, the malaria burden among indigenous populations in tropical regions is now expanding.

While long-standing infectious and parasitic diseases have withstood the best efforts of the international health community, new organisms—so-called emerging infections—are adding to that burden. The pandemic of sexually transmitted diseases proceeds relatively unrestrained, causing 250 million cases per year. One component of this pandemic, namely, HIV/AIDS, is expected to affect 30 million to 40 million persons globally by the year 2000.

In addition to communicable diseases, the number and range of chronic conditions associated with environment and lifestyle are increasing rapidly in the less developed world as the socioeconomic status of countries improves. Each year, for example, approximately seven million new cases of cancer occur, half of them now in the Third World.

Meeting diverse needs

The need for improving the international health picture is evident. What are the characteristics of NGOs that make them so effective in doing so?

- *They are able to reach the areas of most severe need.* NGOs are effective in reaching and improving conditions for the poor, the dispossessed, and the isolated in less developed nations. They work in rural and urban areas and concentrate on poorer communities having few basic resources or lacking an existing health infrastructure. They target parts of the world where, for one reason or another, the local government has been unable to meet needs.
- *They promote local involvement.* NGOs enlist community participation and help coordinate local groups that have disparate interests. Because NGOs are usually committed for the long term—beyond emergencies—they form close bonds with community groups and institutions and engender strong support for the services they provide.

- *They operate at low cost.* NGO staff are typically highly motivated and generally work for a stipend or very modest salaries; some work entirely voluntarily. The agencies also tend to rely on low-cost technology and streamlined services that, combined with minimal staff costs, allow them to operate efficiently on relatively small budgets.
- *They are adaptive and innovative.* To be effective, NGOs must aim their help appropriately. They must be sensitive to the technological sophistication and distinct needs of each particular locale. NGOs generally build on existing services and infrastructures and promote technology transfers that reduce the need for additional resources.
- *They work independently.* Nongovernmental by definition, NGOs can function relatively free from political entanglements. They usually operate within a region with the approval of the host government. Largely apolitical, they enjoy a special nonpartisan status locally, which promotes community acceptance and trust.
- *They strive for sustainability.* An important priority of NGOs is to achieve sustainable outcomes that are not dependent upon continuing external technical assistance and financing. In the health care field, NGOs have been instrumental in establishing primary-care delivery systems that continue to have a major impact upon the general health status of less developed countries long after assistance teams have gone.

Orbiting ophthalmologists

Approximately 42 million people around the world are blind; 90% of them live in less developed countries. For many of the world's blind, proper treatment could cure their problems (or could have prevented it).

Orbis International, a nonprofit organization dedicated to fighting blindness worldwide, flies to less developed countries at the invitation of the national government and local ophthalmologic society. Orbis teams travel on an aircraft that carries a full complement of ophthalmologists, nurses, and technicians. The group began in 1982, flying its eye doctors worldwide on a converted Douglas DC-8 donated by United Airlines. In 1994 that plane was replaced by a DC-10 jumbo jet, converted to a self-sufficient treatment and teaching facility twice the size of the original plane.

The passenger cabin of the aircraft is used as a classroom where host-country doctors watch live surgery and can communicate with the operating surgeon via an audiovisual system. Another section of the cabin has been converted to an examination and laser-treatment room. Here physicians treat diseases such as cataract, trachoma, glaucoma, and onchocerciasis (river blindness). Mid cabin between the wings are surgical facilities linked to the recovery room and nurses station.

Since it began its work, Orbis has provided training for more than 30,000 doctors and nurses and restored the sight of at least 18,000 patients in 70 countries. Orbis' "wings of mercy" offer training that otherwise might not be provided by local governments or international donor agencies. Individuals who suffer from eye diseases and visual impairment are the beneficiaries.

Commitment of a former president

Once you've seen a small child with a two-foot-long live guinea worm protruding from her body, right through a large sore between her toes, you never forget it.

—Jimmy Carter, Ghana, 1988

After leaving the White House in 1981, Jimmy Carter established the Carter Center in Atlanta, Ga., an NGO that works to resolve conflict, promote democracy, preserve human rights, improve health, and fight hunger around the world. In 1986 the center founded Global 2000, a program focusing on disease treatment and prevention in the Third World. One of Global 2000's most important efforts thus far has been its campaign, headed by international health expert Donald R. Hopkins, to eradicate dracunculiasis (guinea worm infection) from the world (*see* page 431).

Guinea worm disease is a debilitating parasitic infection that formerly afflicted nearly five million people annually. The infection results from the drinking of contaminated water from a source that harbors the *Cyclops* water flea. The water fleas release parasites that grow into large worms in the bodies of infected people. While not deadly, dracunculiasis causes enormous human suffering and a major loss of human productivity, which can devastate the economy of a less developed country.

Modern medicine has no treatment for guinea worm disease. Fortunately, however, the infection can be prevented.

An Indian patient is one of many to have his eyesight restored on board Orbis International's flying eye hospital during a three-week mission of Orbis volunteers in Calcutta.

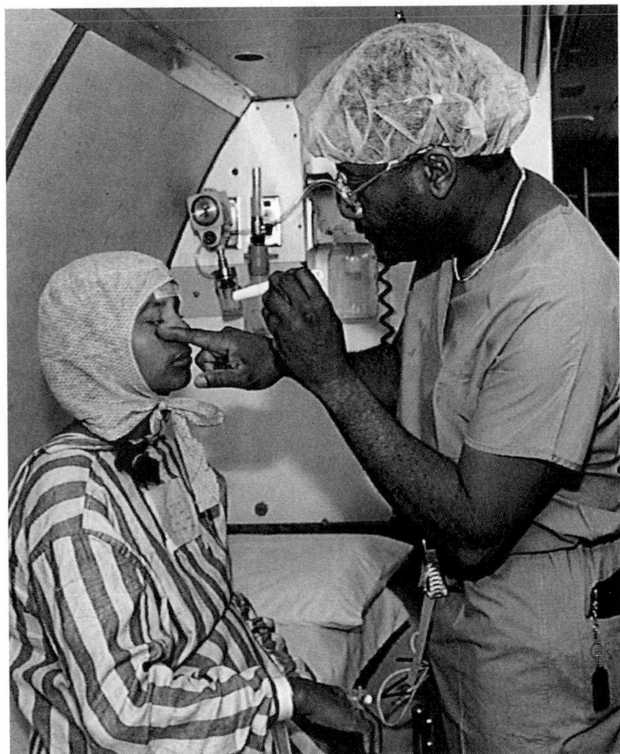

Abbas—Magnum

Courtesy of Project HOPE

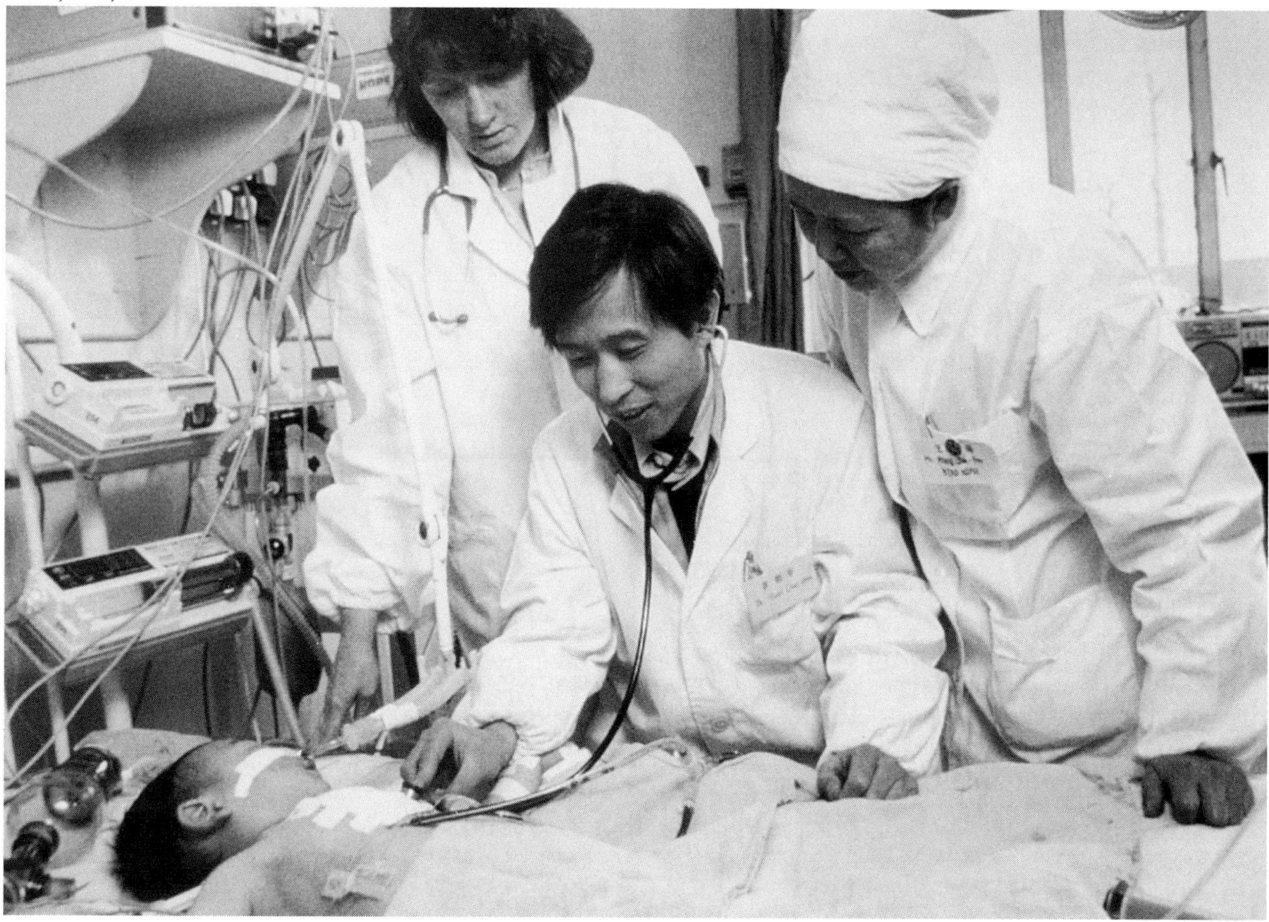

Building upon 12 years of experience in China, Project HOPE is collaborating with the Chinese government to establish the country's first major pediatric referral and teaching hospital. The medical center is scheduled to open in Shanghai in 1996.

The strategy is simple: identify affected villages and help inhabitants prevent infection by (1) installing borehole wells and other safe drinking-water sources, (2) teaching people how to filter their water, and (3) treating stagnant water sources with a chemical larvicide.

Collaborating with international industry, public- and private-sector donors, and the Centers for Disease Control and Prevention, Global 2000 is close to achieving its goal of relegating guinea worm infection to the history books before the end of the century. The projected number of total cases for 1995 was 13,000. E.I. du Pont de Nemours & Co. and Precision Fabrics Group developed a kind of fine-mesh nylon fabric that removes water fleas from contaminated water; these companies have jointly donated 1.4 million reusable filters to the Global 2000's guinea worm eradication effort. American Cyanamid Co. donated more than $2 million worth of the larvicide Abate, which kills the parasites but leaves the water safe for human consumption. In March 1995 private Japanese corporations pledged over $1.5 million for four-wheel-drive vehicles and motorcycles to aid the search for remaining cases.

As chairman of Global 2000, the former president has played a special diplomatic role, enlisting the cooperation and support of national leaders and health ministers in Pakistan and those countries of Africa where the guinea worm is endemic. Carter makes the point that "once they see that this is a popular and relatively easy thing they can do for their people, they are usually quite willing to help."

The guinea worm parasite has several characteristics that make it an ideal eradication candidate. It is easy to determine where it is endemic, and there is no animal reservoir from which humans can be infected once the organism has been eliminated. An important step in the dracunculiasis eradication effort has been the exploitation of naturally occurring declines in incidence by season, which magnify the impact of disease-control measures.

Guinea worm will be only the second infectious disease to be officially eradicated from the world; smallpox was the first, and great strides are being made toward the global elimination of polio. Clearly, the success of Global 2000 and its various partners offers a model for NGOs throughout the international health field. As Carter points out:

> *The world is full of difficult problems that we cannot yet solve. This is one we can solve.... The eradication of guinea worm disease will be a gift whose full value is impossible to measure.*

Reason to hope

The more fortunate among us have the obligation not to take care of the world, but rather, because of our blessings, to help the world take care of itself.

—William B. Walsh, founder, Project HOPE

Unlike some NGOs, Project HOPE is only partially concerned with the provision of immediate humanitarian/medical assistance. The nonprofit organization, begun in 1958, seeks to build lasting health infrastructures by helping health professionals throughout the less developed world become the teachers and providers of state-of-the-art care. Simply put, the goal is to help people help themselves. The project's guiding philosophy is that good health is essential for social and economic development—and ultimately for the dignity of every human being.

In its 37-year history, Project HOPE has conducted special programs in over 80 countries. These are complemented by others that target communities as a whole, such as AIDS prevention and child immunization.

The following are just a few of HOPE's special missions in recent years:

- establishing the Shanghai Children's Medical Center, China's first sophisticated pediatric referral and teaching hospital, in collaboration with the country's government; scheduled to open in 1996, the hospital will be able to care for up to 90,000 pediatric inpatients and 200,000 outpatients annually
- supplying $235.5 million in medical equipment and services to the 15 republics of the former Soviet Union between 1989 and 1994
- training health administrators in the Czech Republic in the principles and strategies of providing medical services in a market economy
- establishing a burn-treatment center—modeled largely on the Boston Shriners Burns Institute—at Moscow's Children's Hospital No. 9

An ailing child receives care from Médecins sans Frontières volunteers in the Cukurca camp in Turkey, where Kurdish refugees from Iraq subsisted without basic necessities following the Persian Gulf War.

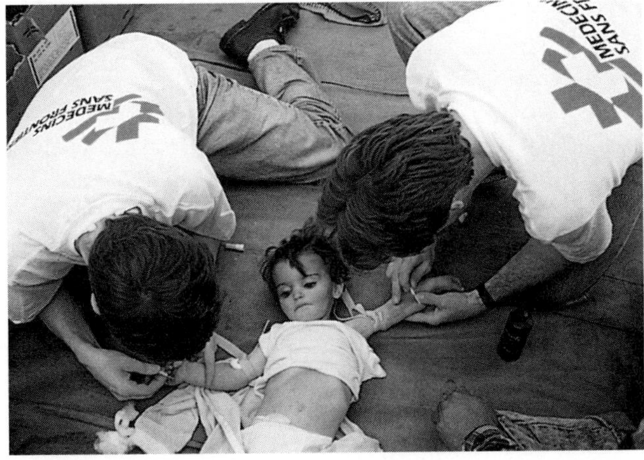

Frank Fournier—Contact Press Images

- providing urgently needed medical supplies and pharmaceuticals to war-torn Bosnia and Herzegovina
- helping establish a national medical emergency system in Costa Rica

Many of Project HOPE's efforts are directed toward issues and problems that are not always perceived as directly related to health. For example, HOPE has implemented income-generation programs tied to its traditional health-education initiatives. Such a strategy recognizes that providing training for the community and health professionals in areas where incomes are low is not enough. If families remain financially unable to make effective changes, health education is doomed to fail. Income-generation programs provide short-term loans, job training, and assistance to mothers so they can become gainfully employed; they generate revenues so that changes in health behavior and reduction of health risks can be achieved and sustained.

Humanitarian goals and political activism

While our medical teams cannot stop the slaughter in Rwanda, or anywhere, we will continue to care for the wounded, the orphans, the displaced.

—Médecins sans Frontières, 1994

Médecins sans Frontières ("Doctors Without Borders"), or MSF, was founded in 1971 by French physicians who had previously treated the sick and wounded during the war in Biafra and responded to the emergency relief needs of the population of East Pakistan (now Bangladesh) when floods devastated the region. Dedicated to the assistance of victims of natural disasters and of catastrophes caused by belligerent or violent conflicts, regardless of race, religion, or political belief, MSF today is among the world's largest NGOs, with sections based in The Netherlands, Belgium, Switzerland, Luxembourg, Spain, and the U.S. Each year about 2,000 MSF doctors, paramedics, nurses, logistics experts, and other personnel travel to crisis-stricken areas, setting up clinics, establishing refugee camps, tracking disease, and providing vital medical care and supplies. MSF was among the first humanitarian-aid teams to respond to the crisis in Rwanda in 1994, and many of its volunteers remained on the scene long after other groups left.

Unlike many other NGOs, MSF does not insist upon maintaining a politically neutral position. Throughout its history the organization has focused on human rights issues as they affect the health of vulnerable populations, in some cases opposing local governments. Its interventions are determined entirely by the population's immediate and long-term needs, not political factors. Thus, MSF teams will enter a country clandestinely if they have to. In order to maintain its independence, MSF does not accept donations from governments or any group or individual with political links.

Future challenges

Increasingly, NGOs are collaborating with international industry. The pharmaceutical industry, for example, has sponsored national immunization campaigns and invested in setting up an infrastructure that makes it possible for countries to assess the impact of widespread vaccination. This clearly meets the interests of pharmaceutical manufacturers in promoting vaccine sales around the world; at the same time, populations of participating countries gain lasting health benefits. While this collaboration is a delicate one, in which clear boundaries must be set so that NGOs do not become vehicles for market development, there are many health care products and technologies with potential for improving the health status of communities in less developed countries.

In the coming years it will be imperative for imaginative new partnerships with business to be considered in battling the many unconquered scourges and addressing the needs of populations for whom there have not been adequate resources thus far. Specific challenges that NGOs will have a major role in meeting include:

- *The smoking-related disease pandemic.* Smoking kills three million people in the world every year. If current smoking patterns continue, by 2025 the toll will be 10 million deaths. Despite great progress in reducing the incidence of cigarette smoking in some industrialized nations (*e.g.,* the U.S.), smoking-prevention programs do not exist in a majority of nations around the world. International tobacco manufacturers have targeted their marketing efforts to nations in the less developed world in order to offset diminishing markets and revenues within Western industrialized nations. They have also taken advantage of the lax regulation of cigarette advertising in these countries. In an increasing number of nations in East and Southeast Asia, Central and Eastern Europe, the former Soviet Union, and Latin America, more than 50% of adults smoke, and rates among adolescents and children are increasing dramatically.

  Epidemics of smoking-caused morbidity and mortality will worsen in coming years as the chronic influence of tobacco begins to have populationwide effects. Antismoking activities have not been a traditional focus of NGOs, but unless they intend to sit idly by and see their success in reducing other kinds of health problems completely undone, they will need to become both active and aggressive in countering this looming public health crisis.
- *Emerging infections and the AIDS epidemic.* In industrialized nations there is evidence of a resurgence of communicable diseases that had once been almost eliminated. In the affluent nations old nemeses, such as tuberculosis, are making new inroads; many previously treatable pathogens are now resistant to antibiotics, and completely new infections are being seen. In the less developed world the disease burden of long-standing infectious diseases is being compounded

A victim of civil war in northern Somalia is fitted for a prosthetic leg at a clinic run by Handicap International, a multinational nongovernmental organization that supports the rehabilitation of physically disabled persons in Third World countries.

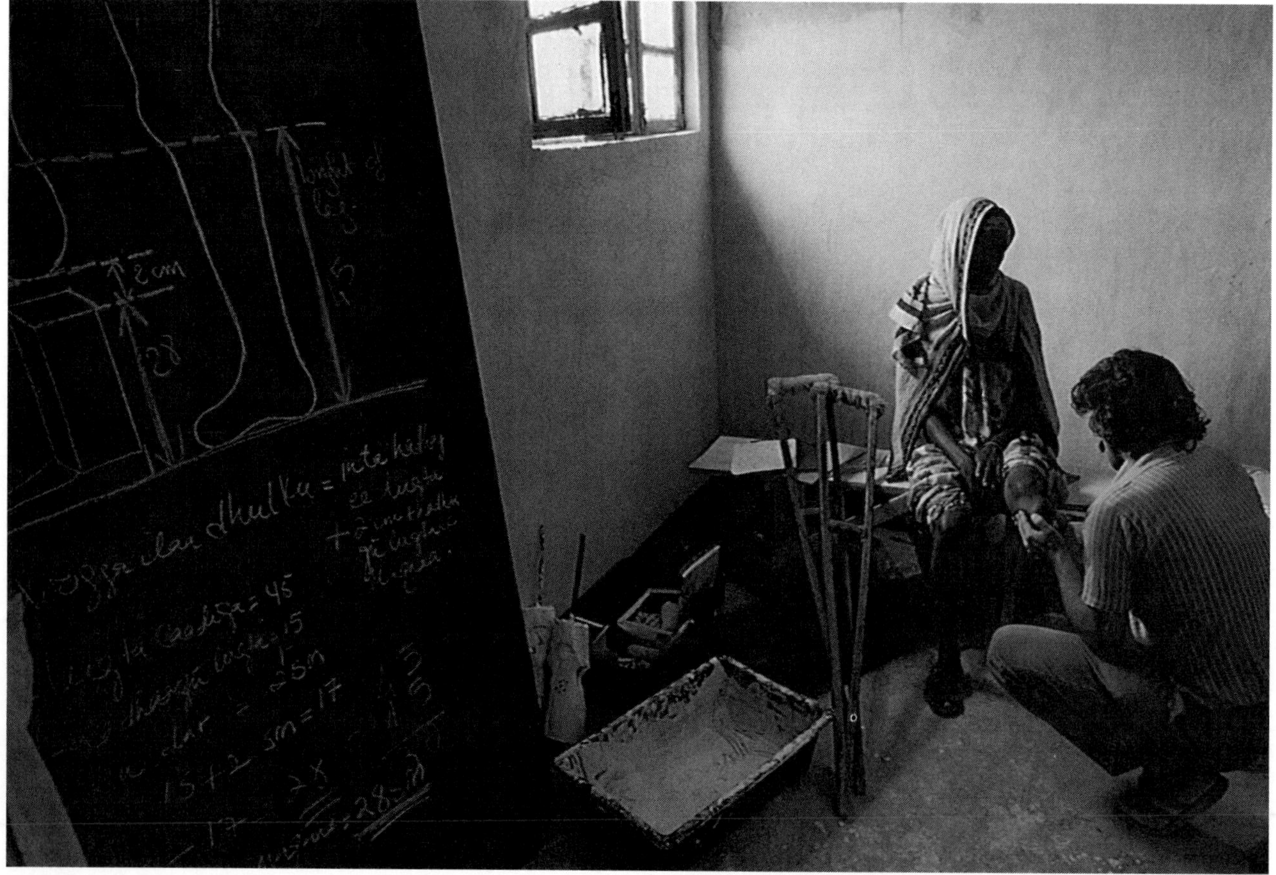

Peter Menzel

by emerging pathogens. For every victory like smallpox eradication, there appear to be new infectious threats to the public health. Thus far, the world community has not been able to respond effectively or fast enough.

There is evidence to suggest that the magnitude of the AIDS problem is considerably greater than reported levels. In most nations, particularly in the less developed world, the systems for HIV/AIDS reporting are in need of major improvement. NGOs will have an ever more critical role in coping with these epidemics. As with other problems NGOs have tackled, they can take an organizational lead to bring together local and humanitarian-aid resources.

- *Women's health.* In the quest to alleviate suffering and reduce unnecessary deaths in the pediatric population, an important area of international health has been neglected. After the neonatal period, female mortality surges ahead of male mortality. Girls die in far greater numbers for many reasons, mostly associated with poverty, poor sanitation and hygiene, malnutrition, infection, and the absence of adequate health care. A perception exists in many parts of the world—and is reinforced by culture—that women have low economic value and are less capable of being contributing, productive members of a household and community. Where resources are scarce, they often do not receive an equal share of existing health services, food, and other necessities.

  Through educational programs NGOs will have a role in reducing discrimination and unnecessarily high female mortality. Central to achieving this objective is the assignment of greater value to women's work. Project HOPE's income-generation programs are examples of the type of effort needed. The deaths of childbearing women can be reduced by the provision of acceptable family-planning services, prenatal care and proper nutrition during pregnancy, and prevention of obstetric complications such as hemorrhage and infection. The provision of relatively simple medical technologies, such as blood transfusions for hemorrhage, antibiotics for infection, and cesareans for obstructed labor, can promote a revolutionary decrease in maternal mortality. NGOs have a vital role to play in eliminating other dangerous and nonscientific cultural practices that harm and disable women, such as female circumcision, which is widely practiced in parts of Africa, the Middle East, and Asia.

  All of these matters were addressed in Cairo in September 1994 at the International Conference on Population and Development, attended by representatives of over 170 nations and thousands of NGOs. Women's health issues would be the central focus of an international world conference near Beijing (Peking) in September 1995.

- *Injury prevention.* Injuries, intentional and unintentional, are leading causes of disability and death in virtually every country in the world. They reduce economic productivity, use up costly health care resources, and contribute substantially to premature loss of life. The implementation of effective programs to reduce the burden of disability and death caused by injuries has been highly successful in industrialized countries. It is time to bring such programs into the international health sphere. Child safety programs are examples.

  As many countries advance and industrialize, the incidence of injuries is likely to increase. This represents a new area of activity for many NGOs, but it is an activity that calls for the kinds of demonstrated capabilities that have made these organizations so effective in responding to other problems.

As the past decades have shown, NGOs have made a valuable contribution to resolving major public health problems and improving health status around the globe. Innovative strategies, rapid organizational responses, and flexibility that promotes local involvement at low cost to achieve sustainable outcomes are all factors that will drive these future international health programs.

—*George A. Gellert, M.D., M.P.H., M.P.A.*

NEWS*CAP*

Good-bye Guinea Worm

Just before catching a flight to Uganda on June 9, 1995, Donald R. Hopkins learned he was the recipient of a coveted John D. and Catherine T. MacArthur Foundation fellowship; the generous cash grants—in Hopkins' case, $320,000—are awarded to a select few individuals whose accomplishments benefit humankind. Hopkins has devoted his public health career to reducing the toll of terrible diseases around the world. He is currently leading the Global 2000 campaign to eradicate dracunculiasis, or guinea worm disease (*see* page 427).

The first disease to be banished from the world was smallpox, and Hopkins was part of that public health triumph. It was he who suggested that guinea worm could be the second human scourge eradicated. Only a decade ago, the devastating parasitic infection afflicted about 10 million people a year. In 1994 that number had been reduced to 164,750. Hopkins' trip to Uganda in June was to attend an international conference on strategies for the last—most exciting—stretch of the eradication effort.

In 1991 Hopkins, a longtime consultant and contributor to the *Medical and Health Annual,* told the editors he had a 2.5-ft guinea worm ("Henrietta") preserved in formaldehyde. He was looking forward to the day "when she would be the last of her kind." That day is now in sight.

Gaza Strip: Health Care Challenges

In September 1993 Israel and the Palestine Liberation Organization (PLO) entered into a historic agreement known as the Declaration of Principles (DOP), which provided for the establishment of limited self-rule in the Gaza Strip and Jericho in the West Bank, Palestinian territories formerly under direct Israeli military occupation. With the signing of the DOP, the possibility of a peaceful resolution to the Palestinian-Israeli conflict became real for the first time since the State of Israel was established. Under the terms of the agreement, Israel would transfer responsibility for several sectors, including that for health, to the newly established Palestinian National Authority (PNA). In May 1994 the parties signed the Cairo Agreement, which, in part, formalized the transfer.

By November 1994 the PNA had established a health authority that had assumed full responsibility for health care in Gaza and Jericho. Yet the implementation of the Gaza-Jericho plan came at a time of unprecedented economic, social, political, and institutional disintegration in the Gaza Strip. Gaza's rapid societal breakdown was due, in part, to many years of occupation by Israelis and, most recently, to a series of prolonged closures of the occupied territories, starting in March 1993. These closures, imposed for security reasons, brought an already weak Palestinian economy to the point of near-total collapse.

Among other things, the need for basic relief—food, water, and other necessities of life—once restricted to a small minority of people in the Gaza Strip and West Bank, had become the concern of a growing majority. By June 1991 the United Nations Relief and Works Agency (UNRWA), whose responsibility had formerly been for the refugee population only, was feeding an unprecedented 120,000 families, both refugee and indigenous, in the Gaza Strip—almost the entire population—and 165,000 families in the West Bank. During 1992 UNRWA distributed an additional 430,000 family food parcels in Gaza and 119,000 in the West Bank. According to UNRWA, in 1995 at least 70,000 Palestinians in Gaza were dependent on food assistance, without which they would have gone hungry.

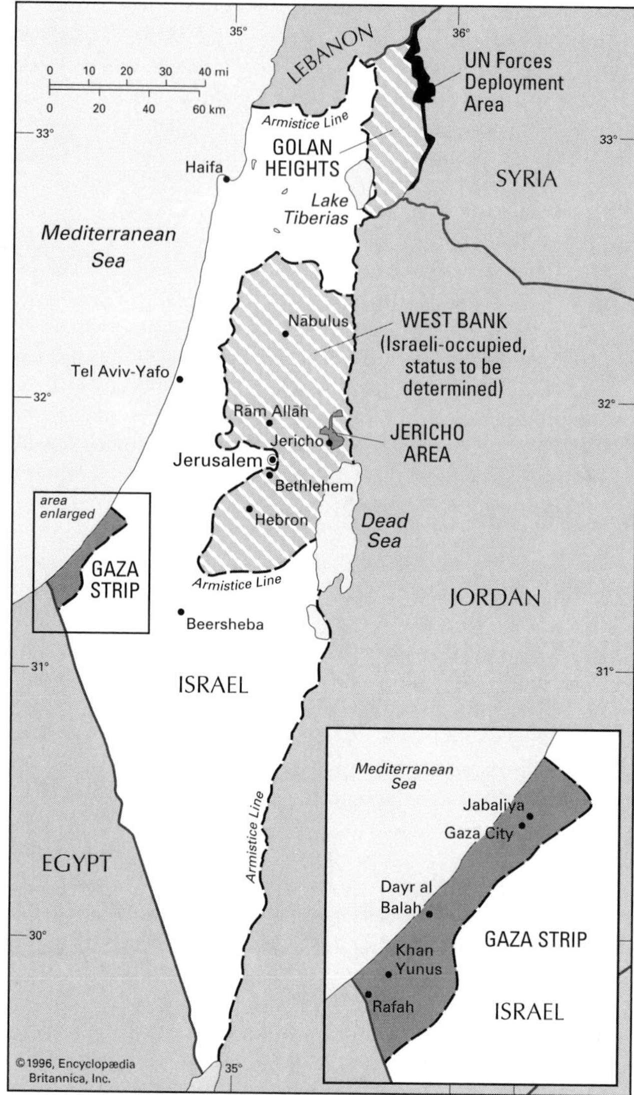

Historical perspective: focus on Gaza

The city of Gaza is one of the oldest in the world, dating to 3200 BC. Its present debilitation belies its remarkable history of resilience in the face of a succession of conquests, first by the Egyptian pharaohs and most recently by the Israeli army. Gaza's geography has clearly shaped its history, in part because it was an important commercial link between Egypt and other ancient empires.

Prior to World War I, Gaza was part of the Ottoman Empire. Traditional attitudes and approaches to medicine and health prevailed, but no records exist from that time. In the years after World War I (1920–48), both the town of Gaza and the Gaza region were under British rule; the Gaza Strip, as such, had no territorial demarcations. During the British Mandate the region was largely rural; the city of Gaza, predominantly Arab, was underdeveloped compared with some other Palestinian towns and cities (particularly those that had a mixed Arab-Jewish or largely Jewish population). Not surprisingly, therefore, health in Gaza and its hinterland was poorer than in many other parts of Palestine.

The Gaza Strip was geographically incorporated after the declaration of Israeli statehood (May 1948) and the ensuing Arab-Israeli war. With an area of 363 sq km (140 sq mi; 45 km [28 mi] long and 8 km [5 mi] wide), it is situated on the eastern Mediterranean, bordered by Israel to the north and east and by Egypt to the south. Within days of its delineation, this tiny territory was besieged by 250,000 refugees fleeing the war in Palestine. Under Egyptian military control from 1948 to 1967, the Gaza Strip's population tripled, and the internal dynamics of the territory were altered forever.

Today the Gaza Strip is one of the most densely populated regions in the world. There are approximately 850,000 people inhabiting the territory, 99% of whom are Sunni Muslims. About 75%—more than 600,000 people—are refugees of the 1948 Arab-Israeli war or their descendants; over half of this population lives in eight overcrowded refugee camps, which were first established in 1950. Inside the camps, where living space is particularly scarce, the density level approaches 75,770 people per square kilometer (197,000 per square mile), which is over three times the population density of Manhattan Island.

The annual population growth rate in Gaza is among the highest in the less developed world, and 60% of the population is under 16 years of age. By the year 2005, Gazans are expected to number 1.7 million. Gazans now live in 13 cities and towns, the most populous being Gaza City, Khan Yunus, Rafah, Jabaliya, and Dayr al Balah. Since 1967 settlement patterns have been shaped largely by the Israeli government, which assumed control of at least 50% of Gaza's land, large portions of which have been allocated to the establishment of 16 Jewish settlements. Although these settlements constituted one-half of 1% of the territory's total population in 1993, Israelis were allotted 84 times more land per capita than Palestinians. Israeli settlers also consumed close to 16 times more water per capita.

Economic collapse

Between 1970 and 1987 the number of Gazans traveling to work in Israel grew from 10% of the total labor force (5,900 people) to over 70% (80,000 Gazans). Wages earned in Israel have been a critical factor in local economic growth, particularly in advancing Gaza's gross national product (GNP), since demand generated by Palestinian workers in Israel increased consumption and trade. This growth was especially pronounced in the first decade of occupation, when Israel's own economy was growing. Because increases in the GNP were largely in the form of external payments (salaries earned in Israel and foreign remittances), economic dependence on Israel became extreme and occurred at the cost of Gaza's own economic development.

Gaza's weakened economy deteriorated rapidly under the combined impact of the Palestinian uprising against Israeli occupation (known in Arabic as the *intifada*) and the Persian Gulf War. Between December 1987 and January 1991, the GNP fell by at least 30%. The cumulative effect of the series of closures in response to heightened levels of Palestinian violence against Jews in Israel was devastating for the economy. By April 1995 the number of Gazans allowed to work in Israel had fallen to 8,000, 10% of 1987 levels. Unemployment stood at nearly 60%. Purchasing power declined, consumption patterns changed, the standard of living fell, and food shortages were widespread.

At odds over statistics

Official Israeli government sources have consistently pointed to improvements in the Gaza health care system under occupation, often citing declines in infant mortality rates (IMR) of the population, increasing immunization rates, and improved medical facilities and access to health care. Palestinian and foreign nongovernmental sources, however, often painted a very different picture—one that was characterized by neglect of the public health infrastructure. According to these sources, health care suffered from discriminatory practices that resulted in poorly equipped and maintained hospitals, inadequate supplies of medicine and medical equipment, poor community outreach programs, and inadequate medical insurance coverage.

During occupation, health care was provided by four main sectors: the Israeli government (40%), UNRWA (40%), and nonprofit nongovernmental organizations (NGOs) and private institutions (20%). Inpatient care was provided in five government hospitals and one private facility with a total of approximately 900 beds. Outpatient services included 27 primary care government clinics scattered throughout the Strip and nine UNRWA primary care health centers in the refugee camps.

Perhaps the most hotly disputed statistics are those concerning the IMR. In 1993 the main causes of infant deaths in Gaza were pneumonia, premature birth, congenital abnormalities, and diarrhea. Some sources report that from 1977 to 1987 the IMR dropped from 100–150 deaths per 1,000 live births to 29. In contrast, however, a study sponsored by the U.S. Agency for International Development (USAID) found an IMR in 1982 of 51–54; the United Nations reported an IMR of 70 in 1985, but the Palestinian Medical Relief Committee suggested that the rate was closer to 100.

The most recent official Israeli statistics, based on death certificates, show that the IMR was 26 in 1990, then increased to 28.3 in 1991 and 31.3 in 1992. The Israeli section of the Defence for Children International found an IMR of 51 per 1,000 live births in 1993. The IMR in Israel, by contrast, was under 10. Because about half of all births occurred at home, however, many infant and maternal deaths may not have been reported.

Public health: successes and failures

Because diarrhea-causing gastrointestinal infections were treated with oral rehydration solution, a low-cost, easily administered, highly effective means of therapy, diarrhea-related mortality was cut by 53% during occupation, and total deaths among children under three years of age were reduced by nearly 42%. Similarly, use of a novel immunization strategy resulted in a drop in the incidence of polio to under one case per 100,000 inhabitants by 1985. Among the refugee population, from 1970 to 1985 the rates of trachoma, an eye infection that commonly results in blindness, fell dramatically from 94 to 0.9 per 100,000, while the rate of tuberculosis was cut in half. Between 1970 and 1985 there also were no reported cases of cholera, diphtheria, leprosy, plague, rabies, relapsing fever, syphilis, or typhus.

Currently, immunization rates for tetanus in Gaza are at least 95%. Over 90% of the population of Gaza is immunized against measles; sporadic epidemics of the disease, however, still occur.

While the Israeli government focused its efforts on preventing epidemics, which it did with considerable success, it failed in a number of other respects. First, there were inadequate government expenditures on health care. In 1993 per capita expenditure on health care was $350 in Israel, $65 in the Gaza Strip and West Bank combined, and $45 in the Gaza Strip alone. The low level of expenditure on health services in Gaza resulted in severe understaffing, inadequate medical equipment (including basic supplies), and poor maintenance of hospital and other health care facilities. In 1993, for example, the Gaza Strip had 0.8 physician per 1,000 people, compared with 2.9 per 1,000 in Israel; Gaza had one hospital bed per 1,000 versus six beds per 1,000 in Israel.

Second, there were numerous official restrictions on health care services. By the time of the Cairo Agreement, Palestinians had little, if any, independent control. Thus, any Palestinian institution wishing to engage in any kind of health-related improvement or expansion had to obtain permission from the Israeli military authorities, and permission was often denied. Restrictions also existed on the importation of various kinds of medical equipment. Before 1994, for example, there was no dialysis machine in the entire Gaza Strip. X-ray machines and electrocardiogram units were in extremely short supply. Prior to 1990 the X-ray department of the government's largest hospital in Gaza had no facilities for angiography or radiotherapy. Basic equipment needed by hospital laboratories was also lacking, and many tests could not be performed at all. In addition, the Israeli military restricted the number of operations performed in Gaza's hospitals and at one point closed the surgical department of the region's main government hospital.

Since the March 1993 closure, almost 75% of the Gaza Strip population has been without any medical insurance. This situation has resulted in death for several seriously ill children who, because of parents' lapsed insurance premiums, could no longer receive treatment.

Finally, the outbreak of the Palestinian uprising in December 1987 had a tremendously detrimental impact on an already marginal, stressed public health infrastructure. The most obvious and direct effect was the sudden, unexpectedly large burden of casualties. Many of the injured were children under 16 years of age; between December 1987 and December 1989, 69 children were killed in Gaza and over 12,000 injured. When so-called plastic bullets (which were actually 70% metal) were introduced, the numbers of injuries and deaths increased. Between December 1987 and December 1992 UNRWA documented 370 fatalities and 59,110 injuries in Gaza. Although these numbers probably underestimate the total number of injured citizens, they suggest the vast number of people that now require rehabilitation services, another vastly underserved sector. All of these events set the stage for a public health crisis.

Water emergency

Perhaps the most urgent public health issue facing the Gaza Strip is the rapidly decreasing supply of fresh water. Water in Gaza is supplied largely by local wells and by the Israeli

An ailing Palestinian child gets urgent care at a clinic in Khan Yunus that is run by the United Nations Relief and Works Agency. The need for basic health services in the fledgling Palestinian territories of the Gaza Strip is enormous.

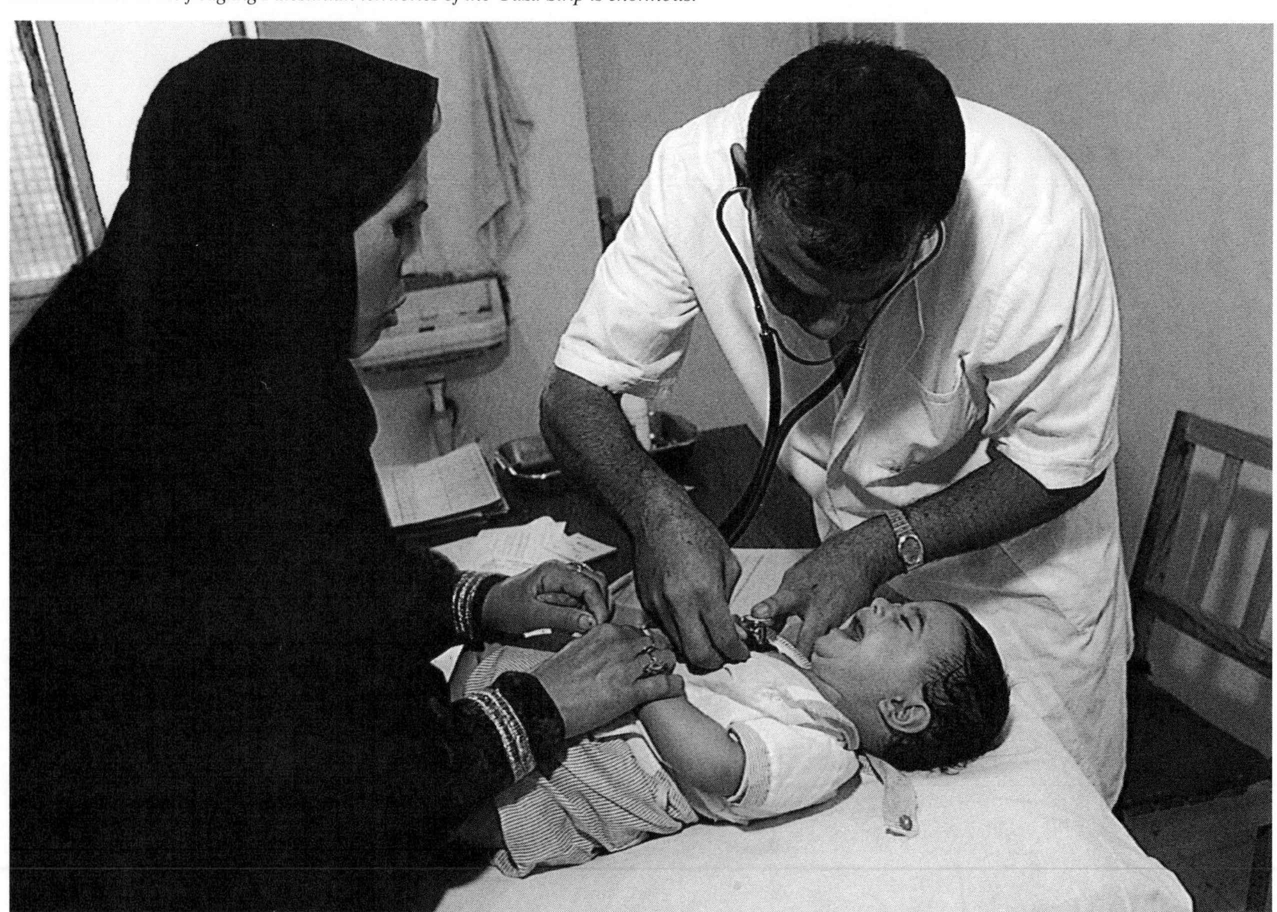

Alon Reininger—Contact Press Images

water company Mekorot. Water quality has deteriorated substantially over the last 10 years. This is primarily due to overpumping, which allows seawater to enter underground reservoirs and causes increased salinity and brackishness. Furthermore, chemical analyses demonstrate leaching of sewage into the groundwater supply. The proper treatment of sewage and wastewater is critical to Gaza's water. Prior to 1992, however, adequate sewage removal and treatment were available in only 3 of 15 localities. Since current demand far exceeds the carrying capacity, raw sewage can be seen flowing down Gaza City streets, even in relatively wealthy areas. Since the time of their creation, the refugee camps have been dependent on open sewers. By 1994 the situation had not appreciably improved, although the international donor community and UNRWA had begun some projects for the rehabilitation of the sewage-disposal infrastructure.

As a result, Gazan water supplies are becoming increasingly unfit for human consumption. In Gaza City, which has the largest population cluster in the territory, a growing number of households no longer consume municipal water. International development experts have estimated that at current levels of domestic and agricultural consumption, the Gaza Strip will be out of fresh water in 10–15 years. The consequences will be disastrous.

Remarkably, for years there had been no widespread epidemics of serious infectious diseases caused by poor sanitation and unsafe water. Good fortune ran out, however, on Nov. 4, 1994, when a case of cholera was reported from the Shejaia neighborhood of Gaza City. The disease-causing organism was characterized by the local laboratory and confirmed by Israeli Ministry of Health and U.S. Centers for Disease Control and Prevention laboratories. The Palestinian Ministry of Health responded quickly by forming a cholera coordinating committee, designating three hospitals as cholera-treatment centers, and contacting USAID for assistance. By November 21 there were 82 cases of cholera, confirmed by laboratory culture, 69 of which were symptomatic. There was one death reported, that of a two-year-old boy who arrived at the hospital severely dehydrated.

Mental health

The psychological effects of disorder, violence, and deprivation should not be underestimated. Everyone in Gaza is traumatized. Children have been the most severely affected. Close to 70% of the Gaza Strip population is 24 years of age and younger and have known nothing but occupation. This is a generation that has never known peace. Moreover, many young people have lost parents and siblings.

Between 1992 and 1993 the Gaza Community Mental Health Programme (GCMHP) surveyed nearly 3,000 Palestinian children aged 8 to 15 and found an extraordinarily high rate of exposure to violence: 93% had been teargassed; 85% had had their homes raided; 55% had witnessed their fathers beaten; 42% had been beaten themselves; 31% had been shot; 28% had had a brother imprisoned; 19% had been detained; 3% had suffered a death in the family; and 69% had been exposed to more than four different types of trauma. For years many children in Gaza had neither home nor classroom, two critical venues of socialization. The impact has been profound. Psychiatrist Eyad as-Sarraj, founder of the GCMHP, reported in early 1995 that 40,000 Gazan children were in need of some form of immediate psychiatric care.

Esais Baitel—Gamma Liaison

Among the Gaza Strip's most pressing public health problems is the fast-decreasing supply of fresh water. At the start of limited self-rule, many Palestinians were already living with water unfit for consumption.

Current health outlook

Diseases reported in Gaza include roundworm, infectious hepatitis, amoebic dysentery, anxiety, depression, hypertension, and blindness. Unfortunately, however, there are no data, but surely the high incidence of these conditions is due in part to severe overcrowding and inadequate infrastructure. Because there are no records, it has not been possible to evaluate demographic patterns of important diseases such as cardiovascular disease, hypertension, cancer, or diabetes, and this will hinder the accuracy of predicting future needs.

In response to the signing of the Israeli-PLO peace agreement, a variety of plans for the development of the Palestinian health sector have emerged. The World Health Organization (WHO) responded with a preliminary plan to develop and implement a program to help transfer health services to an interim Palestinian authority and to provide emergency assistance as needed. A World Bank plan included both long- and short-term objectives based on the premise that a large and probably unsustainable fraction (about 10%) of gross domestic product (GDP) is currently committed to health care in the territories. UNRWA responded with a list of several health projects, appropriately prioritized and each requiring six to nine months for completion. USAID provided an estimated $23 million to assist the Palestinian health authority to build its capacity for primary health care in the Gaza Strip, as well as the West Bank, but owing to a restructuring of USAID's strategy in the Middle East, that program was canceled in March 1995.

The most comprehensive plan to date, the National Health Plan for the Palestinian People, has been prepared under the auspices of the PLO. This plan is based on previously outlined strategies put forward by the Palestine Red Crescent Society (PRCS) and the Palestine Health Council. The PRCS was created by the PLO in 1969, with the responsibility of addressing the health needs of Palestinians in the occupied territories; its president is Fathi Arafat, a physician and a brother of PLO Chairman Yasir Arafat. The PLO's National Health Plan has four guiding principles: (1) behavioral, biological, and environmental factors are the major determinants of health status, (2) promotion of health and prevention of disease are the most effective approaches to health care, (3) the most should be made of what already exists, and (4) barriers to health services need to be eliminated.

NEWS*CAP*

Polio Conqueror Dies

Jonas Salk, the creator of the first effective vaccine against poliomyelitis (infantile paralysis), died on June 23, 1995, in La Jolla, Calif. Early in the 20th century, epidemics of polio began intensifying until the disease came to be considered the scourge of summer. Fearful parents kept their children away from public swimming pools and other crowded places. In 1952, the worst year, about 58,000 cases were reported in the United States alone; more than 3,000 died from the disease.

Salk, who was born on Oct. 28, 1914, in New York City, first conducted research on viruses in the 1930s when he was a medical student at New York University, and in the 1940s he helped develop flu vaccines at the University of Michigan. He began his studies of polio at the University of Pittsburgh, Pa., where in 1947 he had become head of viral research.

March of Dimes Birth Defects Foundation

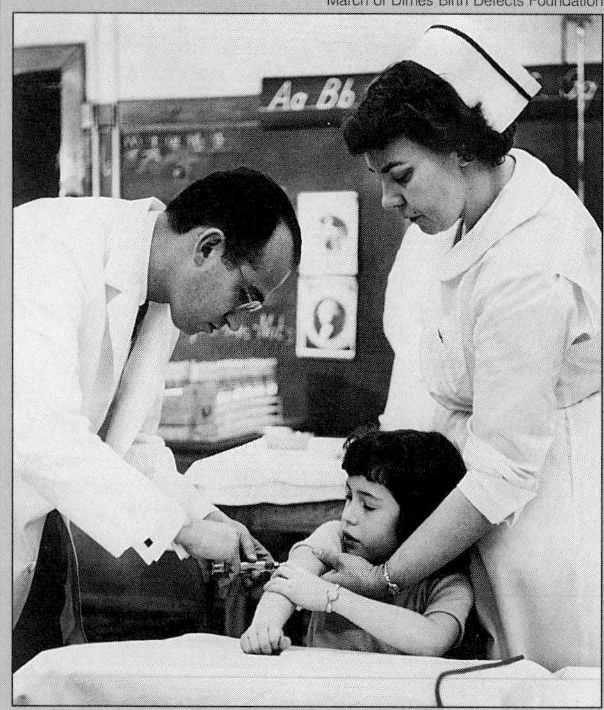

It had been thought that live forms of the poliovirus were necessary for successful immunization, but Salk was convinced that inactivated virus would work. With financial help from the March of Dimes campaign of the National Foundation for Infantile Paralysis, he developed an injectable inactivated vaccine. He conducted the first human trials on former polio patients and on himself and his family, and then in 1954 clinical trials began on 1.8 million U.S. schoolchildren. On April 12, 1955, the announcement was made that the vaccine was effective and safe. A nationwide inoculation campaign began, and by 1962 the number of new cases had dropped to 1,000. Although in the U.S. the Salk vaccine was superseded that year by the live-virus oral vaccine developed by Albert B. Sabin, the former remained in use in many countries. By 1995 polio had been eliminated from the entire Western Hemisphere and was targeted for global eradication.

In 1963 Salk founded what became the Salk Institute for Biological Studies in La Jolla. In the 1980s he began research aimed at developing vaccines for multiple sclerosis and AIDS, and at the time of his death a vaccine to prevent the development of AIDS in HIV-infected persons was being tested in a small clinical trial. Among the many awards Salk received during his career were the French Legion of Honor (1955 and 1976), the Albert Lasker Award (1956), and the Presidential Medal of Freedom (1977).

Urgent needs

Actual strategies for improving health care have yet to be implemented, and adequate funding needs to be found. In early 1995 WHO launched a $13 million appeal for "funds for meeting the urgent health needs of the Palestinian people." The lack of a system for collecting and evaluating health data is something that requires immediate attention by the new leadership. Other needs are:

- to attend to the emergent water crisis
- to coordinate the four existing health care sectors, at least in the short term
- to continue all successful programs, such as those for childhood immunizations, prenatal care, newborn nutrition, and appropriate pediatric rehydration therapy
- to maintain critical primary health care services provided by NGOs
- to make the best use of health care professionals and leaders from the medical community, regardless of their political affiliation (in particular, these should include physicians from the occupied territories who are the most conversant with the problems of their respective communities)
- to ensure that donated medical equipment and health care technology are carefully matched to the technological sophistication of Palestinian society (health authorities should avoid being seduced by complex, expensive, state-of-the-art gadgetry)
- to establish medical education and training at all levels: college, nursing schools, paramedical training programs, medical schools, and postgraduate residency programs (well-trained personnel functioning even in mediocre facilities are likely to provide much better patient care than mediocre personnel in state-of-the-art facilities)
- to establish financial mechanisms (*e.g.,* a banking system and currency) that allow the absorption of development funds and will reduce the fraction of GDP devoted to health care to a sustainable level

When Riyad Zanoun was appointed minister of health services in Gaza and Jericho in 1994, he commented, "Medicine is a humanitarian matter that bridges even enemies." Avoiding a health care disaster in the fledgling Palestinian entity will require humanitarian efforts from all sides. While the above needs are not the only ones, they deserve the highest priority. The future of health care in Gaza depends upon it.

—*Sara M. Roy, Ed.D., and Jay J. Schnitzer, M.D., Ph.D.*

Aid for Rwandans: Report from Goma

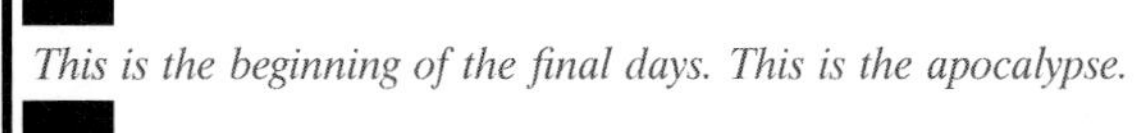

This is the beginning of the final days. This is the apocalypse.

So a resident of Goma, Zaire, described the sudden influx of almost a million Rwandan refugees into his quiet, once prosperous little town. Even in a continent where mass refugee migrations have been startlingly common in the last decade, the desperate flight of hundreds of thousands of Rwandan refugees into Zaire in July 1994 shocked the world.

On the evening of April 6, 1994, the Hutu presidents of Rwanda and Burundi were flying home from a negotiation meeting in Tanzania aimed at reconciling differences with Tutsi foes. The plane that was carrying them was shot down as it approached the airport in Rwanda's capital, Kigali. The following morning, radical elements of the Rwandan military set up roadblocks throughout the capital, captured Hutu and Tutsi politicians who favored reconciliation, and summarily killed them. Fueled by messages broadcast by the Hutu militia's radio station Radiotélévision Libre des Mille Collines, the violence spread to other parts of the country. Groups of Hutu armed with grenades and machetes brutally killed Tutsi. The resulting death toll (April through June) was estimated at between 500,000 and one million.

During those terrible three months, the international community did virtually nothing to stop the systematic genocide of the Tutsi. The well-armed Rwandan Patriotic Front (RPF), comprising Tutsi formerly in exile in Uganda, steadily gained territory and by July 4 was able to capture Rwanda's two main cities, Kigali and Butare. As the RPF advanced, hundreds of thousands of Hutu refugees fled either across the border into Tanzania and Burundi or toward a "safe haven" created by the French military in southwestern Rwanda. The arrival of 280,000 refugees in the Tanzanian district of Benaco and more than 100,000 in northern Burundi in April 1994 was handled relatively well by relief organizations. No one, however, was prepared for what would happen on Rwanda's border with Zaire.

Roots of disaster

The roots of this tragic exodus lie deep in Rwanda's past. Rwanda is a small, densely populated central African nation of nearly eight million people. Its political destiny has been intimately tied to relations between the majority Hutu and minority Tutsi. On the eve of Rwanda's independence from Belgium in 1961, a Hutu-led revolution swept away the power of the Tutsi elite, and the Hutu dominated the government for three decades. During this time the two ethnic groups launched numerous violent attacks against each other. In the early 1990s the well-armed rebel RPF attacked and occupied parts of northeastern Rwanda. Although in the spring of 1994 internationally sponsored negotiations in neighboring Tanzania sought reconciliation—in the form of a revised constitution and a transitional government that would precede democratic elections—those efforts were doomed to failure by events in April.

Exodus

Goma was a small border town at the northern end of Lake Kivu with a population of approximately 15,000 until, on July 14, the first refugees approached on a bridge from the Rwandan town of Gisenyi. Zairean officials initially attempted to stem the flow, but the situation rapidly deteriorated as hundreds of thousands of Hutu surged across the bridge. On several occasions panicking refugees stampeded and crushed countless people to death. Upon arriving in Goma, the refugees camped on traffic circles, occupied schools and

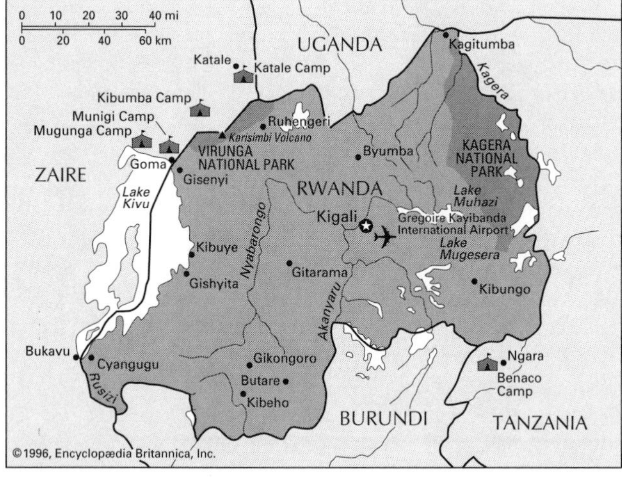

warehouses, and soon took over every open space available. Although Goma is situated beside a large freshwater lake, the water rapidly became contaminated as thousands of people bathed, collected water, and washed clothes along the shore.

Other refugees crossed the border north of Goma and settled in makeshift camps in the Katale and Kibumba areas; both refugee camps lacked clean water. When the Zairean government insisted that refugees be removed from Goma, the Office of the United Nations High Commissioner for Refugees (UNHCR) helped move the Rwandans to Katale, Kibumba, and two other camps, Munigi and Mugunga.

Public health crisis

An influx of that magnitude had never been anticipated; thus, virtually no preparations had been made. Predictably, a public health emergency developed rapidly. The most critical threat to public health was the lack of drinking water, a situation worsened by the rocky, volcanic ground, which made the digging of latrines for sanitation purposes difficult or impossible. One million people living in crowded conditions—with inadequate shelter, relying on contaminated water sources, with virtually no sanitation, in a region where both cholera and dysentery were known to be endemic—was a formula for disaster.

On July 20, less than a week after the arrival of the first refugees, the first case of suspected cholera was identified. A diagnostic laboratory in The Netherlands quickly identified the causative organism as particular strain of cholera that was known to be resistant to readily obtainable antibiotics such as tetracycline and doxycycline. The next day a surveillance system was established whereby all patients with diarrhea or dehydration were recorded by workers at Goma clinics; the numbers were totaled each day and reported at a nightly medical-coordination meeting. More than 3,000 cases were reported the first day; by July 26 the number had increased to approximately 6,000. By this time a number of volunteer relief workers had arrived in the area and joined local Zairean health care workers in battling the epidemic. They labored under extraordinarily difficult conditions, attempting to care for sick and dying refugees in tents, in local government-run clinics, and on open, unshaded ground strewn with thousands of bodies. Initially medical workers lacked even the most basic therapeutic tools—beds, bedpans, buckets, drugs, clean water, oral rehydration salts, intravenous (IV) solutions, and IV needles.

Between July 21 and August 12, 62,000 cases of diarrheal disease were reported by clinics in the area. Most cholera cases were reported in the town of Goma; during the peak of the epidemic, almost 80% of cases were reported from Goma clinics and the Munigi camp (about 10 km [6 mi] from town). The World Health Organization (WHO) suggests that with simple treatment the case fatality rate (CFR) for cholera should be as low as 1%; in most cholera epidemics in refugee camps during the past decade, however, the CFR has been between 2% and 3%. The proportion of cholera patients who died in Goma and its environs during those first few days reached a peak of 22% on July 23. Overall, almost 7% of Rwandan refugees treated in July and August for diarrheal disease (including cholera) died.

International aid in high gear

During the first week after the influx, the international community was almost completely absent. The Dutch branch of the international relief organization Médecins sans Frontières (MSF; Doctors Without Borders) was among the first on the scene; before the Rwandans' arrival the agency already had a team of two doctors and three nurses working in the Goma area. Within 48 hours, however, this small team was joined by other MSF colleagues, who were flown in from adjacent countries in Africa and from Europe. By the second week, other early arrivals included MSF Belgium, Care International, the International Committee of the Red Cross, and the French military medical group Bioforce.

By late July the international response was in high gear. UNHCR sent in an emergency management team that established itself as the lead coordinating body. UNICEF sent in a team to address the plight of more than 10,000 "unaccompanied" children. The World Food Programme began to transport tons of food by truck from neighboring Uganda and by plane from other countries in the region. UNHCR and Oxfam began the challenging task of purifying, transporting, and storing water from Lake Kivu; during the final week of July, they were joined by the U.S. military, which provided expensive purification plants and water tankers. Eventually there were dozens of nongovernmental organizations (NGOs) ranging from the most reputable and experienced, such as MSF, the New York-based International Rescue Committee, and Irish Concern, to small fly-by-night agencies that sent in inexperienced personnel and inappropriate donated supplies. One well-meaning U.S. agency sent a planeload of Gatorade to help treat patients with diarrhea when much cheaper packets of oral rehydration salts would have been far more helpful. In early August there was a risk that too many relief workers—some too inexperienced to contribute effectively—would saturate the area. More than 30 relief agencies and 400 expatriate relief workers were operating in the Goma camps by the second week of August, many of them struggling to find a useful role in the relief effort. The task of coordinating

Mark Peters—Sipa

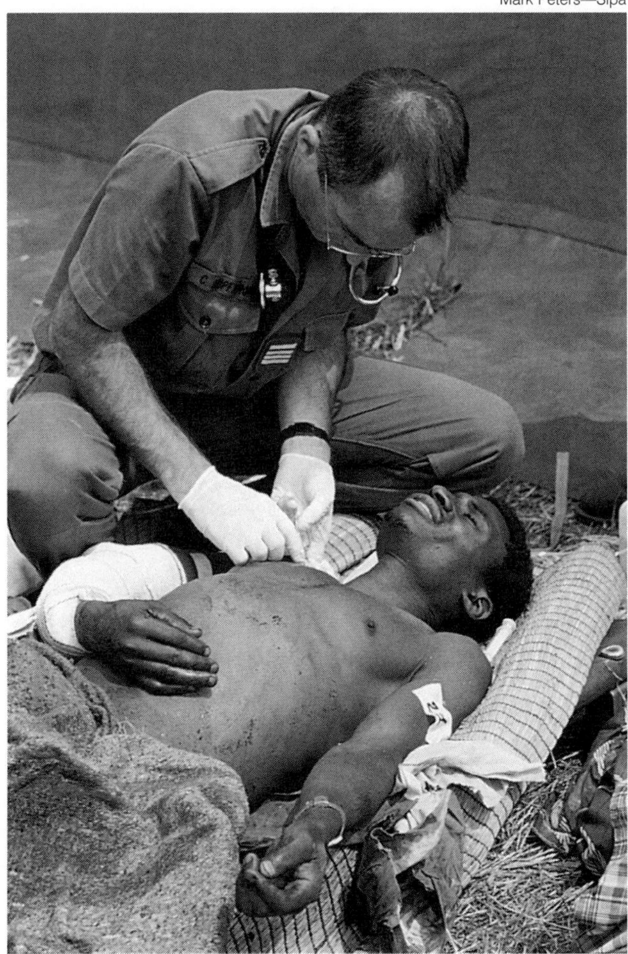

Summer 1994: in the midst of an unprecedented humanitarian crisis, a French doctor attempts to save a wounded victim of the mass exodus of refugees from Rwanda to Zaire.

this vast array of agencies and individuals was a daunting one; the general consensus, however, was that UNHCR performed the job well.

Death toll

By the second week of the cholera epidemic, medical personnel and supplies had begun arriving, and conditions in the health centers improved. Both the French and Israeli military forces established referral hospitals and laboratories in the town, and the U.S. military commenced work on improving the water supply. Consequently, the death figures announced at the evening meetings were more encouraging; by July 26 the CFR for cholera patients was between 3% and 5%.

Although the death rate among patients in clinics was high, even more people died in the camps without ever having gained access to clinics. In contrast to many other emergency situations, the number of deaths among the Goma refugees was distressingly simple to estimate. Because the earth consists of volcanic rock, it was almost impossible to dig graves to bury the dead; therefore, bodies were left by the road and collected by trucks that took them to mass graves for burial. UNHCR calculated the number of bodies collected between July 14 and August 14 at 48,347. Though *numbers* of the dead could be recorded, calculating death *rates* was another matter, owing to the unreliable estimates of the total number of refugees in the Goma area. Nonetheless, using a consensus population figure of 800,000, officials estimated that at least 6% of the refugee population died, equivalent to an average daily crude death rate (CDR) of 20 per 10,000. By comparison, the baseline prewar death rate in Rwanda was approximately 0.6 per 10,000 per day. Surveys conducted in the three main camps during the second week of August (by then, the Munigi camp had been closed) confirmed the high death rate; these surveys estimated that between 7% and 9% of refugees died during that first month, which made this the most lethal refugee crisis in recent history.

Once the cholera outbreak was quelled, an epidemic of dysentery quickly followed. The illness, caused by the organism *Shigella dysenteriae* type 1, produced severe bloody diarrhea, fever, and abdominal cramps. Studies in central Africa had documented the recent and rapid spread of this highly lethal disease, especially among refugees and others displaced by war. Those studies showed that the organism was rapidly becoming resistant to antibiotics commonly used to treat the illness, such as trimethoprim-sulfamethoxazole and nalidixic acid. The use of antibiotics is far more critical in the treatment of dysentery than it is in cholera; therefore, the news from laboratories in Goma that the organism was totally resistant to these drugs was greeted with dismay by medical workers. The only effective drug available was ciprofloxacin, which cost almost $20 per patient for a full-treatment course, a formidable sum in a situation where thousands of people were infected. A committee of infectious disease experts from WHO, UNHCR, the U.S. Agency for International Development, the Centers for Disease Control and Prevention, and the Paris-based aid organization Epicentre was convened to consider treatment options. The committee recommended that dysentery patients be treated with ciprofloxacin only if they were under 5 years of age, older than 55 years, or pregnant or had severe symptoms—the groups at highest risk of death. These guidelines could be implemented when the U.S. military donated one million capsules of the drug. During the week of August 8–14, more than 15,000 cases of dysentery were reported; surveys found that approximately 40% of the refugee deaths were associated with dysentery.

Another condition that emerged in the Goma camps was cerebrospinal meningitis, a communicable disease that spreads rapidly in crowded settings and may cause death in 10–30% of infected patients. An active surveillance system was established to identify and report patients with symptoms associated with the disease, such as fever, severe headache, stiff neck, vomiting, and changes in mental status. A number of patients suspected of having the disease were detected, and samples of their cerebrospinal fluid were taken by spinal tap and sent to local laboratories, where most were confirmed to be infected by *Neisseria meningitidis* group A.

On the basis of experience elsewhere in Africa, relief doctors used a threshold incidence of 15 meningitis cases per 100,000 population in a single week to predict a full-blown epidemic. During the week of August 8–14, the incidence

Mark Peters—Sipa

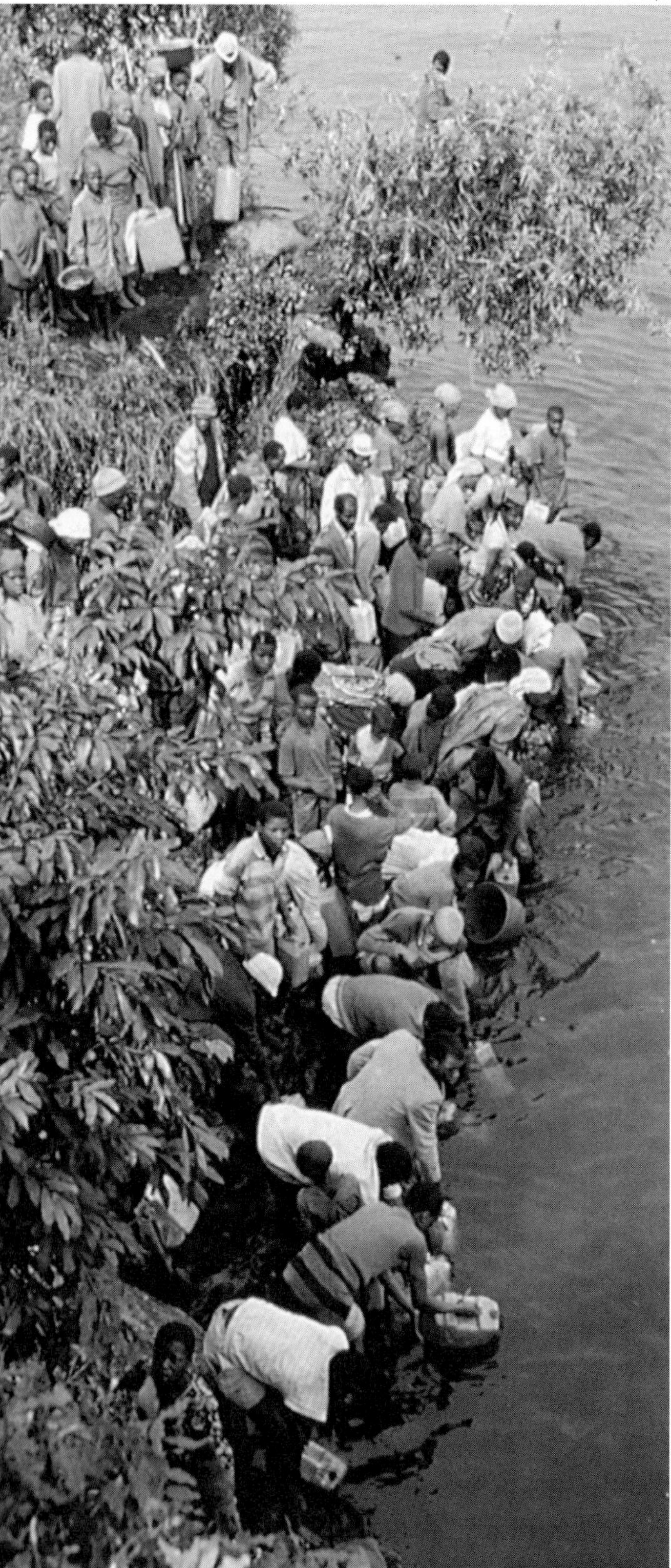

Dead bodies and human waste pollute Goma's Lake Kivu. A public health crisis quickly emerged as millions of Rwandan refugees attempted to subsist without fresh water and other basic necessities of life.

reached 19 per 100,000 in the Kibumba camp. A mass vaccination campaign was then undertaken, which successfully averted a more massive epidemic. After August 20 the number of meningitis cases began to decrease. Other severe illnesses of concern to health workers in Goma included malaria and pneumonia; relatively few deaths, however, were attributed to these diseases during the month or two following the influx.

By the second week of August, the CDR for all diseases had fallen to an average of 5 per 10,000 per day, down from 34 per 10,000 during the week begun July 18. This decline was due to improvements in the quality and quantity of water supplies, improved sanitation, better medical services, and an extension of health services into the community. According to information gathered in surveys, only 50% of refugees who died had ever reached a health clinic, and 77% of all deaths occurred at home. UNHCR was aware of the need to develop outreach services that would enable health workers to identify sick refugees promptly, commence early treatment in their homes, and refer the severely ill to treatment centers.

In addition, a system of health surveillance was developed; diseases of public health importance were recorded on standardized forms and routinely reported to UNHCR, which issued weekly bulletins. These reports of disease trends enabled agencies to focus on the most pressing public health problems. The information system was instrumental in detecting the meningitis epidemic, responding to the high cholera CFR, and identifying dysentery as a major public health threat. Data collected routinely in clinics were complemented by valuable health statistics gathered by the three camp surveys previously mentioned.

Starving women and children

In early August health workers began to see increasing numbers of malnourished children (as indicated by a low weight-for-height index). A sample of 1,984 children under age five in the three camps were weighed and measured; 399 (20%) were acutely malnourished. Normally, fewer than 5% of African children are acutely malnourished. Several reasons for the elevated rate were identified. Children who lived in households where there was no male adult had malnourishment rates that were double those in households where a male resided. This was attributed to the food-distribution system in the camps, which was controlled by a group of former Rwandan government officials and soldiers. Under the system, a single or widowed woman usually did not have the influence or tenacity to obtain a fair share of rations for her children. Female-headed households were also 25% less likely to have stored food or to be protected by adequate water-resistant shelters than were male-headed households. Moreover, single mothers were the least likely to have any money for purchasing food at local markets. The health personnel who weighed and measured the children also found that those who had recently been ill with dysentery were more than four times as likely to be malnourished as those who had not had dysentery.

In response to the high malnutrition rate, UNHCR attempted to reform the food-distribution process. The overall quantity of food arriving in the area was probably adequate by the second week in August; since there had been no registration of refugees, however, the total population size was unknown and, therefore, the average caloric value of an individual ration could not be calculated. While the food rations, consisting of corn (maize) flour, beans, and vegetable oil, were consistent with the traditional Rwandan diet, the refugees lacked foods such as fresh fruit and vegetables containing essential vitamins. The daily food-distribution system remained firmly in the control of former Rwandan political leaders, many of whom had been implicated in the massacre of Tutsi. Aid workers' efforts to implement a registration system that would allow all families equal access to relief items were strongly and often violently resisted by the Rwandan leaders. On several occasions relief personnel were evacuated from the camps when the situation became dangerous.

Those problems highlight the insecure circumstances that frequently surround relief programs. The situation in Goma made a strong case for the deployment of UN security forces to ensure that relief supplies are not systematically diverted from their intended beneficiaries. Experience around the world has demonstrated that distribution systems need to be designed so that relief items are handed directly to family members and so that vulnerable groups in the community receive equitable shares.

The most vulnerable group of Rwandan refugees comprised the estimated 12,000 unaccompanied children. Given the widespread violence in Rwanda prior to the refugee exodus and the high death rate experienced by the refugees in Goma, it is not surprising that many children lost both parents. In addition to true orphans, there were probably many thousands of other children who were separated from their parents during the flight from their homeland. One of the most moving sights in the camps was the daily trickle of helpless young children who drifted alone into clinics and hospitals seeking shelter. Several centers, each caring for between 50 and 1,000 of these children, were hastily established by various NGOs, with UNICEF providing technical support, coordination, and medical supplies.

Despite those efforts, the large numbers of unaccompanied children, the inadequate facilities and unhygienic environment, and the outbreaks of cholera and dysentery led to a very high death rate. During the last two weeks of July, for example, the daily death rate for unaccompanied children ranged between 25 and 60 per 10,000. The care of infants under one year of age was especially challenging since those infants would normally have been somewhat protected from disease through immunity from breast-feeding. During late July the daily death rate among infants in the orphanages was between 1% and 8%. Eventually the standard of care improved, and by the end of August, the death rate had been reduced to fewer than 5 per 10,000 per day.

Hard lessons learned

The most important lesson from this tragedy was that the international community must intervene early in the evolution of civil conflicts such as the one that developed in Rwanda in 1994. The massive population migration was a direct result of the terrible massacres that took place between April and June, during which time the world's leaders merely wrung their hands and took no effective action to stop the slaughter. Another lesson was the lack of global preparedness for emergencies on the scale of Rwanda. Western military forces probably possess the sole capacity to respond to a sudden exodus of a million people in a remote corner of the world like Goma. In this instance, however, even the military was too slow in its response. It took two weeks, for example, before the U.S. military was able to provide an average of even one liter (about 1.1 qt) of potable water per refugee per day (WHO recommends a minimum of 15 liters). Another problem was that military forces need to wait for a political decision by their commander in chief. Though military personnel are needed for providing disaster relief on a large scale, they usually cannot be included in emergency planning because their involvement is often politically driven.

NGOs and individual relief workers learned another important lesson in Goma. Disaster-aid experts now widely acknowledge that there is an urgent need to change the approach of relief agencies from one of benevolent voluntarism (in which the effort, not the outcome, counts) to one of professionalism—in which well-trained personnel provide appropriate interventions. The quantity of goods provided

Peter Turnley—Black Star

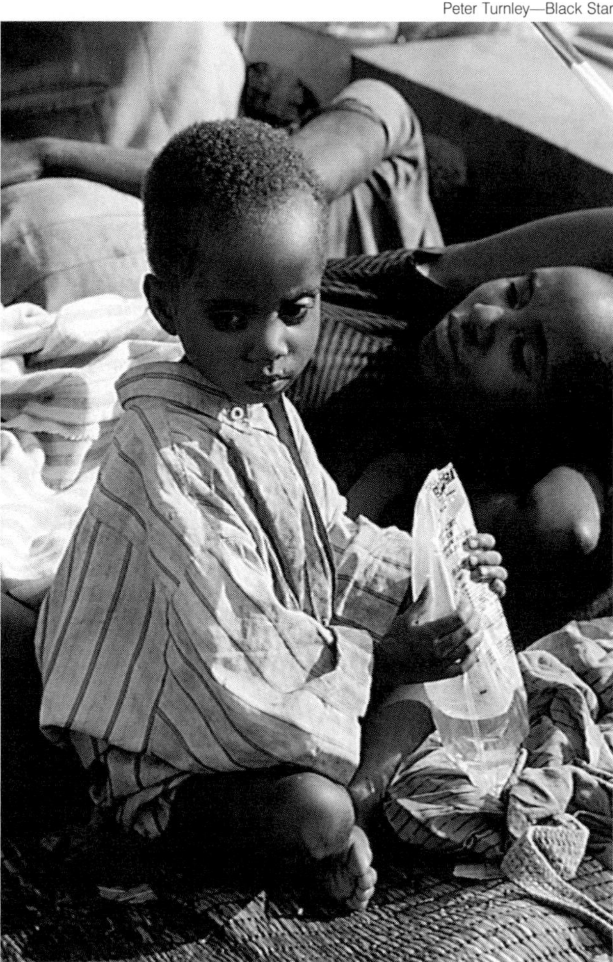

Both cholera and dysentery struck the vast Rwandan refugee populations living in camps near Goma. The young camp resident above receives oral rehydration solution for diarrhea.

Sebastião Salgado

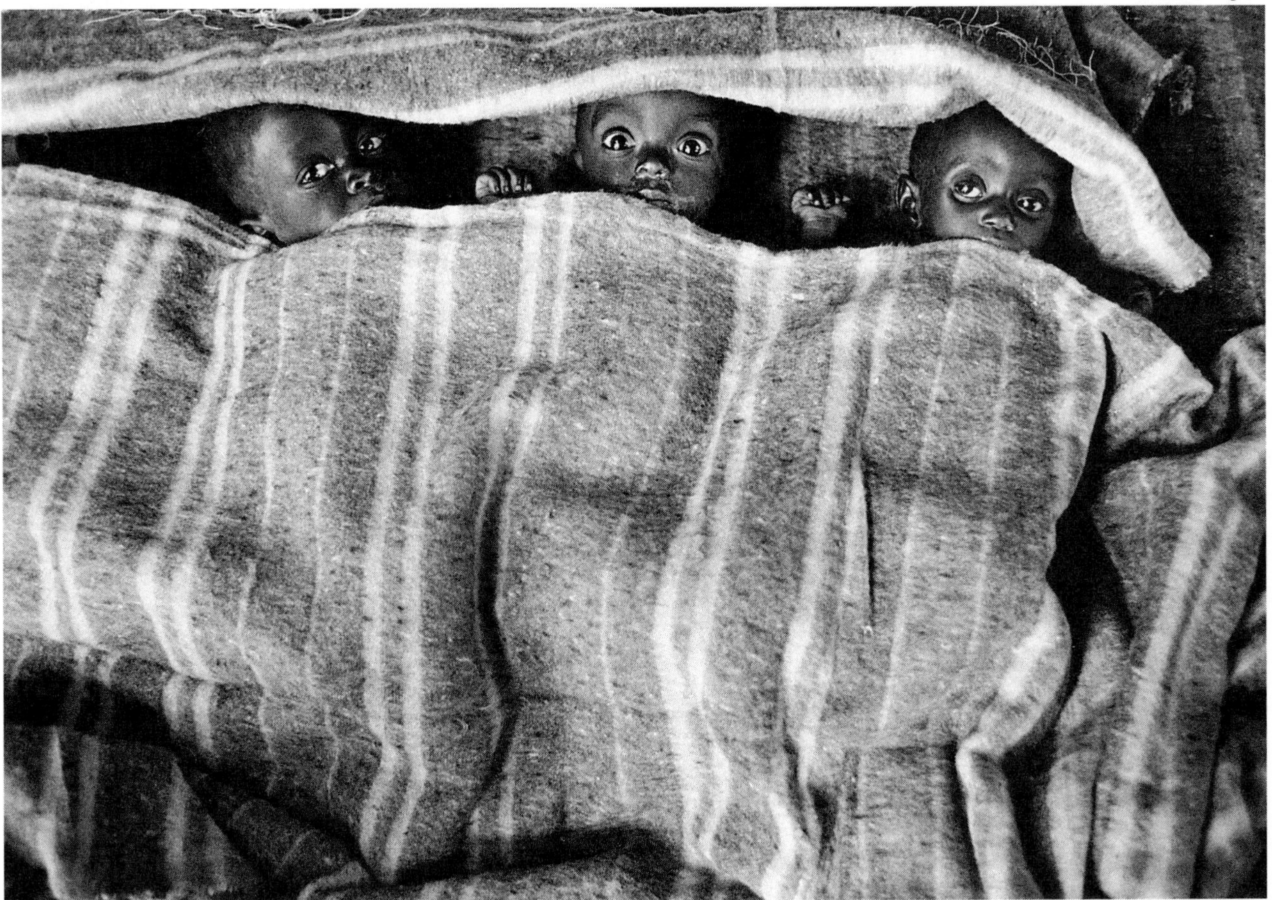

August 1994: orphaned babies in a refugee camp in Zaire, photographed by Sebastião Salgado. The award-winning Brazilian photojournalist has devoted his career to documenting the plight of the world's most disadvantaged peoples.

should not be the sole indicator of success; rather, efforts should focus on providing aid that has a clearly beneficial impact on the human lives saved.

Although the initial death rate from cholera and dysentery in and around Goma, was exceptionally high, it dropped dramatically once an effective program was established during the third week after the influx. The coordinated approach to information gathering was encouraging, as was the use of that information to guide decision making and to concentrate on the most critical priorities.

Aftermath

At the peak of the Goma emergency, on a small field adjacent to the airport, dozens of journalists from the world's leading media organizations pitched tents, set up their high-tech equipment, and beamed graphic pictures and words into the living rooms of the world. The saturated media coverage helped mobilize the global response to the crisis and encouraged a stream of VIP visitors that included the chairman of the U.S. Joint Chiefs of Staff and the vice president's wife. As is often the case in acute humanitarian crises, however, the intense media coverage was short-lived; by the first week of August, the journalists' "tent city" had been abandoned. The loss of publicity inevitably led to a decrease in the availability of public funds for the relief program and a gradual withdrawal of relief agencies. The Israeli, French, and U.S. military withdrew their forces in mid-August. In Goma insecurity in the camps and threats to relief workers added to the momentum to withdraw from the area. In September, 15 of the NGOs signed a joint statement threatening to leave the camps en masse if the UN did not ensure adequate security. The threat was never carried out; however, some agencies, including MSF France, did leave the area. The multilateral relief organizations UNHCR and UNICEF and the NGOs CARE, the International Federation of Red Cross and Red Crescent Societies, MSF Belgium and Holland, Irish Concern, and the International Rescue Committee are among the agencies that continued to provide assistance long after the media spotlight was turned away from Goma.

Nine months after the emergency, the three main Goma camps remained; the health situation had greatly improved, with death rates comparable to prewar rates in Rwanda. Because Hutu leaders continued to threaten violence against people who attempted—or even talked about—returning to their homeland, fewer than 20% of the refugees had returned to Rwanda. The future of more than 12,000 unaccompanied children remained uncertain. While these children were, for the most part, relatively healthy and living in fairly comfortable conditions, fewer than 10% had been reunited with their families. UNICEF and other relief agencies established a tracing service in the belief that most of the children could eventually find a home with relatives.

Inside Rwanda there was a period of relative peace from August 1994; nevertheless, the country had been devastated. The new government, formed by the victorious RPF, had been severely constrained by its lack of funds, a shortage of skilled manpower, and the lack of any genuine reconciliation between the two rival ethnic groups. More than 500,000 Rwandans had been killed between April 1994 and April 1995; at least two million were refugees in neighboring countries, and at least a million additional persons were displaced within the country. At the same time, ethnic tensions were running high in adjacent Burundi, where almost 50,000 Hutu refugees from Rwanda in Burundian camps were fleeing violence and attempting to enter Tanzania.

The horror of the first few weeks of the Goma disaster will remain forever in the memories of those who were there; the most experienced relief workers had never seen a situation so bad. While their immediate picture of Goma was of starving, dehydrated people stricken with and dying of disease, the more overwhelming horror stemmed from an awareness of inhumane behavior that had led to the exodus in the first place. Fortunately, those memories will be tempered by the eventual success of a technically focused and well-coordinated relief effort. What was most troubling, almost a year after the disaster, was that a similar violent confrontation between Hutu and Tutsi was rapidly evolving in Burundi, yet the world's efforts to prevent a catastrophic escalation of violence were as passive and ineffectual as they first had been in Rwanda in 1994.

—*Michael J. Toole, M.D., D.T.M. & H.*

NEWS*CAP*

James Grant: Every Child's Best Friend

On Feb. 16, 1995, Hillary Rodham Clinton announced that the United States would become the 178th country to sign the 1989 Convention on the Rights of the Child. The occasion for the long-overdue announcement was a memorial service for James P. Grant, UNICEF's executive director for 15 years. The 2,500 who filled the New York City cathedral where the special service was held heard the first lady thank Grant for being "our conscience, our example, and our spur." Even after cancer forced him to retire from UNICEF only a week before his death on Jan. 28, 1995, Grant had continued to campaign for the ratification of the convention, a legal guarantee of children's basic rights.

Grant, who considered his work a great privilege, campaigned tirelessly worldwide to bring easy, low-cost solutions to children's health problems. One example of his dedication was that he never traveled without a supply of oral rehydration salts—a simple mixture of baking soda, glucose, and salt that is a cheap and highly effective treatment for diarrhea, a leading child killer. The UN has said that thanks to Grant's leadership, some 25 million young lives were saved. In 1994 Pres. Bill Clinton awarded Grant the Presidential Medal of Freedom.

Grant was born in Beijing (Peking) on May 12, 1922. He earned a degree in economics at the University of California at Berkeley and a law degree from Harvard and served in a number of international service positions before becoming head of UNICEF in 1980. Beginning that year he issued *The State of the World's Children,* an annual report spotlighting the successes and failures in meeting children's needs.

Of the many highlights of his career, perhaps the greatest was in 1990 when he organized the World Summit for Children, the largest gathering of world leaders ever assembled to discuss a single topic. The summit adopted as goals: reducing child mortality, increasing availability of primary education in less developed countries, reducing maternal mortality, cutting malnutrition, and providing clean water to all. More than 100 countries made a commitment to achieving these goals by the year 2000.

Gerard Rancinan—Sygma

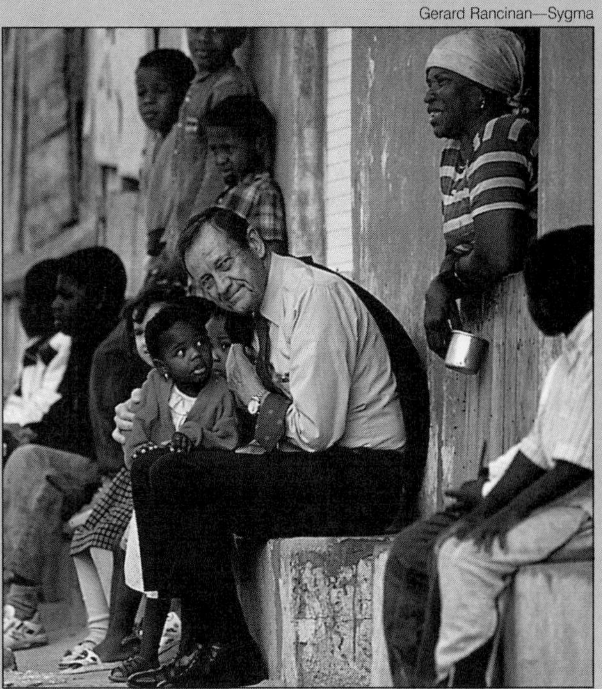

Contributors to the World of Medicine

Stanley J. Bigos, M.D.
New Outlook on Back Pain
Professor, Department of Orthopaedics and Environmental Health, University of Washington, Seattle; Chairman, Panel on Acute Low Back Problems in Adults, Agency for Health Care Policy and Research, U.S. Department of Health and Human Services

Lester E. Block, D.D.S., M.P.H.
U.S. Health Reform: Dead but Not Buried
Director of Graduate Studies, Division of Health Management and Policy, School of Public Health, University of Minnesota, Minneapolis

Ann M. Charbonneau
Oral Health 2000: An American Initiative
Manager of Programs and Development, Oral Health America, America's Fund for Dental Health, Chicago

Gerald W. Chodak, M.D.
Focus on Prostate Cancer
Professor of Surgery, University of Chicago Hospitals; Director, Prostate and Urology Center, Louis A. Weiss Memorial Hospital, Chicago

Susan D. Conley
A Future for Irradiated Food? (coauthor)
Acting Director, Information and Legislative Affairs, Food Safety and Inspection Service, United States Department of Agriculture, Washington, D.C.

Bradley A. Connor, M.D.
Medical Sleuths in Kathmandu (coauthor)
Assistant Attending Physician, The New York Hospital–Cornell University Medical College; Adjunct Faculty, Rockefeller University; Medical Director, Travel Health Services, New York City

John H. Dirckx, M.D.
What's in a Name?
Medical Director, C.H. Gosiger Memorial Health Center, University of Dayton, Ohio

Alexander Dorozynski
Report from France
Science Writer and Book Author, Recloses, France

Alvin N. Eden, M.D.
Fundamentals of Feeding Infants
Chairman and Director, Department of Pediatrics, Wyckoff Heights Medical Center, Brooklyn, N.Y.; Associate Clinical Professor of Pediatrics, The New York Hospital–Cornell Medical Center, New York City

Marc K. Effron, M.D.
Cardiovascular Health Update
Senior Cardiologist and Director of Echocardiography, Scripps Memorial Hospital, La Jolla, Calif.; Assistant Clinical Professor, University of California at San Diego School of Medicine, La Jolla

Weylin G. Eng, O.D.
Contemporary Contacts (coauthor)
Director of Professional Affairs and Associate Clinical Professor, University of California at Berkeley School of Optometry

Daniel L. Engeljohn
A Future for Irradiated Food? (coauthor)
Branch Chief, Processed Products Inspection Division, Institute of Food Technology, Washington, D.C.

H. Perry Fell, Ph.D.
Targeted Cancer Treatment (coauthor)
Director, Molecular Immunology Department, Bristol-Myers Squibb Pharmaceutical Research Institute, Seattle, Wash.

Danielle Foullon
New Drugs Approved by the Food and Drug Administration, January 1994–July 1995
Biotechnology Editor, F-D-C Reports, Inc., Chevy Chase, Md.

Barry A. Franklin, Ph.D.
Rejuvenation Through Exercise (coauthor)
Director, Cardiac Rehabilitation and Exercise Laboratories, William Beaumont Hospital, Royal Oak, Mich.; Professor of Physiology, Wayne State University School of Medicine, Detroit, Mich.

George A. Freedman, D.D.S.
Technology for Teeth
Dentist in Private Practice, Markham, Ont.; Adjunct Associate Professor, Case Western Reserve University School of Dentistry, Cleveland, Ohio; Past President, American Academy of Cosmetic Dentistry

Andrew Friede, M.D., M.P.H.
Medical Informatics (coauthor)
Chief, Public Health Information Systems Branch, Information Resources Management Office, Centers for Disease Control and Prevention, Atlanta, Ga. (article was not written as part of official duties and does not necessarily represent the views of the Department of Health and Human Services)

George A. Gellert, M.D., M.P.H., M.P.A.
Thinking Globally
Director, Medical Programs, Epidemiology and Public Health, Project HOPE, Millwood, Va.; Adjunct Associate Professor, George Washington University School of Medicine and Health Sciences, Washington, D.C.

Gareth M. Green, M.D.
Service and Sickness: Persian Gulf Puzzle
Professor of Environmental Health, Associate Dean for Professional Education, and Director, Master of Public Health Program, Harvard School of Public Health, Boston

Daniel R. Kuritzkes, M.D.
AIDS Update
Assistant Professor of Medicine, Microbiology, and Immunology, University of Colorado Health Sciences Center, Denver

John La Puma, M.D.
Managed Care: Raising New Issues
Internist in Private Practice, Elk Grove, Ill.; Clinical Associate Professor of Medicine, Department of Medicine, University of Chicago Pritzker School of Medicine

Stephen Lock, M.D.
Bedside Reading: An Opus from Oxford
Research Fellow, The Wellcome Institute for the History of Medicine, London

Charles-Gene McDaniel, M.S.J.
NewsCaps
Head, Faculty of Journalism and Communication Studies, Roosevelt University, Chicago

Beverly Merz
Women's Health Update (coauthor)
Editor, *Harvard Women's Health Watch,* Boston

Mark Messina, Ph.D.
Vegetables: Rating the Healthiest (coauthor)
Nutrition Consultant, Port Townsend, Wash.; formerly a Program Director, National Cancer Institute, National Institutes of Health, Bethesda, Md.

Virginia Kisch Messina, M.P.H., R.D.
Vegetables: Rating the Healthiest (coauthor)
Nutrition Consultant, Port Townsend, Wash.; Coauthor, *The No Cholesterol Vegetarian Barbecue Cookbook*

Laura J. Miller, M.D.
Birth and the Blues
Assistant Professor, Department of Psychiatry, University of Illinois at Chicago

J. Ian Morrison, Ph.D.
The Changing World of Medicine and Health
President, Institute for the Future, Menlo Park, Calif.

Frances Munnings
Rejuvenation Through Exercise (coauthor)
Freelance Writer, Minneapolis, Minn.

Thomas H. Murray, Ph.D.
Aid-in-Dying: Society's Dilemma
Professor and Director, Center for Biomedical Ethics, Case Western Reserve University, Cleveland, Ohio

Josephine E. Newell, M.D.
Commemorating the Country Doctor
Retired Physician, Raleigh, N.C.; Former President, North Carolina Medical Society; Founder, The Country Doctor Museum, Bailey, N.C.

Dale Nordenberg, M.D.
Medical Informatics (coauthor)
Assistant Professor, Department of Pediatrics, Emory University School of Medicine; Director, Office of Medical Informatics, Egleston Children's Hospital at Emory University, Atlanta, Ga.

Richard M. Restak, M.D.
It's a Dog's Job
Neurologist in Private Practice; Associate Clinical Professor of Neurology, Georgetown University School of Medicine, Washington, D.C.

Sara M. Roy, Ed.D.
Gaza Strip: Health Care Challenges (coauthor)
Research Scholar, Center for Middle Eastern Studies, Harvard University, Cambridge, Mass.

Jay J. Schnitzer, M.D., Ph.D.
Gaza Strip: Health Care Challenges (coauthor)
Assistant Surgeon, Massachusetts General Hospital; Assistant Professor of Surgery, Harvard Medical School, Boston

Arnold Schussheim, M.D.
Children's Care Comes Home (coauthor)
Pediatrician and Pediatric Gastroenterologist in Private Practice, Bayside, N.Y.; Associate Professor of Pediatrics, Albert Einstein College of Medicine, New York City

Lynn Gardiner Seim, R.N., M.S.N.
Children's Care Comes Home (coauthor)
National Director, Pediatric Clinical Practice, Olsten Kimberly QualityCare, Melville, N.Y.

David R. Shlim, M.D.
Medical Sleuths in Kathmandu (coauthor)
Medical Director, the Canadian International Water and Energy Consultants Clinic, Kathmandu, Nepal; Medical Director of the Himalayan Rescue Association, Nepal; Chairman, Medicine for Adventure Travel, Jackson Hole, Wyo.

Clay B. Siegall, Ph.D.
Targeted Cancer Treatment (coauthor)
Principal Scientist, Molecular Immunology Department, Bristol-Myers Squibb Pharmaceutical Research Institute, Seattle, Wash.

Dennis L. Stevens, Ph.D., M.D.
Strep: Growing Deadlier?
Chief, Infectious Diseases Section, Veterans Affairs Medical Center, Boise, Idaho; Professor of Medicine, University of Washington School of Medicine, Seattle

Ashley Melton Stinson
Women's Health Update (coauthor)
Associate Editor, *Harvard Women's Health Watch,* Boston

Richard Stone
Hormones, Hormones Everywhere
Staff Reporter, *Science* magazine, Washington, D.C.

Michael J. Toole, M.D., D.T.M. & H.
Aid for Rwandans: Report from Goma
Medical Epidemiologist, Macfarlane Burnet Centre for Medical Research, Melbourne, Australia

Jeff Wallenfeldt
NewsCaps
Copy Editor, Encyclopædia Britannica, Chicago

Caroline Wang, Dr.P.H.
Injury-Prevention Messages: View from the Other Side
Assistant Professor, School of Public Health, University of Michigan, Ann Arbor

Barbara Whitney
NewsCaps
Copy Supervisor, Encyclopædia Britannica, Chicago

Myron Winick, M.D.
Coffee: Filtering Out the Facts
Emeritus R.R. Williams Professor of Nutrition, Columbia University College of Physicians and Surgeons, New York City

Michael D. Yapko, Ph.D.
Hypnosis: Treatment in a Trance
Clinical Psychologist in Private Practice; Director, The Milton H. Erikson Institute of San Diego, Solana Beach, Calif.

Robert C. Yeager, M.J.
Contemporary Contacts (coauthor)
Senior Editor, Chevron Corp., San Francisco; Book Author

Zae Zatoon, Ph.D.
Eating Disorders Update
Psychotherapist in Private Practice, Kailua-Kona, Hawaii; Member, National Association of Anorexia Nervosa and Associated Disorders and National Eating Disorders Organization

Glossary

A

abortifacient: an agent such as a drug that induces termination of a pregnancy

adenoma: a non-life-threatening tumor of a glandular structure or of glandular origin

adrenal medulla: the inner or deepest part of the adrenal gland (as opposed to the adrenal cortex, or outer covering of the gland); produces epinephrine, which is the body's principal blood-pressure-raising hormone

adrenaline: *see* epinephrine

aerobic activity: any sustained, moderately strenuous effort carried on at an intensity level just high enough that the heart and lungs can keep pace with the muscles' increased need for oxygen

aerobic capacity: the maximum amount of oxygen one's respiratory system can deliver to the muscles during the most strenuous activity one is able to do

afferent: conveying nervous impulses inward toward a nerve center such as the brain or spinal cord

agonist *1:* a chemical substance capable of combining with a receptor on a cell and initiating a reaction or activity; *2:* a muscle that on contracting is automatically checked and controlled by the opposing simultaneous contraction of another muscle; *cf.,* antagonist

allele: any of the different forms of a gene that can occur at a given locus, or site, on a chromosome

amenorrhea: the abnormal absence or suppression of the menstrual flow

anaerobic activity: any sudden vigorous action (as sprinting) involving an intense burst of muscle activity that outstrips the ability of the heart and lungs to supply the oxygen needed to perform the action

analgesic: an agent for producing insensibility to pain without loss of consciousness

androgen: a male sex hormone

angina pectoris: a disease marked by brief, sudden attacks of chest pain precipitated by a deficient supply of oxygen to the heart muscles

angioplasty: a procedure used to enlarge the lumen (inner hollow portion) of a partly closed artery by passing a catheter through the narrowed area, where the tip of a balloon device is inflated

animal model: an animal similar to humans in its anatomy, physiology, or response to a pathogen and used in medical research to obtain results that can be applied in human medicine

antagonist *1:* a chemical that acts within the body to reduce the normal activity of another chemical substance; *2:* a muscle that contracts with and limits the action of another muscle with which it is paired; *cf.,* agonist

anthrax: an infectious disease of warm-blooded animals caused by a spore-forming bacterium, transmissible to humans especially by the handling of infected products; characterized by external ulcerated masses of tissue or by lesions in the lungs

antibody: any of a large number of proteins that are produced by specialized cells to act against an antigen (as a toxin or enzyme) in an immune response

anticonvulsant: a drug used to control or prevent convulsions

antigen: any substance (as a toxin or enzyme) capable of stimulating an immune response

antioxidant: a substance that opposes combination with oxygen or inhibits reactions promoted by oxygen or peroxides

aphasia: a loss or impairment of the power to use or comprehend words, usually resulting from a brain lesion

apoptosis: the process of programmed cell death

arthroscopy: a visual examination of the interior of a joint (as a knee) using a specialized instrument (arthroscope)

assay: a detailed analysis (as of a drug) to determine the presence, absence, or quantity of certain components or characteristics

astigmatism: a defect of vision due to irregular curvature of the cornea and characterized by blurring and distortion

atherosclerosis: a condition characterized by fatty deposits in the inner layer of the arteries and an increase in arterial fibrous tissue

atrophy: a decrease in size or wasting away of a body part or tissue; also, arrested development or loss of a part or organ incidental to the normal development or life of an animal or plant

aura: a subjective sensation, such as voices, colored lights, or numbness, experienced before an attack of a medical disorder (as a migraine headache)

autologous bone marrow transplantation: a procedure in which bone marrow is removed from a patient, frozen, stored, and then reimplanted after the patient has received treatment

autonomic nervous system: a part of the vertebrate nervous system that activates muscle and glandular tissues and governs involuntary actions; made up of the sympathetic and parasympathetic nervous systems

Gopal Murti—Phototake

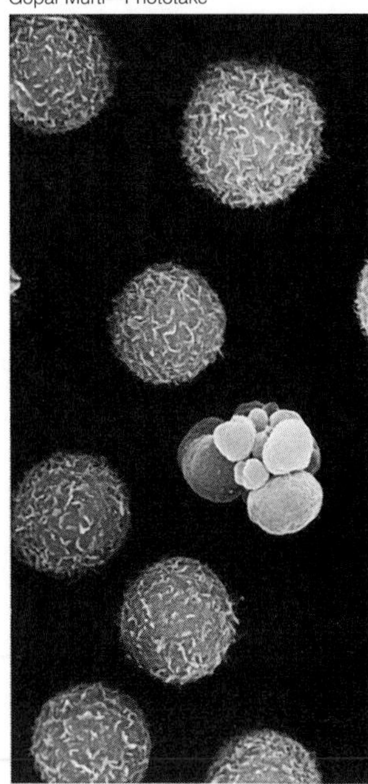

apoptosis

B

bacteremia: transient presence of bacteria in the blood

benign: of a mild type or character, not threatening to health or life; also, nonmalignant

beta-carotene: a compound found in plant foods, mainly dark green and deep yellow vegetables and fruits such as sweet potatoes, spinach, and cantaloupe; in the body beta-carotene is converted into vitamin A (retinol), an essential vitamin that aids in the prevention of night blindness and promotes healthy hair, teeth, gums, bones, skin, and mucous membranes

biopsy: the removal and examination of tissues, cells, or fluids from the living body

blood-brain barrier: a barrier created by the modification of capillaries that prevents many substances from leaving the blood and crossing the capillary walls into the brain tissues

blood poisoning: an invasion of the bloodstream by virulent microorganisms from a focus of infection; accompanied by chills, fever, and exhaustion and often by the formation of secondary abscesses in various organs; *also called* septicemia

bone marrow: a soft, highly vascular connective tissue that occupies the cavities of most bones and occurs in two forms: whitish or yellowish marrow made up mostly of fat cells and reddish marrow containing little fat and producing red blood cells

botulin: a toxin that is the by-product of a spore-forming bacterium and directly causes acute food poisoning (botulism) characterized by muscle weakness and paralysis, disturbances of vision, swallowing, and speech, and a high mortality rate

Illustration by Jody Williams

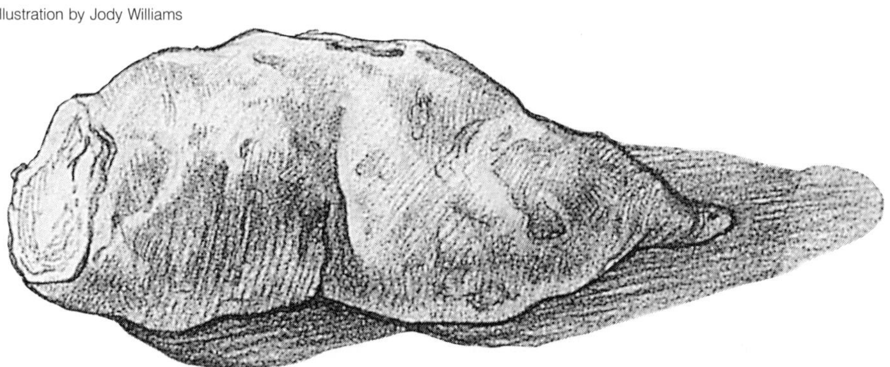

beta-carotene

brain death: the final cessation of activity in the central nervous system

brain stem: the part of the brain that connects the spinal cord with the forebrain and cerebrum

bronchopulmonary dysplasia: the abnormal growth or development of the bronchial tubes

calorie: a unit of measurement expressing the heat-producing or energy-producing value of food when oxidized in the body; *also called* kilocalorie

carbohydrate: any of various compounds of carbon, hydrogen, and oxygen (as sugars, starches, and celluloses), most of which are formed by green plants and constitute a major class of foods

carcinogen: an agent producing or inciting cancer

carcinoma: a tumor arising from epithelial tissue

caries: the progressive destruction of bone or tooth, especially, tooth decay

carotenoid: any of various pigments, usually yellow to red, found widely in plants and animals

cataract: a clouding of the lens of the eye or its surrounding transparent membrane that obstructs the passage of light and may eventually result in blindness

catatonia: a state of marked psychomotor disturbance that may involve stupor, inability to speak, rigidity, purposeless excitement, and inappropriate or bizarre posturing; occurs especially in schizophrenia

central nervous system (CNS): the part of the nervous system that consists of the brain and spinal cord, to which sensory impulses are transmitted and from which motor impulses pass out; coordinates the activity of the entire nervous system

cerebral cortex: the surface layer of gray matter of the cerebrum; functions chiefly in coordination of higher nervous activity

chemotherapy: the utilization of chemical agents in the treatment of disease; often associated with cancer treatment

cholesterol: a fatlike substance manufactured by animal cells, present in body cells and fluids, important in normal physiological processes, and implicated as a factor in atherosclerosis

cingulate gyrus: one of the middle convoluted ridges of each cerebral hemisphere that partly surrounds the band of fibers uniting the hemispheres of the brain

cleft lip: a deformity existing from birth in which the upper lip is split

cleft palate: a fissure of the roof of the mouth, existing from birth and produced by a failure of the two sections of the jaw to unite during embryonic development; often associated with cleft lip

clinical trial: a test of the quality, value, or usefulness of a treatment or procedure involving or depending upon direct observation of a living patient

CNS: *see* central nervous system

computed tomography (CT): an imaging technique in which a three-dimensional picture of a body structure is constructed by a computer from a series of cross-sectional views; *also called* computerized tomography

control group: subjects in a clinical trial or an experiment who are treated or followed as a comparison group in whom an event or disease has not occurred or who do not receive any treatment during the investigation

Alexander Tsiaras—Science Source/Photo Researchers

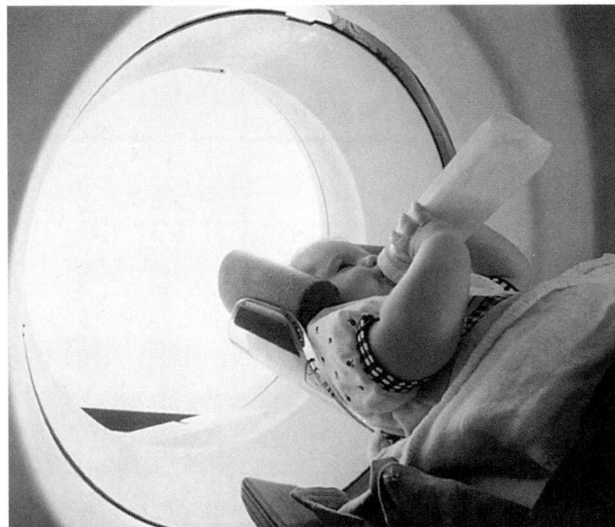

computed tomography

congestive heart failure: a condition in which the heart is unable to maintain adequate circulation of blood in the tissues or to pump out the blood returned to it by the venous circulation

conjunctivitis: inflammation of the mucous membrane that lines the inner surface of the eyelids and continues over the front of the eyeball

contracture: a permanent shortening (as of muscle, tendon, or scar tissue) producing deformity or distortion

contraindication: something (as a symptom or condition) that makes a particular treatment or procedure inadvisable

corticosteroid: any of various chemical compounds secreted by the outer layer, or cortex, of the adrenal glands

cot death: *see* sudden infant death syndrome

crib death: *see* sudden infant death syndrome

cryoprobe: a blunt chilled instrument used to freeze tissue in cryosurgery

cryosurgery: surgery in which the tissue to be treated or operated on is frozen, usually with liquid nitrogen

CT: *see* computed tomography

cyanotic heart disease: any of several heart disorders in which blood is insufficiently oxygenated; manifestations include a bluish or purplish discoloration of the skin

cystic fibrosis: a common hereditary disease that usually appears in early childhood and involves a generalized disorder of exocrine glands; manifestations include excess salt loss in sweat and digestive and respiratory problems

cytokine: any of a class of substances involved in the regulation of the immune system and secreted by immune system cells

D

delusion: an abnormal mental state characterized by a false belief regarding the self or persons or objects outside the self, which persists despite actuality; occurs in some psychotic states

dendrite: any of the branching outgrowths extending from a nerve cell that conduct nerve impulses toward the body of the cell

depolarize: to subject a cell to a loss of the difference in charge between the inside and outside of the plasma membrane due to a change in the permeability of the membrane and the migration of sodium to the interior of the cell

double-blind: an experimental procedure in which neither the subjects nor the researchers know the makeup of the test and control groups during the course of the study

E

echocardiography: a noninvasive and painless diagnostic procedure for making a record of the cardiac structure and functioning by means of high-frequency sound waves reflected back from the heart

ectopic pregnancy: gestation elsewhere than in the uterus (as in a fallopian tube)

eczema: an inflammatory condition of the skin, characterized by redness, itching, and oozing blisters that become scaly, crusted, or hardened

electrophysiology: the electrical phenomena associated with bodily functions; also, the branch of study that deals with these phenomena

Hank Morgan—Rainbow

cryoprobe

encode: in genetics, to dictate the genetic code for specific amino acids, which are the building blocks of protein

endogenous: related to or produced by metabolic synthesis in the body; also, caused by factors within the body or mind or arising from internal structural or functional causes

endometriosis: a condition characterized by the presence of uterine-lining tissue in places in the abdominal cavity where it is not normally found

endorphin: any of a group of proteins with potent analgesic (pain-blocking) properties that occur naturally in the brain

endoscopy: a procedure performed by means of a flexible tube for visualizing the interior of a hollow organ or structure (as of the gastrointestinal or urinary tract)

epidemic: an outbreak of disease affecting many individuals within a population, community, or region at the same time

epidemiology: a branch of medical science that deals with the incidence, distribution, and control of disease in a population

epinephrine: a colorless crystalline sympathetic-nervous-system-stimulating hormone that is secreted by the inner portion of the adrenal gland and functions as the principal blood-pressure raising hormone; *also called* adrenaline

epizootic: an outbreak of disease affecting many animals of one kind at the same time

erythrocyte: any of the nonnucleated (*i.e.,* lacking a nucleus) hemoglobin-containing cells of human blood that transport oxygen to the tissues and are responsible for the red color of human blood; *also called* red blood cell

estradiol: an estrogenic hormone, usually made synthetically, a form of which is often used in the treatment of menopausal symptoms

estrogen: a substance (as a sex hormone) that stimulates the development of female secondary sex characteristics and tends to promote sexual excitement during ovulation

euthanasia: the act or practice of killing hopelessly sick or injured individuals in a relatively painless way for reasons of mercy or allowing a hopelessly ill patient to die by taking less-than-complete measures to prolong life

exogenous: introduced from or produced outside the organism or system

expression: something that manifests, represents, reflects, embodies, or symbolizes something else; in genetics, the detectable effect of a gene

exudate: the material composed of serum, fibrin, and white blood cells that escapes from blood vessels into a superficial lesion or area of inflammation

F

fibrin: a white insoluble protein formed in the clotting of blood

farsightedness: *see* hyperopia

free radical: an especially reactive atom or group of atoms that has one or more unpaired electrons

G

G protein: any of many natural substances found at a cell's surface that function as "on-off" switches for cells; also, the specialized proteins that help cells convert signals from the environment and within the body into messages that direct fundamental bodily processes

gastroenteritis: inflammation of the lining of the stomach and the intestines

generic name: a name not protected by trademark

Swapan Parekh—Black Star

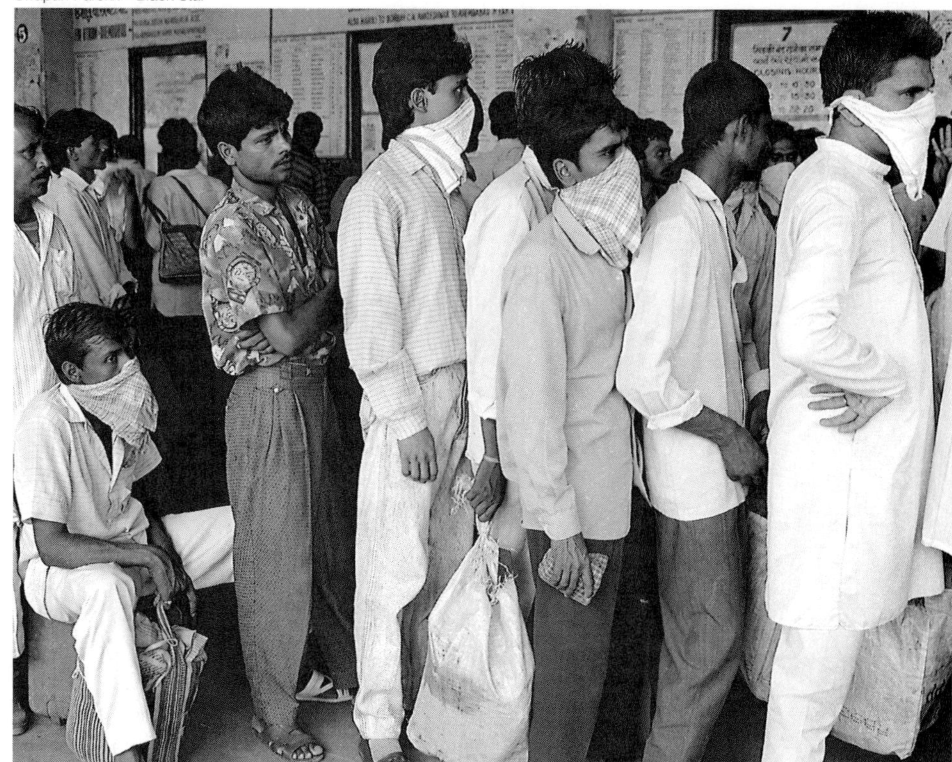

epidemic

Kevin Horan

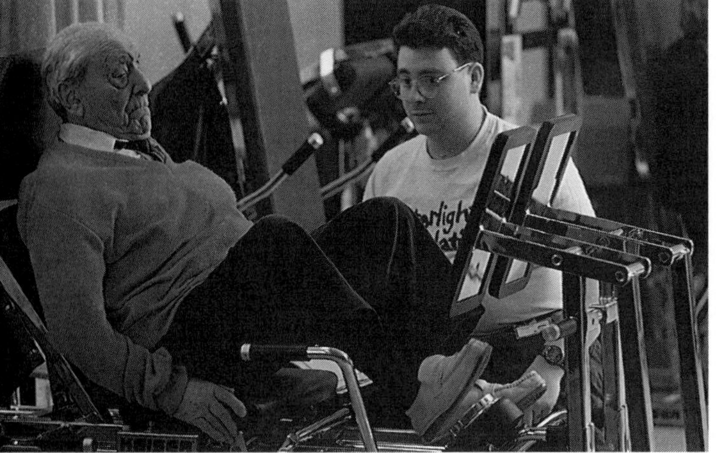

geriatrics

genome: the entire genetic complement of a given species

geriatrics: a branch of medicine that deals with the problems and diseases of old age and aging people

gerontology: the specific study of aging and its phenomena

gingivitis: an inflammation of the gums

glutamate: a major neuro-transmitter in the central nervous system

graft: to surgically transplant living tissue from one site to another; also, the trans-planted tissue itself

H

half-life: the time required for the activity of a substance (as a radioactive agent) to reduce to half its original level; in pharmacol-ogy, the length of time taken by the body to eliminate half the quantity of a drug in the bloodstream

hallucination: the perception of something (as a visual im-age or a sensation of sound) with no external cause, usu-ally arising from a disorder of the nervous system or in response to drugs or other stimulants

health maintenance organi-zation (HMO): an institution or group that provides comprehensive health care to voluntarily enrolled individuals and families in a particular geographic area; served by physicians with limited referral to outside specialists; financed through fixed periodic payments by enrollees

hematology: a branch of biology that deals with the blood and blood-forming organs

hemorrhage: a copious discharge of blood from the blood vessels that results in heavy or uncontrollable bleeding

histology: a branch of the study of anatomical science that deals with the minute structure of animal and plant tissues as discernible by means of microscopic examination

HMO: *see* health mainte-nance organization

hospitalism: the factors and influences that adversely affect the mental or physical health of hospitalized persons; also, the deleterious mental and physical effects on infants and children resulting from their living in institutions without the ben-efit of a home environment and parents

Huntington's disease: a hereditary degenerative nervous system disorder characterized by involuntary, uncontrollable, purposeless movements of body and face and marked incoordination of limbs; *also called* Hunt-ington's chorea

hyperopia: a condition in which visual images come to a focus behind the retina of the eye, which results in better vision for distant than for near objects; *also called* farsightedness

I

immunocompetent: possess-ing the capacity for a normal immune response

immunocompromised: having the immune system impaired or weakened (as by drugs or illness)

informed consent: consent to surgery or to participation in a medical experiment by a patient or subject after learning about the potential risks and benefits of the procedure

innervate: to arouse or stim-ulate (a nerve or an organ) to activity

inoculate: to introduce (usu-ally by injection) a harmless quantity of a causative agent of disease into the body in order to build resistance or prevent disease, as in vac-cination; also, to introduce an organism into a culture medium in order to study, reproduce, or grow the organism

insoluble fiber: an essentially indigestible plant material (as bran) that is found mostly in whole grains and is incapable of being dissolved in liquid; tends to promote bowel regularity; has been shown to protect against colon or rectal cancer; *cf.,* soluble fiber

intervention: the act of in-terfering with a condition to modify it or with a disease process to change its course or progress

intravenous: situated within, performed within, occurring within, or administered via a vein

invasive: involving entry into the living body, especially healthy tissue; also, tending to spread within the body

iron-deficiency anemia: a blood condition caused by a lack of iron and character-ized by red blood cells that are low in hemoglobin and tend to be abnormally small

F.M. Kearney—Impact Visuals

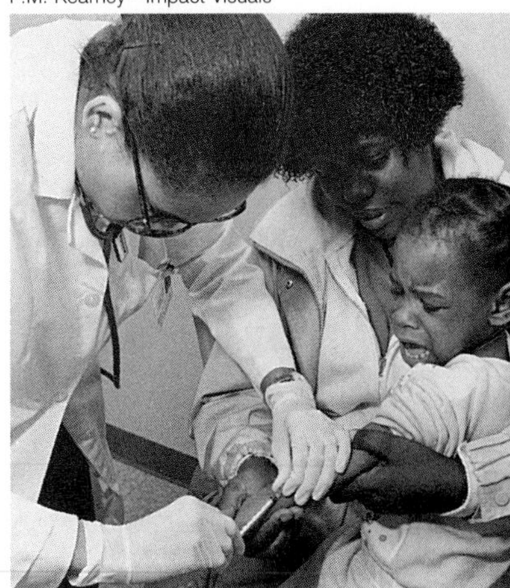

inoculate

K

kilocalorie: *see* calorie

L

Lamaze method: an approach to childbirth that involves psychological and physical preparation by the mother (and often the father) in order to suppress pain and facilitate delivery without drugs; named for the French obstetrician Fernand Lamaze

Joseph Nettis—Stock, Boston

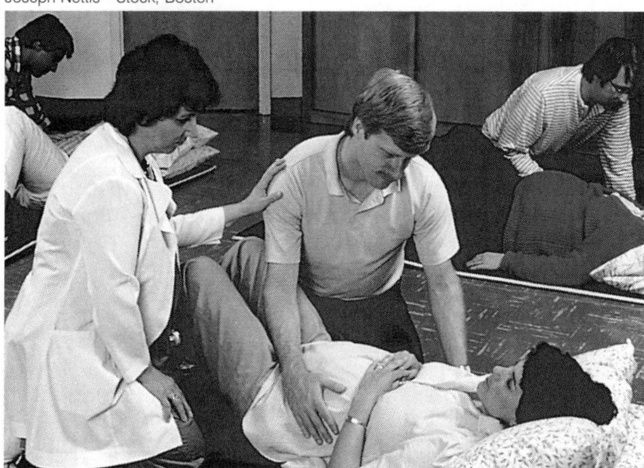

Lamaze method

leishmaniasis: an infection caused by parasites of the genus *Leishmania,* which are usually transmitted by insects; may be a severe infectious disease (visceral leishmaniasis) marked by fever, progressive anemia, and enlargement of the spleen and liver or a skin disease (cutaneous leishmaniasis) marked by ulcerated lesions

leukemia: an acute or chronic cancer of the blood-forming organs characterized by abnormal proliferation and development of white blood cells in the circulating blood and the bone marrow; classified by cell type

leukocyte: any of several kinds of white or colorless cells of human blood that function in body defense and repair; *also called* white blood cell

limbic system: a group of nerve centers below the cerebral cortex of the brain that are concerned especially with emotion and motivation

longevity: long life

lumbar puncture: the introduction of a hollow needle into the fluid-filled area of the spinal column in the lumbar region of the spine either to withdraw cerebrospinal fluid for diagnostic purposes or to inject anesthetic drugs; *also called* spinal tap

lymphocyte: any of the colorless weakly motile cells produced in lymph tissue that are the cellular mediators of the immune system and constitute one-fifth to one-third of the white blood cells of human blood

lymphoma: a usually cancerous tumor of the lymph tissue

M

macrophage: an immune-system cell that engulfs foreign material and consumes debris and foreign bodies and that functions in the protection of the body against infection and destructive substances

magnetic resonance imaging (MRI): a noninvasive diagnostic technique that produces computerized images of internal body tissues and is based on the response to a magnetic field induced by the application of radio waves

malignant: tending to produce death or deterioration by infiltration into tissue; having an unfavorable prognosis; cancerous

mediator: an agent (as an enzyme or hormone) that moderates or influences a chemical or biological process

menarche: the beginning of the menstrual function, usually marked by a woman's first menstrual period

meningitis: inflammation of any of the three membranes that envelop the brain and spinal cord

meningomyelocele: a birth defect characterized by protrusion of the spinal cord and its enveloping membranes through an abnormal opening in the spinal column

meta-analysis: a method of combining data from many experiments or studies to obtain statistical results that represent a synthesis of all data on a specific scientific question

metastasis: the spread or transfer of a disease (as cancer) from an original site to another part of the body (as in the spread of malignant cells), involving development of a similar lesion in the new location

mitosis: a process that takes place in the nucleus of a dividing cell and results in the formation of two new nuclei, each having the same number of chromosomes as were contained in the parent nucleus

monoclonal antibody: a highly specific antibody targeted against a single antigen (as a toxin or an enzyme); produced in great quantity in the laboratory by artificially contrived hybrid cells made by fusing normal antibody-producing cells with cancer cells

morbidity: a disease state or symptom; also, the rate of illness in a specific community or group

morphine: a bitter crystalline substance that is derived from the opium poppy and is used in the form of soluble salt for sedation or for treatment of severe pain; may produce tolerance

David Spector, M.D.—Peter Arnold, Inc.

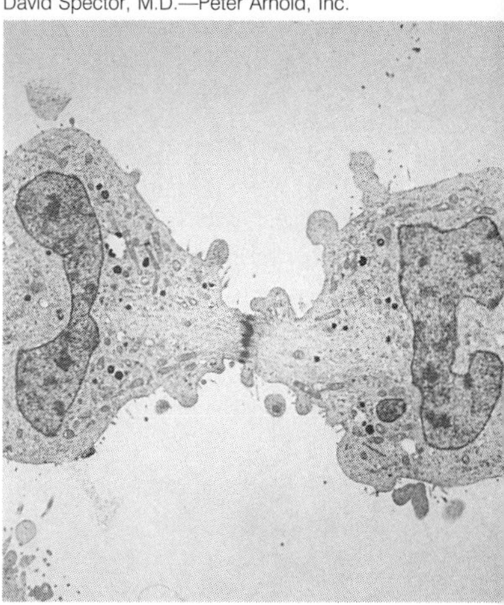

mitosis

morphology: a branch of biology that deals with the form and structure of organs apart from their function

MRI: *see* magnetic resonance imaging

myopia: a condition in which visual images come to a focus in front of the retina of the eye owing to a defect in the eye's refraction or an abnormality in the length of the eyeball, resulting in sharper vision for near than for far objects; *also called* nearsightedness

myositis: a muscular discomfort or pain from infection or an unknown cause

N

nearsightedness: *see* myopia

neonatology: a branch of medicine concerned with the care, development, and diseases of newborn infants

neoplasm: a new growth of tissue serving no function in the maintenance of an organism's processes

neuron: the basic cell of the nervous system, the function of which is to transmit nerve impulses; *also called* nerve cell

neuroscience: a branch of the life sciences that is concerned with the anatomy, physiology, biochemistry, and molecular biology of nerves and nervous tissue, especially their relation to behavior and learning

neurotransmitter: a chemical substance that conveys nerve impulses across the synapses, or junctions, between the neurons

neutrophil: a type of leukocyte that is essential for removing and destroying bacteria, cellular debris, and other foreign material

nonproprietary name: a name used to connote a product that is not used, produced, or marketed under exclusive legal right

nonsteroidal anti-inflammatory drug (NSAID): a drug such as aspirin, ibuprofen, or acetaminophen used to counteract inflammation

norepinephrine: a hormone that transmits impulses between neurons of the sympathetic nervous system, as well as between some neurons of the central nervous system; a precursor of epinephrine

NSAID: *see* nonsteroidal anti-inflammatory drug

oncogene: a gene having the potential to cause a normal cell to become cancerous

opportunistic infection: a severe illness in a person whose immune function is impaired, produced by a microorganism that is usually harmless

otitis media: inflammation of the middle ear marked by pain, fever, dizziness, and abnormalities of hearing; common in childhood

oxidation: the act or process of combining with oxygen

oxytocin: a pituitary hormone that stimulates the contraction of uterine muscle, hastening childbirth, and the secretion of milk

P

pandemic: a disease occurring globally or over a wide geographic area and affecting an exceptionally high proportion of the population

parasympathetic nervous system: a part of the autonomic nervous system that tends to induce secretion, increase the tone and contractility of smooth muscle, slow heart rate, and cause the stretching of blood vessels beyond normal dimensions; *cf.*, sympathetic nervous system

pathophysiology: the functional changes that accompany a particular syndrome or disease

PCR: *see* polymerase chain reaction

periodontitis: the inflammation of the supporting structures of the teeth and gums, especially the fibrous connective-tissue layer that holds the teeth in place in the jawbone; *also called* periodontal disease

peripheral nervous system (PNS): the part of the nervous system that is outside the central nervous system; includes the cranial nerves (with the exception of the optic nerve), spinal nerves, and nerves of the autonomic nervous system

PET: *see* positron-emission tomography

phytochemical: any of various plant substances that have no known nutrient value but may have an important role in health; examples include carotenoids and flavonoids

placebo: a medication prescribed more for the state of a patient's mental well-being than for its effect on the disorder; also, an inert or innocuous substance used especially in controlled experiments to test the effectiveness of an active substance

placebo effect: an improvement in a disease or condition that occurs in response to the patient's belief in the effectiveness of a given treatment

plasma: the fluid part of a liquid (as blood, lymph, or milk) as distinguished from material suspended in the liquid

platelet: a small disk-shaped component in the blood that contributes to the clotting process

Illustration by Harwin Studios

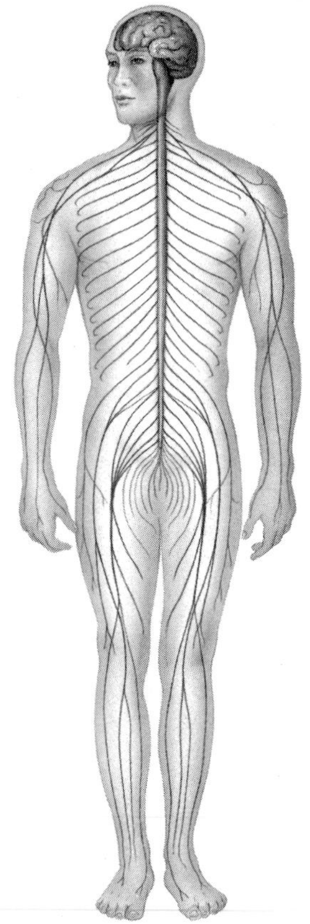

PNS and CNS

PNS: *see* peripheral nervous system

polymerase chain reaction (PCR): a technique for rapidly synthesizing large quantities of a given segment of DNA

positron-emission tomography (PET): a diagnostic technique based on the detection of positrons (positively charged electrons) emitted by radioisotopes (radioactive forms of elements) introduced into the body; produces three-dimensional images that reflect and characterize the metabolic and chemical activity of tissues

potassium: an essential mineral found in foods (*e.g.,* bananas, meats, bran) that facilitates muscle contraction and the transmission of nerve impulses; helps regulate fluid and electrolyte balance in cells; and promotes the release of energy from carbohydrates, proteins, and fats

potentiate: to make effective or active; also, to make more effective or more active

PPO: *see* preferred provider organization

precursor: a substance, cell, or cellular component from which another substance, cell, or cellular component is formed, especially by natural processes

preferred provider organization (PPO): a health care plan that offers economic incentives to consumers who patronize certain physicians, laboratories, and hospitals that agree to be supervised by the plan and to accept scheduled fees

presbyopia: a visual condition in which loss of elasticity of the lens of the eye causes an inability to focus sharply for near vision; becomes apparent especially in middle age

prolactin: a hormone produced by the pituitary gland that induces the secretion of milk by the mammary gland and maintains the corpora lutea (the reddish-yellow masses of endocrine tissue that persist throughout a pregnancy) in a functional state

prospective study: a research protocol in which subjects who are healthy or untreated are followed over time and monitored for the development of a particular illness or the effects of a particular treatment; *cf.,* retrospective study

prostaglandin: any of various active fatty acid derivatives that are present in many tissues and organs of the body and have a variety of hormonelike actions

protease inhibitor: an agent that slows or interferes with the chemical decomposition of proteins

protein *1:* any of numerous combinations of amino acids occurring naturally in the body and linked to form long chains that are one of the most essential components of living cells; *2:* a nutrient found in many foods; broken down into its component parts (amino acids) and absorbed into the bloodstream to be utilized by tissues throughout the body

proto-oncogene: a gene that has the potential to become a cancer-causing gene, or oncogene

proton: an elementary particle that is identical with the nucleus of a hydrogen atom, that along with neutrons is a constituent of all other atomic nuclei, and that carries a positive charge numerically equal to the charge of an electron

psychoneuroimmunology: the study of the connections between the brain and the immune system

psychosis: a serious mental illness characterized by defective or absent contact with reality, often marked by hallucinations or delusions

R

radioisotope: a radioactive version of an element that has two or more atomic forms with different masses; used in nuclear medicine in the diagnosis or treatment of illness

receptor: a cell or group of cells that receives a stimulus

red blood cell: *see* erythrocyte

retinoblastoma: a hereditary malignant tumor of the retina of the eye

retrospective study: a formal study based on past events; a research protocol in which individuals who have a particular disorder are compared with unaffected individuals with respect to their previous exposure to a possible risk factor; also, research in which persons who have taken a particular drug or undergone a particular procedure are compared with untreated persons with respect to outcome; *cf.,* prospective study

retrovirus: any of a group of viruses (as HIV) that carry their genetic blueprint in the form of RNA and, by means of a special enzyme, use RNA to synthesize DNA—a reversal of the process used by most other viruses and all cellular organisms

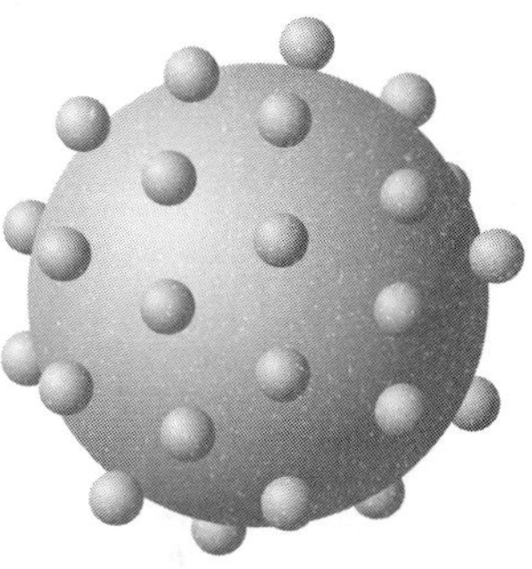

retrovirus

rheumatoid arthritis: a usually chronic disease of unknown cause that is characterized by pain, stiffness, inflammation, swelling, and sometimes destruction of the joints

RU-486: a drug taken orally to induce abortion; functions by blocking the body's use of the hormone progesterone

S

saphenous vein: either of two chief superficial veins of the leg that are sometimes surgically removed and grafted to other parts of the body (as the coronary arteries)

saturated fat: a fatty acid in its most complex, solid form; constitutes a large proportion of the fat in foods high in cholesterol (as butter, milk, cheese, eggs, meat, and chocolate)

sclera: the dense, fibrous, opaque white outer coat of the eye

screening: testing of a population or group in order to detect or calculate the prevalence of a specific disease

septicemia: *see* blood poisoning

serotonin: a natural chemical that constricts blood vessels, inhibits gastric secretion, stimulates smooth muscle, and serves as a central nervous system neurotransmitter; thought to be important in many neurological and psychiatric conditions

serum: the clear yellowish fluid that remains after blood has solidified or after suspended material (as blood cells) has been removed from blood

sickle-cell disease: a chronic inherited blood condition in which an individual inherits a pair of abnormal genes for hemoglobin (the oxygen-carrying protein in the blood), which results in red blood cells that are crescent- rather than disk-shaped; characterized by tissue damage due to insufficient oxygen; *also called* sickle-cell anemia

sickle-cell trait: an inherited blood condition in which an individual inherits a single abnormal hemoglobin gene (along with one normal gene), which causes some red blood cells to mutate into a crescent shape but usually not enough to produce anemia or the tissue injury characteristic of sickle-cell disease

Johnson & Johnson Interventional Systems Co.

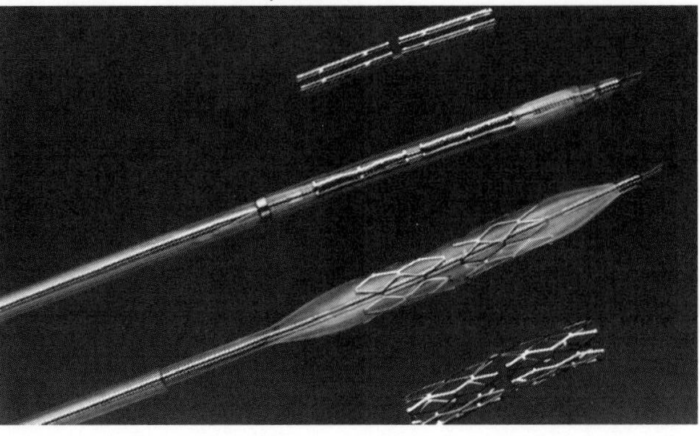

stent

SIDS: *see* sudden infant death syndrome

smooth muscle: muscle tissue, such as that found in the stomach and bladder, that performs functions not subject to conscious control

sodium: an element that functions within the body primarily to regulate fluid balance and preserve the structural integrity and function of body cells

soluble fiber: a plant material found primarily in fruits and vegetables that is capable of dissolving in liquid and may reduce blood cholesterol and help to regulate blood glucose

somatotropin: a hormone that is secreted by the front portion of the pituitary gland and regulates growth

spinal tap: *see* lumbar puncture

stain: a dye or mixture of dyes used in microscopy to make minute and transparent structures visible, to differentiate tissue elements, or to produce specific chemical reactions

stem cell: an unspecialized cell capable of giving rise to different types of cells

stenosis: a narrowing or constriction of the diameter of a bodily passage or orifice

stent: a metal device implanted in an artery to hold it open and help prevent the buildup that leads to artery damage and obstruction

streptococcus: any of a group of bacteria (genus *Streptococcus*) that are important pathogens in humans, causing many illnesses

sudden infant death syndrome (SIDS): death of an apparently healthy infant, usually before one year of age, that is of unknown cause and occurs especially during sleep; *also called* crib death or cot death

sympathetic nervous system: the part of the autonomic nervous system that is concerned especially with preparing the body to react to situations of stress or emergency; *cf.,* parasympathetic nervous system

synapse: the site where a nervous impulse passes from one neuron to another

T

thalamus: the part of the brain that serves as a relay station to and from the cerebral cortex and functions especially in sensation and arousal

tolerance: the ability to endure the effects of a drug or food or of a physiological insult without displaying the usual unfavorable effects; increased resistance to the usual effects of a drug due to continued use

total fat: the amount of fat (in grams) listed on a nutritional label on packaged foods that includes the amount of the three types of fat (saturated, polyunsaturated, and monounsaturated) in a serving

U

ultrasound imaging: a diagnostic or therapeutic technique that uses vibrations of frequencies above the audible range to produce a two-dimensional image; often used to examine and measure internal body structures and to detect bodily abnormalities

V

vasodilation: widening of the lumen (inner hollow portion) of a blood vessel

venous: made up of or carried on by the veins

W

white blood cell: *see* leukocyte

Z

zoonosis: a disease communicable to humans from other vertebrate animals

Main source: *Webster's Medical Desk Dictionary,* 1993

From the Pages of the 1995 Encyclopædia Britannica

The editors of the *Medical and Health Annual* include this section to share with readers articles that have been written by distinguished scholars and revised for the most recent printing of *Encyclopædia Britannica.* The following is a comprehensive overview, prepared for the 1995 *Britannica,* of medicine's rapidly advancing means of diagnosing and treating human illness. (Like all *Encyclopædia Britannica* articles, this selection uses British spellings.)

—*The Editors*

Diagnosis and Therapeutics

Diagnosis, from the Greek *gnosis* meaning knowledge, is the art of determining the nature of a disease and distinguishing one disease from another. The diagnostic process is the method by which health professionals select one disease over another, identifying one as the most likely cause of a person's symptoms. Symptoms that appear early in the course of a disease are often more vague and undifferentiated than those that arise as the disease progresses, making this the most difficult time to make an accurate diagnosis. Reaching an accurate conclusion depends on the timing and the sequence of the symptoms, past medical history and risk factors for certain diseases, and a recent exposure to disease. The physician, in making a diagnosis, also relies on various other clues such as physical signs, nonverbal signals of distress, and the results of selected laboratory and radiological tests. From the large number of facts obtained, a list of possible diagnoses can be determined, which are referred to as the differential diagnosis. The physician organizes the list with the most likely diagnosis given first. Additional information is identified, and appropriate tests are selected that will narrow the list or confirm one of the possible diseases.

Therapeutics is the art and science of treating disease. It comes from the Greek *therapeutikos,* which means "inclined to serve." In a broad sense therapeutics means serving and caring for the patient in a comprehensive manner, preventing disease as well as managing specific problems. Exercise, diet, and mental factors are therefore integral to the prevention, as well as the management of disease processes. More specific measures that are employed to treat specific symptoms include the use of drugs to relieve pain or treat infection, surgery to remove diseased tissue or replace poorly functioning or nonfunctioning organs with fully operating ones, and counseling or psychotherapy to relieve emotional distress. Confidence in the physician and in the method selected enhances effectiveness.

DIAGNOSIS

Historical aspects

Traditionally, diagnosis has been defined as the art of identifying a disease from its signs and symptoms. Formerly, few diagnostic tests were available to assist the physician who depended on medical history, observation, and examination. Only recently, with the many technological advances in medicine, have tests become available to assist in making specific diagnoses.

Medicine and personal hygiene reached new heights in the 5th century BC at the time of the Greek physician Hippocrates. The Greeks recognized the salubrious effects of bathing, fresh air, a good diet, and exercise, which have received renewed attention today. Illness was thought to result from an imbalance between the four humours of the body: blood, phlegm, yellow bile, and black bile. The Greeks emphasized the value of observation, including bodily signs and excretions. The focus, however, was more on predicting the outcome of an illness (*i.e.,* prognosis) and less on its diagnosis. A physician's reputation depended on accurate prognostic skills, predicting who would recover and who would die or how long an illness would last.

The Greeks

Hippocrates is credited with establishing the ethical basis of the physician's behaviour, and graduating physicians still recite the oath ascribed to him. His writings document the value of objectively evaluating all aspects of the patient's symptoms, diet, sleep patterns, and habits. No finding was considered insignificant, and physicians were encouraged to employ all their senses—sight, hearing, smell, taste, and touch—in making a diagnosis. These principles hold just as true today.

The Romans made significant advances in supplying and purifying water and in improving sanitation.

Galen (AD 130–200) is considered the most influential physician after Hippocrates because of his extensive studies in anatomy and physiology. His voluminous writings in anatomy and physiology rendered him the ultimate authority in these fields until the 16th century. As the first experimental neurologist, he described the cranial nerves and the sympathetic nervous system. He showed that the heart will continue beating when removed from the body and thus does not depend on the nervous system. Many of his views, however, contained fallacies, which remained unchallenged for centuries. His description of the heart and its chambers and valves, in which he contended that blood passes from the right to the left ventricle by means of invisible pores in the interventricular septum, delayed the discovery of blood circulation for 14 centuries. The true nature of the circulation of blood was not recognized until the time of William Harvey (1578–1657), who published his findings in *Exercitatio anatomica de motu cordis et sanguinis in animalibus* (translated as *An Anatomical Dissertation Upon the Movement of the Heart and Blood in Animals* and usually referred to as *De Motu Cordis*).

From the Middle Ages to the 18th century, uroscopy (examination of the urine) was a common method for diagnosing illness. The colour of the urine, as well as cloudiness, precipitates, and particles in the urine, was believed to indicate the cause of the disorder.

Diagnostic tools

One of the greatest advances in diagnostic tools was the invention of the compound microscope toward the end of the 16th century by the Dutch spectacle makers Hans Jansen and his son Zacharias. In the early 17th century Galileo constructed a microscope and a telescope. One of the great early microscopists, Antonie van Leeuwenhoek (1632–1723), was the first to see protozoa and bacteria and the first to describe red blood cells. He also demonstrated the capillary anastomosis (network) between arteries and veins that proved Harvey to be correct.

Although the mercury thermometer of Daniel Fahrenheit (1686–1736) appeared about 1714, it was not until 1866 that it came into general use as a clinical tool. It was initially 25.4 centimetres (10 inches) long and took five minutes to register a temperature. A pocket version was developed by Sir Thomas Clifford Allbutt in 1866. The thermometer was popularized by Karl August Wunderlich who thought, incorrectly, that every disease had its own characteristic fever pattern.

Another significant medical advance, which greatly improved the ability to diagnose diseases of the chest and heart, was the invention of the stethoscope in 1816 by René-Théophile-Hyacinthe Laënnec (1781–1826). Before this, the lungs and heart were examined by applying the ear to the chest wall. Laënnec initially used a roll of papers to enhance sounds from the chest and later replaced this "instrument" with a wooden cylinder. He improved the original monaural (one-ear) stethoscope with the binaural device still in current use. Tuberculosis was prominent at the time, and the stethoscope allowed Laënnec to diagnose this condition at an earlier stage than was previously possible.

Another significant diagnostic aid was the ophthalmoscope developed by Hermann von Helmholtz (1821–94), a physician best known for his knowledge of physics and mathematics. With this device, the retina and blood vessels could be seen through the pupil, allowing the inner eye to provide information not only concerning diseases of the eye but also about those pertaining to cardiovascular abnormalities and complications of diabetes mellitus.

Perhaps the greatest modern anatomic diagnostic tool is the X ray, discovered in 1895 by the German physicist Wilhelm Conrad Röntgen. X rays have since been commonly referred to as roentgen rays, and their application eventually led to the development of computerized tomography and magnetic resonance imaging, two techniques that are extremely useful modern diagnostic tools.

Medical training

The training of physicians also has undergone significant change over the years. Until the end of the 19th century, physicians were trained through lectures and rarely were taught at the patient's bedside. This practice was altered by Sir William Osler, one of the most renowned physicians of the early 20th century, who introduced the practice of instructing students at the bedside of the patient. He emphasized the importance of taking an accurate medical history, providing a thorough examination of a patient, and closely observing the patient's behaviour to gather clues for a diagnosis before resorting to laboratory testing.

Medical history

The medical history of a patient is the most useful and important element in making an accurate diagnosis, much more valuable than either physical examinations or diagnostic tests. The medical interview is the process of gathering data that will lead to an understanding of the disease and the underlying physiological process. To be effective, an interviewer must possess good communication skills and be alert to nonverbal clues as well as to the verbal message. Often, more information is conveyed by nonverbal actions and tone of voice than by words. The objective is to obtain an accurate and comprehensive picture of the patient's situation, including the nature and timing of symptoms, emotional factors (including types of stress), and past medical conditions that may place the patient at greater risk for certain diseases.

The medical interview

The accuracy and usefulness of the medical interview depend on the physician's ability to elicit information pertinent to the problem at hand and on the patient's accurate recall and articulation of the sequence of symptoms. This may be difficult because meaningful data may be forgotten if the patient is experiencing pain or emotional distress. The skilled interviewer knows when to use silence, open-ended questions, or specific closed-ended questions to explore avenues in which the most useful information may be found. The real reason for the patient's visit may not be apparent until a rapport has been established and the person feels comfortable describing what is most bothersome. Problems that are emotionally threatening may not be voiced until adequate courage is summoned—sometimes not until the end of the appointment when the patient's hand is on the doorknob.

A complete medical history consists of an account of the present illness, the past medical history, family history, occupational background, psychosocial history, and a review of body systems.

An account of the present illness, which includes the circumstances surrounding the onset of recent health changes and the chronology of subsequent events that have led the patient to seek medical care, is essential to understanding the course of the disease process. Current medications are listed in the medical history because they may play a role in the current illness.

The past medical history is an overall view of the patient's health prior to the present illness. It should include previous hospitalizations, injuries, operations, and any significant illness that may not have required hospitalization. Allergies are included here if not listed separately.

Family history

Included in a family history are the age and state of health of each immediate family member as well as the cause of death of any parents, grandparents, and other close relatives. Of particular importance are genetic or environmental diseases that have known risks. If a close relative such as a father died of a heart attack (acute myocardial infarction) before the age of 60, all his children are at greater risk of suffering an early heart attack. This risk increases if other factors such as hypertension (high blood pressure) or elevated serum cholesterol are present. Similarly, a history of some cancers (*e.g.,* colon cancer) increases the risk for offspring to develop that type of cancer. The development of lung cancer in a parent provides even greater impetus for close relatives to avoid smoking. Other diseases that may have hereditary or environmental roots are diabetes, hypertension, tuberculosis, depression and other forms of mental illness, arthritis, and epilepsy. Actually, any disease that arises in two or more members of a family suggests a possible predisposing factor, and the patient should be considered to be at increased risk for this condition.

The occupational history is important because the workplace may be a source of toxins, such as chemicals or cigarette smoke, that place one at higher risk of cancer or other diseases.

The psychosocial history—information on education, lifestyle, marital status, and religious beliefs—may influence future medical decisions, as may the patient's smoking history, alcohol intake, and use of such controlled substances as marijuana or cocaine.

The review of body systems allows the physician to identify any other symptoms that have not been noted previously and that may influence the patient's current state of health or provide subtle clues to the diagnosis. All major body systems are reviewed in an orderly manner, usually from the head down to the extremities. The intent is to uncover any past illnesses or problems that have not been previously identified and that may now or later influence the patient's health. For example, the patient may describe leg pain while walking, which could be an early indication of blood vessel occlusion and increase the physician's concern about possible coronary artery disease that otherwise may not have been suspected.

Physical examination

MANUAL PROCEDURES

The physical examination continues the diagnostic process, adding information obtained by inspection, palpation, percussion, and auscultation (see below). When data accumulated from the history and physical examination are complete, a working diagnosis is established, and tests are selected that will help to retain or exclude that diagnosis.

Patients are usually apprehensive and anxious when being examined because they feel exposed, vulnerable, and afraid of discomfort. The physician attempts to allay that anxiety by explaining which examinations are to be performed and the degree of discomfort that will be entailed. Throughout the examination, concern for the patient's dignity must be maintained.

Inspection. A wide array of sophisticated instruments is available to assist with examinations, but a well-performed visual inspection can often reveal more information. Osler admonished physicians to closely observe patients before touching them, to cultivate the power of observation, as it is one of the greatest diagnostic tools. Wasting and hallmarks of poor nutrition may indicate chronic disease; poor grooming or slack posture may suggest depression or low self-esteem.

Visual inspection

Inspection begins with the patient's general appearance, state of nutrition, symmetry, and posture. The physician then proceeds to more specific examination of the skin—looking for redness or other signs of infection, hair loss, nail thickening, and moles or other areas of pigmentation—and inquires about any recent changes in skin lesions that could indicate early cancer.

Examination of the nails can provide important clues about systemic disease. Clubbing of the nails (broadening of the nailbeds, with curved and shiny nails) may indicate congenital heart disease, chronic obstructive pulmonary disease, bronchogenic carcinoma, or another cardiac or pulmonary condition. Pitting of the nails occurs in about 50 percent of patients with psoriasis.

Inspection should encompass, in particular, areas that the patient normally would not be able to see, such as the scalp, back, and buttocks.

The skin should always be inspected for cancer, though it is sometimes difficult to differentiate a benign mole (nevus) from a cancer. The most dangerous skin cancer, malignant melanoma, occurs in about 1 in 10,000 people and can spread readily throughout the body. A squamous-cell carcinoma also may spread but is slow to do so and can be completely cured by early detection and removal. Basal-cell cancer is the most common form of skin cancer, and, though it is locally invasive, it does not spread. Suspicious lesions are those that have recently enlarged, started to bleed, become darker, or developed an irregular outline. Most skin cancers occur on areas of the body that have been exposed to the sun; they are more common in light-skinned individuals with blond hair and blue eyes who sunburn easily.

The most common premalignant (precancerous) skin lesion is actinic keratosis, a rough, scaling, red or brown papule that appears on sun-exposed areas such as a bald scalp, ears, the forehead, and the back of the hands. These lesions can be easily removed by cryotherapy (therapeutic use of cold) or electrodesiccation (dehydration of tissue by electric current).

Palpation. Palpation is the act of feeling the surface of the body with the hands to determine the characteristics of the organs beneath the surface. It can be performed with one hand or two and can be light or deep.

Types of palpation

Light palpation is used to detect tenderness, muscle spasm, or rigidity of the abdomen. If abdominal pain is present, gentle palpation begins farthest away from the pain to localize the point of maximum tenderness. Acute inflammation in the abdomen, as in acute appendicitis, causes peritoneal irritation, resulting in not only localized tenderness in the right lower abdomen but also a guarding reaction (tightening and rigidity) by the muscles in that area to protect the inflamed organ from the external pressure.

Deep palpation of the abdomen is used to determine the size of the liver, spleen, or kidneys and to detect an abnormal mass. An abdominal aortic aneurysm can be detected by palpating a pulsatile mass in the upper abdomen. An acutely tender mass in the right upper abdomen that is more painful on inspiration is probably an inflamed gallbladder. An unexplained nontender abdominal mass could be as nonthreatening as a hard stool or as serious as a tumour.

Palpation also is used to detect and evaluate abnormal lesions in the breast, prostate, lymph nodes, or testicles. Proper breast examination includes frequent (at least monthly) self-examinations and an annual examination by a physician. Palpation should be methodical and performed over the entire breast; the method of action is done either in concentric circles or outward from the nipple using a spokes-of-a-wheel approach. Suspicious breast lesions are hard and fixed rather than movable. Skin retraction or breast asymmetry can indicate an underlying, potentially serious lesion. Cancers are usually not tender, and benign lesions are more likely to be round, elastic or firm, movable, and well-defined. Similarly, suspicious prostate lesions are hard, irregular nodules within the prostate, whereas benign prostatic hyperplasia (BPH) is a soft symmetrical enlargement of the gland.

Palpation also can detect cardiac enlargement if the point of maximal impulse (PMI) of the heart is farther left than normal. Other cardiac abnormalities can be suspected if a thrill is felt using light palpation over the chest wall. A thrill is a vibratory sensation felt on the skin overlying an area of turbulence and indicates a loud heart murmur usually caused by an incompetent heart valve.

Percussion. Percussion is a diagnostic procedure used to determine the density of a part by tapping the surface with short, sharp blows and evaluating the resulting sounds. In the abdomen it can be used to detect fluid (ascites), a gaseous distention of the intestine as occurs in bowel obstruction, or an enlargement of the liver. It is used most often to evaluate the chest. Percussion produces a resonant note when the area over a healthy lung is struck; a dull sound, however, will emanate if the lung contains fluid, as in pneumonia, or when a region over a solid mass such as the heart is tapped. A lung that is diseased with emphysema contains more air than a healthy lung and produces hyperresonance. A stomach distended with air will produce a high-pitched, hollow tympanic sound.

Body sounds provide diagnostic clues

Auscultation. Auscultation is performed with a stethoscope to evaluate sounds produced by the heart, lungs, blood vessels, or bowels. The lack of bowel sounds indicates a nonfunctioning or paralyzed bowel, and high-pitched "tinkling" bowel sounds suggest bowel obstruction. The "growling" of the stomach is an accentuation of these sounds during periods of bowel hyperactivity.

Bruits are blowing vascular sounds resembling heart murmurs that are perceived over partially occluded blood vessels. When detected over the carotid arteries, a bruit may indicate an increased risk of stroke; when produced by the abdomen, it may indicate partial obstruction of the aorta or other major arteries such as the renal, iliac, or femoral arteries.

Listening to the sound of air passing in and out of the lungs can be useful in detecting an obstruction as in asthma or an inflammation as in bronchitis or pneumonia. Adventitious sounds are those heard in addition to normal breathing sounds and include crackles, wheezes, and rubs. Crackles (also called rales) resemble the sound made by rubbing hair between the fingers next to the ear. They are caused by fluid in the small passageways that adheres to the walls during respiration. Crackles are heard in congestive heart failure and pneumonia. Wheezes, musical sounds heard mostly during expiration, are caused by rapid airflow through a partially obstructed airway as in asthma or bronchitis. Pleural rubs sound like creaking leather and are caused by pleural surfaces roughened by inflammation moving against each other, which occurs in patients with pneumonia and pulmonary infarction.

Cardiac auscultation is the evaluation of the sounds made by the heart valves—namely, the aortic, pulmonary, tricuspid, and mitral—for murmurs that may be due to turbulent blood flow or vibrations from a heart valve deformity. Murmurs may be physiological (unimportant clinically) or pathological, indicating a problem that needs attention, especially if they reflect obstruction of normal blood flow. Heart murmurs vary according to their timing in the cardiac cycle (systole, the period of contraction when blood is pumped from the heart, and diastole, the period of heart expansion between pumping), location, duration, intensity, pitch, and quality. Intensity is graded on a scale from 1 to 6, with 6 being the loudest. Heart murmurs are described as "grade 2/6"—the numerator represents the intensity of the murmur, and the denominator indicates the highest grade of the scale being used. However, the intensity of the murmur alone provides little information about the clinical severity of the problem. An ejection murmur caused by turbulence across the aortic valve during systole can be either serious or nonthreatening depending on its cause, even though the intensity of the murmur may be the same. Therefore, the pitch and quality of the murmur also are described. Pitch is usually reported as high or low, and quality is described as harsh, soft, blowing, musical, or rumbling. For example, the murmur of mitral stenosis may be described as a grade 3/6, low-pitched, rumbling, presystolic murmur heard best at the apex and having an increased first heart sound at the apex.

SPECIAL EXAMINATIONS

Evaluation of body systems

Emergency. Of greatest importance in an emergency is the evaluation of systems that are essential to sustaining life—namely, the circulatory, respiratory, and central nervous systems.

First, the person in distress should be checked to determine whether breathing is normal or at least whether there is adequate exchange of air to ensure oxygenation of the blood. If the person is unconscious, the first maneuver is to tilt the head back and lift the chin (unless a neck injury is suspected) to prevent the tongue and jaw from obstructing the airway and then to provide artificial respiration. If the person has eaten recently, the cause may be obstruction by a foreign body (usually food), and the Heimlich maneuver (subdiaphragmatic abdominal thrust) should be performed.

Second, the circulation should be evaluated. Is the heart beating, and is the output adequate to provide oxygenated blood to the tissues, or has this been compromised by excessive bleeding? A blood pressure greater than 100/60 millimetres of mercury (mm Hg) indicates adequate perfusion.

Shock occurs when the blood pressure falls to extremely low levels because of inadequate blood volume (hypovolemic shock), poor heart function (cardiogenic shock), or malfunction of the vascular system that results in lost peripheral vascular tone, vasodilation, and pooling of the blood (neurogenic shock). Signs of shock are a rapid and weak pulse, pale complexion, sweating, and confusion. Organs particularly sensitive to injury if the shock is not corrected are the brain, heart, lungs, kidneys, and liver.

Examination of the unconscious patient

An unconscious person may not respond to external stimulation, in which case the person would be in a coma, or the patient may exhibit varying levels of unconsciousness, responding only to painful stimuli (deep level of unconsciousness) or when shaken or called by name (light level). Pupil size and reactivity to light can provide clues to the status of the nervous system. Bilateral dilated pupils that do not contract when a light is placed on one of them indicate death or severe damage to the nervous system. Small pupils that do react to light are seen in narcotic overdose. If one pupil is larger than the other, a brain lesion on one side or hemorrhage should be suspected.

Pediatric. Examinations to assess the well-being of children begin at birth. The Apgar score, named for the anesthesiologist Virginia Apgar, is obtained at one and five minutes after birth and indicates the condition of the newborn. A score of 0 (absent), 1, and 2 is given for each of the five parameters, which are heart rate, respiratory effort, muscle tone, reflex irritability, and colour. Infants scoring between 7 and 10 at one minute will likely do well with no special treatment; those scoring between 4 and 6 may require stimulation or brief respiratory support; those scoring 3 or below will probably need extended resuscitative efforts. Infants who have a score of 7 or above at five minutes will continue to do well. The Apgar score is usually reported as two numbers, from 1 to 10, that are separated by a virgule, the first number being the score at one minute, the second the score at five minutes.

Developmental assessment is measured with growth charts developed by the National Center for Health Statistics. A child's length (or height) and weight are plotted over time on standard graphs constructed from data gathered from a large number of average-sized children. The average length of a newborn infant is 50 centimetres (20 inches). The length increases by 50 percent at 12 months of age and doubles to 100 centimetres when the child is 4 years old. The average weight at birth is 3.4 kilograms (7.5 pounds), which doubles in 4 to 5 months and triples when the child is 12 months old. After 2 years of age, height increases by 5 centimetres and weight increases by 2.3 kilograms per year until the growth spurt during adolescence.

Psychosocial development can be measured using the Denver Developmental Screening Test. This test evaluates motor, language, and social development skills in children up to 6 years of age.

Adolescent growth

The adolescent growth spurt is closely associated with the development of the reproductive system. Puberty occurs in American girls starting at 10 or 11 years of age (average) and in American boys at age 11. In girls the first sign of puberty is the breast bud followed by breast and pubic hair development. In boys it is growth of the testes with reddening and wrinkling of the scrotum. Pubic hair appears within six months of these first signs of puberty, followed in another six months or so by enlargement of the penis.

Hearing is evaluated early, and a disorder should be suspected if speech is delayed or abnormal. Vision testing is begun in the newborn to detect strabismus and other congenital abnormalities. Visual acuity can be evaluated in children 2 to 3 years of age. Dental appointments should begin when the child is 2 or 3, because the eruption of primary teeth is usually complete by 2 years of age. Permanent teeth begin erupting about age 6 and are all in place by age 12 or 13 years.

Geriatric. The number of people in the United States older than 65 years of age is increasing rapidly, and demographers project that soon 50 percent of the American population will live to 85 years or older. As the body ages there is a steady loss in organ reserve (ability to function beyond the level normally required, which may be called upon in an emergency), which leads to decreasing functional capacity and increasing vulnerability to disease and disability. Age-related changes include the following:

1. Cellular changes occur, including decreased function and number.
2. Increased collagen results in greater stiffness and decreased tissue elasticity.
3. Muscle mass decreases, as does the mass of the liver, brain, and kidneys.
4. Cardiac output is reduced, the ability to respond to stress diminishes, and blood flow to the kidneys and other organs decreases.
5. Pulmonary function decreases because the number of alveoli lessens, expiratory muscles weaken, and there is a reduction in elastic recoil.
6. Gastrointestinal changes occur, including decreased secretion of stomach acid; decreased intestinal motil-

ity, resulting in constipation and dehydration of the stools; slower metabolism of drugs by the liver; increased incidence of gallstones; and loss of teeth, impairing proper chewing and digestion. Diverticulosis occurs in more than 50 percent of persons by age 80.
7. Excretory function diminishes because of a decrease in kidney mass and in the number of functioning nephrons.
8. Endocrine changes are noted and can include decreased functioning of thyroid and adrenal glands and decreased insulin production by the pancreas along with increasing insulin resistance that results in diabetes mellitus.
9. Neurological changes occur, including a slowing of nerve conduction velocity, a loss of brain substance, a reduction in the amount of deep sleep and an increase in the number of brief arousals, and a decrease in cerebral blood flow.
10. Visual acuity, hearing, taste, and smell decline. Vision is much more limited in dim light. The incidence of glaucoma and cataracts increases.
11. Height decreases because of the narrowing of the intervertebral disks and narrowing of the vertebrae, resulting in the loss of five centimetres by the age of 70 years.

Osteoporosis, which is demineralization of bone and loss of bone mass, results in an increased risk of fracture, especially of the hip, wrist, and spine. Bone loss is accelerated in women during menopause but can be prevented by administration of estrogen and calcium. Progesterone is added to prevent endometrial cancer if the uterus is still present.

Cancers occur most frequently in the elderly. Carcinoma of the colon is predominantly a disease of the geriatric population and is the second leading cause of death from cancer in the United States.

Depression and other mood disorders are more common among older individuals than among younger persons. The symptoms of depression may be more vague and are more likely to occur as physical symptoms than in other age groups.

Dementia (loss of intellectual function) is common among the elderly, and Alzheimer's disease is thought to account for more than 60 percent of these cases. Alzheimer's disease is characterized by a slowly progressive cognitive decline, in the absence of other causes of dementia. It affects about 10 percent of all persons older than 65 years of age.

Psychiatric. Psychological dysfunction and stress-related illness are a significant problem in today's increasingly complex society. Anxiety and depression represent the two most common mental health disorders and are responsible for a high degree of morbidity and mortality.

Anxiety disorders. The most common anxiety disorders are panic disorder, generalized anxiety disorder, post-traumatic stress disorder, phobic disorder, and obsessive-compulsive disorder.

Panic disorder

Panic disorder is characterized by four panic attacks within a four-week period or one or more panic attacks followed by at least a month of persistent fear of having another attack. A panic attack is the sudden onset of intense apprehension, fear, or terror and at least four of the following conditions: shortness of breath or a smothering sensation, palpitations or accelerated heart rate, chest pain or discomfort, choking, dizziness or faintness, trembling or shaking, sweating, nausea or abdominal distress, a feeling of unreality, numbness or tingling, hot flashes or chills, fear of dying, and fear of "going crazy," or losing control. A panic attack is unexpected and does not immediately precede or follow a stressful situation, although the person who experiences the attack usually is in a period of increased stress. Because somatic symptoms play a prominent role in a panic attack, it is easy to mistake the attack for other problems such as heart disease or a gastrointestinal problem. Fortunately, the condition responds well to treatment consisting of pharmacotherapy and supportive counseling by the family physician.

There is a close association between panic disorder and depression, and a large percentage of persons suffering from panic disorder go on to experience a major depression within the next few years. Such antidepressants as imipramine and desipramine are the most effective treatment for panic disorder and may also provide effective relief of any associated depressive symptoms.

Agoraphobia, which literally means "fear of the marketplace" and indicates fear of being away from the safety of home, commonly occurs with panic disorder. Although the person avoids being alone, the only desired companions are those to whom no explanation of the agoraphobic behaviour is required. Places where crowds or situations would complicate a swift and unnoticed escape in the event of a panic attack are avoided.

Generalized anxiety disorder is the unrealistic or excessive worry about two or more life circumstances that is experienced more days than not for a period of six months or longer. Examples would be excessive worry about finances or danger to one's child when there is no reason for this concern. The anxious behaviour indicative of this disorder includes symptoms of motor tension (*e.g.,* trembling or shaky feeling, muscle soreness or tension, and restlessness), autonomic hyperactivity (*e.g.,* shortness of breath, palpitations, and dizziness), and vigilance and scanning, which includes difficulty concentrating, an exaggerated startle response, and a tense, keyed-up feeling.

Post-traumatic stress disorder

Post-traumatic stress disorder can result after exposure to a very distressing event that elicits feelings of intense terror, fear, or helplessness. Traumatic events such as having witnessed a murder or the sudden destruction of one's home or having participated in a military battle are cited as causes of this disorder. The person experiences frequent flashbacks and may exhibit increased irritability, have exaggerated startle reactions, and have sleeping difficulties, including nightmares. Intense anxiety can result when the person is exposed to environmental stimuli that symbolize or resemble the event.

Phobic disorder involves the persistent and irrational fear of a specific object, activity, or situation that results in a compulsion to avoid that object or situation. The person recognizes the fear as excessive or unreasonable but cannot control the anxiety associated with it. Agoraphobia is one of the most severe phobias. Other phobias include the fear of heights (acrophobia), confined spaces (claustrophobia), animals, insects, snakes, and flying in airplanes. Social phobia is the fear of social situations in which the person dreads being criticized or humiliated. Performance anxiety is a form of social phobia.

Obsessive-compulsive disorder is marked by recurrent obsessions or compulsions that cause extreme distress and interfere with the normal activities of daily life. Obsessions are persistent ideas, thoughts, impulses, or images that are experienced as intrusive, senseless, and generally repugnant but which cannot be ignored or suppressed. Compulsions are repetitive, intentional behaviours performed in a ritualized manner in an attempt to neutralize the obsession and control the anxiety associated with it.

Disorders of mood. Major depression and other mood disorders such as dysthymia, bipolar disorder, and cyclothymia are common and very treatable forms of psychiatric problems. Depression is one of the most common conditions encountered in medical practice and affects up to 25 percent of women and 12 percent of men. Untreated depression can persist for two years or longer. Sixty percent of patients who receive treatment and recover will experience a recurrence of depression within three years. Fortunately, most episodes of major depression respond well to treatment.

Major depression

For the diagnosis of major depression to be made, a depressed mood or loss of interest or pleasure in almost all activities must be present for at least two weeks and at least four of the following symptoms must be experienced: sleep disturbance (usually early morning awakening), fatigue or loss of energy, feelings of worthlessness or excessive guilt, diminished ability to concentrate or make decisions, agitation (anxiety or restlessness) or slowed movements, change in appetite with or without weight loss, and recurrent thoughts of death or suicide.

Dysthymia, or minor depression, is the presence of a depressed mood for most of the day for two years with no more than two months' freedom from symptoms. In addition at least two of the following symptoms must occur concurrently with the depression: disruption in eating habits—poor appetite or overeating; disturbed sleeping pattern—insomnia or hypersomnia; low energy or fatigue; low self-esteem; poor concentration or difficulty making decisions; and a feeling of hopelessness.

Bipolar disorder (manic-depressive disorder) is characterized by recurrent episodes of mania and major depression. Most of those who suffer from this condition (60 to 80 percent) initially manifest a manic phase, followed by depression. Manic symptoms consist of feelings of inflated self-esteem or grandiosity, a decreased need for sleep, unusual loquacity, an unconnected flow of ideas, distractibility, or excessive involvement in pleasurable activities that have a high potential for painful consequences, such as buying sprees or sexual indiscretions. Lithium is an effective drug for controlling these symptoms, although additional medications such as a benzodiazepine are needed to counteract an acute manic phase, and other antidepressants are necessary to treat bouts of major depression.

Cyclothymia is a chronic mood disturbance and is a milder form of bipolar disorder. For this diagnosis to be made, the patient will have exhibited at least two years of hypomania (moderate mania) and numerous periods of depressed mood that do not meet the criteria for major depression.

Tests and diagnostic procedures

CLINICAL LABORATORY TESTS

Laboratory tests can be valuable aids in making a diagnosis, but, as screening tools for detecting hidden disease in asymptomatic individuals, their usefulness is limited. The value of a test as a diagnostic aid depends on its sensitivity and specificity. Sensitivity is the measure of the percentage of individuals with the disease who have a positive test result (*i.e.*, people with the disease who are correctly identified by the procedure), and specificity is the measure of the percentage of people without the disease who have a negative test result (*i.e.*, healthy individuals correctly identified as free of the disease). If a test is 100 percent sensitive and the test result is negative, it can be said with certainty that the person does not have the disease, because there will be no false-negative results. If the test is not specific enough, however, it will yield a large number of false-positive results (positive test results for those who do not have the disease). The ideal test would be 100 percent sensitive and 100 percent specific; an example would be an early pregnancy test that was so accurate that it was positive in every woman who was pregnant and was never positive in a woman who was not pregnant. Unfortunately no such test exists. The normal value for a test is based on 95 percent of the population tested being free of disease, meaning that 1 out of every 20 test results in healthy individuals will be outside the normal range and therefore positive for the disease.

Sensitivity and specificity of tests

In the past, physicians would order selected tests based on the likelihood that the person had a certain disease. With the advent of automated analyzers, an increasing number and variety of tests have been made available at greatly reduced cost so that as many as 18 or more tests can be performed for what it previously cost to carry out three or four individual tests. A panel of chemical tests for blood and urine have become routine components of the basic medical workup. A disadvantage of this strategy is that each test produces some false-positive results and requires additional tests to rule out these diseases. The trend is reversing to perform only those tests most likely to be cost-effective.

A normal laboratory value is one that falls within a range that represents most healthy individuals. It is clear, however, that some healthy persons will have values outside that range and some individuals with disease will have values within the normal range. Thus, no sharp line divides normal and abnormal values. Tables of normal reference values must be updated regularly to react to changes in laboratory technique. Many normal values vary dramatically with age and gender.

Worldwide, the standard for reporting laboratory measurements is the International System of Units (SI units). The United States is the only major industrialized country that has not adopted the International System and continues to use customary units of measurement. Most tables provide both units to facilitate communication and understanding.

SI units

Body fluid tests. *Blood.* Blood is composed of plasma and blood cells. The blood cells—erythrocytes (red blood cells), leukocytes (white blood cells), and thrombocytes (platelets)—are suspended in the plasma with other particulate matter. Plasma is a clear, yellowish fluid that makes up more than half the volume of blood. It is distinguished from serum, which is the clear, cell-free fluid from which fibrinogen has been removed. Tests to measure the concentration of substances in the blood may use plasma, serum, or whole blood that has been anticoagulated to keep all the contents in suspension.

A complete blood count (CBC) is a measure of the hematologic parameters of the blood (see the table for reference values). Included in the CBC is the calculation of the number of red blood cells (red blood cell count) or white blood cells (white blood cell count) in a cubic millimetre (mm³) of blood, a differential white blood cell count, a hemoglobin assay, a hematocrit, calculations of red cell volume, and a platelet count.

Complete blood count

The differential white blood cell count includes measurements of the different types of white blood cells that constitute the total white blood cell count: the band neutrophils, segmented neutrophils, lymphocytes, monocytes, eosinophils, and basophils. A specific infection can be suspected based on the type of leukocyte that has an abnormal value. Viral infections usually affect the lymphocyte count, whereas bacterial infections increase the percentage of band neutrophils. Eosinophils are increased in those with allergic conditions and parasitic infection. Infection with the human immunodeficiency virus (HIV), which causes acquired immunodeficiency syndrome (AIDS), damages the body's ability to fight infection. The immune system of a healthy individual responds to infection by increasing the number of white blood cells, while the immune system of a person infected with HIV is unable to mount a defense of white blood cells (namely, lymphocytes) and cannot defend the body against viral or bacterial assault.

Of the calculations of red cell volume, the mean corpuscular volume (MCV) is the most useful for indicating anemia. The reticulocyte count, which measures the number of young red blood cells being produced, is used to distinguish between anemias resulting from a decrease in production of erythrocytes and those caused by an increase in destruction or loss of erythrocytes. An increase in the number of red blood cells (polycythemia) is normal

Reference Values in Hematology*

component	SI units	conventional units
Red blood cell count		
Female	$4.2–5.4 \times 10^{12}$/l	$4.2–5.4 \times 10^{6}$/mm³
Male	$4.6–6.2 \times 10^{12}$/l	$4.6–6.2 \times 10^{6}$/mm³
White blood cell count	$4.5–11.0 \times 10^{9}$/l	4,500–11,000/mm³
Differential white blood cell count		
Band neutrophils	150–400/mm³	3%–5%
Segmented neutrophils	3,000–5,800/mm³	54%–62%
Lymphocytes	1,500–3,000/mm³	25%–33%
Monocytes	300–500/mm³	3%–7%
Eosinophils	50–250/mm³	1%–3%
Basophils	15–50/mm³	0%–1%
Hemoglobin		
Female	120–160 g/l	12.0–16.0 g/dl
Male	130–180 g/l	13.0–18.0 g/dl
Hematocrit		
Female	0.37–0.47	37%–47%
Male	0.40–0.54	40%–54%
Mean corpuscular volume	80–96 femtolitres	80–96 μm³
Reticulocyte count	$25–75 \times 10^{9}$/l	25,000–75,000/mm³
Platelet count	$150–350 \times 10^{9}$/l	$150–350 \times 10^{3}$/mm³
Prothrombin time	12–14 seconds	12–14 seconds
Partial thromboplastin time	20–35 seconds	20–35 seconds
Plasma fibrinogen	2.0–4.0 g/l	200–400 mg/dl
Erythrocyte sedimentation rate		
Female	0–20 mm/h	0–20 mm/h
Male	0–15 mm/h	0–15 mm/h

*All values given for adults.

for persons living at high altitudes, but in most of the population it indicates disease.

Platelets, small structures that are two to four micrometres in diameter, play a role in blood clotting. A decrease in the platelet count can result in bleeding if the number falls to a value below 50×10^3 per cubic millimetre.

Hematopoiesis (the production of blood cells) occurs in the bone marrow, and many types of blood disorders can be diagnosed best by analyzing a sample of bone marrow removed by a needle from the centre of the pelvic bone or the sternum (bone marrow biopsy).

Bleeding disorders are suspected when blood is seen in the skin (purpura) or a wound is delayed in clotting. In addition to a low platelet count in the peripheral blood, there may be a decrease in megakaryocytes, cells in the bone marrow that form platelets. A bleeding time greater than 20 minutes indicates an abnormality of platelet function. Other screening tests for coagulation disorders include the prothrombin time (PT) test, the partial thromboplastin time (PTT) test, and the plasma fibrinogen assay (see the table). Blood factors, which are protein elements essential to the clotting of blood, should be assayed if a disorder associated with one of them is suspected. For example, factor VIII or IX can be assayed if the patient is thought to have hemophilia.

The erythrocyte sedimentation rate (ESR) is the rate at which red blood cells settle in a column of blood in one hour. It is a nonspecific indicator of inflammatory disease that is also increased in anemia (see the table).

The Coombs, or antiglobulin, test (AGT) is used to test blood cells for compatibility when doing a cross match to detect antibodies that would interfere with a blood transfusion. It also is used to detect antibodies to red blood cells in hemolytic disease of the newborn and drug-induced hemolytic anemias.

Urine. Examining the urine is one of the oldest forms of diagnostic testing, extending back to the days of Hippocrates. Physicians observed the urine (uroscopy) to diagnose all forms of illness because direct examination of a patient, or at least disrobing the patient, was socially unacceptable (see above *Historical aspects*).

Urinalysis

Urinalysis is the most commonly performed test in the physician's office. It consists of (1) a gross examination, in which the colour, turbidity, and specific gravity of the urine are assessed, (2) the use of a dipstick (a plastic strip containing reagent pads) to test for bilirubin, blood, glucose, ketones, leukocyte esterase, nitrite, pH, protein, and urobilinogen, and (3) a microscopic examination of a centrifuged specimen to detect red or white blood cells, casts, crystals, and bacteria. The urine is collected using a "clean-catch" technique to eliminate contamination with bacteria from skin or vaginal secretions.

Dipstick tests are available that contain from 2 to 10 different tests. The test for glucose, which indicates diabetes, and the test for protein, which indicates kidney disease, tumours of the urinary tract, or hypertensive disorders of pregnancy, are two of the most important assays available.

The microscopic examination is the most valuable urinalysis test. It will show a variety of cells that are normally shed from the urinary tract. Usually up to five white blood cells per high-power field (HPF) are present; more than 10 white blood cells per HPF indicates a urinary tract infection. More than two red blood cells per HPF is abnormal, although in women this is often due to vaginal contamination from menstruation. Cylindrically shaped urinary casts, shed from the kidney's tubules, consist of protein mixed with cells or other materials and may indicate renal disease if present in large numbers. Various crystals also are found in the urinary sediment, but these are generally of little clinical significance.

Feces. The tests most commonly performed on feces are the fecal occult blood test (FOBT), stool cultures, and the examination for parasites. The fecal occult blood test is a low-cost method for detecting bleeding, which may be the first sign of carcinoma of the colon or rectum. Although the false-positive rate for this test is low, the false-negative rate is high. It is more likely to detect lesions in the right (ascending) colon because they bleed more than those in the left (descending) colon. Routine surveillance for colorectal cancer depends on periodic fecal occult blood testing combined with direct visualization of the lower colon with a sigmoidoscope (see below).

Fecal occult blood test

Individuals who are at increased risk for colon cancer and should be screened regularly are identified by any of the following criteria: age greater than 50 years, previous colorectal cancer or adenoma, family history of colon cancer or polyps in a first-degree relative or another genetic predisposition (*e.g.,* cancer family syndrome), history of ulcerative colitis or Crohn's disease, or personal or family history of genital or breast cancer.

Stool cultures are obtained when diarrhea is severe and particular bacteria such as *Salmonella, Shigella,* or *Giardia* are suspected. If a parasitic infection is suspected, the stool is examined under the microscope for the eggs or cysts of parasites such as pinworms (*Enterobius vermicularis*) or roundworms (*Ascaris lumbricoides*).

Cerebrospinal fluid. Examination of the cerebrospinal fluid, obtained by lumbar puncture (*i.e.,* a needle inserted into the lower back), is performed if meningitis or hemorrhage into the central nervous system (subarachnoid hemorrhage) is suspected. The fluid is normally crystal clear and colourless. It will contain blood if subarachnoid hemorrhage has occurred.

Tests give clues to various disease processes. Viral meningitis can be differentiated from bacterial meningitis by the type of white blood cells identified, although a bacterial culture is the definitive test. The glucose value will usually be normal in patients with viral meningitis but low in those with bacterial and fungal meningitis. The protein level is increased in individuals with meningitis and tumour. The pressure of the fluid within the spinal canal is measured after the needle is inserted. The pressure is elevated in the presence of infection and tumour.

Gastric fluid. By passing a tube through the nose and into the stomach, gastric fluid can be obtained from the stomach for examination. The most common reason for this test is to look for blood in the upper gastrointestinal tract. Gastric fluid also can be cultured to test for tuberculosis if an adequate sputum sample cannot be obtained for culture.

Semen. More than 10 percent of couples in the United States have difficulty establishing a pregnancy. In addition to obtaining a complete history, performing a physical examination of both partners, and verifying that ovulation does occur in the woman, the physician will perform a semen analysis. Normal semen contains more than 60 million sperm per millilitre. More than 60 percent of the sperm are motile two hours after ejaculation, and 80 to 90 percent will have normal form and structure. Possible causes of infertility are a low sperm count, low motility, or a low percentage of normal forms.

Infertility in men

Miscellaneous tests. *Immunologic procedures.* Immunologic blood tests demonstrate abnormalities of the immune system. Immunity to disease depends on the body's ability to produce antibodies (immunoglobulins) when challenged by foreign substances (antigens). Antibodies bind to and help eliminate antigens from the body. The inability of the body to produce certain classes of immunoglobulins (IgG, IgA, IgM, IgD, IgE) can lead to disease. Complexes formed by the antigen-antibody reaction can be deposited in almost any tissue and can lead to malfunction of that organ. Immunofluorescence assays to detect antinuclear antibodies (antibodies that will bind to antigens within the nucleus) can be used to diagnose systemic lupus erythematosus and rheumatoid arthritis.

The inability of the body to develop antibodies to invading bacteria may result from infection with HIV, which invades white blood cells—primarily monocytes, macrophages, and helper T lymphocytes. Helper T cells are a subgroup of T lymphocytes that are the primary regulators of the immune response and proliferate in response to antigenic stimulation. Testing for HIV is performed with an enzyme-linked immunosorbent assay (ELISA) and the western immunoblotting antibody test (western blot).

Oral glucose tolerance test. The glucose tolerance test is used to confirm or exclude the diagnosis of diabetes mellitus when a fasting blood glucose test result is not definitive (*i.e.,* greater than the upper range of the normal

Diabetes mellitus

value, 115 milligrams per decilitre [mg/dl; 6.4 mmol/l], but less than the diagnostic level for diabetes, 140 mg/dl [7.8 mmol/l]). Even if a blood glucose test is obtained after fasting 10 to 12 hours and the level is above 140 mg/dl, it is important to confirm the result with a second determination to rule out other factors that may have given a one-time abnormal test result.

The oral glucose tolerance test measures the response of the body to a challenge load (an amount calculated to evoke a response) of glucose. It most often is used during pregnancy to detect early glucose intolerance that could pose a significant risk to the infant. After a fasting blood glucose test result is obtained, 75 grams of glucose (100 grams if the patient is pregnant) is administered and blood samples are taken every 30 minutes for two hours. In patients with diabetes, the blood glucose value will rise to a higher level and remain higher longer than in individuals who do not have diabetes.

A simpler but less reliable screening test is the two-hour postprandial blood glucose test performed two hours after intake of a standard glucose solution or a meal containing 100 grams of carbohydrates. A plasma glucose level above 140 mg/dl indicates the need for a glucose tolerance test.

Gastrointestinal absorption tests. Malabsorption of nutrients can result from surgical alterations or physiological disturbances of the gastrointestinal tract: removal of a significant portion of the bowel can cause the malabsorption condition short-bowel syndrome, a diffuse mucosal disease such as sprue can interfere with absorption, and diseases of the liver or pancreas may prevent digestive enzymes from reaching the intestines. Bacterial overgrowth in the intestines can interfere with glucose absorption, and the stomach's failure to produce intrinsic factor will prevent the absorption of vitamin B_{12} (cobalamin), which leads to pernicious anemia.

Persons who have a low serum vitamin B_{12} level and who are suspected of having pernicious anemia usually are required to undergo the Schilling test. Radioactive vitamin B_{12} is administered orally, and the amount excreted in the urine over the next 24 hours is measured. Malabsorption is confirmed if less than eight percent of the vitamin B_{12} is excreted in the urine.

Steatorrhea is the excretion of an excessive amount of fat in the stool, which is diagnostic of fat malabsorption when the amount of fat in the diet is normal. Stool specimens are collected for three days following two days of a diet containing 100 grams of fat per day. The excretion of more than six grams of fat daily indicates fat malabsorption, which may occur in persons with pancreatic disease, in those with diffuse mucosal disease, and in those who have undergone massive small-bowel resection.

A five-carbon sugar, D-xylose, is absorbed in the duodenum and proximal jejunum. It is not metabolized and is excreted unchanged in the urine. The D-xylose absorption test measures the absorption ability of the jejunum. Lowered excretion indicates diminished intestinal absorption usually caused by a decreased absorptive surface, infiltrative intestinal disease, or bacterial overgrowth.

Toxicological tests. Toxicology is the study of poisons—their action, detection, and the treatment of conditions they produce. Many substances are toxic only at high concentrations. Lithium, for example, is used to treat manic-depressive disorder but can be toxic at high levels. Another example is acetaminophen, which is valuable in controlling fever and discomfort but is toxic in large doses.

Levels of toxicity

The concentration of an element in the blood is the usual measure of toxicity. The therapeutic blood range is the concentration of the drug that provides therapeutic benefit, whereas the toxic blood range is the concentration at which toxic manifestations are likely.

Some substances such as insecticides are toxic to one individual and not to another. Many environmental substances as well as some encountered in the workplace are toxic in high doses; these include organic solvents, heavy metals, mineral dusts, dyes, and cigarette smoke. Acceptable exposure levels are controlled by government standards.

The nervous system is most sensitive to toxicological damage. Common toxins that cause damage to peripheral nerves are the six-carbon solvents, such as *n*-hexane, in glues or solvents and organophosphorus compounds. Carbon disulfide, used in the production of rayon fibres and cellophane, is a potent neurotoxin. Because no specific treatment is available for most of these toxic manifestations, preventing overexposure is important.

GENETIC TESTING

The diagnostic evaluation of a genetic disorder begins with a medical history, a physical examination, and the construction of a family pedigree documenting the diseases and genetic disorders present in the past three generations. This pedigree aids in determining if the problem is sex-linked, dominant, recessive, or not likely to be genetic.

Chemical, radiological, histopathologic, and electrodiagnostic procedures can diagnose basic defects in patients suspected of genetic disease. These include chromosome karyotyping (in which chromosomes are arranged according to a standard classification scheme), enzyme or hormone assays, amino acid chromatography of blood and urine, gene and deoxyribonucleic acid (DNA) probes, blood and Rh typing, immunoglobulin determination, electrodiagnostics, and hemoglobin electrophoresis.

As a result of genetic mutation, a genetic disorder can occur in a child with parents who are not affected by this disorder. This mutation can occur when the egg or sperm form (germinal mutation), or it can occur later following conception, when chromosomes from the egg and sperm combine. Mutations can occur spontaneously or be stimulated by such environmental factors as radiation or carcinogenic (cancer-causing) agents. Mutations occur with increasing frequency as people age. In men this may result from errors that occur throughout a lifetime as DNA replicates to produce sperm. In women nondisjunction of chromosomes becomes more common later in life, increasing the risk of aneuploidy (too many or too few chromosomes). Long-term exposure to ambient ionizing radiation may cause genetic mutations in either gender.

Cyto-genetics

Cytogenetics is the microscopic study of chromosomes and the transmission of genetic material from parent to offspring. Humans have 22 pairs of identical chromosomes plus a pair of sex chromosomes (one inherited from each parent). There are 50,000 to 100,000 genes arranged along the chromosomes in linear order, each having a precise location, or locus. The location of about 3,000 genes is known, and the locus of another 3,000 is strongly suspected. The goal of the international human genome project is to map the location of all genes by the year 2005; a rough map has already been produced.

Two broad classes of genes have been implicated in the development of cancer—oncogenes, which promote tumour growth, and tumour-suppressor genes. Both types of cancer-related genes, usually more than one variation of each type, are involved in a particular cancer, such as that of the colon or breast.

Prenatal diagnosis. Prenatal screening is performed if there is a family history of inherited disease, the mother is at an advanced age, a previous child had a chromosomal abnormality, or there is an ethnic indication of risk (Ashkenazic Jews and French Canadians are at increased risk for Tay-Sachs disease; blacks, Arabs, Turks, and others for sickle-cell anemia; and those of Mediterranean descent for thalassemia [hereditary anemia]). Parents can be tested before or after conception to determine whether they are carriers.

Alpha-fetoprotein screening

The most common screening test is an assay of alpha-fetoprotein (AFP) in the maternal serum. Elevated levels are associated with neural tube defects in the fetus such as spina bifida (defective closure of the spine) and anencephaly (absence of brain tissue). When alpha-fetoprotein levels are elevated, a more specific diagnosis is attempted using ultrasonography and amniocentesis to analyze the amniotic fluid for the presence of alpha-fetoprotein and acetylcholinesterase. Fetal cells contained in the amniotic fluid also can be cultured and the karyotype (chromosome morphology) determined to identify chromosomal abnormality. Cells for chromosome analysis also can be obtained by chorionic villus sampling, the direct needle aspiration of cells from the chorionic villus (future placenta). (See *Macropædia* REPRODUCTION AND REPRODUCTIVE SYSTEMS: *Human reproduction from conception to birth: The normal events of pregnancy: Prenatal care and testing*.)

Chromosomal analysis. To obtain a person's karyotype, laboratory technicians grow human cells in tissue culture media. After being stained and sorted, the chromosomes are counted and displayed. The cells are obtained from the blood, skin, or bone marrow or by amniocentesis or chorionic villus sampling. The standard karyotype shown in the figure has approximately 400 visible bands, and each band contains up to several hundred genes.

When a chromosomal aberration is identified, it allows for a more accurate prediction of the risk of its recurrence in future offspring. Karyotyping can be used not only to diagnose aneuploidy, which is responsible for Down, Turner's, and Klinefelter's syndromes, but also to identify the chromosomal aberrations associated with solid tumours such as Wilms' tumour, meningioma, neuroblastoma, retinoblastoma, renal-cell carcinoma, small-cell lung cancer, and certain leukemias and lymphomas.

DNA probes. Karyotyping requires a great deal of time and effort and may not always provide conclusive information. It is most useful in identifying very large defects involving hundreds or even thousands of genes.

Newer techniques such as fluorescent in situ hybridization (FISH) have much higher rates of sensitivity and specificity. FISH also provides results more quickly because no cell culture is required. This technique can detect smaller genetic deletions involving one to five genes. It is also useful in detecting moderate-sized deletions such as those causing Prader-Willi syndrome, which is characterized by a rounded face, low forehead, and mental retardation.

Gene analysis with recombinant DNA

The analysis of individual genes has been greatly enhanced by the development of recombinant DNA technology. Small DNA fragments can be isolated, and unlimited amounts of cloned material can be produced. Once cloned, the various genes and gene products can be used to study gene function in healthy individuals and those with disease. Recombinant DNA methods can detect any change in DNA, down to a one-base-pair change out of the three billion base pairs in the genome. DNA probes are labeled with radioactive isotopes or fluorescent dyes and used to identify persons who are carriers for autosomal recessive conditions. Disorders that can be detected using this technique include hemophilia A, polycystic kidney disease, sickle-cell disease, Huntington's chorea, cystic fibrosis, and hemochromatosis.

Biochemical tests. Biochemical tests primarily detect enzymatic defects such as phenylketonuria, porphyria, and glycogen-storage disease. Although testing of newborns for all these abnormalities is possible, it is not cost-effective, because some are quite rare. Screening requirements for these disorders vary from state to state and depend on whether the disease is sufficiently common, has severe consequences, and can be treated or prevented if diagnosed early and whether the test can be applied to the entire population at risk.

INSTRUMENTAL SCREENING

Scopes. *Sigmoidoscopy.* Colorectal cancer is the second leading cause of death from cancer in the United States. This disease is preventable if adenomatous polyps, protruding growths from the mucosal surface that can progress to cancer, are identified and removed. Although most adenomatous polyps are not cancerous, this possibility can only be discounted by histologic examination, which requires their removal. Fifty percent of all lesions occur in the rectum and sigmoid colon; they can be detected and removed using a 60-centimetre flexible sigmoidoscope. This instrument consists of a bundle of optical fibres that carry the visual image; it can be bent at the tip in four directions using controls at the base so that it can be maneuvered through the contorted sigmoid colon. The scope also contains a light source at the tip for illuminating the bowel, as well as separate passageways for instilling air and water, for suctioning fluid, and for inserting such instruments as biopsy forceps and snares. This scope has a smaller diameter than do rigid scopes and causes the patient less discomfort because of its flexibility. The operator can see the organ directly through a magnifying eyepiece or indirectly by a video monitor. The latter allows videotaping of suspicious lesions. Both rigid and flexible scopes can be fitted with a still camera.

The flexible fibre-optic sigmoidoscope comes in lengths of 35 and 60 centimetres. When fully inserted, the 60-centimetre scope can reach to the mid-descending colon and is the more frequently used scope. The colonoscope is a similar flexible fibre-optic scope that is longer and can reach the cecum, thus allowing evaluation of the entire colon. Its use requires that the patient be sedated because its passage through the entire colon is more uncomfortable.

A rigid, 25-centimetre sigmoidoscope is less expensive and allows direct visualization of the bowel, but it is less popular because of the greater discomfort its rigidness causes. The proctoscope and anoscope, shorter rigid instruments used to visualize the lower rectum and anus, are used to diagnose and treat hemorrhoids and other lesions in the anorectal area.

Screening for colon cancer

The incidence of colon cancer increases sharply after the age of 50. Asymptomatic individuals should have a sigmoidoscopy at age 50 and, if the result is negative, the test should be repeated every three to five years. Symptomatic persons and those with a family history of colon cancer should start regular examinations at age 40 or younger.

Esophagogastroduodenoscopy. As the lengthy name implies, esophagogastroduodenoscopy (EGD) is an endoscopic examination in which a scope is passed through the esophagus, stomach, and duodenum for a visual examination. This flexible fibre-optic scope contains the same channels as the flexible fibre-optic sigmoidoscope described above and usually has a camera attached to record visually recognizable abnormalities.

This procedure is indicated when symptoms of peptic ulcer disease persist despite an adequate trial of treatment or when there is upper gastrointestinal bleeding or a suspicion of upper gastrointestinal cancer. It is also indicated if there is an esophageal stricture or obstruction or persistent vomiting of unknown cause. Esophageal strictures, if benign, can be successfully dilated, and upper gastrointestinal bleeding can be controlled using electrocoagulation. If the bleeding is from esophageal varices, they can be injected with a sclerosing (hardening) agent. A tissue sample can be removed and examined (a biopsy) from any suspicious lesion of the esophagus, stomach, or duodenum to make the specific tissue diagnosis that is necessary when deciding on the most appropriate therapy.

Endoscopic retrograde cholangiopancreatoscopy. The flexible fibre-optic scope used in endoscopic retrograde cholangiopancreatography (ERCP) is similar to the scopes described above. It is passed through the stomach into the duodenum to visualize the ampulla of Vater, the opening of the common bile duct into the duodenum. It enables injection of a radiopaque dye into the common bile duct to permit radiographic visualization of the common bile duct and the pancreatic duct. This test is used to evaluate the patient with jaundice whose biliary tract is suspected to be obstructed because of a gallstone or tumour. It is also used to evaluate persistent pancreatitis of unknown cause. If there is stricture of the ampulla or another area in the common bile duct, a sphincterotomy (incision of the sphincter) or balloon dilatation can be used to enlarge the opening.

Alternative to major surgery

Laparoscopy. Fibre-optic technology has greatly expanded the procedures that can be performed by laparoscopy. By using local anesthesia and mild sedation, the abdominal wall can be punctured and the laparoscope inserted to examine the contents of the abdomen, obviating the need for major surgery and general anesthesia. Instruments are inserted through multiple ports in the abdomen, and surgeons can visualize abdominal organs without making an open incision into the abdomen. Valuable diagnostic information can be obtained by examining a biopsy specimen of the liver or abdominal lesions. Surgeons also can perform a variety of procedures with this method, such as removing the gallbladder and ligating the fallopian tubes. In orthopedic surgery the same technique is called arthroscopy, and it simplifies the treatment of many disorders that previously required a large surgical incision and a lengthy period of rehabilitation.

Nasopharyngolarygoscopy. The use of fibre-optic nasopharyngolaryngoscopes permits visualization of structures inside the nasal passages such as the sinus openings, larynx, and vocal cords. A more thorough examination can be performed than is possible using indirect visualization with a mirror.

Colposcopy. The colposcope is a lighted magnifying scope used to directly visualize the vulva, vagina, and cervix and to evaluate suspicious areas. Colposcopy is used when the Papanicolaou test suggests the possibility of cancer; it helps to detect precancerous abnormalities and identifies in which areas a biopsy should be performed for a definitive diagnosis to be made.

Graphing and miscellaneous instrumental screening. *Electroencephalogram.* The electroencephalogram (EEG) is a record of electrical activity of the brain recorded by 8 to 16 pairs of electrodes attached to the scalp. It is useful in the diagnosis of epilepsy, brain tumours, and sleep disorders and in the assessment of patients with suspected brain death. The latter use is particularly important if organs are to be saved for transplantation as soon as brain death is confirmed. Sleep deprivation and other provocative tests, including photic stimulation and hyperventilation, can be used to accentuate borderline findings. The EEG is of no use in diagnosing psychiatric illness.

Electrocardiogram. The electrocardiogram (ECG) is a graphic recording of the electrical activity of the heart detected at the body surface and amplified. It was invented by the Dutch physiologist Willem Einthoven (1860–1927) and for many years was called an EKG after the German *Elektrokardiogramm.* Electrodes to record the electrical activity of the heart are placed at 10 different locations, one on each of the four limbs and six at different locations on the anterior chest wall. Twelve different leads, or electrical pictures, are generated, each having its own normal configuration.

Evaluating the heart

The ECG is of greatest use in diagnosing cardiac arrhythmias, acute and prior myocardial infarctions, pericardial disease, cardiac enlargement (atrial and ventricular), and various electrolyte disturbances and drug effects. The exercise electrocardiogram, or ECG stress test, is used to assess the ability of the coronary arteries to deliver oxygen while the heart is undergoing strain imposed by a standardized exercise protocol. If the blood supply to the heart is jeopardized during exercise, the inadequate oxygenation of the heart muscle is recorded by typical changes in the electrocardiogram that indicate coronary artery disease (narrowing of the coronary arteries).

Echocardiography. The echocardiogram is a noninvasive technique used to record the structure of the heart by using ultrahigh-frequency sound waves. A transducer placed on the chest wall emits a short burst of ultrasound waves and then measures the reflection, or echo of the sound as it bounces back from such cardiac structures as valves and the muscle wall. It is used to evaluate chamber size, wall thickness, wall motion, valve structure, and valve motion. It is the method of choice for detecting infection of the valves (endocarditis), intracardiac tumours, and pericardial fluid. Mitral valve prolapse is easily visualized by this noninvasive technique.

Myocardial perfusion imaging. Myocardial perfusion imaging uses radioactive thallium to detect myocardial ischemia, myocardial infarction, and coronary artery disease. Injected intravenously, radioactive thallium is rapidly absorbed by the myocardium and is normally distributed evenly in heart muscle. Deficient blood flow to a portion of the myocardium is readily detectable by decreased uptake in that area. Evidence of recent and not-so-recent myocardial infarcts will be visible, but most persons with coronary artery disease who have not had a previous infarction will have normal perfusion patterns when they are at rest. In such a patient a thallium stress test is performed in which the substance is injected while the individual is exercising so that areas of transient ischemia can be identified and the patient treated to prevent myocardial infarction. An alternative means of stressing the heart that can provide information comparable with exercise is the injection of dipyridamole, a vasodilator. This test is used to diagnose coronary artery disease when the resting electrocardiogram is abnormal or the exercise electrocardiogram is equivocal.

Another method for evaluating the heart without the stress of exercise involves the intravenous injection of the drug dobutamine, while monitoring the effects using echocardiography. By using dobutamine echocardiography, the heart condition of frail patients and those who have heart disease or physical limitations that preclude exercise can be evaluated. Dobutamine induces the same changes in the heart that would occur during a standard exercise test. Two-dimensional echocardiography shows areas of the left ventricle that function abnormally. This technique uses no X-ray or radioactive material and is useful in diagnosing heart disease during pregnancy (see above *Echocardiography*).

Cardiac catheterization and angiography. A more specific measurement of coronary artery narrowing is carried out by placing a catheter into the heart though which a radiopaque dye is injected, allowing the cardiac chambers and coronary arteries to be directly visualized. This test is more expensive and more hazardous than the noninvasive procedures and is usually performed after the others to quantify the severity of disease present and to establish whether the person is a candidate for surgical intervention with balloon angioplasty or coronary bypass surgery. It is also used to evaluate patients with suspected valvular disease and those with angina who do not respond to treatment.

Diagnosing muscle disorders

Electromyography. Electromyography (EMG), the graphing and study of the electrical characteristics of muscles, is used to differentiate disease of the muscles from disease of the peripheral nerves. A needle electrode is inserted into the muscle, and the electrical activity of the muscle is measured. Resting muscle is normally electrically silent. The electrical potential is measured with the muscle at rest and during contraction. The response to electrical stimulation allows the physician to determine whether muscle weakness is the result of a disease in the muscle, such as a myositis (inflammation of the muscle), or a disease of nerves leading to muscle (neuropathy), such as Guillain-Barré syndrome.

SURGICAL EXAMINATION

Biopsy. A biopsy is the removal of tissue for microscopic examination to establish a precise diagnosis. Tissue can be obtained from any organ by excision, incision, removal by a needle, or scraping. Glass slides of the tissue are prepared and examined microscopically to define the characteristic nature of the lesion.

An excisional biopsy is the total removal of the lesion to be examined and is most often used to diagnose skin lesions. The major advantage of excisional biopsy is that it provides the pathologist with the entire lesion and minimizes the chance that a cancer in part of the lesion would be missed. This technique is practical only when the lesion is accessible and is less than two or three centimetres in diameter.

An incisional biopsy involves the removal of only a portion of the lesion for pathological examination and is used when the size or location of the tumour prohibits its complete excision. This technique also is used when a needle biopsy does not provide adequate information for a diagnosis to be made.

A needle biopsy is the simplest and least disruptive way to obtain tissue for pathological examination. This procedure can be performed using either a large cutting needle to obtain a "core" of tissue or a small-gauge needle. The latter technique, termed fine-needle aspiration biopsy, is accomplished by inserting the needle into the area of interest and applying suction to draw the tissue into the needle. A needle biopsy is often used to obtain specimens from breast masses. It is less expensive and involves less morbidity than does an open biopsy. The main disadvantages include the missing of deep lesions with the needle and the need for a specially trained pathologist to accurately interpret the specimen. As noted above, often more cells are needed for a precise diagnosis than are provided by a fine-needle biopsy.

Fine-needle aspiration biopsy

Another form of aspiration biopsy is the endometrial biopsy, in which the specimen is obtained by applying suction through a curette inserted into the uterus to obtain cells from the internal lining.

Abrasion is a method by which cells are obtained from the surface of lesions using a brush or spatula. Cells from epithelial-lined body cavities and surfaces such as the vagina, bronchus, and stomach are examined using the Papanicolaou technique. The Papanicolaou test or smear, commonly called the Pap smear, is the examination of cervical cells that have been fixed and stained on a slide according to the technique developed by the Greek physician George Nicolas Papanicolaou. This technique also can be applied to cells obtained from other surfaces.

Exploratory surgery. When a specific diagnosis is not possible using noninvasive or simple biopsy techniques, it may be necessary to surgically explore the area in question. If the lesion is in the abdomen, this involves a laparotomy or incision into the abdomen to observe the lesion. If possible a biopsy sample is removed. It may be apparent that the lesion is inoperable because of its location or attachment to vital structures from which it cannot be separated.

RADIOLOGICAL SCREENING

Named after Wilhelm Conrad Röntgen, the roentgenogram is the photograph of internal structures made by passing X rays through the body to produce a shadow image on specially sensitized film. The value of a roentgenogram is considerably enhanced by the use of contrast material, such as barium, to make structures visible on the film that would otherwise not appear. Perhaps the most common procedure employs a barium enema, administered to the patient before the X-ray examination, which allows identification of polyps as small as one centimetre in diameter when air is inserted after the barium (a double-contrast barium enema). This screening is effective if precancerous polyps are identified at an early stage.

Chest film. One of the most common screening roentgenograms is the chest film, taken to look for such infections as tuberculosis and conditions like heart disease and cancer. Treatment of tuberculosis detected by a roentgenogram can prevent more extensive infection, but unfortunately this technique is of little value in screening for lung cancer because the stage at which the disease is detectable by this method is too far advanced for treatment to be of value.

Screening for breast cancer

Mammography. New film screening techniques make it possible to detect lesions in the breast using low doses of radiation. Mammography is never a substitute for a clinical breast examination by a physician, because not all lesions are detectable by X-ray examination; however, lesions often can be detected by mammography before they are palpable in the breast. The primary purpose for mammography is the detection of cancer at the earliest, treatable stage, before the lesion is palpable.

Mammography is most useful in older women whose breast tissue is less dense than that of younger women. Mammography is never a substitute for a biopsy if a suspicious mass is palpated. Some groups recommend an initial mammogram at 35 to 40 years of age to serve as a baseline for subsequent screening. The American Cancer Society recommends a mammogram every one to two years from age 40 to 49 and yearly thereafter. However, women at increased risk for breast cancer should consider initiating annual mammographic screening before the age of 40. The risk of breast cancer is doubled or trebled in women who have a sister with breast cancer or whose mother was diagnosed with breast cancer before the age of 40.

COMPUTERIZED BODY SCANNING

Computed tomography. The introduction of computed tomography (CT scan) in 1972 was a major advance in visualizing almost all parts of the body. Particularly useful in diagnosing tumours and other space-occupying lesions, it uses a tiny X-ray beam that traverses the body in an axial plane. Detectors record the strength of the exiting X rays; this information is then processed by a computer and a cross-sectional image of the body produced.

CT is the preferred examination for evaluating stroke, particularly subarachnoid hemorrhage, as well as abdominal tumours and abscesses.

Ultrasonography. Ultrasonography, or ultrasound imaging, uses pulsed or continuous high-frequency sound waves to image internal structures by recording the differing reflection signals. The sonographic image is not as precise as images obtained through computed tomography or magnetic resonance imaging, but it is used in many procedures because it is quick and relatively inexpensive and has no known biological hazards when used within the diagnostic range.

Advantages of ultrasound

This method is used to diagnose gallstones, heart defects, and tumours. It is used to guide certain procedures such as needle biopsies and the introduction of tubes for drainage. It has become an essential part of obstetric and prenatal assessment, although controversy exists as to its routine use in obstetric care. Ultrasonography plays an integral role in the diagnosis and management of fetal abnormalities; it is also used to guide intrauterine corrective surgery.

Magnetic resonance imaging. Magnetic resonance imaging (MRI) relies on the response of magnetic fields to short bursts of radio-frequency waves to produce computer images that provide structural and biochemical information about tissue. The process uses radio waves and is thus much safer than imaging using X rays or gamma rays. This totally noninvasive but very expensive procedure is particularly useful in detecting cerebral edema, abnormalities of the spine, and early-stage cancer. In examining the brain, spinal cord, urinary bladder, pelvic organs, and cancellous bone, MRI is the superior imaging technique. Because patients must lie quietly inside a narrow tube, MRI may raise anxiety levels in the patients, especially those with claustrophobia. Another disadvantage of MRI is that it has a longer scanning time than CT, which makes it more sensitive to motion artifacts and thus of less value in scanning the chest or abdomen. Because of the strong magnetic field, MRI cannot be used if a pacemaker is present or if metal is present in critical areas such as the eye or brain.

MRI has largely supplanted arthrography, the injection of dye into a joint to visualize cartilage or ligament damage to the knee or shoulder, and myelography, the injection of dye into the spinal canal to visualize spinal cord or intervertebral disk abnormalities.

Multiple sclerosis, a disease with multiple foci of demyelination (loss of the myelin sheath of a nerve) in the brain, sometimes can be diagnosed using MRI. However, because the test is not sufficiently sensitive, a normal MRI cannot exclude the diagnosis.

Magnetic resonance angiography, a unique form of MRI technology, can be used to produce an image of flowing blood. This permits the visualization of arteries and veins without the need for needles, catheters, or contrast agents.

CT and MRI provide two-dimensional views of cross sections of the body, and these images must be viewed in sequence by the radiologist. Computer technology now makes it possible to construct holograms that provide three-dimensional images from digital data obtained by conventional CT or MRI scanners. These holograms can be useful in locating lesions more precisely and in mapping the exact location of coronary arteries when planning bypass surgery or angioplasty.

Three-dimensional images

Digital subtraction angiography. Digital subtraction angiography (DSA), an electronic technique for imaging blood vessels, is useful in diagnosing arterial occlusion, including carotid artery stenosis and pulmonary artery thrombosis, and in detecting renal vascular disease. After contrast material is injected into an artery or vein, a physician produces fluoroscopic images. Using these digitized images, a computer subtracts the image made with contrast material from a postinjection image made without contrast material, producing an image that allows the dye in the arteries to be seen more clearly. In this manner, the images arising from soft tissues, bones, and gas are the same in the initial and subsequent image and are thereby eliminated by the subtraction process. The remaining images of blood vessels containing the contrast material are thus more prominent.

Positron emission tomography. Positron emission tomography (PET) is a highly sensitive technique for diagnosing stroke and other neurological diseases such as multiple sclerosis and epilepsy. Positron-emitting radionuclides with short half-lives are used to detect cerebral blood flow, oxygen utilization, and glucose metabolism, providing both qualitative and quantitative information regarding metabolism and blood flow, such as in the heart.

PSYCHOLOGICAL TESTS

As with all medical testing, psychological testing is used as an aid in diagnosis, but no test stands alone. Each result must be combined with information gathered from the history, clinical evaluation, and other tests to be of greatest value. Testing, usually by a trained psychologist, is used to differentiate psychiatric from organic problems, to measure intelligence, to detect or confirm depression or other emotional abnormalities, and to evaluate personality or cognitive functioning. Some of the most commonly used tests are listed below.

1. The Minnesota Multiphasic Personality Inventory (MMPI) is a questionnaire designed for people older than 16 years of age. The 567 true-false statements require a trained psychologist to interpret the 14 personality scales and to determine the clinical significance of the findings. The test is used to assess psychopathologic status and personality functioning.
2. The Mini-Mental State Examination (MMSE) is the most widely used screening test for impairment of cognitive function. Developed by Marshal F. Folstein and colleagues, this brief and easy-to-administer test is used to identify persons with dementia.
3. Personality functioning and psychopathologic status can be assessed with the 10 inkblot cards of the Rorschach test. The associations these ambiguous images provoke require expert interpretation; results provide useful information on emotional aberrations.
4. The Thematic Apperception Test (TAT) uses 20 pictures of people in different situations to which the viewer ascribes meaning, which reflects areas of anxiety, personal conflict, and interpersonal relationships.
5. Information about a person's concerns and emotional conflicts can be gathered by administering the draw-a-person test and the sentence-completion test.
6. The Beck Depression Inventory (BDI), a 21-item self-administered test, measures subjective experiences and psychological symptoms associated with depression.
7. The Zung Self-Rating Depression Scale, which can be self-administered or given by a trained interviewer, employs 20 items to measure the severity of depression.

Formulating a diagnosis

The differential diagnosis

The process of formulating a diagnosis is called clinical decision making. The clinician uses the information gathered from the history and physical examination to develop a list of possible causes of the disorder, called the differential diagnosis. The clinician then decides what tests to order to help refine the list or identify the specific disease responsible for the patient's complaints. During this process, some possible diseases (hypotheses) will be discarded and new ones added as tests either confirm or deny the possibility that a given disease is present. The list is refined until the physician feels justified in moving forward to treatment. Even after treatment is begun, the list of possible diagnoses may be revised further if the patient does not progress as expected.

The hypotheses are ranked with the most likely disease placed first. Sometimes, however, a less likely disease is addressed first because it is more life-threatening and could lead to serious consequences if not treated promptly. Following this course, the possibility of a heart attack would be eliminated first in a patient experiencing chest pain and appendicitis would be the first condition to be addressed in a child with abdominal pain, even though another less serious disease is more likely.

An algorithm is a sequence of alternate steps that can be taken to solve problems—a decision tree. Starting with a chief complaint or key clue, the physician moves along this decision tree, directed one of two ways by each new piece of information, and eliminates diagnoses. If the wrong path is taken, the physician returns to a previous branching point and follows the other path. Computers can be used to assist in making the diagnosis; however, they lack the intuition of an experienced physician and the nonverbal diagnostic clues obtained during the interview.

Diagnostic tests rarely establish the presence of a disease without doubt. The greater the sensitivity and the specificity of the test, the more useful it will be. Ordering too many tests poses significant danger, not only because of low cost-effectiveness but also because a falsely abnormal test result requires a further series of tests to prove or disprove its accuracy. This further testing may involve additional discomfort, risk, and cost to the patient, which is especially unfortunate if the tests need not have been ordered in the first place. It is just as important to know when not to order a test as to know which tests to order.

Physician-patient relationship

An important feature of clinical decision making is the ongoing relationship between the physician and patient. The knowledge a physician gains in caring for the patient for a long period of time can provide greater insight into the likelihood of a given disease being present. When the symptoms are caused by emotional factors, the familiar personal physician is more likely to accurately diagnose them than is a physician seeing the patient for the first time. Also, a lengthy and trusting association with a physician will often positively influence the patient's outcome. Thus, sporadic visits to the emergency department of a hospital, where physicians who are unfamiliar with the patient are asked to provide diagnoses and treatment without the benefit of this partnership, are more likely to be inefficient, expensive, and less personally satisfying.

Early in the course of a disease, decisions must be made with fewer clues to the diagnosis than are likely to be available later. One of the most difficult tasks in medicine is to separate, in the early stages of an illness, the serious and life-threatening diseases from the transient and minor ones. Many illnesses will resolve without a diagnosis ever being reached. Nevertheless, an illness may remain undiagnosed for months or years before new symptoms appear and the disease advances to a stage that permits diagnosis.

Patients often have undifferentiated complaints that can represent an uncommon serious disorder or a common but not very serious disorder. For example, a patient may experience fatigue. Depending on the patient's family history and personal background, the physician may think initially of depression and next of anemia secondary to gastrointestinal bleeding. A variety of less likely disorders will follow. Anemia is easy to rule out with inexpensive hemoglobin and hematocrit tests. These tests should be ordered even if depression is the correct diagnosis because anemia may contribute to the weariness and should be treated as well. Depression can be diagnosed with appropriate questioning, and a physical examination may eliminate many other diagnostic possibilities.

THERAPEUTICS

Preventive medicine

The rationale for preventive medicine is to identify risk factors in each individual and reduce or eliminate those risks in an attempt to prevent disease. Primary prevention is the preemptive behavior that seeks to avert disease before it develops—for example, vaccinating children against diseases. Secondary prevention is the early detection of disease or its precursors before symptoms appear, with the aim of preventing or curing it. Examples include regular cervical Papanicolaou test screening and mammography. Tertiary prevention is an attempt to stop or limit the spread of disease that is already present. Clearly, primary prevention is the most cost-effective method of controlling disease.

Leading causes of death in the United States

The five leading causes of death in the United States are cardiovascular disease, cancer, cerebrovascular disease, accidental injuries, and chronic lung disease. The single most preventable cause of death in the United States is cigarette smoking, which is linked to cardiovascular disease (heart attack), cancer (lung, larynx, bladder, pancreas, and so on), cerebrovascular disease (stroke), and chronic lung disease (emphysema, chronic bronchitis).

Following earlier work by the Canadian Task Force on the Periodic Health Examination, the U.S. Preventive Services Task Force was established to evaluate the effectiveness of various screening tests, immunizations, and prophylactic regimens based on a critical review of the scientific literature. Its report, *Guide to Clinical Preventive Services,* lists the recommendations for the 60 target conditions evaluated by the panel.

Immunization is the best method for preventing infectious diseases. Standard immunizations of infants and children include those for diphtheria, tetanus, and pertussis (DTP); polio (OPV); measles, mumps, and rubella (MMR); *Haemophilus influenzae* type b (HbCV); and hepatitis B (HBV). A yearly vaccine against the influenza virus should be administered to adults who are older than 65 years of age, to those at risk because of chronic cardiopulmonary disease, and to those in chronic care facilities. Adults also should be immunized once at age 65 years against pneumococcal pneumonia with a vaccine containing 23 of the most common strains of *Streptococcus pneumoniae*.

Acquired immunodeficiency syndrome (AIDS), caused by the human immunodeficiency virus (HIV), is also a major infectious disease problem. Although a vaccine is expected, obstacles to its development are great. The only primary preventive measures currently available are either to abstain from sexual contact or to use condoms and, among intravenous drug users, to avoid sharing needles. Almost 25 percent of adult AIDS cases in the United States are related to infection from needles used to administer illegal drugs.

Preventing the spread of AIDS

The risk factors for coronary artery disease that can be modified to prevent myocardial infarction are cigarette smoking, hypertension, an elevated serum cholesterol level, a sedentary lifestyle, obesity, stress, and excessive alcohol consumption. In addition to an elevated total serum cholesterol level, an elevated low-density lipoprotein (LDL) level and a decreased high-density lipoprotein (HDL) level are significant risk factors. The total cholesterol level and elevated LDL level can be reduced by appropriate diet, whereas a low HDL can be raised by stopping smoking and increasing activity. If these measures do not provide adequate control, a variety of drugs capable of lowering the cholesterol level are available.

The major risk factor for stroke is hypertension, with cigarette smoking and diabetes mellitus significantly increasing the risk. Transient ischemic attacks (TIAs) occur before stroke in 20 percent of patients and consist of sudden onset of one or more of the following symptoms: temporary loss of vision in one eye, unilateral numbness, temporary loss of speech or slurred speech, and localized weakness of an arm or leg. Attacks last less than 24 hours and resolve without permanent damage until the stroke occurs.

Relation of smoking and cancer

The most important preventive behaviour in averting cancer is the avoidance of cigarette smoke. Smoking accounts for 30 percent of all cancer deaths, and there is increasing recognition of the danger of environmental or sidestream smoke to the nonsmoker. Primary prevention of skin cancer includes restricting exposure to ultraviolet light by using sunscreens or protective clothing. Secondary preventive measures include mammography, clinical breast examinations, and breast self-examinations for breast cancer; pelvic examinations and Papanicolaou tests for cervical and ovarian cancer; and sigmoidoscopy, digital rectal examinations, and stool tests for occult blood for colorectal cancer.

Demineralization of bone and a reduction in bone mass (osteoporosis) occur most often in men and women age 70 or older and may result in fractures, low back pain, and loss of stature. Osteoporosis in postmenopausal women that is caused by estrogen deficiency is the most common manifestation. The most effective method for preventing loss of bone mass after menopause is estrogen replacement therapy and increased calcium intake. Primary preventive measures include increasing physical activity and avoiding cigarettes and heavy alcohol consumption.

Alcohol abuse is the primary reason that accidents are the fourth leading cause of death in the United States. Other factors are failure to wear seat belts or motorcycle helmets, sleep deprivation, and guns in the home. Taking reasonable precautions and being aware of the potential dangers of alcohol and firearms can help reduce the number of deaths due to accidents.

Treatment of symptoms

PAIN

Pain is the most common of all symptoms and often requires treatment before its specific cause is known. Pain is both an emotional and a physical experience and is difficult to compare from one person to another. One patient may have a high pain threshold and complain only after the disease process has progressed beyond its early stage, while another with a low pain threshold may complain about pain that would be ignored or tolerated by most people. Pain from any cause can be increased by anxiety, fear, depression, loneliness, and frustration or anger.

Acute and chronic pain

Acute pain serves a useful function as a protective mechanism that leads to the removal of the source of the pain, whether it be localized injury or infection. Chronic pain serves a less useful function and is often more difficult to treat. Although acute pain requires immediate attention, its cause is usually easily found, whereas chronic pain complaints may be more vague and difficult to isolate.

The ideal method for treating pain is to eliminate the cause, such as to surgically remove an inflamed structure, to apply hot compresses to a muscle spasm, or to set a fractured bone in a cast. Alternatives to drug therapy, such as physical therapy, should be relied on whenever possible. The analgesic drugs most often used to alleviate mild and moderate pain are the nonsteroidal anti-inflammatory drugs (NSAIDs) such as aspirin, ibuprofen, acetaminophen, or indomethacin. If these are ineffective, a weak opiate such as codeine, hydrocodone, or oxycodone would be the next choice. Severe pain not controlled by these agents requires a strong opiate such as morphine or meperidine. Because opiates are addictive, their use is controlled by the Controlled Substances Act, and individuals prescribing or dispensing these drugs must register annually with the Drug Enforcement Administration. Each drug is assigned to one of five groups, from schedule I, which includes drugs that have the highest potential for abuse, to schedule V, which includes drugs with a limited dependence-causing potential.

NAUSEA AND VOMITING

Nausea and vomiting are common symptoms that may arise from diseases of the gastrointestinal tract, including gastroenteritis or bowel obstruction, from medications, such as analgesics or digoxin, or from nervous system disturbances such as migraine headaches or motion sickness. Vomiting is controlled by a vomiting centre located in the medulla oblongata of the brain stem.

Identifying and treating the cause is important, especially if the condition responds well to treatment and is serious if not addressed. A bowel obstruction can occur as a result of adhesions from previous abdominal surgery. Obstruction or decreased bowel motility also can occur with constipation and fecal impaction. Such important and treatable causes must be ruled out before resorting to antiemetic (serving to prevent or cure vomiting) drugs. The most frequently used antiemetic agents are the phenothiazines, the most popular being prochlorperazine (Compazine [trademark]). Antihistamines may be useful in motion sickness, but newer and more powerful drugs are needed to control the vomiting associated with cancer chemotherapy.

Nausea and vomiting are experienced by more than 50 percent of pregnant women during the first trimester. These symptoms are referred to as morning sickness, although they can occur at any time of the day. They may be distressing, but they cause no adverse effect on the fetus. Drug therapy is not only unnecessary; it should be avoided unless proved safe for the fetus. Treatment involves rest and intake of frequent small meals and pyridoxine (vitamin B_6).

Treatment of morning sickness

DIARRHEA

Acute diarrhea can result from food poisoning, laxatives, alcohol, and some antacids but usually is caused by an acute infection with bacteria such as *Escherichia coli, Salmonella,* and *Staphylococcus aureus.* In infants, acute diarrhea is usually self-limiting, and treatment consists primarily of preventing dehydration. Traveler's diarrhea affects up to half of those traveling to developing areas of the world. Preventive measures include chewing two tablets of bismuth subsalicylate (Pepto-Bismol [trademark]) four times a day, drinking only bottled water or other bottled or canned beverages, and eating only fruits that may be peeled, canned products, and restaurant food that is piping hot. Avoiding dairy products, raw seafood and vegetables, and food served at room temperature also limits exposure. Severe cases require antibiotic therapy.

COUGH

Coughing is a normal reflex that helps clear the respiratory tract of secretions and foreign material. It also can result from irritation of the airway or from stimulation of receptors in the lung, diaphragm, ear (tympanic membrane), and stomach. The most common cause of acute cough is the common cold. Chronic cough is most often caused by irritation and excessive mucus production that results from cigarette smoking or from postnasal drainage associated with an allergic reaction.

Treatment includes humidification of the air to loosen secretions and to counteract the drying effect of coughing and inflammation. Moist air from a vaporizer or a hot shower helps, as do hot drinks and soups. Antihistamines are often used to treat acute cough, but their value is questionable if an allergy is not present. They may also cause additional drying of the respiratory mucosa. Guaifenesin is widely used in cough preparations to help liquefy secretions and aid expectoration. Decongestants reduce secretions by causing vasoconstriction of the nasopharyngeal mucosa. The most common decongestants found in many cough preparations are pseudoephedrine, phenylephrine, and phenylpropanolamine. They may cause high blood pressure, restlessness, and urinary retention and should be used with caution in anyone being treated for hypertension. Narcotics are powerful cough suppressants, codeine being the most frequently used. Several safer nonnarcotic antitussive (cough-preventing) agents are available such as dextromethorphan, which has almost equal effectiveness but fewer side effects. Most cough preparations containing dextromethorphan also contain a decongestant and an expectorant. Because coughing is an important defense mechanism in clearing secretions from blocked airways, a productive cough (one that produces secretions) should not be suppressed.

Side effects of cough preparations

INSOMNIA

Insomnia is a difficulty in falling asleep or the feeling that sleep is not refreshing. Transient insomnia occurs when there are stressful life events or schedule changes, as shift workers or those who travel across multiple time zones experience. A disturbed sleep can also be related to the intake of stimulating drugs, anxiety, depression, or medical conditions associated with pain. Anxiety usually causes difficulty in falling asleep, whereas depression is associated with early morning awakening. The elderly spend less time sleeping, and their sleep is lighter and marked by more frequent awakenings. This situation is exacerbated by afternoon napping.

The treatment of insomnia involves establishing good sleep hygiene: maintaining a consistent schedule of when to retire and awaken, setting a comfortable room temperature, and minimizing such disruptive stimuli as noise and light. Daily exercise is beneficial but should be avoided immediately before bedtime. Stimulants should be avoided, including nicotine and caffeine. Alcohol disrupts the normal sleep pattern and should also be avoided. Drinkers sleep more lightly and frequently awaken unknowingly, which leaves them feeling unrefreshed the next day.

When medication is required, physicians usually prescribe one of the sleep-inducing benzodiazepines. They may have long-, intermediate-, or ultrashort-acting effects. None should be used regularly for long periods. Various nonbenzodiazepine hypnotics and sedatives are also available, and their usefulness varies according to individual preference.

Designing a therapeutic regimen

Once the physician makes a diagnosis or identifies the most likely cause of the symptoms and decides on the appropriate treatment, an entirely new set of conditions becomes operative. One of the first conditions to be considered is the patient's reason for seeking medical advice and the patient's expectations. The patient's visit may have been precipitated by the discovery that a friend's minor symptom, similar in nature to one the patient has been experiencing, proved to be something serious. If tests can rule out this possibility, reassurance may serve as a therapeutic action. When possible, physicians work to cure a disease and thereby relieve the symptoms, but many times the disease is unknown or chronic and incurable. In either case, relief from or improvement of symptoms or restoration of normal functioning is the goal. When neither a cure nor complete relief of symptoms is possible, an explanation of the disease and knowledge of the cause and what to expect may provide significant relief. Patients often want to know the name of the disease, what caused it, how long it will last, what additional symptoms may occur, and what they can do to assist the physician's treatment to hasten recovery. Providing information about the disease can help to alleviate anxiety and fears that could otherwise impede the patient's progress.

Attention to the patient's emotional well-being

An essential ingredient of any successful therapeutic regimen is the positive attitude of the patient toward the physician. A relationship of trust and respect for the physician based on reputation or years of supportive care is one of the physician's most powerful therapeutic tools.

When selecting a management plan, the physician usually has several options, and the outcomes or consequences of each will vary. Often, the best choice is one made together with the patient, who may have definite preferences for a trial of therapy over further testing or for oral medication rather than an injection, even if the latter would provide more rapid relief. The possible side effects of the medicine or treatment may well influence therapeutic choice, such as if a person would prefer dizziness to nausea. Once a course of therapy is selected, a new decision tree arises that leads to new options, depending on the response. Further testing, increasing the dose of medication, or changing to a new drug may be required. Almost every treatment has some degree of risk, from either unwanted side effects or unexpected complications. The physician describes these risks in terms of probability, expecting the patient to accept or reject the treatment based on these odds and his or her willingness to suffer the side effects or to risk the complications to achieve relief.

Another factor affecting therapeutic success is patient compliance—the degree to which patients adhere to the regimen recommended by their physician. Therapeutic regimens that require significant changes in lifestyle, such as recommendations to follow a special diet, begin an exercise program, or discontinue harmful habits like smoking cigarettes, are likely to result in poor compliance. Also, the greater the number of drugs prescribed and the more complicated the regimen, the poorer is the compliance. A patient is much more likely to successfully follow a regimen of taking a single dose of medication daily than one prescribed four times daily. Patients also may not fully realize the need to continue taking the medication after their symptoms have subsided, despite a physician's instruction

Adhering to the therapeutic regimen

to finish the medicine. Patient compliance may be most difficult to achieve in chronic but generally asymptomatic illnesses such as hypertension. Patients who experience no symptoms may need to be convinced of the necessity of taking their medication daily to prevent the occurrence of an untoward event (in hypertension, a stroke or other cardiovascular problems). Similarly, patients with depression or anxiety may want to discontinue medication once their symptoms abate. Until a relapse occurs, they may not recognize the need to continue taking the medication until instructed to taper the dosage slowly.

In deciding which therapeutic regimen is likely to be most effective, the physician must depend on scientific studies that compare one drug or treatment regimen with others that have been proved effective. The most dependable study is one that is truly objective and removes the possibility of bias on the part of the patient who wants the drug to work and the bias of the physician who may expect a certain outcome and subtly influence the interpretation. Such a study is "double-blind": it controls for both possible tendencies by comparing an active drug with an inactive "look-alike" drug. Neither the patient nor the physician knows which drug the patient is taking, so that neither one's bias can influence the result. Although this is the best way to demonstrate the effectiveness of a drug, it is sometimes very difficult to control for all the variables that could influence the outcome, such as varying degrees of stress one group or another may be under. Physicians will use the results of a wide variety of studies similar to this study to decide whether a regimen or drug is likely to work in a given patient; however, they will depend most heavily on their past experience with drugs or other techniques that have worked under similar circumstances. It is knowledge based on experience and on understanding of the patient that leads to the greatest therapeutic success.

The double-blind study

Diet

PROPHYLACTIC MEASURES OF NUTRITION

General requirements. Adequate nutritional intake is required to maintain health and prevent disease. Certain nutrients are essential; without them a deficiency disease will result. Required nutrients that cannot be synthesized by the body and therefore must be taken regularly are essential amino acids, water-soluble and fat-soluble vitamins, minerals, and essential fatty acids. The U.S. Recommended Dietary Allowances (RDAs), one of many sets of recommendations put out by various countries and organizations, have been established for these essential nutrients by the Food and Nutrition Board of the National Academy of Sciences. These RDAs are guidelines and not absolute minimums. Intake of less than the RDA for a given nutrient increases the risk of inadequate intake and a deficiency disorder. Nutritional requirements are greater during the periods of rapid growth (infancy, childhood, and adolescence) and during pregnancy and lactation. Requirements vary with physical activity, aging, infections, medications, metabolic disorders (*e.g.,* hyperthyroidism), and other medical situations. RDAs do not address all circumstances and are designed only for the average healthy person.

Protein, needed to maintain body function and structure, consists of nine essential amino acids that must be provided from different foods in a mixed diet. Ten to 15 percent of calories should come from protein. The oxidation of 1 gram (0.036 ounce) of protein provides 4 kilocalories of energy. The same is true for carbohydrate, but fat yields 9 kilocalories.

Carbohydrate provides about 45 percent of calories in the American diet, in the form of sugars, starches (complex carbohydrates), and dietary fibre (indigestible carbohydrates). Fibre is not digestible but increases the bulk of the stool and facilitates faster intestinal transit, which some believe reduces the risk of colon cancer by diminishing the time that cancer-producing substances in the diet remain in contact with the bowel wall. Increasing bulk also decreases the concentration of these substances. Dietary fibre can be insoluble (wheat bran) or soluble (oat bran and psyllium). Only the soluble fibres found in oats, fruit, and legumes lower blood cholesterol and benefit individuals with diabetes by delaying the absorption of glucose.

The most concentrated source of energy is fat, the source of fat-soluble vitamins and essential fatty acids. Thirty-seven percent of calories in the American diet come from fat, but the ideal is closer to 30 percent. The average American diet also contains 450 milligrams daily of cholesterol, but less than 300 milligrams is recommended.

Food Guide Pyramid

The recommended daily diet as determined by the U.S. Department of Agriculture is called the Food Guide Pyramid and consists of 6 to 11 servings of bread, cereal, rice, or pasta; 3 to 5 servings of vegetables; 2 to 4 servings of fruit; 2 to 3 servings of fish, meat, poultry, dry beans, eggs, or nuts; and 2 to 3 servings of milk, yogurt, or cheese.

Requirements in infancy. Nutritional needs are greatest during the first year of life. Meeting the energy demands during this period of rapid growth requires 100 to 120 kilocalories per kilogram per day. Breast milk, the ideal food, is not only readily available at the proper temperature, it also contains antibodies from the mother that help protect against disease. Infant formulas closely approximate the contents of breast milk, and both contain about 50 percent of calories from carbohydrate, 40 percent from fat, and 10 percent from protein.

Breast milk or commercial formula is recommended for the first six months of life and may be continued through the first year. Solid foods are introduced at four to six months of age starting with rice cereal and then introducing a new vegetable, fruit, or meat each week. Cow's milk should not be given to infants younger than six months of age, and low-fat milk should be avoided throughout infancy because it does not contain adequate calories and polyunsaturated fats required for development. Additional iron and vitamins should be given, especially to infants at high risk of iron deficiency, such as those with a low birth weight.

Toddlers are usually picky eaters, but attempts should be made to include the following four basic food groups in their diet: meat, fish, poultry, or eggs; dairy products such as milk or cheese; fruits and vegetables; and cereals, rice, or potatoes. Mealtime presents an excellent opportunity for social interaction and strengthening of the family unit. This starts with the bonding between mother and child during breast-feeding and continues as a source of family interaction throughout childhood.

Requirements in adolescence. Nutritional needs during adolescence vary according to activity levels, with some athletes requiring an extremely high-calorie diet. Other adolescents, however, who are relatively sedentary consume calories in excess of their energy needs and become obese. Peer pressure and the desire for social acceptance can profoundly affect the quality of nutrition of the adolescent as food intake may shift from the home to fast-food establishments.

Risks of adolescent pregnancy

Pregnancy during adolescence can present special hazards if the pregnancy occurs before the adolescent has finished growing and if she has established poor eating habits. Pregnancy increases the already high requirements for calcium, iron, and vitamins in these teenagers.

Eating disorders such as anorexia nervosa and bulimia arise predominantly in young women as a result of biological, psychological, and social factors. An excessive concern with body image and a fear of becoming fat are hallmarks of these conditions. The patient with anorexia nervosa has a distorted body image and an inordinate fear of gaining weight; consequently she reduces her nutritional intake below the amount needed to maintain a normal minimal weight. Severe electrolyte disturbances and death can result. Bulimia is a behavioral disorder marked by binge eating followed by acts of purging (*e.g.,* self-induced vomiting, ingestion of laxatives or diuretics, or vigorous exercising) to avoid weight gain.

Requirements of the elderly. The elderly often have decreased intestinal motility and decreased gastric acid secretion that can lead to nutritional deficiencies. The problem can be accentuated by poorly fitting dentures, poor appetite, and a decreased sense of taste and smell. Although lower levels of activity reduce the need for calories, older persons may feel something is wrong if they do not have the appetite of their younger years, even if caloric intake is adequate to maintain weight. The reduction in gastric acid secretion can lead to decreased absorption of vitamins and other nutrients. Nutritional deficiencies can reduce the level of cognitive functioning. Vitamin supplementation, especially with cobalamin (vitamin B_{12}), may be particularly valuable in the elderly.

The diet of the geriatric population is often deficient in calcium and iron, with the average woman ingesting only half the amount of calcium needed daily. Decreased intake of vegetables can also contribute to various nutritional deficiencies.

Constipation, which is common in the elderly, results from decreased intestinal motility and immobility and is worsened by reduced fluid and fibre intake. The multiple medications that the elderly are likely to be taking may contribute to constipation and prevent the absorption of certain nutrients. Some drugs, such as the phenothiazines, may interfere with temperature regulation and lead to problems during hot weather, especially if fluid intake is inadequate.

Requirements in pregnancy. The growing fetus depends on the mother for all nutrition and increases the mother's usual demand for certain substances such as iron, folic acid, and calcium, which should be added as supplements to a balanced diet that contains most of the other required nutrients. The diet of adolescent girls, however, is often deficient in calcium, iron, and vitamins. If poor nutritional habits have been established previously and are maintained during pregnancy, the pregnant adolescent and her fetus are at increased risk.

In addition to avoiding junk foods, the pregnant woman should abstain from alcohol, smoking, and illicit drugs because these all have a detrimental effect on the fetus. Although the average recommended weight gain during pregnancy is approximately 11.3 kilograms (25 pounds), the pregnant woman should be less concerned with a maximum weight gain than she is with meeting the nutritional requirements of pregnancy. Low weight gain (less than 9.1 kilograms) has been associated with intrauterine growth retardation and prematurity in the United States.

Requirements during breast-feeding

Women who are breast-feeding should continue taking vitamin supplements and increasing their intake of calcium and protein to provide adequate breast milk. This regimen will not interfere with the mother's ability to slowly lose the weight gained during pregnancy.

THERAPEUTIC MEASURES OF NUTRITION

Changes in diet can have a therapeutic effect on obesity, diabetes mellitus, hypertension, peptic ulcer, and osteoporosis.

Obesity. About one-fourth of the American population meets the definition of obesity (20 percent above ideal body weight). Obesity occurs when the number of calories consumed exceeds the number that is metabolized, the remainder being stored as adipose (fat) tissue. Many theories address the causes of obesity, but no single cause is apparent. Multiple factors influence weight, including genetic factors, endocrine levels, activity levels, metabolic rates, eating patterns, and stress.

The treatment of obesity requires reducing calorie intake while increasing calorie expenditure (exercise). Because obesity is a chronic illness, it requires long-term lifestyle changes unless surgery is performed to effect permanent changes in the digestion of food. Thus fad diets, no matter how effective they are in the short term, remain inadequate for long-term weight control. A reduction in calorie intake of 500 kilocalories per day should lead to a loss of 0.45 kilogram (1 pound) per week. This reduction can be increased by greater calorie reduction or an accompanying exercise program. With exercise, the weight loss will be primarily fat, whereas without it, muscle is lost as well. Exercise also leads to a "positive" addiction that makes it easier to sustain regular exercising for long periods. It reduces the risk of heart disease and can improve self-esteem.

Weight-reduction diets for the obese individual should be similar to those used by nonobese persons but with fewer calories—namely, a low-fat diet that avoids high-calorie foods. One of the most popular and successful of these diets is the very-low-calorie diet (VLCD) that results in rapid fat loss while minimizing the loss of lean muscle tissue. These diets require supplementation with potassium and a vitamin-mineral complex. Fad diets that eliminate one foodstuff, such as carbohydrate or protein, may give short-term results but fail in the long term to maintain the weight loss. Furthermore, these diets can lead to medically significant problems, such as ketosis (a buildup of ketones in the body).

Very-low-calorie diet

Appetite-suppressing drugs have limited short-term and no long-term effectiveness. Surgery can provide long-term benefits but it is an option only to those at least 45.3 kilograms heavier than their ideal body weight who are willing to suffer the common complications. The most frequently performed procedures are vertical banded gastroplasty and gastric bypass, both of which effectively reduce the size of the stomach.

Diabetes mellitus. Diet is the cornerstone of diabetic treatment whether or not insulin is prescribed. The goal is to regulate the patient's blood glucose level to as close to normal as possible and for the patient to achieve and maintain an ideal weight. Refined and simple sugars are avoided, and saturated fat is reduced by focusing the diet on poultry and fish rather than meat as a major source of protein. Soluble fibre such as that found in beans and oatmeal is recommended in contrast to the insoluble fibre found in wheat and bran. Artificial sweeteners are effective low-calorie replacements for simple sugar. The American Diabetes Association's recommendations are similar to those of the American Heart Association—that is, adhering to a balanced diet with restricted saturated fat intake while maintaining normal weight. Three or four meals of equal caloric content are spaced throughout the day, especially when supplemental insulin is needed.

Hypertension. Many patients with hypertension benefit from a low-sodium diet (reduced sodium chloride [table salt] intake) and physicians often recommend this as part of the initial therapy for hypertension. If alterations in diet fail to counteract the hypertension, drugs such as diuretics may be prescribed along with potassium supplements (because diuretics may deplete potassium). Other dietary measures are directed toward achieving an ideal body weight because obesity contributes to hypertension and increases the risk of cardiovascular disease. An adequate low-sodium diet can be achieved with a no-added-salt diet—that is, no salt is added to food after preparation, and foods with a high-sodium content such as cured meats are avoided. Low-sodium diets should be combined with increased potassium, which can be obtained by eating fruits, especially bananas, and vegetables, or using salt substitutes.

Low-sodium diet

Peptic ulcer. In the past a bland diet and frequent ingestion of milk and cream were the mainstays of ulcer treatment. Today the only dietary regimen is the avoidance of such irritating foods as spicy and highly seasoned foods and coffee. The newer drug therapies decrease gastric acidity much more than antacids and other dietary measures do. The infection of the stomach by *Helicobacter pylori* is now recognzied as a major factor in chronic gastritis and recurrent peptic ulcer in many patients. This bacterial infection requires a treatment regimen consisting of antibiotics and a bismuth-containing compound, which is different from the treatment of an ulcer that is not caused by *H. pylori*.

Osteoporosis. Although little can be done to treat osteoporosis once it is established, a great deal can be accomplished to prevent it, as has been discussed above (see above *Preventive medicine*). Osteoporosis, the loss of bone density, occurs in men and women older than 70 years of age and is manifested primarily in hip and vertebral fractures. It is most noticeable in postmenopausal women who have not taken estrogen. Estrogen replacement therapy, which should be combined with supplemental calcium, is most effective in decreasing bone resorption when begun during menopause, although it will provide some benefit if started later. In women who have an intact uterus, estrogen must be taken with progesterone to reduce the risk of endometrial cancer.

Biological therapy

BLOOD AND BLOOD CELLS

Blood transfusions

Blood transfusions were not clinically useful until about 1900 when the blood types A, B, and O were identified and cross-matching of the donor's blood against that of the recipient to prove compatibility became possible. When blood with the A antigen (type A or AB) is given to someone with anti-A antibodies (type B or O blood), lysis of the red blood cells occurs, which can be fatal. Persons with blood type O are universal donors because this blood type does not contain antigen A or B; however, because type O blood contains antibodies against both A and B, patients with this blood type can receive only type O blood. Fortunately, type O is the most common blood type, occurring in 40 to 60 percent of people, depending on the selected population (*e.g.,* 40 percent of the white population has blood type O, while 60 percent of Native Americans have it). Conversely, persons with type AB blood are universal recipients. Having no antibodies against A or B, they can receive type O, A, or B red blood cells.

Most individuals are Rh-positive, which means they have the D antigen; less than 15 percent of the population lack this antigen and are Rh-negative. Although anti-D antibodies are not naturally present, the antigen is so highly immunogenic (able to provoke an immune response) that anti-D antibodies will develop if an Rh-negative person is transfused with Rh-positive blood. Severe lysis of red blood cells will occur at any subsequent transfusion. The condition erythroblastosis fetalis, or hemolytic disease of the newborn, occurs when Rh-positive babies are born to Rh-negative mothers who have developed anti-D antibodies either from a previous transfusion or by maternal-fetal exchange during a previous pregnancy.

Whole blood transfusions are infrequently used because most transfusions only require one or more specific blood components. Whole blood, which contains red blood cells, plasma, platelets, and coagulation factors, is used mainly during cardiac surgery and when there is moderate or massive hemorrhage. It can be used only up to 35 days after it has been drawn and is not always available, because most units of collected blood are used for obtaining components.

Packed red blood cells are what remains of whole blood after the plasma and platelets have been removed. A 450-millilitre unit of whole blood is reduced to a 220-millilitre volume. Packed red blood cells are used most often to raise a low hemoglobin or hematocrit level in patients with chronic anemia or mild hemorrhage.

Leukocyte-poor red blood cells are obtained by employing a filter to remove white blood cells (leukocytes) from a unit of packed red blood cells. This type of transfusion is used to prevent febrile reactions in patients who have had multiple febrile transfusion reactions in the past, presumably to white blood cell antigens.

Platelet transfusions are used to prevent bleeding in patients with very low platelet counts, usually less than 20,000 cells per microlitre, and in those undergoing surgery whose counts are less than 50,000 cells per microlitre.

Autologous transfusion is the reinfusion of one's own blood. The blood is obtained before surgery and its use avoids transfusion reactions and transfusion-transmitted diseases. Donation can begin one month before surgery and be repeated weekly, depending on the number of units likely to be needed.

PLASMA

Coagulation factors

Plasma, the liquid portion of the blood, is more than 90 percent water. It contains all the noncellular components of whole blood including the coagulation factors, immunoglobulins, electrolytes, and proteins. When frozen, the coagulation factors remain stable for up to one year but must be used within 24 hours when thawed. Fresh frozen plasma is used in patients with multiple clotting factor deficiencies, such as in those with severe liver disease or massive hemorrhage.

Cryoprecipitate is prepared from fresh frozen plasma and contains about half the coagulation factors in $^{1}/_{15}$ the volume. It is used to treat patients with deficiencies of factor VIII, von Willebrand factor, factor XIII, and fibrinogen.

Specific clotting factor concentrates are prepared from pooled plasma or pooled cryoprecipitate. Factor VIII concentrate, the antihemophilic factor, is the preferred treatment for hemophilia A. A monoclonal antibody–purified human factor VIII is also available. Factor IX complex, the prothrombin complex, is also available for treating hemophilia B (factor IX deficiency).

IMMUNOGLOBULINS

Immune serum globulin (ISG), obtained from the plasma of unselected donors, contains a mixture of immunoglobulins, mainly IgG, with lesser amounts of IgM and IgA. It is used to provide passive immunity to a variety of diseases such as measles, hepatitis A, and hypogammaglobulinemia. Intravenous immunoglobulins (IVIGs) provide immediate antibody levels and avoid the need for painful intramuscular injections.

Hyperimmune serum globulin is prepared in the same way as the nonspecific immunoglobulin above but from patients who are selected because of their high titres of specific antibodies. Rh-immune globulin is given to pregnant Rh-negative women to prevent hemolytic disease of the newborn. Other hyperimmune serum globulins are used to prevent hepatitis B, tetanus, rabies, and varicella-zoster in exposed individuals.

BONE MARROW TRANSPLANTATION

Graft-versus-host disease

Bone marrow transplantation does not involve the transfer of a discrete anatomic organ as occurs in other forms of transplantation, but it entails the same risk of rejection by the recipient, which is called graft-versus-host disease (GVHD). The main indications for bone marrow transplantation are leukemia, aplastic anemia, and congenital immunologic defects.

Immunosuppressive drugs and irradiation are usually used to prepare the recipient. Close matching of tissue between donor and recipient is also essential to minimize GVHD, with autologous transplantation being the best method (the patients donate their own marrow at times of remission to be used later). Allogeneic (homologous) bone marrow transplants by a matched donor (preferably a sibling) are the most common.

Bone marrow transplantation is not recommended for patients older than 50 years of age, because of the higher mortality that results. The incidence of graft-versus-host disease increases in those older than 30 years of age. Those who donate bone marrow incur no risk, because they generate new marrow to replace that which has been removed. General anesthesia is required, however, to aspirate the bone marrow from the iliac crests, which is then infused into the recipient.

HEMATOPOIETIC GROWTH FACTORS

The hematopoietic growth factors are potent regulators of blood cell proliferation and development in the bone marrow. They are able to augment hematopoiesis when bone marrow dysfunction exists. Recombinant DNA technology has made it possible to clone the genes responsible for many of these factors. Some are commercially available and can be used to stimulate white blood cell development in patients with neutropenia (a decrease in the number of neutrophilic leukocytes) associated with cancer chemotherapy.

The first to be developed was erythropoietin, which stimulates red blood cell production. It is used to treat the anemia associated with chronic renal failure and that related to therapy with zidovudine (AZT) in patients infected with HIV. It may also be useful in reversing anemia in cancer patients receiving chemotherapy. Filgrastim (granulocyte colony-stimulating factor [G-CSF]) is used to stimulate the production of white blood cells, which prevents infection in patients whose white blood cells are diminished because of the effects of anticancer drugs. Another is sargramostim (granulocyte-macrophage colony-stimulating factor [GM-CSF]), which is used to increase the white blood cell count in patients with Hodgkin's disease or acute lymphoblastic leukemia who are undergoing autologous bone marrow transplantation.

BIOLOGICAL RESPONSE MODIFIERS

Biological response modifiers, used to treat cancer, exert their antitumour effects by improving host defense mechanisms against the tumour. They have a direct antiproliferative effect on tumour cells and also enhance the ability of the host to tolerate damage by toxic chemicals that may be used to destroy the cancer.

Biological response modifiers include monoclonal antibodies, immunomodulating agents such as the bacille Calmette-Guérin (BCG) vaccine used against tuberculosis, lymphokines and cytokines such as interleukin-2, and the interferons.

The three major classes of interferons are interferon-α, produced by white blood cells; interferon-β, produced by fibroblasts; and interferon-γ, produced by lymphocytes. The interferons are proteins produced by these cells in response to viral infections or other stimuli; they have antiviral, antiproliferative, and immunomodulatory properties that make them useful in treating some viral infections and cancers. They do not act directly on the viruses but rather indirectly, increasing the resistance of cells to viral infections. This can be particularly useful in patients who have an impaired immune system and a diminished ability to fight viral infections, especially those with AIDS.

Role of interferon

Interferon-α is produced by a recombinant DNA process using genetically engineered *Escherichia coli.* Recombinant interferon-α appears to be most effective against hairy-cell leukemia and chronic myelogenous leukemia, lymphoma, multiple myeloma, AIDS-associated Kaposi's sarcoma, and chronic type C hepatitis. It is moderately effective in treating melanoma, renal cell carcinoma, and carcinoid. It also can enhance the effectiveness of chemotherapy in some cancers. Unfortunately, treatment with this drug can be quite toxic.

Interferon-γ may prove useful in treating a different set of diseases—for example, chronic conditions such as rheumatoid arthritis.

HORMONES

The term hormone is derived from the Greek *hormaein,* meaning "to set in motion." It refers to a chemical substance that has a regulatory effect on a certain organ or organs. There are sex hormones such as estrogen and progesterone, thyroid hormones, insulin, adrenal cortical and pituitary hormones, and growth hormones.

Estrogens (estradiol, estone, and estriol) promote the growth and development of the female reproductive system—the vagina, uterus, fallopian tubes—and breasts. They are responsible for the development of secondary sex characteristics—growth of pubic and axillary hair, pigmentation of the nipples and genitals—and contribute to bone formation. The decrease in estrogen after menopause contributes to bone demineralization and osteoporosis, and hormone replacement therapy is often recommended to counteract this occurrence (see above *Preventive medicine*). Postmenopausal estrogen also prevents atrophic vaginitis, in which the vaginal mucosa becomes thin and friable. Estrogens can be administered orally, through the skin (transdermally), vaginally, and intramuscularly.

Progestins combined with estrogens comprise the oral contraceptives that inhibit ovulation by affecting the hypothalamus and pituitary. Progestin-only pills and injections are also effective contraceptives that work by forming a thick cervical mucus that is relatively impenetrable to sperm. Although the mortality associated with all forms of birth control is less than that associated with childbirth, this is not true for women older than the age of 35 years who smoke cigarettes. Their risk of stroke, heart attacks, and other cardiovascular problems is greatly increased, and the use of oral contraceptives is contraindicated. Levonorgestrel is a synthetic progestin that is implanted beneath the skin of the upper arm in six Silastic (trademark) capsules and provides birth control for five years.

Androgens

Androgens consist of testosterone and its derivatives, the anabolic steroids. Testosterone is produced in the testes in males, and small amounts are produced by the ovary and adrenal cortex in females. Testosterone is used to stimulate sexual organ development in androgen-deficient males and to initiate puberty in selected boys with delayed growth. The anabolic steroids are testosterone derivatives that provide anabolic activity with less stimulation of growth of the sexual organs. The use of anabolic steroids to increase muscle strength and endurance has been universally deplored by the medical community. This practice may have serious long-term effects such as the development of atherosclerotic disease because of effects on the blood lipids, especially the lowering of high-density lipoproteins. Their use in juvenile athletes can cause premature epiphyseal closure (early ossification of the growth zone of bones), compromising the attainment of their full adult height.

Human chorionic gonadotropin (HCG) is a hormone produced by cells of the placenta that can be extracted from the urine of pregnant women days after fertilization and thus is used in the early detection of pregnancy. It is also used to stimulate descent of the testicles in boys with prepubertal cryptorchidism and to treat infertility in men with underdeveloped testicles. Because it can stimulate the thyroid, it was inappropriately thought to be useful in treating obesity; there is no clinical proof of its effectiveness in this application.

Growth hormone, produced by the pituitary gland, stimulates linear growth and regulates metabolic functions. Inadequate secretion of this hormone by the pituitary will impair growth in children, which is evidenced by their poor rate of growth and delayed bone age (*i.e.,* slowed bone development). A synthetic preparation of the hormone is used to treat children who have a congenital deficiency of growth hormone.

Adrenal corticosteroids are any of the steroid hormones produced by the adrenal cortex except for the sex hormones. These include the mineralocorticoids (aldosterone) and glucocorticoids (cortisol), the secretion of which is regulated by the adrenocorticotrophic hormone (ACTH) produced in the anterior pituitary. Overproduction of ACTH leads to excessive secretion of glucocorticoids (Cushing's syndrome), which also can result from an increased concentration of corticosteroids secreted by tumours of the adrenal gland; conversely, the production of an insufficient amount of adrenal corticosteroids results in primary adrenocortical insufficiency (Addison's disease). The glucocorticoids are used primarily for their potent anti-inflammatory effects in rheumatic disorders, collagen diseases, dermatologic diseases, allergic disorders, and respiratory diseases and for the palliative management of leukemia and lymphoma. Cortisone and hydrocortisone are less potent than prednisone and triamcinolone, but dexamethasone and betamethasone have the greatest anti-inflammatory potency. Disadvantages of corticosteroid use include the masking of signs of infection, an increase in the risk of peptic ulcer, and the development of edema and muscle weakness.

Manufacture of insulin

Insulin, secreted by the pancreas, is the principal hormone governing glucose metabolism. Insulin preparations were extracted from beef or pork pancreas until recombinant DNA technology made it possible to manufacture human insulin. Three preparations are available: rapid-acting (Regular, Semilente [trademark]), intermediate-acting (NPH, Lente [trademark]), and long-acting (PZI, Ultralente [trademark]). Other antidiabetic agents are available for treating non-insulin-dependent diabetes mellitus (NIDDM), also referred to as adult-onset diabetes, or type II diabetes. The sulfonylureas are oral hypoglycemic agents used as adjuncts to diet and exercise in the treatment of NIDDM.

Thyroid hormones include thyroxine and triiodothyronine, which regulate tissue metabolism. Natural desiccated thyroid produced from beef and pork and the synthetic derivatives levothyroxine and liothyronine are used in replacement therapy to treat hypothyroidism that results from any cause.

Drug therapy

GENERAL FEATURES

Principles of drug uptake and distribution. Study of the factors that influence the movement of drugs throughout the body is called pharmacokinetics, which includes the absorption, distribution, localization in tissues, biotransformation, and excretion of drugs. The study of the actions of the drugs and their effects is called pharmacodynamics. Before a drug can be effective, it must be absorbed and distributed throughout the body. Drugs taken orally may be absorbed by the intestines at different rates, some being absorbed rapidly, some more slowly. Even rapidly absorbed drugs can be prepared in ways that slow the degree of absorption and permit them to remain effective for 12 hours or longer. Drugs administered either intravenously or intramuscularly bypass problems of absorption, but dosage calculation is more critical.

Variation in drug response

Individuals respond differently to the same drug. Elderly persons, because of reduced kidney and liver function, may metabolize and excrete drugs more slowly. Because of this and other factors, the elderly usually require lower doses of medication than do younger people.

Other factors that affect the individual's response to drugs are the presence of disease, degree of nutrition or malnutrition, genetics, and the presence of other drugs in the system. Furthermore, just as the pain threshold varies among individuals, so does the response to drugs. Some people need higher-than-average doses; some, being very sensitive to drugs, cannot tolerate even average doses, and they experience side effects when others do not.

Infants and children may have different rates of absorption than adults because bowel motility is irregular or gastric acidity is decreased. Drug distribution may be different in some people, such as premature infants who have little fatty tissue and a greater proportion of body water. Metabolic rates, which affect pharmacokinetics, are much higher during childhood, as anyone with a two-year-old can attest. The dosages of drugs for children are usually calculated on the basis of weight (milligrams per kilogram) or on the basis of body surface area (milligrams per square metre). If a drug has a wide margin of safety, it may be given as a fraction of the adult dose based on age, but the great variation in size among children of the same age complicates this computation. Children are not small adults, and drug dosages may be quite different than they are for adults.

The elderly are particularly susceptible to adverse drug effects because they often have multiple illnesses that require their taking various medications, some of which may be incompatible with others. In addition to decreased renal and hepatic function, gastric acid secretion decreases with age, and arteriosclerosis narrows the arteries, decreasing blood flow to the intestines and other organs. The precautions followed in prescribing medication for the elderly are an excellent example of the principle that should govern all drug therapy—drugs should be used in the lowest effective dose, especially because side effects increase with concentration. Because of illness or frailty, elderly people often have less reserve and may not be able to tolerate minor side effects that younger adults might not even notice.

When drugs are given in repeated doses, a steady state is achieved: the amount being administered equals the amount being excreted or metabolized. With some drugs, however, it may be difficult to determine the proper dose because of individual variations. In these cases, determining the plasma level of the drug may be useful, especially if the therapeutic window (*i.e.,* the concentration above which the drug is toxic and below which it is ineffective) is relatively small. Plasma levels of phenytoin, used to control epilepsy; digitalis, prescribed to combat heart failure; and lithium, used to moderate bipolar disorder (traditionally called manic-depressive disorder), should be monitored.

Indications for use. The purpose of using drugs is to relieve symptoms, treat infection, reduce the risk of future disease, and destroy selected cells such as in the chemotherapeutic treatment of cancer. The best treatment, however, may not require a drug at all. Recognizing that no effective medication exists is just as important as knowing which one to select. When more than one drug is useful, physicians should select the one that is most effective, least hazardous, and least expensive. A recently developed drug may promise better results, yet it will be less predictable and possibly more expensive.

Judicious prescription of medication

Every drug has multiple actions: it will affect organs and systems beyond those to which it is specifically targeted. Some patients may also experience idiosyncratic effects (abnormal reactions peculiar to that individual) as well as allergic reactions to certain drugs—additional reasons to select drugs carefully and avoid their use altogether when simpler measures will work just as well. A case in point is the belief that penicillin or other antibiotics will cure viral infections—they will not. While new antiviral drugs are under development, using antibiotics unnecessarily is unwise and potentially dangerous. The number of drug-resistant organisms is growing and must be counteracted by the judicious prescribing of these chemicals.

Unnecessary drug use also increases the possibility of drug interactions that may interfere with drug effectiveness. Interaction can occur in the stomach or intestinal tract where the presence of one drug may interfere with the absorption of another. Antacids, for example, reduce the absorption of the popular antibiotic tetracycline by forming insoluble complexes. Of greater importance is the interference of one drug with another. Some drugs can inhibit metabolism, which allows the amount of the drug to accumulate in the system, leading to potential toxicity if the dose is not decreased. Cimetidine, a drug used to treat peptic ulcers, causes few side effects by itself, but it does inhibit drug-metabolizing microsomal enzymes in the liver, increasing concentrations of many drugs that depend on these enzymes to be metabolized. This inhibition can be serious if the other drug is the anticoagulant warfarin. Bleeding can result if the dose is not reduced. Many other drugs are affected, such as antihypertensives (calcium channel blockers), antiarrhythmics (quinidine), and anticonvulsants (phenytoin). One drug can also decrease the renal excretion of another. Sometimes this effect is used to advantage, as, for example, when probenecid is given with penicillin to decrease its removal and thereby increase its concentration in the blood. But this type of interaction can be deadly: quinidine, for instance, can reduce the clearance of digoxin, a drug used to treat heart failure, potentially increasing its concentration to dangerous levels. Two drugs can also have additive effects, leading to toxicity, though either one alone would be therapeutic.

Problems with drug interactions can occur when a patient is being treated by different physicians, and one physician is not aware of the drug(s) that another has prescribed. Sometimes a physician may prescribe a drug to treat a symptom that actually is a side effect of another drug. Of course, discontinuing the first drug is preferable to adding another that may have side effects of its own. When a new symptom occurs, a recently initiated drug should be suspected before other causes are investigated. Patients should inform their physicians of any new drugs they are taking, as well as consult with the pharmacist about possible interactions that a nonprescription drug might have with a prescription drug already being taken. Having a personal physician who monitors all the drugs, both prescription and nonprescription, that the patient is taking is a wise course to follow.

Monitoring intake of prescription and nonprescription drugs

In the United States, responsibility for assuring the safety and efficacy of prescription drugs is delegated to the Food and Drug Administration (FDA). This includes the approval of new drugs, identification of new indications, official labeling (to prevent unwarranted claims), surveillance of adverse drug reactions, and approval of methods of manufacture. Before an investigational new drug (IND) can be tested in humans, it must be submitted to and approved by the FDA. If clinical trials are successful, a new drug application (NDA) must be approved before it can be licensed and sold. This process usually takes years, but if the drug provides benefit to patients with life-threatening illnesses when existing treatments do not, then accelerated approval is possible. Physicians can receive permission to use an unapproved drug for a single patient. This consent, called emergency use and sometimes referred to as single-patient compassionate use, is granted if the situation is desperate and no other treatment is available. The FDA also sometimes grants approval to acquire drugs from other countries that are not available in the United States if a life-threatening situation seems to warrant this action.

Another way to gain access to an investigational drug is to participate in a clinical trial. If it is a well-controlled, randomized, double-blind trial rather than an "open trial"—in which the investigator is not "blinded" and knows who is the subject and who is the control—the patient runs the risk of being given a placebo rather than the active drug.

The Federal Trade Commission (FTC) has responsibility for "truth in advertising" to assure that false or misleading claims are not made about foods, over-the-counter drugs, or cosmetics.

A rare disease presents a unique problem in treatment because the number of patients with the disease is so small (fewer than 200,000 in the United States) that it is not worthwhile for companies to go through the lengthy and expensive process required for approval and marketing. Drugs produced for such cases are made available under the Orphan Drug Act of 1983, which was intended to stimulate the development of drugs for rare diseases. More than 400 orphan drugs have been designated, but there are about 5,000 rare diseases that remain without treatment.

Controlled substances

Controlled substances are drugs that foster dependence and have the potential for abuse. The Drug Enforcement Administration (DEA) regulates their manufacture, prescribing, and dispensing. Controlled substances are divided into five classes, or schedules, based on their potential for abuse or physical and psychological dependence. Schedule I encompasses heroin and other drugs with a high potential for abuse and no accepted medical use in the United States. Schedule II drugs, including narcotics such as opium and cocaine and stimulants such as amphetamines, have a high potential for abuse and dependence. Schedule III includes those drugs such as certain stimulants, depressants, barbiturates, and preparations containing limited amounts of codeine that cause moderate dependence. Schedule IV contains drugs that have limited potential for abuse or dependence, and includes some sedatives, antianxiety agents, and nonnarcotic analgesics. Schedule V drugs have an even lower potential for abuse than do schedule IV substances. Some, such as cough medicines and antidiarrheal agents containing limited amounts of codeine, can be purchased without a prescription. Physicians must have a DEA registration number to prescribe any controlled substance. Special triplicate prescription forms are required in certain states for schedule II drugs, and a patient's supply of these drugs cannot be replenished without a new prescription.

SYSTEMIC DRUG THERAPY

Systemic drug therapy involves treatment that affects the body as a whole or that acts specifically on systems that involve the entire body, such as the cardiovascular, respiratory, gastrointestinal, or nervous systems. Psychiatric disorders also are treated systemically.

Cholesterol deposits lead to athero-sclerosis

The cardiovascular system. Atherosclerosis, the most common form of arteriosclerosis (generally called hardening of the arteries), is the thickening of large and medium-size arterial walls by cholesterol deposits that form plaques, causing the size of the arterial lumen to diminish. This narrowing compromises the artery's ability to supply blood to tissues and is most serious when the coronary arteries (those feeding the heart muscle) become clogged. A heart attack, with the death of a portion of the heart muscle, results; if the damage is extensive, sudden death will follow. The arteriosclerotic process can be slowed or even reversed by lowering serum cholesterol, especially the low-density lipoprotein (LDL) component. Cholesterol-reducing drugs, a low-cholesterol diet, exercise, and weight control can help. One form of cholesterol, high-density lipoprotein (HDL), is actually beneficial and helps to carry the harmful cholesterol out of the arterial wall. While some drugs will raise blood levels of high-density lipoprotein cholesterol, the most effective means of increasing it is to avoid cigarette smoke and increase exercise.

Narrowing of the coronary arteries can reduce the flow of blood to the heart and cause chest pain (angina pectoris). This condition can be treated with drugs such as nitroglycerin that primarily dilate the coronary arteries or by those such as the beta-blockers and calcium channel blockers that primarily reduce myocardial oxygen requirements.

Drugs that increase the strength of the heart muscle have been used to treat congestive heart failure for more than 200 years. Digitalis, derived from the foxglove plant, was the first drug found to have a positive inotropic effect (affects the force of muscular contraction) on the heart. Digoxin, the most commonly used form of this substance, can be given orally or intravenously. Digitalis has a relatively narrow therapeutic range: too much is toxic and can cause cardiac arrhythmias. Because toxicity is increased if the patient's serum potassium is low, close attention is paid to maintaining adequate potassium levels.

Drugs that dilate arterial smooth muscle and lower peripheral resistance (vasodilators) are also effective in treating heart failure by reducing the workload of the heart. The angiotensin converting enzyme (ACE) inhibitors are vasodilators used to treat heart failure. They also lower blood pressure in patients who are hypertensive.

Treatment of hyper-tension

The majority of cases of hypertension are due to unknown causes and are called essential, or primary, hypertension. Approximately five percent of all patients have secondary hypertension, which is high blood pressure that results from a known cause (*e.g.,* kidney disease). While the first treatment of hypertension should be to have the patient achieve normal weight, exercise, and reduce sodium in the diet, a wide variety of drugs are available to lower blood pressure, whether it be the systolic or diastolic measurement that is too high. A stepped-care approach has traditionally been used, starting with a single, well-tolerated drug, such as a diuretic. If it proves inadequate, a second drug is added and the combination manipulated until the most effective regimen with the fewest side effects is found. Occasionally, a third drug may be necessary.

The respiratory system. The drugs most frequently used for respiratory treatment are those that relieve cough in acute bronchitis. Antibiotics are effective only if the cause is bacterial. Most often, however, a virus is responsible, and the symptoms rather than the cause of the disease are treated, primarily with drugs that loosen or liquefy thick mucus (expectorants) and humidification (steam) that soothes the irritated mucous lining. While these treatments are widely prescribed, they have not been proven effective clinically. Cough suppressants are used to reduce unnecessary coughing but should not be employed excessively to subvert the cough's natural protective mechanism of ridding the airway of secretions and foreign substances. Dextromethorphan is a nonopioid cough suppressant nearly as effective as codeine and is available in over-the-counter preparations. If nasal congestion and postnasal drainage are present, an antihistamine and decongestant may be useful (see above *Treatment of symptoms: Cough*).

Asthma is a narrowing of the airways characterized by episodic wheezing. Bronchodilators are effective in a mild to moderate attack. Frequent attacks require long-term treatment with anti-inflammatory drugs such as cromolyn sodium, nedocromil sodium, or a corticosteroid.

Chronic obstructive pulmonary disease (COPD) manifests itself late in life with chronic cough and shortness of breath. Although most of the damage has already occurred, some benefit can still be obtained by stopping smoking, using bronchodilators, and administering antibiotics early when superimposed infection occurs. Supplemental oxygen therapy is used in severe cases.

The gastrointestinal system. Drugs are frequently used to reduce lower bowel activity when diarrhea occurs or to increase activity if constipation is the problem. Laxatives in the form of stimulants (cascara sagrada), bulk-forming agents (psyllium seed), osmotics (milk of magnesia), or lubricants (mineral oil) are commonly used. Diarrhea must be treated with appropriate antibiotics if the cause is bacterial, as in traveler's diarrhea, or with an antiparasitic agent if a parasite is to blame. Antidiarrheal agents include narcotics (codeine, paregoric), nonnarcotic analogs (loperamide hydrochloride), and bismuth subsalicylate (Pepto-Bismol [trademark]; see above *Treatment of symptoms: Diarrhea*).

Ulcers and chronic gastritis

Chronic gastritis and recurrent peptic ulcer often result from infection with *Helicobacter pylori* and are treated with antibiotics and bismuth. Ulcers not caused by *H. pylori* are treated with drugs that reduce the secretion of gastric acid, such as the H_2-receptor antagonists (cimetidine), or agents that form a barrier protecting the stomach against the acid (sucralfate). Antacids are used for additional symptomatic relief.

Nausea and vomiting are protective reflexes that should not be totally suppressed without the underlying cause being known. They may be psychogenic or caused by gastrointestinal or central nervous system disorders, medications, or systemic conditions (pregnancy or diabetic acidosis). Among the most widely used antiemetics are the phenothiazines (Compazine [trademark]), but new drugs continue to be developed that help control the vomiting related to cancer chemotherapy.

The nervous system. Alzheimer's disease is the most prevalent form of dementia (loss of intellectual function), and treatment had been primarily supportive until drugs that show modest promise for improving cognition (tacrine) were developed. Evidence that the continual use of cognitive faculties slows memory loss in the elderly has been supported by research showing that older persons who are stimulated regularly with memory exercises retain information better than those who are not.

Parkinsonism is named after James Parkinson, the English surgeon who in 1817 described "the shaking palsy." Although no treatment is known to halt the advance of the disease, levodopa and other drugs can significantly relieve the symptoms of tremor, muscular rigidity, and postural instability.

Migraine headache can be alleviated by one of the many forms of ergotamine and nonsteroidal anti-inflammatory drugs. Sumatriptan is a drug that has significantly improved the treatment of severe migraine attacks, causing fewer side effects than ergotamine or dihydroergotamine, but it is expensive.

Psychiatric disorders. Some of the greatest recent advances in pharmacotherapy have been in the treatment of anxiety disorders and depression. The benzodiazepines have been the mainstay of treatment for anxiety disorders since the 1960s, although their prolonged use incurs the risk of mild dependence. The azaspirodecanediones (buspirone) have little potential for producing dependency and are not affected by alcohol intake. Newer and safer medications are also available for treating panic disorder and obsessive-compulsive disorder.

Depression is among the most common life-threatening diseases, and considerable advances have been made in managing this very treatable disorder. The selective serotonin reuptake inhibitors (SSRIs) match previous antidepressants in effectiveness and have fewer unpleasant side effects. They also are safer if an overdose is taken, which is a significant threat in the case of severely depressed patients.

LOCAL DRUG THERAPY

Local anesthetics produce loss of sensation and make it possible for many surgical procedures to be performed without a general anesthetic. Barring any complications, the need for the patient to remain overnight in the hospital is obviated. Local anesthetics are also used to anesthetize specific peripheral nerves or larger nerve trunks. These nerve blocks can provide relief in painful conditions like rib fractures, but they are most frequently used to anesthetize an extremity during hand or foot surgery. Spinal anesthesia and epidural anesthesia, in which a local anesthetic is injected into the subarachnoid or epidural space of the lumbar (lower back) area of the spinal canal, provide pain relief during childbirth or surgery that involves the pelvic area yet lack the problems associated with a general anesthetic. Topical anesthetics, a type of local anesthetic, are also used on the skin, in the eye's conjunctiva and cornea, and in the mucous membranes of the nose, mouth, larynx, vagina, or urethra.

Topical anesthetics

Medications prescribed for dermatologic disorders account for a large amount of local drug therapy, whether it be a substance to stimulate hair growth or to soothe a burning and itching rash. Many different corticosteroid preparations are available to treat eczema, allergic reactions to substances like poison ivy, or seborrheic dermatitis. Sunblocks are used to protect the skin against ultraviolet rays and prevent skin cancer that can result from exposure to such radiation. Acne is controlled with skin cleansers, keratolytics to promote peeling, and topical antibiotics to prevent or treat infection. Physicians use various wet dressings, lotions, gels, creams, and ointments to treat acutely inflamed weeping and crusting sores and to moisturize and protect dry, cracked, and scaling skin. Burns heal more rapidly and with less scarring when treated appropriately with topical preparations like silver sulfadiazine. *Candida* infections of the mucous lining of the mouth (*i.e.,* thrush) or the vagina respond to nystatin or one of the imidazole drugs. The traditional treatment of genital warts has been the topical application of podophyllin, a crude resin, but new technology has made available interferon-α, which is 70 percent effective when injected into the lesion itself or subcutaneously below it.

Most ophthalmic drugs are local—eye drops to treat glaucoma, steroid-antibacterial mixtures to treat infection, artificial tears for dry-eye syndromes, or mydriatics (drugs causing dilation of the pupil), like atropine, that facilitate refraction and internal examination of the eye.

CHEMOTHERAPY

Chemotherapy is the treatment of disease using chemical agents that are intended to eliminate the causative organism without harming the patient. In the strict sense, this applies to the use of antibiotics to treat such invading organisms as bacteria, viruses, fungi, or parasites. The term is commonly used, however, to describe the use of drugs to treat cancer, in which case the target is not a causative organism but wildly multiplying cells. The purpose of the therapy is to selectively kill tumour cells and leave normal cells unharmed—a very difficult task because most drugs have a narrow therapeutic zone beyond which they harm normal cells as well as cancer cells. Approximately 50 different anticancer drugs are available, and an equal number are currently being tested. Anticancer drugs are only relatively selective for cancer cells, and the toughest task for the physician is to select a drug that will destroy the most cancer cells, leave normal cells unharmed, and cause the fewest unpleasant and undesirable side effects. The therapeutic goal is to favourably balance the risk-benefit ratio in which the morbidity of the treatment is weighed against its potential benefits. If a treatment causes patients to be miserable and has only a slight chance of prolonging life, many patients will forego further treatment. However, if the potential for significantly prolonging survival by aggressive therapy exists, the patient may decide to continue with the therapy.

Cancer treatment

The effectiveness of chemotherapy depends on the highest possible concentration of the drug being at the tumour site sufficiently long to kill the tumour cells. The maximal opportunity for a cure exists in the early stage of the disease when the tumour is small and localized. The larger and more disseminated the tumour, the more difficult it is to eradicate. The stage the tumour is in will also determine the route of administration, which can be oral, intravenous, intra-abdominal, intrathecal (into the subarachnoid space of the spinal cord), or intra-arterial—specifically, into the artery feeding the tumour.

Suppression of bone marrow activity, which results in a decrease in blood cell production, represents the most limiting factor in chemotherapy. Because chemotherapy is most effective when used at the highest nontoxic dose, the interval between treatments may need to be prolonged to prevent complete bone marrow suppression. Supportive measures undertaken when bone marrow suppression occurs include repeated platelet transfusions (to combat bleeding caused by diminished platelet production) and white blood cell transfusions (to control infection).

Adjuvant chemotherapy is the use of drugs to eradicate or suppress residual disease after surgery or irradiation has been used to treat the tumour. This is necessary because distant micrometastases often occur beyond the primary tumour site. Adjuvant chemotherapy reduces the rate of recurrence of some cancers, especially ovarian cancer, osteogenic sarcoma, colon cancer, and Wilms' tumour. The antiestrogen drug tamoxifen has been effective in selected patients with breast cancer.

Surgical therapy

MAJOR CATEGORIES OF SURGERY

Wound treatment. Wounds, whether caused by accidental injury or a surgical scalpel, heal in three ways: (1) primary intention (wound edges are brought together, as in a clean surgical wound), (2) secondary intention (the wound is left open and heals by epithelization), or (3) third intention, or delayed closure (the wound is identified as potentially infected, is left open until contamination is minimized, and is then closed).

Choosing which method is best depends on whether excessive bacterial contamination is present, whether all necrotic material and foreign bodies can be identified and removed, and whether bleeding can be adequately controlled. Normal healing can occur only if the wound edges are clean and can be closely opposed without undue stress on the tissue. An adequate blood supply to the wound is essential. If the tissue is tight and the edges cannot be closed without tension, the blood supply will be compromised. Cutting under the skin to free it from the underlying subcutaneous tissue may allow the edges to be brought together without tension. If direct approximation is still not possible, then skin grafts or flaps are used for closure.

Cleansing the wound

Wound closure begins with a thorough cleansing of the wound and the installation of a local anesthetic, usually lidocaine, which takes effect quickly and lasts for one to two hours. If the wound is contaminated, further cleansing is performed after instilling the local anesthetic, especially if foreign material is present. If the injury resulted from a fall on gravel or asphalt as in some motorcycle accidents, then aggressive scrubbing is needed to remove the many small pieces imbedded beneath the skin. High-pressure irrigation with saline solution will remove most foreign material and reduce the risk of subsequent infection. Contaminated wounds must be considered to be prone to infection with *Clostridium tetani,* which causes tetanus, and appropriate immunization should be given.

Sutures are the most commonly used means of wound closure, although staples and adhesive tissue tape may be more appropriate in certain circumstances. Silk sutures were originally used to close skin wounds, but nylon is stronger and causes less tissue reaction. Ideally, sutures are of the smallest possible diameter that will still maintain approximation of the wound edges. Absorbable sutures made of catgut (made not from cat but from sheep intestines) or a synthetic material such as polyglycolic acid are used to approximate the deeper layers of tissue beneath the skin so that tissue reaction will be lessened. The objective is to eliminate any unfilled space that could delay healing or allow fluid to accumulate. Drains connected to closed suction are used to prevent the collection of fluid when it is likely to accumulate, but drains serve as a source of contamination and are used infrequently. Staples permit faster closure of the skin but are less precise than sutures. When the edges can be brought together easily and without tension, tape is very useful. Although it is comfortable, easy to apply, and avoids the marks left by sutures, tape may come loose or be removed by the patient and is less successful if much wound edema occurs.

Sutures are removed after 3 to 14 days depending on the area involved, the cosmetic result desired, the blood supply to the area, and the amount of reaction that occurs around the sutures. Sutures on the face should be removed in three to five days to avoid suture marks. Tape is often used to provide support for the remainder of the time the wound needs to heal. Sutures on the trunk or leg will be removed after 7 to 10 days or longer if there is much tension on the wound. Tension and scarring are minimized in surgical procedures by making an incision parallel to normal skin lines, as in the horizontal neck incision for thyroidectomy.

Dressings protect the wound from external contamination and facilitate absorption of drainage. Because a surgical wound is most susceptible to surface contamination during the first 24 hours, an occlusive dressing is applied, consisting of gauze held in place by tape. Materials like transparent semipermeable membranes permit the wound to be observed without removal of the dressing and exposure of the wound to contamination. Dressings support the wound and, by adding compression, aid healing, as skin grafts do.

Wound healing

The healing of a wound results in scar formation; a strong yet minimally apparent scar is desirable. In some individuals a keloid, or thick overgrowth of scar, occurs no matter how carefully the wound was closed. The four phases of wound healing are inflammatory, migratory, proliferative, and late. The first, or inflammatory, phase occurs in the first 24 hours when platelets form a plug by adhering to the collagen exposed by damage to blood vessels. Fibrin joins the platelets to form a clot, and white blood cells invade the area to remove contamination by foreign material. Local blood vessels dilate to increase blood supply to the area, which hastens healing. In the second, or migratory, phase, fibroblasts and macrophages infiltrate the wound to initiate reconstruction. Capillaries grow in from the periphery, and epithelial cells advance across the clot to form a scab. In the proliferative phase, the fibroblasts produce collagen that increases wound strength, new epithelial cells cover the wound area, and capillaries join to form new blood vessels. In the late phase, the production of new and stronger collagen remodels the scar, blood vessels enlarge, and the epithelium at the surface heals.

Many factors, including diabetes mellitus or medications, can affect wound healing. In a patient whose diabetes is well controlled, wound healing is essentially normal, but, if the blood glucose level is elevated, it can impair healing and predispose the wound to infection. Kidney or liver failure and malnutrition also will delay wound healing, as will poor circulation owing to arteriosclerosis. Having steroids or anticancer or other drugs in the system can adversely affect the normal healing process.

Surgical extirpation. Extirpation is the complete removal or eradication of an organ or tissue and is a term usually used in cancer treatment or in the treatment of otherwise diseased or infected organs. The aim is to completely remove all cancerous tissue, which usually involves removing the visible tumour plus adjacent tissue that may contain microscopic extensions of the tumour. Excising a rim of adjacent, seemingly normal tissue ensures a complete cure unless there has been extension through the lymphatic system, which is the primary route for cancer to spread. For this reason, local lymph nodes are often removed with the tumour. Pathological examination of the nodes will show whether the cancer has spread. This indicates the likelihood of cure and whether additional treatment such as radiation or chemotherapy is needed.

Palliative surgery

If complete removal of a tumour is not possible, palliative surgery, which provides relief but is not a cure, may be useful to relieve pain or pressure on adjacent structures. Radical surgery may not always be best, as in the early stages of breast cancer. Removal of the entire breast and surrounding structures, including the axillary lymph nodes, has been shown to provide no greater benefit than a lumpectomy (removal of the tumour only) followed by radiation to the area in early stages of breast cancer, while it often causes the patient increased psychological distress. However, because of improvements in breast reconstruction techniques, the trauma of a radical mastectomy is becoming less severe.

Reconstructive surgery. Reconstructive surgery is employed when a significant amount of tissue is missing as a result of trauma or surgical removal. A skin graft may be required if the wound cannot be closed directly. If a large surface area is involved, a thin split-thickness skin graft, consisting of epidermis only, is used. Unfortunately, although these grafts survive transplantation more successfully and heal more rapidly than other types of grafts, they are aesthetically displeasing because their appearance differs markedly from that of normal skin. In a small defect, especially one involving the face or hand, a full-thickness skin graft, consisting of epidermis and dermis, is used, and skin is generally donated from the ear, neck, or groin. Exposure of bone, nerve, or tendon requires a skin flap. This can be a local flap, in which tissue is freed and rotated from an adjacent area to cover the defect, or a free flap, in which tissue from another area of the body is used. An example of a local flap is the rotation of adjacent tissue (skin and subcutaneous tissue) to cover the defect left from removing a skin cancer. A free flap is used when the amount of tissue needed is not available locally, as in an injury to the lower leg from an automobile bumper. The amount and type of tissue needed and the blood supply available determine the type of flap to be used. The blood supply must be adequate to supply the separated flap and wound edge with nourishment.

Tissue expanders are another way of creating extra tissue that can be used to cover a defect. Inflatable plastic reservoirs are implanted under the normal skin of an adjacent area. For several weeks the reservoir is expanded with saline to stretch the overlying skin, which is then used to cover the defect.

Reconstructive surgery is performed for a variety of surgical conditions. It may require the fashioning of a new "organ," as in an artificial bladder, or may involve insertion of prosthetic devices such as artificial heart valves, pacemakers, joints, blood vessels, or bones.

Prosthetic devices

Prosthetic devices can be used to replace diseased tissue. They usually perform better than donated tissue because they are made of material that does not stimulate rejection. The first prosthetic device to be used was the Dacron aortic graft developed by Michael E. De Bakey in 1954 to replace aortic aneurysms (dilated vessels that risk rupture and death) or vessels obstructed by arteriosclerotic plaques. Grafts made of similar materials are now employed to replace diseased arteries throughout the body. Other prosthetic devices include heart valves (made of plastic or taken from a pig) and metal joints (*e.g.,* hip, knee, or shoulder).

Transplantation surgery. The success of organ transplantation has greatly improved since the advent of the immunosuppressive drug cyclosporine. New and improved immunosuppressive drugs are currently being developed.

Kidney transplants are the most common, with those donated from living relatives ensuring the greatest prospects of long-term survival. The best survival rates are between identical twins. Cadaver transplants are often used, and one-year graft survival rate is 75 to 90 percent. Approximately 50 percent of grafts cease to function after 8 to 11 years, but others last 20 years or more. Kidneys removed from living donors can be preserved for up to 72 hours before they must be implanted, but most are implanted within 24 hours because successful transplantation decreases with time.

Heart and heart-lung organs can be preserved for four to six hours, and the success rate with this procedure continues to improve. Extensive blood and tissue matching is performed to minimize the risk of rejection. The size of the donor and donated organ should match the size of the recipient and the recipient's organ, and the time between pronouncement of death and procurement of the organ should be kept as short as possible.

In selected patients, liver transplantation has become an accepted treatment for end-stage liver disease. Mortality following surgery is 10 to 20 percent, and survivors still require long-term immunosuppressive therapy.

SURGICAL TECHNIQUES

Laser surgery. A laser is a device that produces an extremely intense monochromatic, nondivergent beam of light capable of generating intense heat when focused at close range. Its applications in the medical field include the surgical welding of a detached retina and the stanching of bleeding (called laser photocoagulation) in the gastrointestinal tract that can result from a peptic ulcer. Because a laser beam is absorbed by pigmented lesions, it can be used to treat pigmented tumours, remove tattoos, or coagulate a hemangioma (a benign but disfiguring tumour of blood vessels). Laser surgery has also been found to be effective in treating superficial bladder cancer and can be combined with ultrasonography for transurethral ultrasound-guided laser-induced prostatectomy (TULIP). More recent uses include the treatment of glaucoma and lesions of the cervix and vulva, including carcinoma in situ and genital warts.

Transurethral ultrasound-guided laser-induced prostatectomy

Cryosurgery. Cryosurgery is the destruction of tissue using extreme cold. Warts, precancerous skin lesions (actinic keratoses), and small cancerous skin lesions can be treated using liquid nitrogen. Other applications include removing cataracts, extirpating central nervous system lesions (including hard-to-reach brain tumours), and treating some heart conduction disorders.

Stereotaxic surgery. Stereotaxis (precise positioning in space) is a valuable neurosurgical technique that enables lesions deep in the brain that cannot be reached otherwise to be located and treated using cold (as in cryosurgery), heat, or chemicals. In this procedure, the head is held motionless in a head ring (halo frame), and the lesion or area to be treated is located using three-dimensional coordinates based on information from X rays and electrodes.

Stereotaxic techniques are also used to focus high-intensity radiation on localized areas of the brain to treat tumours or to obliterate arteriovenous malformations. This technique is also employed to guide fine-needle aspiration biopsies of brain lesions; it requires that only one burr hole be made in the skull with the patient under local anesthesia. Stereotaxic fine-needle biopsy also is used to evaluate breast lesions that are not palpable but are detected by mammography.

Minimally invasive surgery. Traditional open surgical techniques are being replaced by new technology in which a small incision is made and a rigid or flexible endoscope is inserted, enabling internal video imaging. Endoscopic procedures are commonly performed on nasal sinuses, intervertebral disks, fallopian tubes, shoulders, and knee joints, as well as on the gall bladder, appendix, and uterus. Although it has many advantages over traditional surgery, endosurgery may be more expensive and have higher complication rates than traditional approaches.

Trauma surgery. Trauma is one of the leading causes of loss of potential years of life. The explosion in the development of medical instrumentation and technology has made it possible for surgeons to save more lives than ever before thought possible. The intensive care unit contains a complex assortment of monitors and life-support equipment that can sustain life in situations that previously proved fatal, such as adult respiratory distress syndrome, multiorgan failure, kidney failure, and sepsis.

Radiation and other nonsurgical therapies

RADIATION THERAPY

Ionizing radiation is the transmission of energy by electromagnetic waves (*e.g.,* X rays) or by particles such as electrons, neutrons, or protons. Interaction with tissue produces free radicals and oxidants that damage or break cellular DNA, leading to cell death. When used properly, radiation may cause less damage than surgery and can often preserve organ structure and function. The type of radiation used depends on the radiosensitivity of the tumour and which healthy organs are within the radiation field. High-energy sources, such as linear accelerators, deposit their energy at a greater depth, sparing the skin but treating the deep-seated tumour. The radiation beam can also come from multiple directions, each beam being focused on the deep tumour, delivering a smaller dose to surrounding organs and tissues. Electron-beam radiation has low penetration and is useful in treating some skin cancers.

Radiation versus surgery

The basic unit of absorbed radiation is the gray (Gy): one gray equals 100 rads. Healthy organs have varying tolerance thresholds to radiation, bone marrow being the most sensitive and skin the least. The nervous system can tolerate much more radiation than the lungs or kidneys. Total body irradiation with approximately 10 Gy causes complete cessation of development of the bone marrow, and physicians use it to destroy defective tissue before performing a bone marrow transplant.

Radiation therapy can also be palliative if a cure is not possible; the size of the tumour can be reduced, thereby relieving pain or pressure on adjacent vital structures. It also can shrink a tumour to allow better drainage of an area, such as the lung, which can help to prevent infection and decrease the chance of bleeding.

Radioactive implants in the form of metal needles or "seeds" are used to treat some cancers, such as those of the prostate and uterine cervix. They can deliver high doses of radiation directly into the tumour with less effect on distant tissues.

An organ can also be irradiated by the ingestion of a radioactive substance. Hyperthyroidism can be treated with iodine-131, which collects in the thyroid gland and destroys a percentage of glandular tissue, thereby reducing function to normal. The drawback to this procedure is the difficulty in calculating the correct dose.

Irradiation is less effective in treating tissues that are poorly oxygenated (hypoxic) because of inadequate blood supply than it is in treating those that are well oxygenated. Some drugs enhance the toxic effect of radiation on tumour cells, especially those that are hypoxic.

OTHER NONINVASIVE THERAPIES

Non-ionizing radiation therapy

Hyperthermia. Some tumours are more sensitive than the surrounding healthy tissue to temperatures around 43° C (109.4° F). Sensitivity to heat is increased in the centre of tumours, where the blood supply is poor and radiation is less effective. A tumour may be heated using microwaves or ultrasound. Hyperthermia may enhance the effect of both radiation and chemotherapy; it is one form of nonionizing radiation therapy.

Photodynamic therapy. Another form of nonionizing radiation therapy is photodynamic therapy (PDT). This experimental technique involves administering a light-absorbing substance that is selectively retained by the tumour cells. The cells are killed by exposure to intense light, usually laser beams of appropriate wavelengths. Lesions amenable to PDT include tumours of the bronchus, bladder, skin, and peritoneal cavity.

Extracorporeal shock wave lithotripsy. The use of focused shock waves to pulverize stones in the urinary tract, usually the kidney or upper ureter, is called extracorporeal shock wave lithotripsy (ESWL). The resultant stone fragments or dust particles are passed through the ureter into the bladder and out the urethra. The patient is given a general, regional, or sometimes even local anesthetic and is immersed in water, and the shock wave is applied to the flank over the kidney. If the stone is small, submersion in a water bath is not necessary; shock waves are transmitted through the skin via a water-filled rubber bulb positioned over the stone site. Stones that are too large to be treated in this manner are removed by passing an endoscope into the ureter.

Psychotherapy

DRUG THERAPY

The use of drugs to treat emotional disorders has expanded dramatically with the development of new and more effective medications for a variety of disorders that formerly were not treatable. Drugs that affect the mind are called psychotropic and can be divided into three categories: antipsychotic drugs, antianxiety agents, and antidepressant drugs.

Antipsychotic agents. The advent of antipsychotic, or neuroleptic, drugs such as Thorazine (trademark) enabled many patients to leave mental hospitals and function in society. The primary indication for the use of antipsychotics is schizophrenia, erroneously called split personality. This is a severe mental disorder characterized by delusions, hallucinations, and sometimes bizarre behaviour. One form, paranoid schizophrenia, is marked by delusions that are centred around a single theme, often accompanied by hallucinations. The most effective drug to use may depend on an individual patient's metabolism of the drug or the severity and nature of the side effects.

Antianxiety agents. Drugs that combat anxiety have been called tranquilizers, an inexact term in that they do not tranquilize as much as reduce anxiety and enable dysfunctional patients to cope more effectively with life's vicissitudes and lead more rewarding lives. This class of drugs include the barbiturates, benzodiazepines, nonbenzodiazepine-nonbarbiturates, and hypnotics. The barbiturates phenobarbital, amobarbital, pentobarbital, and secobarbital have been around the longest and are used primarily as sedatives or for seizure disorders (phenobarbital).

Usefulness of benzodiazepines

The benzodiazepines have become the drugs of choice for acute anxiety. The first to be developed was chlordiazepoxide (Librium [trademark]), followed by a large variety of benzodiazepines that each has slightly different properties. Some are used primarily as sleeping pills (hypnotics) to treat insomnia. Before the development of the benzodiazepines, the only available antianxiety drugs were the barbiturates and meprobamate. The benzodiazepines have fewer unfavourable side effects and less abuse potential and have replaced barbiturates and meprobamate in the treatment of anxiety. They also are useful in treating alcohol withdrawal, calming muscle spasm, and preparing a patient for anesthesia. Drug dependency is a potential problem, however, especially in persons with a history of dependence on alcohol or other psychoactive drugs.

The nonbenzodiazepine-nonbarbiturate drugs include meprobamate (see above), which is rarely used today, and a new class of drugs, the azaspirodecanediones (buspirone), that have some advantages over the benzodiazepines. The most significant advantage is the absence of the potential for abuse, which renders these drugs safe in the long-term treatment of chronic problems such as generalized anxiety disorder. They also have no sedative effects and thus are safe for patients to use when driving or operating machinery. New drugs like buspirone that are effective but avoid many of the unfavourable side effects of earlier agents will continue to be developed.

Hypnotic agents

Hypnotic agents (nonbenzodiazepines) include chloral hydrate, some sedating antidepressants, and sedating antihistamines, such as diphenhydramine (Benadryl [trademark]) and hydroxyzine (Atarax [trademark]). These are used less frequently than the benzodiazepine hypnotics because of an increased morning hangover effect and other side effects. The distinction between antianxiety drugs and hypnotics is not clear, because many can serve both functions. Small doses of hypnotic benzodiazepines are effective antianxiety agents, and in many persons, especially the elderly, antianxiety benzodiazepines can induce sleep.

Antidepressant drugs. Depression, the most common emotional disorder, is classified as an affective disorder, the term affect referring to emotions and feelings. Affective disorders, also called mood disorders, include major depression and bipolar (manic-depressive) disorder.

Many drugs are available to treat depression effectively. One is selected over another based on side effects or safety. The main classes of antidepressants are the tricyclics, selective serotonin reuptake inhibitors (SSRIs), monoamine oxidase inhibitors (MAOIs), and others that are often called heterocyclics (trazodone, bupropion). The most recently developed antidepressants are the SSRIs, such as fluoxetine (Prozac [trademark]), sertraline, and paroxetine. They have no sedating effect, anticholinergic activity, associated weight gain, or cardiac toxicity, but they can cause nervousness. The oldest and best-studied class is the tricyclics, which are divided into tertiary amines and secondary amines. Most tricyclics have a sedating effect, cardiac toxicity, and varying degrees of anticholinergic side effects, which some individuals, especially the elderly, have difficulty tolerating. Anticholinergic effects, which result from the blockage of parasympathetic nerve impulses, include dry mouth, constipation, difficulty urinating, and confusion. Monoamine oxidase inhibitors have the potential to produce dangerous drug interactions. This is especially true of tyramine, which can cause hypertension and severe headache. Tyramine is found in many foods, which forces patients who take it to adhere to a specific diet.

Bipolar disorder is characterized by severe mood swings, from excessive elation and talkativeness to severe depression. The predominantly favoured mood-stabilizing drug is lithium, which requires regular monitoring of blood concentrations to achieve optimum effect. If the patient experiences episodes of mania or depression while taking lithium, additional drugs may be necessary.

BEHAVIORAL THERAPY

Behavioral therapy, also called behavioral modification, uses psychological counseling to change activity that is undesirable or potentially harmful. Treatment most often is directed toward changing harmful habits, such as discontinuing cigarette smoking, dieting to lose weight, controlling alcohol abuse, or managing stress more effectively.

Several types of behavioral therapy are used. Rational emotive therapy aims at altering inaccurate or irrational thoughts that lead to negative emotions or maladaptive behaviour. Other behavioral approaches attempt to modify physical responses. Biofeedback, for example, uses sensitive electronic devices and the principles of reinforcement to provide continuous visual or auditory "feedback," which helps patients learn to control subtle physical processes. Relaxation training, like deep muscle relaxation exercises, is a stress-reducing technique that can be used conveniently any time of the day. These cognitive behavioral techniques have been used to treat insomnia, hypertension, headaches, chronic pain, and phobias.

Modification of physical responses

Behavioral therapies have been developed for common problems of both childhood (*e.g.,* academic performance, enuresis, stuttering) and adulthood (*e.g.,* marital discord).

GROUP THERAPY

Psychotherapy in which an experienced therapist—a psychiatrist, psychologist, social worker, or member of the clergy—works with a group of patients or relatives is called group therapy. The process uses the interaction of group members to benefit each member of the group. Behavioral modification through group interaction and support can be used to change eating behaviours, which can lead to a reduction in weight. Support groups are available to assist patients and families in dealing with cancer, alcoholism, abuse, bereavement, and many other crises.

FAMILY AND SYSTEMIC THERAPY

General systems theories emerged in the biological and social sciences following World War II. This led to the conceptualization of the individual as an interdependent part of larger social systems. Systemic therapy does not focus on how problems start, but rather on how the dynamics of relationships influence the problem. The therapist's goal is to alter the dynamics of the relationships rather than to focus only on the behaviour or internal dynamics of individuals. For example, if a child is having temper tantrums, attention would be given to the stage of family development, the quality of communication between its members, and the clarity and flexibility of family roles.

Family therapy

Family counseling brings the entire family together to discuss specific problems of one or more family members, including adolescent discipline problems, marital discord, drug abuse, or relationship problems in families that can arise from remarriage.

PSYCHODYNAMIC THERAPIES

Sigmund Freud held that all behaviour is influenced by unconscious motivations and conflicts. Personality characteristics are thought to be shaped from the earliest childhood experiences. Psychological defenses are seen mainly as unconscious coping responses, the purpose of which is to resolve the conflicts that arise between basic desires and the constraints of external reality. Emotional problems are seen as maladaptive responses to these unconscious conflicts.

Psychodynamic therapies emphasize that insight is essential to lasting change. Insight means understanding how a problem emerged and what defensive purpose it serves. A classic form of psychodynamic therapy is psychoanalysis, in which the patient engages in free association of ideas and feelings and the psychoanalyst offers interpretations as to the meaning of the associations. Another form is brief, dynamic psychotherapy, in which the clinician makes recommendations based on an understanding of the situation and the reasons for resisting change.

Psychotherapy, the use of mental rather than physical means to achieve behavioral or attitudinal change, employs suggestion, persuasion, education, reassurance, insight, and hypnosis. Supportive psychotherapy is used to reinforce a patient's defenses, but avoids the intensive probing of emotional conflicts employed in psychoanalysis and intensive psychotherapy.

Experienced clinicians usually draw on various counseling theories and techniques to design interventions that fit a patient's problem. The format of therapy (*e.g.,* individual, couple, family, or group) will vary with each patient. Many patients respond best to a combination approach. Depression, for example, is frequently alleviated by medication and cognitive-behavioral therapy. There is growing interest in primary prevention to increase the coping abilities and resilience of children, families, and adults who are at risk for mental health problems.

BIBLIOGRAPHY. RALPH H. MAJOR, *A History of Medicine,* 2 vol. (1954), covers medical history from its beginnings to modern times; unlike many history books, it is easy reading. MARK H. SWARTZ, *Textbook of Physical Diagnosis: History and Examination,* 2nd ed. (1994), an excellent illustrated text, covers the techniques of physical diagnosis. PAUL EKMAN and WALLACE V. FRIESEN, *Unmasking the Face: A Guide to Recognizing Emotions from Facial Clues* (1975, reprinted 1984), is a classic text in facial expression and emotion that uses composite photographs to show the importance of such areas as the brow, eyes, or mouth. AMERICAN PSYCHIATRIC ASSOCIATION, *Diagnostic and Statistical Manual of Mental Disorders: DSM-IV,* 4th ed. (1994), the standard reference, contains the diagnostic criteria for mental diseases as determined by the American Psychiatric Association. PAUL CUTLER, *Problem Solving in Clinical Medicine: From Data to Diagnosis,* 2nd ed. (1985), covers the fundamentals of problem solving and includes many examples. An unusual reference containing technical information not found in standard medical dictionaries is JAMES L. BENNINGTON, *Dictionary & Encyclopedia of Laboratory Medicine and Technology* (1984). ROBERT E. RAKEL, *Textbook of Family Practice,* 4th ed. (1990), is the standard textbook for family physicians covering the breadth of the discipline and emphasizing clinical diagnosis and treatment. A handy pocket reference presented in outline format containing diagnostic essentials for most medical conditions is DAVID C. DUGDALE and MICKEY S. EISENBERG, *Medical Diagnostics* (1992). ROBERT R. EDELMAN and STEVEN WARACH, "Magnetic Resonance Imaging," *The New England Journal of Medicine,* 328(10):708–716 (Mar. 11, 1993) and 328(11):785–791 (Mar. 18, 1993), provide a complete discussion of MRI including physical principles, uses, and cost-benefit considerations. Annually an issue of *JAMA,* the journal of the American Medical Association, is devoted to recent discoveries in every medical discipline and is an excellent source of up-to-date information on new developments in medicine; one such development is treated in RICHARD C. REBA, "Nuclear Medicine," *JAMA,* 270(2):230–232 (July 14, 1993). An expert panel reviewed the scientific literature and developed recommendations for prevention in 60 conditions that represent the leading causes of death and disability in the United States; these recommendations are found in U.S. PREVENTIVE SERVICES TASK FORCE, *Guide to Clinical Preventive Services* (1989). *Manual of Clinical Dietetics,* 4th ed. (1992), published by the American Dietetic Association, is an excellent reference for diets and nutritional contents of foods. *Drug Facts and Comparisons* (annual), contains detailed information about all prescription drugs. *Drug Evaluations Annual* is a well-written evaluation of the clinical use of specific drugs, including comparative evaluations. *Conn's Current Therapy* (annual), provides a concise reference for the treatment of most medical and surgical diseases. *Scientific American Medicine* (monthly), published in loose-leaf format, covers all major areas of internal medicine. DOUGLAS WILMORE (ed.), *Care of the Surgical Patient,* 2 vol. (1989), is a regularly updated loose-leaf publication from the Committee on Pre and Postoperative Care of the American College of Surgeons; vol. 1 is devoted to critical care and vol. 2 to elective surgery. *Current Medical Diagnosis & Treatment* (annual), contains concise diagnostic information and treatment for a large number of medical diseases. JAMES B. WYNGAARDEN, LLOYD J. SMITH, JR., and J. CLAUDE BENNETT, *Cecil Textbook of Medicine,* 19th ed. (1992), is one of the best standard textbooks of medicine, compiled by leading authorities and containing thorough information on common and rare diseases. RICHARD D. DESHAZO and DAVID L. SMITH (eds.), "Primer of Allergic and Immunologic Diseases," *JAMA,* 268(20):2785–2996 (Nov. 25, 1992), is an entire issue devoted to allergy and immunology, containing articles ranging from the basics of the immune response to autoimmune diseases and immunization; prepared by the American Academy of Allergy and Immunology, it provides complete coverage of the subject.

ROBERT E. RAKEL. Professor and Chair, Department of Family Medicine, and Associate Dean for Academic and Clinical Affairs, Baylor College of Medicine, Houston, Texas. Author and editor of numerous textbooks, including *Conn's Current Therapy, 1994.*

Index

This is a three-year cumulative index. Index entries to World of Medicine articles in this and previous editions of the *Medical and Health Annual* are set in boldface type, *e.g.,* **AIDS.** Entries to other subjects are set in lightface type, *e.g.,* alcohol. Additional information on any of these subjects is identified with a subheading and indented under the entry heading. The numbers following headings and subheadings indicate the year (boldface) of the edition and the page number (lightface) on which the information appears. The abbreviation *il.* indicates an illustration.

AIDS, *or* acquired immune deficiency syndrome **96**–268; **95**–52, 215; **94**–235
alternative medicine **94**–243
American Indians **96**–106
celebrity deaths **94**–9
hemophiliacs **95**–459
Hispanic Americans **96**–137
alcohol
cancer risk factor **94**–419
cultural behavior **96**–146

All entry headings are alphabetized word by word. Hyphenated words and words separated by dashes or slashes are treated as two words. When one word differs from another only by the presence of additional characters at the end, the shorter precedes the longer. In inverted names, the words following the comma are considered only after the preceding part of the name has been alphabetized.
Examples:

Lake
Lake, Simon
Lake Charles
Lakeland

Names beginning with "Mc" and "Mac" are alphabetized as "Mac"; "St." is alphabetized as "Saint."

a

Dark-type numbers refer to the year of the edition, *e.g.*, **96**–264 for the 1996 edition, page 264.

b

Dark-type numbers refer to the year of the edition, *e.g.,* **96**–264 for the 1996 edition, page 264.

d

Dark-type numbers refer to the year of the edition, *e.g.,* **96**–264 for the 1996 edition, page 264.

e

f

g

Dark-type numbers refer to the year of the edition, *e.g.,* **96**–264 for the 1996 edition, page 264.

Dark-type numbers refer to the year of the edition, *e.g.*, **96**–264 for the 1996 edition, page 264.

i

j

k

Dark-type numbers refer to the year of the edition, *e.g.*, **96**–264 for the 1996 edition, page 264.

l

Dark-type numbers refer to the year of the edition, *e.g.*, **96**–264 for the 1996 edition, page 264.

O

Dark-type numbers refer to the year of the edition, *e.g.*, **96**–264 for the 1996 edition, page 264.

p

q

r

S

t

Dark-type numbers refer to the year of the edition, *e.g.*, **96**–264 for the 1996 edition, page 264.

Dark-type numbers refer to the year of the edition, *e.g.*, **96**–264 for the 1996 edition, page 264.